Hardanger filling stitches

This edition published in Great Britain in 2024 by
Search Press Ltd
Wellwood
North Farm Road
Tunbridge Wells
Kent TN2 3DR
www.searchpress.com

Reprinted 2024.

Originally published in 2023 in Australia by
Vetty Creations
PO Box 1723, Hornsby Westfield NSW 1635, Australia
www.vettycreations.com.au

ISBN: 978-1-80092-201-3

This book was conceived, designed and produced by Yvette Stanton, Vetty Creations

Printed in China.

cataloguing-in-publication data

Stanton, Yvette, 1974—

Hardanger filling stitches: A step-by-step handbook

280 p. : b/w & col. ill ; 28cm
Bibliography.
Includes index.
ISBN 978-1-80092-201-3

1. Hardanger needlework
2. Hardanger needlework – Patterns
3. Hardanger needlework – Handbooks, manuals, etc.
4. Embroidery – Norway
5. Embroidery – Norway –Hardanger Region
6. Embroidery – Handbooks, manuals, etc.

746.44

acknowledgements

Thank you to Donna Ruettimann Finley, who suggested that I should write this book!

Thank you to the Hardanger Folkesmuseum, Agnete Sivertsen, The Embroiderers' Guild of NSW Library, Brian Curtis, Marianne Mäder (*Double twisted cross and Soleil stitch*), Joan Elsley, Virginia Foster, Carmen Gartshore, Ki Es, John Stanton and Beth Harwood. Thank you to my family and friends for cheering me on while I wrote this book.

image credits

All photographs copyright © Yvette Stanton 2023, except as detailed following. Page 6 and 7 Top: Mittet & Co. AS, 1960. Hordaland, Norway. Collection: National Library of Norway. Photograph in public domain. Bottom: Torstein Lofthus. Hardanger, Hordaland, Norway. Collection: National Library of Norway. Photograph in public domain.

bibliography

Arias Ruiz, Mamen. *La Broderie Hardanger*. Éditions de Saxe, Chaponost, France. 2020.

de Dillmont, Therese. *Hardanger Embroideries, 1st Series*. Editions Th. de Dillmont. 1921.

de Dillmont, Therese. *Hardanger Embroideries, 2nd Series*. Editions Th. de Dillmont. 1921.

Geldens, Janny. *The Complete Book of Hardanger*. Little Hills Press, Crows Nest, Australia. NSW. 1997.

Love, Janice. *Fundamentals Made Fancy*. Love 'N Stitches, Athens GA, USA. 1993.

Love, Janice. *Hardanger Basics and Beyond*. Love 'N Stitches, Athens GA, USA. 1990.

Marfaing, Frédérique. *Hardanger Embroidery*. Stackpole Books, Mechanicsburg PA, USA. 2014.

Meier, Susan L, & Watnemo, Rosalyn K. *Advanced Charted Hardanger Embroidery*. Nordic Needle. 1982.

Stanton, Yvette. *Early-Style Hardanger*. Vetty Creations, Sydney Australia. 2016.

Stanton, Yvette. *Elegant Hardanger Embroidery*. Vetty Creations, Sydney Australia. 2002.

Stanton, Yvette. *Frisian Whitework*. Vetty Creations, Sydney Australia. 2021.

Stuland, Gudrun. *Hardangersaum*, Fabritius and Sønners, Oslo 1960. Reprinted 2013 by Hordaland Husflidslag, Bergen.

Valevatn, Kirsten. *Hardanger Embroidery... stitch by stitch*, self-published, Voss 1996.

Valevatn, Kirsten. *Teljesaum til bunad... sting for sting*, self-published, Voss 1991.

other books by Yvette Stanton

Elegant Hardanger Embroidery
Early-Style Hardanger: Traditional Norwegian Whitework Embroidery
Frisian Whitework: Dutch Embroidery from Friesland
Portuguese Whitework: Bullion Embroidery from Guimarães
Sardinian Knotted Embroidery: Whitework from Teulada
Smøyg: Norwegian Pattern Darning
The Left-Handed Embroiderer's Companion: a Step-by-Step Stitch Dictionary
The Right-Handed Embroiderer's Companion: a Step-by-Step Stitch Dictionary
Ukrainian Drawn Thread Embroidery: Merezhka Poltavska
With Prue Scott:
Mountmellick Embroidery: Inspired by Nature

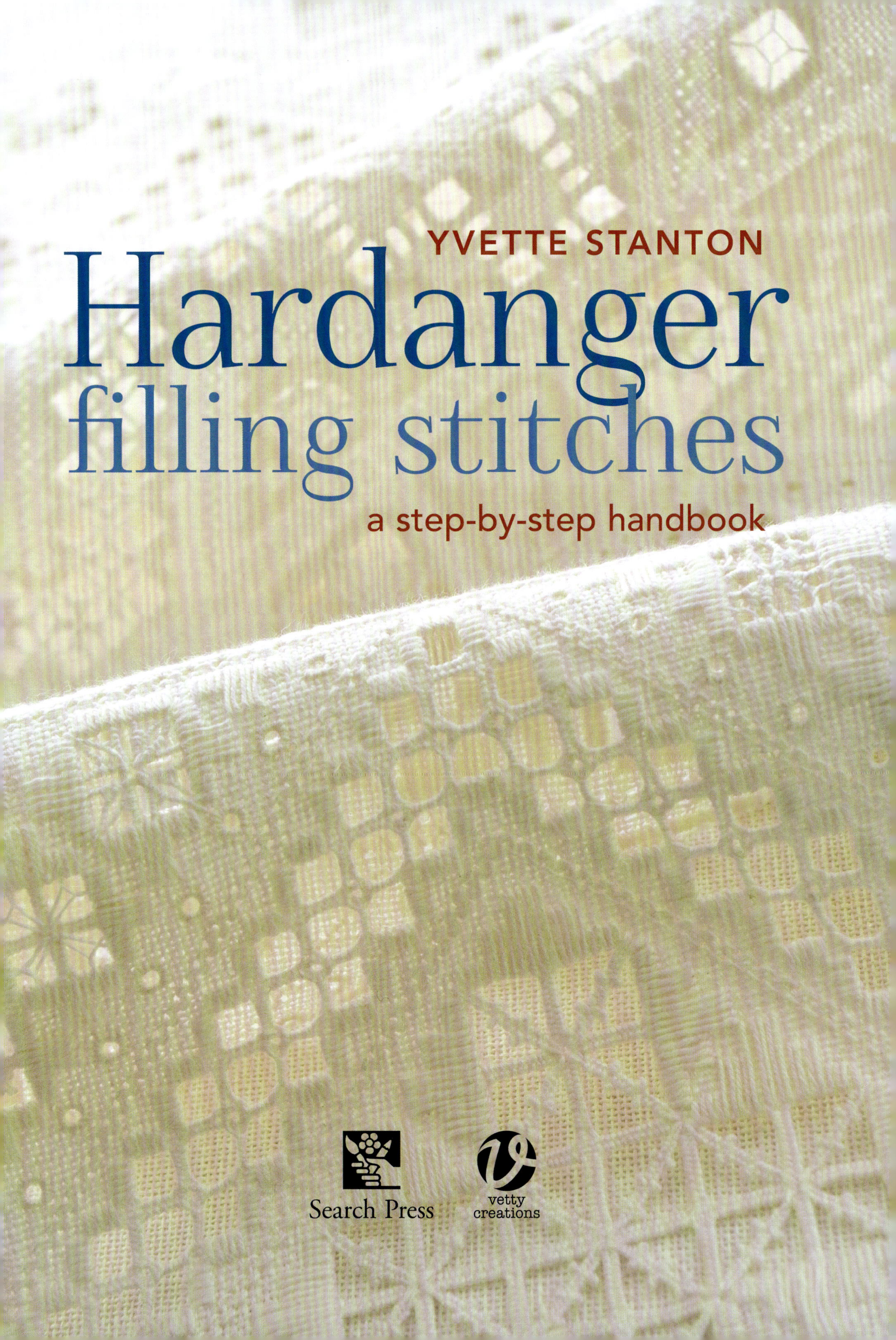

YVETTE STANTON

Hardanger filling stitches

a step-by-step handbook

Search Press

vetty creations

contents

Numbers in *italics* indicate the start of the left-handed instructions; numbers in **bold** indicate the start of the right-handed instructions.

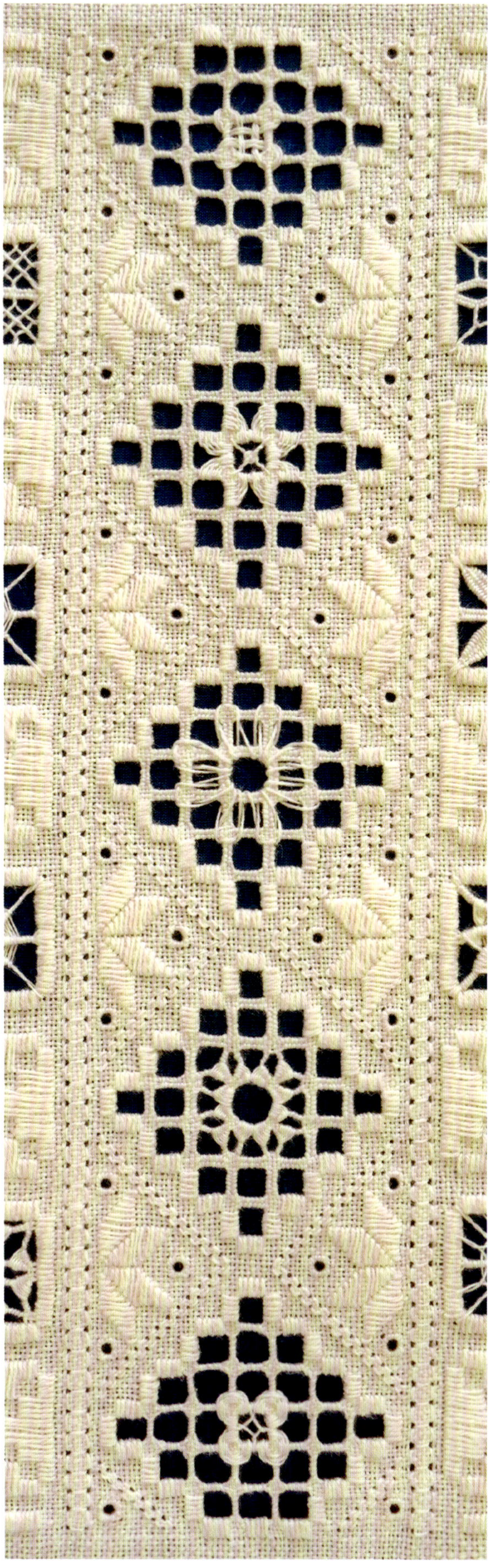

introduction

Hardanger filling stitches are some of the main elements that create the lacy effect of Hardanger embroidery. Along with the more understated and demure pulled thread stitches, it is the cutwork that creates drama.

In Hardanger embroidery, cutwork areas are edged with satin stitch. Fabric threads are cut and withdrawn from the cutwork area, leaving a network of threads. These remaining fabric threads need stabilisation, so are sewn back together with introduced threads. This can be as simple as wrapping or weaving those threads together. More and more elaborate ways of stabilising those threads have been developed so that the stabilisation is no longer purely utilitarian, but is now also decorative. It is these stabilisation stitches which fill the cutwork areas – hence *filling stitches* – both purely functional and highly decorative, that are the focus of this book.

Hardanger embroidery comes from the Hardangerfjord region of Norway, and most likely developed out of the Italian needlelace, reticella. The embroidery is likely an attempt by women in the region to create their own version of reticella, which in time became its own distinctive style.

While reticella had quite elaborate needleweaving, early pieces of Hardanger embroidery generally had relatively simple cutwork fillings. The filling stitches used in that period included woven diagonals, knotted picots, twisted crosses and Xs, and dove's eyes.

As time has gone on, and as Hardanger embroidery spread to other parts of the world, newer filling stitches have been created and added to the tradition. At times, people also work very elaborate fillings, in the style of reticella, in Hardanger embroidery.

This book seeks to teach and explain as many Hardanger filling stitches as possible, from the very simple, single hole fillings, through to the highly ornamental, even reticella in style, multiple hole fillings. It does not, however, teach all Hardanger stitches; rather it teaches just the basics which either can or need to be worked with filling stitches.

historical examples

In historical Hardanger embroidery, the palette of filling stitches was far more limited than what we have available to us today, and some that were used in times past have dropped out of regular usage.

Hardanger embroidery was traditionally worked on parts of the bunad (folk dress) of the Hardangerfjord region. It was often found on the collar, cuffs and front

Traditional Hardanger shirt featuring cutwork of woven bars with knotted picots.

Decorative band worn on a traditional pleated headdress from the Hardanger region of Norway. The needleweaving is knotted picots and woven bars.

The cuff of a traditional Hardanger shirt with woven bars, woven diagonals, dove's eyes and knotted picots.

Left: Hardanger bride with two friends in traditional clothing. Right: detail of the aprons shown left.

yoke of the shirts, on the bands around the pleated headdresses, and on the aprons. The shirt and headdress bands were relatively narrow and therefore usually only had simple filling stitches such as knotted picots. Usually, the more elaborate filling stitches were found on the wider bands of the aprons.

The photo, left, shows a bride and two of her friends. While the two friends have Hardanger embroidery on their shirts, and are likely to have it on the bands around their headdresses, the filling stitches used there are usually quite plain, so it is the aprons we will concentrate on and identify what is possible.

In the photo right, we can see the apron bands in more detail. The apron on the left has plain woven bars, knotted picots, woven diagonals, wrapped bars and a more filigree stitch which is possibly twisted cross. The middle apron has plain

woven bars, woven diagonals with knotted picots, wrapped bars and dove's eyes. It is harder to identify the stitches on the apron on the right, but as far as I can see, it has plain woven bars, twisted crosses, buttonholed circles, dove's eyes, dove's eyes with crosses, woven diagonals, and possibly some type of spider's webs. The cutwork shapes they are worked in include diamonds, triangles, Xs, crosses and squares.

Below, far left: Women in traditional clothing from Kvam, Vestland (previously Hordaland) county, Norway.
Below: detail of the aprons, far left.

The photo below left is of a group of women wearing traditional clothing from the Kvam area, which is on the northern side the Hardangerfjord. The photo below shows the apron bands enlarged, so that we can somewhat see more of the detail.

While it is difficult to see clearly, it appears that the fillings are not particularly elaborate on these aprons. I suspect that there are plain woven bars, knotted picots, dove's eyes, and twisted crosses. In this case, it is the cutwork shapes they are worked in that create the major elements of the design. A number of cutwork shapes are

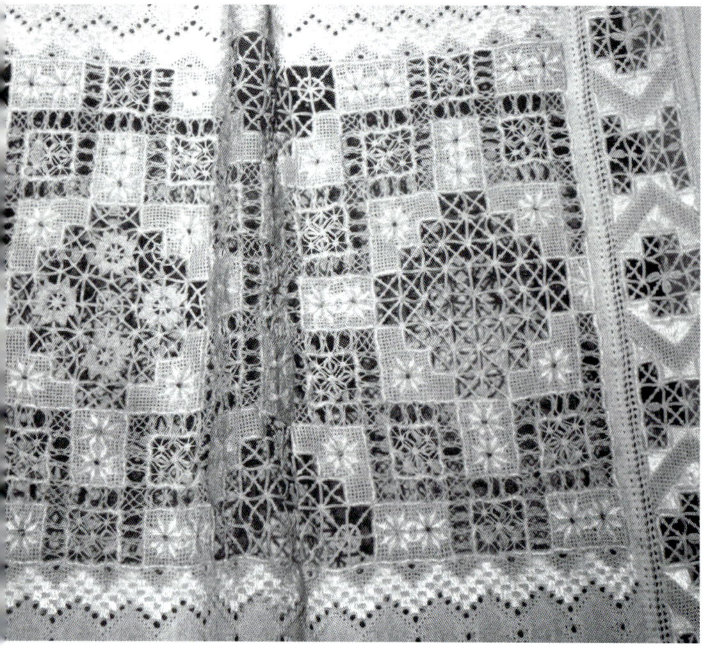

Above and left: Apron made for the 1900 Paris World Fair by Brita Skåltveit.

used. What looks like an eight-pointed star is known as an eight-petalled rose, or *åttebladrose*, in Norway. This shape is used in both positive and negative. There are also triangles, diamonds, Xs, squares, and zig-zags.

The apron above and above right was made for the 1900 Paris World Fair by Brita Skåltveit, representing Norway. It has incredibly elaborate fillings, which are clearly linked to reticella lace. This apron should not be taken as being wholly representative of the style. It was worked as a 'wow' piece, not necessarily as typical. The apron should be seen as an outlier, but does show us what can be done with Hardanger fillings.

contemporary examples

Contemporary examples of filling stitches range from very simple to very elaborate. In Norway, Hardanger remains quite traditional, but outside of Norway stitchers continue to push the boundaries to devise new filling stitches. Often these are a combination of existing stitches into larger conglomerate stitches, or appropriations of stitches and motifs from reticella.

One particularly notable example of a contemporary application of filling stitches is the lacy edge. This is not a traditional edge but has become a very important part of contemporary Hardanger embroidery that many stitchers aspire to be able to stitch.

Another contemporary filling stitch that many aspire to stitch is the looped picot. Traditionally picots were knots, but this picot has a lacy open loop.

creating new stitches

Some of the stitches in this book are very old, and some are very new. All stitches had to be devised somehow. Sometimes new stitches come about by accident: someone is trying to make a stitch, gets it wrong and comes up with something new. Sometimes someone sets out to create something new by experimentation. Other new stitches come about because people wonder, "What would happen if I put such and such a stitch with another stitch?" And then they try it to find out.

There are an infinite number of possible filling stitches. So feel free to experiment with combining stitches to create something new. It may not be completely new – someone else may have done it before you – but it shouldn't stop you from experimenting, trying things and generally being creative!

Hardanger embroidery featuring the lacy edge, with dove's eye and looped picot filling stitches.

Foundations for fillings

The foundations for filling stitches are incredibly important. Without them, there is nowhere to work the filling stitches. Satin stitch bounds the edges of cutwork areas. It needs to be worked correctly so that the fabric threads can be successfully cut and withdrawn from the cutwork areas.

All stitching other than filling stitches should also be worked before any threads are cut. This ensures that everything is in the right place and successfully stitched, before cutting, which is often seen as the point of no return.

before you begin

Traditionally, white high count linen fabric and white linen thread were used for Hardanger embroidery.

fabric

Evenweave fabric is any fabric that has the same number of threads over the same distance for both the warp (up and down the length of the fabric) and weft (left and right across the fabric, from selvedge to selvedge). Any evenweave fabric is suitable for Hardanger and can be any fibre – whether linen, cotton, viscose blend, etc – as long as it is evenweave. You do not have to use so-called 'Hardanger' fabric for Hardanger.

'Evenweave' does not refer to the uniformity of fabric threads or whether there are slubs in the fabric.

how to check fabric count

Fabric thread count is most often measured across an inch of fabric. If your ruler or measuring tape doesn't show inches, 2.5 cm is approximately equal to 1 inch.

To determine the thread count of a fabric:

1 Insert a pin anywhere in the fabric.

2 Measure 1 inch (2.5 cm) from the pin, in line with the threads of the fabric. At the end of the 1 inch (2.5 cm), insert another pin. Do this for both the warp and the weft, from the original pin.

3 Count the threads between the first and second pins. If there are 38 threads, then it has a thread count of 38. If there are 25 threads, the fabric is 25 count, sometimes expressed as 25 threads per inch.

4 Count the threads between the first pin and third pins to find the thread count for the fabric's other dimension.

Matching numbers mean the fabric is evenweave. A square design worked on such fabric will be square. If the numbers differ only by one or two, it is nearly evenweave. A square design on such fabric will be nearly square. If the numbers are very different, it is not evenweave. A square design on such fabric will not be square. Over longer distances, any disparity between the two lengths is magnified.

thread

Traditionally, linen thread was used for Hardanger. These days many people use pearl cotton, which is a mercerised, single strand thread. Some use stranded floss as it comes in more colours than pearl cotton. Specialty threads such as overdyed or sparkly threads can also be used.

Two weights of thread are used for Hardanger embroidery. The heavier weight is used for satin stitching and buttonhole stitching. Everything else – pulled thread stitches, surface stitches, and filling stitches – is worked in the lighter weight. In contemporary work, some stitchers use a third, even lighter weight for the filling stitches, to give an even more pronounced lacy effect.

a note on colour

When working any sort of openwork, including filling stitches, you want the stitches to dazzle, rather than the fabric or thread distracting you from them. Use caution in employing colour or specialty threads for anything other than the plainest filling stitches, otherwise they will compete for attention. Openwork is best worked in the same or a very similar colour as the fabric so that you see the stitches, rather than the colour.

needles

Hardanger is a counted thread embroidery: the stitches are positioned by counting the fabric threads. They need to sit in the fabric's holes; the needle must not split fabric threads, because then the stitches won't sit in the right place. The best needles to use are those that have a blunt tip – tapestry needles – as these will not easily split fabric threads, but instead pass between them.

If you can find a tapestry needle that works well for both your heavier weight thread and your lighter weight thread, you can use the one size of needle. Otherwise you will want one for each weight of thread.

choosing the correct needle size

A threaded needle has thread coming out both sides of the eye. This means the thickest thread that goes through the fabric is double thickness thread.

A needle's purpose is to make a hole large enough for the thread to easily pass through the fabric. A needle that is too thin wears the thread each time it goes through the fabric, quickly creating a fluffy, worn looking thread.

Use a needle where the shaft is the same thickness as the doubled thread. The easiest way to do this is to try your thread in different needles and see which matches the doubled thickness best.

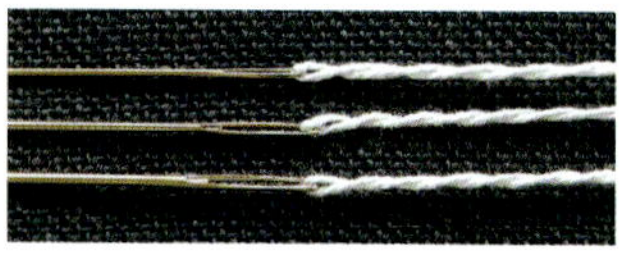

Needle too small (top). The middle or lower needle would be suitable for this thread.

Many people choose a needle size that is too small, which wears the thread much more quickly. The correct size needle for the thread will give a superior result.

scissors

Fine, sharp-pointed embroidery scissors are required for accurate cutting of fabric threads. When not sharp enough, they will make a messy, shaggy cut. Poor quality scissors can make your work appear to be lower quality.

Blades that are too thick will not easily pass between the fabric threads to isolate the correct ones to cut.

Looking from the side, scissor blades should be narrow (a ten degree angle from the tip, or less). Looking from the top, the blades should be narrow. The smaller the girth of each blade as you move away from the tip, the less thickness you have to pass between the fabric threads, and the easier it will be to get a good cut.

hoops

Hardanger embroidery is not traditionally worked in a hoop or frame. Many stitchers use them, though, so it is a matter of personal preference.

For this book, I found a hoop helped to provide good tension for cutwork areas. A small hoop is good for single motifs. Use a larger hoop for large areas or move a small one around.

The fabric grain must be square, meaning that warp and weft threads should be perpendicular. Without this, the stitching could be distorted.

top tip using a hoop

For cutwork, it is vital that fabric mounted in a hoop should have squared grain and regular – not taut or loose – tension. Stretched fabric, when released from the hoop, will relax and the diagonal stitches particularly, may be too loose. Relaxed fabric can result in puckering when stitches are pulled too tight.

magnification

Magnification can make needlework easier. There are many types of magnifiers available. Some mount onto spectacles. Others are worn on a cord around the neck and balanced against your chest. Some are freestanding on the table or floor and others are combined with lamps. Use whichever makes you feel most comfortable.

lighting

Good lighting helps to reduce eye strain. Daylight is best, however, many like to stitch at night. Daylight coloured light globes provide light close to daylight. A daylight globe will have a temperature of around 6400 Kelvin, (6400K). Daylight coloured globes can go in a regular lamp.

sewing or stabbing?

This book shows the needle in a sewing or scooping motion (where the needle is parallel to the fabric surface), rather than a stabbing motion (where the needle is perpendicular to the fabric surface). Beginners to counted thread work often do better with a sewing/scooping motion than with a stabbing motion.

'Stabbing' style, usually worked in a hoop, means you have to think about where to bring the needle out every single time. You can easily make the mistake of bringing the needle out directly next to where you just inserted it while working satin stitch, because if it looks okay on the front, it must be okay, right?

When 'sewing', keeping the same needle angle and motion as for the rest of, say, a kloster, means you're less likely to make stitch direction reversal errors, because inserting the needle incorrectly is going to feel wrong.

Once the process and mechanics of working a stitch have been mastered and understood, more experienced stitchers could change to using a stabbing motion, as it can provide better control when stitching.

left-handed or right-handed?

Both left- and right-handed stitch instructions are provided in this book. Left-handed are red, and right-handed are blue. Instructions for suitable for both are purple. A tab at the top outer edge of each page indicates the handedness, by colour and an L, R or an L&R.

It is also noted whether a stitch is traditional or contemporary. When there are variations on the same page, this classification applies to the main stitch only.

stitching order

Cutwork should always be worked last. Everything else should be correctly positioned before any threads are cut, otherwise you may cut in the wrong place. When cutting and withdrawing threads, the fabric is destabilised and pulled thread stitches near cut threads can cause threads to pull too far and even come out.

To minimise the chance of errors, first work satin stitch including klosters. Work pulled thread stitches, and then any surface stitchery. Only when all elements are positioned correctly should you cut fabric threads and work fillings.

Many people find it helpful to start at or near the centre of a design and work outwards.

reading a chart

Hardanger embroidery is worked from a chart or pattern which shows motifs and stitches, and their position. Each grid line equates to a fabric thread. There is no universal style of notation of motifs, so each filling stitch in this book has a diagram of how it *may* look on a chart.

This chart shows the fabric thread grid. The thick black lines are the thicker thread and the lines indicate thinner thread. The greyed areas are where threads have been removed. The bars shown are woven.

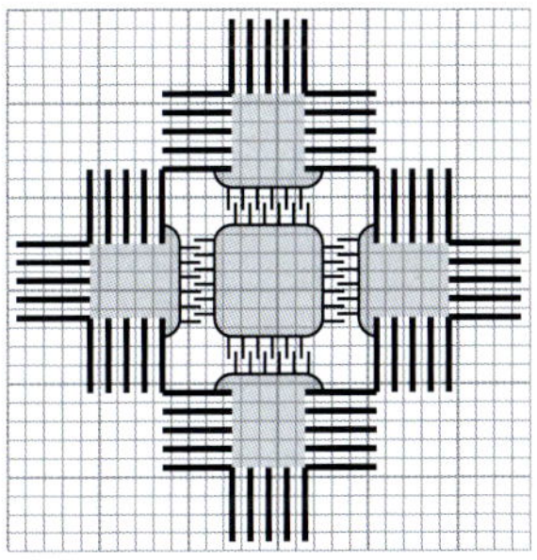

starting new threads

away waste knot

A waste knot is used to secure a thread in an area where there is no previous stitching. This method works best when the fabric is mounted in a hoop.

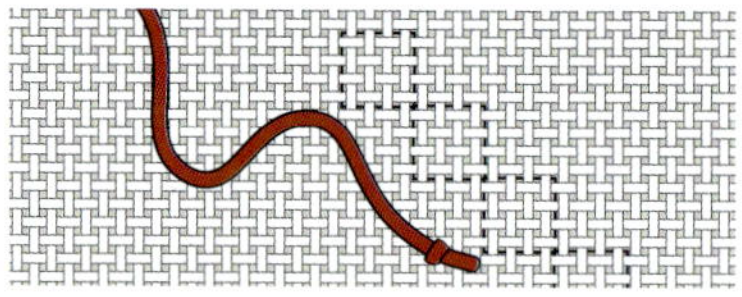

1 Work out where the new stitching needs to begin and where the stitching line will continue. Tie a knot in the end of the thread, large enough not to slip between the fabric threads.

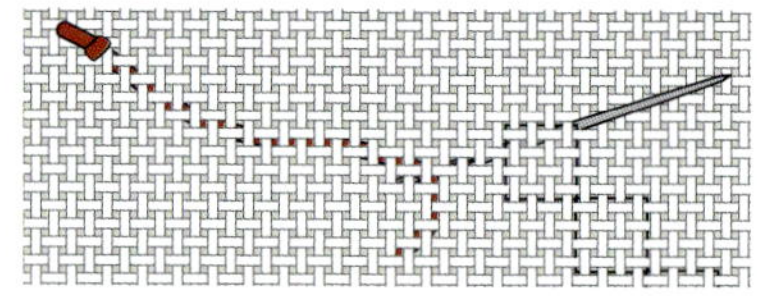

2 From the front, insert the needle about 8 cm (3 in) from the starting point. Bring it out at the starting point.
❶ *The knot sits on the front. Ensure the thread is not under the stitching path.*

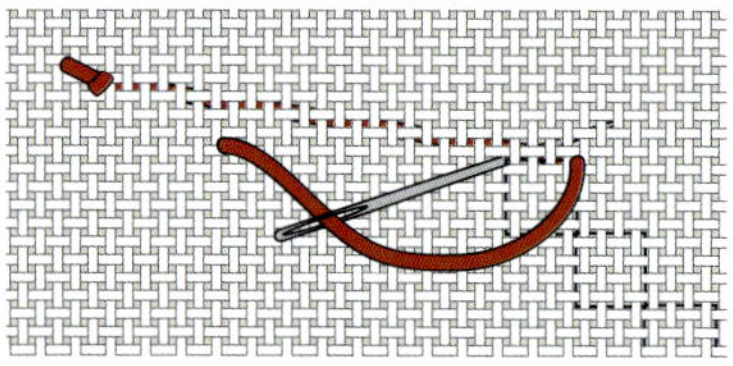

3 Pull the needle and thread through. Begin stitching.

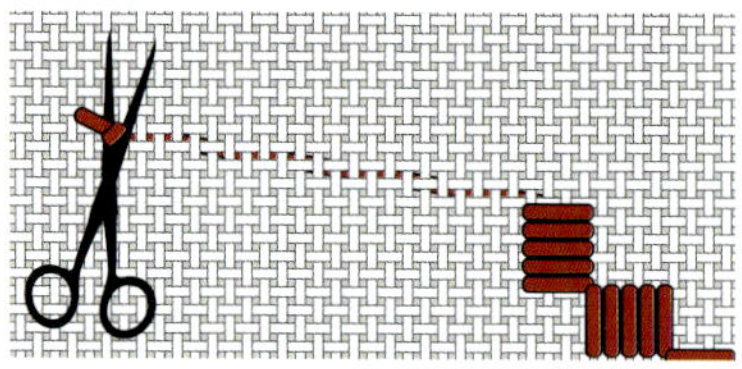

4 When a good amount of stitching has been completed, cut off the knot and ease the end through to the back.

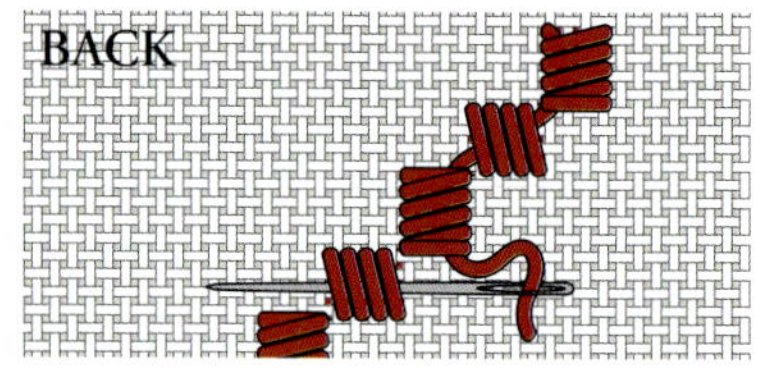

5 On the back, thread the end into the needle and run it under the stitches for about 4 cm (1¾ in) to secure it. Keep stitching as before.

covered waste knot

This method of starting with a waste knot works well when stitching long straight lines, in a hoop.

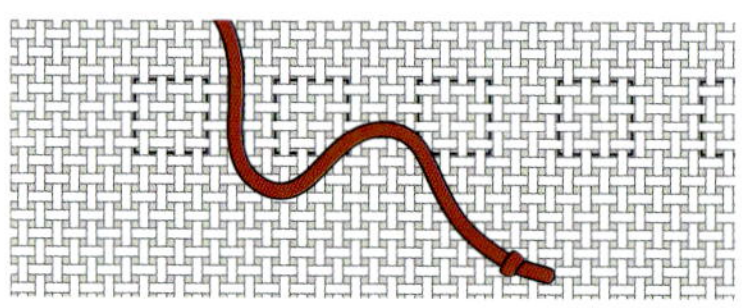

1 Work out where the new stitching needs to begin and where the stitching line will continue. Tie a knot in the end of the thread, large enough not to slip through the fabric holes.

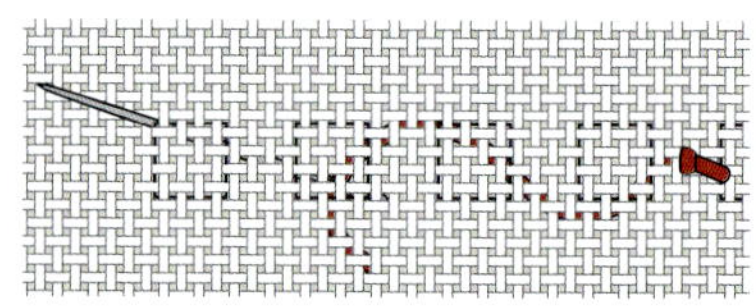

2 On the front, insert the needle about 5 cm (2 in) away from the starting point, so the thread lies under the stitching path. Bring it out at the starting point.
❶ *The knot sits on the front of the fabric.*

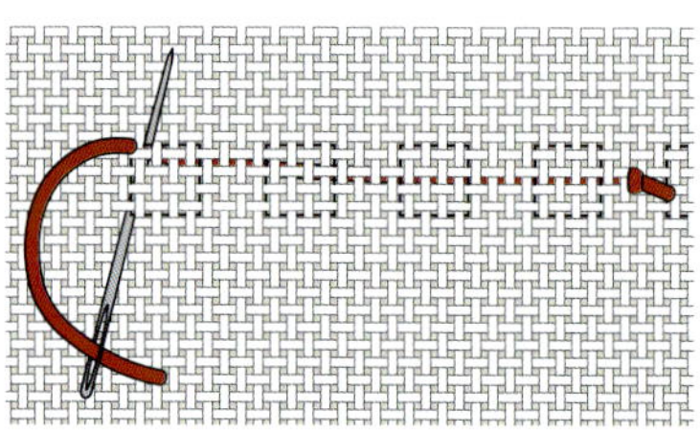

3 Begin stitching, making sure that the stitching covers the waste knot thread on the back.

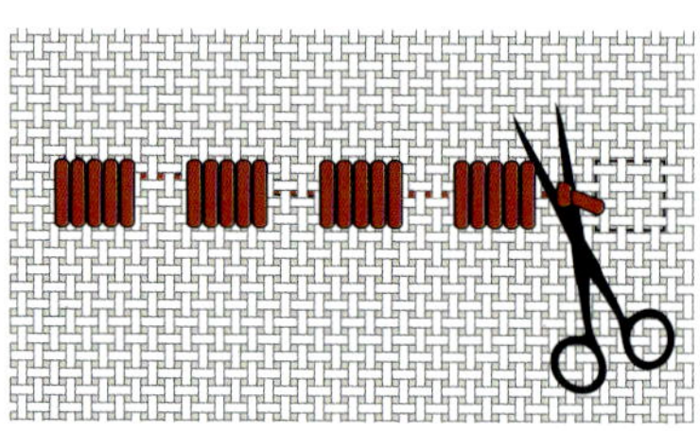

4 When the stitching passes the waste knot, carefully cut off the knot. Ease the thread end through to the back of the fabric.

❶ *Nothing further is needed to finish the thread, as it has already been secured. Continue stitching with the main thread. The back is shown here.*

pin stitch

This method of starting can be used where there is no stitching nearby. It is secure, despite not looking like it would be!

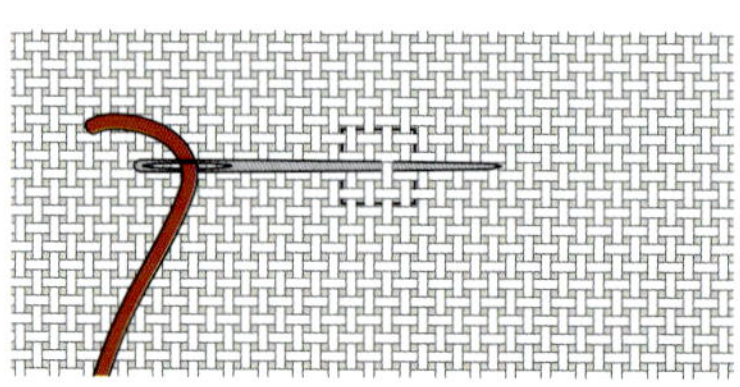

1 Underneath where the first stitches will be, insert the needle and bring it out one thread to the right.

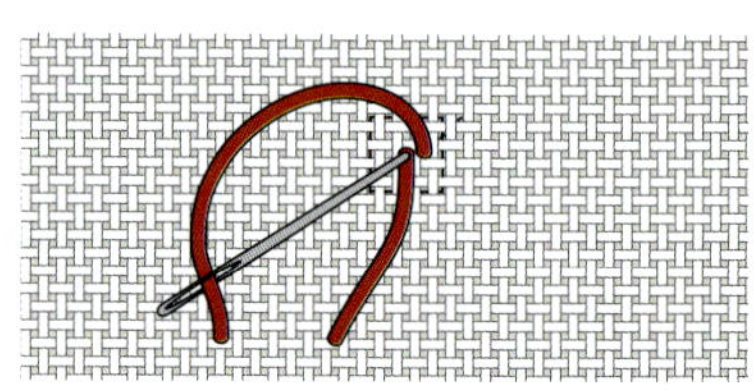

2 Pull the needle through, and leave a tail hanging. Insert the needle back in the same hole, piercing the tail.

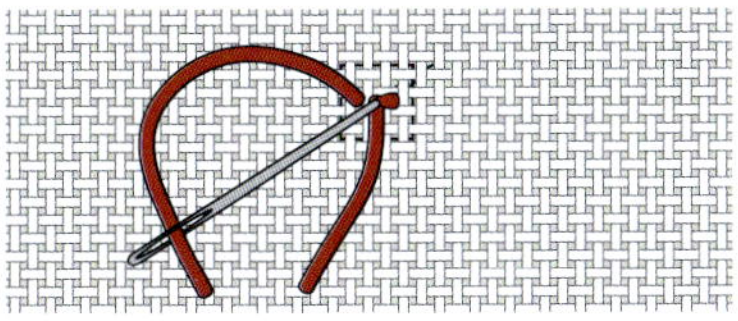

3 Bring the needle out one thread to the left. Insert it in the same centre hole, piercing the tail again.

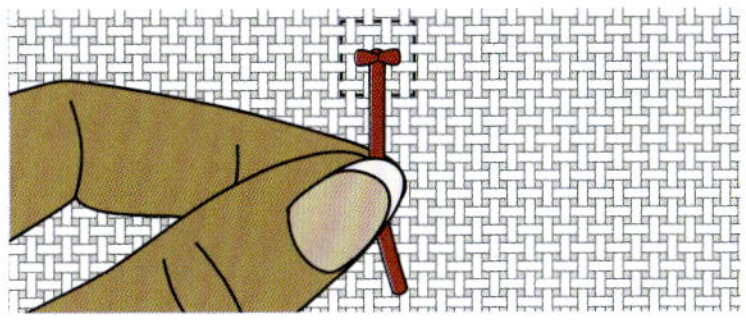

4 Pull the tail to check that everything is locked into place. If it isn't, ensure the stitches pierce the tail.

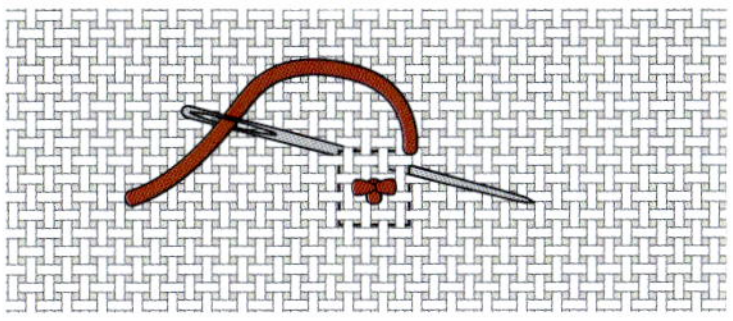

5 Trim the tail very close to the stitches, then stitch as required, over the top.

running the thread under the back

This method is useful when there is existing stitching adjacent.

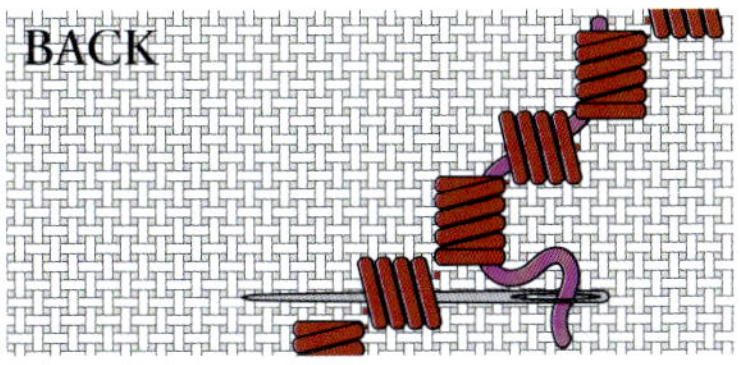

1 On the back, about 5 cm (2 in) away from starting point, take the new thread (shown in purple) under the back of about half the distance.

❶ *If the old thread was finished under the same stitching, hold its end as you sew in the new one to ensure the new one does not unthread it.*

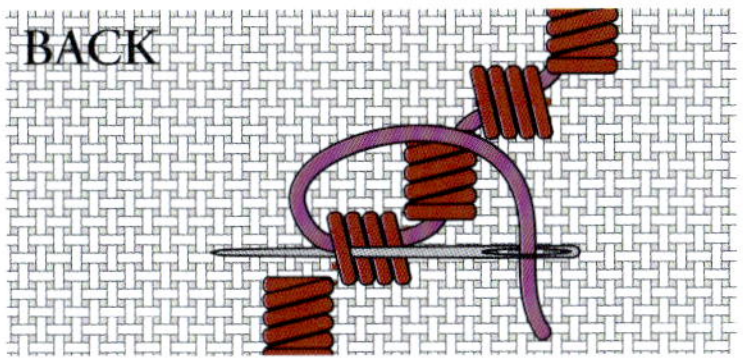

2 Take a backstitch under the last stitch of the kloster you have just gone under.

❶ *When working pulled thread stitches, make sure the new thread is well secured with a number of backstitches. Otherwise it will come out as soon as you put any tension on the thread.*

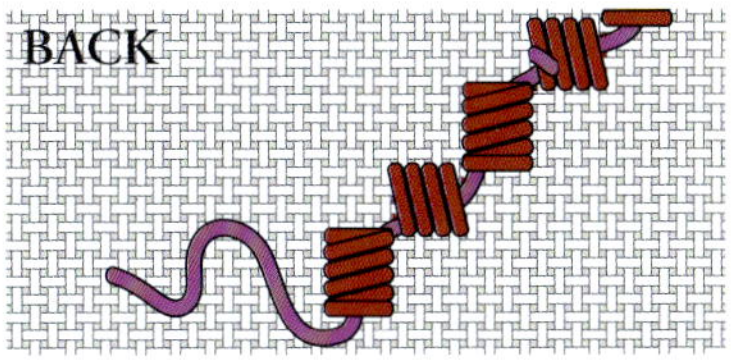

3 Continue taking the needle under the back of the stitches, bringing it out where the stitching will need to recommence.

over the tail

In this method, for more advanced stitchers, you hold the tail in place on the back, while stitching over it.

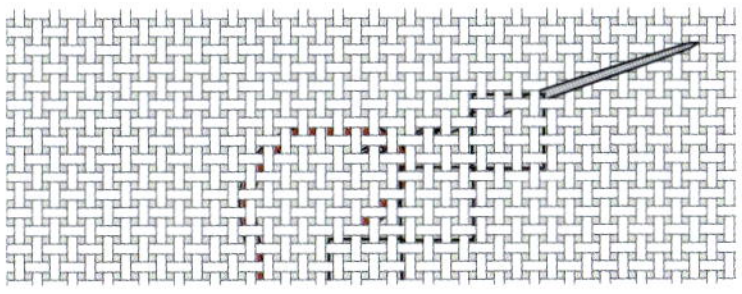

1 Bring the needle out where you need to start stitching.

❶ *No knot is required.*

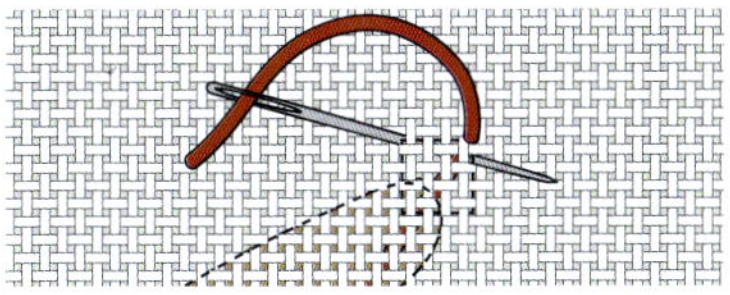

2 On the back, hold a thread tail of about 4 cm (1⅝ in) under the stitching path.

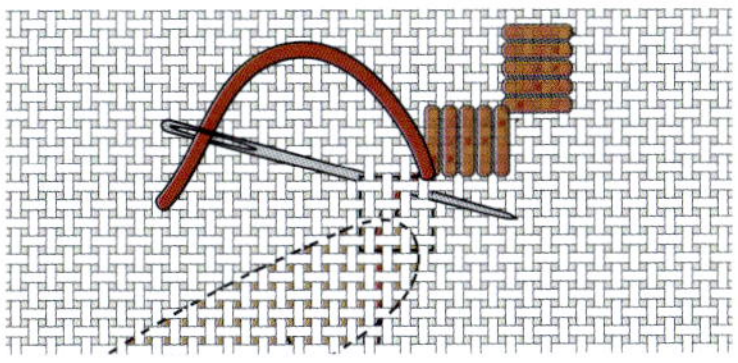

3 Stitch, continuing to hold the tail in place, and ensuring that it is covered by the stitching on the back.

❶ *Periodically check that it is being covered successfully.*

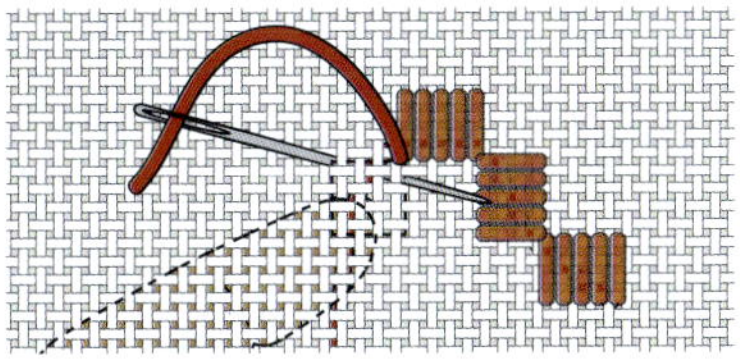

❶ *When you need to change directions, make sure you move the thread tail to underneath where the stitching will lie.*

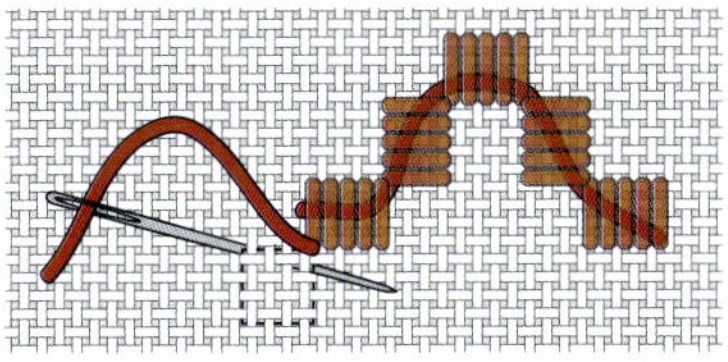

4 Stitch over about five kloster blocks' worth of tail, then trim any excess. Continue stitching.

finishing threads

To finish threads, run them under the back of the stitching, similar to starting, except you do not need any back stitches. Do not run the thread back and forth as this will be messy and create unnecessary lumps.

For satin stitch, I like to go under the equivalent of at least five klosters. For tighter, pulled thread stitches such as cable stitch, I go under 2–4 cm (1–2 inches) worth of stitches.

I have successfully laundered pieces that have been finished in these ways. If in doubt, just go a bit further than you otherwise might!

starting new threads

away waste knot

A waste knot is used to secure a thread in an area where there is no previous stitching. This method works best when the fabric is mounted in a hoop.

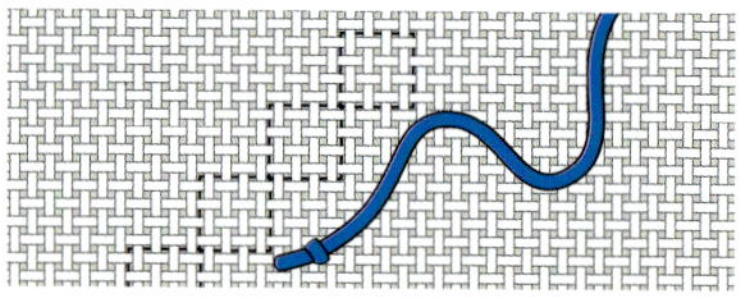

1 Work out where the new stitching needs to begin and where the stitching line will continue. Tie a knot in the end of the thread, large enough not to slip between the fabric threads.

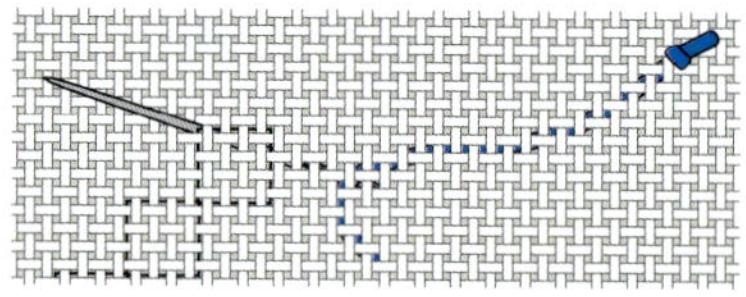

2 From the front, insert the needle about 8 cm (3 in) from the starting point. Bring it out at the starting point.
! *The knot sits on the front. Ensure the thread is not under the stitching path.*

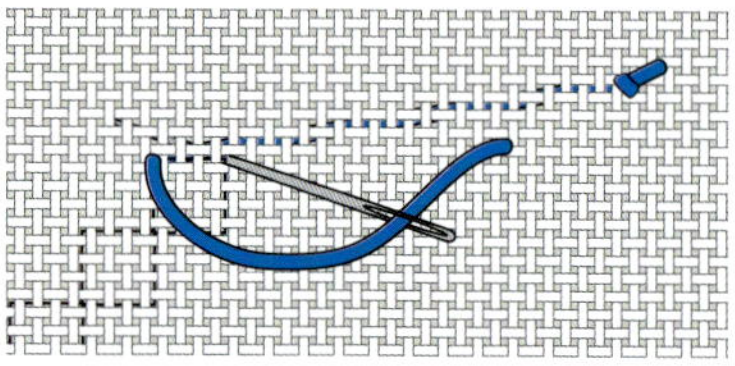

3 Pull the needle and thread through. Begin stitching.

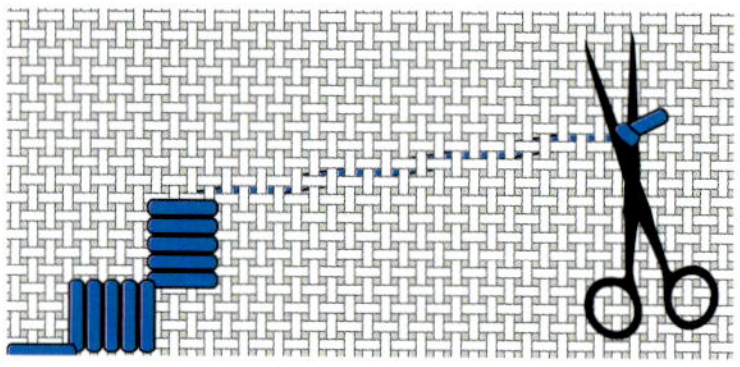

4 When a good amount of stitching has been completed, cut off the knot and ease the end through to the back.

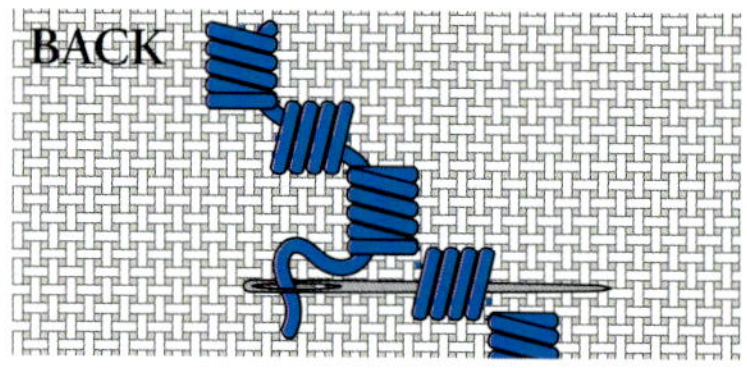

5 On the back, thread the end into the needle and run it under the stitches for about 4 cm ($1\frac{3}{4}$ in) to secure it. Keep stitching as before.

covered waste knot

This method of starting with a waste knot works well when stitching long straight lines, in a hoop.

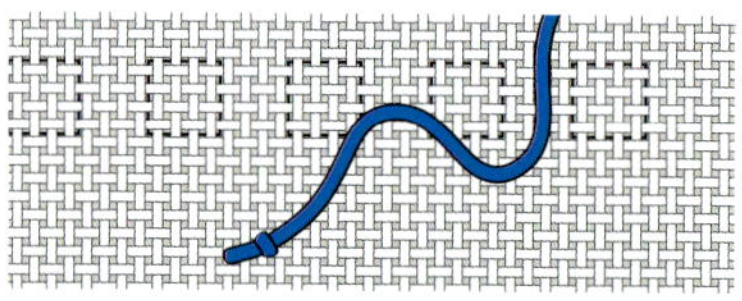

1 Work out where the new stitching needs to begin and where the stitching line will continue. Tie a knot in the end of the thread, large enough not to slip through the fabric holes.

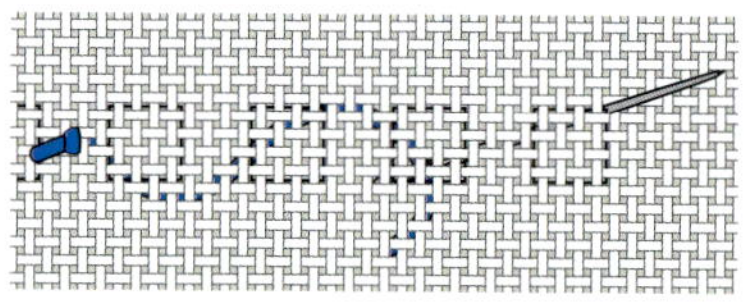

2 On the front, insert the needle about 5 cm (2 in) away from the starting point, so that the thread lies under the stitching path. Bring it out at the starting point.
! *The knot sits on the front of the fabric.*

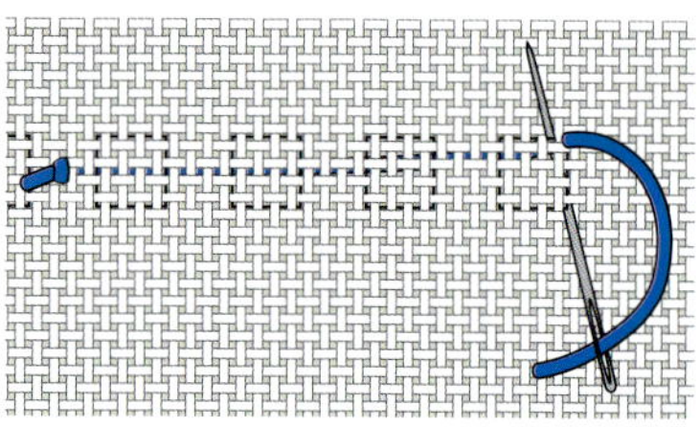

3 Begin stitching, making sure that the stitching covers the waste knot thread on the back.

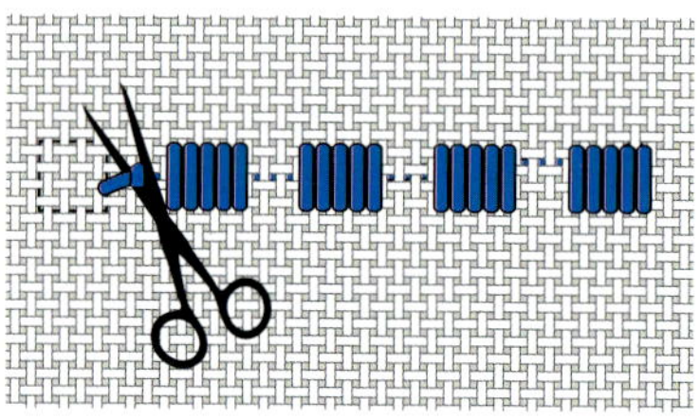

4 When the stitching passes the waste knot, carefully cut off the knot. Ease the thread end through to the back of the fabric.

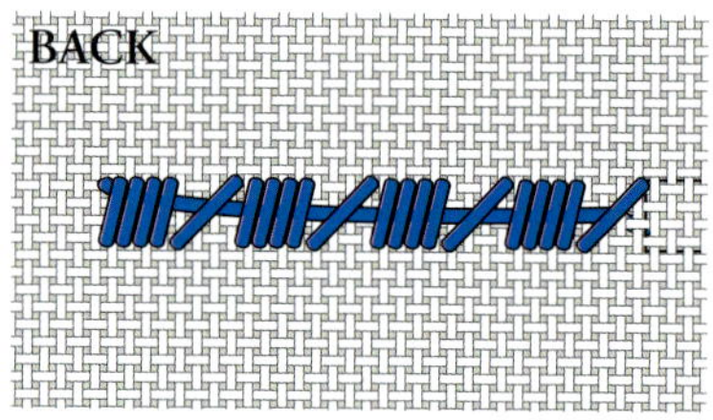

! *Nothing further is needed to finish the thread, as it has already been secured. Continue stitching with the main thread. The back is shown here.*

pin stitch

This method of starting can be used where there is no stitching nearby. It is secure, despite not looking like it would be!

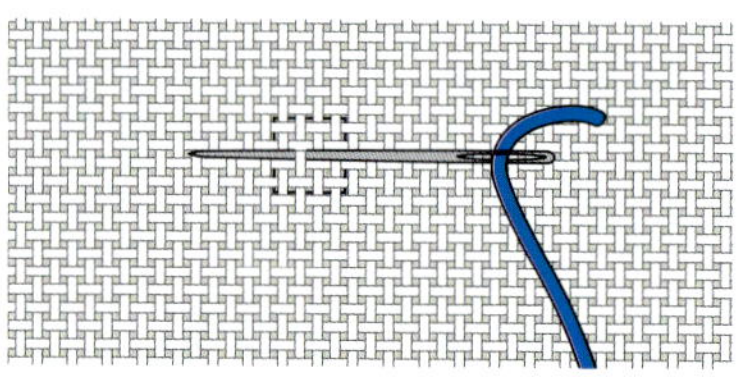

1 Underneath where the first stitches will be, insert the needle and bring it out one thread to the left.

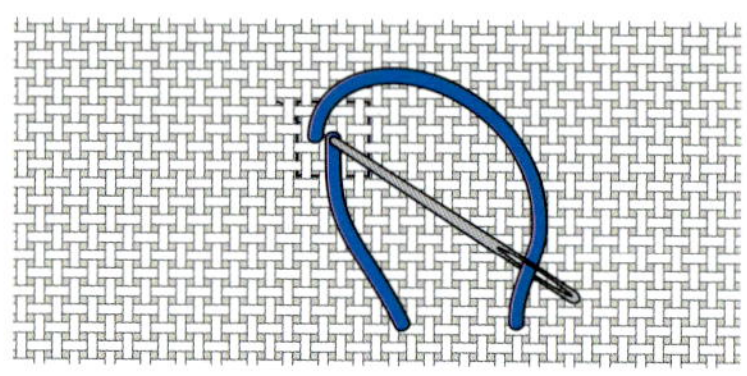

2 Pull the needle through, and leave a tail hanging. Insert the needle back in the same hole, piercing the tail.

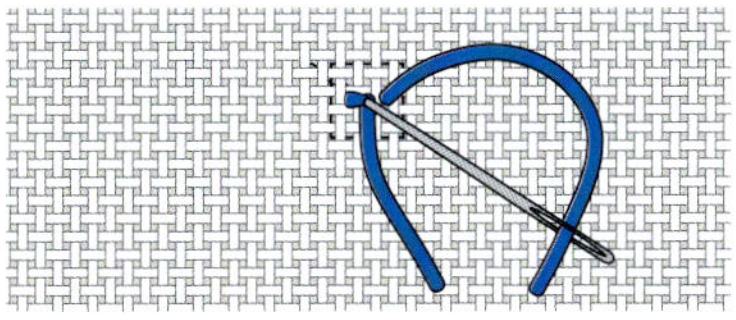

3 Bring the needle out one thread to the right. Insert it in the same centre hole, piercing the tail again.

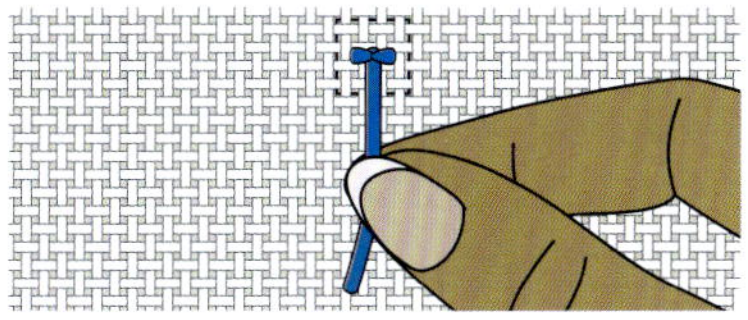

4 Pull the tail to check that everything is locked into place. If it isn't, ensure the stitches pierce the tail.

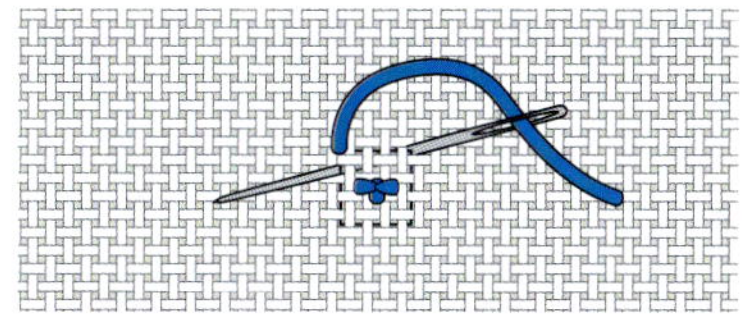

5 Trim the tail very close to the stitches, then stitch as required, over the top.

running the thread under the back

This method is useful when there is existing stitching adjacent.

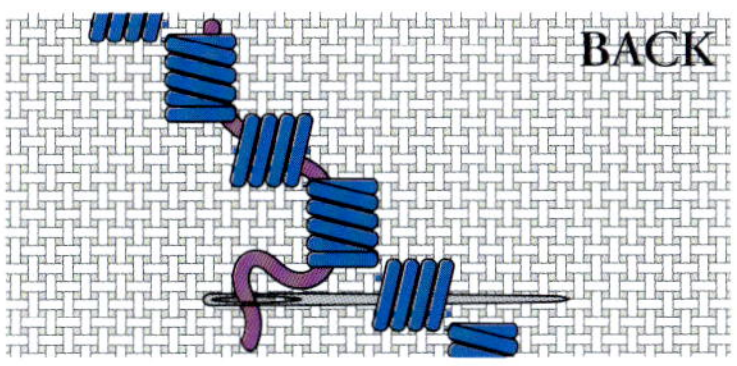

1 On the back, about 5 cm (2 in) away from the starting point, take the new thread (shown in purple) under the back of about half the distance.

❶ *If the old thread was finished under the same stitching, hold its end as you sew in the new one to ensure the new one does not unthread it.*

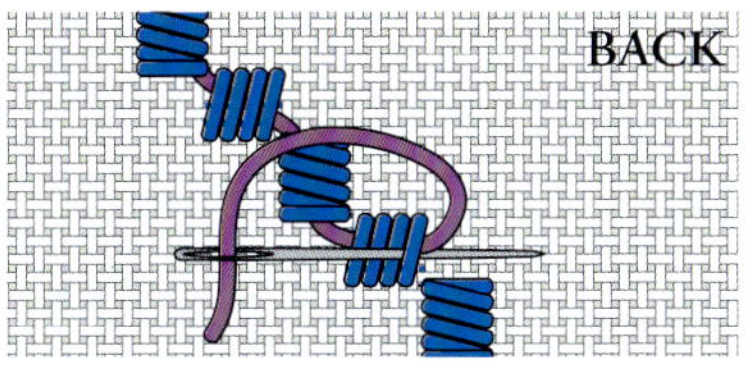

2 Take a small backstitch under the last stitch of the kloster you have just gone under.

❶ *When working pulled thread stitches, make sure the new thread is well secured with a number of backstitches. Otherwise it will come out as soon as you put any tension on the thread.*

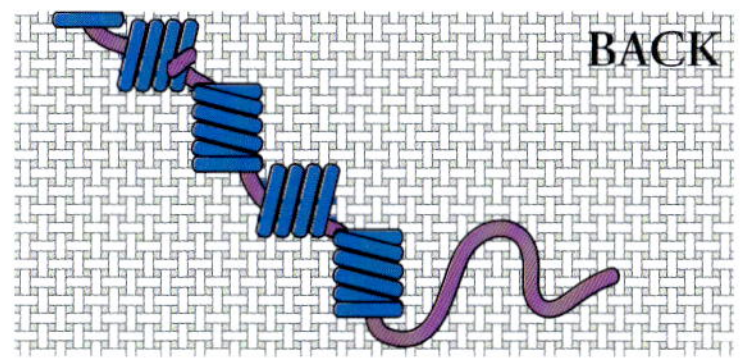

3 Continue taking the needle under the back of the stitches, bringing it out where the stitching will need to recommence.

over the tail

In this method, for more advanced stitchers, you hold the tail in place on the back, while stitching over it.

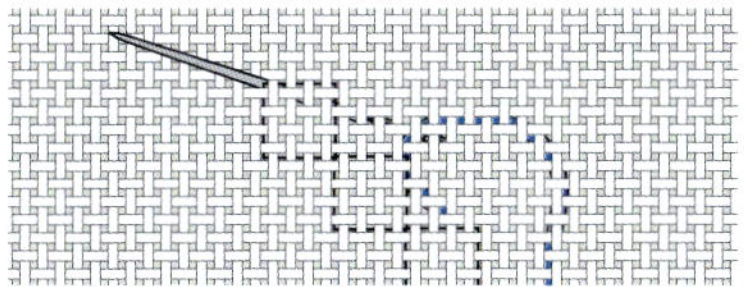

1 Bring the needle out where you need to start stitching.

❶ *No knot is required.*

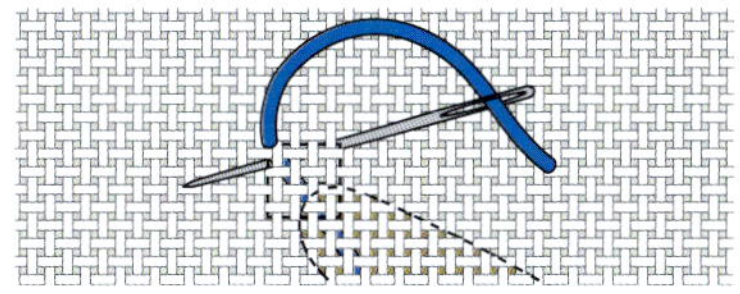

2 On the back, hold a thread tail of about 4 cm ($1\frac{5}{8}$ in) under where the stitching will go.

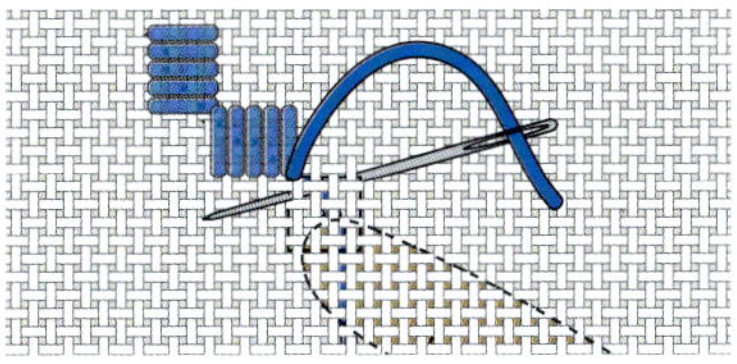

3 Stitch, continuing to hold the tail in place, and ensuring that it is covered by the stitching on the back.

❶ *Periodically check that it is being covered successfully.*

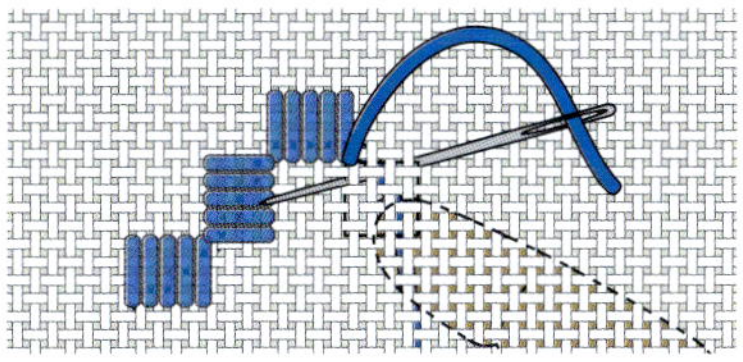

❶ *When you need to change directions, make sure you move the thread tail to underneath where the stitching will lie.*

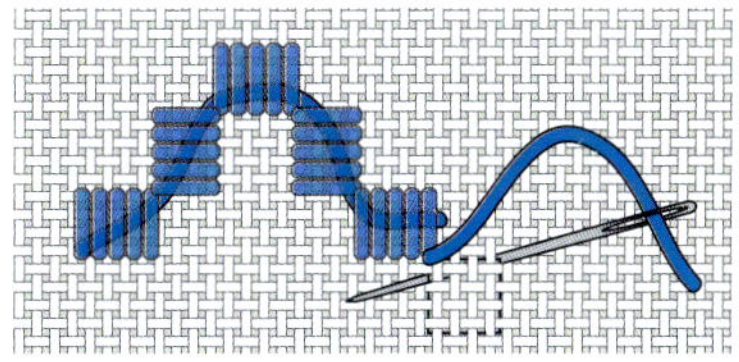

4 Stitch over about five kloster blocks' worth of tail, then trim any excess. Continue stitching.

finishing threads

To finish threads, run them under the back of the stitching, similar to starting, except you do not need any back stitches. Do not run the thread back and forth as this will be messy and create unnecessary lumps.

For satin stitch, I like to go under the equivalent of at least five klosters. For tighter, pulled thread stitches such as cable stitch, I go under 2–4 cm (1–2 inches) worth of stitches.

I have successfully laundered pieces that have been finished in these ways. If in doubt, just go a bit further than you otherwise might!

satin stitch

Satin stitch creates the framework for all Hardanger embroidery, particularly the cutwork, as well as adding decorative elements. It is worked in the heavier weight of thread.

There are many satin stitch motifs used in Hardanger embroidery. The most basic is a block of five parallel stitches that span a width and length of four threads. These blocks are known as klosters or kloster blocks.

Klosters and longer satin stitch blocks can be put together to form cutwork areas in the shapes of diamonds, triangles, squares and zig-zags. We will cover each of these as they are foundational to filling stitches.

klosters in diagonal lines

TRADITIONAL

When working klosters in diagonal lines, the klosters go across the fabric in steps like a staircase, with a rise (or fall) then a flat, then a rise/fall then a flat.

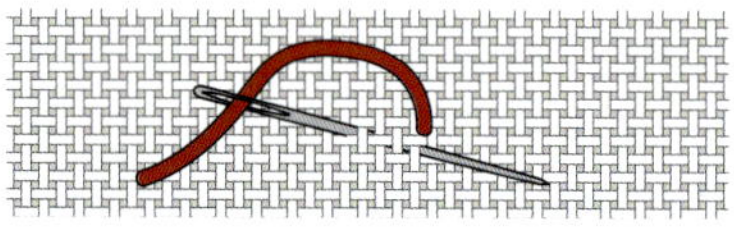

1 Bring the needle out in the starting position. Insert the needle four threads to the left, and bring it out four threads right and one down.

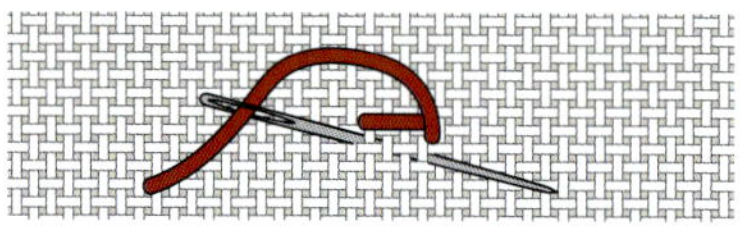

2 Pull the needle through to tighten the stitch so that it lies flat on the fabric. Insert the needle four threads to the left and bring it out four threads right and one down.

! *Don't tighten the stitch so much that the ends pull inward. Don't leave it so loose that the stitch looks slack.*

3 Complete four parallel stitches, all the same length and tension. Continuing down, bring the needle out for the fifth stitch. Insert it four threads to the left, and bring it out in the same hole from which the thread just emerged.

! *Klosters span four fabric threads in each direction, with four under the width and four under the length.*

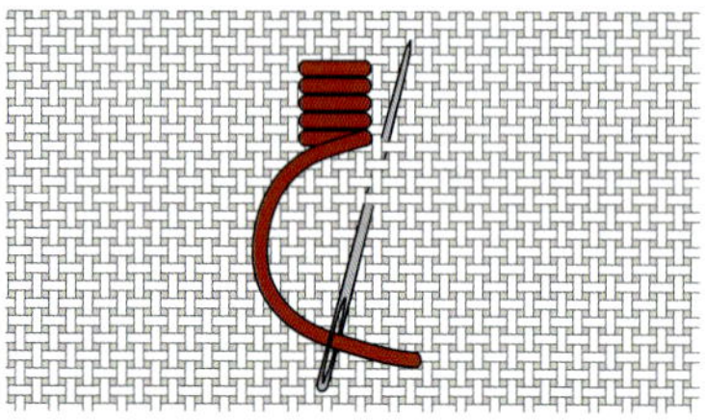

4 Pull the needle through to tighten the stitch. Insert the needle four threads below, and bring it out one right of where it previously emerged.

! *There must be no gap between blocks.*

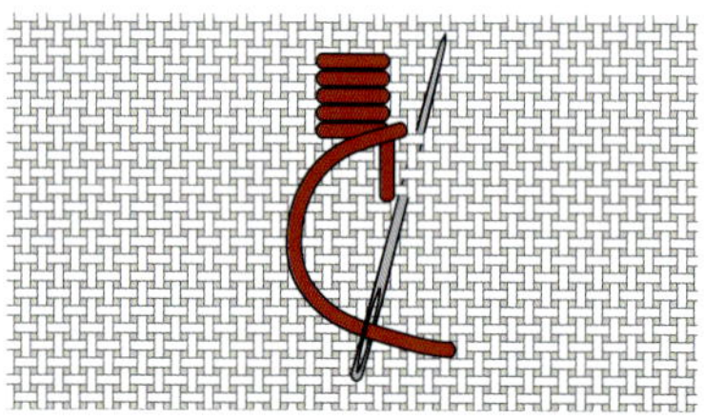

5 Pull the needle through to tighten the stitch so that it lies flat on the fabric. Insert the needle four threads below, and bring it out one thread right of where it previously emerged.

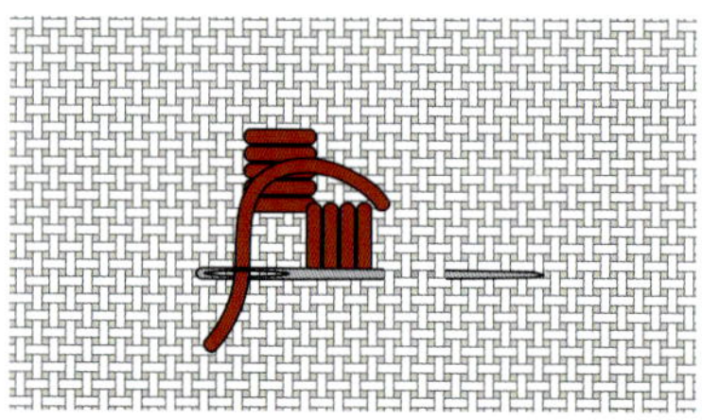

6 Work three more stitches, all the same length and tension. Continuing right, bring the needle out for the next stitch. Insert it four threads below. Bring it out four to the right.

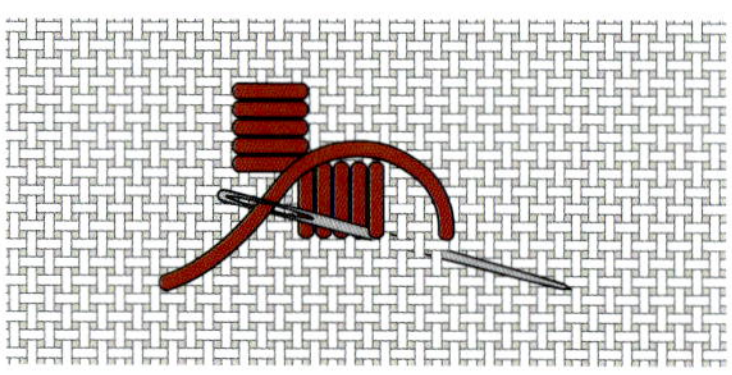

7 Pull the needle through to tighten the stitch. Insert the needle four threads to the left, in the same hole as the bottom of the previous stitch. Bring it out four threads right and one down.

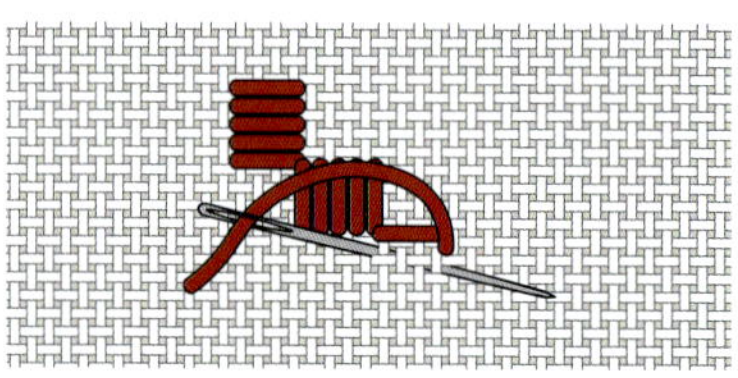

8 Pull the needle through to tighten the stitch. Insert the needle four threads to the left and bring it out four threads right and one down.

! *Blocks must alternate between horizontal and vertical.*

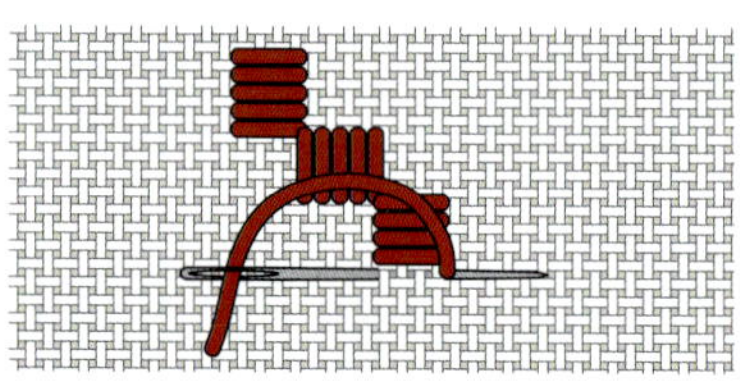

9 Work four parallel stitches, all the same length and tension. Bring the needle out for the fifth stitch. Insert it four threads to the left. Bring it out in the same hole as where the thread just emerged.

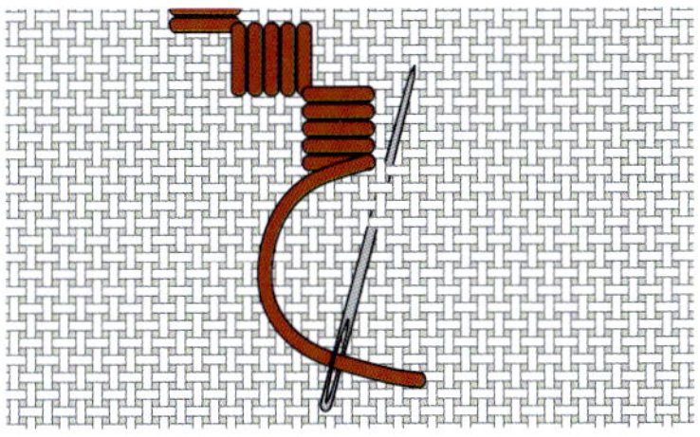

10 Pull the needle through to tighten the stitch. Insert it four threads below. Bring it out one thread right of where it previously emerged.

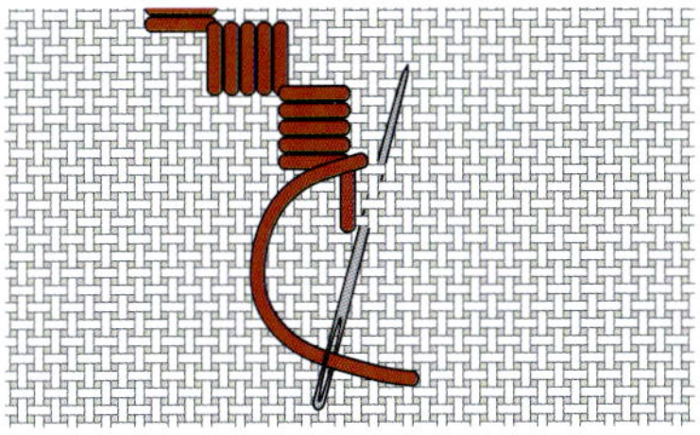

11 Pull the needle through to tighten the stitch. Insert it four threads below. Bring it out one thread right of where it previously emerged.

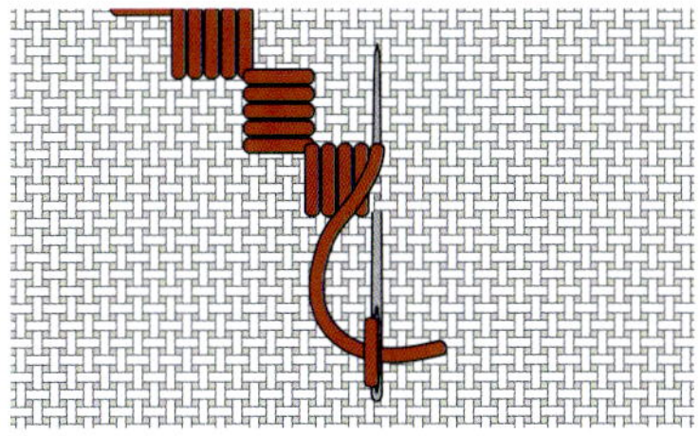

12 Continue similarly. To turn the corner, insert the needle for the last stitch of the block and bring it out in the same hole as it last emerged.

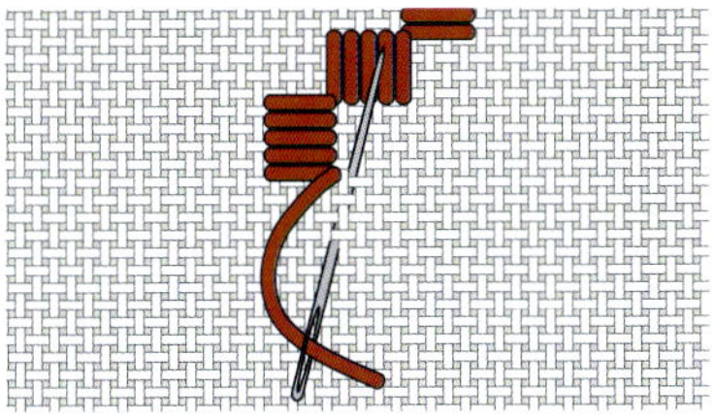

13 Turn the work 90° clockwise. Pull the needle and thread through. Continue stitching as before.

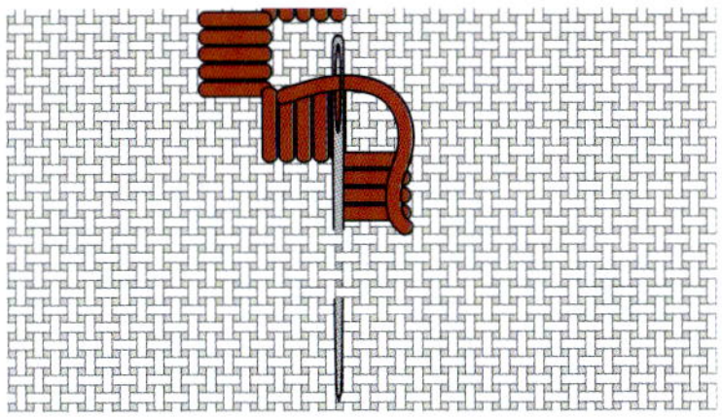

14 To turn the corner the other direction, insert the needle to complete the last stitch of the block and bring it out four threads below.

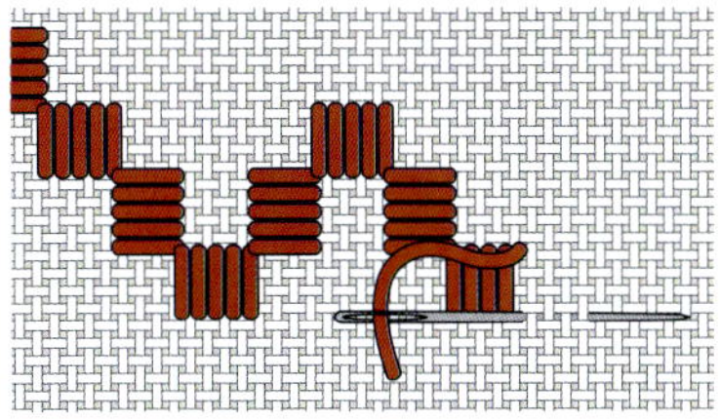

15 Turn the work 90° anticlockwise, and continue working as before to build up a line of stitching.

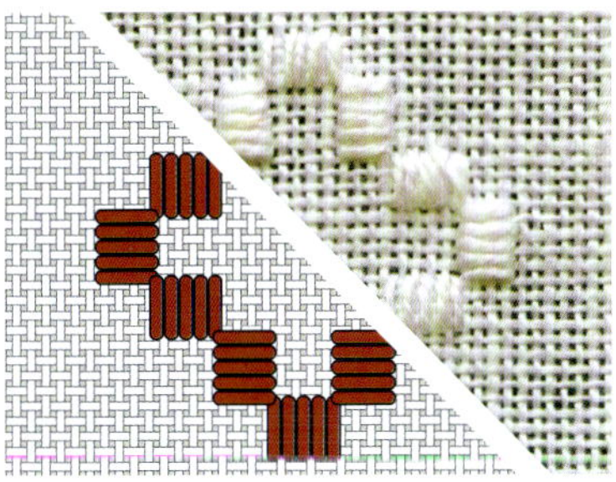

❶ *To complete a circuit, the first and last klosters must share a corner hole. If they don't, there is at least one mistake.*

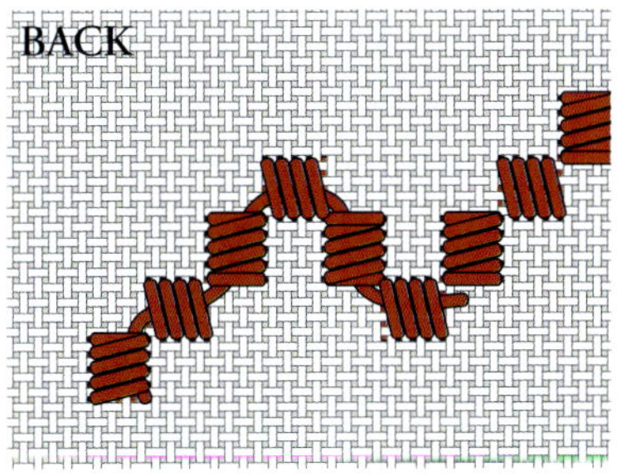

16 To finish, run the thread under the back of about 5 cm (2 in) of stitching. Trim any remaining thread.

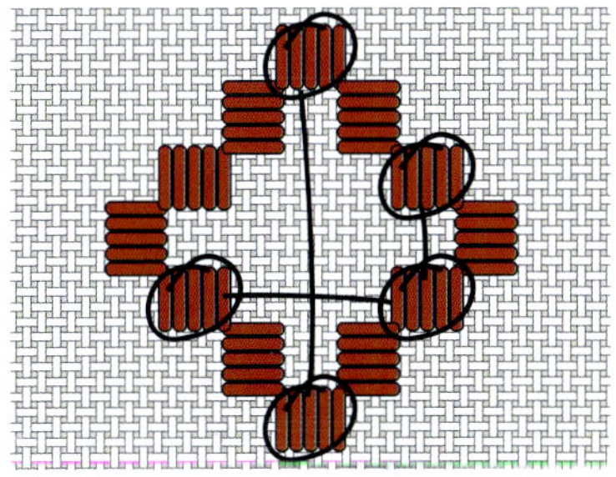

❶ *In cutwork motifs, each kloster should be paired with one in the same orientation on the far side.*

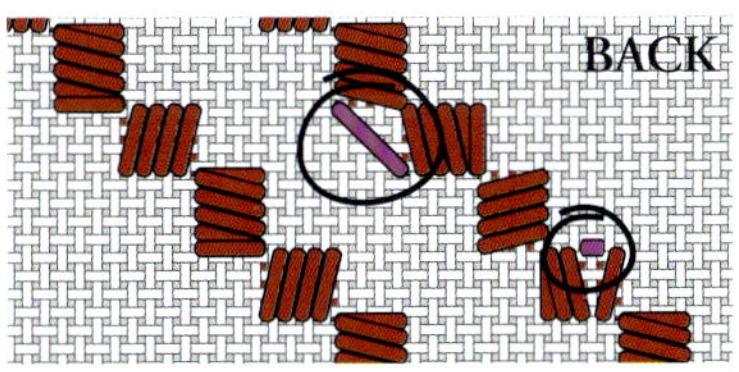

❶ *The back of the work is correct in the left line. The right line has two errors, where the direction has been reversed in error. Such errors can cause the stitching to unravel when the adjacent fabric threads are cut.*

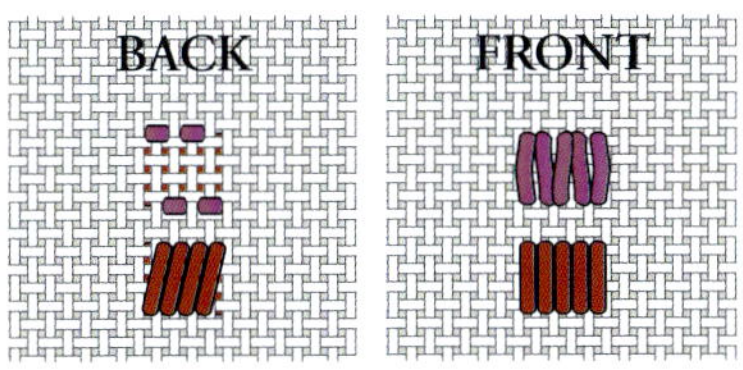

❶ *The stitches must spiral the fabric's threads (lower left). Never bring the needle out next to the hole just entered (upper left) as the stitches will flip up when adjacent fabric threads are cut. The stitches also sit incorrectly (upper right).*

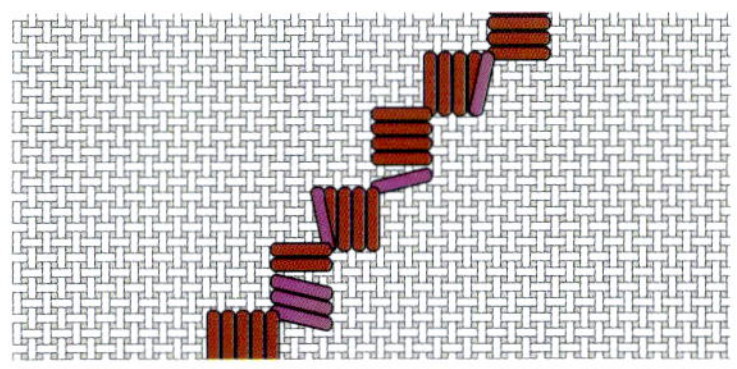

❶ *All stitches should be parallel to the fabric threads on the front. All the purple stitches are incorrect and will cause counting mistakes and are likely to be problematic when cutting threads.*

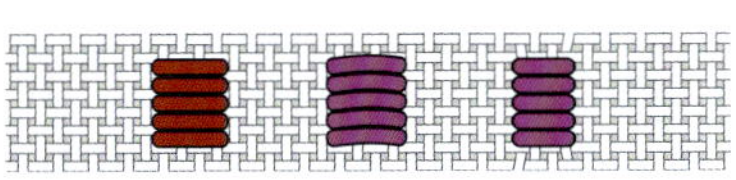

❶ *Good stitch tension is important. Loose stitches (centre) may accidentally be cut. Stitches that are too tight (right) distort the fabric.*

❶ *Never change threads in the middle of a block, as the difference in thread shine and wear will be obvious. Finish a block with the old thread and start a new thread for the next block.*

satin stitch

Satin stitch creates the framework for all Hardanger embroidery, particularly the cutwork, as well as adding decorative elements. It is worked in the heavier weight of thread.

There are many satin stitch motifs used in Hardanger embroidery. The most basic is a block of five parallel stitches that span a width and length of four threads. These blocks are known as klosters or kloster blocks.

Klosters and longer satin stitch blocks can be put together to form cutwork areas in the shapes of diamonds, triangles, squares and zig-zags. We will cover each of these as they are foundational to filling stitches.

klosters in diagonal lines

TRADITIONAL

When working klosters in diagonal lines, the klosters go across the fabric in steps like a staircase, with a rise (or fall) then a flat, then a rise/fall then a flat.

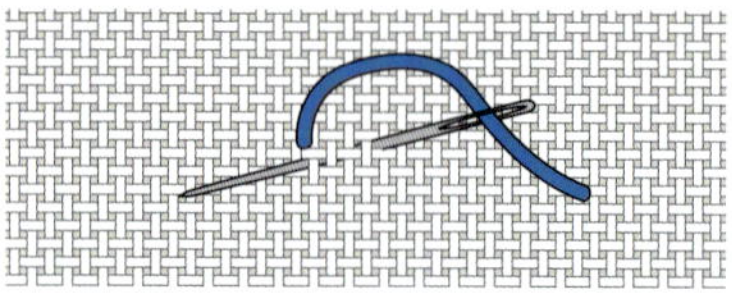

1 Bring the needle out in the starting position. Insert the needle four threads to the right, and bring it out four threads left and one down.

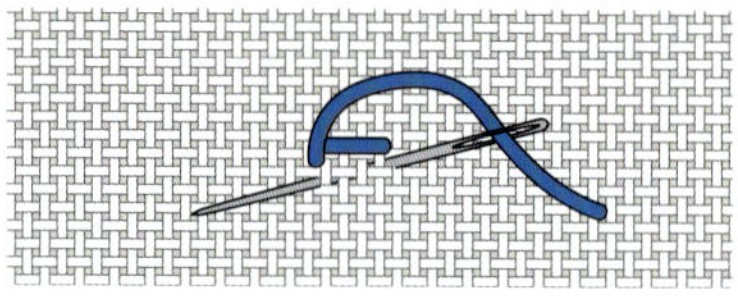

2 Pull the needle through to tighten the stitch so that it lies flat on the fabric. Insert the needle four threads to the right and bring it out four threads left and one down.

❶ *Don't tighten the stitch so much that the ends pull inward. Don't leave it so loose that the stitch looks slack.*

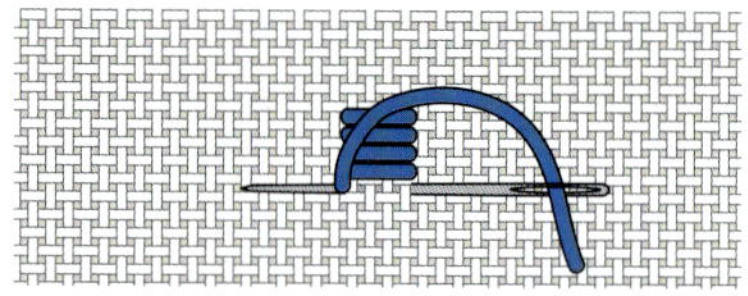

3 Complete four parallel stitches, all the same length and tension. Continuing down, bring the needle out for the fifth stitch. Insert it four threads to the right, and bring it out in the same hole from which the thread just emerged.

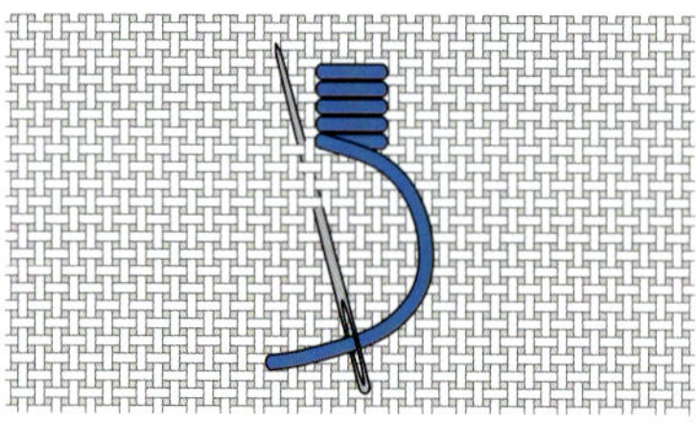

4 Pull the needle through to tighten the stitch so that it lies flat on the fabric. Insert the needle four threads below, and bring it out one thread left of where it previously emerged.

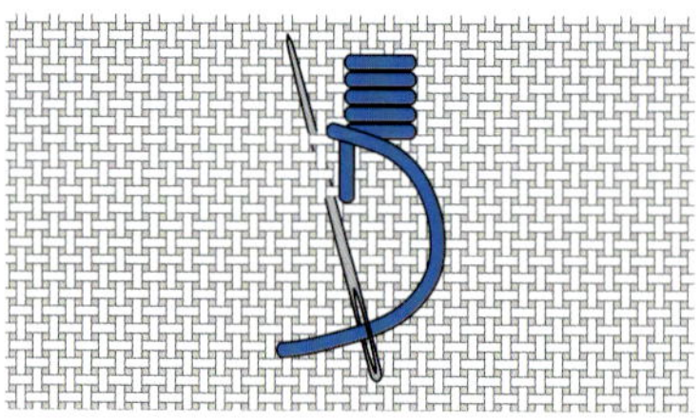

5 Pull the needle through to tighten the stitch so that it lies flat on the fabric. Insert the needle four threads below, and bring it out one thread left of where it previously emerged.

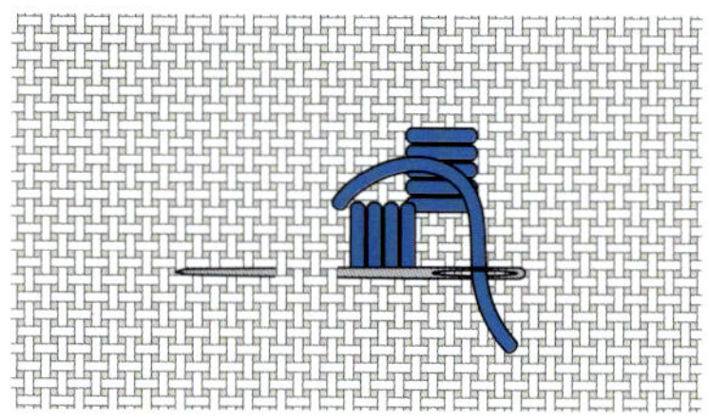

6 Work three more stitches, all the same length and tension. Continuing left, bring the needle out for the next stitch. Insert it four threads below. Bring it out four to the left.

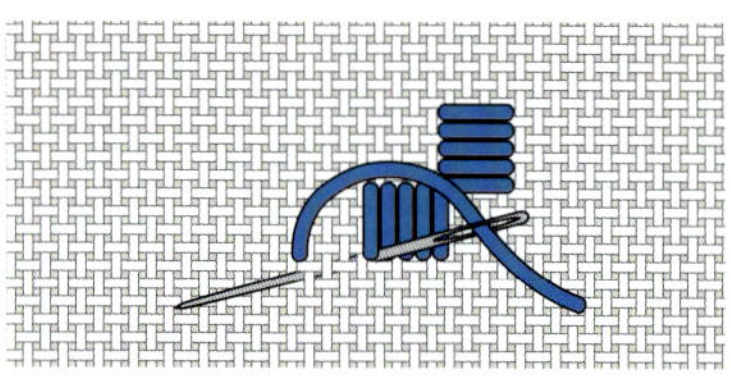

7 Pull the needle through to tighten the stitch. Insert the needle four threads to the right, in the same hole as the bottom of the previous stitch. Bring it out four threads left and one down.

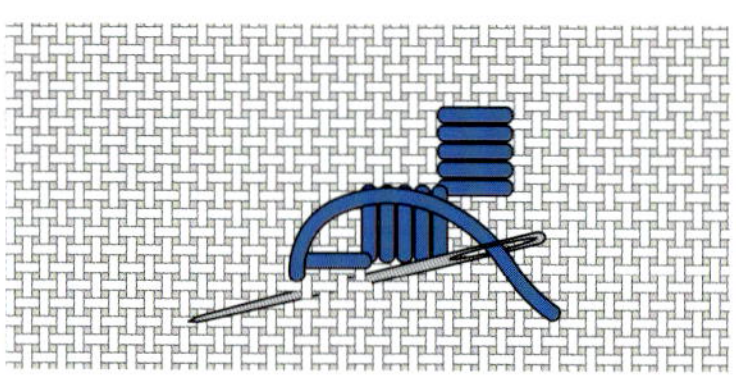

8 Pull the needle through to tighten the stitch. Insert the needle four threads to the right and bring it out four threads left and one down.

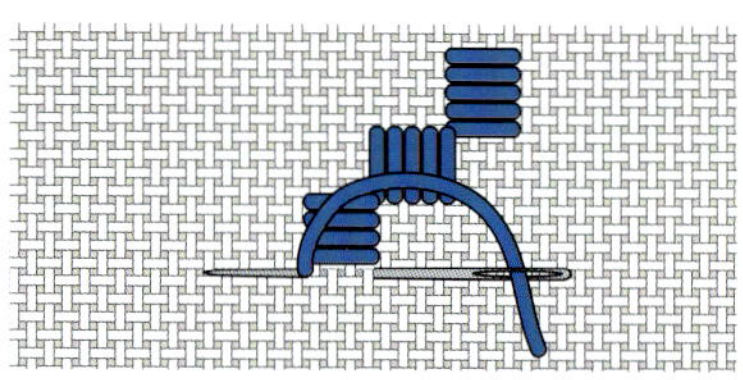

9 Work four parallel stitches, all the same length and tension. Continuing down, bring the needle out for the fifth stitch. Insert it four threads to the right. Bring it out in the same hole as where the thread just emerged.

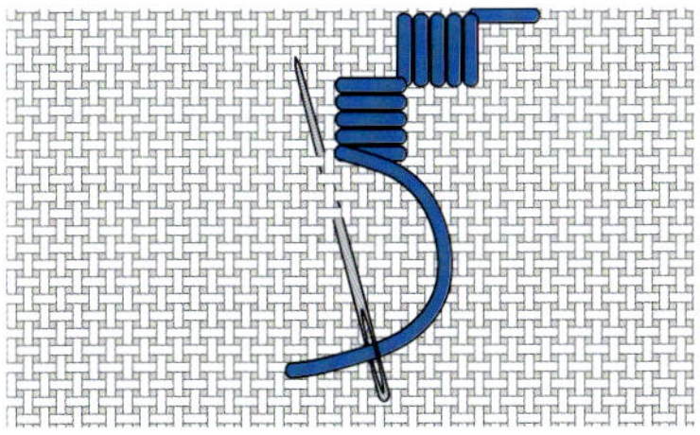

10 Pull the needle through to tighten the stitch. Insert it four threads below. Bring it out one thread left of where it previously emerged.

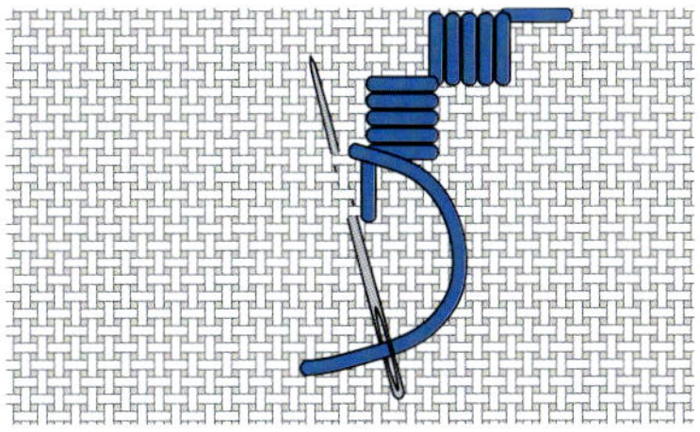

11 Pull the needle through to tighten the stitch. Insert it four threads below. Bring it out one thread left of where it previously emerged.

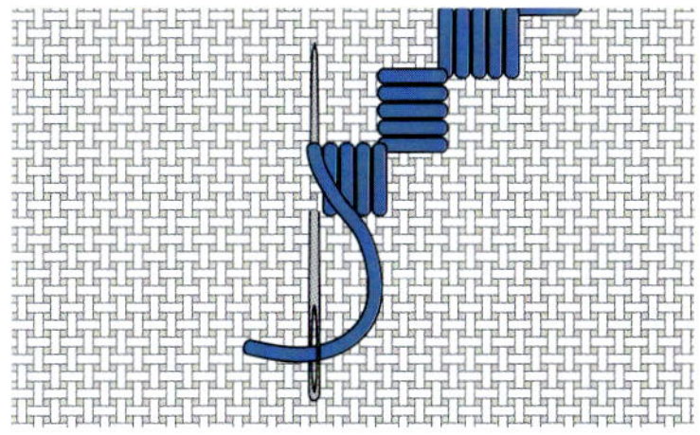

12 Continue similarly. To turn the corner, insert the needle for the last stitch of the block and bring it out in the same hole as it last emerged.

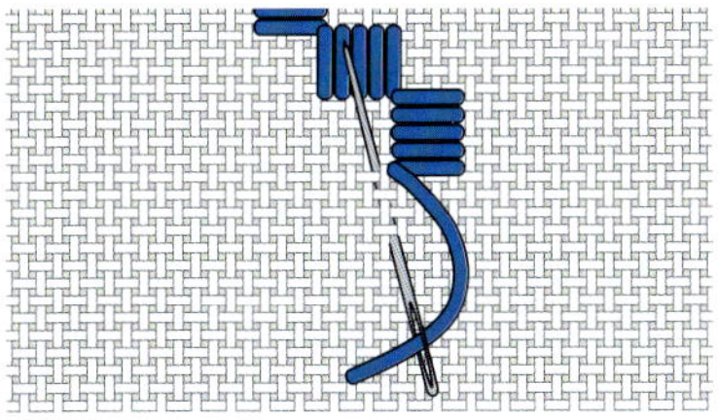

13 Turn the work 90° anticlockwise. Pull the needle and thread through. Continue stitching as before.

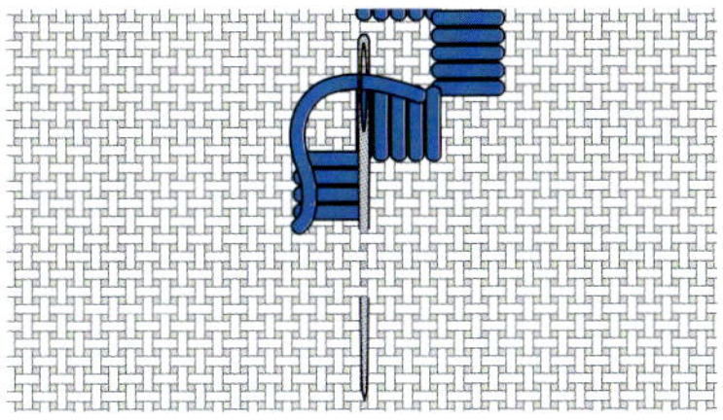

14 To turn the corner the other direction, insert the needle to complete the last stitch of the block and bring it out four threads below.

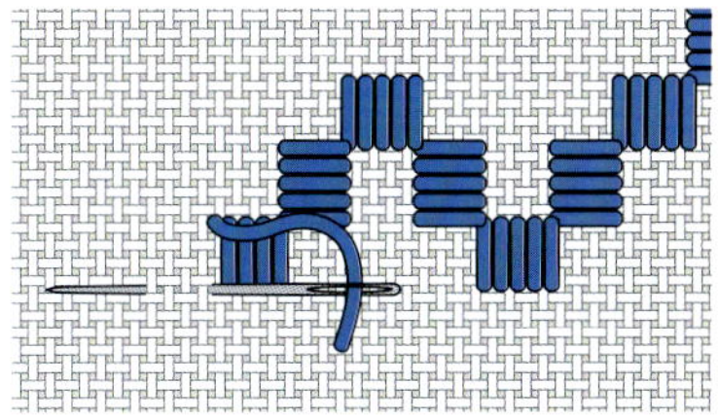

15 Turn the work 90° clockwise, and continue working as before to build up a line of stitching.

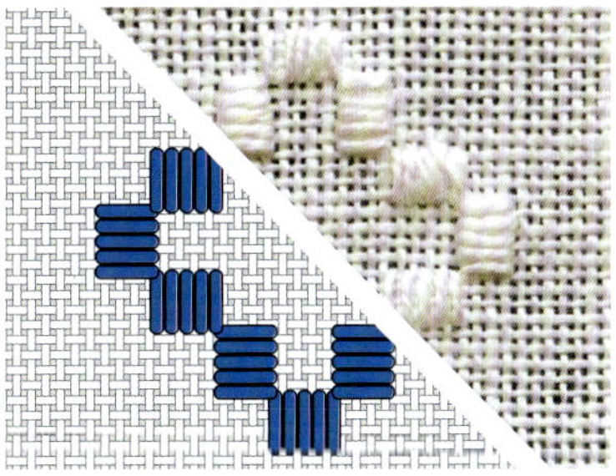

❶ *To complete a circuit, the first and last klosters must share a corner hole. If they don't, there is at least one mistake.*

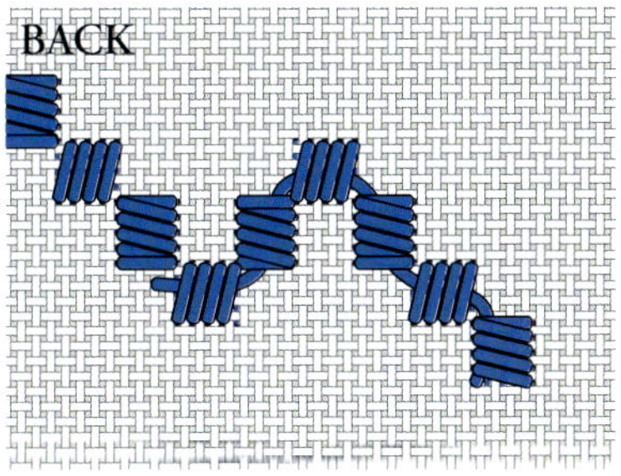

16 To finish, run the thread under the back of about 5 cm (2 in) of stitching. Trim any remaining thread.

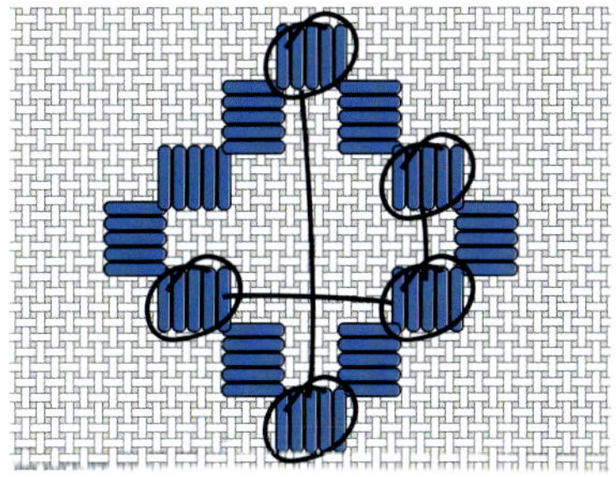

❶ *In cutwork motifs, each kloster should be paired with one in the same orientation on the far side.*

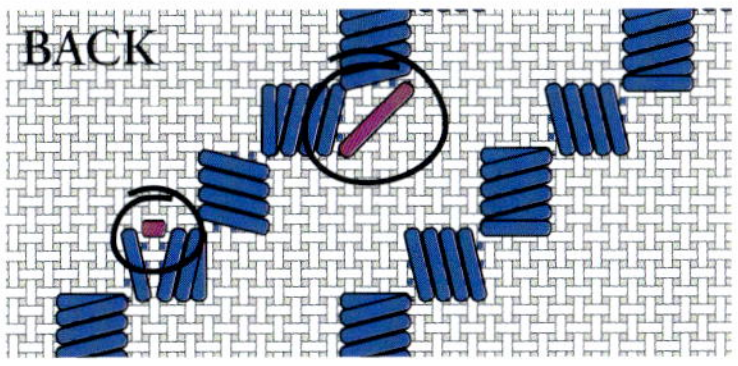

❶ *The back of the work is correct in the right line. The left line has two errors, where the direction has been reversed in error. Such errors can cause the stitching to unravel when the adjacent fabric threads are cut.*

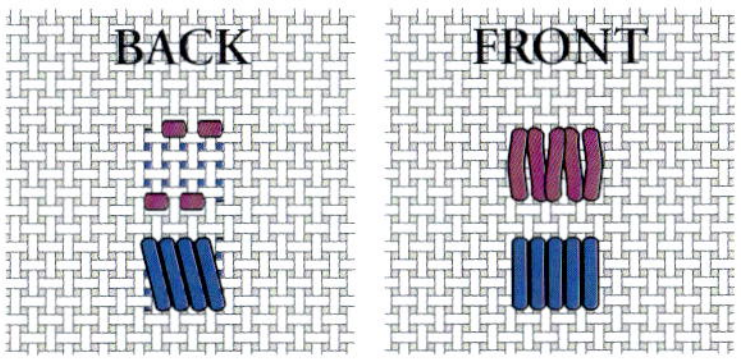

❶ *The stitches must spiral the fabric's threads (lower left). Never bring the needle out next to the hole just entered (upper left) as the stitches will flip up when adjacent fabric threads are cut. The stitches also sit incorrectly (upper right).*

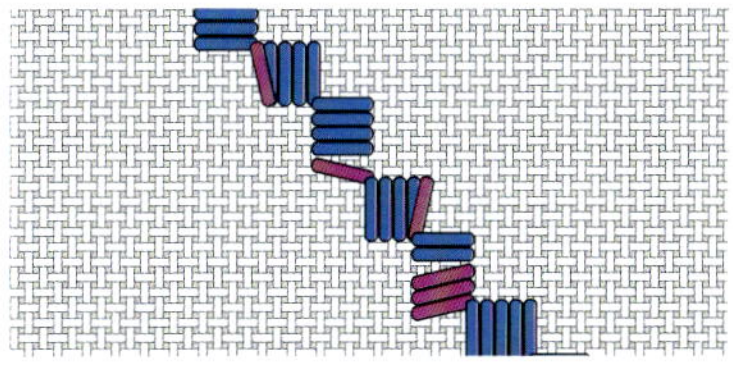

❶ *All stitches should be parallel to the fabric threads on the front. All the purple stitches are incorrect and will cause counting mistakes and are likely to be problematic when cutting threads.*

❶ *Good stitch tension is important. Loose stitches (centre) may accidentally be cut. Stitches that are too tight (right) distort the fabric.*

❶ *Never change threads in the middle of a block, as the difference in thread shine and wear will be obvious. Finish a block with the old thread and start a new thread for the next block.*

klosters in straight lines

When klosters are worked in straight lines, count the threads between them carefully.

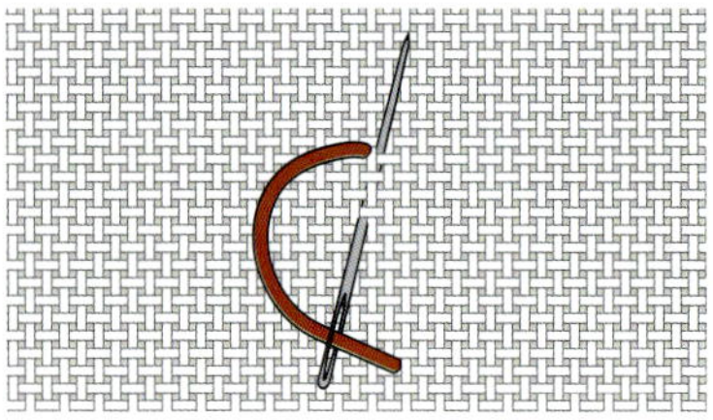

1 Bring the needle out in the starting position. Insert it four threads down, and bring it out four threads up and one right.

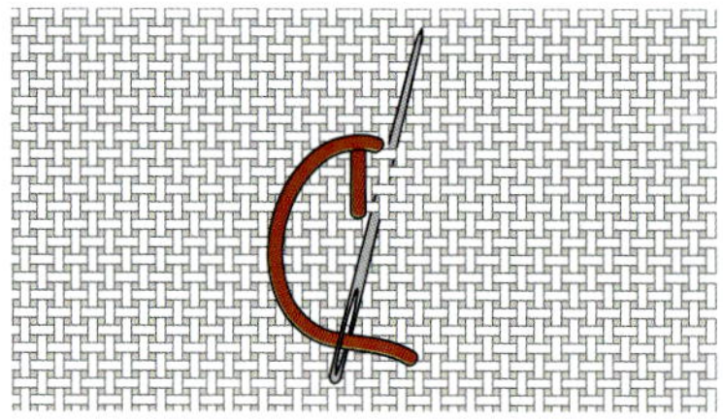

2 Pull the needle through to tighten the stitch so that it lies flat on the fabric. Insert it four threads down, and bring it out four threads up and one right.

❶ *Don't tighten the stitch so much that the ends pull inward. Don't leave it so loose that the stitch looks slack.*

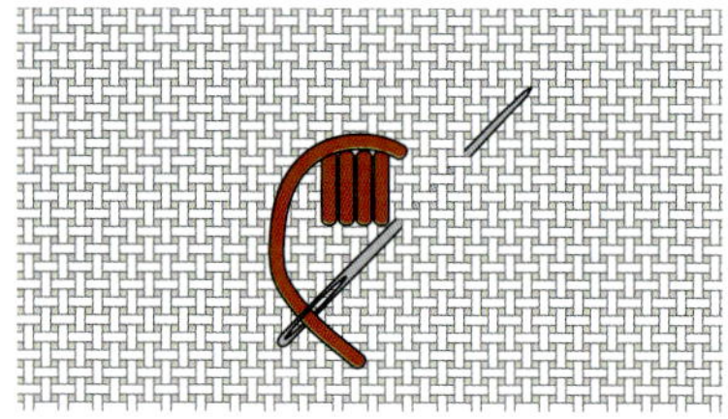

3 Complete four parallel stitches, all the same length and tension. Continuing to move right, bring the needle out for the fifth stitch. Insert it four threads down. Bring it out four threads up and right.

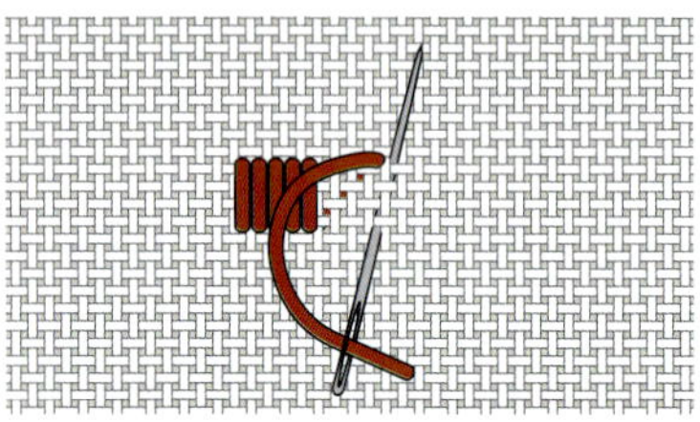

4 Pull the needle through to tighten the stitch so that it lies flat on the fabric. Insert it four threads down, and bring it out one thread right of where it previously emerged.

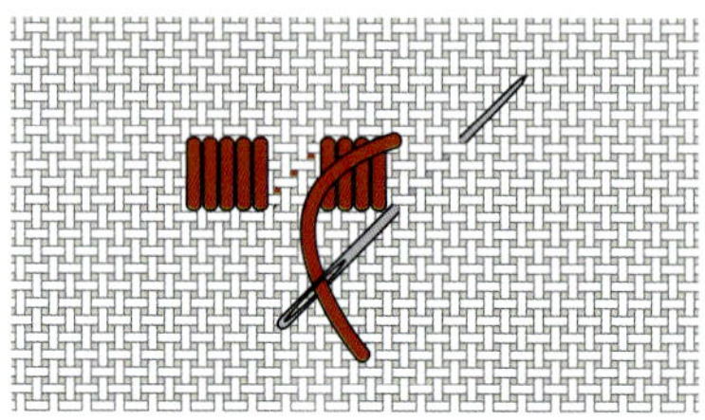

5 Work four parallel stitches and bring the needle out for the fifth stitch. Insert it to complete the block. Bring it out four threads up and right.

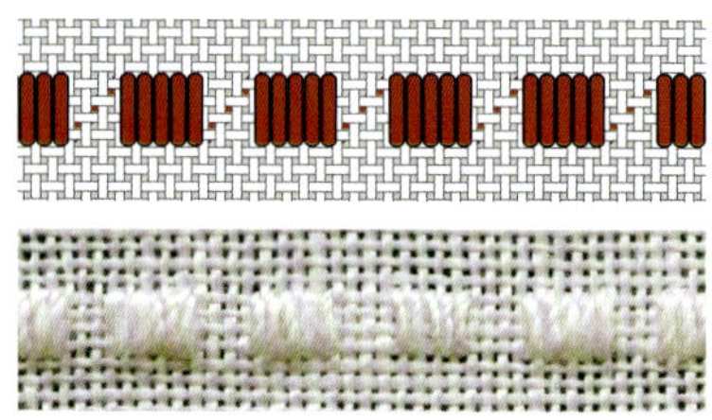

6 Continue in the same manner to build up a line of stitching.

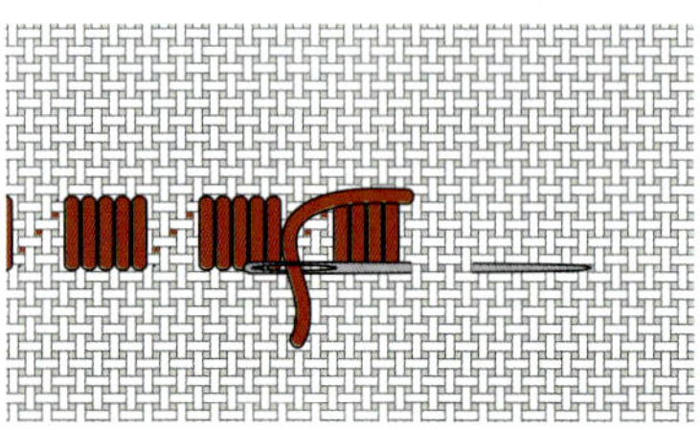

7 To turn a corner to the right, insert the needle to finish the fifth stitch of the block. Bring it out four threads to the right.

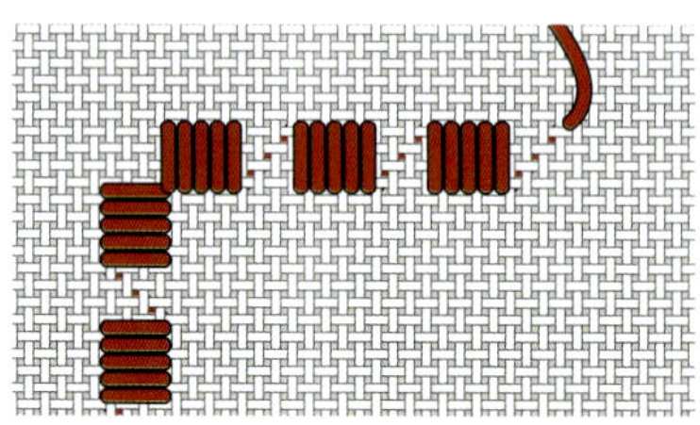

8 Turn the work 90° anticlockwise and continue stitching as before.

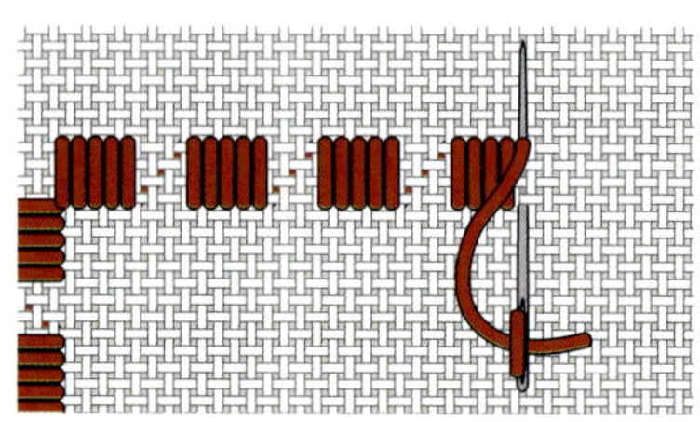

9 To turn a corner to the left, insert the needle to finish the fifth stitch of the block. Bring it out four threads up.

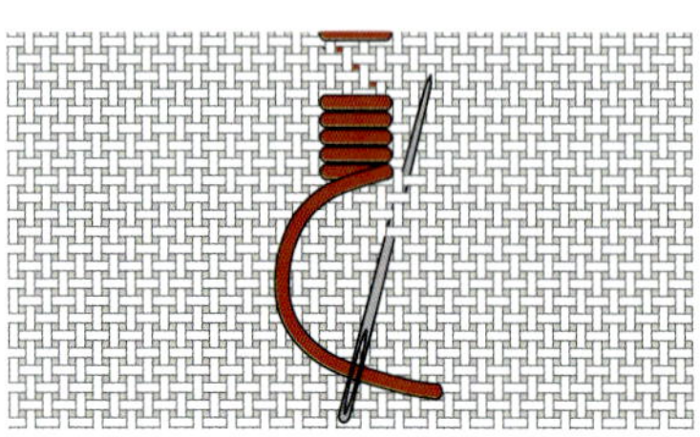

10 Turn the work 90° clockwise. Insert the needle four threads down. Bring it out again four threads up and one right.

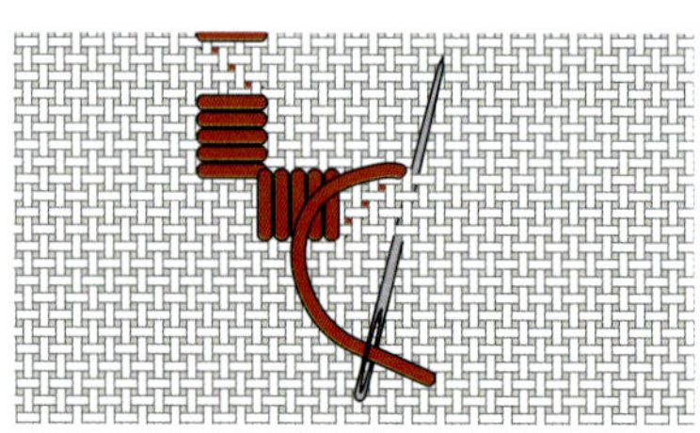

11 Continue on, in the same way as before.

❶ *For finishing and changing of threads use the same methods as for klosters in diagonal lines. Most of the mistakes to watch for with diagonal lines apply as well.*

klosters in straight lines

When klosters are worked in straight lines, count the threads between them carefully.

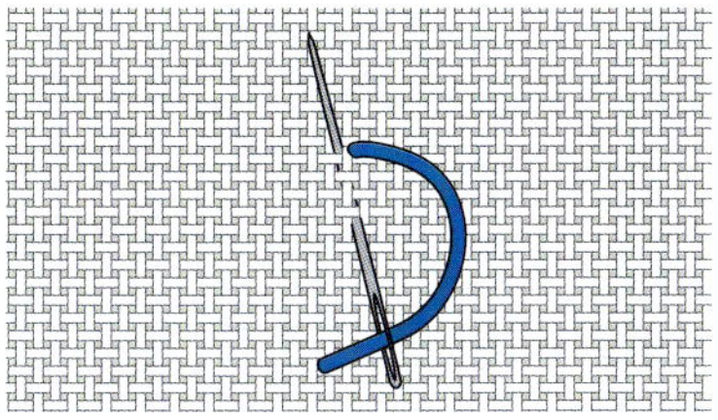

1 Bring the needle out in the starting position. Insert it four threads down, and bring it out four threads up and one left.

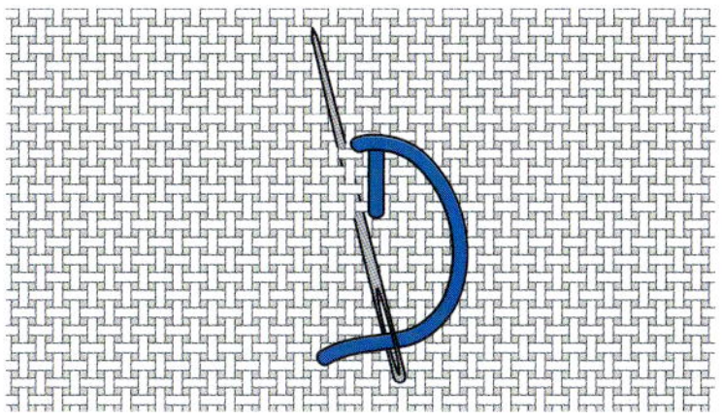

2 Pull the needle through to tighten the stitch so that it lies flat on the fabric. Insert it four threads down, and bring it out four threads up and one left.

❶ *Don't tighten the stitch so much that the ends pull inward. Don't leave it so loose that the stitch looks slack.*

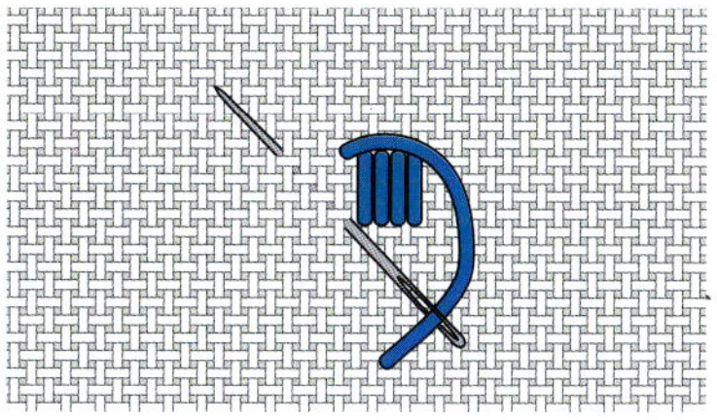

3 Complete four parallel stitches, all the same length and tension. Continuing to move left, bring the needle out for the fifth stitch. Insert it four threads down. Bring it out four threads up and left.

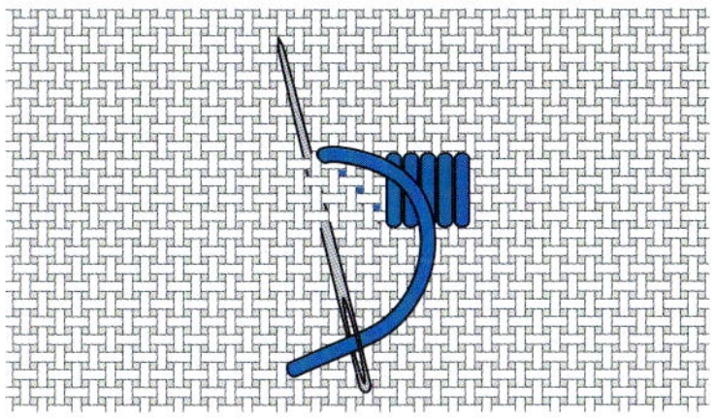

4 Pull the needle through to tighten the stitch so that it lies flat on the fabric. Insert it four threads down, and bring it out one thread left of where it previously emerged.

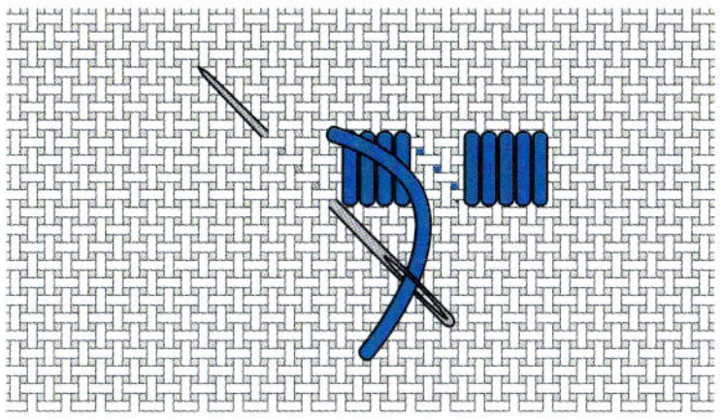

5 Work four parallel stitches and bring the needle out for the fifth stitch. Insert it to complete the block. Bring it out four threads up and left.

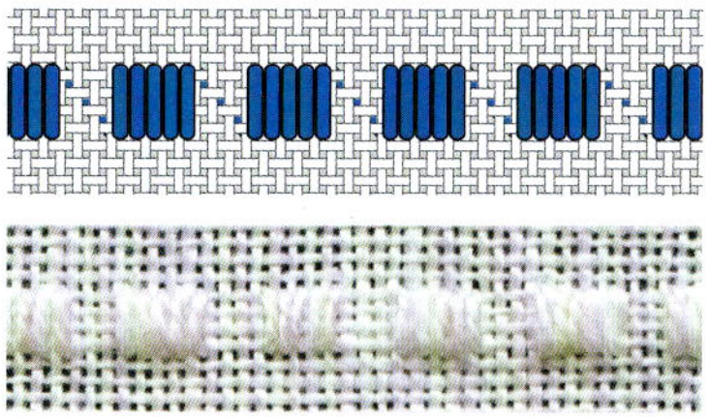

6 Continue in the same manner to build up a line of stitching.

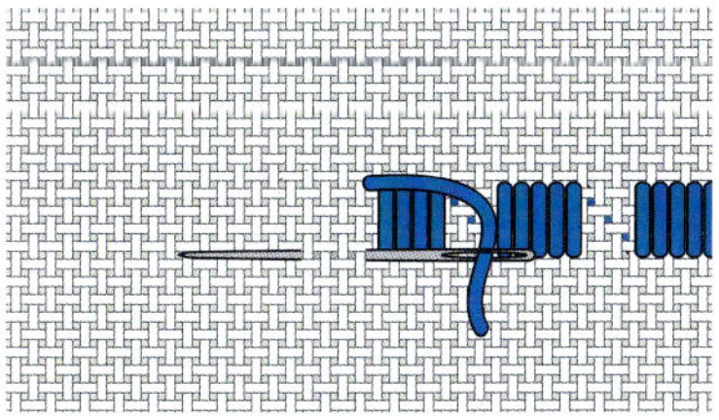

7 To turn a corner to the left, insert the needle to finish the fifth stitch of the block. Bring it out four threads to the left.

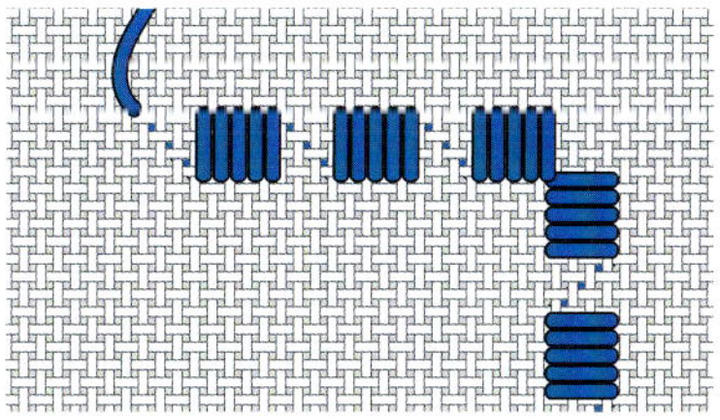

8 Turn the work 90° clockwise and continue stitching as before.

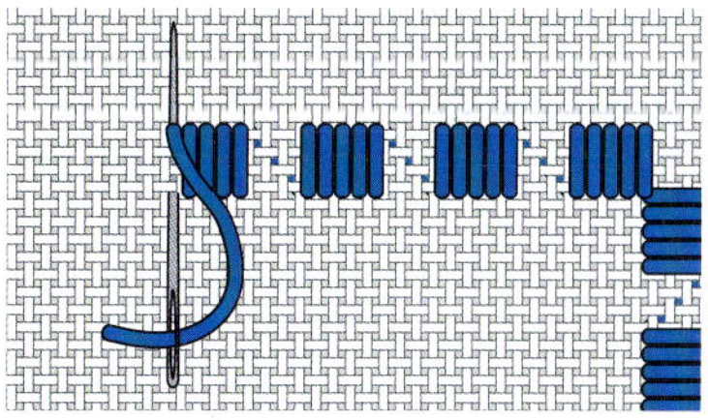

9 To turn a corner to the right, insert the needle to finish the fifth stitch of the block. Bring it out four threads up.

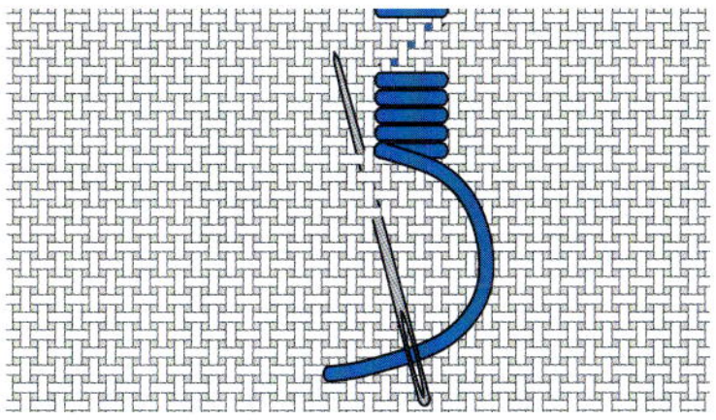

10 Turn the work 90° anticlockwise. Insert the needle four threads down. Bring it out again four threads up and one left.

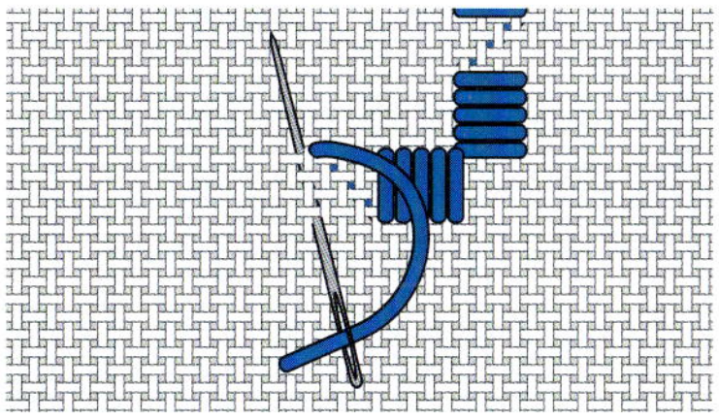

11 Continue on, in the same way as before.

❶ *For finishing and changing of threads use the same methods as for klosters in diagonal lines. Most of the mistakes to watch for with diagonal lines apply as well.*

L

kloster square

Kloster squares combine straight lines with the corners of diagonal lines.

TRADITIONAL

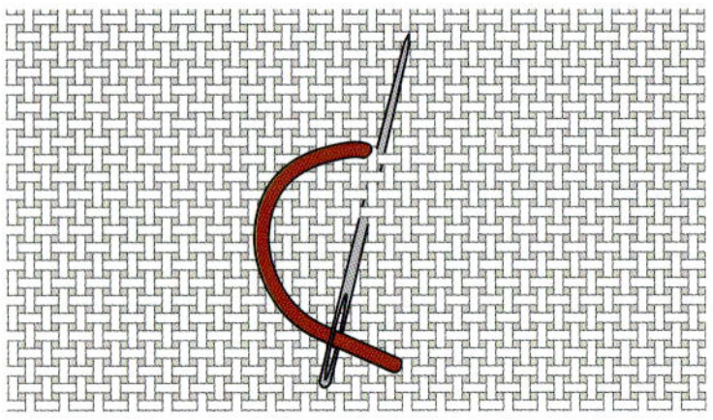

1 Bring the needle out in the starting position. Insert it four threads down, and bring it out four threads up and one right.

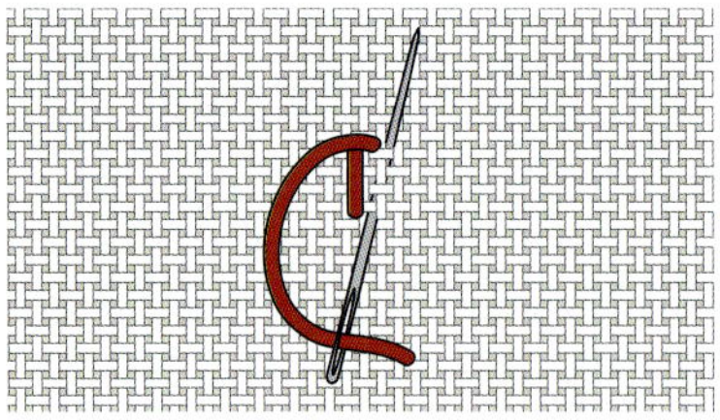

2 Pull the needle through to tighten the stitch so that it lies flat on the fabric. Insert it four threads down, and bring it out four threads up and one right.

❶ *Don't tighten the stitch so much that the ends pull inward. Don't leave it so loose that the stitch looks slack.*

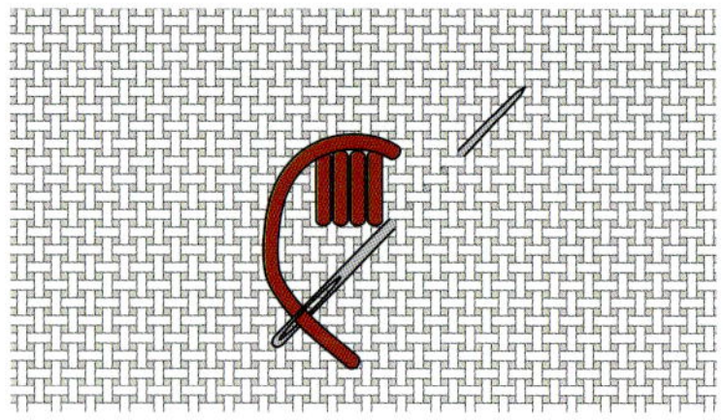

3 Complete four parallel stitches, all the same length and tension. Continuing to move right, bring the needle out for the fifth stitch. Insert it four threads down. Bring it out four threads up and right.

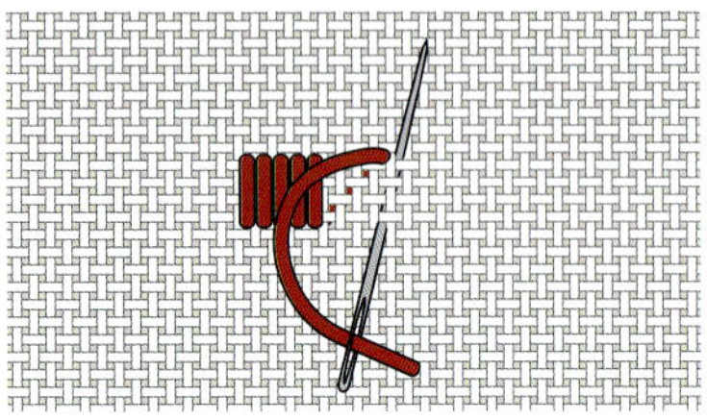

4 Pull the needle through to tighten the stitch so that it lies flat on the fabric. Insert it four threads down, and bring it out one thread right of where it previously emerged.

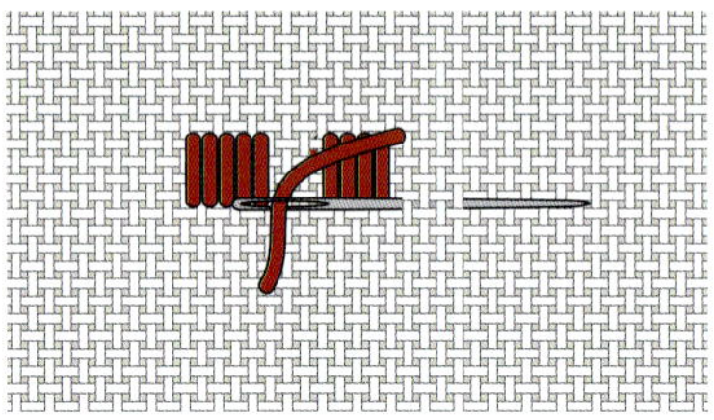

5 Work four parallel stitches and bring the needle out for the fifth stitch. Insert it to complete the block. Bring it out four threads to the right.

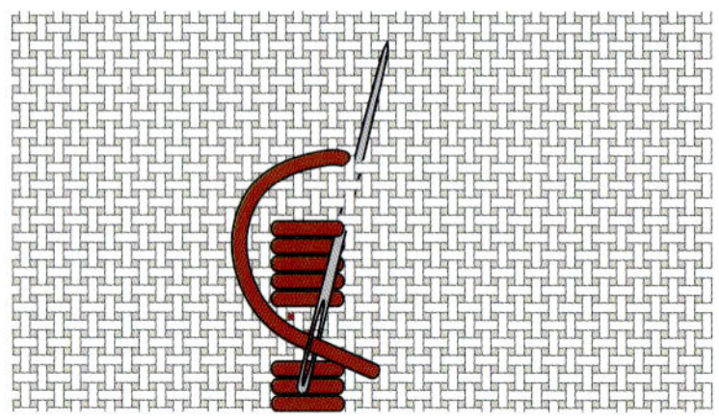

6 Turn the work 90° anticlockwise and pull the needle through. Insert it four threads down and bring it out again four threads up and one to the right.

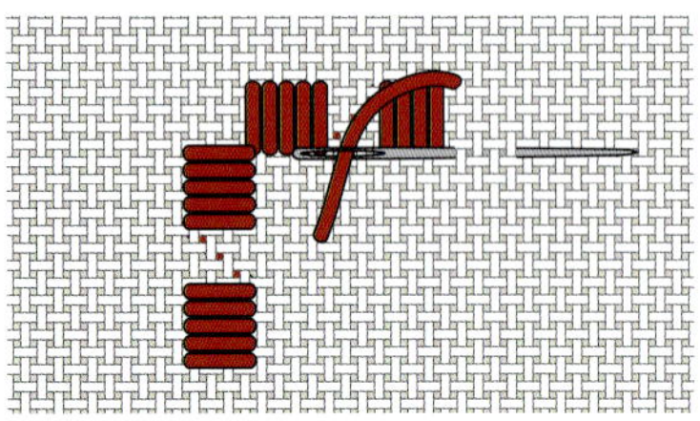

7 Work two more kloster blocks and insert the needle to turn the next corner.

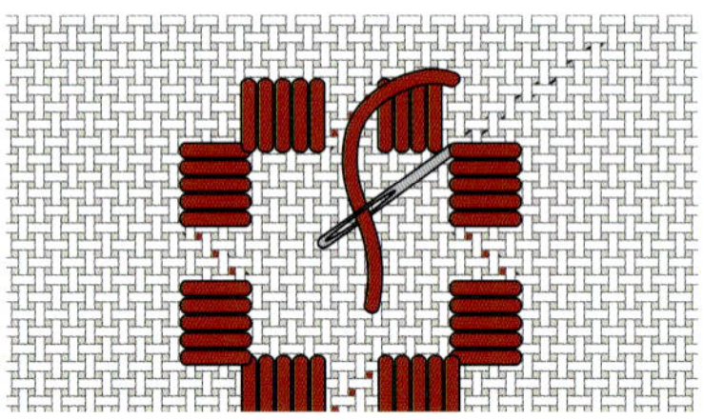

8 Repeat the first two sides to complete the kloster square. Finish by taking the needle to the back at the completion of the final stitch.

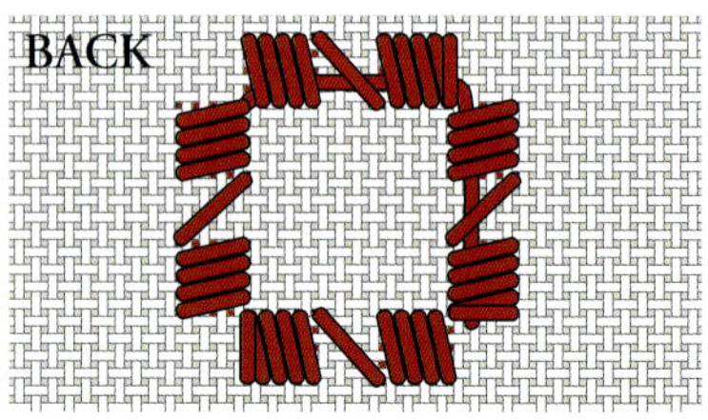

9 To finish, run the needle under the back of four klosters and trim any excess thread.

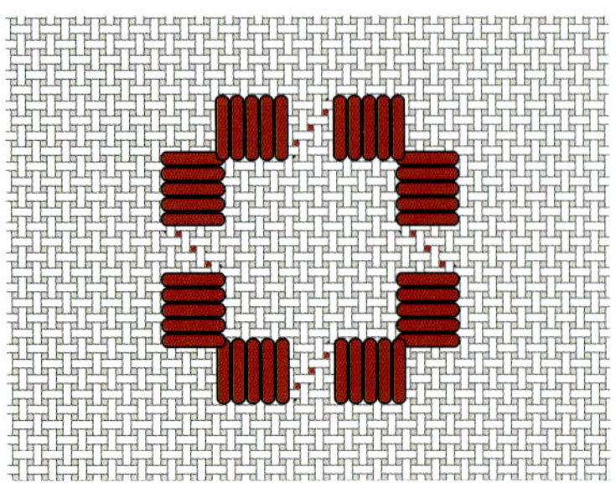

10 The completed kloster square.

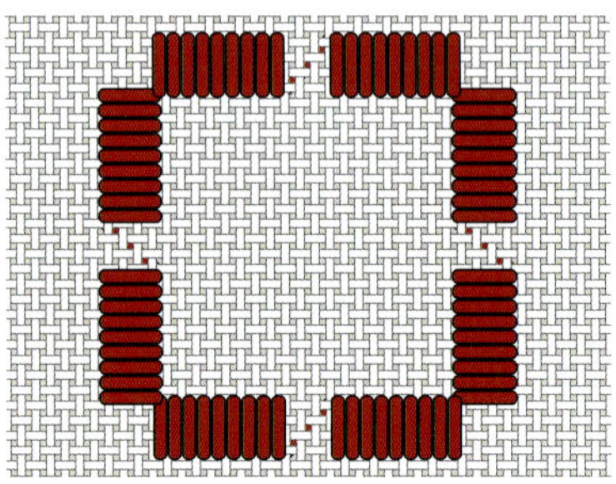

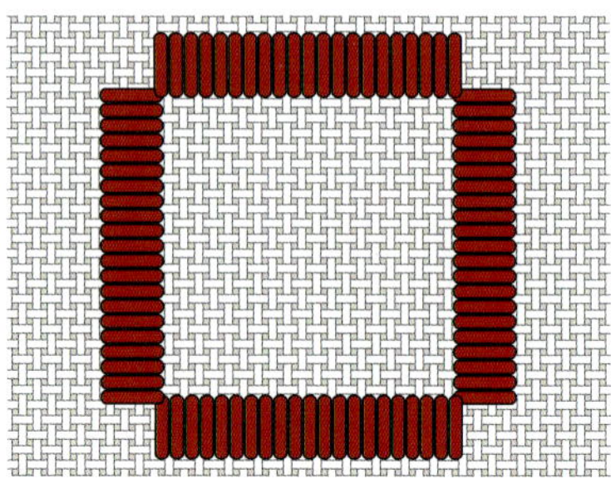

❶ *Some squares (above, and above right) are larger and have more stitches in each satin stitch block. Follow your chart for stitch quantity and placement.*

kloster square

Kloster squares combine straight lines with the corners of diagonal lines.

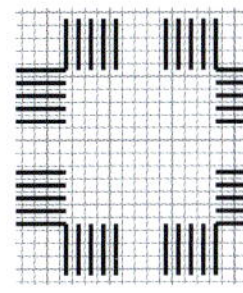

TRADITIONAL

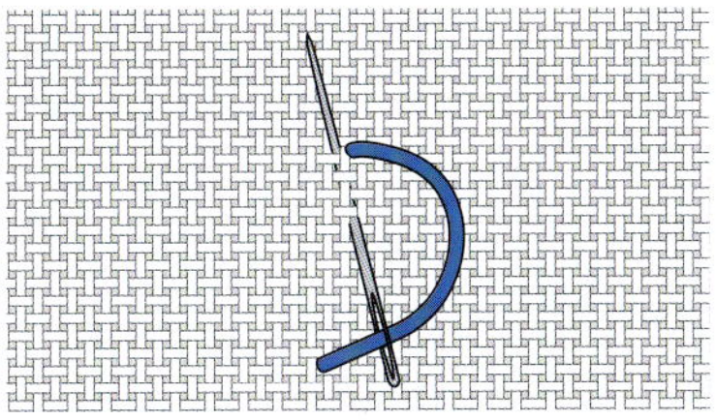

1 Bring the needle out in the starting position. Insert it four threads down, and bring it out four threads up and one left.

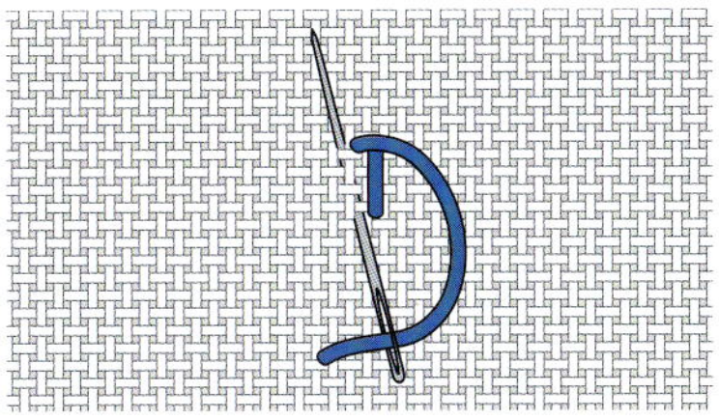

2 Pull the needle through to tighten the stitch so that it lies flat on the fabric. Insert it four threads down, and bring it out four threads up and one left.

❶ *Don't tighten the stitch so much that the ends pull inward. Don't leave it so loose that the stitch looks slack.*

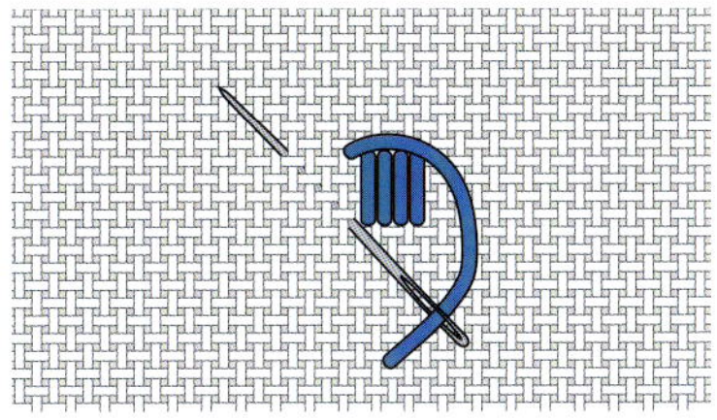

3 Complete four parallel stitches, all the same length and tension. Continuing to move left, bring the needle out for the fifth stitch. Insert it four threads down. Bring it out four threads up and left.

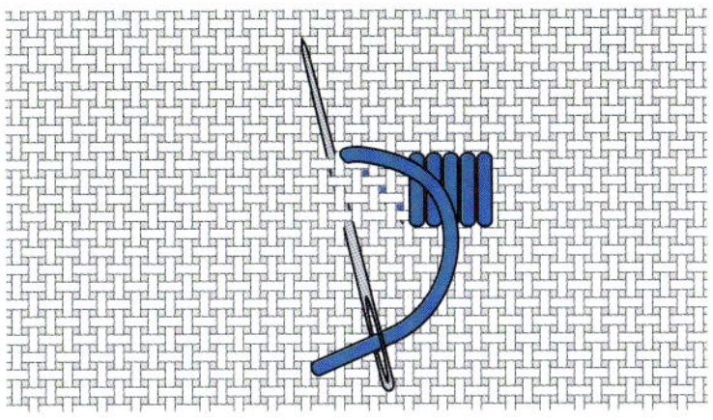

4 Pull the needle through to tighten the stitch so that it lies flat on the fabric. Insert it four threads down, and bring it out one thread left of where it previously emerged.

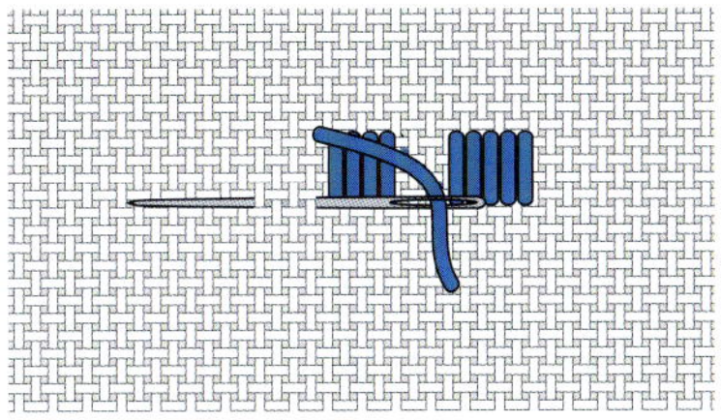

5 Work four parallel stitches and bring the needle out for the fifth stitch. Insert it to complete the block. Bring it out four threads to the left.

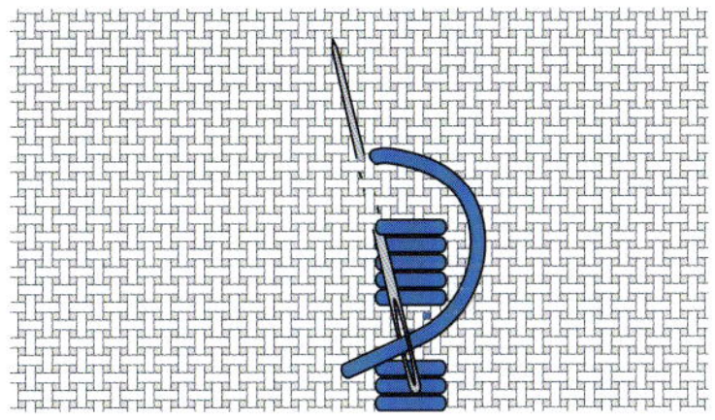

6 Turn the work 90° clockwise and pull the needle through. Insert it four threads down and bring it out again four threads up and one to the left.

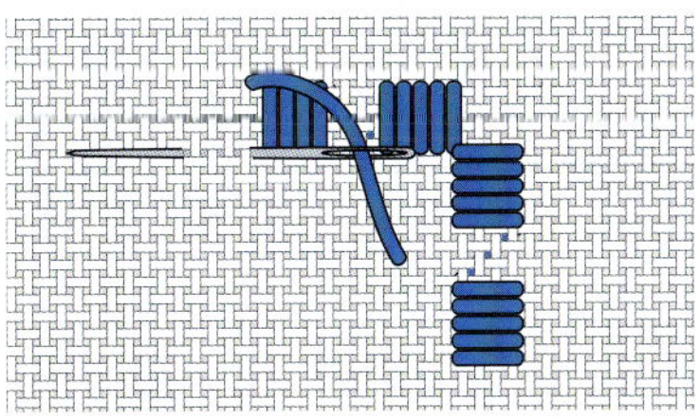

7 Work two more kloster blocks and insert the needle to turn the next corner.

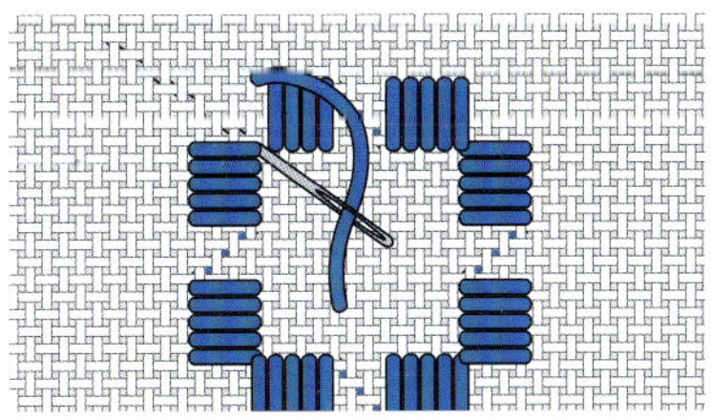

8 Repeat the first two sides to complete the kloster square. Finish by taking the needle to the back at the completion of the final stitch.

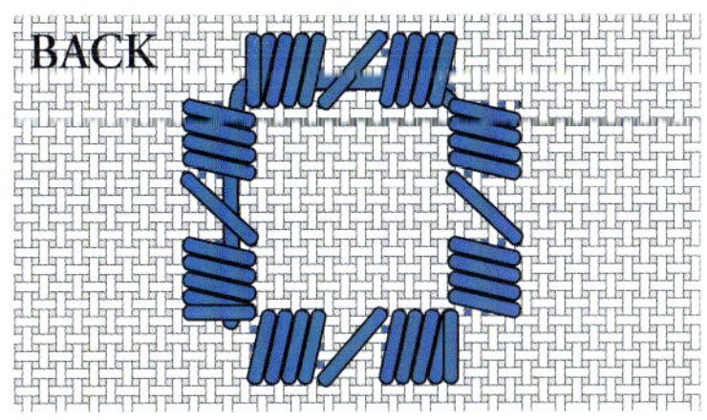

9 To finish, run the needle under the back of four klosters and trim any excess thread.

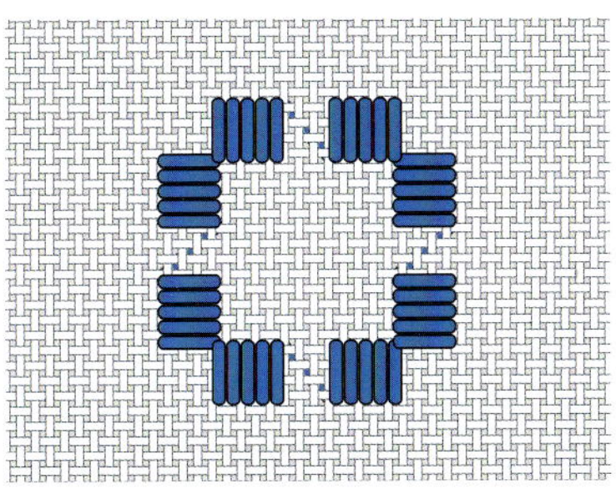

10 The completed kloster square.

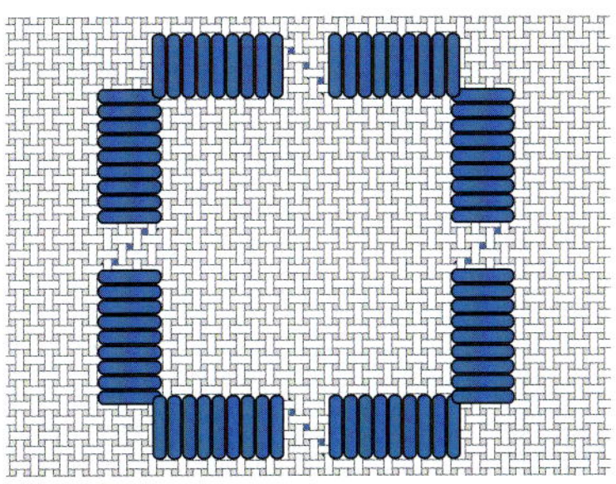

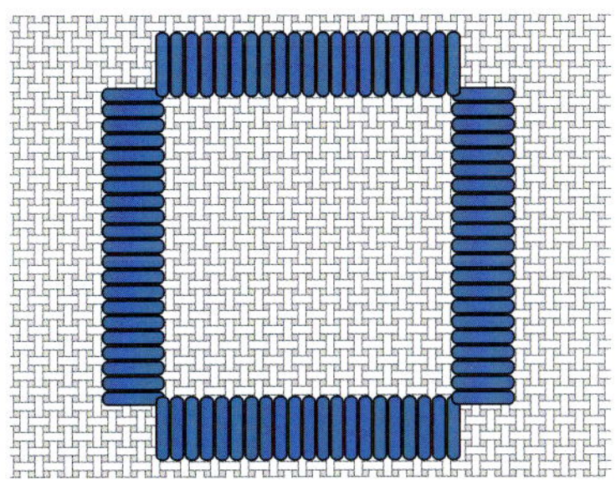

❶ *Some squares (above, and above right) are larger and have more stitches in each satin stitch block. Follow your chart for stitch quantity and placement.*

L

satin stitch stepped triangles

TRADITIONAL

in a square

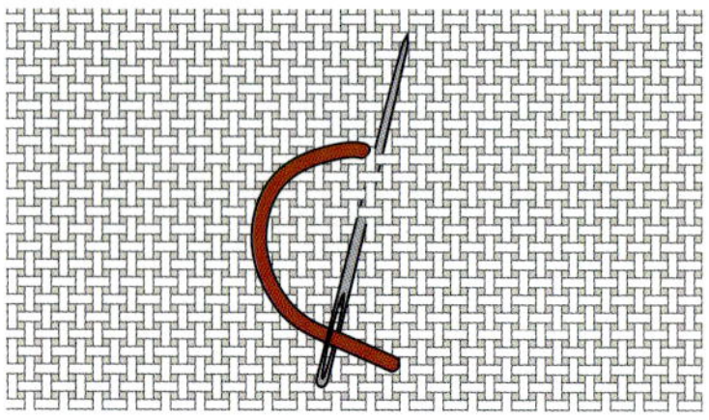

1 Bring the needle out. Insert it four threads down, and bring it out four threads up and one right.

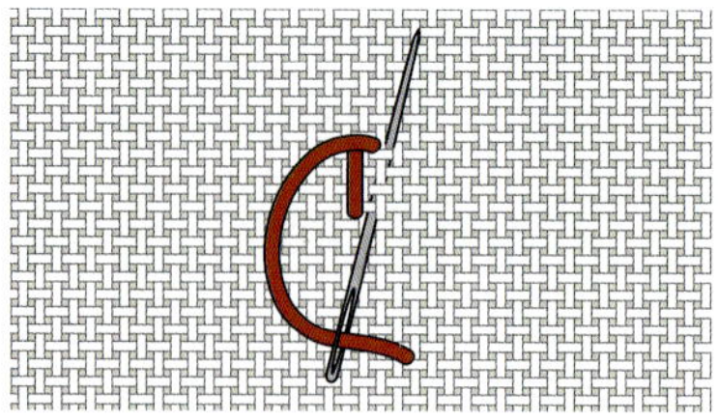

2 Pull the needle through. Tighten the stitch to have gentle tension. Insert the needle four threads down. Bring it out four up and one right.

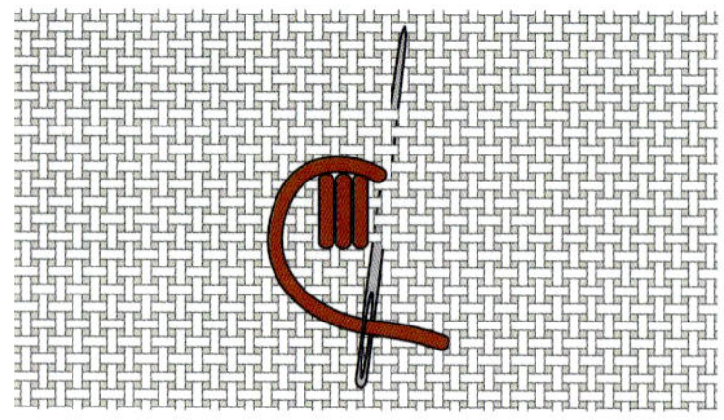

3 Make three parallel stitches. Bring the needle out for the fourth stitch. Insert it four threads down. Bring it out eight up and one right.

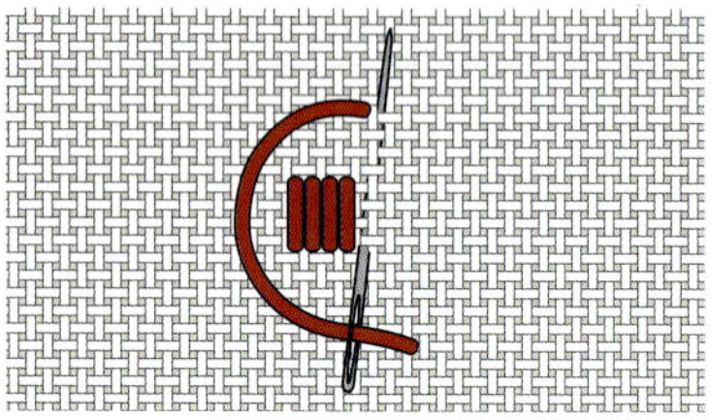

4 Pull the needle through. Insert it eight threads down, and bring it out one thread right of where it previously emerged.

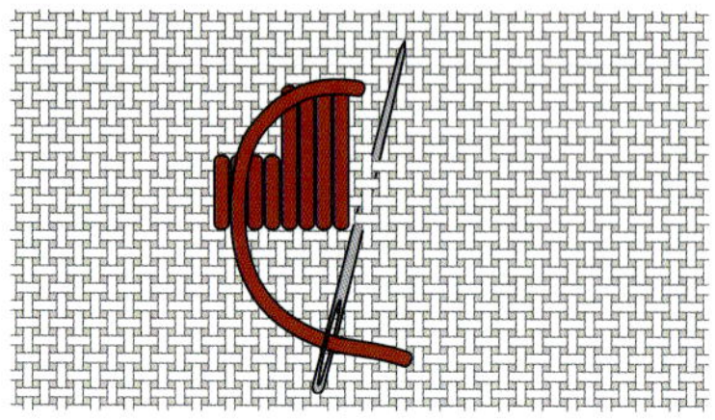

5 Work four longer stitches and bring the needle out for a fifth stitch. Insert it eight threads down. Bring it out four up and one right.

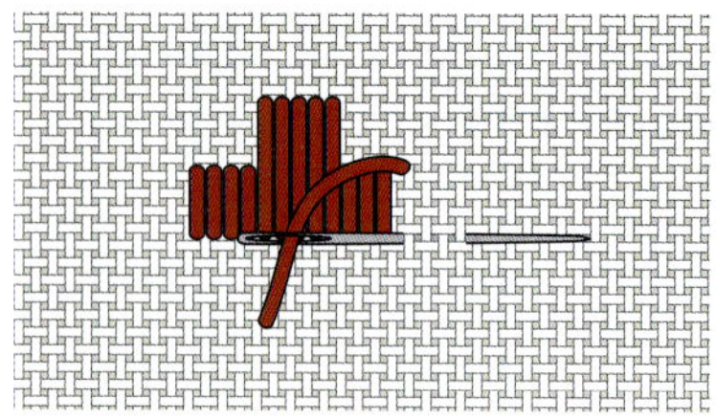

6 Work three shorter stitches. Bring the needle out for the fourth stitch. Insert it four threads down and bring it out four to the right.

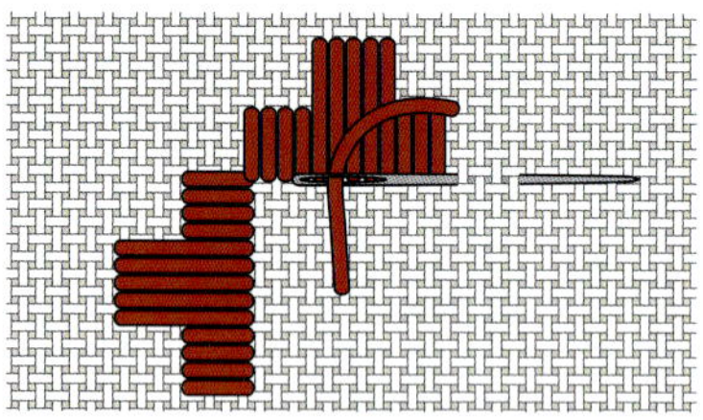

7 Turn the work 90° anticlockwise and work another stepped triangle.

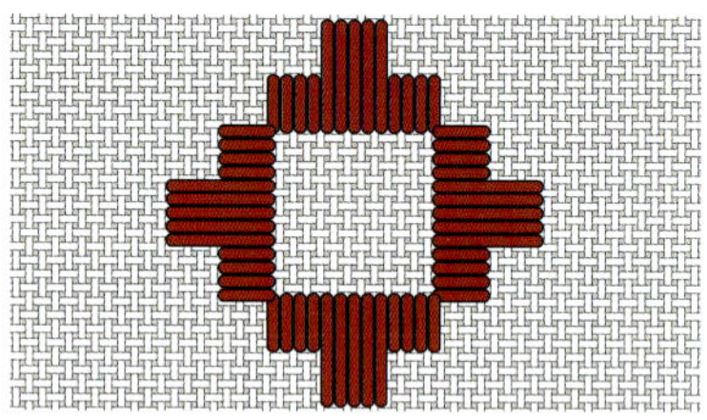

8 Work two more triangles to complete the square.

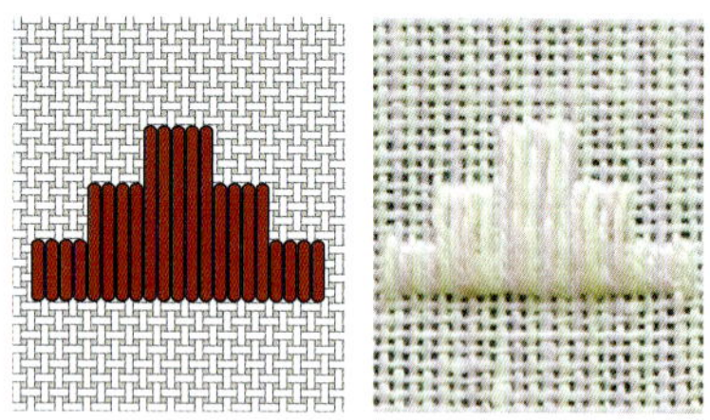

❶ *Larger triangles have another, longer section in the centre. The side sections have four stitches; the centre has five.*

in a diagonal line

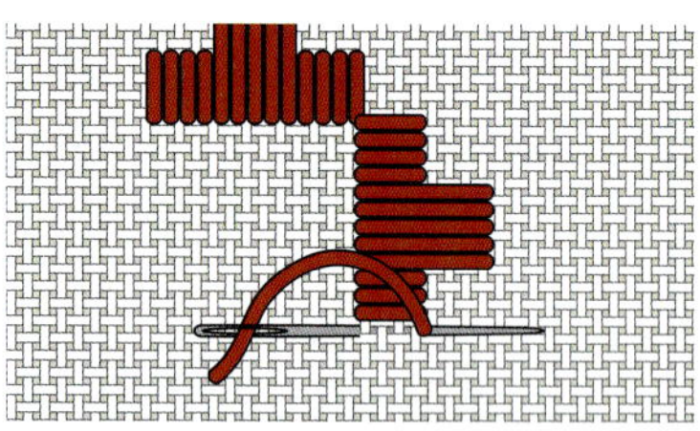

1 After Step 6, work another triangle. Insert the needle to complete the last stitch, then bring it out in the same hole as it just emerged from.

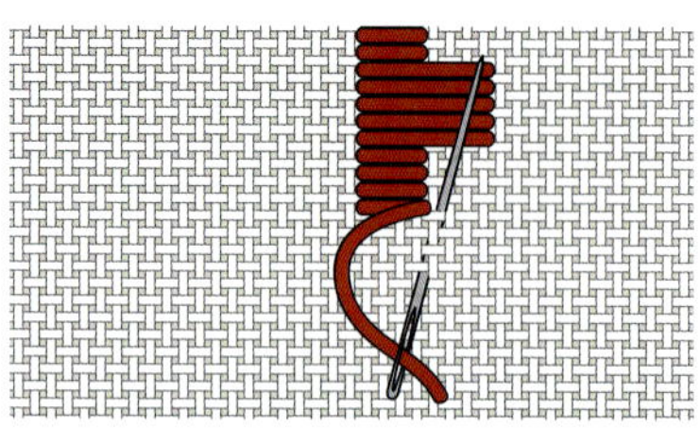

2 Pull the needle through. Insert it four threads down and bring it out four threads up and one to the right.

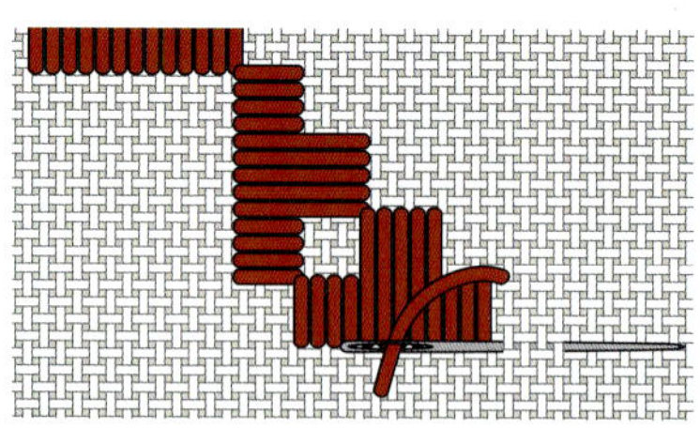

3 Complete another triangle. Insert the needle for the last stitch, then bring it out four threads to the right. Continue, making a line of triangles.

❶ *These triangles are sawtooth rather than stepped. There are many variations that can be made.*

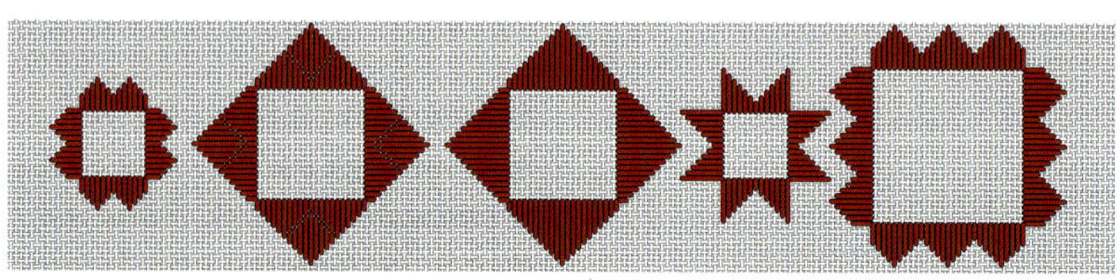

satin stitch stepped triangles

in a square

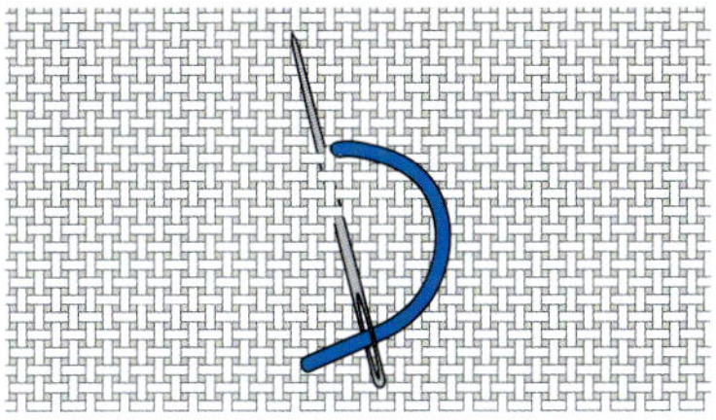

1 Bring the needle out. Insert it four threads down, and bring it out four threads up and one left.

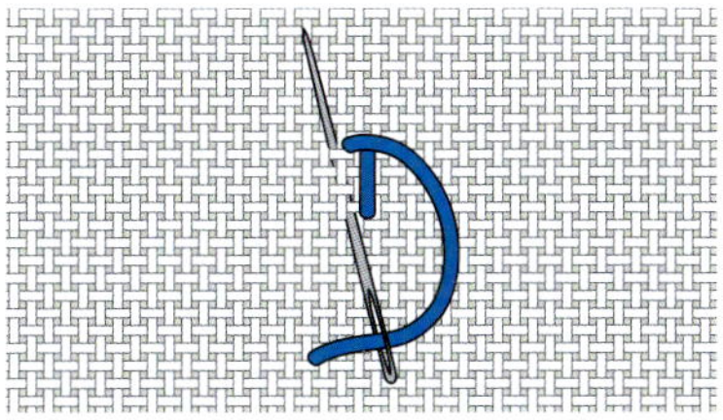

2 Pull the needle through. Tighten the stitch to have gentle tension. Insert the needle four threads down. Bring it out four up and one left.

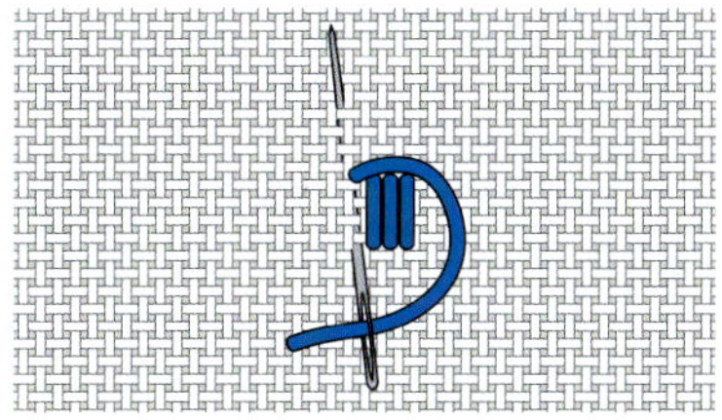

3 Make three parallel stitches. Bring the needle out for the fourth stitch. Insert it four threads down. Bring it out eight up and one left.

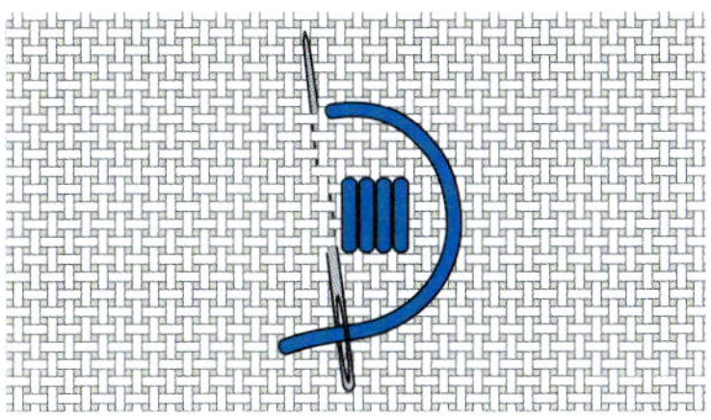

4 Pull the needle through. Insert the needle eight threads down, and bring it out one thread left of where it previously emerged.

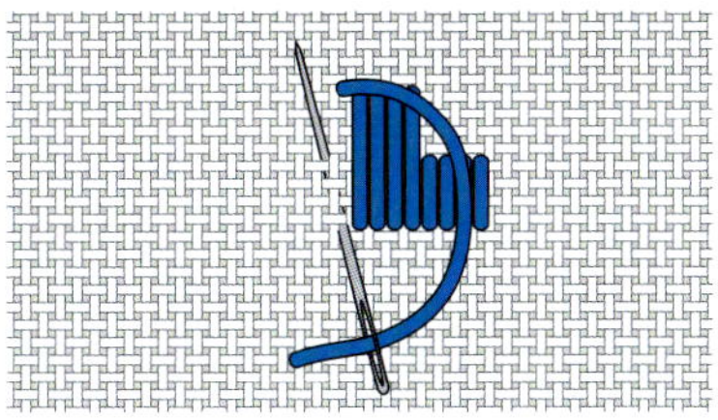

5 Work four longer stitches and bring the needle out for a fifth stitch. Insert it eight threads down. Bring it out four up and one left.

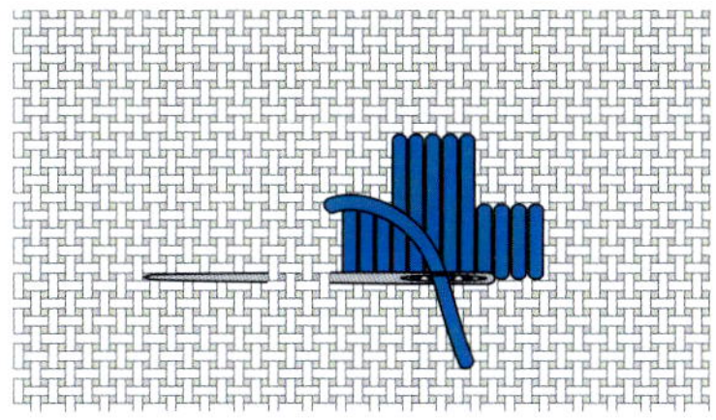

6 Work three shorter stitches. Bring the needle out for the fourth stitch. Insert it four threads down and bring it out four to the left.

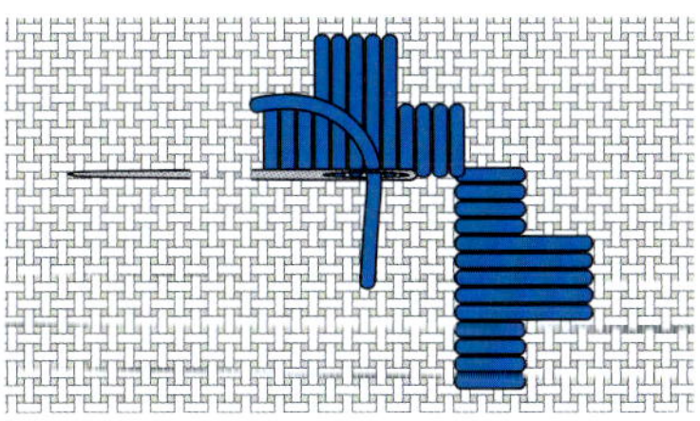

7 Turn the work 90° clockwise and work another stepped triangle.

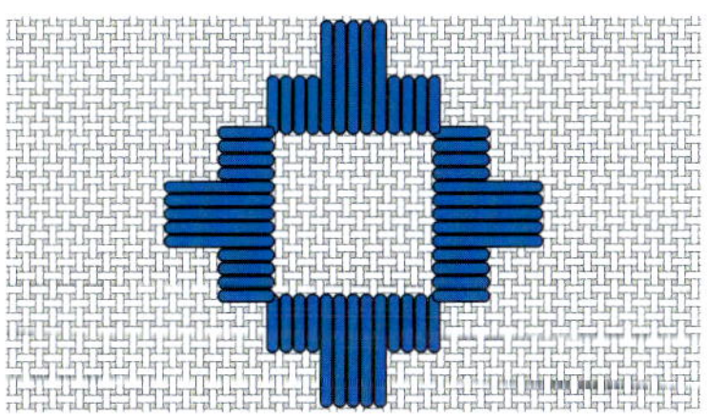

8 Work two more triangles to complete the square.

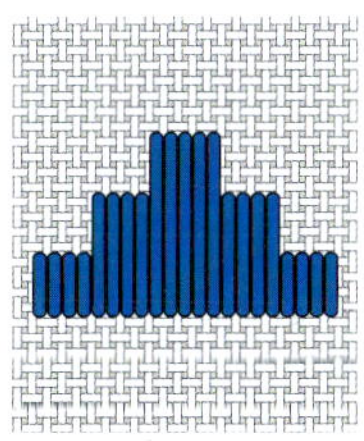

❶ *Larger triangles have another, longer section in the centre. The side sections have four stitches; the centre has five.*

in a diagonal line

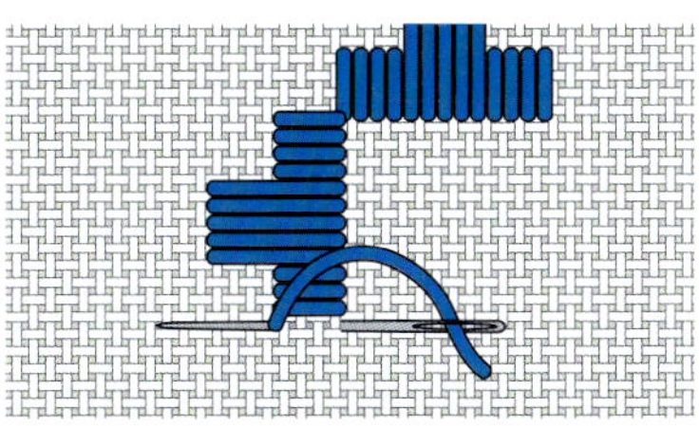

1 After Step 6, work another triangle. Insert the needle to complete the last stitch, then bring it out in the same hole as it just emerged from.

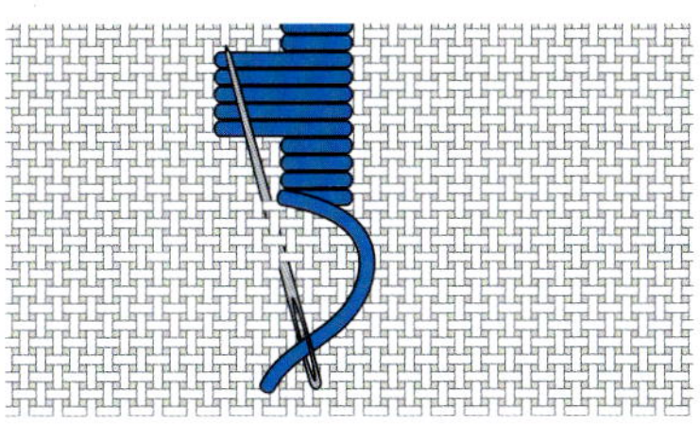

2 Pull the needle through. Insert it four threads down and bring it out four threads up and one to the left.

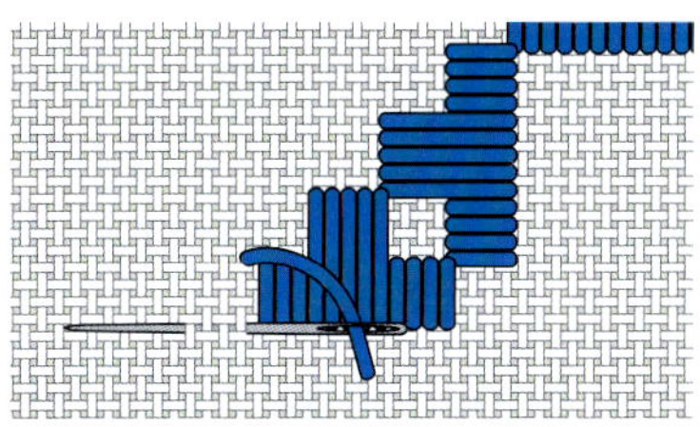

3 Complete another triangle. Insert the needle for the last stitch, then bring it out four threads to the left. Continue, making a line of triangles.

❶ *These triangles are sawtooth rather than stepped. There are many variations that can be made.*

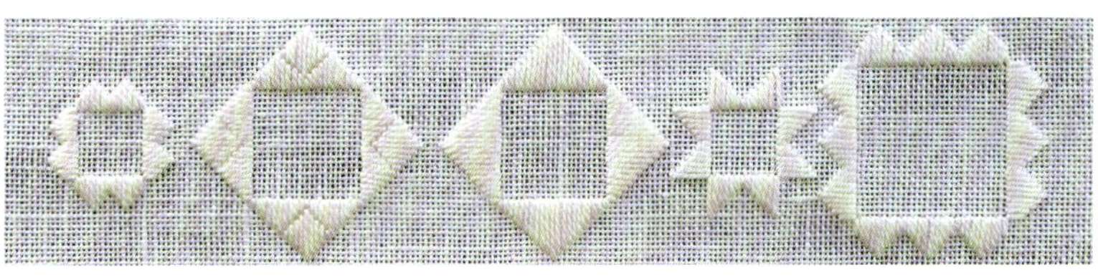

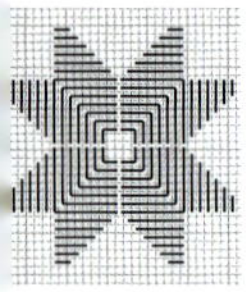

TRADITIONAL

satin stitch star *also known as eight-petalled rose*

This traditional motif is stitched in satin stitch. The size can vary, so follow your chart.

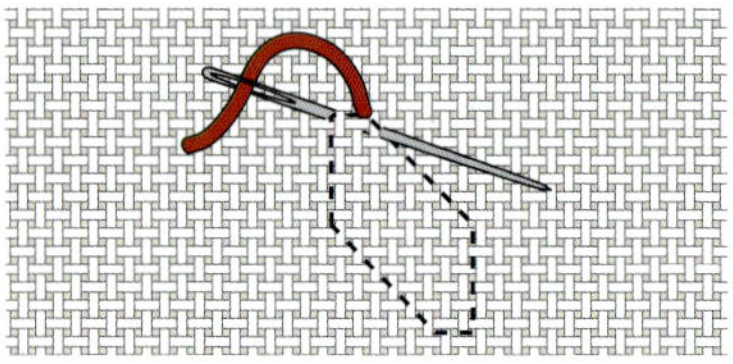

1 Bring the needle out of the fabric. Insert it two threads to the left. Bring the needle out one thread down and three threads to the right.

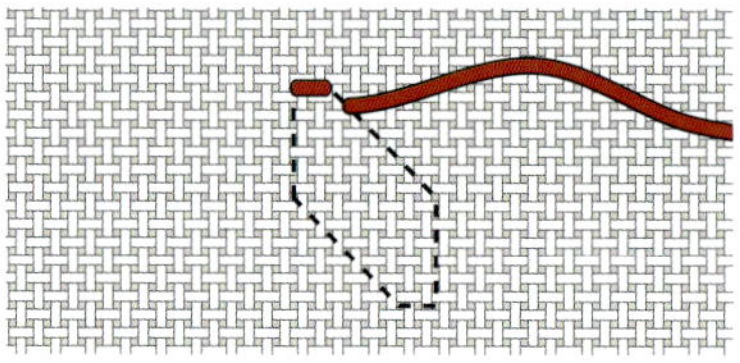

2 Gently pull the needle and thread through so that the stitch lies flat on the fabric surface.

❶ *Don't tighten it so much that the ends pull inward. Don't leave it so loose that the stitch looks slack.*

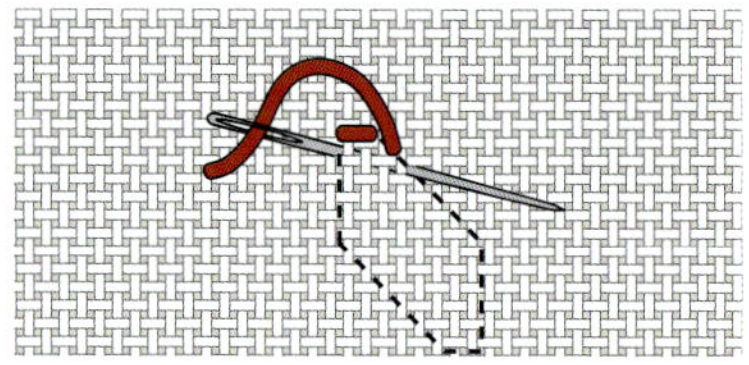

3 Insert the needle below the left end of the previous stitch. Bring the needle out one thread down and four threads right. Gently tighten the stitch to lie flat on the fabric.

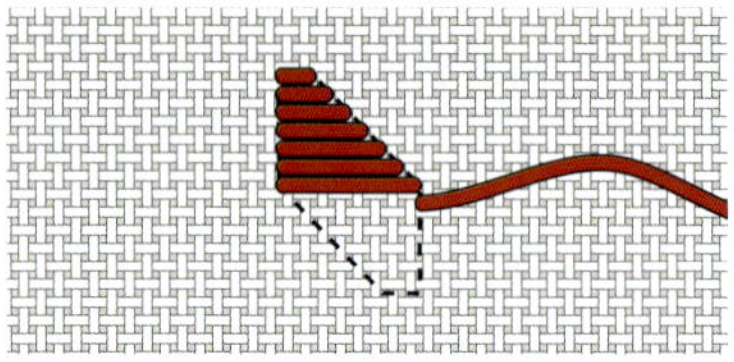

4 Continue increasing the length of the stitches, according to your chart. To begin decreasing, bring the needle out immediately below the beginning of the last, longest stitch.

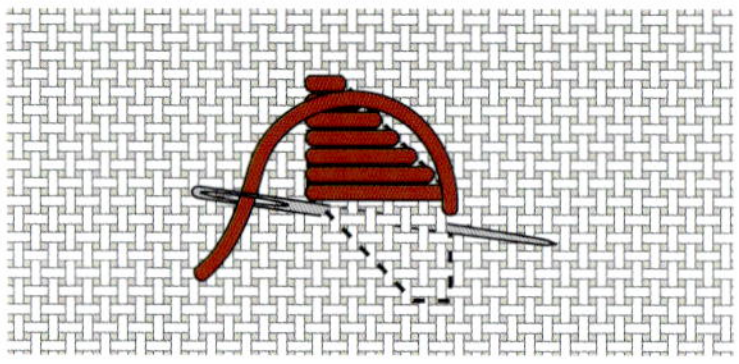

5 Insert the needle one thread right and down from where the previous stitch ended. Bring the needle out one thread below the right end of the previous stitch.

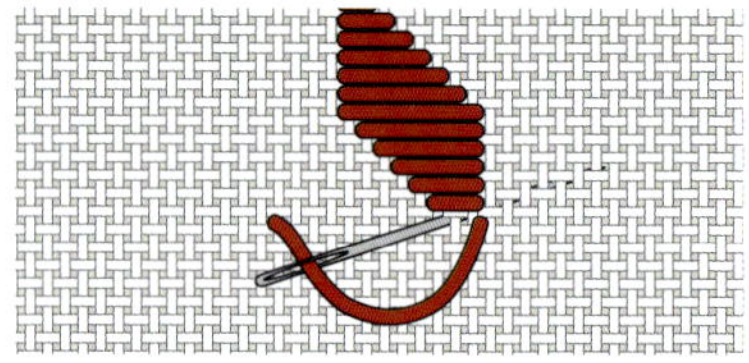

6 Pull the needle and thread through. Continue decreasing the length of each subsequent stitch. To finish the segment, take the needle through to the back when the stitch spans only two fabric threads.

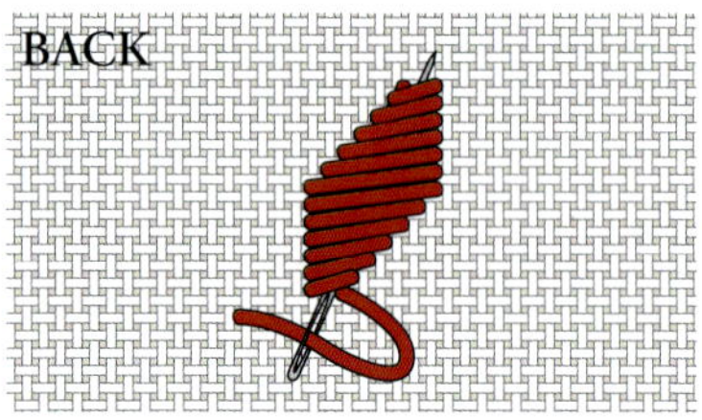

7 Turn the fabric over and run the thread under the back of the stitching, ready to work the next segment.

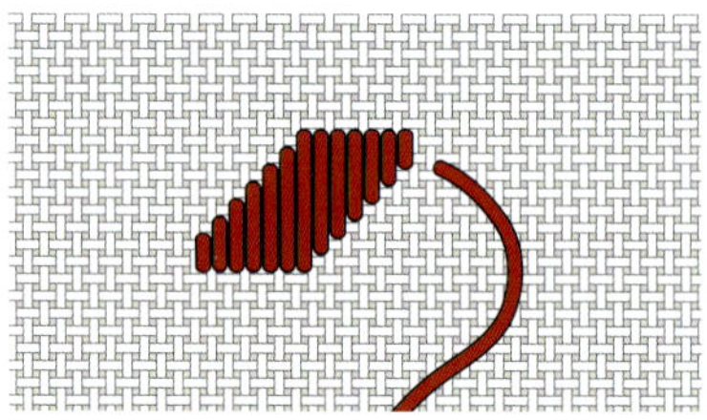

8 Turn back to the front. Turn the work 90° anticlockwise. Bring the needle out two threads to the right of the bottom of the first stitch.

❶ *Subsequent segments are flipped, and increase and decrease on opposite sides.*

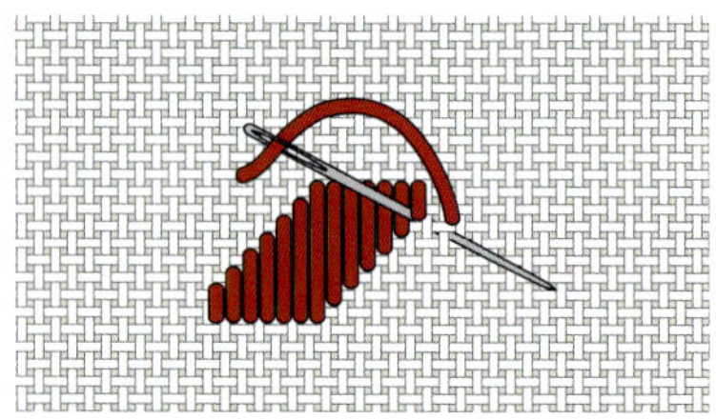

9 Insert the needle two threads left, into the same hole as the first stitch of the previous segment. Bring it out one thread below the previous stitch.

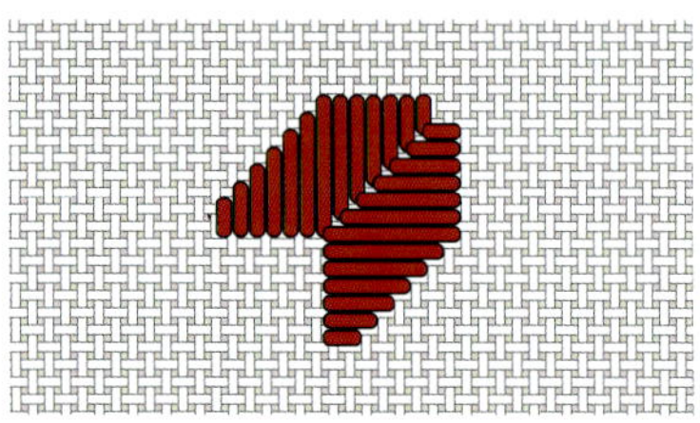

10 Continue working the segment, following the chart, increasing and decreasing similarly to before.

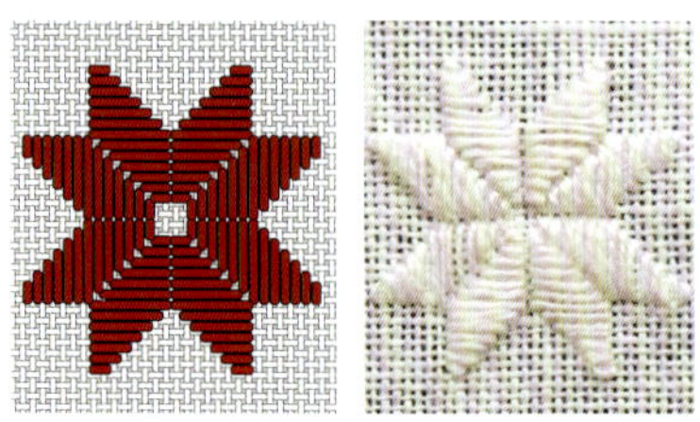

11 Complete the star by following the chart for stitch placement.

❶ *Turn the work for each subsequent segment, so you are stitching in the same orientation as for the previous ones.*

❶ *Never start a new thread in the middle of a segment. If you do, the change in thread will be extremely obvious.*

If there is not enough thread to complete a segment, undo it to the end of the previous segment, finish the thread and start a new one.

satin stitch star *also known as eight-petalled rose*

This traditional motif is stitched in satin stitch. The size can vary, so follow your chart.

R

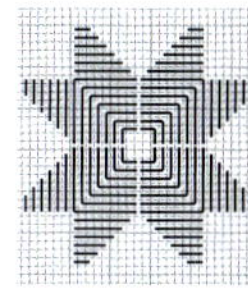

TRADITIONAL

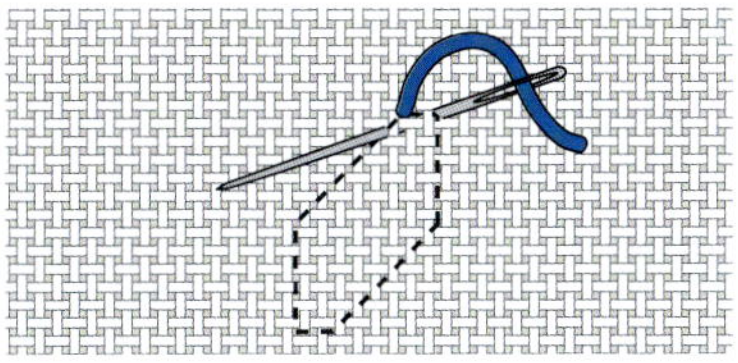

1 Bring the needle out of the fabric. Insert it two threads to the right. Bring the needle out one thread down and three threads to the left.

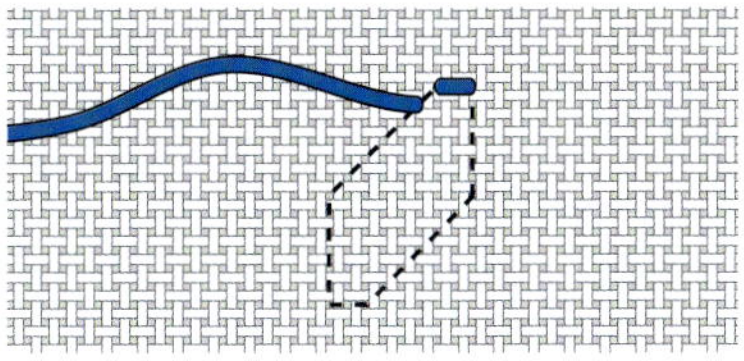

2 Gently pull the needle and thread through so that the stitch lies flat on the fabric surface.

❶ *Don't tighten it so much that the ends pull inward. Don't leave it so loose that the stitch looks slack.*

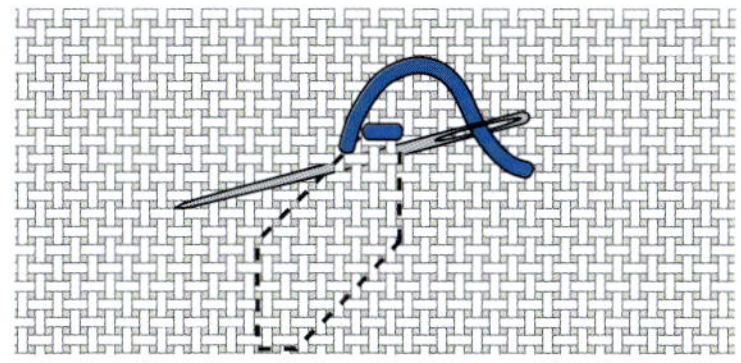

3 Insert the needle below the right end of the previous stitch. Bring the needle out one thread down and four threads left. Gently tighten the stitch to lie flat on the fabric.

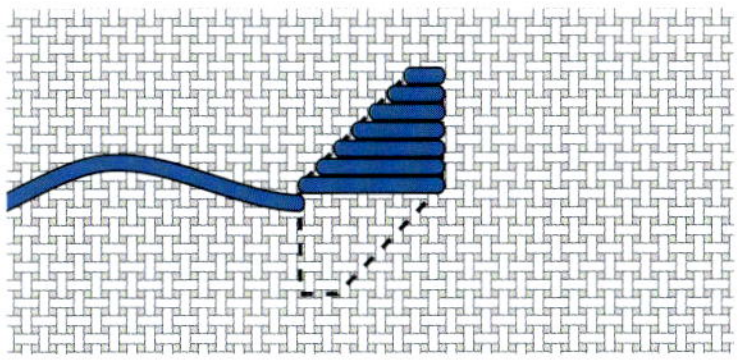

4 Continue increasing the length of the stitches, according to your chart. To begin decreasing, bring the needle out immediately below the beginning of the last, longest stitch.

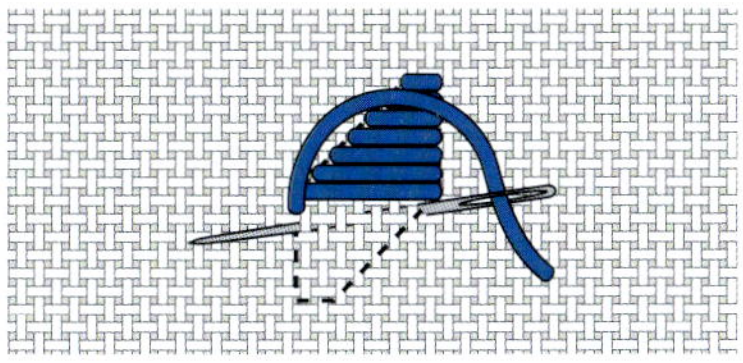

5 Insert the needle one thread left and down from where the previous stitch ended. Bring the needle out one thread below the left end of the previous stitch.

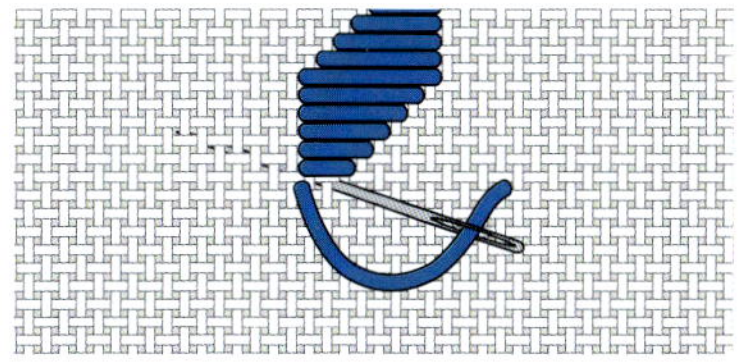

6 Pull the needle and thread through. Continue decreasing the length of each subsequent stitch. To finish the segment, take the needle through to the back when the stitch spans only two fabric threads.

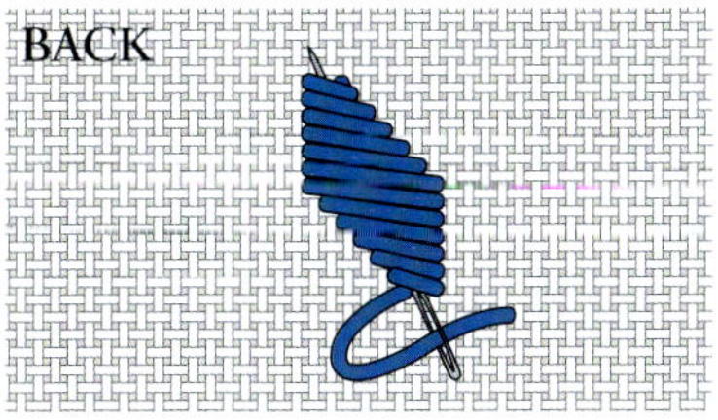

7 Turn the fabric over and run the thread under the back of the stitching, ready to work the next segment.

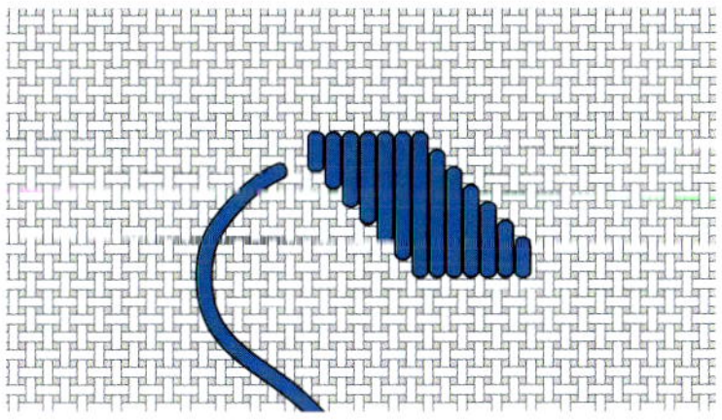

8 Turn back to the front. Turn the work 90° clockwise. Bring the needle out two threads to the left of the bottom of the first stitch.

❶ *Subsequent segments are flipped, and increase and decrease on opposite sides.*

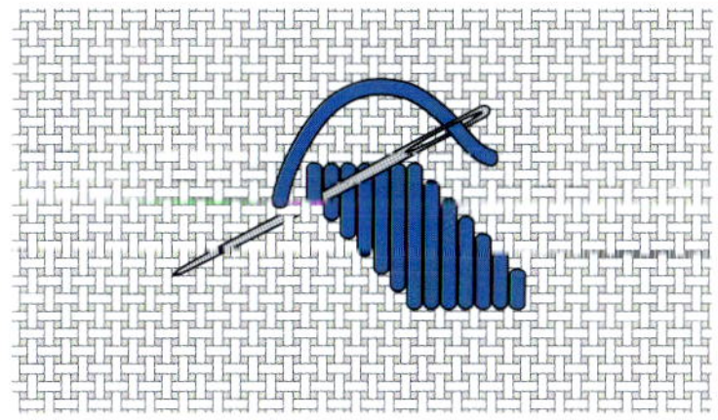

9 Insert the needle two threads right, into the same hole as the first stitch of the previous segment. Bring it out one thread below the previous stitch.

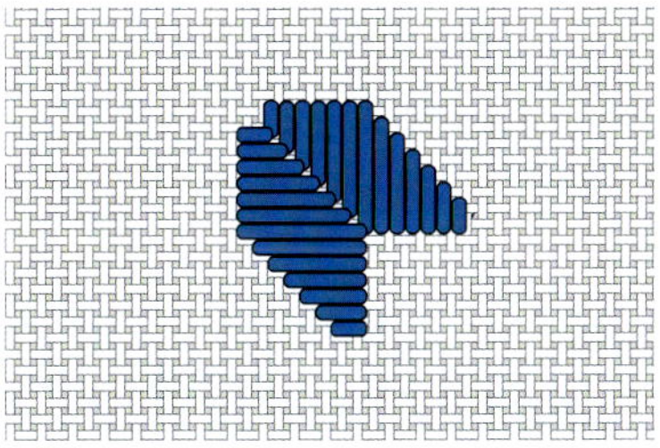

10 Continue working the segment, following the chart, increasing and decreasing similarly to before.

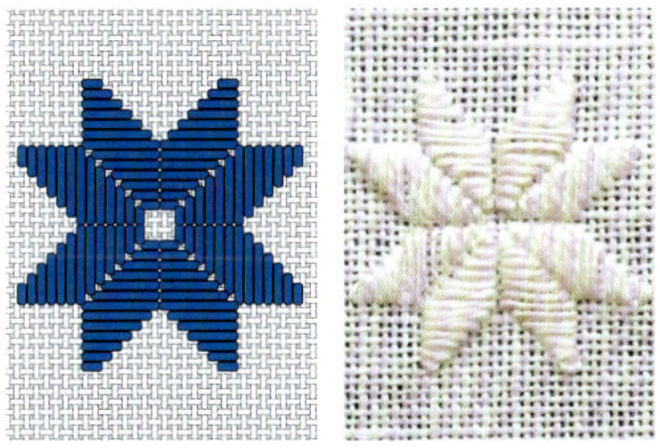

11 Complete the star by following the chart for stitch placement.

❶ *Turn the work for each subsequent segment, so you are stitching in the same orientation as for the previous ones.*

❶ *Never start a new thread in the middle of a segment. If you do, the change in thread will be extremely obvious.*

If there is not enough thread to complete a segment, undo it to the end of the previous segment, finish the thread and start a new one.

cable stitch

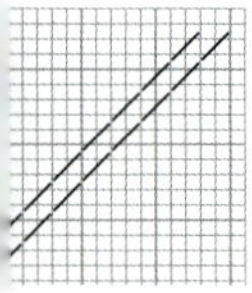

TRADITIONAL

Cable stitch is a pulled thread stitch, useful for creating texture and lines. Use the thinner thread.

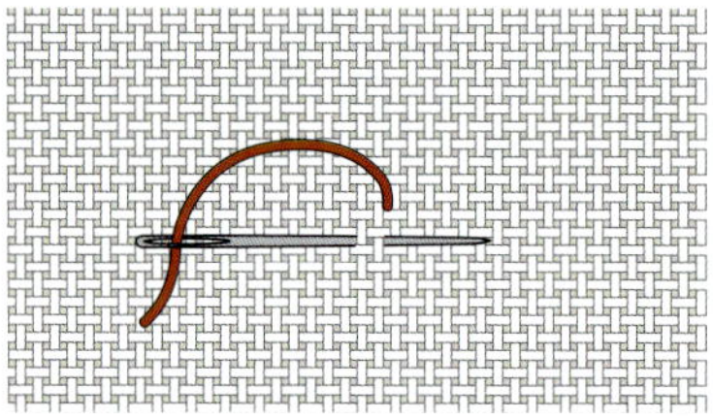

1 Bring the needle out of the fabric. Insert it two threads down and left. Bring it out again two threads to the right.

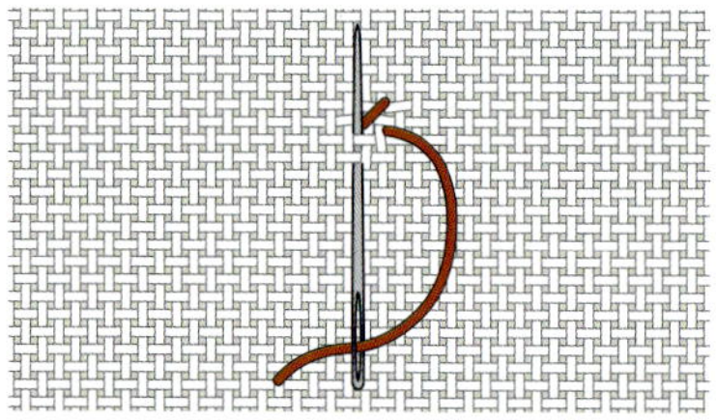

2 Pull the needle through to tighten the stitch and pull the fabric threads together. Insert the needle two threads down and left. Bring it out two up.

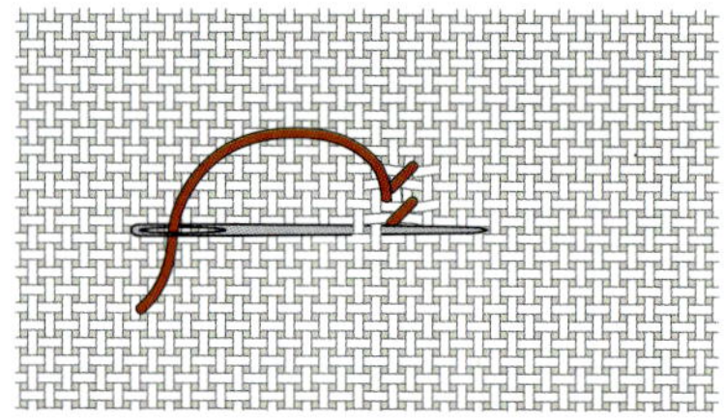

3 Pull the needle through to tighten the stitch. Insert it two threads down and left. Bring it out again two threads to the right.

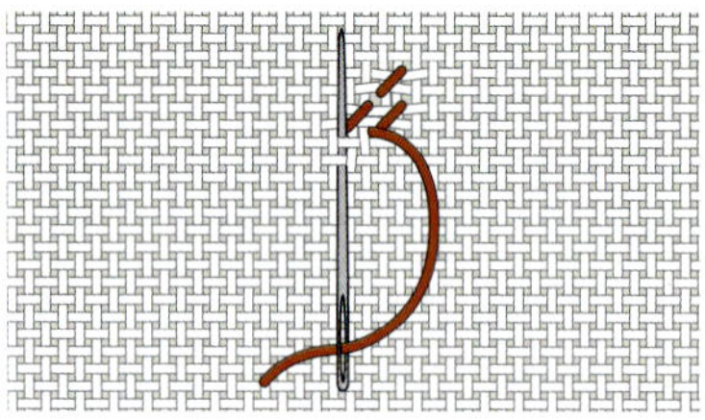

4 Pull the needle through and tighten the stitch. Insert it two threads down and left. Bring it out two up.

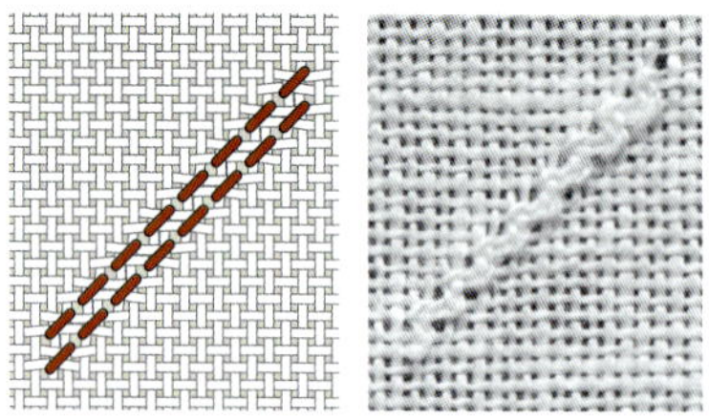

5 Continue in the same way. To finish, run the thread under the back of eight to ten stitches.

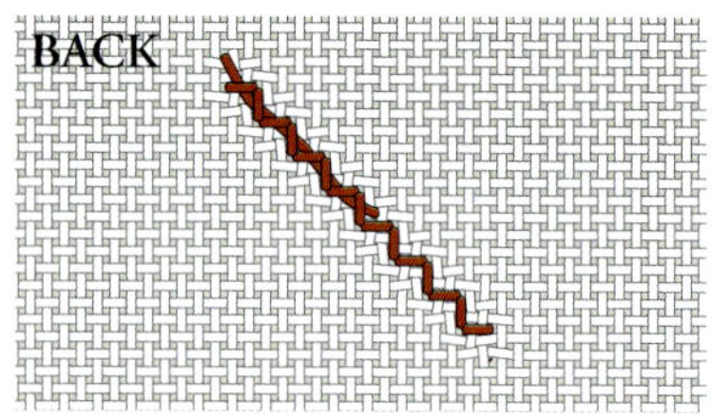

❶ *On the back, the stitches appear as steps zig-zagging across surface of the fabric. The top end shows the tail.*

turning corners

To turn a corner with a point, an extra stitch needs to be placed in the sequence.

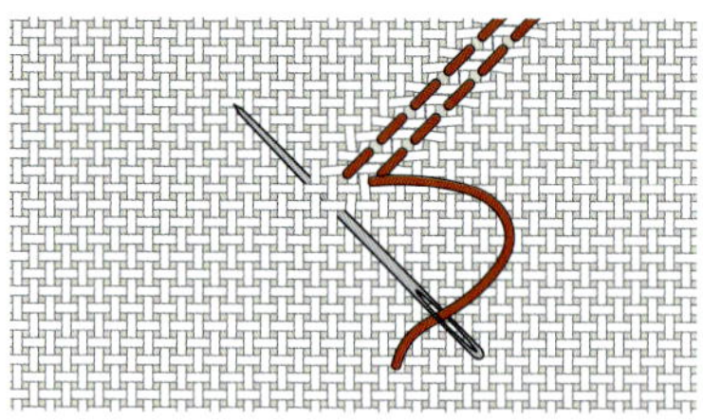

1 At the corner, insert the needle. Bring it out up and left two threads. ❶ *A corner is the only time that a diagonal stitch on the back is correct.*

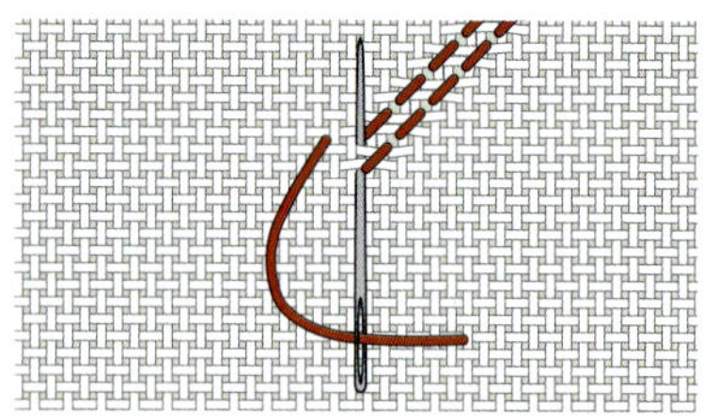

2 Pull the needle and through and tighten the stitch. Insert the needle into the corner hole again, and take it under two threads vertically.

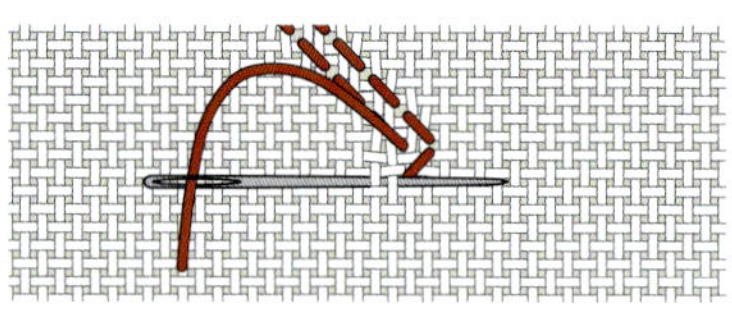

3 Turn the work 90° anticlockwise and continue stitching as before, in the new direction.

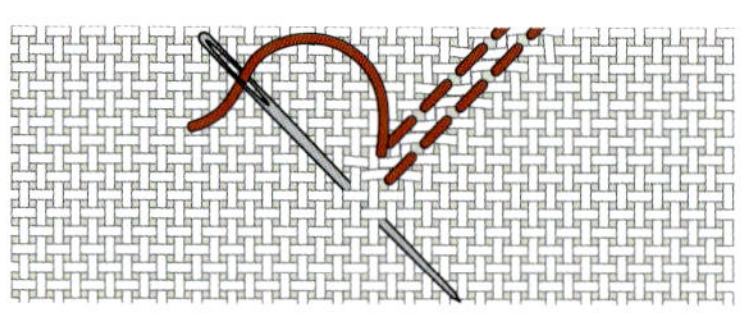

4 To turn the other direction, insert the needle in the corner. Bring it out two threads down and right.

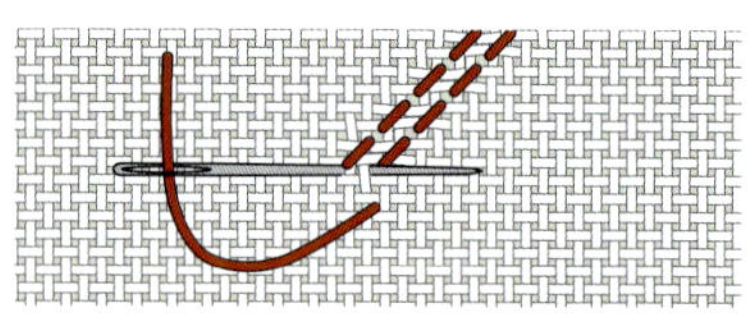

5 Pull the needle to tighten. Insert the needle in the corner again. Take it under two threads horizontally.

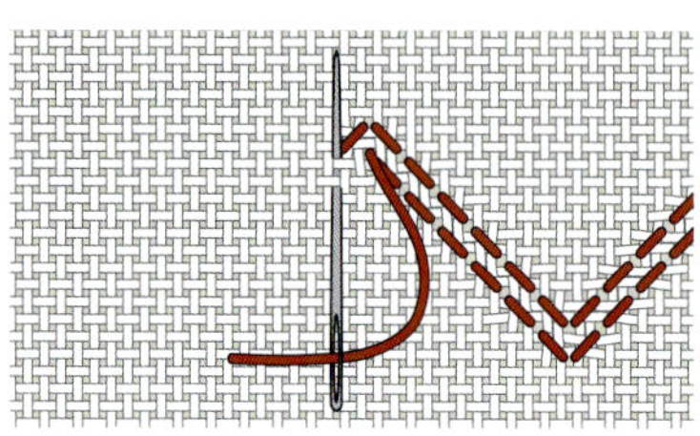

6 Turn the work 90° clockwise. Continue stitching as before.

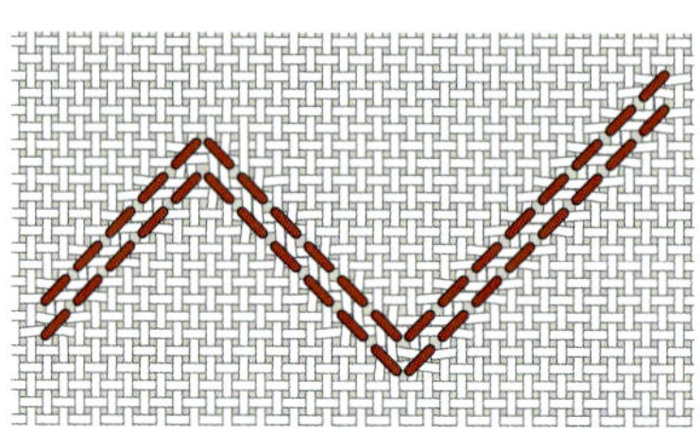

7 The completed corners and stitching.

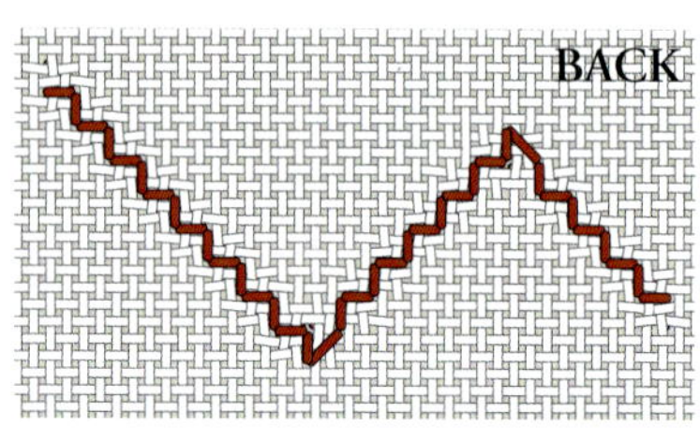

❶ *The back of the work has diagonal stitches in the corner.*

cable stitch

Cable stitch is a pulled thread stitch, useful for creating texture and lines. Use the thinner thread.

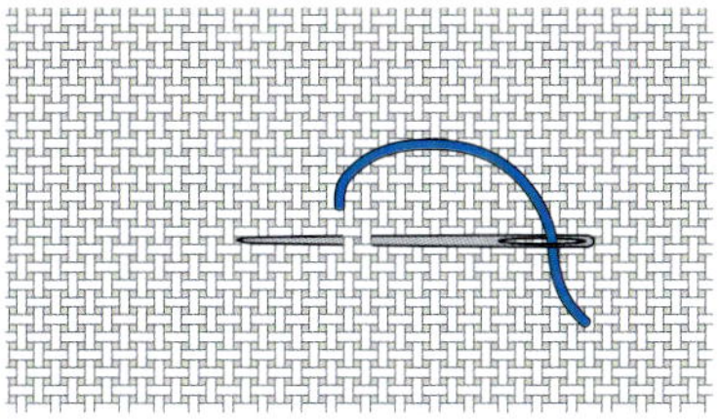

1 Bring the needle out of the fabric. Insert it two threads down and right. Bring it out again two threads to the left.

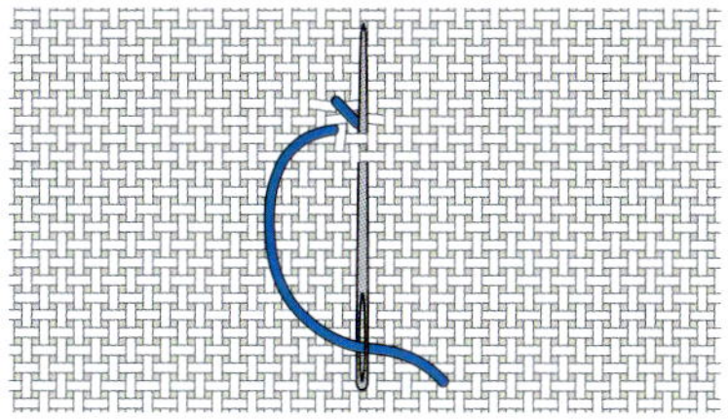

2 Pull the needle through to tighten the stitch and pull the fabric threads together. Insert the needle two threads down and right. Bring it out two up.

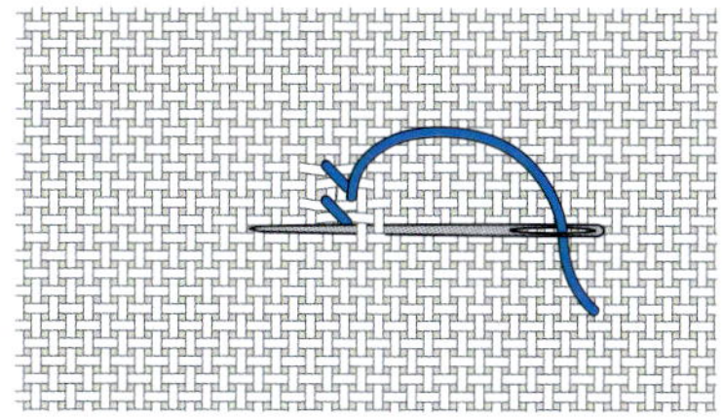

3 Pull the needle through and tighten the stitch. Insert it two threads down and right. Bring it out again two threads to the left.

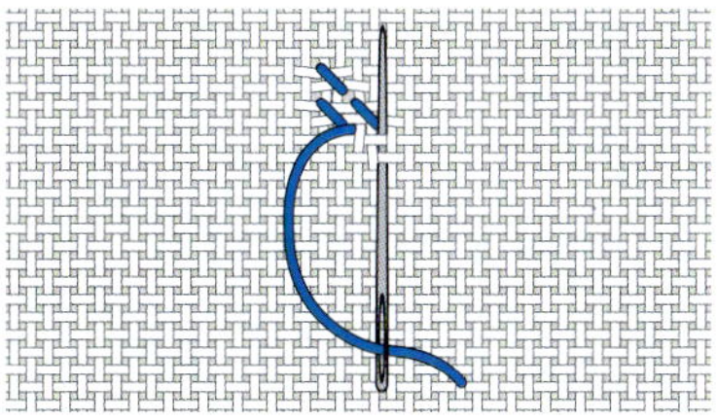

4 Pull the needle through and tighten the stitch. Insert it two threads down and right. Bring it out two up.

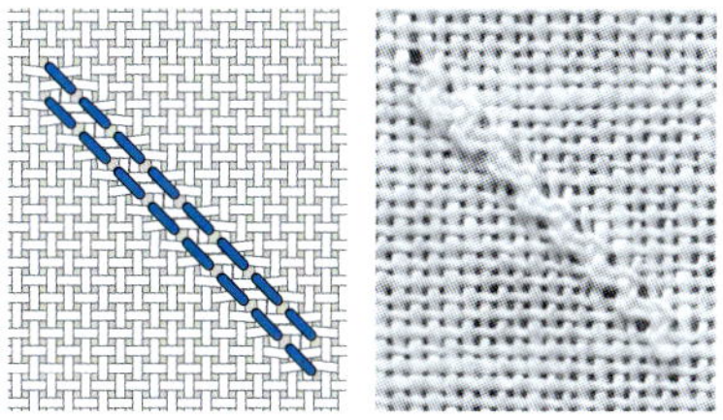

5 Continue in the same way. To finish, run the thread under the back of eight to ten stitches.

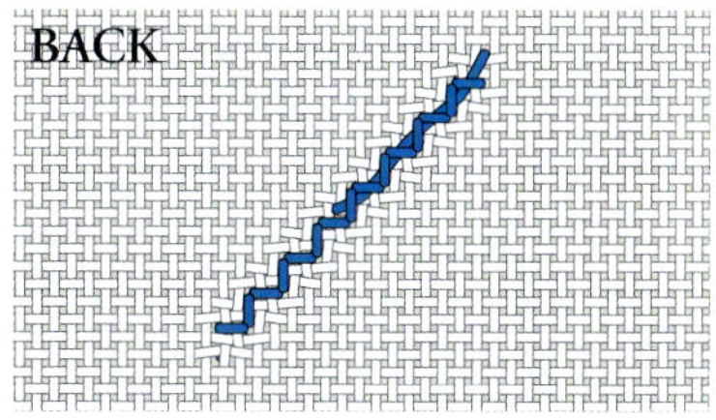

❶ *On the back, the stitches appear as steps zig-zagging across surface of the fabric. The top end shows the tail.*

turning corners

To turn a corner with a point, an extra stitch needs to be placed in the sequence.

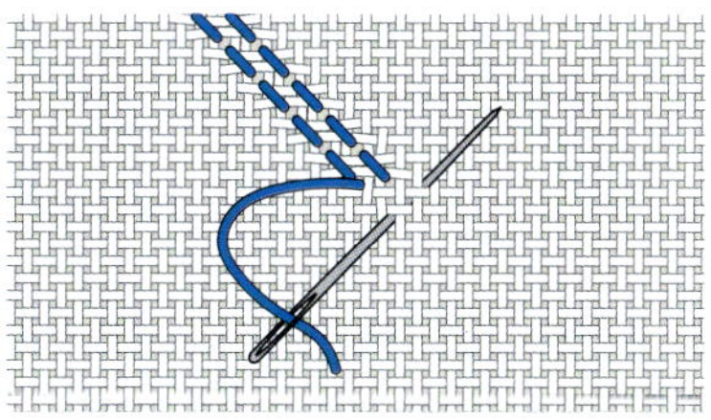

1 At the corner, insert the needle. Bring it out up and right two threads. ❶ *A corner is the only time that a diagonal stitch on the back is correct.*

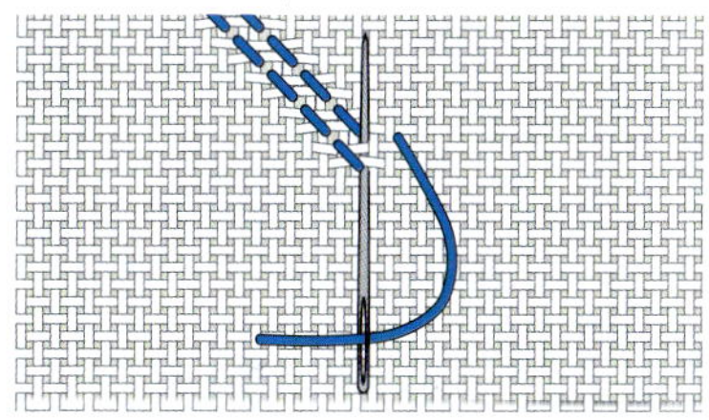

2 Pull the needle and through and tighten the stitch. Insert the needle into the corner hole again, and take it under two threads vertically.

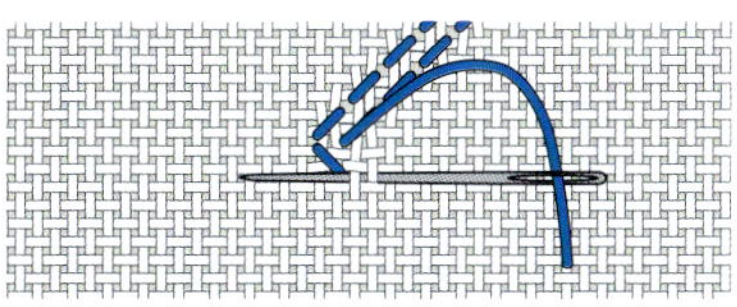

3 Turn the work 90° clockwise and continue stitching as before, in the new direction.

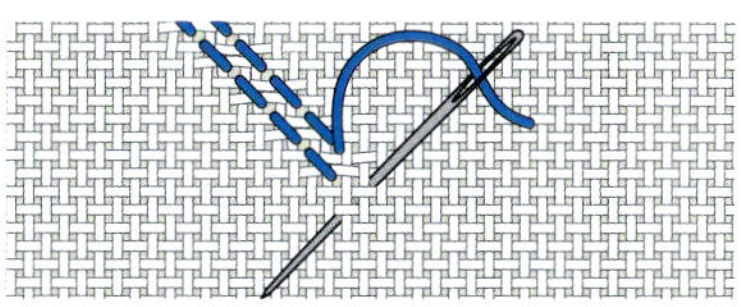

4 To turn the other direction, insert the needle in the corner. Bring it out two threads down and left.

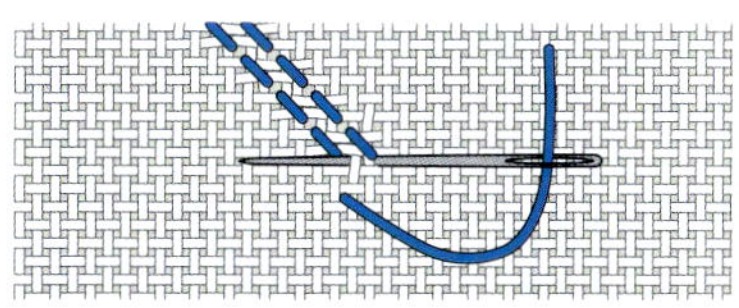

5 Pull the needle to tighten. Insert the needle in the corner again. Take it under two threads horizontally.

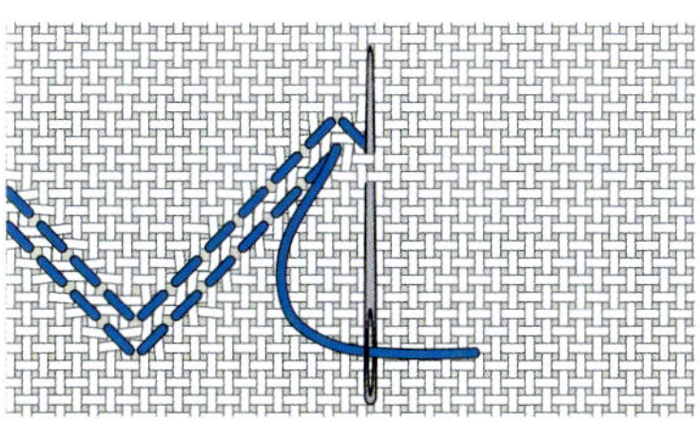

6 Turn the work 90° anticlockwise. Continue stitching as before.

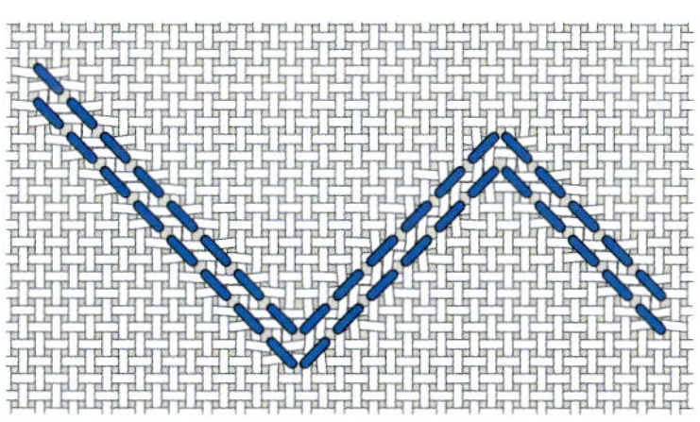

7 The completed corners and stitching.

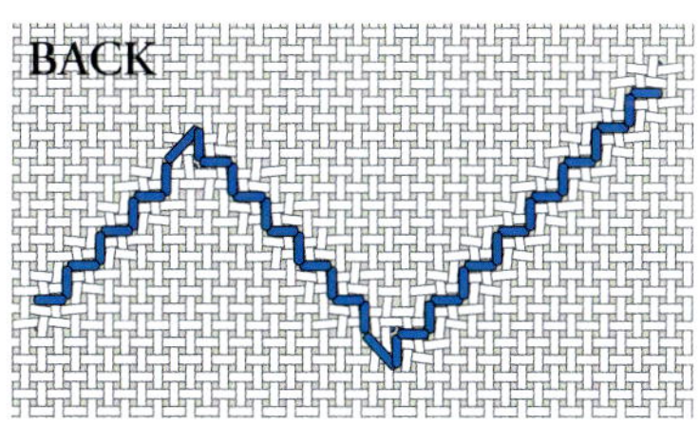

❶ *The back of the work has diagonal stitches in the corner.*

four-sided stitch

L

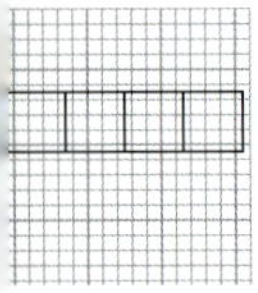

TRADITIONAL

This pulled thread stitch is useful for borders. It can be worked with regular, rather than tight, tension as a counted stitch if holes are not desired. Use the thinner thread.

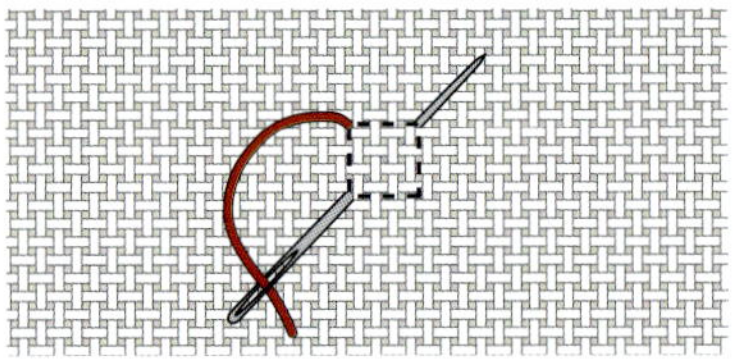

1 Bring the needle out of the left top of the four by four thread square. Insert it in the bottom left corner. Bring it out in the top right corner.

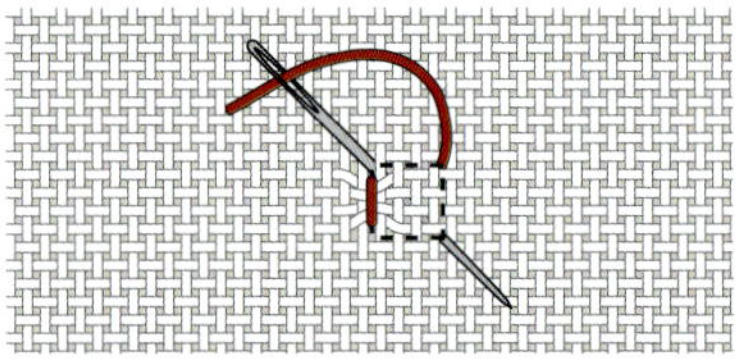

2 Pull the needle through. Tighten the stitch. Insert the needle in the top left corner and bring it out in the bottom right corner.

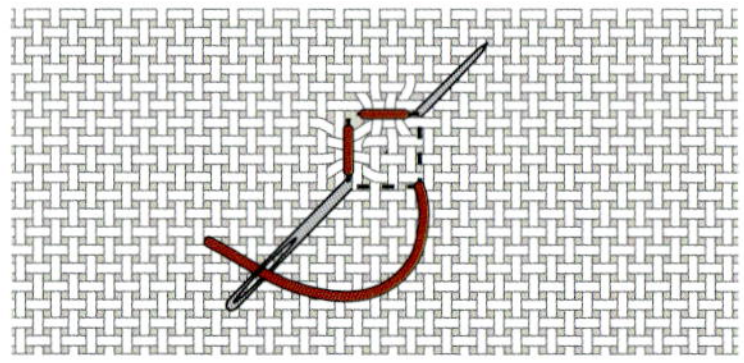

3 Pull the needle through. Tighten the stitch. Insert the needle in the bottom left corner, bringing it out in the top right corner.

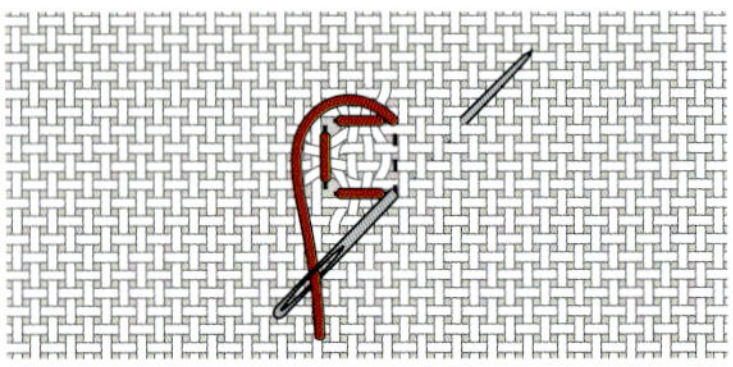

4 Pull the needle through. Tighten the stitch. Insert the needle in the bottom right to finish the square. Bring it out in the top right of the next square.

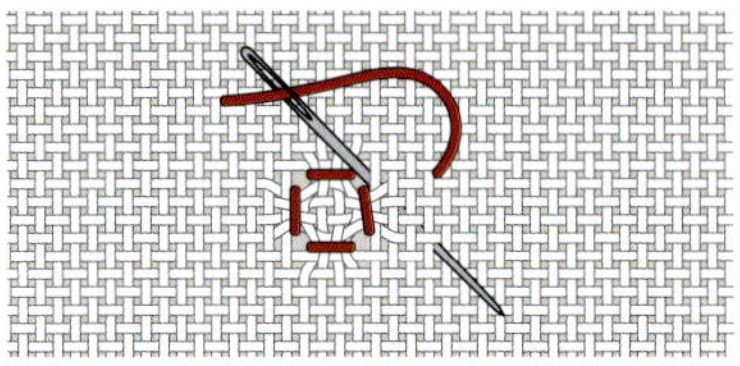

5 Pull the needle through. Tighten the stitch. Insert the needle in the top left. Bring it out in the bottom right.

❶ *Except for the first one, the vertical stitches slope due to the thread tension.*

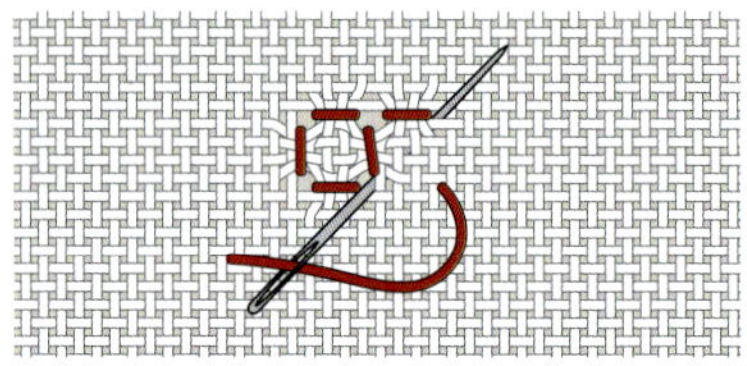

6 Pull the needle through and tighten the stitch. Insert the needle in the bottom left corner, bringing it out in the top right corner.

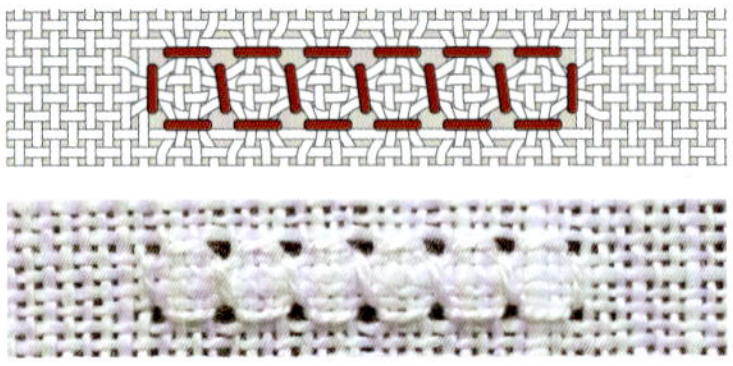

7 Cycle through the steps. Work a vertical stitch to finish. Take the needle to the back. Run it under the back of the stitching to secure the end.

❶ *Think of this as making little boxes. First, work the left side of the box. Then work the top, the bottom and finally, the right side of the box (which is also the left side of the next box). Work the top of the box, then the bottom of the box. Keep cycling through.*

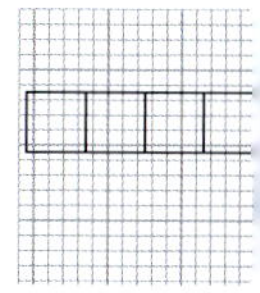

TRADITIONAL

four-sided stitch

This pulled thread stitch is useful for borders. It can be worked with regular, rather than tight, tension as a counted stitch if holes are not desired. Use the thinner thread.

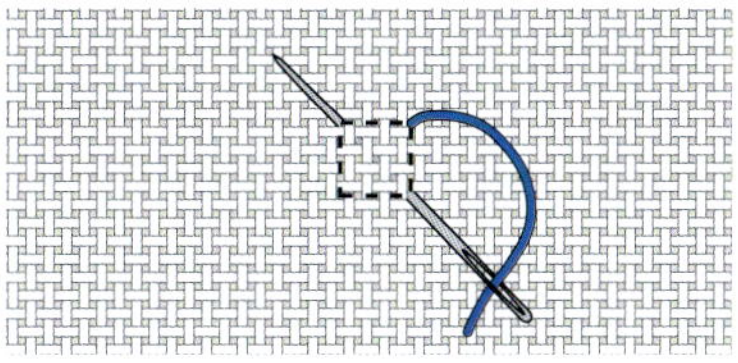

1 Bring the needle out of the right top of the four by four thread square. Insert it in the bottom right corner. Bring it out in the top left corner.

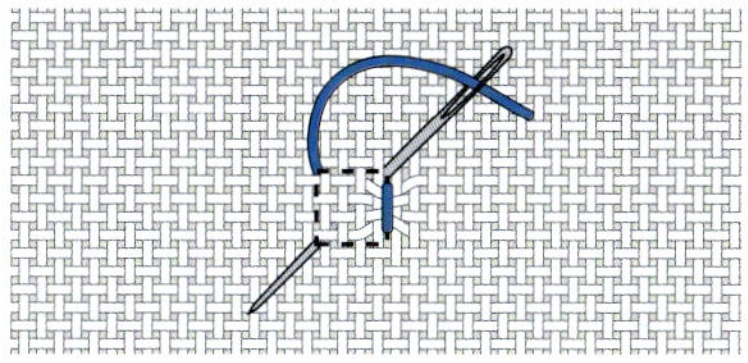

2 Pull the needle through. Tighten the stitch. Insert the needle in the top right corner and bring it out in the bottom left corner.

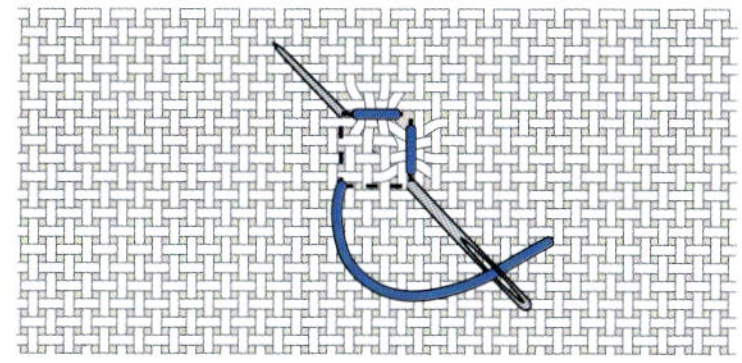

3 Pull the needle through. Tighten the stitch. Insert the needle in the bottom right corner, bringing it out in the top left corner.

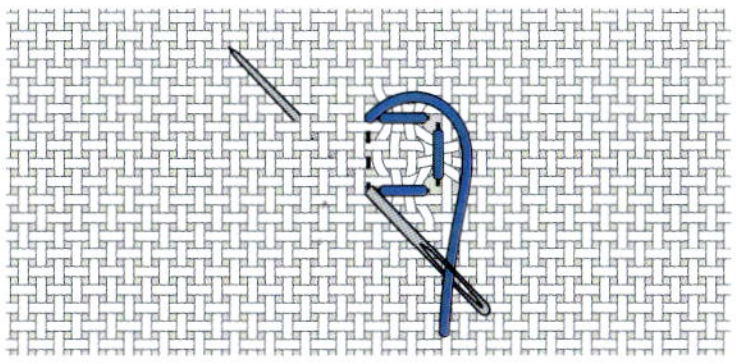

4 Pull the needle through. Tighten the stitch. Insert the needle in the bottom left to finish the square. Bring it out in the top left of the next square.

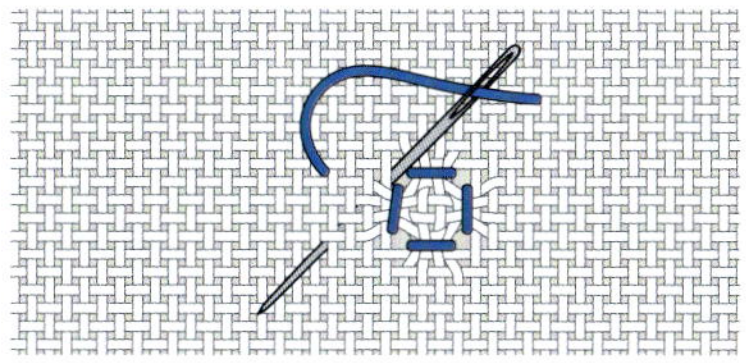

5 Pull the needle through. Tighten the stitch. Insert the needle in the top right. Bring it out in the bottom left.

❶ *Except for the first one, the vertical stitches slope due to the thread tension.*

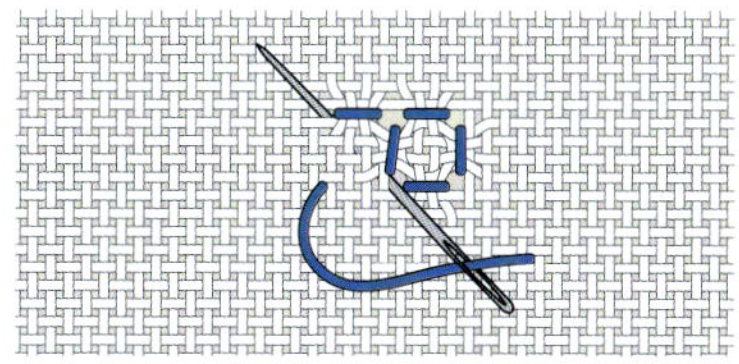

6 Pull the needle through and tighten the stitch. Insert the needle in the bottom right corner, bringing it out in the top left corner.

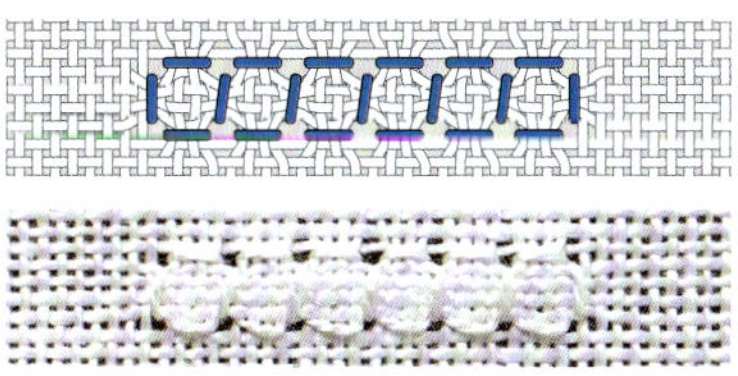

7 Cycle through the steps. Work a vertical stitch to finish. Take the needle to the back. Run it under the back of the stitching to secure the end.

❶ *Think of this as making little boxes. First, work the right side of the box. Then work the top, the bottom and finally, the left side of the box (which is also the right side of the next box). Work the top of the box, then the bottom of the box. Keep cycling through.*

L

eyelets

These eyelets do not need any stitching nearby in which to anchor the ends, making them very versatile. Use the thinner thread.

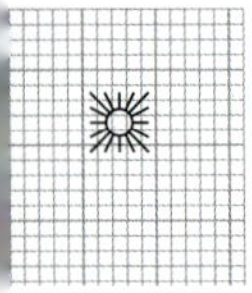

TRADITIONAL

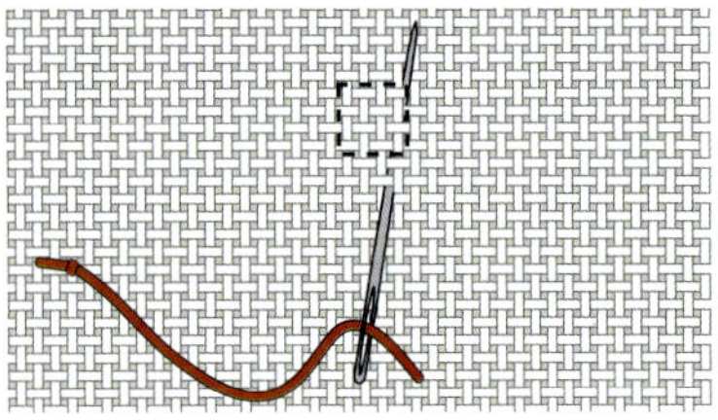

1 Make a knot in the thread. Insert the needle two threads down and one thread left of the bottom right corner of the eyelet which is about to be stitched. Bring it out in the top right corner.

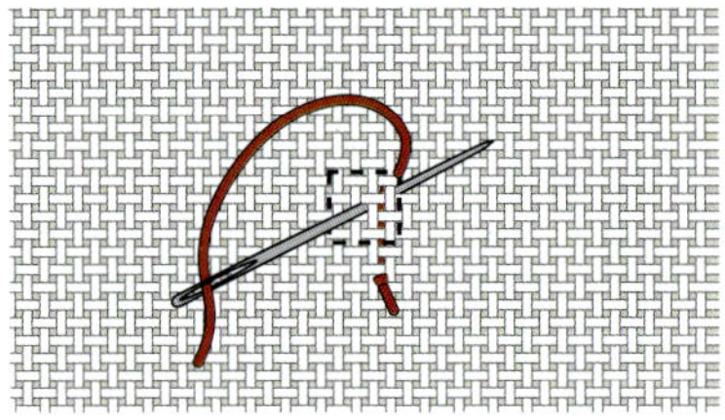

2 Pull the needle and thread through. The knot will sit on the front of the fabric. Insert the needle in the centre of the eyelet. Take the needle behind the thread leading to the knot, and bring it out again one thread below where it last emerged.

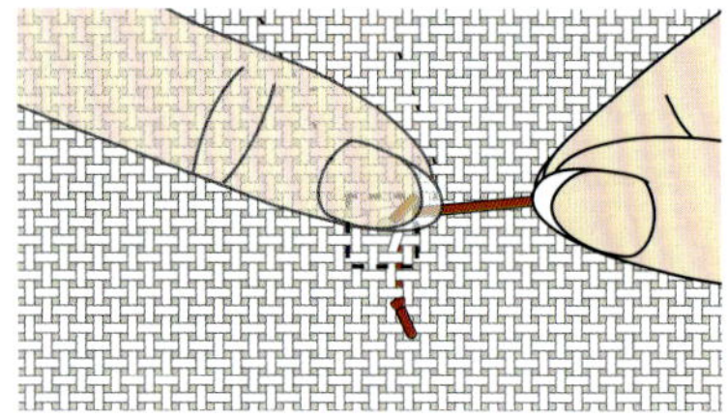

3 Pinch the stitch between your finger and thumb with one hand. With the other hand, pull the thread away from the centre to tighten the stitch and enlarge the centre hole.

Strong, even tension throughout creates an open, evenly shaped hole.

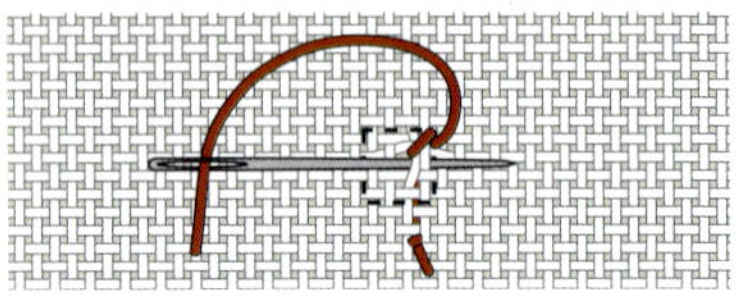

4 Insert the needle in the centre of the eyelet. Take the needle behind the thread leading to the knot, and bring it out again one thread down from where it last emerged.

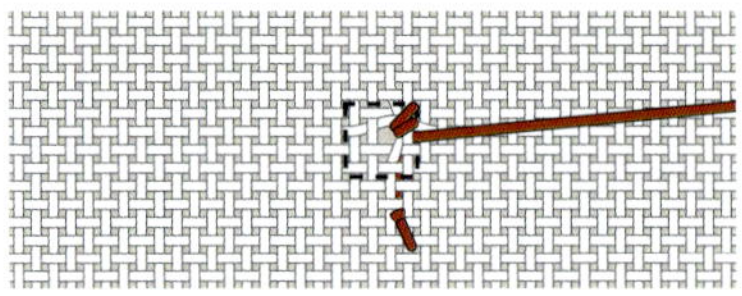

5 Pull the needle through and pinch and pull to tighten the stitch. Insert the needle at the centre and bring it out again one thread further around the edge of the eyelet.

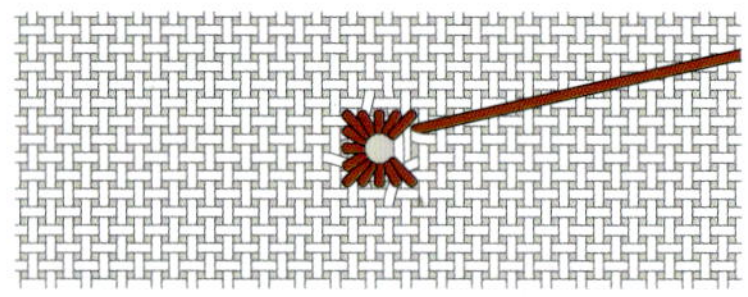

6 Keep working around the eyelet, to complete the first three sides, with five stitches on each side. Turn the work as necessary to make it easier to insert the needle.

On passing the knot, it can be cut off.

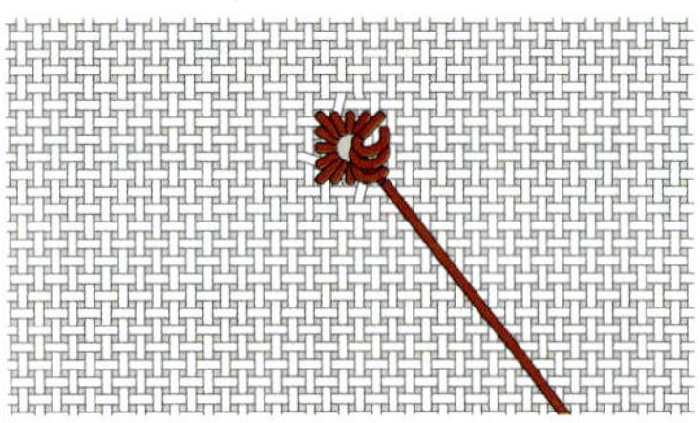

7 For the final three stitches, work them as loose loops, and bring the needle out in the corner.

The loose tension means the previous stitches can accidentally get caught on the needle. Ensure they don't.

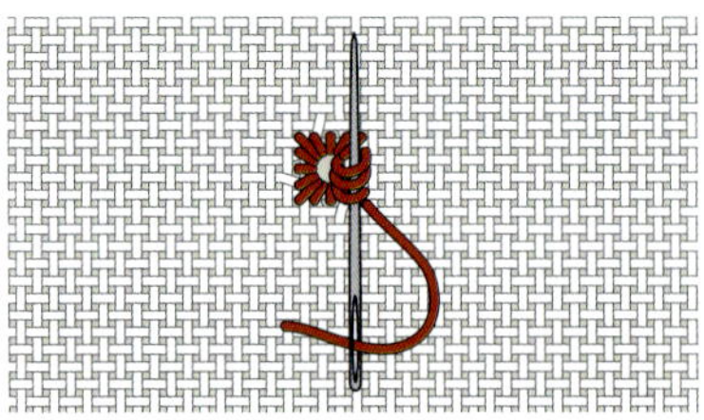

8 From the corner, insert the needle under the three loose loops. Leave it sitting in the loops.

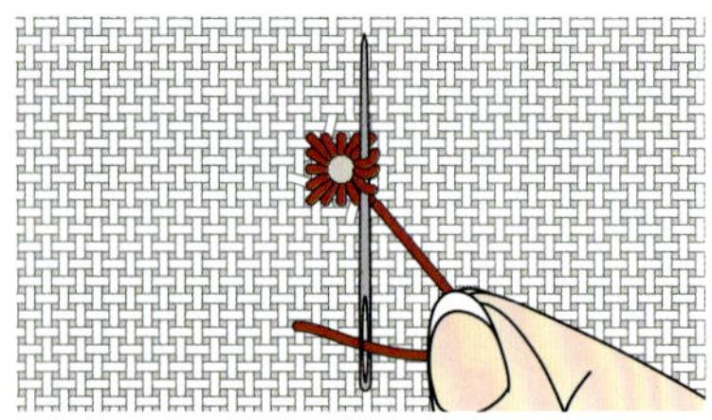

9 Pull the thread coming out of the corner to tighten the three stitches around the needle shaft.

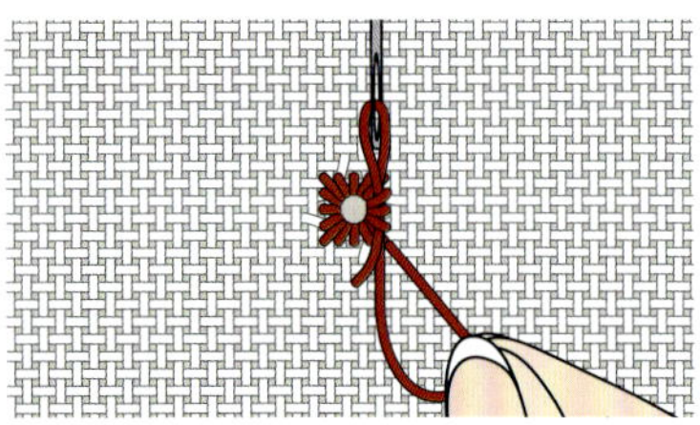

10 Pull the needle further so the doubled thread sits within the stitches. Pull the thread to tighten further.

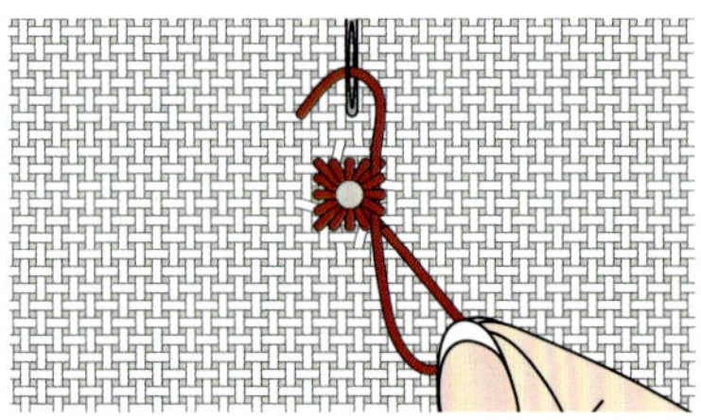

11 Pull the needle further so the single thread sits within the stitches. Pull the thread to tighten further.

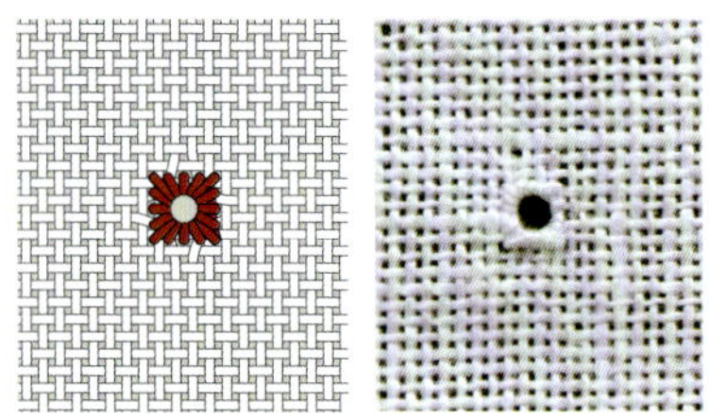

12 Pull the needle through to finally tighten the last stitch and finish the eyelet. Trim the thread end.

If there is no hole or a tiny hole, it is not a real eyelet. Use tight tension and pull your eyelet open.

eyelets

These eyelets do not need any stitching nearby in which to anchor the ends, making them very versatile. Use the thinner thread.

R

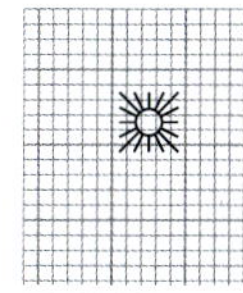
TRADITIONAL

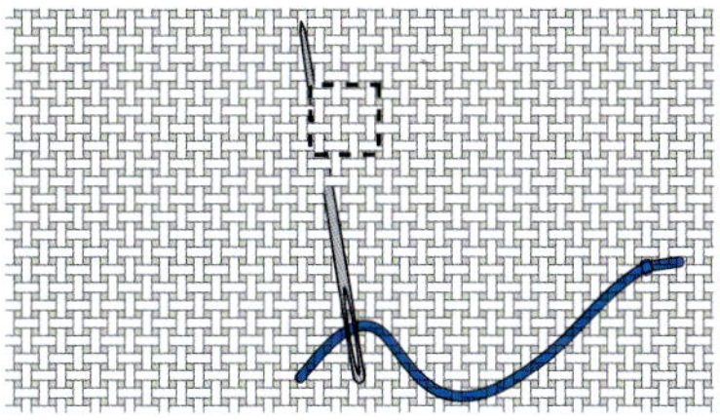

1 Make a knot in the thread. Insert the needle two threads down and one thread right of the bottom left corner of the eyelet which is about to be stitched. Bring it out in the top left corner.

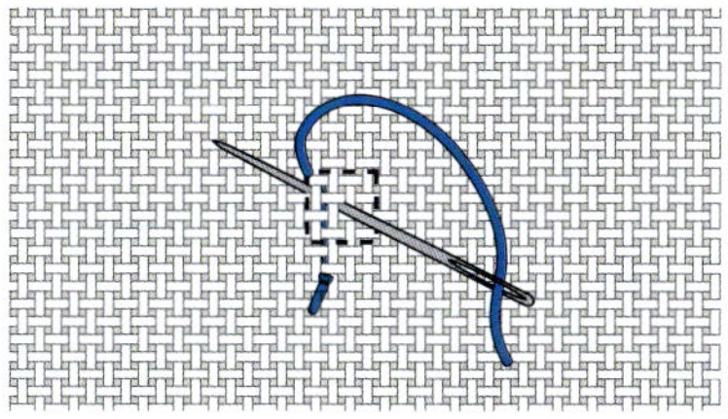

2 Pull the needle and thread through. The knot will sit on the front of the fabric. Insert the needle in the centre of the eyelet. Take the needle behind the thread leading to the knot, and bring it out again one thread below where it last emerged.

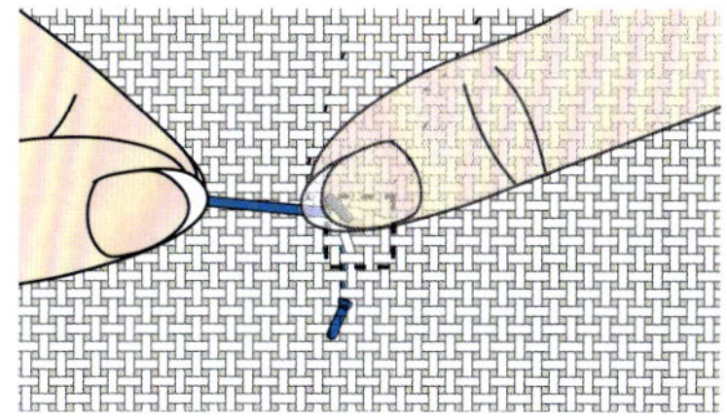

3 Pinch the stitch between your finger and thumb with one hand. With the other hand, pull the thread away from the centre to tighten the stitch and enlarge the centre hole.

! *Strong, even tension throughout creates an open, evenly shaped hole.*

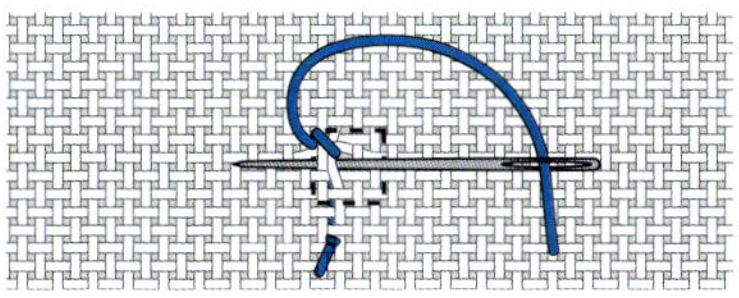

4 Insert the needle in the centre of the eyelet. Take the needle behind the thread leading to the knot, and bring it out again one thread down from where it last emerged.

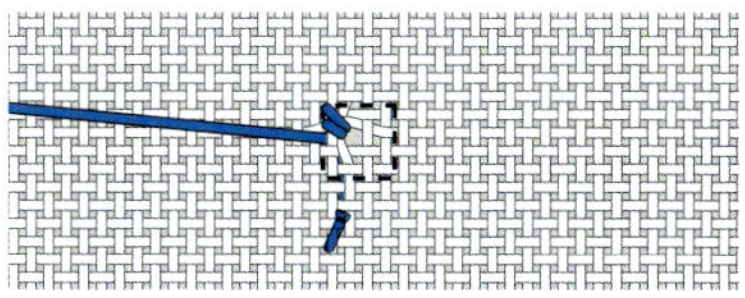

5 Pull the needle through and pinch and pull to tighten the stitch. Insert the needle at the centre and bring it out again one thread further around the edge of the eyelet.

6 Keep working around the eyelet, to complete the first three sides, with five stitches on each side. Turn the work as necessary to make it easier to insert the needle.

! *On passing the knot, it can be cut off.*

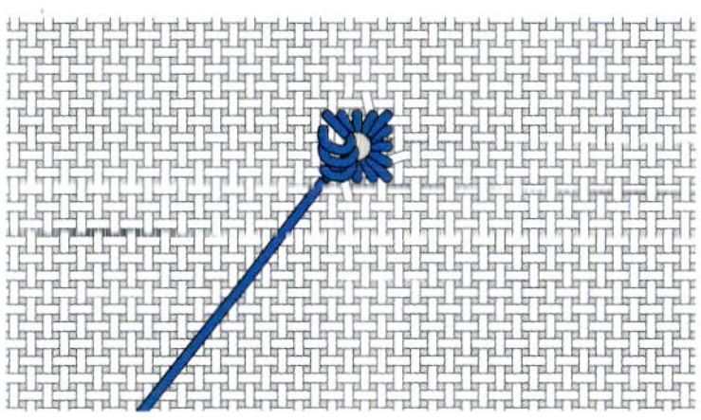

7 For the final three stitches, work them as loose loops, and bring the needle out in the corner.

! *The loose tension means the previous stitches can accidentally get caught on the needle. Ensure they don't.*

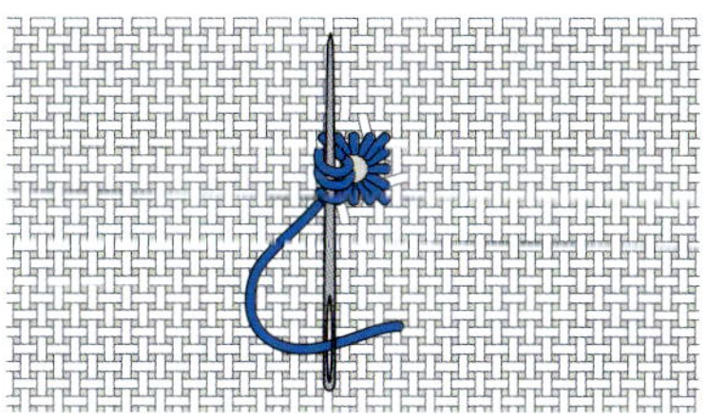

8 From the corner, insert the needle under the three loose loops. Leave it sitting in the loops.

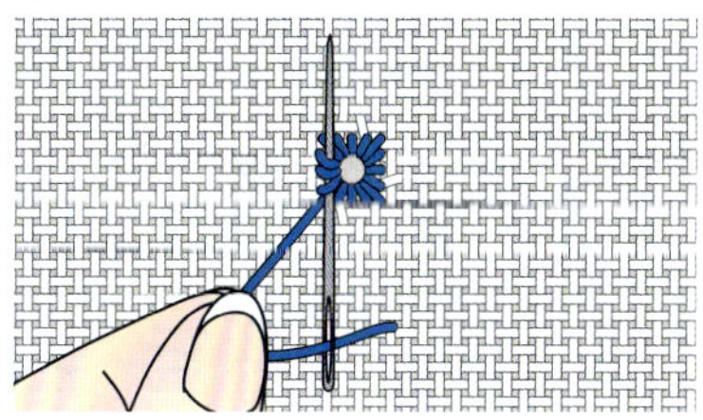

9 Pull the thread coming out of the corner to tighten the three stitches around the needle shaft.

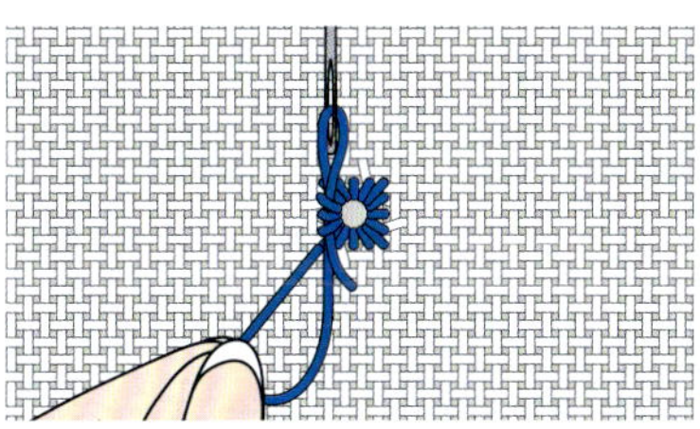

10 Pull the needle further so the doubled thread sits within the stitches. Pull the thread to tighten further.

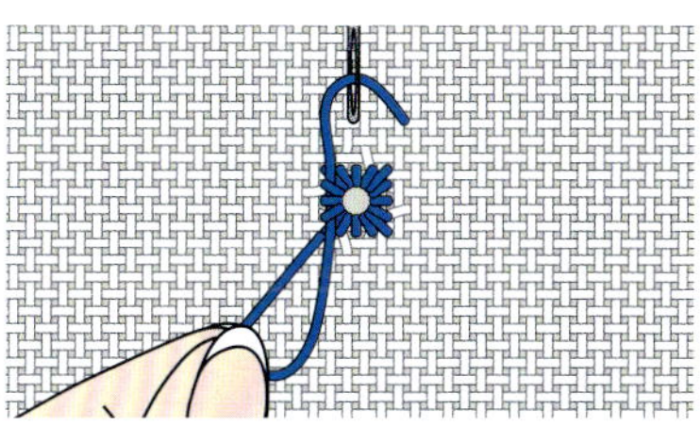

11 Pull the needle further so the single thread sits within the stitches. Pull the thread to tighten further.

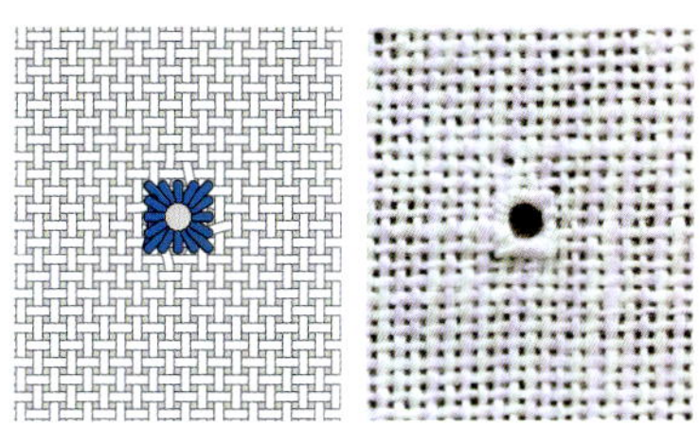

12 Pull the needle through to finally tighten the last stitch and finish the eyelet. Trim the thread end.

! *If there is no hole or a tiny hole, it is not a real eyelet. Use tight tension and pull your eyelet open.*

cutting fabric threads

Fabric threads are cut and withdrawn between cutwork's satin stitch boundaries. Only ever cut threads once all the other stitching is worked, because pulled thread stitches worked after the threads are cut could cause the cut ends to fray.

top tip cutting

Only cut when you are feeling fresh; not tired or rushed, as it is easy to make mistakes. Take care and use good lighting. Remember to breathe!

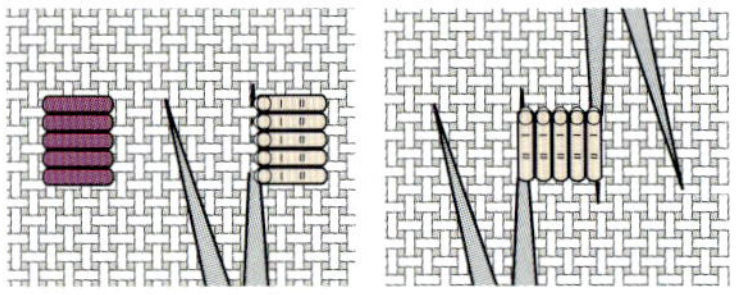

❶ *Imagine each kloster is a hand, with each stitch a finger. Cuts always trim the fingernails (left). The cut is never made on the sides of the hand (right).*

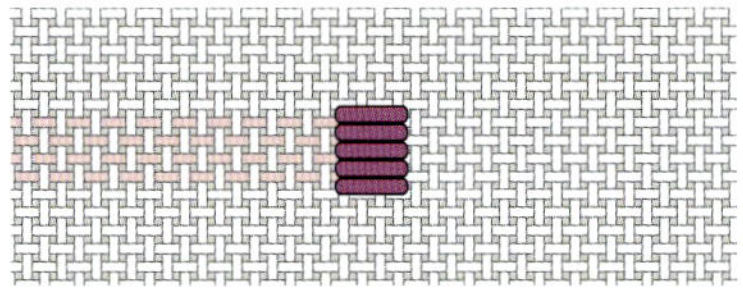

❶ *The four threads that extend from between the five stitches of the kloster block need to be cut. Cut all four at once, singly, or in pairs.*

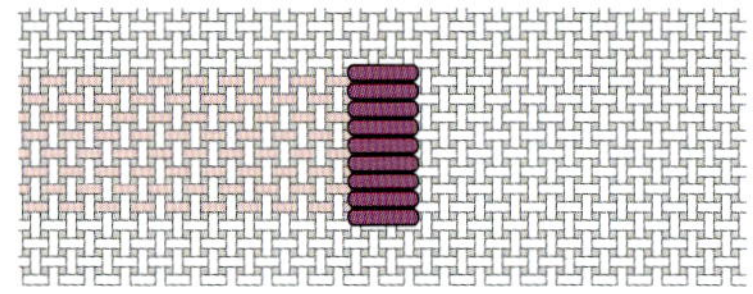

❶ *Sometimes there are more than five satin stitches to cut beside. Refer to your project instructions for the correct number of threads to cut.*

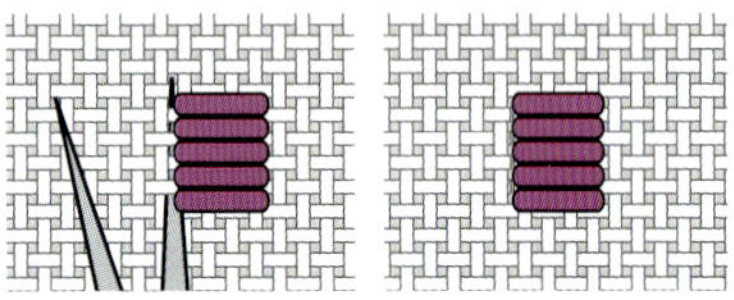

❶ *Always keep the scissors on the left, and the kloster on the right. This will result in a closer cut because of the way the blades are mounted.*

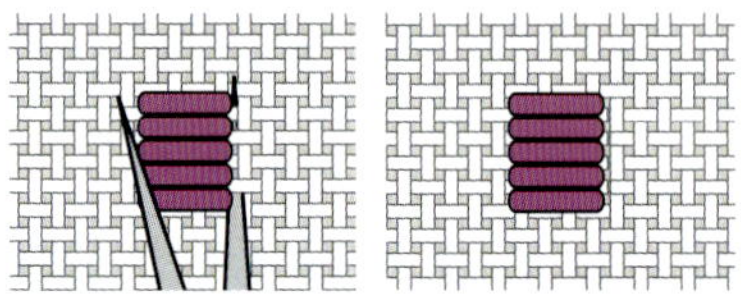

❶ *If the kloster is on the left, the lower blade will push the scissors further away from the stitches and will result in 'whiskers' at the end of the stitches.*

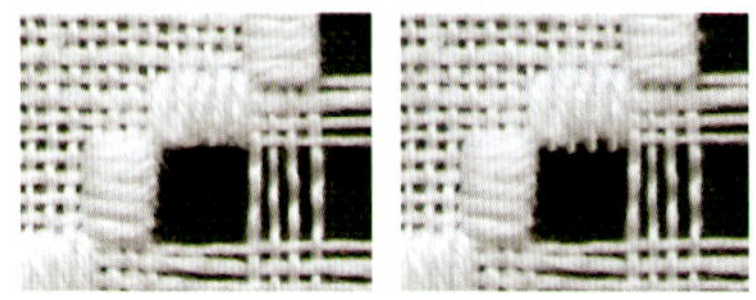

❶ *A good cut will be clean like the one on the left. A poor cut will have whiskers showing, as on the right.*

scissors for cutting

Fine, sharp-pointed embroidery scissors are required for accurate cutting. They should be sharply pointed and have sharp cutting blades. Looking from the side, the blades should have an angle of ten degrees or less. Looking from the top, the blades should be narrow. The smaller the girth of each blade as you move away from the tip, the less that has to pass between the fabric threads, and the easier it will be to get a good cut.

A poor quality pair of scissors will lower the quality of your work because they won't give a clean enough cut.

in a square

The square shown is a common size, however squares with longer sides are possible, so refer to your project instructions for how many threads to cut.

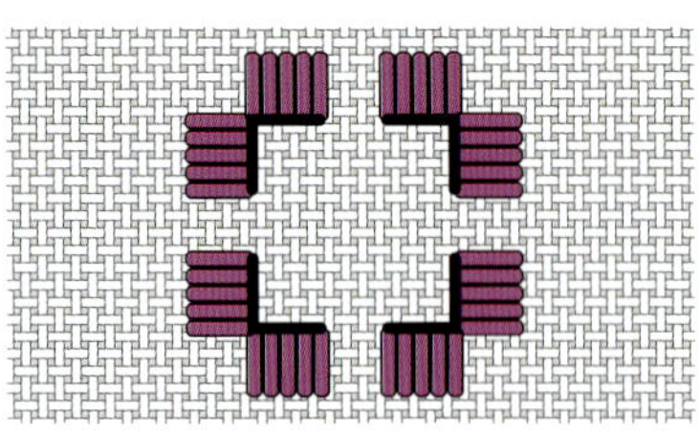

1 For this motif, the parts that need to be cut are marked with thick lines.

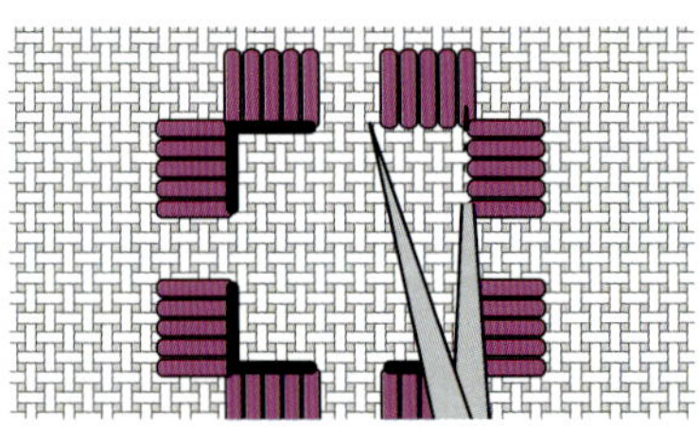

2 Insert the scissor blade left of the kloster. When the point has passed all four threads to be cut, return it to the front through the next fabric hole.

❶ *By returning the blade to the fabric front, you can't accidentally cut too many threads.*

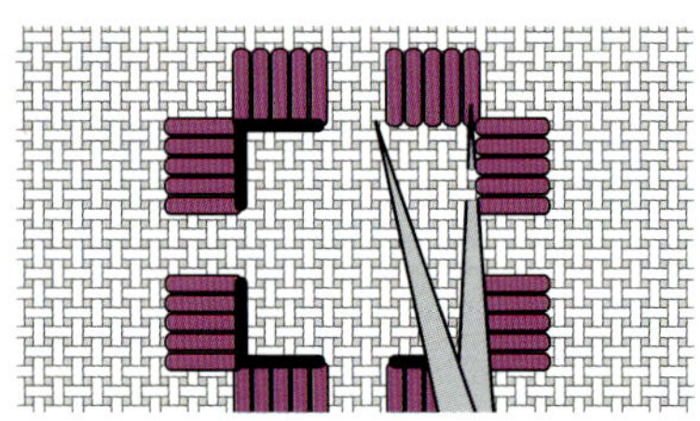

❶ *If you prefer, you can cut two threads, and then two threads, rather than trying to take the blade under all four at once. This can be helpful when your scissors are not particularly fine-pointed.*

❶ *Cutting threads singly makes it hard to get a clean cut without whiskers.*

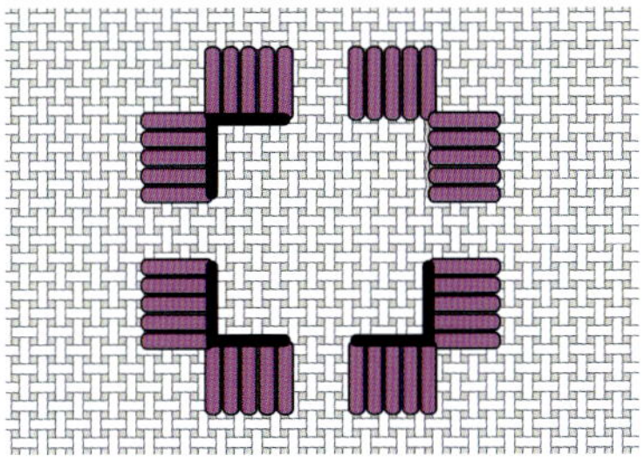

3 Check that the correct threads will be cut. Wiggle the scissors to ensure no stitches are caught. Carefully cut as close as possible to the stitches.

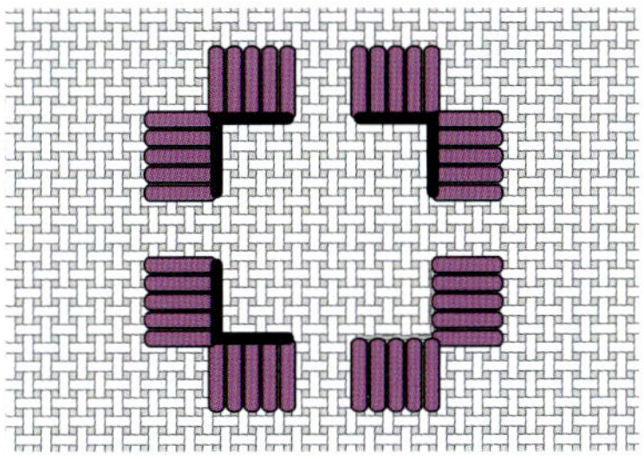

4 Turn the work 90° clockwise, and cut the four threads to the left of the next kloster.

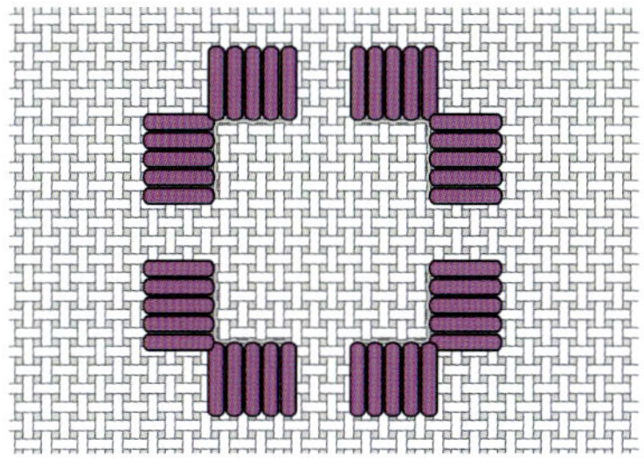

5 Continue around the drawn thread area until all the required threads are cut.

in a diamond

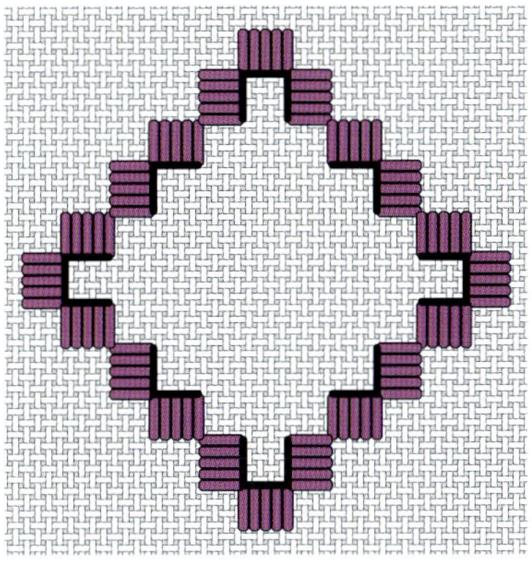

1 For this motif, the parts that need to be cut are marked with thick lines.

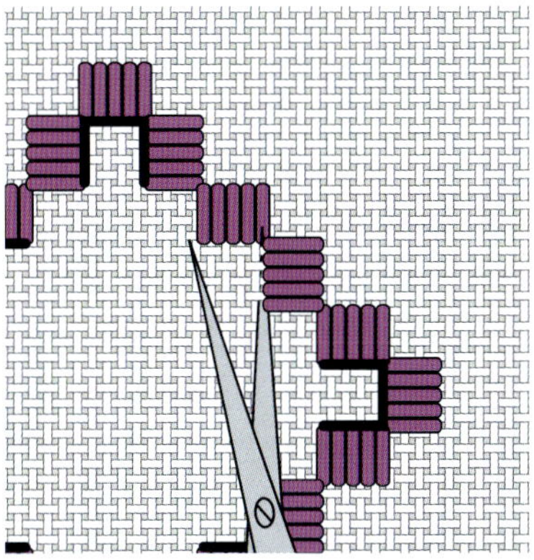

2 Insert the scissor blade on the left of the kloster. Carefully slip the blade under the four threads that need to be cut. When the blade point has passed the fourth thread, return it to the front through the next fabric hole.

! *By returning the blade to the fabric front, you won't cut too many threads.*

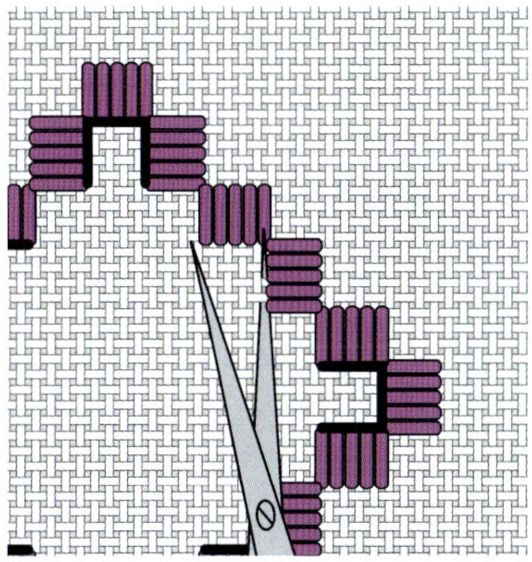

! *If you prefer, you can cut two threads, and then two threads, rather than trying to take the blade under all four at once. This can be helpful when your scissors are not particularly fine pointed.*

! *Cutting threads singly makes it hard to get a clean cut without whiskers.*

3 Check that the four threads are the ones that need to be cut. Wiggle the scissors to ensure no stitches are caught. Carefully cut as close as possible to the stitches.

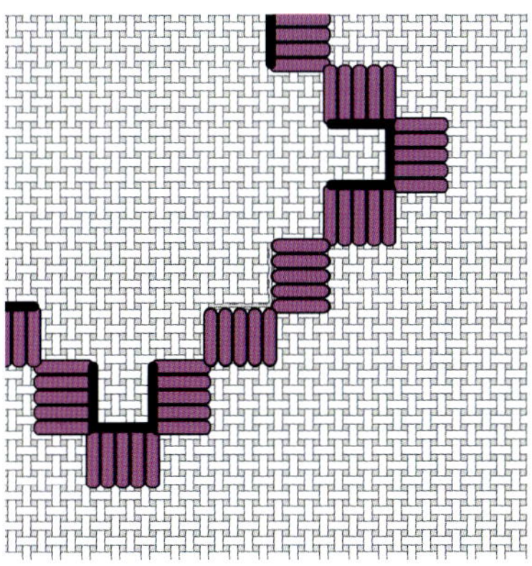

4 Turn the work 90° clockwise, and cut the four threads to the left of the next kloster.

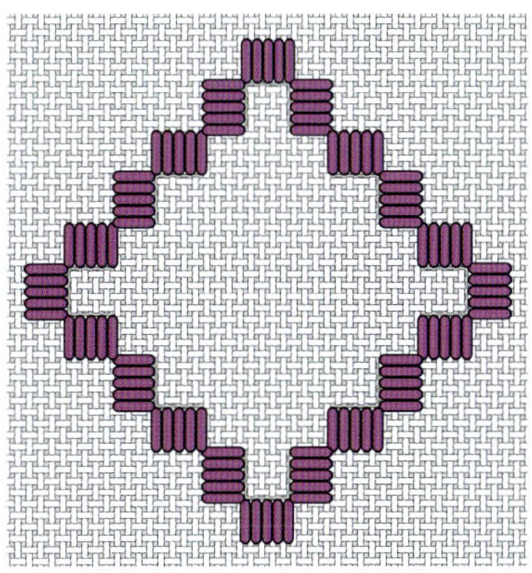

5 Continue around the drawn thread area until all the required threads are cut.

troubleshooting cutting-related errors

replacing a fabric thread cut in error

If you accidentally cut a thread, it can be mended. Use a thread from the fabric's unhemmed edge if possible, or embroidery thread of the same colour and weight as the fabric threads. This may be a somewhat visible mend, but it may be better than starting again!

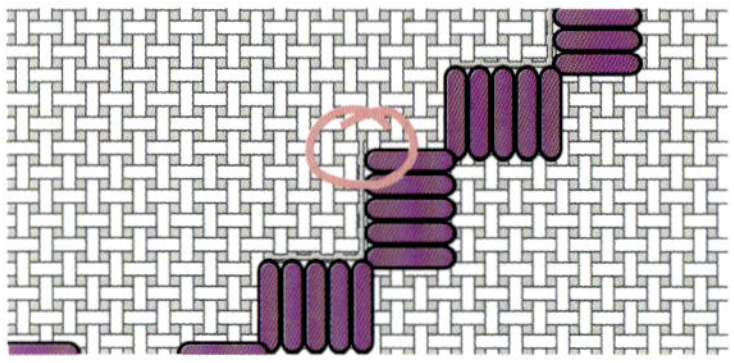

! *It is very easy to accidentally cut the wrong threads. Shown above is a common error: cutting too far.*

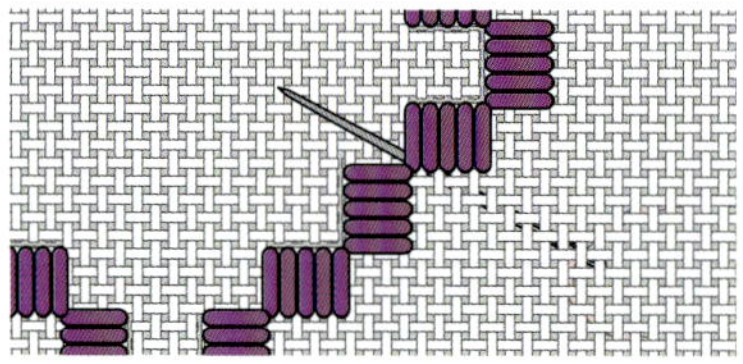

1 Thread a new thread into the needle. Anchor it in the back of the klosters and bring the needle out from underneath the kloster further on from the cut in the thread.

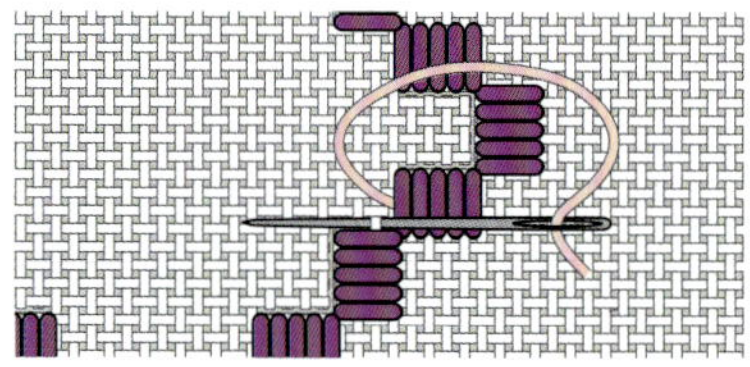

2 Following the thread which was mistakenly cut, take the needle under the first thread that vertically crosses over it.

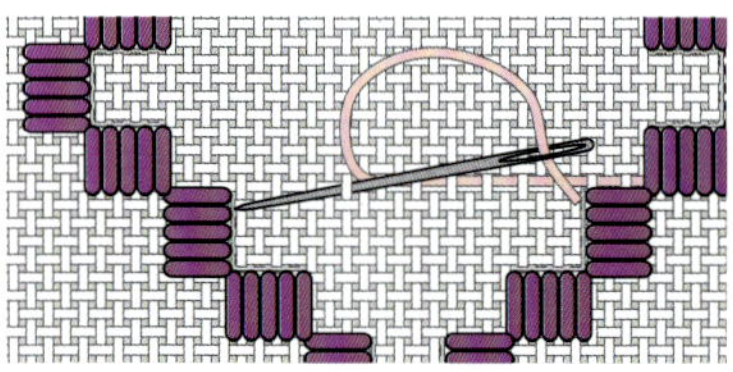

3 Pull the needle through. Continue along the cut thread, past the cut, weaving the needle underneath each of the vertically crossing threads.

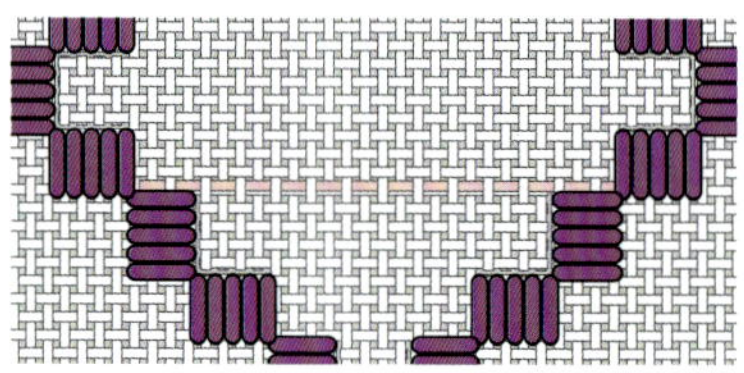

4 At the far side of the satin stitch boundary, take the thread in under the satin stitch to finish it off.

! *The cut thread remains in place for strength. The new thread extends well past the cut point to increase strength.*

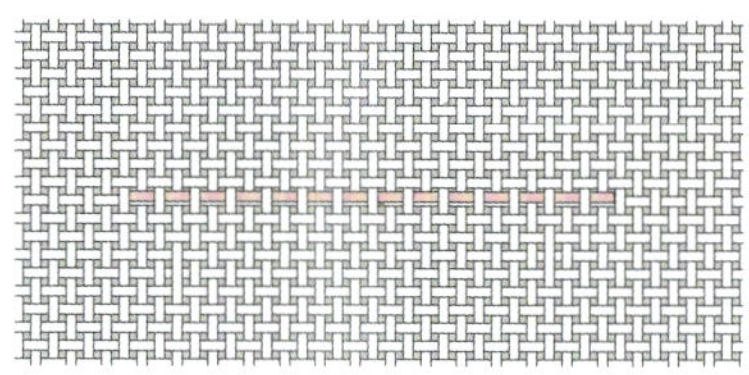

! *If there is no satin stitch nearby under which to anchor the thread, it can just be started and finished well beyond each side of the cut. With good care of the finished piece, it should not come undone.*

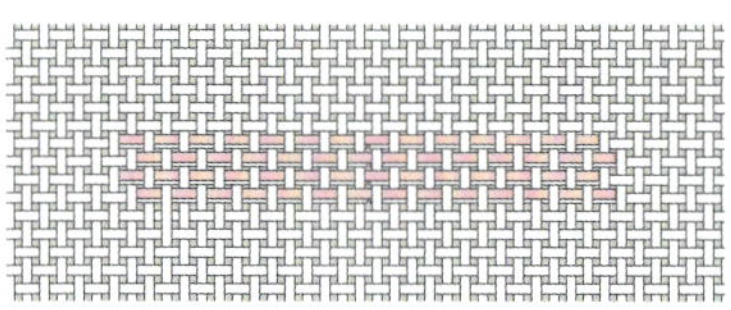

! *If more than one thread is cut, note that the fabric will be much weakened. Weave an extra thread for each of the cut threads.*

replacing a satin stitch cut in error

Sometimes one (or more) of the satin stitches is accidentally cut while cutting alongside them. Care must be taken while mending because you'll be working over fabric threads that have already been cut. A mend like this can be done, but will never be as satisfactory as it would have been without the cut.

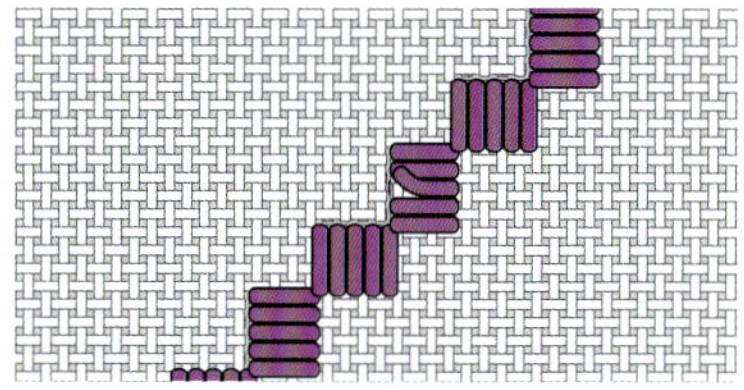

! *Despite care, sometimes some of the satin stitch is accidentally cut.*

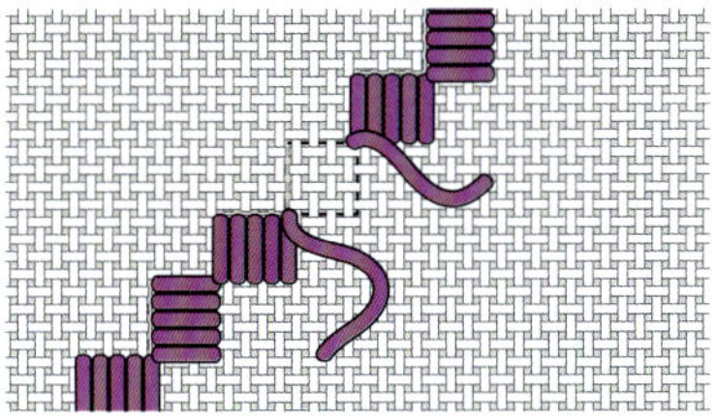

1 Undo the kloster with the cut.

! *You will be left with very short ends of threads.*

! *Take care when undoing because the cut fabric threads will be unstable.*

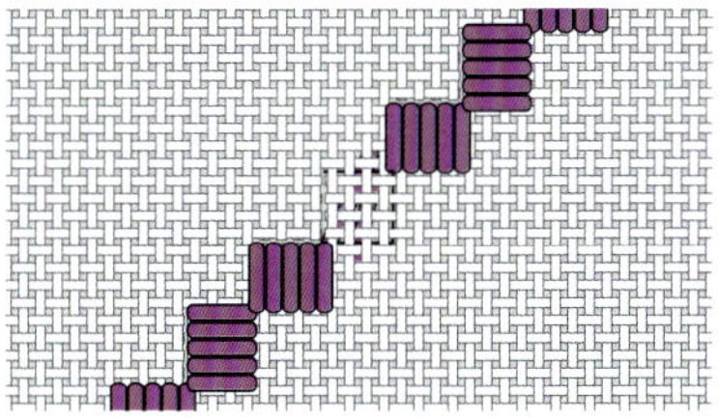

2 Take the thread ends to the back and lay them across the back of the space where the kloster has been removed.

! *As you restitch the kloster, ensure that these thread ends are covered by the new thread on the back.*

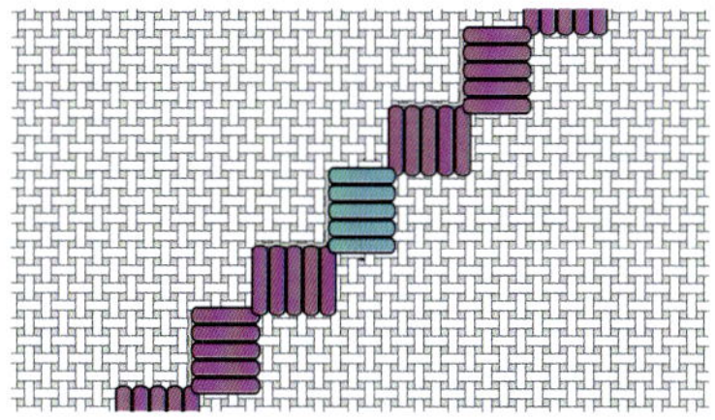

3 Start a new thread under the back of the adjacent kloster blocks. Carefully re-stitch the block. Finish the thread in the back of the stitching.

! *Take particular care when stitching over the cut edge. It will not be easy, so take your time.*

! *Trim the ends of the old thread.*

tacking down a flipping-up stitch

When a reversal error has been made in the satin stitching, cutting alongside it can cause the satin stitch to flip up, since the fabric thread is not holding it down any longer.

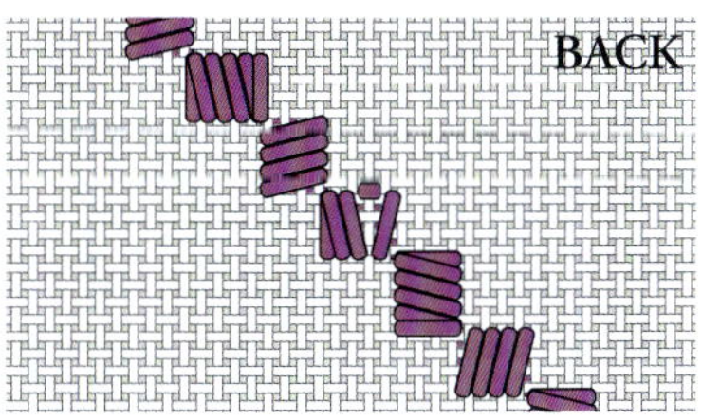

! *The reversal error from the back.*

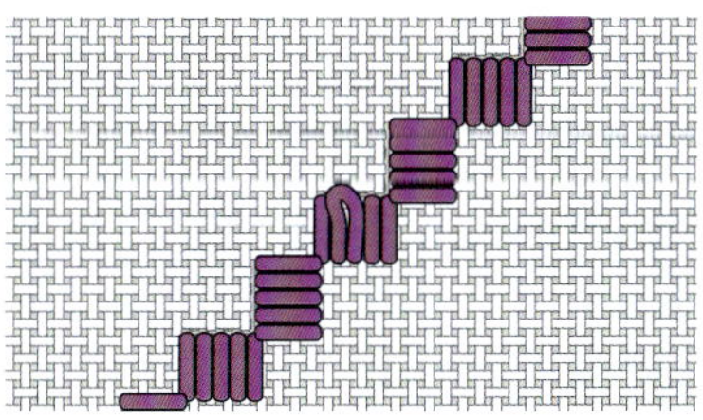

! *What it looks like from the front when the fabric threads alongside are cut.*

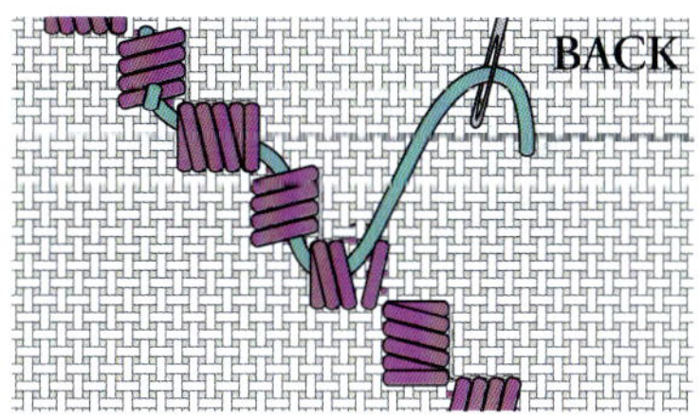

1 Anchor a new thread (of the same colour – different colour shown for illustration purposes only) in the back of the adjacent satin stitch blocks.

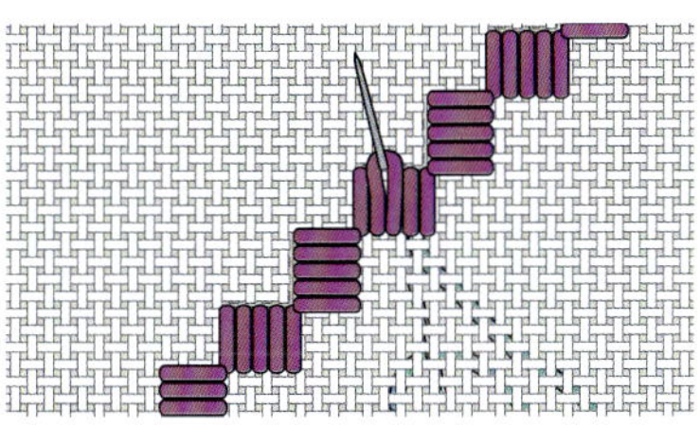

2 On the front, bring the needle up through the cut in the fabric, and through the looped stitch.

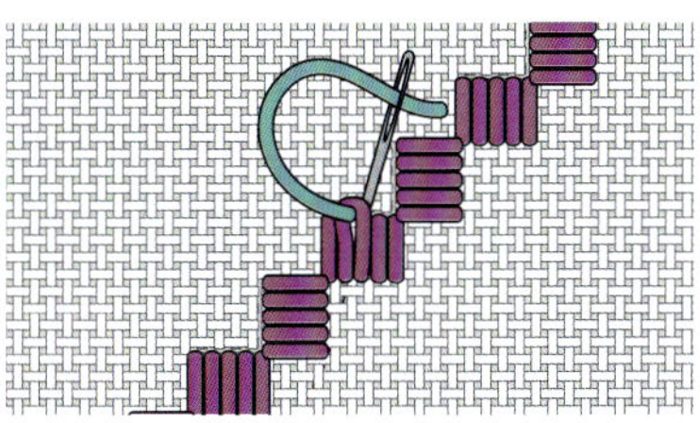

3 Pull the needle through. Take the needle down again through the cut in the fabric outside the loop.

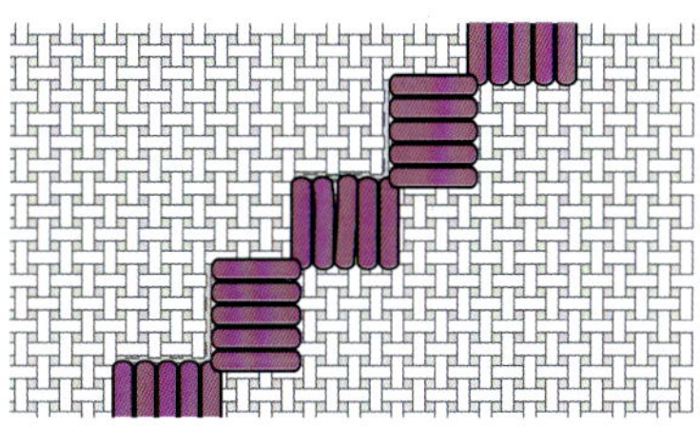

4 Pull the needle through, so that the new thread holds down the looped stitch with similar tension to the other stitches. Finish the new thread in the back of nearby stitching.

withdrawing fabric threads

In order for the drawn thread fillings to be worked, cut threads need to be withdrawn, leaving a mesh on which to work the next stage of stitching. The withdrawing for two standard shapes is shown, however there are very many other shapes and possibilities for the placement and quantity of withdrawn threads within a cutwork shape.

in a square

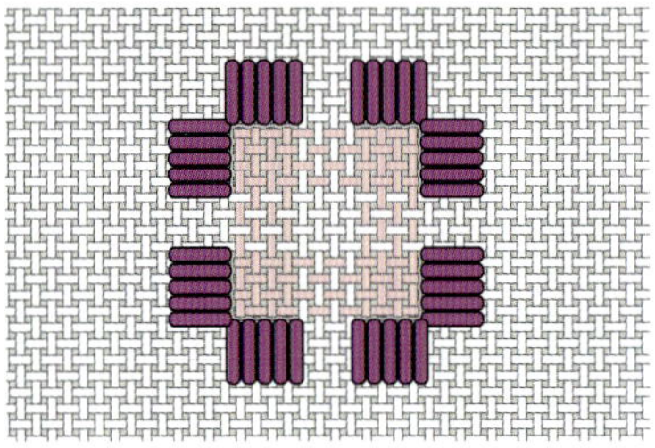

1 Within the drawn thread area, all the threads with cut ends need to be withdrawn. They are shown here in pink.

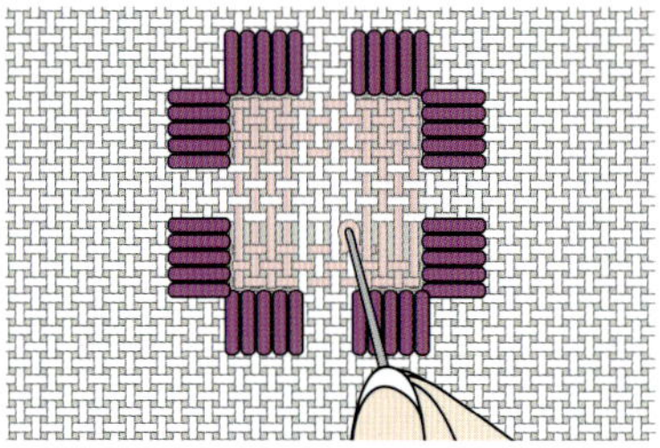

2 Carefully remove the threads one at a time.

❶ *A pair of tweezers, or lifting the threads up with a tapestry needle can help. Nimble fingers can work fine too!*

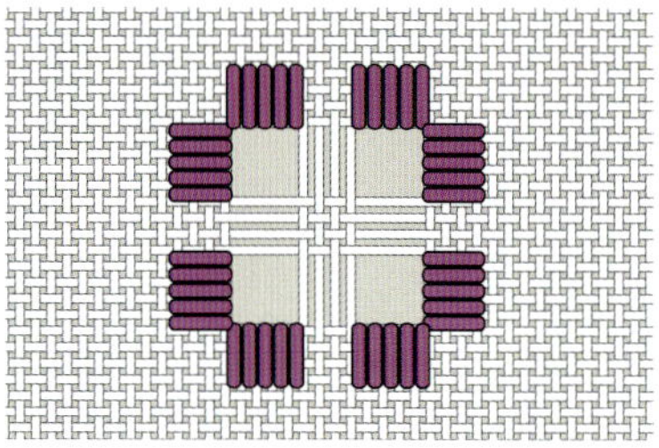

3 Continue withdrawing threads until they are all removed.

❶ *If there is a large cutwork area, only remove the threads where you will be immediately working. Otherwise the fabric may become destabilised.*

in a diamond

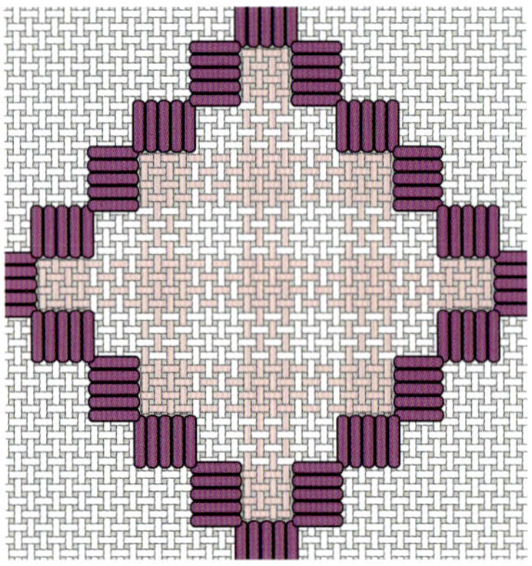

1 Within the drawn thread area, all the threads with cut ends need to be withdrawn. They are shown here in pink.

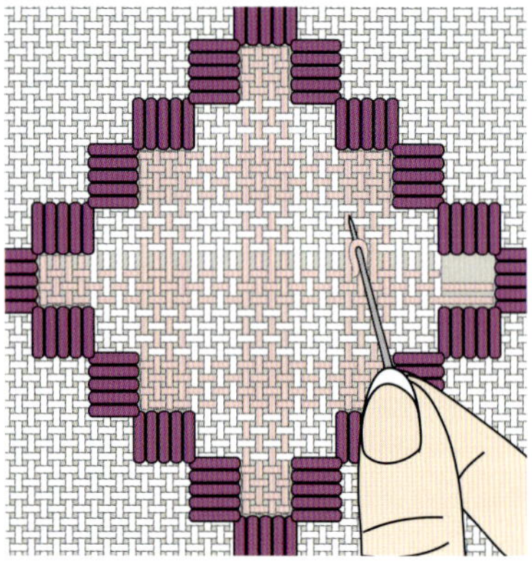

2 Carefully remove the threads one at a time.

❶ *A pair of tweezers, or lifting the threads up with a tapestry needle can help. Nimble fingers can work fine too!*

3 Continue withdrawing threads until they are all removed.

❶ *If there is a large cutwork area, only remove the threads where you will be immediately working. Otherwise the fabric will become destabilised.*

ready for filling stitches

Once you have cut and withdrawn the threads, for many filling stitches it is recommended that you mount the fabric in a hoop or frame. Make sure the fabric threads are square. This will help with tension, particularly if there are diagonal stitches as part of the filling stitch.

If you are dealing with multiple complicated fillings in the one area, work out a stitching path before you start if one is not provided. Lay a piece of tracing paper over the chart, and with a pencil, draw a path through, noting when various parts of filling stitches will need to be worked, and if there are any parts that will need to be laced behind or dead ends that will need to be avoided. Work in straight line paths where possible. You may need to try more than one option to create the best path.

Filling stitches

Use the thinner of the two weights of thread for all filling stitches, except in rare cases where the thicker one is specified.

The filling stitches in this book which are worked with woven bars assume that the needle in the weaving comes up in the centre of the bar. If your needle goes down at the centre, the fillings will not work in the same way.

Don't try to cram too many stitches in. Many stitchers think the more stitches they cram in, the better the result will be. On the contrary: more stitches can mean tension is harder to control, and it can look like there wasn't enough room for them all, because often there isn't! Don't be afraid to reduce the number of stitches. It will likely make things easier for you and provide a better result.

Be consistent! If you have identical parts of stitches or are working the stitch more than once, make sure you use the same tension, and the same number of wraps or weaves throughout. Make a note of the number of wraps or weaves on the pattern or chart, so that when you come back to it after a break, you are able to maintain consistency.

The early part of this chapter is organised into stitch family groupings, such as dove's eyes, spider webs, Greek crosses and picots. The later part has more elaborate orphan stitches that don't easily fit within families.

starting & finishing threads for cutwork

These methods work for wrapped and woven bars.

starting under satin stitch

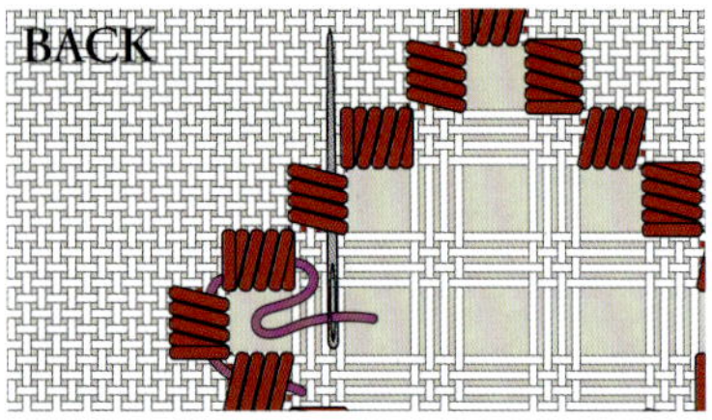

1 On the back, about 5 cm (2 in) away from starting point, take the new thread (shown in purple) under the back of about half the stitches.

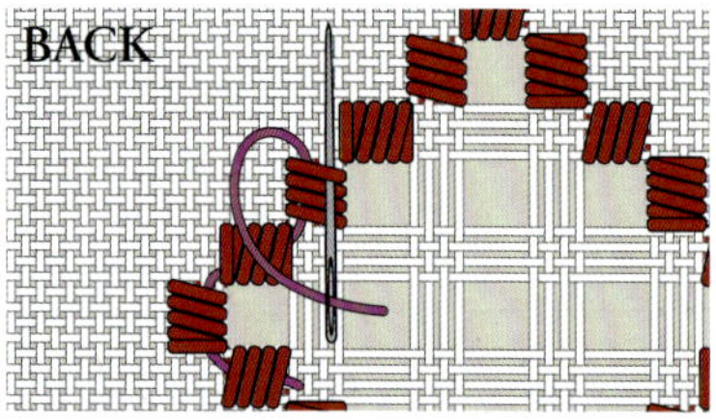

2 Take a backstitch under the last stitch of the kloster you have just gone under.

! *The backstitch helps to secure the thread so that when you put tension on it, it doesn't pull straight out again.*

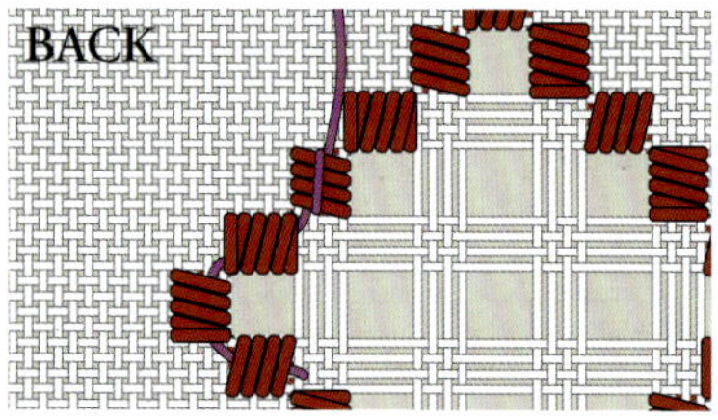

! *Do not take the backstitch under the whole block. It will be too noticeable, and one of the features of Hardanger embroidery is its very neat back. It also isn't as secure as under a single stitch, because a single stitch wraps tighter.*

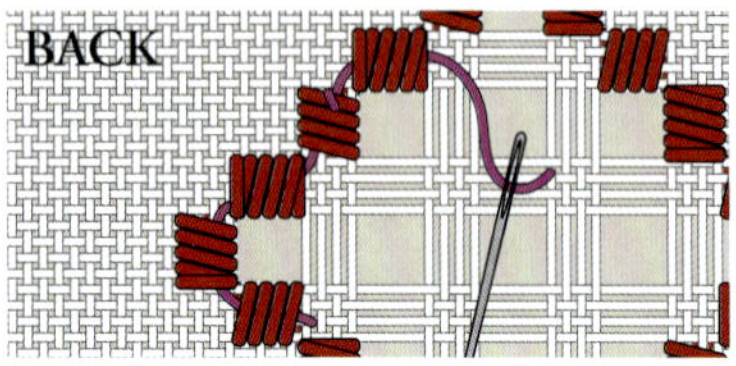

3 Continue taking the needle under the back of the stitches, bringing it out where the stitching will need to commence.

self-covered start

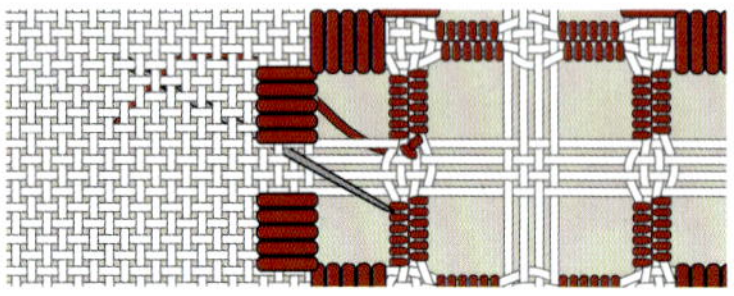

1 From the front, insert a needle with a knotted thread, one thread up from the centre of the woven square at the end of the first bar. Bring it out one thread up from the centre of the woven square at the edge.

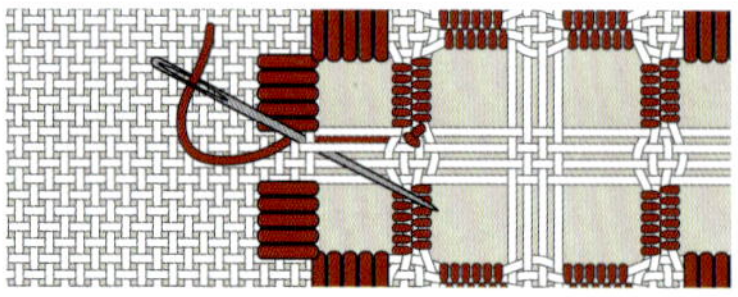

2 Insert the needle one thread to the right, and bring it out ready to begin the bar.

! *The thread sits underneath one side of the bar, to make it easier to cover.*

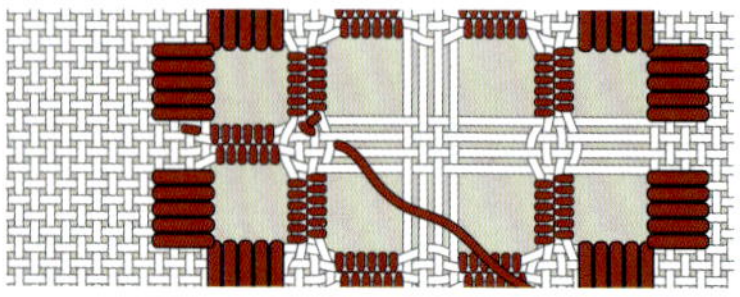

3 Pull the thread through. Stitch the bar, making sure the thread is enclosed in the stitching, on the back. Then stitch as required.

! *Trim the knot once you have passed it.*

finishing threads

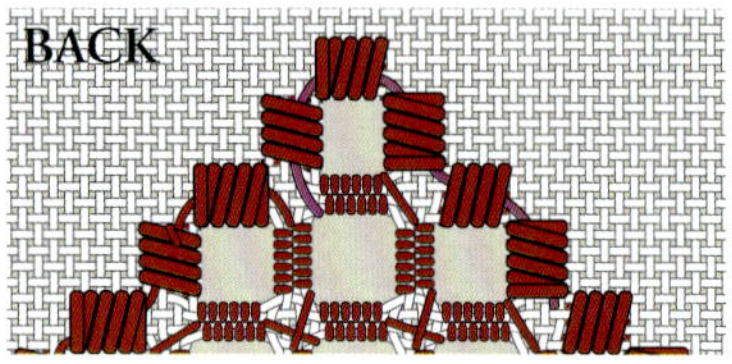

4 To finish, run the thread under the back of about five klosters.

! *There is no need to use backstitches to finish.*

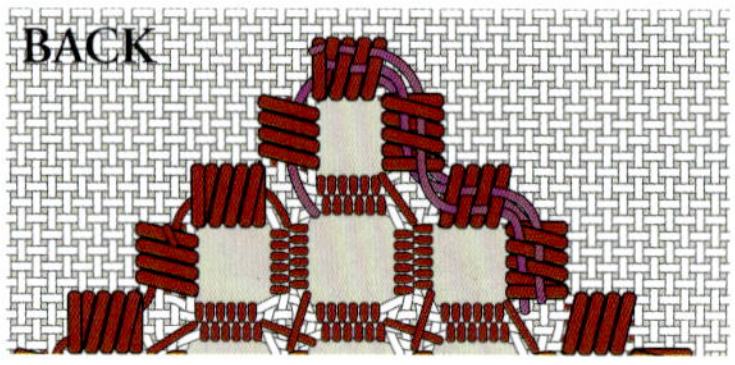

! *Do not weave the thread back and forth under the klosters. It will just make it messy and lumpy for no added benefit.*

starting & finishing threads for cutwork

These methods work for wrapped and woven bars.

starting under satin stitch

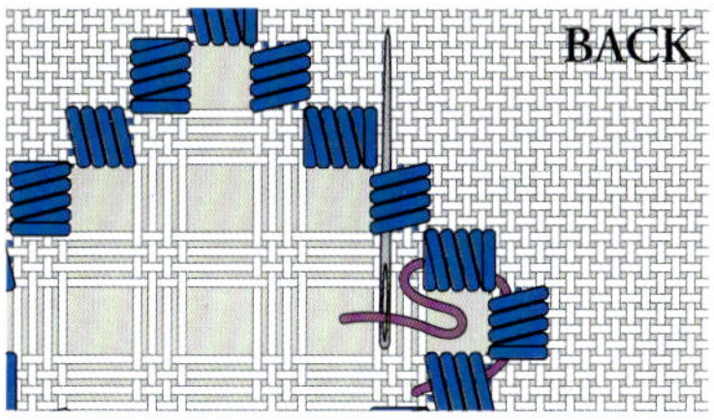

1 On the back, about 5 cm (2 in) away from starting point, take the new thread (shown in purple) under the back of about half the stitches.

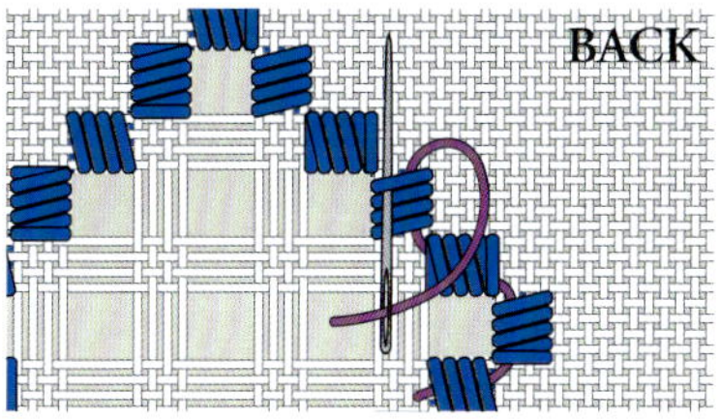

2 Take a backstitch under the last stitch of the kloster you have just gone under.

❶ *The backstitch helps to secure the thread so that when you put tension on it, it doesn't pull straight out again.*

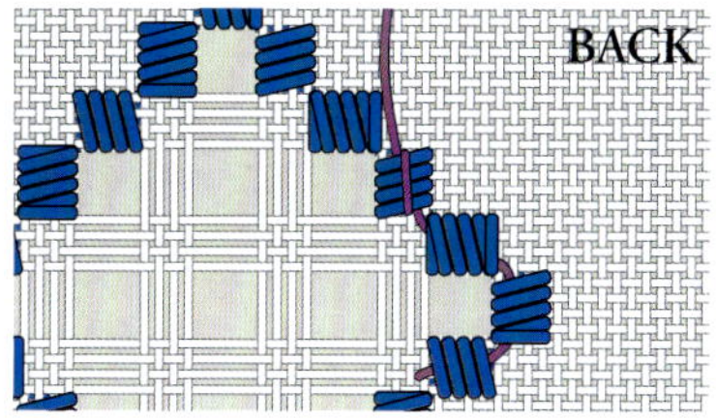

❶ *Do not take the backstitch under the whole block. It will be too noticeable, and one of the features of Hardanger embroidery is its very neat back. It also isn't as secure as under a single stitch, because a single stitch wraps tighter.*

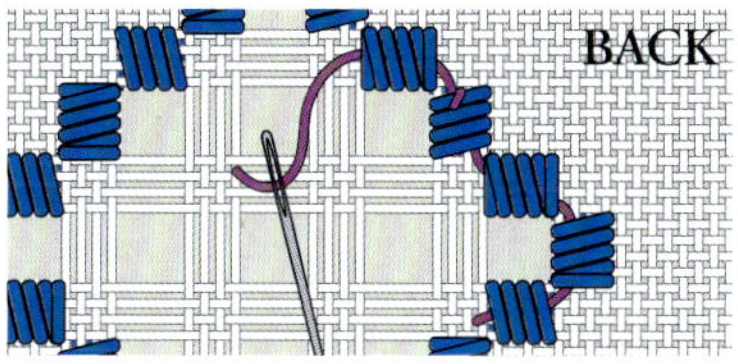

3 Continue taking the needle under the back of the stitches, bringing it out where the stitching will need to commence.

self-covered start

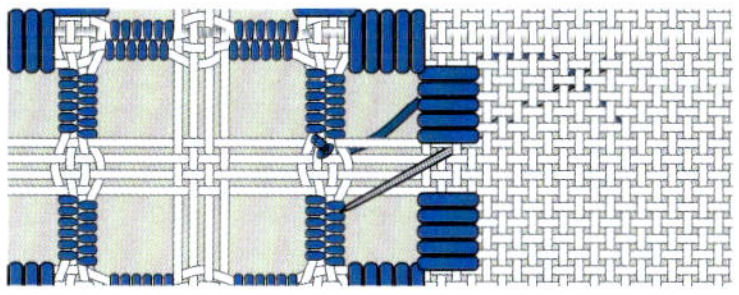

1 From the front, insert a needle with a knotted thread, one thread up from the centre of the woven square at the end of the first bar. Bring it out one thread up from the centre of the woven square at the edge.

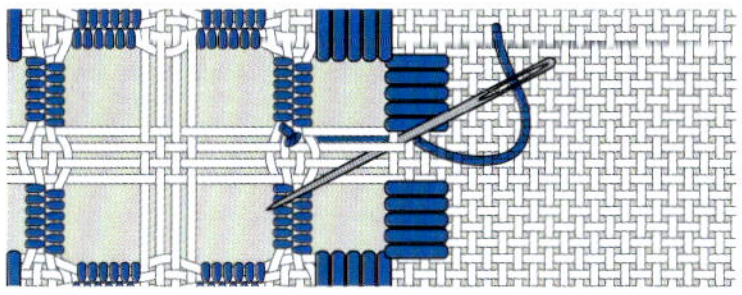

2 Insert the needle one thread to the left, and bring it out ready to begin the bar.

❶ *The thread sits underneath one side of the bar, to make it easier to cover.*

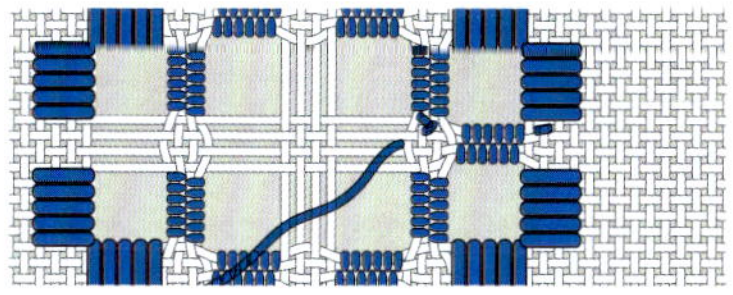

3 Pull the thread through. Stitch the bar, making sure the thread is enclosed in the stitching, on the back. Then stitch as required.

❶ *Trim the knot once you have passed it.*

finishing threads

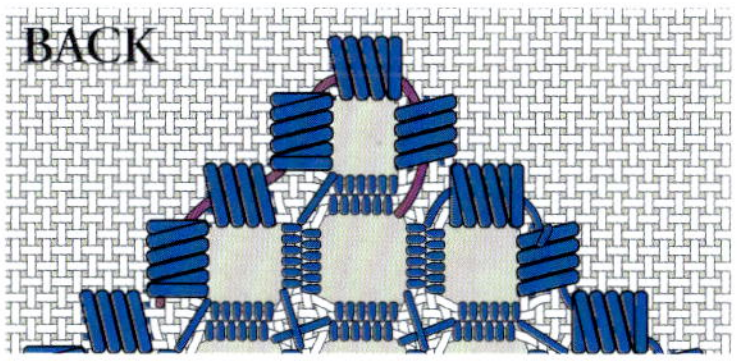

4 To finish, run the thread under the back of about five klosters.

❶ *There is no need to use backstitches to finish.*

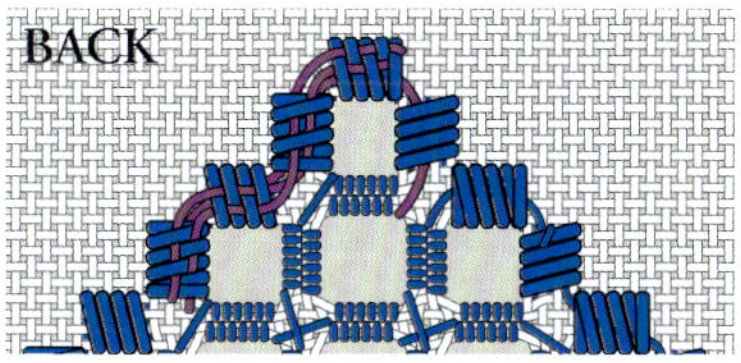

❶ *Do not weave the thread back and forth under the klosters. It will just make it messy and lumpy for no added benefit.*

the importance of tension

Stitch tension can make or break a stitch. With correct tension, your work will sing. Without it, your work will look sloppy or strained. Good tension comes with practice. Don't expect to get a stitch right the first time. Work on it, adjusting your tension until you get it right.

For stitches with tight tension, people often don't pull their stitches tight enough. It is rare to find someone who pulls too tight. Many are scared they will break their thread by pulling too tight, however this rarely happens!

Curved stitches can be difficult. It is easy to make them too tight, so that they lose their curve. These stitches often need to be relaxed.

If your stitch doesn't turn out well the first time, unless you know you're a tight stitcher, make the assumption that what you've done is too loose. When stitches are too loose, it can be difficult to maintain even tension. Try it again, tighter. Does that look better? Could it go tighter? If not, maybe you're a 'too tight' person. Relax. Try it again, looser. Or maybe some parts are too tight, and some are too loose. Compare your work with the stitched example, and try to identify the differences. Maybe your stitching is too tight. Maybe it is too loose. Maybe the tension is uneven. Once you've identified the problems, work to rectify them.

Closely related to tension problems is that some people try to cram too many stitches in. There is no prize for having the most stitches on a woven bar! Often people can fit way too many in because their stitches are not tight enough. Tighten your stitches and you will fit fewer in.

When learning a stitch and your first attempt is unsuccessful, leave it intact and work a new sample so you can see any improvement. If you've undone and redone it, you won't be able to compare.

In this book, I often talk about using 'gentle tension'. This means that it has been pulled a little bit, but not too tight. There's still some relaxation in that stitch. It's how I would describe the sweet spot of tension.

too loose | too tight | uneven | just right

*The most common problems with **woven bars** are stitching too loose and cramming in too many stitches.*

*The 'too tight' **Greek cross** looks fine but as it distorts the fabric, it's too tight. Too loose and the lovely curves between stitches disappear.*

*When stitches are pulled too tight in **wrapped divided bars with dove's eyes**, the fabric distorts. Too loose it looks sloppy and overly loopy.*

*It is difficult to work **corner eyelets with square filet** too tight, but too loose and the stitch loses all definition.*

removing the slack

With some stitches, when they're too loose, you can use your needle to move the slack further through the stitching path to remove some of it to the working part of the thread.

1 In this festoon stitch example, the pink stitch is a little too loose, causing the inner circle to be misshapen.

! *It isn't off much, but it is off. It is fixing things like this that can make a difference.*

2 Follow the path to the loose end of the thread and insert the needle into the next stitch along. Gently pull on that stitch to move some of the slack along to it and out of the previous stitch.

top tip tension

Don't try to cram in so many stitches!

Some stitchers' work doesn't look as good as it could because they try to cram in too many stitches. Don't be afraid to put in fewer stitches! It will give the stitches room to breathe, and will likely help to improve your tension.

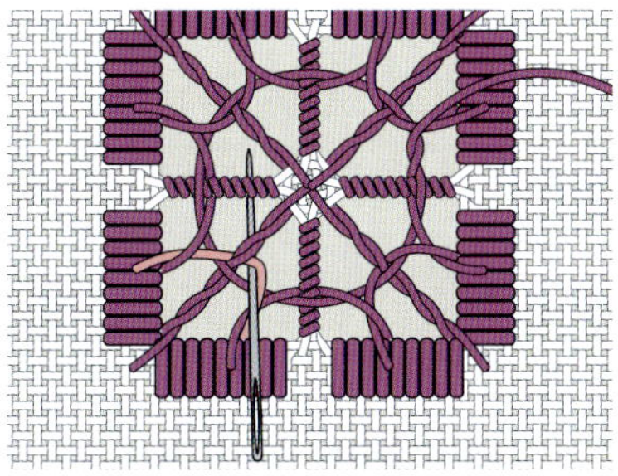

3 Slowly and carefully continue along each of the stitches, easing the extra length along to the next stitch, and to shorten the previous one back to its right tension.

! *It will be slow and laborious.*

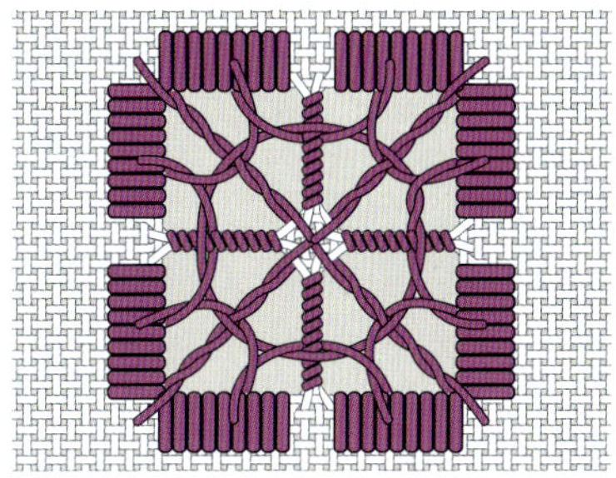

4 Continue right through to the final stitch, easing the extra length out. Or as you go, distribute the extra length amongst each of the stitches to even it all out.

easing tension

With some stitches, when they're too tight, you can use your needle to move some extra thread length through the stitching path from the end of the stitching, to ease the tension.

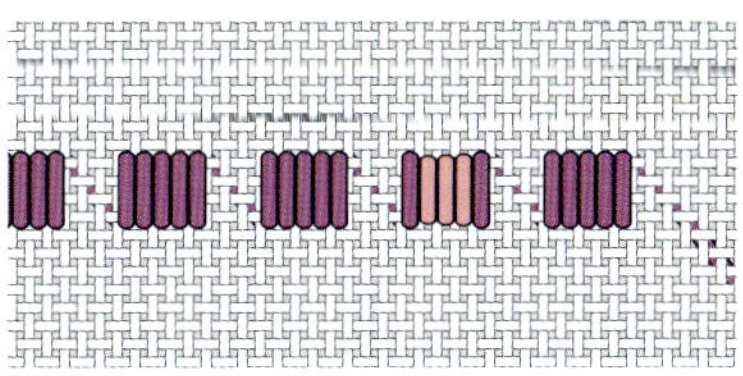

1 In this example, the pink stitches are too tight, with varying degrees of tightness.

! *They aren't off much, but they are off. It is fixing things like this that can make a difference.*

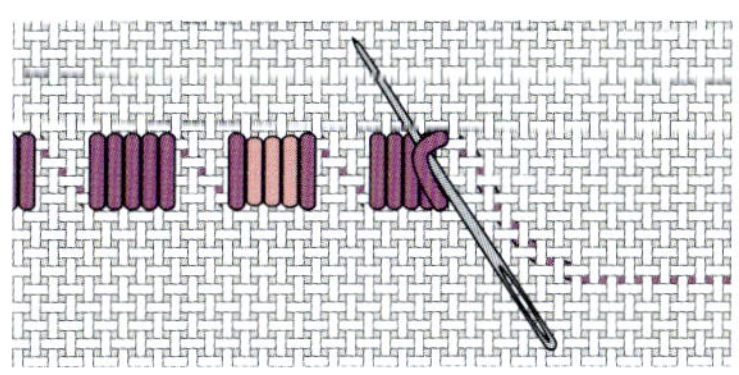

2 At the loose end of the thread, insert the needle into the last stitch. Gently lever it up to lengthen the stitch.

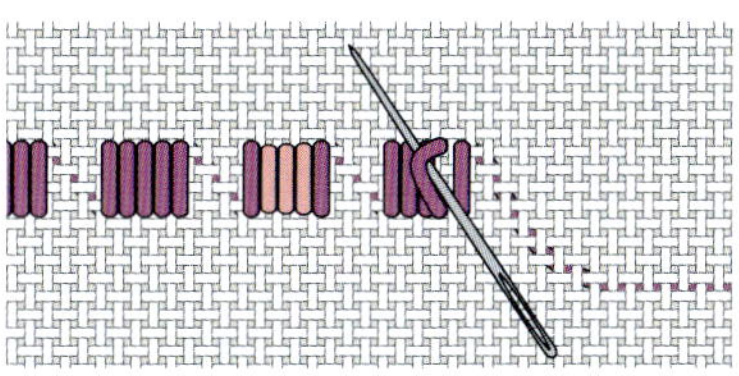

3 Move to the next stitch and lever it up, bringing the extra length into this stitch, thereby bringing the last one back to normal.

! *It will be slow and laborious.*

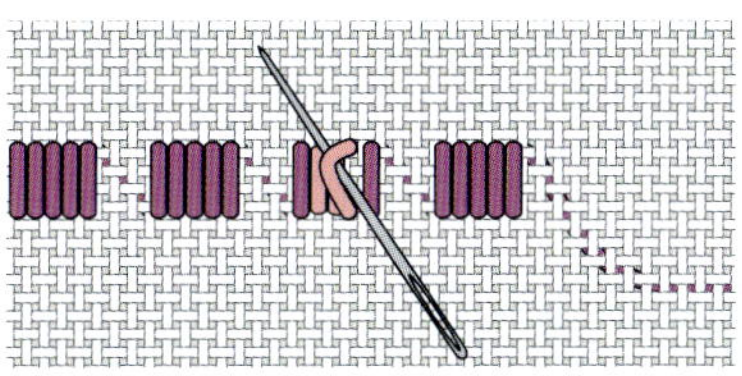

4 Continue along, moving the extra length on to subsequent stitches until you reach the short ones.

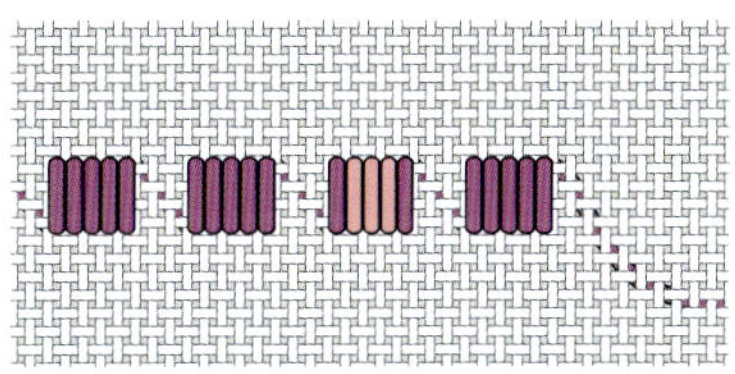

5 Use the extra length to even out the length of the short stitches.

! *If you have too much extra length, you will need to take it back out; if too little, you will need to add more.*

L

woven bars

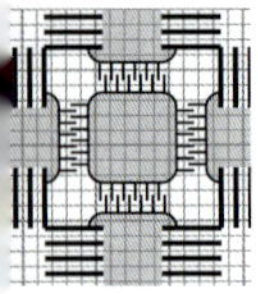

TRADITIONAL

Woven bars are the basic stitch used for filling cutwork areas. Before you begin, plan a path to stitch all the bars. Sometimes using straight lines is more sensible, and sometimes using zig-zagging lines is more sensible.

straight lines

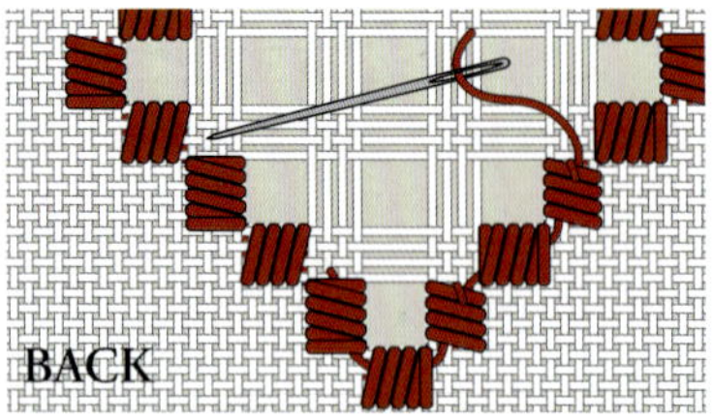

1 Anchor the thread in the back of the satin stitching. Run the thread under the back of four or five klosters, with one or two back-stitches under single threads.

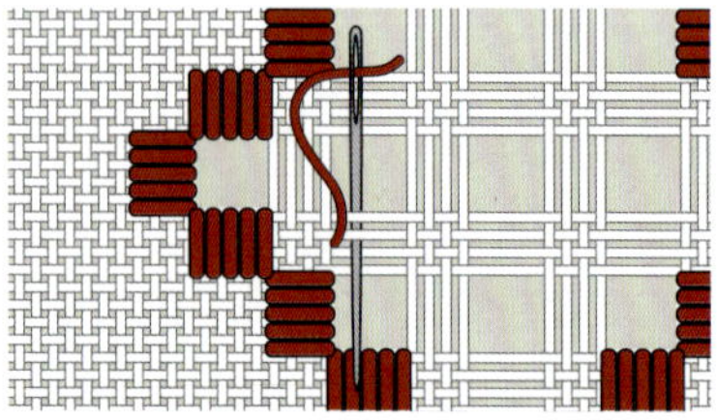

2 On the front, bring the needle out between the four threads at the left end of the first bar. From above, slide it under the upper two threads and bring it up again in the centre.

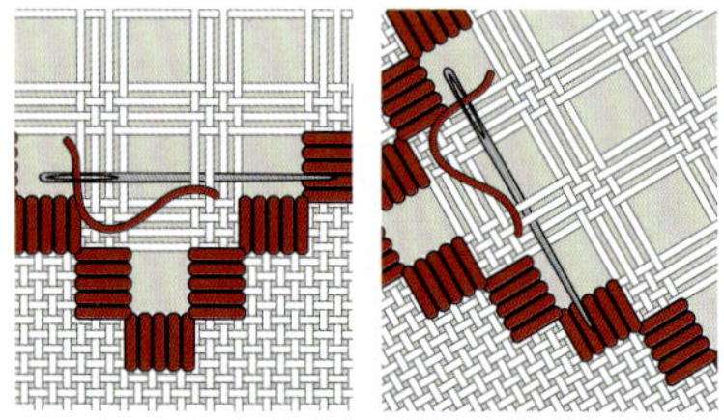

! *Some people prefer to insert their needle horizontally, moving upward to fill the bar. Some prefer to work with their fabric on an angle. Use whatever position suits you best.*

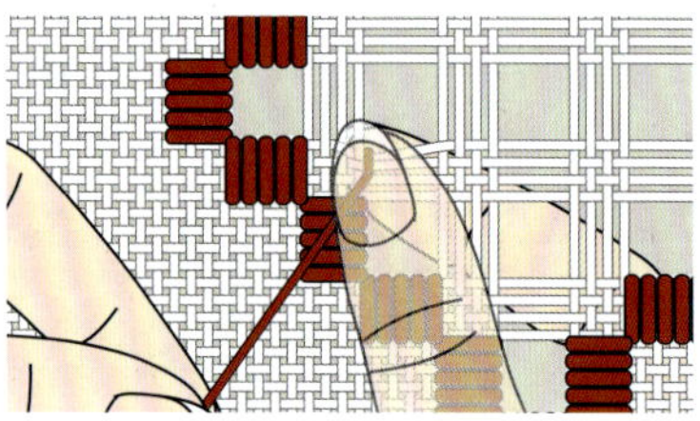

3 Pull the needle through. When the stitch is snug around the side of the bar, pinch the bar between your right forefinger and thumb, and with the other hand, pull the thread to the left and down.

! *Pinching stabilises the bar while you tighten the stitch, giving good tension. Pulling left and down narrows the bar and pulls the stitch snugly down.*

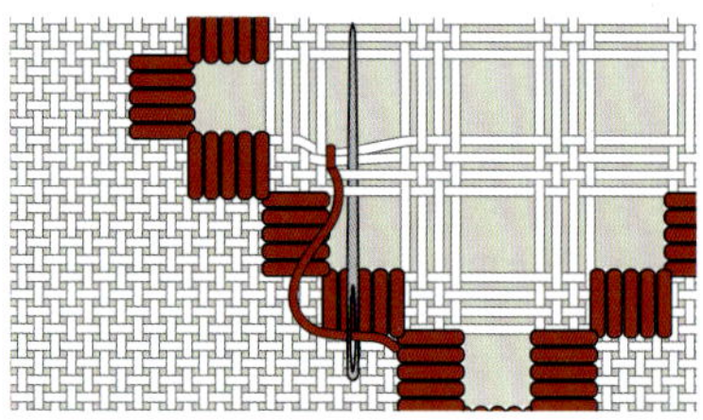

4 From below, slide the needle under the lower two threads and bring it out again in the centre.

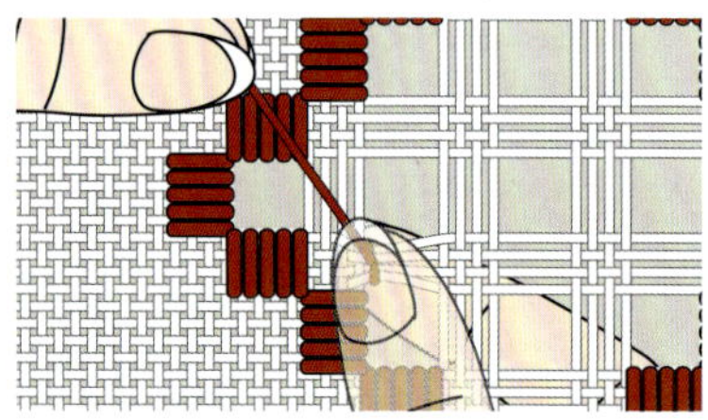

5 Pull the needle through. When the stitch is nearly tight around the side of the bar, pinch the bar between your right forefinger and thumb as you pull the thread to the left and up.

! *Pulling the stitch left and up narrows the bar and nestles the stitch snugly against the first one.*

! *Tighten after each stitch.*

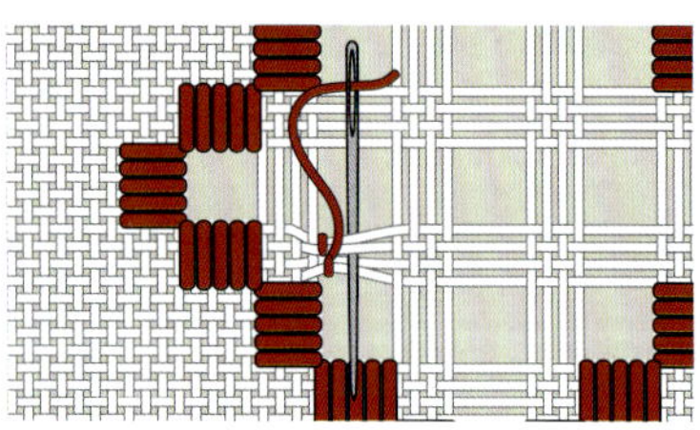

6 From above, slide the needle under the upper two threads and bring it out again in the centre.

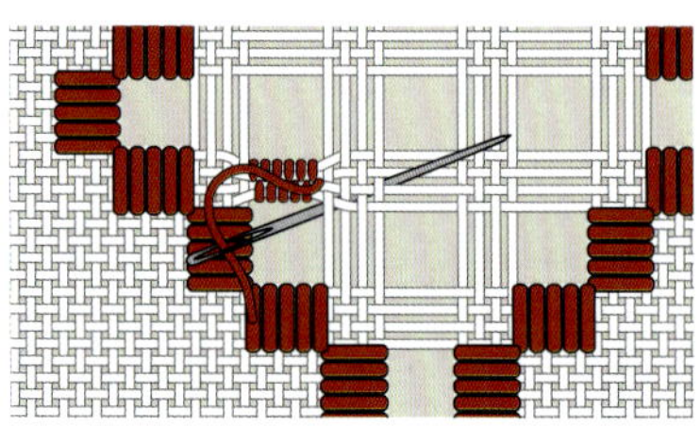

7 Continue weaving the bar, pulling each stitch in snug against the previous ones. Fill the bar with an equal number of stitches on each side. To finish the bar and start the next one, pass the needle behind the adjacent woven square, and bring the needle out in the centre of the next bar.

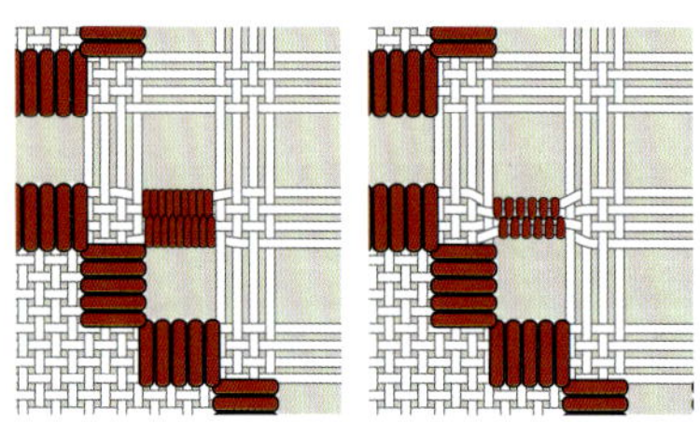

! *Do not cram the bar with stitches as shown left. Five, six, or seven stitches per side is ample, as shown right. If you can fit more in, you're probably not tightening the stitch tension enough. Use as few stitches as you can to fill the bar. Keep the tension and quantity constant throughout the project.*

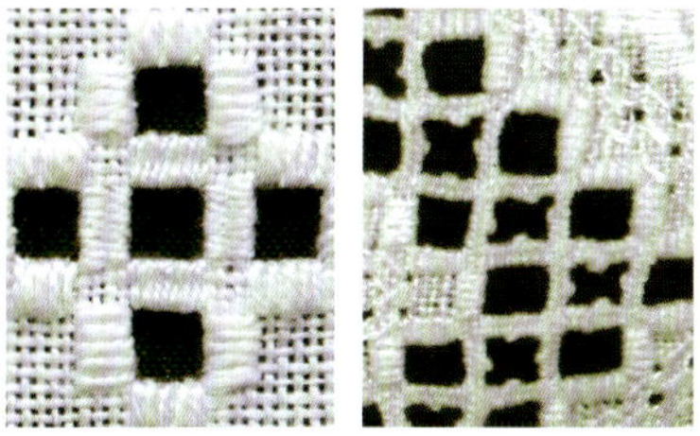

The weaving should pull the threads inward so that the bar is narrower than the adjacent woven square. If it isn't (as shown left), you're not pulling tight enough. Historical examples have bars that are narrow, not wide. If you pinch and pull after each stitch, you will be able to narrow your bars.

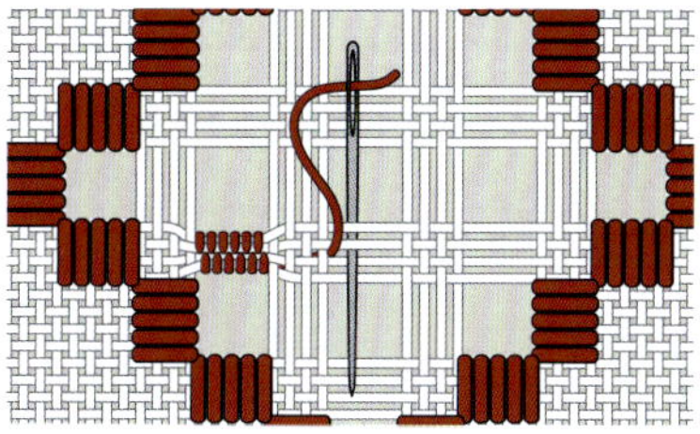

8 Pull the needle through. From above, slide it under the upper two threads. Bring it up again in the centre.

Always start each bar on the same side. If you choose the upper threads for the first bar, use them for each one after that. If you choose the lower threads, always start with them.

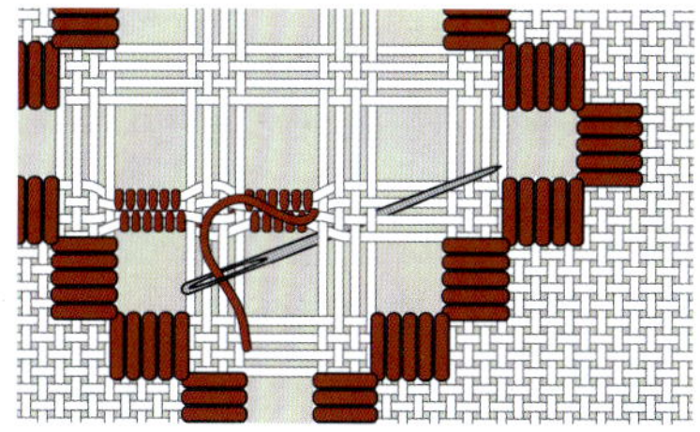

9 Continue weaving from one side of the bar to the other, pulling the stitches in tight. Use the same quantity of stitches as for the first bar. Pass the needle behind the adjacent woven square, and bring the needle out in the centre of the next bar.

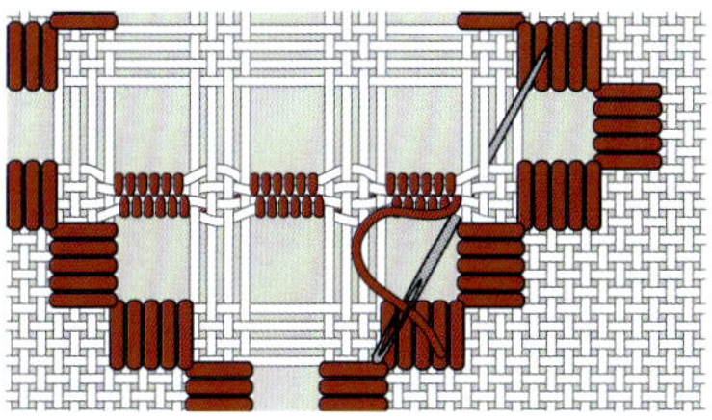

10 Work the next bar similarly. To make a left turn, pass the needle behind the adjacent woven square. Bring the needle out in the centre of the next bar.

Following completion of this side, the next bar is adjacent to the left, so the path will be anticlockwise.

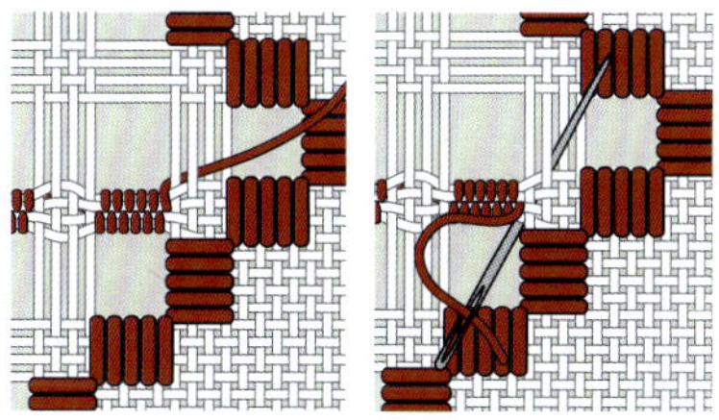

Whether you're turning left or right, make sure the thread goes behind the adjacent woven square and doesn't just slip around the corner (shown above left) which looks like a mistake. This may mean that you need a one-off extra stitch on one side (shown above right).

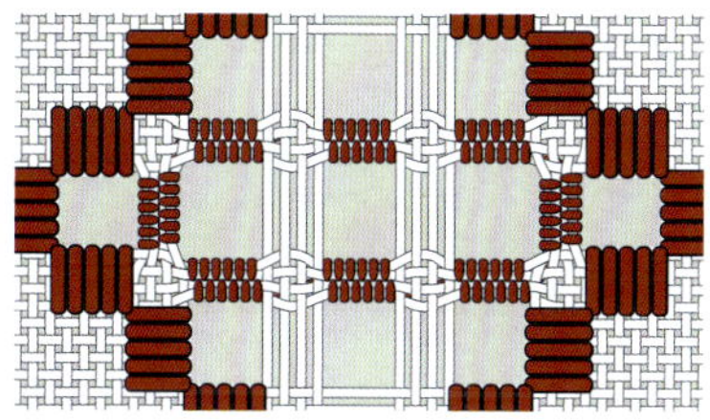

11 Turn the work 90° clockwise and continue around the circuit, working the bars in long lines, in an anticlockwise direction.

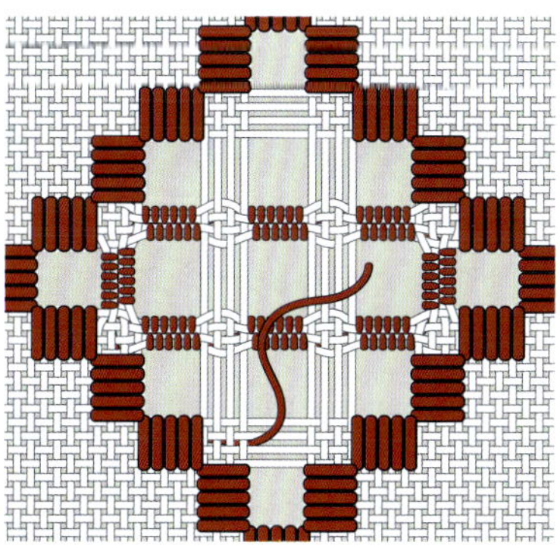

12 Take the needle through the back of the satin stitch to come up next to the closest woven square, ready to start a new circuit.

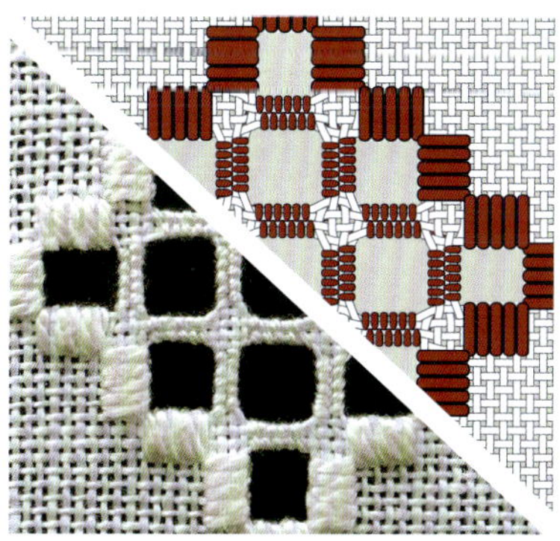

13 Work the circuit similarly to the previous circuit. To finish, run the thread through the back of the satin stitching.

Working bars in long straight lines helps them to sit neatly in straight lines.

For left-handers it makes sense to start stitching on the bar's left side (when the bar stretches away from you). Work circuits anticlockwise where possible. Alternatively, start on the right side and work clockwise. Whichever you choose, be consistent throughout.

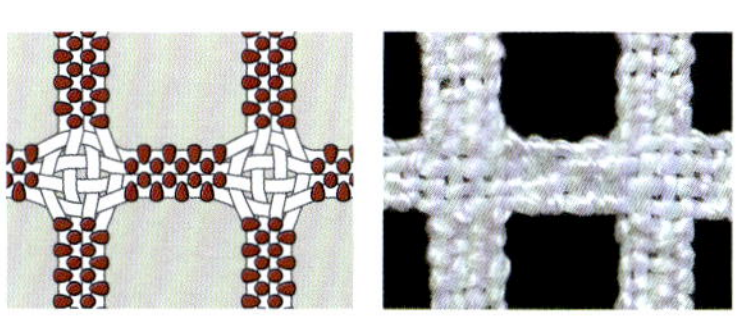

In this variation, the bar's threads are woven singly rather than in pairs. This gives four divisions across the bar. It can be hard to achieve good tension.

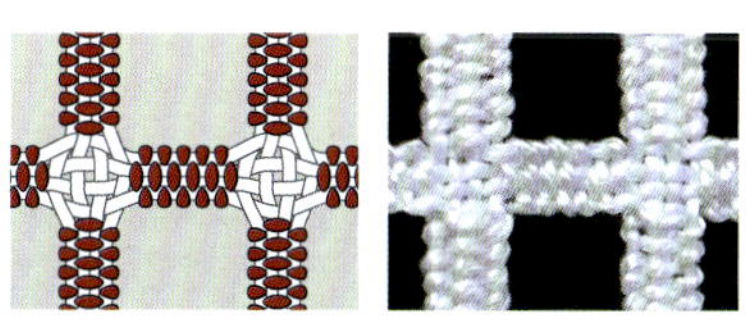

Another unusual variation is for the outer threads to be woven singly, with the inner two worked as a pair. This gives three divisions across the bar.

top tip weaving

Historically, weaving stitches have the needle coming up in the centre of the bar. In this book, all the filling stitches adjacent to weaving are based on this. If you usually go down at the centre, you may need to come up instead, to use the instructions in this book.

zig-zagging lines

Woven bars stitched in zig-zagging lines are often best for filling long and narrow diagonal cutwork areas. When moving from one bar to the next you need to ensure that you do not pull too tightly as the thread goes across the bias and can distort the fabric.

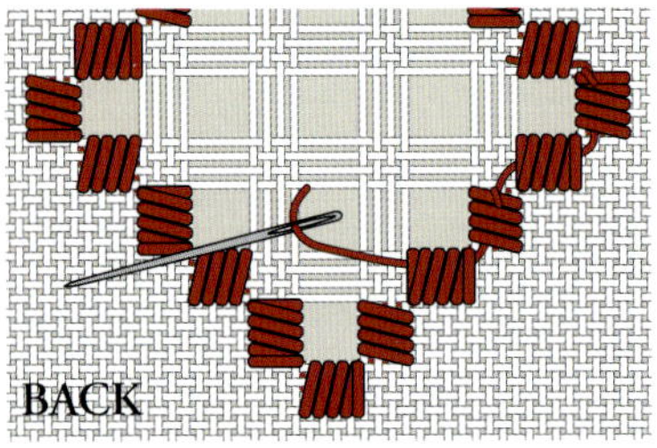

1 Anchor the thread in the back of the satin stitching. Run the thread under the back of four or five klosters, with one or two back-stitches under single threads.

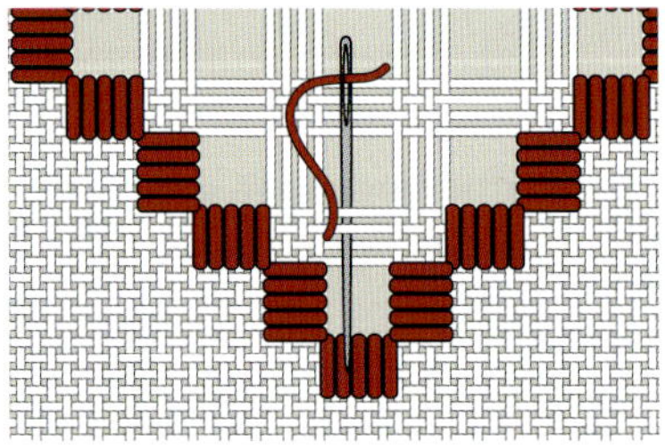

2 On the front, bring the needle out between the four threads at the left end of the first bar. From above, slide it under the upper two threads and bring it up again in the centre.

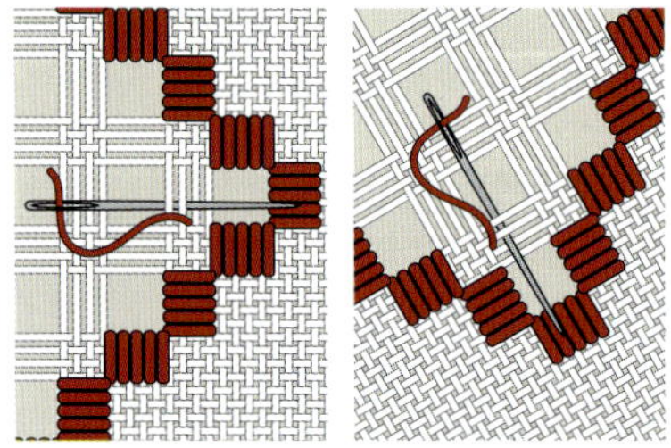

❶ *Some people prefer to insert their needle horizontally, moving upward to fill the bar. Some prefer to work with their fabric on an angle. Use whatever position suits you best.*

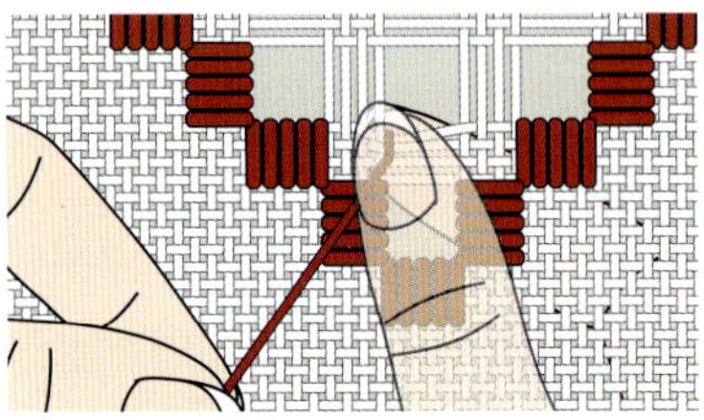

3 Pull the needle through. When the stitch is snug around the side of the bar, pinch the bar between your right forefinger and thumb, and with the other hand, pull the thread to the left and down.

❶ *Pinching stabilises the bar while you tighten the stitch, giving good tension. Pulling left and down narrows the bar and pulls the stitch snugly down.*

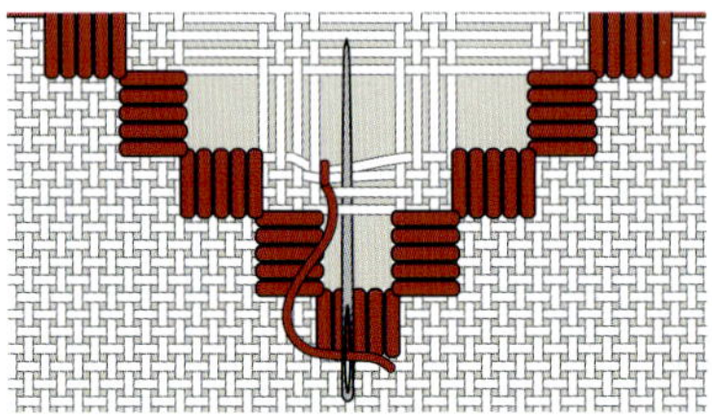

4 From below, slide the needle under the lower two threads and bring it out again in the centre.

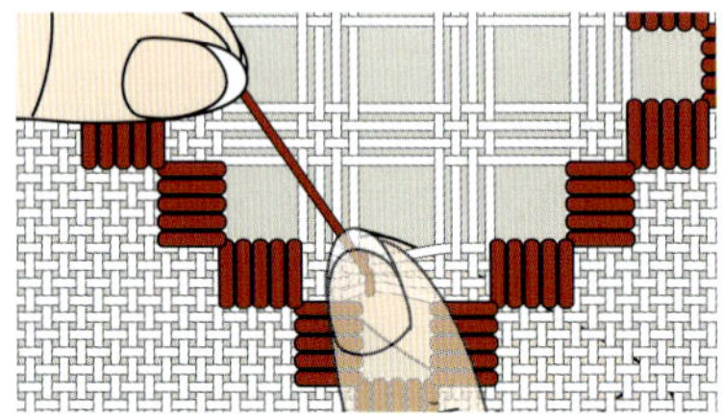

5 Pull the needle through. When the stitch is nearly tight around the side of the bar, pinch the bar between your right forefinger and thumb as you pull the thread to the left and up.

❶ *Pulling the stitch left and up narrows the bar and nestles the stitch snugly against the first one.*

❶ *Tighten after each stitch.*

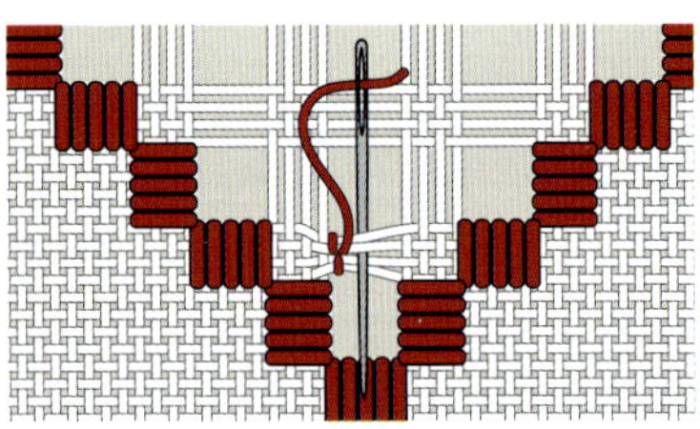

6 From above, slide the needle under the upper two threads and bring it out again in the centre.

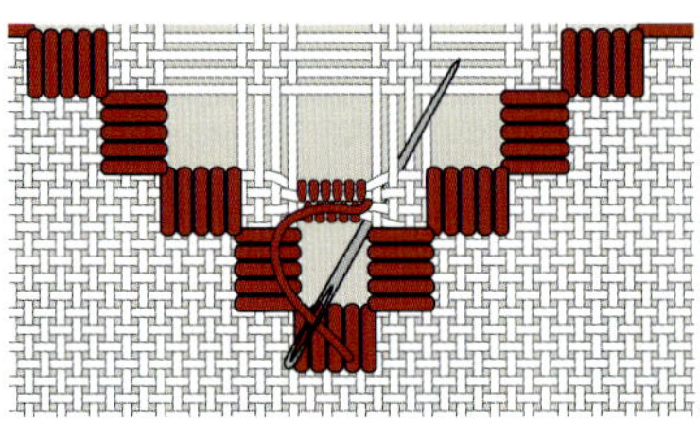

7 Continue weaving the bar, pulling each stitch in snug against the previous ones. Fill the bar with an equal number of stitches on each side. To finish the bar and start the next one, pass the needle behind the adjacent woven square, and bring it out in the centre of the next bar.

❶ *Do not make the stitch behind the woven square too tight.*

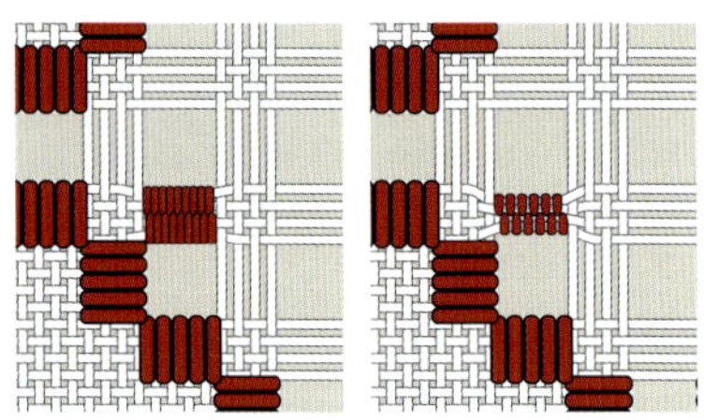

❶ *Do not cram the bar with stitches as shown left. Five, six, or seven stitches per side is ample, as shown right. If you can fit more in, you're probably not tightening the stitch tension enough. Use as few stitches as you can to fill the bar. Keep the stitch tension and quantity constant throughout the project.*

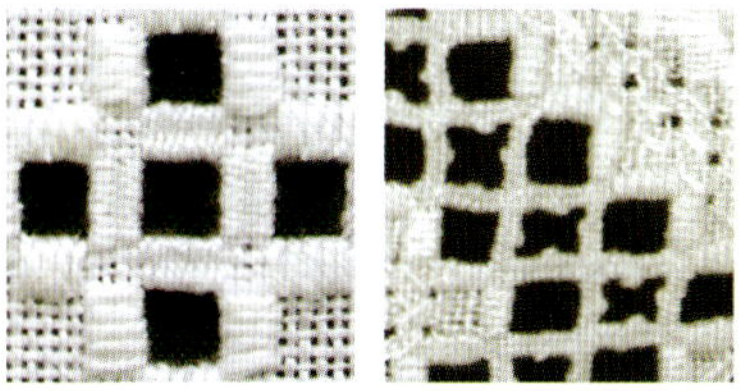

❶ *The weaving should pull the threads inward so that the bar is narrower than the adjacent woven square. If it isn't (as shown left), you're not pulling tight enough. Historical examples have bars that are narrow, not wide. If you pinch and pull after each stitch, you will be able to narrow your bars.*

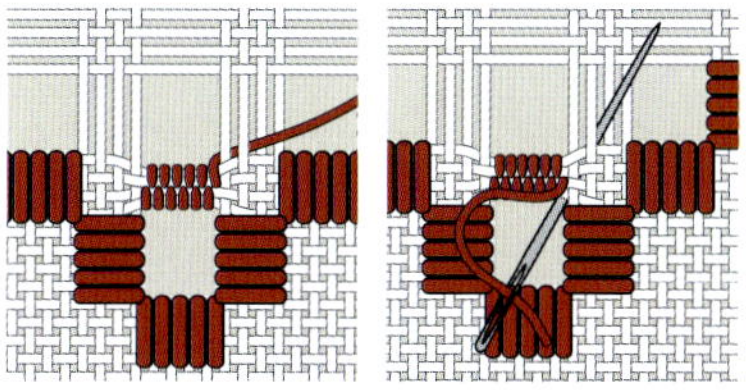

❶ *Whether you're turning left or right, make sure the thread goes behind the adjacent woven square and doesn't just slip around the corner (shown above left) which looks like a mistake. This may mean that you need a one-off extra stitch on one side (shown above right). Don't make the stitch behind too tight.*

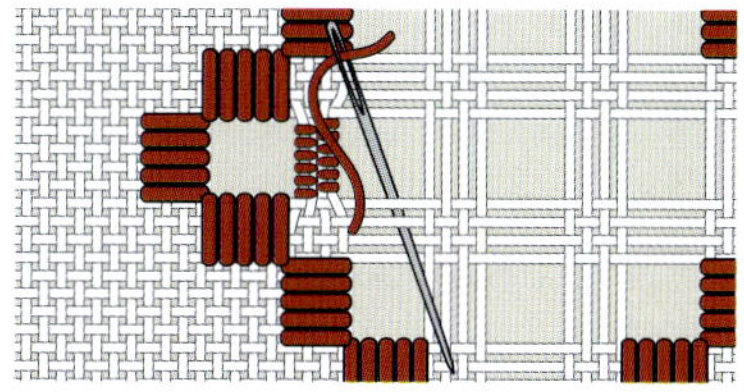

8 Turn the work 90° clockwise. From above, slide the needle under the upper two threads and bring it up again in the centre.

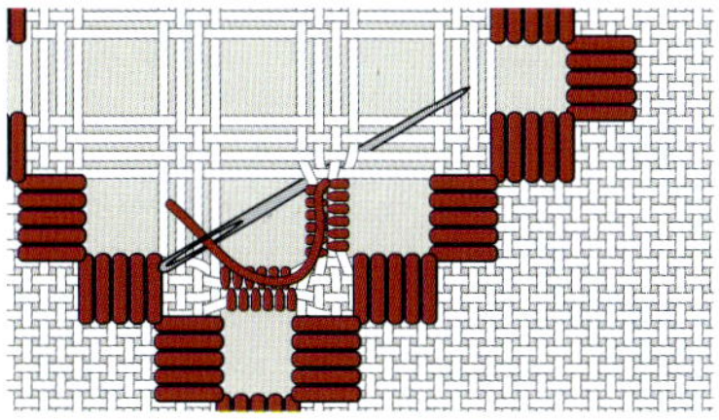

9 Weave the bar. Finish with a stitch on the opposite side to the next bar. Turn the work 90° anticlockwise. Pass the needle behind the woven square. Bring it out in the next bar's centre.

❶ *There will be an extra stitch on this bar so that the needle passes behind the woven square, rather than the thread slipping around the corner.*

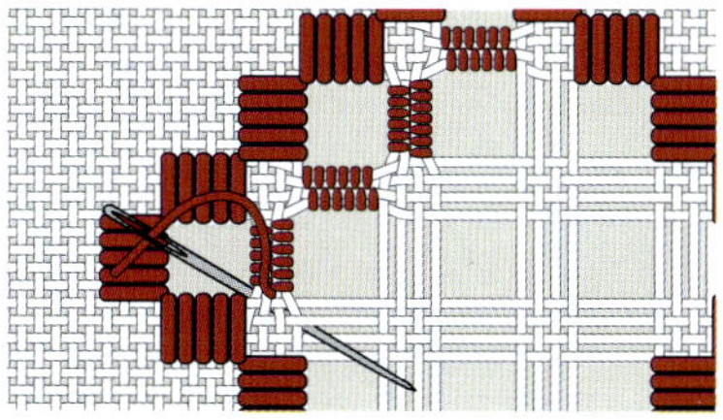

10 Weave the next two bars as for the first two. Finish each bar with a stitch on the side opposite to the next bar you'll stitch. Pass the needle behind the woven fabric square and bring it out in the centre of the next bar.

❶ *Do not make the stitch behind the woven square too tight.*

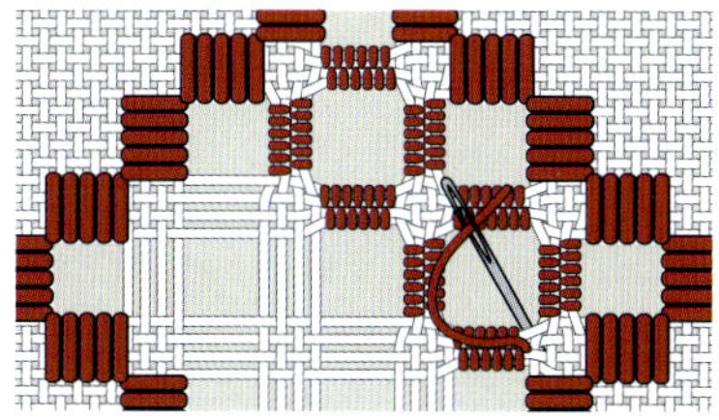

11 Work the next row similarly. If the row's final bar does not have an adjacent bar to continue to (as shown here) finish with a stitch on the opposite side to the edge of the cutwork.

❶ *If the end of the row does have an adjacent bar, turn the corner in the usual way, ensuring the bar's last stitch is on the opposite side to the next bar.*

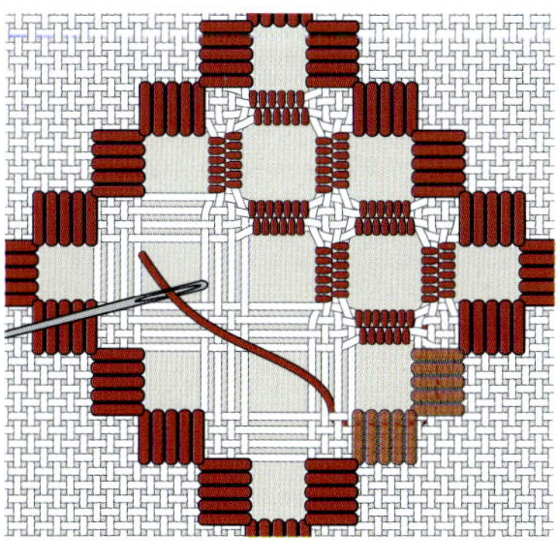

12 On the back, run the thread under the satin stitch to the next bar.

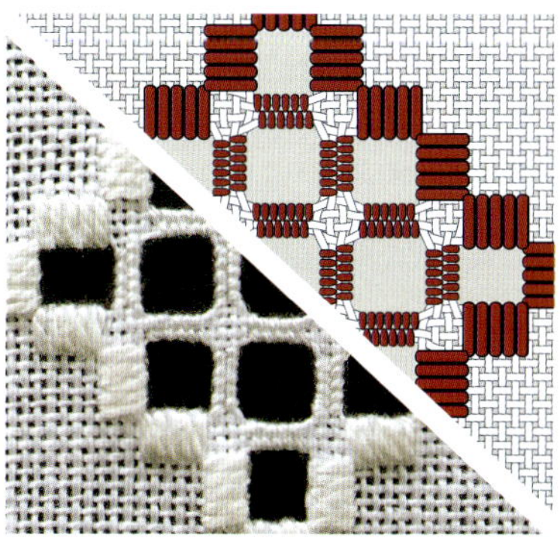

13 Complete the next two rows similarly, finishing the thread under the back of the satin stitching.

❶ *I make a point of always starting my weaving on the same side of the bar. For left-handers it makes sense to start stitching on left side of the bar (if you were looking at it with the bar stretching away from you). Whichever you choose, be consistent throughout.*

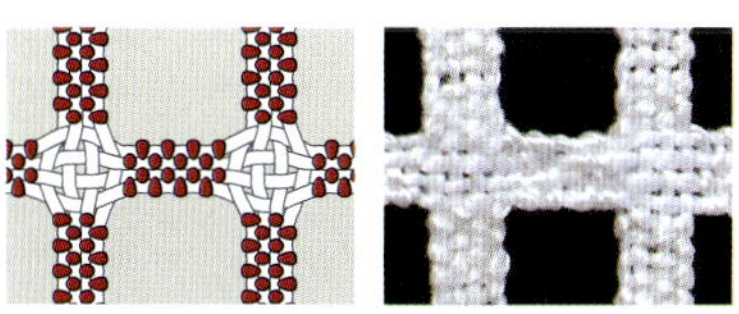

❶ *In this variation, the bar's threads are woven singly rather than in pairs. This gives four divisions across the bar. It can be hard to achieve good tension.*

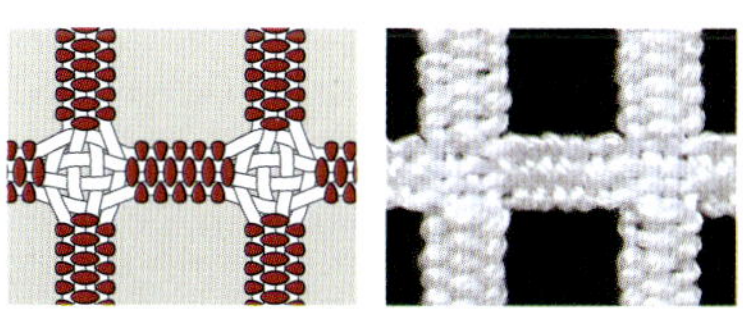

❶ *Another unusual variation is for the outer threads to be woven singly, with the inner two worked as a pair. This gives three divisions across the bar.*

top tip weaving

Historically, weaving stitches have the needle coming up in the centre of the bar. In this book, all the filling stitches adjacent to weaving are based on this. If you usually go down at the centre, you may need to come up instead, to use the instructions in this book.

R

TRADITIONAL

woven bars

Woven bars are the basic stitch used for filling cutwork areas. Before you begin, plan a path to stitch all the bars. Sometimes using straight lines is more sensible, and sometimes using zig-zagging lines is more sensible.

straight lines

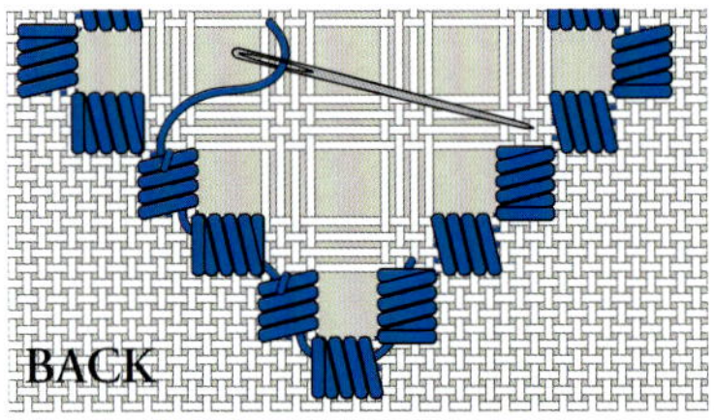

1 Anchor the thread in the back of the satin stitching. Run the thread under the back of four or five klosters, with one or two back-stitches under single threads.

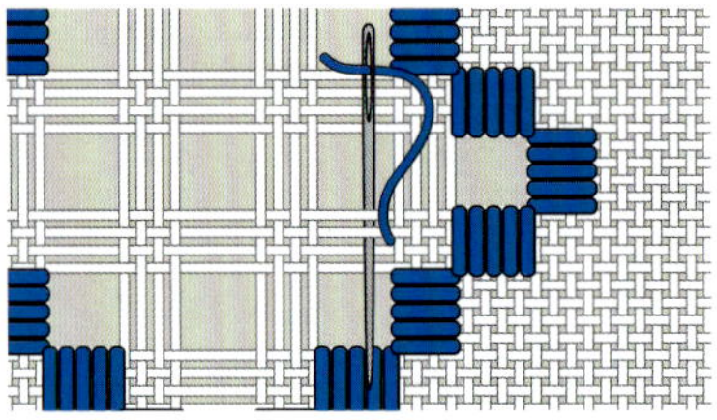

2 On the front, bring the needle out between the four threads at the right end of the first bar. From above, slide it under the upper two threads and bring it up again in the centre.

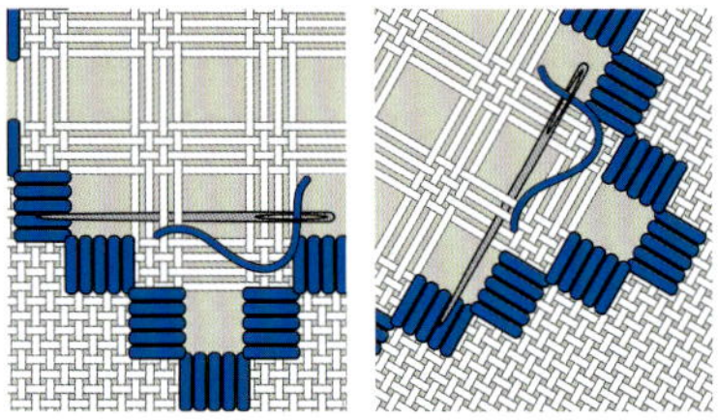

❶ *Some people prefer to insert their needle horizontally, moving upward to fill the bar. Some prefer to work with their fabric on an angle. Use whatever position suits you best.*

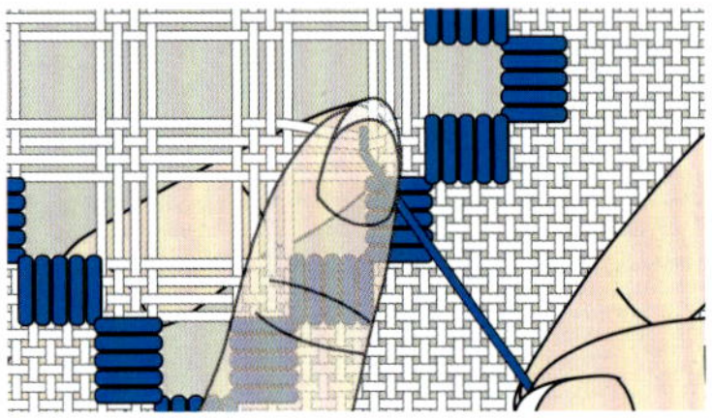

3 Pull the needle through. When the stitch is snug around the side of the bar, pinch the bar between your left forefinger and thumb, and with the other hand, pull the thread to the right and down.

❶ *Pinching stabilises the bar while you tighten the stitch, giving very good tension. Pulling right and down narrows the bar and pulls the stitch snugly down.*

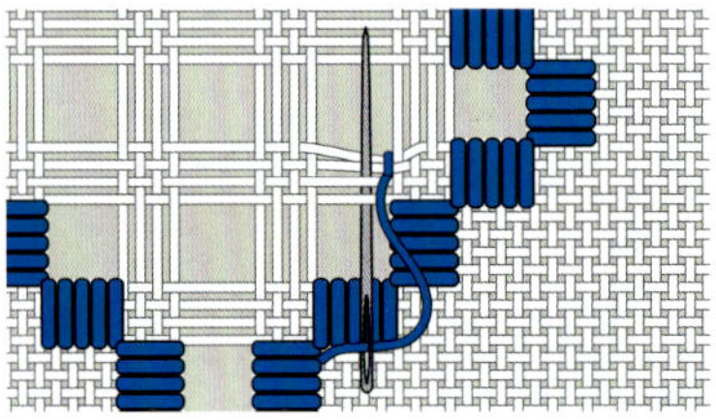

4 From below, slide the needle under the lower two threads and bring it out again in the centre.

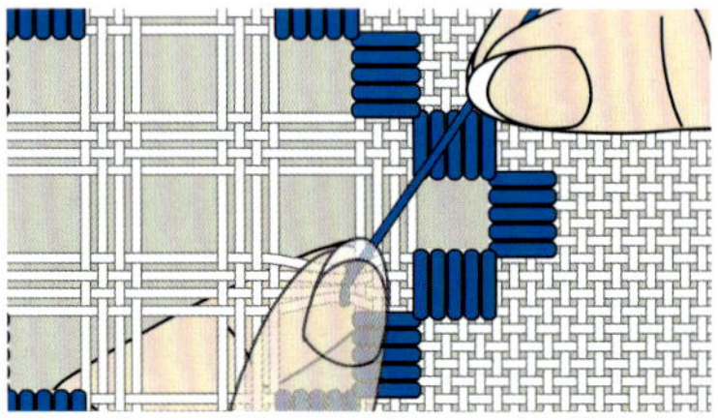

5 Pull the needle through. When the stitch is nearly tight around the side of the bar, pinch the bar between your left forefinger and thumb as you pull the thread to the right and up.

❶ *Pulling the stitch right and up narrows the bar and nestles the stitch snugly against the first one.*

❶ *Tighten after each stitch.*

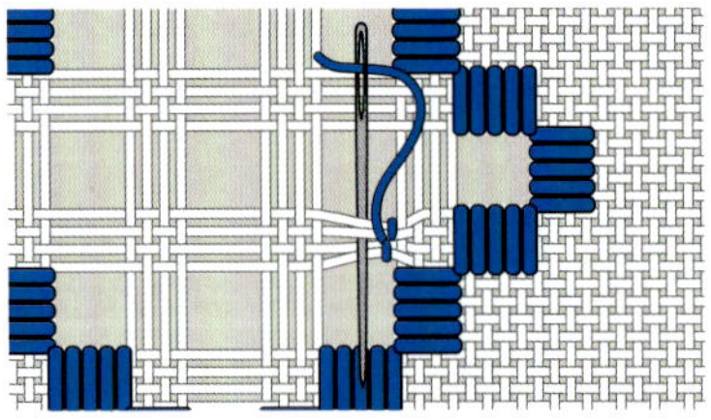

6 From above, slide the needle under the upper two threads and bring it out again in the centre.

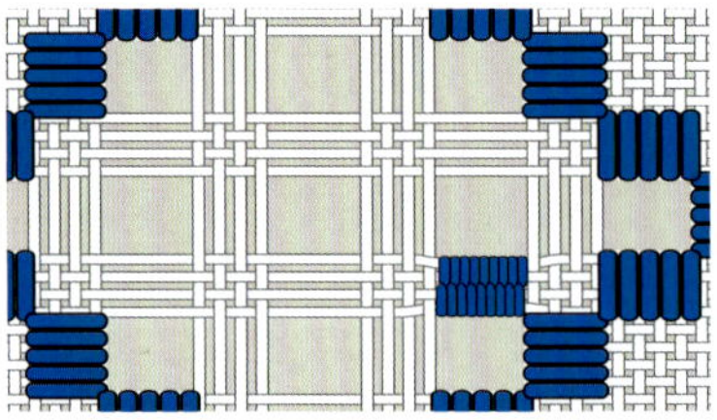

7 Continue weaving the bar, pulling each stitch in snug against the previous ones. Fill the bar with an equal number of stitches on each side. To finish the bar and start the next one, pass the needle behind the adjacent woven square, and bring the needle out in the centre of the next bar.

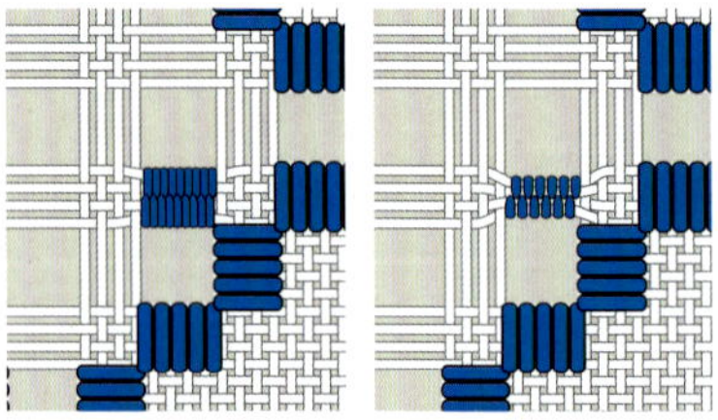

❶ *Do not cram the bar with stitches as shown left. Five, six, or seven stitches per side is ample, as shown right. If you can fit more in, you're probably not tightening the stitch tension enough. Use as few stitches as you can to fill the bar. Keep the tension and quantity constant throughout the project.*

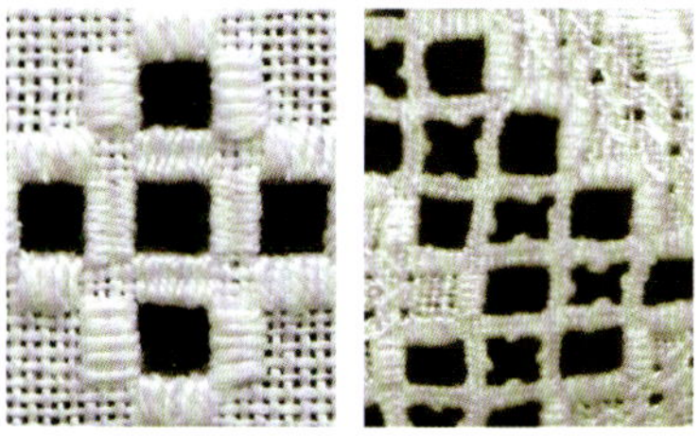

The weaving should pull the threads inward so that the bar is narrower than the adjacent woven square. If it isn't (as shown left), you're not pulling tight enough. Historical examples have bars that are narrow, not wide. If you pinch and pull after each stitch, you will be able to narrow your bars.

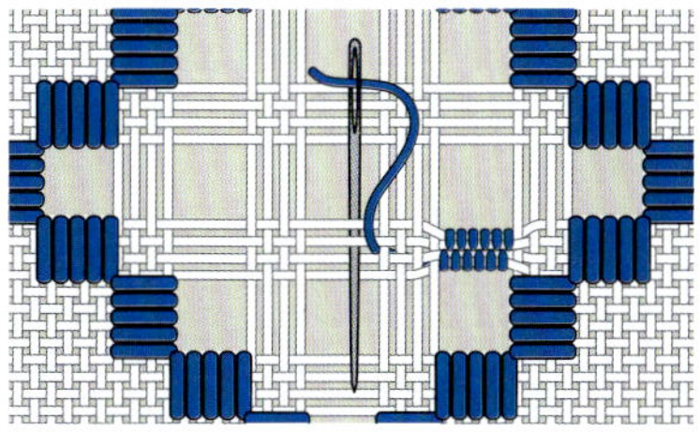

8 Pull the needle through. From above, slide it under the upper two threads. Bring it up again in the centre.

Always start each bar on the same side. If you choose the upper threads for the first bar, use them for each one after that. If you choose the lower threads, always start with them.

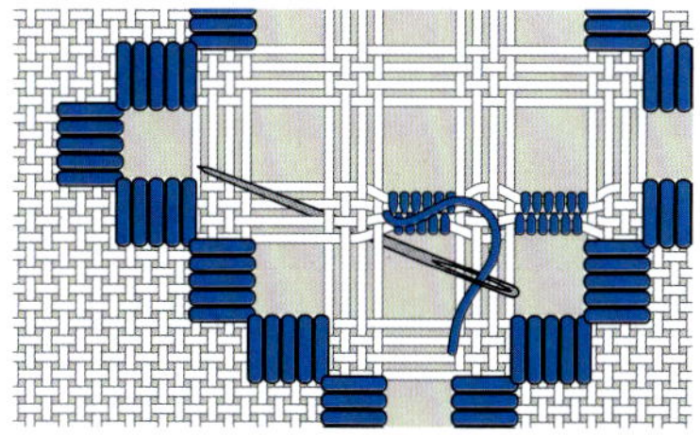

9 Continue weaving from one side of the bar to the other, pulling the stitches in tight. Use the same quantity of stitches as for the first bar. Pass the needle behind the adjacent woven square, and bring the needle out in the centre of the next bar.

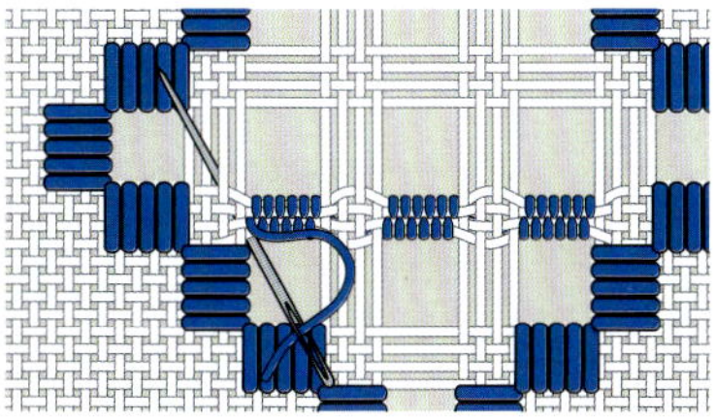

10 Work the next bar similarly. To make a right turn, pass the needle behind the adjacent woven square. Bring it out in the next bar's centre.

Following completion of this side, the next bar is adjacent to the right, so the path will be clockwise.

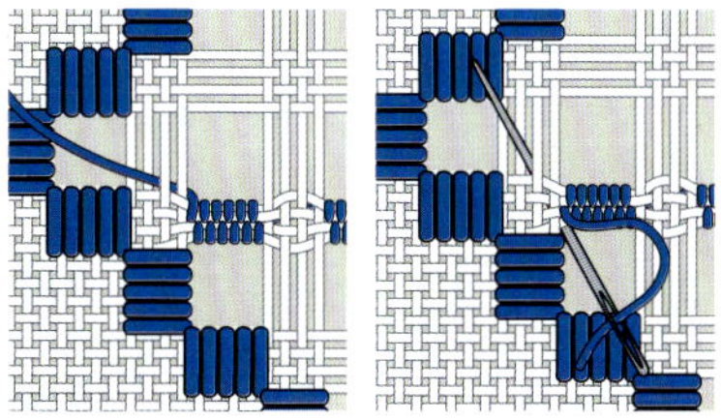

Whether you're turning left or right, make sure the thread goes behind the adjacent woven square and doesn't just slip around the corner (shown above left) which looks like a mistake. This may mean that you need a one-off extra stitch on one side (shown above right).

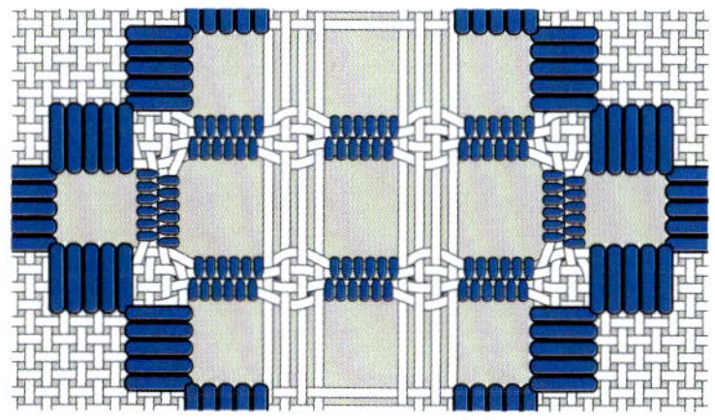

11 Turn the work 90° anticlockwise and continue around the circuit, working the bars in long lines, in a clockwise direction.

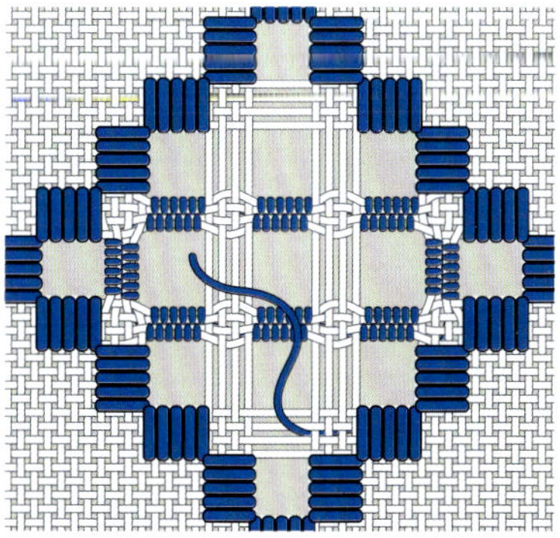

12 Take the needle through the back of the satin stitch to come up next to the closest woven square, ready to start a new circuit.

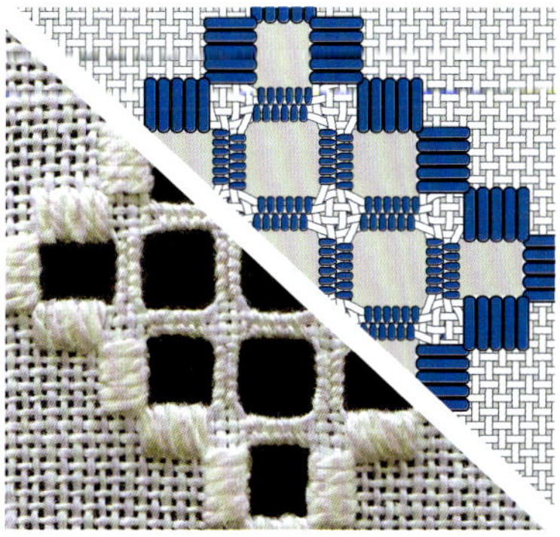

13 Work the circuit similarly to the previous circuit. To finish, run the thread through the back of the satin stitching.

Working bars in long straight lines helps them to sit neatly in straight lines.

For right-handers it makes sense to start stitching on the bar's right side (when the bar stretches away from you). Work circuits clockwise where possible. Alternatively, start on the left side and work anticlockwise. Whichever you choose, be consistent throughout.

top tip weaving

Historically, weaving stitches have the needle coming up in the centre of the bar. In this book, all the filling stitches adjacent to weaving are based on this. If you usually go down at the centre, you may need to come up instead, to use the instructions in this book.

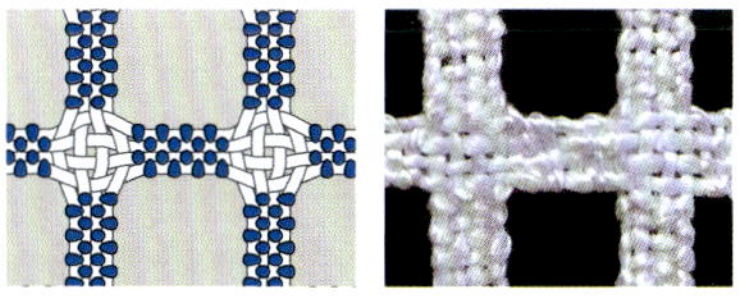

In this variation, the bar's threads are woven singly rather than in pairs. This gives four divisions across the bar. It can be hard to achieve good tension.

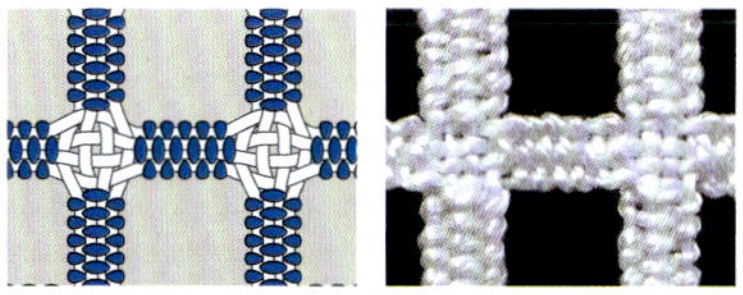

Another unusual variation is for the outer threads to be woven singly, with the inner two worked as a pair. This gives three divisions across the bar.

zig-zagging lines

Woven bars stitched in zig-zagging lines are often best for filling long and narrow diagonal cutwork areas. When moving from one bar to the next you need to ensure that you do not pull too tightly as the thread goes across the bias and can distort the fabric.

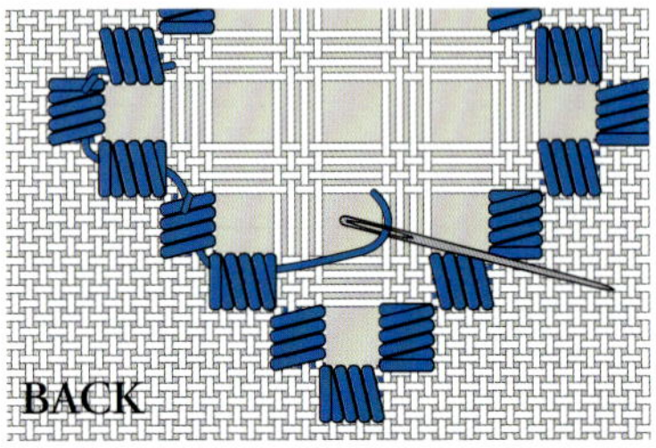

1 Anchor the thread in the back of the satin stitching. Run the thread under the back of four or five klosters, with one or two backstitches under single threads.

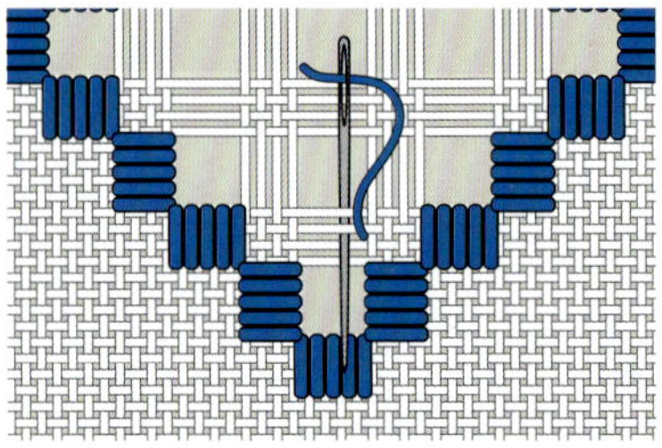

2 On the front, bring the needle out between the four threads at the right end of the first bar. From above, slide it under the upper two threads and bring it up again in the centre.

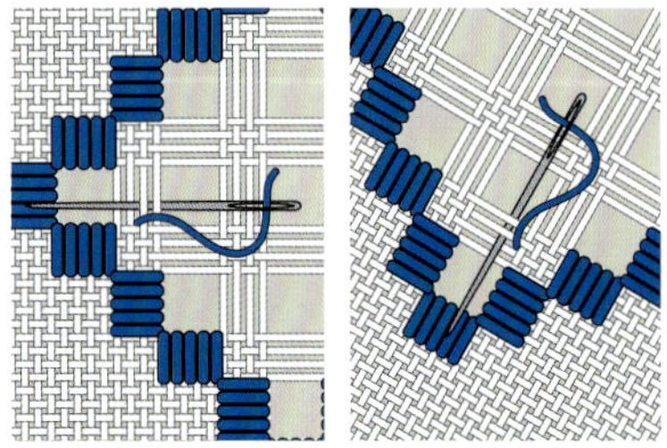

❶ *Some people prefer to insert their needle horizontally, moving upward to fill the bar. Some prefer to work with their fabric on an angle. Use whatever position suits you best.*

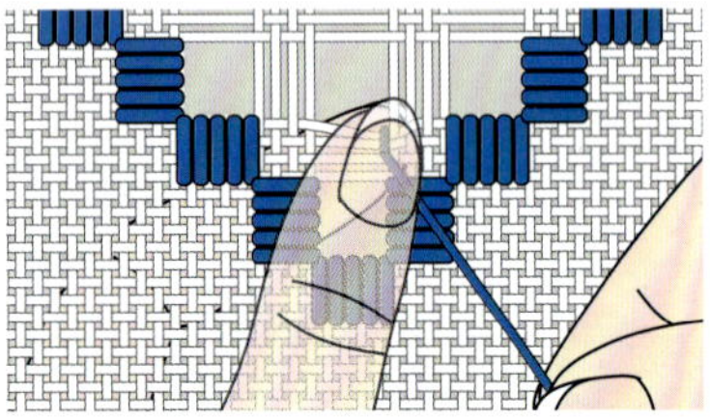

3 Pull the needle through. When the stitch is snug around the side of the bar, pinch the bar between your left forefinger and thumb, and with the other hand, pull the thread to the right and down.

❶ *Pinching stabilises the bar while you tighten the stitch, giving good tension. Pulling right and down narrows the bar and pulls the stitch snugly down.*

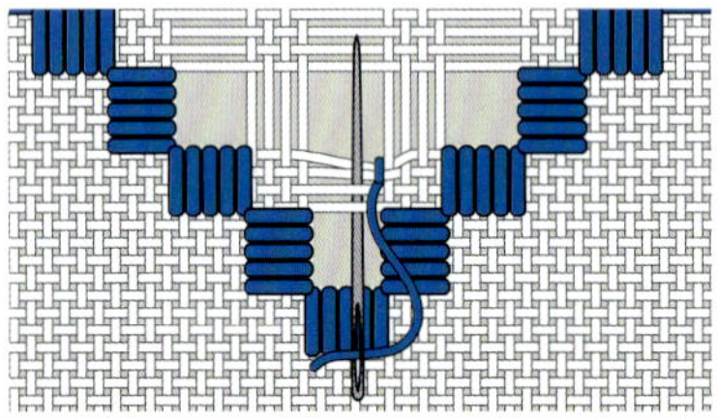

4 From below, slide the needle under the lower two threads and bring it out again in the centre.

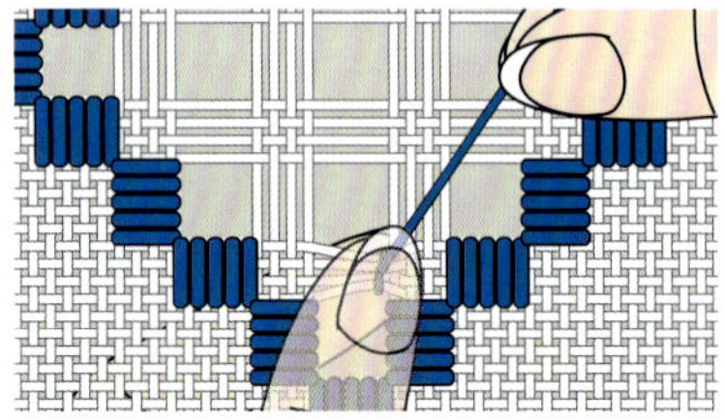

5 Pull the needle through. When the stitch is nearly tight around the side of the bar, pinch the bar between your left forefinger and thumb as you pull the thread to the right and up.

❶ *Pulling the stitch right and up narrows the bar and nestles the stitch snugly against the first one.*

❶ *Tighten after each stitch.*

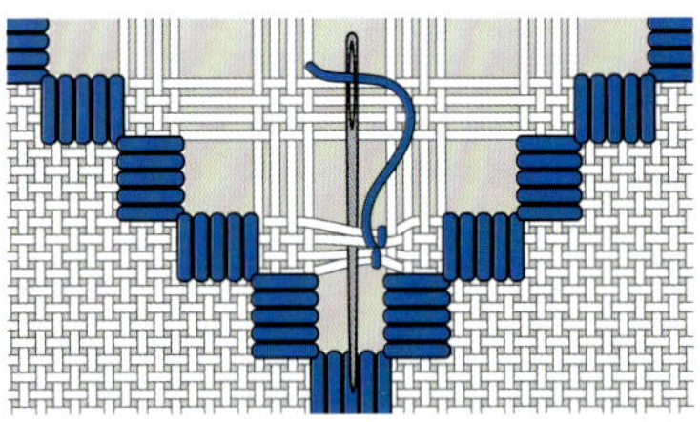

6 From above, slide the needle under the upper two threads and bring it out again in the centre.

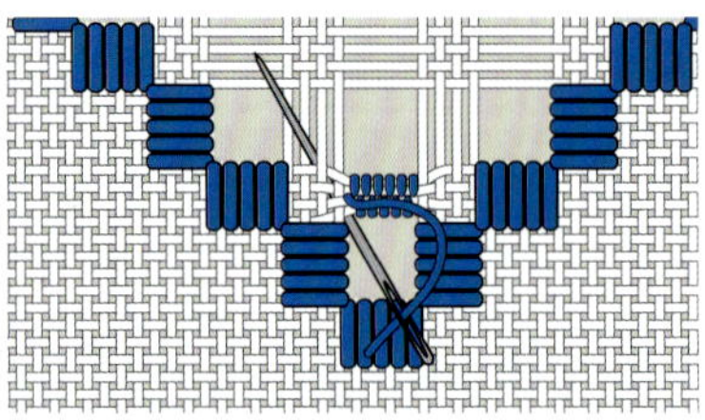

7 Continue weaving the bar, pulling each stitch in snug against the previous ones. Fill the bar with an equal number of stitches on each side. To finish the bar and start the next one, pass the needle behind the adjacent woven square, and bring it out in the centre of the next bar.

❶ *Do not make the stitch behind the woven square too tight.*

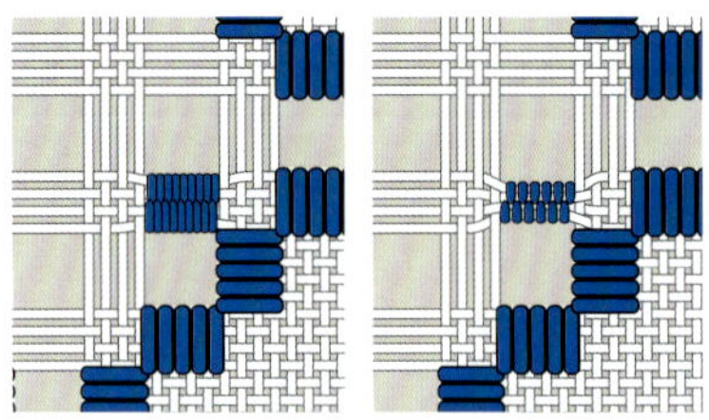

❶ *Do not cram the bar with stitches as shown left. 5, 6, or 7 stitches per side is ample, as shown right. If you can fit more in, you're probably not tightening the stitch tension enough. Use as few stitches as you can to fill the bar. Keep the stitch tension and quantity constant throughout the project.*

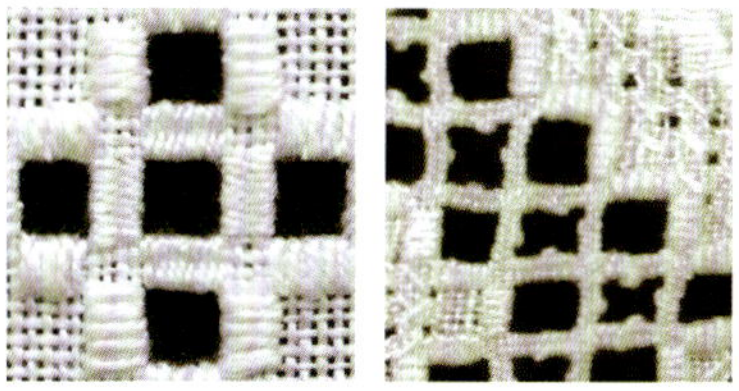

The weaving should pull the threads inward so that the bar is narrower than the adjacent woven square. If it isn't (as shown left), you're not pulling tight enough. Historical examples have bars that are narrow, not wide. If you pinch and pull after each stitch, you will be able to narrow your bars.

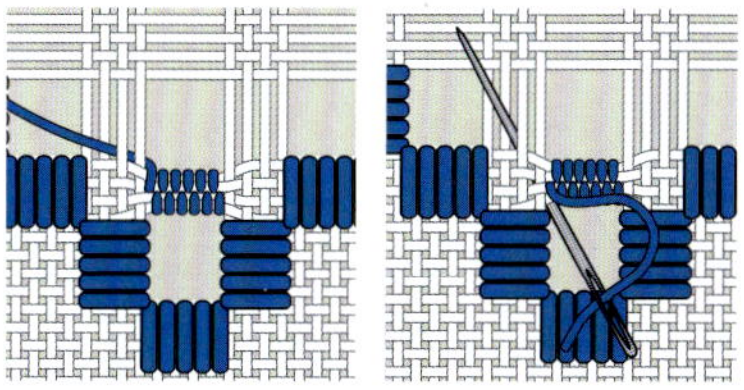

Whether you're turning left or right, make sure the thread goes behind the adjacent woven square and doesn't just slip around the corner (shown above left) which looks like a mistake. This may mean that you need a one-off extra stitch on one side (shown above right).

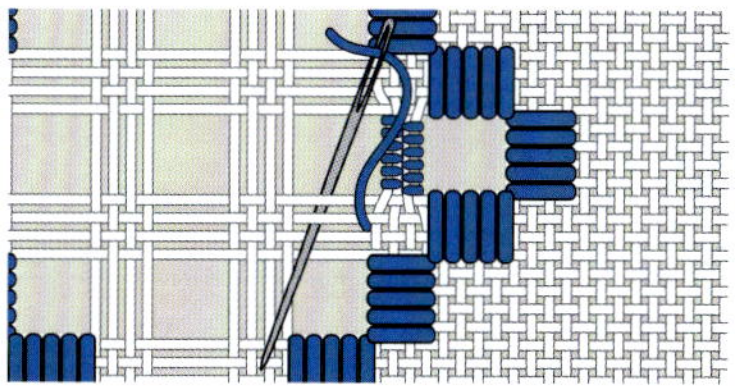

8 Turn the work 90° anticlockwise. From above, slide the needle under the upper two threads and bring it up again in the centre.

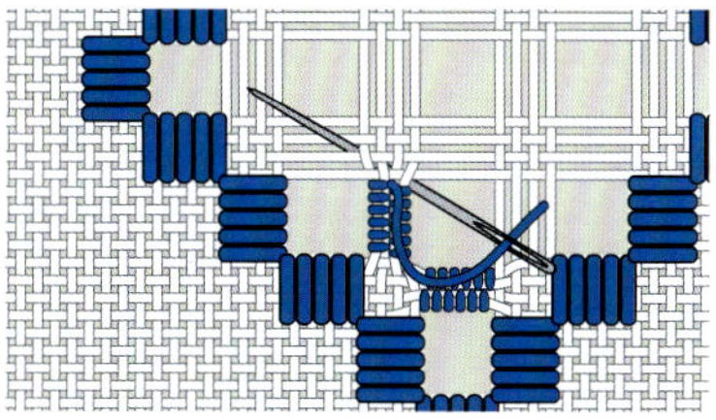

9 Weave the bar. Finish with a stitch on side opposite to the next bar. Turn the work 90° clockwise. Pass the needle behind the woven square. Bring it out in the centre of the next bar.

There will be an extra stitch on this bar so that the needle passes behind the woven square, rather than the thread slipping around the corner.

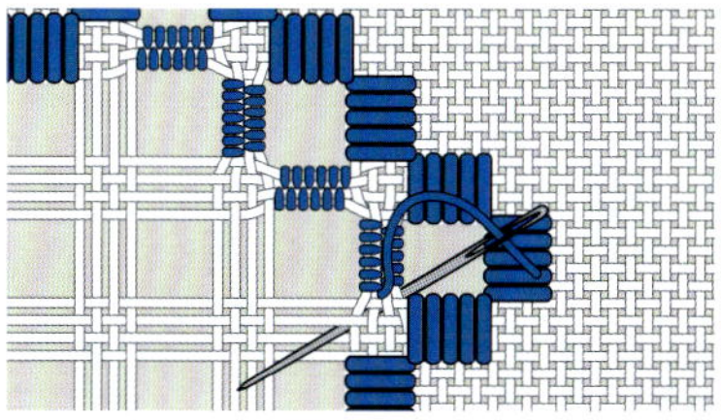

10 Weave the next two bars as for the first two. Finish each bar with a stitch on the side opposite to the next bar you'll stitch. Pass the needle behind the woven fabric square and bring it out in the centre of the next bar.

Do not make the stitch behind the woven square too tight.

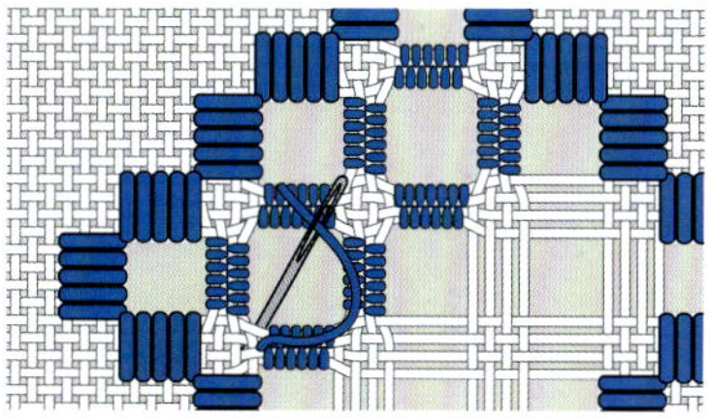

11 Work the next row similarly. If the row's final bar does not have an adjacent bar to continue to (as shown here) finish with a stitch on the opposite side to the edge of the cutwork.

If the end of the row does have an adjacent bar, turn the corner in the usual way, ensuring the bar's last stitch is on the opposite side to the next bar.

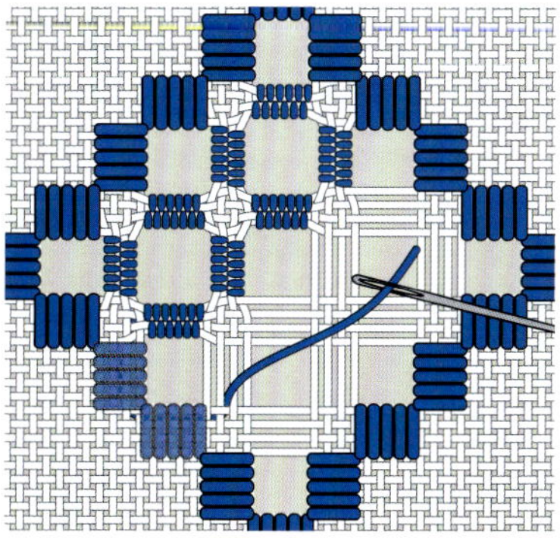

12 On the back, run the thread under the satin stitch to the next bar.

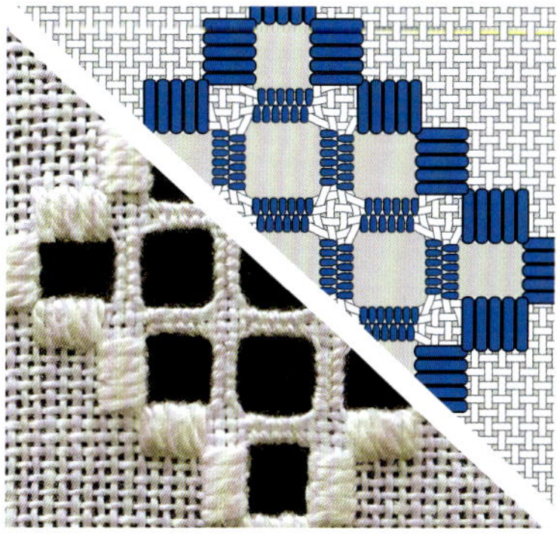

13 Complete the next two rows similarly, finishing the thread under the back of the satin stitching.

I make a point of always starting my weaving on the same side of the bar. For right-handers it makes sense to start stitching on right side of the bar (if you were looking at it with the bar stretching away from you). Whichever you choose, be consistent throughout.

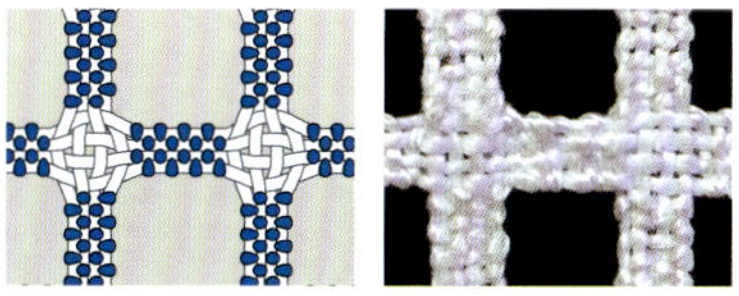

In this variation, the bar's threads are woven singly rather than in pairs. This gives four divisions across the bar. It can be hard to achieve good tension.

Another unusual variation is for the outer threads to be woven singly, with the inner two worked as a pair. This gives three divisions across the bar.

top tip weaving

Historically, weaving stitches have the needle coming up in the centre of the bar. In this book, all the filling stitches adjacent to weaving are based on this. If you usually go down at the centre, you may need to come up instead, to use the instructions in this book.

wrapped bars

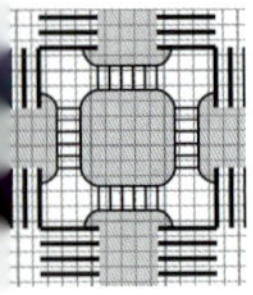

TRADITIONAL

Wrapped bars can be used in place of woven bars in many instances. They need to be stitched with care because it is easy for them to look crooked. They can be such a useful part of many combination stitches that it is worth learning to do them well.

straight lines

I often see wrapped bars stitched extremely poorly; looking crooked and unpleasant. My advice, wherever possible, is to stitch them in straight line paths, rather than zig-zagging paths. This will improve the appearance greatly, as it stops the woven fabric squares between the bars from being distorted.

This is a shape where the wrapped bars have been stitched in a zig-zagging path. They are very crooked and it is an unsatisfactory result.

This is the same shape where the bars have been wrapped in straight line paths. The bars are much straighter and the result is far more satisfactory.

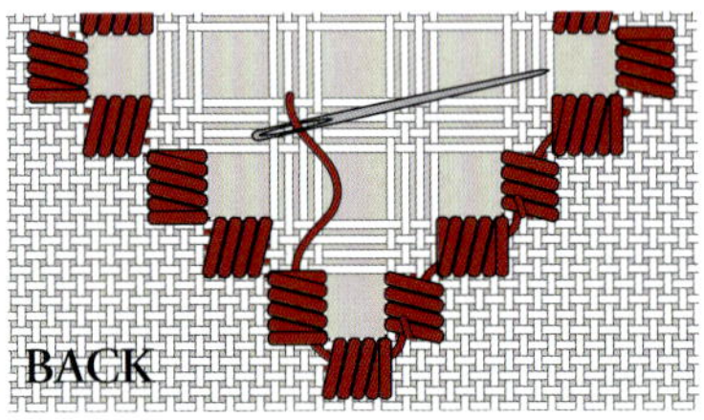

1 Anchor the thread in the back of the satin stitching. Run the thread under the back of four or five klosters, with one or two backstitches under single threads.

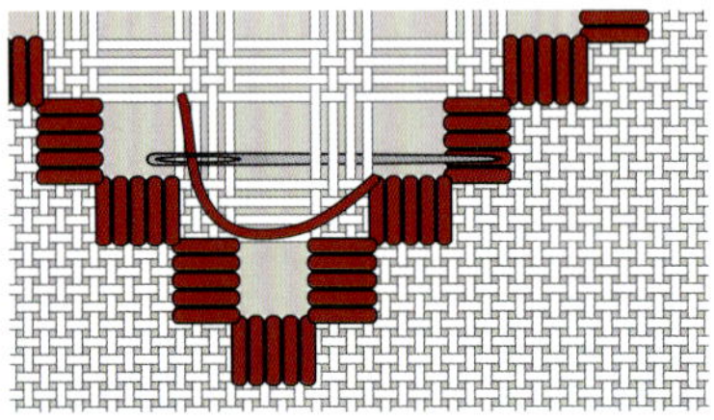

2 On the front, bring the needle out to the right of the first bar to wrap. Slide the needle under the bar from left to right.

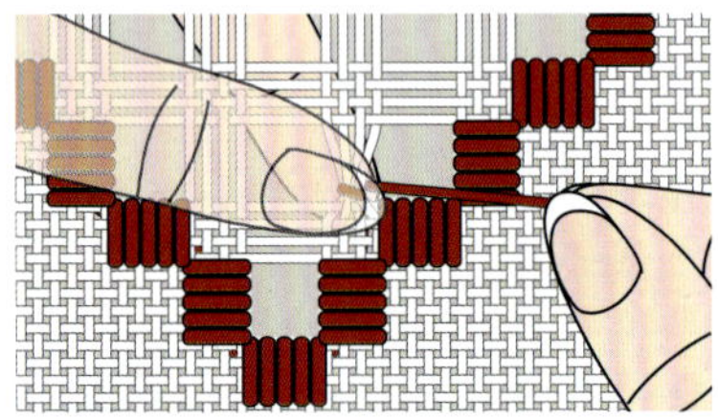

3 Pinch the bar between your left forefinger and thumb, and with the other hand, pull the thread to the right.

Pinching stabilises the bar while you tighten the stitch, giving good tension. Pulling to the right brings the bar in on both sides, making it narrow.

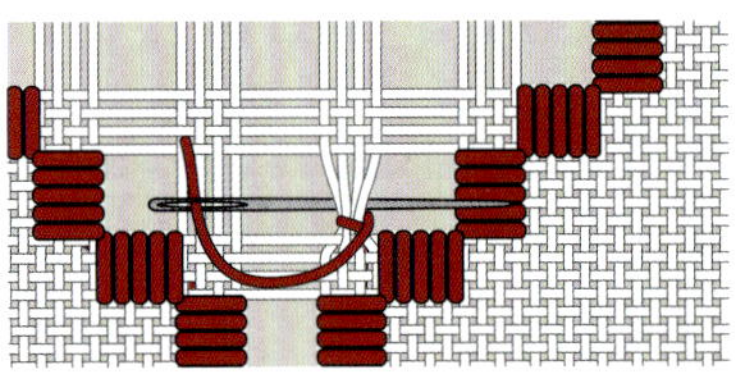

4 Moving up, slide the needle under the bar again. Ensure the new stitch does not overlap the first one.

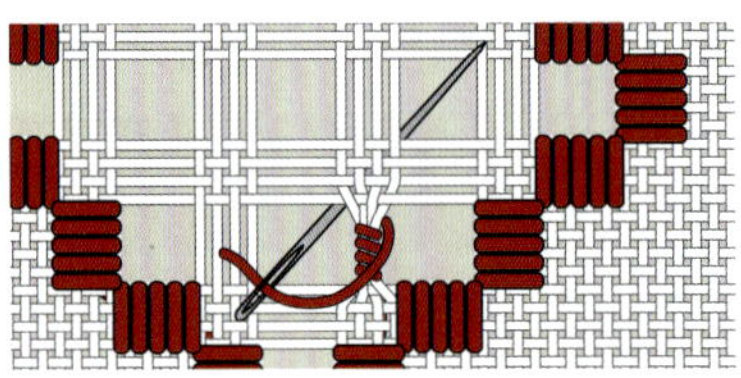

5 Continue wrapping, to fill the bar, pinching and pulling to tighten after each stitch. Pass the needle diagonally behind the woven fabric square and bring it out beside the next bar, which is directly above.

The wraps should lie next to each other on the bar and not overlap. They do not need to be tightly packed.

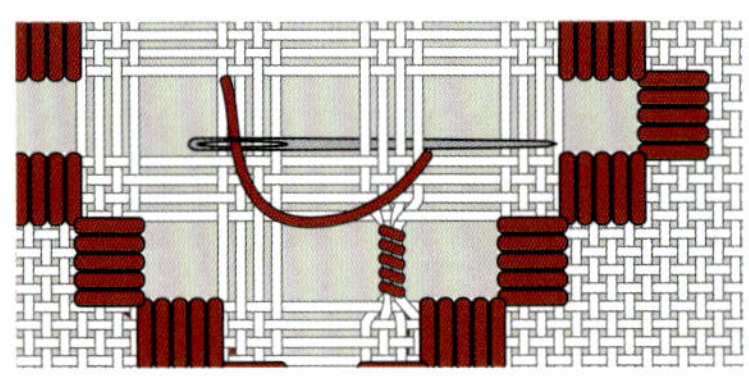

6 Slide the needle under the bar from left to right.

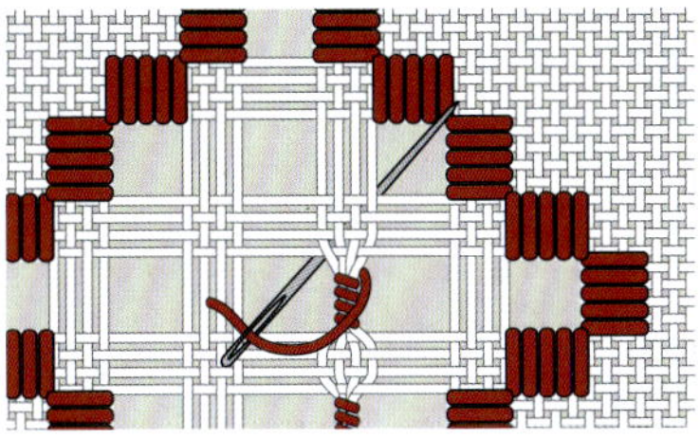

7 Continue wrapping, to fill the bar, pinching and pulling to tighten after each stitch. Pass the needle diagonally behind the woven fabric square and bring it out beside the next bar, which is directly above.

❶ *Each bar should have the same quantity of wraps.*

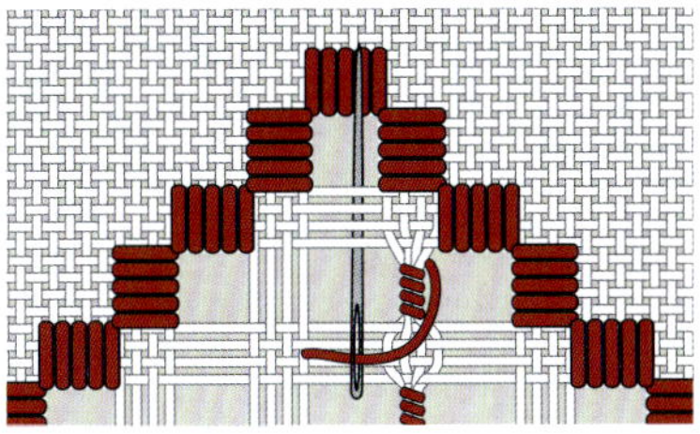

8 Wrap the next bar and slide the needle, from below, under the bar above left.

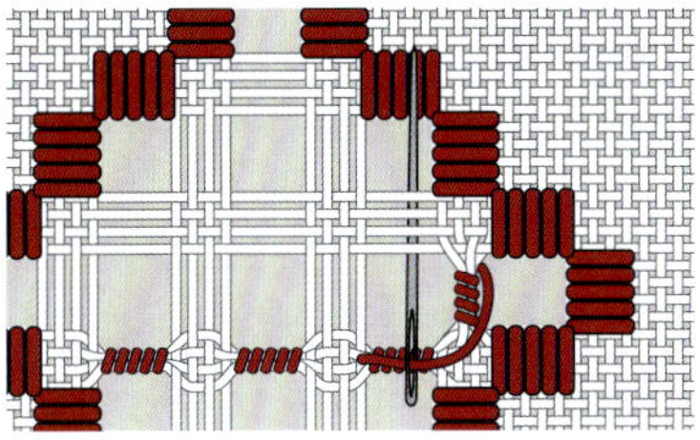

9 Turn the work 90° clockwise and wrap the bar. Slide the needle, from below, under the bar above left.

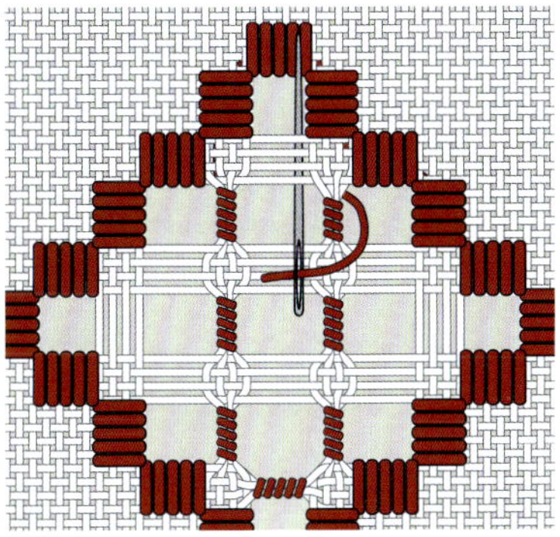

10 Turn the work 90° clockwise and wrap the next three bars. Slide the needle, from below, under the bar above left.

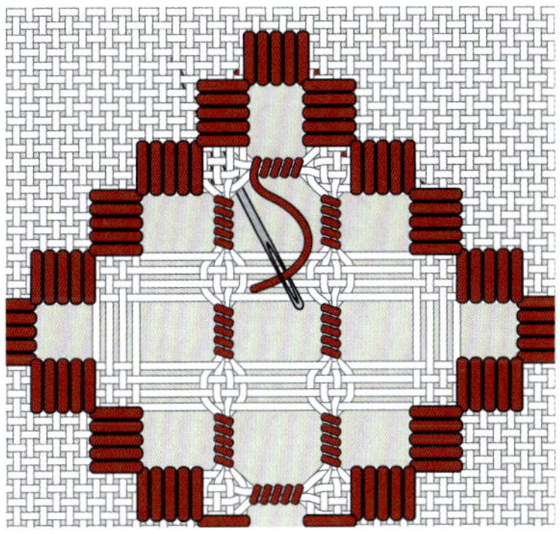

11 Wrap the final bar of the circuit and take the needle to the back.

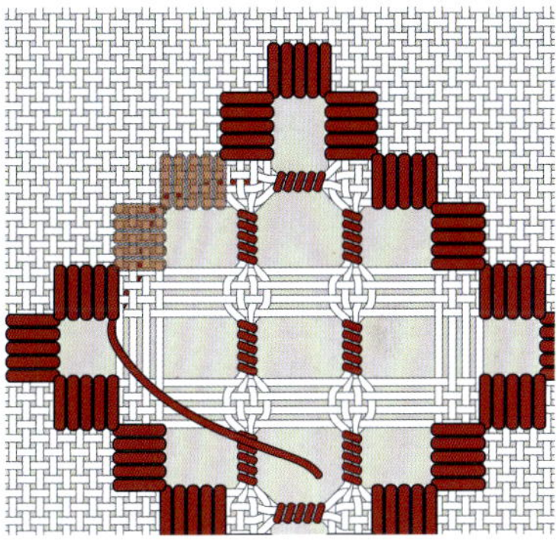

12 On the back, take the needle under the satin stitch to bring it out ready to start the next circuit.

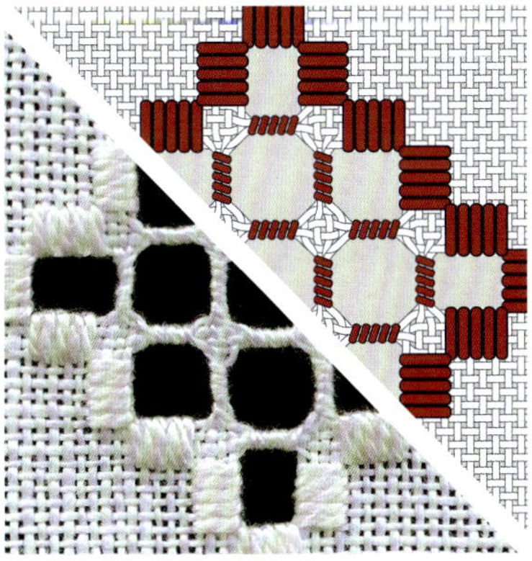

13 Work the second circuit similarly to the first, this time starting with the single bar, then progressing down the side with three in a row and continuing on to complete it.

❶ *Some people don't like to work their bars in straight line paths because it means there are diagonal stitches behind the intervening fabric woven squares. When you work in straight line paths, the front looks far superior. If this means that there are more obvious stitches on the back, then so be it. I'd prefer the front of my work to look exemplary, rather than the back. I still want the back to look neat, but the work is not meant to be reversible.*

L

TRADITIONAL

wrapped zig-zagging lines

While my advice is to use wrapped bars in zig-zagging lines as little as possible, sometimes they are a good choice for a space. An example of this could be a long diagonal cutwork area. (I still would prefer to work in straight lines!)

1 Mount the fabric into a hoop or frame so that the fabric is flat and the grain is square. This will hold the fabric threads taut and straight, and give you the best chance of keeping the bars straight while wrapping.

❶ *Do not stretch the fabric.*

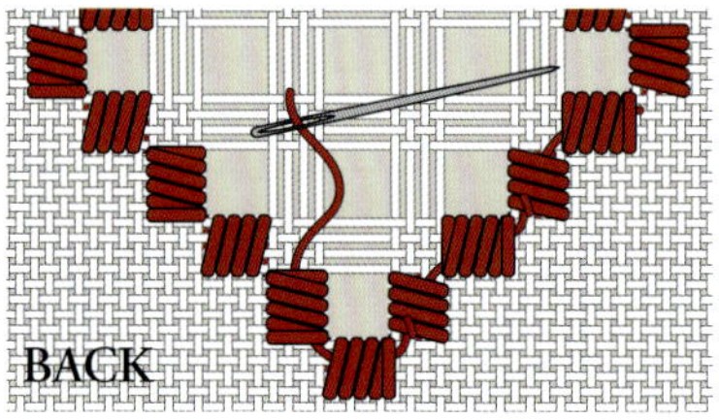

2 Anchor the thread in the back of the satin stitching. Run the thread under the back of four or five klosters, with one or two backstitches under single threads.

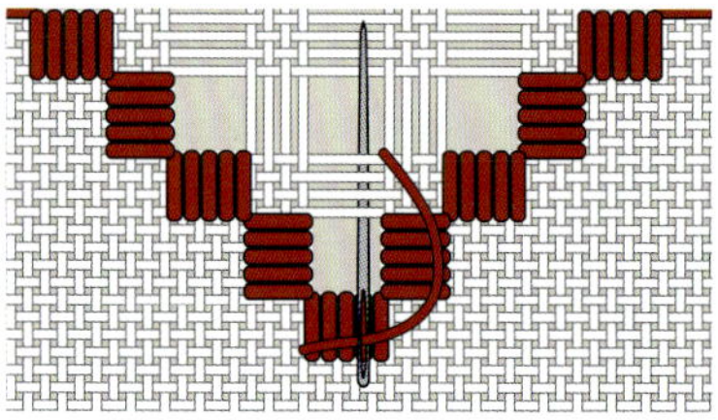

3 On the front, bring the needle out above the first bar to wrap. Slide the needle under the bar from below.

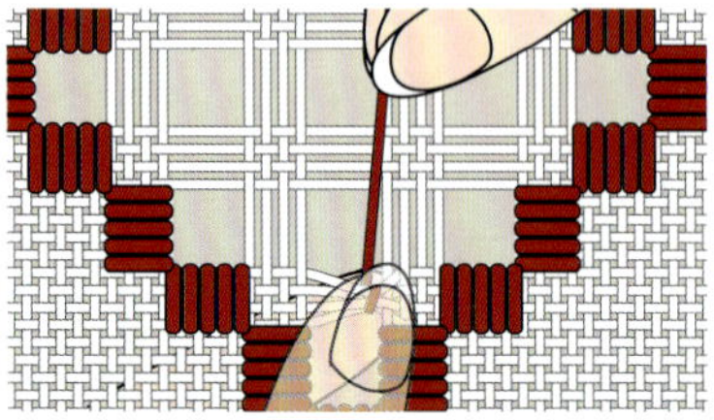

4 Pinch the bar between your forefinger and thumb, and with the other hand, pull the thread upward.

❶ *Pinching stabilises the bar while you tighten the stitch, giving good tension. Pulling upward across the surface of the fabric brings the bar in on both sides, making it narrow.*

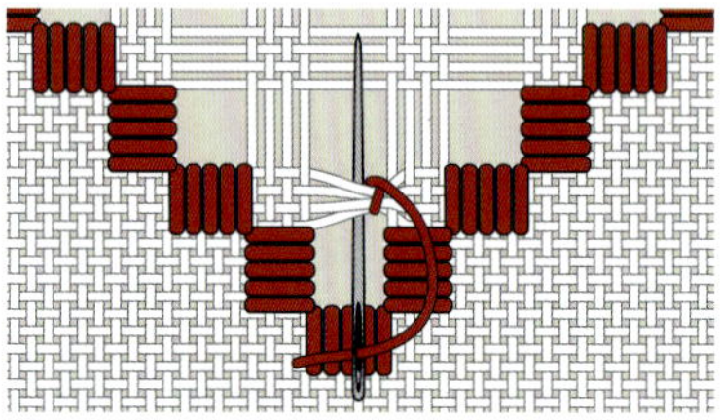

5 Moving left, slide the needle under the bar again. Ensure the new stitch does not overlap the first one.

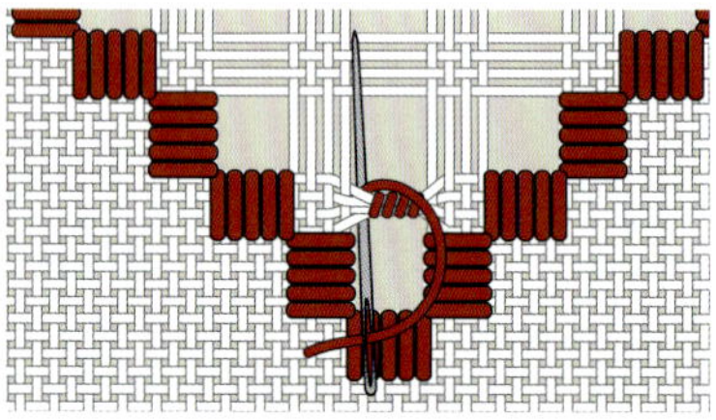

6 Continue wrapping, to fill the bar, pinching and pulling to tighten after each stitch. To complete the bar, slide the needle under the bar one last time.

❶ *The wraps should lie next to each other on the bar and not overlap. They do not need to be tightly packed.*

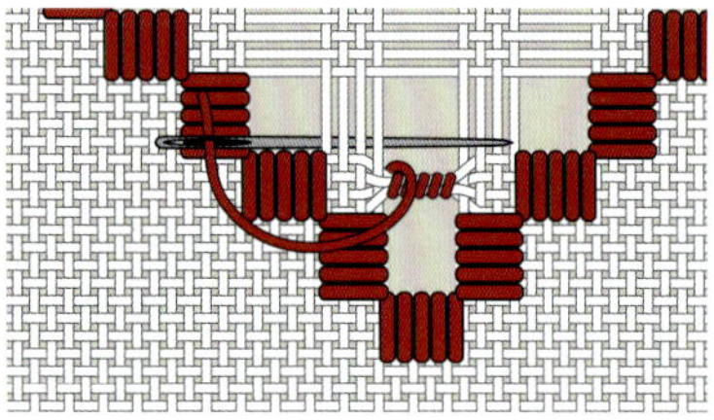

7 From the left, slide the needle under the new bar, just to the left of the previous one.

❶ *When you pull the needle and tighten the stitch, ensure it does not pull the two bars together at an angle. The stitches should be tight without distorting the weave of the fabric.*

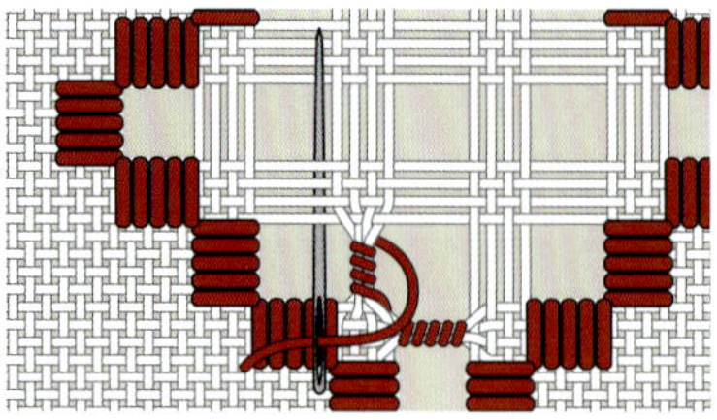

8 Continue wrapping to fill the bar, pinching and pulling to tighten after each stitch. To complete the bar, slide the needle under the next bar to the left, from below.

❶ *Each bar should have the same quantity of wraps.*

❶ *At the corner do not pull the thread so hard that it distorts the fabric.*

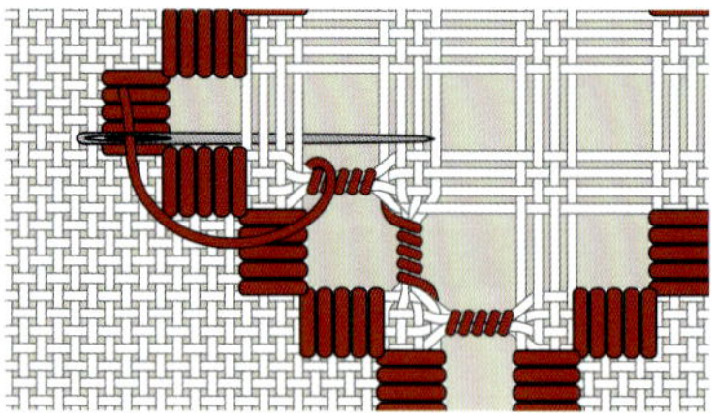

9 Continue wrapping, to fill the bar, pinching and pulling to tighten after each stitch. Complete the bar, then slide the needle from the left under the next bar to the left.

❶ *As you go around the corner, take care to not distort the fabric.*

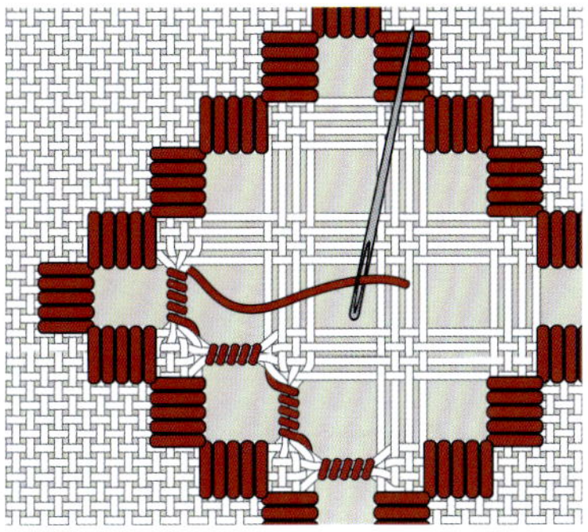

10 Continue wrapping, and finish the bar with the needle emerging beside the completed bar.

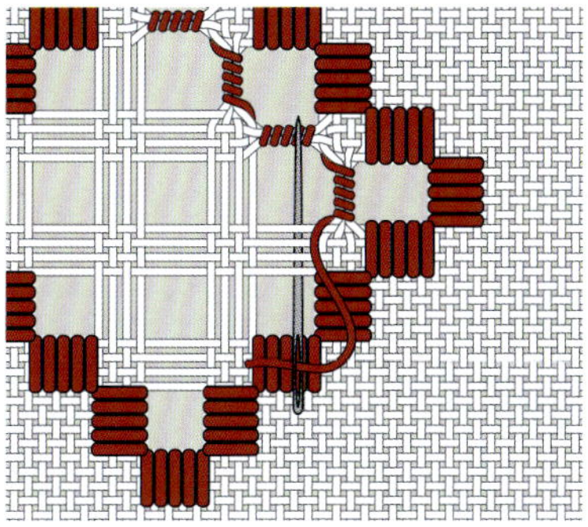

11 Turn the work 180°. Slide the needle under the new bar from below.

❶ *As you go around the corner, take care to not distort the fabric.*

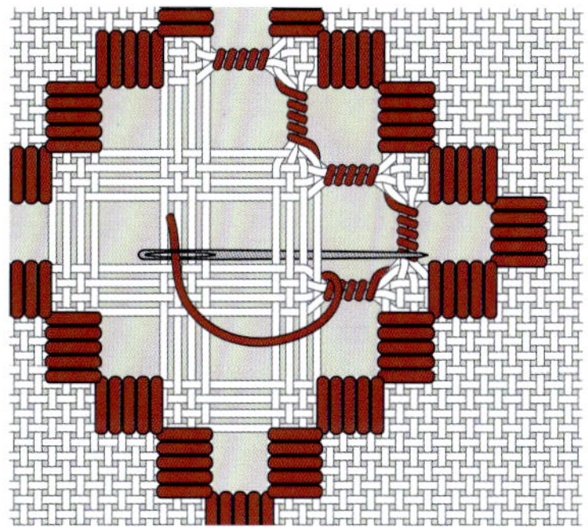

12 Continue wrapping, to fill the bar, pinching and pulling to tighten after each stitch. Complete the bar, then slide the needle from the left under the next bar.

❶ *As you go around the corner, take care to not distort the fabric.*

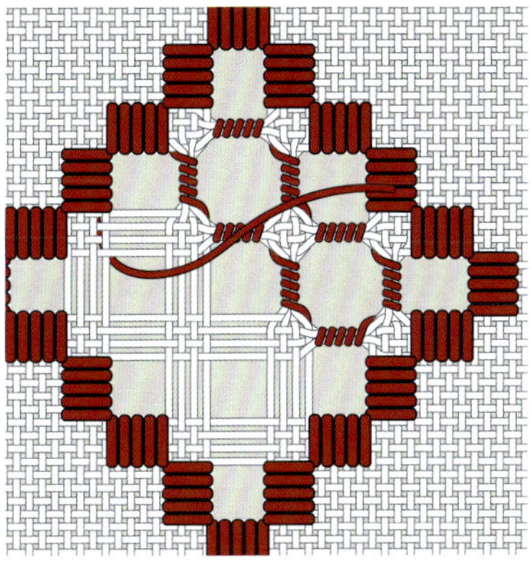

13 Continue wrapping bars. At the end of the row, take the needle to the back and run it under the satin stitch to bring it out ready for the next row.

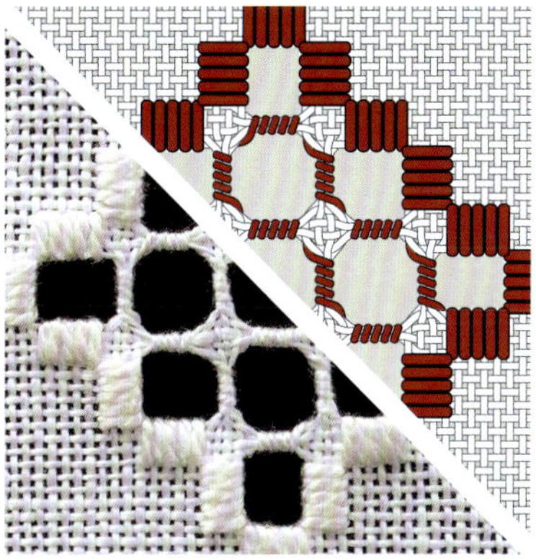

14 Complete the rest of the bars similarly. Finish the thread under the back of the satin stitch.

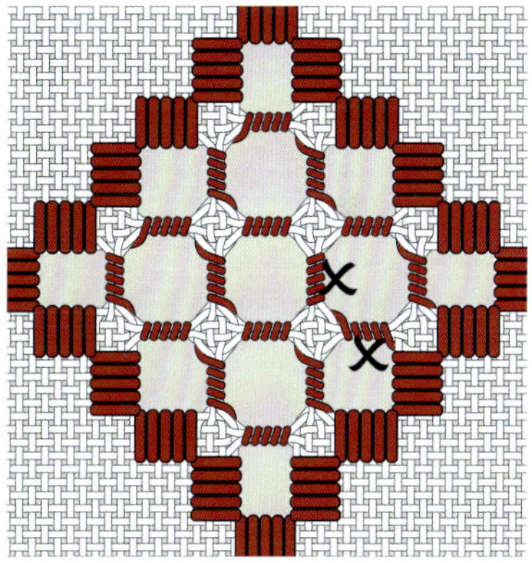

❶ *It is important that all the vertical bars are wrapped in the same way as each other, and all the horizontal ones should be the same as each other. If any have the wraps slanting the opposite way, an error has been made in moving from one bar to the next.*

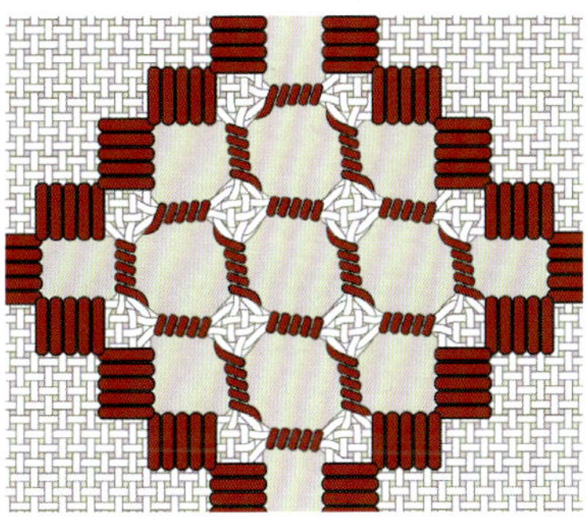

❶ *Be careful that your stitching does not pull too hard when you work the stitches between bars. Because they cross the fabric on the bias, it is easy to accidentally pull things out of kilter. This is why I prefer stitching in straight lines instead of zig-zagging lines.*

top tip wrapped bars

Unless you want to deliberately make use of the way wrapped bars stitched in zig-zagging lines pull things out of shape, (like the stitched example at the top of the opposite page) it is best to stitch them in straight lines wherever possible. It will provide superior results.

R

wrapped bars

Wrapped bars can be used in place of woven bars in many instances. They need to be stitched with care because it is easy for them to look crooked. They can be such a useful part of many combination stitches that it is worth learning to do them well.

TRADITIONAL

straight lines

I often see wrapped bars stitched extremely poorly; looking crooked and unpleasant. My advice, wherever possible, is to stitch them in straight line paths, rather than zig-zagging paths. This will improve the appearance greatly, as it stops the woven fabric squares between the bars from being distorted.

❶ *This is a shape where the wrapped bars have been stitched in a zig-zagging path. They are very crooked and it is an unsatisfactory result.*

❶ *This is the same shape where the bars have been wrapped in straight line paths. The bars are much straighter and the result is far more satisfactory.*

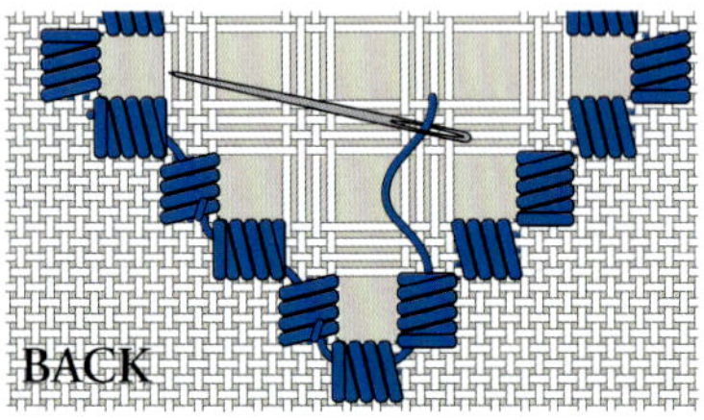

1 Anchor the thread in the back of the satin stitching. Run the thread under the back of four or five klosters, with one or two backstitches under single threads.

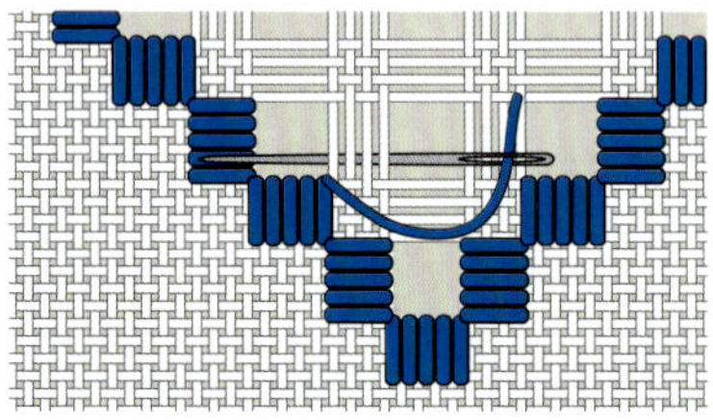

2 On the front, bring the needle out to the left of the first bar to wrap. Slide the needle under the bar from right to left.

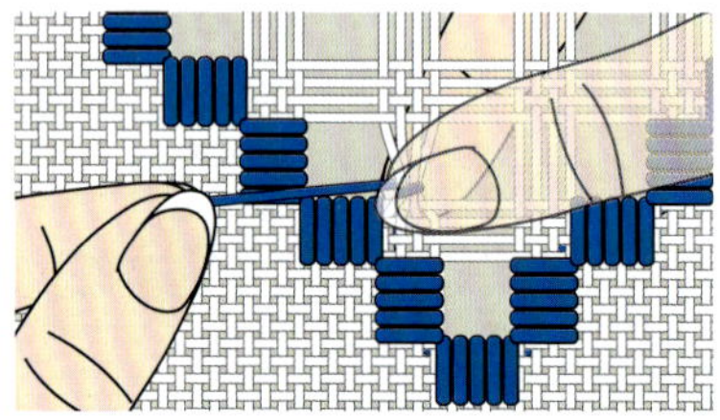

3 Pinch the bar between your right forefinger and thumb, and with the other hand, pull the thread to the left.

❶ *Pinching stabilises the bar while you tighten the stitch, giving good tension. Pulling to the right brings the bar in on both sides, making it narrow.*

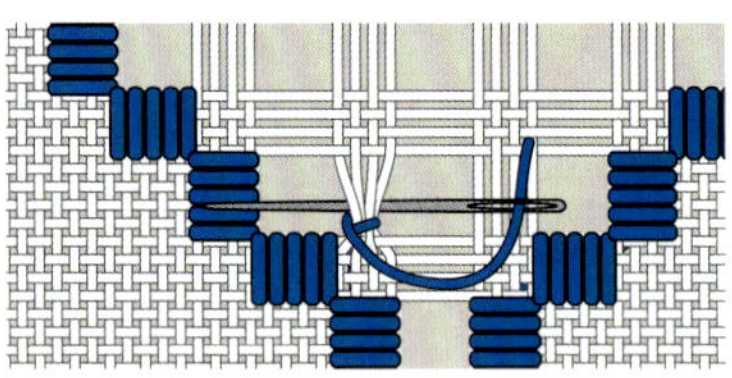

4 Moving up, slide the needle under the bar again. Ensure the new stitch does not overlap the first one.

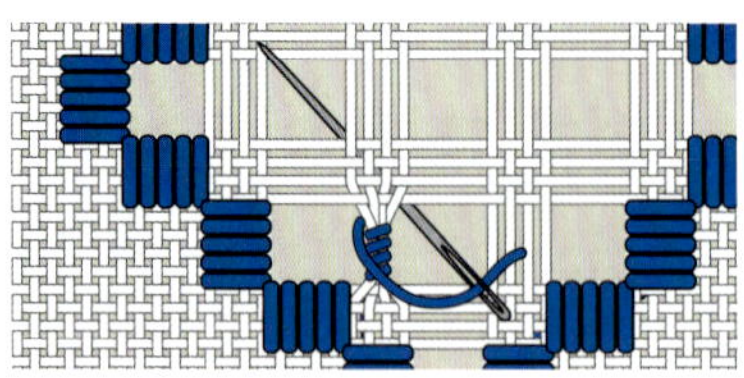

5 Continue wrapping, to fill the bar, pinching and pulling to tighten after each stitch. Pass the needle diagonally behind the woven fabric square and bring it out beside the next bar, which is directly above.

❶ *The wraps should lie next to each other on the bar and not overlap. They do not need to be tightly packed.*

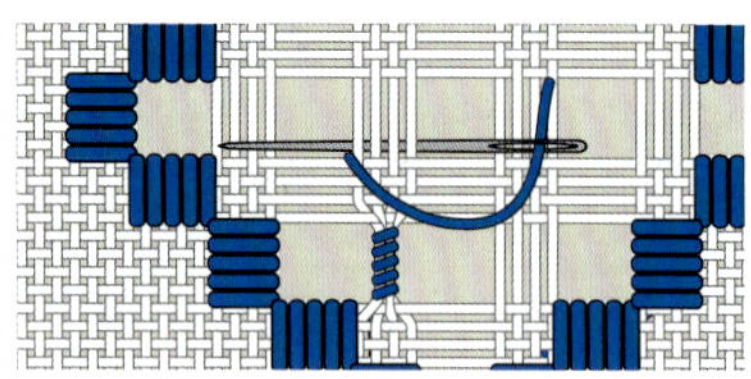

6 Slide the needle under the bar from right to left.

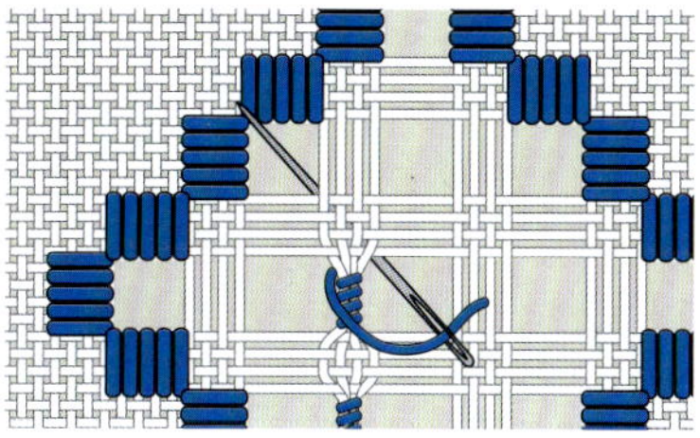

7 Continue wrapping, to fill the bar, pinching and pulling to tighten after each stitch. Pass the needle diagonally behind the woven fabric square and bring it out beside the next bar, which is directly above.

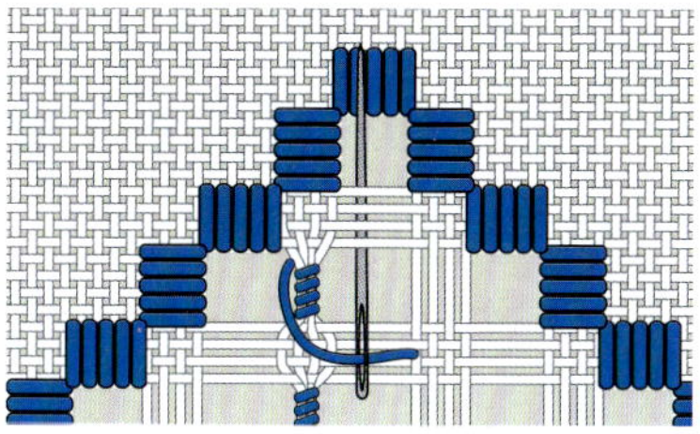

8 Wrap the next bar and slide the needle, from below, under the bar above right.

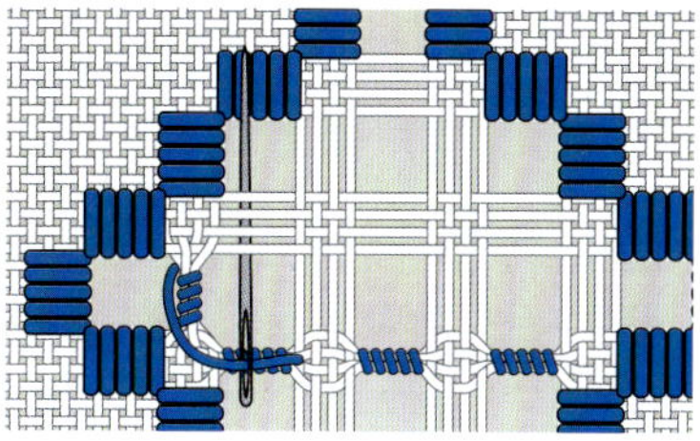

9 Turn the work 90° anticlockwise and wrap the bar. Slide the needle, from below, under the bar above right.

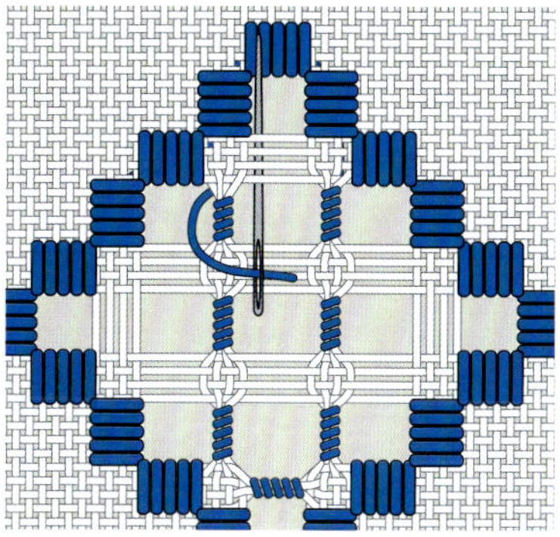

10 Turn the work 90° anticlockwise and wrap the next three bars. Slide the needle, from below, under the bar above right.

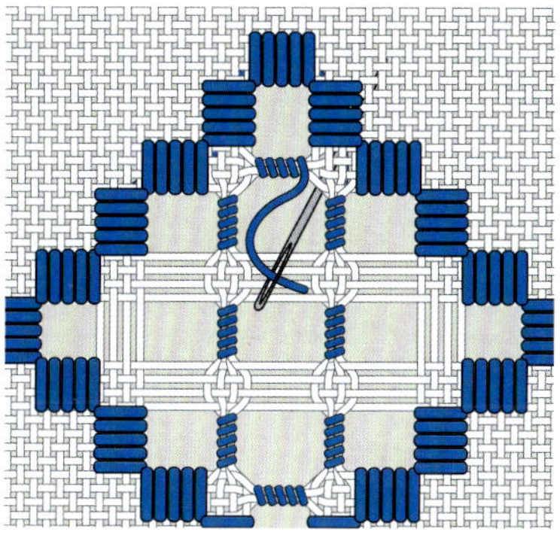

11 Wrap the final bar of the circuit and take the needle to the back.

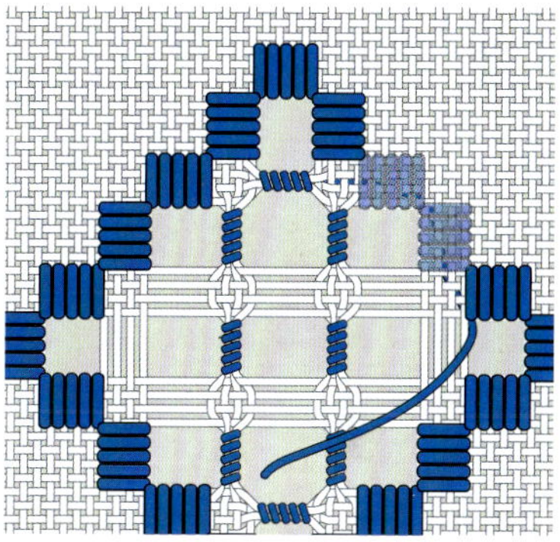

12 On the back, take the needle under the satin stitch to bring it out ready to start the next circuit.

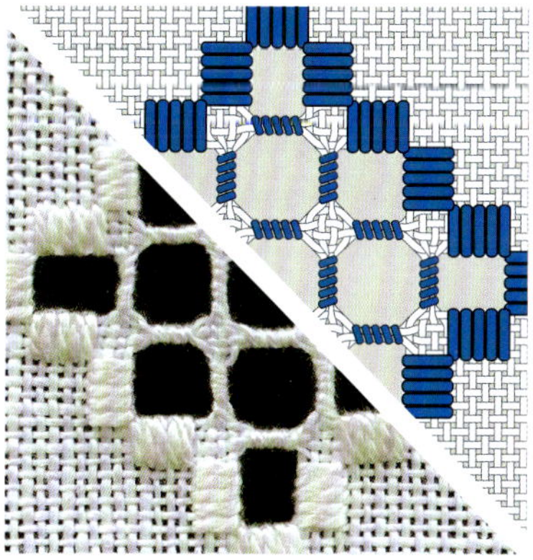

13 Work the second circuit similarly to the first, this time starting with the single bar, then progressing down the side with three in a row and continuing on to complete it.

Some people don't like to work their bars in straight line paths because it means there are diagonal stitches behind the intervening fabric woven squares. When you work in straight line paths, the front looks far superior. If this means that there are more obvious stitches on the back, then so be it. I'd prefer the front of my work to look exemplary, rather than the back. I still want the back to look neat, but the work is not meant to be reversible.

wrapped zig-zagging lines

While my advice is to use wrapped bars in zig-zagging lines as little as possible, sometimes they are a good choice for a space. An example of this could be a long diagonal cutwork area. (I still would prefer to work in straight lines!)

1 Mount the fabric into a hoop or frame so that the fabric is flat and the grain is square. This will hold the fabric threads taut and straight, and give you the best chance of keeping the bars straight while wrapping.

❶ *Do not stretch the fabric.*

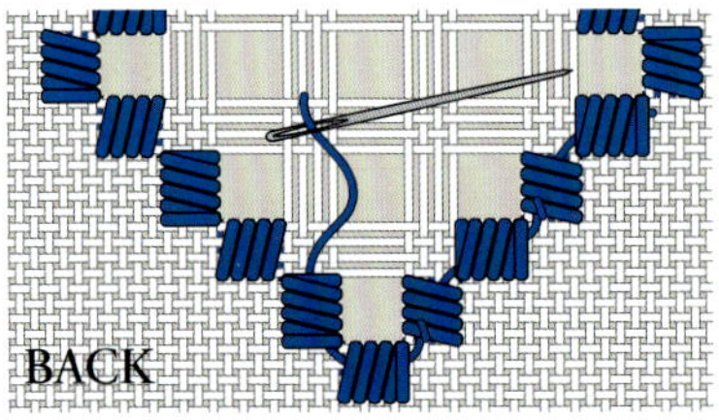

2 Anchor the thread in the back of the satin stitching. Run the thread under the back of four or five klosters, with one or two backstitches under single threads.

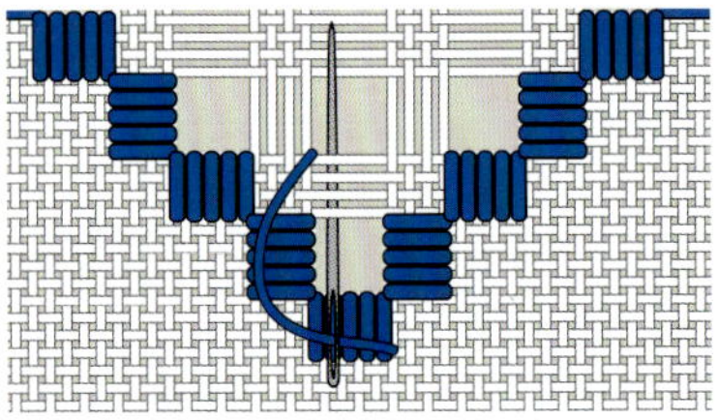

3 On the front, bring the needle out above the first bar to wrap. Slide the needle under the bar from below.

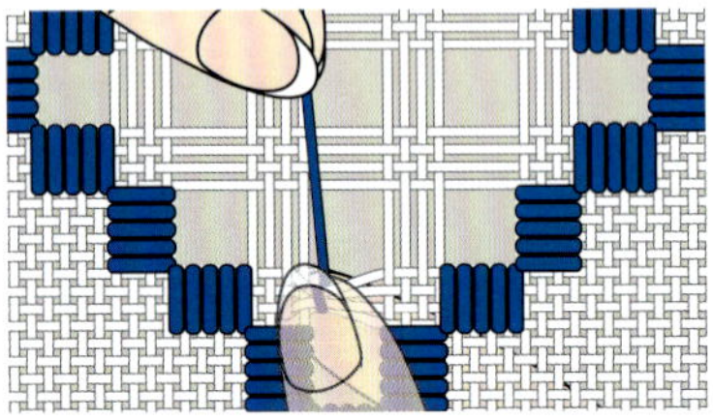

4 Pinch the bar between your forefinger and thumb, and with the other hand, pull the thread upward.

❶ *Pinching stabilises the bar while you tighten the stitch, giving good tension. Pulling upward across the surface of the fabric brings the bar in on both sides, making it narrow.*

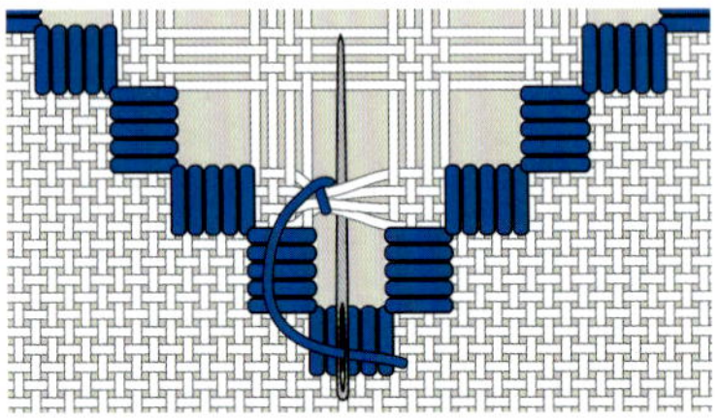

5 Moving right, slide the needle under the bar again. Ensure the new stitch does not overlap the first one.

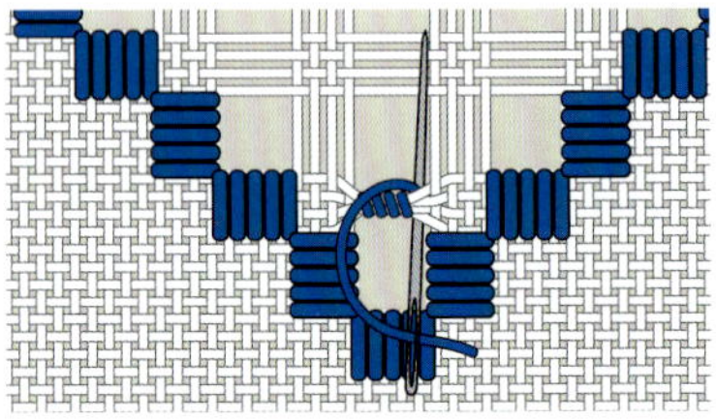

6 Continue wrapping, to fill the bar, pinching and pulling to tighten after each stitch. To complete the bar, slide the needle under the bar one last time.

❶ *The wraps should lie next to each other on the bar and not overlap. They do not need to be tightly packed.*

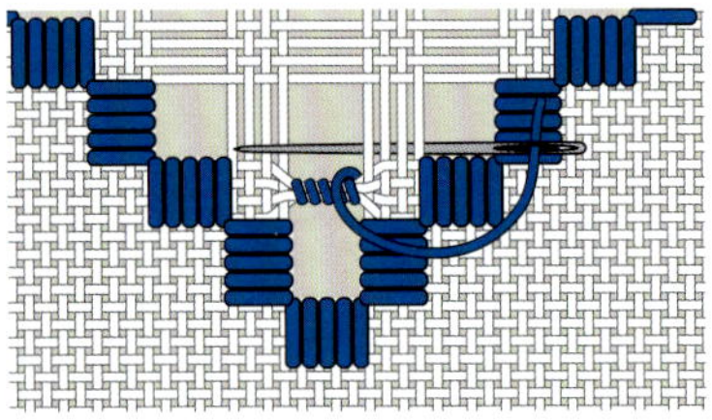

7 From the right, slide the needle under the new bar, just to the right of the previous one.

❶ *When you pull the needle and tighten the stitch, ensure it does not pull the two bars together at an angle. The stitches should be tight without distorting the weave of the fabric.*

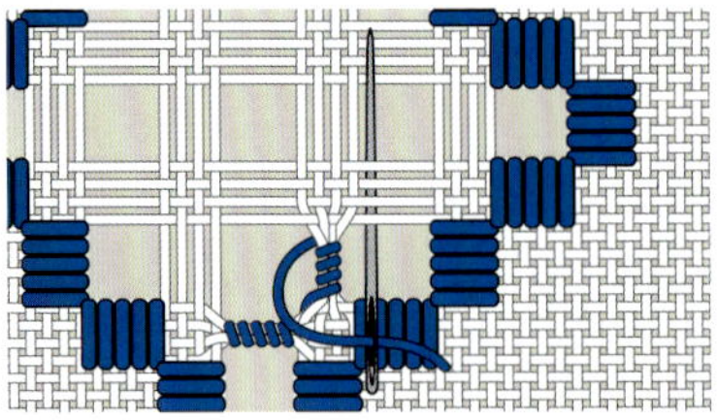

8 Continue wrapping, to fill the bar, pinching and pulling to tighten after each stitch. To complete the bar, slide the needle under the next bar to the right, from below.

❶ *Each bar should have the same quantity of wraps.*

❶ *At the corner do not pull the thread so hard that it distorts the fabric.*

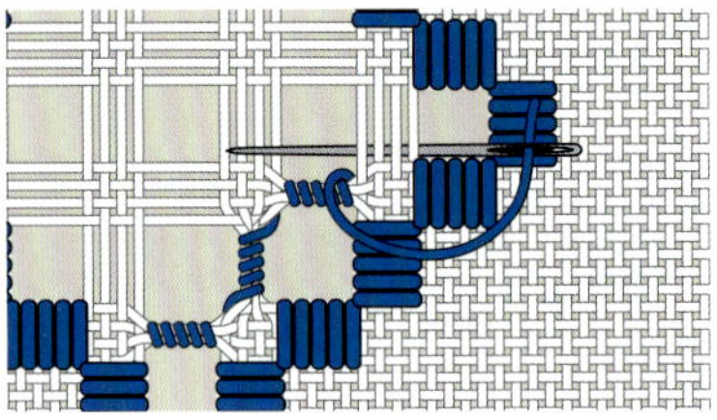

9 Continue wrapping, to fill the bar, pinching and pulling to tighten after each stitch. Complete the bar, then slide the needle from the right under the next bar to the right.

❶ *As you go around the corner, take care to not distort the fabric.*

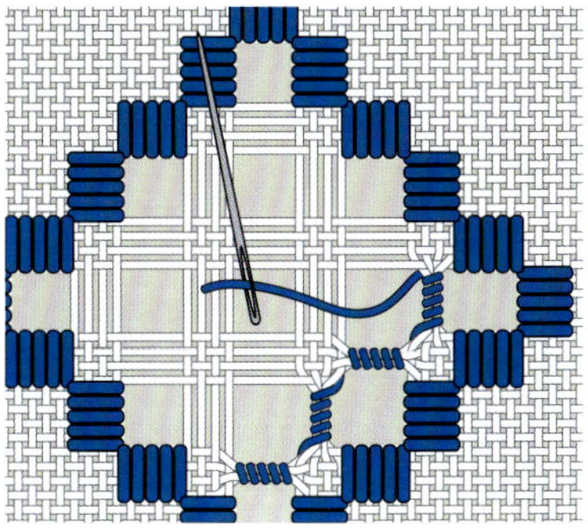

10 Continue wrapping, and finish the bar with the needle emerging beside the completed bar.

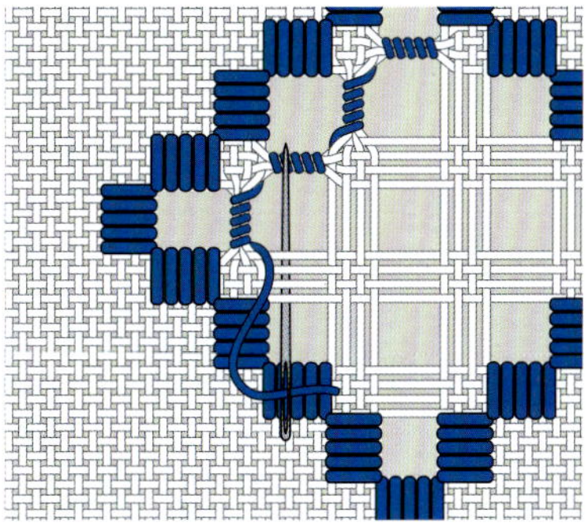

11 Turn the work 180°. Slide the needle under the new bar from below.

❶ *As you go around the corner, take care to not distort the fabric.*

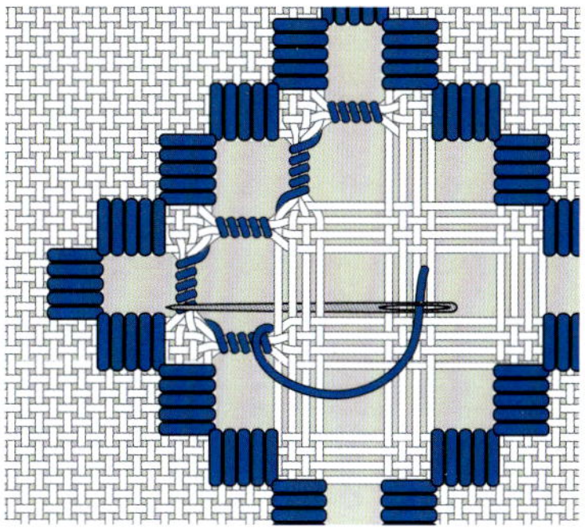

12 Continue wrapping, to fill the bar, pinching and pulling to tighten after each stitch. Complete the bar, then slide the needle from the right under the next bar.

❶ *As you go around the corner, take care to not distort the fabric.*

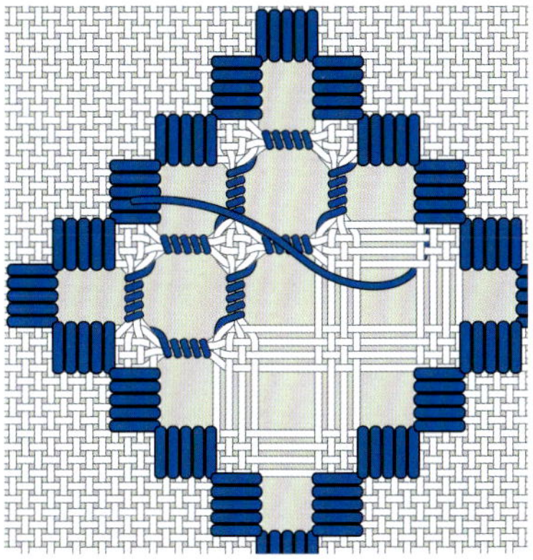

13 Continue wrapping bars. At the end of the row, take the needle to the back and run it under the satin stitch to bring it out ready for the next row.

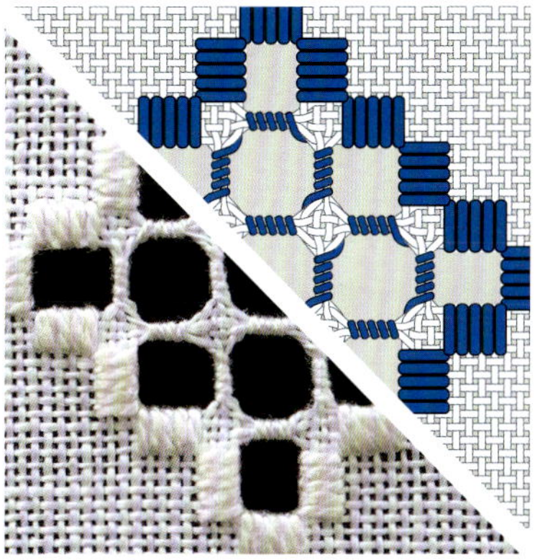

14 Complete the rest of the bars similarly. Finish the thread under the back of the satin stitch.

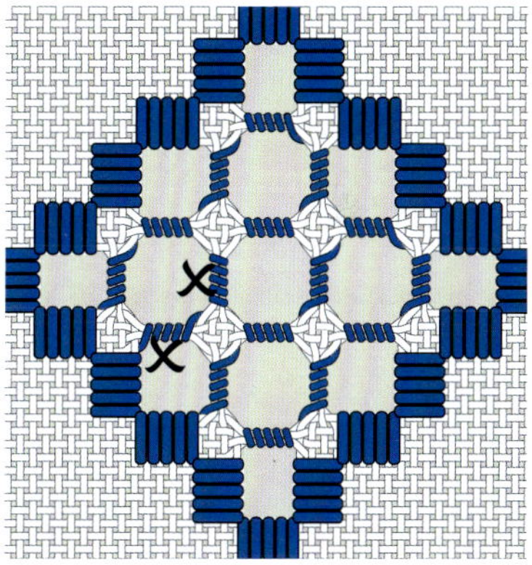

❶ *It is important that all the vertical bars are wrapped in the same way as each other, and all the horizontal ones should be the same as each other. If any have the wraps slanting the opposite way, an error has been made in moving from one bar to the next.*

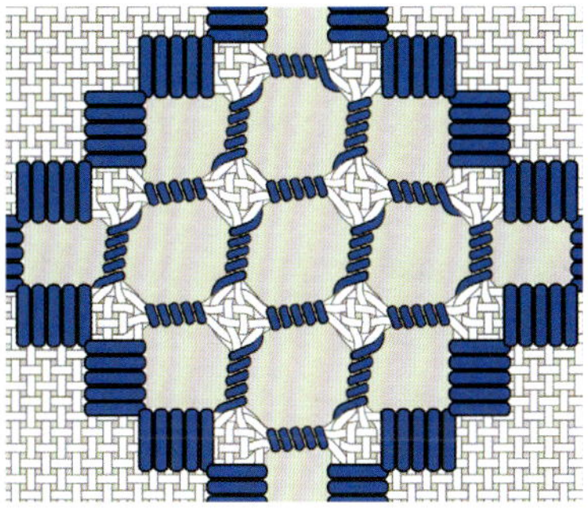

❶ *Be careful that your stitching does not pull too hard when you work the stitches between bars. Because they cross the fabric on the bias, it is easy to accidentally pull things out of kilter. This is why I prefer stitching in straight lines instead of zig-zagging lines.*

top tip wrapped bars

Unless you want to deliberately make use of the way wrapped bars stitched in zig-zagging lines pull things out of shape, (like the stitched example at the top of the opposite page) it is best to stitch them in straight lines wherever possible. It will provide superior results.

lacing behind

When there are specialty stitches within cutwork there may be no easy stitching path without doubling up on some parts. You will need to lace the thread behind the fabric threads and weave or wrap over the top.

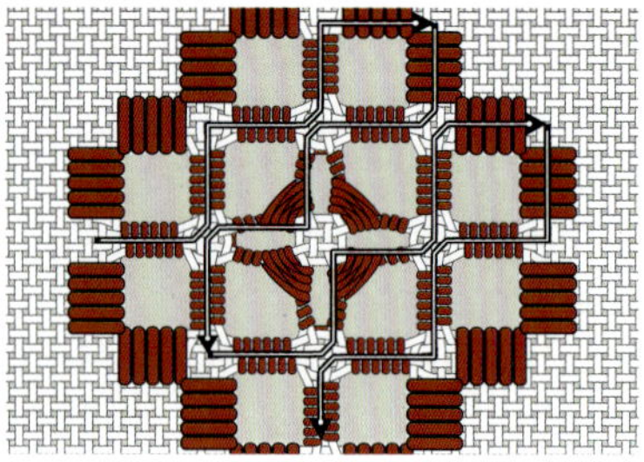

In this example, the zig-zagging path completes most of the weaving. However there are parts you can't get to without doubling back.

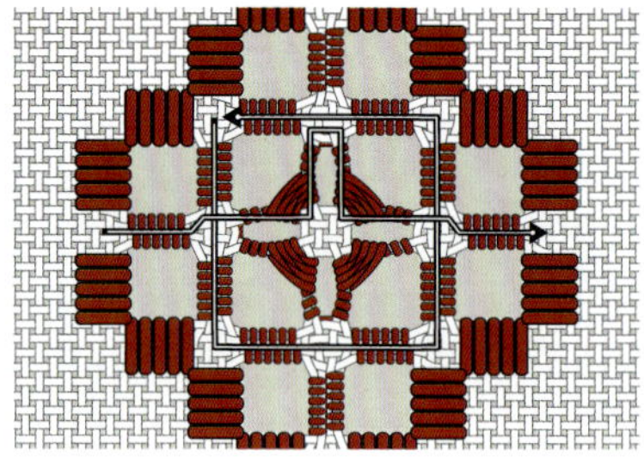

The same example is stitched with straight lines. There are large amounts you can't get to without going over the same section twice.

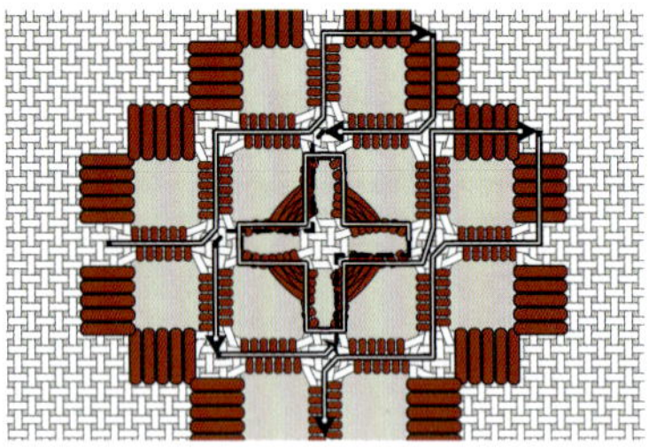

This is the zig-zagging example, with sections laced behind (shown as dotted lines) for the first pass and then stitched over the top of for the second pass.

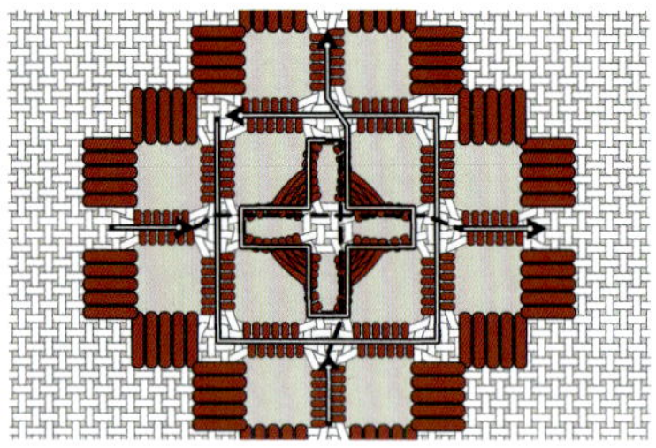

This is the straight lines example, with sections laced behind (shown as dotted lines) for the first pass and then stitched over the top for the second pass.

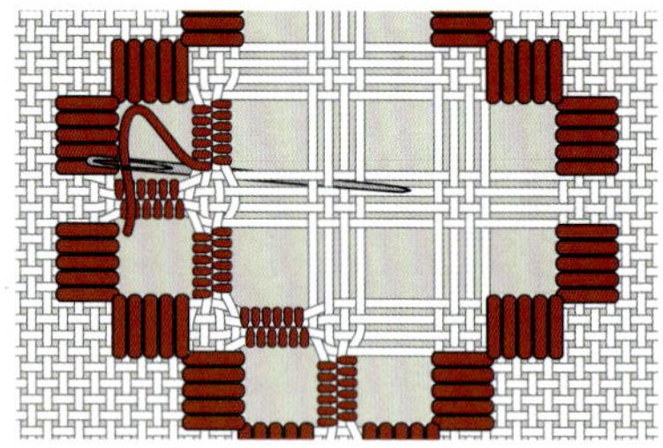

1 Pass the needle under the bar to skip. Bring it out one thread up from the woven square's centre.

A thread on one side is easier to cover.

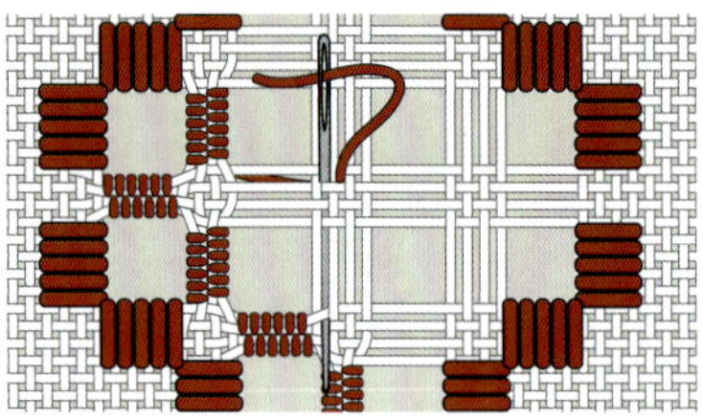

2 Pull the needle through. Insert it one thread to the left, and bring it out in line with that, one thread below the woven square below's top.

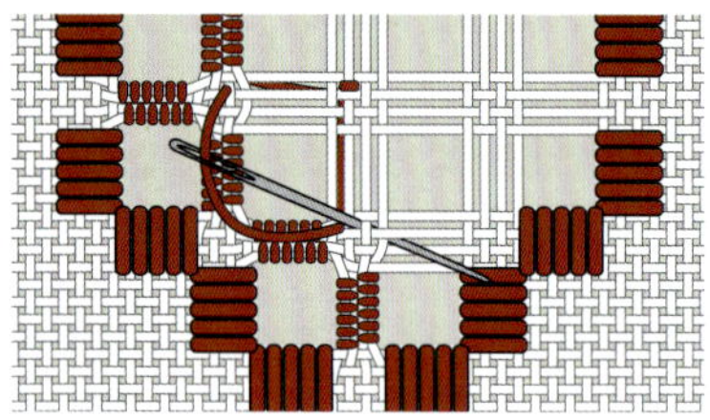

3 Pull the needle through. Insert it one thread to the right and bring it out in the next bar, ready to stitch the bar.

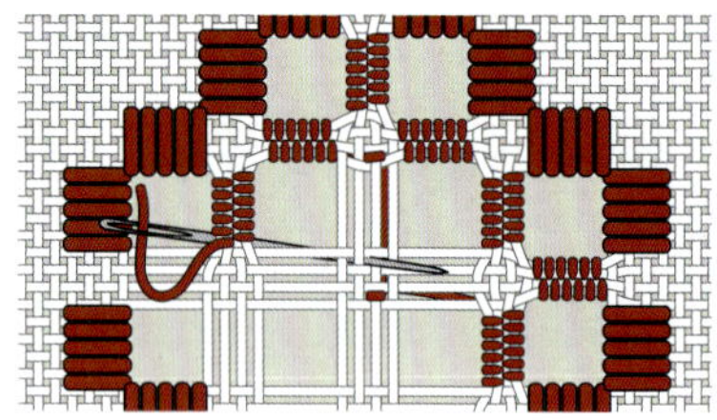

4 Work the next two bars. Turn the work 180°. Pass the needle under the bar to skip. Bring it out one thread up from the woven square's centre.

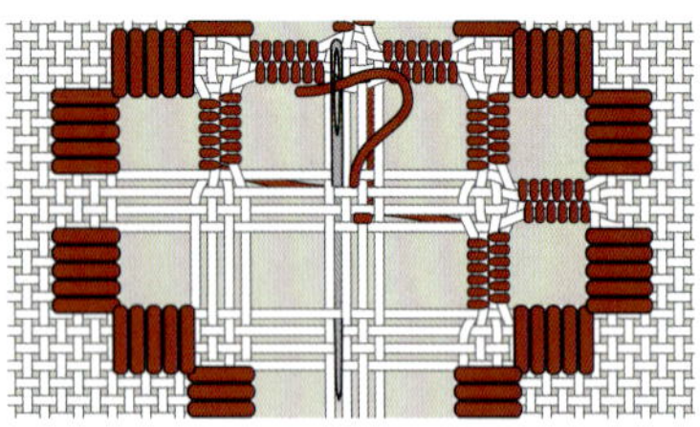

5 Pull the needle through. Insert it one thread to the left. Bring it out in line with that, one thread below the top of the woven square below.

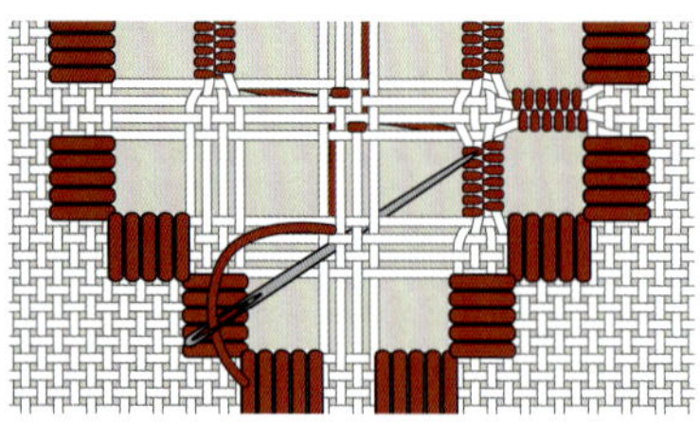

6 Pull the needle through. Insert it one thread below and bring it out in the next bar, ready to stitch.

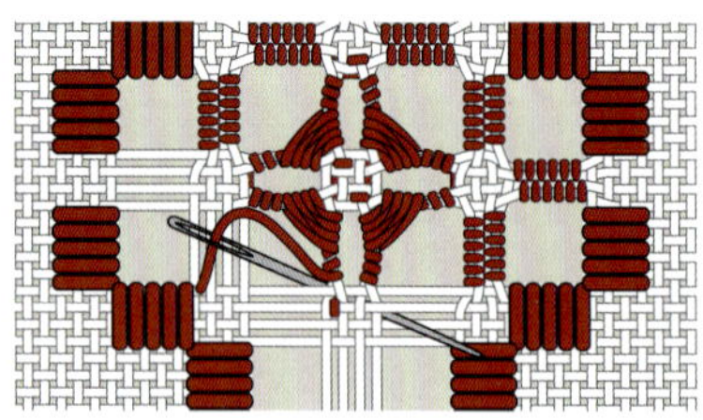

7 Work the specialty stitch in the space. Ensure you cover all laced stitches on the back, as you go. Continue stitching as before.

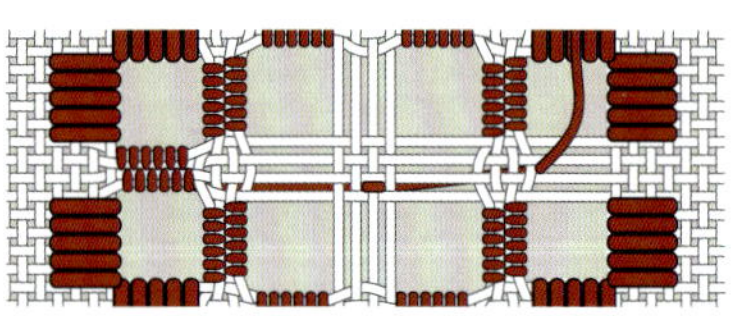

Break up long lengths of lacing with stitches in the woven fabric squares.

If there are two laced threads behind a bar, have one on either side of the centre so that one side does not look thicker than the other.

Lacing looks best when the colour of the thread is the same as or very similar to the colour of the fabric, as the extra stitches on the front will blend in better.

lacing behind

When there are specialty stitches within cutwork there may be no easy stitching path without doubling up on some parts. You will need to lace the thread behind the fabric threads and weave or wrap over the top.

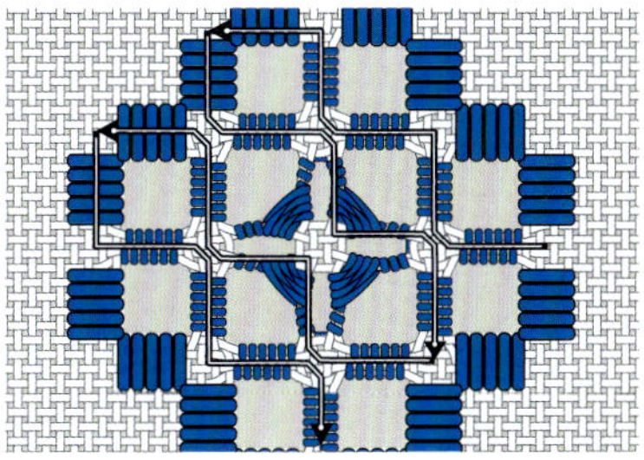

In this example, the zig-zagging path completes most of the weaving. However there are parts you can't get to without doubling back.

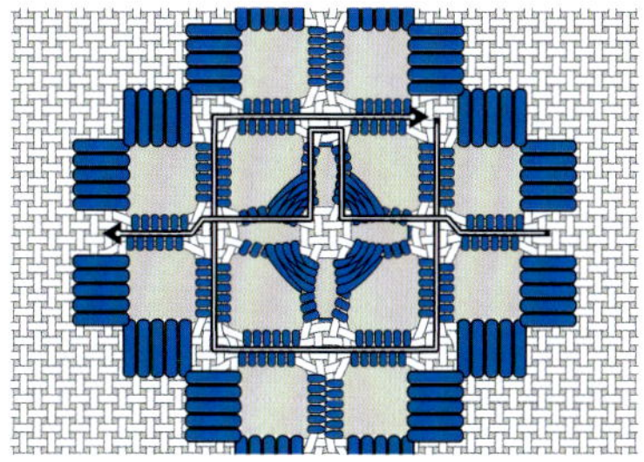

The same example is stitched with straight lines. There are large amounts you can't get to without going over the same section twice.

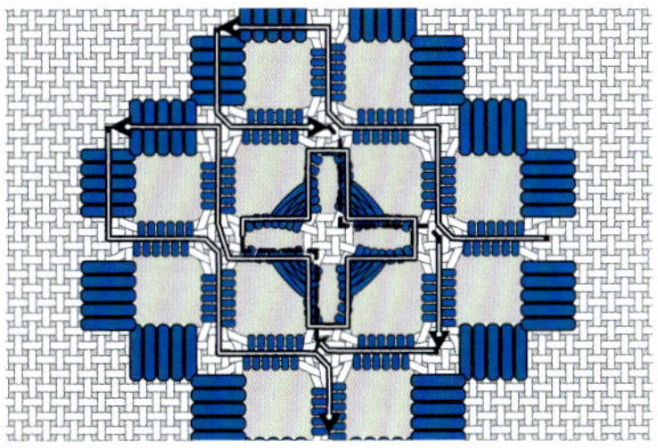

This is the zig-zagging example, with sections laced behind (shown as dotted lines) for the first pass and then stitched over the top of for the second pass.

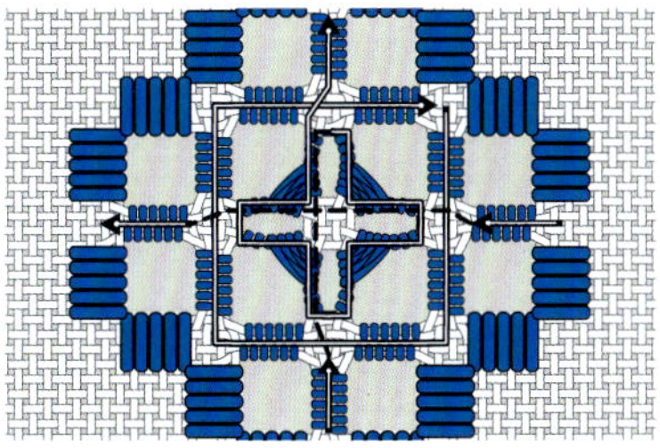

This is the straight lines example, with sections laced behind (shown as dotted lines) for the first pass and then stitched over the top for the second pass.

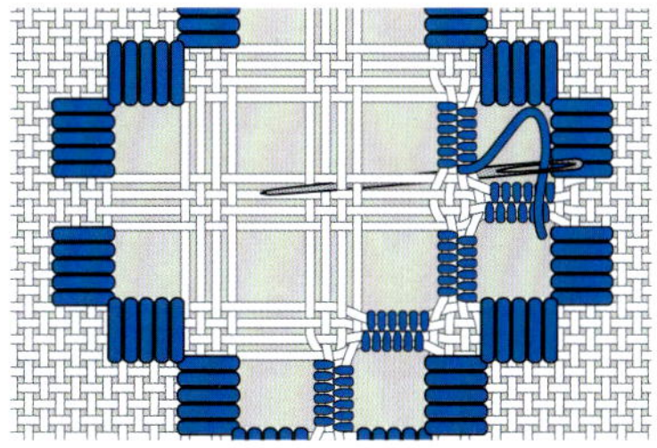

1 Pass the needle under the bar to skip. Bring it out one thread up from the woven square's centre.

A thread on one side is easier to cover.

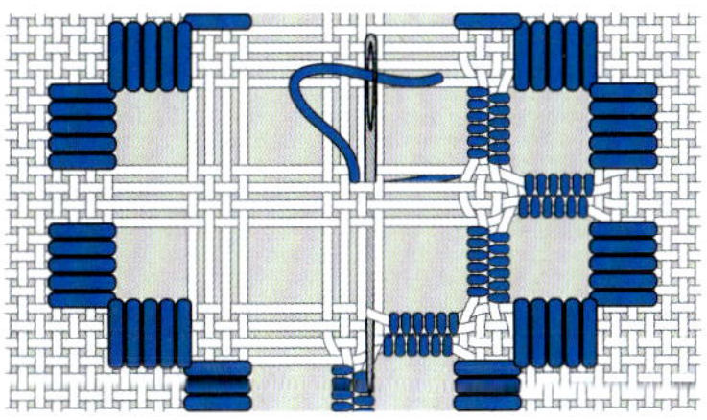

2 Pull the needle through. Insert it one thread to the right, and bring it out in line with that, one thread below the woven square below's top.

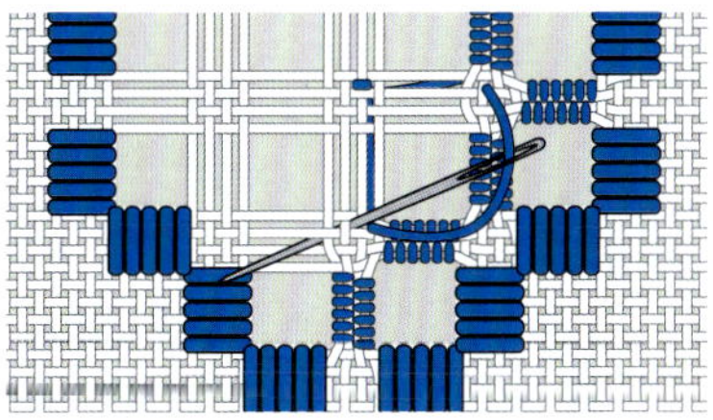

3 Pull the needle through. Insert it one thread to the left and bring it out in the next bar, ready to stitch the bar.

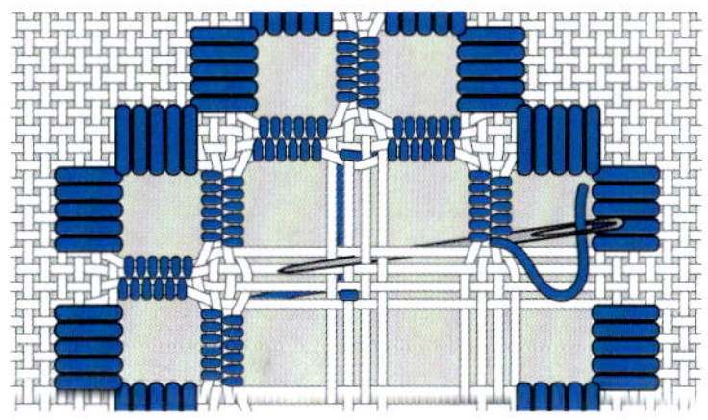

4 Work the next two bars. Turn the work 180°. Pass the needle under the bar to skip. Bring it out one thread up from the woven square's centre.

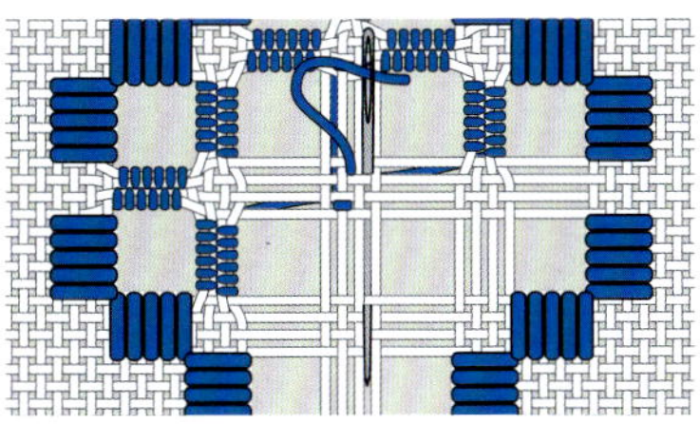

5 Pull the needle through. Insert it one thread to the right. Bring it out in line with that one thread down from the woven square below's top.

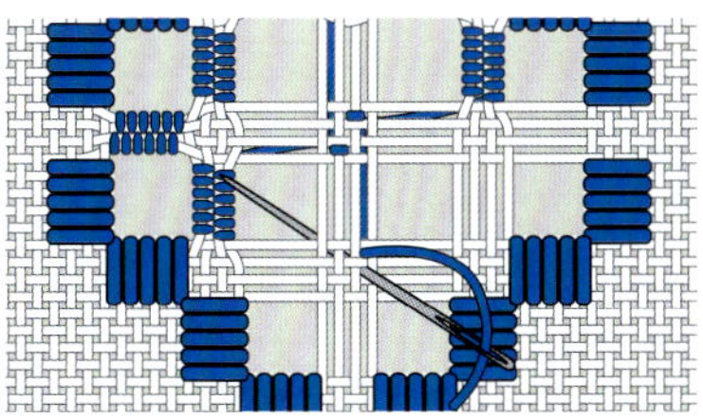

6 Pull the needle through. Insert it one thread below and bring it out in the next bar, ready to stitch.

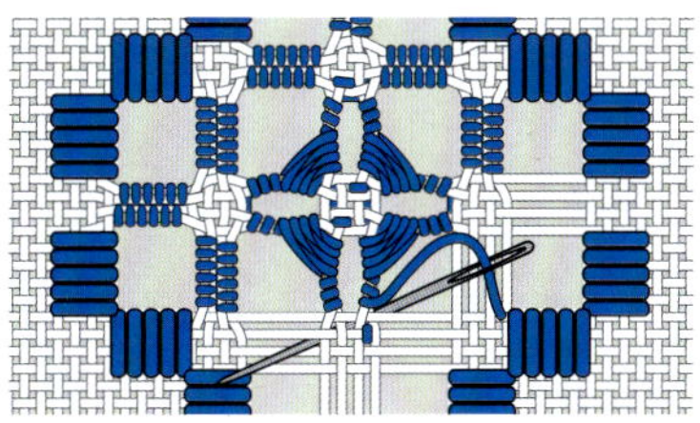

7 Work the specialty stitch in the space. Ensure you cover all laced stitches on the back, as you go. Continue stitching as before.

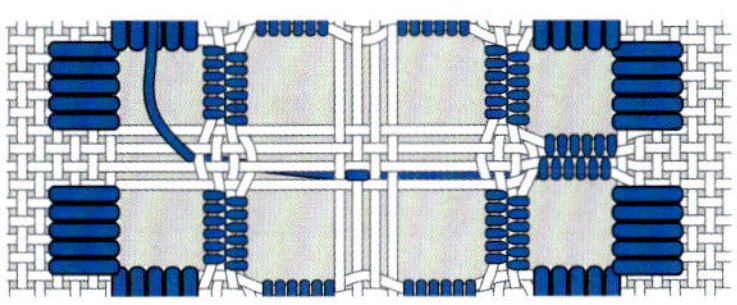

Break up long lengths of lacing with stitches in the woven fabric squares.

If there are two laced threads behind a bar, have one on either side of the centre so that one side does not look thicker than the other.

Lacing looks best when the colour of the thread is the same as or very similar to the colour of the fabric, as the extra stitches on the front will blend in better.

changing threads during cutwork

The easiest place to change threads during cutwork is in the back of the satin stitch edge. However, sometimes you are nowhere near there and need to change over. The old thread is shown in blue. The new thread is shown in red. These techniques also work for wrapped bars.

new under old, old under new

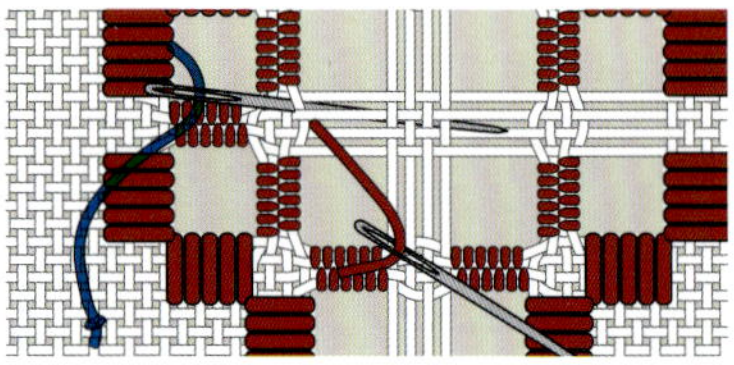

1 When you have enough thread to do one more bar, thread a second needle with a new thread with a knot in the end. Insert the new needle in the woven square before the bar to be stitched, and bring it out at the far end of the one after.

❶ *A thread on one side is easier to cover.*

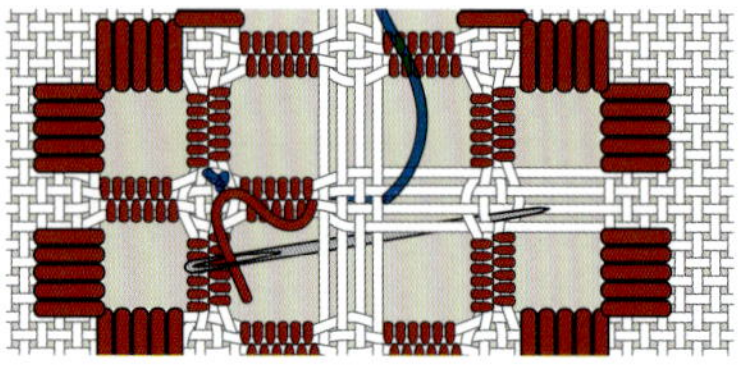

2 Pull the needle through. With the old thread, stitch the bar, making sure the laced new thread is enclosed in the stitching, on the back. Bring the old thread out in the woven square at the far end of the next bar.

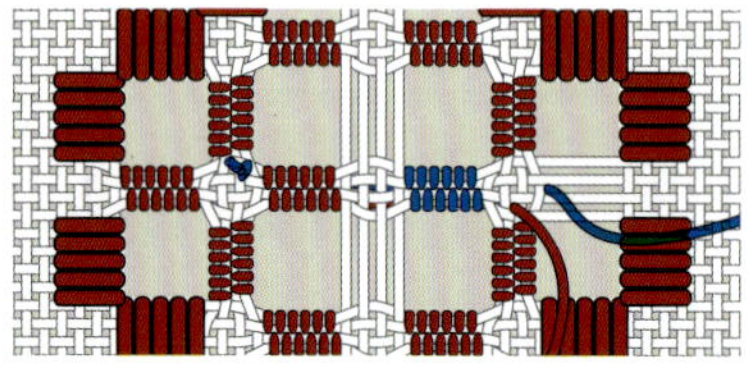

3 Pull the thread through. With the new thread, stitch the bar, making sure the laced old thread is enclosed in the stitching, on the back.

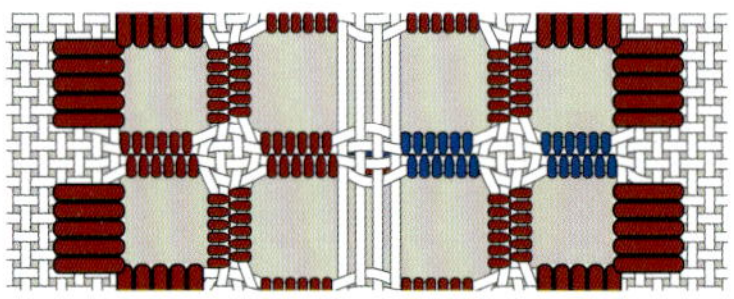

4 Trim the knot and the old thread. Continue with the new thread.

❶ *A similar technique can be used when working wrapped bars, rather than woven bars.*

new and old under new

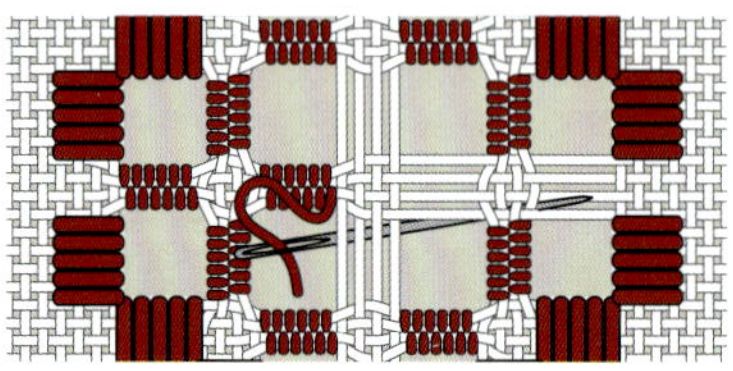

1 Pass the needle under the next bar and bring it out one thread up from the bottom of the following bar.

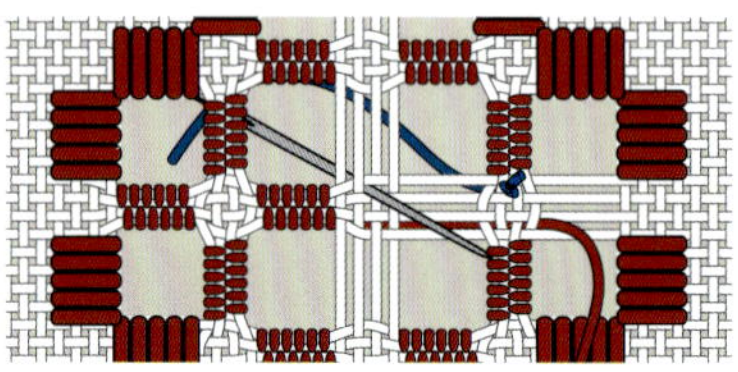

2 Pull the needle through. From the front, insert a needle with the new knotted thread, one thread up from the centre of the woven square at the end of the next bar. Bring it out one thread up from the centre of the woven square next to the current bar.

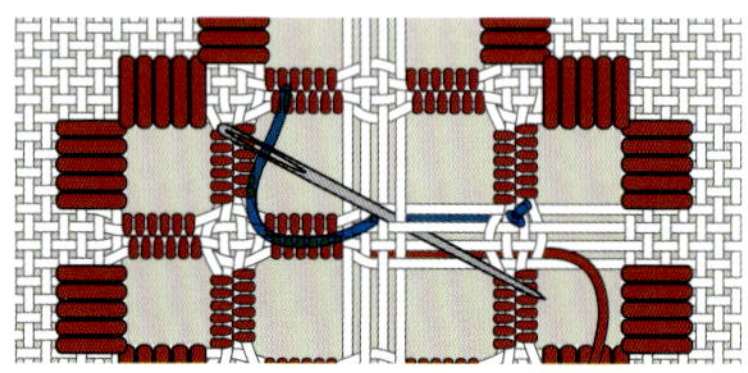

3 Insert the needle one thread to the right, and bring it out ready to begin the next bar.

❶ *The new thread sits underneath one side of the bar, and the old thread sits under the other.*

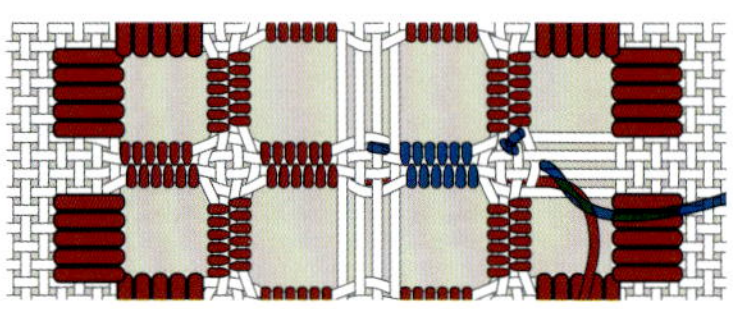

4 Pull the thread through. With the new thread, stitch the bar, making sure the threads are enclosed in the stitching, on the back.

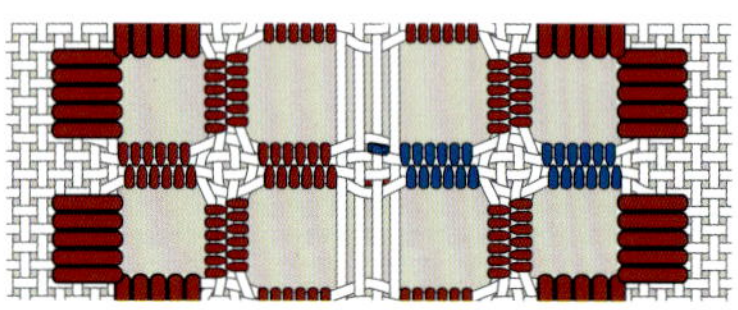

5 Trim the knot and the old thread. Continue with the new thread.

❶ *A similar technique can be used when working wrapped bars, rather than woven bars.*

changing threads during cutwork

The easiest place to change threads during cutwork is in the back of the satin stitch edge. However, sometimes you are nowhere near there and need to change over. The old thread is shown in blue. The new thread is shown in red. These techniques also work for wrapped bars.

new under old, old under new

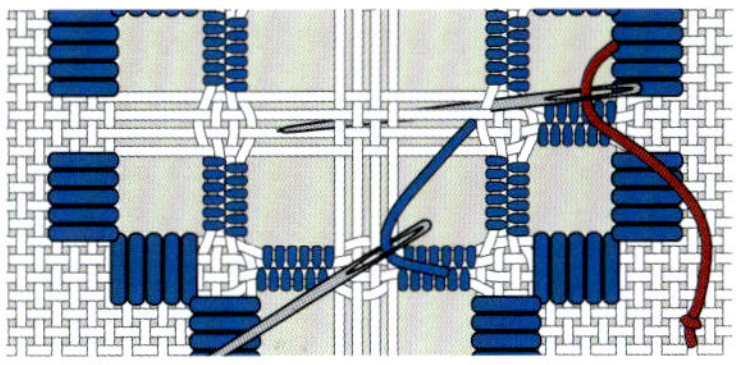

1 When you have enough thread to do one more bar, thread a second needle with a new thread with a knot in the end. Insert the new needle in the woven square before the bar to be stitched, and bring it out at the far end of the one after.

❶ *A thread on one side is easier to cover.*

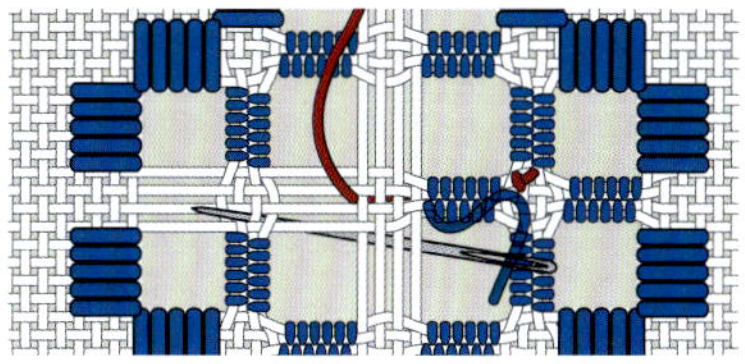

2 Pull the needle through. With the old thread, stitch the bar, making sure the laced new thread is enclosed in the stitching, on the back. Bring the old thread out in the woven square at the far end of the next bar.

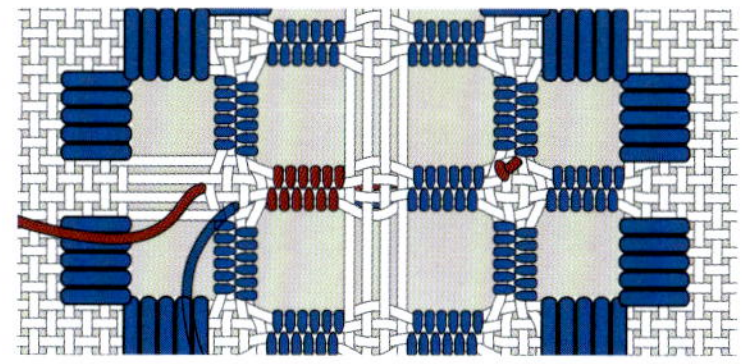

3 Pull the thread through. With the new thread, stitch the bar, making sure the laced old thread is enclosed in the stitching, on the back.

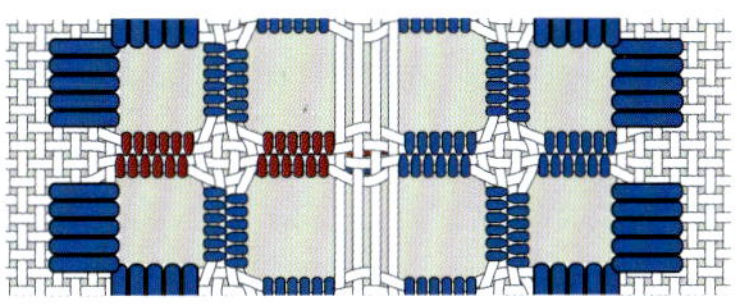

4 Trim the knot and the old thread. Continue with the new thread.

❶ *A similar technique can be used when working wrapped bars, rather than woven bars.*

new and old under new

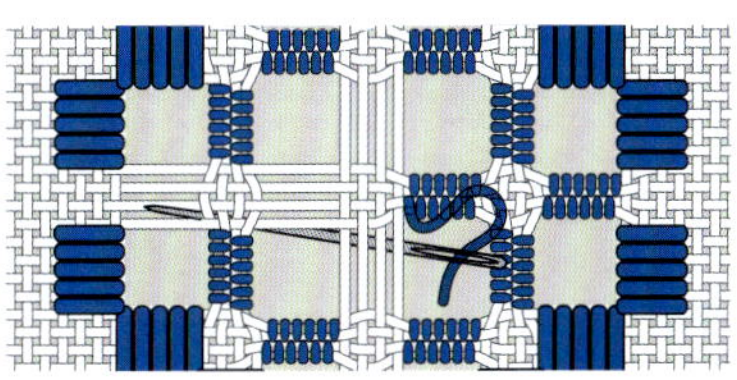

1 Pass the needle under the next bar and bring it out one thread up from the bottom of the following bar.

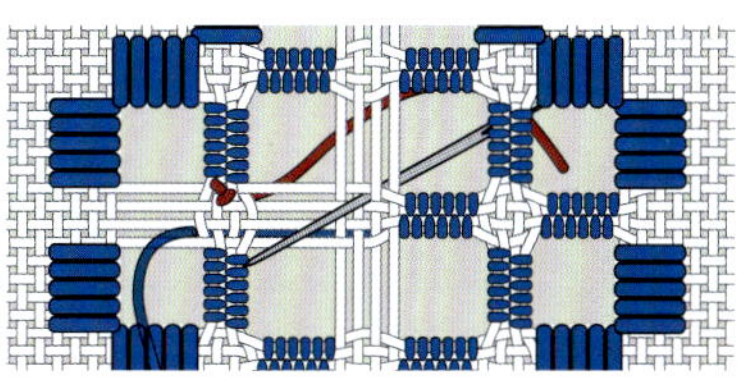

2 Pull the needle through. From the front, insert a needle with the new knotted thread, one thread up from the centre of the woven square at the end of the next bar. Bring it out one thread up from the centre of the woven square next to the current bar.

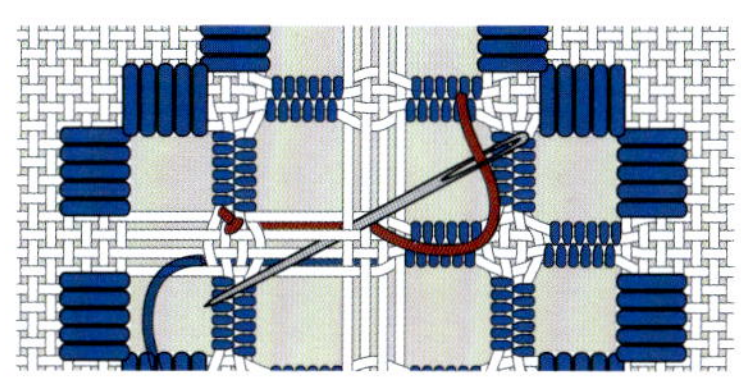

3 Insert the needle one thread to the right, and bring it out ready to begin the next bar.

❶ *The new thread sits underneath one side of the bar, and the old thread sits under the other.*

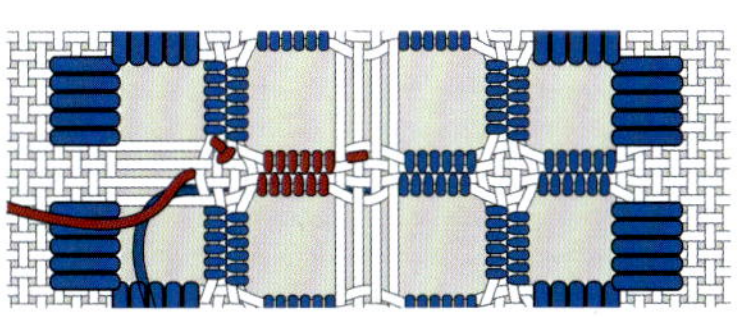

4 Pull the thread through. With the new thread, stitch the bar, making sure the threads are enclosed in the stitching, on the back.

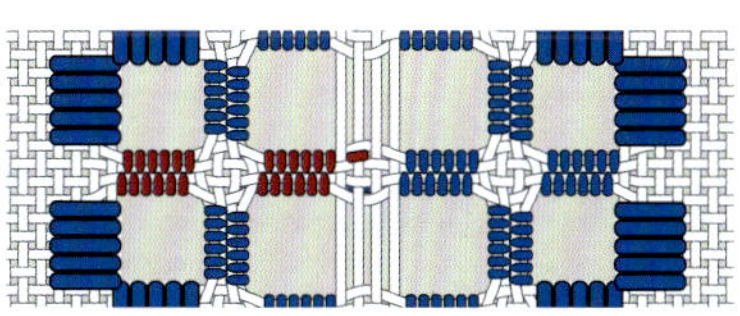

5 Trim the knot and the old thread. Continue with the new thread.

❶ *A similar technique can be used when working wrapped bars, rather than woven bars.*

zig-zagging lines

woven grouped zig-zagging line

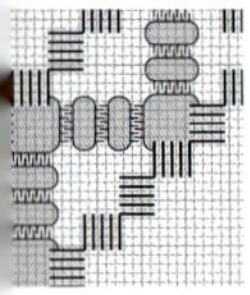

TRADITIONAL

Sometimes long lines of zig-zagging bars in groups of three are used as filling stitches.

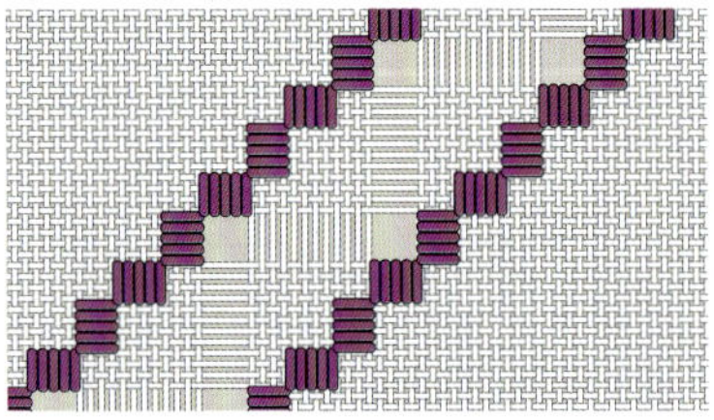

1 Cut inside only every second pair of satin stitch blocks to form a path as shown. Remove the threads ready for stitching.

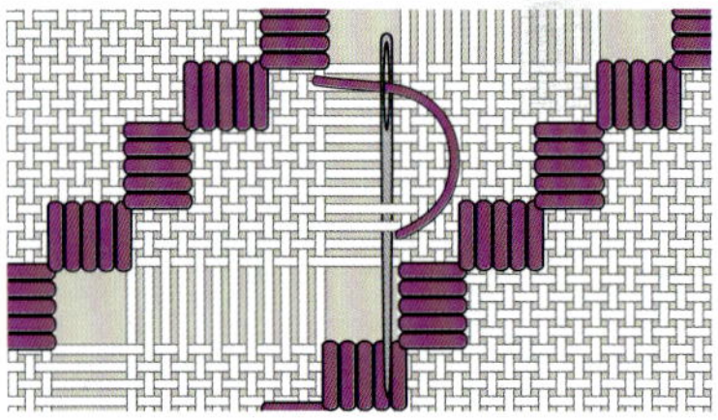

2 Bring the needle out two threads up at the right edge of the drawn thread area. From above, slide it under the next two threads up.

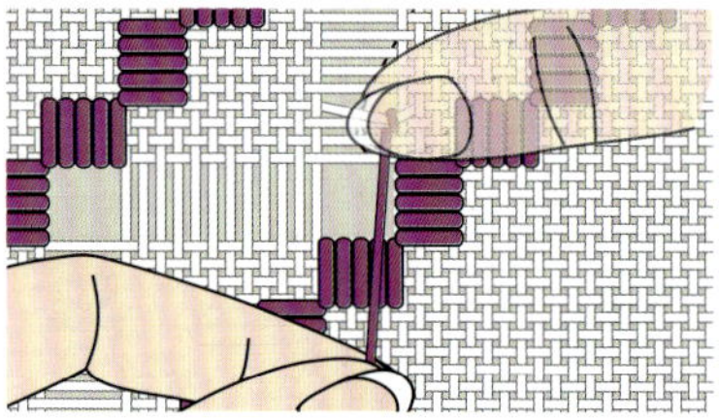

3 Pinch the stitch between your finger and thumb. With the other hand, pull the thread to tighten the stitch.
❶ *Do this after each stitch.*

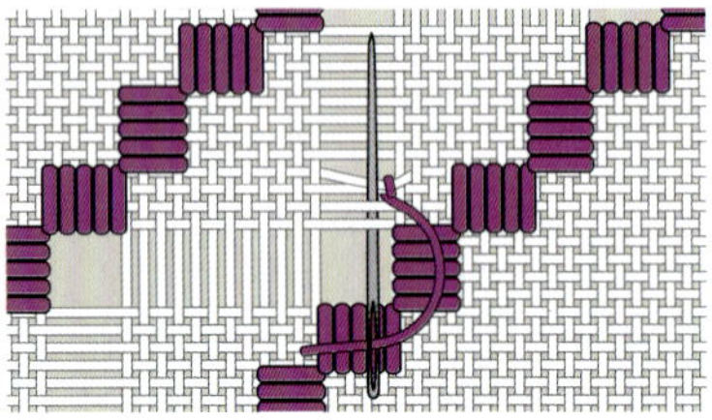

4 Moving left, from below, slide the needle under the lower two threads of the bar.

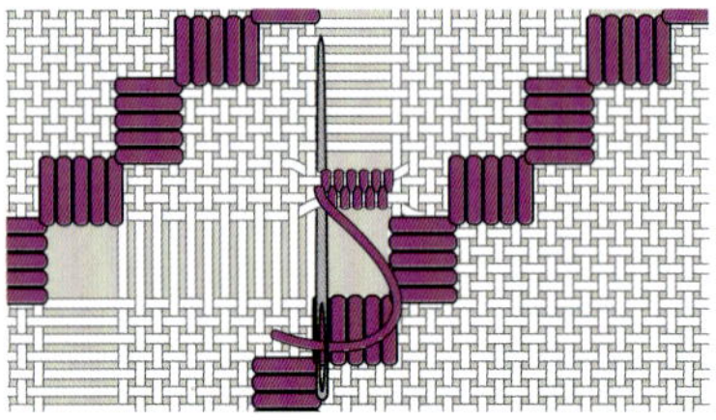

5 Pinch and pull to tighten the stitch. Weave back and forth until the bar is full, finishing with a stitch on the upper group. From below, slide the needle behind the bar.
❶ *Do not cram the stitches in.*

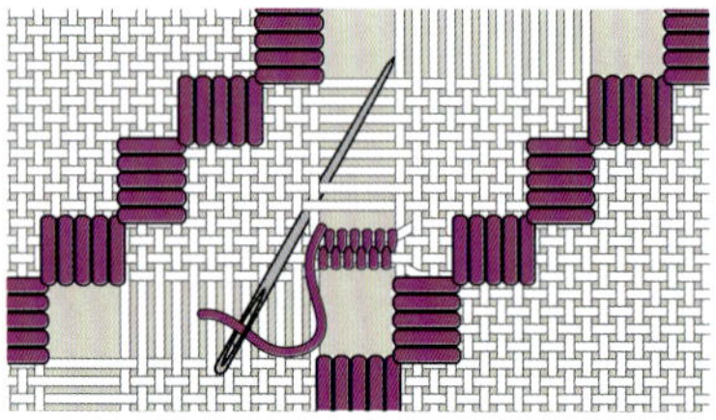

6 Insert the needle one thread to the left above the bar. Bring it out two threads up in the drawn thread area.

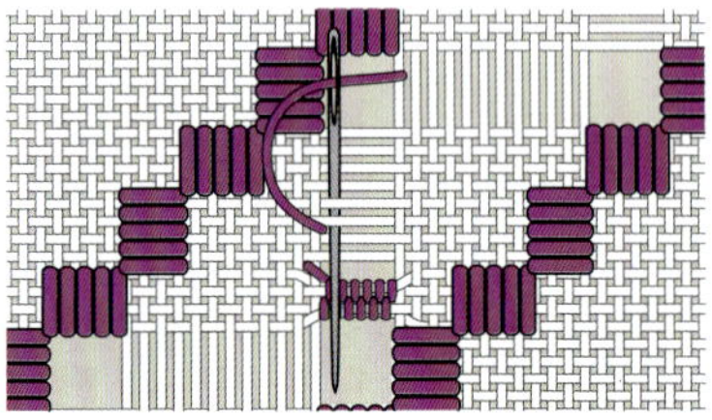

7 Moving right, from above, slide the needle under the upper two threads of the new bar to be woven.

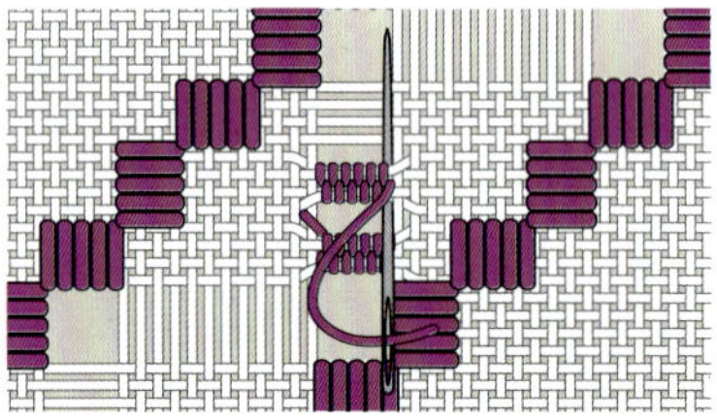

8 Moving right, weave until the bar is full, finishing with a stitch on the upper group. From below, slide the needle behind the bar.

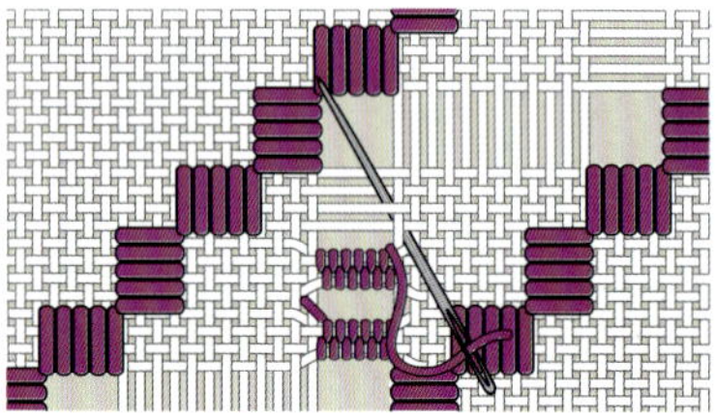

9 Insert the needle one thread to the right above the bar. Bring it out two threads up in the drawn thread area.

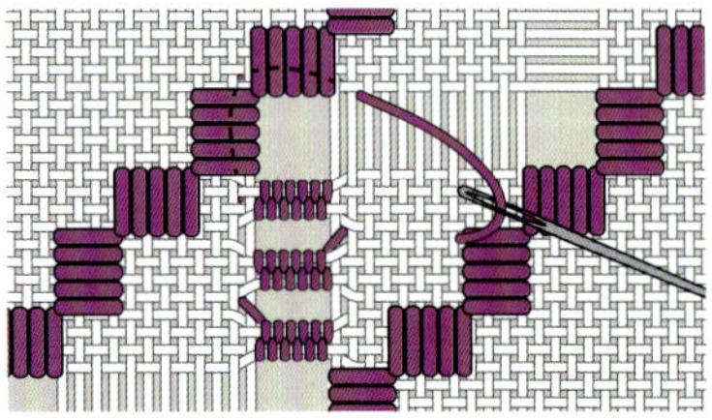

10 Work the third bar as for the first. On the back run the thread under the two intervening klosters. Bring the needle out two threads along at the next drawn thread area's top edge.

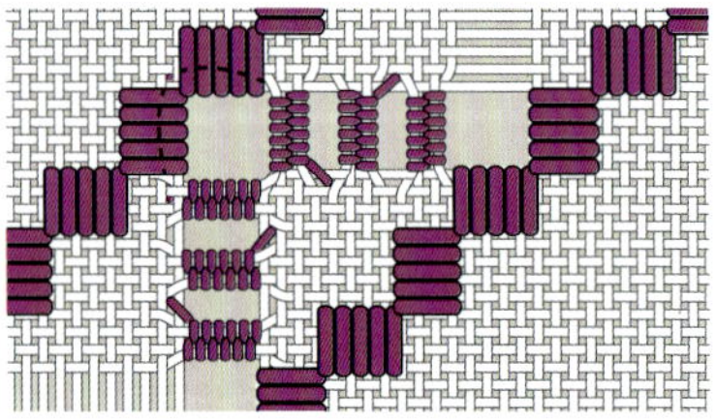

11 Work three bars, zig-zagging from side to side.

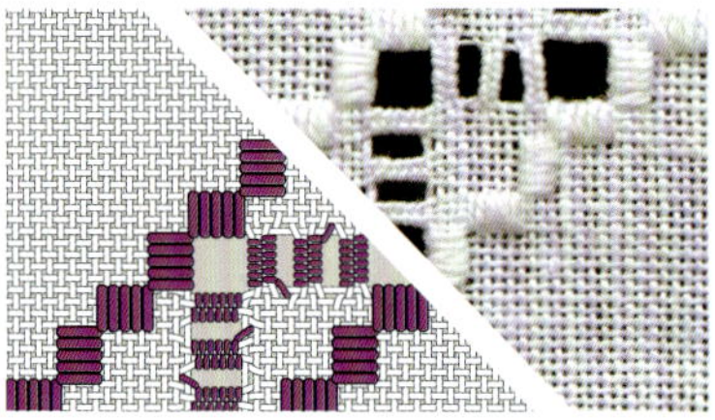

12 Run the thread under the two intervening kloster blocks, and keep working woven bars.

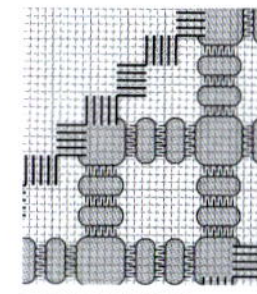

woven grouped double zig-zagging line

For more than one line, where possible work across the width, rather than along the length.

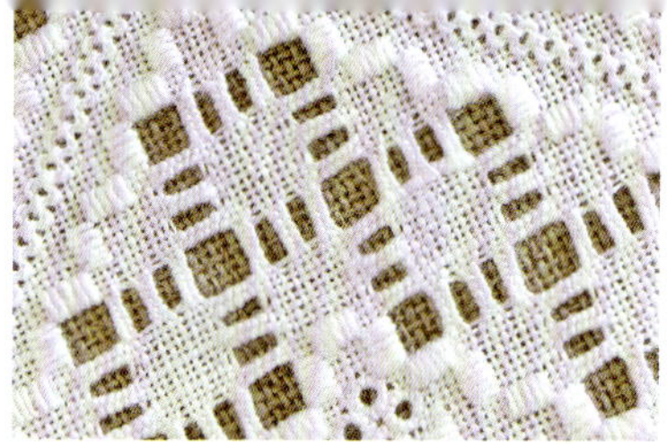

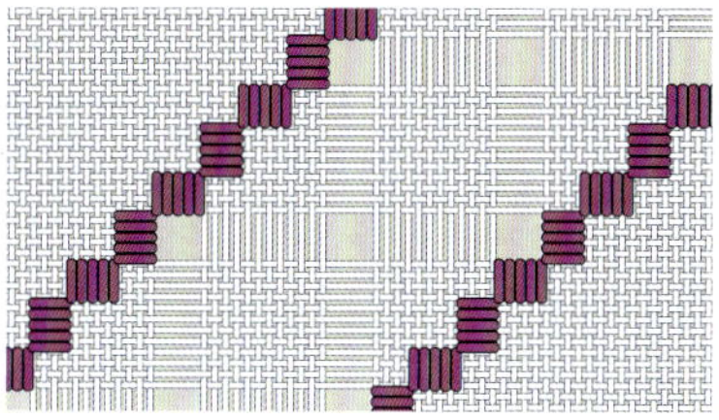

1 Cut inside only every second pair of satin stitch blocks to form a path as shown. Remove the threads ready for stitching.

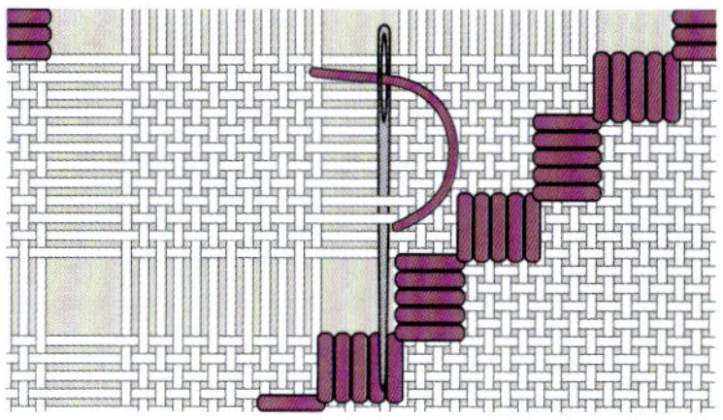

2 Bring the needle out two threads up at the right edge of the drawn thread area. From above, slide it under the next two threads up.

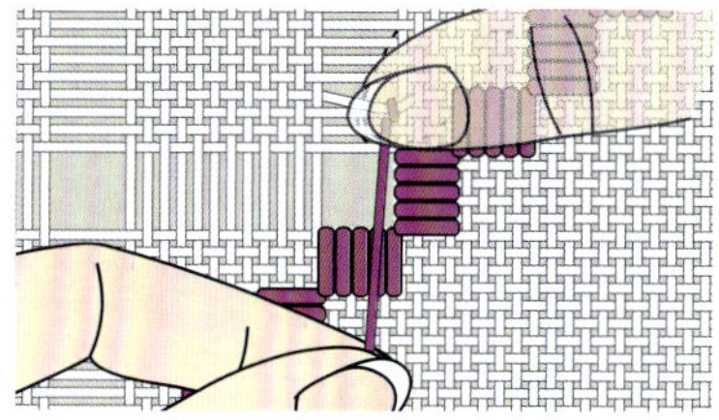

3 Pinch the stitch between your finger and thumb. With the other hand, pull the thread to tighten the stitch.

❶ *Do this after each stitch.*

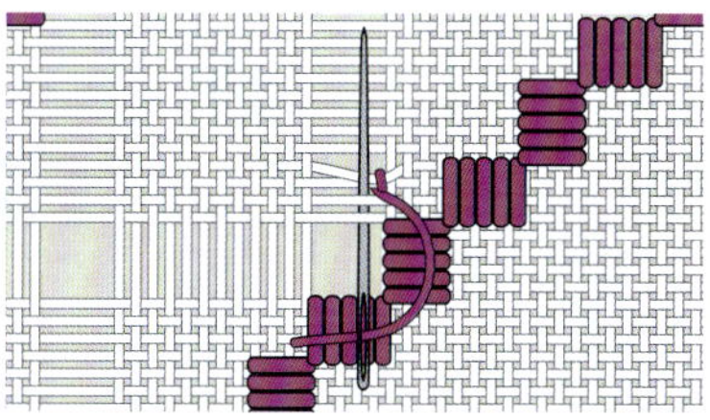

4 Moving left, from below, slide the needle under the lower two threads of the bar.

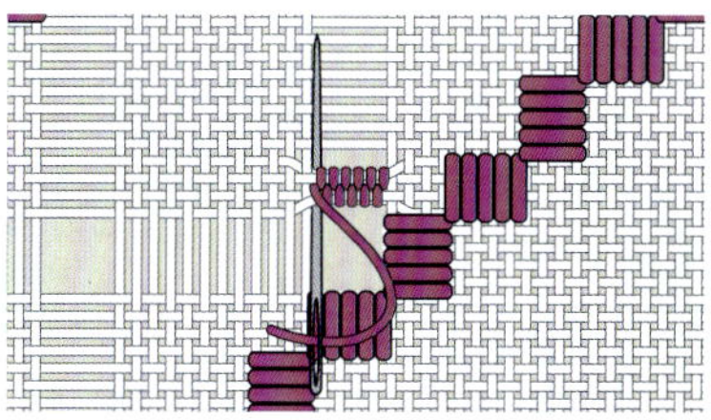

5 Pinch and pull to tighten the stitch. Weave to fill the bar, finishing with a stitch on the upper group. From below, slide the needle behind the bar.

❶ *Use as few stitches as you can to fill the bar.*

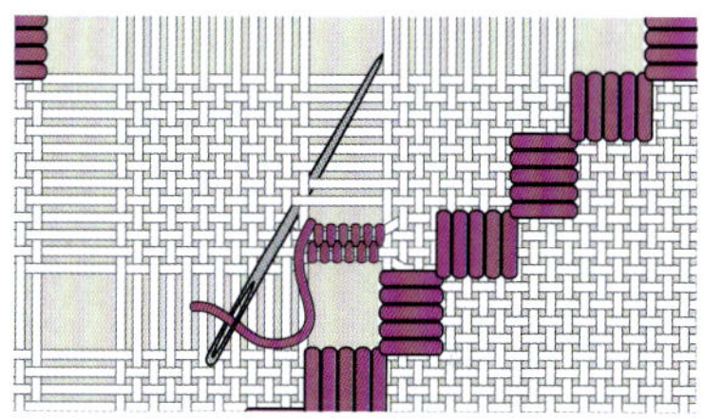

6 Insert the needle one thread to the left above the bar. Bring it out two threads up in the drawn thread area.

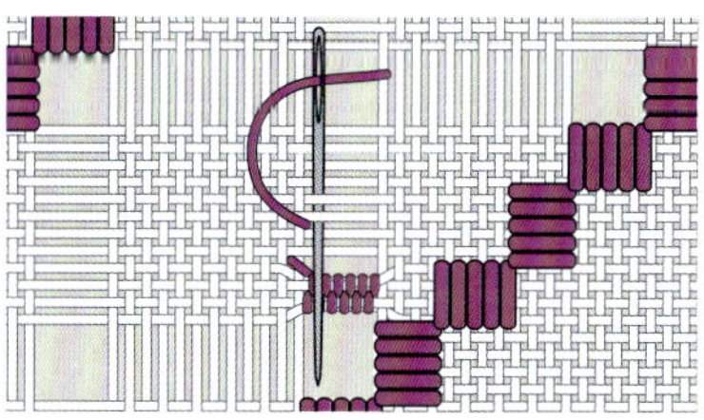

7 Moving right, from above, slide the needle under the upper two threads of the new bar to be woven.

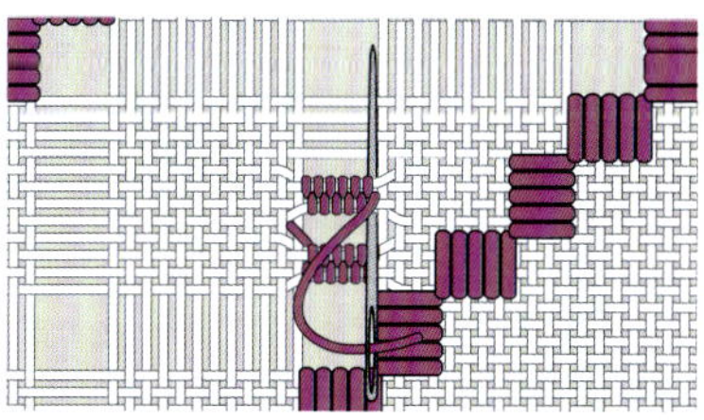

8 Moving right, weave until the bar is full, finishing with a stitch on the upper threads. From below, slide the needle behind the bar.

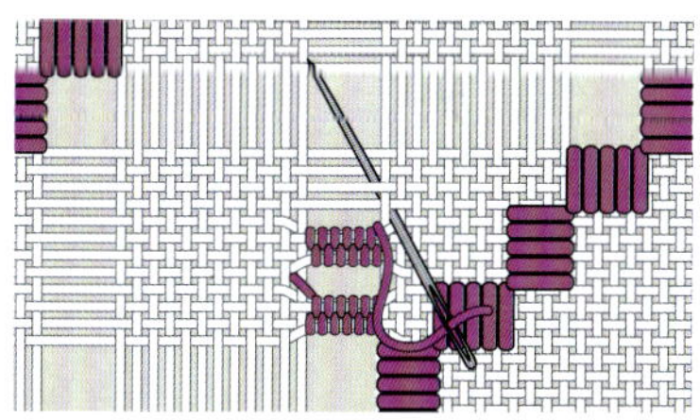

9 Insert the needle one thread to the right above the bar. Bring it out two threads up in the drawn thread area.

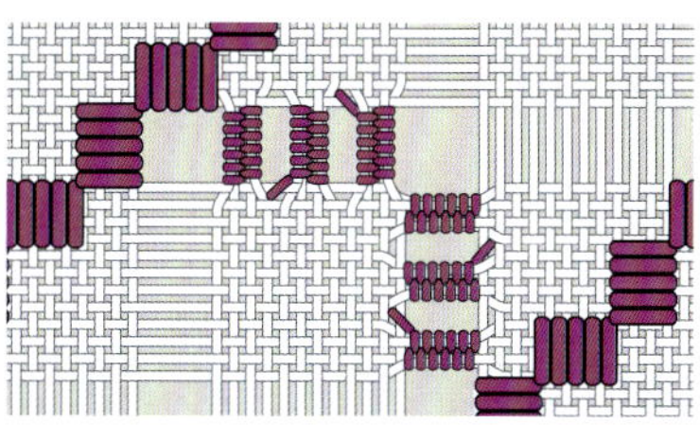

10 Work the third bar as for the first. Pass the needle behind the woven corner, and bring it out two threads along in the adjacent drawn thread area. Work three woven bars, zig-zagging from side to side.

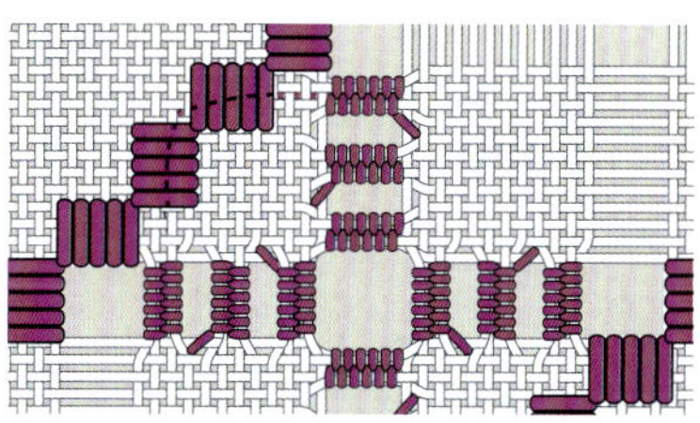

11 Run the thread under the back of the intervening klosters. Work woven bars in the next two drawn thread areas, back to the other side.

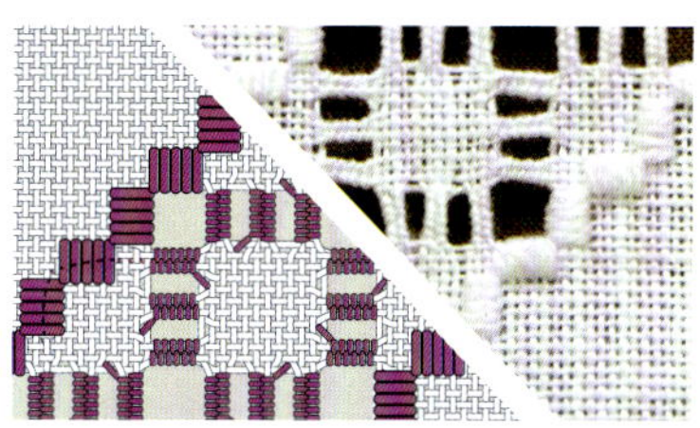

12 Continue working back and forth across the width of the drawn thread area, running the thread under the back of the intervening klosters to move further along.

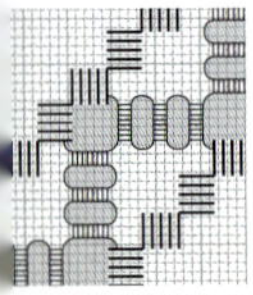

wrapped grouped zig-zagging line

Sometimes long lines of zig-zagging bars in groups of three are used as filling stitches.

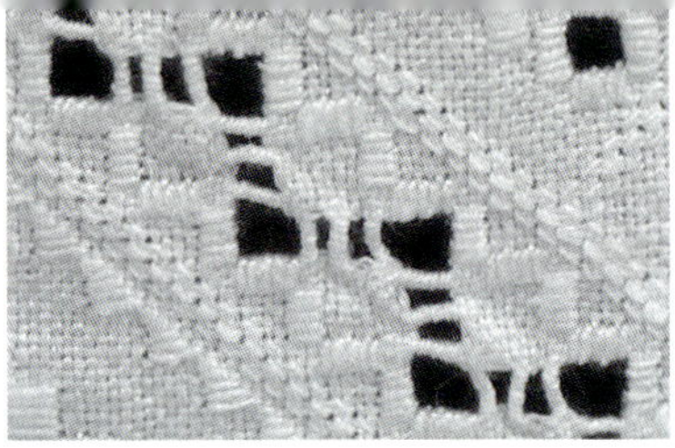

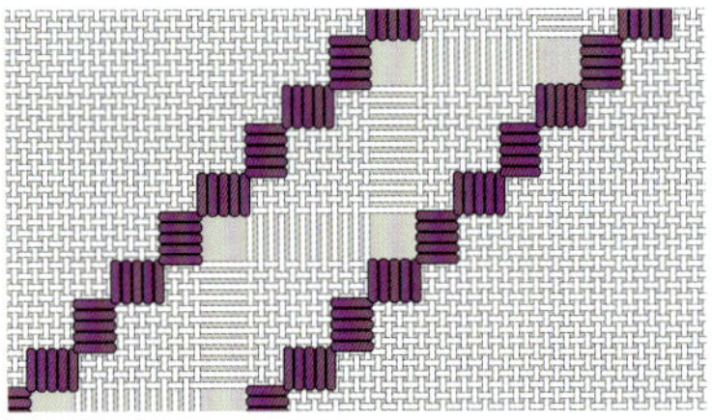

1 Cut inside only every second pair of satin stitch blocks to form a path as shown. Remove the threads ready for wrapping.

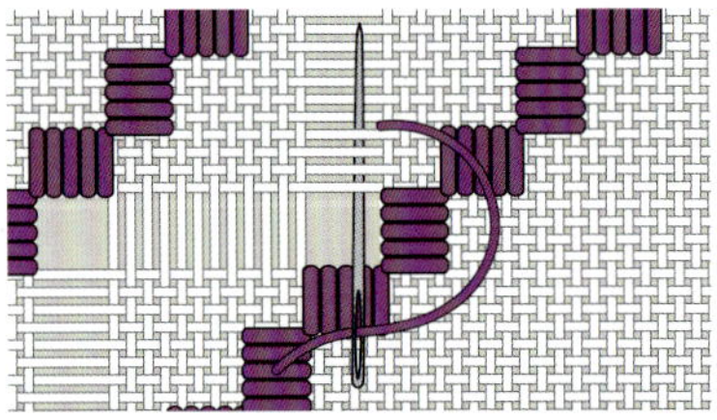

2 Bring the needle out four threads up at the right edge of the drawn thread area. From below, slide the needle under the same four threads.

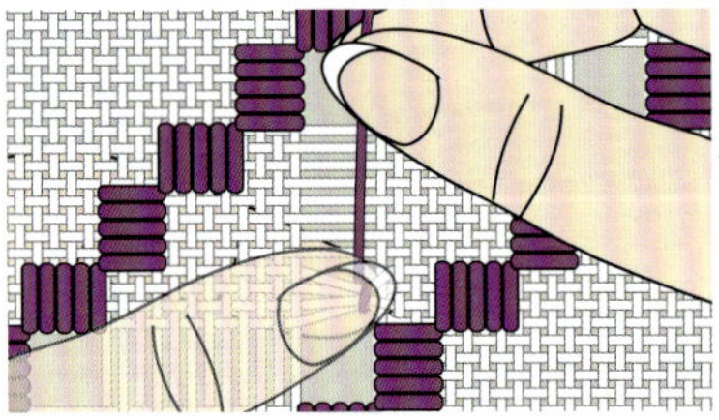

3 Pinch the stitch between your finger and thumb. With the other hand, pull the thread to tighten the stitch.

❶ *Do this after each stitch.*

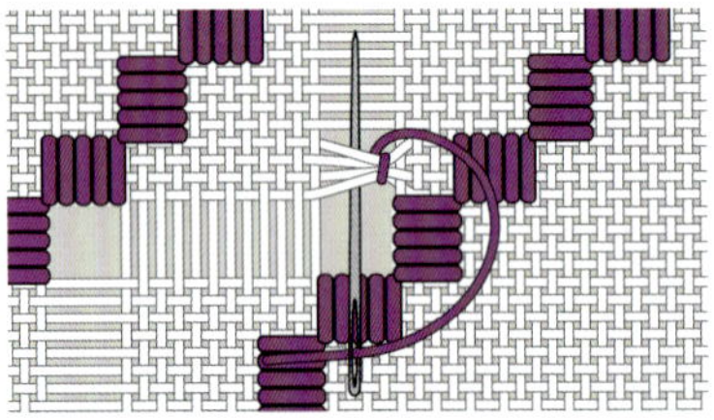

4 Moving left, slide the needle under the four threads, from below. Ensure the new stitch does not overlap the first one. Pinch and pull to tighten.

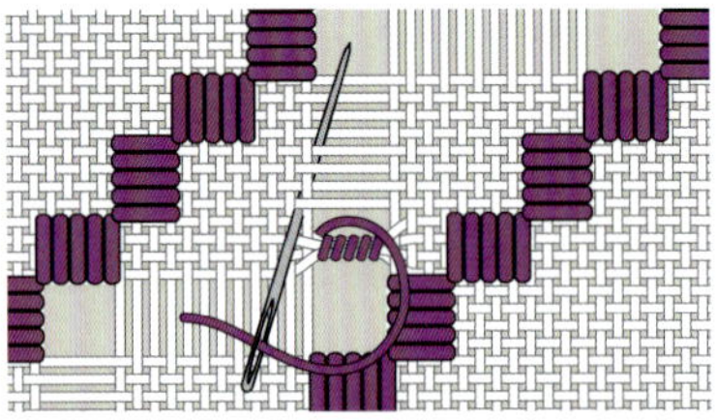

5 Fill the bar. Insert the needle one thread to the left of the gap above the bar. Bring it out four threads up, in the drawn thread area.

❶ *Fill it with as few stitches as possible.*

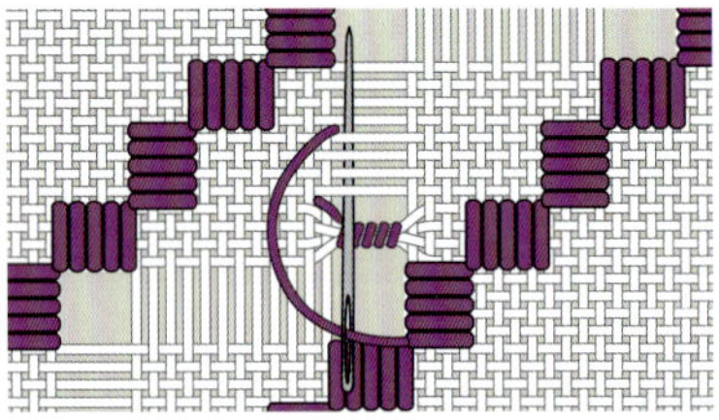

6 From below, slide the needle under these next four threads.

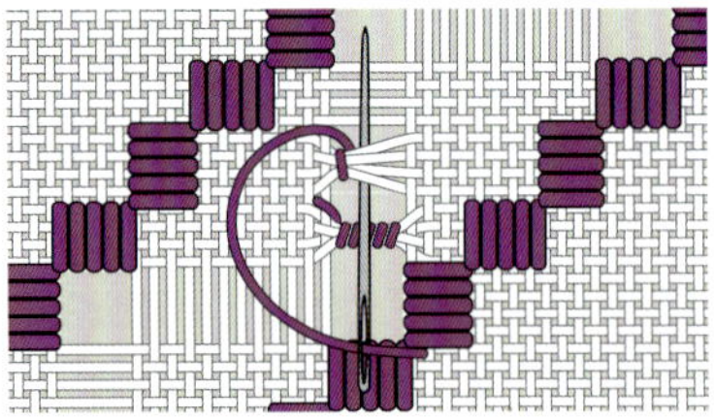

7 Pinch and pull to tighten the stitch. A little to the right, slide the needle under the four threads, from below. Ensure the new stitch does not overlap the first one.

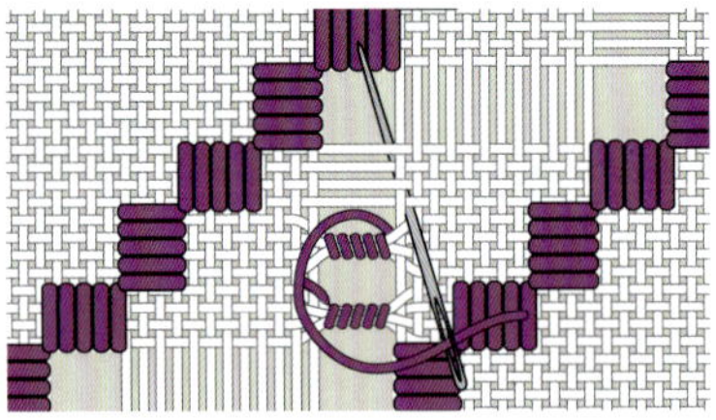

8 Fill the bar with wrapped stitches, tightening after each one. Insert the needle one thread to the right of the gap above the bar. Bring it out four threads up, in the drawn thread area.

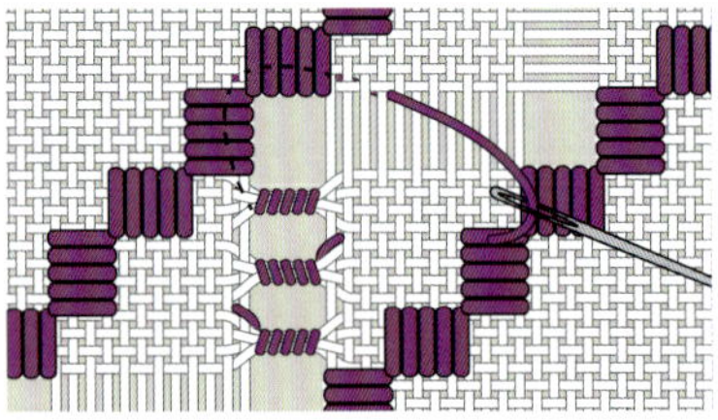

9 Work the third bar as for the first. On the back run the thread under the two intervening kloster blocks. Bring the needle out four threads along at the next drawn thread area's top edge.

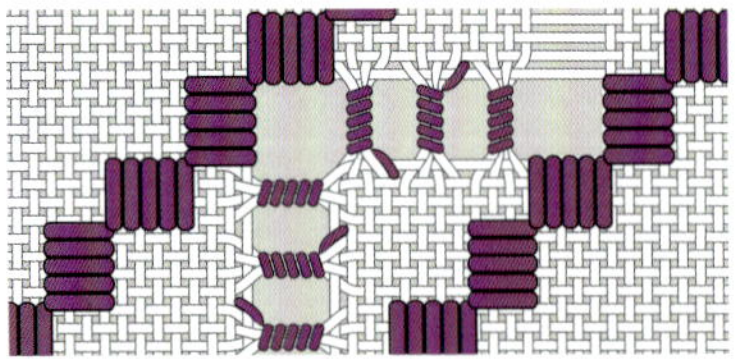

10 Work three bars, zig-zagging from side to side.

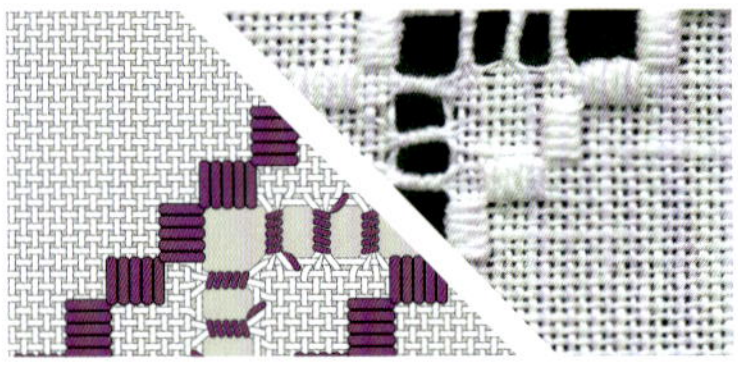

11 Run the thread under the two intervening kloster blocks, and keep working wrapped bars.

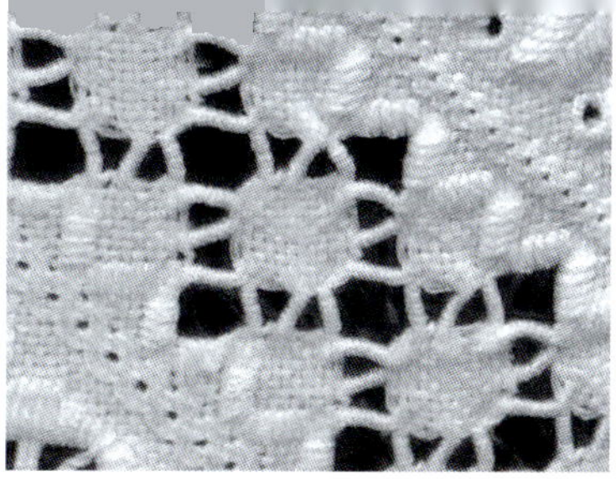

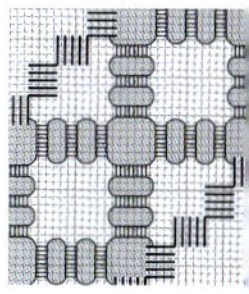

TRADITIONAL

wrapped grouped double zig-zagging line

For more than one line, where possible work across the width, rather than along the length.

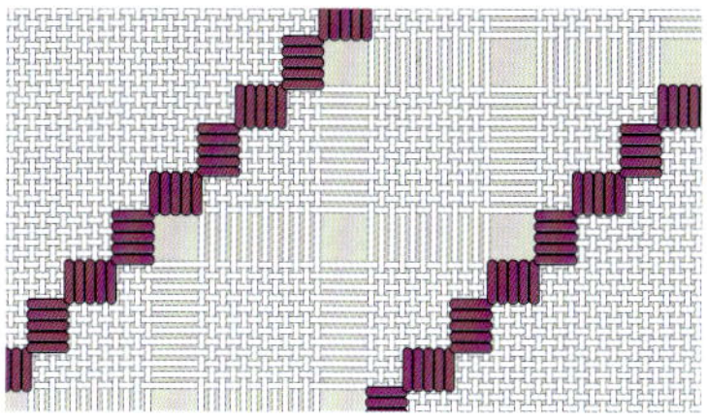

1 Cut inside only every second pair of satin stitch blocks to form a path as shown. Remove the threads ready for wrapping.

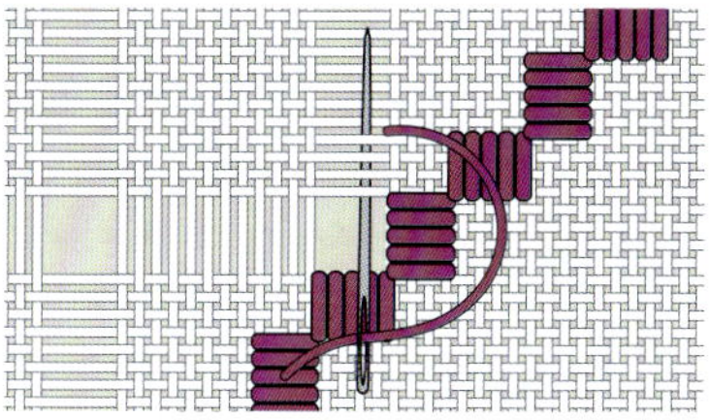

2 Bring the needle out four threads up at the right edge of the drawn thread area. From below, slide the needle under the same four threads.

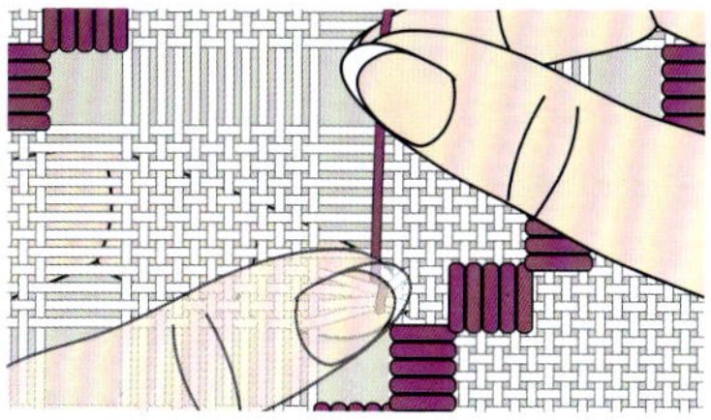

3 Pinch the stitch between your finger and thumb. With the other hand, pull the thread to tighten the stitch.
❶ *Do this after each stitch.*

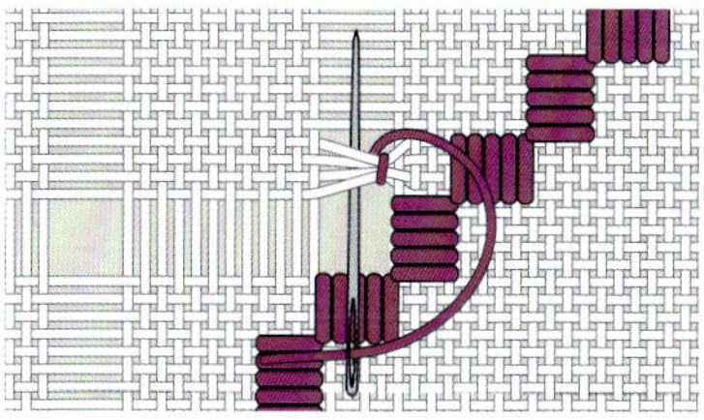

4 Moving left, slide the needle under the four threads, from below. Ensure the new stitch does not overlap the first one. Pinch and pull to tighten.

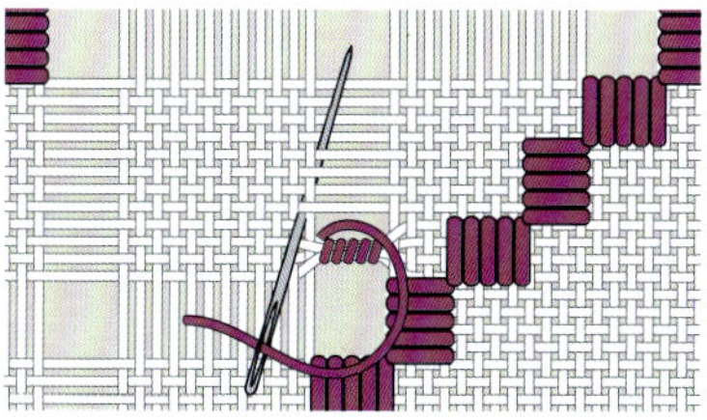

5 Wrap the bar. Insert the needle one thread left, above the bar. Bring it out four up, in the drawn thread area.
❶ *Use as few stitches as you can to fill the bar.*

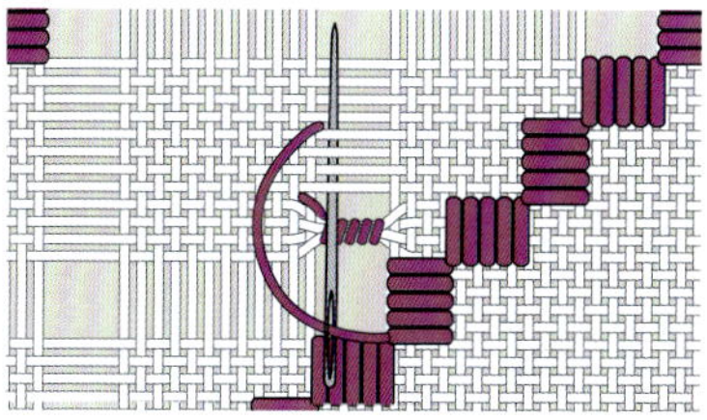

6 From below, slide the needle under these next four threads.

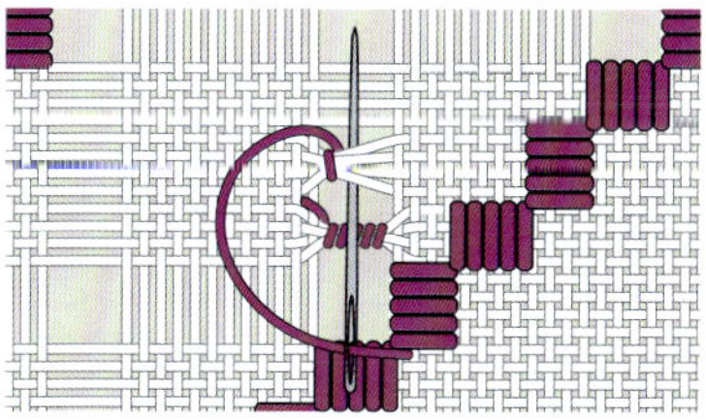

7 Pinch and pull to tighten the stitch. A little to the right, slide the needle under the four threads, from below. Ensure the new stitch does not overlap the first one.

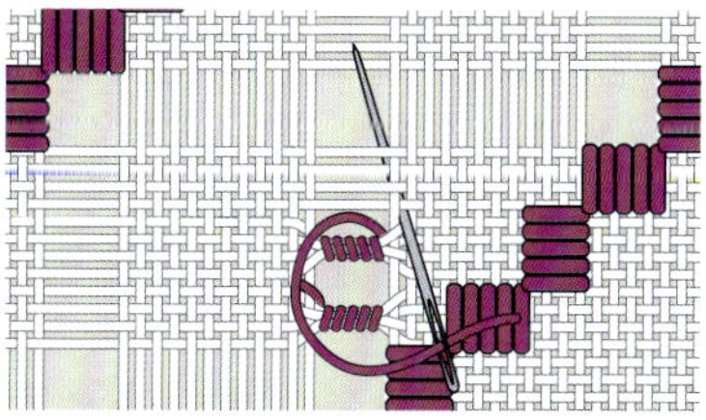

8 Fill the bar with wrapped stitches, tightening after each one. Insert the needle one thread to the right of the gap above the bar. Bring it out four threads up, in the drawn thread area.

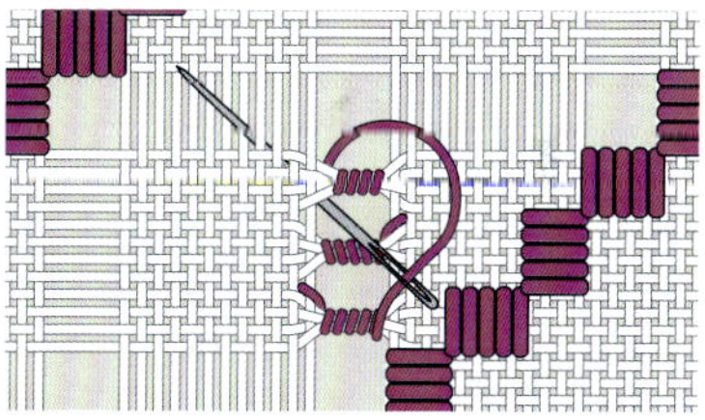

9 Work the third bar as for the first. Pass the needle behind the woven corner, and bring it out four threads along in the adjacent drawn thread area.

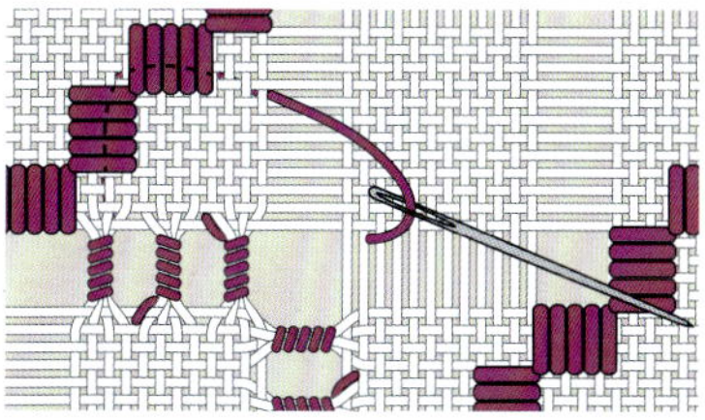

10 Work three wrapped bars. On the back run the thread under the intervening two kloster blocks. Bring the needle out four threads along at the next drawn thread area's left edge.

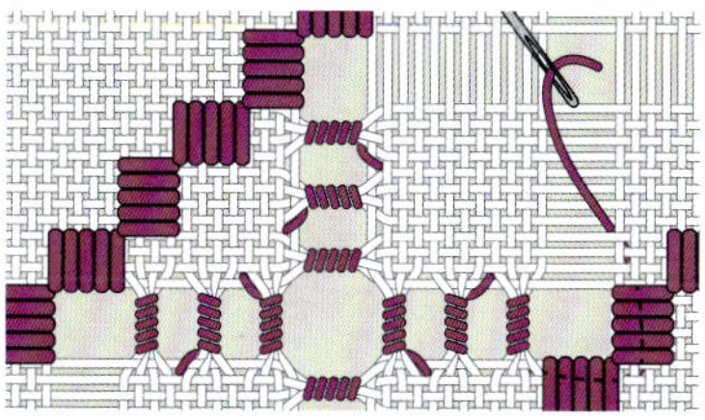

11 Wrap bars in the next two drawn thread areas, back to the other side. On the back run the thread under the intervening two klosters. Bring the needle out four threads along at the next drawn thread area's top edge.

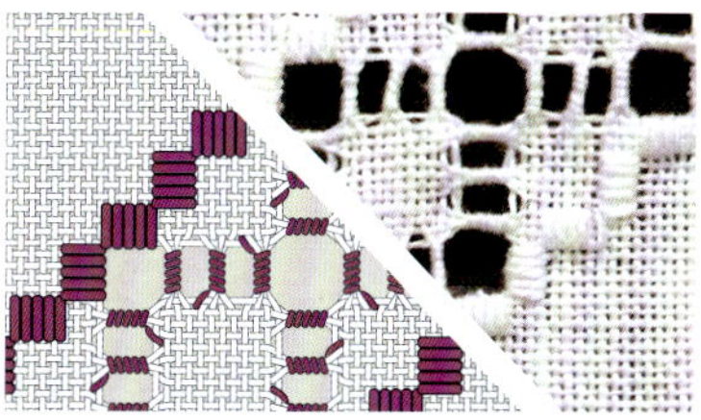

12 Keep zig-zagging back and forth across the drawn thread area.

L

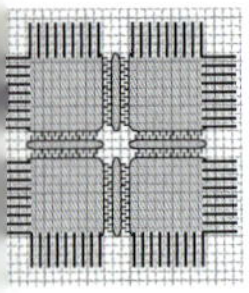

CONTEMPORARY

divided bars

woven

These woven or wrapped paired half-width bars are usually used in combination with other stitches and motifs. Each bar uses only two threads rather than the usual four.

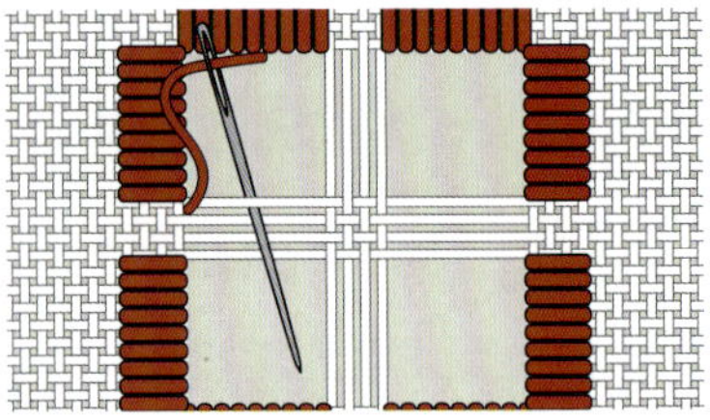

1 Working with the two upper threads only, bring the needle out at the left end of the left bar, between the two threads. From above, slide the needle under the upper thread, and bring it out between the two.

❶ *These bars are half the width of normal bars, using only two threads in each rather than the usual four.*

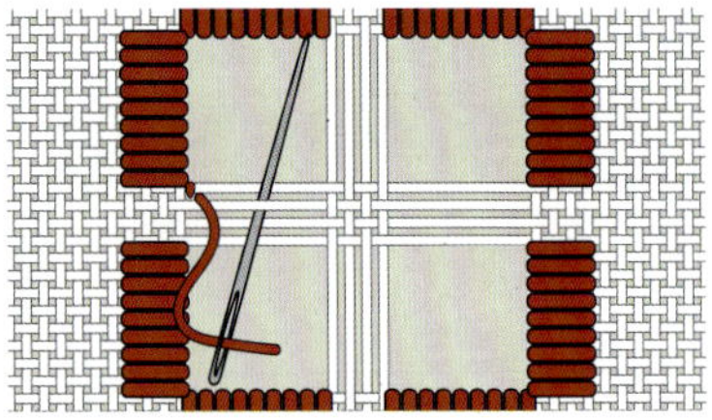

2 Tighten the stitch so that it sits snug against the fabric thread. Slide it under the lower thread, from below. Bring it out between the two.

❶ *Some motifs require overpacked bars to help them to bend. Most people overpack their woven bars, so unless you know you have sparse stitching, do not make too much effort to cram more in.*

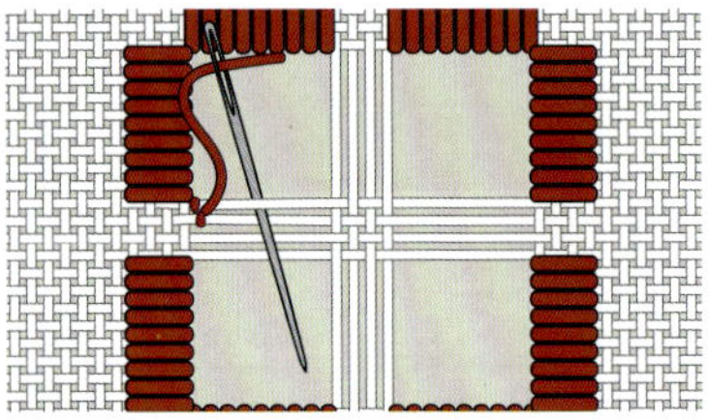

3 Pull the needle through so that the stitch sits snug against the fabric thread. Insert the needle under the other thread of the pair, from above. Bring it out between the two.

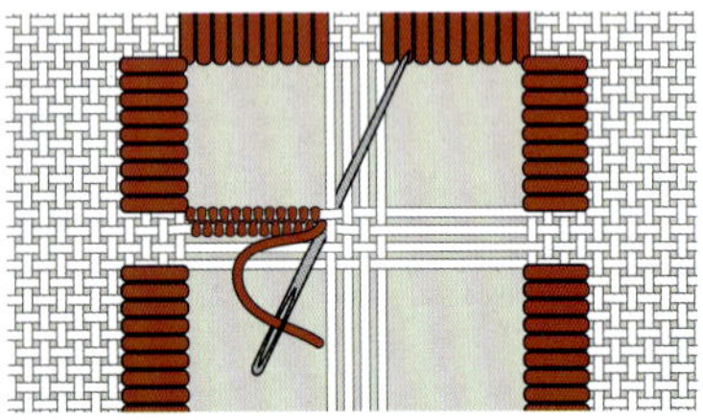

4 Continue weaving. When you reach the end of the bar, insert the needle below the bar and bring it out in the next bar above, one thread from the left.

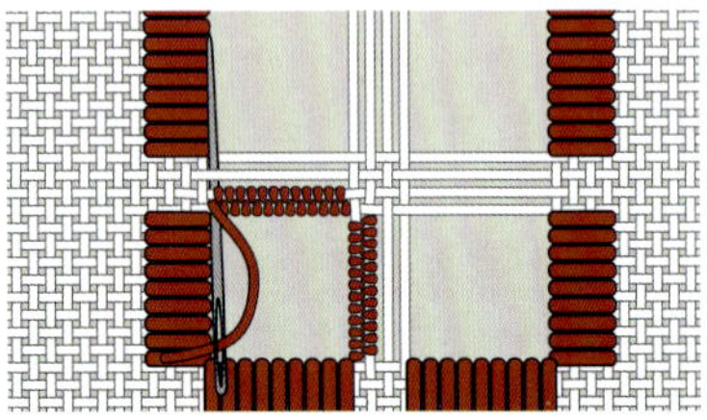

5 Turn the work 90° anticlockwise and weave the bar. To finish with a stitch on the lower thread, take the needle behind the woven bar. Bring it out between the threads of the adjacent bar.

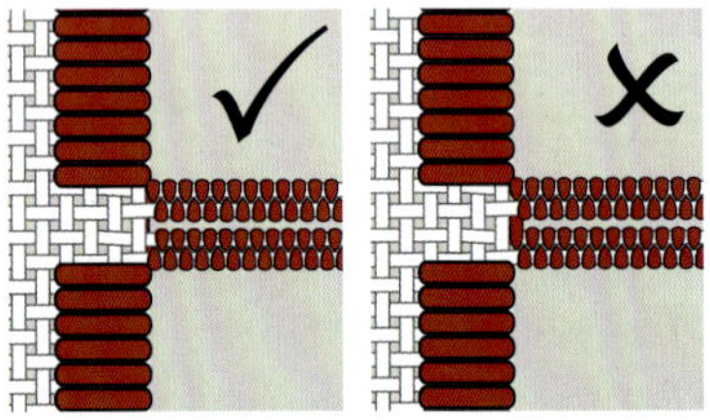

❶ *Finishing on the opposite side to the next bar will improve the appearance. If you finish on the same side, the thread will be visible between the bars.*

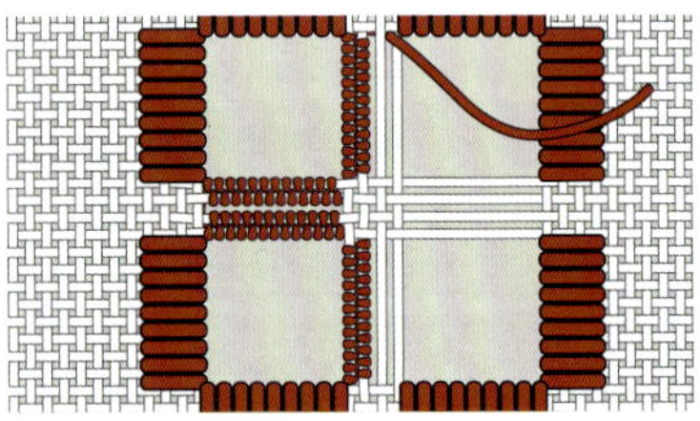

6 Pull the needle through. Weave the next two bars, turning the corner after the first one.

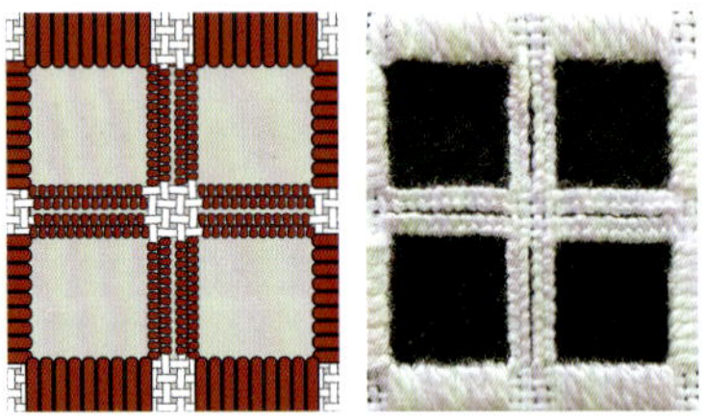

7 Work the remaining bars similarly. Finish the thread in the back of the satin stitching.

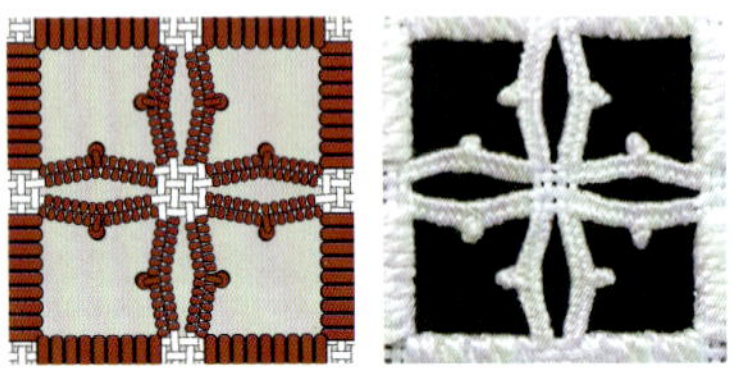

❶ *A variation is to work overpacked bars with any type of picots at the bar's midpoint. Pull the picot to make a bend in the bar.*

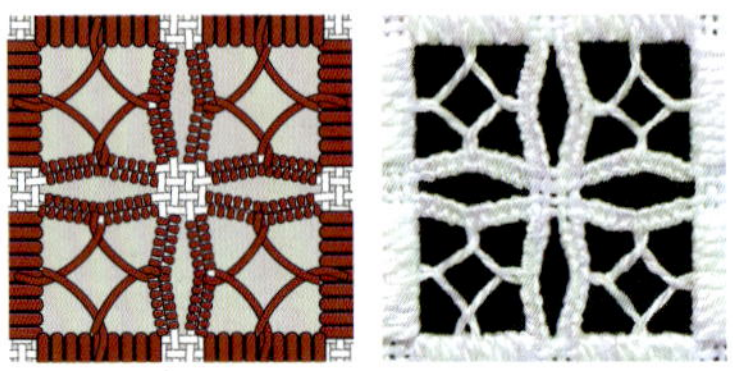

❶ *Another variation is to work dove's eyes in each of the quadrants.*

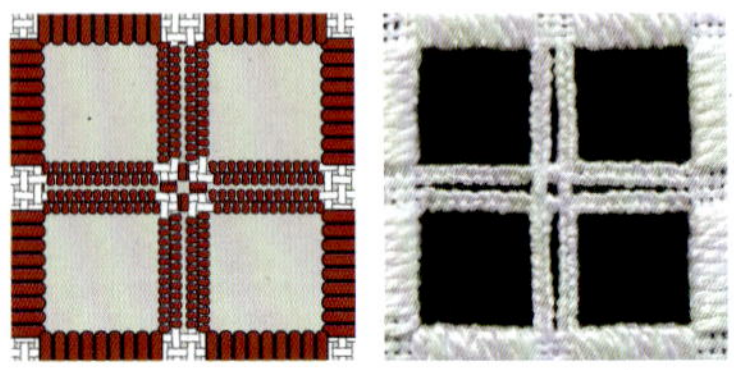

❶ *Another variation is to work a simplified eyelet in the centre woven square: two stitches from between each paired bar to the centre.*

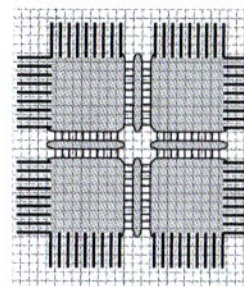

wrapped

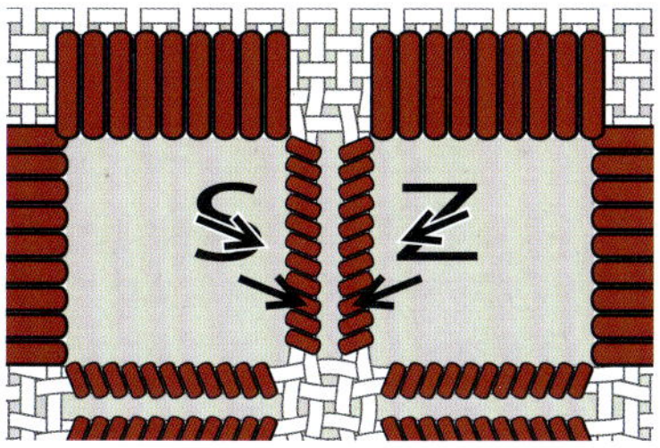

! *The method for wrapping divided bars within a square is different from regular wrapped bars. With full-width bars, the wrapping (or spiralling) direction always stays the same. In squares, they are wrapped as S or Z wraps, which are shown above.*

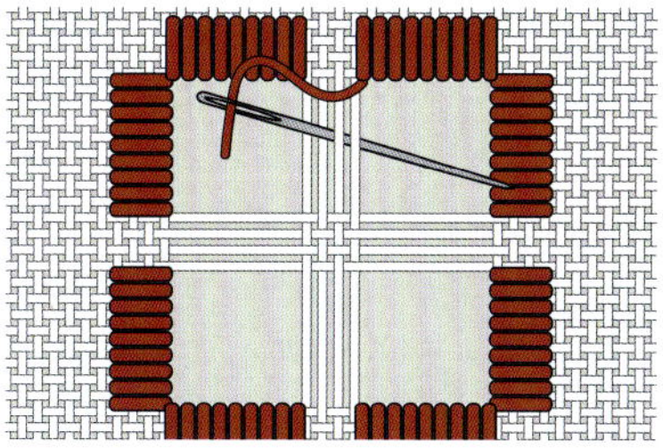

1 Bring the needle out at the top of the uppermost bar, to the right of the four threads. From the left, slide the needle under the right two threads.

! *These bars are half the width of normal bars, using only two threads in each rather than the usual four.*

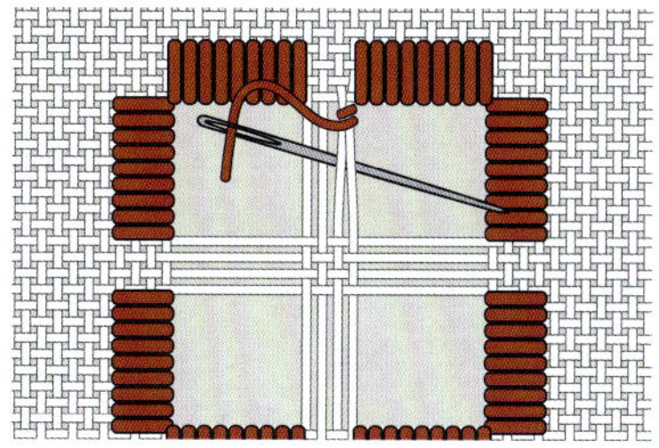

2 Pinch the bar between your forefinger and thumb, and with the other hand, pull the thread to the right, to tighten the stitch. Moving down, slide the needle under the bar again from the left. Ensure the new stitch does not overlap the first one.

! *This bar will have Z wraps.*

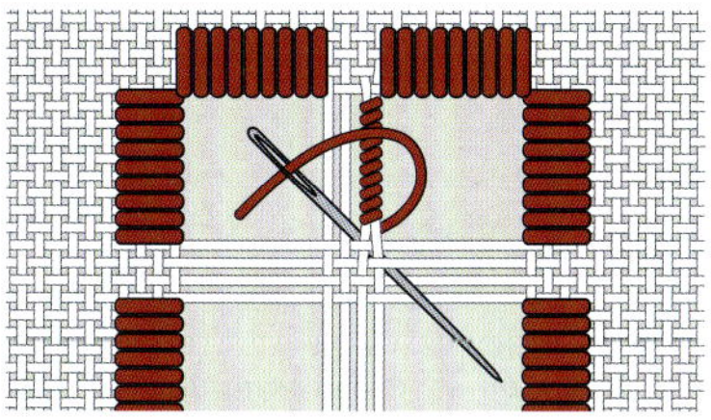

3 Continue wrapping the bar. To complete the bar and start the next one, from the left take the needle under the woven square, and bring it out in the centre of the four threads to the right.

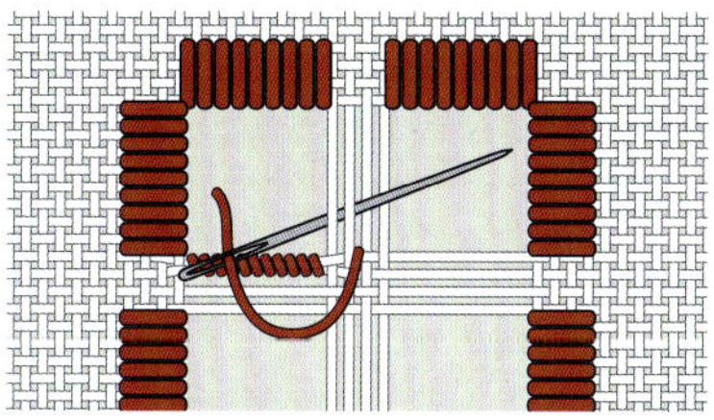

4 Pull the needle through to tighten the stitch but not distort the woven fabric square. Turn the work 90° anticlockwise. From the left, slide the needle under the left two threads.

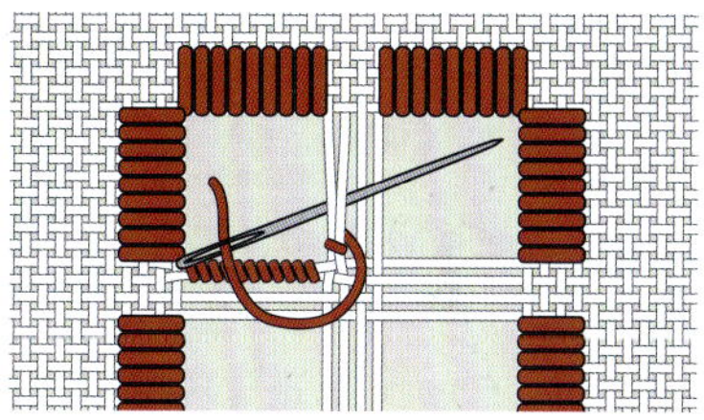

5 Pull to tighten the stitch. Moving up, slide the needle under the bar again. Ensure the new stitch does not overlap the first one.

! *This bar will have S wraps.*

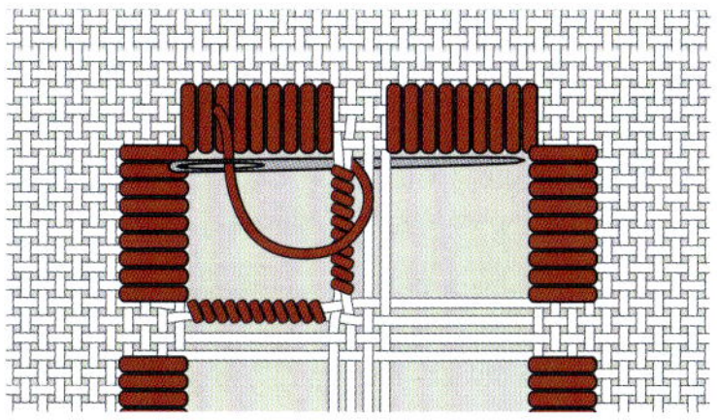

6 Continue wrapping the bar. To complete the bar and start the next one, from the left take the needle under all four fabric threads.

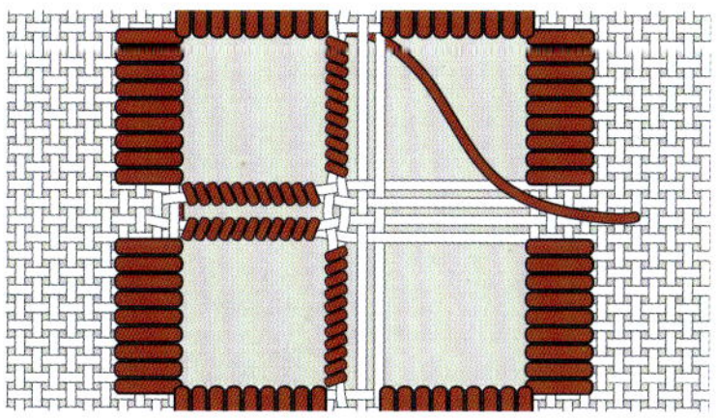

7 Turn the work 90° anticlockwise and repeat the stitching of the first quadrant in this new quadrant.

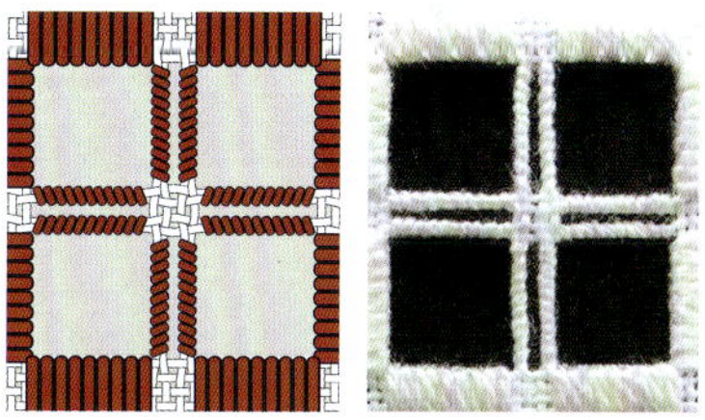

8 Complete the final two quadrants and finish the thread in the back of the satin stitching.

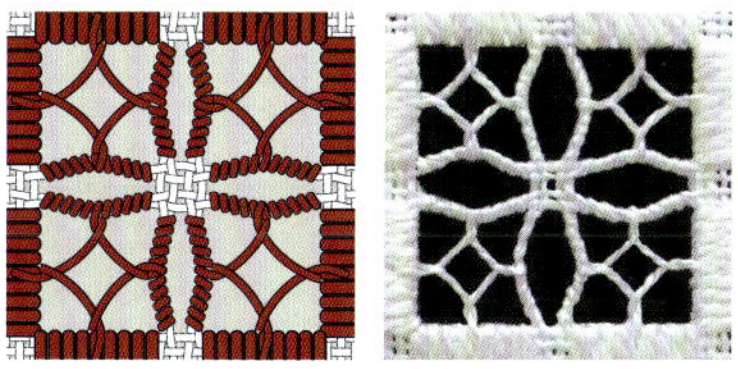

! *A variation is to work dove's eyes in each of the quadrants.*

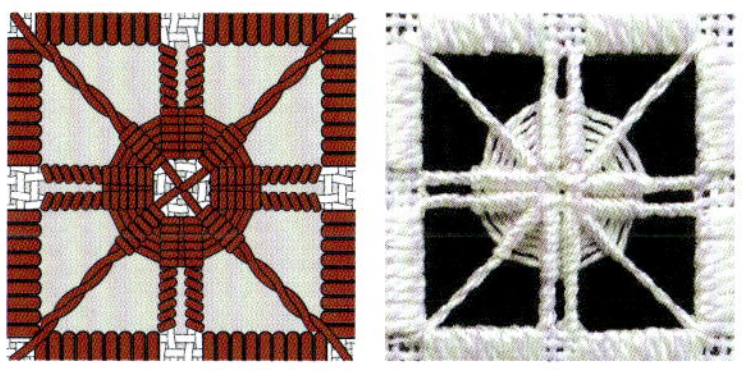

! *Another variation is to work a spider web (woven, ribbed or whipped) over the central intersection using the divided bars as some of the spokes.*

divided bars

woven

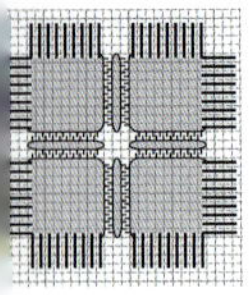

These woven or wrapped paired half-width bars are usually used in combination with other stitches and motifs. Each bar uses only two threads rather than the usual four.

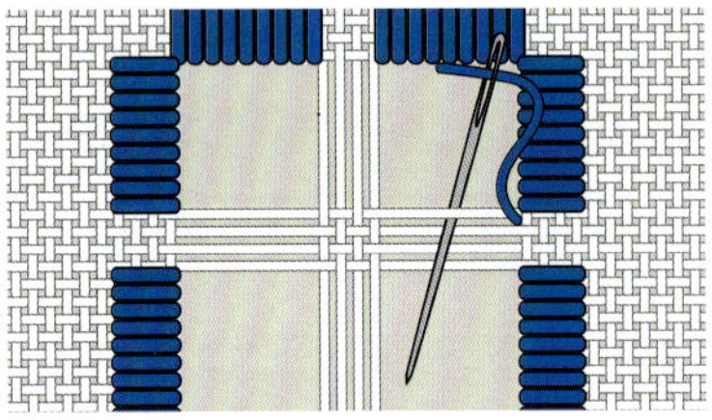

1 Working with the two upper threads only, bring the needle out at the right end of the right bar, between the two threads. From above, slide the needle under the upper thread, and bring it out between the two.

❶ *These bars are half the width of normal bars, using only two threads in each rather than the usual four.*

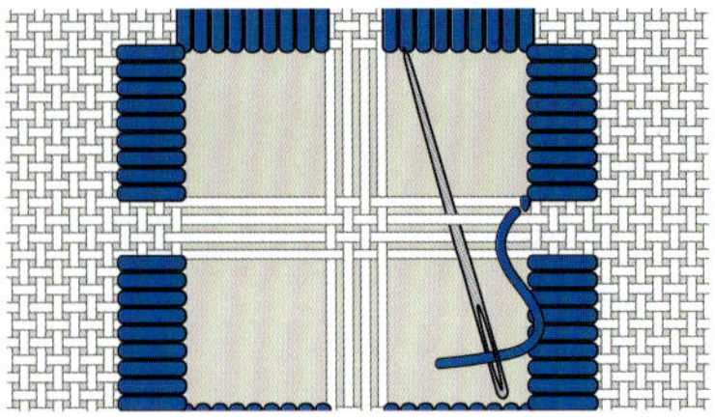

2 Tighten the stitch so that it sits snug against the fabric thread. Slide it under the lower thread, from below. Bring it out between the two.

❶ *Some motifs require overpacked bars to help them to bend. Most people overpack their woven bars, so unless you know you have sparse stitching, do not make too much effort to cram more in.*

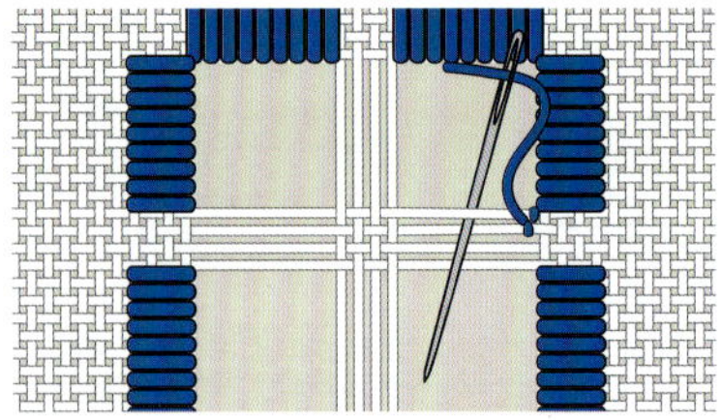

3 Pull the needle through so that the stitch sits snug against the fabric thread. Insert the needle under the other thread of the pair, from above. Bring it out between the two.

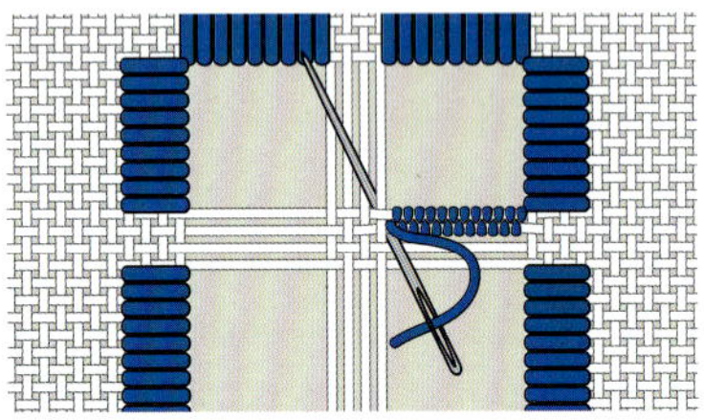

4 Continue weaving. When you reach the end of the bar, insert the needle below the bar and bring it out in the next bar above, one thread from the right.

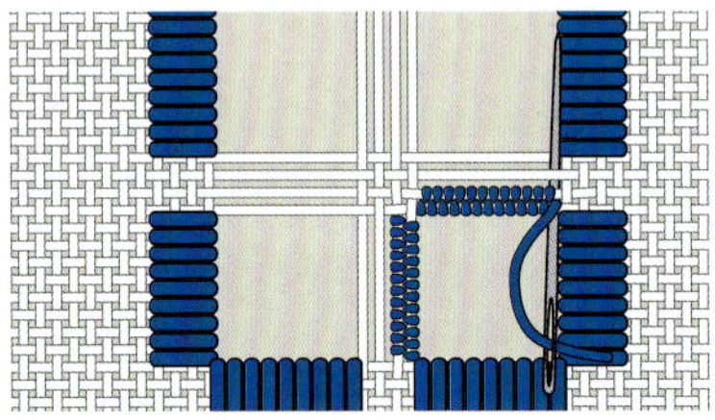

5 Turn the work 90° clockwise and weave the bar. To finish with a stitch on the lower thread, take the needle behind the woven bar. Bring it out between the threads of the adjacent bar.

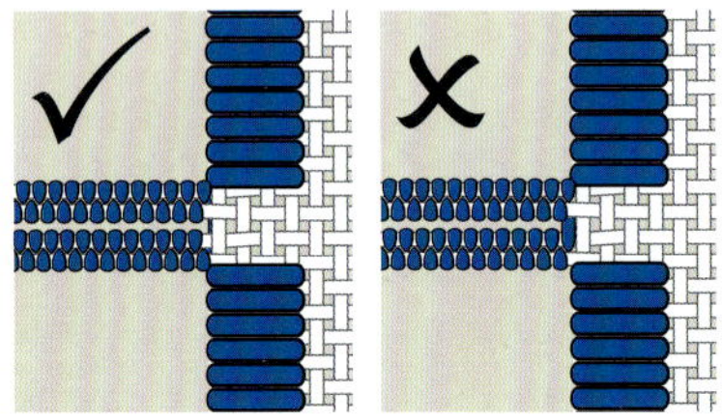

❶ *Finishing on the opposite side to the next bar will improve the appearance. If you finish on the same side, the thread will be visible between the bars.*

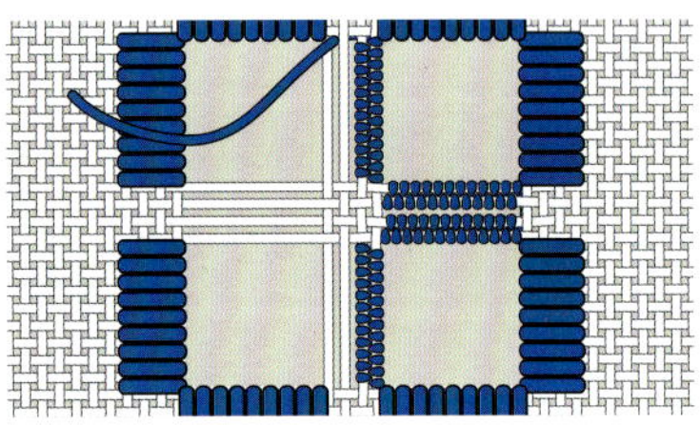

6 Pull the needle through. Weave the next two bars, turning the corner after the first one.

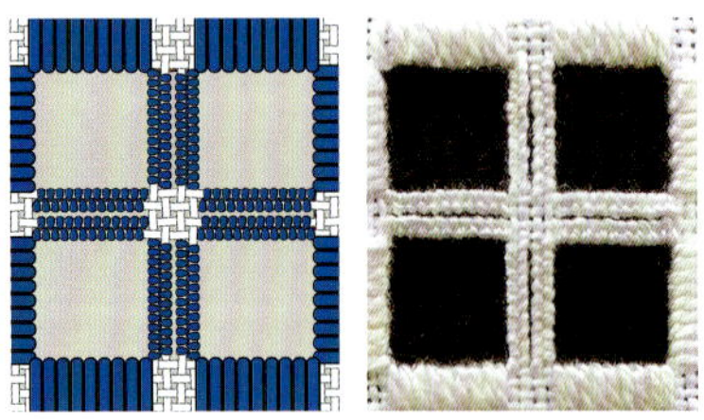

7 Work the remaining bars similarly. Finish the thread in the back of the satin stitching.

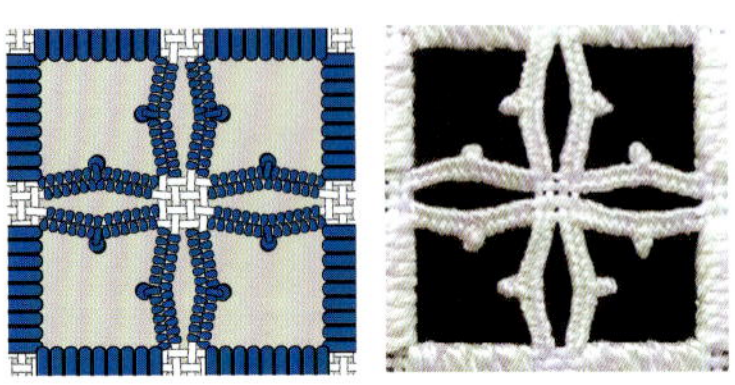

❶ *A variation is to work overpacked bars with any type of picots at the bar's midpoint. Pull the picot to make a bend in the bar.*

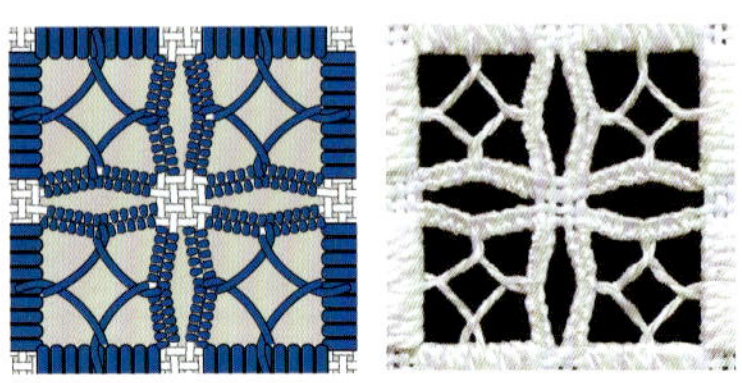

❶ *Another variation is to work dove's eyes in each of the quadrants.*

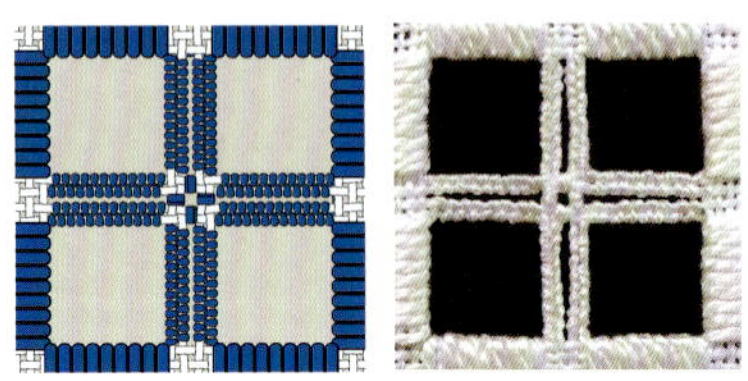

❶ *Another variation is to work a simplified eyelet in the centre woven square: two stitches from between each paired bar to the centre.*

wrapped

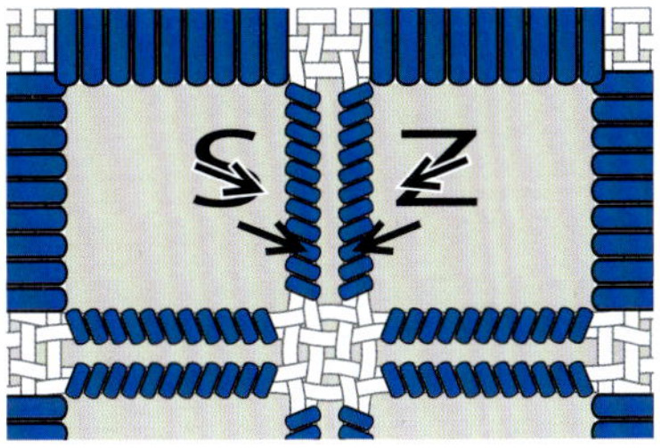

❶ *The method for wrapping divided bars within a square is different from regular wrapped bars. With full-width bars, the wrapping (or spiralling) direction always stays the same. In squares, they are wrapped as S or Z wraps, which are shown above.*

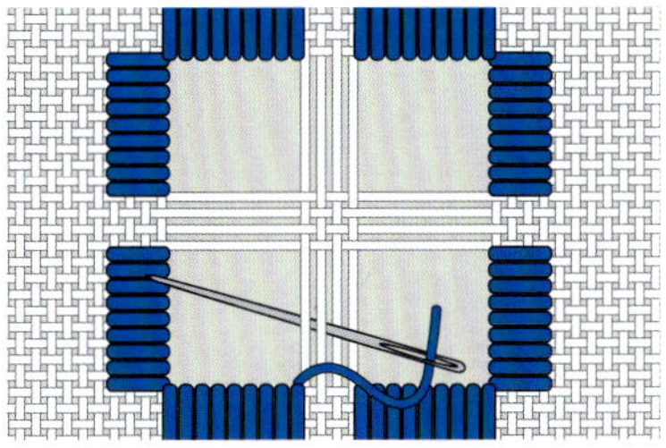

1 Bring the needle out at the top of the uppermost bar, to the left of the four threads. From the right, slide the needle under the left two threads.

❶ *These bars are half the width of normal bars, using only two threads in each rather than the usual four.*

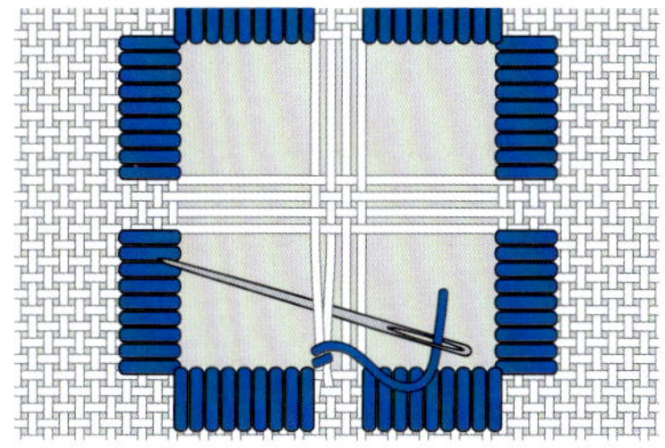

2 Pinch the bar between your forefinger and thumb, and with the other hand, pull the thread to the left, to tighten the stitch. Moving up, slide the needle under the bar again from the right. Ensure the new stitch does not overlap the first one.

❶ *This bar will have Z wraps.*

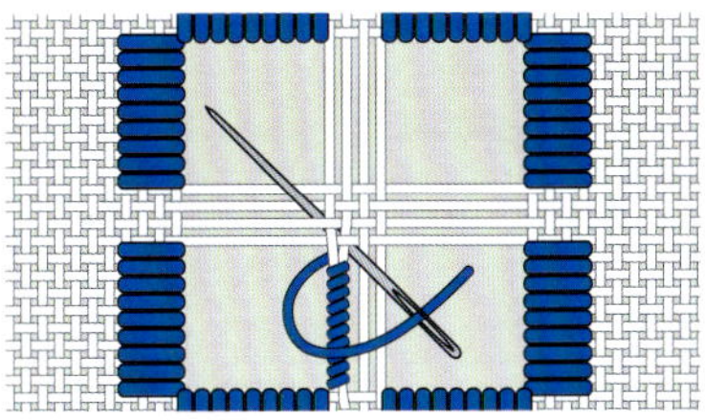

3 Continue wrapping the bar. To complete the bar and start the next one, from the right take the needle under the woven square, and bring it out in the centre of the four threads to the left.

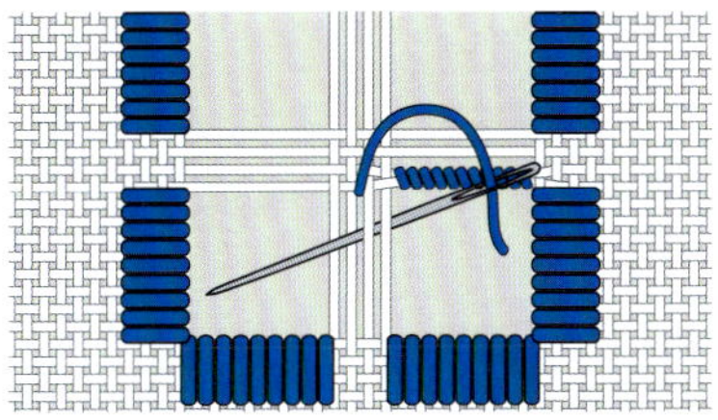

4 Pull the needle through to tighten the stitch but not distort the woven fabric square. Turn the work 90° anticlockwise. From the right, slide the needle under the right two threads.

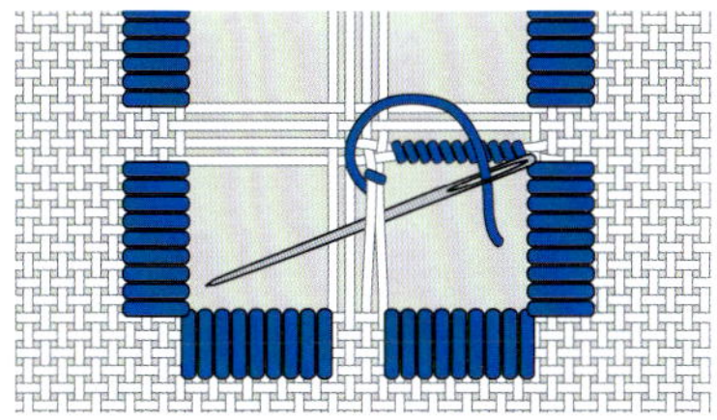

5 Pull to tighten the stitch. Moving down, slide the needle under the bar again. Ensure the new stitch does not overlap the first one.

❶ *This bar will have S wraps.*

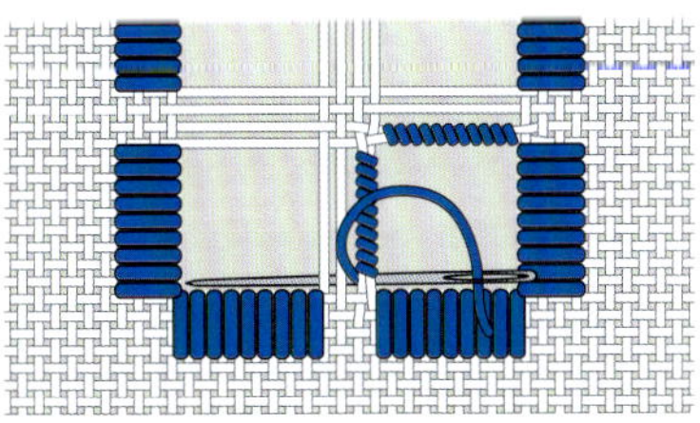

6 Continue wrapping the bar. To complete the bar and start the next one, from the right take the needle under all four fabric threads.

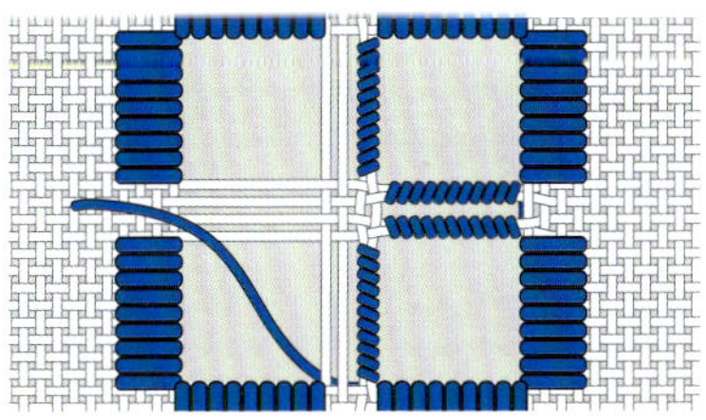

7 Turn the work 90° anticlockwise and repeat the stitching of the first quadrant in this new quadrant.

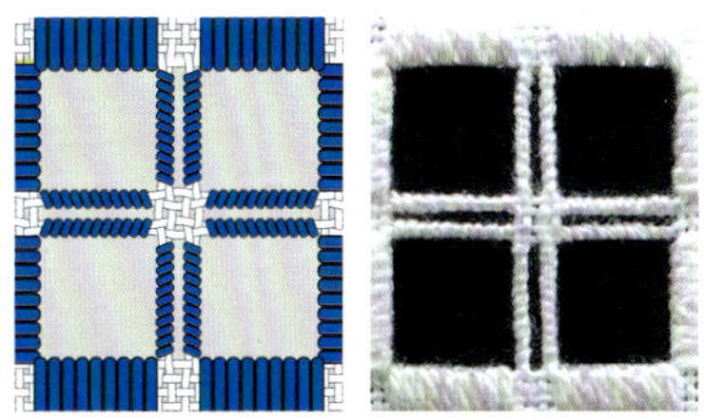

8 Complete the final two quadrants and finish the thread in the back of the satin stitching.

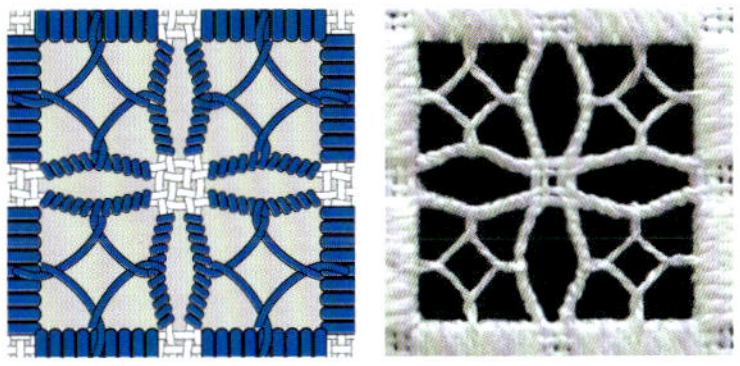

❶ *A variation is to work dove's eyes in each of the quadrants.*

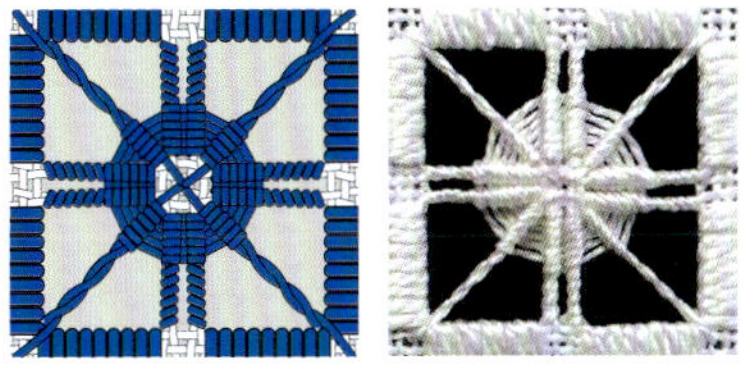

❶ *Another variation is to work a spider web (woven, ribbed or whipped) over the central intersection using the divided bars as some of the spokes.*

L

woven diagonals

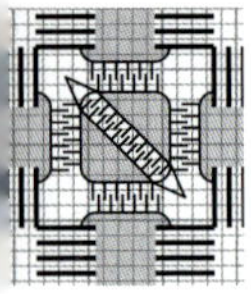

TRADITIONAL

The more sides of the openwork square that are stitched before you work the filling stitches, the more stable the embroidery will be. Stitch the woven diagonal after stitching the third or preferably the fourth edge of the square.

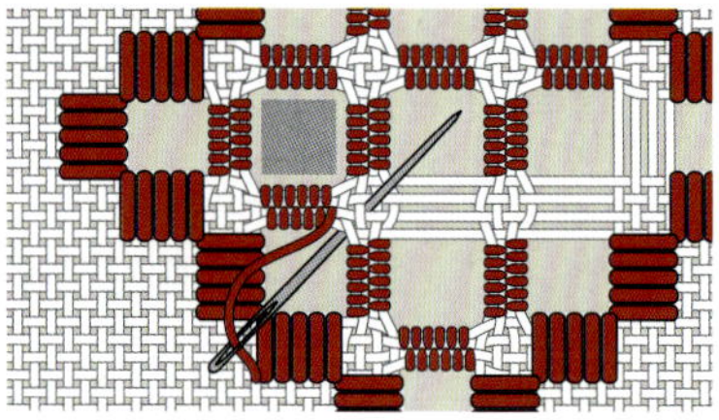

1 Complete the fourth side of the square (shown in grey) to be filled. Bring the needle out in the centre of the adjacent woven square.

Sometimes it may be necessary to work the woven diagonal after the third side.

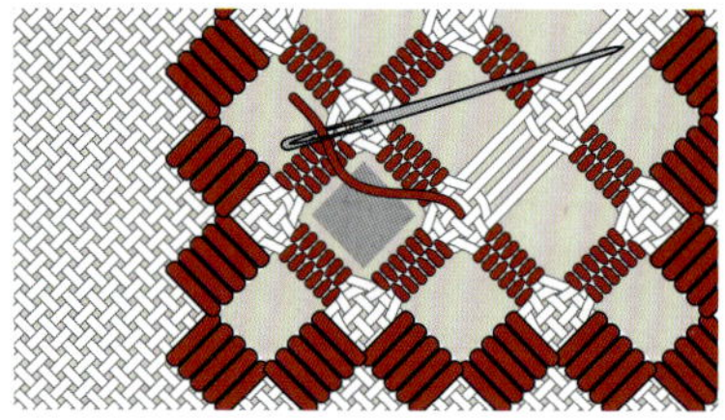

2 Pull the needle through. Turn the work 45° anticlockwise so that the thread emerges at the right of the open square.

3 From the front, insert the needle in the centre of the woven square in the opposite corner. Bring it out in the right corner of the open square, through the same hole as before.

4 Pull the needle through. From the front, insert the needle in the centre of the opposite corner again. Bring the needle out between the laced stitches so that one is above the needle, and two are below.

5 Pull the needle through.

The laced stitches should span the square gently. They should not be too loose or too tight.

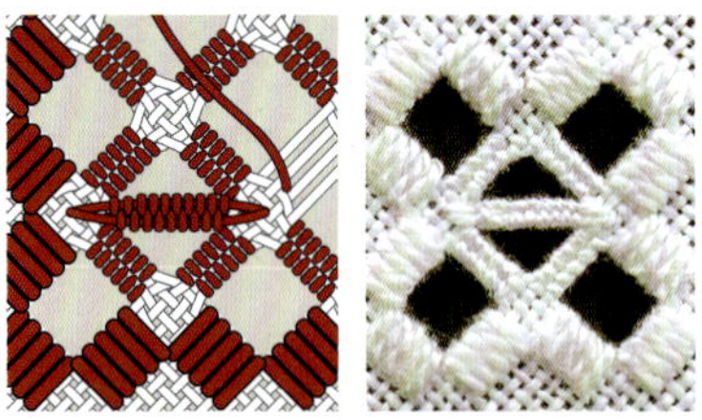

6 Work weaving stitches to fill the bar, keeping one laced thread above the needle, and two below. After completing the bar, bring the thread out ready to continue stitching.

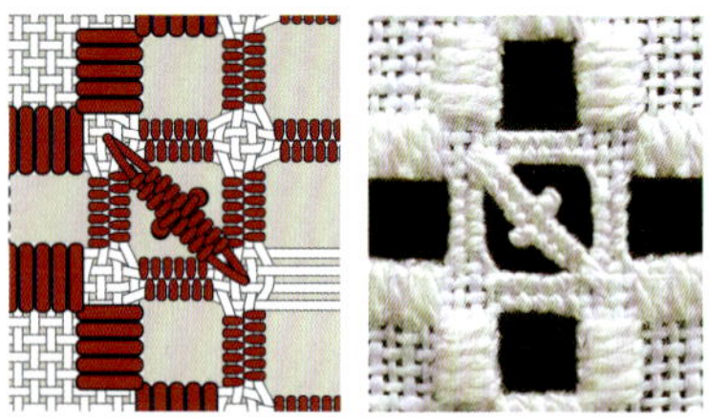

You can also work picots on the sides of the bar.

woven petal

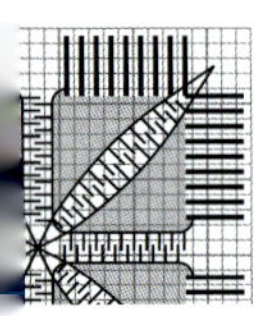

CONTEMPORARY

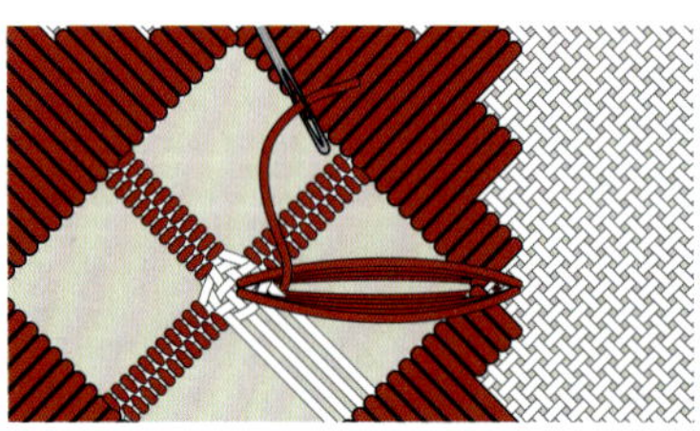

1 In a large square, work similarly to woven diagonals, but use nine foundation stitches rather than the three used for woven diagonals.

Nine stitches make a suitably heavy base for the wider middle stitches.

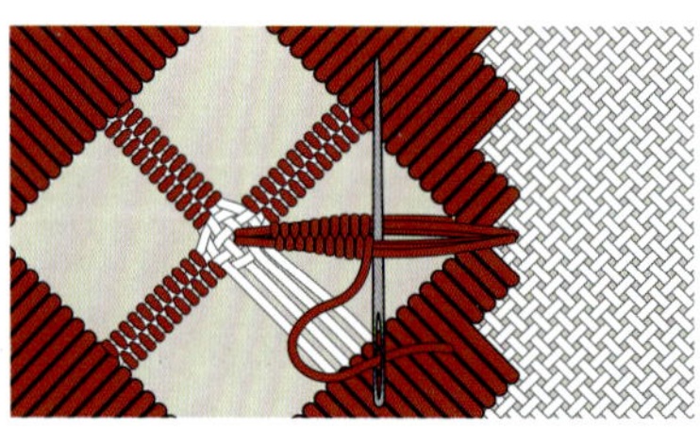

2 Work the first three stitches on each side of the petal very tightly, then carefully and gradually loosen tension to be much wider at the middle.

Stitches should not be markedly different from the ones beside them.

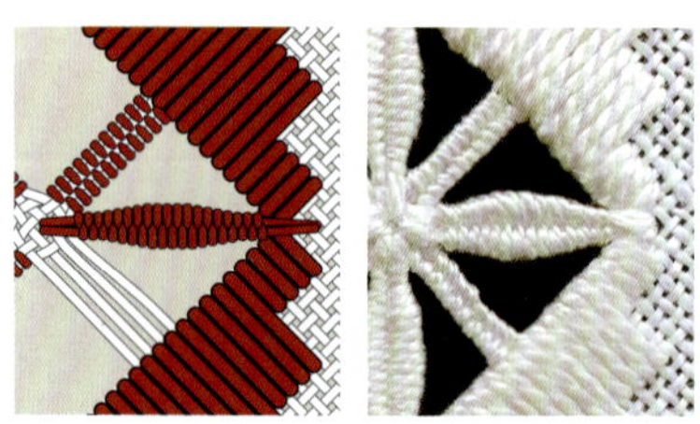

3 Complete the petal by increasing the tension, to make increasingly shorter stitches. Work the last three stitches on each side of the petal really tightly.

The sides should curve smoothly.

woven diagonals

The more sides of the openwork square that are stitched before you work the filling stitches, the more stable the embroidery will be. Stitch the woven diagonal after stitching the third or preferably the fourth edge of the square.

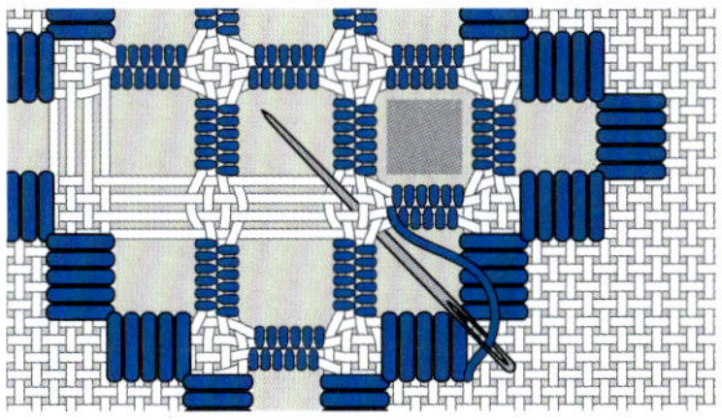

1 Complete the fourth side of the square (shown in grey) to be filled. Bring the needle out in the centre of the adjacent woven square.

❶ *Sometimes it may be necessary to work the woven diagonal after the third side.*

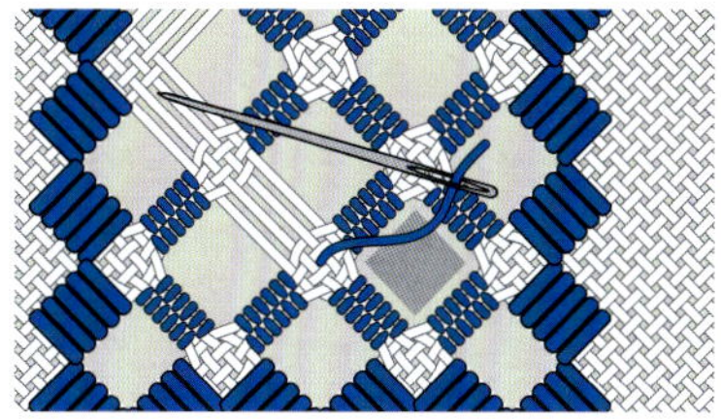

2 Pull the needle through. Turn the work 45° clockwise so that the thread emerges at the left of the open square.

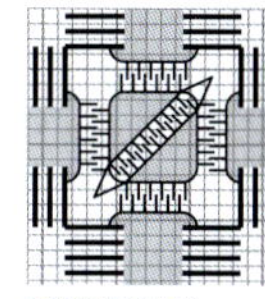

TRADITIONAL

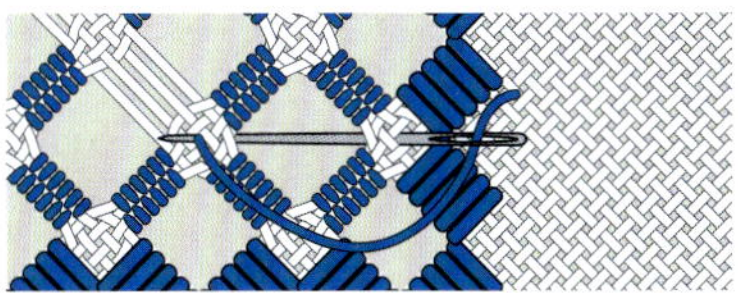

3 From the front, insert the needle in the centre of the woven square in the opposite corner. Bring it out in the left corner of the open square, through the same hole as before.

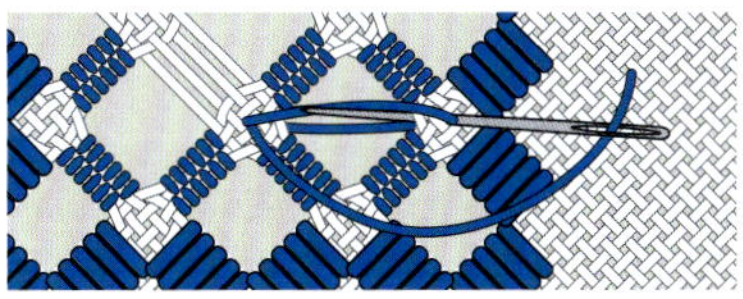

4 Pull the needle through. From the front, insert the needle in the centre of the opposite corner again. Bring the needle out between the laced stitches so that one is below the needle, and two are above.

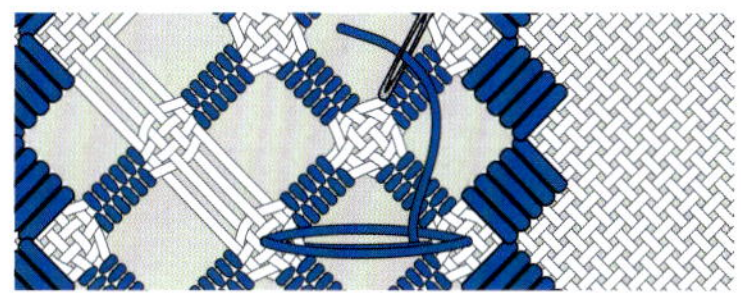

5 Pull the needle through.

❶ *The laced stitches should span the square gently. They should not be too loose or too tight.*

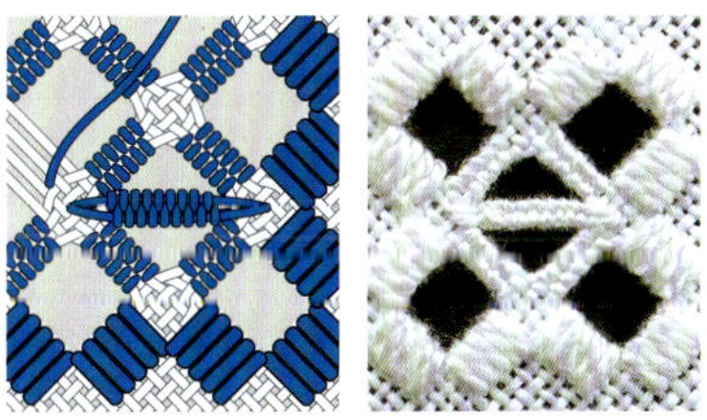

6 Work weaving stitches to fill the bar, keeping one laced thread below the needle, and two above. After completing the bar, bring the thread out ready to continue stitching.

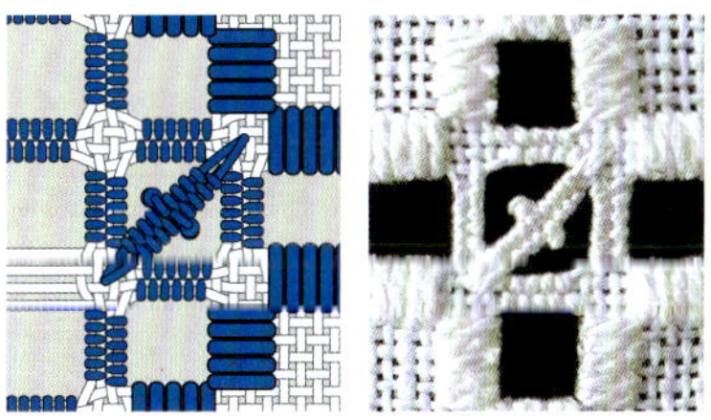

❶ *You can also work picots on the sides of the bar.*

woven petal

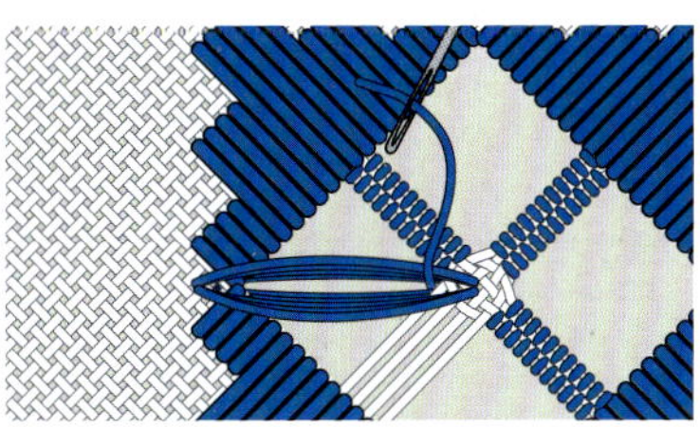

1 In a large square, work similarly to woven diagonals, but use nine foundation stitches rather than the three used for woven diagonals.

❶ *Nine stitches make a suitably heavy base for the wider middle stitches.*

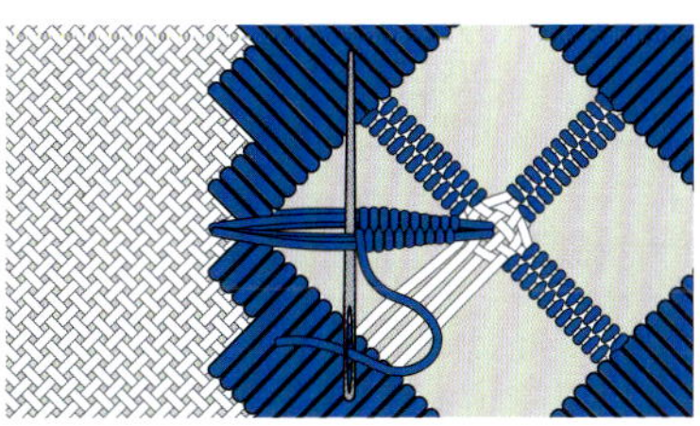

2 Work the first three stitches on each side of the petal very tightly, then carefully and gradually loosen tension to be much wider at the middle.

❶ *Stitches should not be markedly different from the ones beside them.*

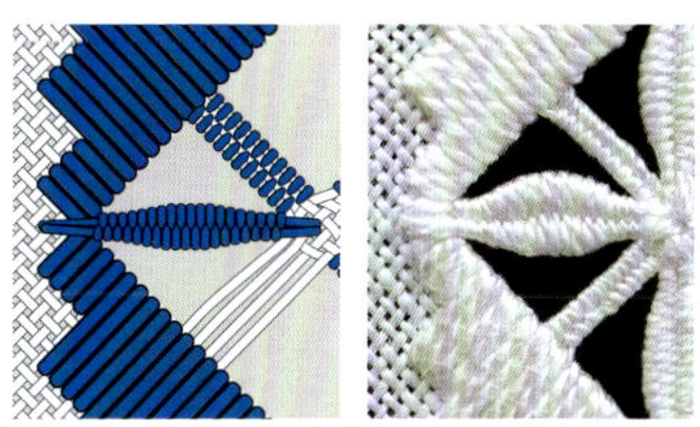

3 Complete the petal by increasing the tension, to make increasingly shorter stitches. Work the last three stitches on each side of the petal really tightly.

❶ *The sides should curve smoothly.*

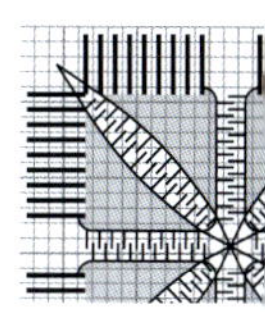

CONTEMPORARY

L

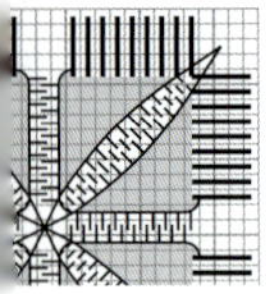

CONTEMPORARY

wide woven petal

This petal differs from the previous one because it is woven across three groups of foundation stitches rather than two.

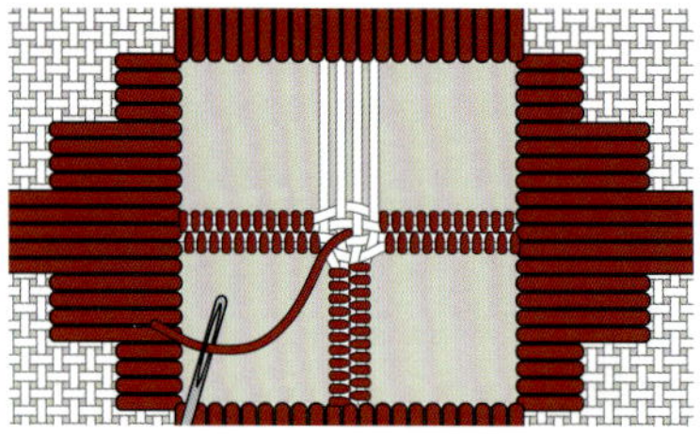

1 In a large square, work three bars ending in the centre. Bring the needle out in the woven square's centre.

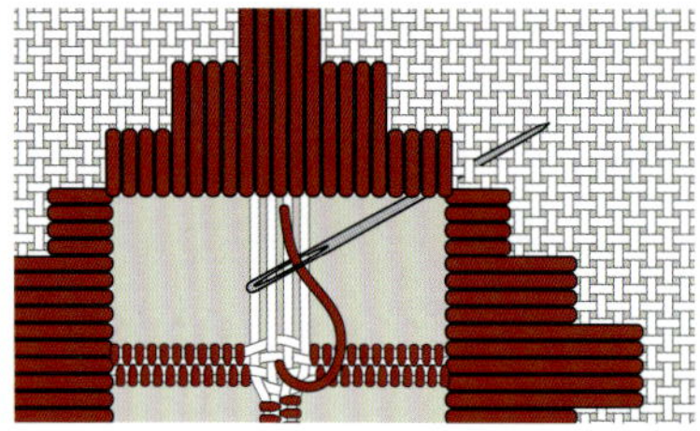

2 In the top right quadrant, bring the needle out in the far corner, two threads away from the cut edges.

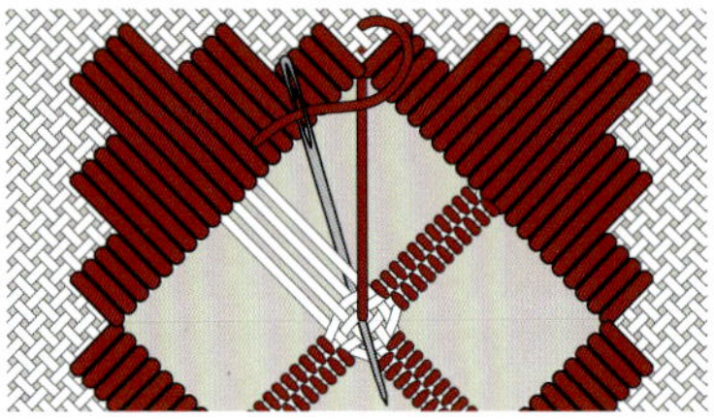

3 Turn the work 45° anticlockwise. Pull the needle through. Tighten the stitch so it lies straight. Bring the needle out in the woven square's centre, inserting it left of the first stitch.

The first stitch will be the tightest, and is the central foundation stitch.

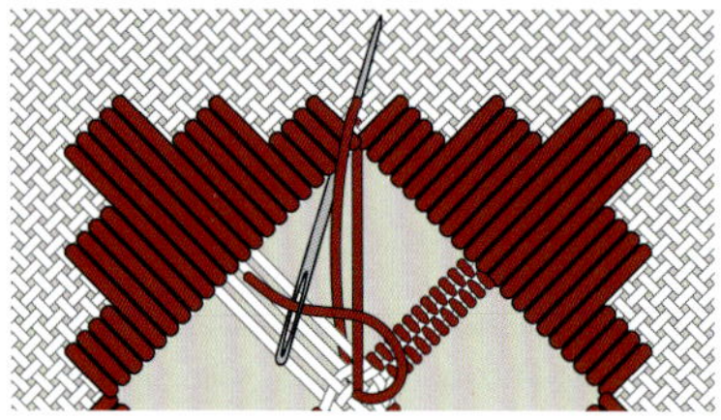

4 Pull the needle through and leave the stitch a little slack. Bring the needle out again in the top corner, inserting left of the first stitch.

The curve of the stitches determines how curved the sides of your petal can be. For wider petals, use longer stitches.

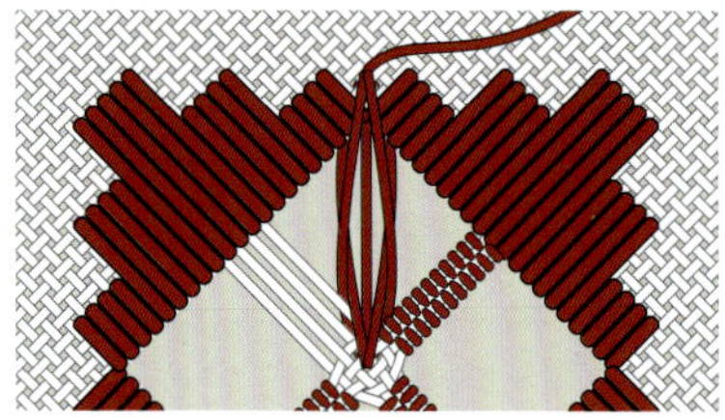

5 Pull the needle through. Make another two stitches with the same tension, on the right-hand side of the first stitch, finishing with the thread coming out in the corner.

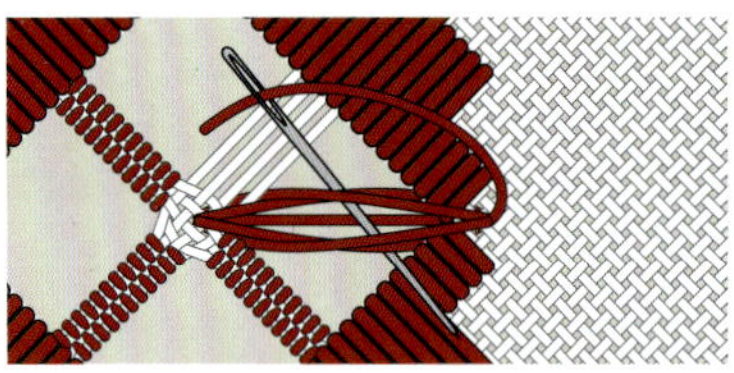

6 Turn the work 90° clockwise. From above, slide the needle under the upper then lower pairs of stitches.

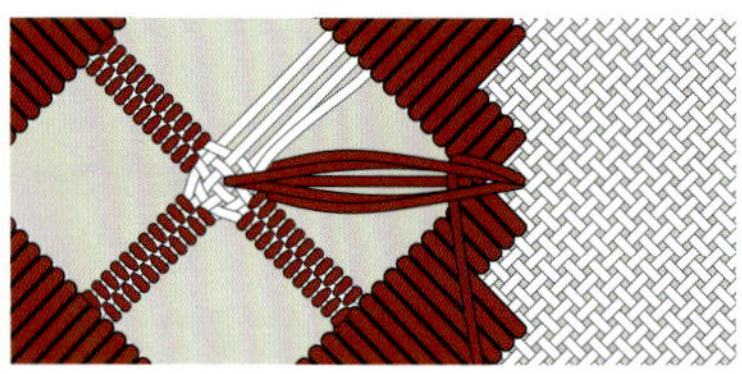

7 Pull the needle through to tighten the stitch against the end of the petal.

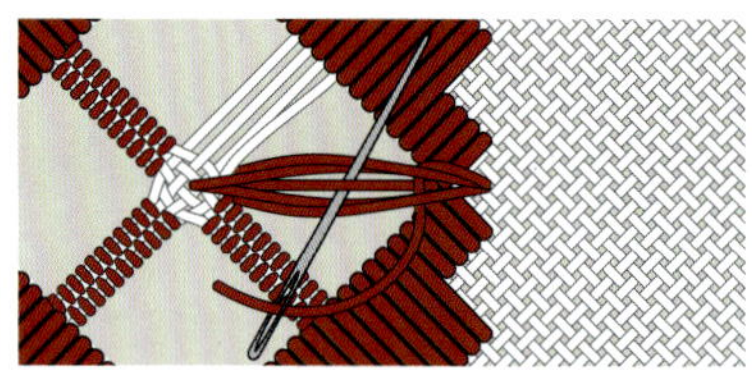

8 From below the petal, slide the needle under the middle stitch.

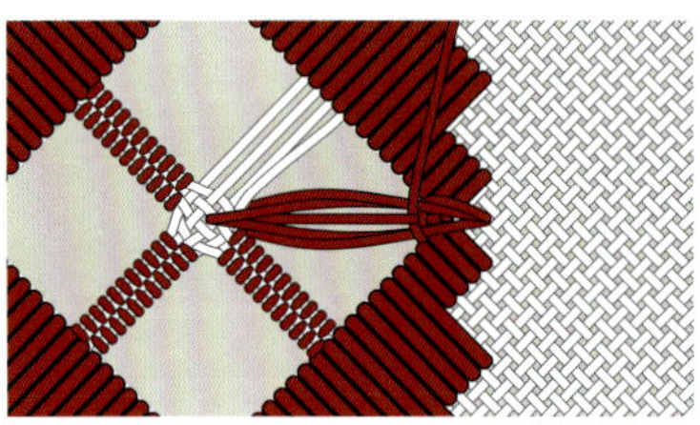

9 Pull the needle through to tighten the stitch.

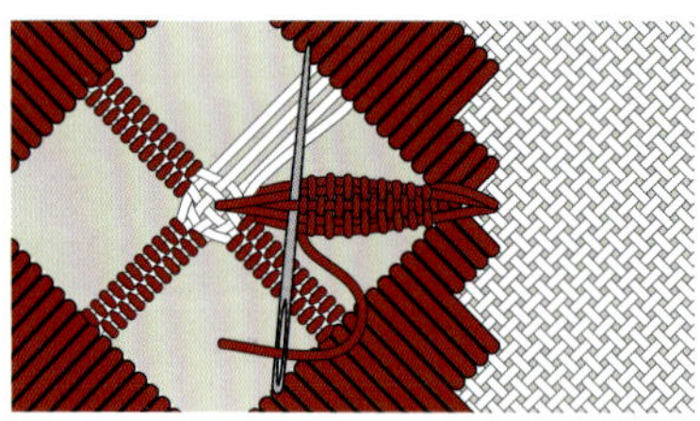

10 Continue weaving. Use tighter tension at the ends, and allow it to relax in the middle to shape the petal.

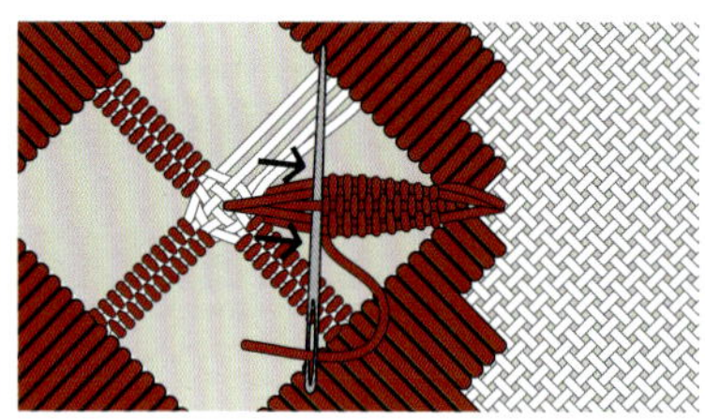

Periodically use the needle to push the stitches back towards the beginning end.

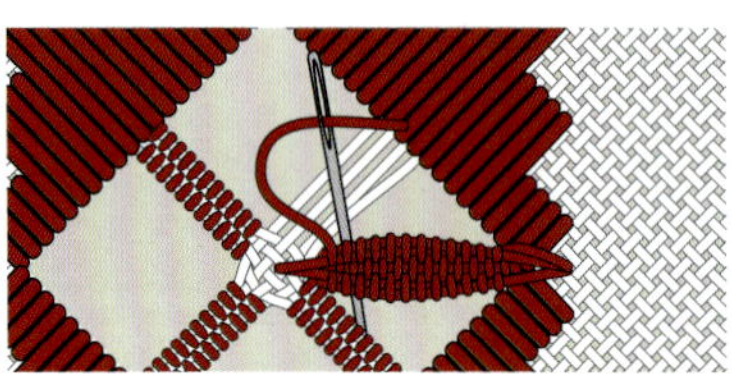

11 To finish the petal, take the needle to the back.

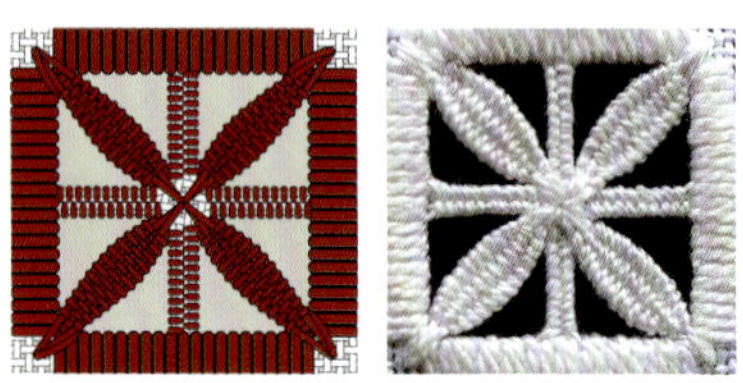

12 Cycle through the steps to work a petal in each quadrant, then weave the final bar.

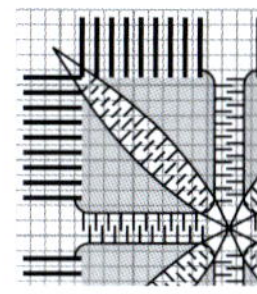

wide woven petal

This petal differs from the previous one because it is woven across three groups of foundation stitches rather than two.

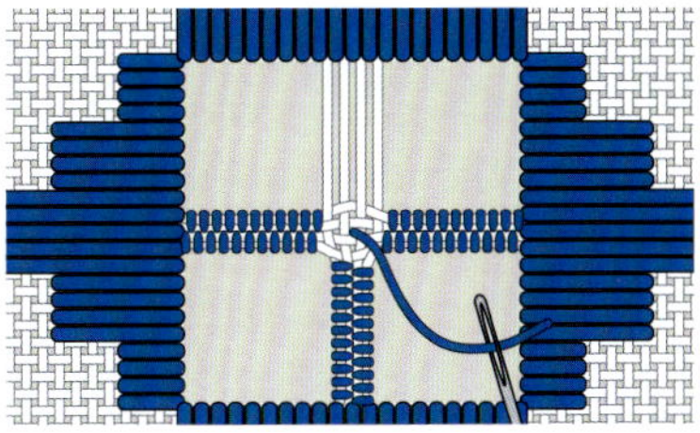

1 In a large square, work three bars ending in the centre. Bring the needle out in the woven square's centre.

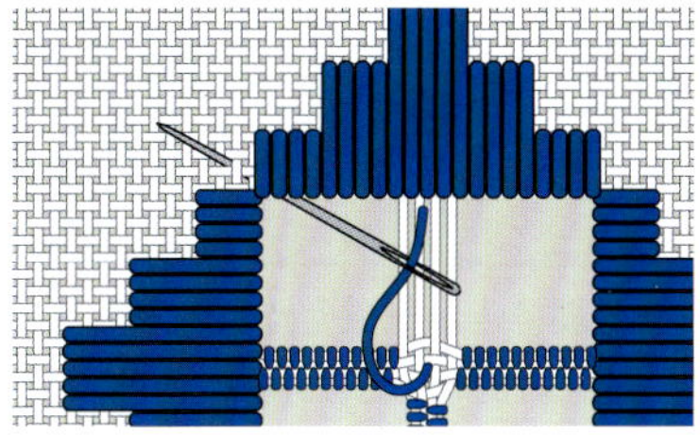

2 In the top left quadrant, bring the needle out in the far corner, two threads away from the cut edges.

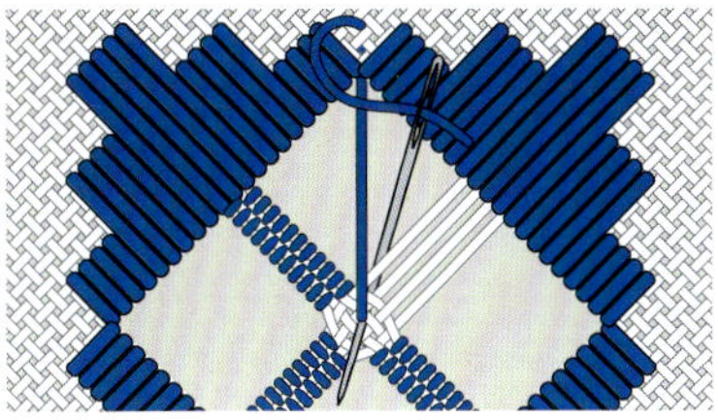

3 Turn the work 45° clockwise. Pull the needle through. Tighten the stitch so it lies straight. Bring the needle out in the woven square's centre, inserting it right of the first stitch.

❶ *The first stitch will be the tightest, and is the central foundation stitch.*

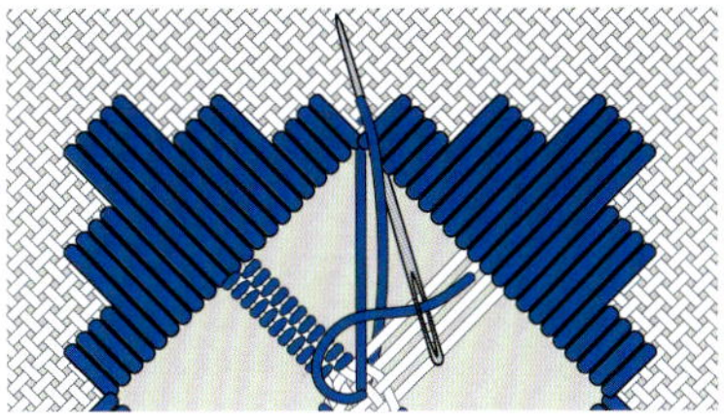

4 Pull the needle through and leave the stitch a little slack. Bring the needle out again in the top corner, inserting right of the first stitch.

❶ *The curve of the stitches determines how curved the sides of your petal can be. For wider petals, use longer stitches.*

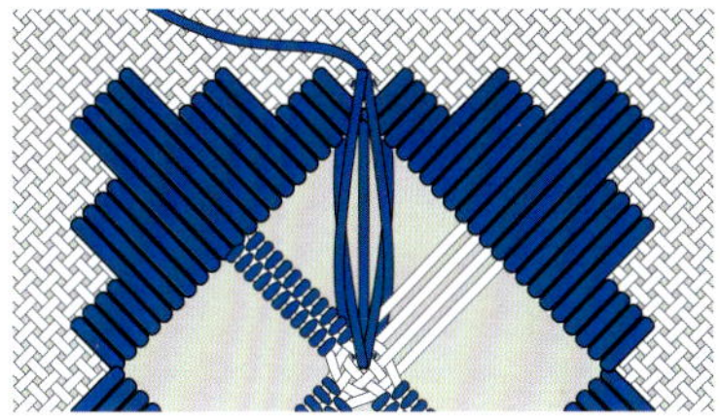

5 Pull the needle through. Make another two stitches with the same tension, on the left-hand side of the first stitch, finishing with the thread coming out in the corner.

6 Turn the work 90° anticlockwise. From above, slide the needle under the upper then lower pairs of stitches.

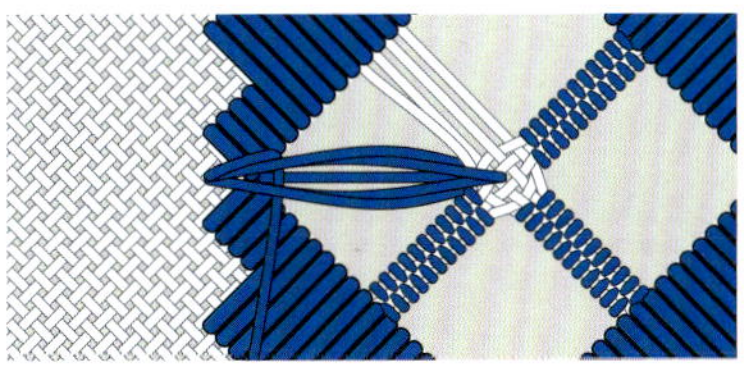

7 Pull the needle through to tighten the stitch against the end of the petal.

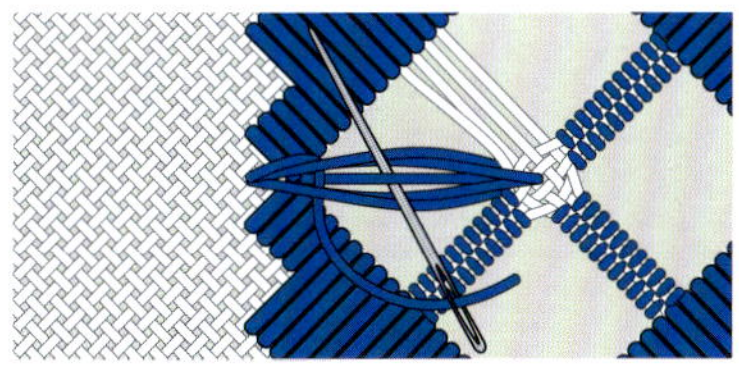

8 From below the petal, slide the needle under the middle stitch.

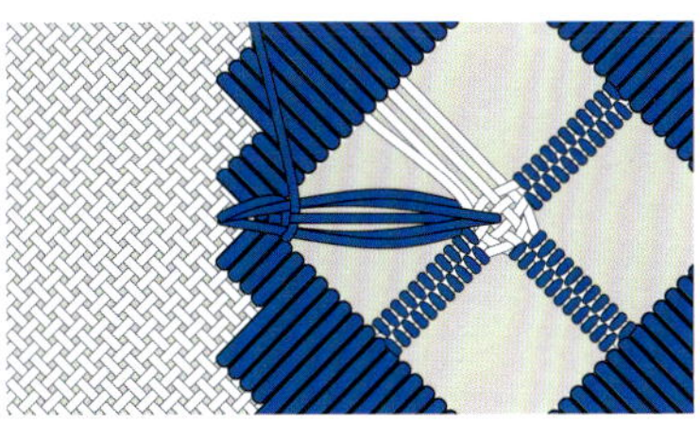

9 Pull the needle through to tighten the stitch.

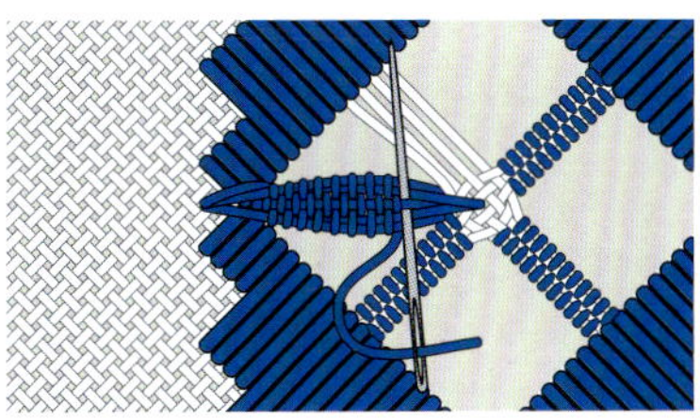

10 Continue weaving. Use tighter tension at the ends, and allow it to relax in the middle to shape the petal.

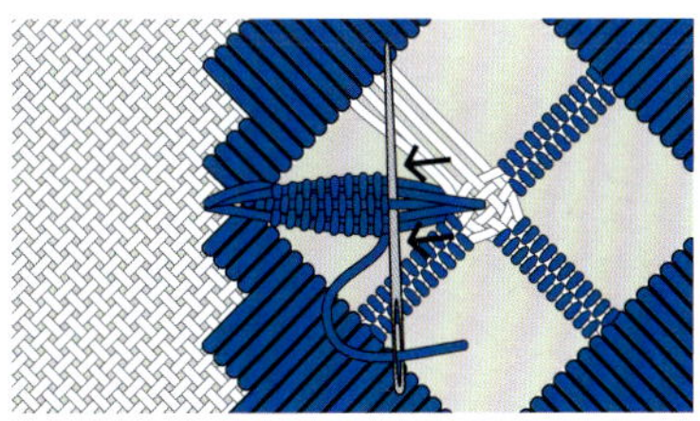

❶ *Periodically use the needle to push the stitches back towards the beginning end.*

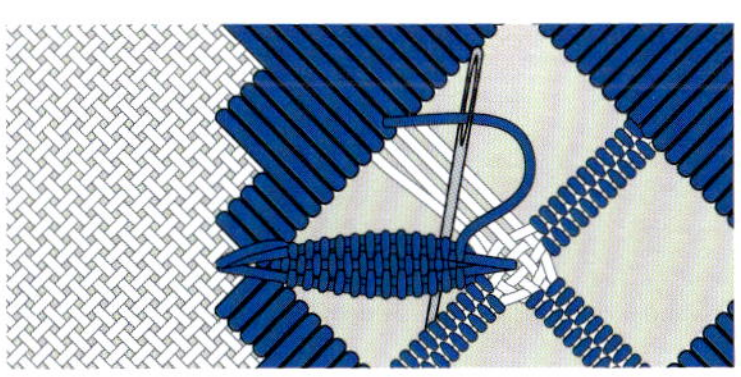

11 To finish the petal, take the needle to the back.

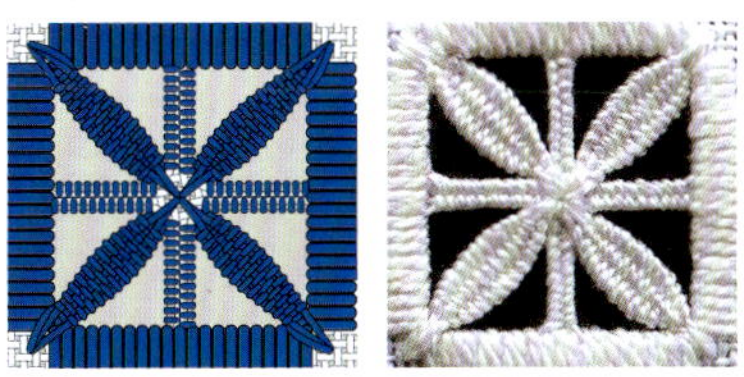

12 Cycle through the steps to work a petal in each quadrant, then weave the final bar.

twists

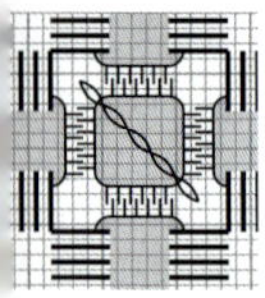

TRADITIONAL

A twisted diagonal stitch can be worked by itself, or another one can be added to make an X.

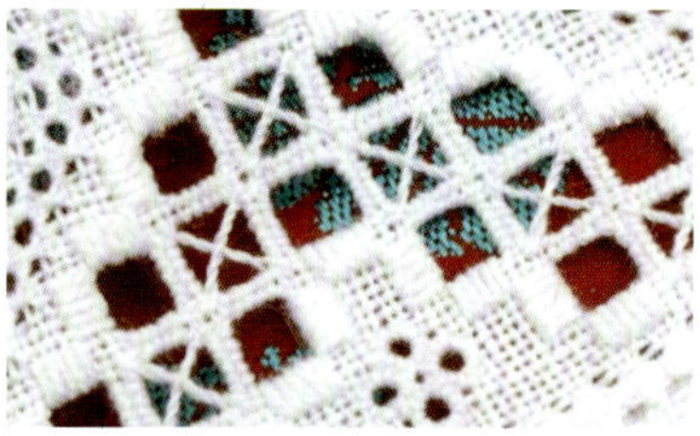

twisted spoke *also known as twisted diagonal*

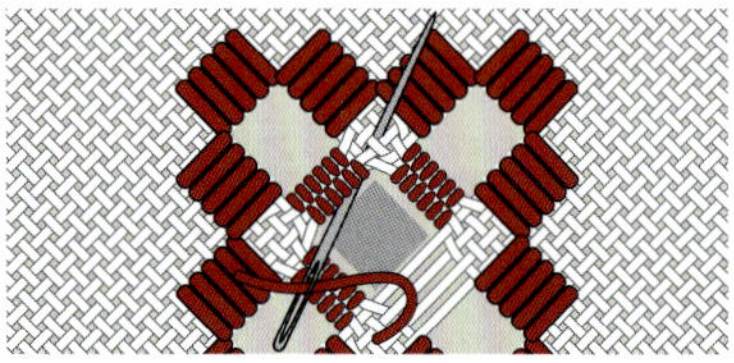

1 After weaving the square's third side, bring the needle out in the next woven square's centre. Turn the work so that the thread emerges at the bottom. Insert the needle in the centre back of the opposite woven square.

2 Pull the needle through. Slide the needle under the stitch, from the left.

❶ *If you're not going to make this an X, you can work the spoke after the third or fourth side.*

3 Pull the thread so that the stitches intertwine. Slide the needle under the stitch again, lower down, from the left.

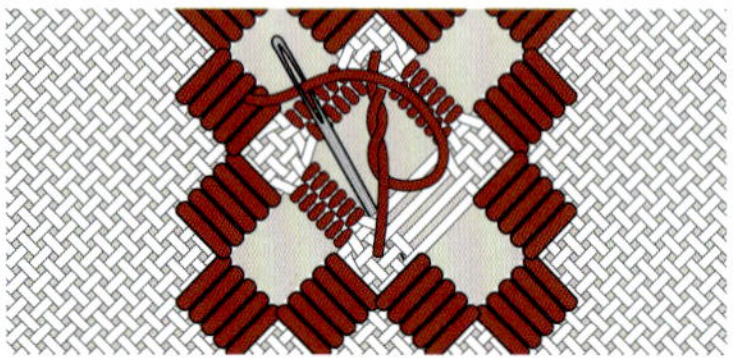

4 Left of the twisted spoke, take the needle through to the back.

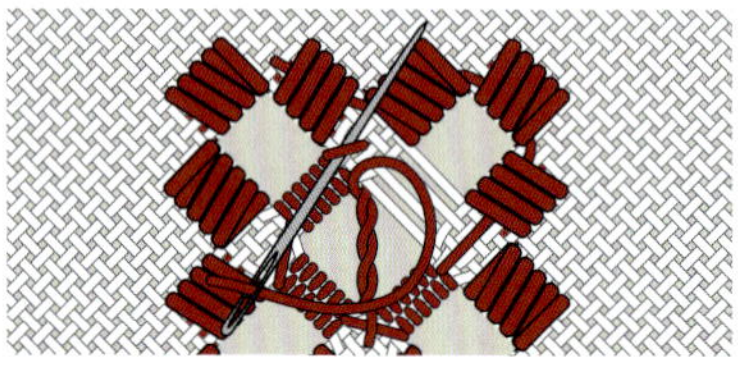

5 Pull to intertwine the stitches. On the back, take the needle under the thread leading to the twisted spoke.

❶ *This keeps the thread twisted properly.*

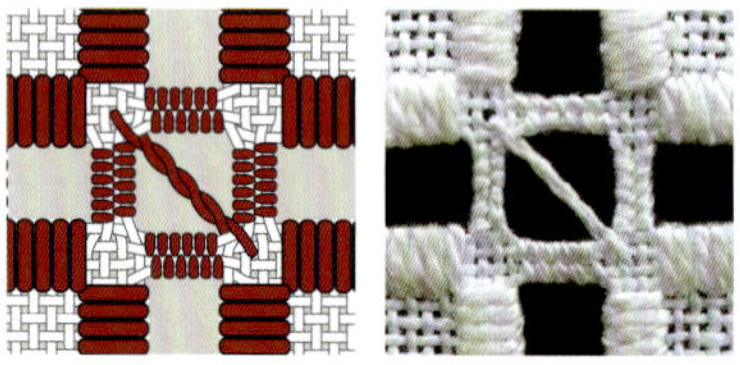

6 Bring the needle out ready for the next bar, and keep on stitching.

❶ *For a twisted spoke sloping the other way, work it after either the second or fourth woven bars, preferably the fourth.*

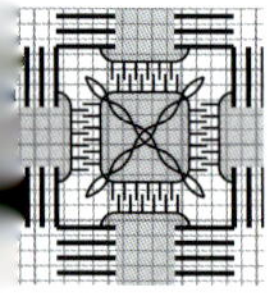

TRADITIONAL

twisted X

After stitching the first, another spoke can be added to make it a twisted X.

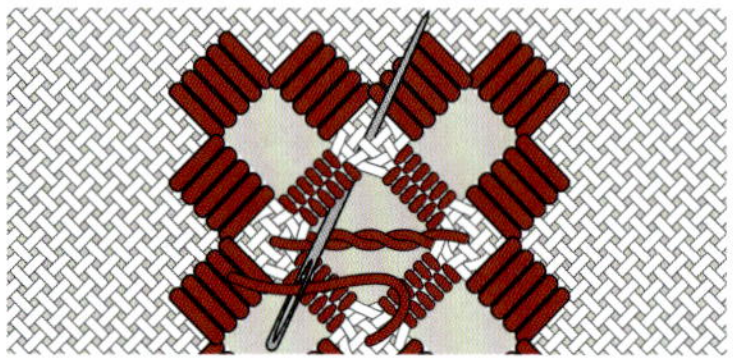

1 After stitching a spoke and a bar, bring the thread out in the next corner. Turn the work so the thread is at the bottom. Take the needle over the spoke. Insert it in the centre back of the opposite woven square.

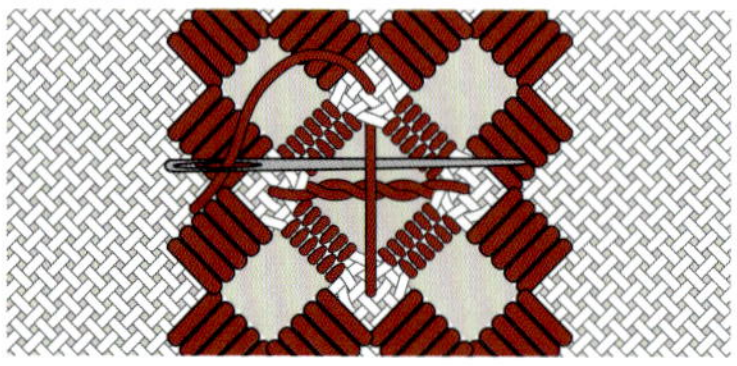

2 Pull the needle through. Slide it under the stitch, from the left.

3 From above left, slide the needle under the crossed stitches in the centre.

4 Pull the thread so that the stitches intertwine. Insert the needle to the left of the spoke, below the cross.

5 On the back, take the needle under the thread leading to the twisted spoke.

❶ *This keeps the thread twisted properly.*

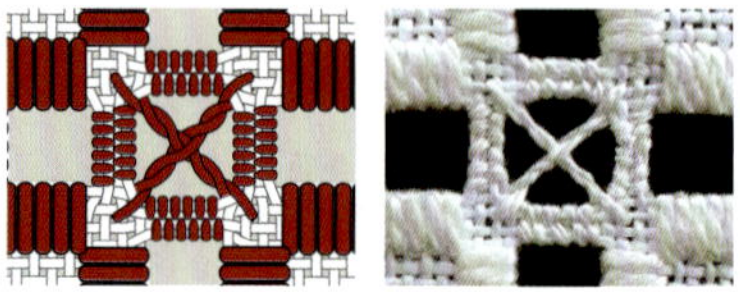

6 Bring the needle out ready for the next bar, and keep on stitching.

twists

A twisted diagonal stitch can be worked by itself, or another one can be added to make an X.

twisted spoke *also known as twisted diagonal*

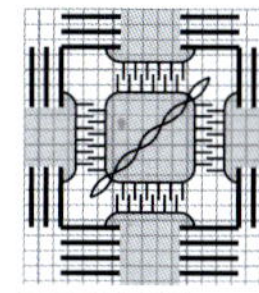

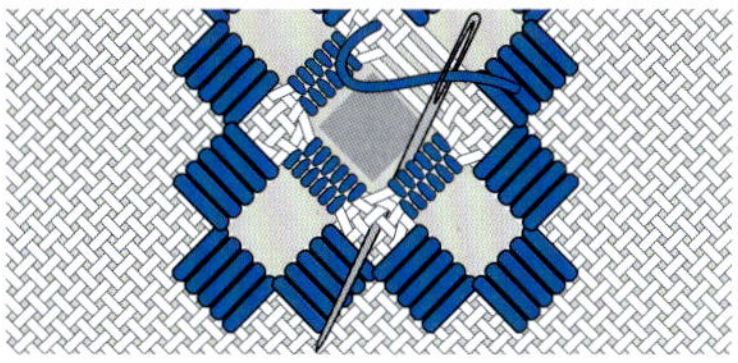

1 After weaving the square's third side, bring the needle out in the next woven square's centre. Turn the work so that the thread emerges at the top. Insert the needle in the centre back of the opposite woven square.

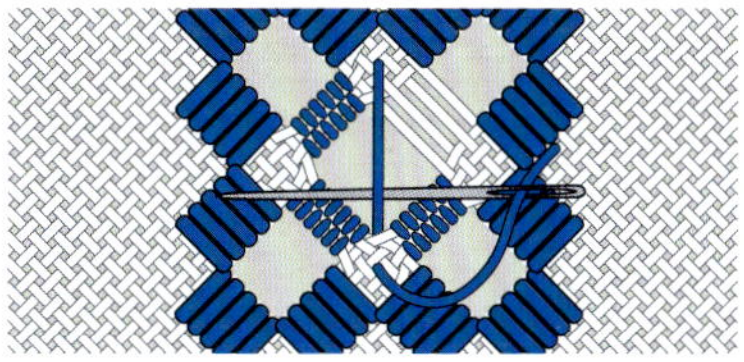

2 Pull the needle through. Slide the needle under the stitch, from the right.

❶ *If you're not going to make this an X, you can work the spoke after the third or fourth side.*

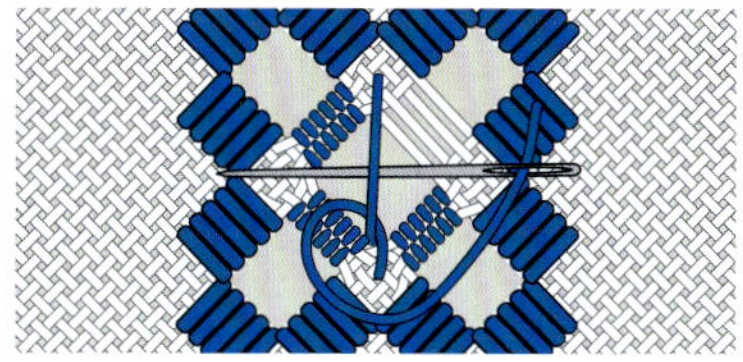

3 Pull the thread so that the stitches intertwine. Slide the needle under the stitch again, a little higher, from the right.

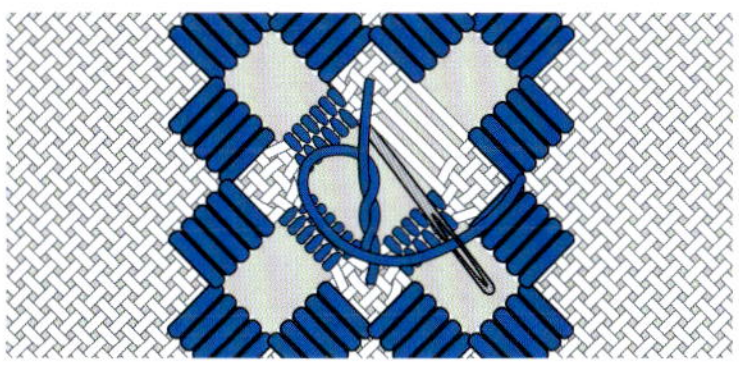

4 Right of the twisted spoke, take the needle through to the back.

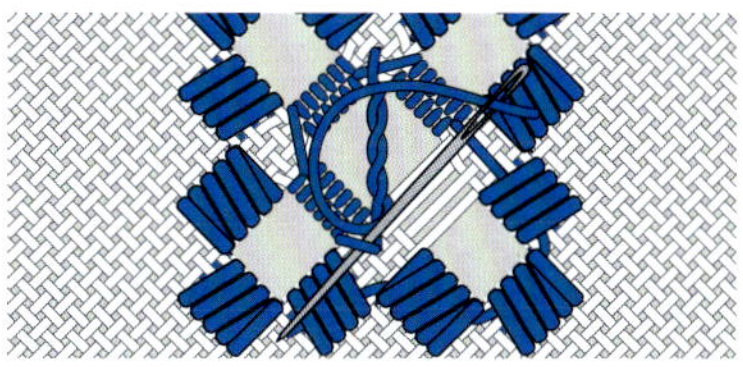

5 Pull to intertwine the stitches. On the back, take the needle under the thread leading to the twisted spoke.

❶ *This keeps the thread twisted properly.*

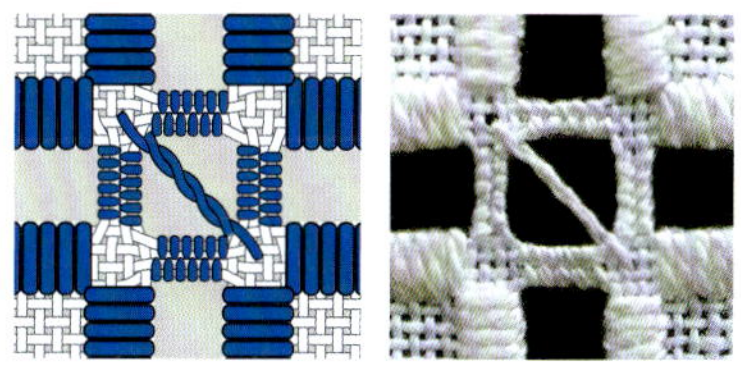

6 Bring the needle out ready for the next bar, and keep on stitching.

❶ *For a twisted spoke sloping the other way, work it after either the second or fourth woven bars, preferably the fourth.*

twisted X

After stitching the first, another spoke can be added to make it a twisted X.

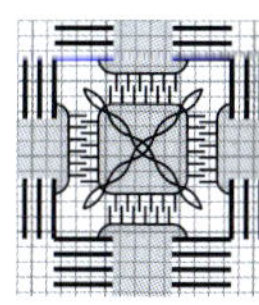

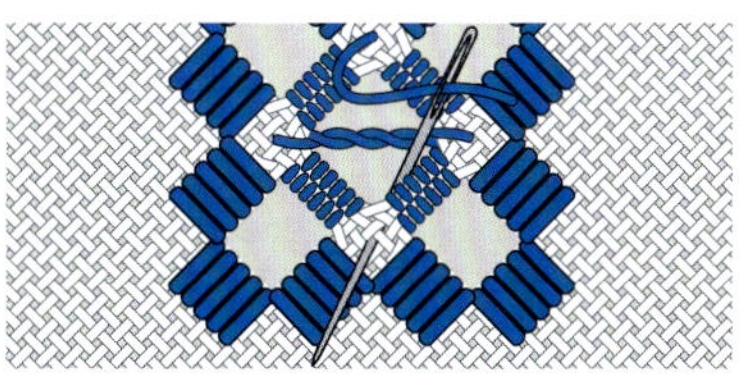

1 After stitching a spoke and a bar, bring the thread out in the next corner. Turn the work so the thread is at the top. Take the needle over the spoke. Insert it in the centre back of the opposite woven square.

2 Pull the needle through. Slide it under the stitch, from the right.

3 From below right, slide the needle under the crossed stitches in the centre.

4 Pull the thread so that the stitches intertwine. Insert the needle to the right of the spoke, above the cross.

5 On the back, take the needle under the thread leading to the twisted spoke.

❶ *This keeps the thread twisted properly.*

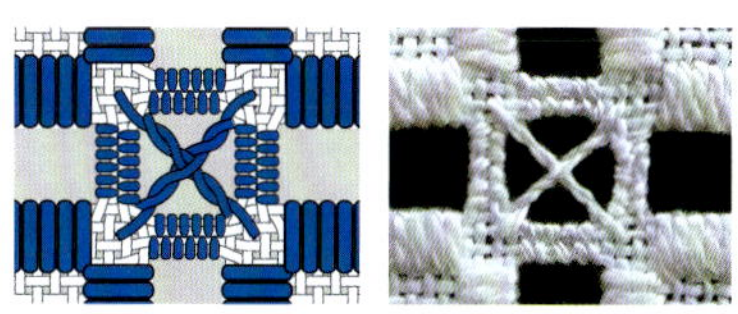

6 Bring the needle out ready for the next bar, and keep on stitching.

twisted cross

This looks similar to a dove's eye, but is constructed like twisted spokes.

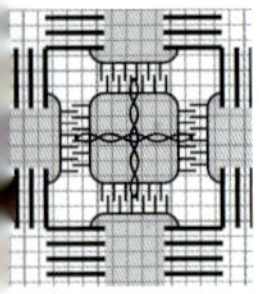

TRADITIONAL

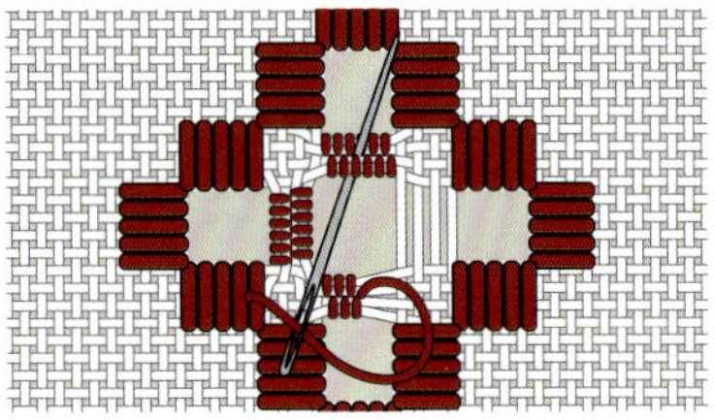

1 Stitch half of the third side of the square where the twisted cross will be worked. From below, insert the needle in the centre back of the bar on the opposite side of the square.

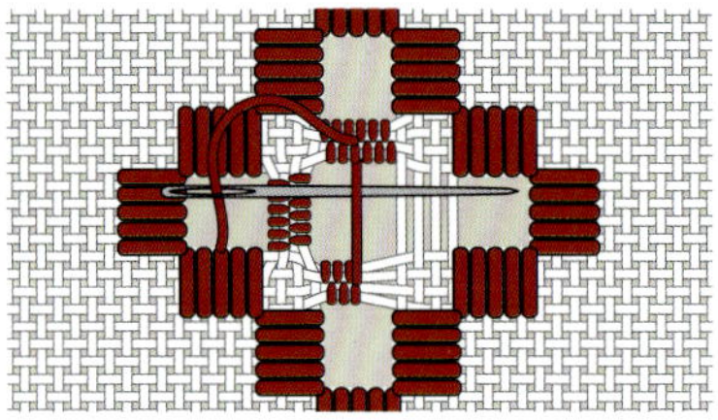

2 Pull the needle through. Slide the needle under the stitch, from the left.

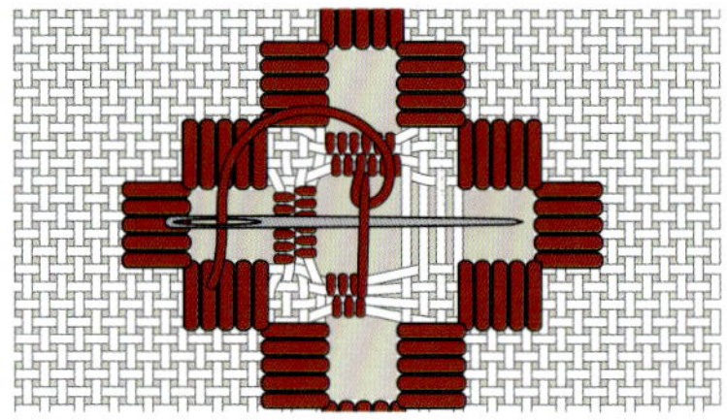

3 Slide the needle under the stitch again, lower down, from the left.

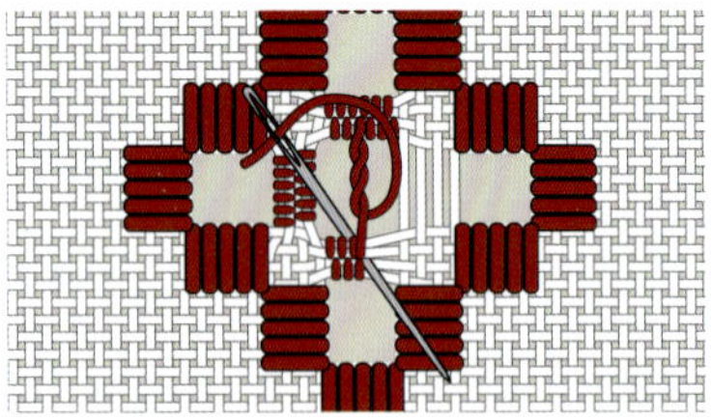

4 Left of the twisted spoke, take the needle to the back. Bring it out in the bar, ready to continue.

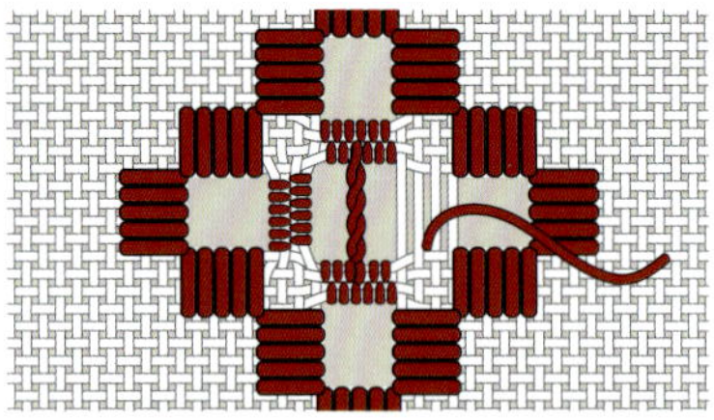

5 Pull the thread so that the stitches intertwine. Complete the bar.

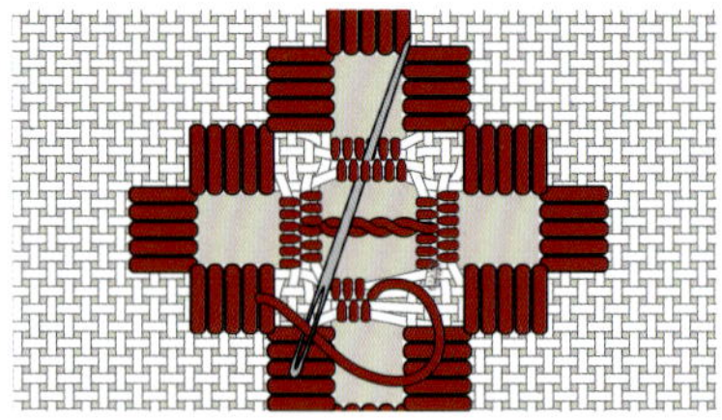

6 Turn the work 90° clockwise. Work half of the next bar. Take the needle over the spoke. From below, insert it in the centre back of the bar on the opposite side of the square.

❶ *If the twisted cross is worked as part of a large drawn thread area, it may be that you do not return to work the second twisted spoke for some time.*

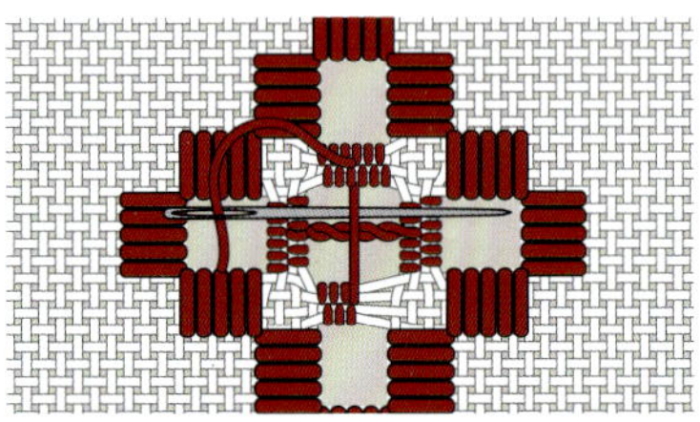

7 Pull the needle through. Slide the needle under the stitch, from the left.

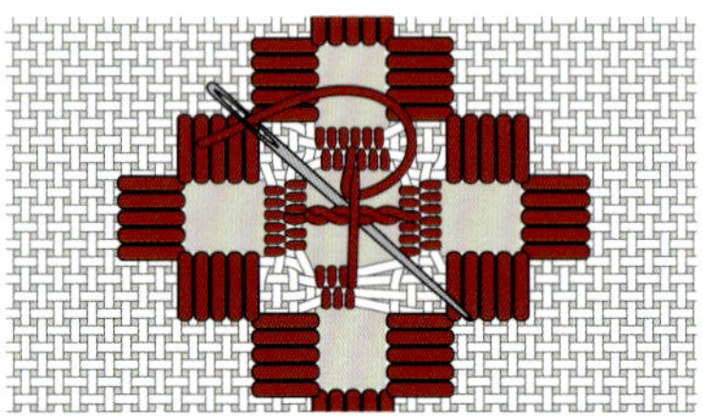

8 Slide the needle under the crossing stitches in the centre, from above left.

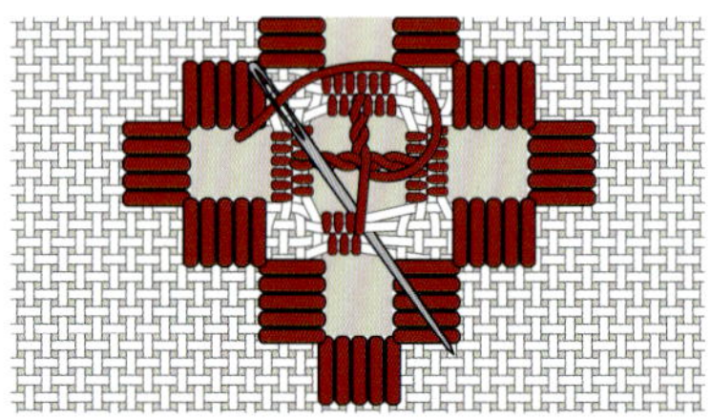

9 Pull the thread so that the stitches intertwine. Left of the twisted spoke, take the needle through to the back, and bring it out in the bar, ready to keep stitching.

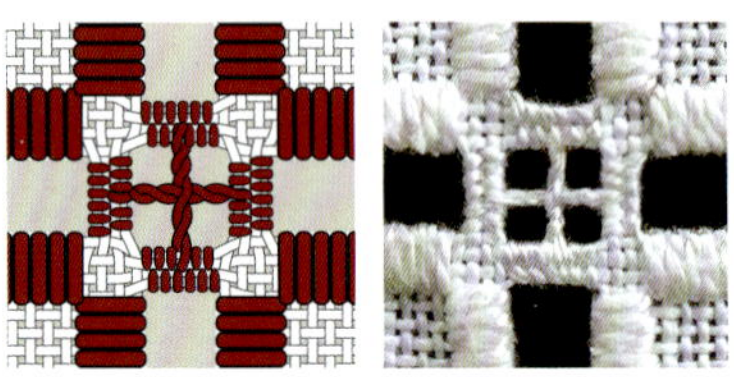

10 Complete the bar.

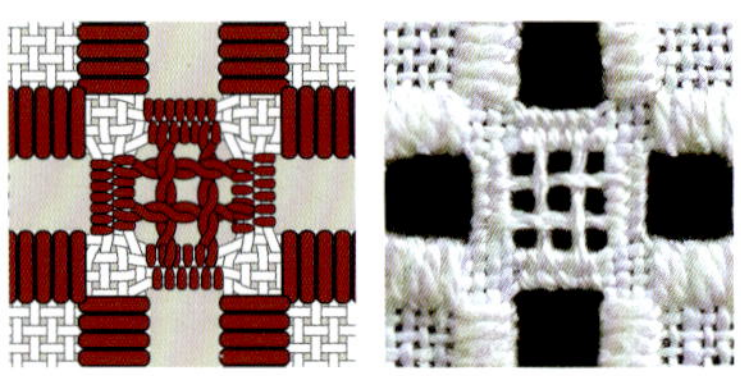

❶ *This variation, Double Twisted Cross, has multiple twisted spokes and which overlap in a special manner rather than being interlocked.*

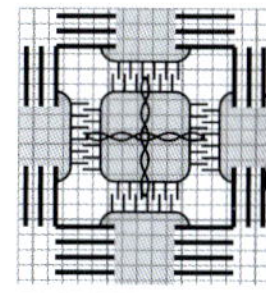

twisted cross

This looks similar to a dove's eye, but is constructed like twisted spokes.

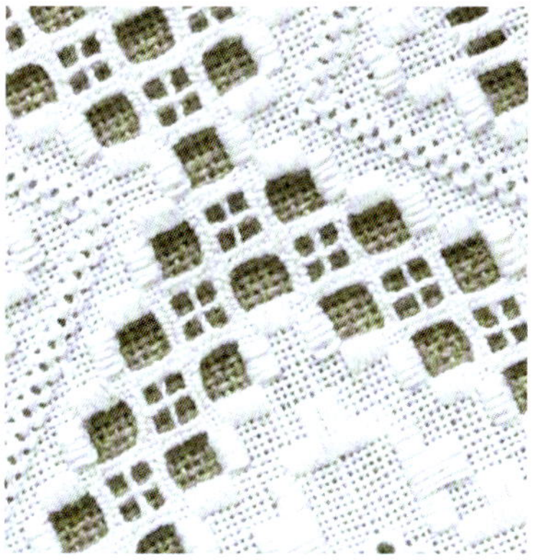

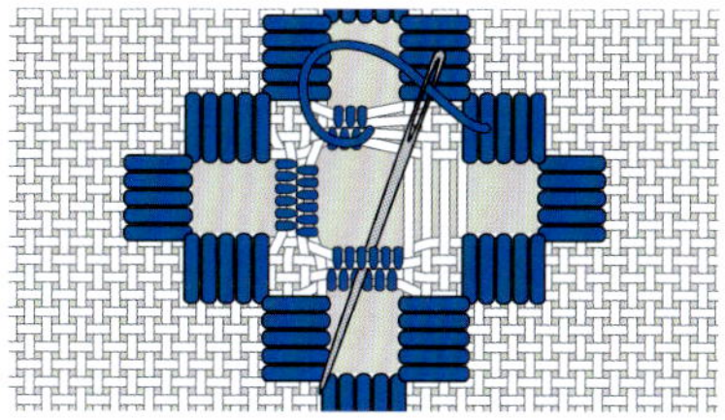

1 Stitch half of the third side of the square where the twisted cross will be worked. From above, insert the needle in the centre back of the bar on the opposite side of the square.

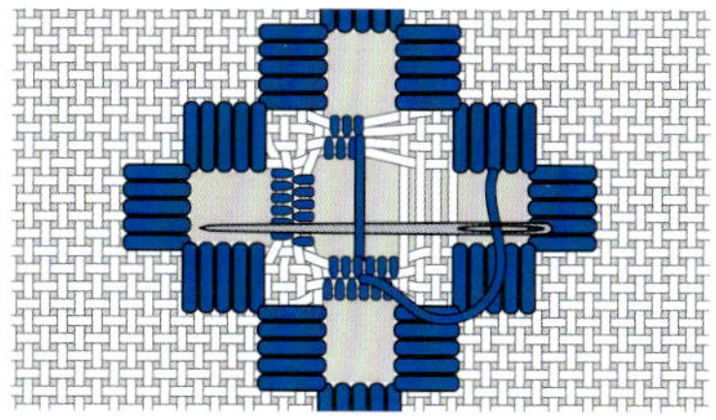

2 Pull the needle through. Slide the needle under the stitch, from the right.

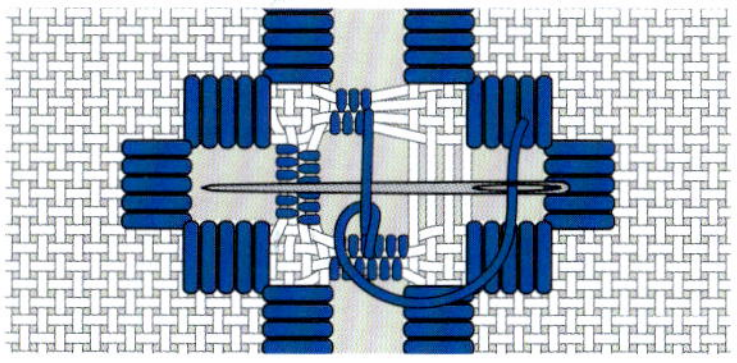

3 Slide the needle under the stitch again, a little higher, from the right.

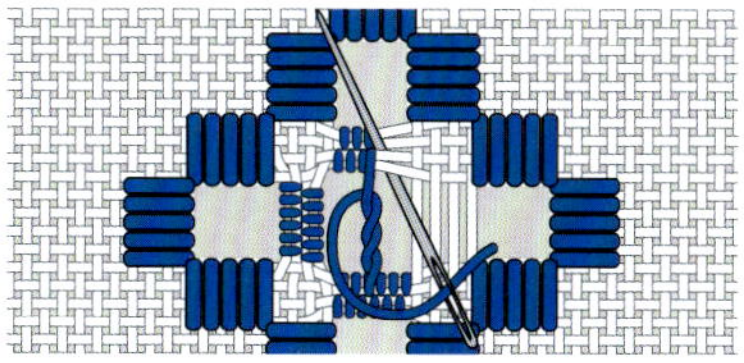

4 Right of the twisted spoke, take the needle through to the back, and bring it out in the bar, ready to keep stitching.

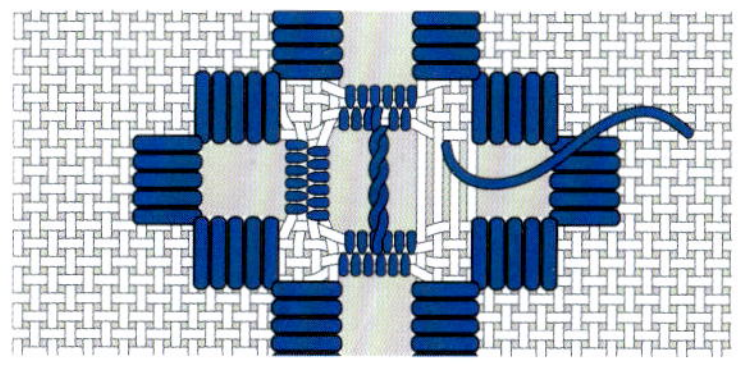

5 Pull the thread so that the stitches intertwine. Complete the bar.

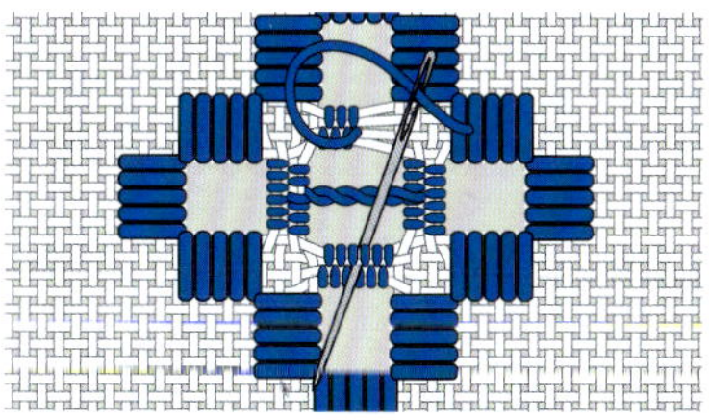

6 Turn the work 90° anticlockwise. Work half of the next bar. Take the needle over the spoke. From above, insert it in the centre back of the bar on the opposite side of the square.

❶ *If the twisted cross is worked as part of a large drawn thread area, it may be that you do not return to work the second twisted spoke for some time.*

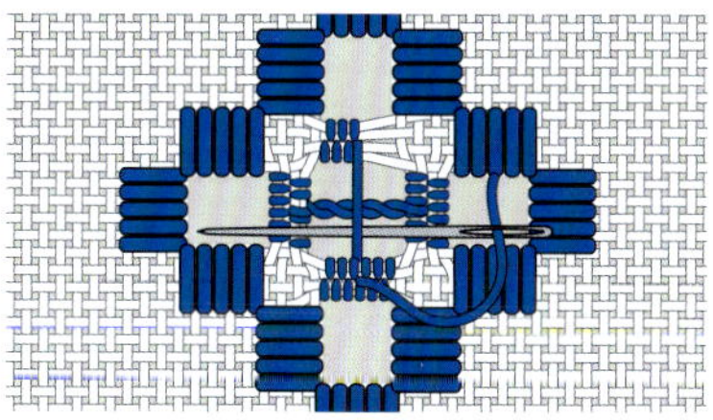

7 Pull the needle through. Slide the needle under the stitch, from the right.

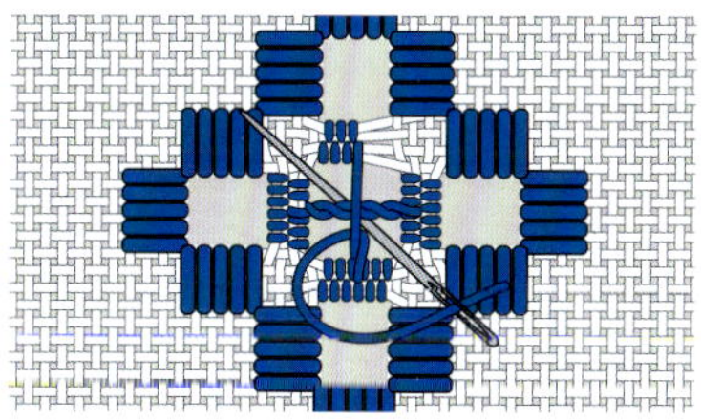

8 Slide the needle under the crossing stitches in the centre, from below right.

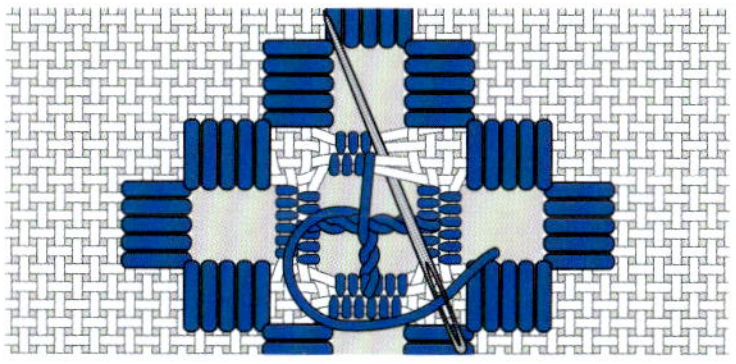

9 Pull the thread so that the stitches intertwine. Take the needle through to the back, just right of the twisted spoke, and bring it out in the bar, ready to keep stitching.

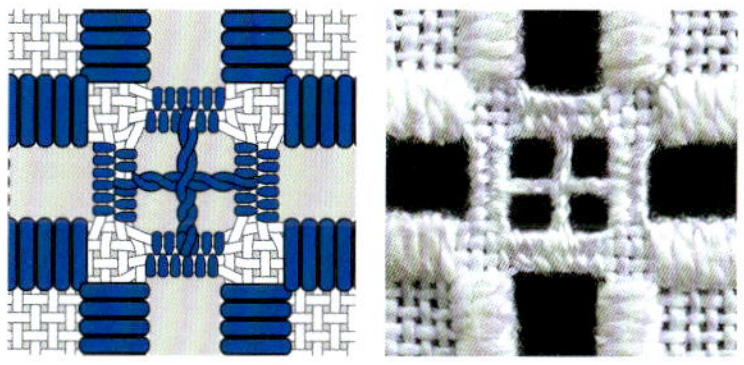

10 Complete the bar.

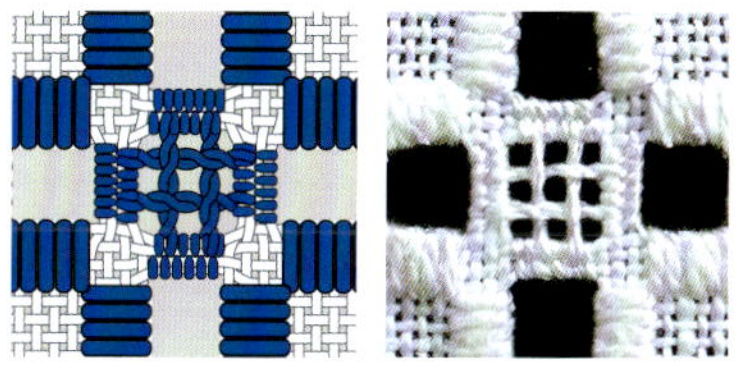

❶ *This variation, Double Twisted Cross, has multiple twisted spokes and which overlap in a special manner rather than being interlocked.*

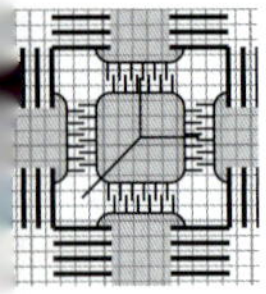

CONTEMPORARY

twisted Y

also called divided branches

This stitch is shown worked in a regular sized square, but can be worked in larger ones or other shapes. They can be worked singly or in four quadrants together. They are often used in combination with other stitches.

❶ *Usually you would work a filling stitch as late as possible during the weaving sequence, however, depending on where you want the bottom of the Y, you may need to work it earlier in the sequence than normal. This may mean stitching into as yet unwoven bars.*

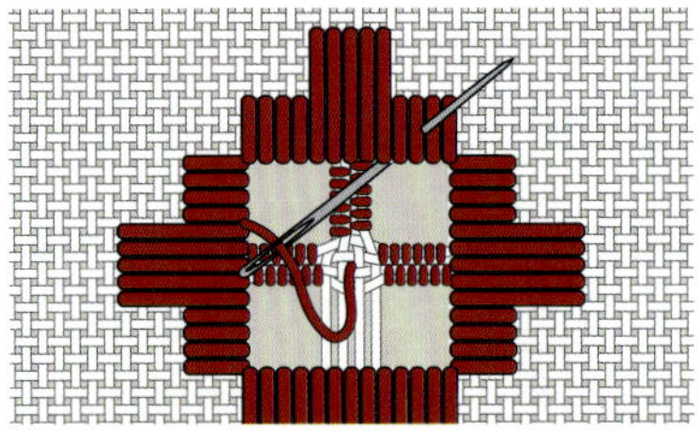

1 Work three bars and bring the needle out in the centre of the woven square. Bring the needle out of the left side opposite, two stitches from the corner, and two fabric threads from the cut edge.

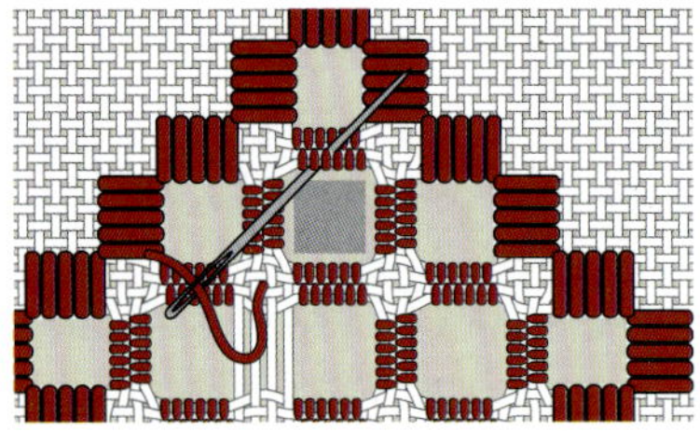

❶ *If working in the middle of an area of cutwork, bring the needle out centrally in the woven bar.*

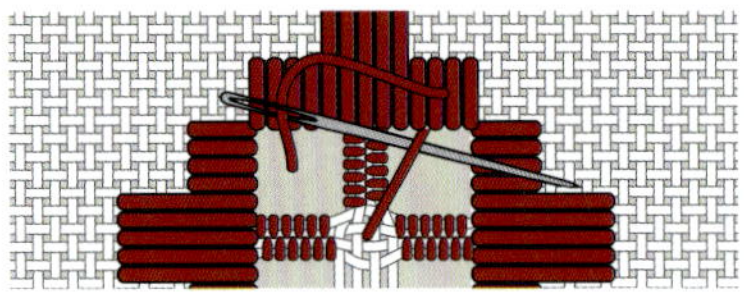

2 Pull the needle through. Slide the needle under the diagonal stitch, from left to right.

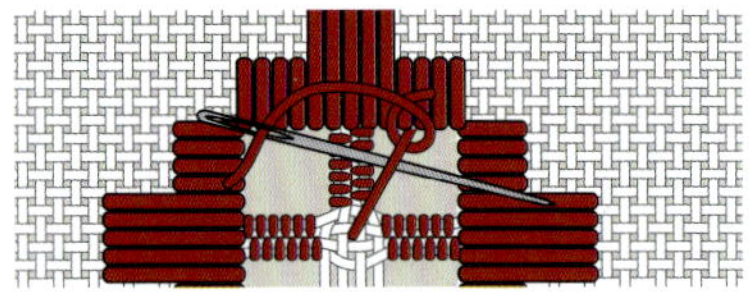

3 Moving down, slide the needle under the diagonal stitch again, then pull to intertwine the stitches.

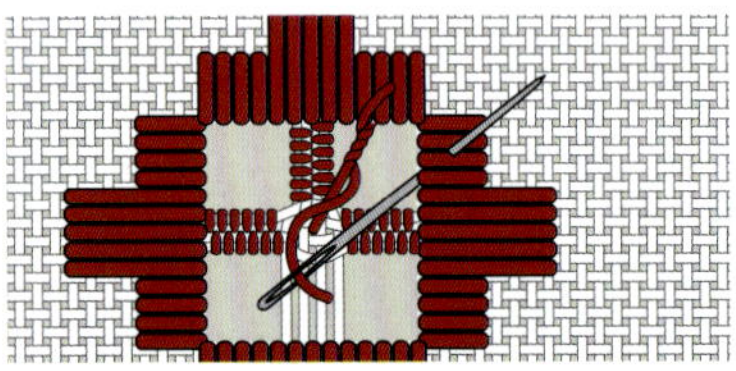

4 Bring the needle out halfway across the next side, two stitches down.

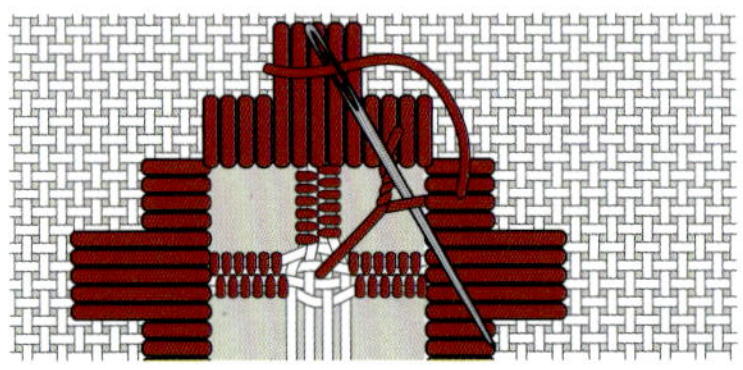

5 Pull the needle through. Slide the needle under the stitch, from above.

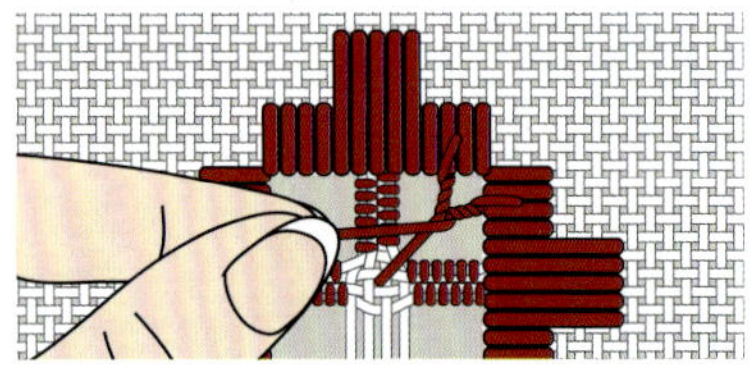

6 Slide the needle under again and pull to intertwine the stitches.

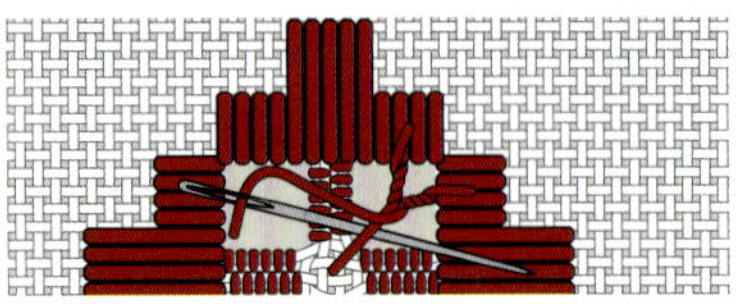

7 Slide the needle under the stem of the Y from the left.

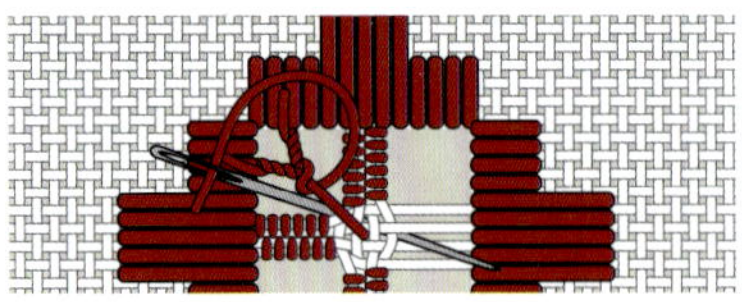

8 Turn the work 90° anticlockwise. Insert the needle below the Y and bring it out ready to keep stitching.

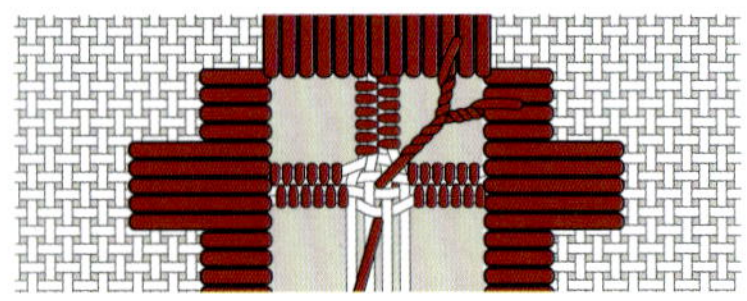

9 Pull the thread to intertwine the stitches. Continue to stitch as required.

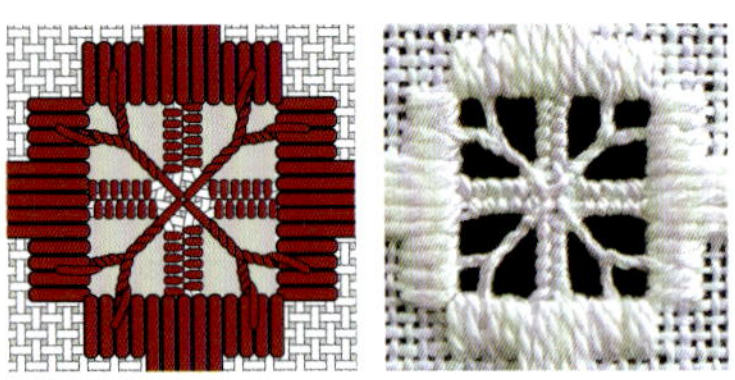

❶ *Work the motif in the other corners if required.*

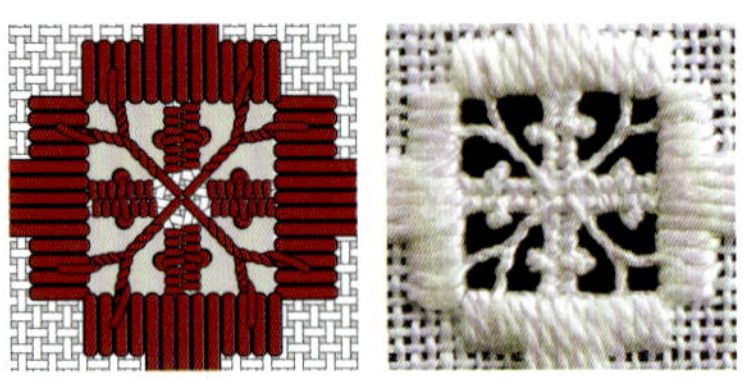

❶ *This variation has picots on the woven bars.*

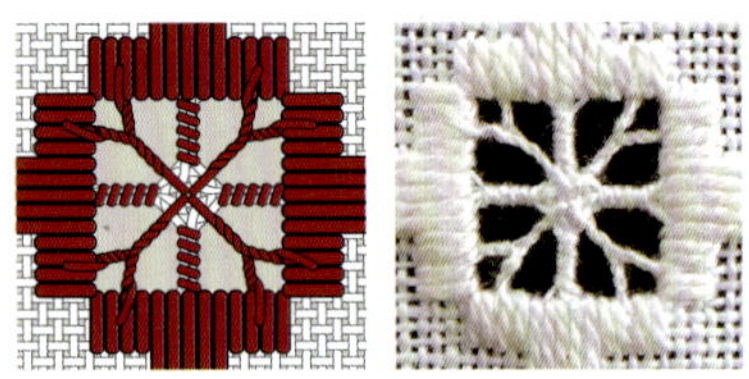

❶ *This variation has wrapped bars instead of woven bars.*

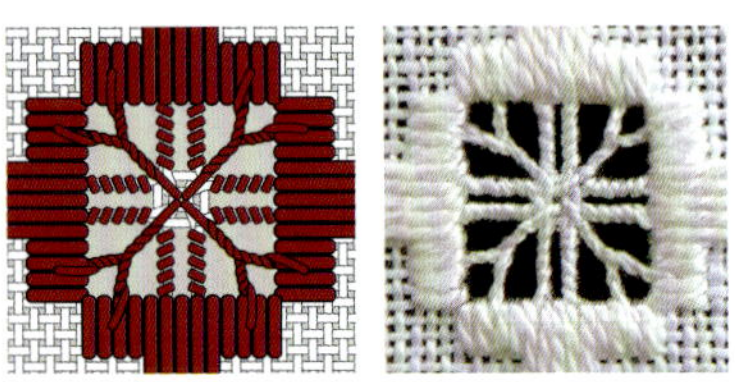

❶ *This variation has divided wrapped bars instead of woven bars.*

twisted Y

also called divided branches

This stitch is shown worked in a regular sized square, but can be worked in larger ones or other shapes. They can be worked singly or in four quadrants together. They are often used in combination with other stitches.

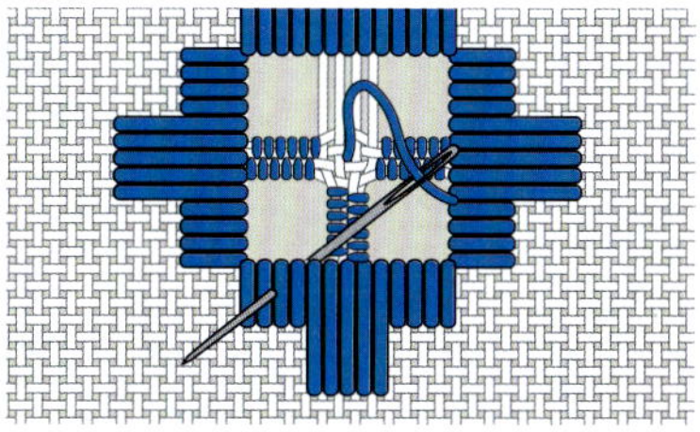

1 Work three bars and bring the needle out in the centre of the woven square. Bring the needle out of the lower side opposite, two stitches from the corner, and two fabric threads from the cut edge.

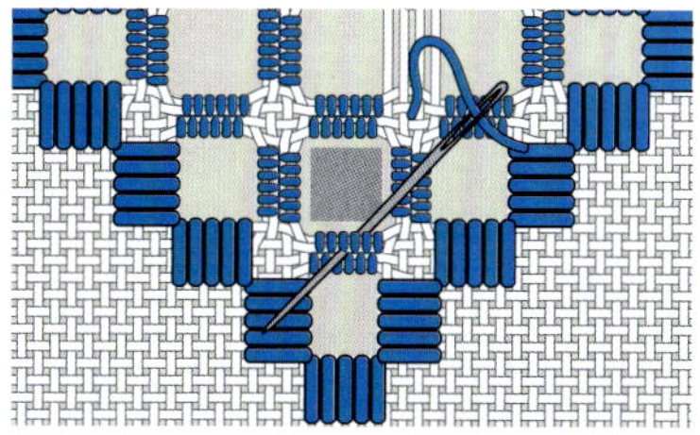

❶ *If working in the middle of an area of cutwork, bring the needle out centrally in the woven bar.*

R

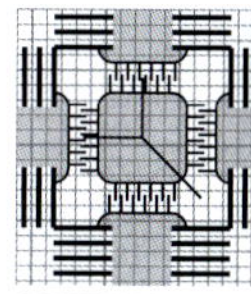

CONTEMPORARY

❶ *Usually you would work a filling stitch as late as possible during the weaving sequence, however, depending on where you want the bottom of the Y, you may need to work it earlier in the sequence than normal. This may mean stitching into as yet unwoven bars.*

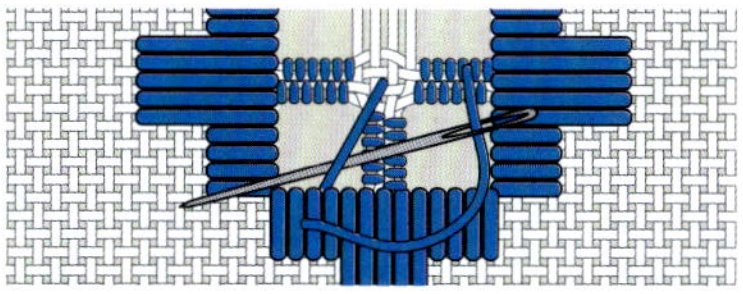

2 Pull the needle through. Slide the needle under the diagonal stitch, from the right.

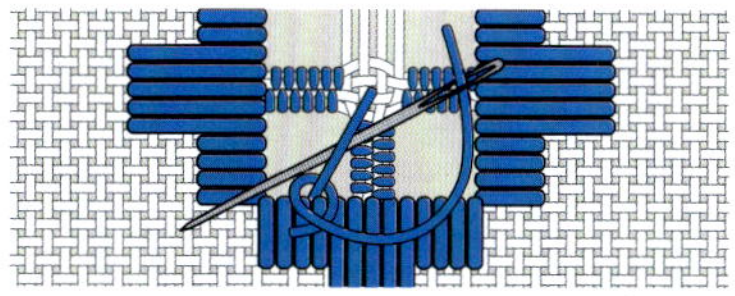

3 Moving up, slide the needle under the diagonal stitch again, then pull to intertwine the stitches.

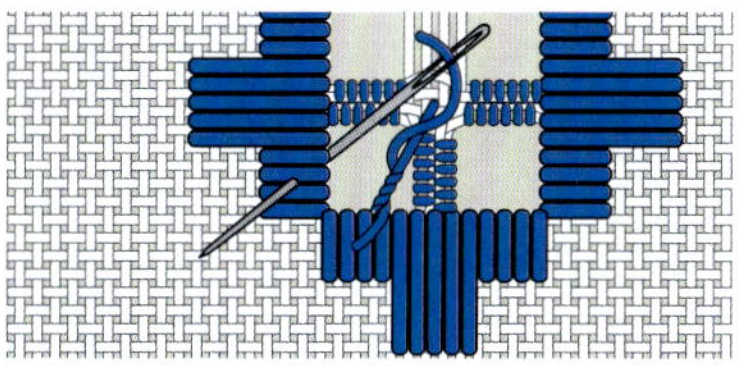

4 Bring the needle out in the next side, halfway across, two stitches up.

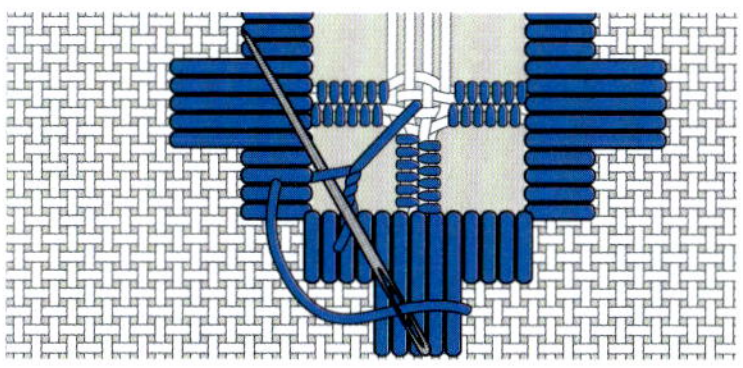

5 Pull the needle through. Slide the needle under the stitch, from below.

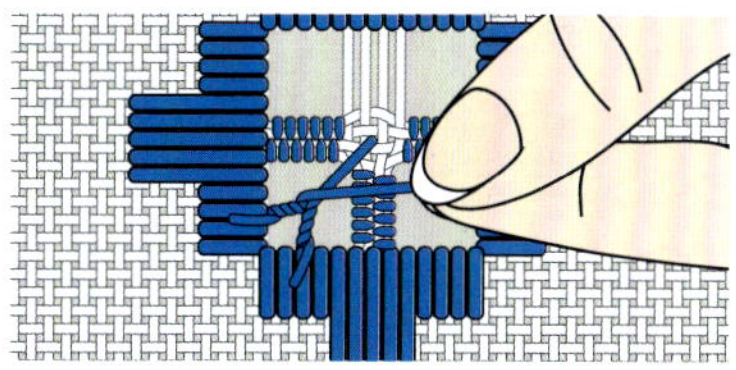

6 Slide the needle under again and pull to intertwine the stitches.

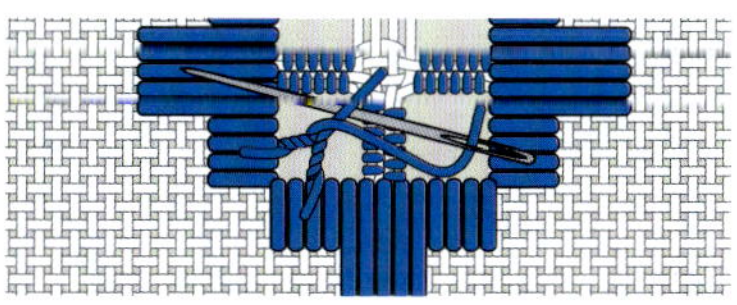

7 Slide the needle under the stem of the Y from the right.

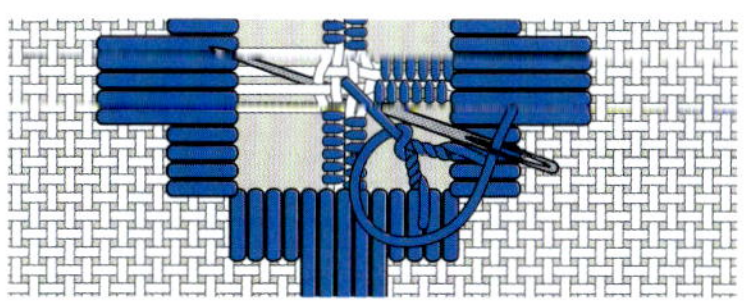

8 Turn the work 90° anticlockwise. Insert the needle above the Y and bring it out ready to keep stitching.

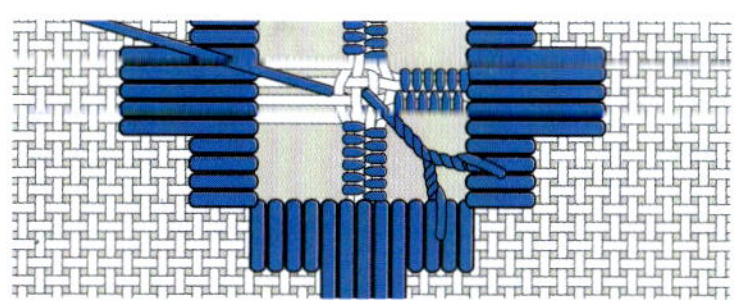

9 Pull the thread to intertwine the stitches. Continue to stitch as required.

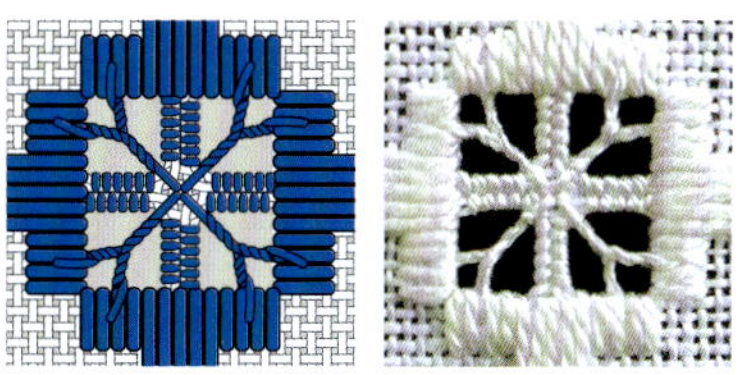

❶ *Work the motif in the other corners if required.*

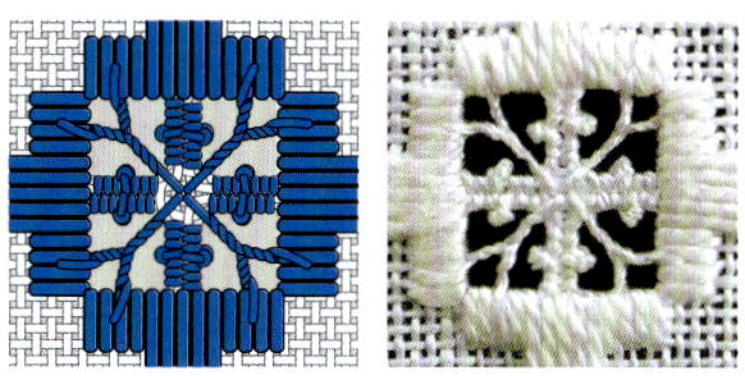

❶ *This variation has picots on the woven bars.*

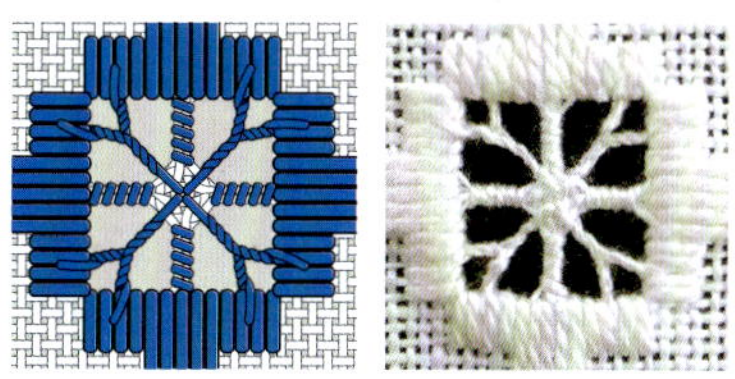

❶ *This variation has wrapped bars instead of woven bars.*

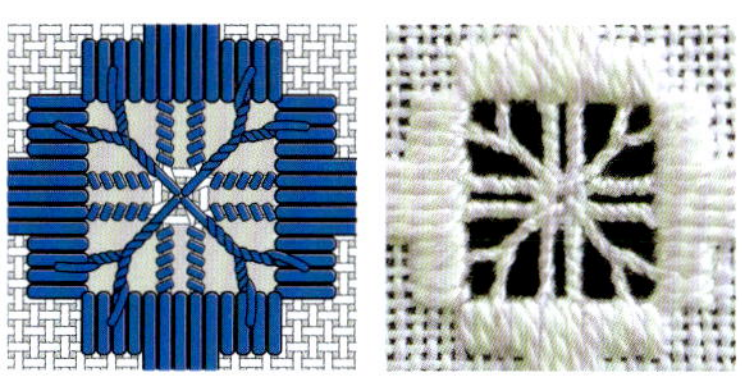

❶ *This variation has divided wrapped bars instead of woven bars.*

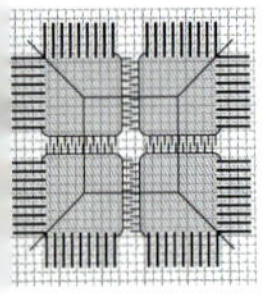

inverse twisted Y *also called reverse twisted Y*

These twisted Ys start with the arms rather than the leg. Their arms point inwards, rather than out to the edges.

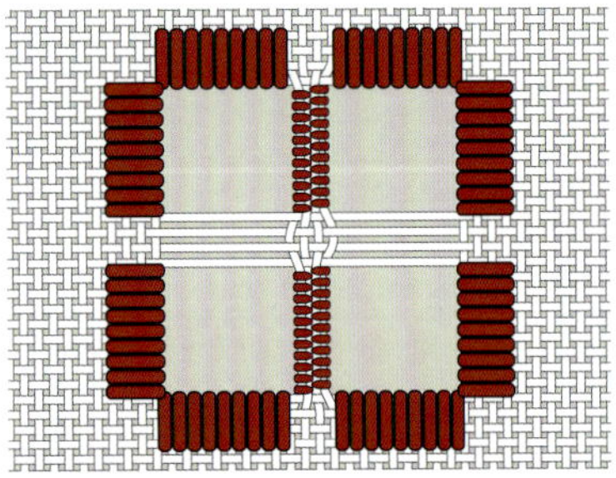

1 Weave from one side to the other along two of the bars within a large satin stitch square.

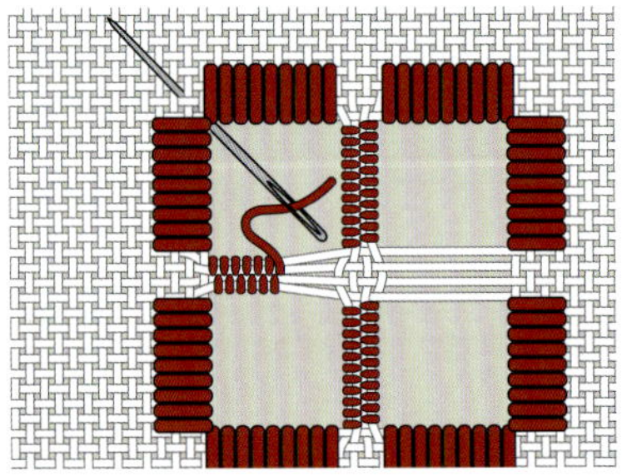

2 Work half the next bar towards the centre. Insert the needle into the centre back of the corner of the quadrant above.

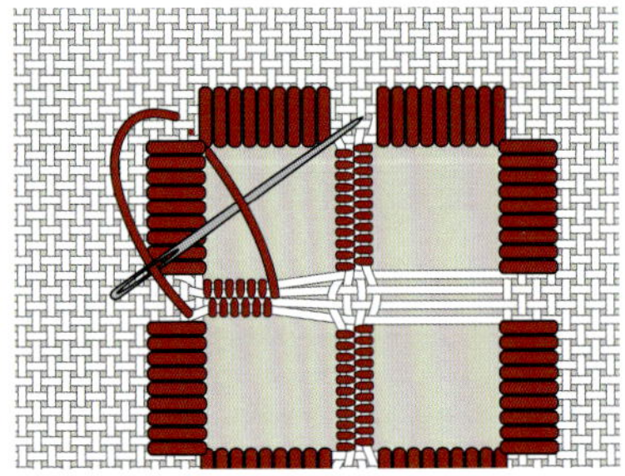

3 Pull the needle through so that the stitch has gentle tension, and slide the needle under the stitch from below left.

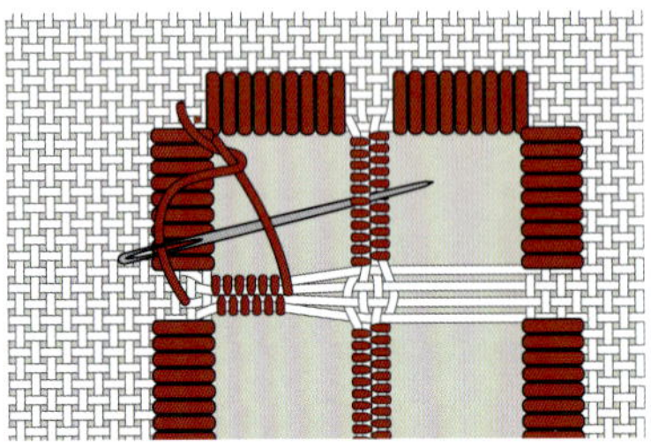

4 Slide the needle under the stitch again, from below left. Bring it out in the adjacent woven bar's centre.

! *When working in a smaller square use fewer twists; for larger, use more.*

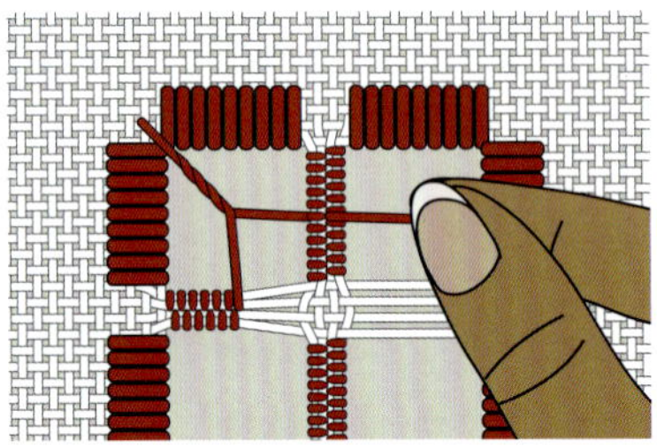

5 Pull the needle through and pull the thread to intertwine the stitches.

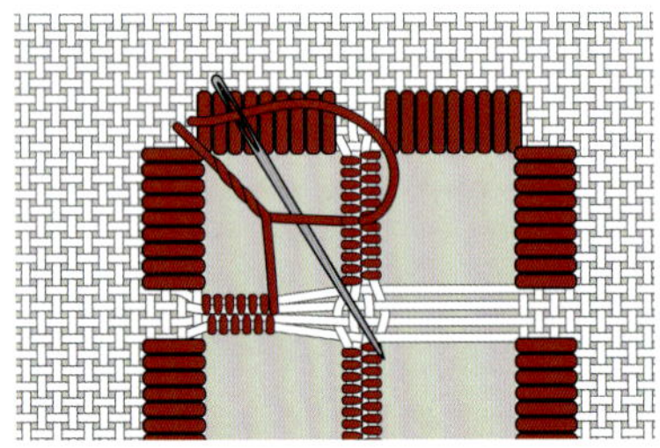

6 Slide the needle under the stitch just made, from above.

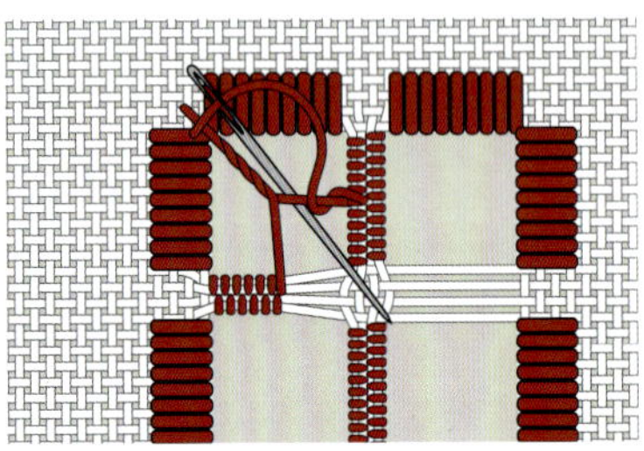

7 Moving left, slide the needle under the stitch again.

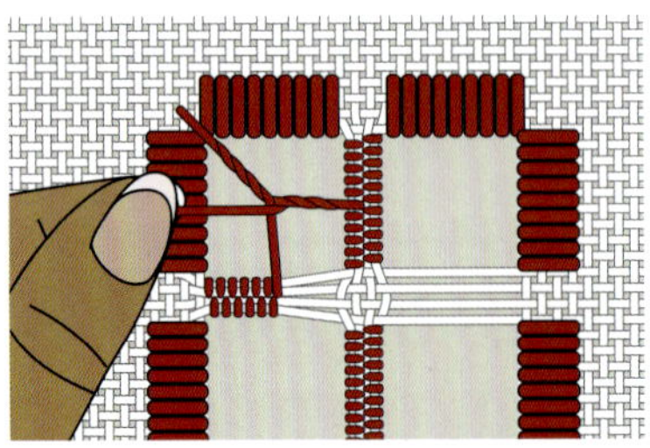

8 Pull the thread to intertwine the stitches.

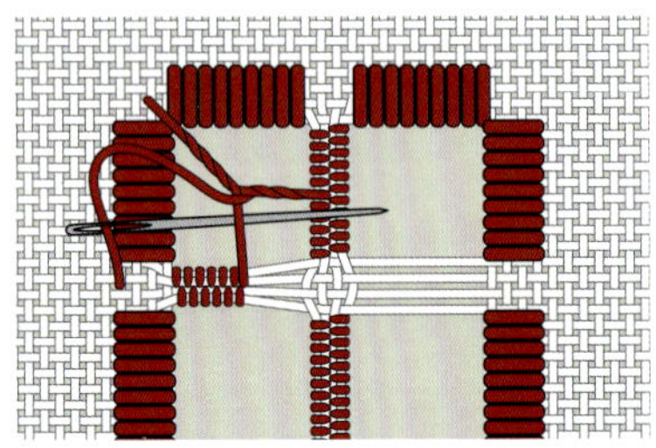

9 Slide the needle under the other arm, from the left.

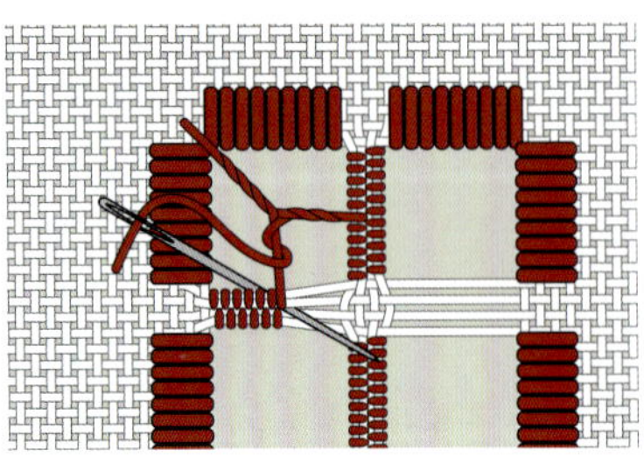

10 Insert the needle under the stitch again and bring it out ready to complete the woven bar.

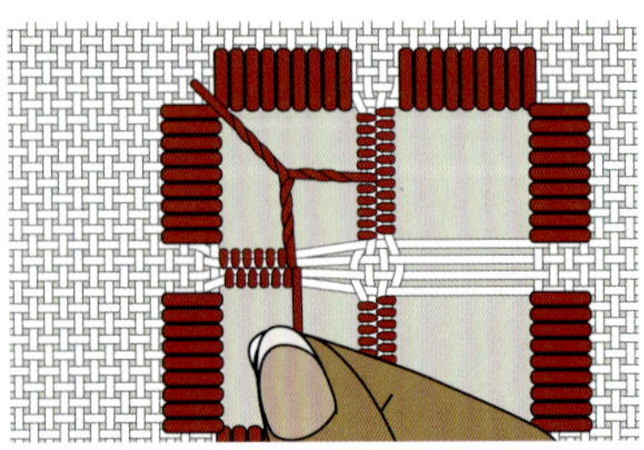

11 Pull the needle through and pull the thread to intertwine the stitches.

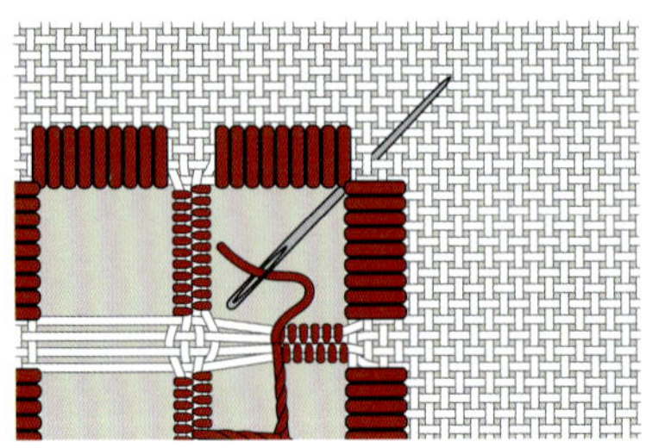

12 Turn the work 180°. Insert the needle into the corner of the adjacent quadrant's centre back.

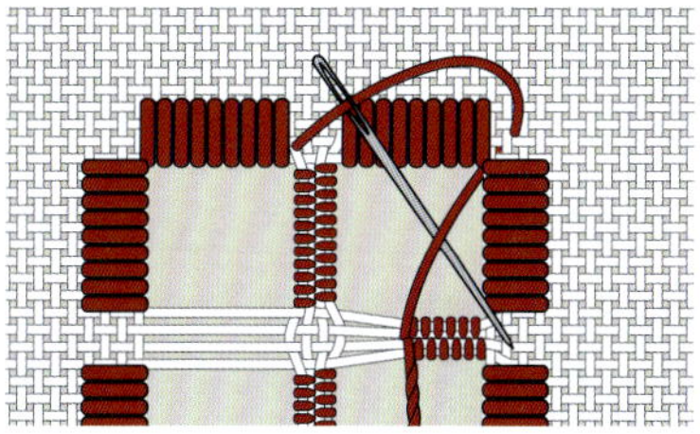

13 Pull the needle through so that the stitch has gentle tension. Slide it under the stitch from the left.

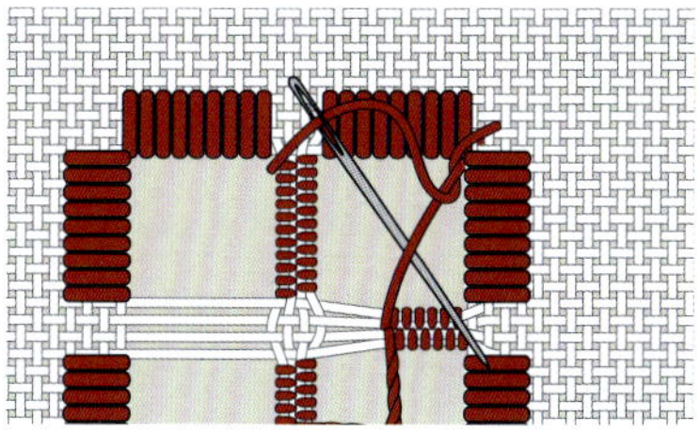

14 Moving slightly down, slide the needle under the stitch again.

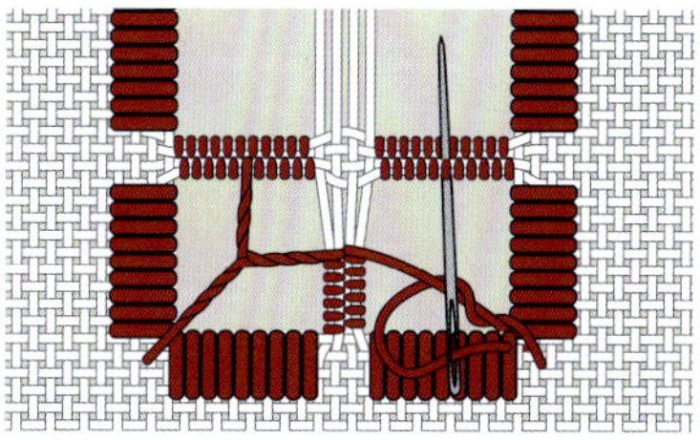

15 Turn the work 90° clockwise. Insert the needle in the centre back of the fully woven bar.

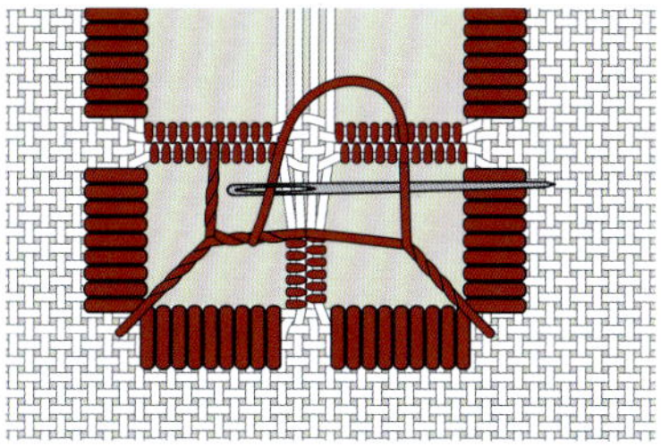

16 Pull the needle through and pull the thread to intertwine the stitches. Slide the needle under the right arm, from left to right.

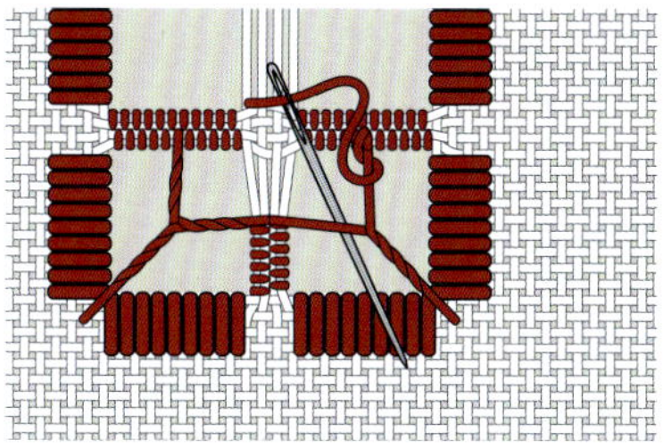

17 Slide the needle under the other arm, from above.

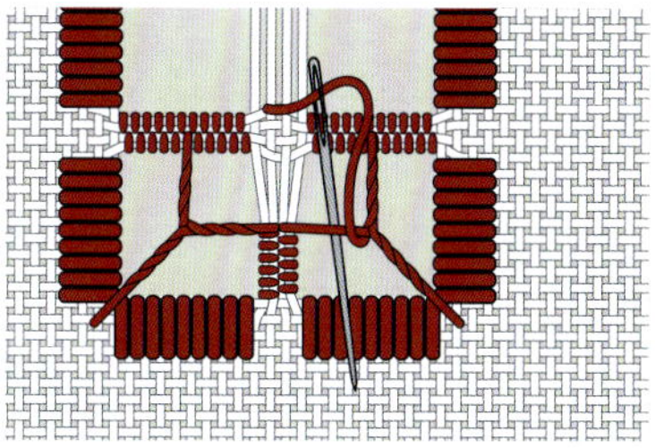

18 Pull the thread downward to intertwine the stitches. Slide the needle under the arm again, from above.

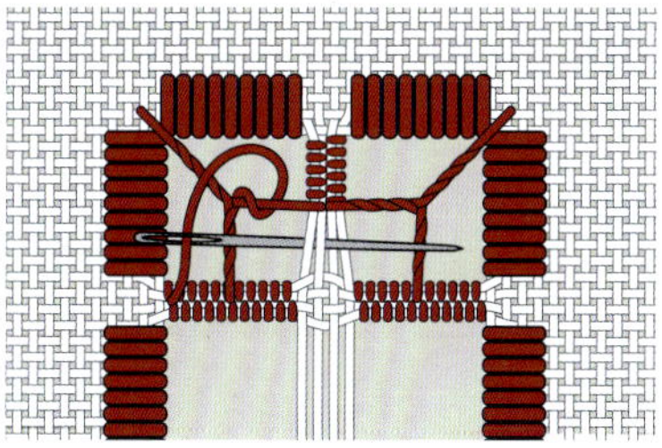

19 Turn the work 180°. Insert the needle ready to continue weaving the bar.

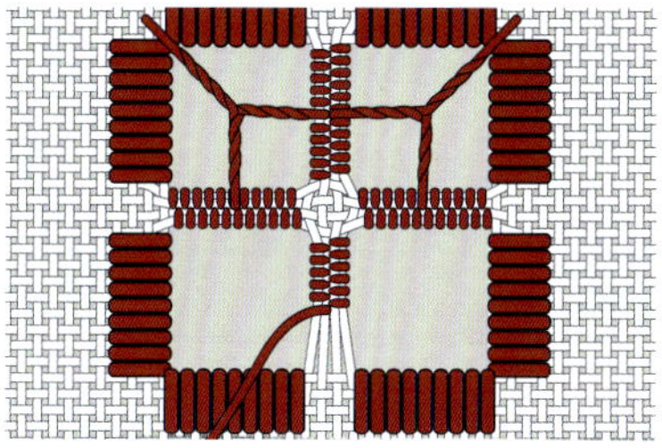

20 Pull the thread to intertwine the stitches, then weave the rest of the bar and half the remaining bar.

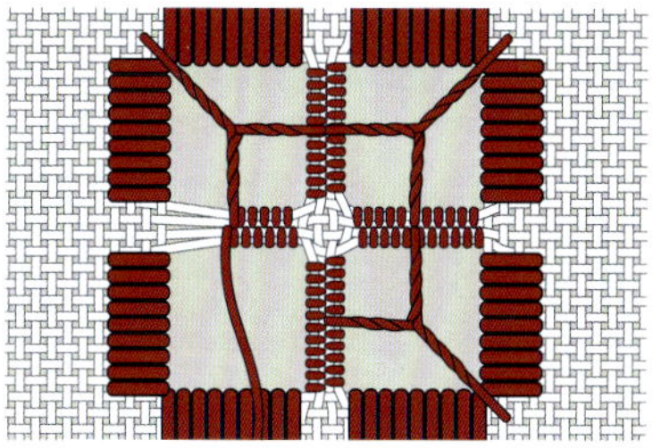

21 Turn the work 90° clockwise. Work through Steps 2 to 11 to stitch an inverted Y in the upper left quadrant.

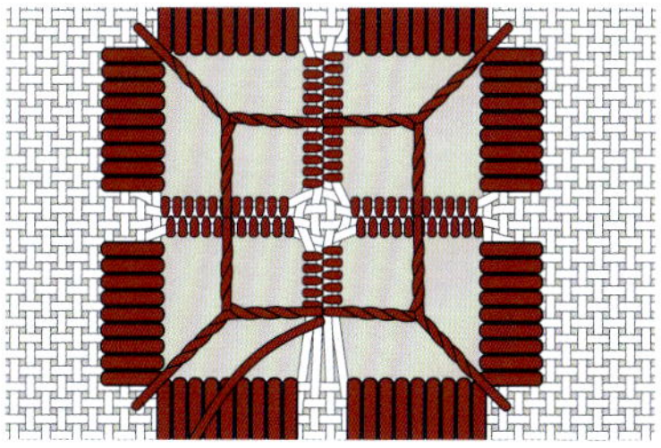

22 Turn the work 180° and work through Steps 12 to 19 to complete the final quadrant.

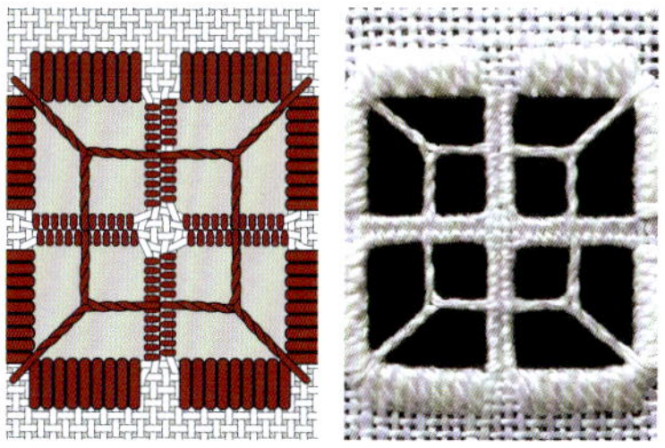

23 Weave the final section of the bar to complete the motif.

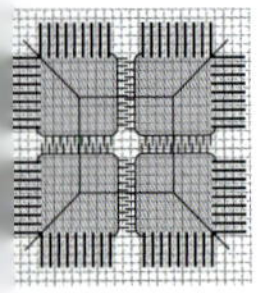

CONTEMPORARY

inverse twisted Y *also called reverse twisted Y*

These twisted Ys start with the arms rather than the leg. Their arms point inwards, rather than out to the edges.

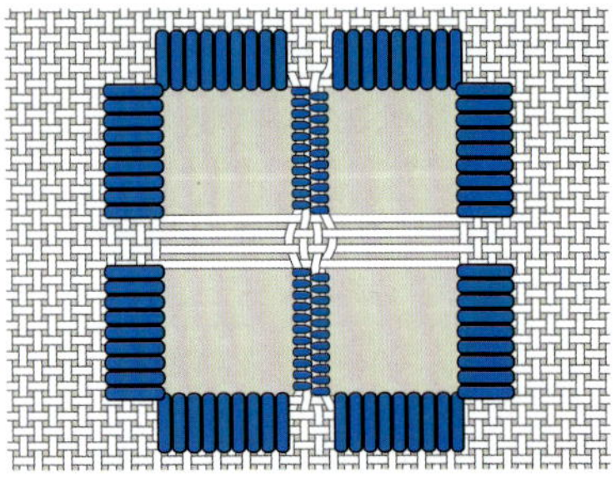

1 Weave from one side to the other along two of the bars within a large satin stitch square.

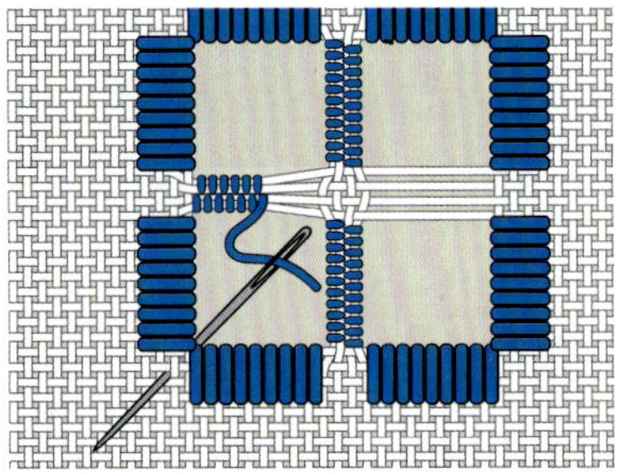

2 Work half the next bar towards the centre. Insert the needle into the centre back of the corner of the quadrant below.

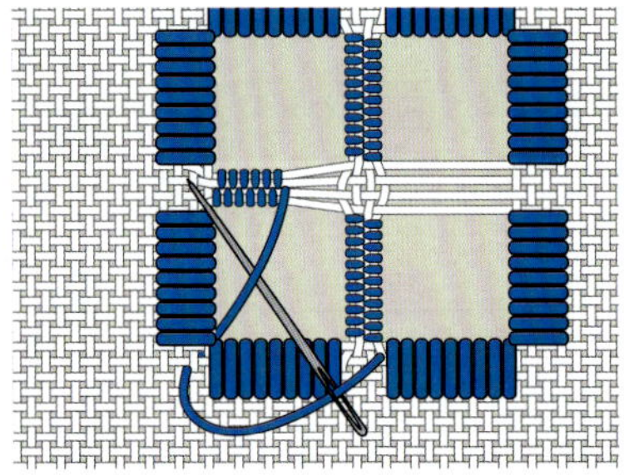

3 Pull the needle through so that the stitch has gentle tension, and slide the needle under the stitch from below right.

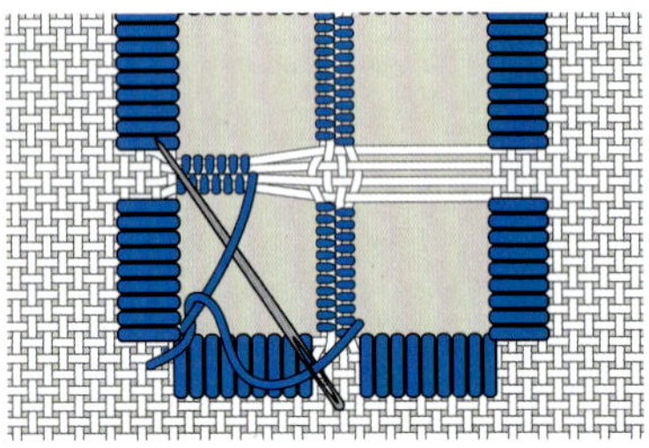

4 Slide the needle under the stitch again, from below right.

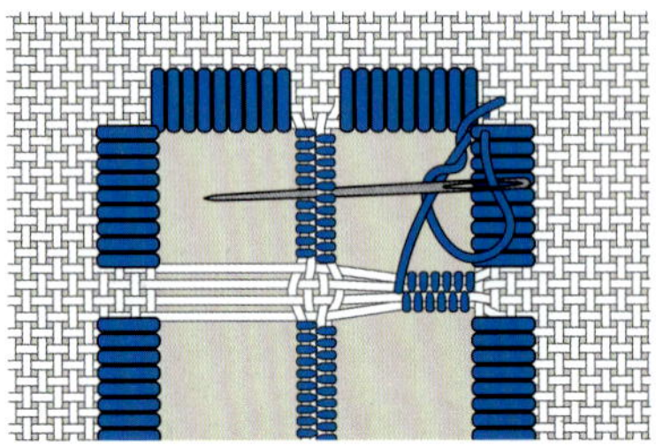

5 Turn the work 180°. Bring the needle out in the adjacent woven bar's centre.

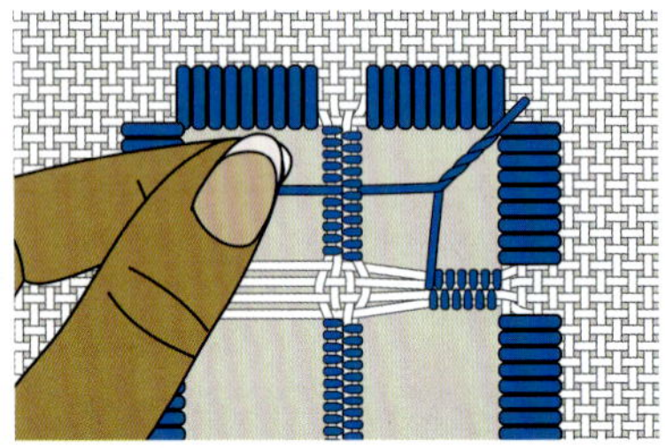

6 Pull the needle through and pull the thread to intertwine the stitches. ❶ *When working in a smaller square use fewer twists; for larger, use more.*

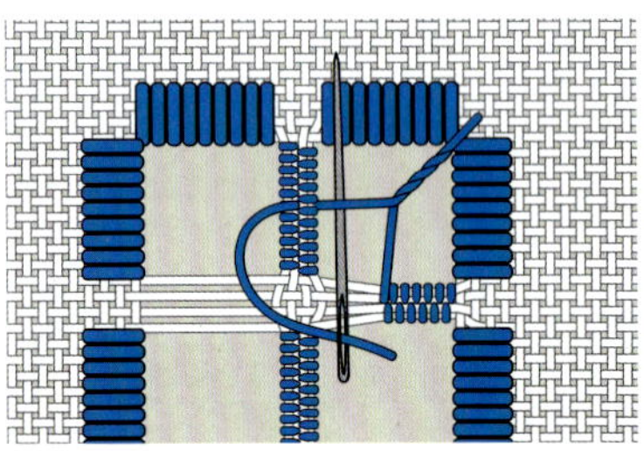

7 Slide the needle under the closest Y arm, from below.

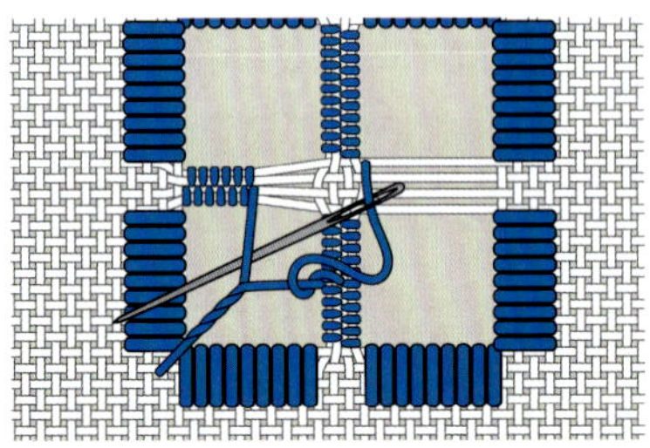

8 Turn the work 180°. From the right, slide the needle under the other arm.

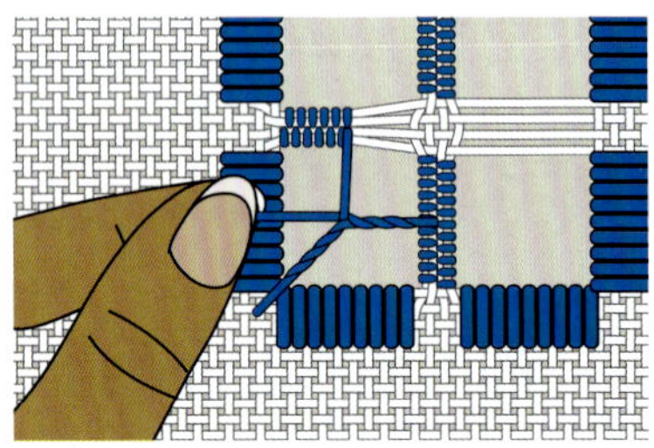

9 Pull the needle through and pull the thread to intertwine the stitches.

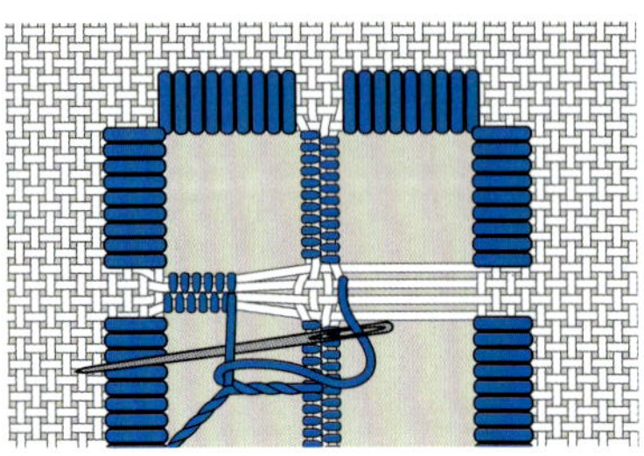

10 Moving up slightly, slide the needle under the arm again.

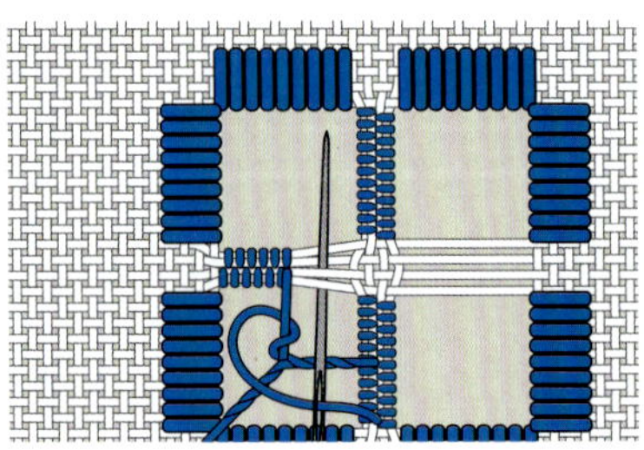

11 Insert the needle in the back of the woven bar and bring it out ready to complete the bar.

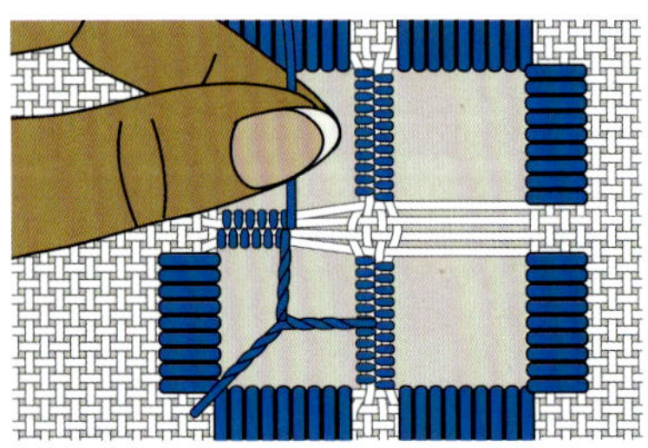

12 Pull the needle through and pull the thread to intertwine the stitches.

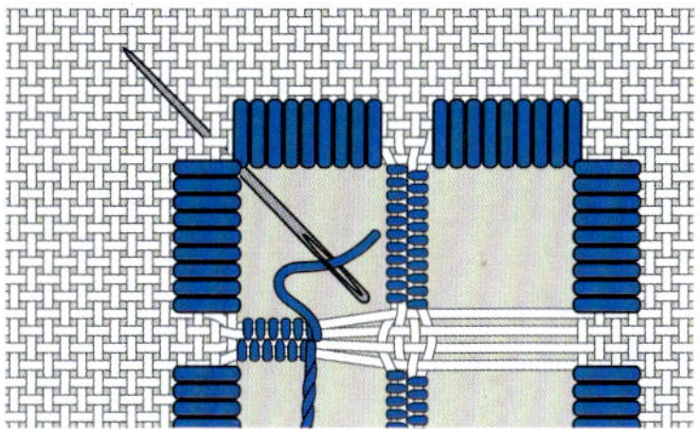

13 Insert the needle into the corner of the adjacent quadrant's centre back.

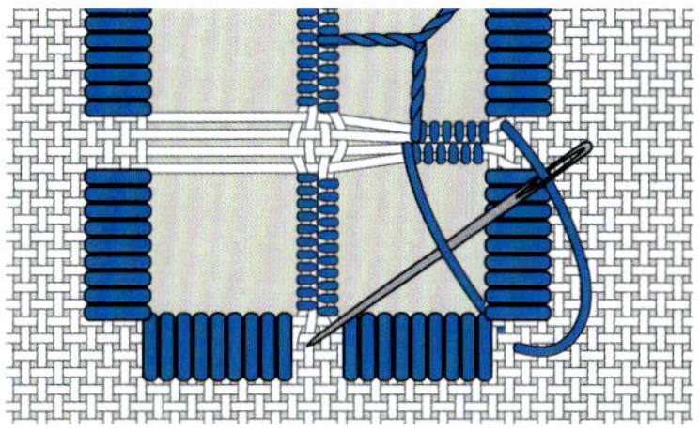

14 Turn the work 180°. Pull the needle through so that the stitch has gentle tension. Slide it under the stitch from the right.

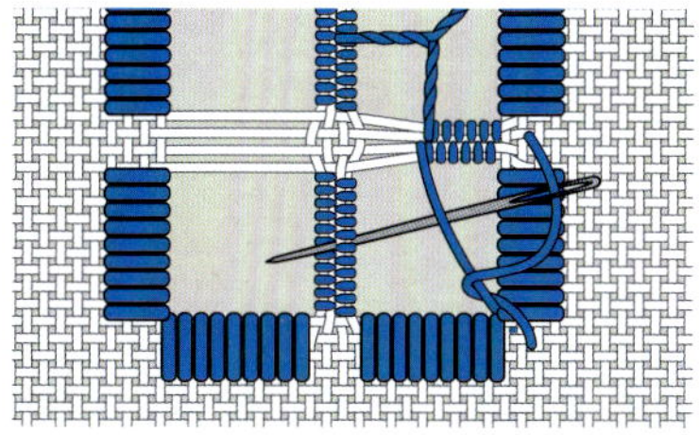

15 Slide the needle under the stitch again, from the right. Bring it out in the adjacent woven bar's centre.

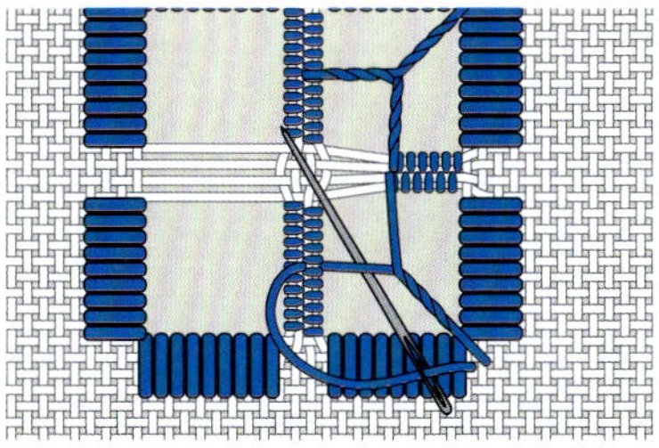

16 Pull the needle through and pull the thread to intertwine the stitches. From below, slide the needle under the closest Y arm.

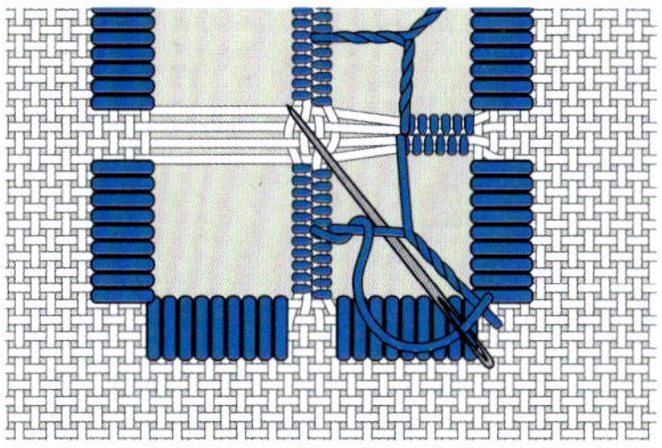

17 Moving right, slide the needle under the arm again, from below.

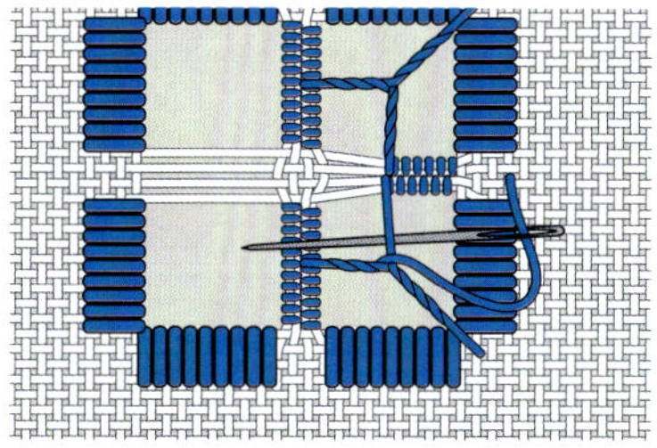

18 Pull the thread to intertwine the stitches. Slide the needle under the other arm, from the right.

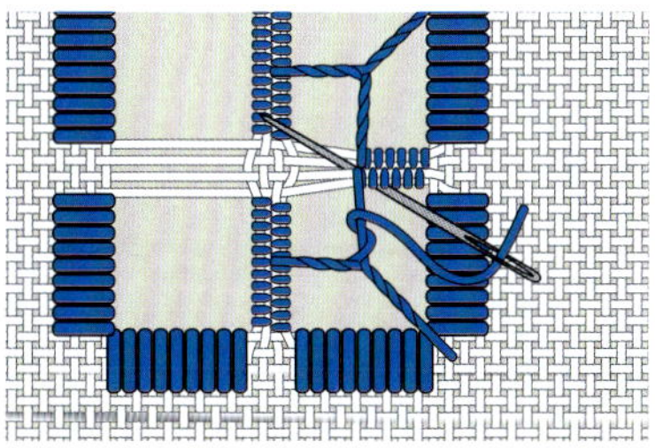

19 Insert the needle ready to continue weaving the bar.

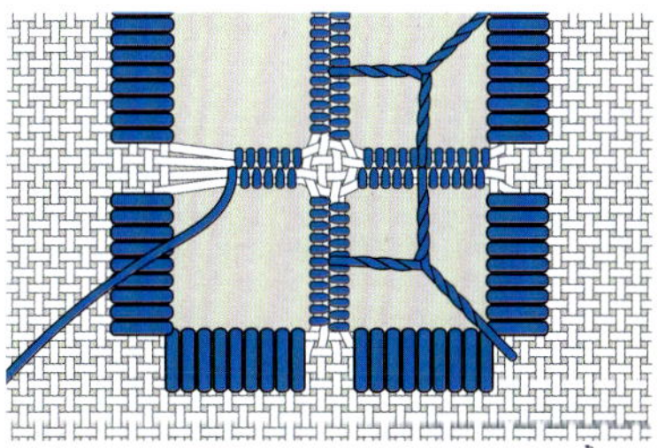

20 Pull the thread to intertwine the stitches, then weave the rest of the bar and half the remaining bar.

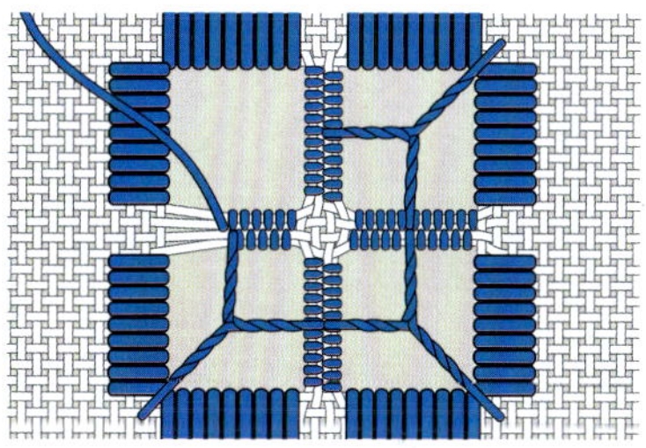

21 Work through Steps 2 to 11 to stitch an inverted Y in the upper left quadrant.

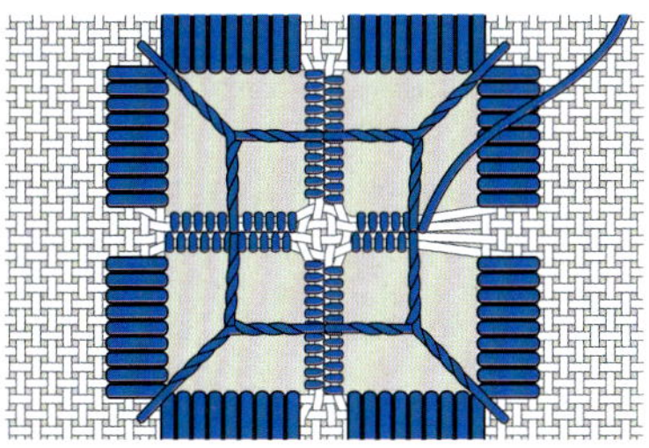

22 Turn the work 180° and work through Steps 12 to 19 to complete the final quadrant.

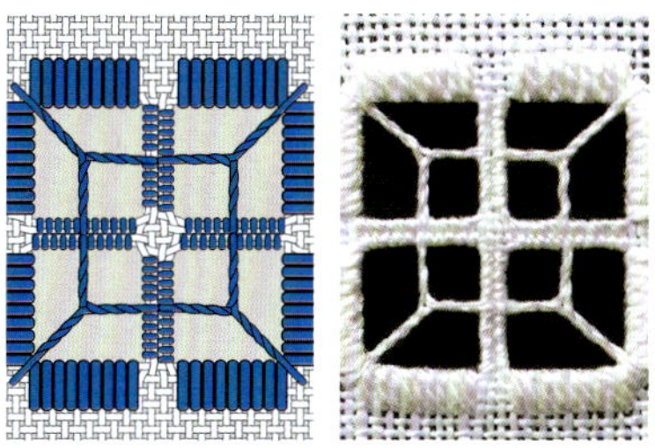

23 Weave the final section of the bar to complete the motif.

L

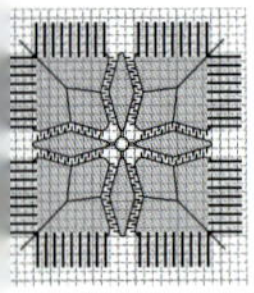

CONTEMPORARY

rosette

also called struvor

This motif is a combination of divided bars (paired half-width bars) with inverse twisted Ys. It is worked in a large square. The bars are usually woven, but they could also be wrapped or even buttonholed.

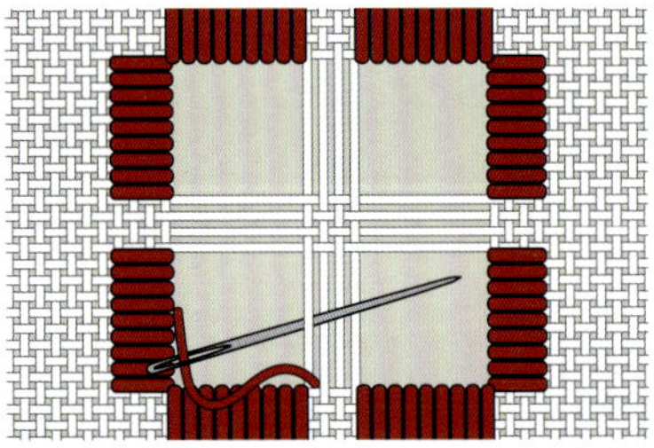

1 In a large square, bring the needle out in the lower vertical bar, one thread from the left. Working with the two left threads only, from the left, insert the needle under the left thread, and bring it out between them.

❶ *These bars are half the width of regular bars, using only two threads in each rather than the usual four.*

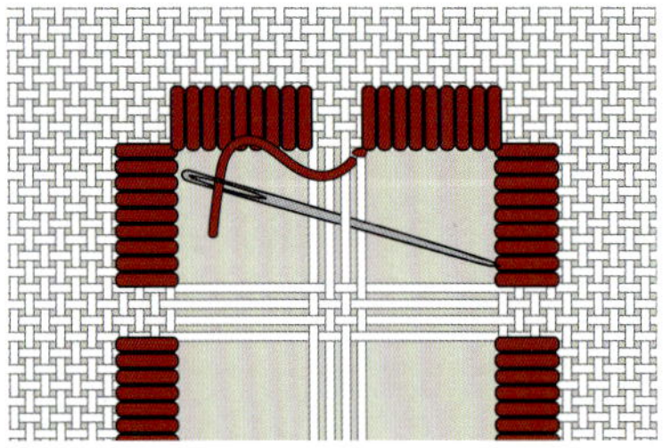

2 Turn the work 180°. Pull the needle through. Insert the under the other thread of the pair, from the left. Bring it out between the two.

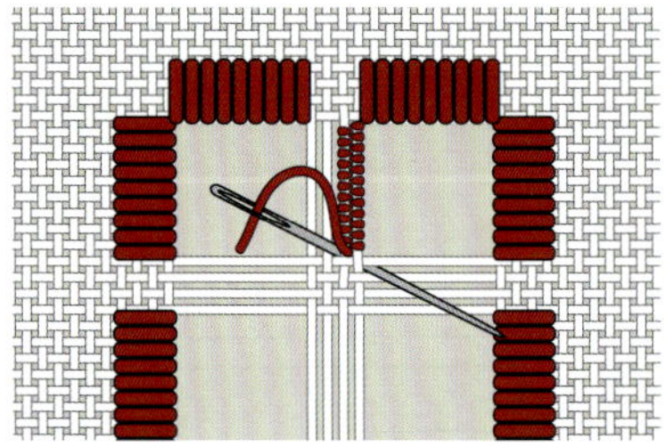

3 Continue weaving. When you reach the end of the bar, insert the needle left of the bar and bring it out in the next bar to the right, one thread down.

❶ *This is one instance where it is acceptable to squeeze a few too many stitches into a bar, as it helps it to bend later.*

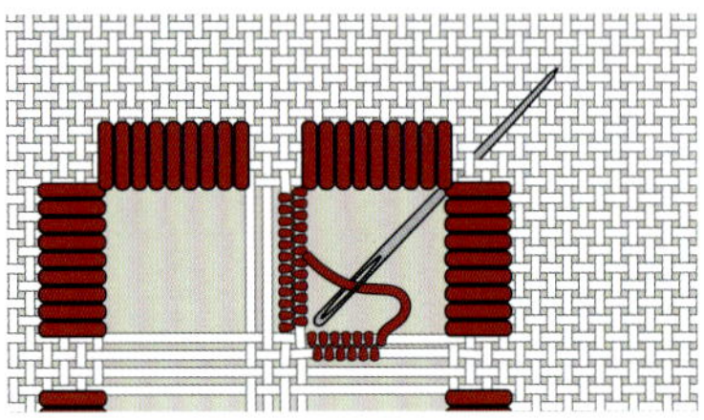

4 Weave half the next bar. Insert the needle in the far corner of the quadrant, two threads from the cut edge.

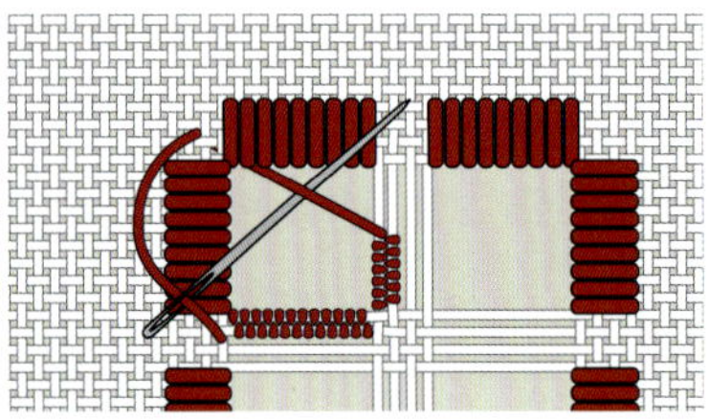

5 Turn the work 90° anticlockwise. Pull the needle through. From below, slide the needle under the stitch.

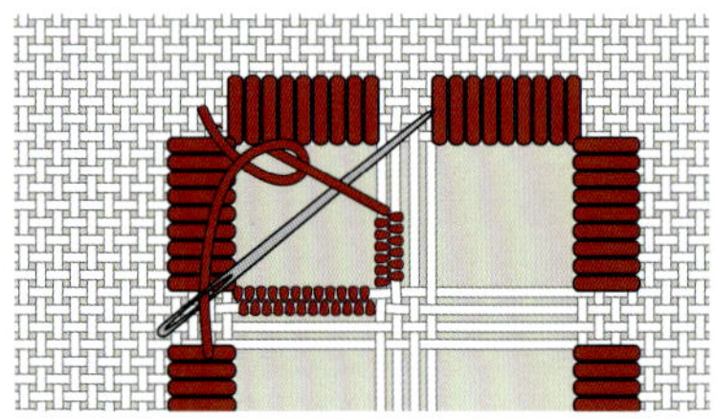

6 Moving right, slide the needle under the stitch again.

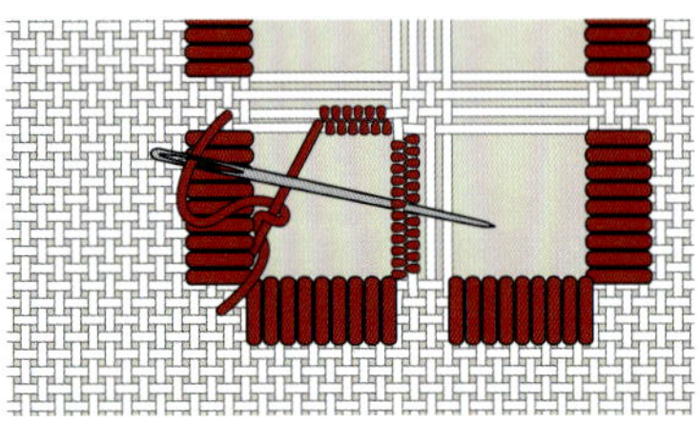

7 Turn the work 90° anticlockwise. Bring the needle out in the centre of the first woven bar.

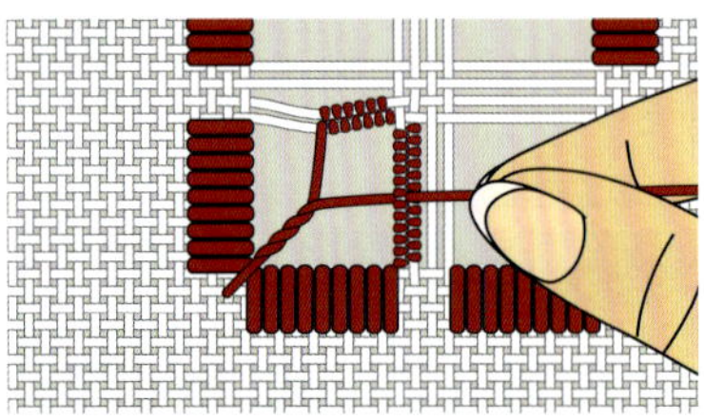

8 Pull the needle through. Pull the thread to tighten the stitches and intertwine them, and to pull the half woven bar inward.

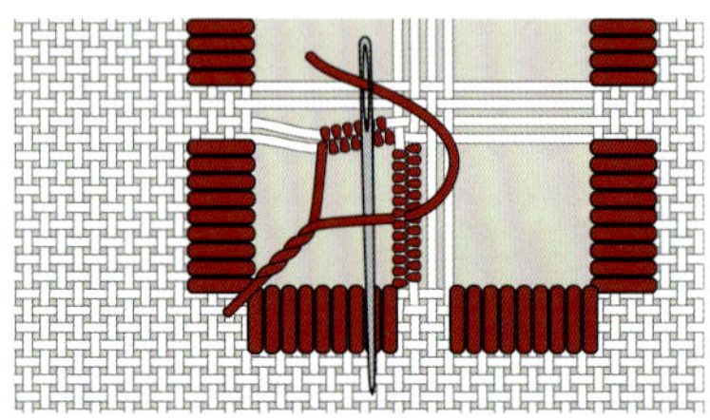

9 From above, slide the needle under the right-hand arm of the Y.

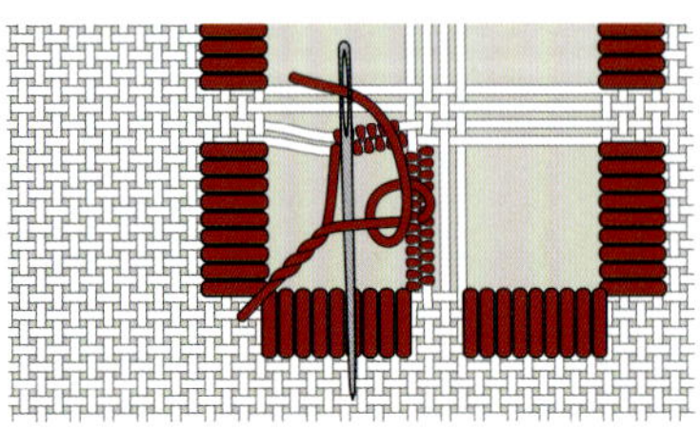

10 Moving left, and from above, slide the needle under the stitch again.

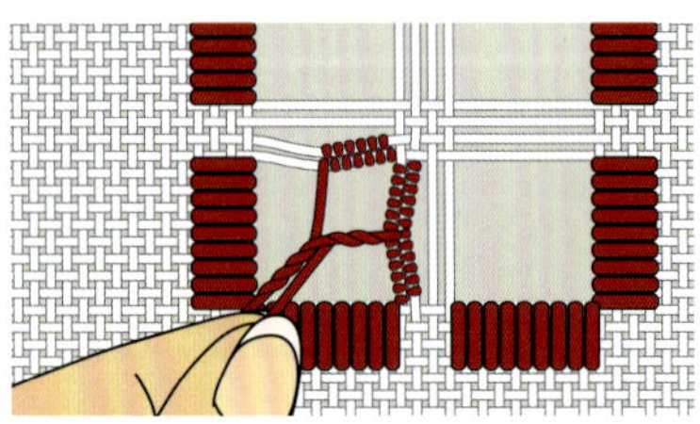

11 Pull the thread to tighten the stitches and intertwine them, and to pull the first woven bar inward to the same degree as the other woven bar.

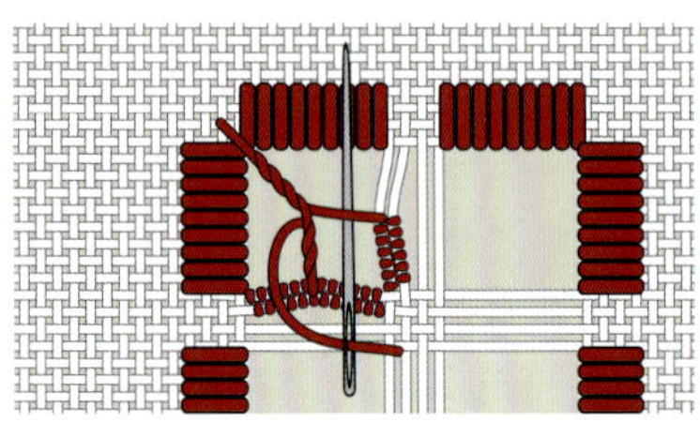

12 Turn the work 90° clockwise. From below, slide the needle under the other arm of the Y.

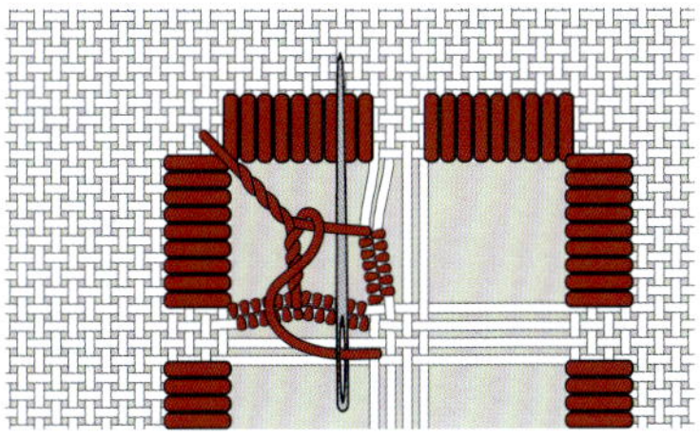

13 Moving to the right, and from below, slide the needle under the stitch again.

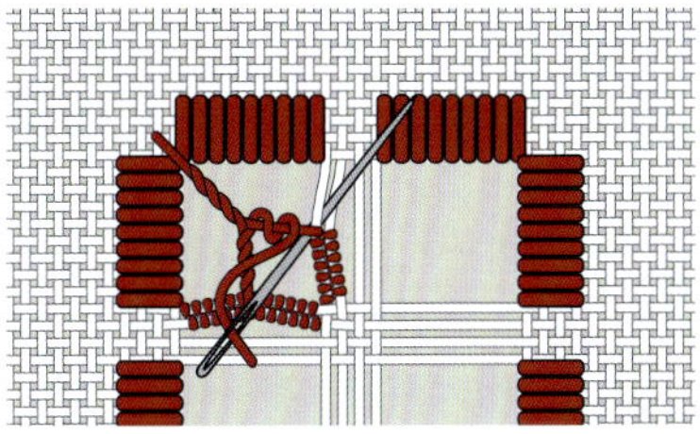

14 Take the needle under the stitch and bring it out in the middle of the bar, ready to continue weaving.

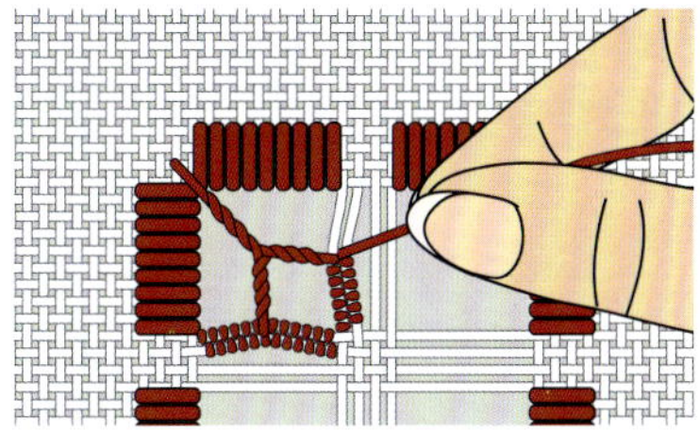

15 Pull the needle through. Pull the thread to intertwine the stitches.

❶ *If the length of the branches is uneven, use your needle to help tighten things up (taking extra slack out) or loosen things off.*

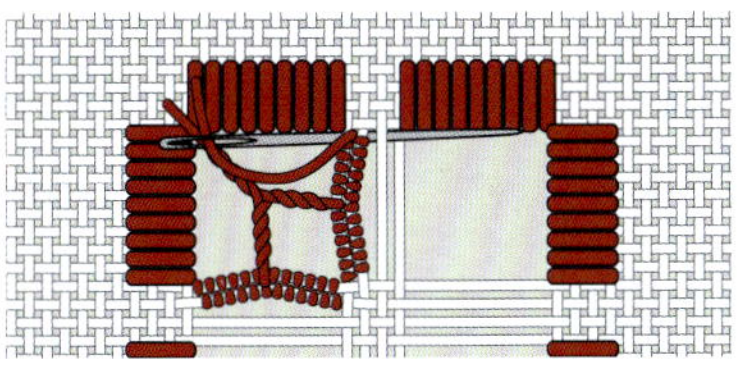

16 Weave the rest of the bar. Finish with a stitch on the left and take the needle behind the woven bar, bringing it out between the two threads of the adjacent bar.

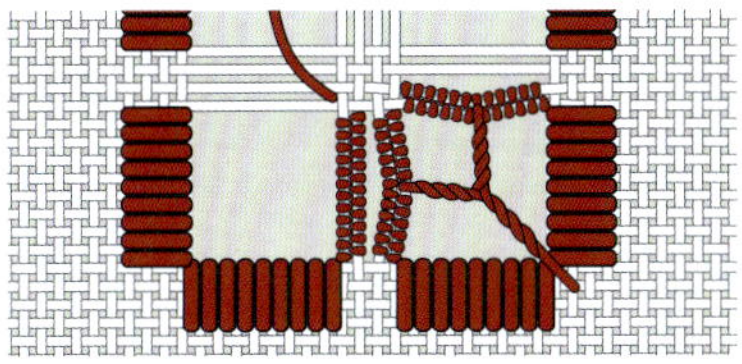

17 Pull the needle through. Turn the work 180° and weave the next bar.

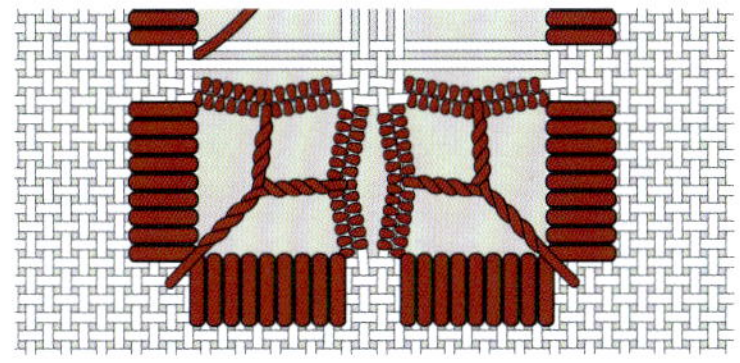

18 Turn the corner and weave half the new bar. Work a twisted Y. Then weave the remainder of the bar. Bring the needle out ready to start the next bar.

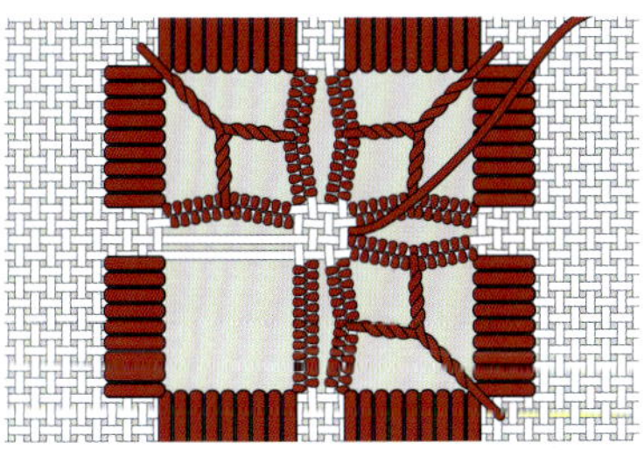

19 Repeat the process in the next corner. Work the first bar for the final corner. Bring the needle out between the second and third quadrants.

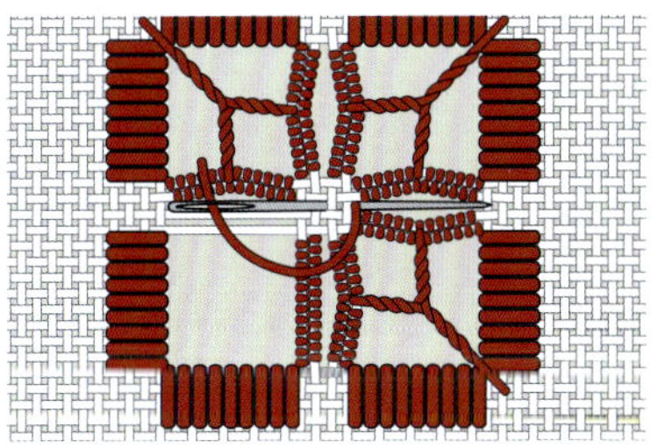

20 Insert the needle two threads to the left and bring the needle out two threads to the right.

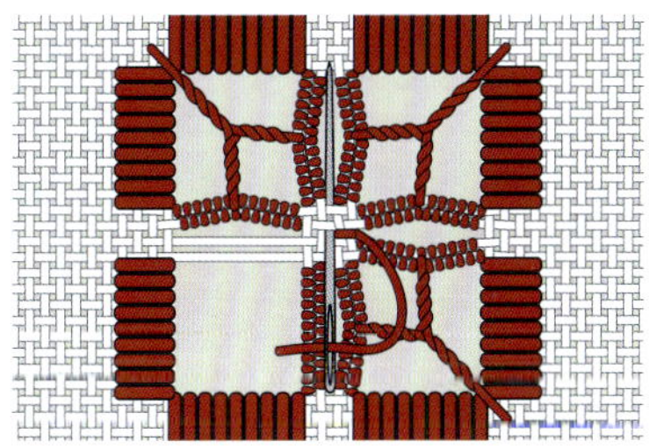

21 Pull the needle through and tighten the stitch. Insert the needle two threads to the left. Bring it out two threads up.

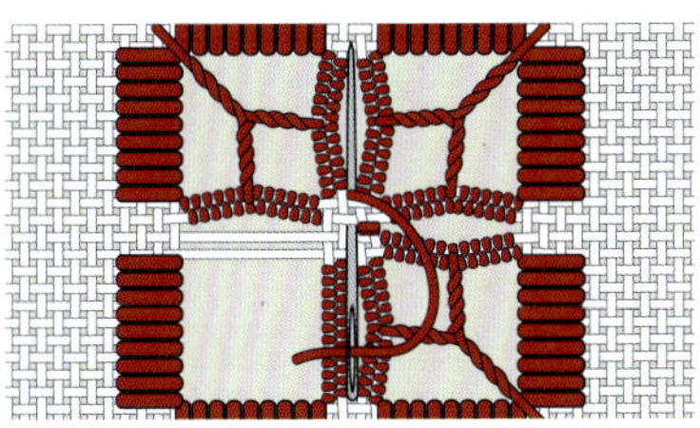

22 Pull the needle through to tighten the stitch. Insert the needle in the same place again.

❶ *Tighten the stitches as you go. You are creating a small eyelet in the centre of the motif.*

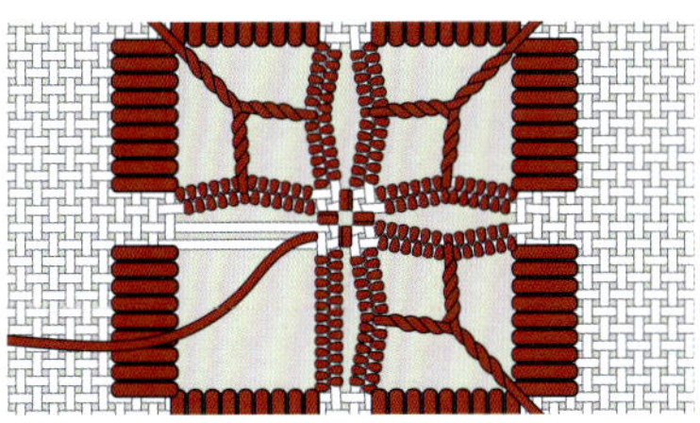

23 Continue around the centre woven square, working two stitches on each side. To finish bring the needle out ready to stitch the final bar.

24 Complete the final quadrant and finish the thread in the back of the satin stitch.

rosette

also called struvor

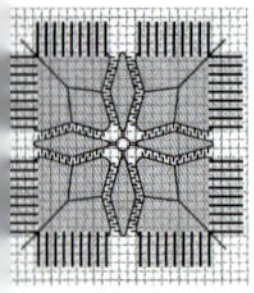

CONTEMPORARY

This motif is a combination of divided bars (paired half-width bars) with inverse twisted Ys. It is worked in a large square. The bars are usually woven, but they could also be wrapped or even buttonholed.

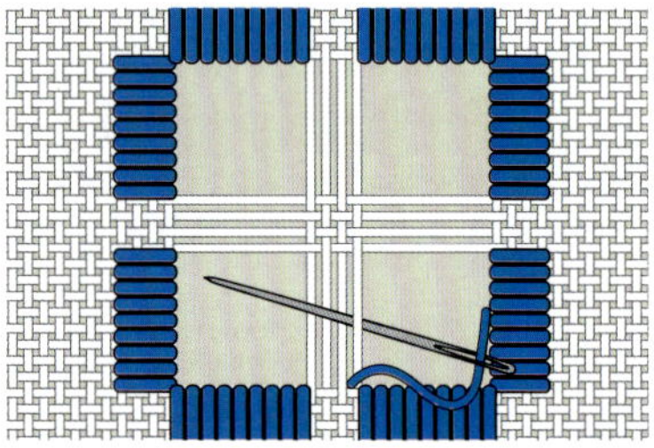

1 In a large square, bring the needle out in the lower vertical bar, one thread from the right. Working with the two right threads only, from the right, insert the needle under the right thread, and bring it out between them.

❶ *These bars are half the width of regular bars, using only two threads in each rather than the usual four.*

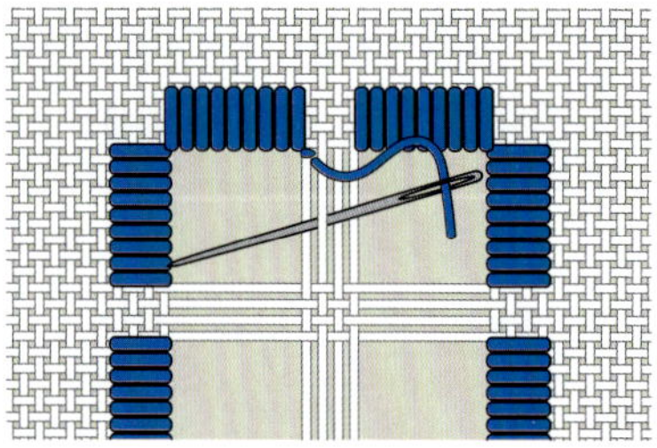

2 Turn the work 180°. Pull the needle through. Insert the under the other thread of the pair, from the left. Bring it out between the two.

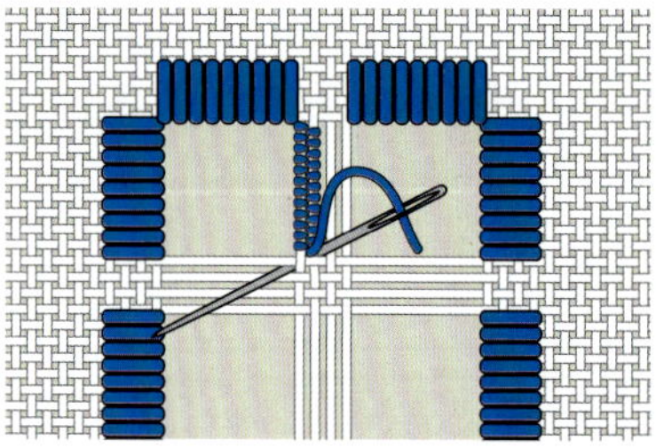

3 Continue weaving. When you reach the end of the bar, insert the needle right of the bar and bring it out in the next bar to the left, one thread down.

❶ *This is a time where it is acceptable to squeeze a few too many stitches into a bar, as it helps it to bend later.*

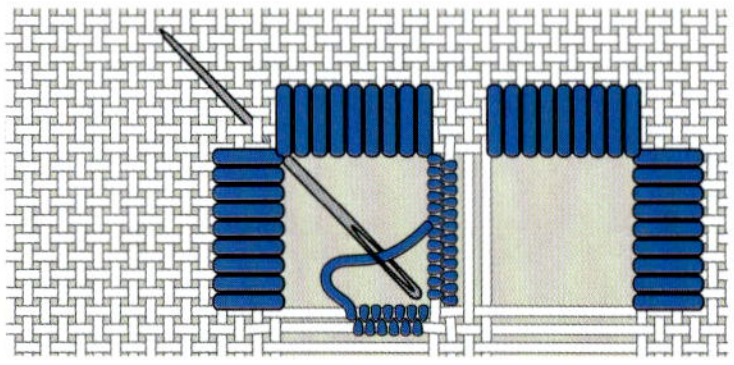

4 Weave half the next bar. Insert the needle in the far corner of the quadrant, two threads from the cut edge.

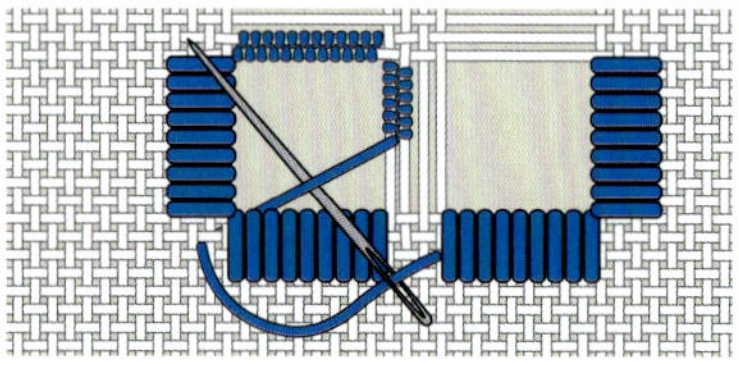

5 Turn the work 90° anticlockwise. Pull the needle through. From below, slide the needle under the stitch.

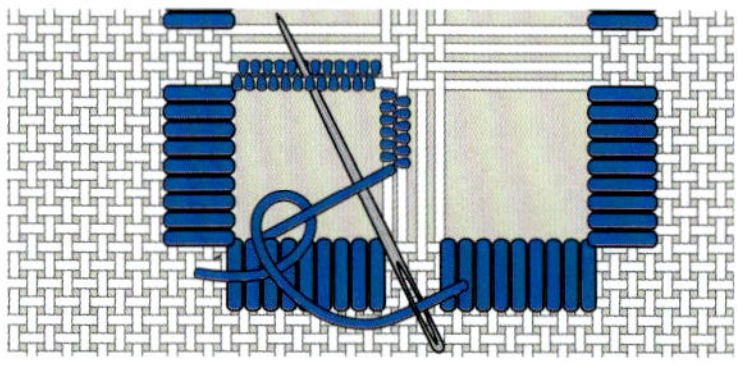

6 Slide the needle under the stitch again. Bring the needle out in the centre of the first woven bar.

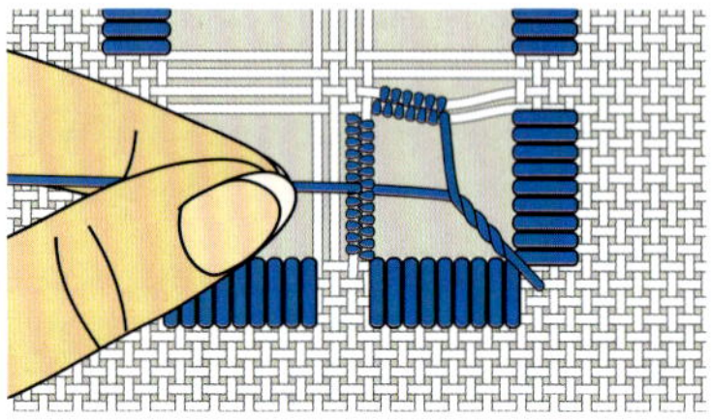

7 Turn the work 90° anticlockwise. Pull the needle through. Pull the thread to tighten the stitches and intertwine them, and to pull the half woven bar inward.

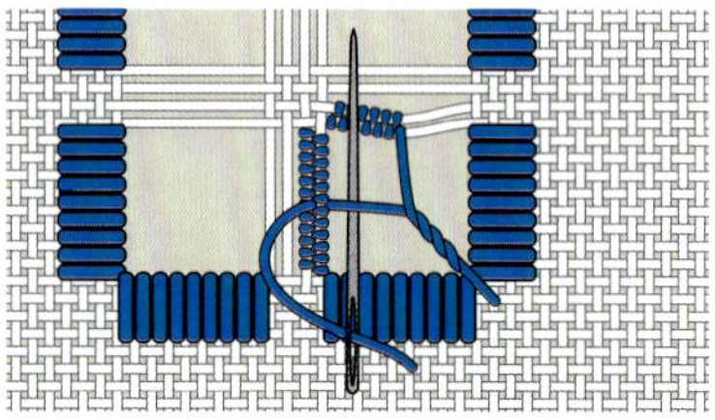

8 From below, slide the needle under the left-hand arm of the Y.

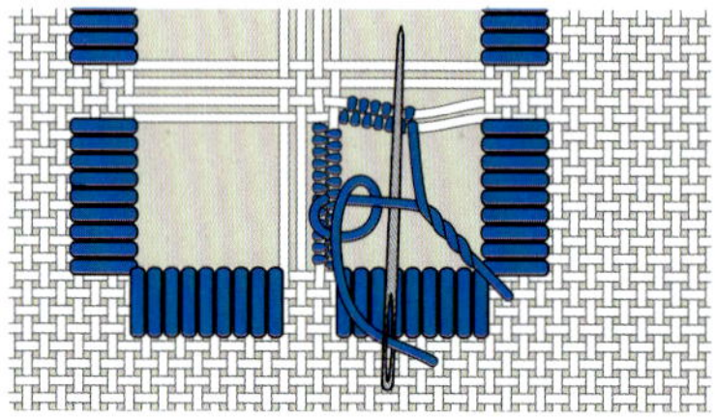

9 Moving right, and from below, slide the needle under the stitch again.

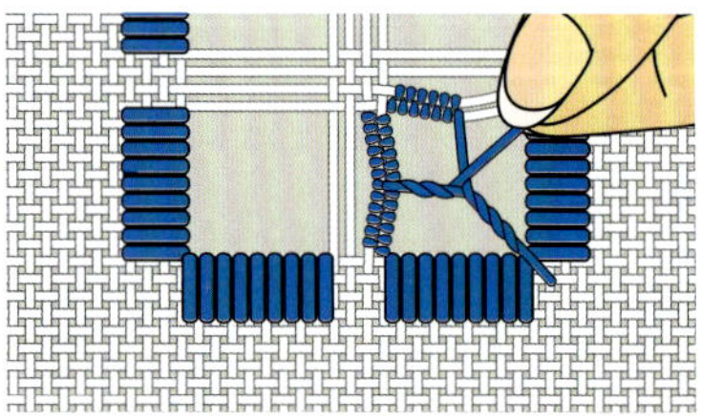

10 Pull the thread to tighten the stitches and intertwine them, and to pull the first woven bar inward to the same degree as the other woven bar.

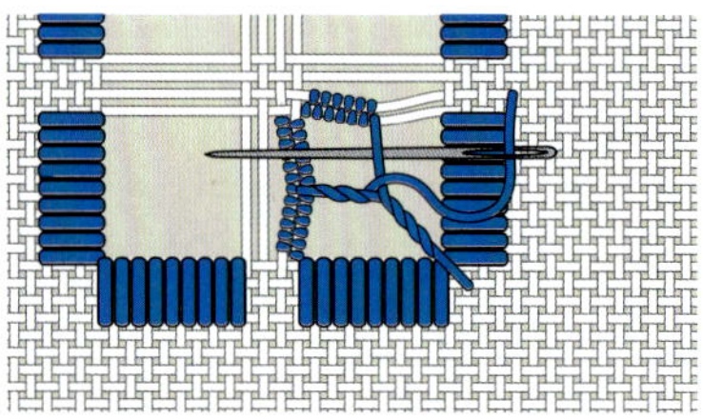

11 From the right, slide the needle under the other arm of the Y.

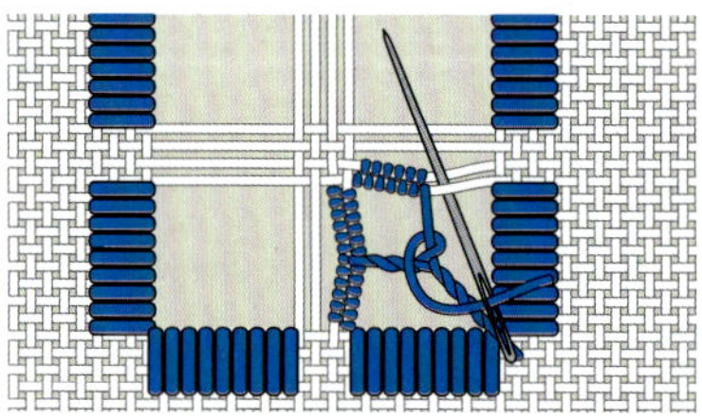

12 Bring the needle out ready to continue weaving the bar.

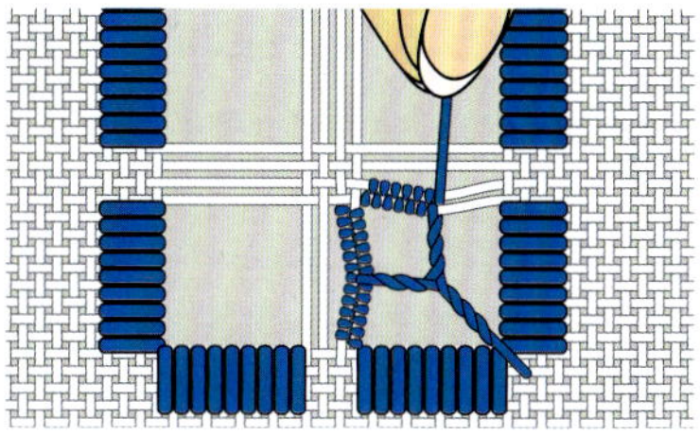

13 Pull the needle through. Pull the thread to intertwine the stitches.

❶ *If the length of the branches is uneven, use your needle to help tighten them up (taking extra slack out) or loosen them off.*

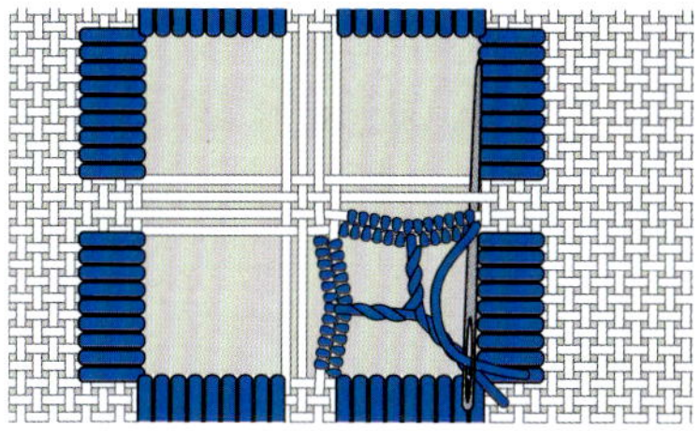

14 Weave the rest of the bar. Finish with a stitch on the lower edge and take the needle behind the woven bar, bringing it out between the two threads of the adjacent bar.

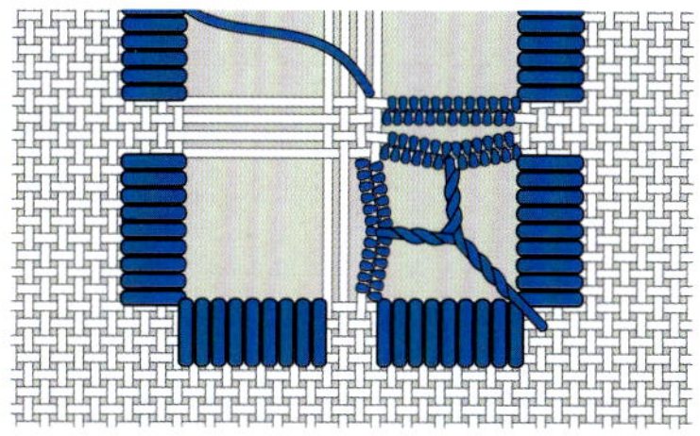

15 Pull the needle through. Weave the next bar.

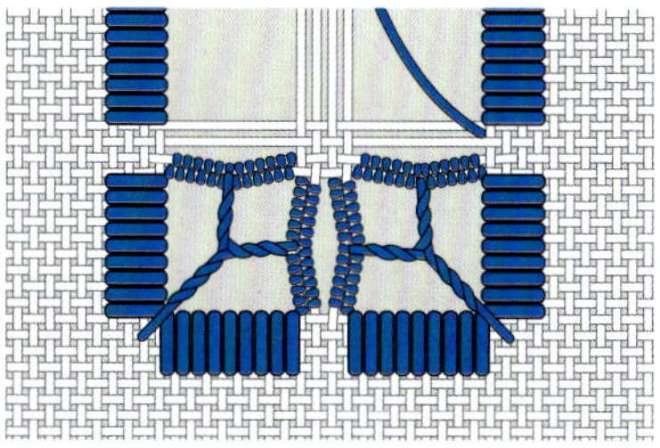

16 Turn the work 90° clockwise. Turn the corner and weave half the new bar. Work a twisted Y. Then weave the remainder of the bar. Bring the needle out ready to start the next bar.

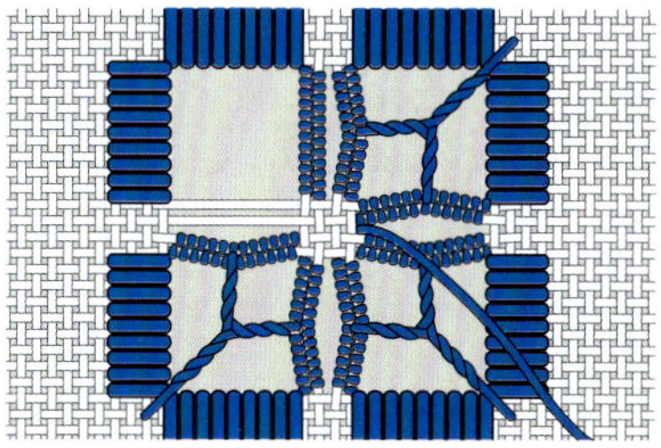

17 Repeat the process in the next corner. Work the first bar for the final corner. Bring the needle out between the second and third quadrants.

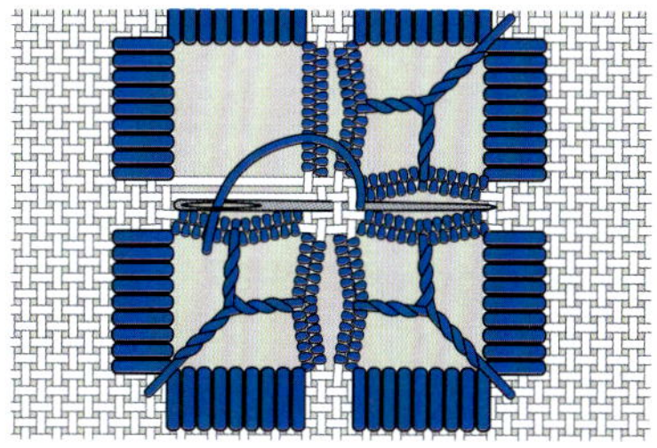

18 Insert the needle two threads to the left and bring the needle out two threads to the right.

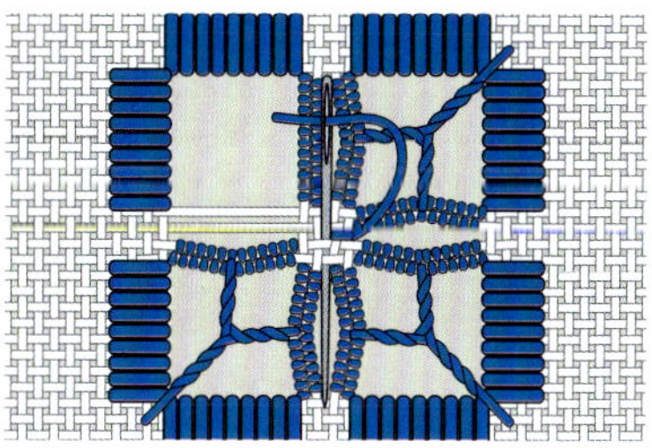

19 Pull the needle through and tighten the stitch. Insert the needle two threads to the left. Bring it out two threads down.

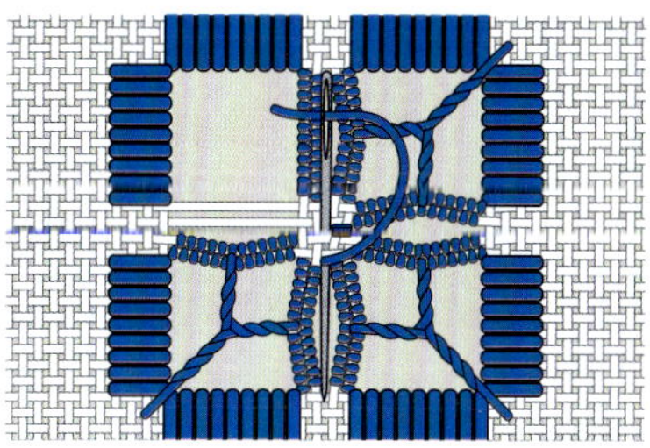

20 Pull the needle through to tighten the stitch. Insert the needle in the same place again.

❶ *Tighten the stitches as you go. You are creating a small eyelet in the centre of the motif.*

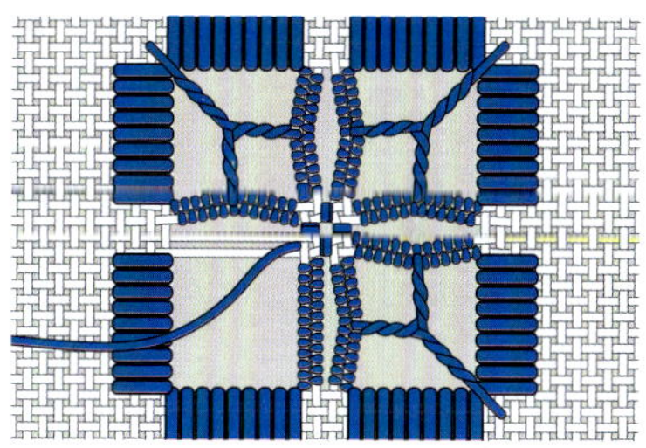

21 Continue around the centre woven square, working two stitches on each side. To finish bring the needle out ready to stitch the final bar.

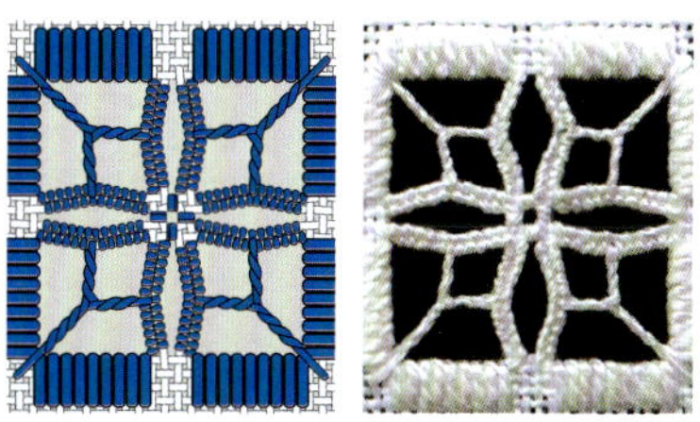

22 Complete the final quadrant and finish the thread in the back of the satin stitch.

curled V

This stitch can be worked with woven or wrapped bars. It can be used singly or in four quadrants of a square. Depending on the orientation of the curled V, you may need to work it into as yet unstitched bars.

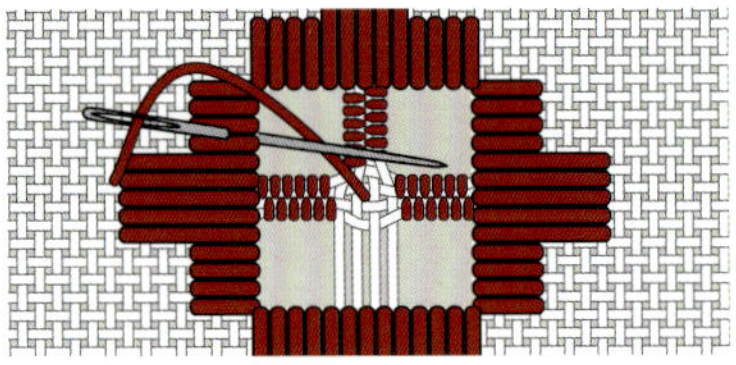

1 Weave three bars. Bring the needle out in the woven square's centre. From the left, insert it halfway across the left satin stitch block; three stitches from the top. Take it over the thread.

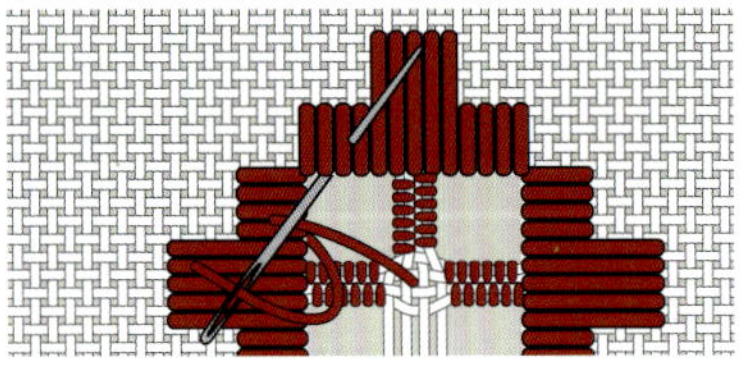

2 Pull the needle through so the stitch curves gently. Bring the needle out halfway up the satin stitch at the upper edge of the quadrant, three stitches from the left.

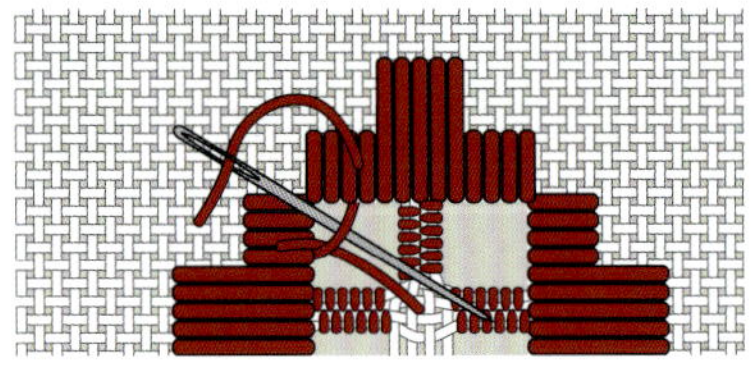

3 Pull the needle through so the stitch curves gently. Slide the needle under the second stitch.

❶ *Continue to any of the endings below.*

ending 1 – no twist

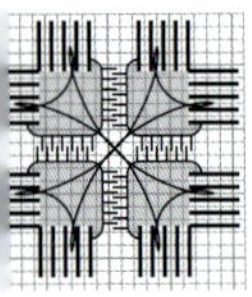

CONTEMPORARY

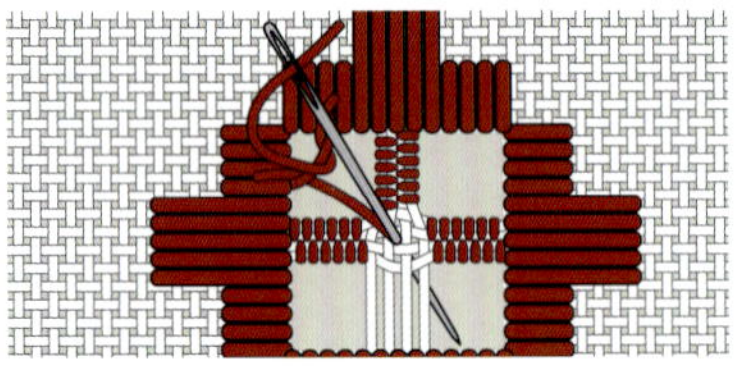

4 Insert the needle in the centre of the woven square.

❶ *When working this in four quadrants of a square, anchor the thread under some stitching on the back of the woven square, so that when starting the next curled V, it does not come straight out of the same hole as where it just entered.*

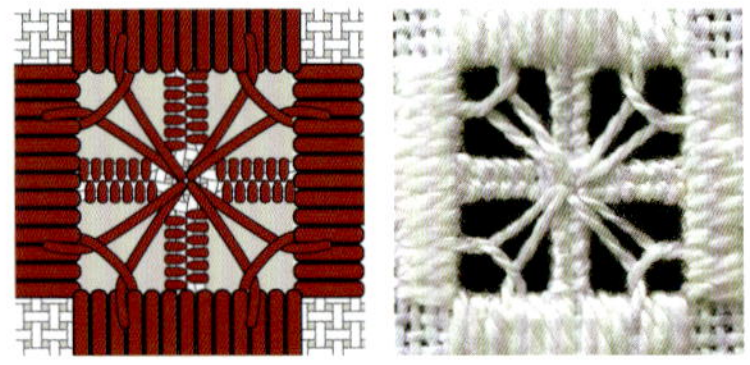

5 Work curled Vs in the other quadrants, then weave the final bar.

ending 2 – single twist

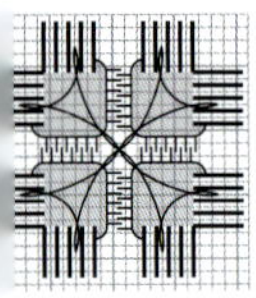

CONTEMPORARY

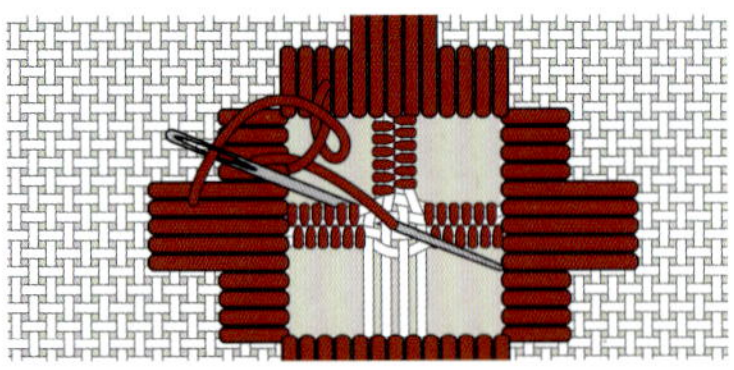

4 Insert the needle below the first stitch and bring it out in the centre of the woven square.

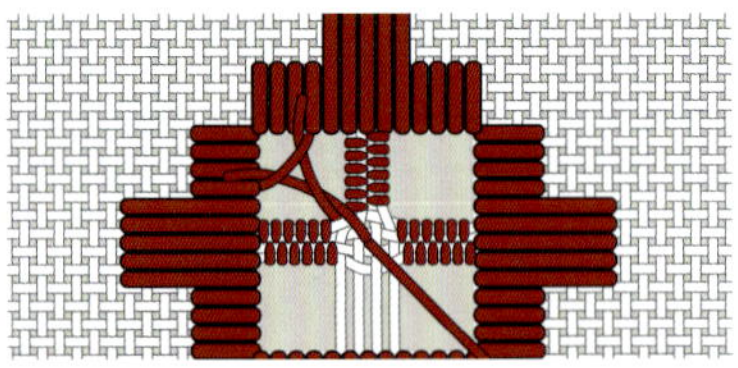

5 Pull the needle through. Pull the thread down and right to intertwine the stitches.

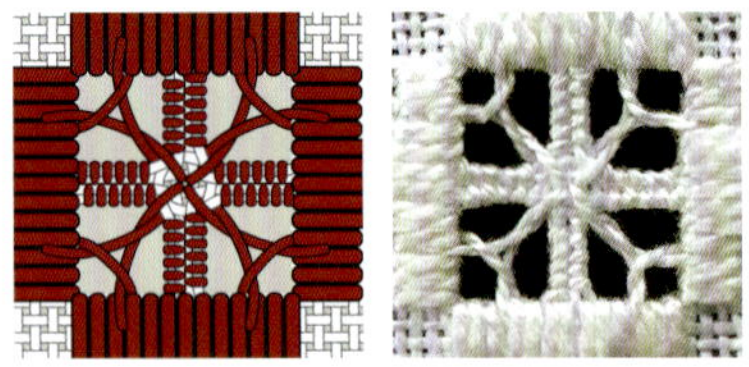

6 Work curled Vs in the other quadrants, then weave the final bar.

ending 3 – double twist

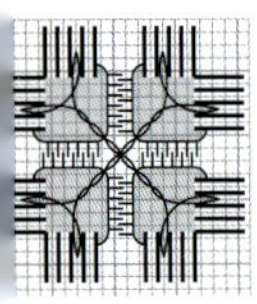

CONTEMPORARY

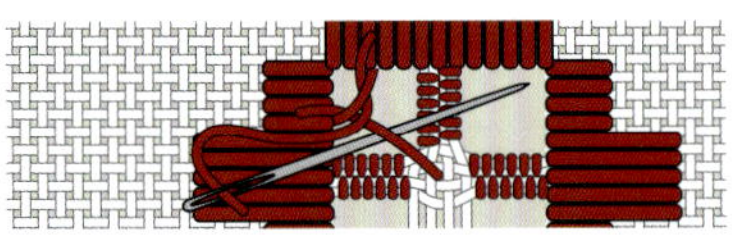

4 From below, slide the needle under the first stitch.

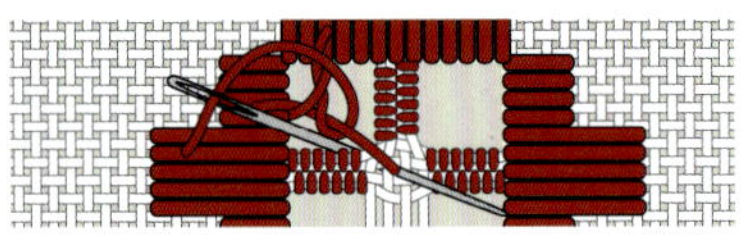

5 Insert the needle below the first stitch and bring it out in the centre of the woven square.

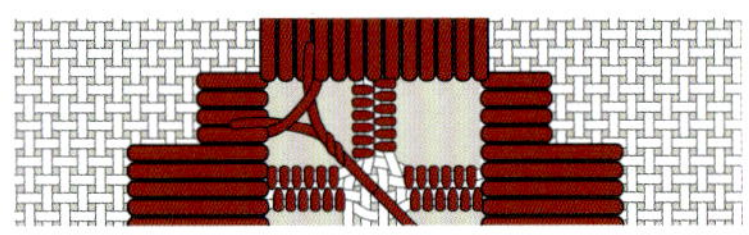

6 Pull the needle through. Pull the thread down and right to intertwine the stitches.

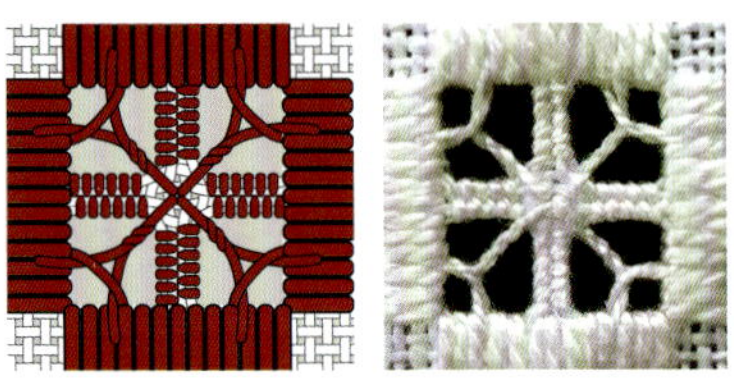

7 Work curled Vs in the other quadrants, then weave the final bar.

curled V

This stitch can be worked with woven or wrapped bars. It can be used singly or in four quadrants of a square. Depending on the orientation of the curled V, you may need to work it into as yet unstitched bars.

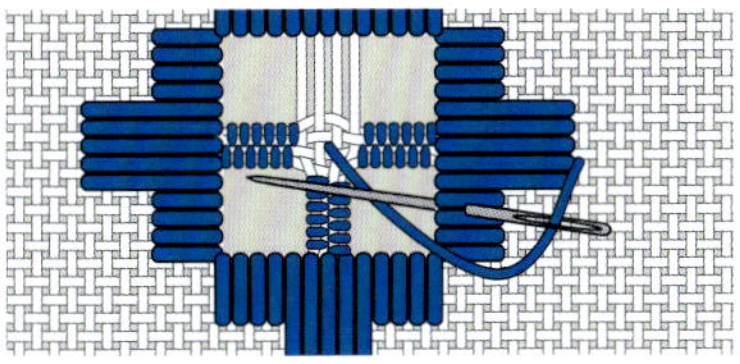

1 Weave three bars. Bring the needle out in the woven square's centre. From the right, insert it halfway across the right satin stitch, three stitches from the bottom. Take it over the thread.

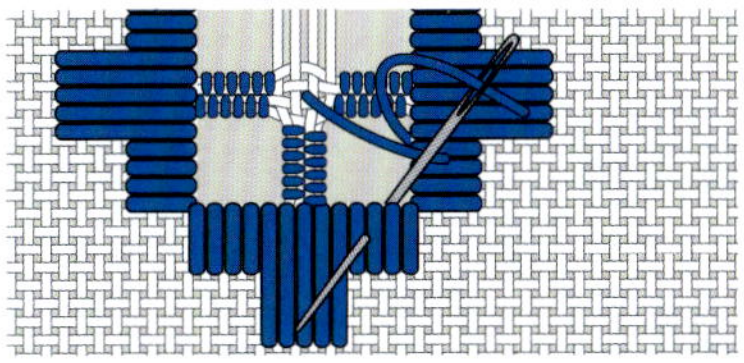

2 Pull the needle through so the stitch curves gently. Bring the needle out halfway across the satin stitch at the lower edge of the quadrant, three stitches from the right.

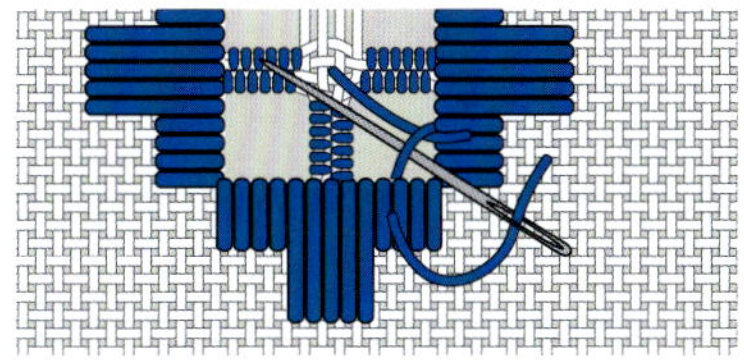

3 Pull the needle through so the stitch curves gently. Slide the needle under the second stitch.

❶ *Continue to any of the endings below.*

ending 1 – no twist

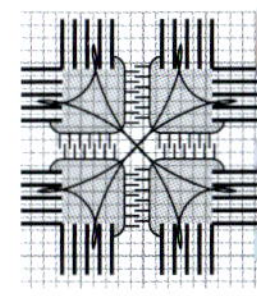

CONTEMPORARY

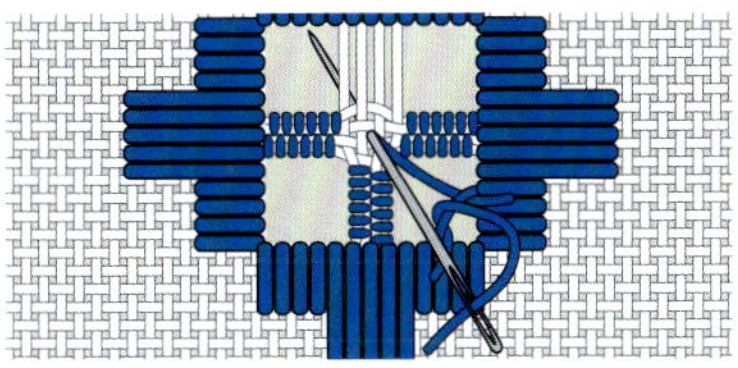

4 Insert the needle in the centre of the woven square.

❶ *When working this in four quadrants of a square, anchor the thread under some stitching on the back of the woven square, so that when starting the next curled V, it does not come straight out of the same hole as where it just entered.*

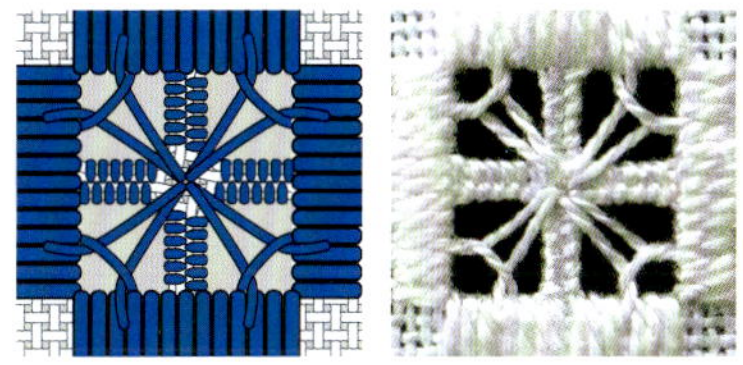

5 Work curled Vs in the other quadrants, then weave the final bar.

ending 2 – single twist

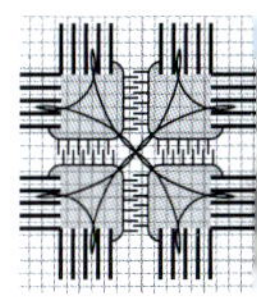

CONTEMPORARY

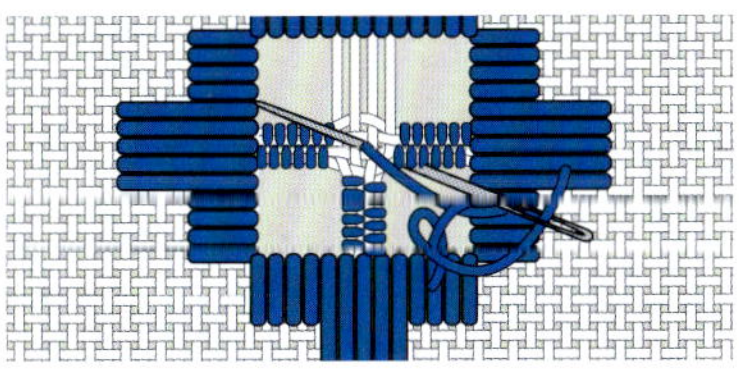

4 Insert the needle above the first stitch and bring it out in the centre of the woven square.

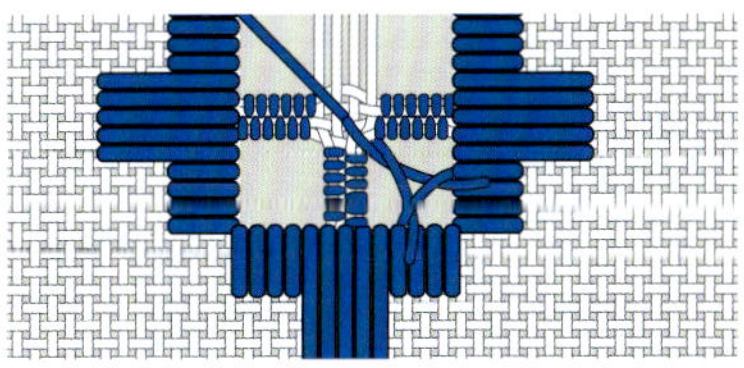

5 Pull the needle through. Pull the thread up and left to intertwine the stitches.

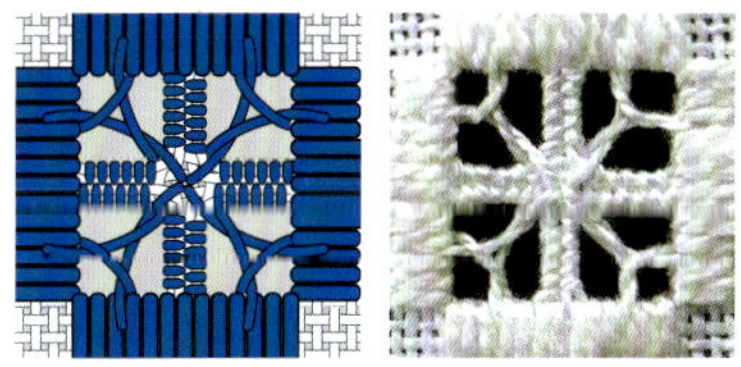

6 Work curled Vs in the other quadrants, then weave the final bar.

ending 3 – double twist

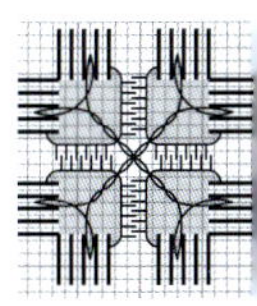

CONTEMPORARY

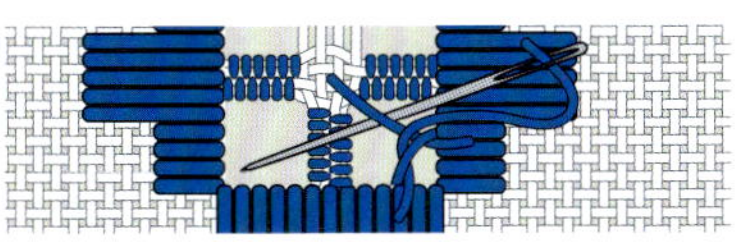

4 From above, slide the needle under the first stitch.

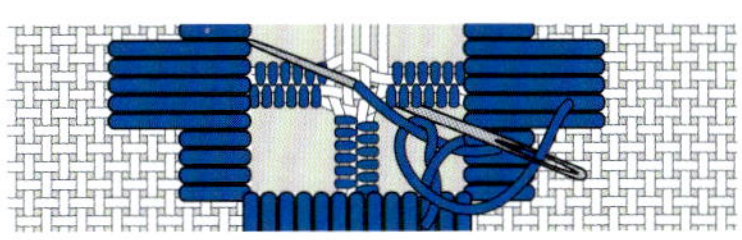

5 Insert the needle above the first stitch and bring it out in the centre of the woven square.

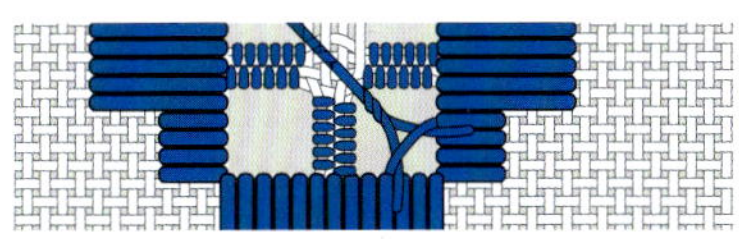

6 Pull the needle through. Pull the thread up and left to intertwine the stitches.

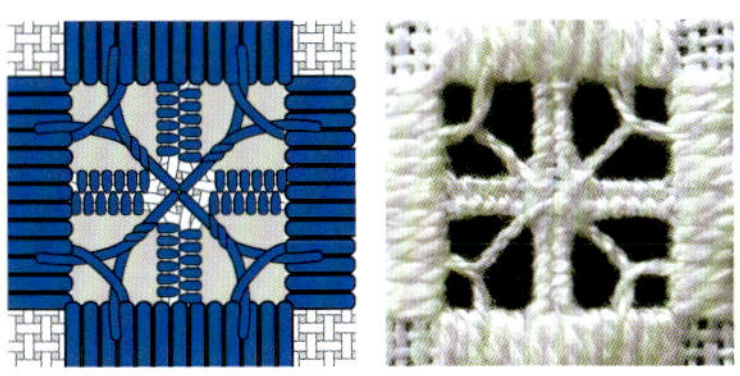

7 Work curled Vs in the other quadrants, then weave the final bar.

L dove's eye

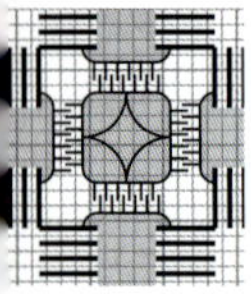

TRADITIONAL

The dove's eye filling stitch is stitched as part of the fourth side of the square in which the filling is worked. Dove's eyes can be worked either clockwise or anticlockwise – just be consistent throughout.

clockwise dove's eye

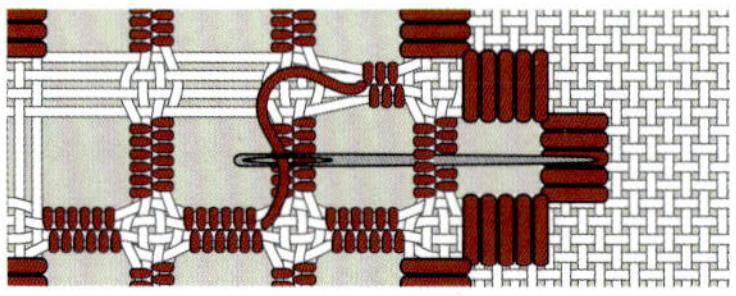

1 Stitch half of the fourth side of the square. Working in a clockwise direction, insert the needle into the centre back of the next woven bar.

! *The needle is always inserted in the back of the bar.*

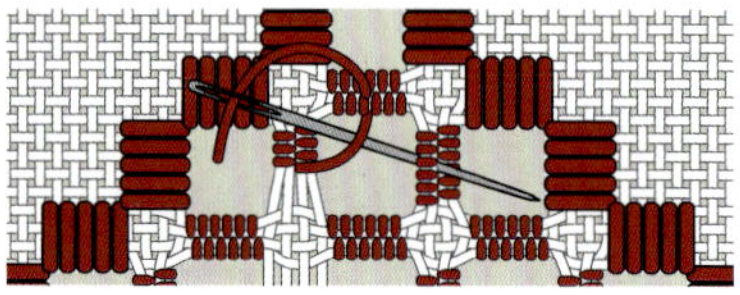

2 Pull the needle through so the stitch gently curves between the two bars. Turn the work 90° anticlockwise. Insert the needle under the previous stitch and into the back of the next woven bar.

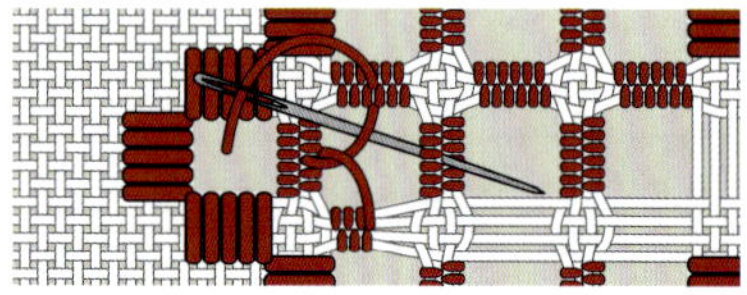

3 Pull the needle through so the stitch gently curves between the two bars. Turn the work 90° anticlockwise. Insert the needle under the previous stitch and into the back of the next woven bar.

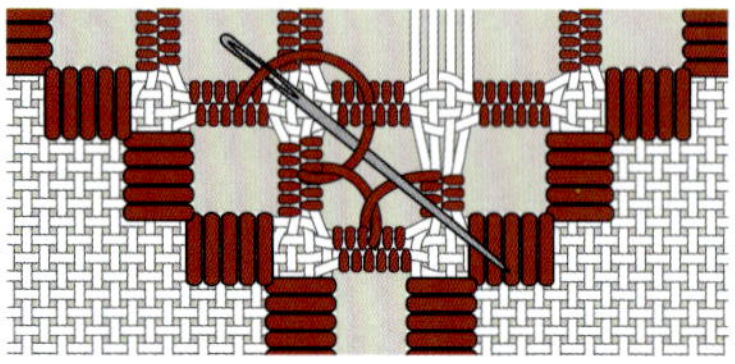

4 Pull the needle through so the stitch gently curves. Turn the work 90° anticlockwise. Take the needle under the previous stitch.

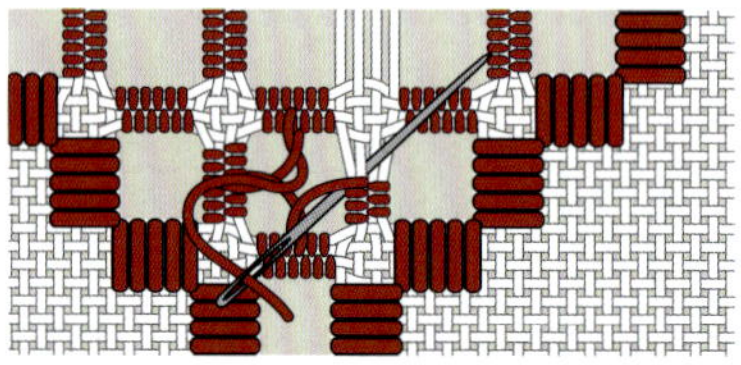

5 Take the needle over the initial curved thread, and insert the needle in the bar ready to continue stitching.

6 Finish the bar. Continue stitching.

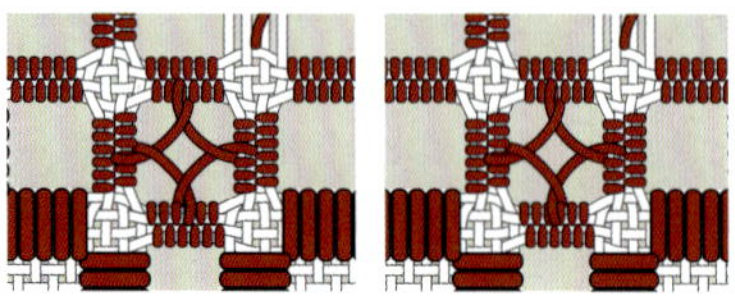

! *Ensure that all the stitches cross the same way: under at one end and over at the other (see left). If a stitch is 'over' or 'under' at both ends (see right), it is incorrect.*

! *The needle should always be inserted in the back of the bar.*

! *The threads should only cross once in the corners, and not have any extra twists.*

dove's eye within satin stitch

Sometimes between one and all four of the sides of the open square in which the filling is to be worked, are satin stitch, rather than woven bars.

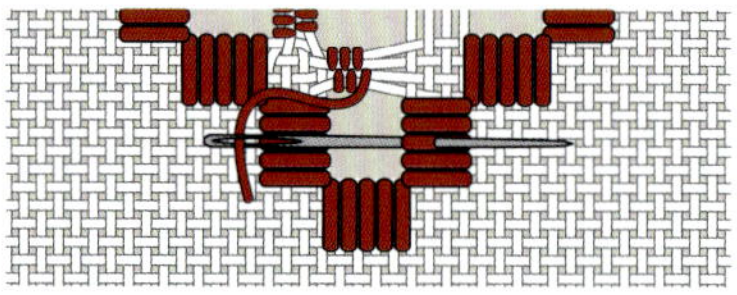

1 Work half the bar on the fourth side of the square. Insert the needle into the back of the kloster, coming out in the centre of the middle stitch.

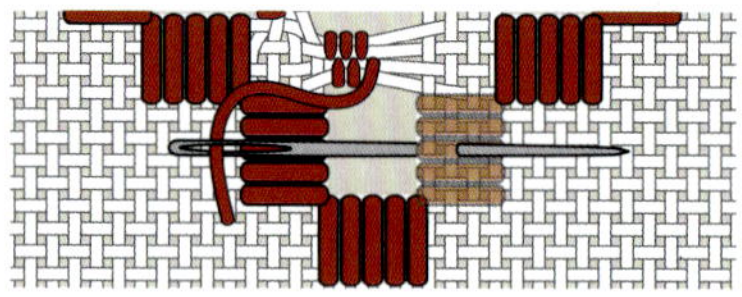

! *The needle should pierce the stitch.*

! *The needle comes out in the centre of the four by four thread block over which the satin stitch is worked.*

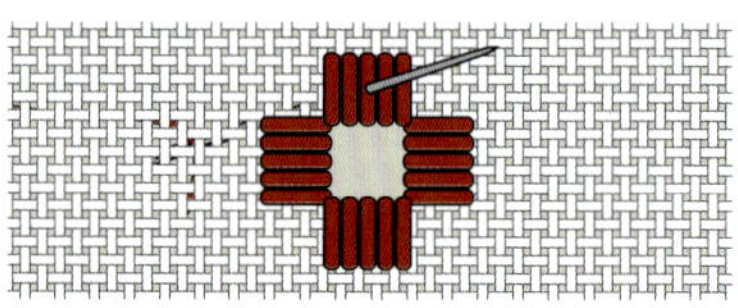

! *If all the sides are satin stitch, start by bringing the needle out in the centre of the middle stitch in one of the blocks.*

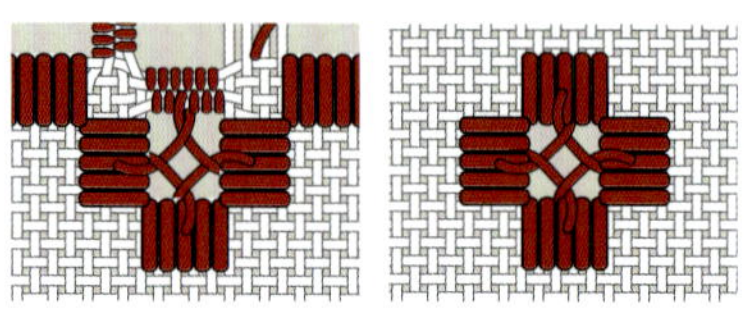

2 Following the same method as above, complete the remainder of the dove's eye filling.

anticlockwise dove's eye

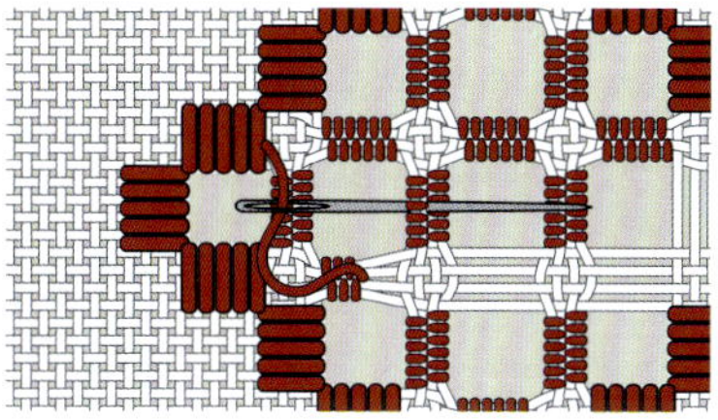

1 Stitch half of the fourth side of the square. Working around the square in an anticlockwise direction, insert the needle into the centre back of the next woven bar.

❶ *The needle is always inserted in the back of the bar.*

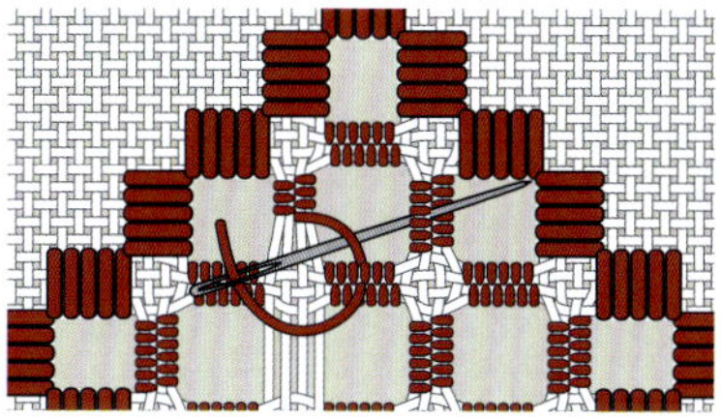

2 Pull the needle through so the stitch gently curves between the two bars. Turn the work 90° clockwise. Insert the needle under the previous stitch and into the back of the next woven bar.

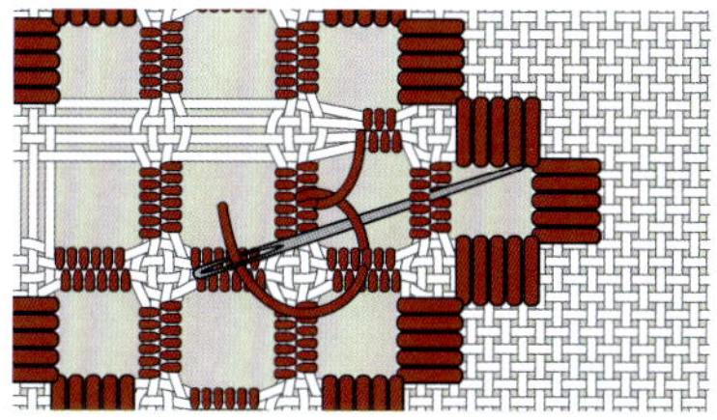

3 Pull the needle through so the stitch gently curves between the two bars. Turn the work 90° clockwise. Insert the needle under the previous stitch and into the back of the next woven bar.

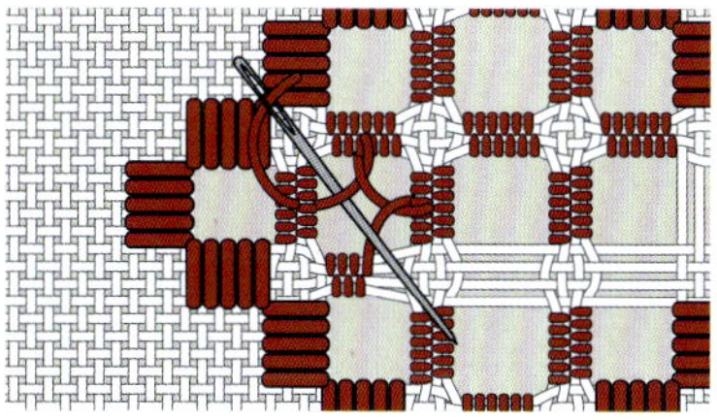

4 Pull the needle through so the stitch gently curves between the two bars. Turn the work 180°. Take the needle under the previous stitch.

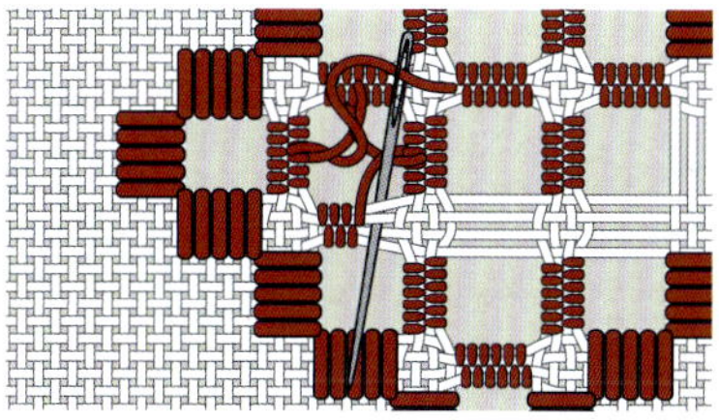

5 Take the needle over the initial curved thread, and insert the needle in the bar ready to continue stitching.

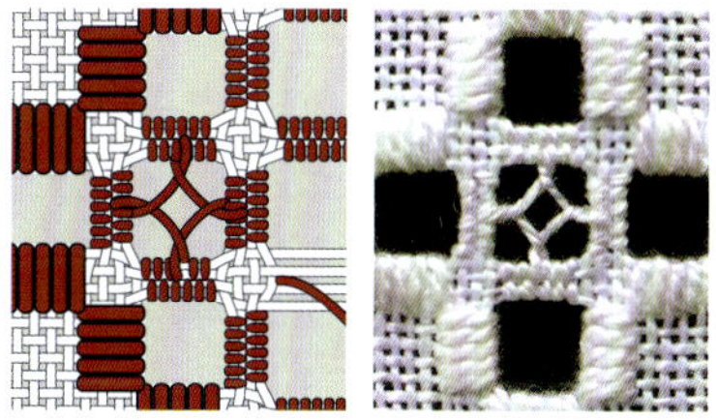

6 Finish the bar. Continue stitching.

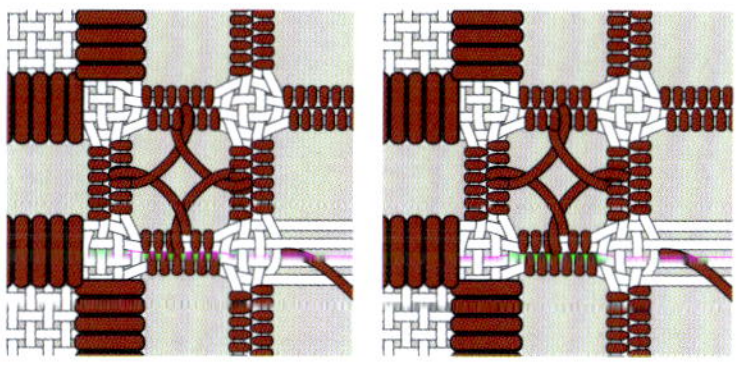

❶ *Ensure that all the stitches cross the same way: under at one end and over at the other (see left). If a stitch is 'over' or 'under' at both ends (see right), it is incorrect.*

❶ *The needle should always be inserted in the back of the bar.*

❶ *The threads should only cross once in the corners, and not have any extra twists.*

dove's eye within satin stitch

Sometimes between one and all four of the sides of the open square in which the filling is to be worked, are satin stitch, rather than woven bars.

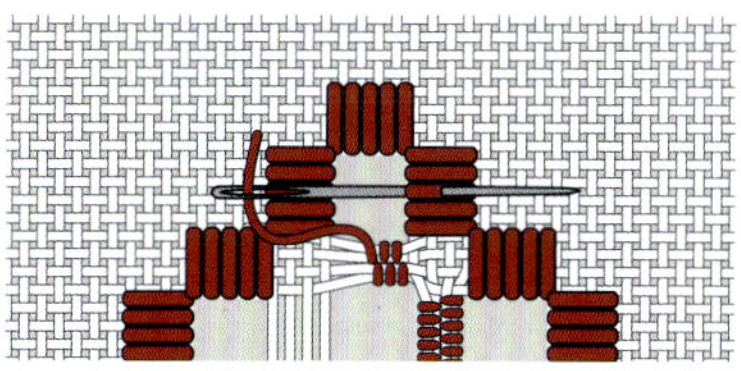

1 Work half the bar on the fourth side of the square. Insert the needle into the back of the kloster, coming out in the centre of the middle stitch.

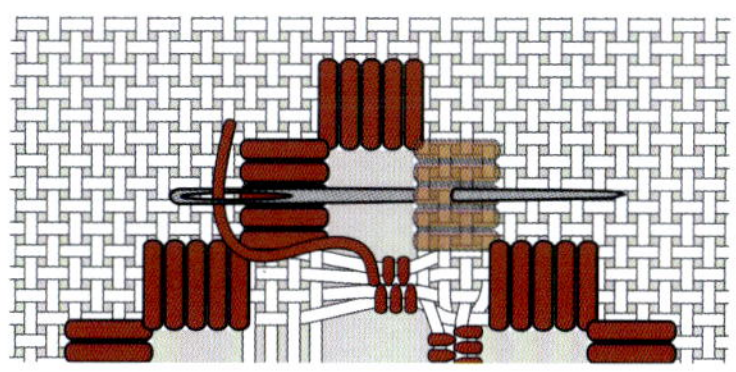

❶ *The needle should pierce the stitch.*

❶ *The needle comes out in the centre of the four by four thread block over which the satin stitch is worked.*

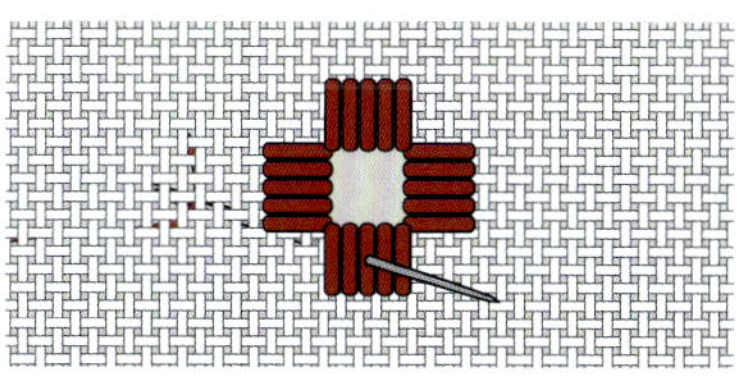

❶ *If all the sides are satin stitch, start by bringing the needle out in the centre of the middle stitch in one of the blocks.*

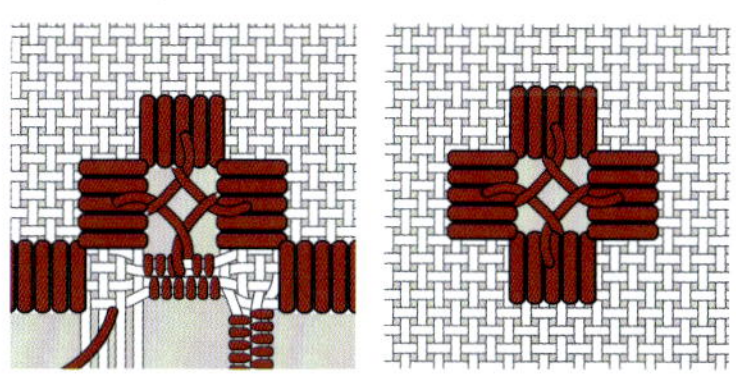

2 Following the same method as above, complete the remainder of the dove's eye filling.

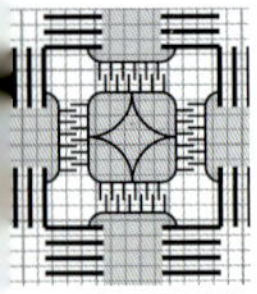

TRADITIONAL

dove's eye

The dove's eye filling stitch is worked as part of the fourth side of the square in which the filling is worked. Dove's eyes can be worked either clockwise or anticlockwise – just be consistent throughout.

clockwise dove's eye

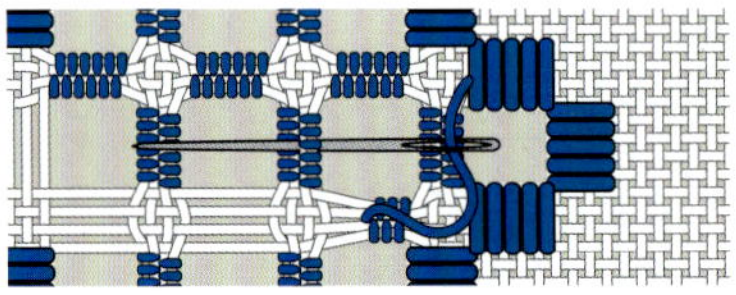

1 Stitch half of the fourth side of the square. Working in a clockwise direction, insert the needle into the centre back of the next woven bar.

❶ *The needle is always inserted in the back of the bar.*

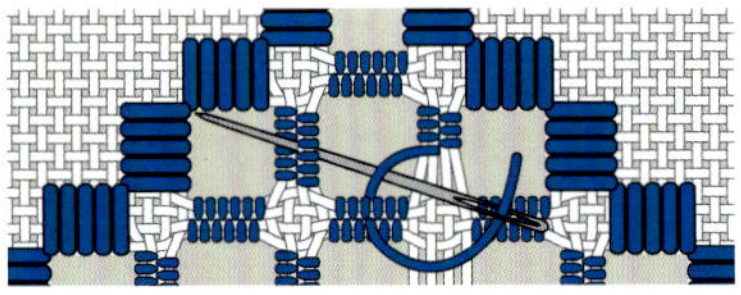

2 Pull the needle through so the stitch gently curves between the two bars. Turn the work 90° anticlockwise. Insert the needle under the previous stitch and into the back of the next woven bar.

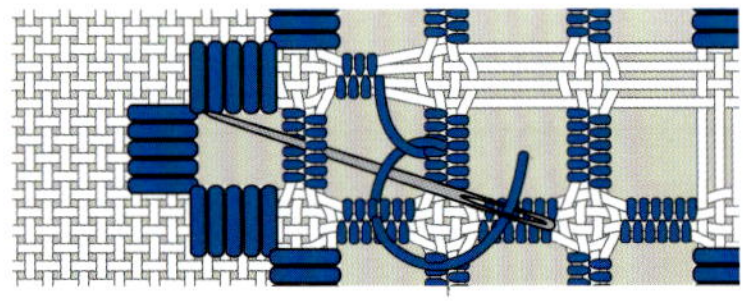

3 Pull the needle through so the stitch gently curves between the two bars. Turn the work 90° anticlockwise. Insert the needle under the previous stitch and into the back of the next woven bar.

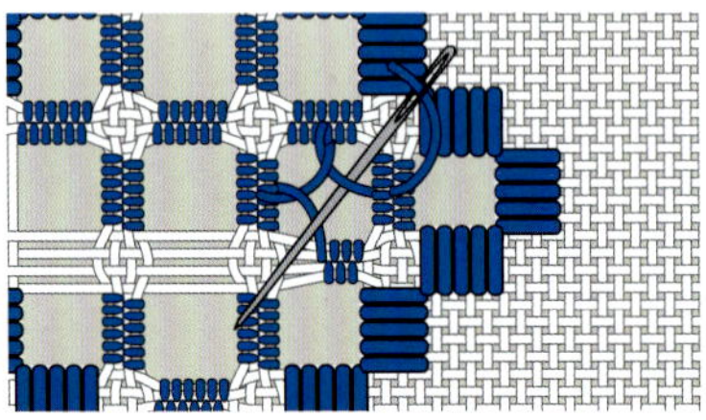

4 Pull the needle through so the stitch gently curves between the two bars. Turn the work 180°. Take the needle under the previous stitch.

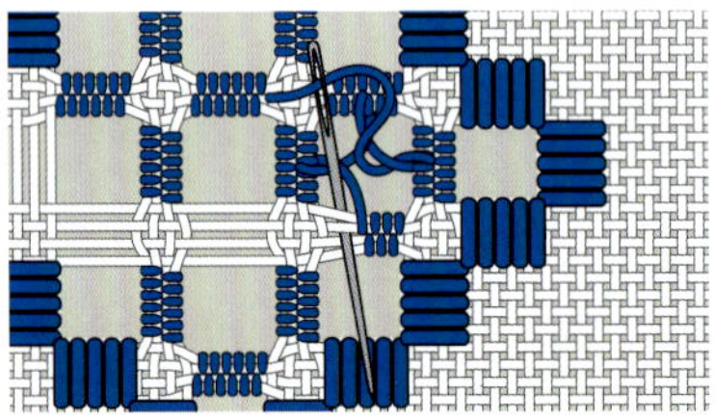

5 Take the needle over the initial curved thread, and insert the needle in the bar ready to continue stitching.

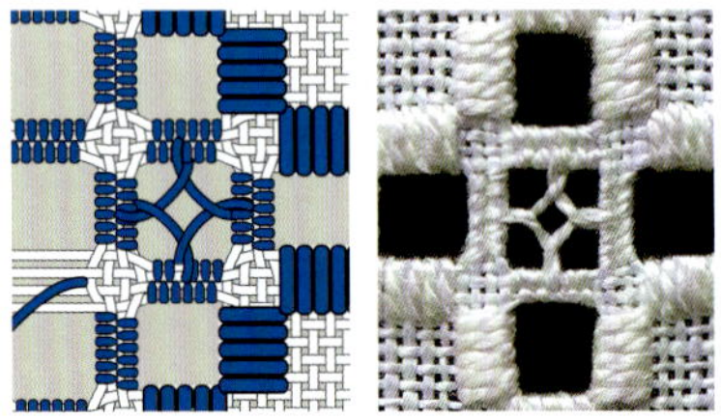

6 Finish the bar. Continue stitching.

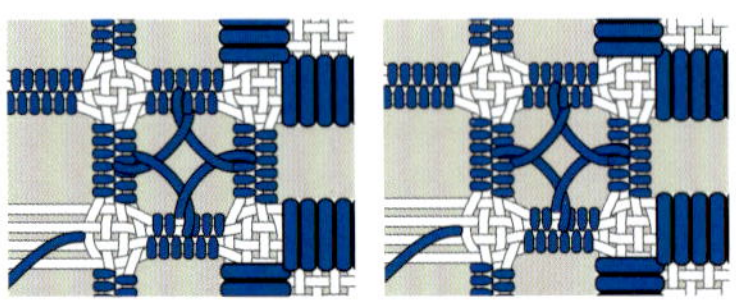

❶ *Ensure that all the stitches cross the same way: under at one end and over at the other (see left). If a stitch is 'over' or 'under' at both ends (see right), it is incorrect.*

❶ *The needle should always be inserted in the back of the bar.*

❶ *The threads should only cross once in the corners, and not have any extra twists.*

dove's eye within satin stitch

Sometimes between one and all four of the sides of the square to be filled are satin stitch, rather than woven bars.

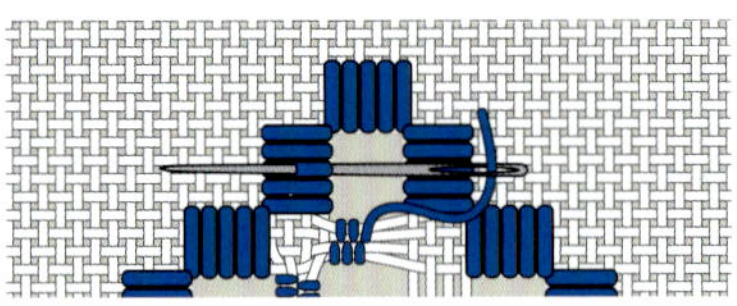

1 Work half the bar on the fourth side of the square. Insert the needle into the back of the kloster, coming out in the centre of the middle stitch.

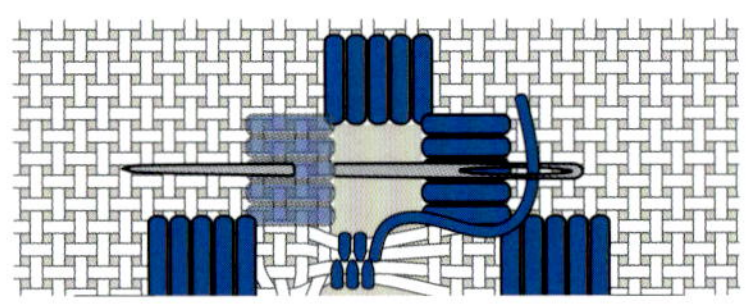

❶ *The needle should pierce the stitch.*

❶ *The needle comes out in the centre of the four by four thread block over which the satin stitch is worked.*

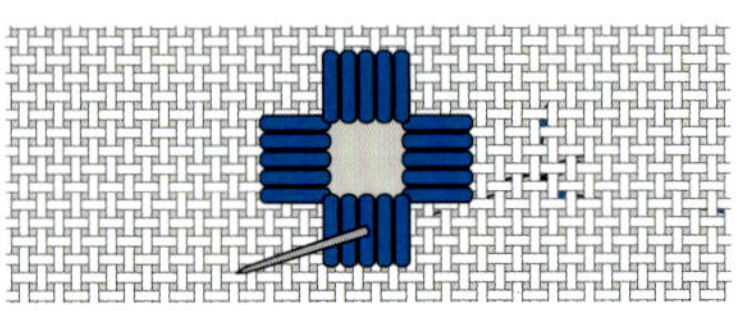

❶ *If all the sides are satin stitch, bring the needle out in the centre of the middle stitch in one of the blocks.*

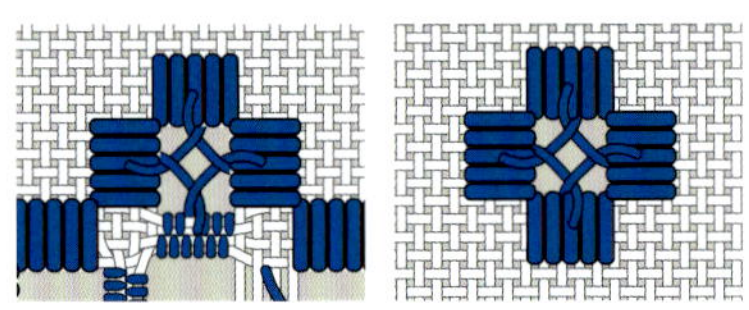

2 Following the same method as above, complete the remainder of the dove's eye filling.

anticlockwise dove's eye

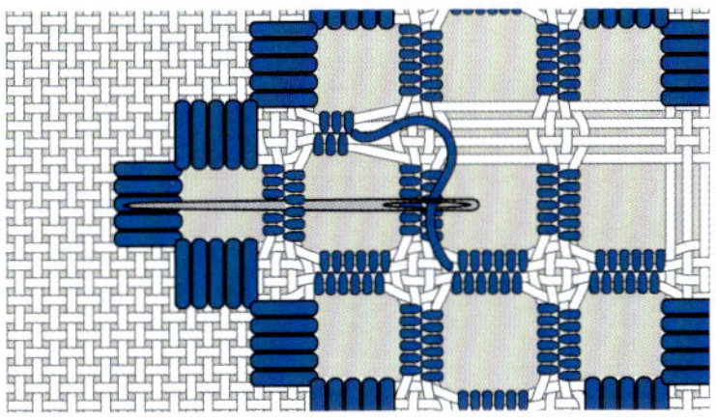

1 Stitch half of the fourth side of the square. Working around the square in an anticlockwise direction, insert the needle into the centre back of the next woven bar.

! *The needle is always inserted in the back of the bar.*

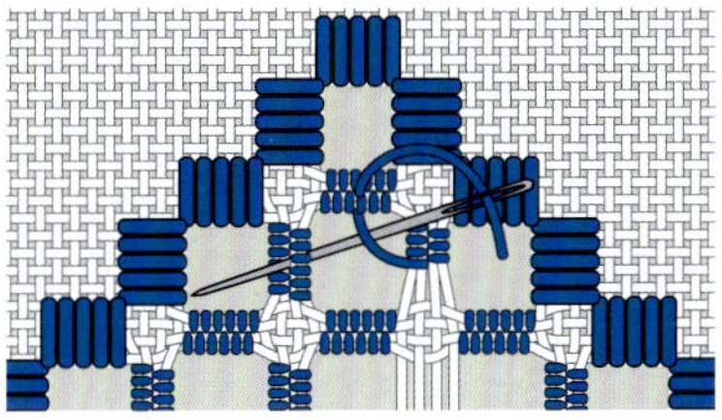

2 Pull the needle through so the stitch gently curves between the two bars. Turn the work 90° clockwise. Insert the needle under the previous stitch and into the back of the next woven bar.

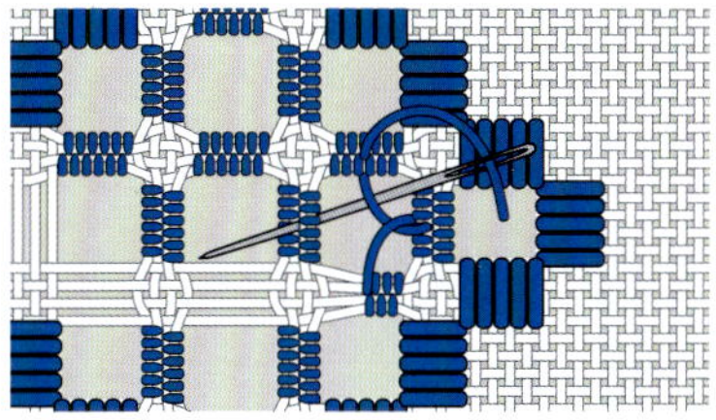

3 Pull the needle through so the stitch gently curves between the two bars. Turn the work 90° clockwise. Insert the needle under the previous stitch and into the back of the next woven bar.

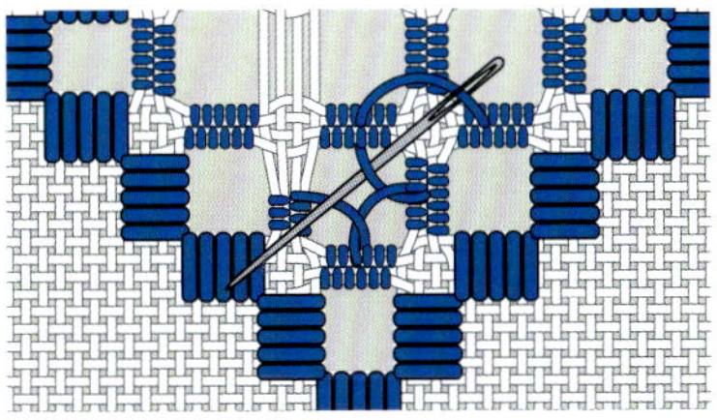

4 Pull the needle through so the stitch gently curves between the two bars. Turn the work 180°. Take the needle under the previous stitch.

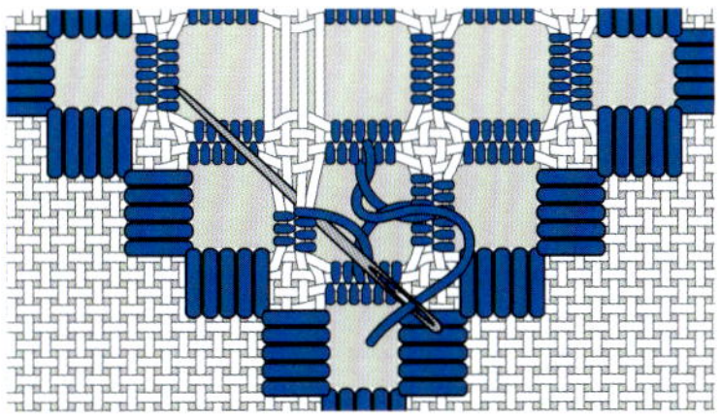

5 Take the needle over the initial curved thread, and insert the needle in the bar ready to continue stitching.

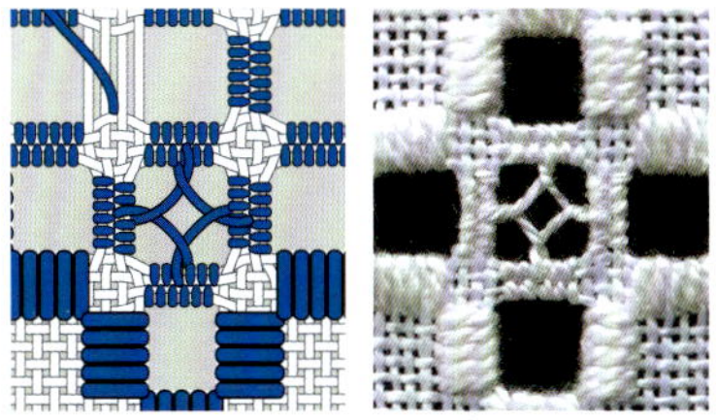

6 Finish the bar. Continue stitching.

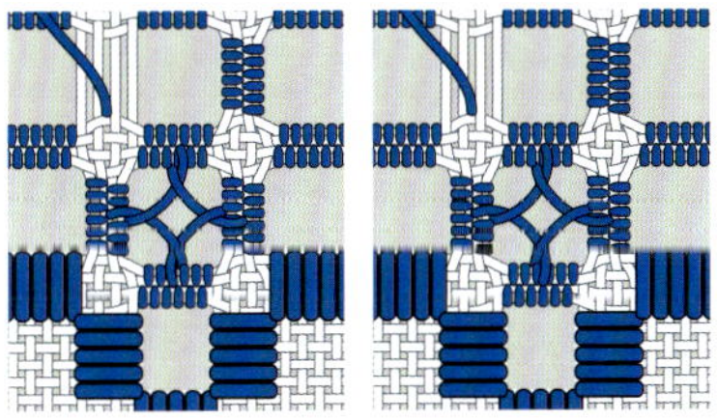

! *Ensure that all the stitches cross the same way: under at one end and over at the other (see left). If a stitch is 'over' or 'under' at both ends (see right), it is incorrect.*

! *The needle should always be inserted in the back of the bar.*

! *The threads should only cross once in the corners, and not have any extra twists.*

dove's eye within satin stitch

Sometimes between one and all four of the sides of the open square in which the filling is worked are satin stitch, rather than woven bars.

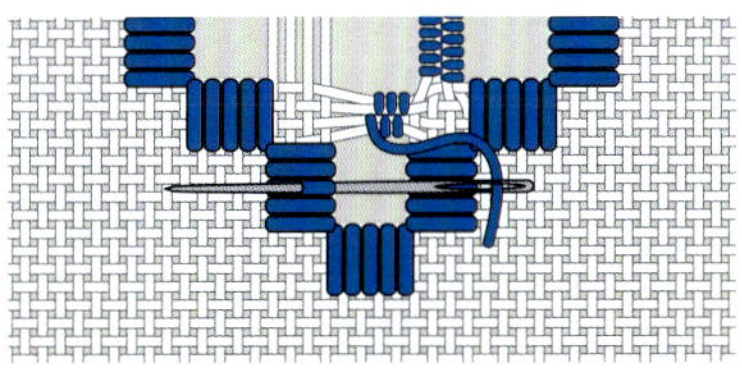

1 Work half the bar on the fourth side of the square. Insert the needle into the back of the kloster, coming out in the centre of the middle stitch.

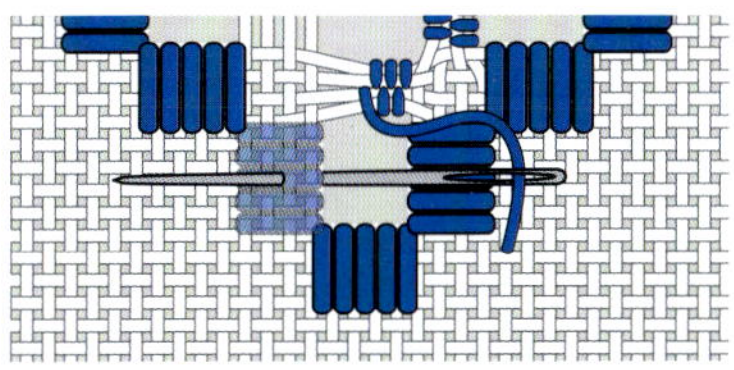

! *The needle should pierce the stitch.*

! *The needle comes out in the centre of the four by four thread block over which the satin stitch is worked.*

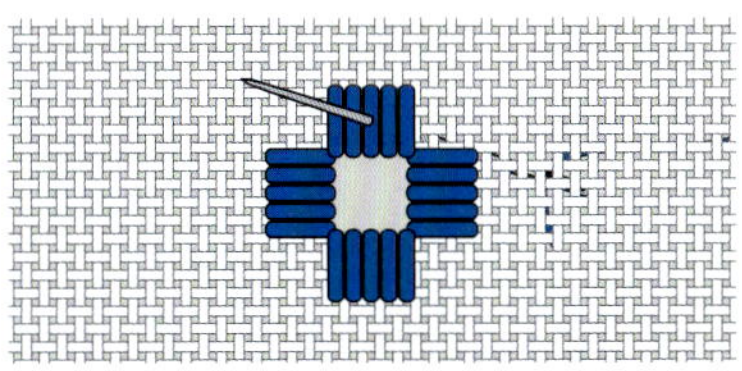

! *If all the sides are satin stitch, bring the needle out in the centre of the middle stitch in one of the blocks.*

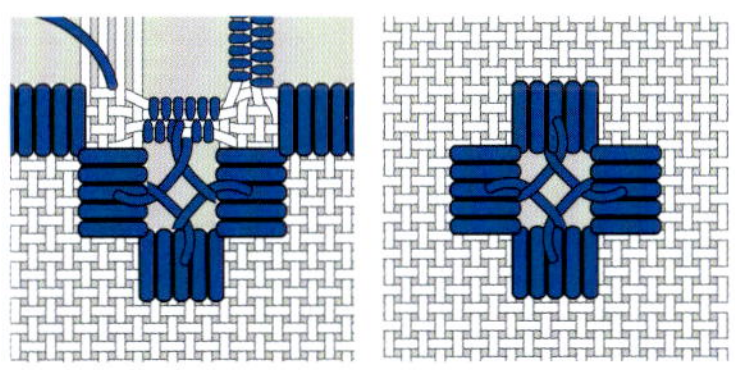

2 Following the same method as above, complete the remainder of the dove's eye filling.

triangular dove's eye *also known as crow's foot*

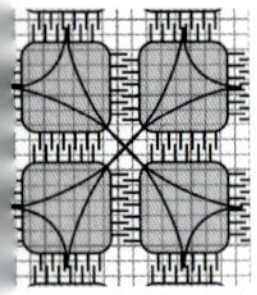

CONTEMPORARY

This stitch is similar to regular dove's eyes, but has only three points rather than four. Two are worked into bars, and one is in a corner woven square. It can be worked in a group, or singly. While the motif looks similar to Curled V it is different.

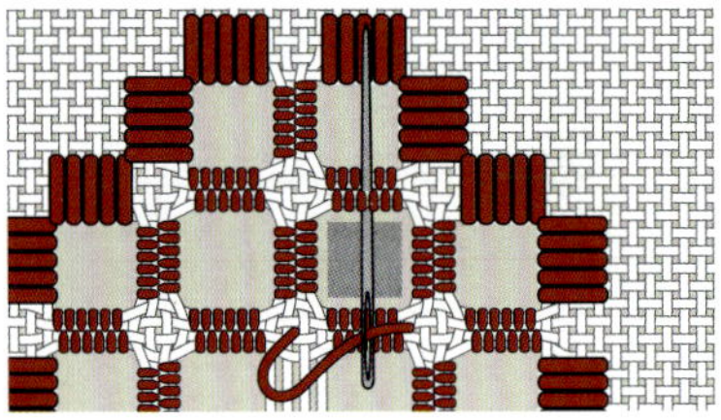

1 Weave the bars of a square. Bring the needle out in the adjacent woven square's centre. Moving in a clockwise direction, skip the first bar, then insert it into the centre back of the next woven bar, from below.

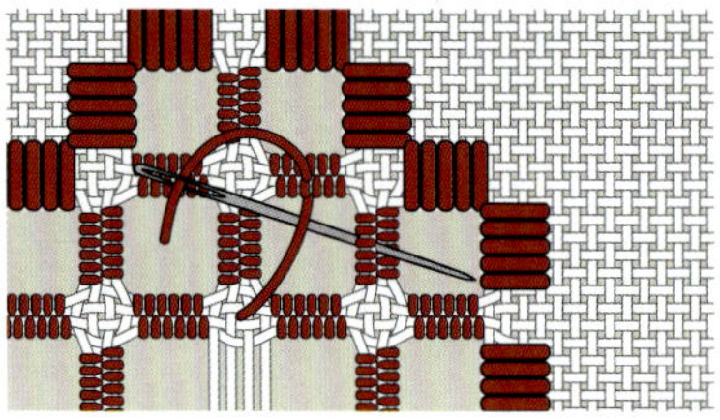

2 Pull the needle through so the stitch curves gently. Insert the needle under the previous stitch and into the back of the next woven bar from the left.

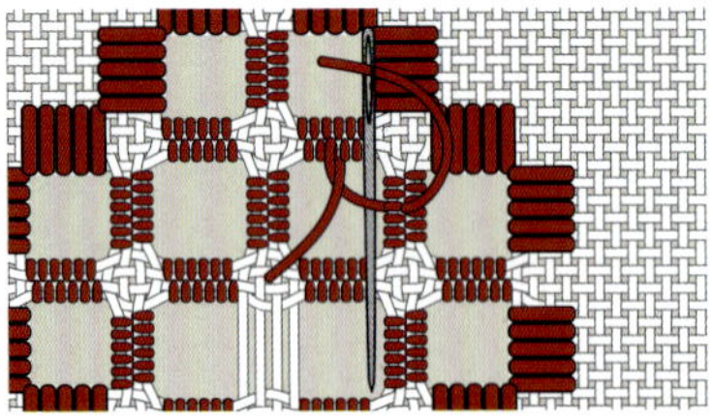

3 Pull the needle through so the stitch curves gently. Slide the needle under the previous stitch from above.

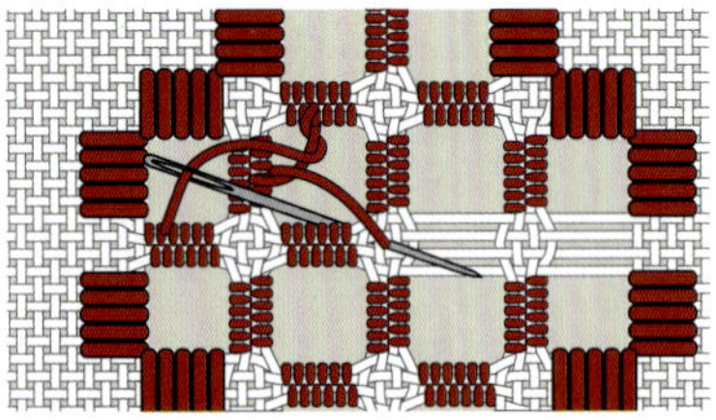

4 Turn the work 90° anticlockwise. Take the needle over the first stitch and to the back. Bring it out in the centre of the woven square.

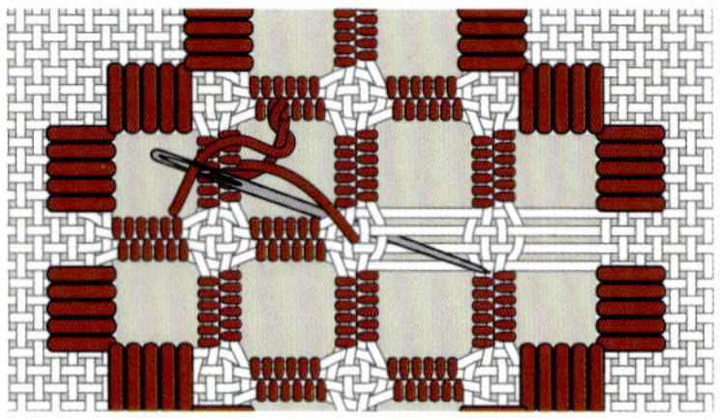

If working a single dove's eye only, take the needle over the first stitch and to the back. Bring it out ready to weave the next bar, then continue on.

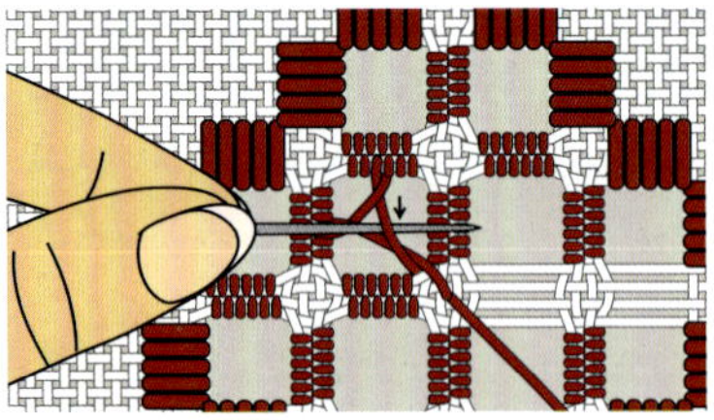

5 Pull the needle through and tighten the stitches of the dove's eye. *Use your needle to adjust the tension of the stitches, if needed, by taking extra tension out to the end (as shown), or adding extra length in from the end.*

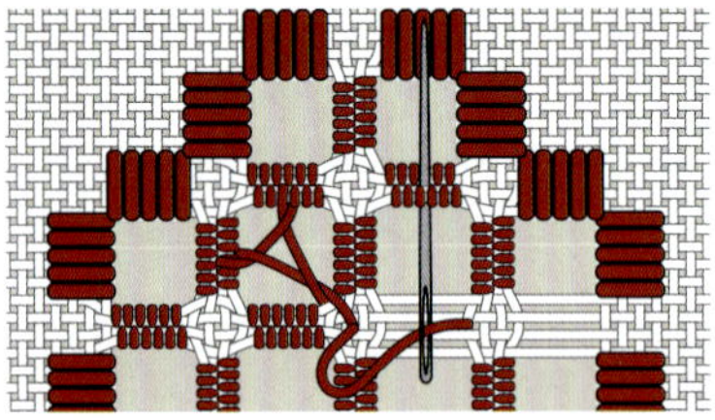

6 Move to an adjacent open square. Moving in a clockwise direction, skip the first bar, then insert it into the centre back of the next woven bar, from below.

7 Work Steps 2 to 5 to complete the next triangular dove's eye, turning the work as required for ease of needle insertion.

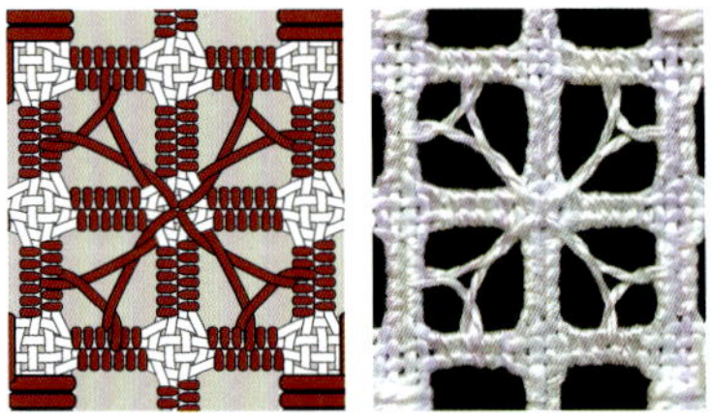

8 Weave the bars to complete the sequence of four triangular dove's eyes.

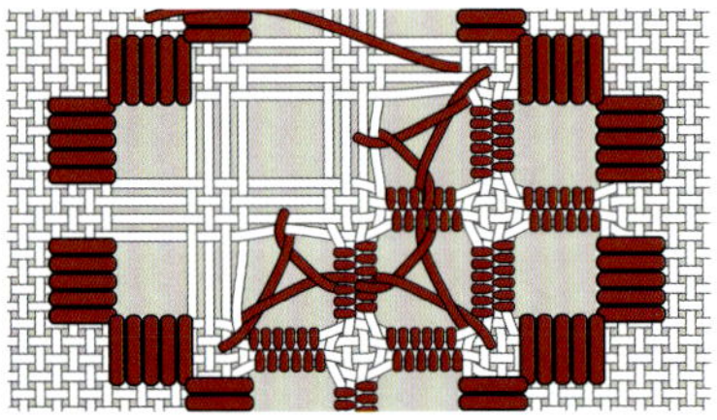

Usually filling stitches are worked as late as possible during the process. However, depending on the path taken and the triangle's orientation, you may need to work it earlier. This may mean stitching into not yet woven bars, so take extra care with tension.

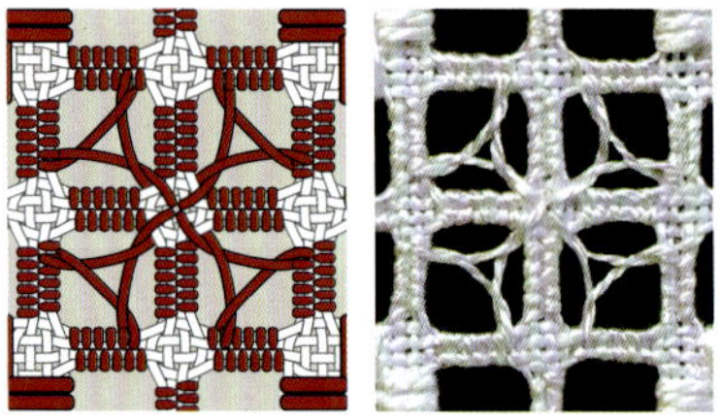

By moving the position of the stitches that go into the bars, you can change the shape of the triangles and the look of the stitch.

triangular dove's eye *also known as crow's foot*

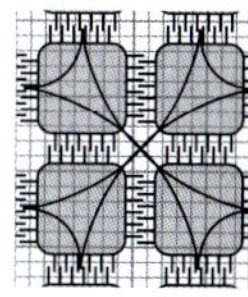

CONTEMPORARY

This stitch is similar to regular dove's eyes, but has only three points rather than four. Two are worked into bars, and one is in a corner woven square. It can be worked in a group, or singly. While the motif looks similar to Curled V it is different.

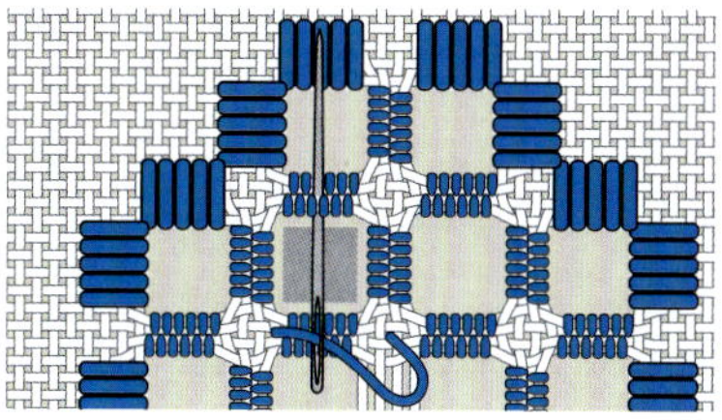

1 Weave the bars of a square. Bring the needle out in the adjacent woven square's centre. Moving in an anticlockwise direction, skip the first bar, then insert it into the centre back of the next woven bar, from below.

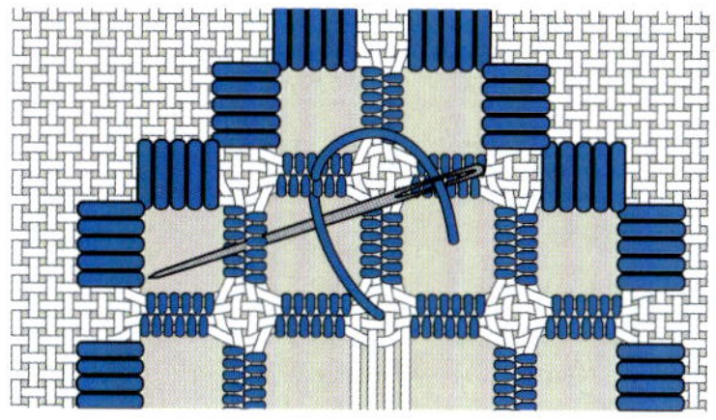

2 Pull the needle through so the stitch curves gently. Insert the needle under the previous stitch and into the back of the next woven bar from the right.

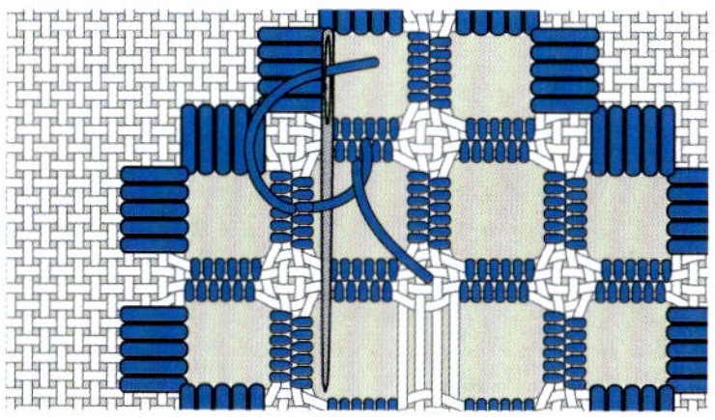

3 Pull the needle through so the stitch gently curves between the two bars. Slide the needle under the previous stitch from above.

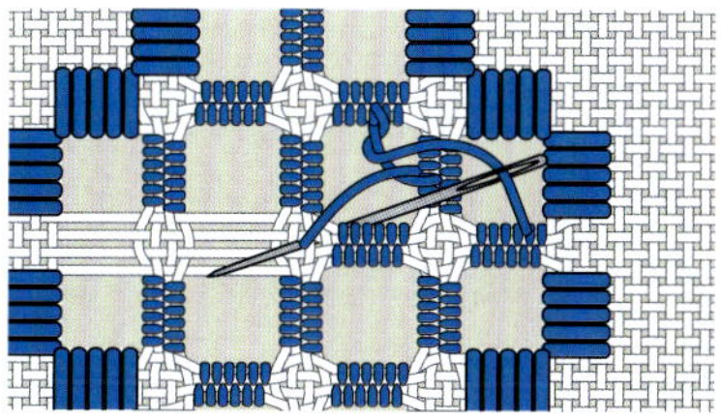

4 Turn the work 90° clockwise. Take the needle over the first stitch and to the back. Bring it out in the centre of the woven square.

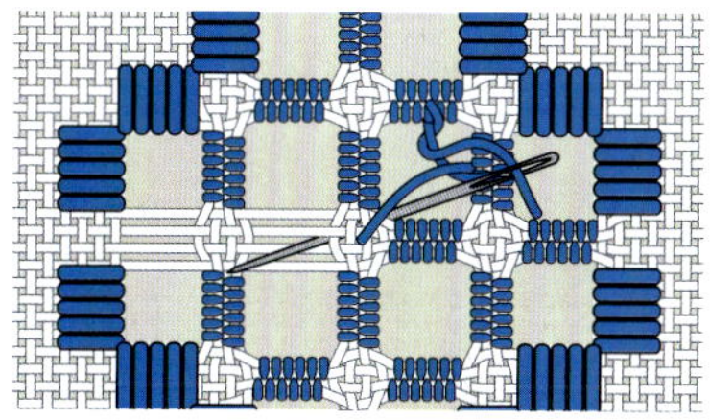

❶ *If working a single dove's eye only, take the needle over the first stitch and to the back. Bring it out ready to weave the next bar, then continue on.*

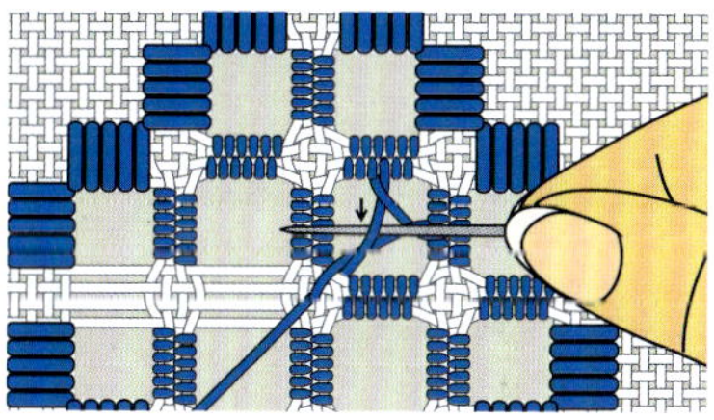

5 Pull the needle through and tighten the stitches of the dove's eye. ❶ *Use your needle to adjust the tension of the stitches, if needed, by taking extra tension out to the end (as shown), or adding extra length in from the end.*

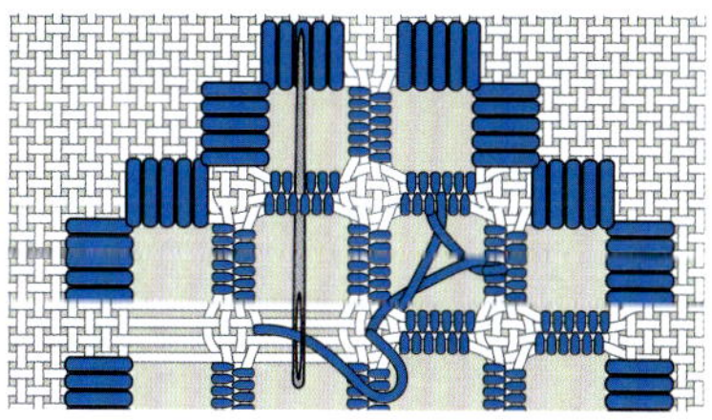

6 Move to an adjacent open square. Moving in an anticlockwise direction, skip the first bar, then insert it into the centre back of the next woven bar, from below.

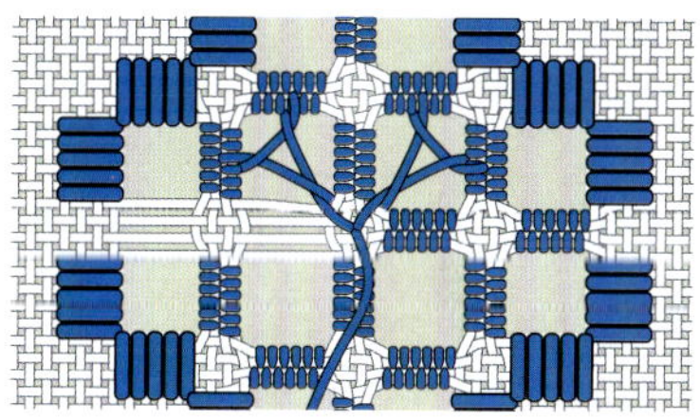

7 Work Steps 2 to 5 to complete the next triangular dove's eye, turning the work as required for ease of needle insertion.

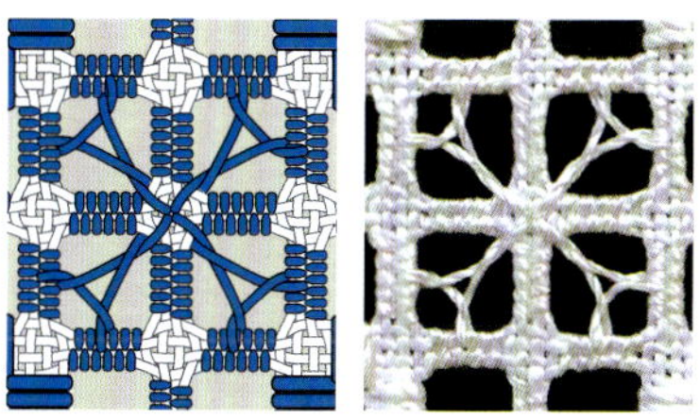

8 Weave the bars to complete the sequence of four triangular dove's eyes.

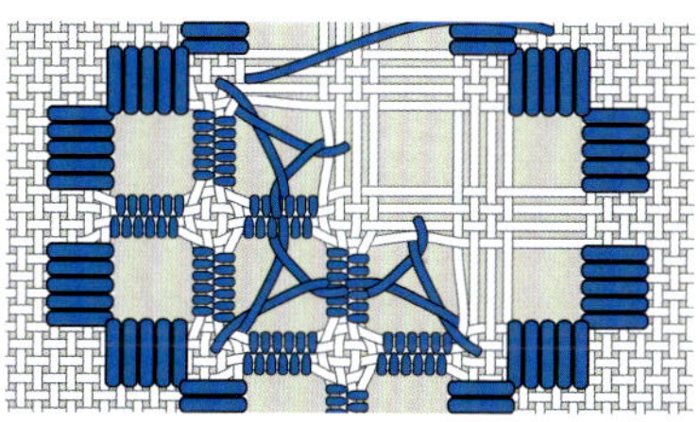

❶ *Usually filling stitches are worked as late as possible during the process, however, depending the path taken and the triangle's orientation, you may need to work it earlier than normal. This may mean stitching into not yet woven bars, so take extra care with tension.*

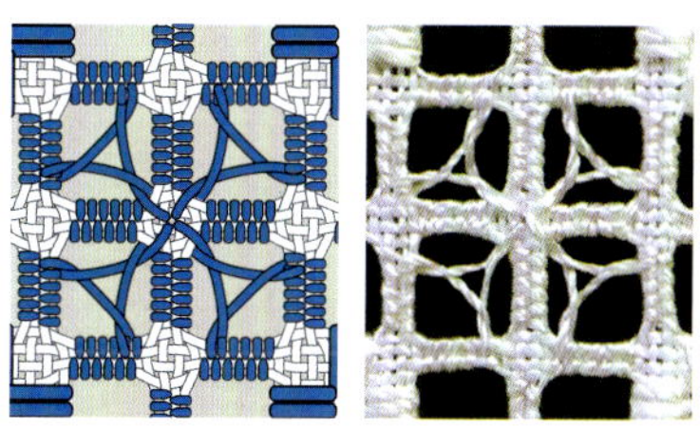

❶ *By moving the position of the stitches that go into the bars, you can change the shape of the triangles and the look of the stitch.*

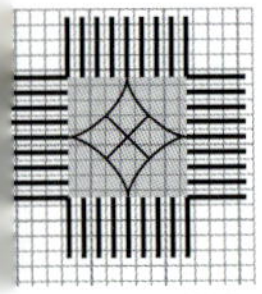

TRADITIONAL

dove's eye with cross

This larger dove's eye has a cross in the centre. It is worked in a square spanning eight by eight threads (nine stitches in each satin stitch block).

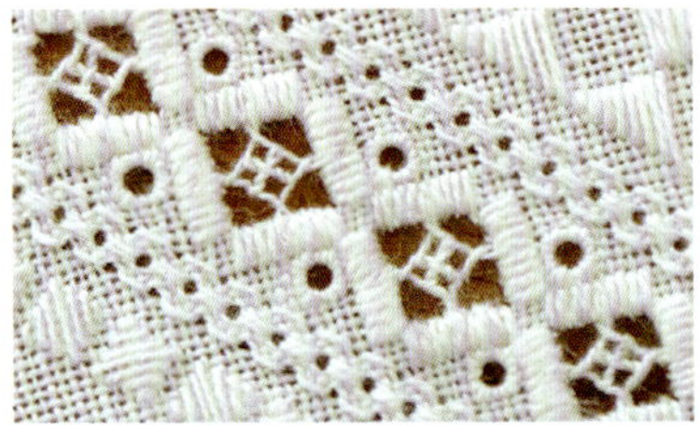

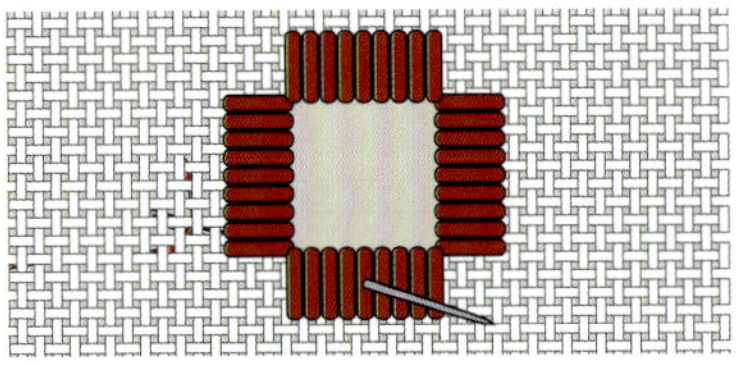

1 Anchor the thread in the back of the satin stitch. Bring the needle out in the centre of the middle stitch in the bottom satin stitch block.

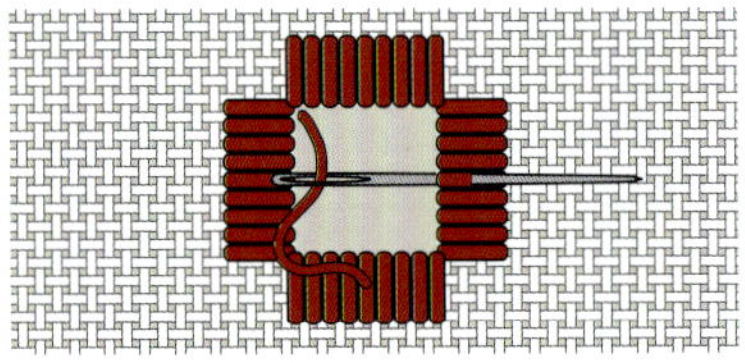

2 Working around the square in an anticlockwise direction, insert the needle into the centre back of the next satin stitch block's middle stitch.

❶ *The needle is always inserted in the back of the block.*

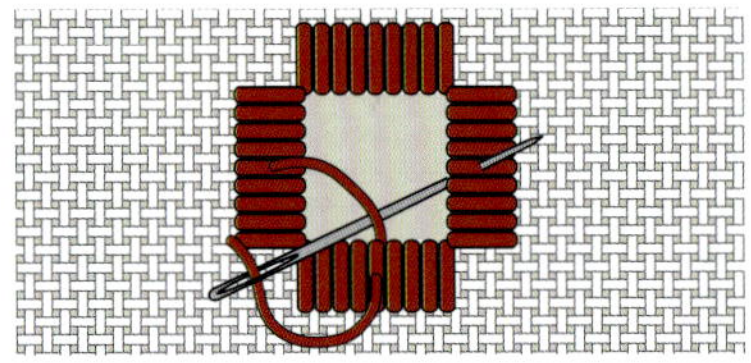

3 Pull the needle through so the stitch gently curves between the two blocks. Turn the work 90° clockwise. Insert the needle under the previous stitch and into the centre back of the next block's middle stitch.

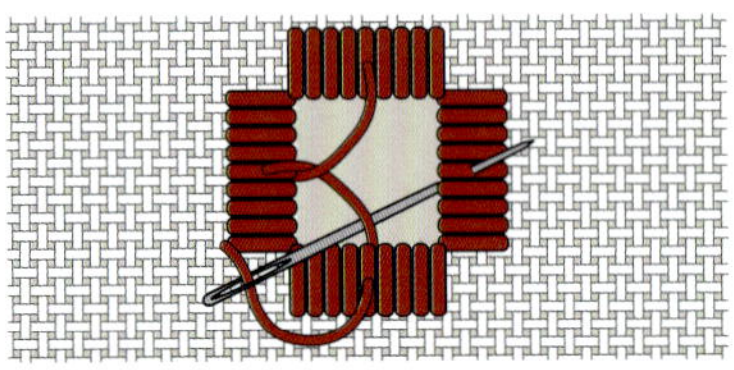

4 Pull the needle through so the stitch curves gently. Turn the work 90° clockwise. Insert the needle under the previous stitch and into the back of the middle of the next block.

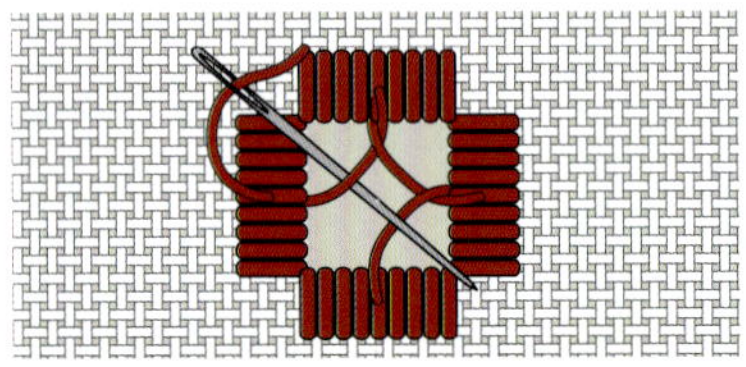

5 Pull the needle through so the stitch curves gently. Turn the work 180°. Take the needle under the previous stitch.

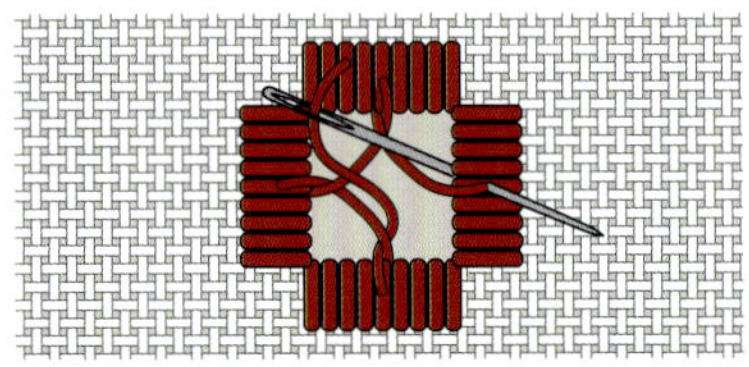

6 Turn the work 90° anticlockwise. Take the needle over the first stitch, and insert it in the back of the next block, bringing it out in the same place as where it first emerged.

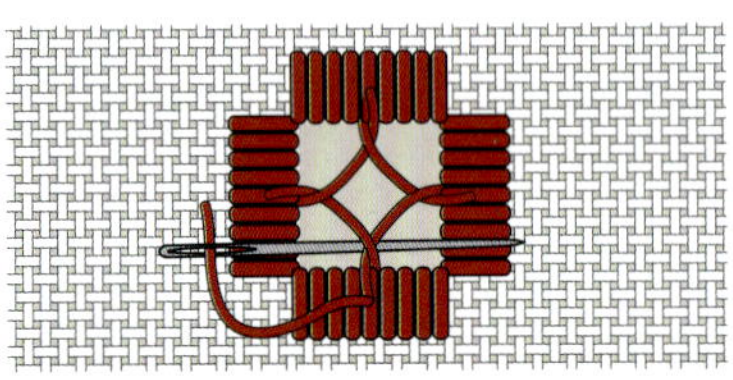

7 Pull the needle through. Turn the work 90° clockwise. From the left, slide the needle under the two stitches at the bottom of the dove's eye.

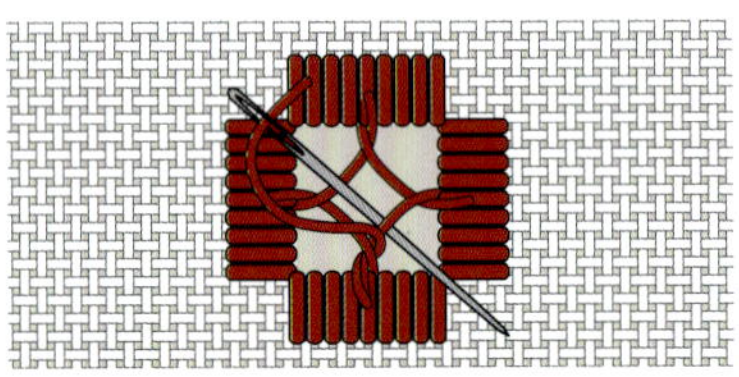

8 From above left, slide the needle under the bottom right part of the dove's eye.

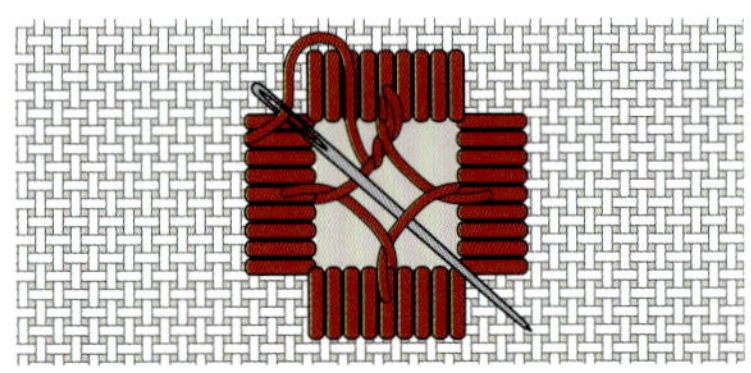

9 Pull the thread so that it intertwines with the dove's eye. Turn the work 180°. From above left, slide the needle under the bottom right part of the dove's eye.

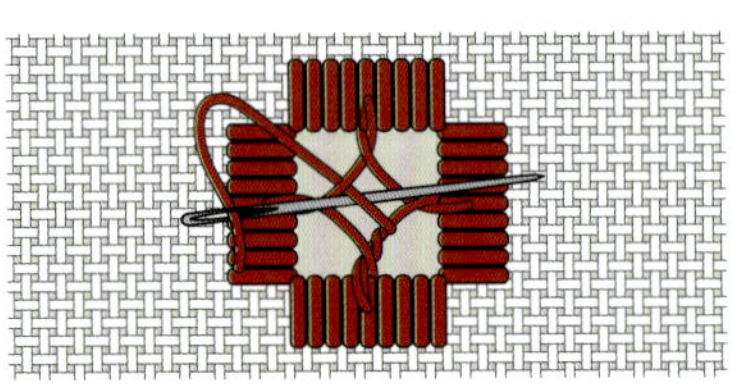

10 Turn the work 180°. From below left, slide the needle under the stitch that goes across the centre.

❶ *When you tighten this stitch, do not pull the dove's eye further inward.*

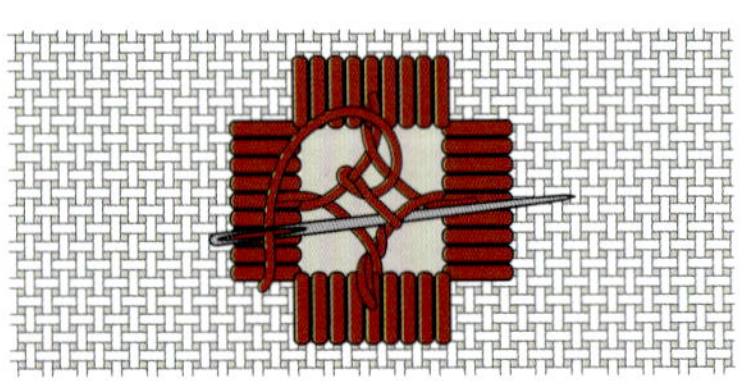

11 Pull the thread so that it intertwines with the stitch across the middle. From the left, slide the needle under the centre crossing stitch and the bottom right part of the dove's eye.

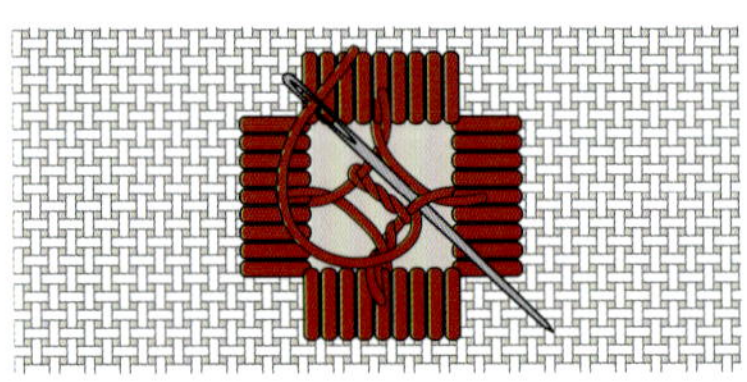

12 Pull the thread so that it intertwines. From above left, slide the needle under the upper section of the bottom right part of the dove's eye.

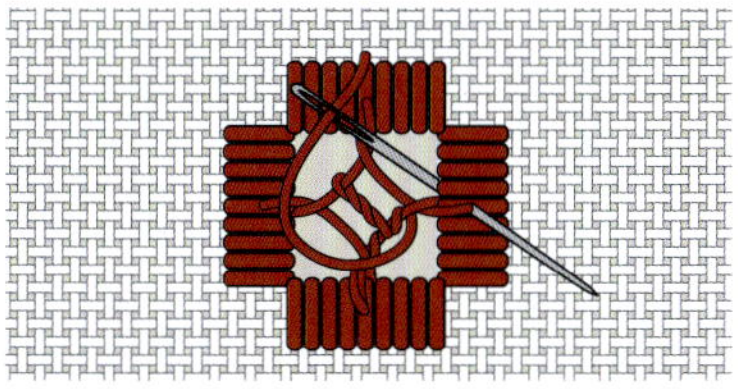

13 Pull the thread so that it intertwines. From above the dove's eye stitch, insert the needle in the back of the next block. Bring it out where the dove's eye stitch emerged.

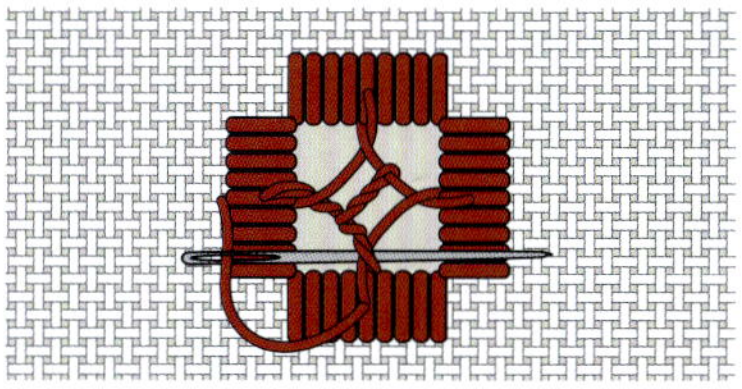

14 Turn the work 90° clockwise. From the left, slide the needle under the stitches at the bottom of the dove's eye.

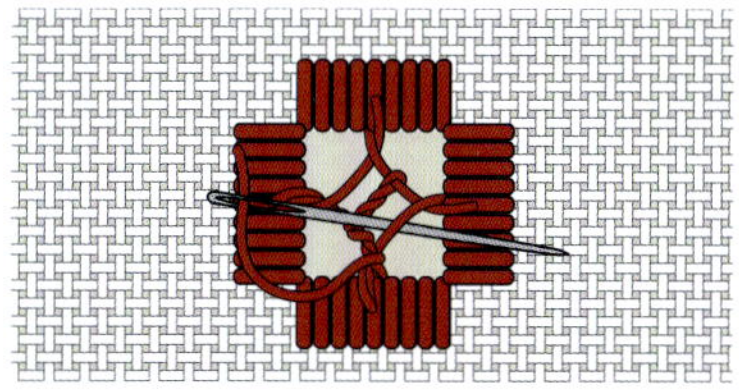

15 From above left, slide the needle under the bottom right part of the dove's eye.

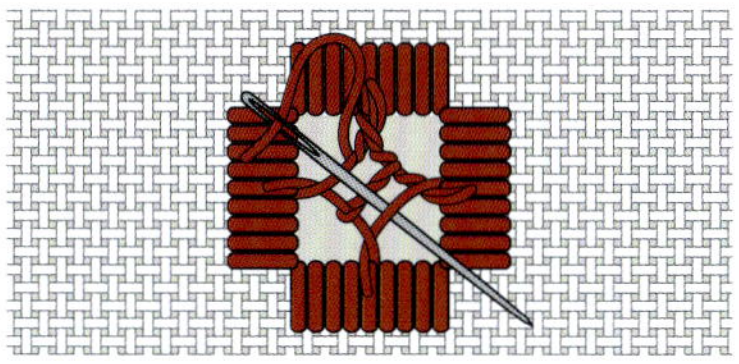

16 Pull the thread so that it intertwines with the dove's eye. Turn the work 180°. From above left, slide the needle under the bottom right part of the dove's eye.

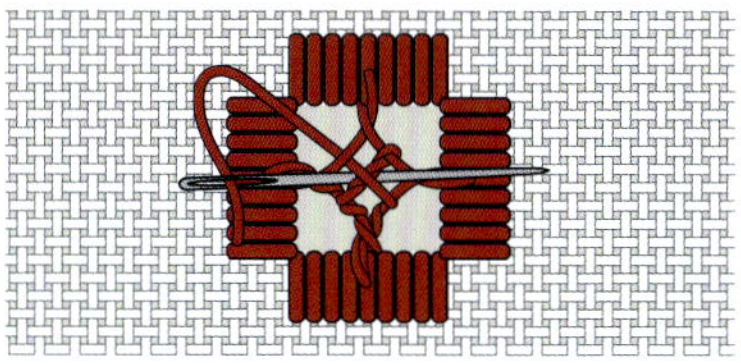

17 Turn the work 180°. From the left, slide the needle under the stitches that cross in the centre.

❶ *When you tighten this stitch, do not pull the dove's eye further inward.*

18 Pull the thread so that it intertwines with the centre stitches. From the left, slide the needle under the current centre crossing stitch and the bottom right part of the dove's eye.

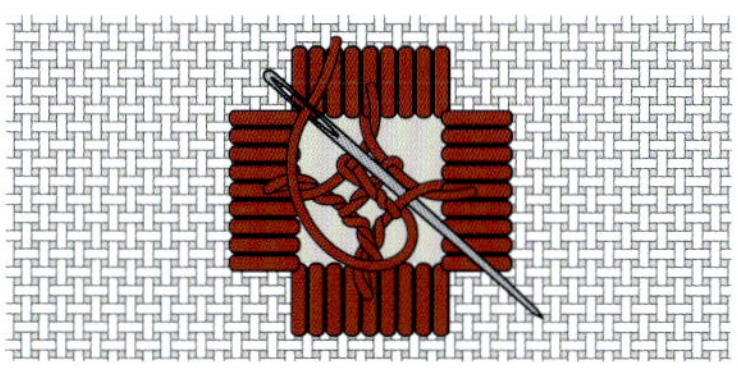

19 Pull the thread so that it intertwines. From above left, slide the needle under the upper section of the bottom right part of the dove's eye.

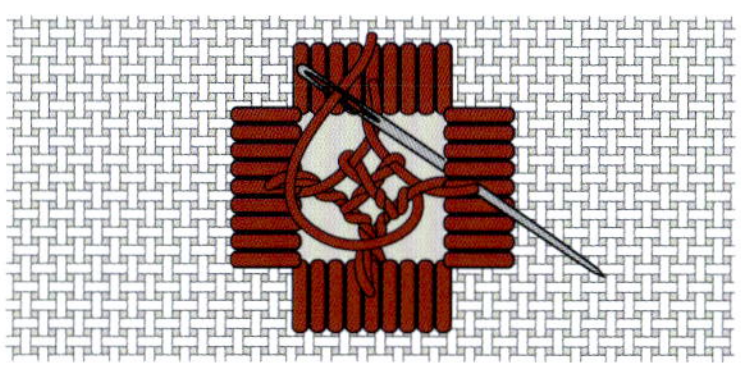

20 Pull the thread so that it intertwines. From above the dove's eye stitch, insert the needle in the back of the next block. Bring it out where the dove's eye stitch emerged.

21 Turn the work 90° clockwise. From the left, slide the needle under the stitches at the bottom of the dove's eye.

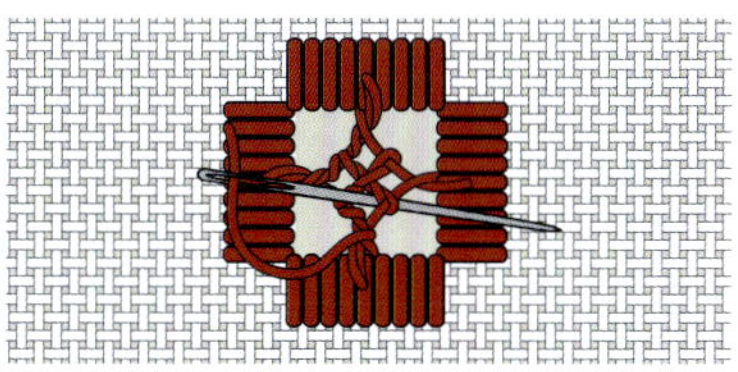

22 Pull the thread so that it intertwines. From the left, slide the needle under the end of the centre crossing stitch and the bottom right part of the dove's eye.

23 Pull the thread so that it intertwines. From above left, slide the needle under the upper section of the bottom right part of the dove's eye.

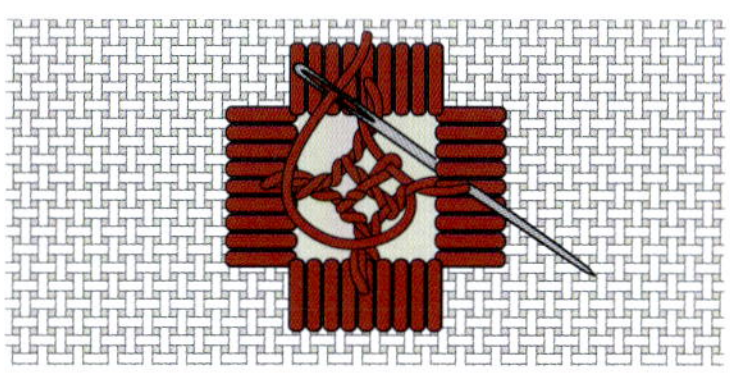

24 Pull the thread so that it intertwines. From above the dove's eye stitch, insert the needle in the back of the next block. Bring it out where the dove's eye stitch emerged.

25 Work the last side in the same way as the previous side. Finish the thread in the back of the stitching.

R

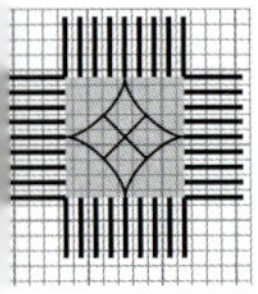

TRADITIONAL

dove's eye with cross

This larger dove's eye has a cross in the centre. It is worked in a square spanning eight by eight threads (nine stitches in each satin stitch block).

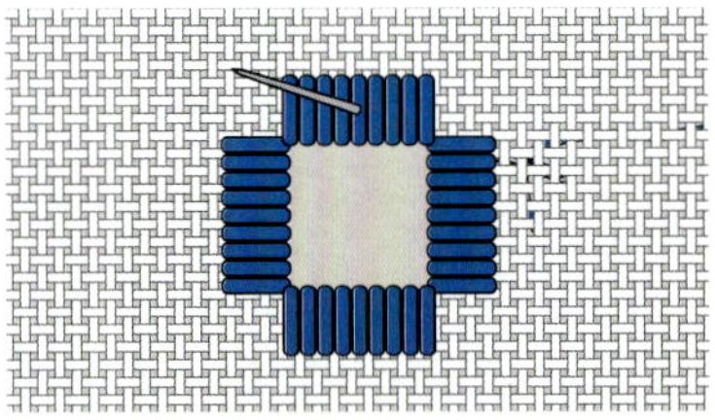

1 Bring the needle out in the centre of the middle stitch in the top satin stitch block.

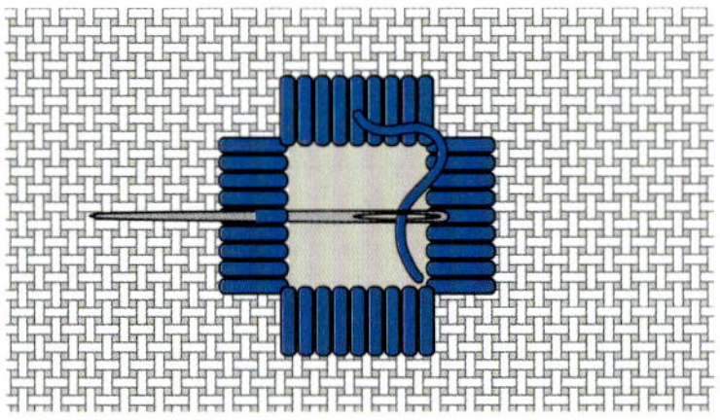

2 Working around the square in an anticlockwise direction, insert the needle into the centre back of the next satin stitch block's middle stitch.

❶ *The needle is always inserted in the back of the block.*

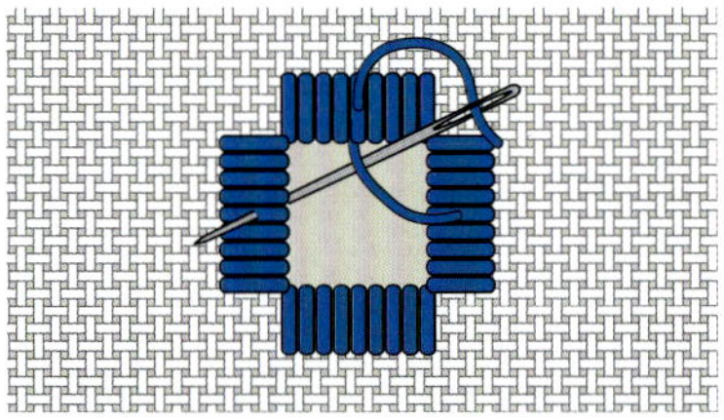

3 Pull the needle through so the stitch gently curves between the two blocks. Turn the work 90° clockwise. Insert the needle under the previous stitch and into the centre back of the middle stitch of the next block.

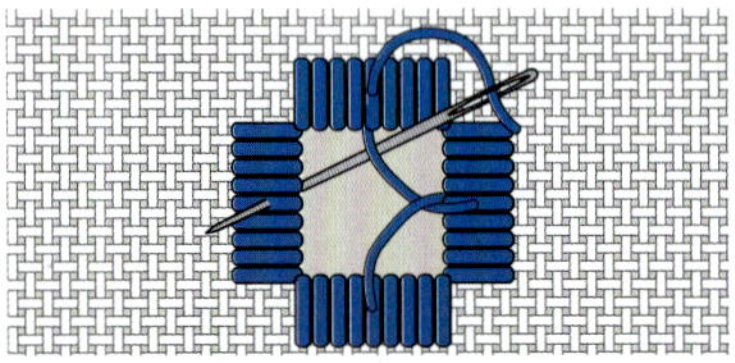

4 Pull the needle through so the stitch curves gently. Turn the work 90° clockwise. Insert the needle under the previous stitch and into the back of the middle of the next block.

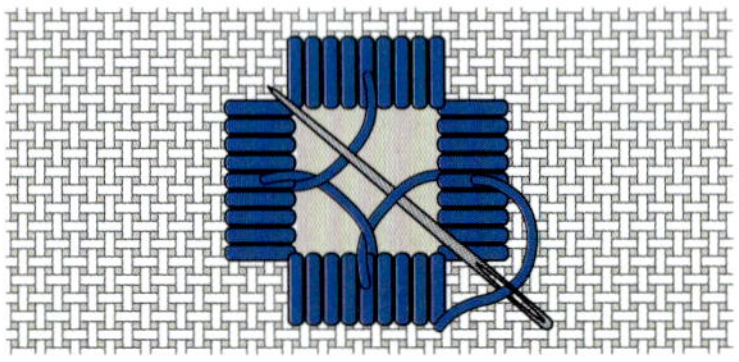

5 Pull the needle through so the stitch curves gently. Turn the work 180°. Take the needle under the previous stitch.

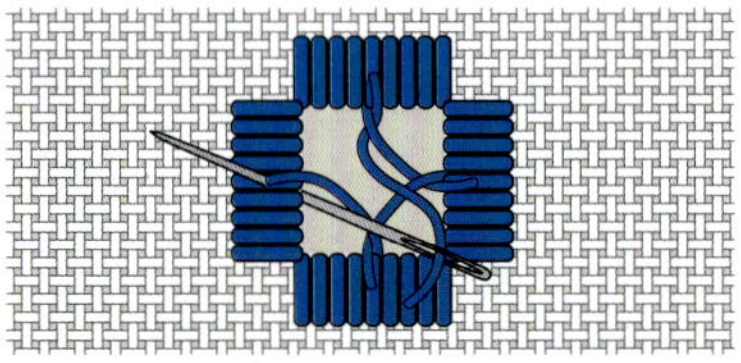

6 Turn the work 90° anticlockwise. Take the needle over the first stitch, and insert it in the back of the next block, bringing it out in the same place as where it first emerged.

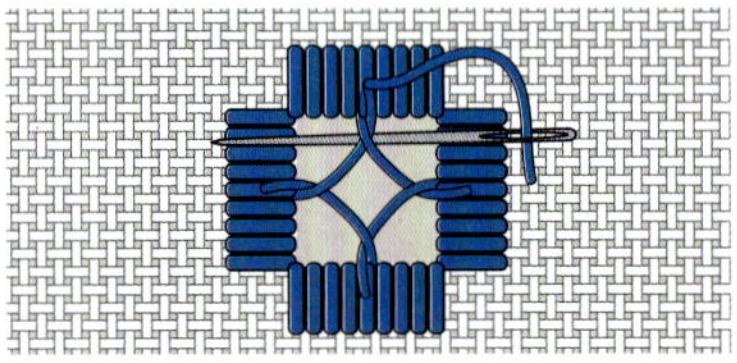

7 Pull the needle through. Turn the work 90° clockwise. From the right, slide the needle under the two stitches at the top of the dove's eye.

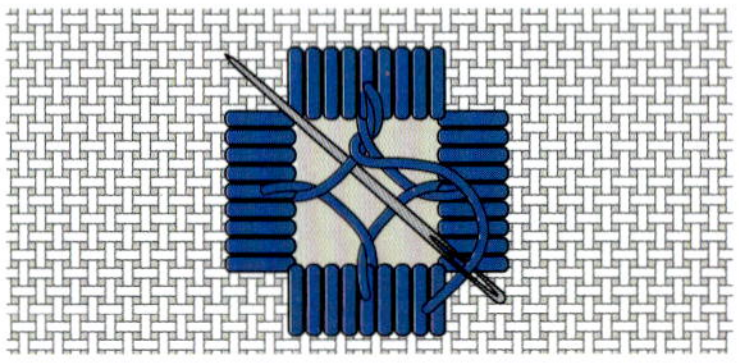

8 From below right, slide the needle under the top left part of the dove's eye.

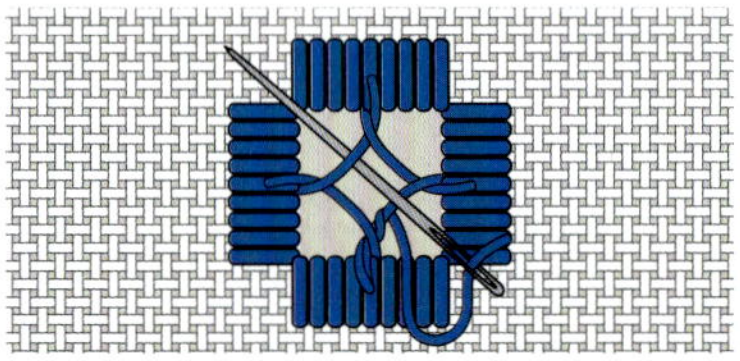

9 Pull the thread so that the new stitches intertwine with the dove's eye. Turn the work 180°. From below right, slide the needle under the top left part of the dove's eye.

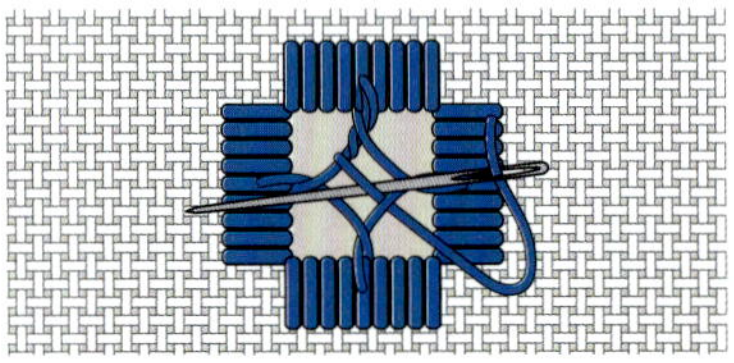

10 Turn the work 180°. From above right, slide the needle under the stitch that goes across the centre.

❶ *When you tighten this stitch, do not pull the dove's eye further inward.*

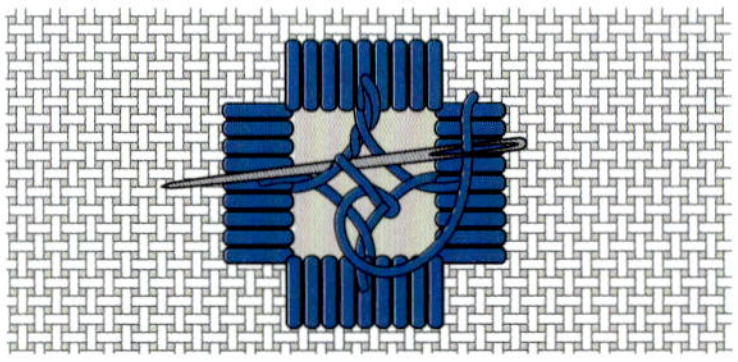

11 Gently pull the thread so that it intertwines with the stitch across the middle. From the right, slide the needle under the centre crossing stitch and the top left part of the dove's eye.

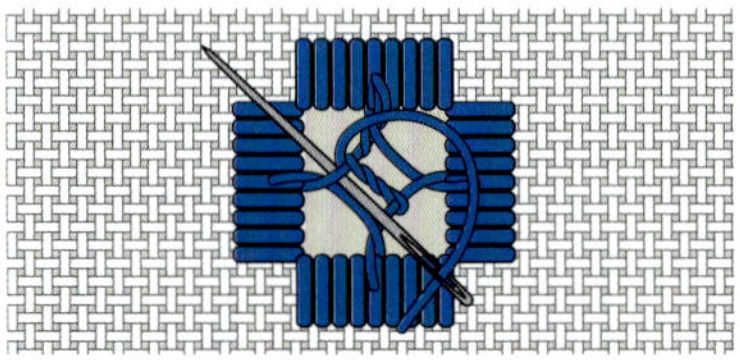

12 Pull the thread so that it intertwines. From below right, slide the needle under the lower section of the top left part of the dove's eye.

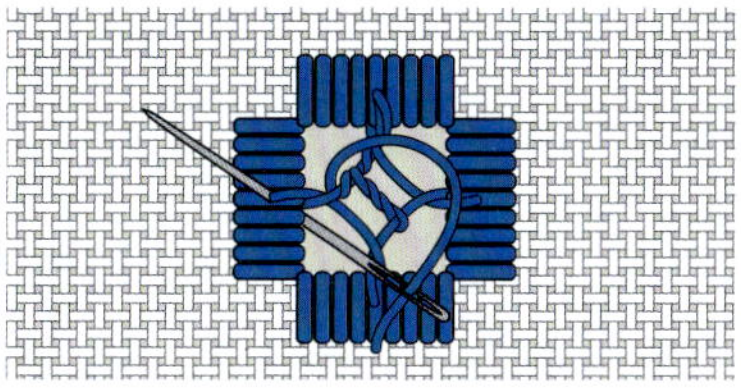

13 Pull the thread so that it intertwines. From below the dove's eye stitch, insert the needle in the back of the next block. Bring it out where the dove's eye stitch emerged.

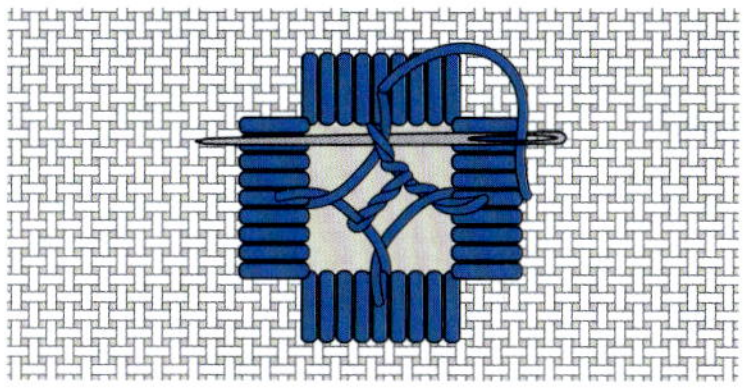

14 Turn the work 90° clockwise. From the right, slide the needle under the stitches at the top of the dove's eye.

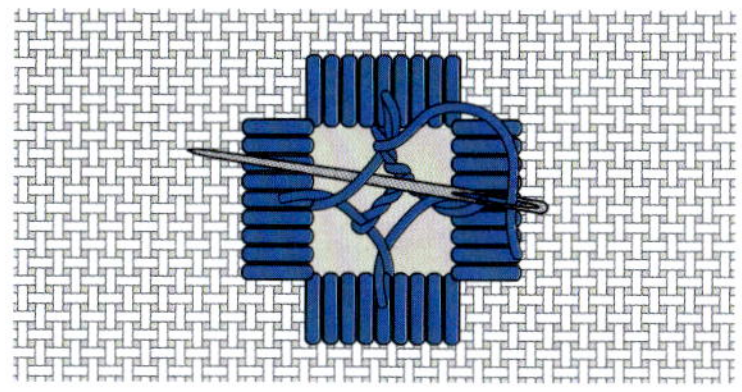

15 From below right, slide the needle under the top left part of the dove's eye.

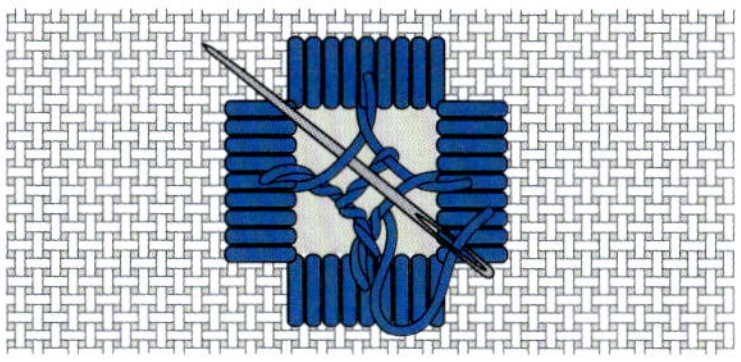

16 Pull the thread so that it intertwines with the dove's eye. Turn the work 180°. From below right, slide the needle under the top left part of the dove's eye.

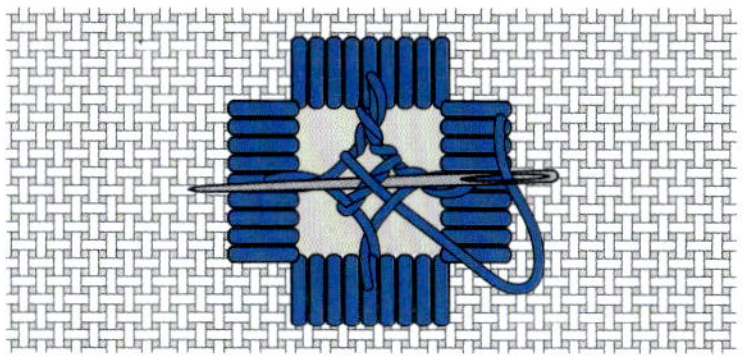

17 Turn the work 180°. From the right, slide the needle under the stitches that cross in the centre.

❶ *When you tighten this stitch, do not pull the dove's eye further inward.*

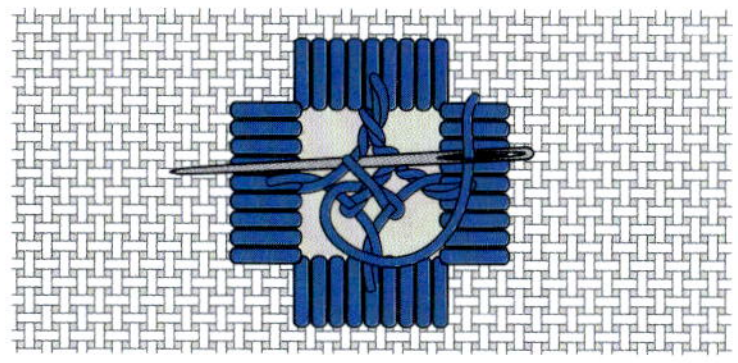

18 Pull the thread so that it intertwines with the centre stitches. From the right, slide the needle under the current centre crossing stitch and the top left part of the dove's eye.

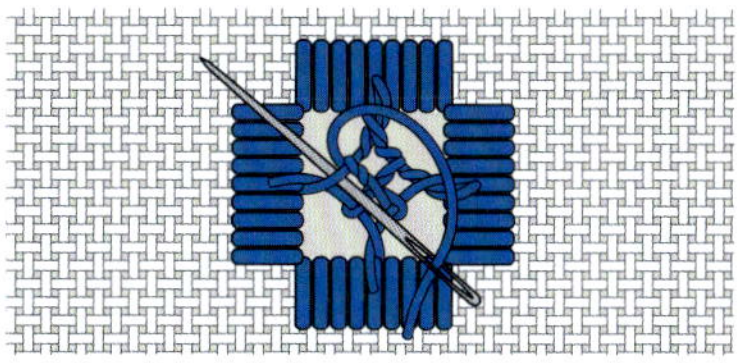

19 Pull the thread so that it intertwines. From below right, slide the needle under the lower section of the top left part of the dove's eye.

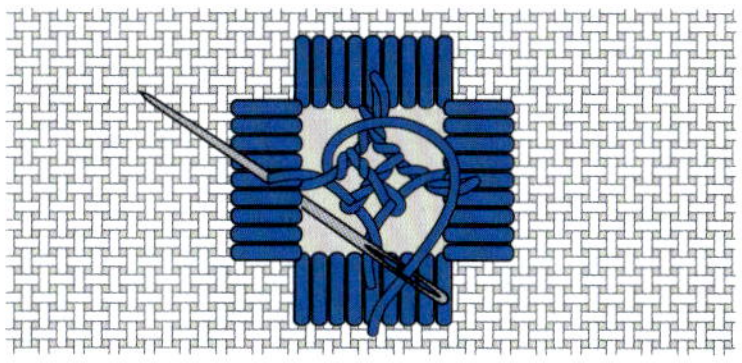

20 Pull the thread so that it intertwines. From below the dove's eye stitch, insert the needle in the back of the next block. Bring it out where the dove's eye stitch emerged.

21 Turn the work 90° clockwise. From the right, slide the needle under the stitches at the top of the dove's eye.

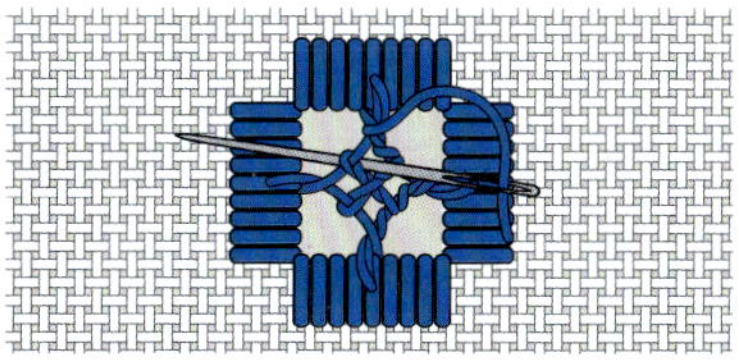

22 Pull the thread so that it intertwines. From the right, slide the needle under the end of the centre crossing stitch and the top left part of the dove's eye.

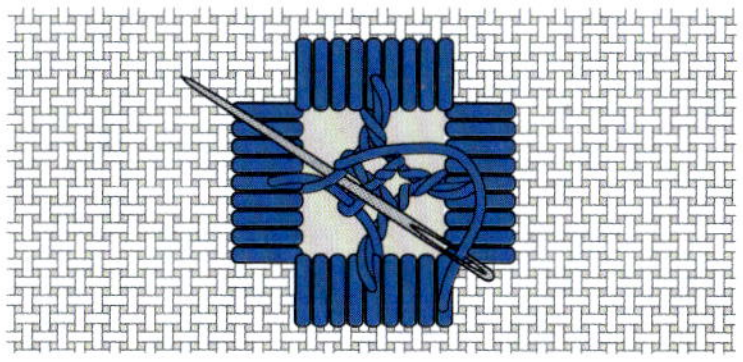

23 Pull the thread so that it intertwines. From below right, slide the needle under the lower section of the top left part of the dove's eye.

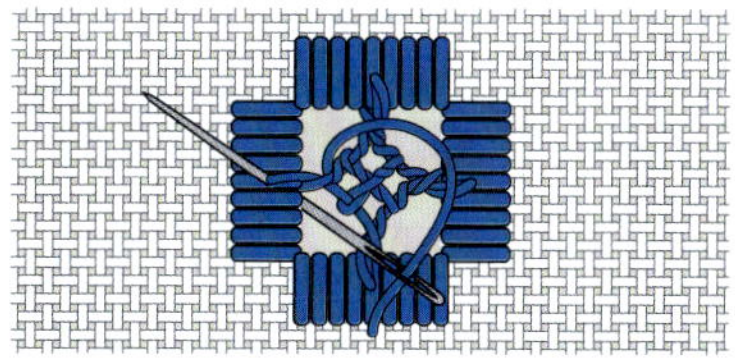

24 Pull the thread so that it intertwines. From below the dove's eye stitch, insert the needle in the back of the next block. Bring it out where the dove's eye stitch emerged.

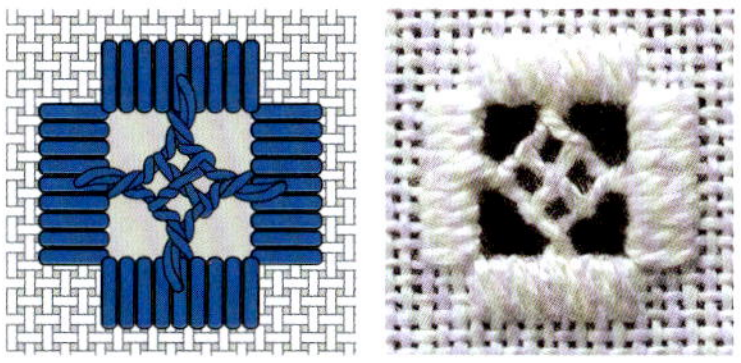

25 Work the last side in the same way as the previous side. Finish the thread in the back of the stitching.

dove's eye cobweb

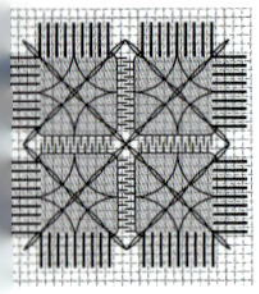

TRADITIONAL

Known as finare spindelvev, or 'finer cobwebs' in Norwegian, this stitch features a dove's eye with a twisted X, worked inside a large square with four quadrants. The cobweb could also be worked singly.

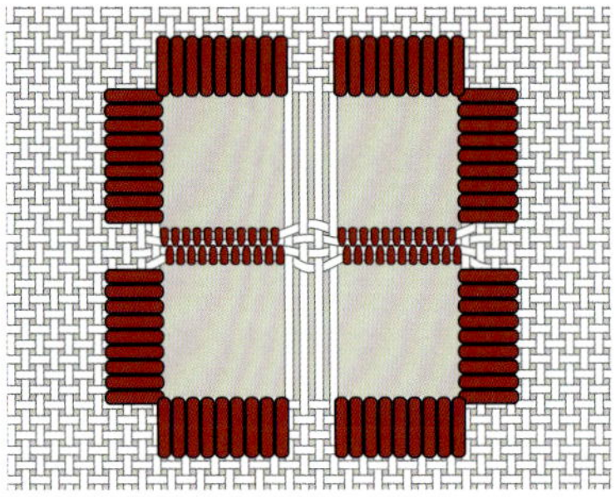

1 In a large square, weave two bars across the middle.

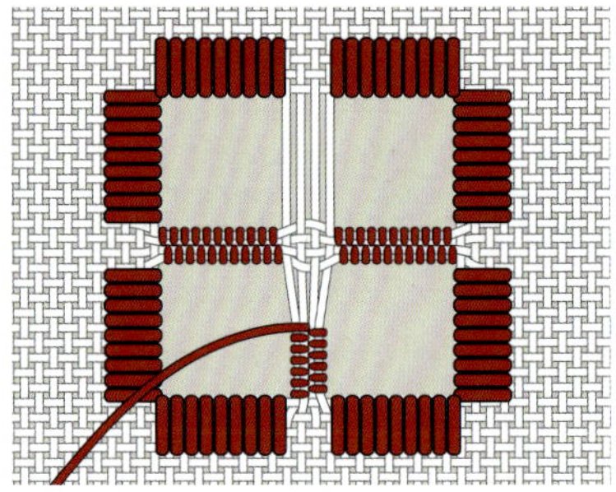

2 On the back, take the thread behind the intervening satin stitch. Work half of the next bar towards the centre.

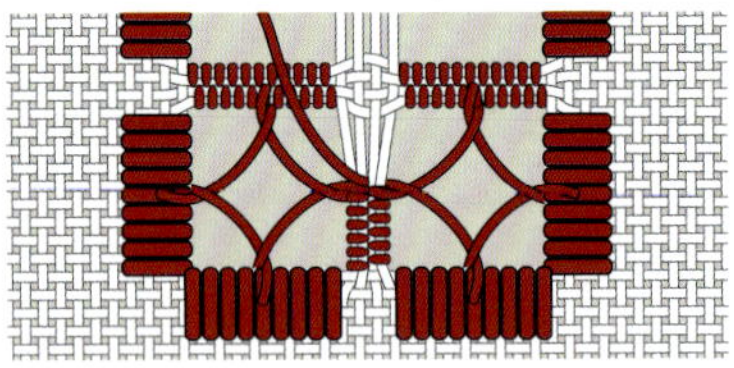

3 Work a dove's eye in each of the bottom two quadrants.

❶ *'Dove's eye' instructions on pages 92–93.*

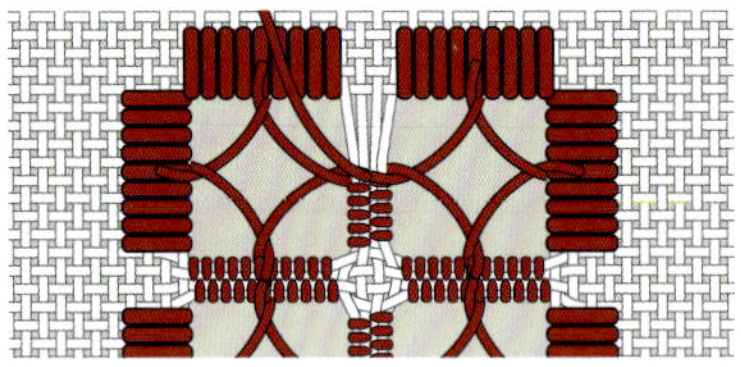

4 Complete the weaving of the bar and work half the remaining bar. Work a dove's eye in each of the top quadrants.

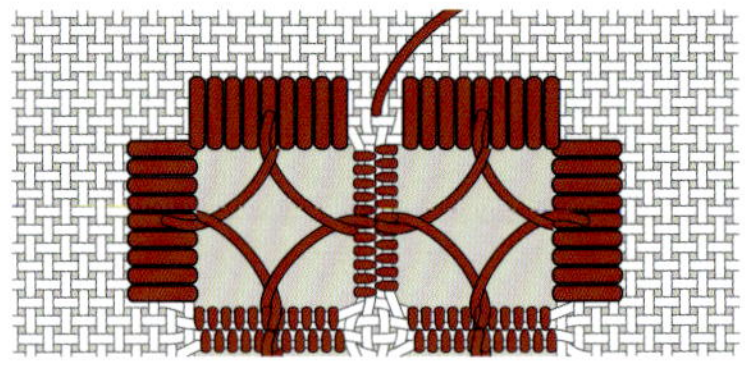

5 Complete the weaving of the bar then bring the needle out in the centre of the woven square between the two satin stitch blocks.

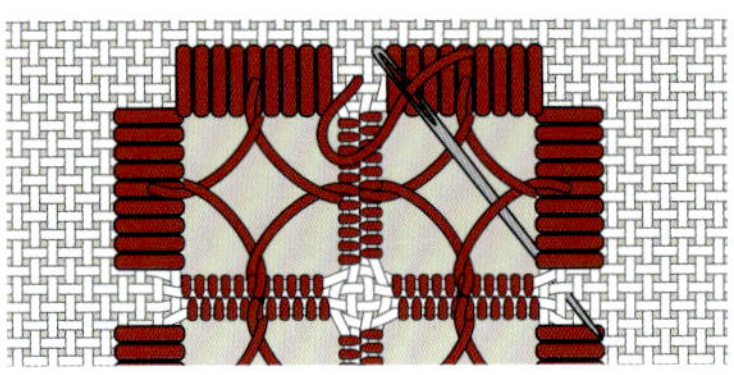

6 Working clockwise, take the needle over the first dove's eye stitch and under the next. Bring it out in the woven square at the side's centre.

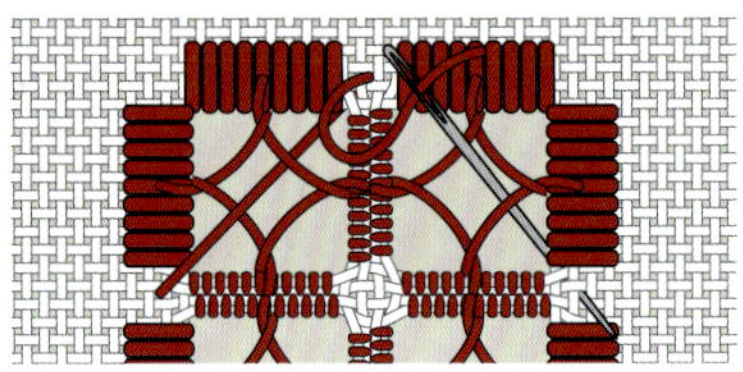

7 Pull the needle through. Turn the work 90° anticlockwise. Take the needle over the first dove's eye stitch, and under the next. Bring it out in the woven square at the side's centre.

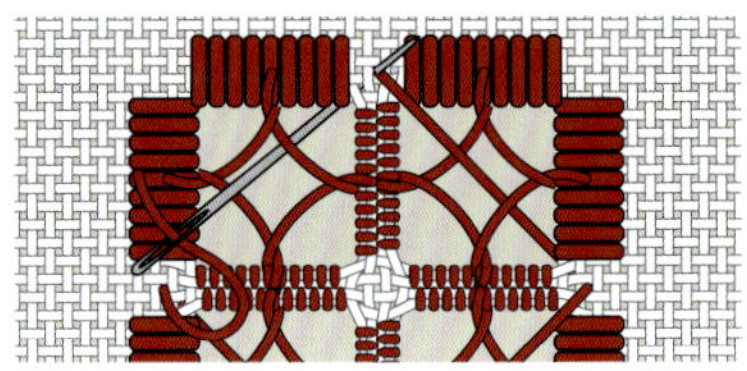

8 Repeat for the remaining two quadrants.

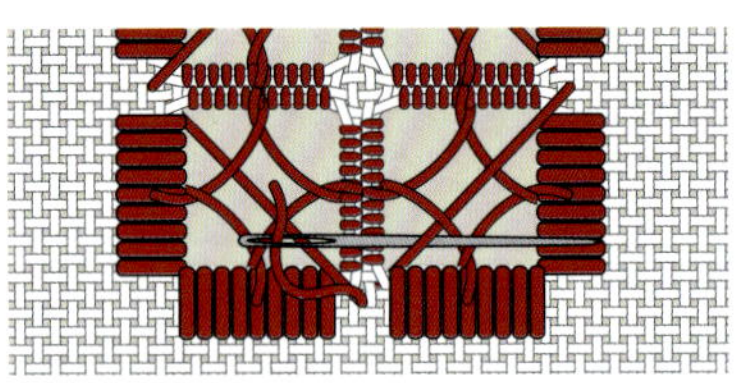

9 Pull the needle through. Turn the work 180°. From the left, slide the needle under the lowest part of the previous diagonal stitch.

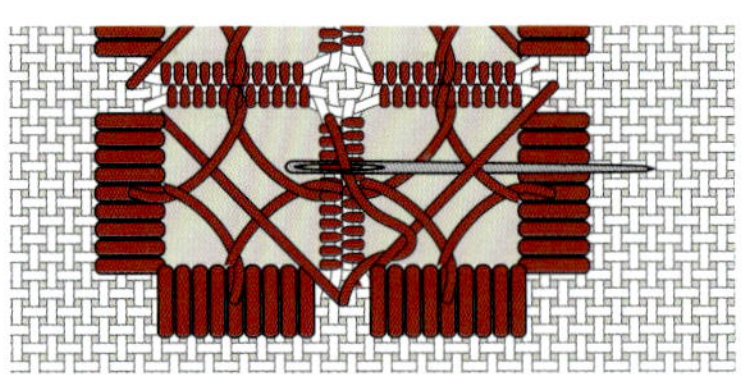

10 From the left, slide the needle under the next section of the diagonal stitch and the dove's eye that it crosses.

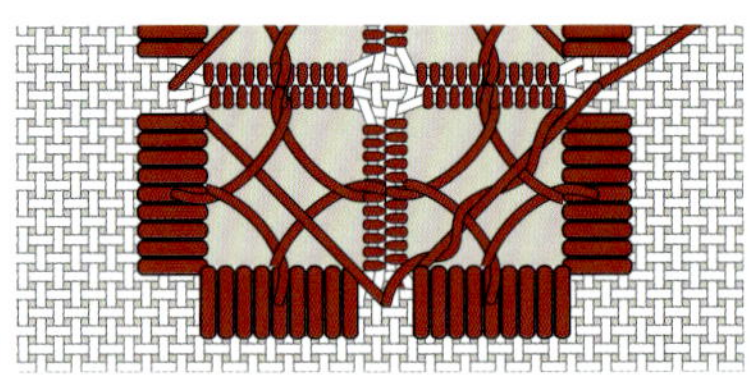

11 Insert the needle on the upper side of the diagonal. Bring it out in the same hole as the end of the diagonal stitch.

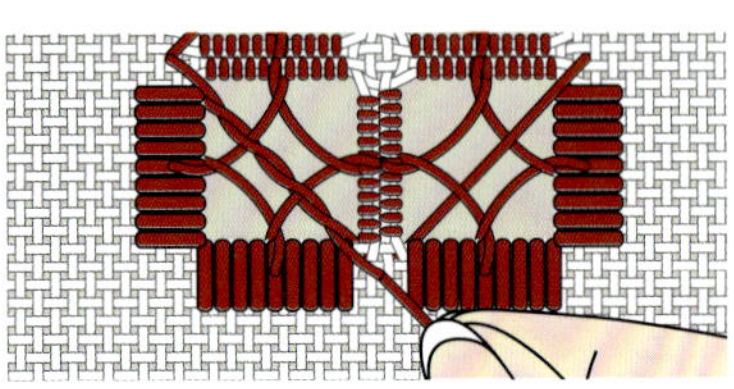

12 Turn the work 90° clockwise. Pull the thread down and right to intertwine the stitches.

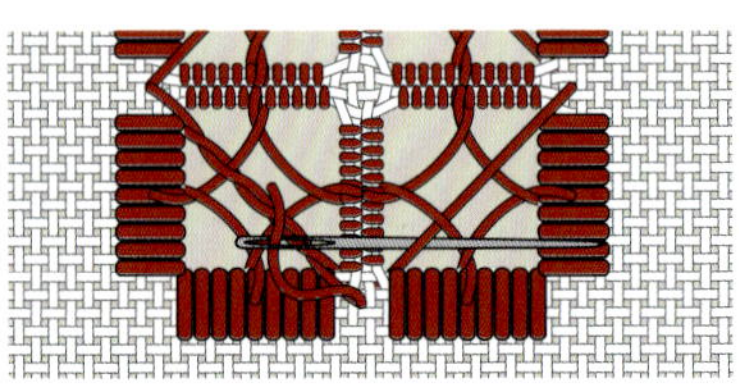

13 From the left, slide the needle under the lowest part of the next diagonal stitch.

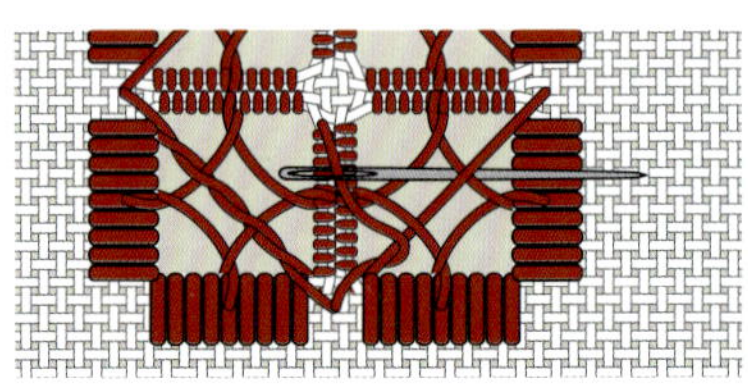

14 From the left, slide the needle under the next section of the diagonal stitch and the dove's eye that it crosses.

15 Insert the needle above the diagonal. Bring it out in the same hole as the end of the diagonal stitch. Pull the thread to intertwine the stitches.

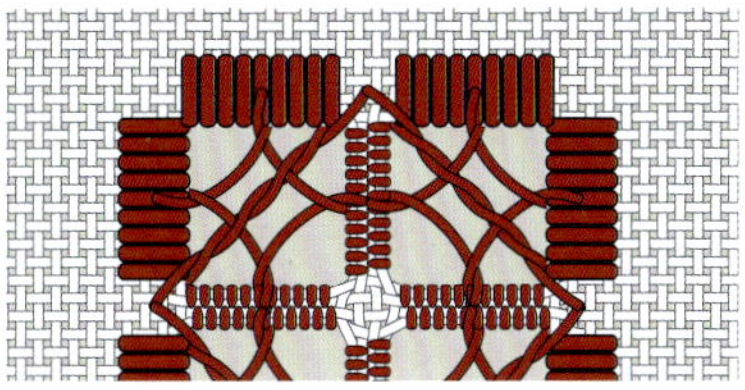

16 Repeat for the other two quadrants, finishing with the thread on the back. Pull the thread to intertwine the stitches.

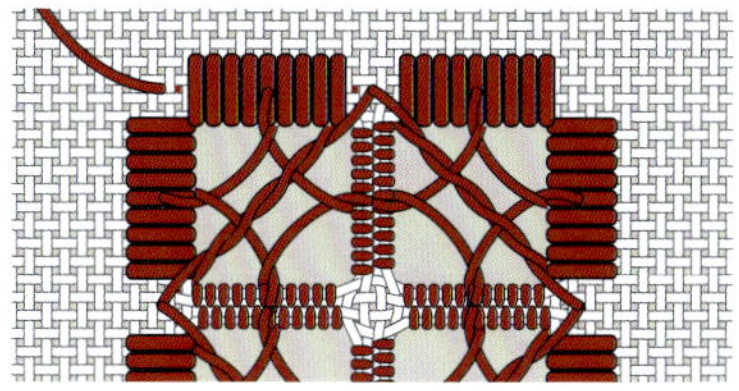

17 On the back, take the thread under the back of the satin stitching to bring it out in the corner woven fabric square's centre.

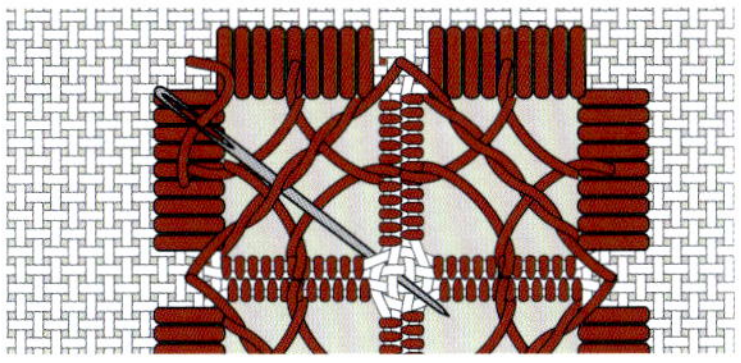

18 From above left, slide the needle under the centre section of the quadrant's twisted stitches, over the dove's eye stitch, and bring it out in the centre of the central woven square.

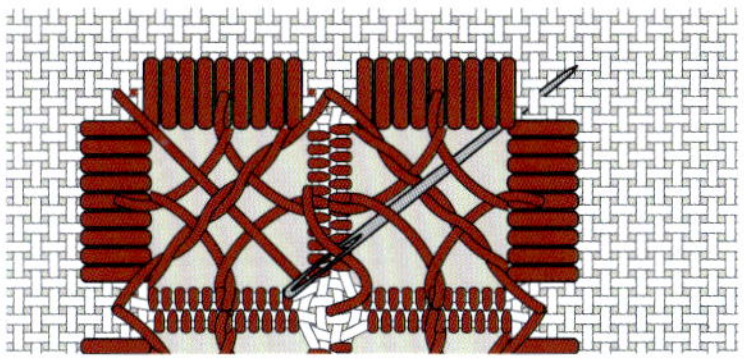

19 Pull the needle through. Moving to the next quadrant, from below left, take the needle under, over, and under the stitches. Bring it out in the corner square's centre.

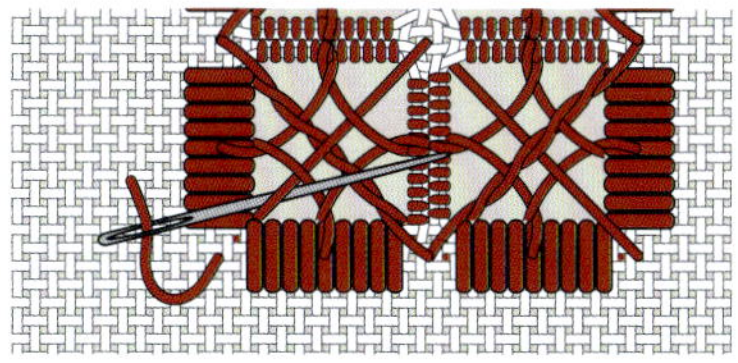

20 Pull the needle through. Turn the work 180°. From the left, slide the needle under the bottom section of the previous diagonal stitch.

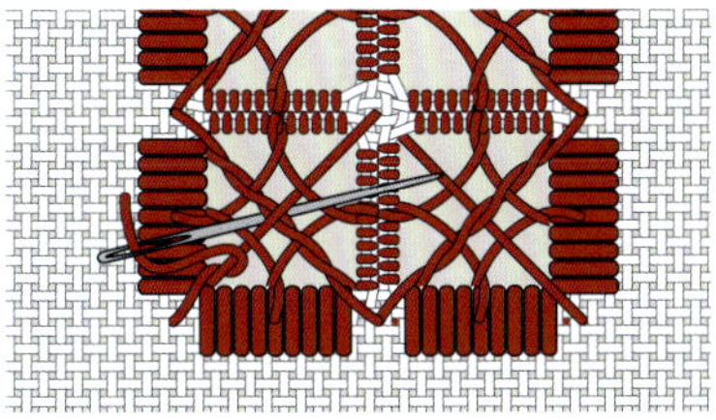

21 From the left, slide the needle under the centre twist and the diagonal stitch.

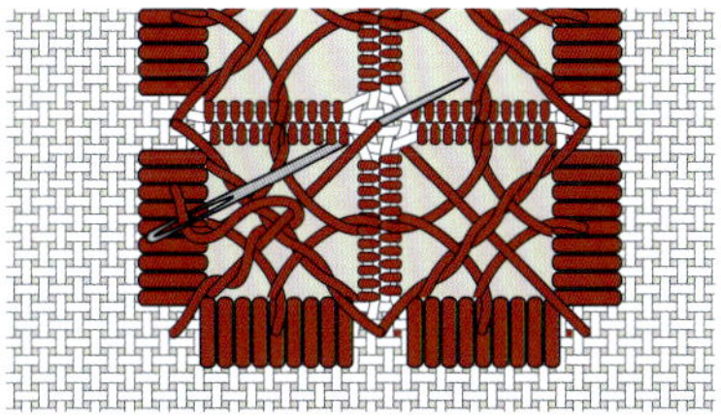

22 Insert the needle above the diagonal and bring it out in the centre of the central woven square.

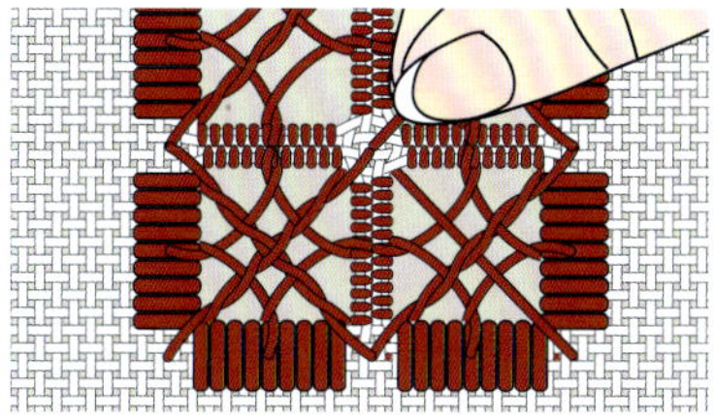

23 Pull the needle to intertwine the stitches.

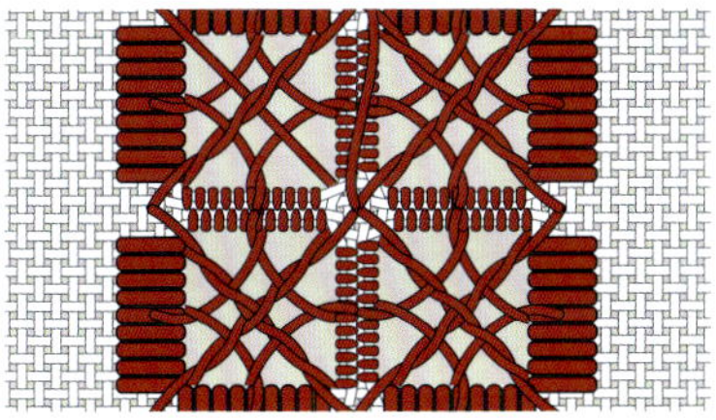

24 Repeat Steps 19 to 23 in the next two quadrants.

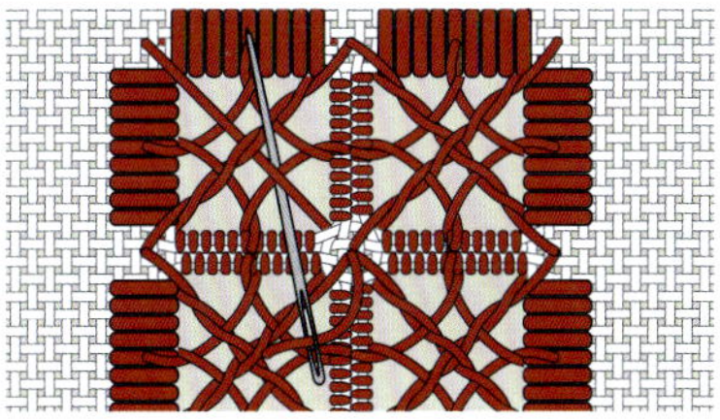

25 From below, slide the needle under the crossing diagonal and lower dove's eye stitch.

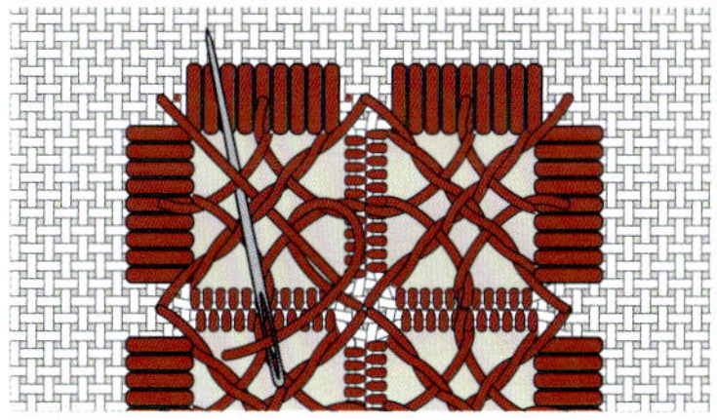

26 From below, slide the needle under the crossing diagonal and upper dove's eye stitch.

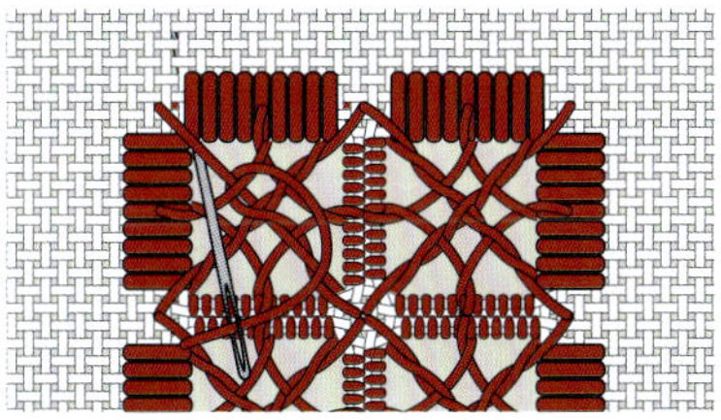

27 From below the diagonal, take the needle to the back in the corner. Pull to intertwine the stitches. Run the thread under the back of the satin stitches to finish it.

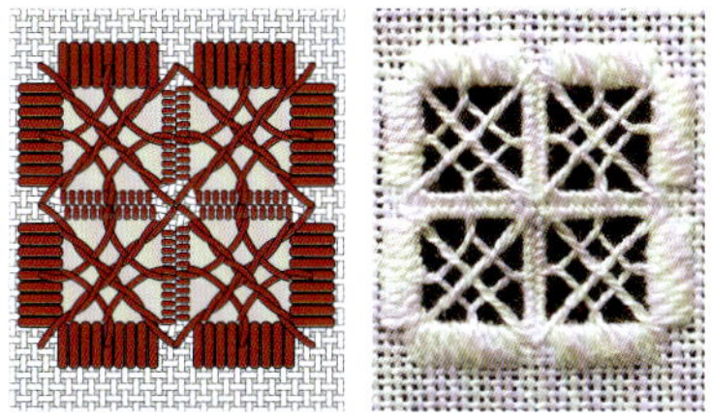

28 The completed dove's eye cobwebs.

R

dove's eye cobweb

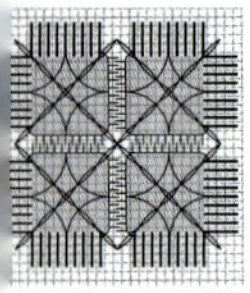

TRADITIONAL

Known as finare spindelvev, or 'finer cobwebs' in Norwegian, this stitch features a dove's eye with a twisted X, worked inside a large square with four quadrants. The cobweb could also be worked singly.

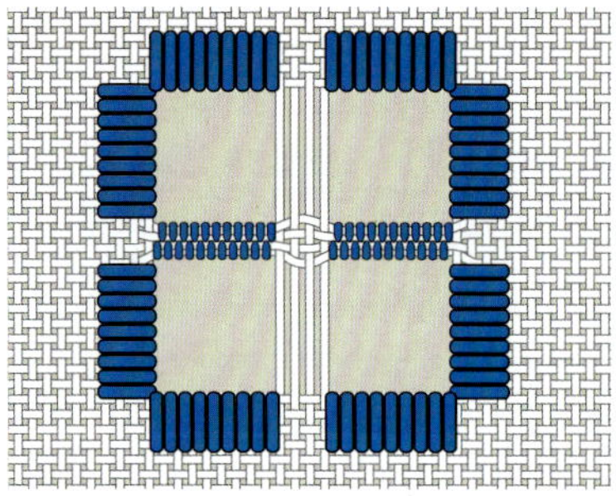

1 In a large square, weave two bars across the middle.

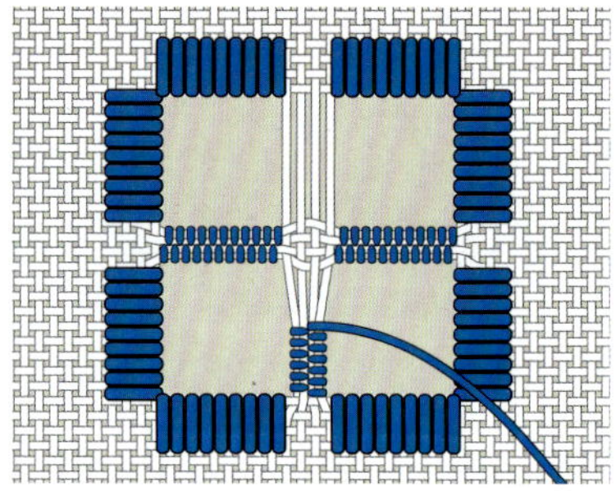

2 On the back, take the thread behind the intervening satin stitch. Work half of the next bar towards the centre.

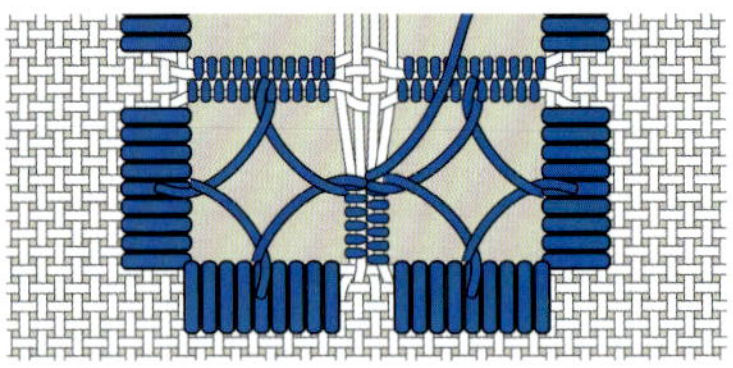

3 Work a dove's eye in each of the bottom two quadrants.

❶ *'Dove's eye' instructions on pages 94–95.*

4 Complete the weaving of the bar and work half the remaining bar. Work a dove's eye in each of the top quadrants.

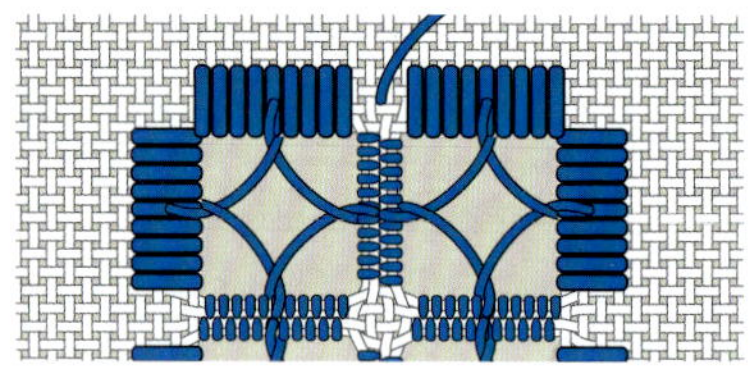

5 Complete the weaving of the bar then bring the needle out in the centre of the woven square between the two satin stitch blocks.

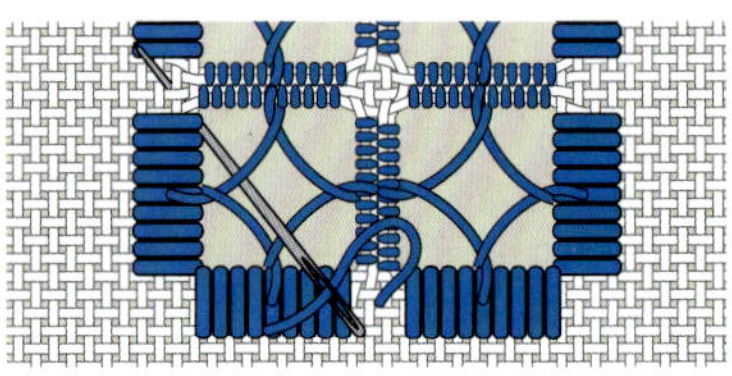

6 Turn the work 180°. Working clockwise, take the needle over the first dove's eye stitch and under the next. Bring it out in the woven square at the side's centre.

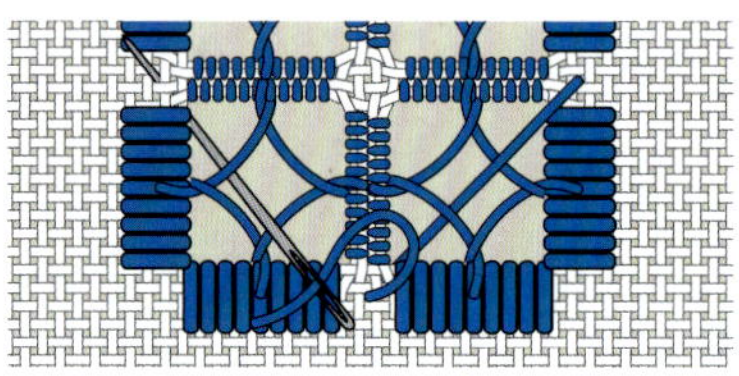

7 Pull the needle through. Turn the work 90° anticlockwise. Take the needle over the first dove's eye stitch, and under the next. Bring it out in the woven square at the side's centre.

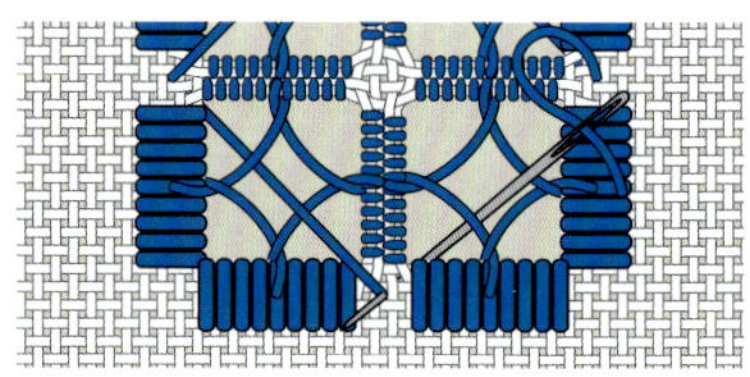

8 Repeat for the remaining two quadrants.

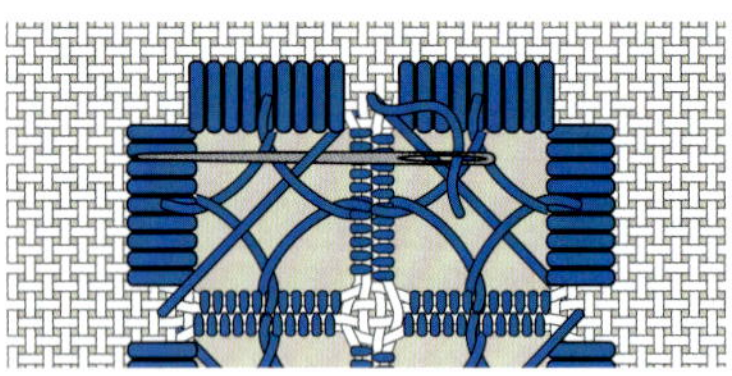

9 Pull the needle through. Turn the work 180°. From the right, slide the needle under the upper part of the previous diagonal stitch.

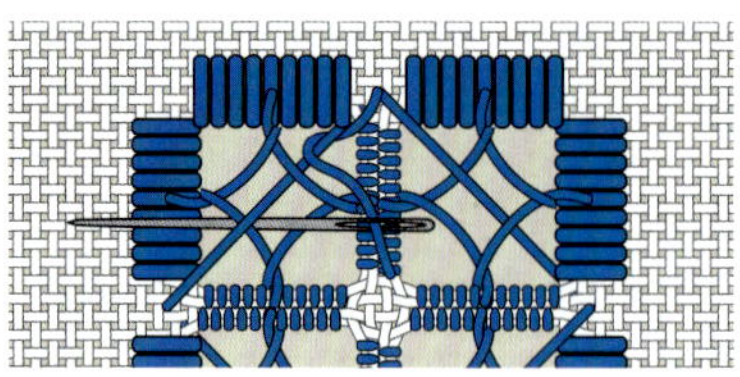

10 From the right, slide the needle under the next section of the diagonal stitch and the dove's eye that it crosses.

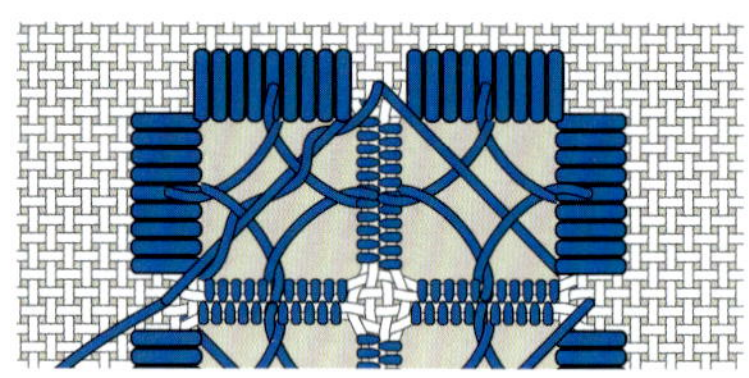

11 Insert the needle on the lower side of the diagonal. Bring it out in the same hole as the end of the diagonal stitch.

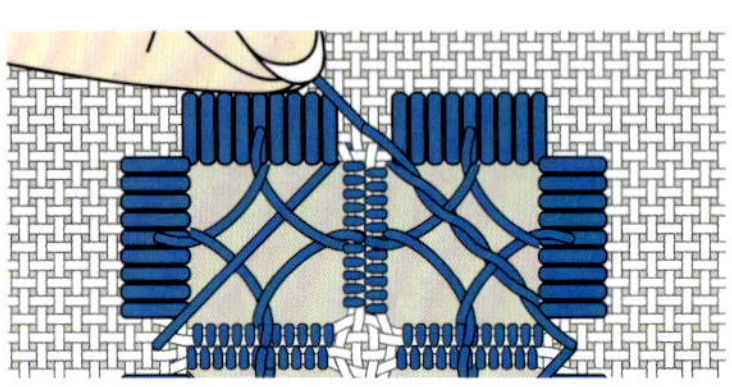

12 Turn the work 90° clockwise. Pull the thread up and left to intertwine the stitches.

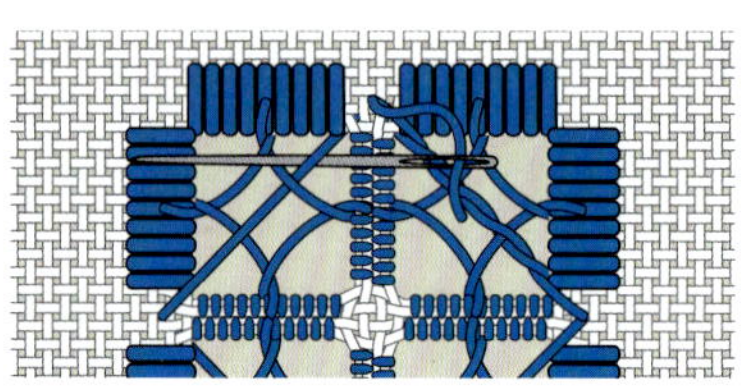

13 From the right, slide the needle under the upper right part of the next diagonal stitch.

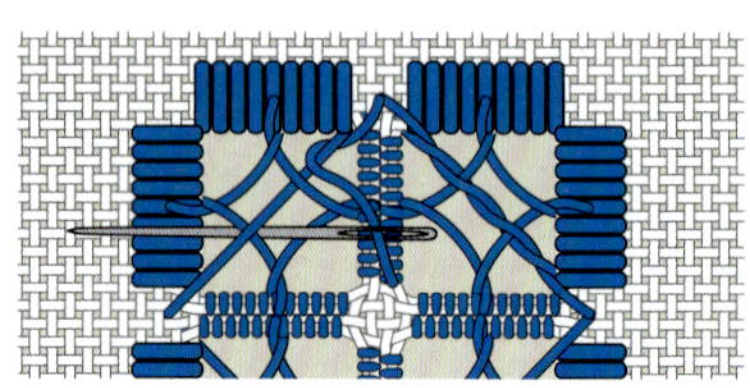

14 From the right, slide the needle under the next section of the diagonal stitch and the dove's eye that it crosses.

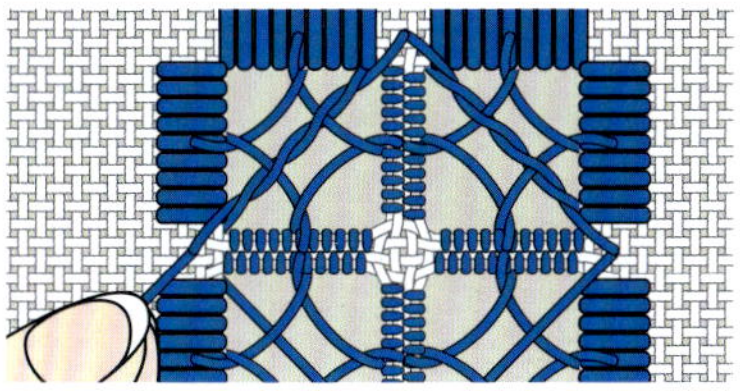

15 Insert the needle below the diagonal. Bring it out in the same hole as the end of the diagonal stitch. Pull the thread to intertwine the stitches.

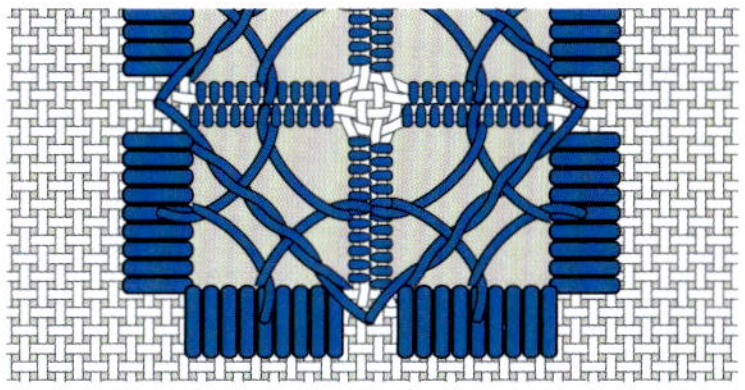

16 Repeat for the other two quadrants, finishing with the thread on the back. Pull the thread to intertwine the stitches.

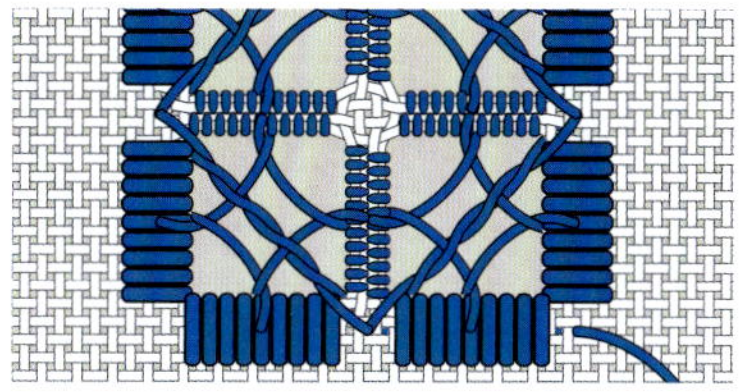

17 On the back, take the thread under the back of the satin stitching to bring it out in the corner woven fabric square's centre.

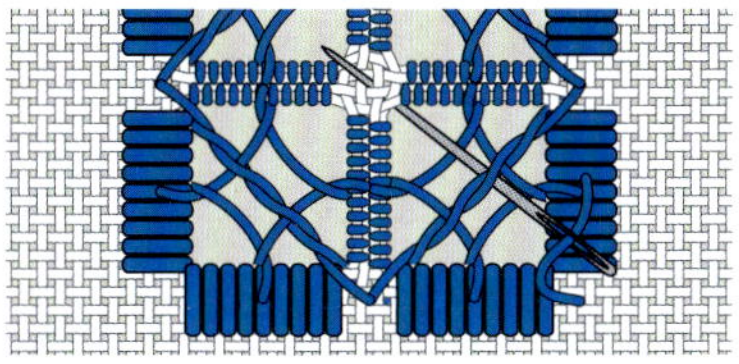

18 From below right, slide the needle under the centre twisted stitches, and bring the needle out in the centre of the woven square.

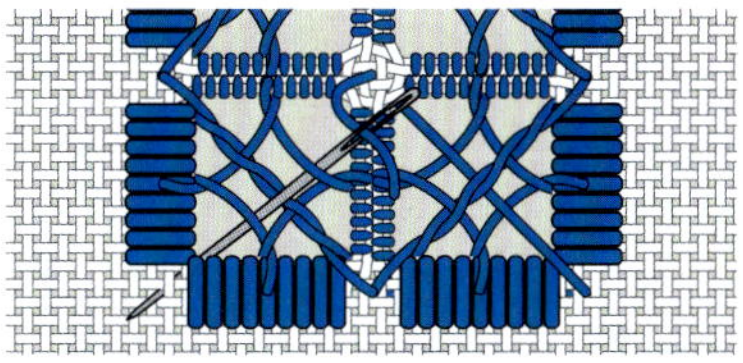

19 Pull the needle through. Moving to the next quadrant, from above right, take the needle under, over, and under the stitches. Bring it out in the corner square's centre.

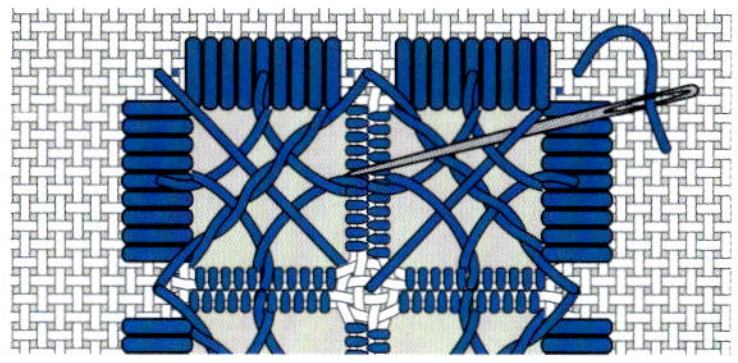

20 Pull the needle through. Turn the work 180°. From the right, slide the needle under the upper part of the previous diagonal stitch.

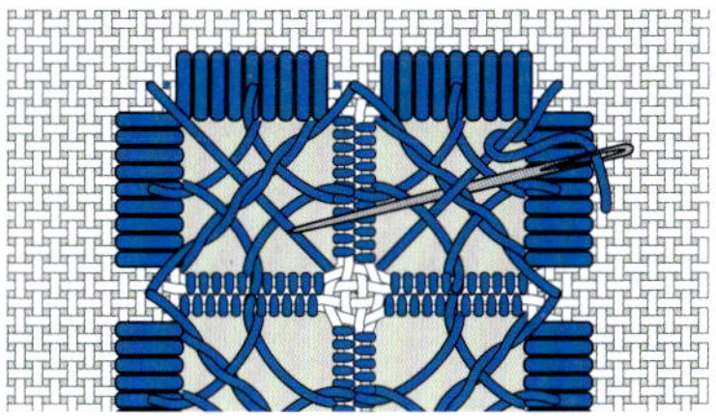

21 From the right, slide the needle under the centre twist and the diagonal stitch.

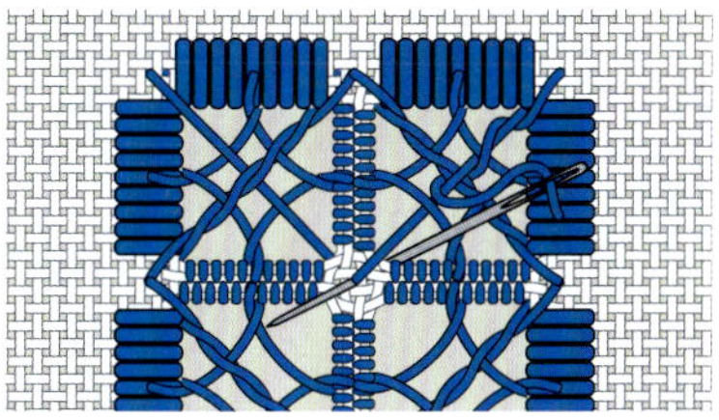

22 Insert the needle below the diagonal and bring it out in the centre of the woven square.

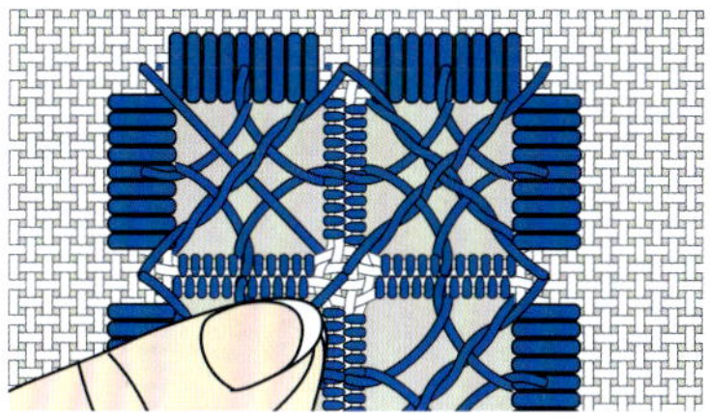

23 Pull the needle to intertwine the stitches.

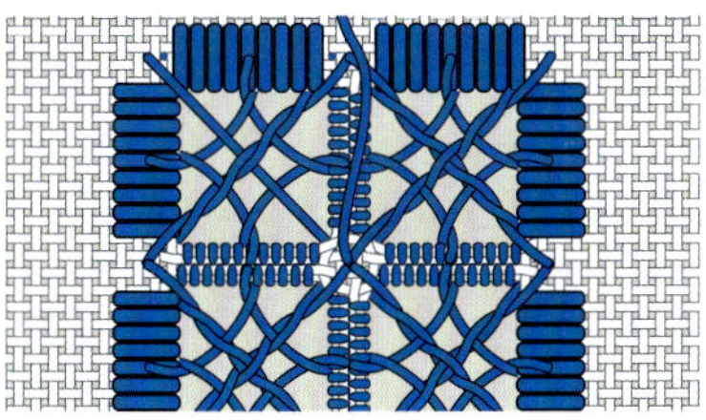

24 Repeat Steps 19 to 23 in the next two quadrants.

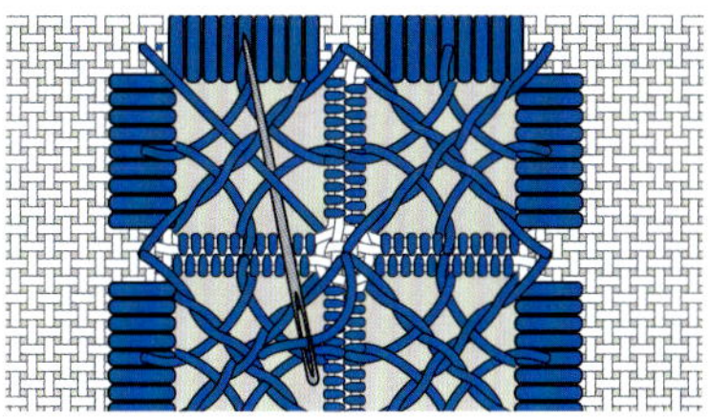

25 From below, slide the needle under the crossing diagonal stitch and dove's eye.

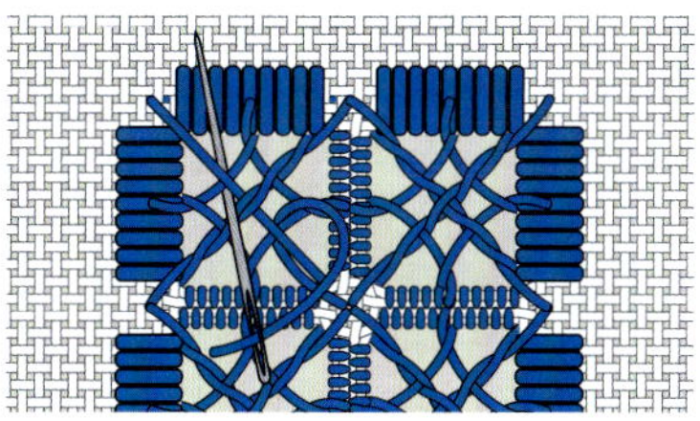

26 From below, slide the needle under the crossing diagonal and twisted stitches.

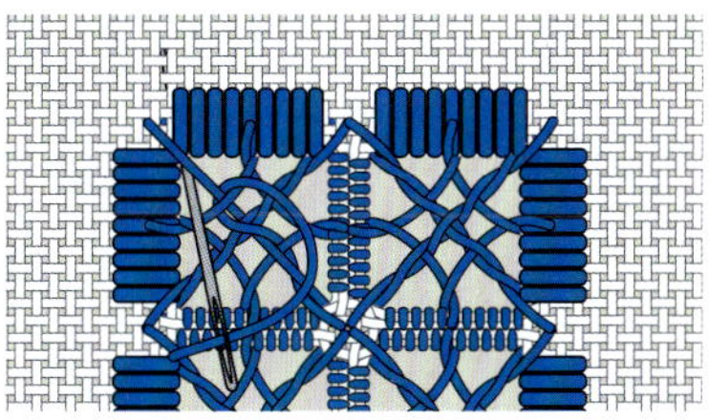

27 From below the diagonal, take the needle to the back in the corner. Pull to intertwine the stitches. Run the thread under the back of the satin stitches to finish it.

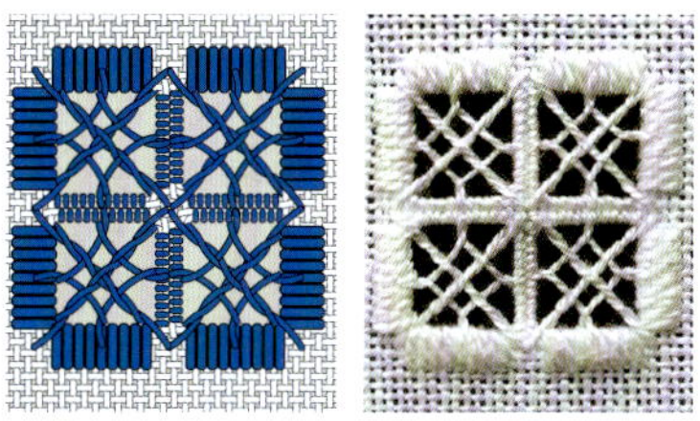

28 The completed dove's eye cobwebs.

dove's eye in a wrapped circle

This motif can be worked as a single filling in a shape as shown here, or incorporated into a larger area of needleweaving.

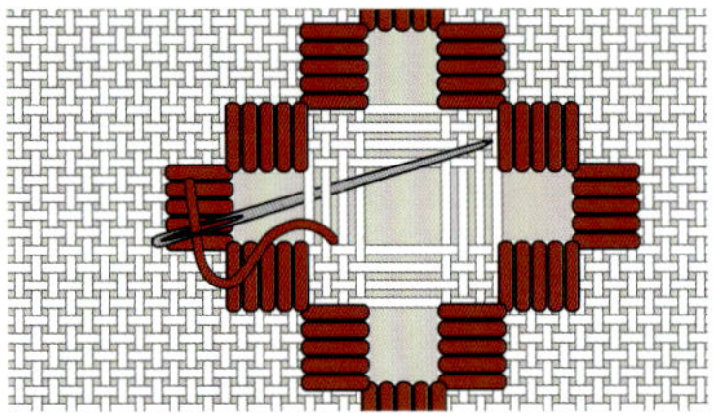

1 Bring the needle out in the centre of the first bar. Slide the needle under the left two threads, from the left.

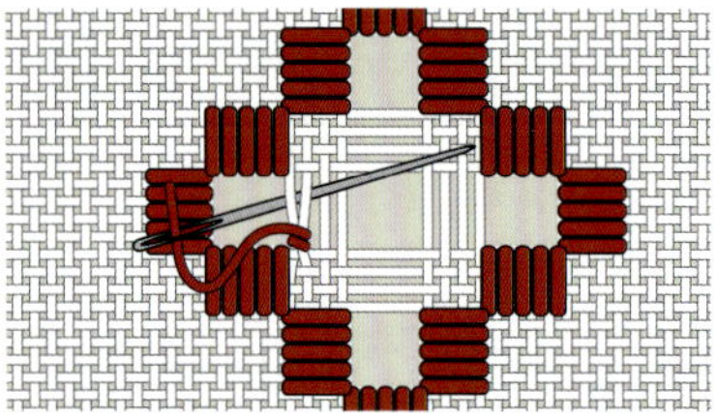

2 Tighten the stitch. Moving up, slide the needle under the left two threads again.

❶ *All stitches should sit next to each other and not overlap.*

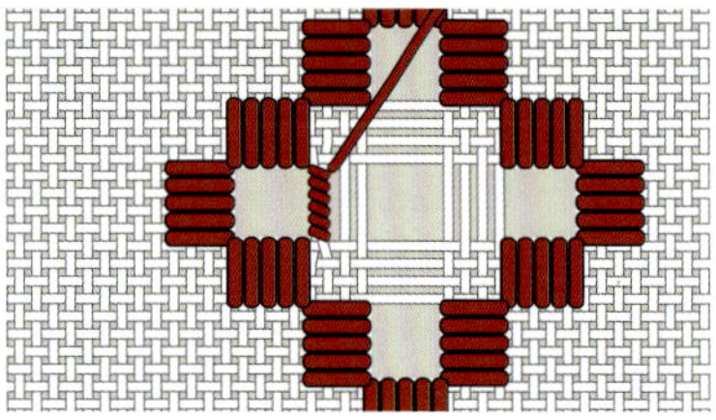

3 Continue tightly wrapping the threads, until you have filled the bar.

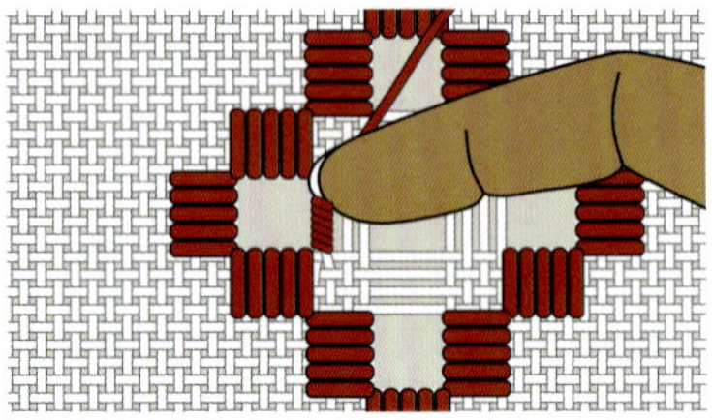

4 Push the stitches down to create more space for more wraps.

❶ *This bar needs to be overwrapped; that is, have too many stitches for the distance.*

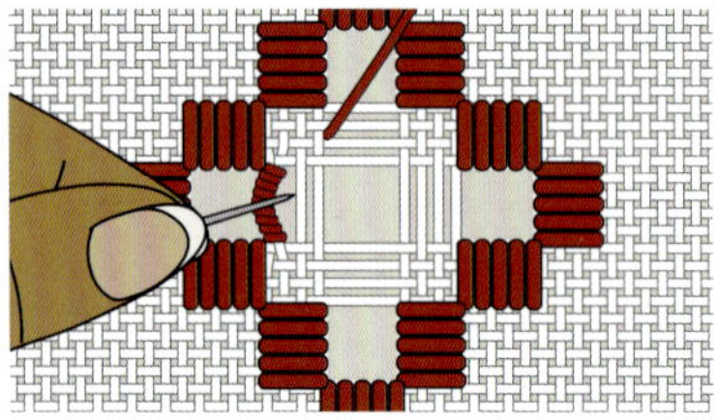

5 Fill the space with wraps again, bringing the thread out ready to start the next bar. Use the tip of the needle to push the wrapped bar outwards to give it a curve.

6 Work a curved overwrapped bar on each of the outer two threads of the square. Finish by bringing the thread out between the bar you've just wrapped and its pair.

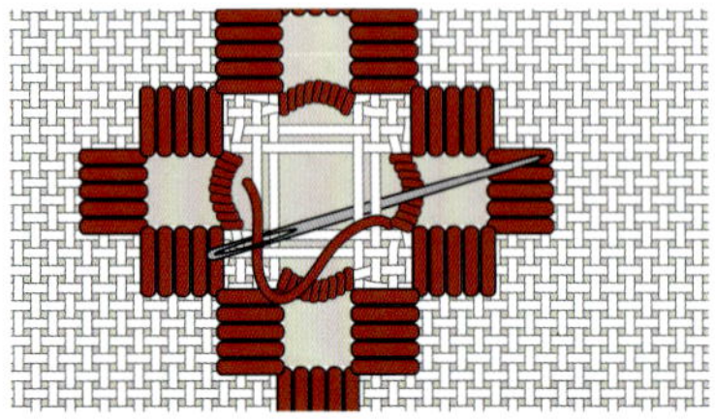

7 Turn the work 90° anticlockwise. From the left, slide the needle under the two threads to the left of where the working thread emerges.

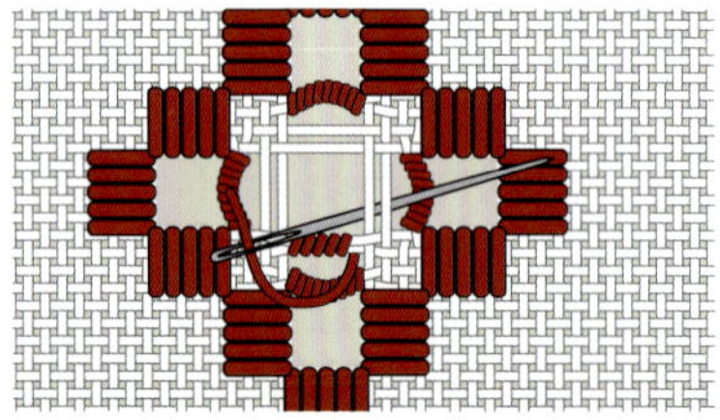

8 Tightly wrap the bar up to the last stitch. Turn the work 90° clockwise. Move to the next bar by inserting the needle, from the left, under the next bar.

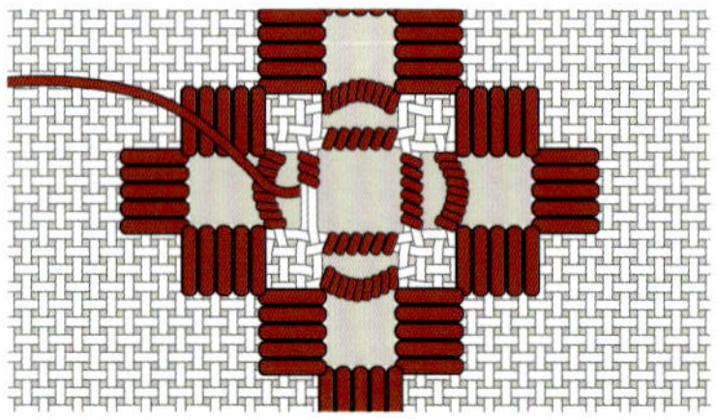

9 Wrap this bar and the next one, turning the work as required. Wrap half the remaining bar.

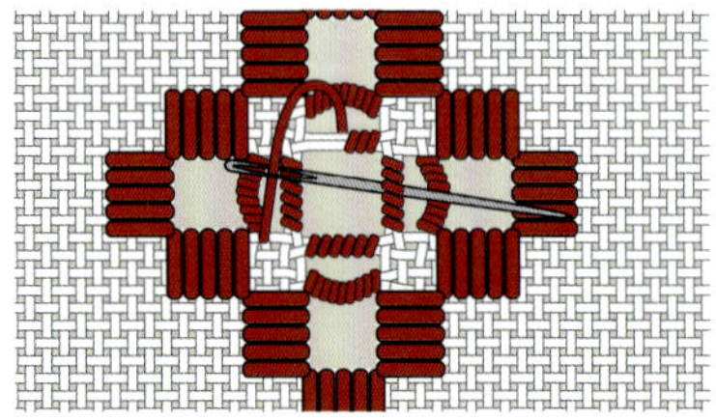

10 Turn the work so the half bar is at the top. Working around the square in a clockwise direction, insert the needle under the adjacent wrapped bar.

11 Turn the work 90° anticlockwise. Tighten the stitch so that it sits with a gentle curve. Slide the needle under the curved stitch and the next bar.

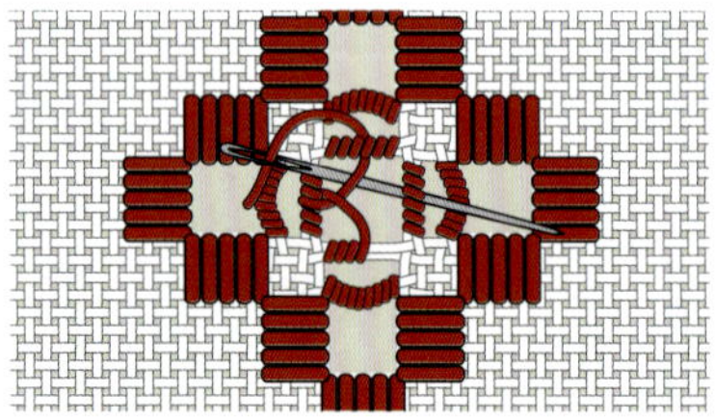

12 Turn the work 90° anticlockwise. Tighten the stitch so it curves gently. Slide the needle under the newest curved stitch and under the next bar.

13 Turn the work 90° anticlockwise. Tighten the stitch so it curves gently. Slide the needle under the newest curved stitch.

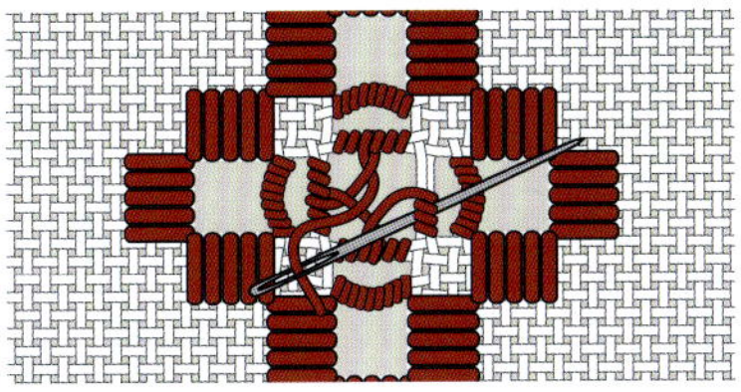

14 Pass the needle over the first curved stitch. From below the curved stitch, insert it under the half wrapped bar.

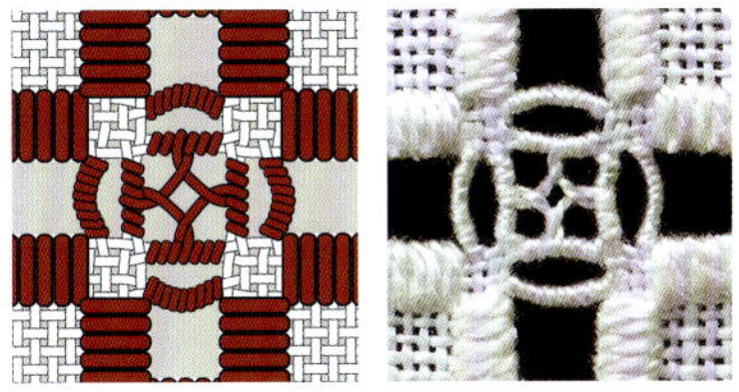

15 Finish wrapping the bar to complete the motif.

dove's eye in a wrapped circle rows *also known as dove's eye in a wrapped circle ribbon*

When worked as rows of dove's eyes in wrapped circles, the process is a little different than for single motifs.

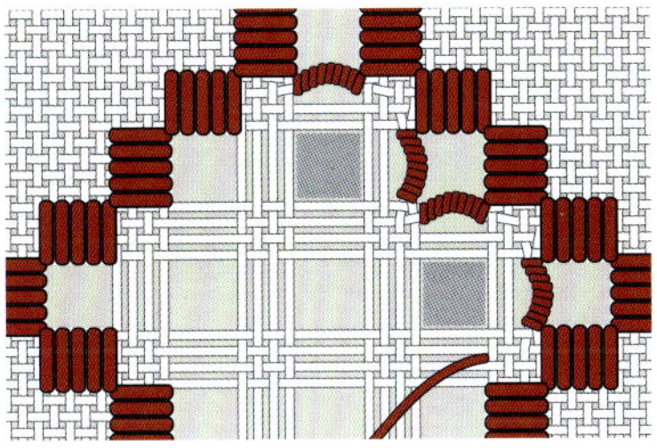

1 Referring to the method of working a single dove's eye in a wrapped circle motif, work overwrapped bars along the outer two threads of the upper side of the row.

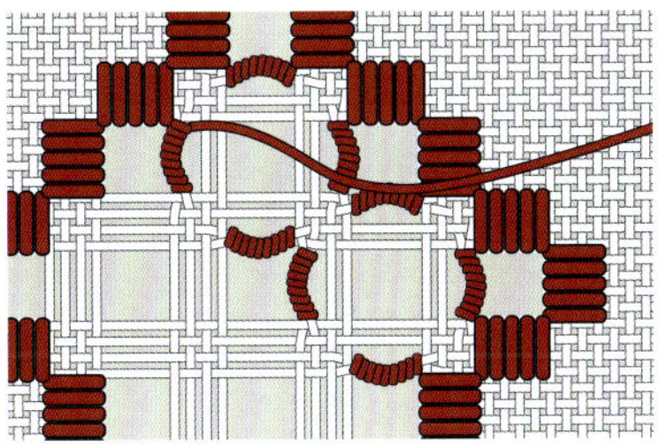

2 Travelling back towards the beginning, work overwrapped bars along the outer two threads of the lower side of the row.

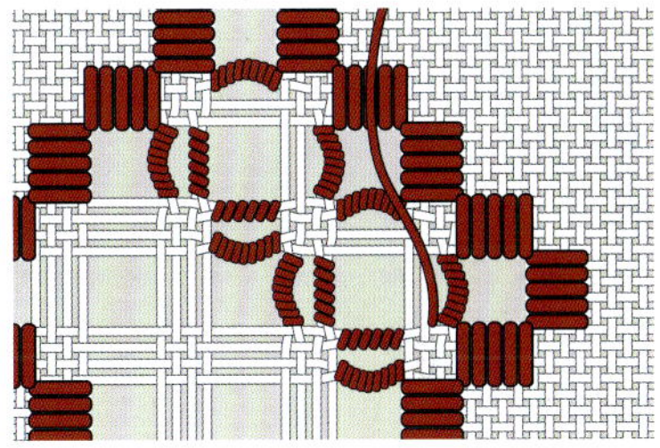

3 Work regular wrapped bars along the inner two threads of the lower side of the row.

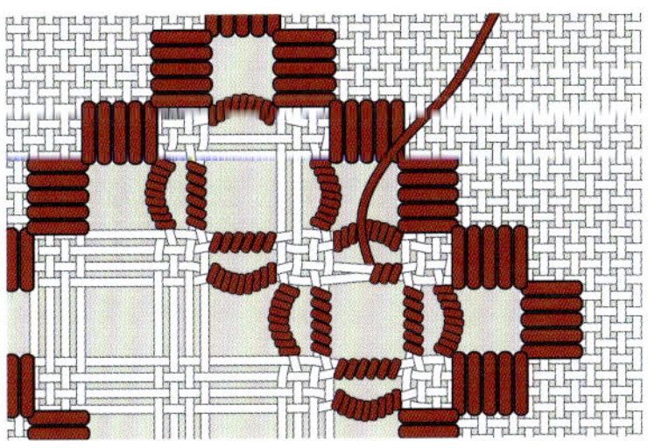

4 Travelling back towards the beginning, wrap the row's first bar and half of the next bar.

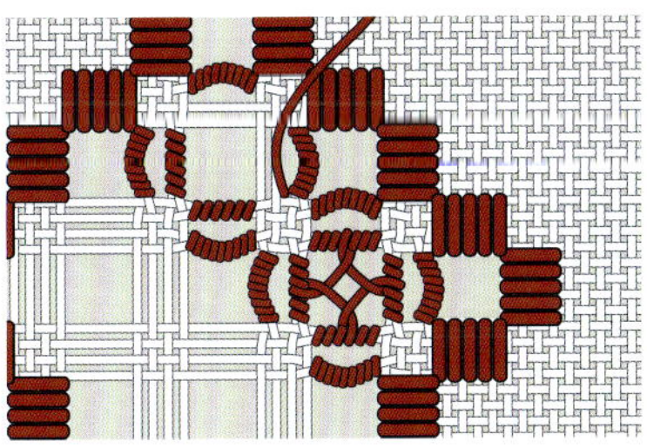

5 Work a dove's eye in the centre of the square, then finish wrapping the bar.

6 Repeat for the next square.

7 Work the next row in the same way.

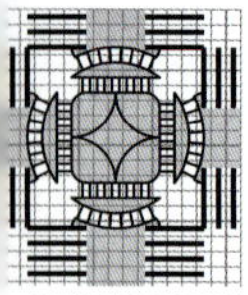

dove's eye in a wrapped circle

This motif can be worked as a single filling in a shape as shown here, or incorporated into a larger area of needleweaving.

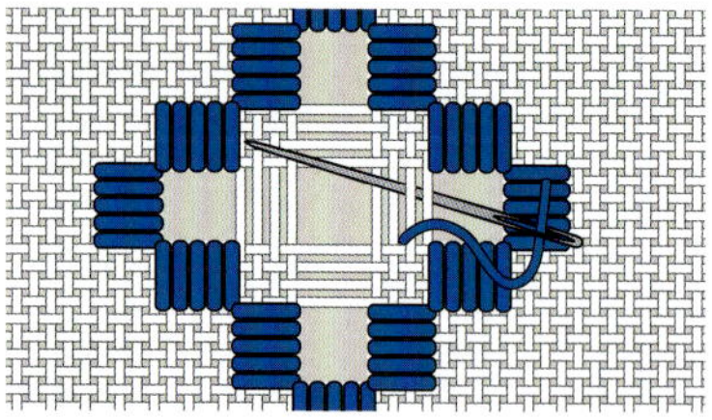

1 Bring the needle out in the centre of the first bar. Slide the needle under the right two threads, from the right.

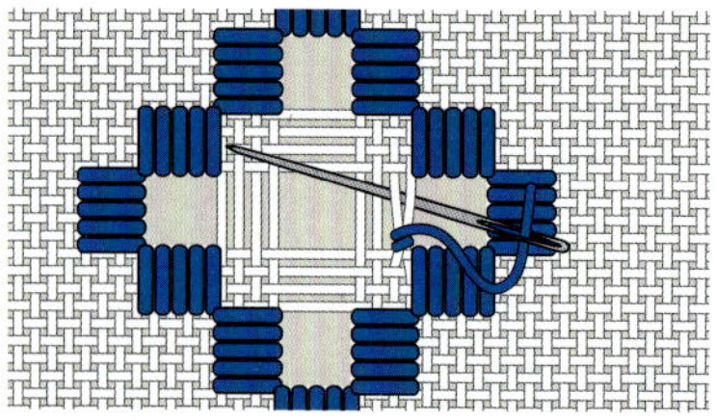

2 Tighten the stitch. Moving up, slide the needle under the right two threads again.

❶ *All stitches should sit next to each other and not overlap.*

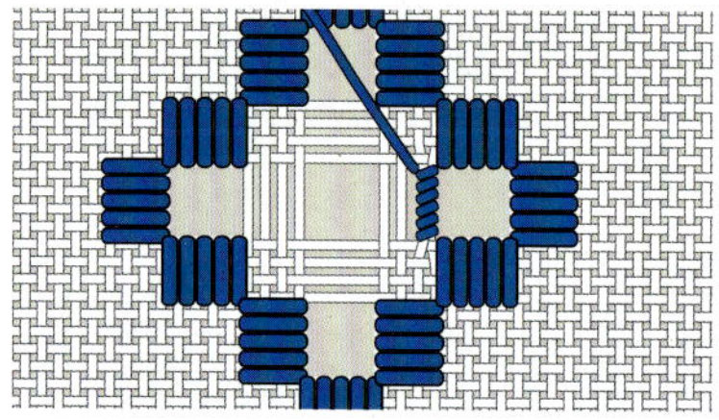

3 Continue tightly wrapping the threads, until you have filled the bar.

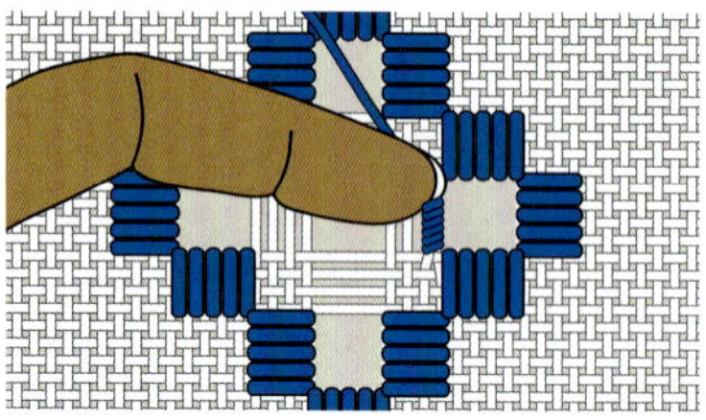

4 Push the stitches down to create more space for more wraps.

❶ *This bar needs to be overwrapped; that is, have too many stitches for the distance.*

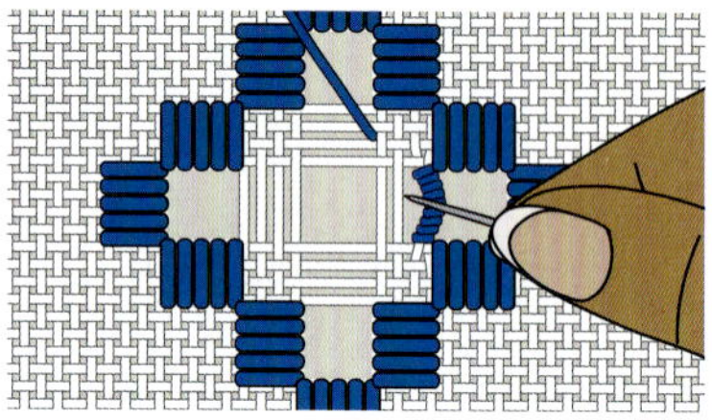

5 Fill the space with wraps again, bringing the thread out ready to start the next bar. Use the tip of the needle to push the wrapped bar outwards to give it a curve.

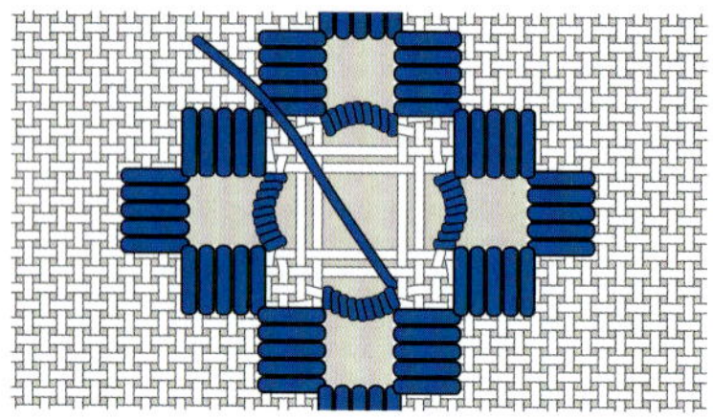

6 Work a curved overwrapped bar on each of the outer two threads of the square. Finish by bringing the thread out between the bar you've just wrapped and its pair.

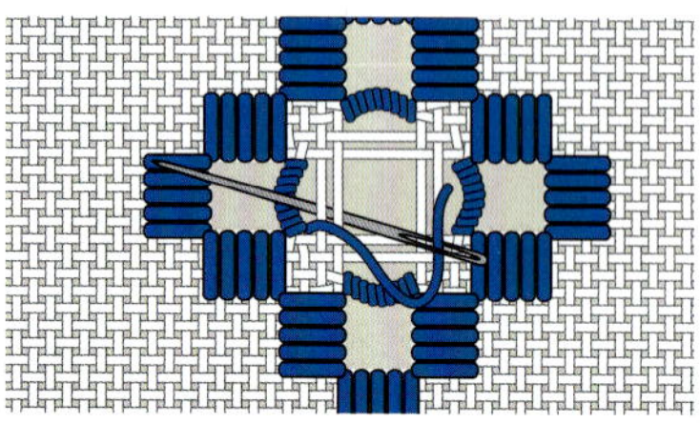

7 Turn the work 90° clockwise. From the right, slide the needle under the two threads to the right of where the working thread emerges.

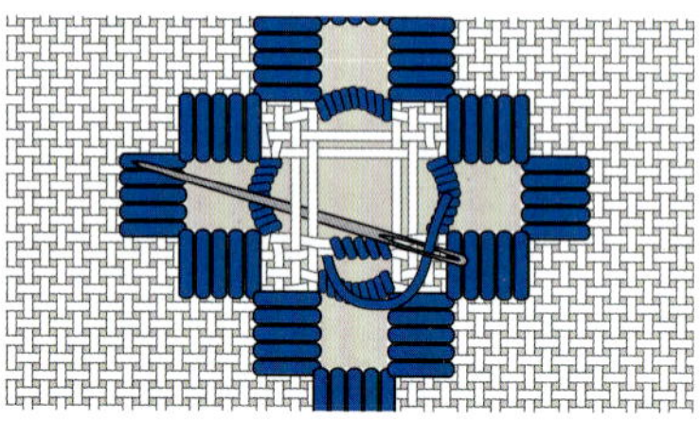

8 Tightly wrap the bar up to the last stitch. Turn the work 90° anticlockwise. Move to the next bar by inserting the needle, from the right, under the next bar.

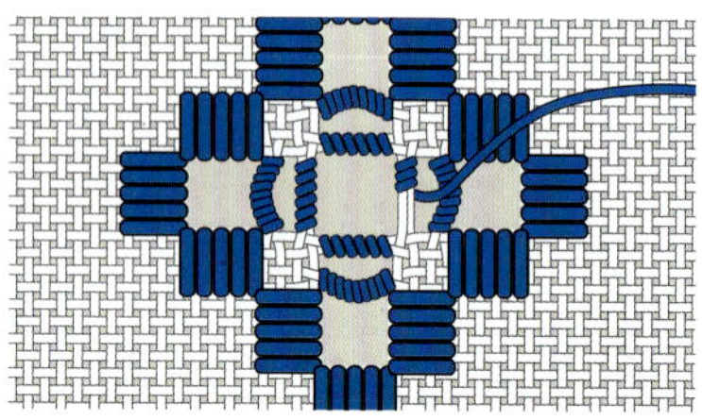

9 Wrap this bar and the next one, turning the work as required. Wrap half the remaining bar.

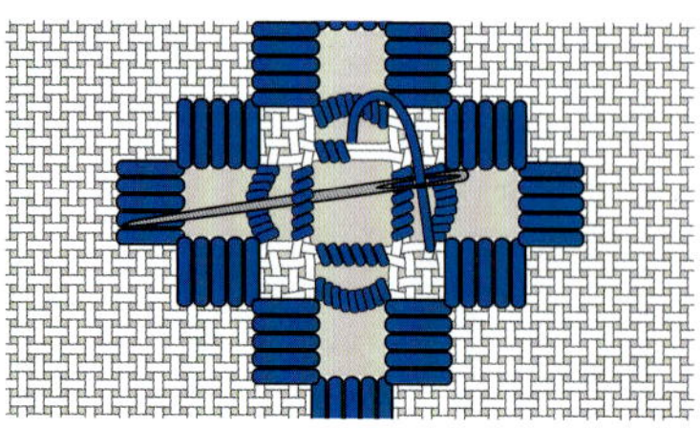

10 Turn the work so the half bar is at the top. Working around the square in an anticlockwise direction, insert the needle under the adjacent wrapped bar.

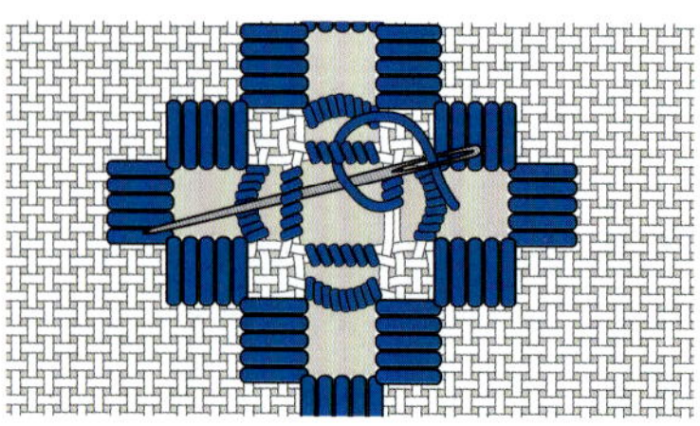

11 Turn the work 90° clockwise. Tighten the stitch so that it sits with a gentle curve. Slide the needle under the curved stitch and the next bar.

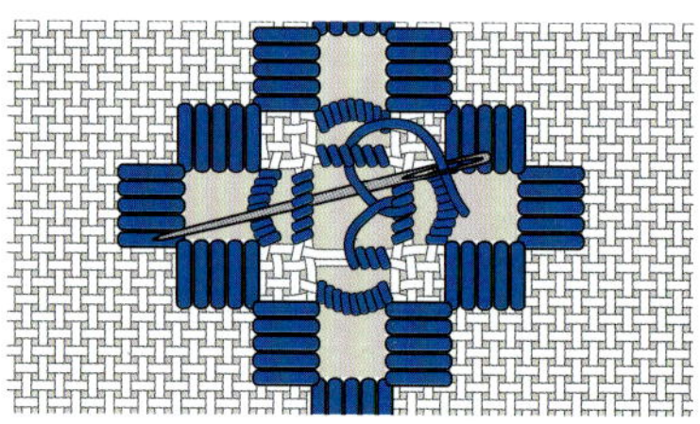

12 Turn the work 90° clockwise. Tighten the stitch so it curves gently. Slide the needle under the newest curved stitch and under the next bar.

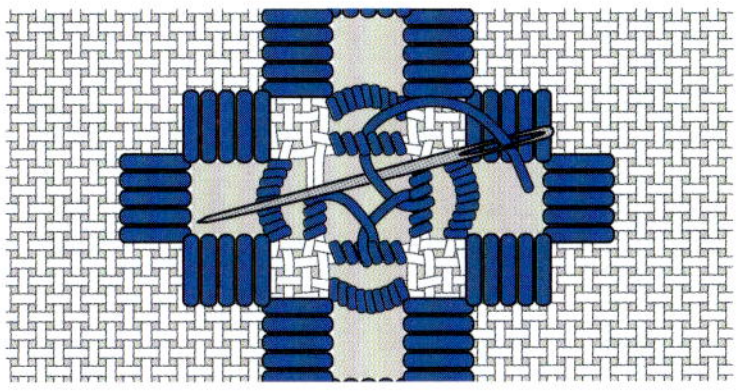

13 Turn the work 90° clockwise. Tighten the stitch so it curves gently. Slide the needle under the newest curved stitch.

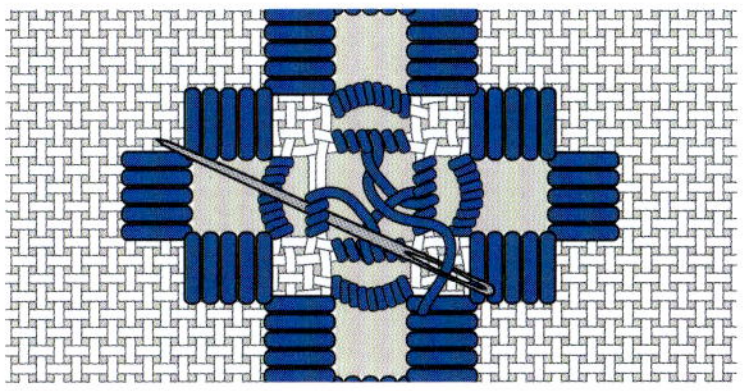

14 Pass the needle over the first curved stitch. From below the curved stitch, insert it under the half wrapped bar.

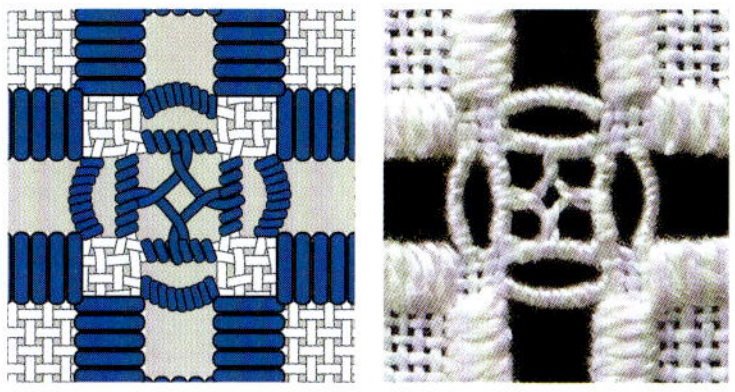

15 Finish wrapping the bar to complete the motif.

dove's eye in a wrapped circle rows *also known as dove's eye in a wrapped circle ribbon*

When worked as rows of dove's eyes in wrapped circles, the process is a little different than for single motifs.

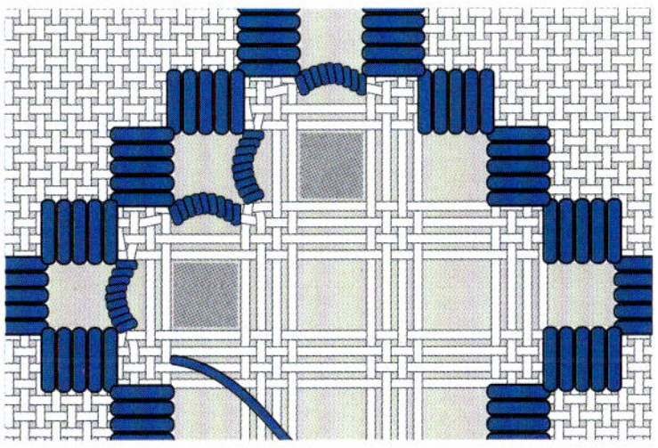

1 Referring to the method of working a single dove's eye in a wrapped circle motif, work overwrapped bars along the outer two threads of the upper side of the row.

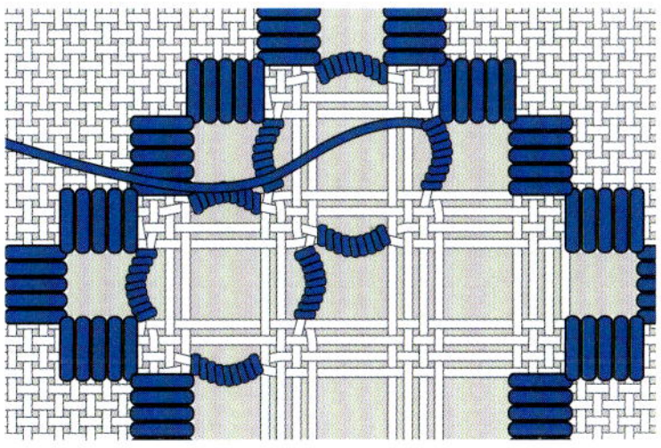

2 Travelling back towards the beginning, work overwrapped bars along the outer two threads of the lower side of the row.

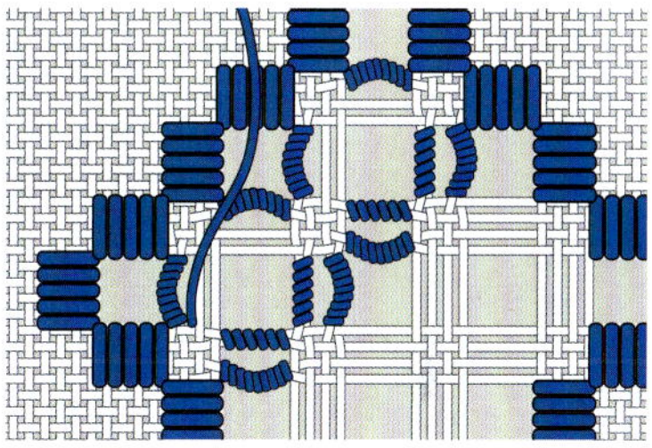

3 Work regular wrapped bars along the inner two threads of the lower side of the row.

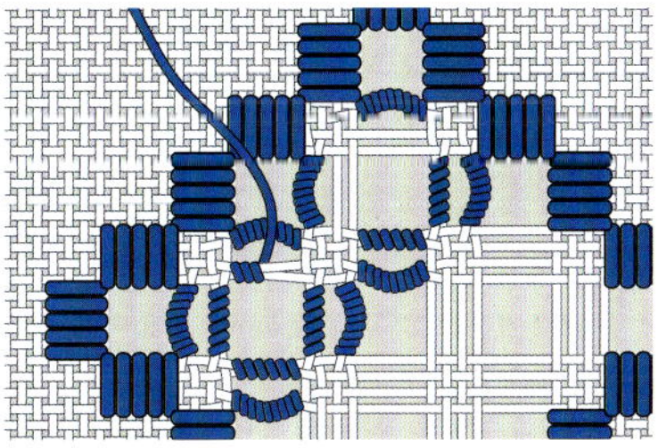

4 Travelling back towards the beginning, wrap the row's first bar and half of the next bar.

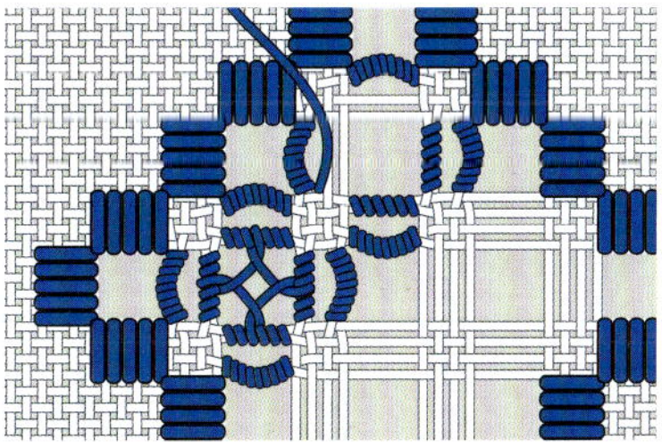

5 Work a dove's eye in the centre of the square, then finish wrapping the bar.

6 Repeat for the next square.

7 Work the next row in the same way.

dove's eyes with wrapped bars

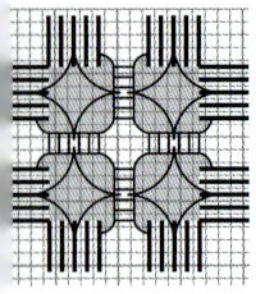

TRADITIONAL

When working with wrapped bars, some dove's eyes start with the thread above the bar and some start with it below. They are handled differently so that they end up looking the same.

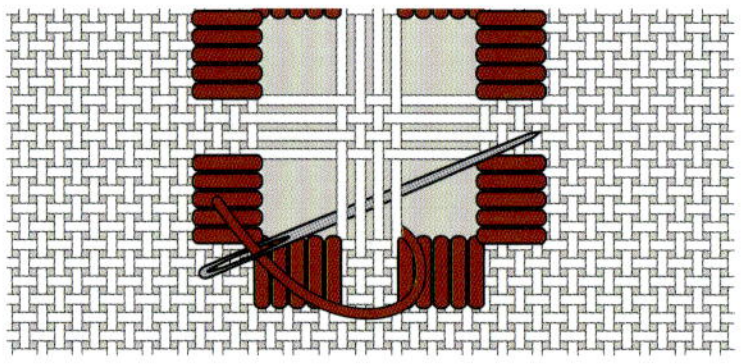

1 Bring the needle out at the square's base, on the right side of the bar. From the left, slide it under the bar.

2 Tightly wrap both bars across the square. Take the thread under the back of the satin stitch, then wrap a half bar.

3 Working with the lower left quadrant, slide the needle, from below, under the upper wrapped bar.

❶ *This dove's eye is worked anticlockwise.*

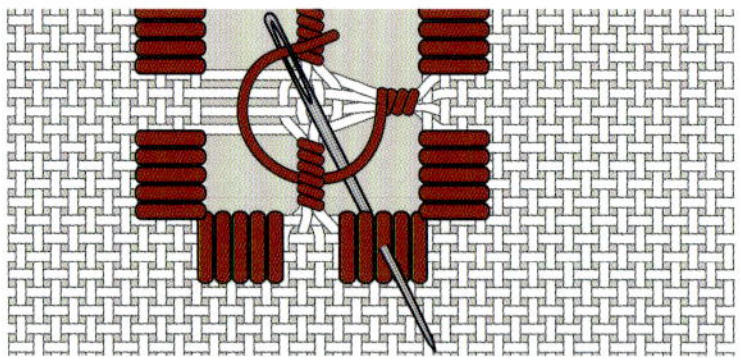

4 Turn the work 90° anticlockwise. Pull the thread so the stitch curves gently. Slide the needle under the stitch and bring it out in the centre of the lower satin stitch block.

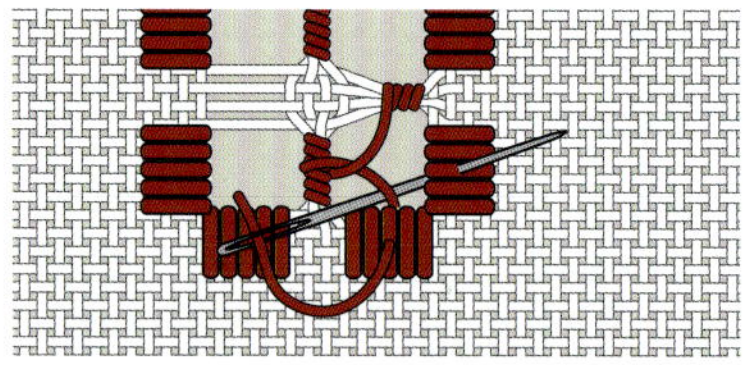

5 Slide the needle under the stitch and bring it out in the centre of the right satin stitch block.

❶ *Each time you pull the needle through, let the stitch curve gently.*

6 Turn the work 90° clockwise. Slide the needle under the stitch, over the first curving stitch and under the not yet wrapped portion of the bar.

7 Working with the lower right quadrant, from above, slide the needle under the upper wrapped bar.

❶ *This dove's eye is worked clockwise.*

8 Turn the work 180°. From the left, insert the needle in the centre of the left satin stitch block. Take the needle over the thread.

9 Pull the needle through. From above, insert it in the centre of the upper satin stitch block. Take it over the thread and under the first stitch.

10 Turn the work 180°. Pull the needle through. Wrap the rest of the bar and half the remaining bar.

11 Work a clockwise dove's eye in the top left quadrant, noting the bars and satin stitch blocks are in different places this time.

12 Work an anticlockwise dove's eye in the top right quadrant, noting the bars and satin stitch blocks are in different places this time.

13 Complete the bar and finish the thread in the back of the satin stitching.

❶ *If the thread comes from the wrapped bar above the bar, work the dove's eye anticlockwise. If the thread comes from the wrapped bar beneath the bar, work the dove's eye clockwise. This way, they will all look the same.*

R

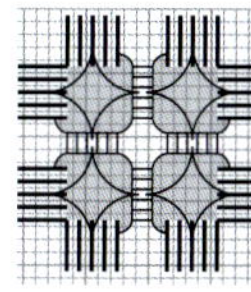

TRADITIONAL

dove's eyes with wrapped bars

When working with wrapped bars, some dove's eyes start with the thread above the bar and some start with it below. They are handled differently so that they end up looking the same.

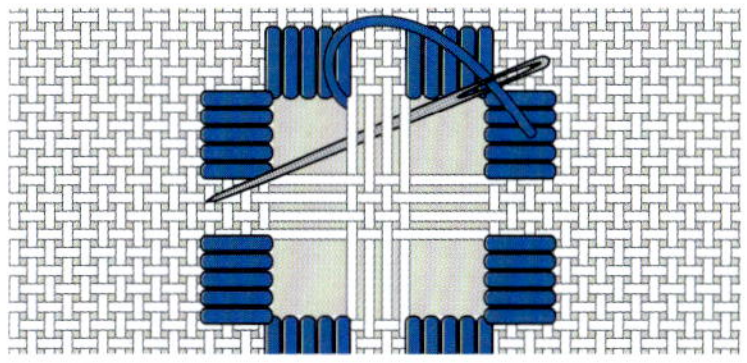

1 Bring the needle out at the square's top, on the left side of the bar. From the right, slide it under the bar.

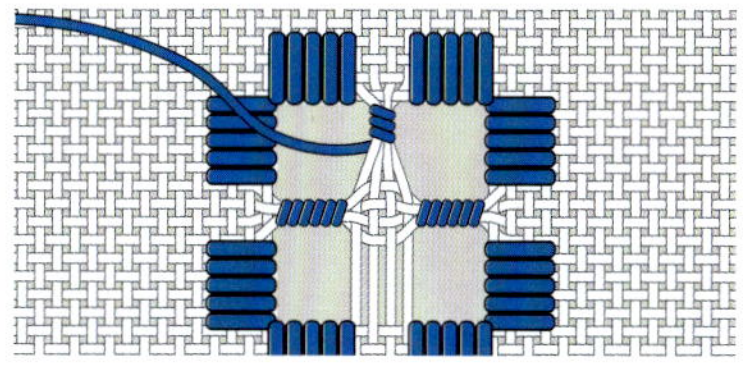

2 Tightly wrap both bars across the square. Take the thread under the back of the satin stitch, then wrap a half bar.

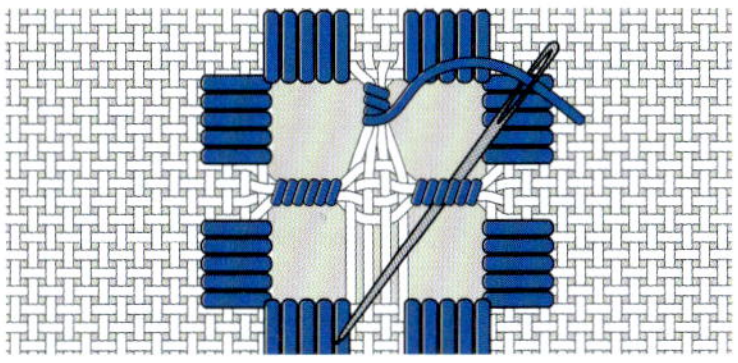

3 Working with the upper right quadrant, slide the needle, from above, under the upper wrapped bar.

❶ *This dove's eye is worked anticlockwise.*

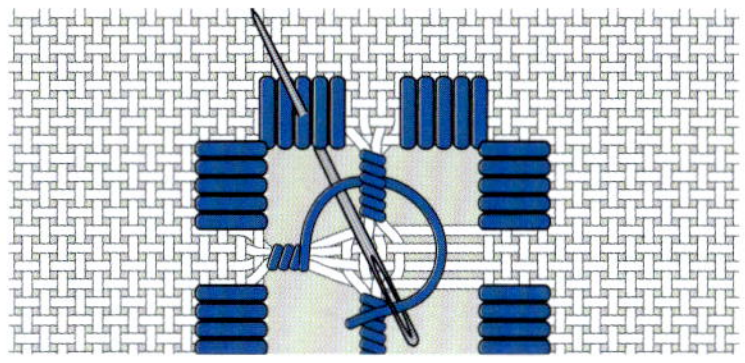

4 Turn the work 90° anticlockwise. Pull the thread so the stitch curves gently. Slide the needle under the stitch and bring it out in the centre of the upper satin stitch block.

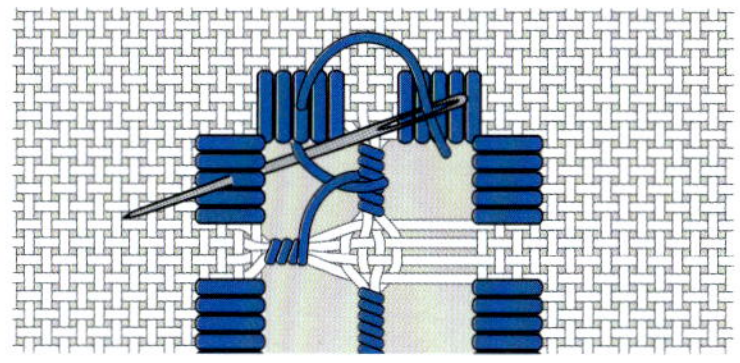

5 Slide the needle under the stitch and bring it out in the centre of the left satin stitch block.

❶ *Each time you pull the needle through, let the stitch curve gently.*

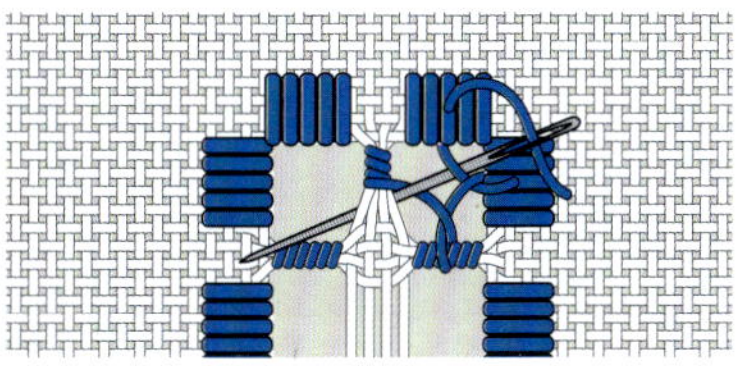

6 Turn the work 90° clockwise. Slide the needle under the stitch, over the first curving stitch and under the not yet wrapped portion of the bar.

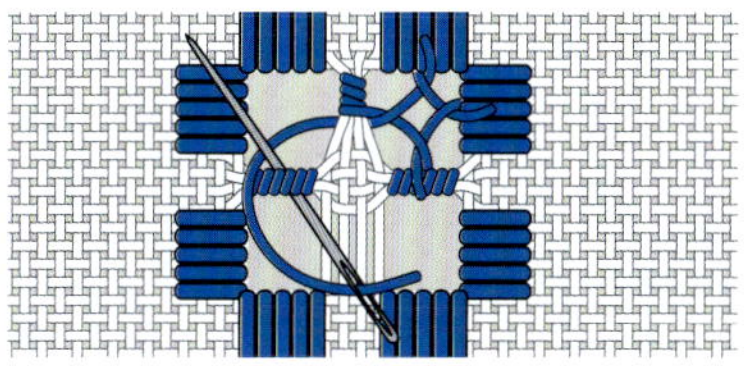

7 Working with the upper left quadrant, from below, slide the needle under the upper wrapped bar.

❶ *This dove's eye is worked clockwise.*

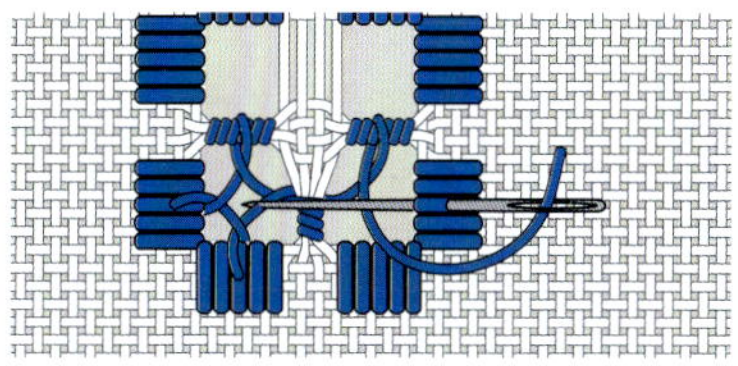

8 Turn the work 180°. From the right, insert the needle in the centre of the right satin stitch block. Take the needle over the thread.

9 Pull the needle through. From below, insert it in the centre of the upper satin stitch block. Take it over the thread and under the first stitch.

10 Turn the work 180°. Pull the needle through. Wrap the rest of the bar and half the remaining bar.

11 Work a clockwise dove's eye in the bottom right quadrant, noting the bars and satin stitch blocks are in different places this time.

12 Work an anticlockwise dove's eye in the bottom left quadrant, noting the bars and satin stitch blocks are in different places this time.

13 Complete the bar and finish the thread in the back of the satin stitching.

❶ *If the thread comes from the wrapped bar above the bar, work the dove's eye anticlockwise. If the thread comes from the wrapped bar beneath the bar, work the dove's eye clockwise. This way, they will all look the same.*

ringed crossed dove's eye

also known as ringed diagonal filet

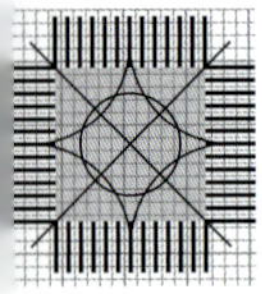

CONTEMPORARY

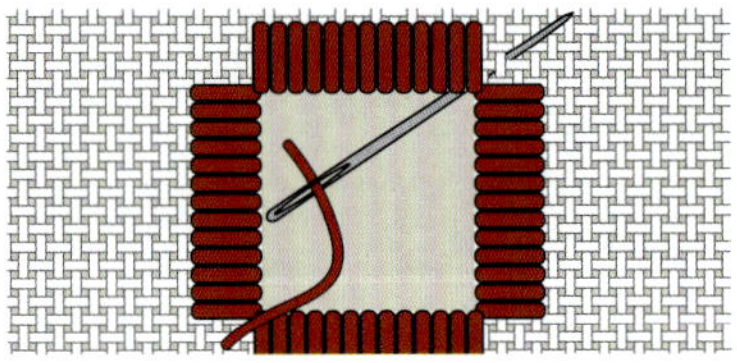

1 Remove all the fabric threads in the square. Bring the needle out in the bottom left corner, two threads away from the edges, then in the far corner.

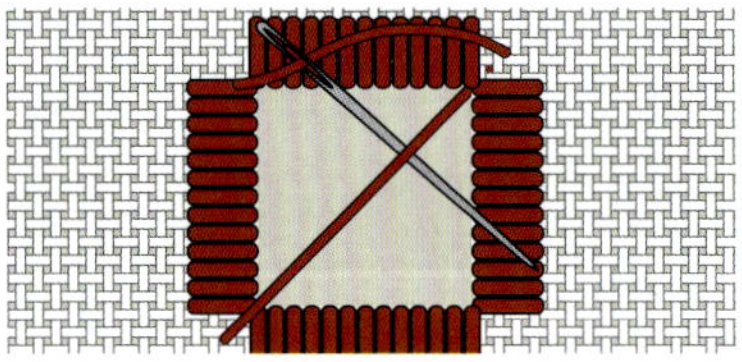

2 Pull the needle through. From above left, slide the needle under the diagonal stitch.

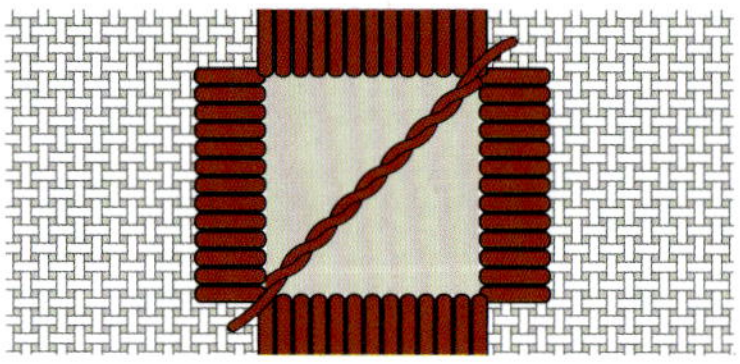

3 Slide the needle under the stitch three more times. Take it to the back. Pull to intertwine the stitches.

❶ *If the square is larger, add more twists.*

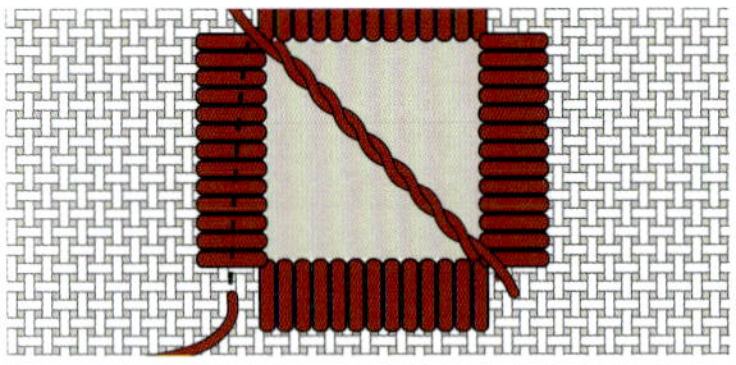

4 Run the thread under the satin stitch on the back. Turn the work 90° clockwise. Bring the needle out in the centre of the corner square.

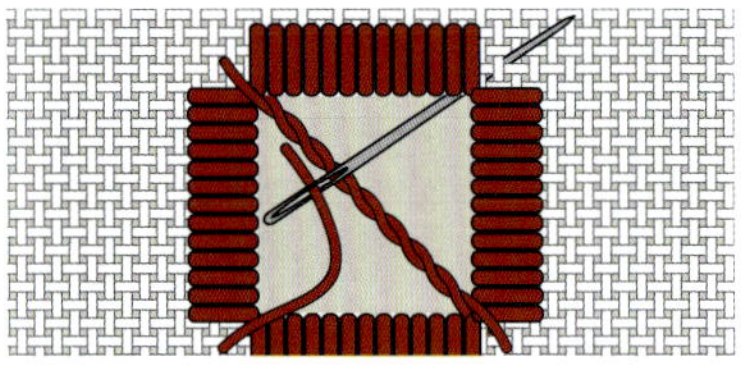

5 Take the needle over the twisted diagonal and bring it out in the opposite corner, two threads away from the cut edges.

6 From above, slide the needle under the stitch twice above the twisted diagonal, once diagonally under it, and once below it. Take it to the back and pull to intertwine the stitches.

7 Run the thread under the satin stitch on the back and bring the needle out halfway along the satin stitch, two threads away from the cut edge, splitting the stitch.

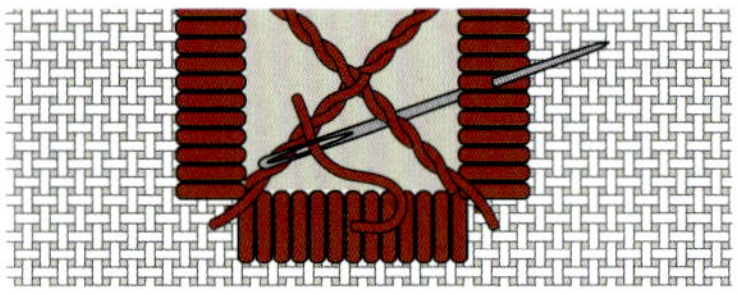

8 Working anticlockwise, take the needle under the twisted diagonal and bring it out in the middle of the satin stitch on the next side, splitting the stitch.

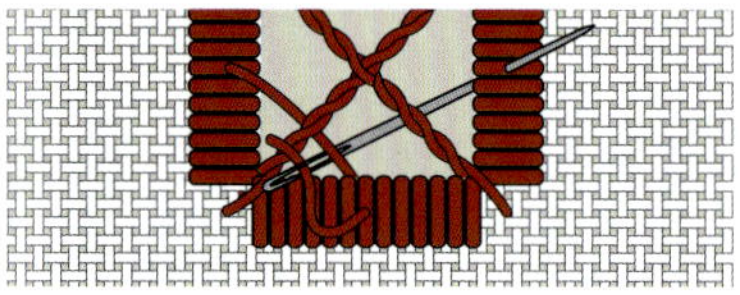

9 Turn the work 90° clockwise. Pass the needle under the previous stitch and the diagonal. Bring it out in the next side's centre, splitting the middle stitch.

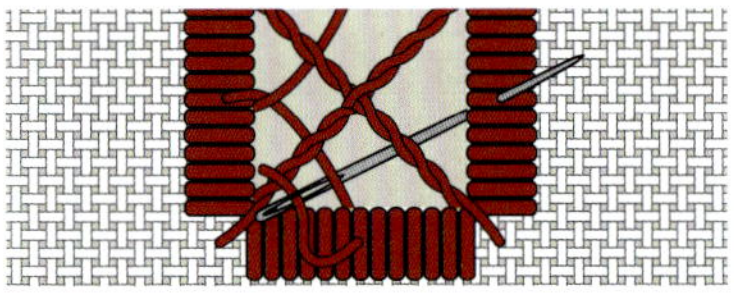

10 Repeat Step 9.

❶ *These dove's eye stitches should be reasonably tight.*

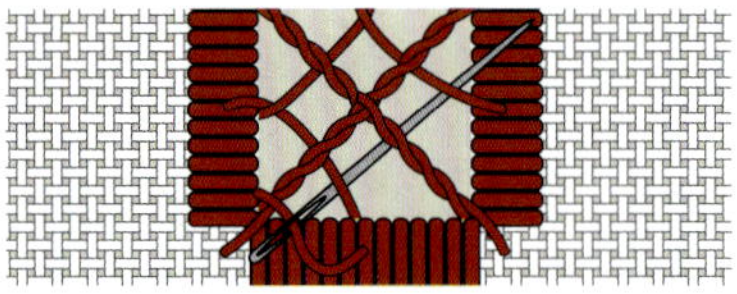

11 Turn the work 90° clockwise. Pull the needle through. Pass it under the previous stitch, the twisted diagonal and the first dove's eye stitch.

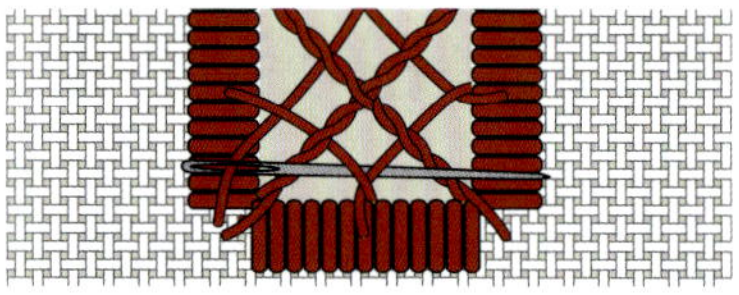

12 Turn the work 180°. Pass the needle over the next diagonal, and under both the dove's eye stitches.

❶ *Work with gentle tension.*

13 Turning as needed, pass the needle over the diagonal and under the dove's eye stitches on the next two sides.

14 Take the needle under the first part of the ring and over the first part of the first dove's eye, and to the back.

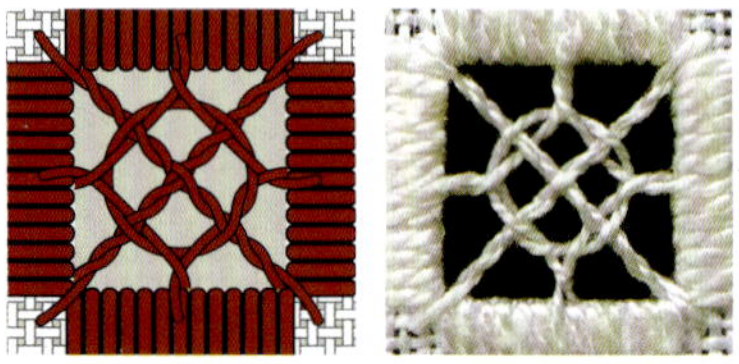

15 Adjust the tension of the dove's eye and ring so they sit well, and the circle is not too small. Finish the thread in the back of the satin stitch.

ringed crossed dove's eye *also known as ringed diagonal filet*

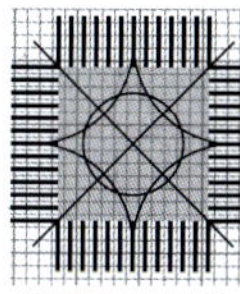

CONTEMPORARY

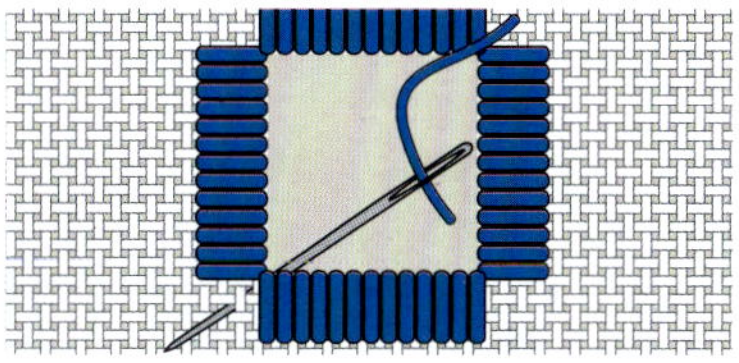

1 Remove all the fabric threads in the square. Bring the needle out in the top right corner, two threads away from the edges, then in the far corner.

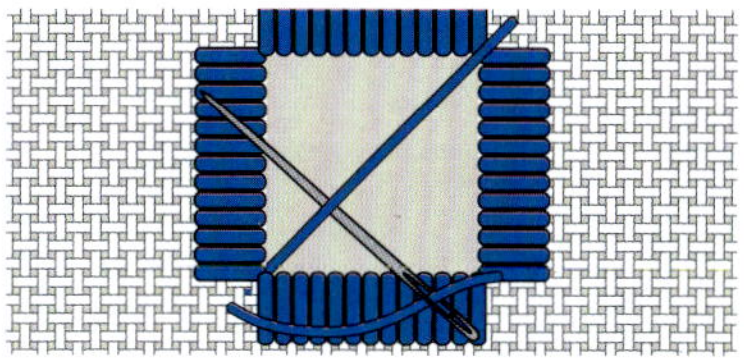

2 Pull the needle through. From below right, slide the needle under the diagonal stitch.

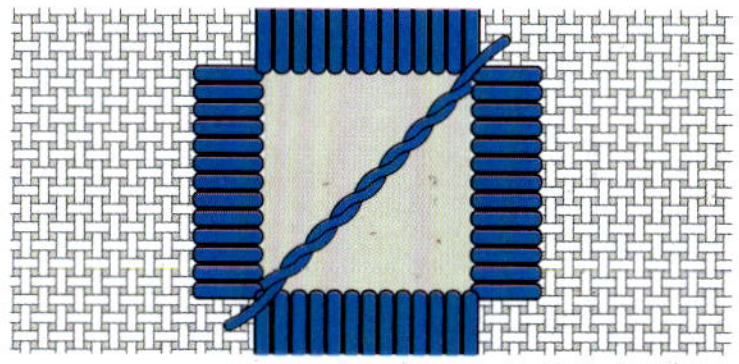

3 Slide the needle under the stitch three more times. Take it to the back. Pull to intertwine the stitches.

❶ *If the square is larger, add more twists.*

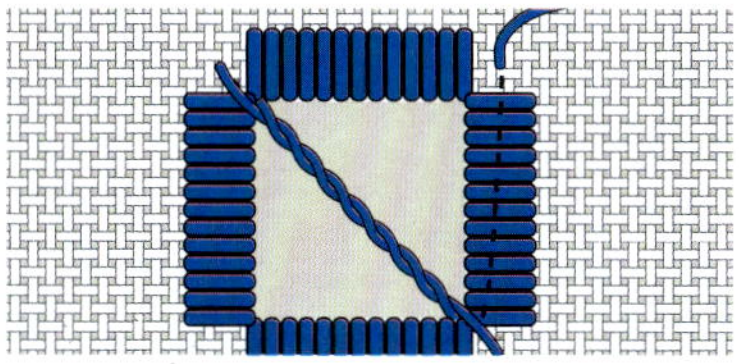

4 Run the thread under the satin stitch on the back. Turn the work 90° clockwise. Bring the needle out in the centre of the corner square.

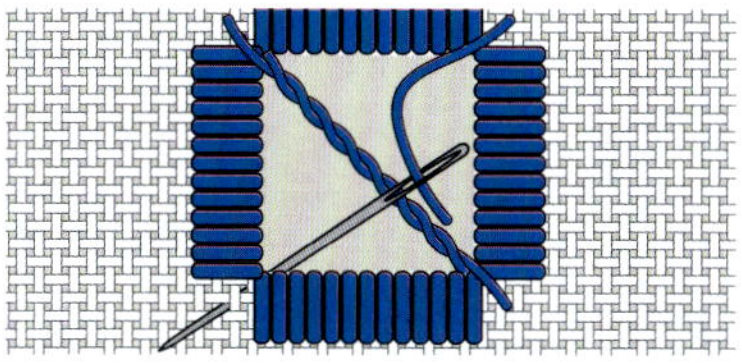

5 Take the needle over the twisted diagonal and bring it out in the opposite corner, two threads away from the cut edges.

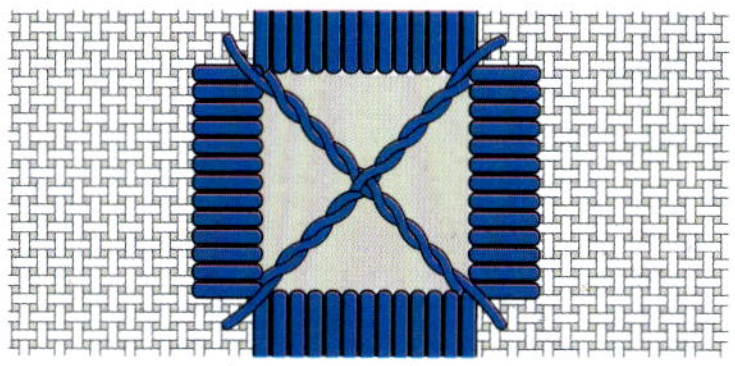

6 From below, slide the needle under the stitch twice below the twisted diagonal, once diagonally under it, and once above it. Take it to the back and pull to intertwine the stitches.

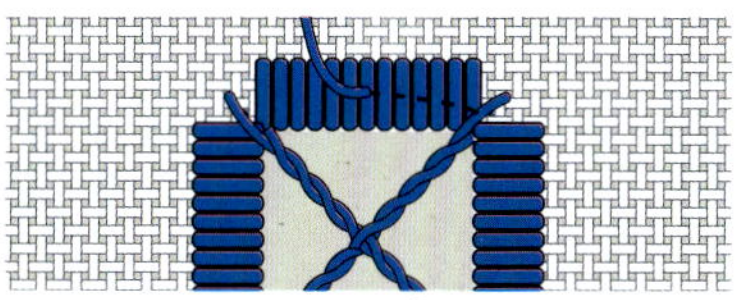

7 Run the thread under the satin stitch on the back and bring the needle out halfway along the satin stitch, two threads away from the cut edge, splitting the stitch.

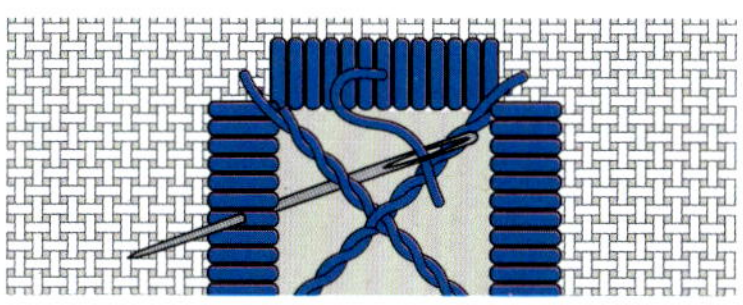

8 Working anticlockwise, take the needle under the twisted diagonal and bring it out in the middle of the satin stitch on the next side, splitting the stitch.

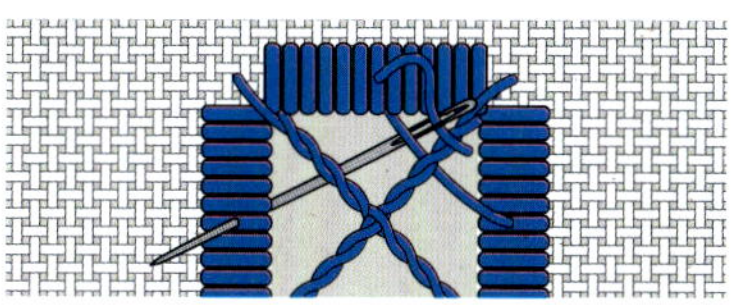

9 Turn the work 90° clockwise. Pass the needle under the previous stitch and the diagonal. Bring it out in the next side's centre, splitting the middle stitch.

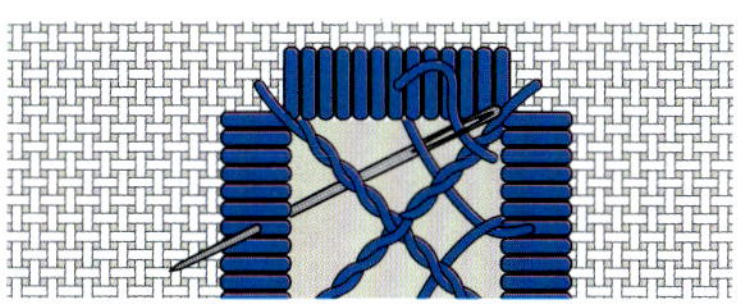

10 Repeat Step 9.

❶ *These dove's eye stitches should be reasonably tight.*

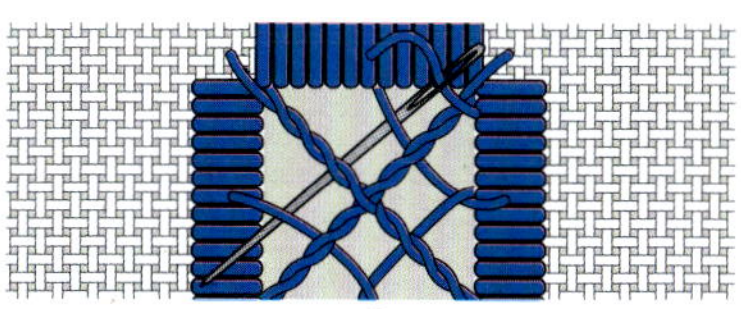

11 Turn the work 90° clockwise. Pull the needle through. Pass it under the previous stitch, the twisted diagonal and the first dove's eye stitch.

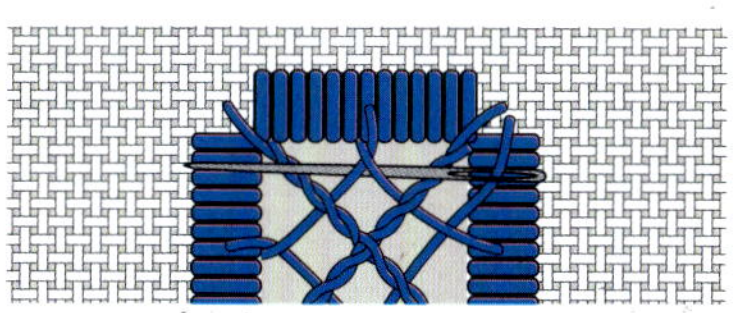

12 Turn the work 180°. Pass the needle over the next diagonal, and under both the dove's eye stitches.

❶ *Work with gentle tension.*

13 Turning as needed, pass the needle over the diagonal and under the dove's eye stitches on the next two sides.

14 Take the needle under the first part of the ring and over the first part of the first dove's eye, and to the back.

15 Adjust the tension of the dove's eye and ring so they sit well, and the circle is not too small. Finish the thread in the back of the satin stitch.

L

square filet

This stitch is worked after weaving or wrapping all sides of the square to be filled. It can be worked either clockwise or anticlockwise – just be consistent throughout.

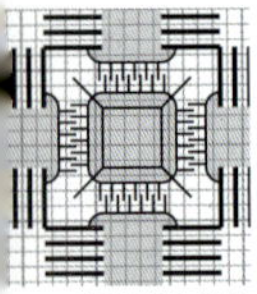

TRADITIONAL

clockwise square filet

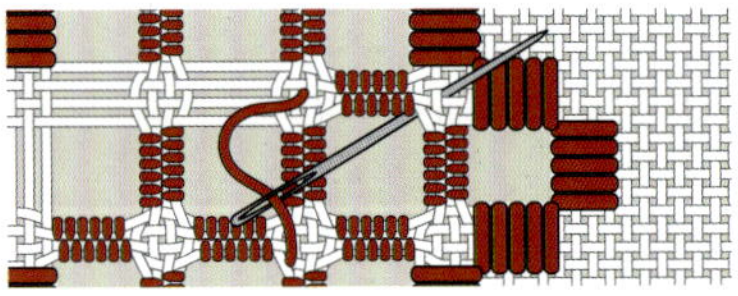

1 After working the fourth side of the square, bring the needle out in the adjacent woven square's centre. Working clockwise, insert the needle in the centre back of the next woven square.

❶ *Always insert the needle in the back.*

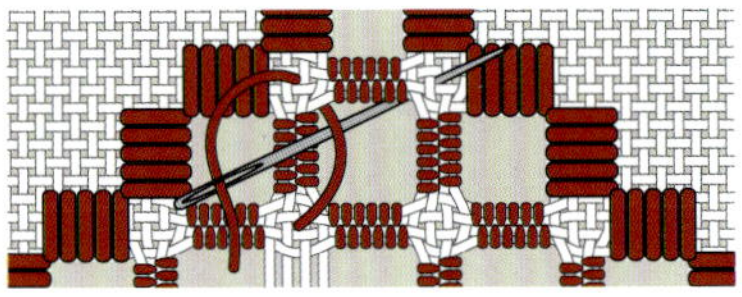

2 Pull the needle through so the stitch gently curves between the two corners. Turn the work 90° anticlockwise. Insert the needle under the previous stitch and into the centre back of the next woven square.

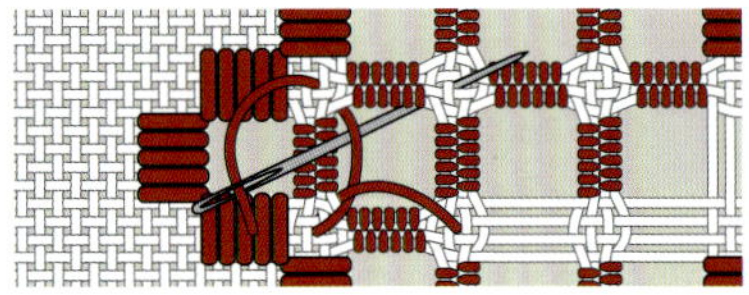

3 Pull the needle through so the stitch gently curves. Turn the work 90° anticlockwise. Insert the needle under the previous stitch and into the centre back of the next woven square.

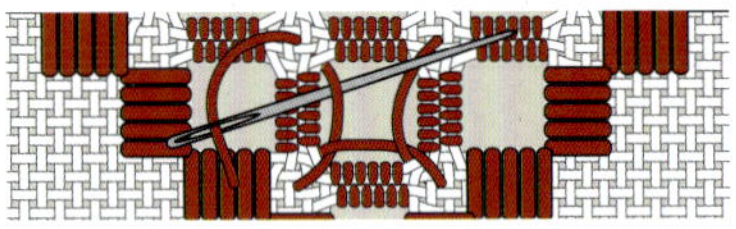

4 Pull the needle through so the stitch gently curves. Turn the work 90° anticlockwise. Slide the needle under the previous stitch.

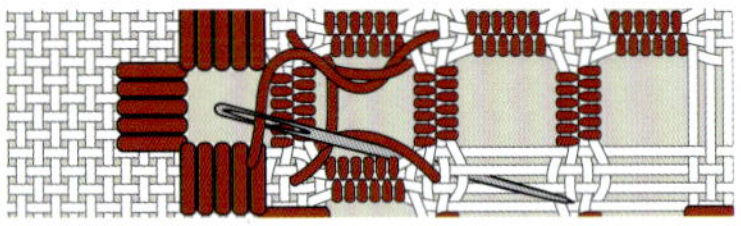

5 Turn the work 90° clockwise. Take the needle over the initial curved stitch, then behind the woven square. Bring it out ready to continue.

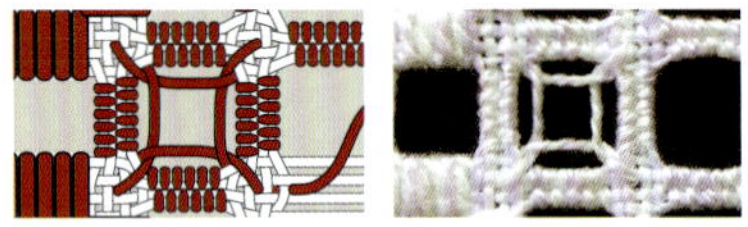

6 The completed square filet stitch ready for continued stitching.

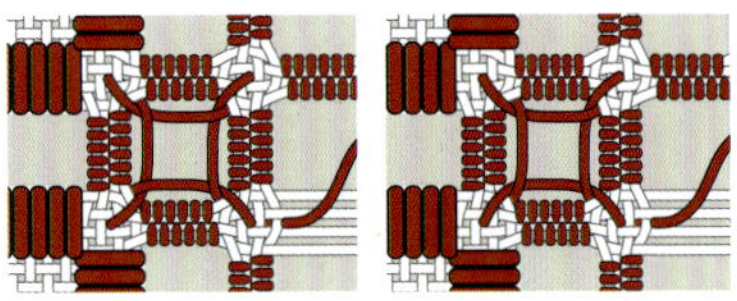

❶ *Ensure that all the stitches cross the same way: under at one end and over at the other (see left). If a stitch is 'over' or 'under' at both ends (see right), it is incorrect.*

❶ *The threads should only cross once in the corners, and not have any extra twists.*

anticlockwise square filet

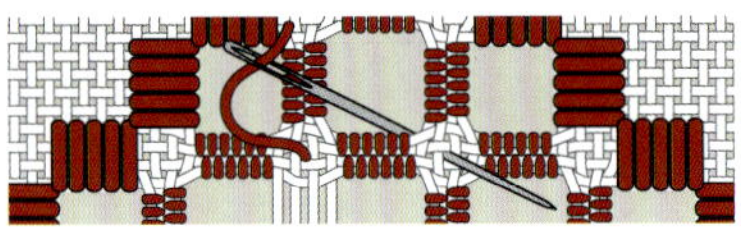

1 After working the fourth side of the square, bring the needle out in the adjacent woven square's centre. Working in an anticlockwise direction, insert the needle in the centre back of the next woven square.

❶ *Always insert the needle in the back.*

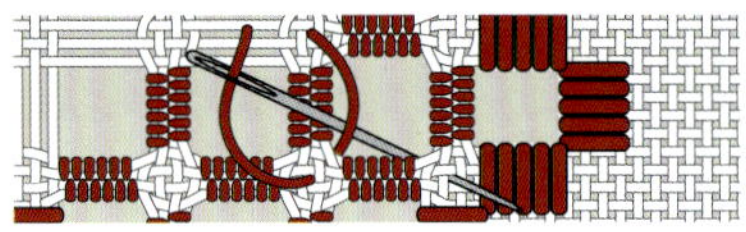

2 Pull the needle through so the stitch gently curves between the two corners. Turn the work 90° clockwise. Insert the needle under the previous stitch and into the centre back of the next woven square.

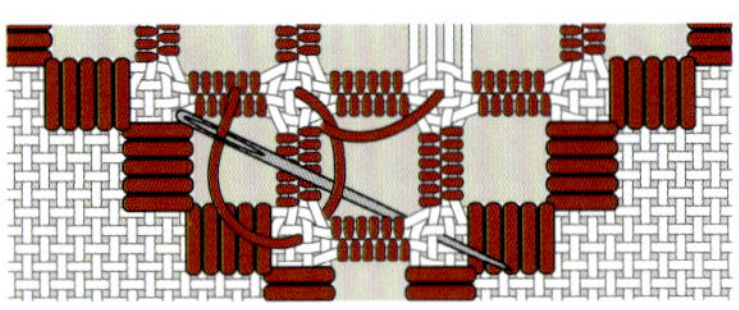

3 Pull the needle through. Turn the work 90° clockwise. Insert the needle under the previous stitch and into the centre back of the next woven square.

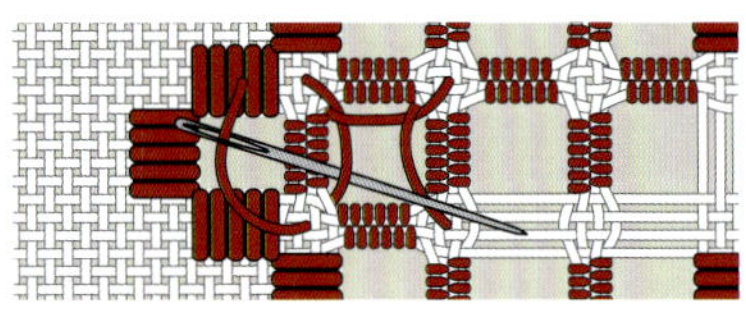

4 Pull the needle through. Turn the work 90° clockwise. Slide the needle under the previous stitch.

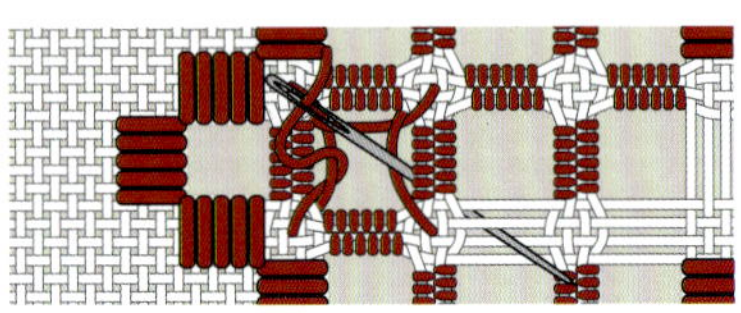

5 Take the needle over the initial curved stitch, then behind the woven square. Bring it out ready to continue.

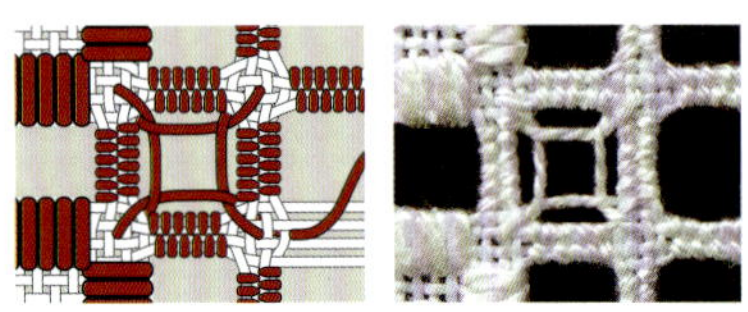

6 The completed square filet stitch ready for continued stitching.

square filet

This stitch is worked after weaving or wrapping all sides of the square to be filled. It can be worked either clockwise or anticlockwise – just be consistent throughout.

R

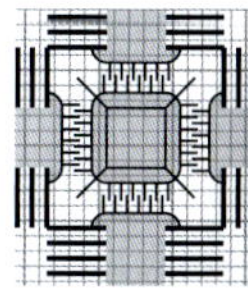

TRADITIONAL

clockwise square filet

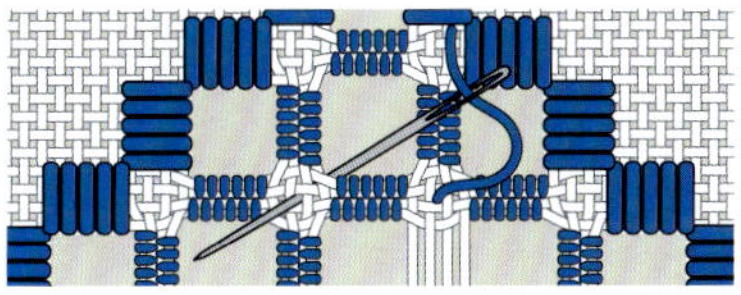

1 After working the fourth side of the square, bring the needle out in the adjacent woven square's centre. Working clockwise, insert the needle in the centre back of the next woven square.
❶ *Always insert the needle in the back.*

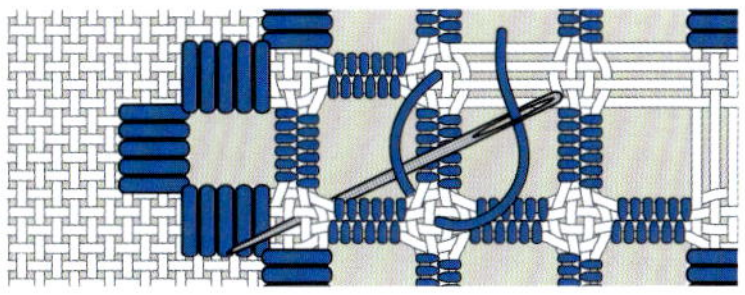

2 Pull the needle through so the stitch gently curves between the two corners. Turn the work 90° anticlockwise. Insert the needle under the previous stitch and into the centre back of the next woven square.

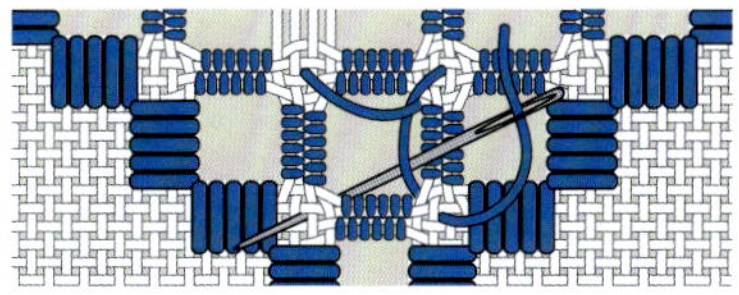

3 Pull the needle through so the stitch gently curves. Turn the work 90° anticlockwise. Insert the needle under the previous stitch and into the centre back of the next woven square.

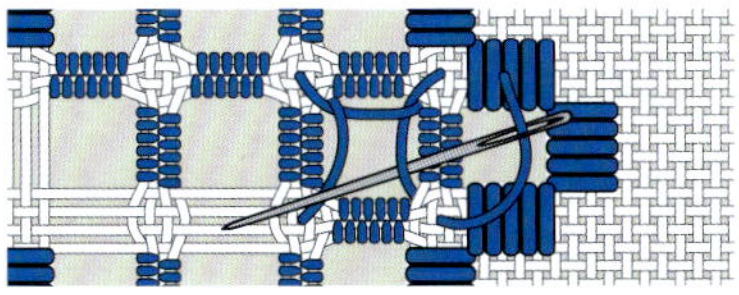

4 Pull the needle through so the stitch gently curves. Turn the work 90° anticlockwise. Slide the needle under the previous stitch.

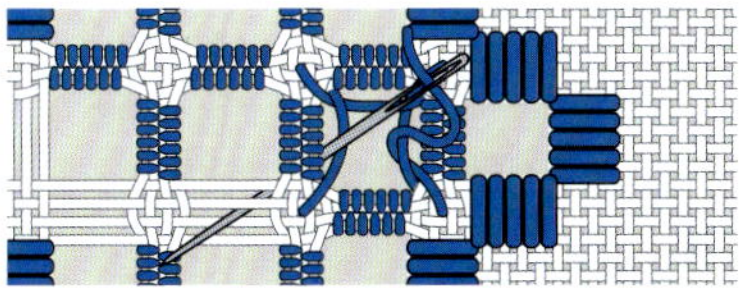

5 Take the needle over the initial curved stitch, then behind the woven square. Bring the needle out ready to continue.

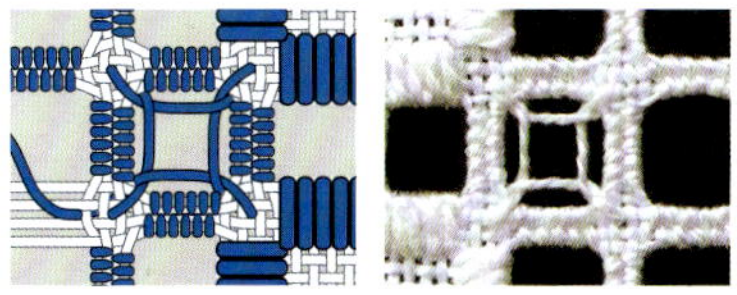

6 The completed square filet stitch ready for continued stitching.

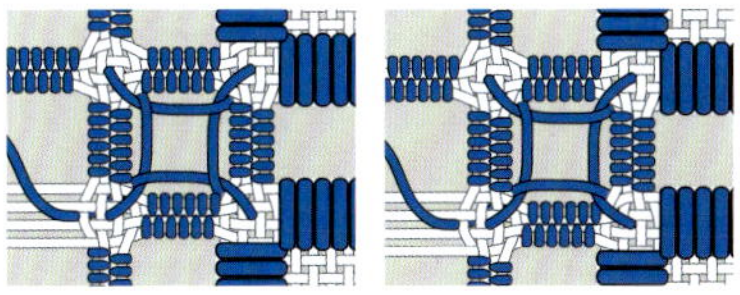

❶ *Ensure all stitches cross the same way: under at one end and over at the other (see left). If a stitch is 'over' or 'under' at both ends (see right), it is incorrect.*
❶ *The threads should only cross once in the corners, and not have any extra twists.*

anticlockwise square filet

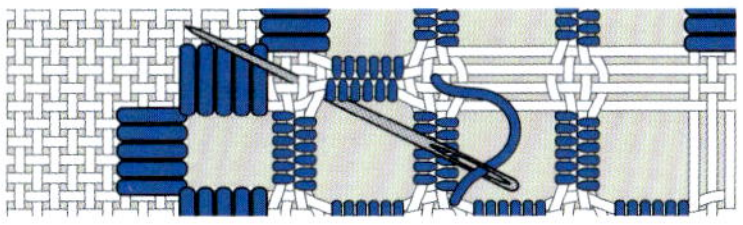

1 After working the fourth side of the square, bring the needle out in the adjacent woven square's centre. Working in an anticlockwise direction, insert the needle in the centre back of the next woven square.
❶ *Always insert the needle in the back.*

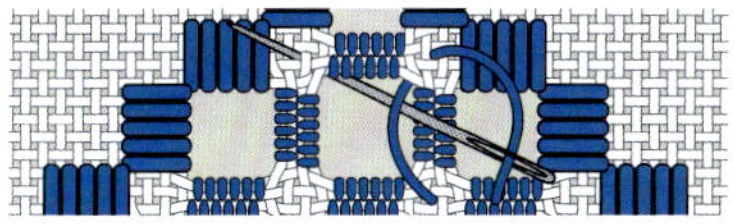

2 Pull the needle through so the stitch gently curves between the two corners. Turn the work 90° clockwise. Insert the needle under the previous stitch and into the centre back of the next woven square.

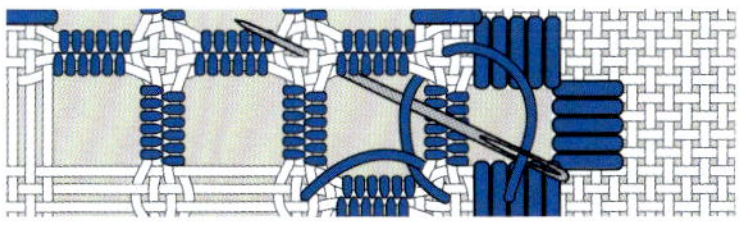

3 Pull the needle. Turn the work 90° clockwise. Insert the needle under the previous stitch and into the centre back of the next woven square.

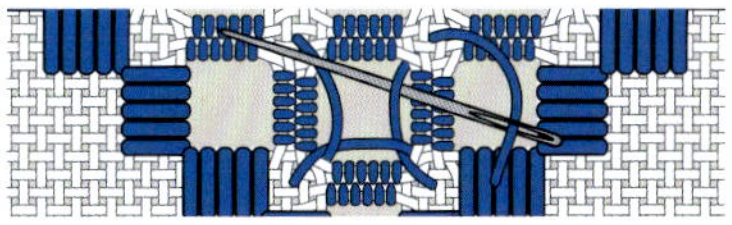

4 Pull the needle through. Turn the work 90° clockwise. Slide the needle under the previous stitch.

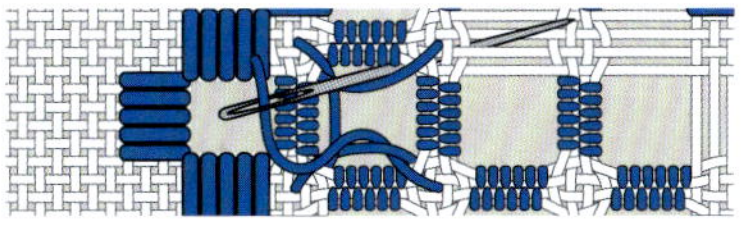

5 Turn the work 90° clockwise. Take the needle over the initial curved stitch, then behind the woven square. Bring it out ready to continue.

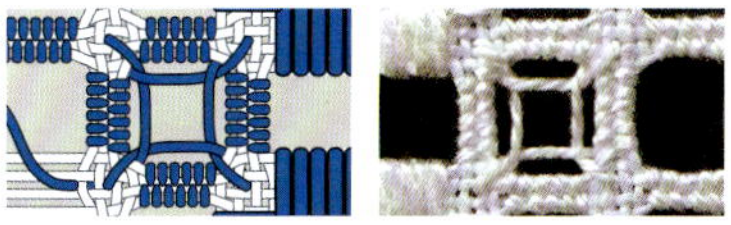

6 The completed square filet stitch ready for continued stitching.

L

double twist square filet

Use a square with at least twelve fabric threads. Cut and remove all the threads inside.

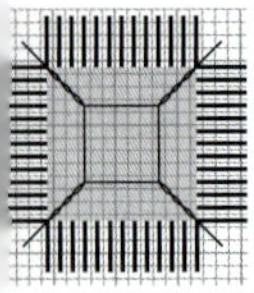

CONTEMPORARY

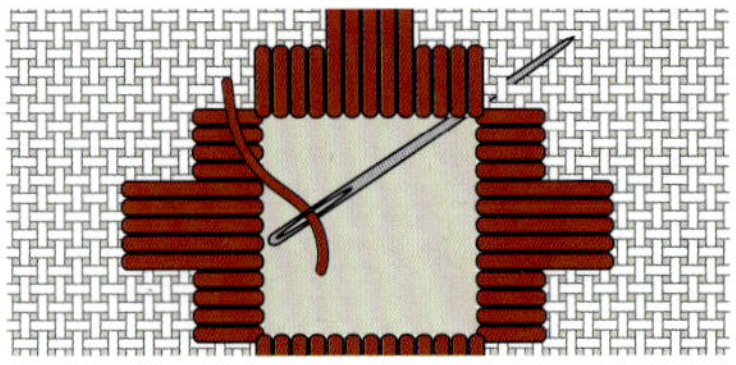

1 Bring the needle out in a corner, two threads away from the cut edges. Working clockwise, insert the needle in the centre back of the next corner.

❶ *Always insert the needle in the back.*

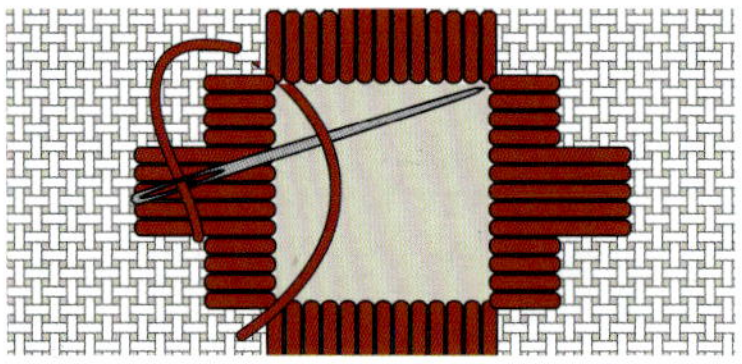

2 Pull the needle through so the stitch gently curves between the two corners. Turn the work 90° anticlockwise. Slide the needle under the curving stitch from the left.

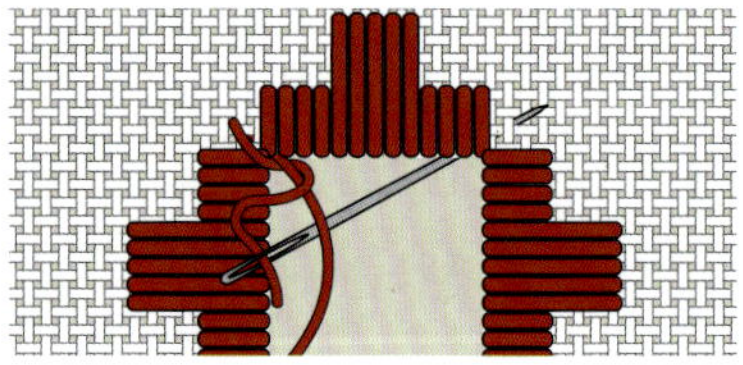

3 Take the needle under the previous stitch again and insert it into the centre back of the next corner.

❶ *If the square is larger than 12 threads across, you can add an extra twist.*

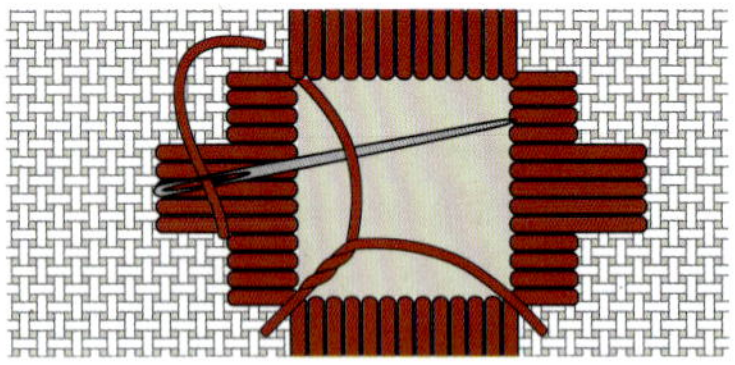

4 Pull the needle through to intertwine the stitches. Turn the work 90° anticlockwise. Slide the needle under the curving stitch, from the left.

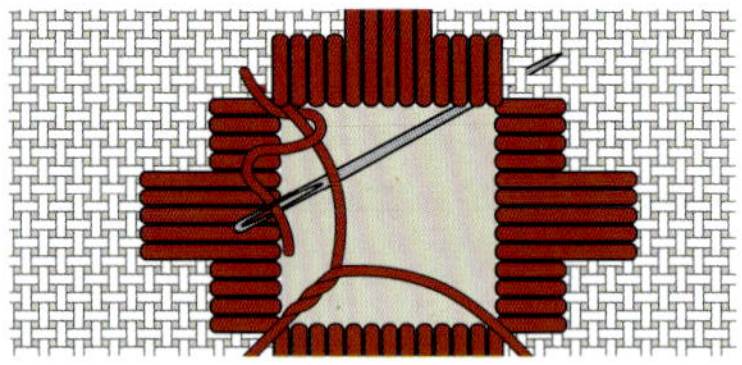

5 Take the needle under the previous stitch again and insert it into the centre back of the next corner.

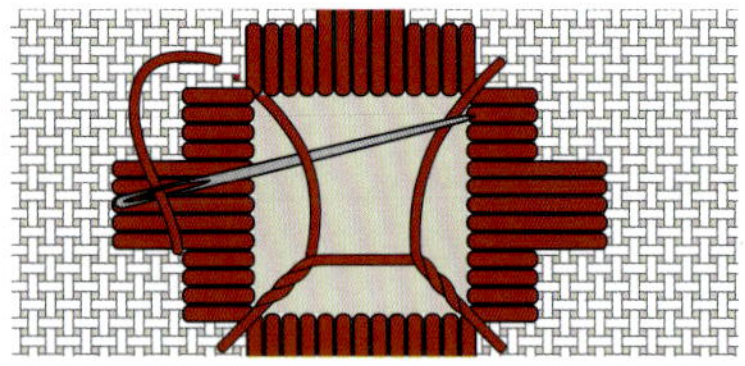

6 Pull the needle through and intertwine the stitches. Turn the work 90° anticlockwise. Slide the needle under the stitch, from the left.

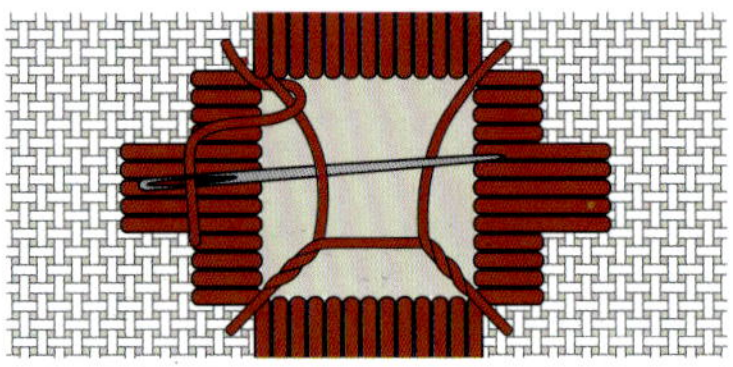

7 Take the needle under the previous stitch again.

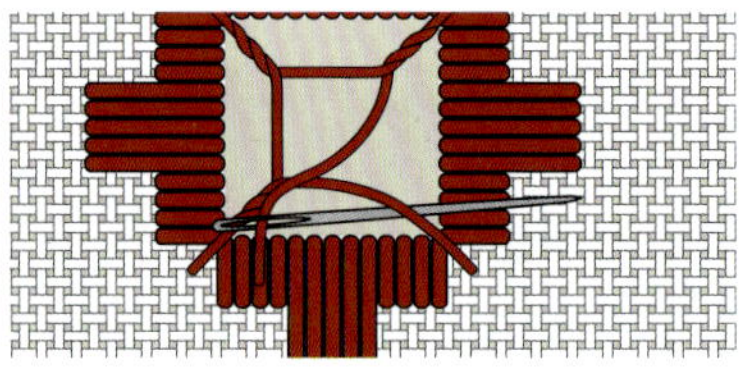

8 Pull the needle through and intertwine the stitches. Turn the work 90° clockwise. Slide the needle under the first stitch, from below left.

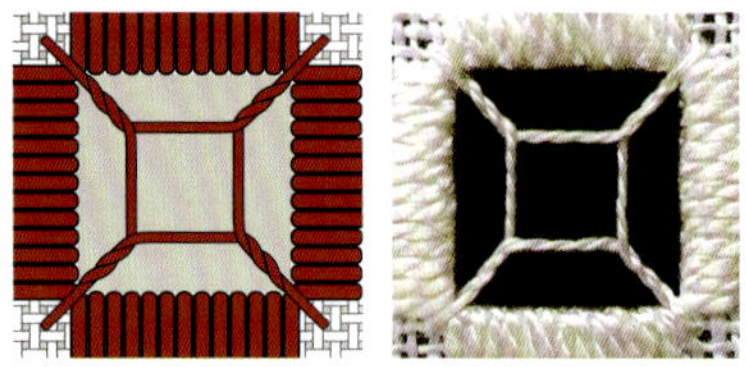

9 Take the needle over the first stitch again, and to the back. Pull the thread to intertwine the stitches. Finish the thread on the back.

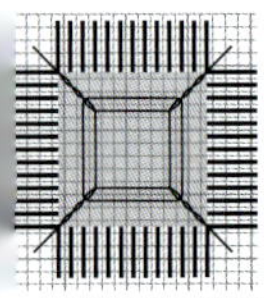

CONTEMPORARY

enclosed square filet

also known as enclosed web

This motif follows on from a double twist square filet.

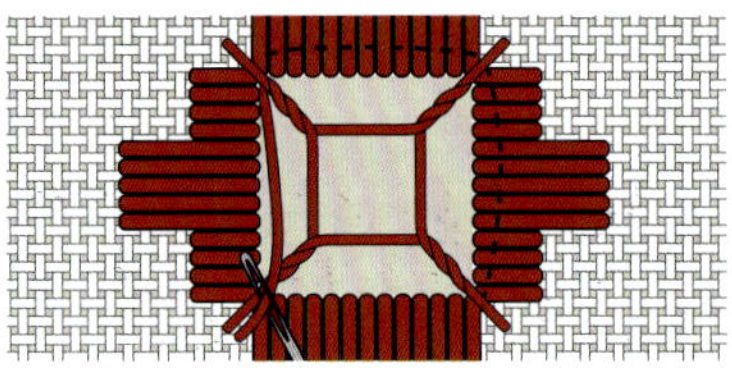

1 Having taken the thread under the back of at least one satin stitch block, bring it out in a corner, behind the stitching.

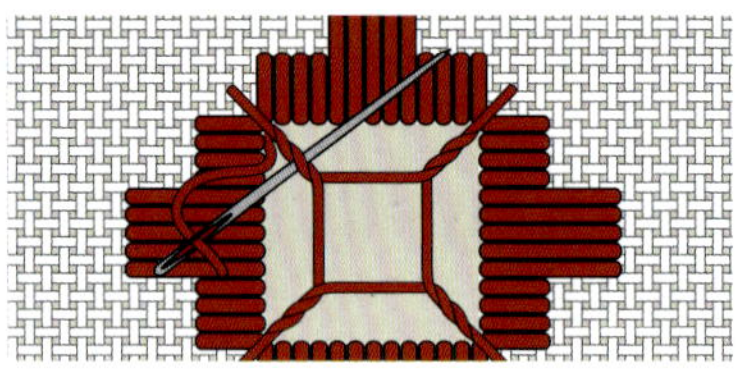

2 Pass the needle through the twist, close to the square filet.

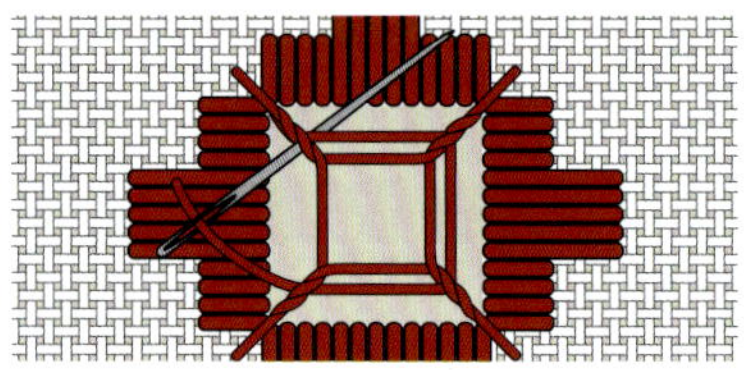

3 Pass the needle through each of the twists in turn. Go through the first one again, bringing it out above the stitch at the start of the circuit.

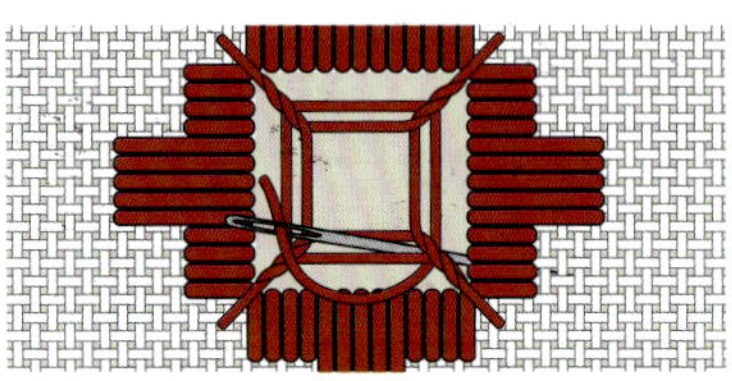

4 Turn the work 180°. Insert the needle between the circuits.

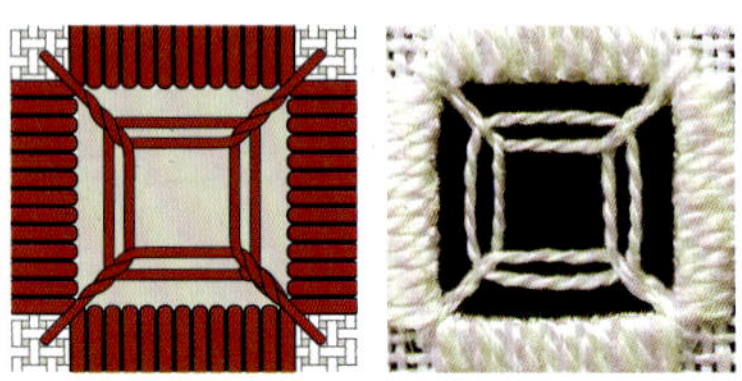

5 Take the thread to the corner and finish it in the back of the satin stitch.

double twist square filet

Use a square with at least twelve fabric threads. Cut and remove all the threads inside.

R

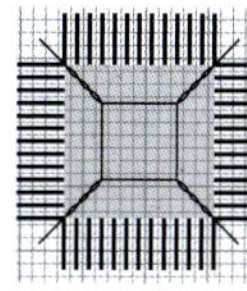

CONTEMPORARY

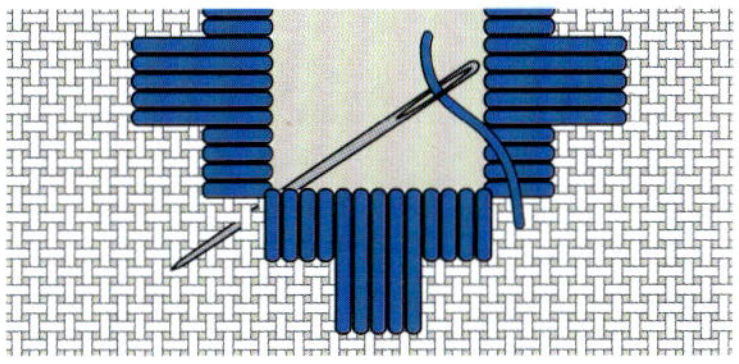

1 Bring the needle out in a corner, two threads away from the cut edges. Working clockwise, insert the needle in the centre back of the next corner. ❶ *Always insert the needle in the back.*

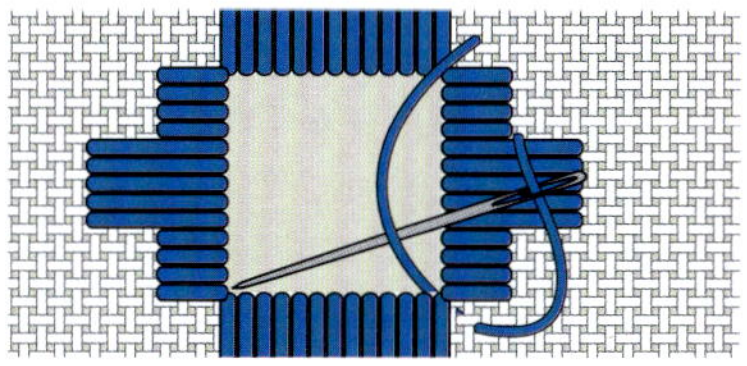

2 Pull the needle through so the stitch gently curves between the two corners. Turn the work 90° anti-clockwise. Slide the needle under the curving stitch from the right.

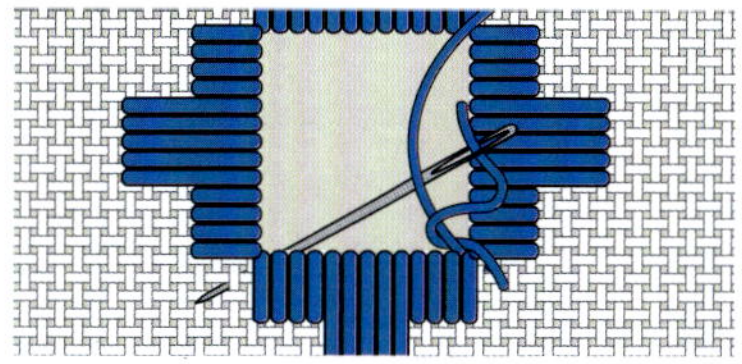

3 Take the needle under the previous stitch again and insert it into the centre back of the next corner. ❶ *If the square is larger than 12 threads across, you can add an extra twist.*

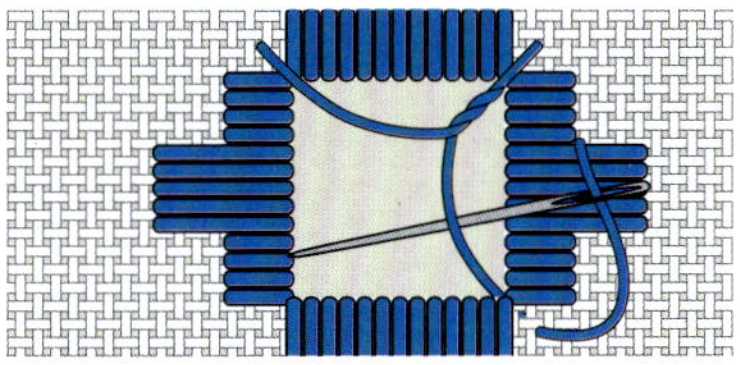

4 Pull the needle through to intertwine the stitches. Turn the work 90° anticlockwise. Slide the needle under the curving stitch, from the right.

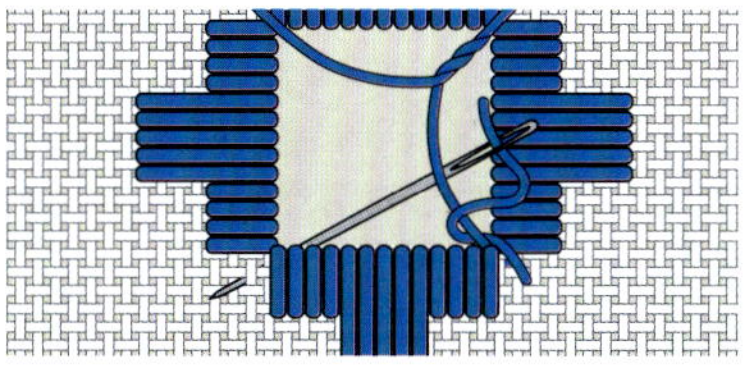

5 Take the needle under the previous stitch again and insert it into the centre back of the next corner.

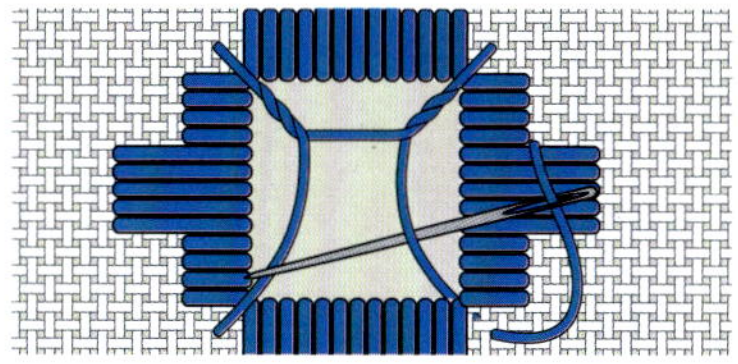

6 Pull the needle through and intertwine the stitches. Turn the work 90° anticlockwise. Slide the needle under the stitch, from the right.

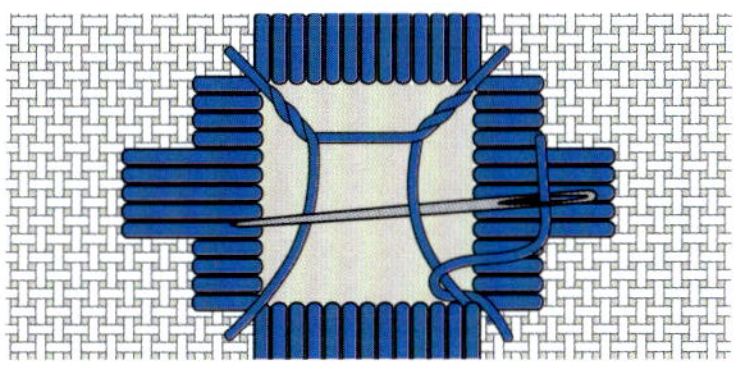

7 Take the needle under the previous stitch again.

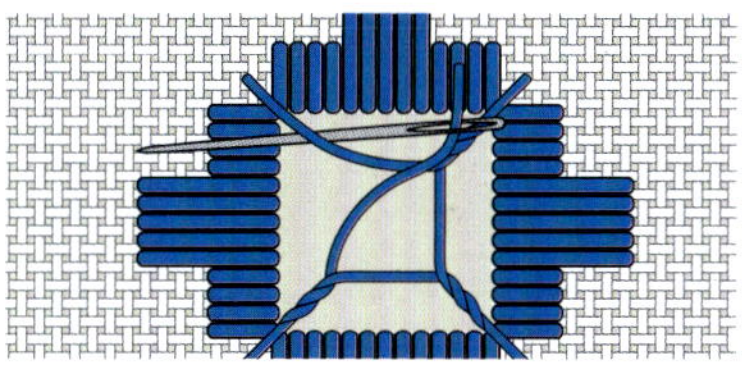

8 Pull the needle through and intertwine the stitches. Turn the work 90° clockwise. Slide the needle under the first stitch, from above right.

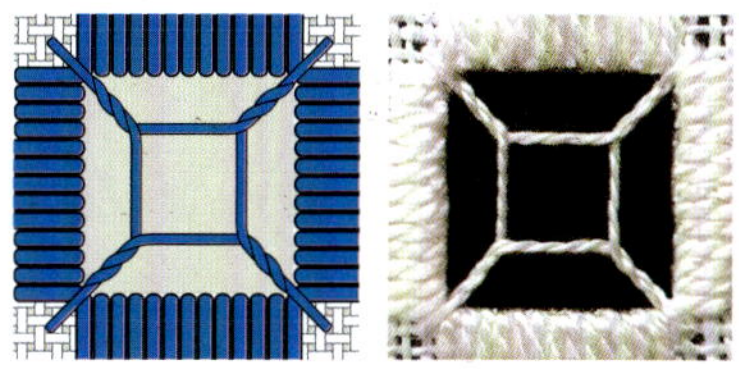

9 Take the needle over the first stitch again, and to the back. Pull the thread to intertwine the stitches. Finish the thread on the back.

enclosed square filet

also known as enclosed web

This motif follows on from a double twist square filet.

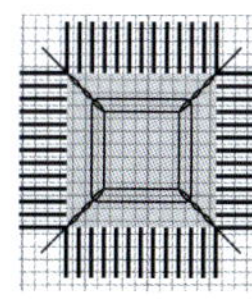

CONTEMPORARY

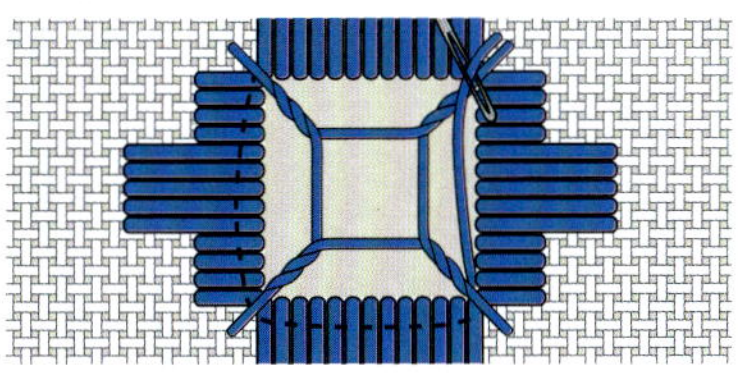

1 Having taken the thread under the back of at least one satin stitch block, bring it out in a corner, behind the stitching.

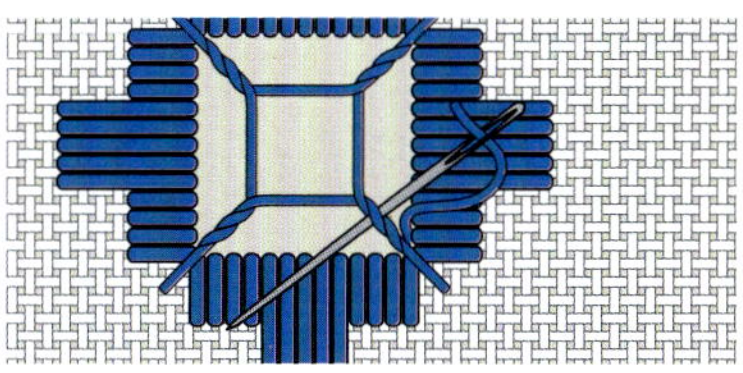

2 Pass the needle through the twist, close to the square filet.

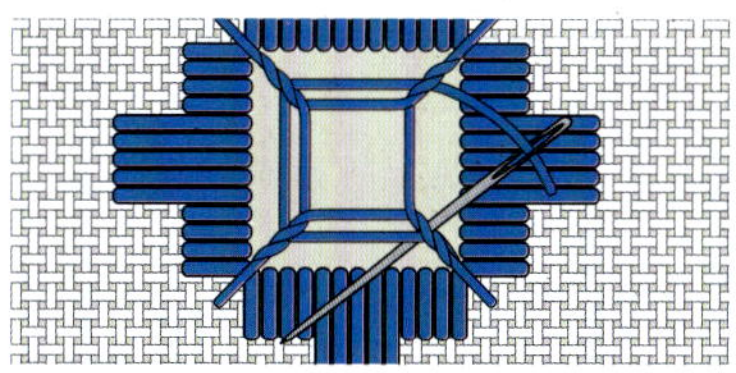

3 Pass the needle through each of the twists in turn. Go through the first one again, bringing it out below the stitch at the start of the circuit.

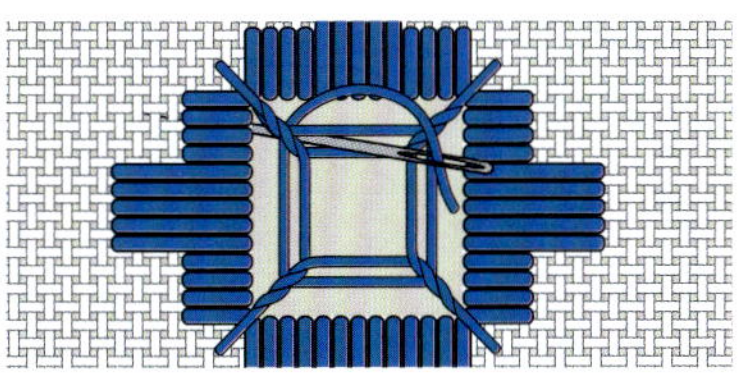

4 Turn the work 180°. Take the needle to the back below the twist

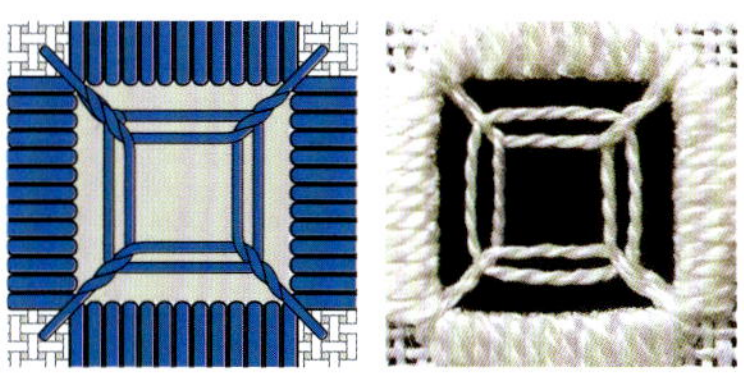

5 Finish the thread in the back of the satin stitch.

beaded square

L

This beaded square is similar to a square filet, but because of the bead's position, the stitching method is adapted. A dove's eye could be similarly adapted.

CONTEMPORARY

❶ *It is important to choose beads that are large enough for the threaded tapestry needle to go through, as a tapestry needle's eye is relatively large. You may choose to use a slightly smaller needle than normal when beading, if you can thread it with your thread. As a warning, a smaller needle will wear the thread more quickly, so only use it for the beaded section.*

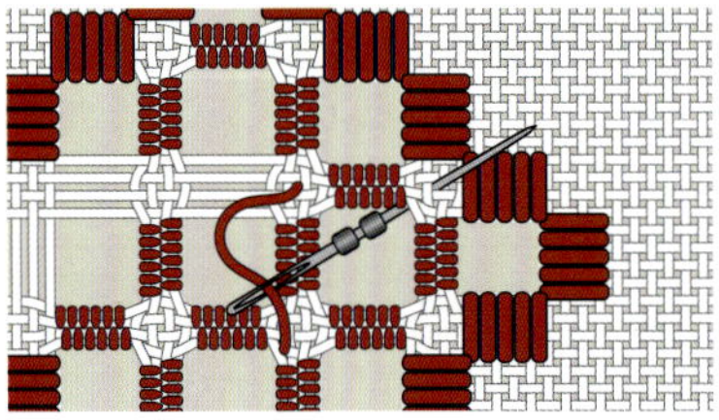

1 After working the fourth side of the square, bring the needle out in the adjacent woven square's centre. Thread two beads onto the needle. Working in a clockwise direction, insert the needle in the centre back of the adjacent corner.

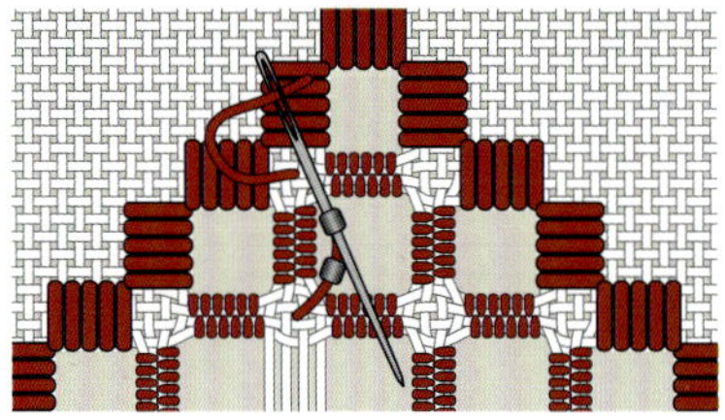

2 Pull the needle through and leave the stitch curving gently. Turn the work 90° anticlockwise. Slide the needle through the closest bead, in the opposite direction to before.

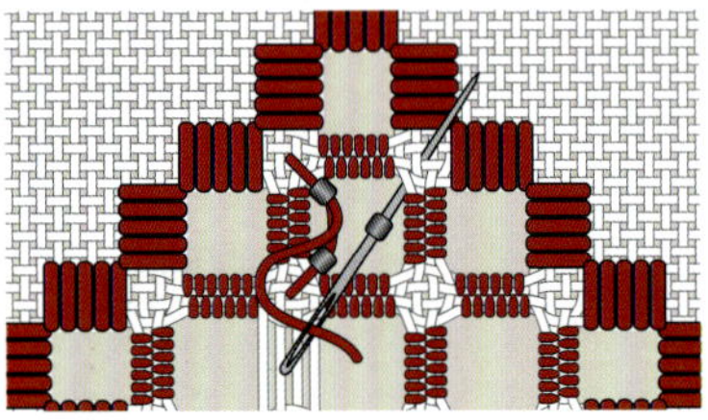

3 Thread another bead on the needle. Insert the needle in the centre back of the next corner.

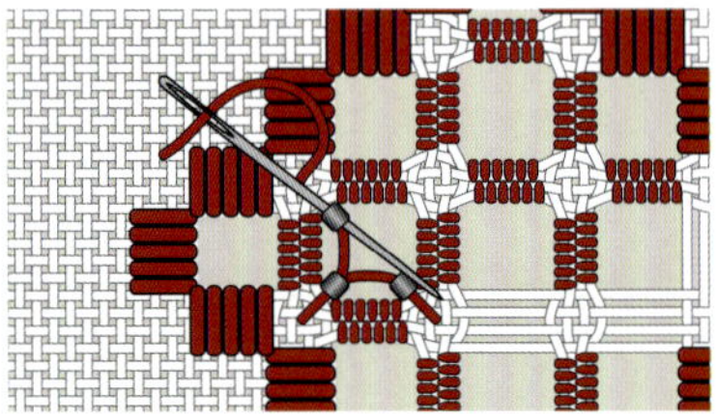

4 Pull the needle through and leave the stitch curving gently. Turn the work 90° anticlockwise. Slide the needle through the closest bead, in the opposite direction to before.

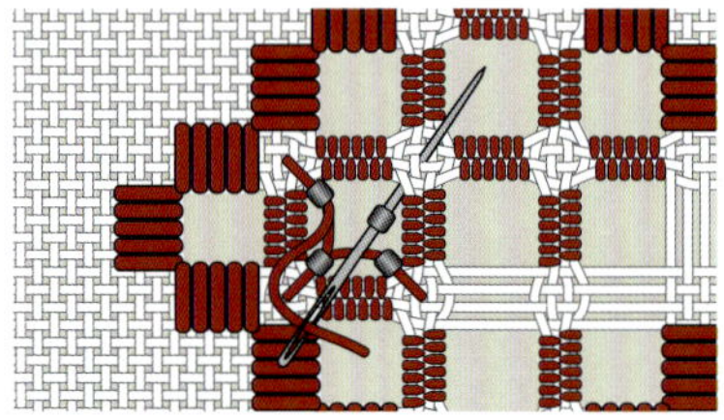

5 Thread another bead on the needle. Insert the needle in the centre back of the next corner.

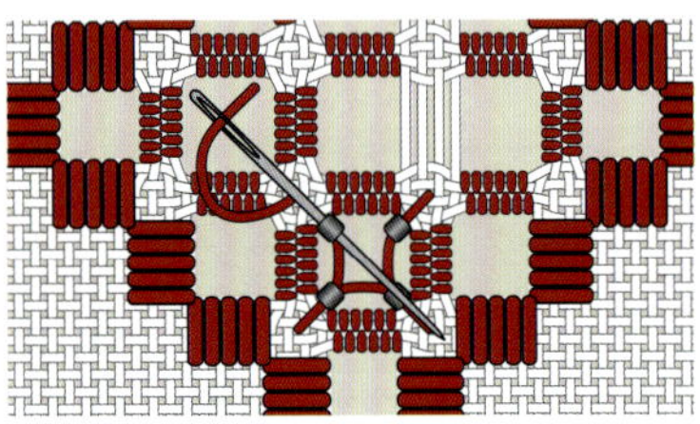

6 Pull the needle through and leave the stitch curving gently. Turn the work 90° anticlockwise. Slide the needle through the closest bead, in the opposite direction to before.

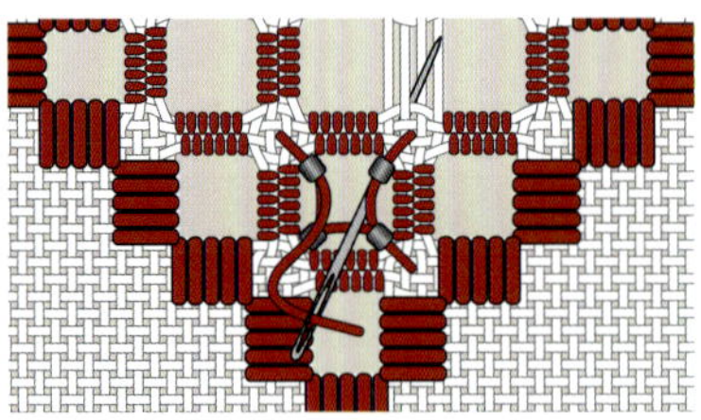

7 Insert the needle in the first bead, and bring it out ready to begin stitching the next bar.

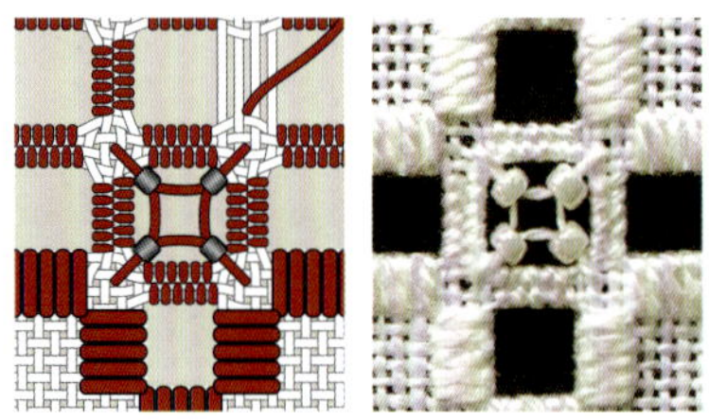

8 Pull the needle through so that the last stitch has the same tension as previous stitches.

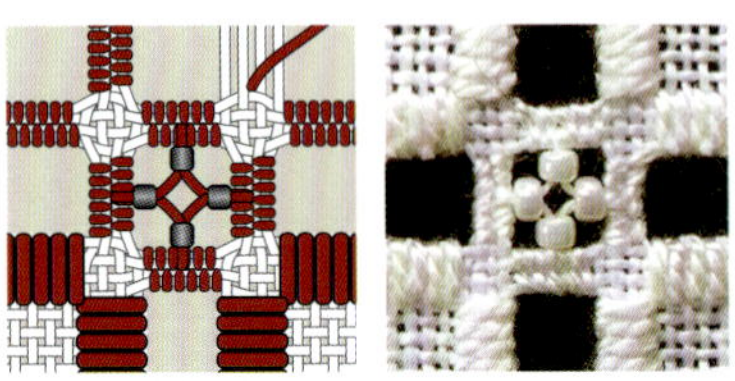

❶ *A similarly stitched beaded diamond, based on a dove's eye.*

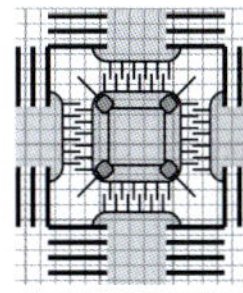

beaded square

This beaded square is similar to a square filet, but because of the bead's position, the stitching method is adapted. A dove's eye could be similarly adapted.

It is important to choose beads that are large enough for the threaded tapestry needle to go through, as a tapestry needle's eye is relatively large. You may choose to use a slightly smaller needle than normal when beading, if you can thread it with your thread. As a warning, a smaller needle will wear the thread more quickly, so only use it for the beaded section.

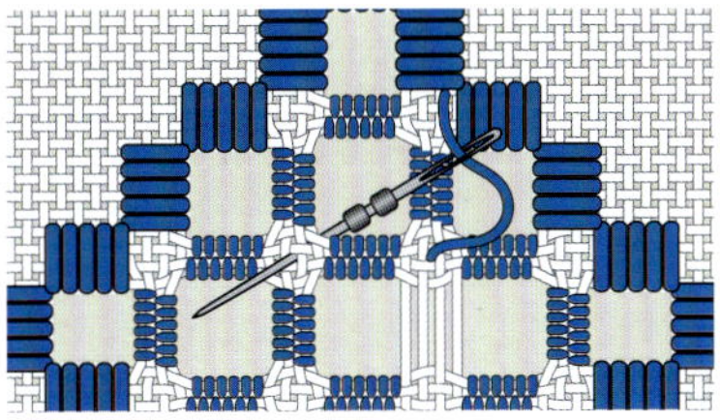

1 After working the fourth side of the square, bring the needle out in the adjacent woven square's centre. Thread two beads onto the needle. Working in a clockwise direction, insert the needle in the centre back of the adjacent corner.

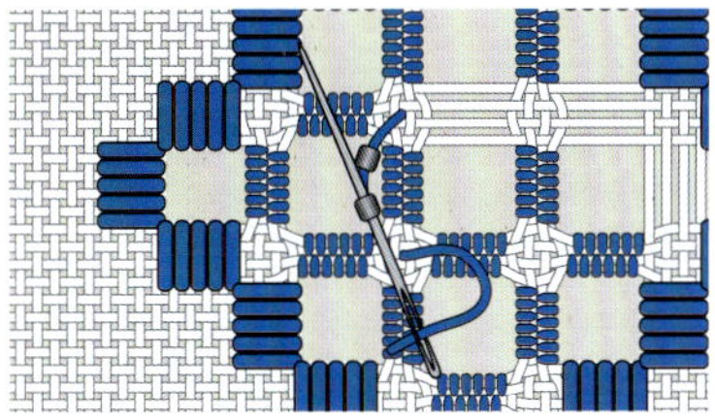

2 Pull the needle through and leave the stitch curving gently. Turn the work 90° anticlockwise. Slide the needle through the closest bead, in the opposite direction to before.

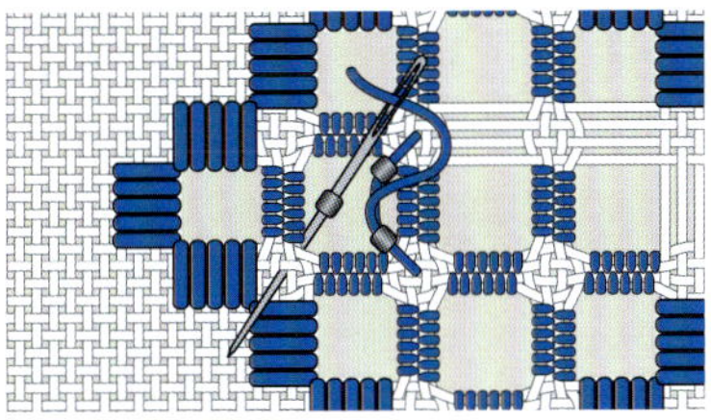

3 Thread another bead on the needle. Insert the needle in the centre back of the next corner.

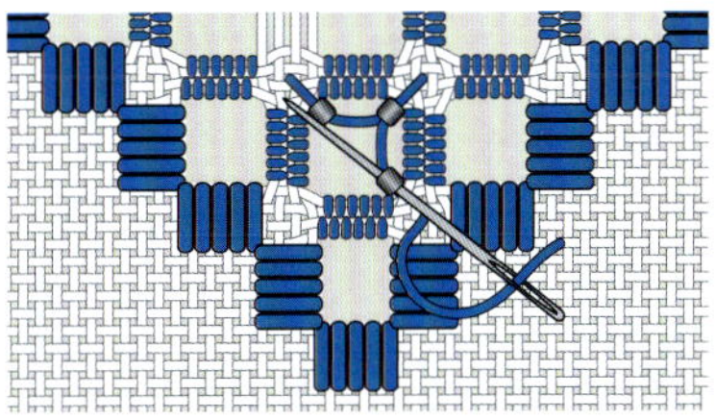

4 Pull the needle through and leave the stitch curving gently. Turn the work 90° anticlockwise. Slide the needle through the closest bead, in the opposite direction to before.

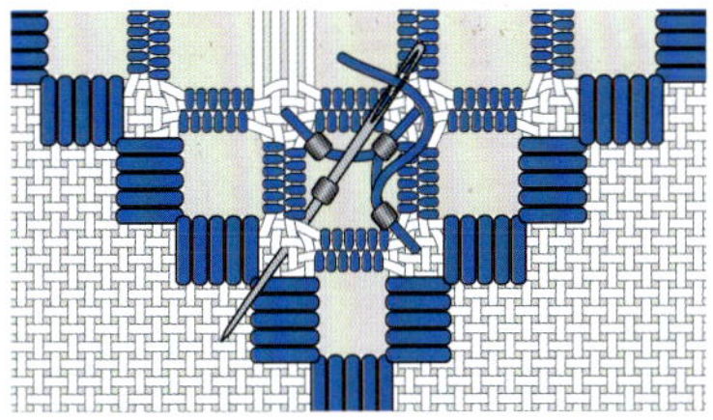

5 Thread another bead on the needle. Insert the needle in the centre back of the next corner.

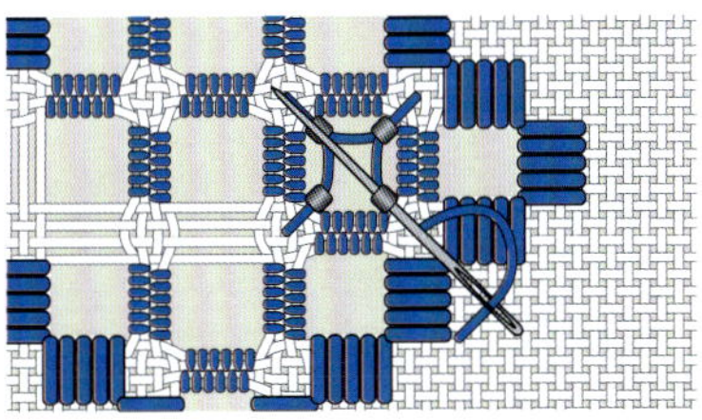

6 Pull the needle through and leave the stitch curving gently. Turn the work 90° anticlockwise. Slide the needle through the closest bead, in the opposite direction to before.

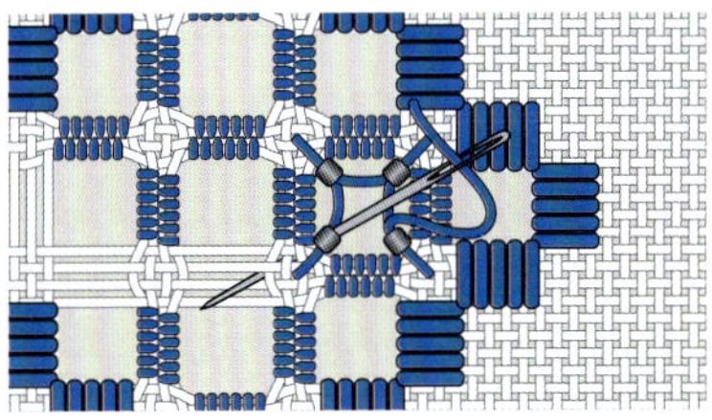

7 Insert the needle in the first bead, and bring it out ready to begin stitching the next bar.

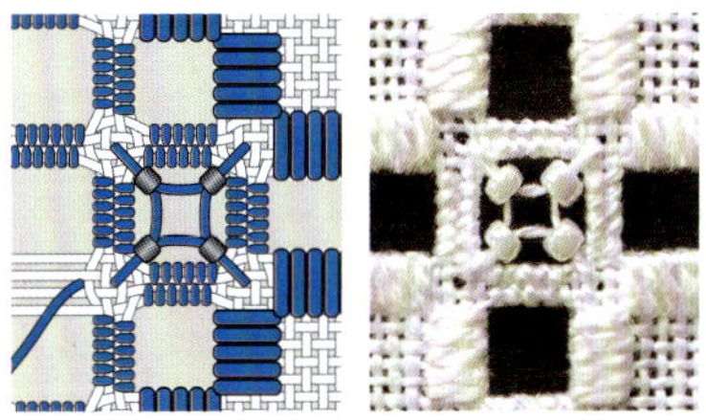

8 Pull the needle through so that the last stitch has the same tension as previous stitches.

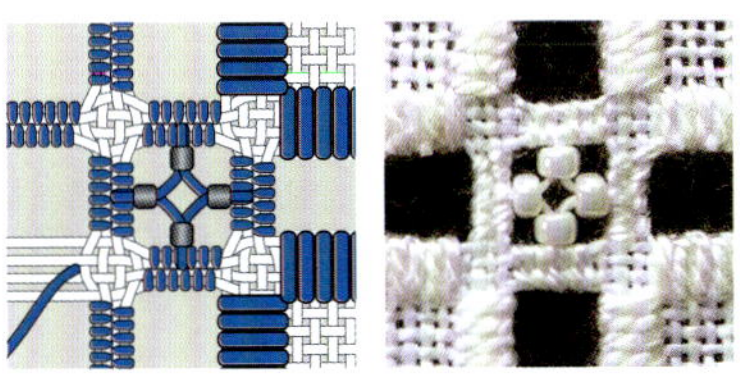

A similarly stitched beaded diamond, based on a dove's eye.

L

nutmeg stitch

CONTEMPORARY

This stitch has an interlocking dove's eye and square filet. When using S twist thread (most thread), work clockwise as the twists work better in a small space with clockwise stitching.

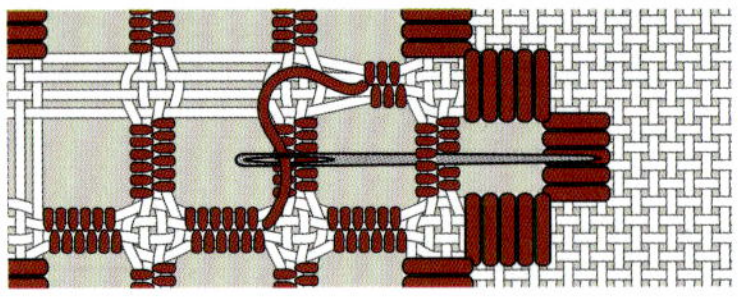

1 Stitch half of the fourth side of the square. Working in a clockwise direction, insert the needle into the centre back of the next woven bar.

The needle is always inserted in the back of the bar.

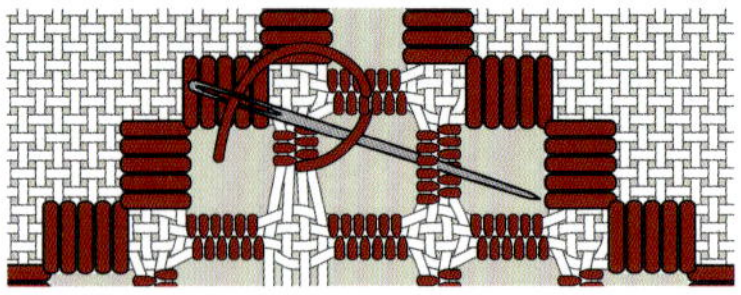

2 Pull the needle through so the stitch curves slightly between the two bars. Turn the work 90° anticlockwise. Insert the needle under the previous stitch and into the back of the next woven bar.

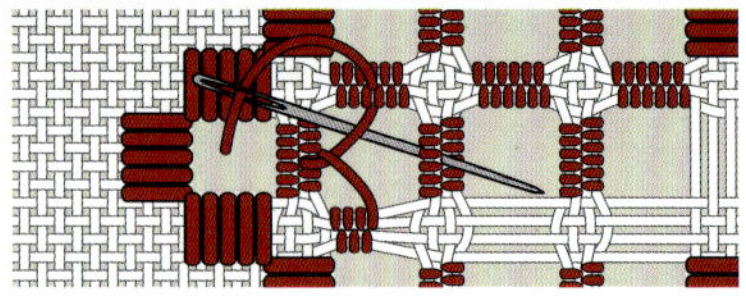

3 Pull the needle through so the stitch curves slightly between the two bars. Turn the work 90° anticlockwise. Insert the needle under the previous stitch and into the back of the next woven bar.

4 Pull the needle through so the stitch curves slightly. Turn the work 90° anticlockwise. Take the needle under the previous stitch.

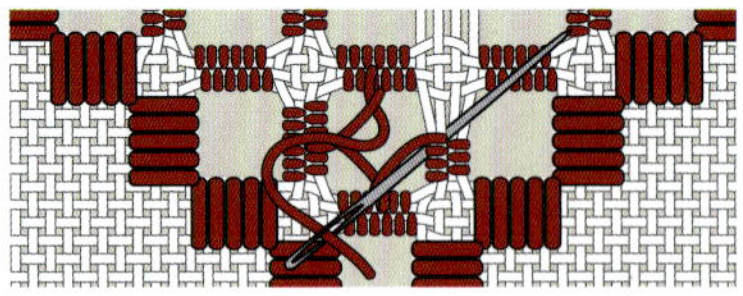

5 Take the needle over the initial curved thread, and insert the needle in the bar ready to continue stitching.

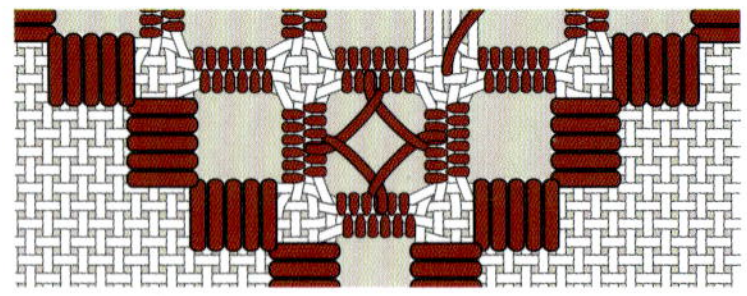

6 Finish weaving the bar to complete the dove's eye section. Bring the thread out in the centre of the next woven fabric square.

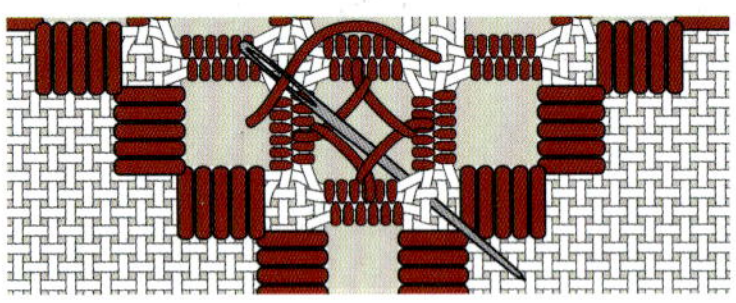

7 Working clockwise, take the needle over the closest dove's eye stitch, then under the next one. Insert it in the centre back of the closest woven square.

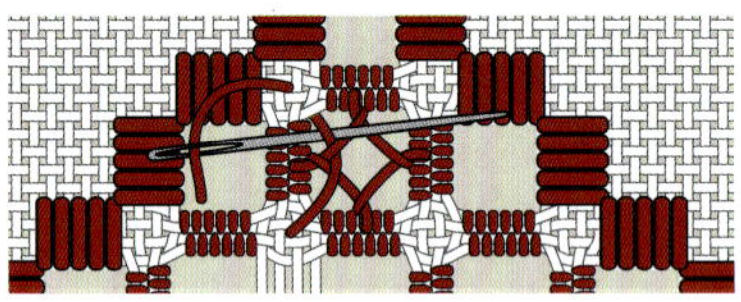

8 Pull the needle through. Turn the work 180°. Slide the needle under the top part of the previous stitch.

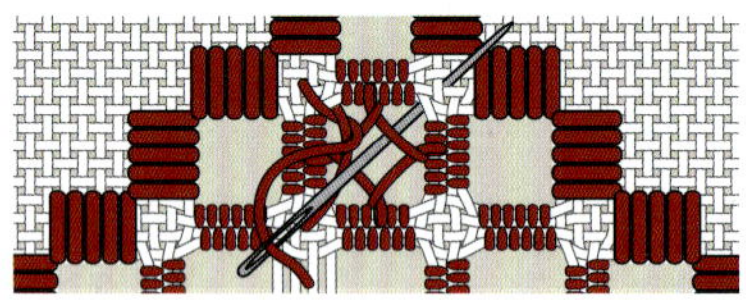

9 Take the needle over the closest dove's eye stitch, then under the next one and insert it into the centre back of the closest woven square.

10 Pull the needle through. Turn the work 90° anticlockwise. Slide the needle under the top part of the previous stitch.

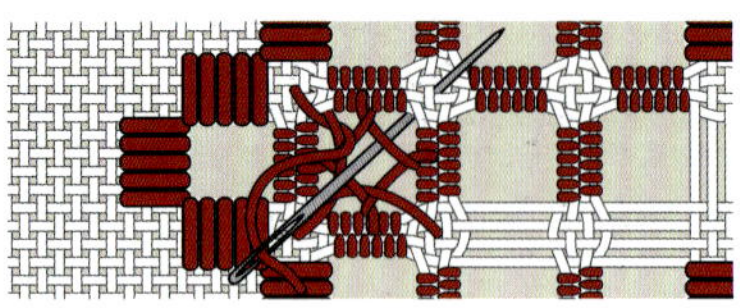

11 Take the needle over the closest dove's eye stitch, then under the next one and insert it into the centre back of the closest woven square.

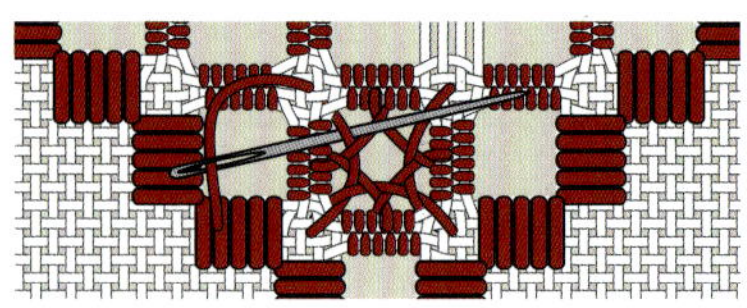

12 Pull the needle through. Turn the work 90° anticlockwise. Slide the needle under the top part of the previous stitch.

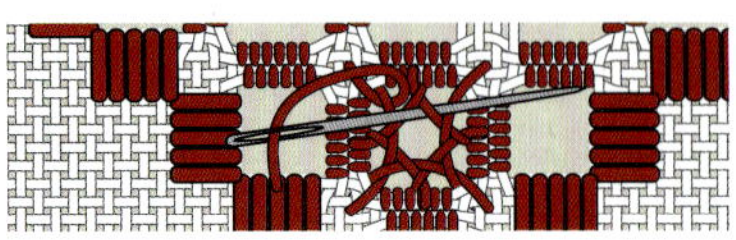

13 Take the needle over the closest dove's eye stitch, then under the next one.

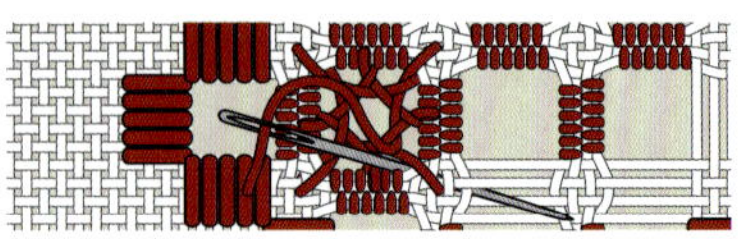

14 Turn the work 90° clockwise. Take the needle over the first square filet stitch and under the woven square. Bring it out in the next bar.

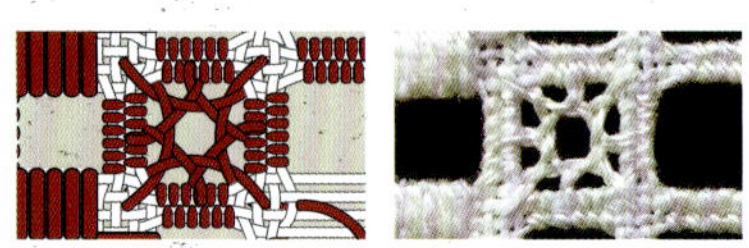

15 The completed nutmeg stitch.

nutmeg stitch

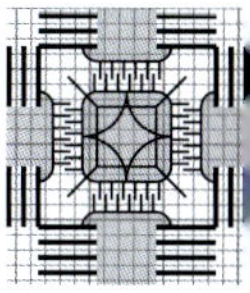

This stitch has an interlocking dove's eye and square filet. When using S twist thread (most thread), work clockwise as the twists work better in a small space with clockwise stitching.

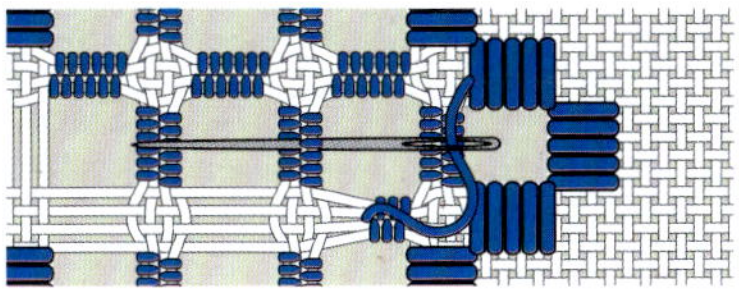

1 Stitch half of the fourth side of the square. Working in a clockwise direction, insert the needle into the centre back of the next woven bar.

❶ *The needle is always inserted in the back of the bar.*

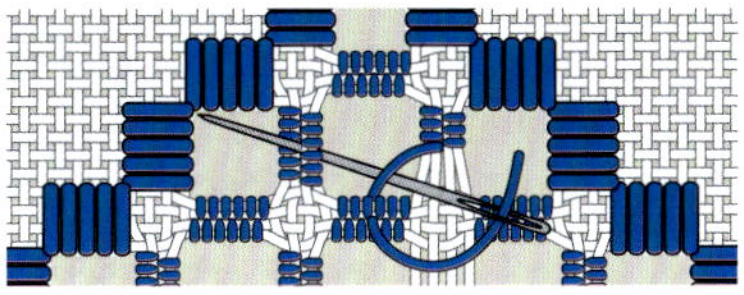

2 Pull the needle through so the stitch curves slightly between the two bars. Turn the work 90° anticlockwise. Insert the needle under the previous stitch and into the back of the next woven bar.

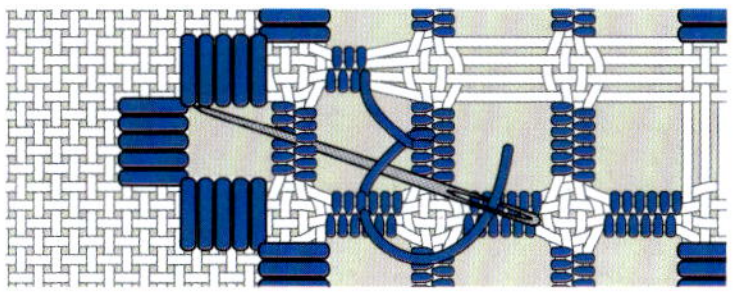

3 Pull the needle through so the stitch curves slightly between the two bars. Turn the work 90° anticlockwise. Insert the needle under the previous stitch and into the back of the next woven bar.

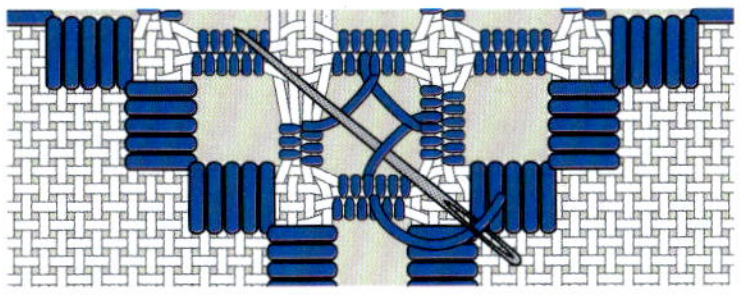

4 Pull the needle through so the stitch curves slightly. Turn the work 90° anticlockwise. Take the needle under the previous stitch.

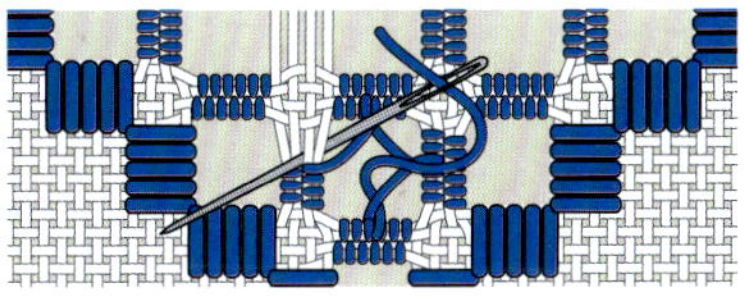

5 Take the needle over the initial curved thread, and insert the needle in the bar ready to continue stitching.

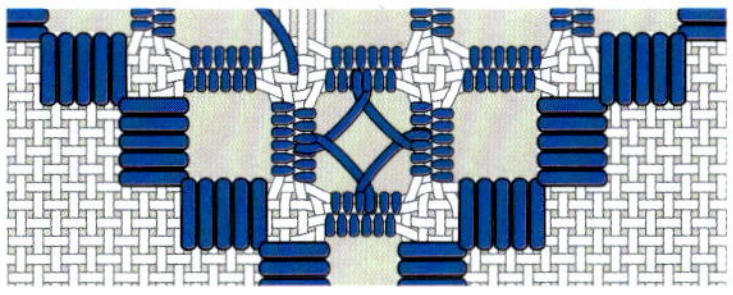

6 Complete the weaving of the bar to complete the dove's eye section. Bring the thread out in the centre of the next woven fabric square.

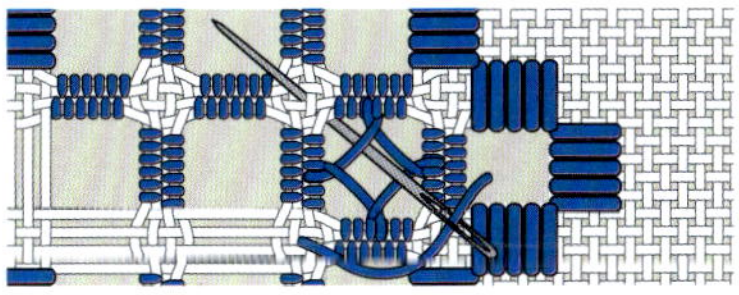

7 Turn the work 90° anticlockwise. Working clockwise, take the needle over the closest dove's eye stitch, then under the next one. Insert it in the closest woven square's centre back.

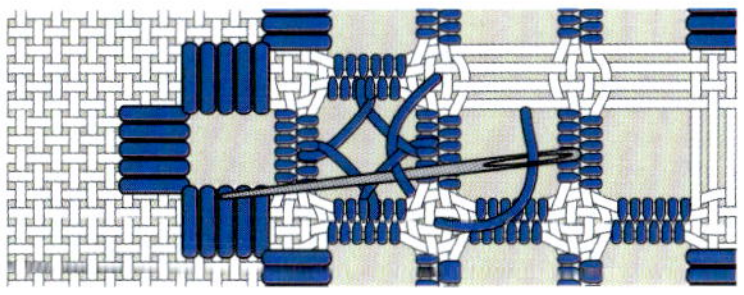

8 Pull the needle through. Turn the work 180°. Slide the needle under the bottom part of the previous stitch.

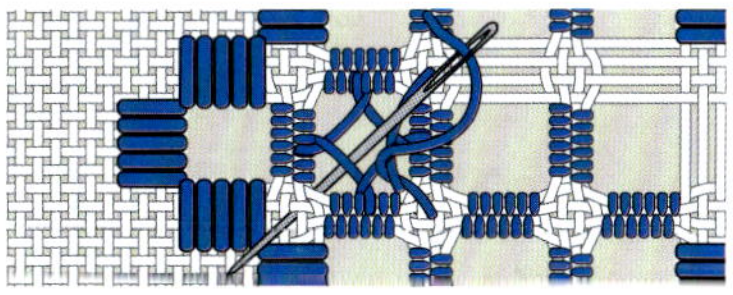

9 Take the needle over the closest dove's eye stitch, then under the next one and insert it into the centre back of the closest woven square.

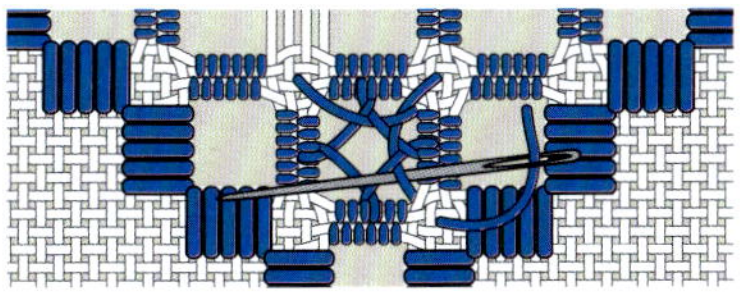

10 Pull the needle through. Turn the work 90° anticlockwise. Slide the needle under the bottom part of the previous stitch.

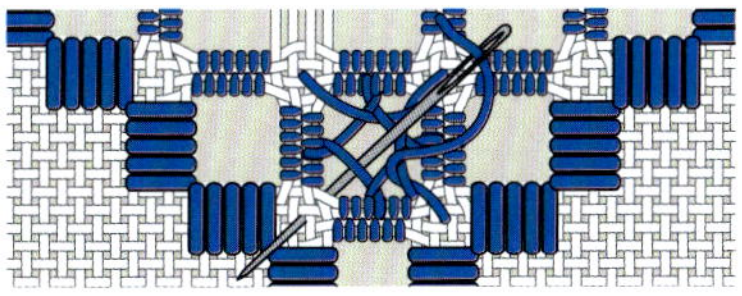

11 Take the needle over the closest dove's eye stitch, then under the next one and insert it into the centre back of the closest woven square.

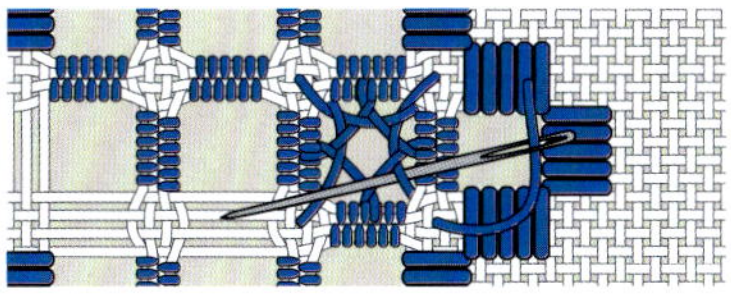

12 Pull the needle through. Turn the work 90° anticlockwise. Slide the needle under the bottom part of the previous stitch.

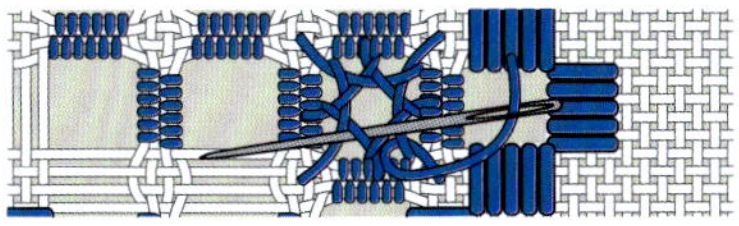

13 Turn the work 90° clockwise. Take the needle over the closest dove's eye stitch, then under the next one.

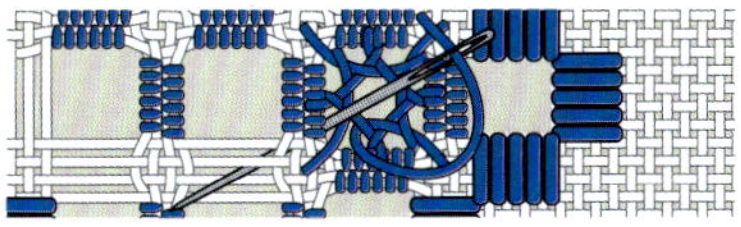

14 Take the needle over the first square filet stitch and under the woven square. Bring it out ready to stitch the next bar.

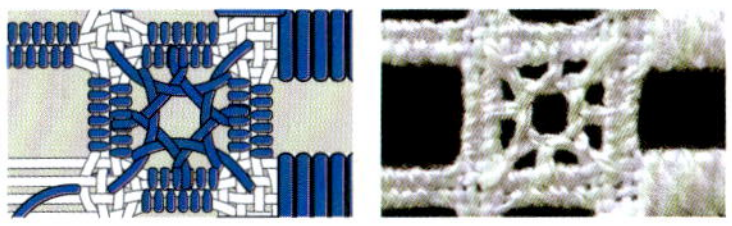

15 The completed nutmeg stitch.

picots

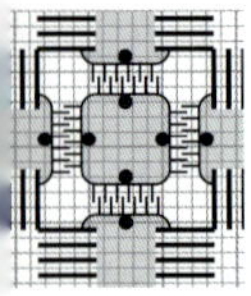

TRADITIONAL

knotted picots

Knotted picots are worked as part of the bar on which they are positioned. They can be worked on one or both sides of the bar.

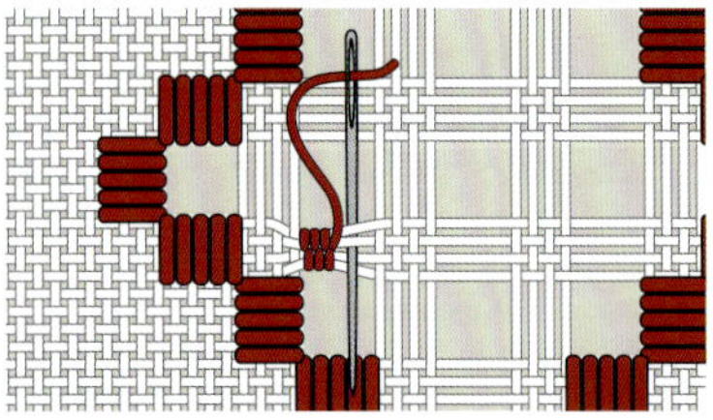

1 Weave half the bar. Insert the needle for the middle stitch.

❶ *The picot is usually worked as the middle stitch of the length of the bar. If you have five stitches on each side, work the picot as part of the third stitch on each side. If you have six stitches, work the picot as part of the fourth stitch, and work extra stitches to make seven stitches per side just for the bars with picots.*

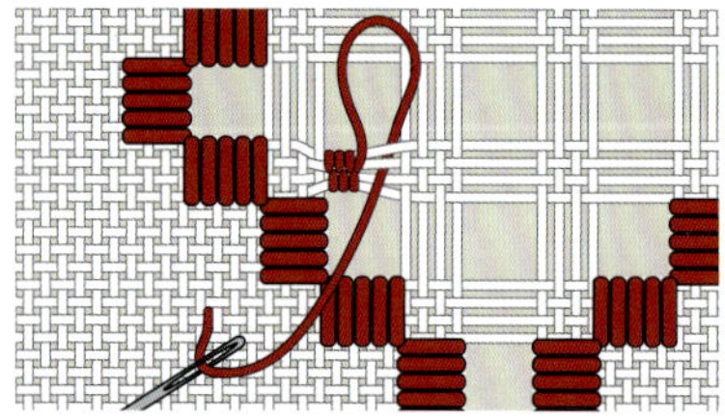

2 Pull the needle through and leave the stitch sitting out from the bar as a loop rather than pulling it in tight.

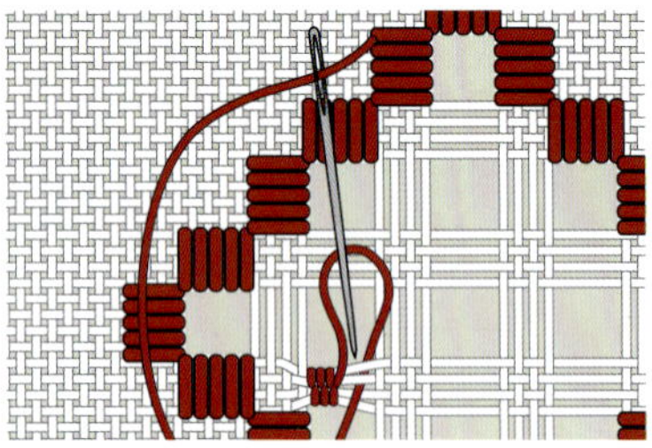

3 Bring the needle around and place the needle over the top edge of the loop as shown.

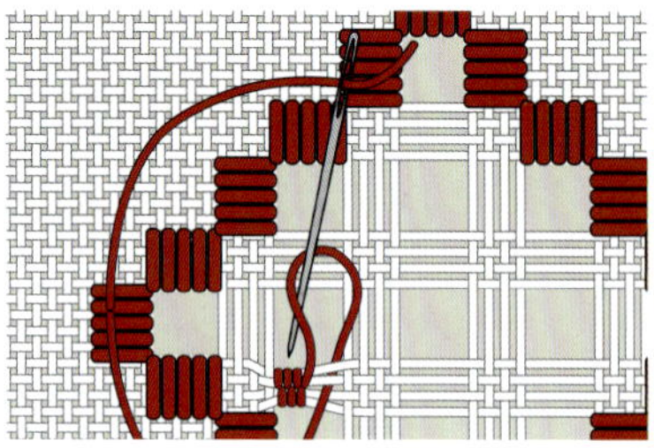

4 Move the needle point to the left behind the left section of the loop.

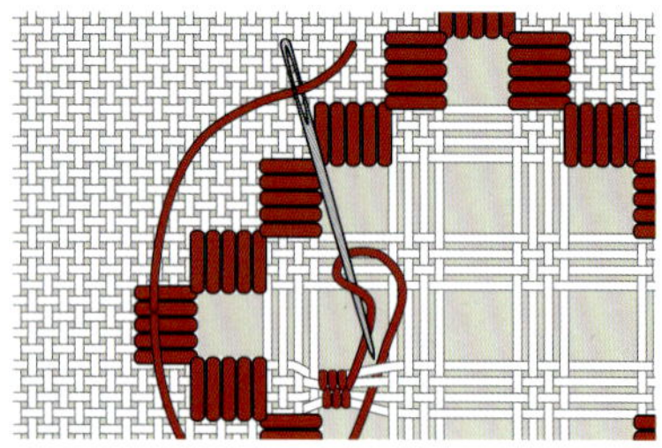

5 Move the needle point to the right over the left section of the loop.

❶ *This makes a wrap around the needle.*

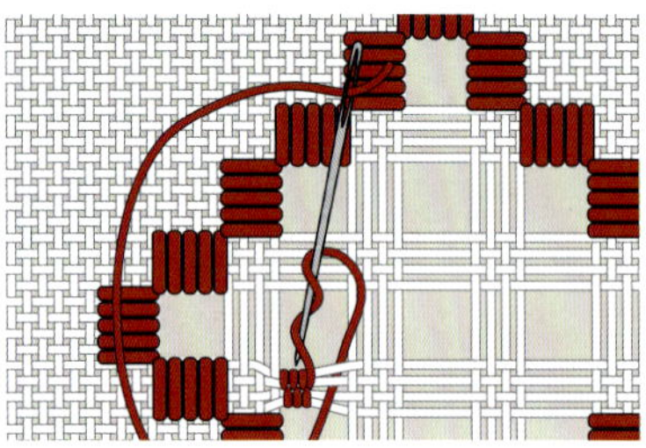

6 Again move the needle point to the left behind the left section of the loop.

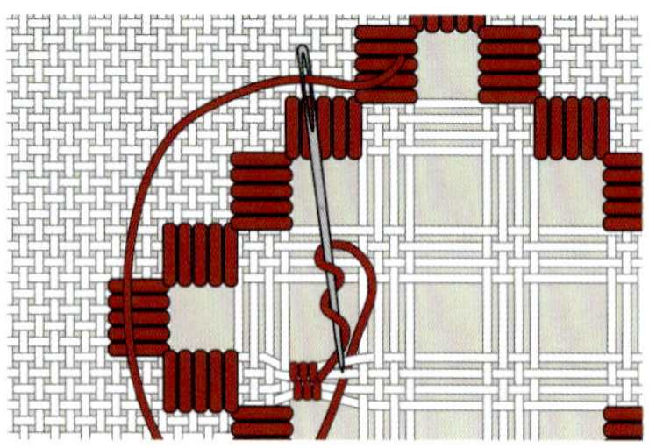

7 Move it to the right over the left section of the loop.

❶ *There are now two wraps around the needle.*

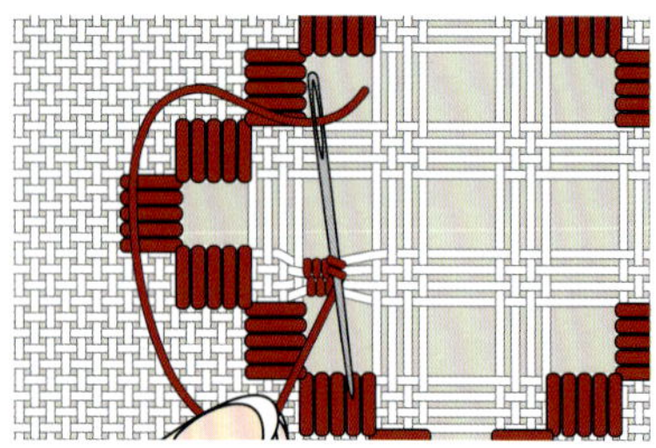

8 Slide the needle further into the wraps. Pull the thread down and left to tighten the wraps around it.

❶ *The wraps stay tight as you pull the needle through. If they are not tight now, they never will be.*

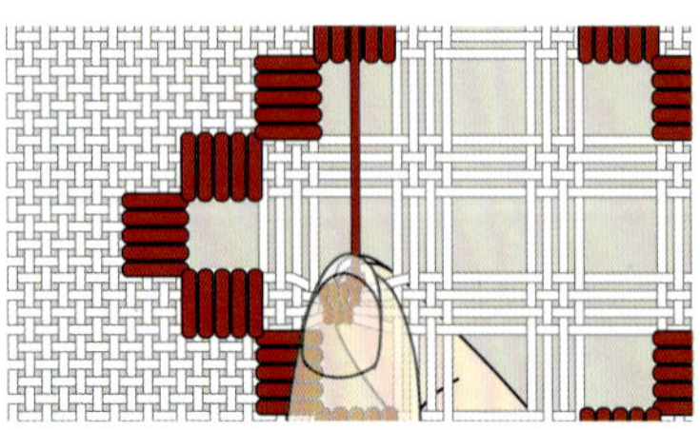

9 Stabilising the wraps with a finger and thumb on each side, pull the needle through and up to tighten the knot at the side of the bar.

❶ *The knot should be tight. If it looks like little loops, tighten it further.*

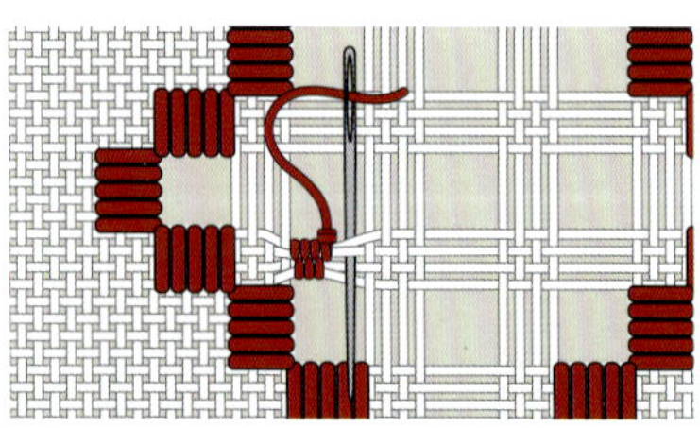

10 From above, slide the needle under the upper two threads of the bar.

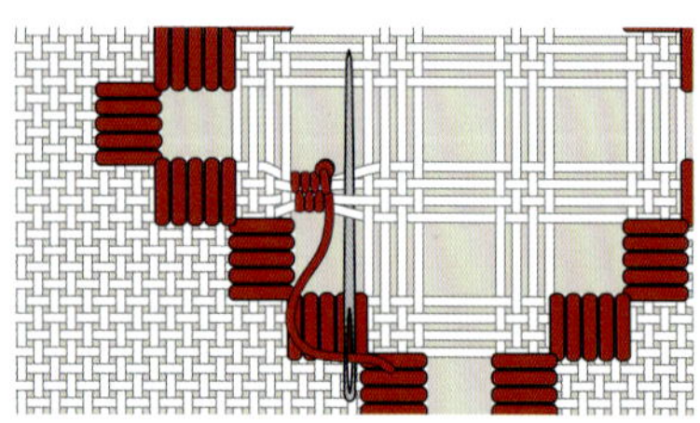

11 From below, slide the needle under the lower two threads of the bar.

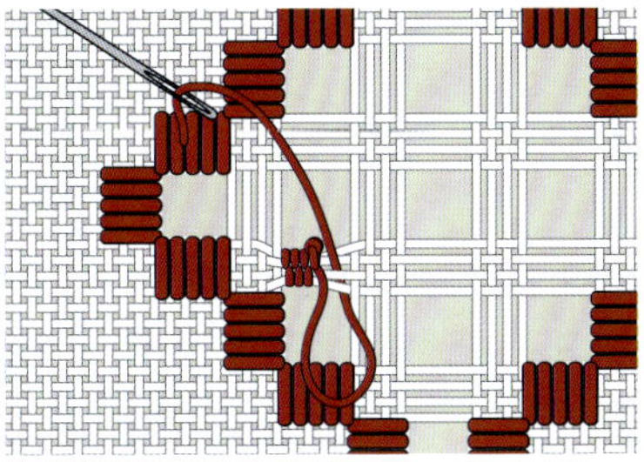

12 Leave the stitch sitting out from the bar as a loop.

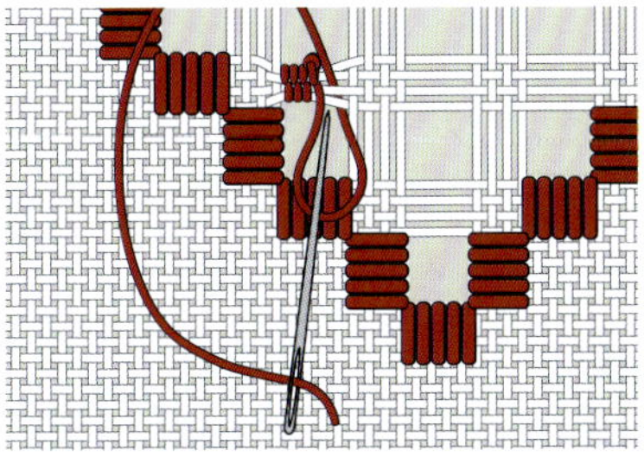

13 Bring the needle around and place the needle over the lower edge of the loop as shown.

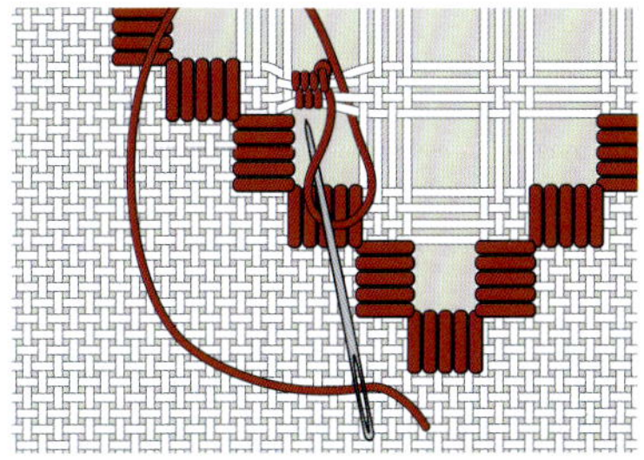

14 Move the needle point to the left behind the left section of the loop.

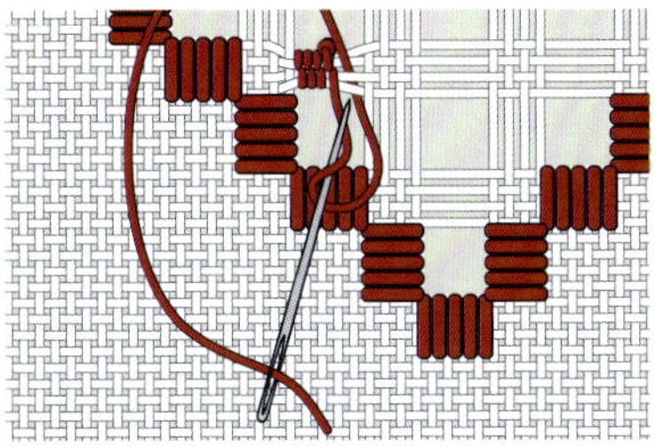

15 Move the needle point to the right over the left section of the loop.

❶ *This makes a wrap around the needle.*

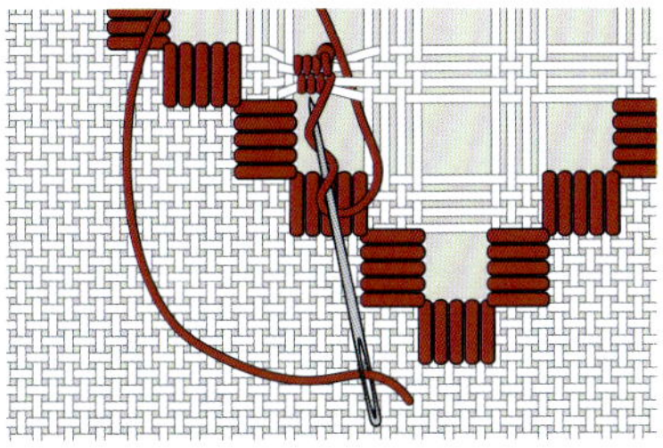

16 Again move the needle point to the left behind the left section of the loop.

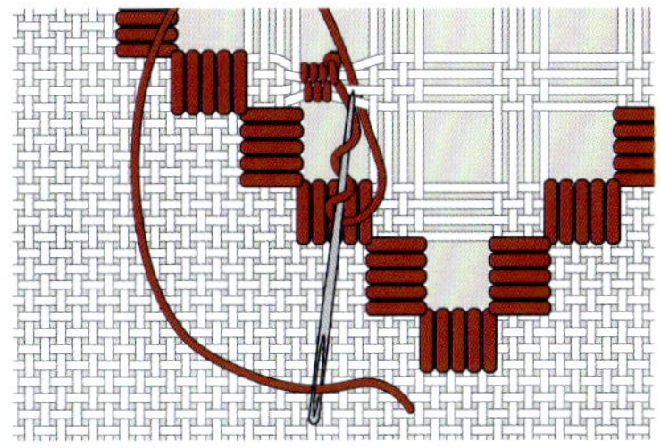

17 Move the needle point to the right over the left section of the loop.

❶ *There are now two wraps around the needle.*

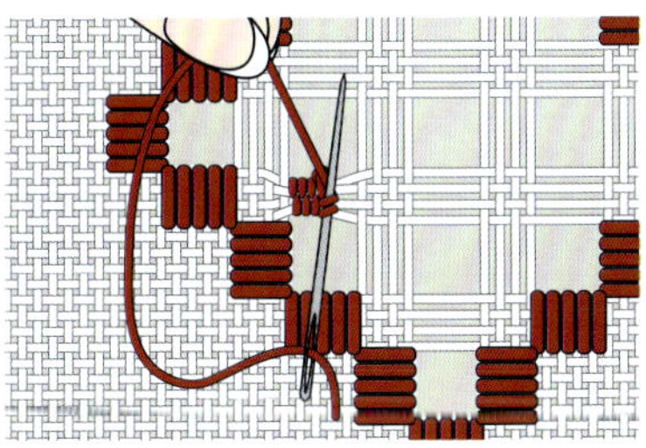

18 Slide the needle further into the wraps. Pull the thread up and left to tighten the wraps around it.

❶ *Ensure the wraps stay tight as you pull the needle through. If they are not tight now, they never will be.*

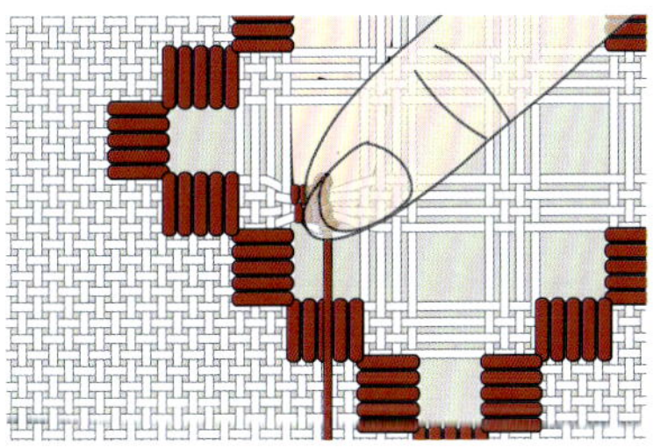

19 Stabilising the wraps with a finger and thumb on each side, pull the needle through and down to tighten the knot at the side of the bar.

❶ *The knot should be tight. If it looks like little loops, you need to pull tighter to make it into a knot.*

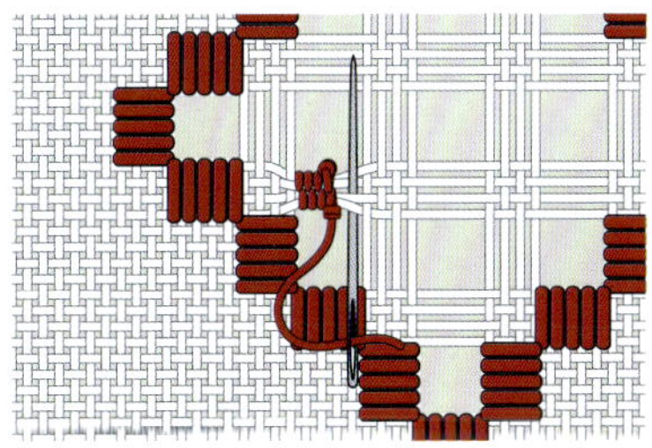

20 From below, slide the needle under the two lower threads of the bar.

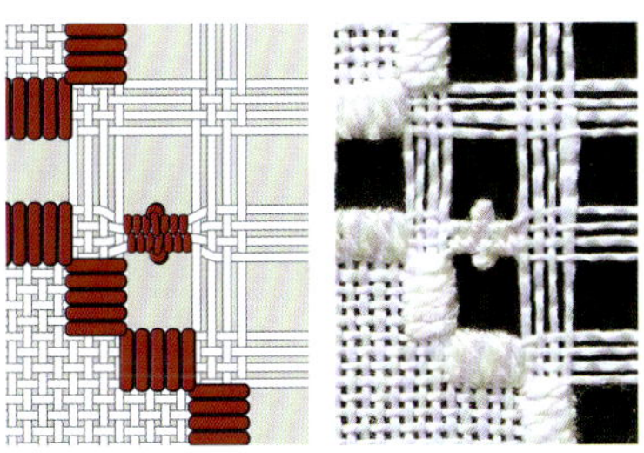

21 Weave the remainder of the bar.

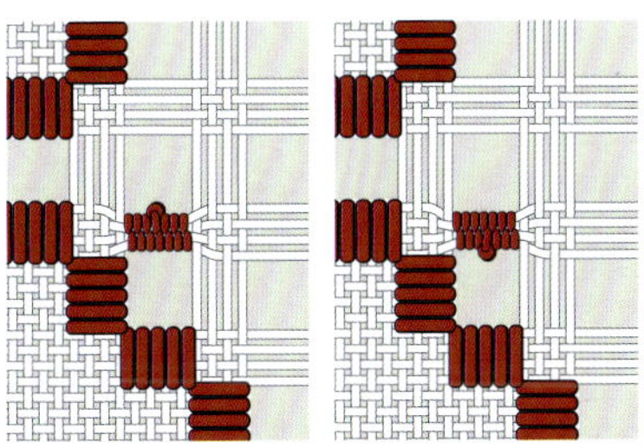

❶ *If a picot is only required on one side of the bar, work a normal woven stitch in place of the missing picot.*

R

picots

TRADITIONAL

knotted picots

Knotted picots are worked as part of the bar on which they are positioned. They can be worked on one or both sides of the bar.

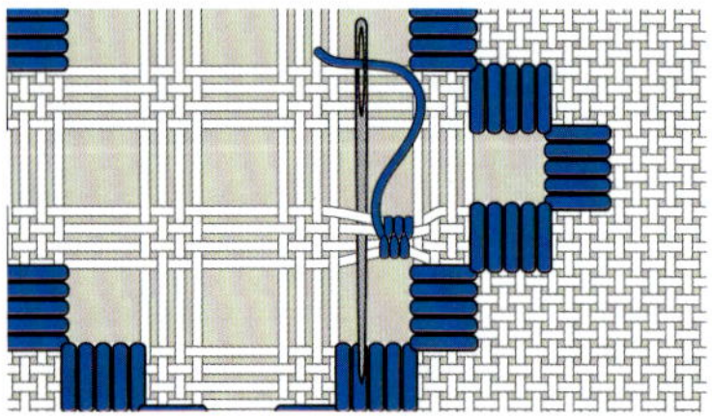

1 Weave half the bar. Insert the needle for the middle stitch.

❶ *The picot is usually worked as the middle stitch of the length of the bar. If you have five stitches on each side, work the picot as part of the third stitch on each side. If you have six stitches, work the picot as part of the fourth stitch, and work extra stitches to make seven stitches per side just for the bars with picots.*

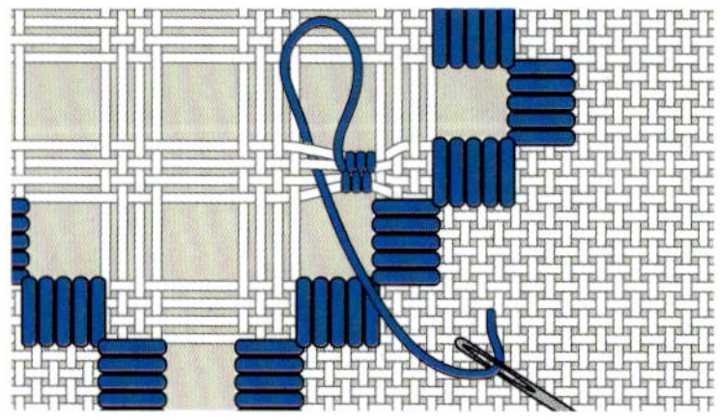

2 Pull the needle through and leave the stitch sitting out from the bar as a loop rather than pulling it in tight.

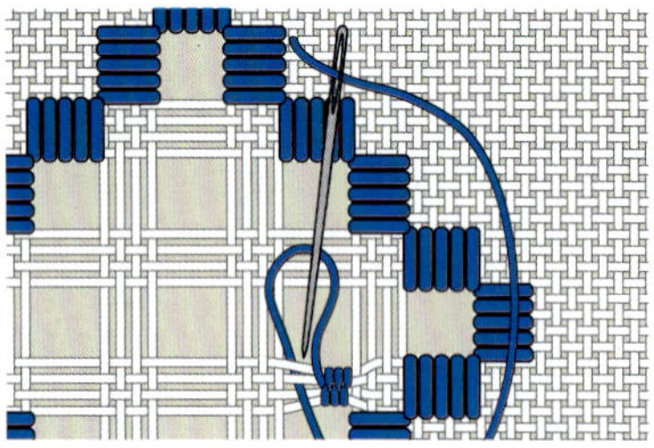

3 Bring the needle around and place the needle over the top edge of the loop as shown.

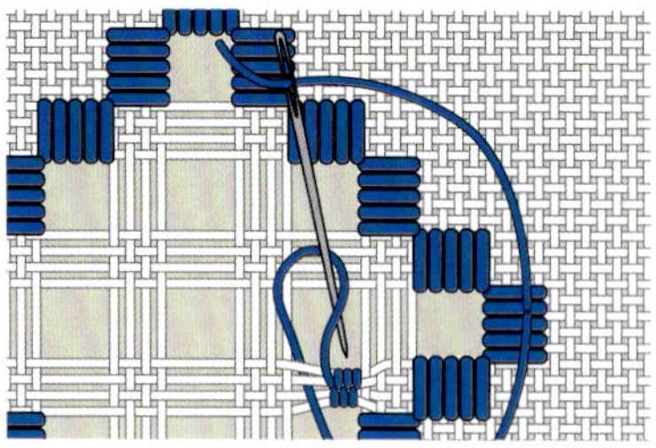

4 Move the needle point to the right behind the right section of the loop.

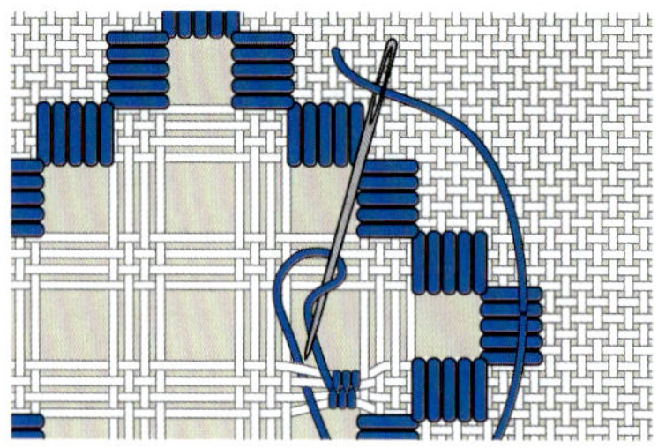

5 Move the needle point to the left over the right section of the loop.

❶ *This makes a wrap around the needle.*

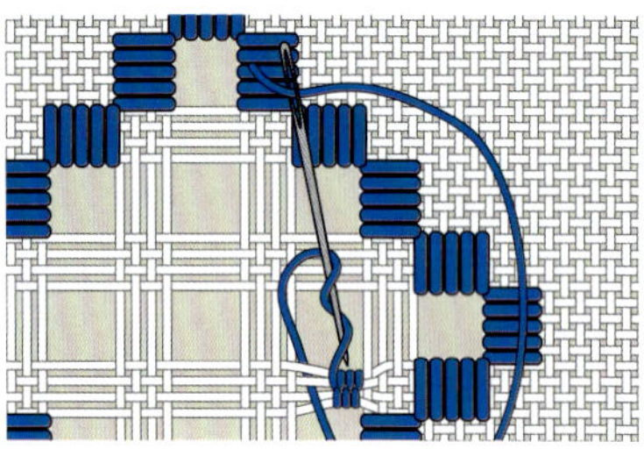

6 Again move the needle point to the right behind the right section of the loop.

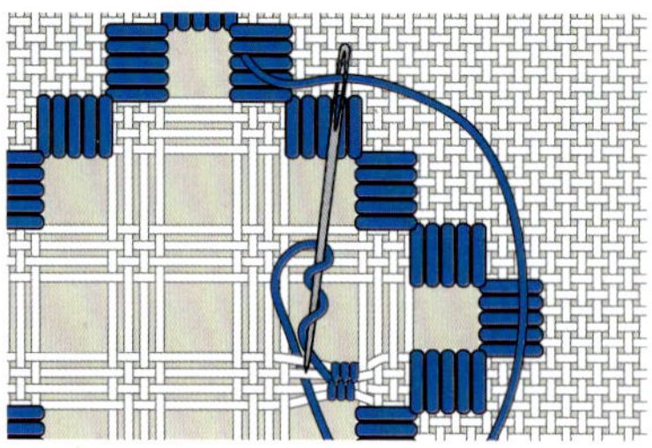

7 Move it to the left over the right section of the loop.

❶ *There are now two wraps around the needle.*

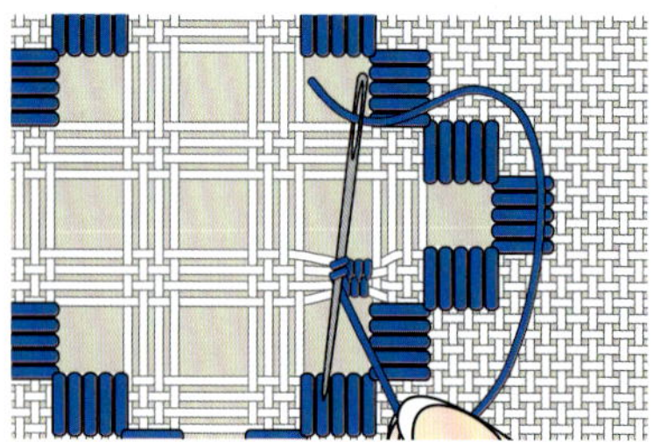

8 Slide the needle further into the wraps. Pull the thread down and right to tighten the wraps around it.

❶ *Ensure the wraps stay tight as you pull the needle through. If they are not tight now, they never will be.*

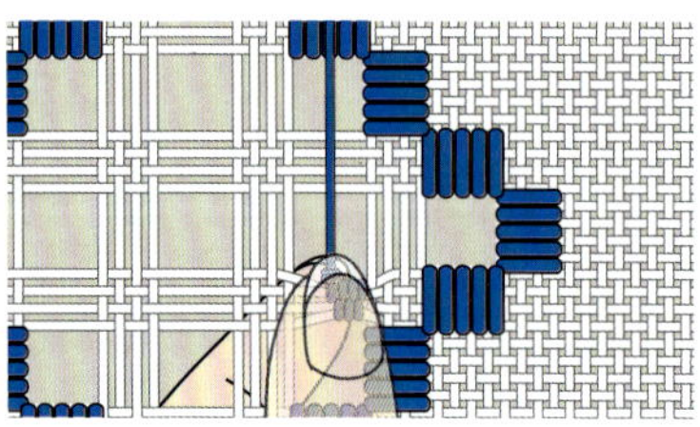

9 Stabilising the wraps with a finger and thumb on each side, pull the needle through and up to tighten the knot at the side of the bar.

❶ *The knot should be tight. If it looks like little loops, tighten it further.*

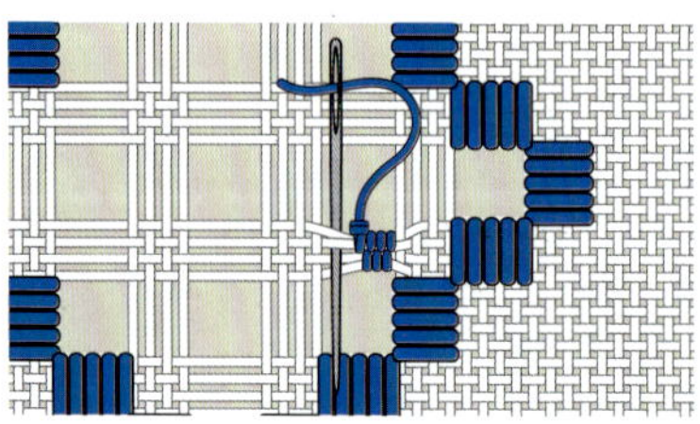

10 From above, slide the needle under the upper two threads of the bar.

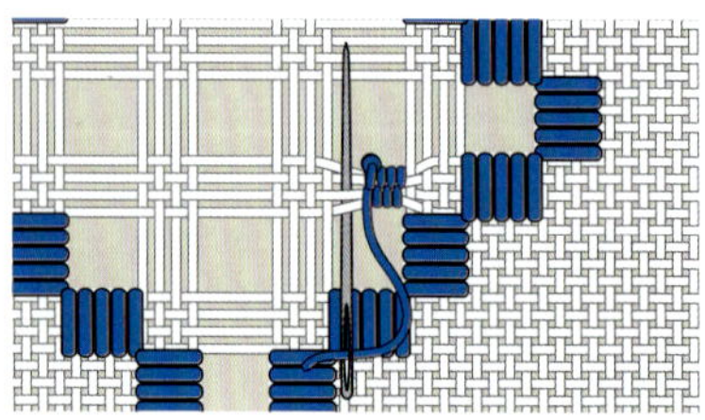

11 From below, slide the needle under the lower two threads of the bar.

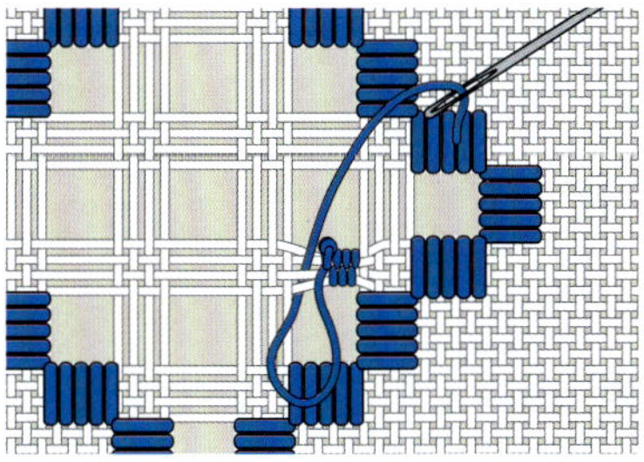

12 Leave the stitch sitting out from the bar as a loop.

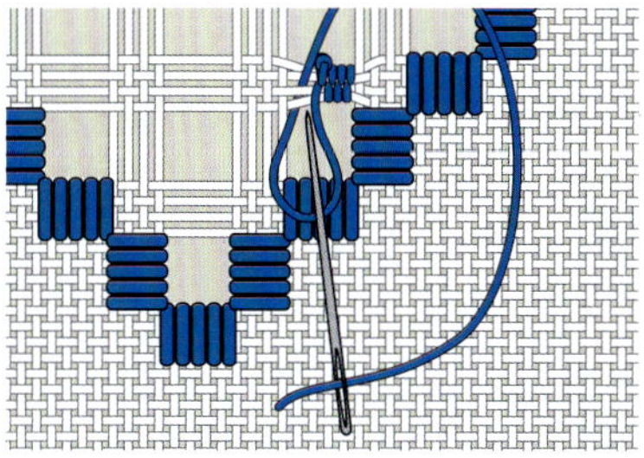

13 Bring the needle around and place the needle over the lower edge of the loop as shown.

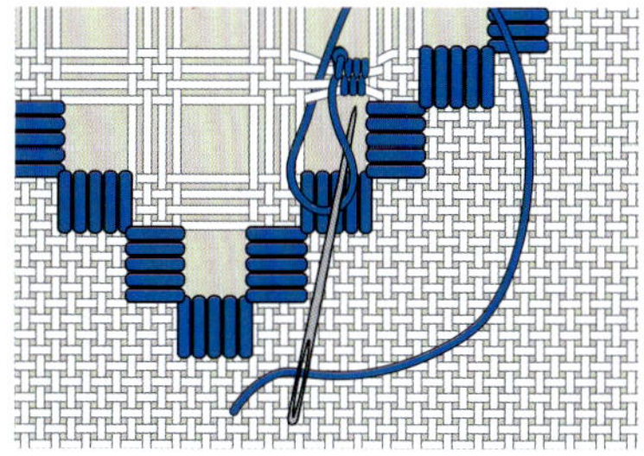

14 Move the needle point to the right behind the right section of the loop.

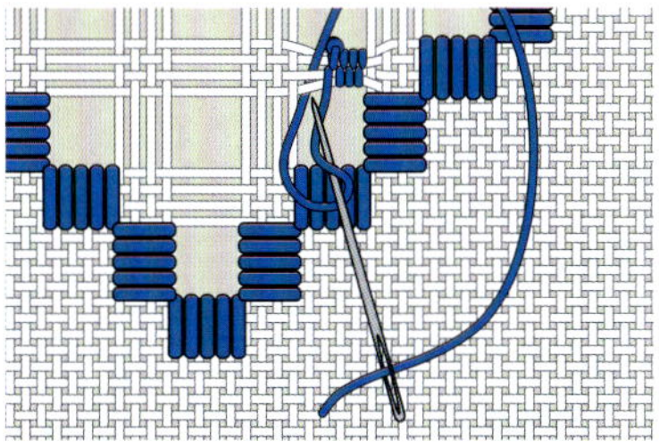

15 Move the needle point to the left over the right section of the loop.

❶ *This makes a wrap around the needle.*

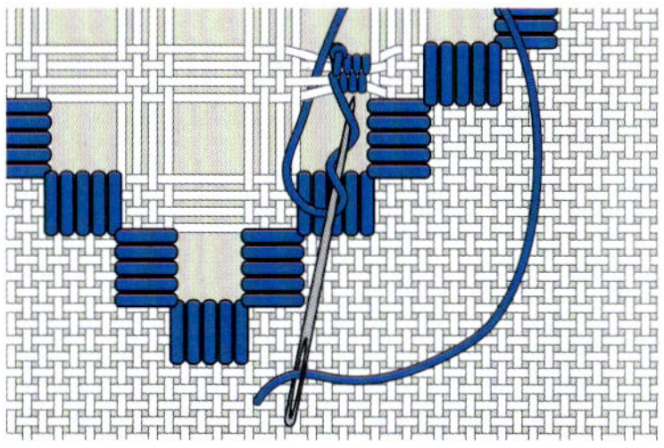

16 Again move the needle point to the right behind the right section of the loop.

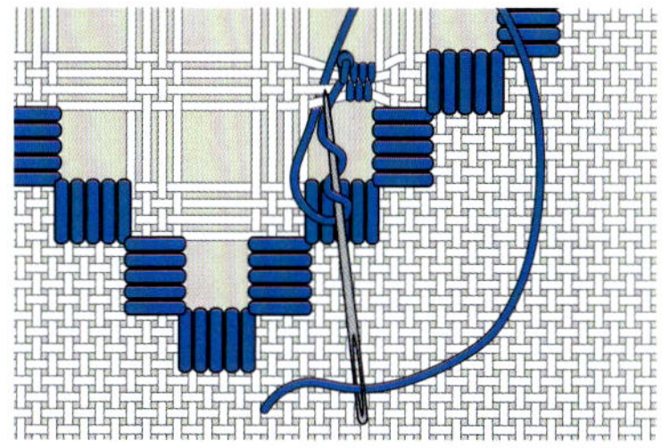

17 Move the needle point to the left over the right section of the loop.

❶ *There are now two wraps around the needle.*

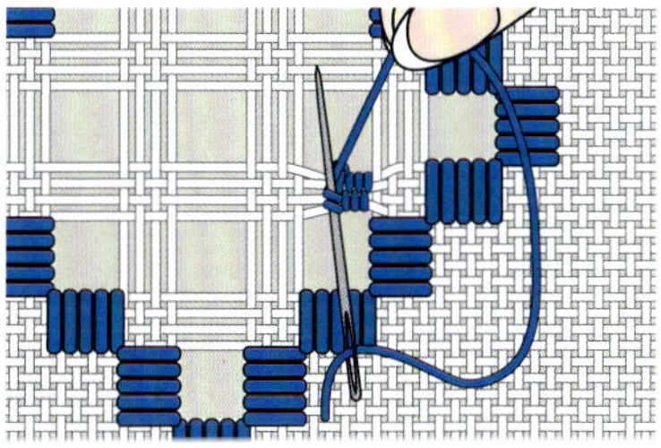

18 Slide the needle further into the wraps. Pull the thread up and right to tighten the wraps around the needle.

❶ *Ensure the wraps stay tight as you pull the needle through. If they are not tight now, they never will be.*

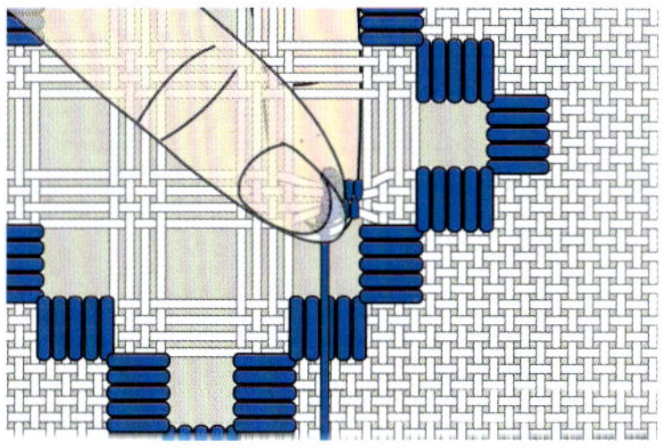

19 Stabilising the wraps with a finger and thumb on each side, pull the needle through and down to tighten the knot at the side of the bar.

❶ *The knot should be tight. If it looks like little loops, you need to pull tighter to make it into a knot.*

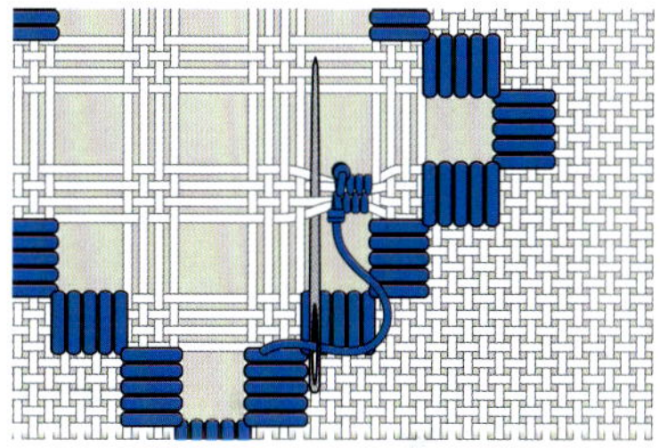

20 From below, slide the needle under the two lower threads of the bar.

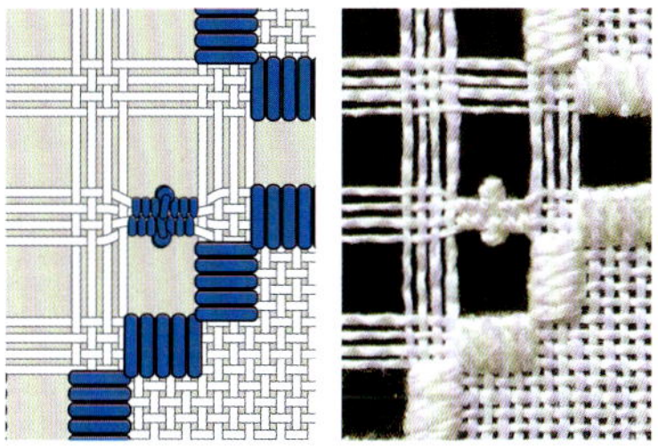

21 Weave the remainder of the bar.

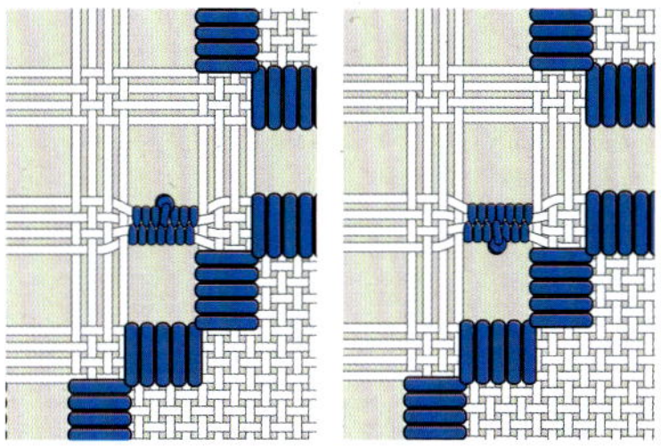

❶ *If a picot is only required on one side of the bar, work a normal woven stitch in place of the missing picot.*

looped picots

Instead of a knot, looped picots have an open loop. They are worked as part of the bar on which they are positioned. They can be worked on one or both sides of the bar.

CONTEMPORARY

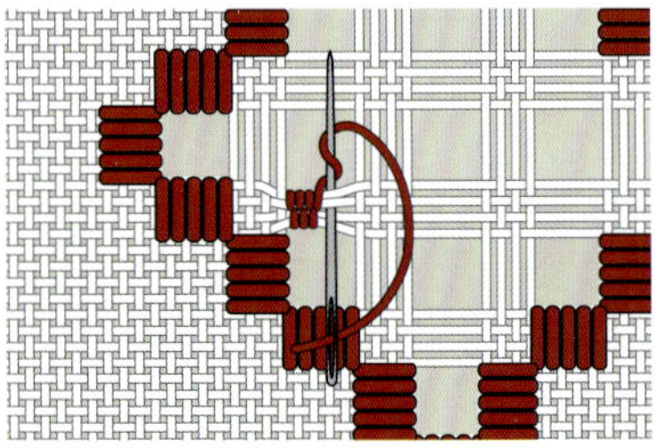

1 Weave half the bar. The next stitch will be on the upper side. From below, insert the needle under the upper two fabric threads. Take the thread to the right behind it and wrap it once.

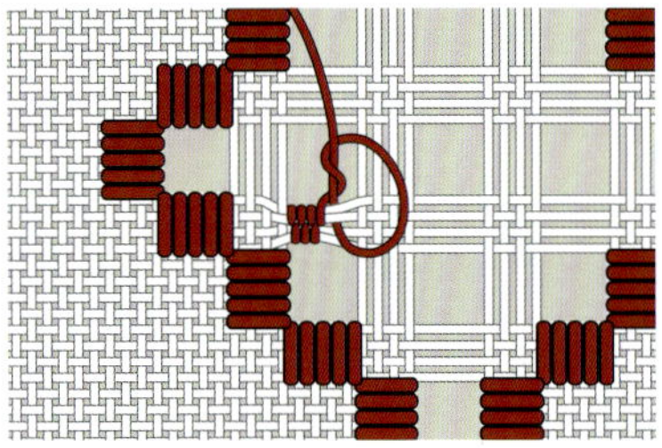

2 Pull the needle through and leave the loop very open.

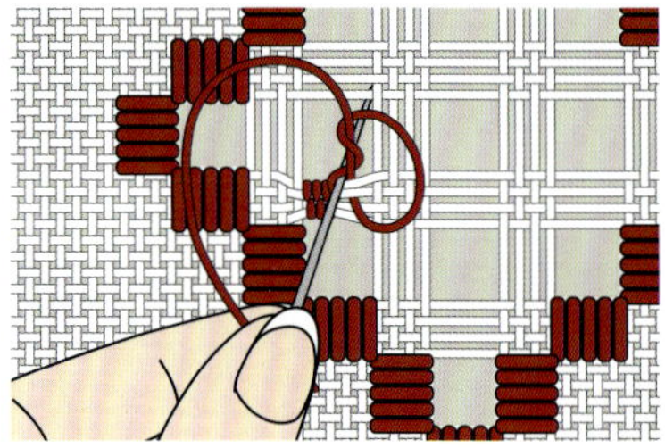

3 Insert the needle, temporarily, under the thread leading to the previous stitching.

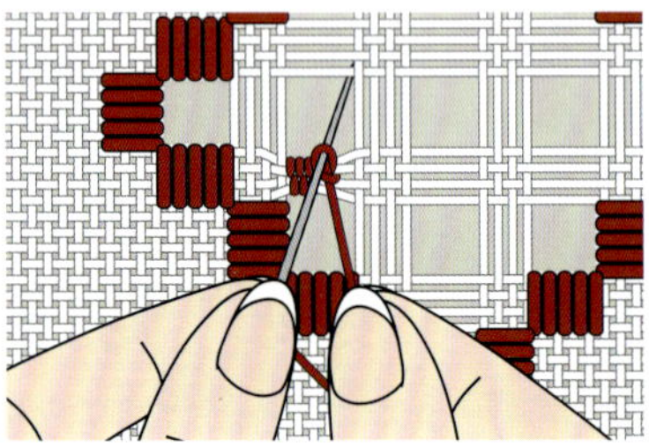

4 Keeping the needle in place, pull the working end of the thread to tighten it next to the needle.

! *The needle keeps the loop open, while tightening the knot beside it.*

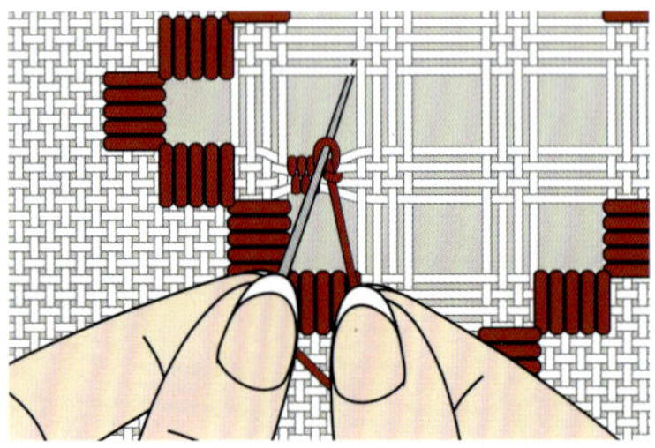

! *If you want your loop to be larger, use the needle to pull the loop a little more open. When you are not using the size of the needle to regulate the loop size, you'll have to be more careful with your tension, to ensure the loops maintain a regular size.*

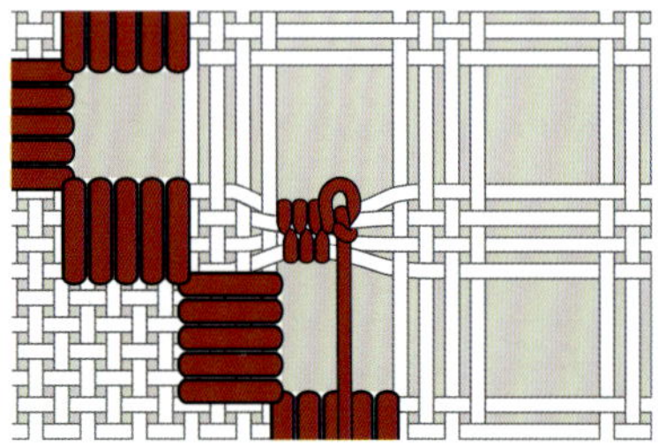

! *Most instructions complete the picot at this step. However, I don't like how the left side of the loop sits forward and is not stabilised. I add another two steps to make it look more even.*

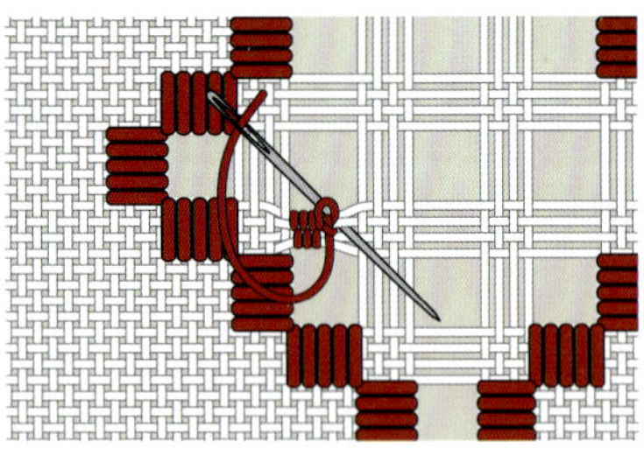

5 Take the needle out of the loop and insert it to the left of the loop, behind the fabric threads. Bring it out in the centre of the bar, ready to continue stitching.

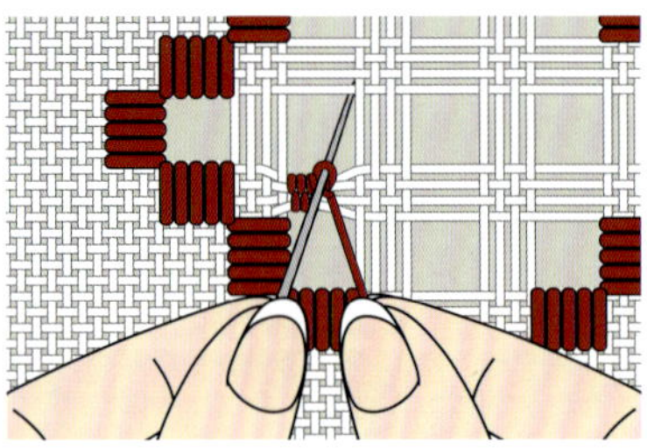

6 Pull the needle through. Insert it, temporarily, in the loop. Pull the thread down, while holding the needle in place, to lock the stitch in place.

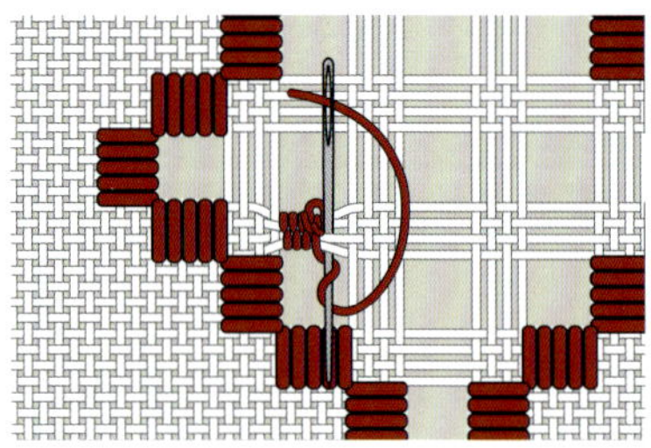

7 From above, insert the needle under the lower two threads. Take the thread to the right behind it and wrap it once.

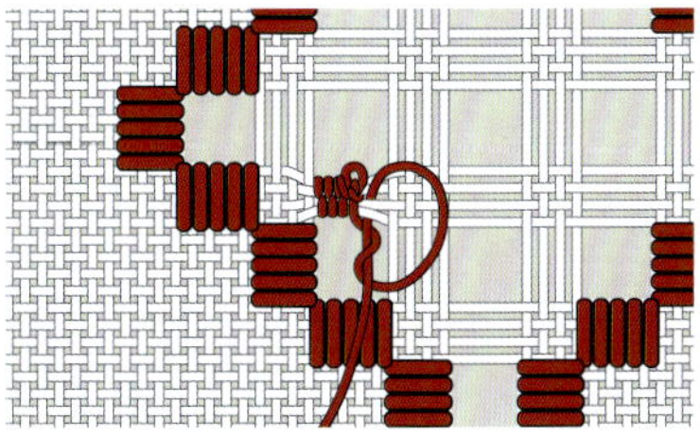

8 Pull the needle through and leave the loop very open.

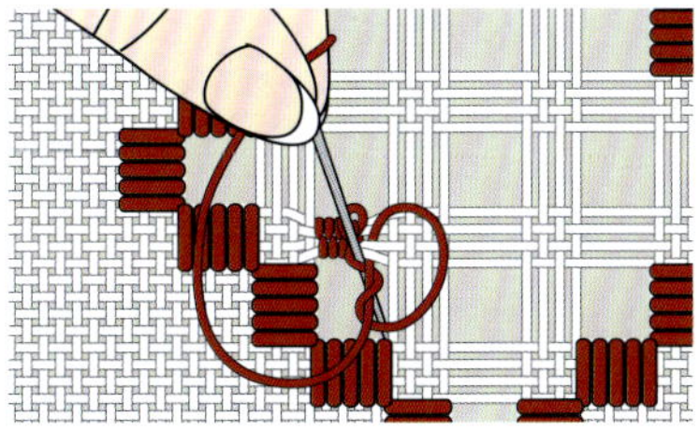

9 Insert the needle, temporarily, under the thread leading to the previous stitching.

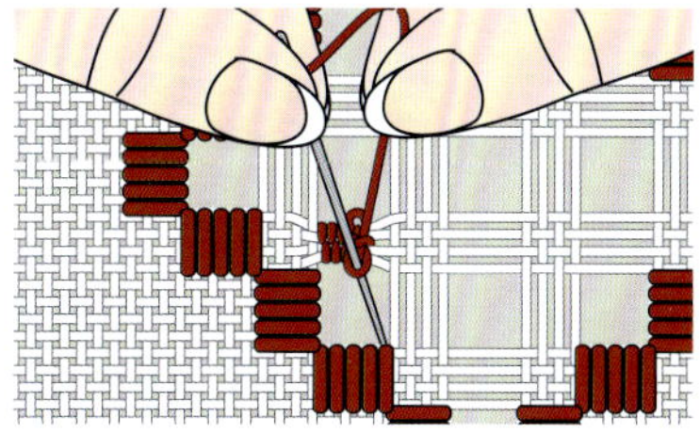

10 Keeping the needle in place, pull the working end of the thread to tighten it next to the needle.

❶ *The needle keeps the loop open, while tightening the knot beside it.*

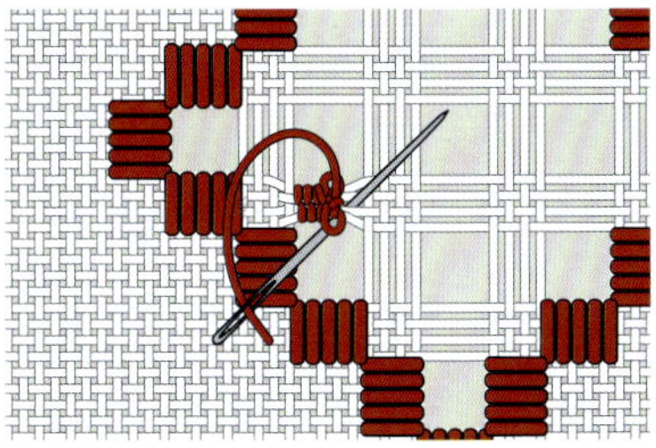

11 Take the needle out of the loop and insert it to the left of the loop, behind the fabric threads. Bring it out in the centre of the bar, ready to continue stitching.

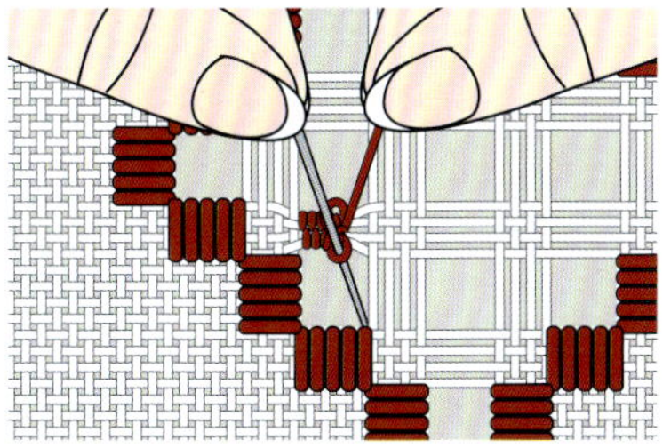

12 Pull the needle through. Insert it, temporarily, in the loop. Pull the thread up, while holding the needle in place, to lock the stitch in place.

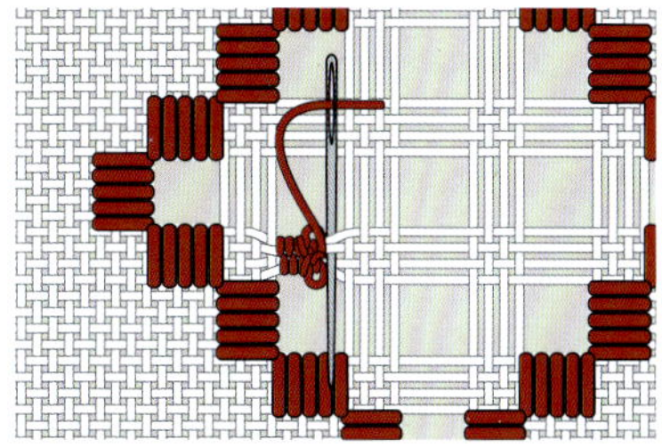

13 From above, insert the needle under the upper two fabric threads, bringing it out in the centre.

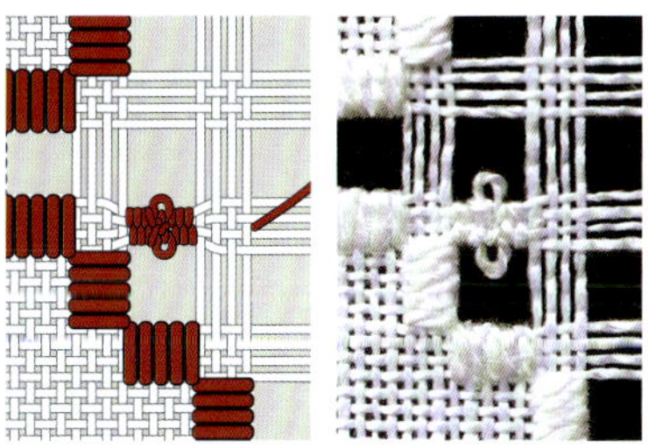

14 Weave the remainder of the bar.

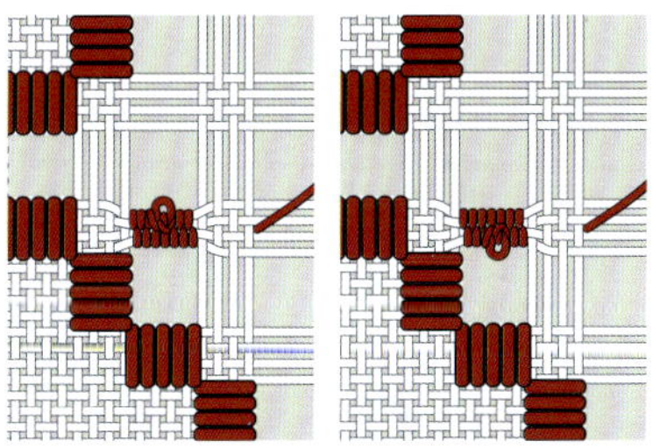

❶ *If a picot is only required on one side of the bar, work a normal woven stitch in place of the missing picot.*

top tip picots

Picots are difficult!

Like all difficult things, picots, whether knotted, looped or chain stitch, can take repeated practice to master. If you don't succeed the first time, keep trying. First master the method, then work on perfecting the tension and regularity of your stitches so that they look as uniform as possible.

looped picots

Instead of a knot, looped picots have an open loop. They are worked as part of the bar on which they are positioned. They can be worked on one or both sides of the bar.

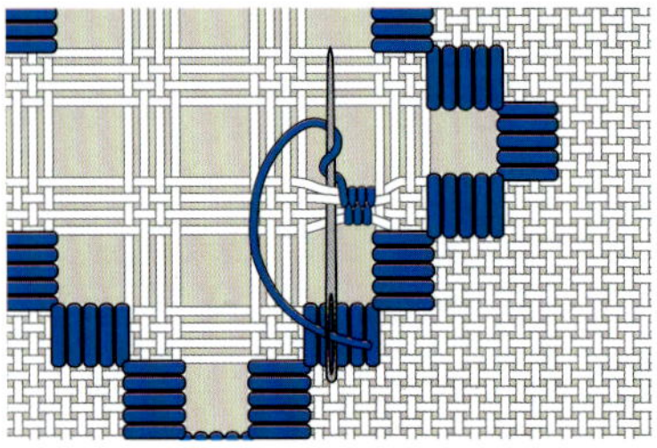

1 Weave half the bar. The next stitch will be on the upper side. From below, insert the needle under the upper two fabric threads. Take the thread to the left behind it and wrap it once.

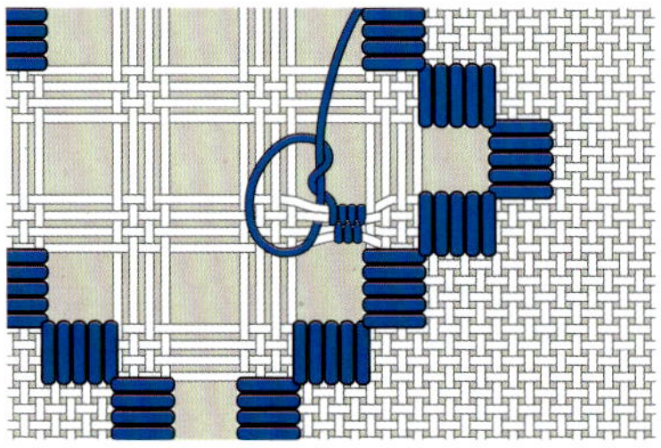

2 Pull the needle through and leave the loop very open.

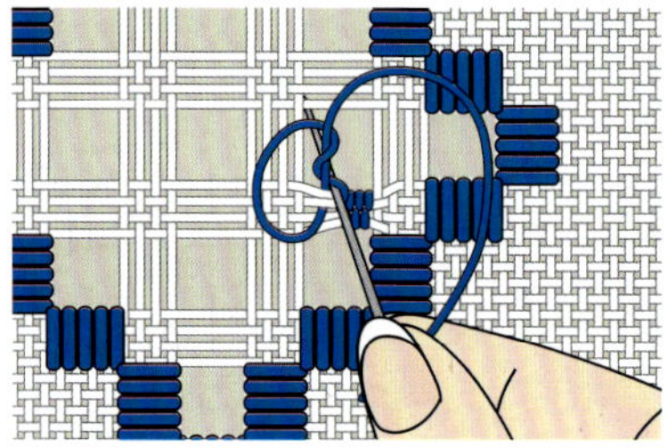

3 Insert the needle, temporarily, under the thread leading to the previous stitching.

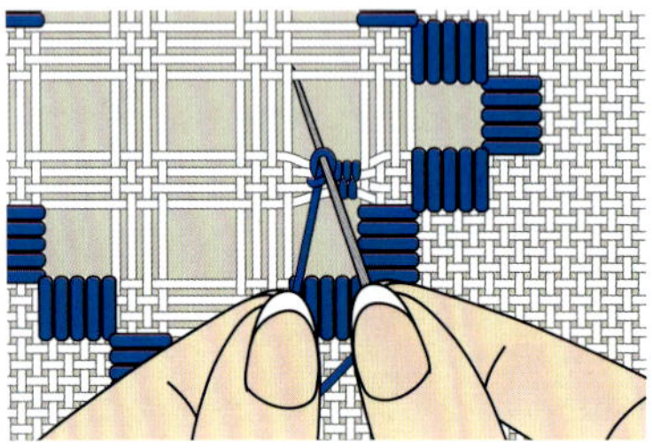

4 Keeping the needle in place, pull the working end of the thread to tighten it next to the needle.

❶ *The needle keeps the loop open, while tightening the knot beside it.*

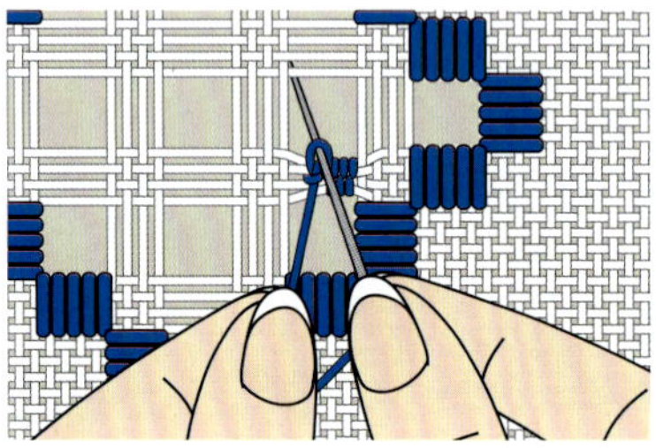

❶ *If you want your loop to be larger, use the needle to pull the loop a little more open. When you are not using the size of the needle to regulate the loop size, you'll have to be more careful with your tension, to ensure the loops maintain a regular size.*

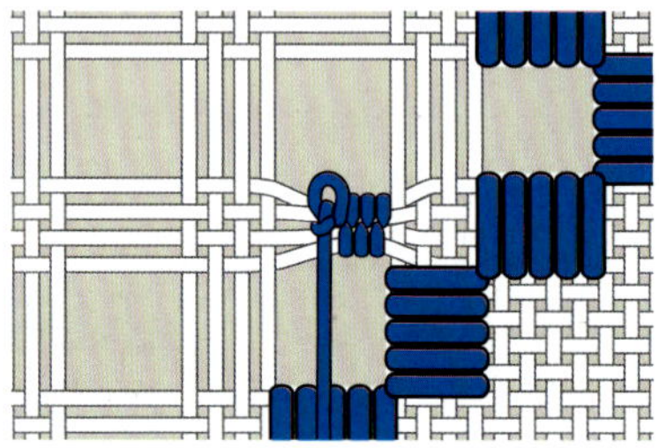

❶ *Most instructions complete the picot at this step. However, I don't like how the right side of the loop sits forward and is not stabilised. I add another two steps to make it look more even.*

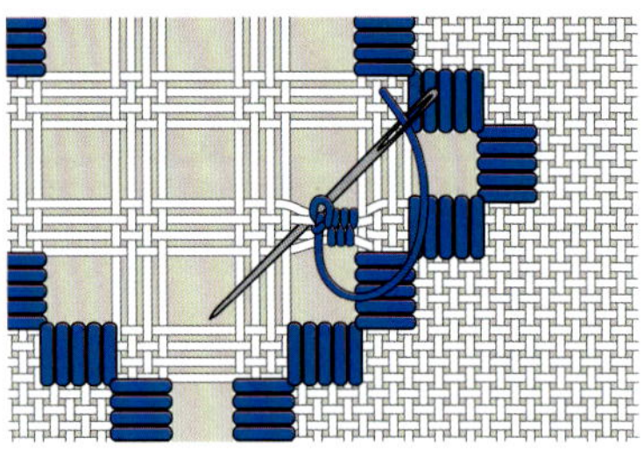

5 Take the needle out of the loop and insert it to the right of the loop, behind the fabric threads. Bring it out in the centre of the bar, ready to continue stitching.

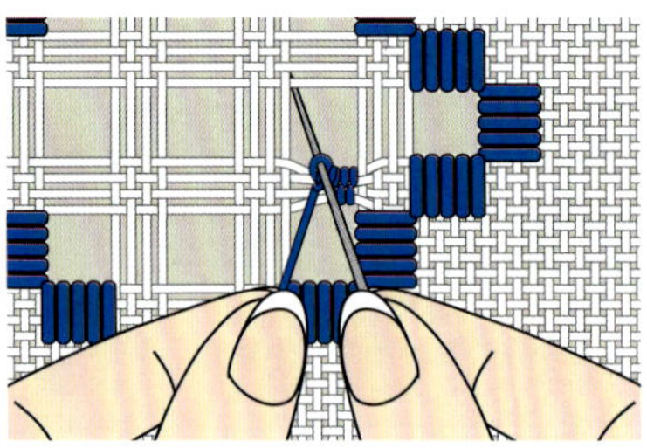

6 Pull the needle through. Insert it, temporarily, in the loop. Pull the thread down, while holding the needle in place, to lock the stitch in place.

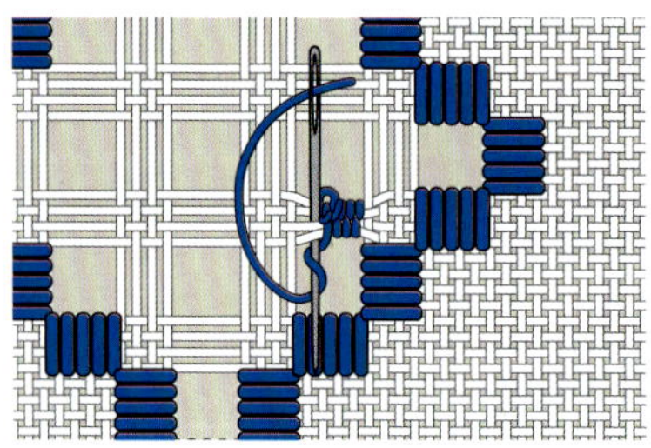

7 From above, insert the needle under the lower two threads. Take the thread to the left behind it and wrap it once.

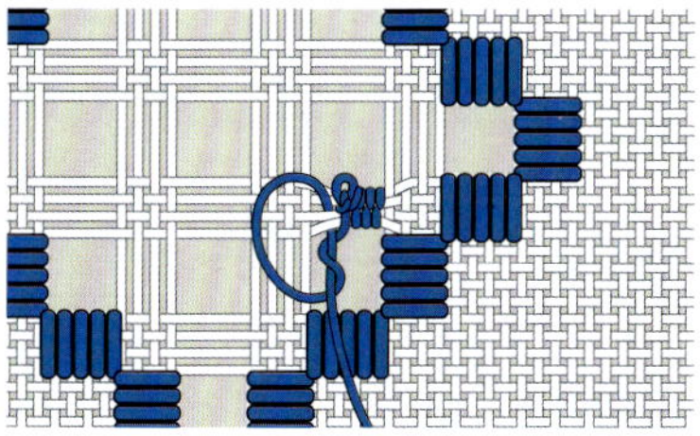

8 Pull the needle through and leave the loop very open.

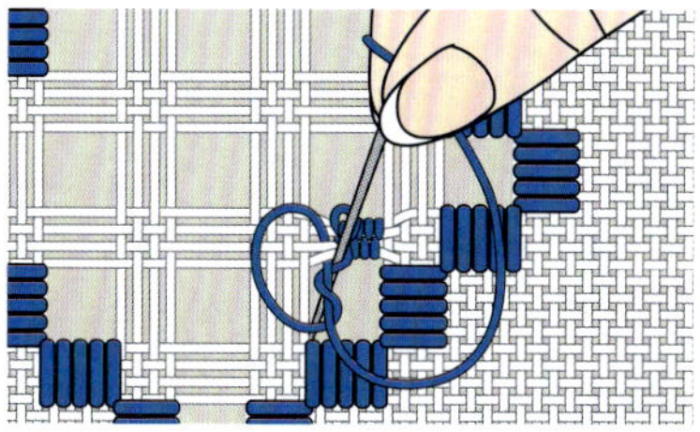

9 Insert the needle, temporarily, under the thread leading to the previous stitching.

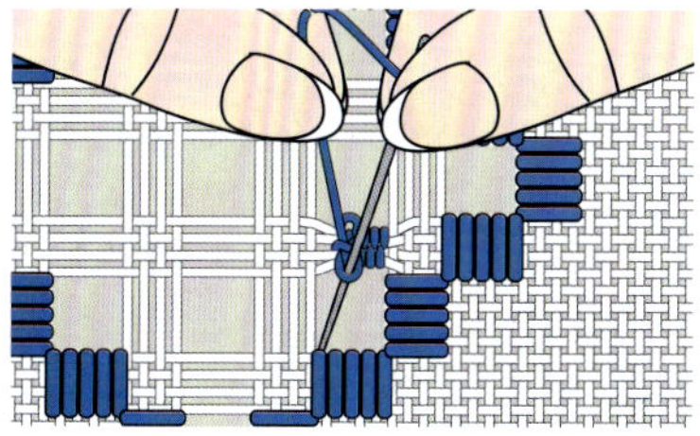

10 Keeping the needle in place, pull the working end of the thread to tighten it next to the needle.

❶ *The needle keeps the loop open, while tightening the knot beside it.*

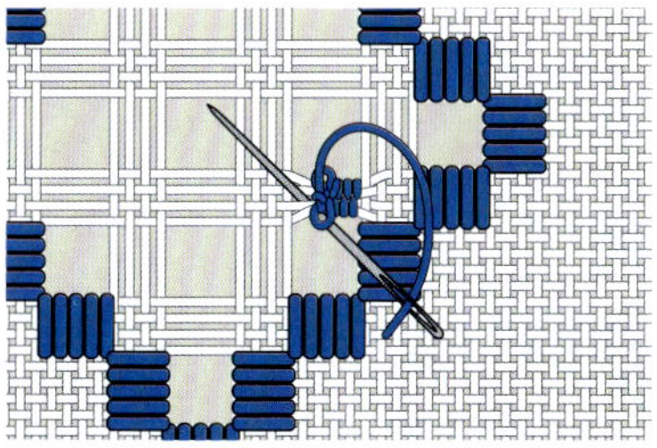

11 Take the needle out of the loop and insert it to the right of the loop, behind the fabric threads. Bring it out in the centre of the bar, ready to continue stitching.

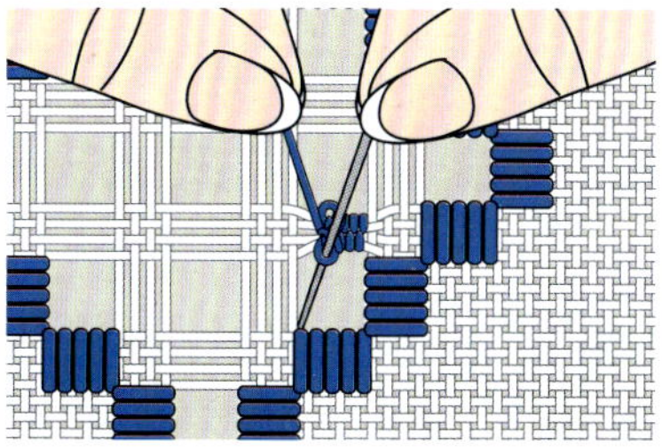

12 Pull the needle through. Insert it, temporarily, in the loop. Pull the thread up, while holding the needle in place, to lock the stitch in place.

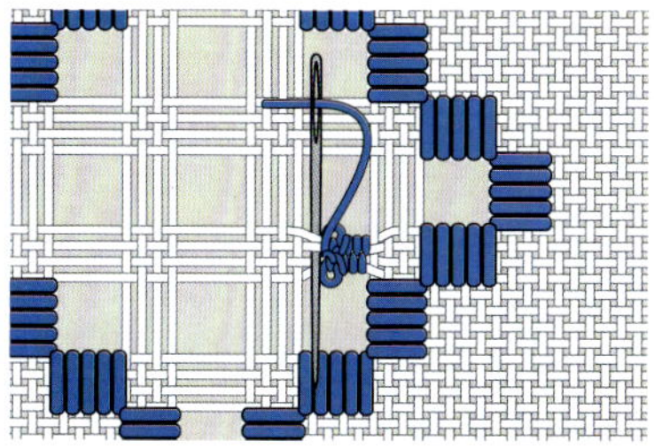

13 From above, insert the needle under the upper two fabric threads, bringing it out in the centre.

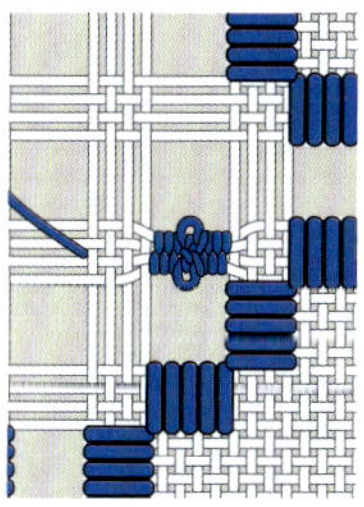

14 Weave the remainder of the bar.

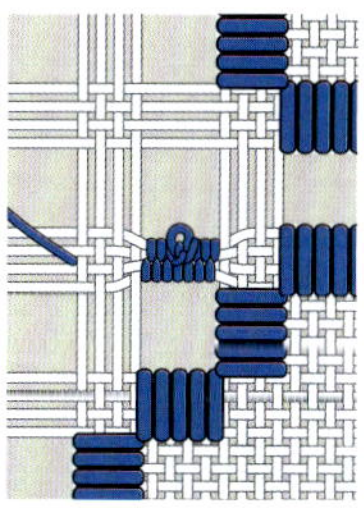

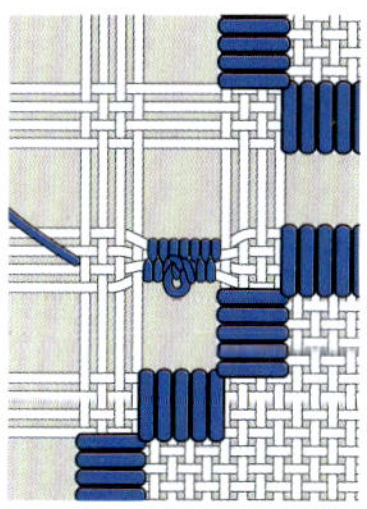

❶ *If a picot is only required on one side of the bar, work a normal woven stitch in place of the missing picot.*

top tip picots

Picots are difficult!

Like all difficult things, picots, whether knotted, looped or chain stitch, can take repeated practice to master. If you don't succeed the first time, keep trying. First master the method, then work on perfecting the tension and regularity of your stitches so that they look as uniform as possible.

chain stitch picots

This is simplest form of picot, being a chain stitch out the side of a woven bar.

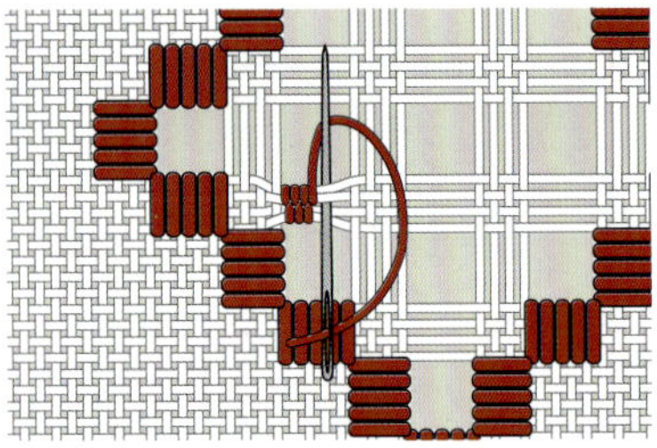

1 Weave half the bar. The next stitch will be on the upper side. From below, insert the needle under the upper two fabric threads. Take the thread behind the needle point from left to right.

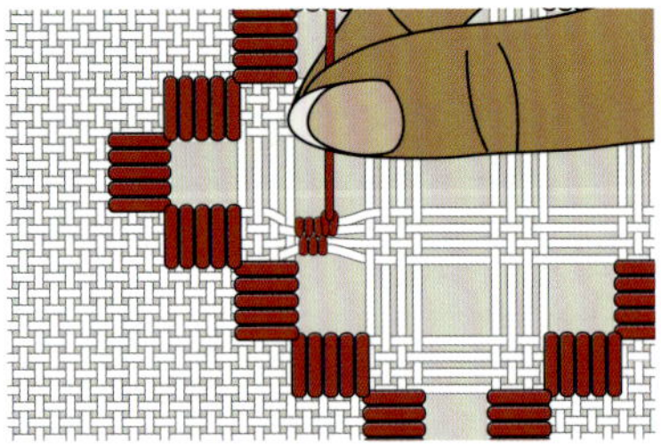

2 Pull the needle through and tighten the stitch so that it has gentle tension.

❶ *If you tighten it too much, it will disappear into the weave of the bar.*

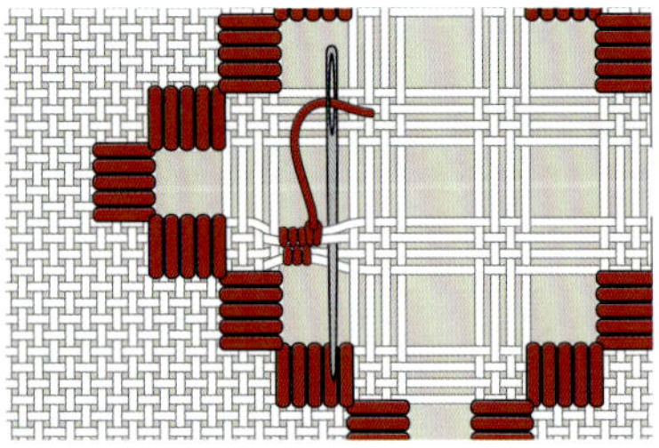

3 Insert the needle under the top two threads and bring it out in the centre of the bar.

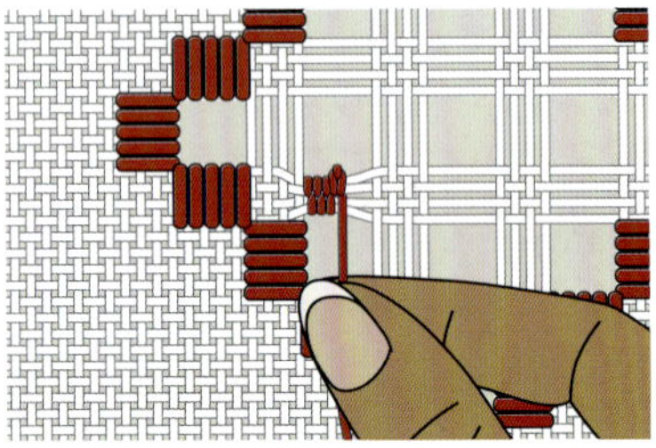

4 Pull the needle through so that the thread folds down behind the chain without shortening the chain at all.

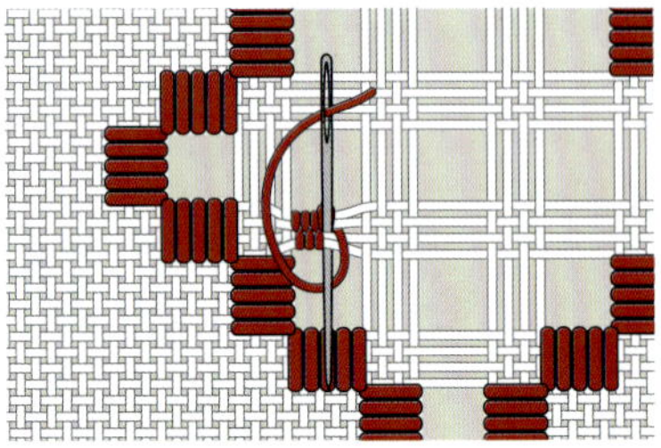

5 From above, insert the needle between the working thread and the stitching, under the lower two fabric threads. Take the thread behind the needle point from right to left.

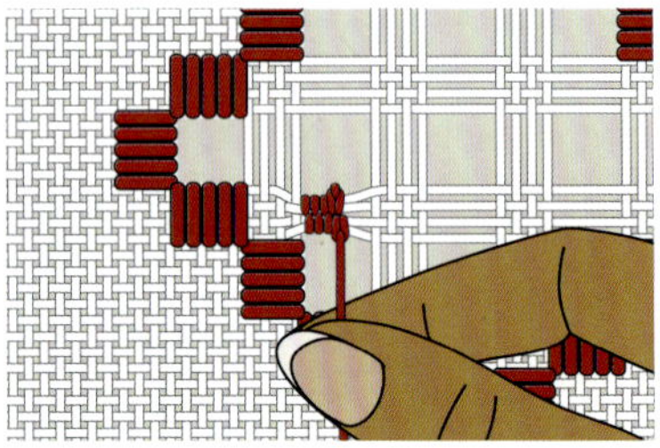

6 Pull the needle through and tighten the stitch so that it has gentle tension.

❶ *If you tighten it too much, it will disappear into the weave of the bar.*

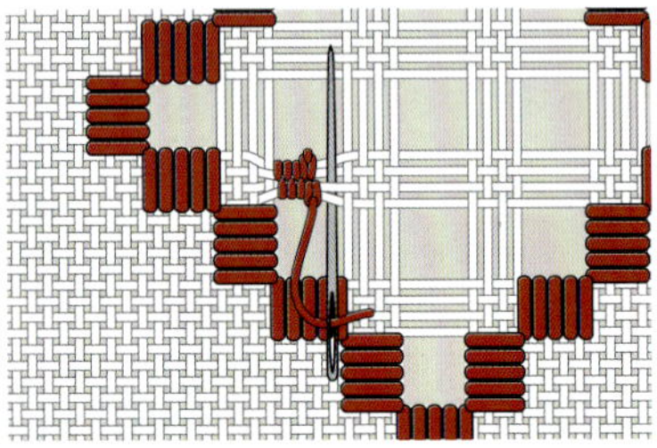

7 Insert the needle under the lower two threads and bring it out in the centre of the bar.

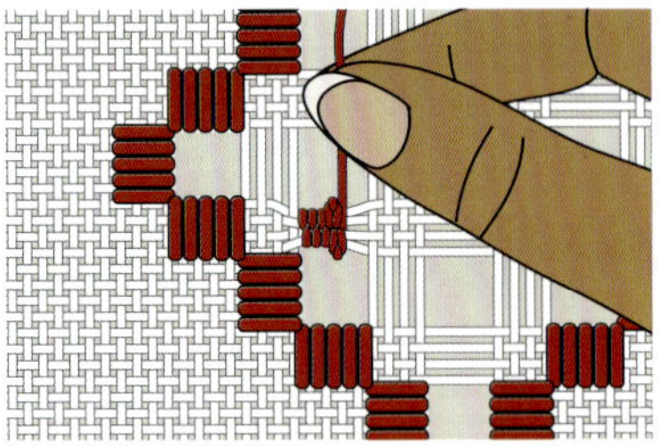

8 Pull the needle through so that the thread folds up behind the chain without shortening the chain at all.

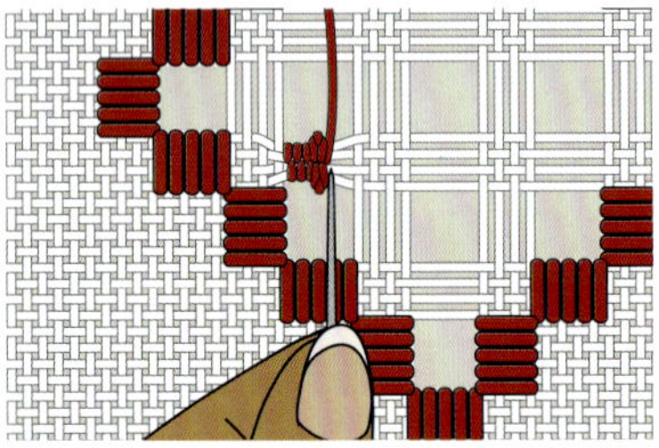

9 Use the tip of the needle to push the lower chain back in line with the upper one.

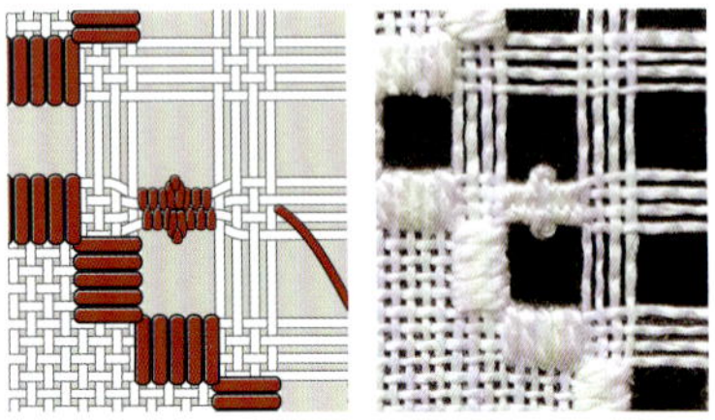

10 Weave the rest of the bar.

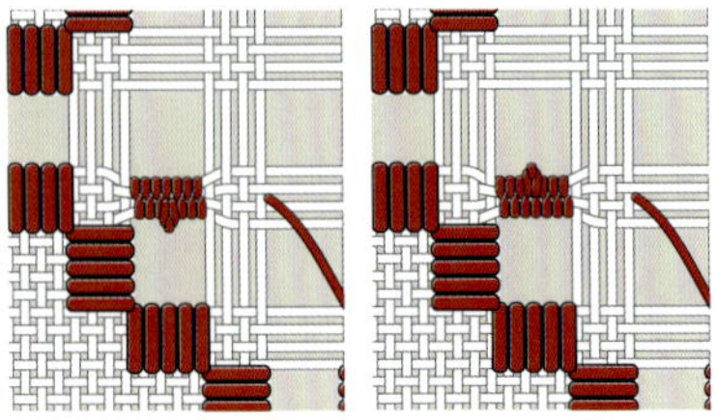

❶ *A single chain stitch picot can be worked on one side of the bar only.*

❶ *Another form of chain stitch picot is worked on buttonhole stitch. The instructions are found on page 191.*

chain stitch picots

This is simplest form of picot, being a chain stitch out the side of a woven bar.

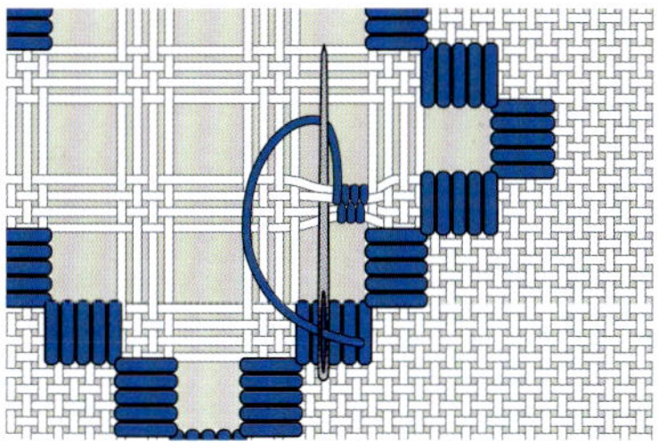

1 Weave half the bar. The next stitch will be on the upper side. From below, insert the needle under the upper two fabric threads. Take the thread behind the needle point from right to left.

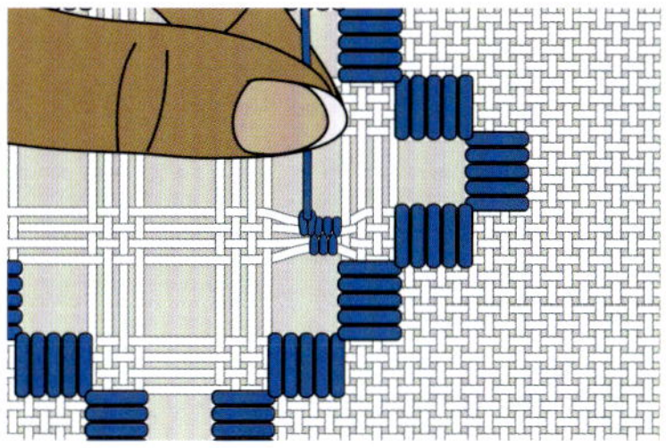

2 Pull the needle through and tighten the stitch so that it has gentle tension.

❶ *If you tighten it too much, it will disappear into the weave of the bar.*

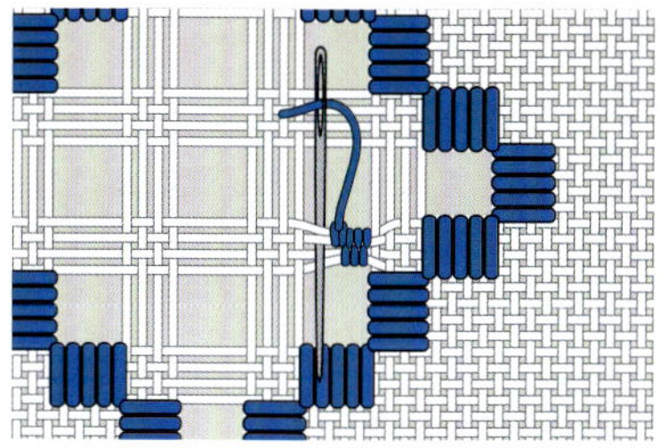

3 Insert the needle under the top two threads and bring it out in the centre of the bar.

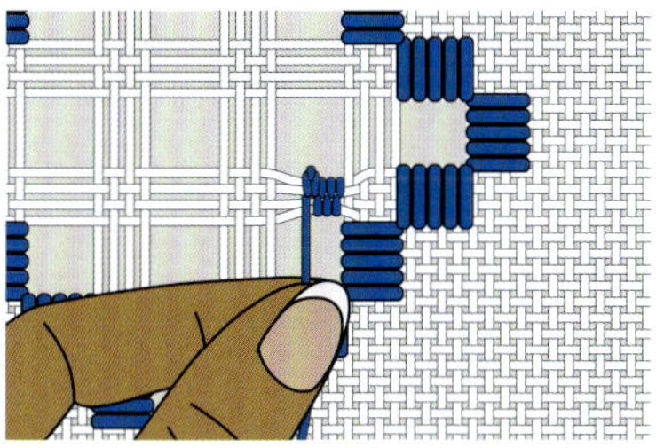

4 Pull the needle through so that the thread folds down behind the chain without shortening the chain at all.

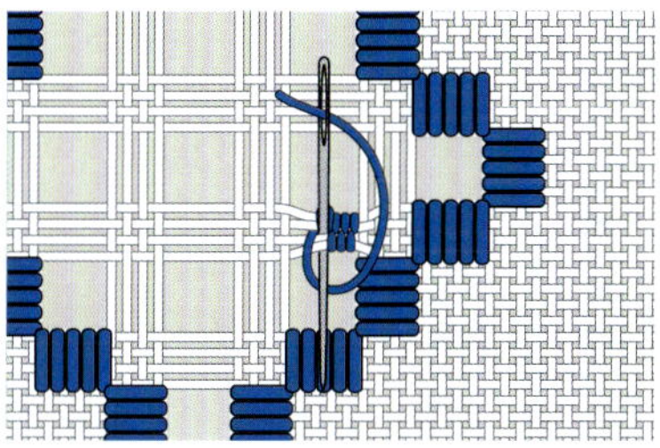

5 From above, insert the needle between the working thread and the stitching, under the lower two fabric threads. Take the thread behind the needle point from left to right.

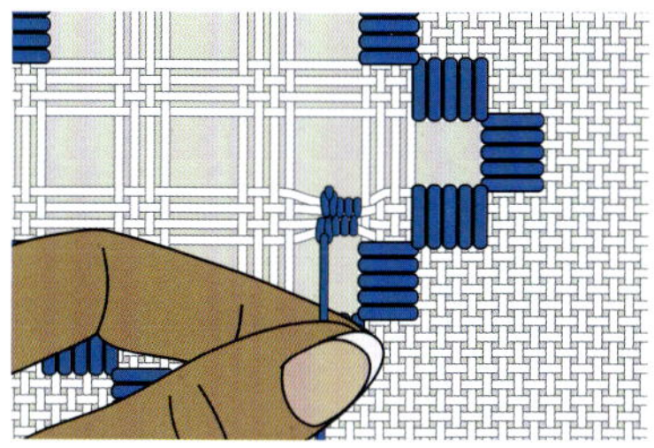

6 Pull the needle through and tighten the stitch so that it has gentle tension.

❶ *If you tighten it too much, it will disappear into the weave of the bar.*

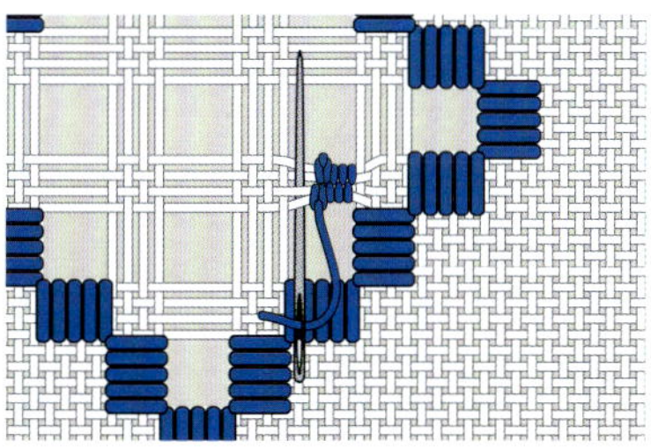

7 Insert the needle under the lower two threads and bring it out in the centre of the bar.

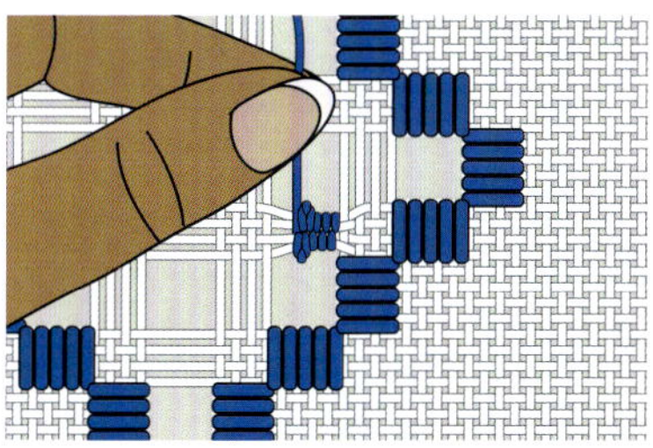

8 Pull the needle through so that the thread folds up behind the chain without shortening the chain at all.

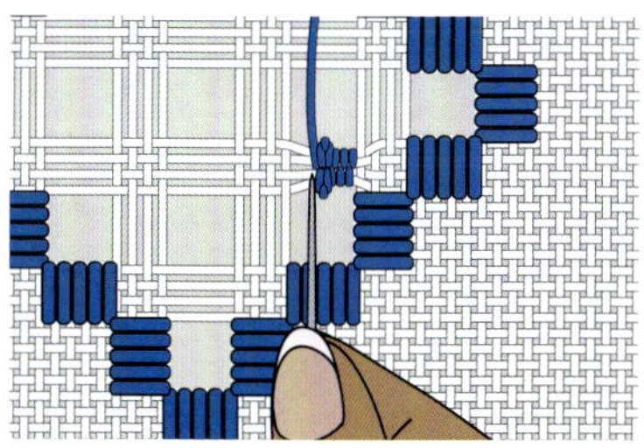

9 Use the tip of the needle to push the lower chain back in line with the upper one.

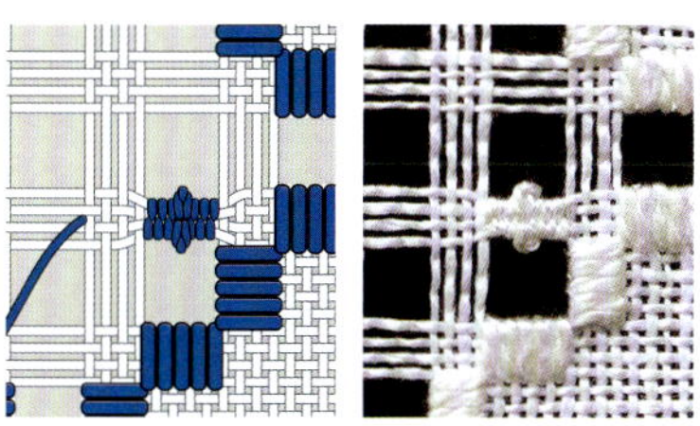

10 Weave the rest of the bar.

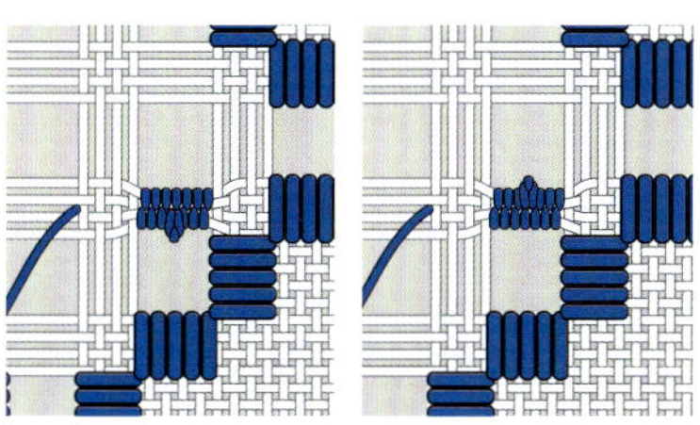

❶ *A single chain stitch picot can be worked on one side of the bar only.*

❶ *Another form of chain stitch picot is worked on buttonhole stitch. The instructions are found on page 193.*

bead picots

It is important to choose beads that are large enough for the threaded tapestry needle to go through, as a tapestry needle's eye is relatively large. You may choose to use a slightly smaller needle than normal when beading, if you can thread it with your thread. As a warning, a smaller needle will wear the thread more quickly, so only use it for the beaded section.

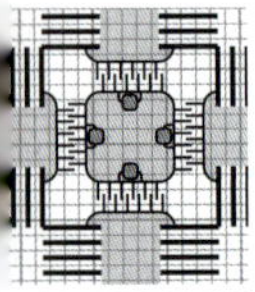

CONTEMPORARY

bead side-on

Of the two methods shown here, this is the stronger and more stable one, as the thread passes through the bead twice. It does mean that the bead may need to be slightly bigger than for the other method.

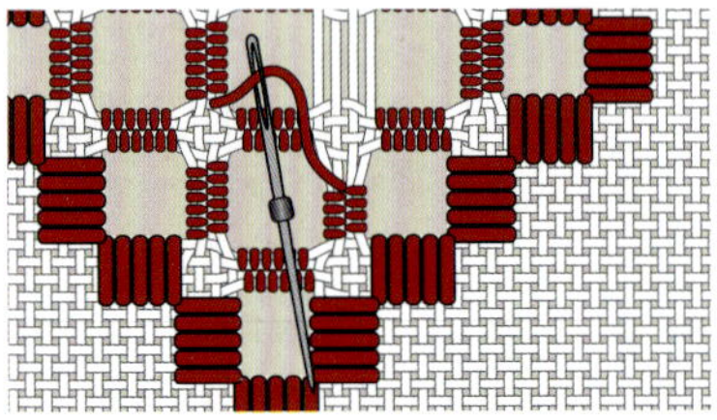

1 Weave the bar just past halfway. Bring the needle out on the side for the bead. Thread the bead onto the needle.

2 Push the bead along the thread to the bar, and lay it back towards the direction you've come from.

❶ *This will help to gauge where to insert the needle next. You want the bead to sit halfway along the bar.*

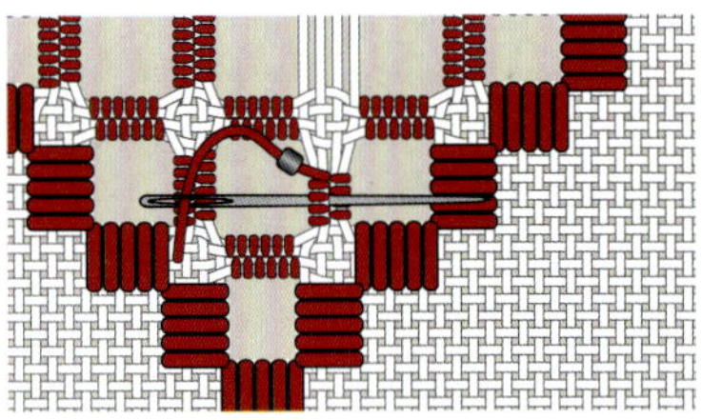

3 Insert the needle in the back of the bar, right next to the bead.

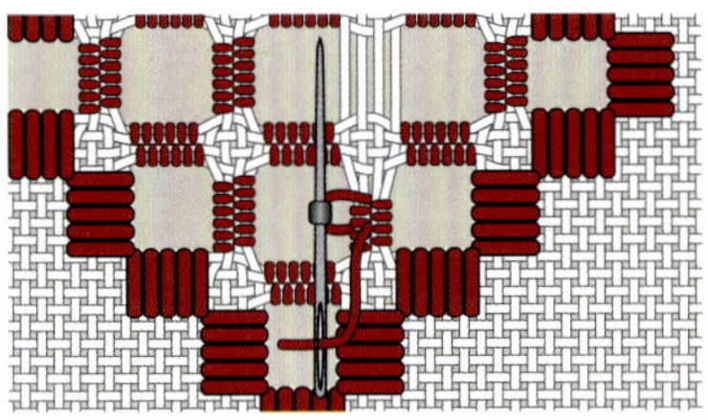

4 Pull the needle through. Slide the needle through the bead again.

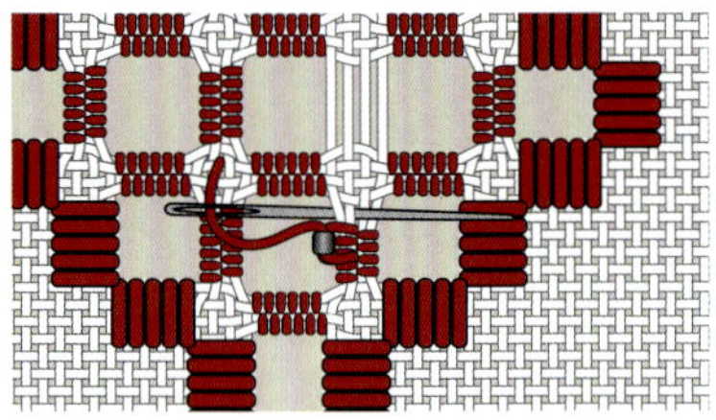

5 Tighten the two stitches so that the bead sits snugly against the side of the bar. Insert the needle to continue weaving as before.

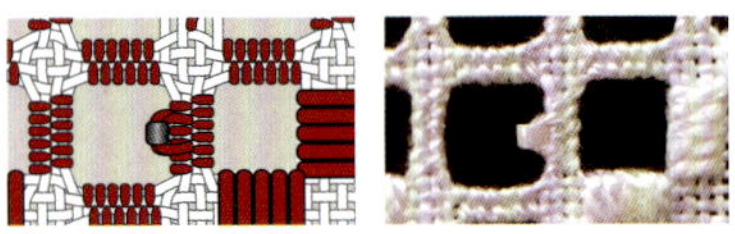

6 The completed bead picot.

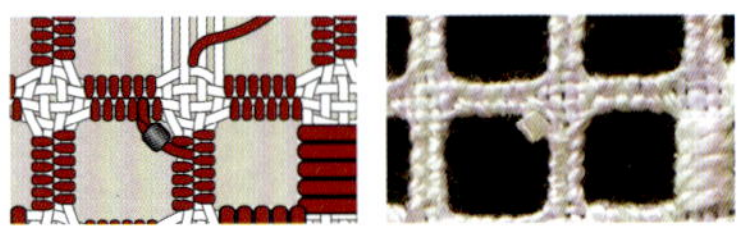

❶ *These bead picots can also be worked in the corner, between bars.*

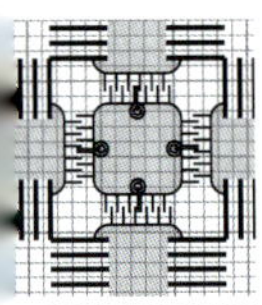

CONTEMPORARY

bead end-on

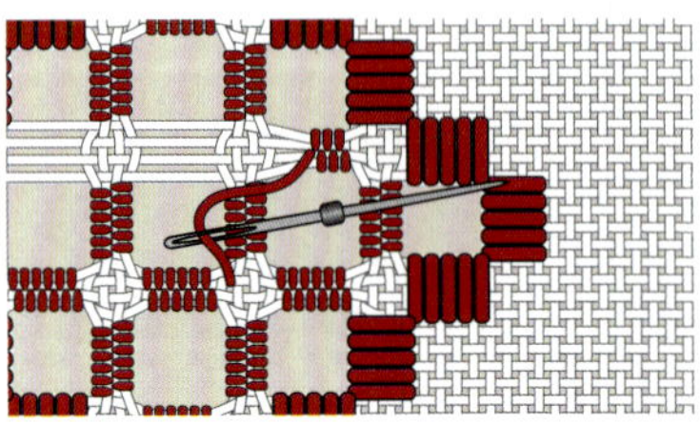

1 Weave to halfway along the bar. Bring the needle out on the side for the bead. Thread the bead onto the needle.

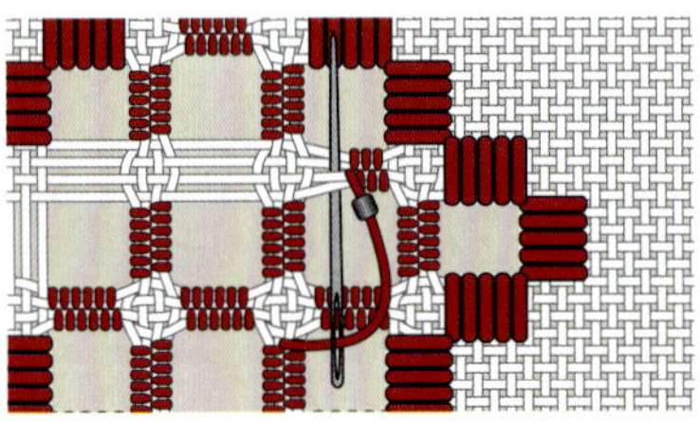

2 Push the bead along the thread to the bar. Continue weaving.

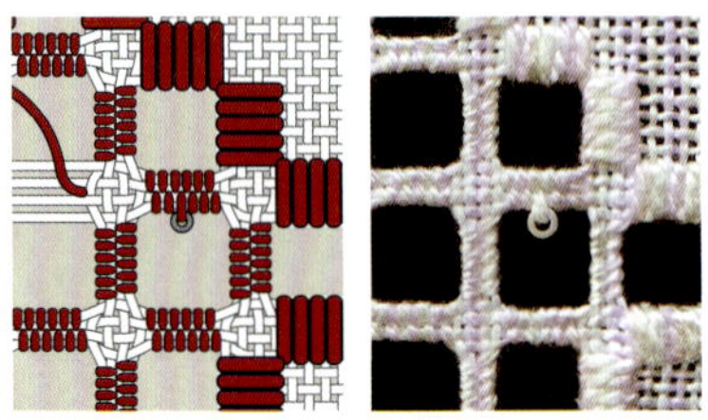

3 Carefully position the bead so that it sits at the side of the bar.

bead picots

It is important to choose beads that are large enough for the threaded tapestry needle to go through, as a tapestry needle's eye is relatively large. You may choose to use a slightly smaller needle than normal when beading, if you can thread it with your thread. As a warning, a smaller needle will wear the thread more quickly, so only use it for the beaded section.

bead side-on

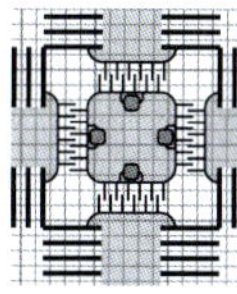

CONTEMPORARY

Of the two methods shown here, this is the stronger and more stable one, as the thread passes through the bead twice. It does mean that the bead may need to be slightly bigger than for the other method.

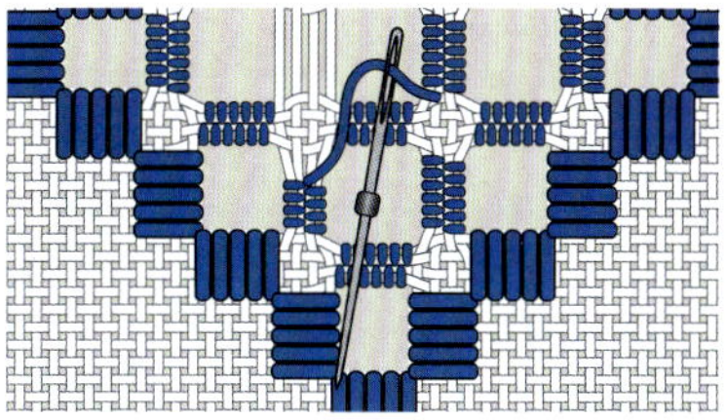

1 Weave the bar just past halfway. Bring the needle out on the side for the bead. Thread the bead onto the needle.

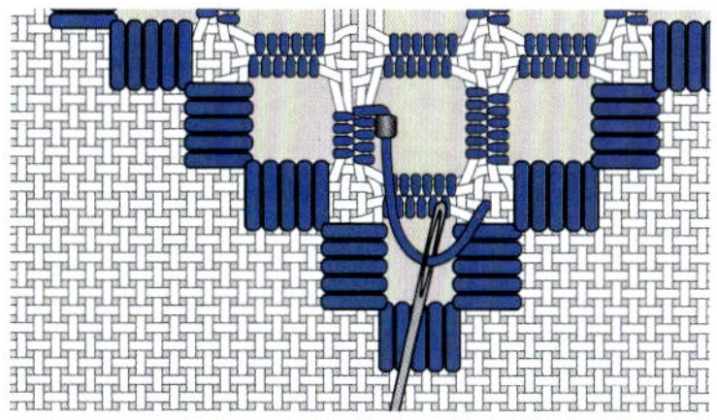

2 Push the bead along the thread to the bar, and lay it back towards the direction you've come from.

! *This will help to gauge where to insert the needle next. You want the bead to sit halfway along the bar.*

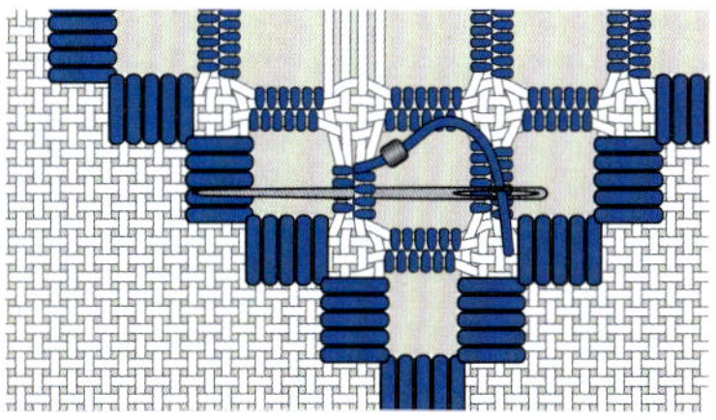

3 Insert the needle in the back of the bar, right next to the bead.

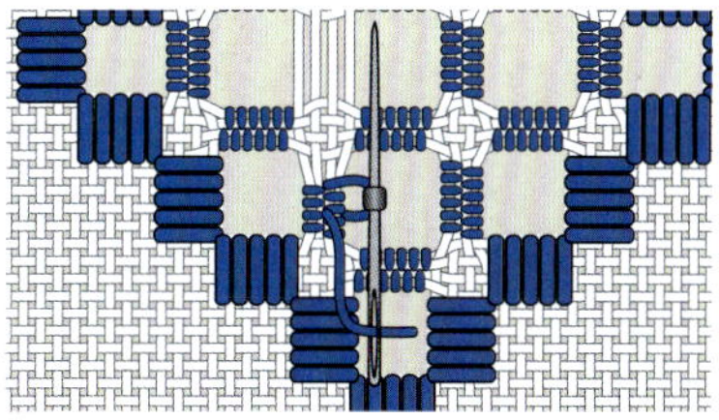

4 Pull the needle through. Slide the needle through the bead again.

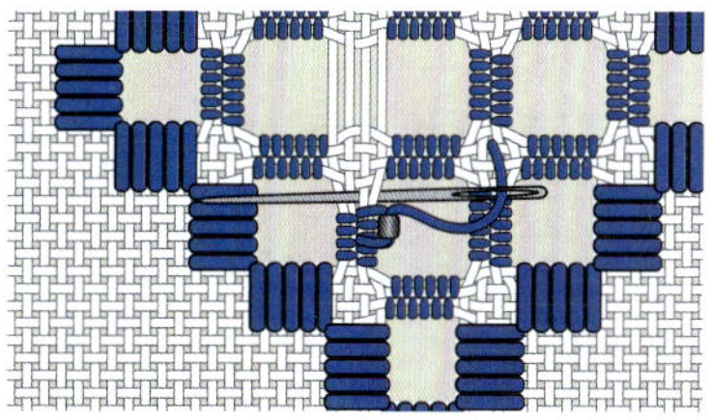

5 Tighten the two stitches so that the bead sits snugly against the side of the bar. Insert the needle to continue weaving as before.

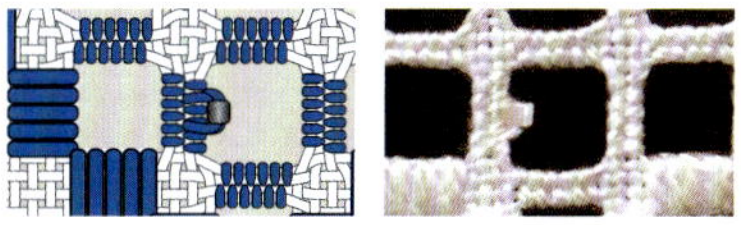

6 The completed bead picot.

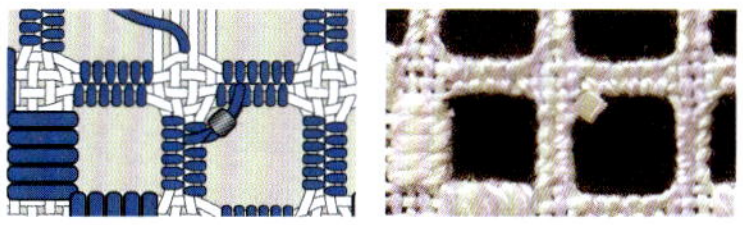

! *These bead picots can also be worked in the corner, between bars.*

bead end-on

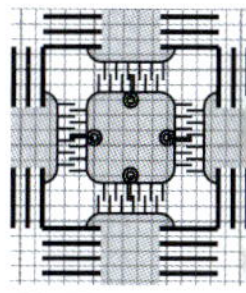

CONTEMPORARY

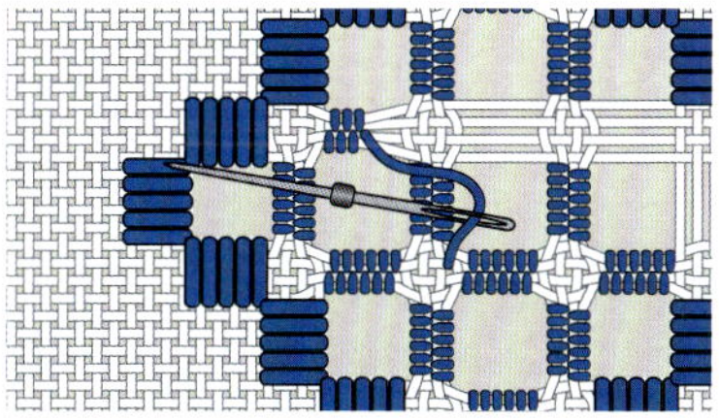

1 Weave to halfway along the bar. Bring the needle out on the side for the bead. Thread the bead onto the needle.

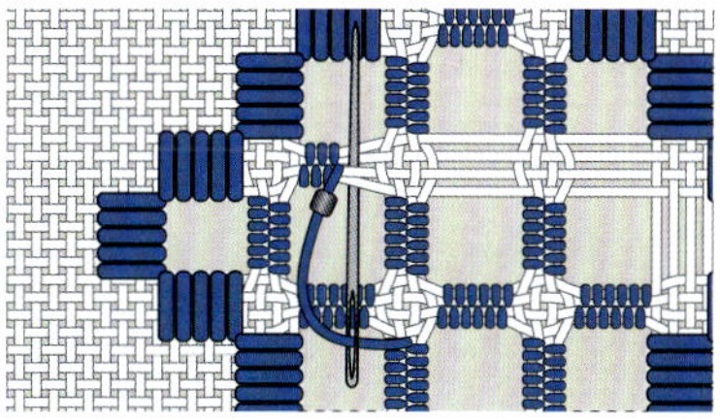

2 Push the bead along the thread to the bar. Continue weaving.

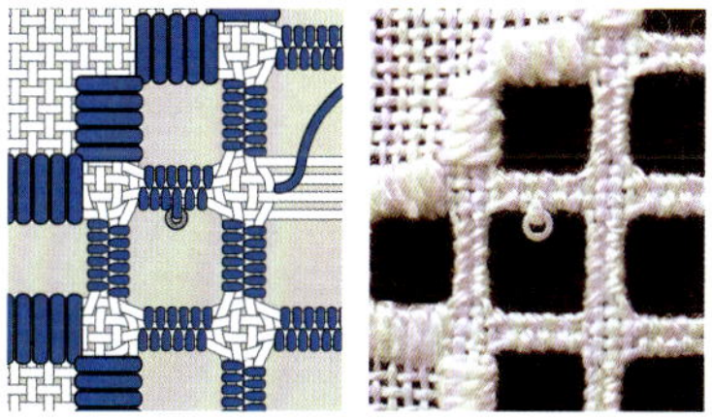

3 Carefully position the bead so that it sits at the side of the bar.

L

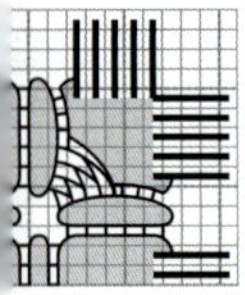

CONTEMPORARY

greek cross *also known as Maltese cross*

The Greek cross can be used singly, in a group, in a row, or in reverse. It can be used in conjunction with other stitches to create elaborate combinations.

quarter cross

The quarter cross forms the basis of all the Greek cross variations.

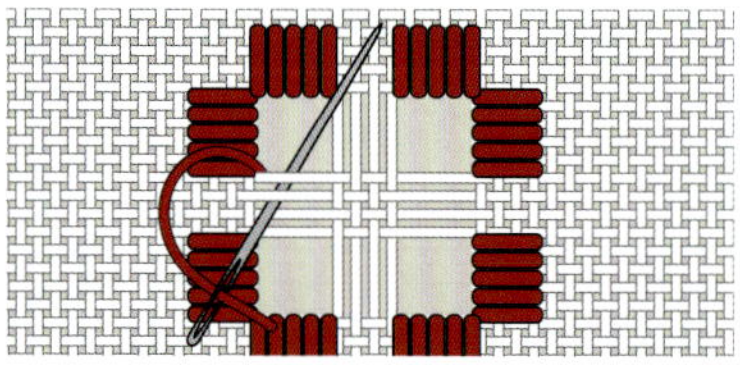

1 Bring the needle out of the fabric above a bar as shown. From below, slide the needle under the top two fabric threads.

2 Tighten the stitch around the fabric threads. Moving right and from below, slide the needle under the same two fabric threads.

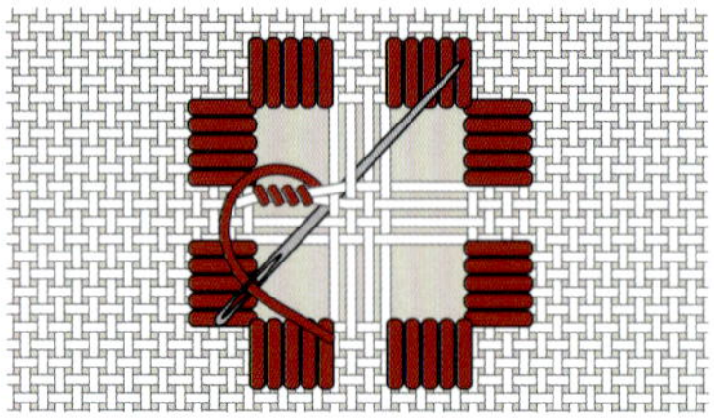

3 Keep wrapping. When there is space for one more stitch, insert the needle below the wrapped bar. Bring it out in the middle of the next bar.

❶ *The wraps should lie next to each other on the bar and not overlap. They do not need to be tightly packed.*

4 Turn the work 45° anticlockwise. From above, slide the needle under the wrapped bar.

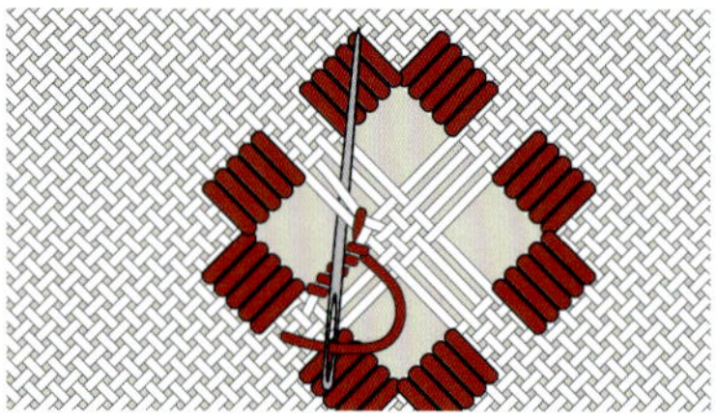

5 Pull the needle through and down to tighten the stitch. From below, slide the needle under the upper two threads as before.

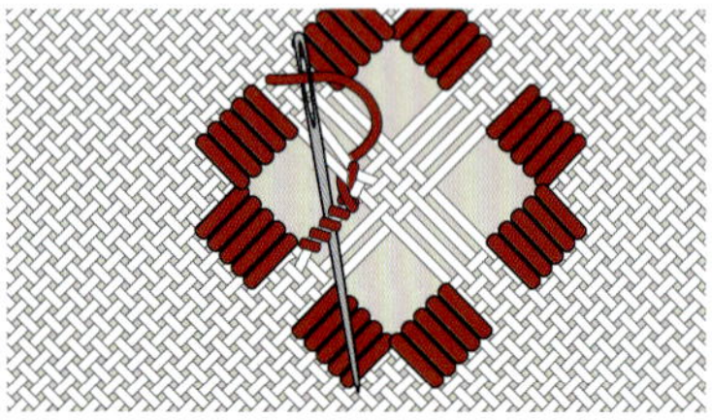

6 Pull the needle through and up to tighten the stitch. From above, slide the needle under the wrapped bar.

❶ *Pull the stitches to tighten them. This pulls the two bars together, and makes gaps on either side of the weaving. The first few stitches should be very tight.*

7 Weave between the two bars, until just over half the distance along the bars is covered. Finish with the needle underneath the upper two threads.

❶ *Each subsequent stitch should be longer than the previous ones. They should not overlap. There should be a smooth curve at the sides.*

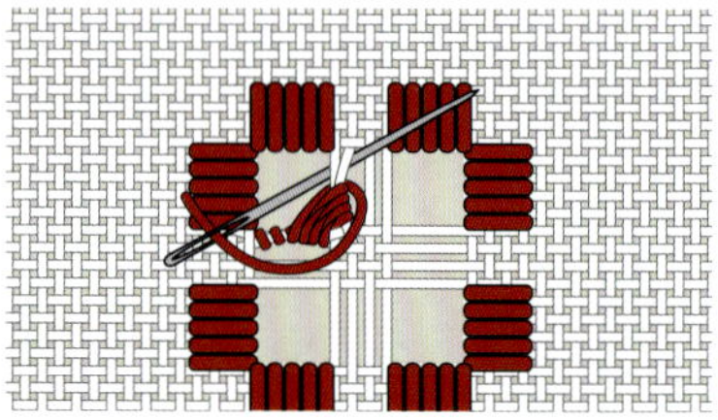

8 Pull the needle through. Turn the work 45° clockwise. From the left, slide the needle under the two unwrapped threads again.

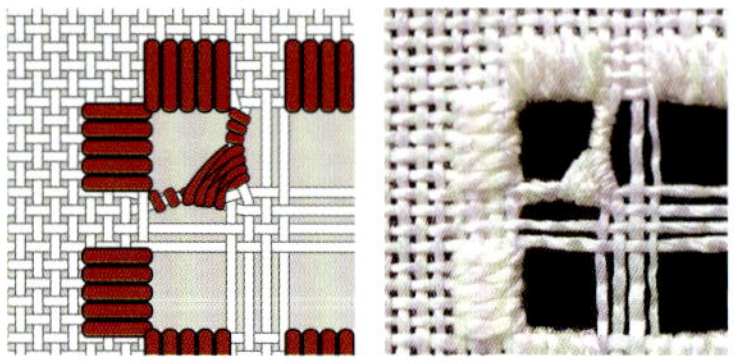

9 Wrap the remainder of the bar, and take the needle to the back.

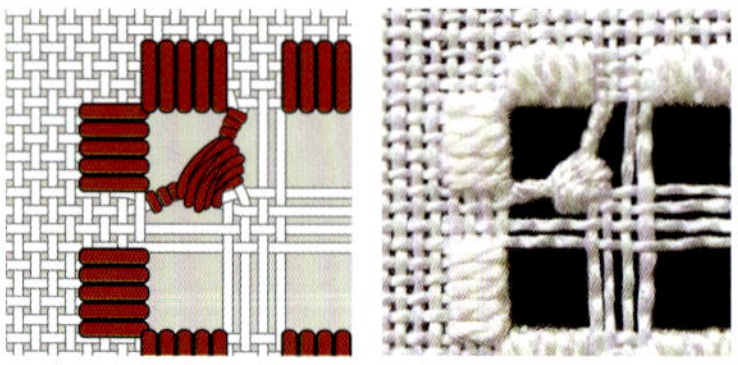

❶ *Stitch tension should not be lumpy and uneven as is shown here.*

greek cross

To make a full Greek cross, work a quarter cross in each quadrant.

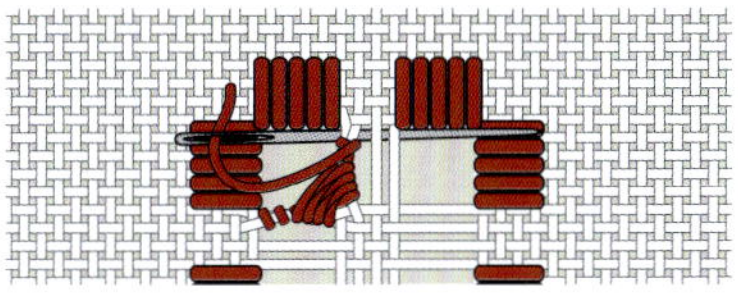

1 Work a quarter cross in the first quadrant. Take the needle behind the four fabric threads and bring it out in the next quadrant.

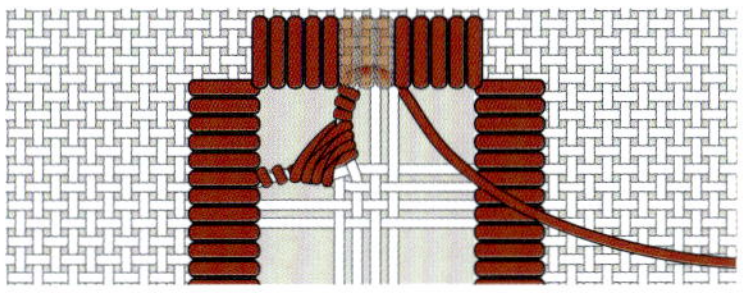

❗ *If the satin stitch square has no gaps at the side, take the needle through the intervening satin stitching on the back and bring it out in the next quadrant.*

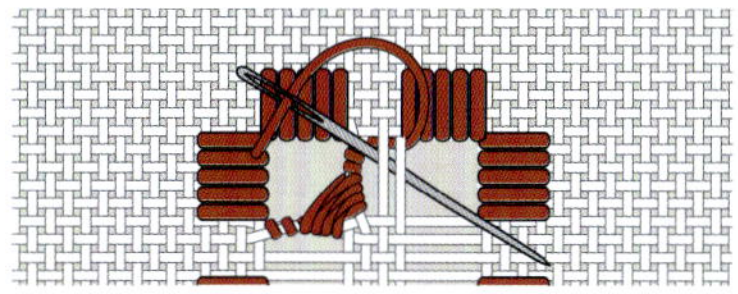

2 From the left, slide the needle under the right two fabric threads.

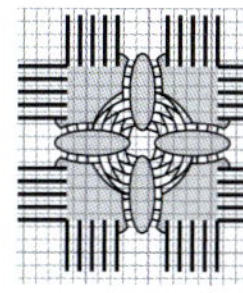

CONTEMPORARY

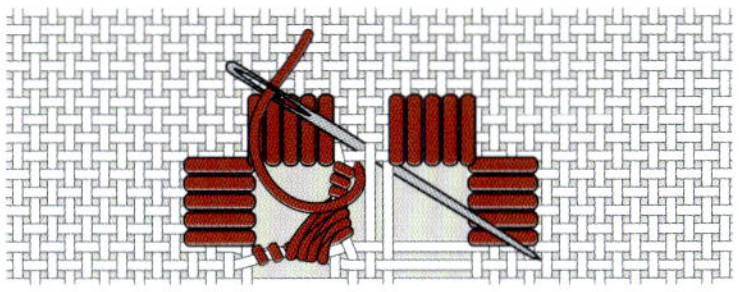

❗ *If preferred, bring the needle up between the bars and insert it one above before bringing it out ready to continue. This 'extra stitch' can be useful for 'hiding' thread movements.*

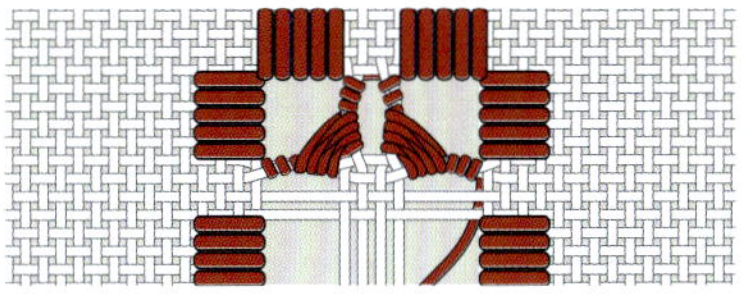

3 Work another quarter cross, using the same stitch quantity as before.

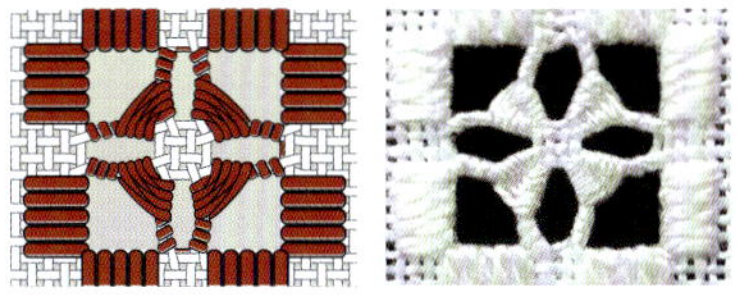

4 Continue until the square is filled.

reverse greek cross

In this Greek cross variation, the quarter crosses face inward rather than outward.

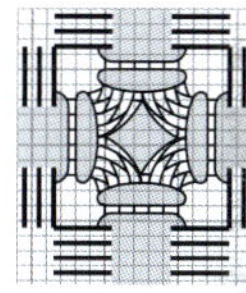

CONTEMPORARY

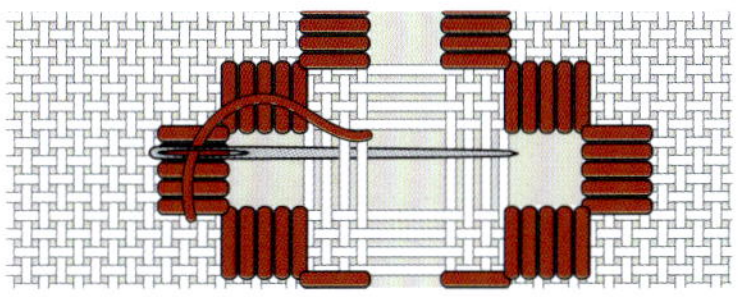

1 Bring the needle and thread out in the top left inner corner. From the left, slide the needle under the two threads just left of this.

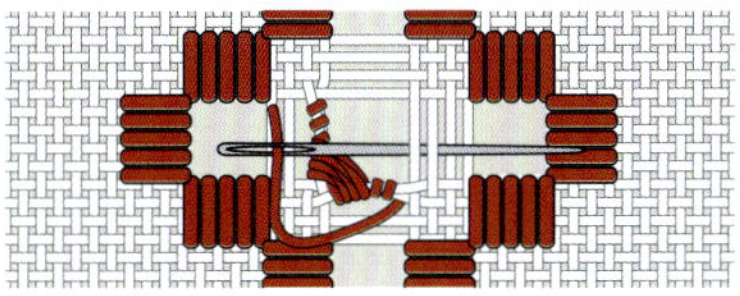

2 Pull the needle through and work a quarter cross. Moving on to the next one, slide the needle under the two closest threads of the adjacent bar.

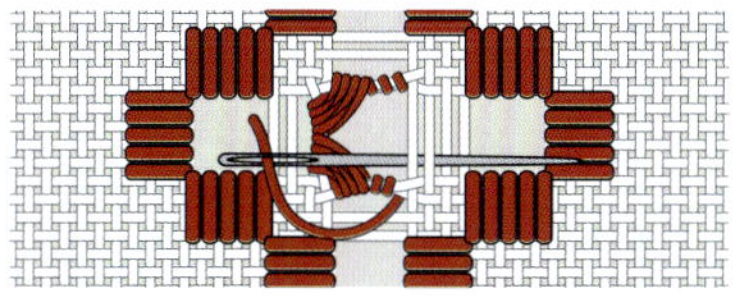

3 Turn the work 90° clockwise. Work a quarter cross between the next two bars. Slide the needle under the two closest threads of the adjacent bar.

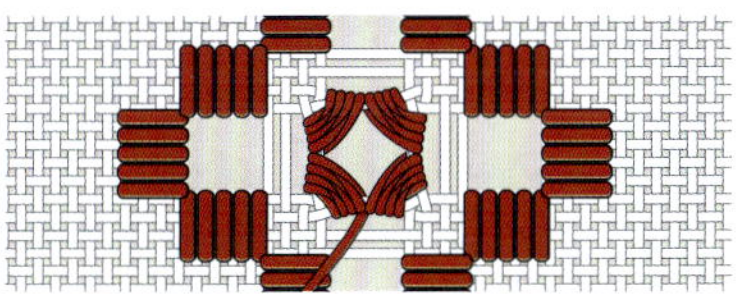

4 Turn the work as required and work a quarter cross in the next two corners.
❗ *You won't be able to wrap the final section of bar because there is already stitching there.*

5 From the centre, insert the needle into the closest side of the first quarter cross, and bring the needle out in the first corner, on the back.
❗ *It goes through the first quarter cross.*

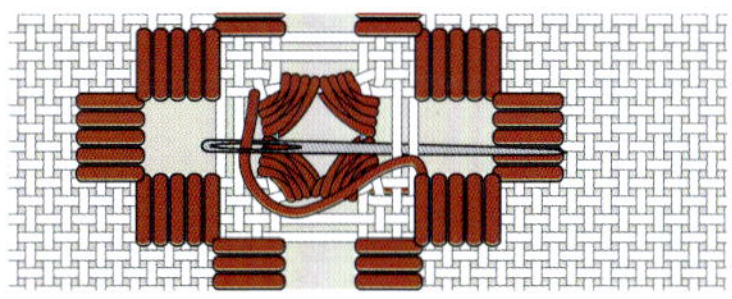

6 Bring the needle out on the far side of the adjacent bar. Slide the needle under the two fabric threads.

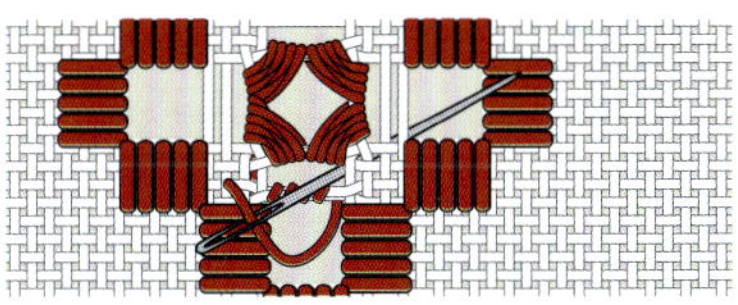

6 Wrap the rest of the bar. Turn the work 90° clockwise. Insert the needle in the gap above the bar and bring it out on the far side of the next two fabric threads.
❗ *Don't overwrap the bar.*

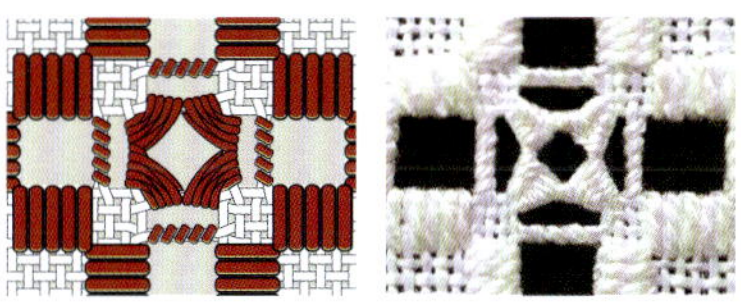

7 Wrap the rest of the bars. To finish take the needle to the back and finish the thread under the satin stitching on the back.
❗ *To work in rows, adapt 'Dove's Eye in a Wrapped Circle Rows' on page 107.*

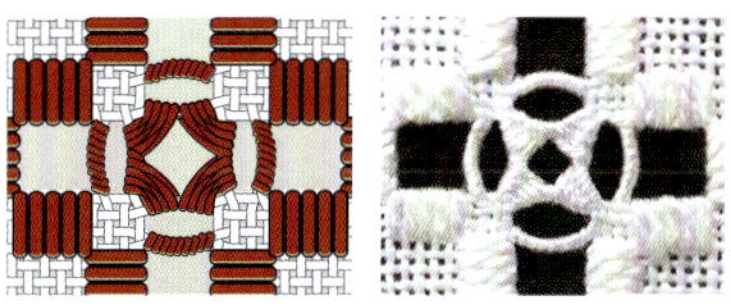

❗ *By overwrapping the bars (cramming in too many wraps), you can force them to bend outwards, making a circle around the reverse Greek cross.*
❗ *To work in rows, adapt 'Dove's Eye in a Wrapped Circle Rows' on page 107.*

R

greek cross *also known as Maltese cross*

The Greek cross can be used singly, in a group, in a row, or in reverse. It can be used in conjunction with other stitches to create elaborate combinations.

CONTEMPORARY

quarter cross

The quarter cross forms the basis of all the Greek cross variations.

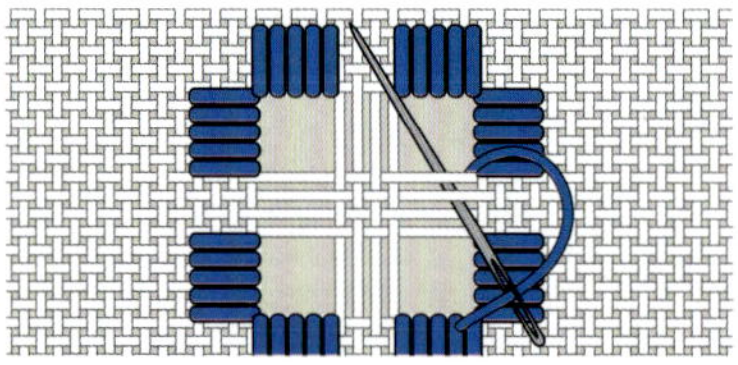

1 Bring the needle out of the fabric above a bar as shown. From below, slide the needle under the top two fabric threads.

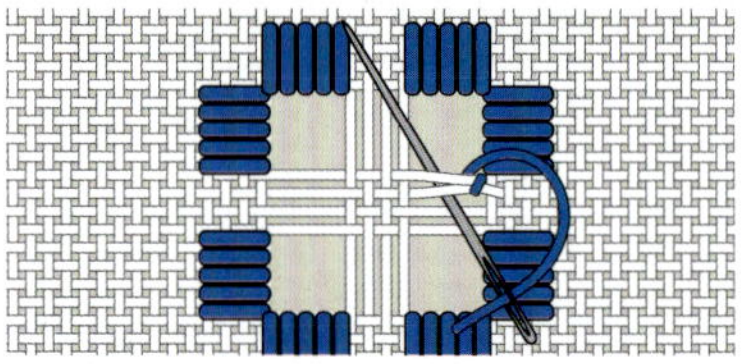

2 Tighten the stitch around the fabric threads. Moving left and from below, slide the needle under the same two fabric threads.

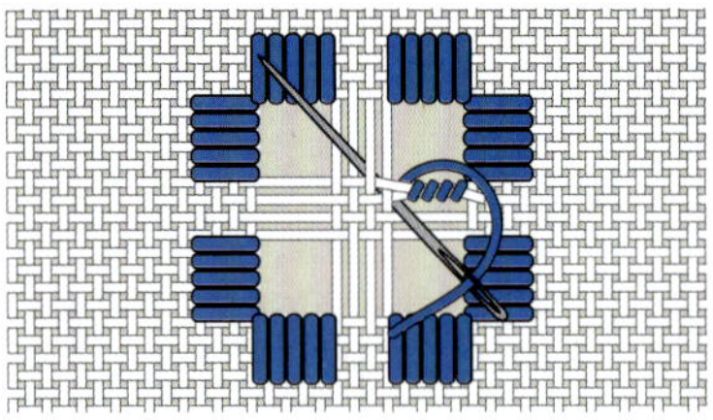

3 Keep wrapping. When there is space for one more stitch, insert the needle below the wrapped bar. Bring it out in the middle of the next bar.

❶ *The wraps should lie next to each other on the bar and not overlap. They do not need to be tightly packed.*

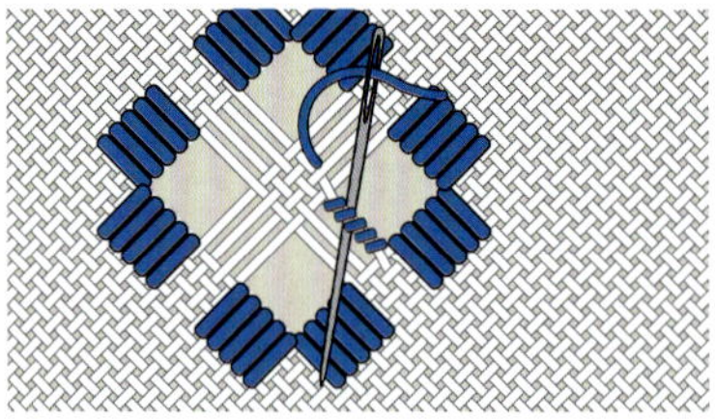

4 Turn the work 45° clockwise. From above, slide the needle under the wrapped bar.

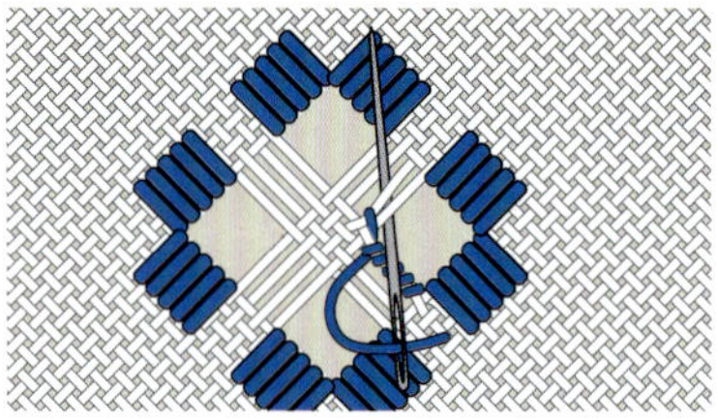

5 Pull the needle through and down to tighten the stitch. From below, slide the needle under the upper two threads as before.

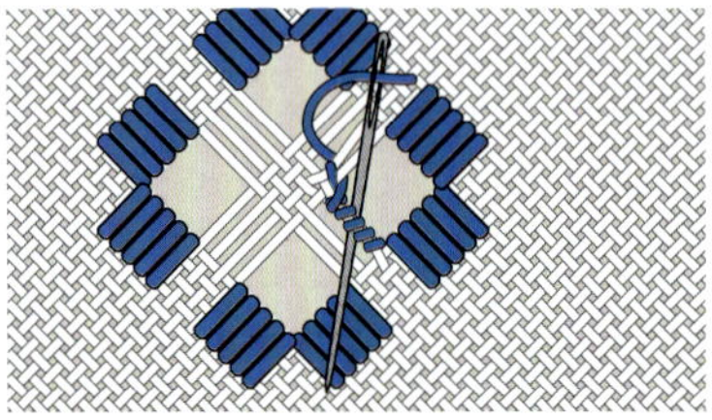

6 Pull the needle through and up to tighten the stitch. From above, slide the needle under the wrapped bar.

❶ *Pull the stitches to tighten them. This pulls the two bars together, and makes gaps on either side of the weaving. The first few stitches should be very tight.*

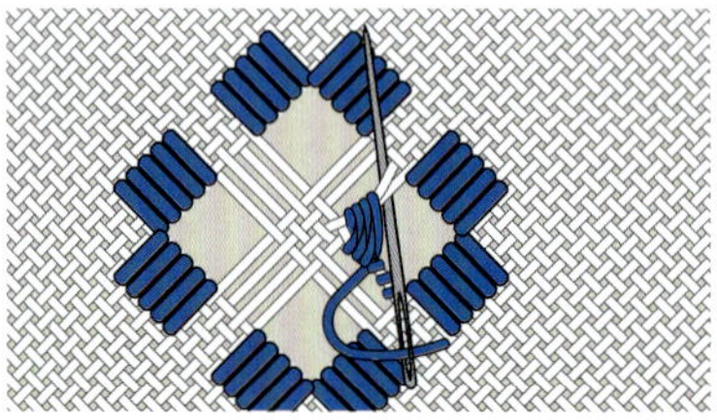

7 Weave between the two bars, until just over half the distance along the bars is covered. Finish with the needle underneath the upper two threads.

❶ *Each subsequent stitch should be longer than the previous ones. They should not overlap. There should be a smooth curve at the sides.*

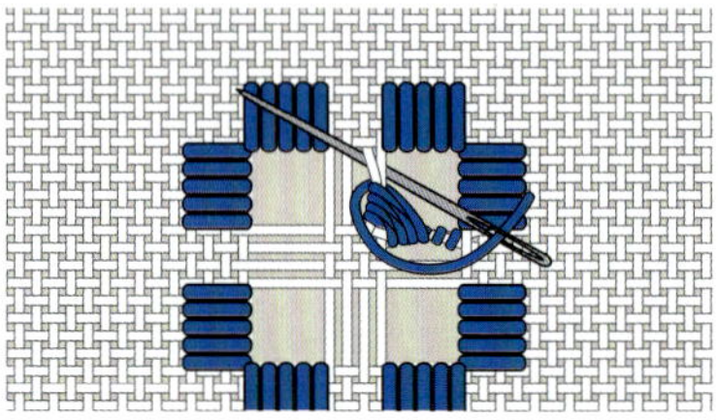

8 Pull the needle through. Turn the work 45° anticlockwise. From the left, slide the needle under the two unwrapped threads again.

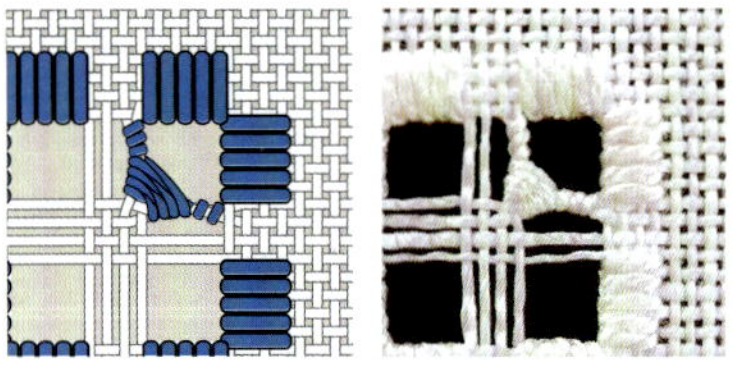

9 Wrap the remainder of the bar, and take the needle to the back.

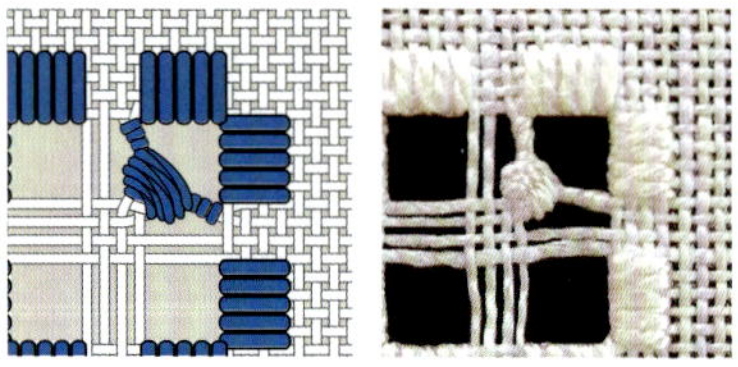

❶ *Stitch tension should not be lumpy and uneven as is shown here.*

greek cross

To make a full Greek cross, work a quarter cross in each quadrant.

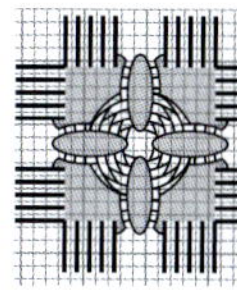

CONTEMPORARY

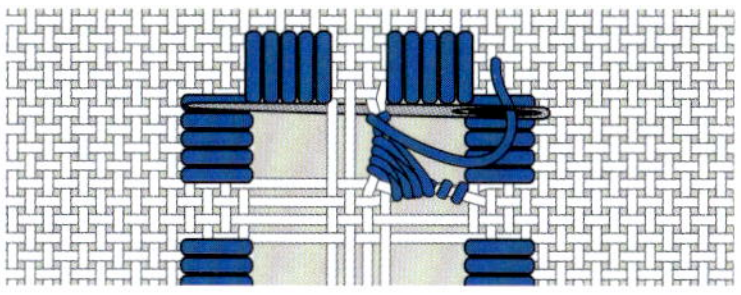

1 Work a quarter cross in the first quadrant. Take the needle behind the four fabric threads and bring it out in the next quadrant.

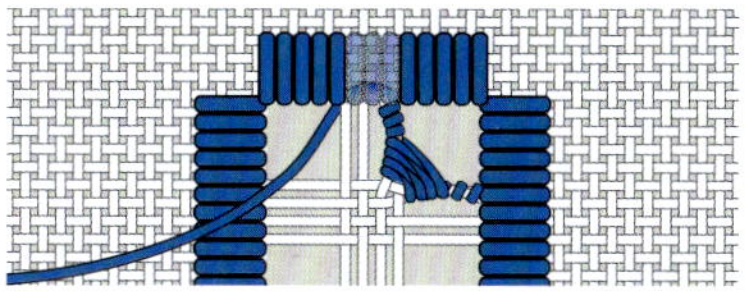

❶ *If the satin stitch square has no gaps at the side, take the needle through the intervening satin stitching on the back and bring it out in the next quadrant.*

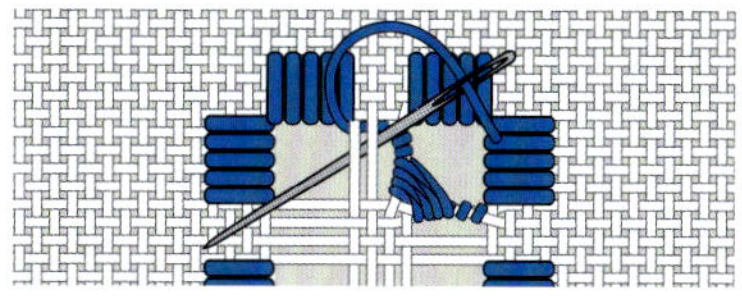

2 From the right, slide the needle under the left two fabric threads.

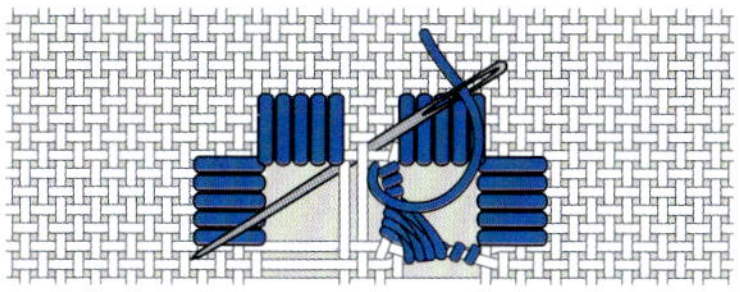

❶ *If preferred, bring the needle up between the bars and insert it one above before bringing it out ready to continue. This 'extra stitch' can be useful for 'hiding' thread movements.*

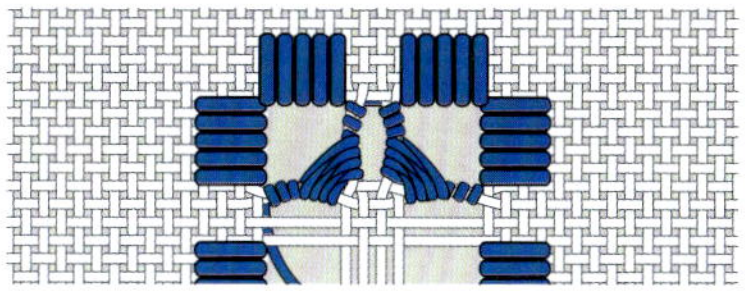

3 Work another quarter cross, using the same stitch quantity as before.

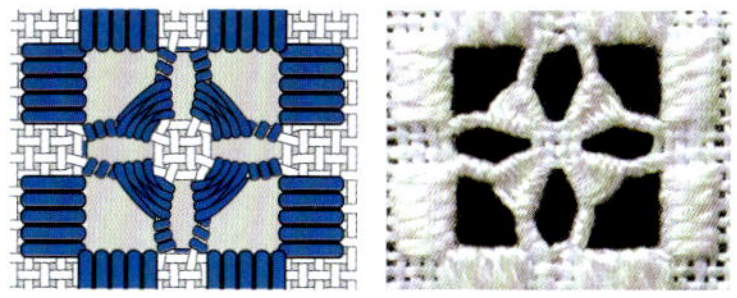

4 Continue until the square is filled.

reverse greek cross

In this Greek cross variation, the quarter crosses face inward rather than outward.

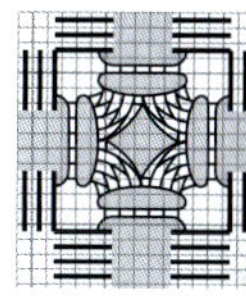

CONTEMPORARY

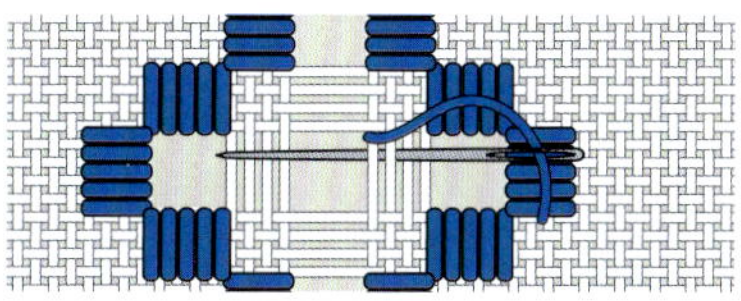

1 Bring the needle and thread out in the top right inner corner. From the right, slide the needle under the two threads just right of this.

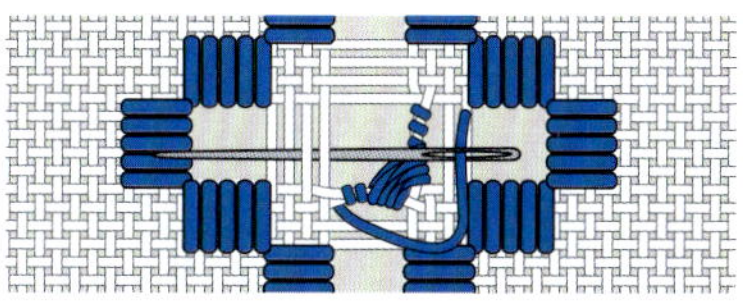

2 Pull the needle through and work a quarter cross. Moving on to the next one, slide the needle under the two closest threads of the adjacent bar.

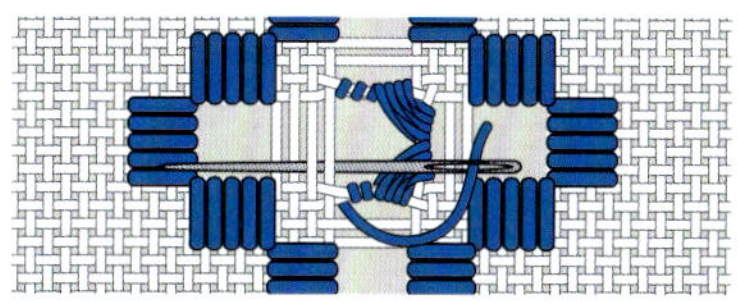

3 Turn the work 90° anticlockwise. Work a quarter cross between the next two bars. Slide the needle under the two closest threads of the adjacent bar.

4 Turn the work as required and work a quarter cross in the next two corners.
❶ *You won't be able to wrap the final section of bar because there is already stitching there.*

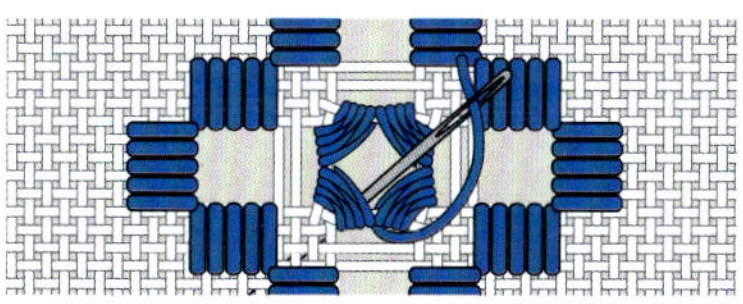

5 From the centre, insert the needle into the closest side of the first quarter cross, and bring the needle out in the first corner, on the back.
❶ *It goes through the first quarter cross.*

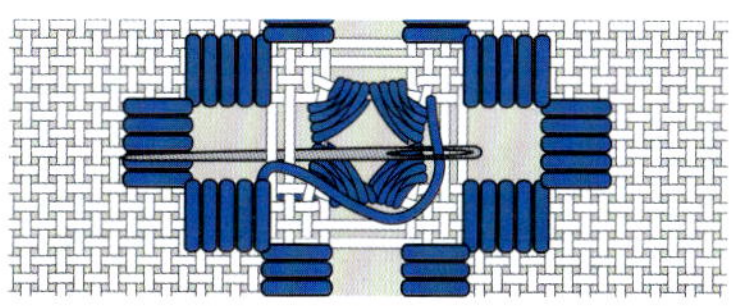

6 Bring the needle out on the far side of the adjacent bar. Slide the needle under the two fabric threads.

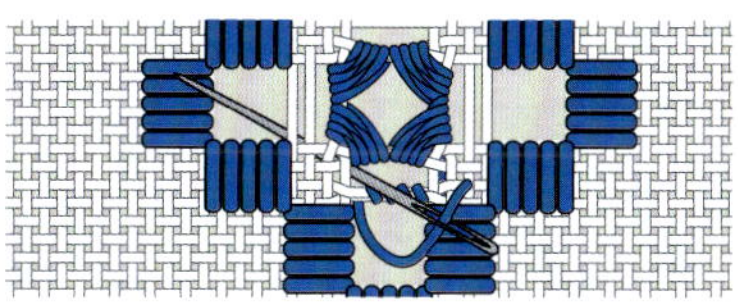

7 Wrap the rest of the bar. Turn the work 90° anticlockwise. Insert the needle in the gap above the bar and bring it out on the far side of the next two fabric threads.
❶ *Don't overwrap the bar.*

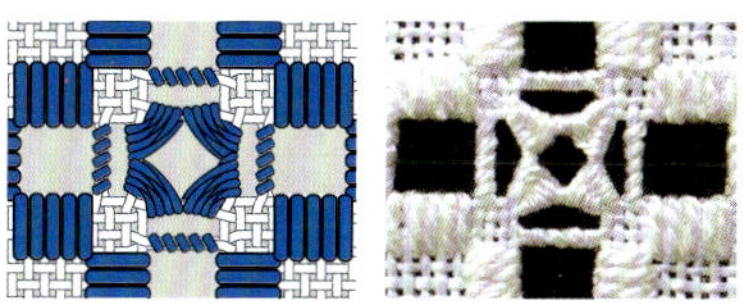

7 Wrap the rest of the bars. To finish take the needle to the back and finish the thread under the satin stitching on the back.
❶ *To work in rows, adapt 'Dove's Eye in a Wrapped Circle Rows' on page 109.*

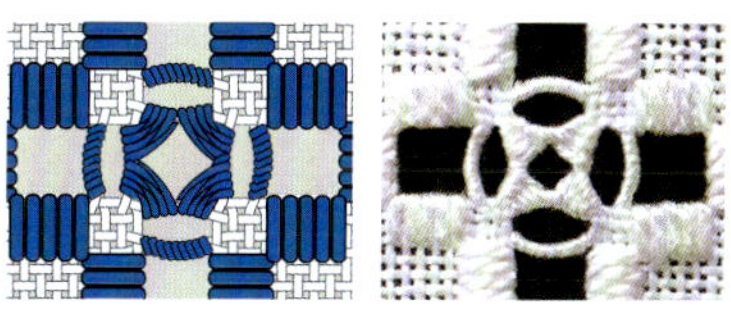

❶ *By overwrapping the bars (cramming in too many wraps), you can force them to bend outwards, making a circle around the reverse Greek cross.*
❶ *To work in rows, adapt 'Dove's Eye in a Wrapped Circle Rows' on page 109.*

L

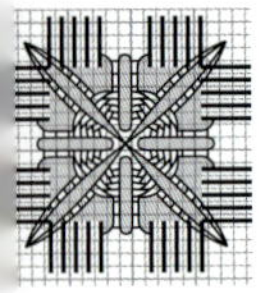

CONTEMPORARY

greek eighth cross

Each section is half the width of a Greek quarter cross, giving it the name Greek eighth cross.

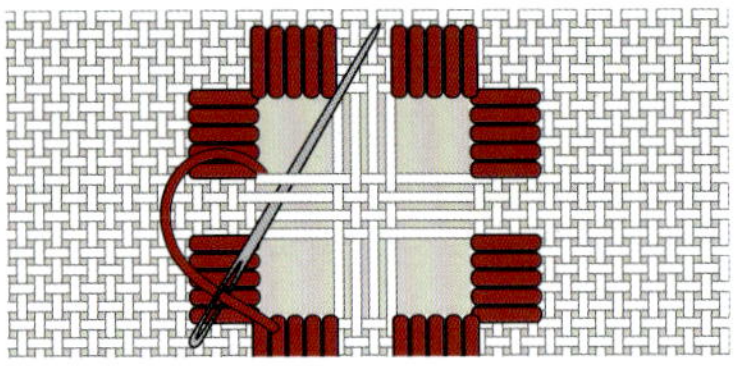

1 Bring the needle out of the fabric above a bar as shown. From below, slide the needle under the upper two fabric threads.

2 Moving right, keep wrapping. To complete the bar, insert the needle below the wraps. Bring it out in the woven square's centre.

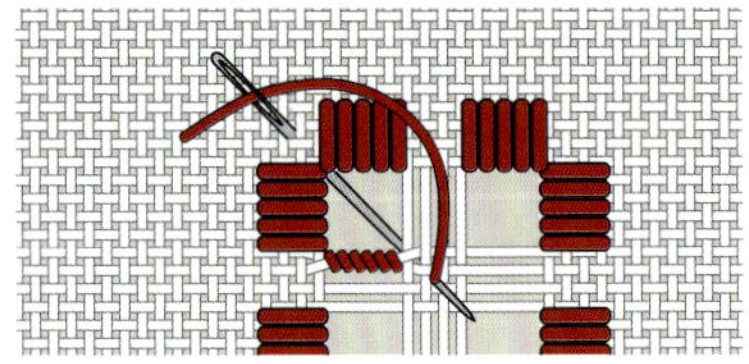

3 In the top left quadrant, insert the needle in the far corner's front, two threads from the cut edges. Bring it out in the woven square's centre.

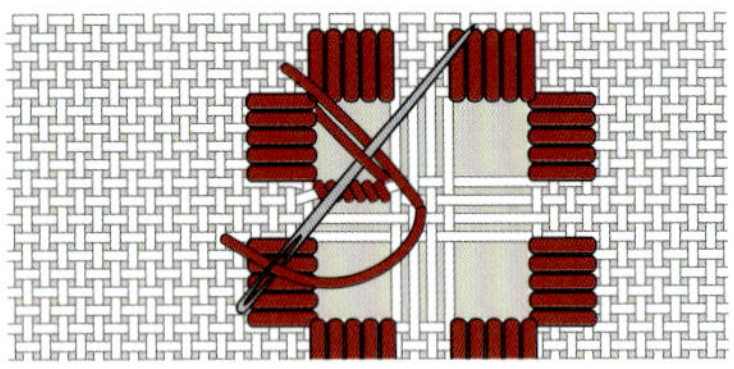

4 Pull the needle through to tighten the stitches. Keeping the tension, from below, slide the needle under the diagonal stitch which sits beneath the fabric.

! *The diagonal stitch becomes one side of the eighth cross.*

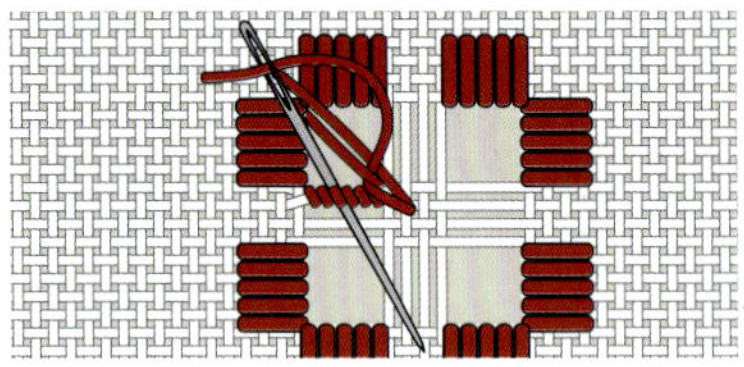

5 From above, slide the needle under the wrapped threads, making sure both diagonal stitches stay tight.

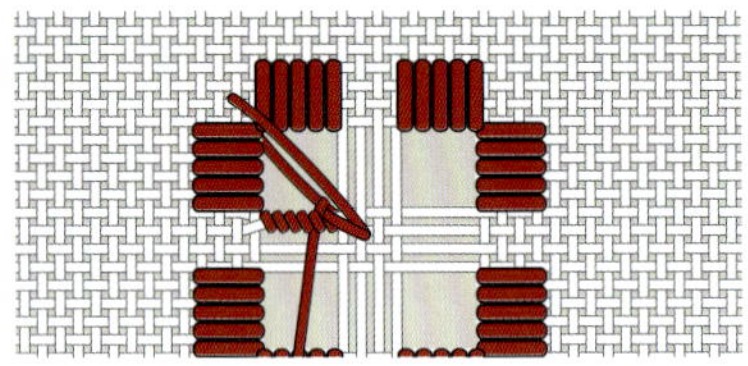

6 Pull the thread to tighten the stitch in towards the woven square, allowing the diagonal to pull inward slightly, and no more.

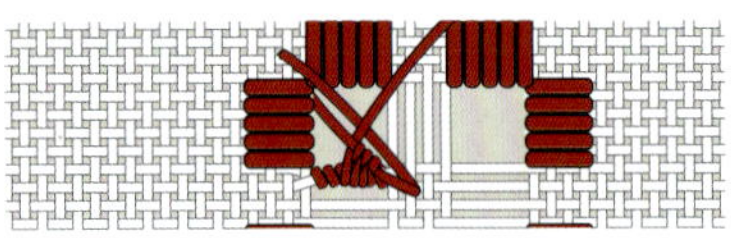

7 Continue to weave back and forth, so just over half the wrapped bar is covered, ensuring the sides have smooth curves and no bumps.

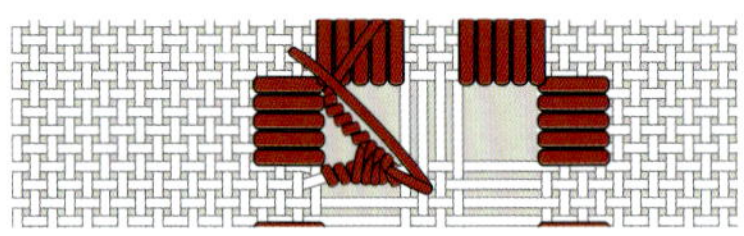

8 Wrap the remainder of the diagonal stitch, and bring the thread out on the far side of the other diagonal stitch.

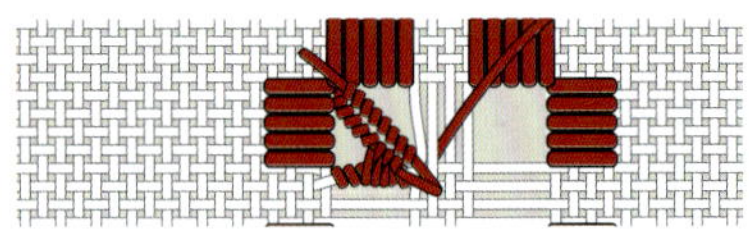

9 Wrap the upper diagonal stitch and bring the thread out in the middle of the adjacent bar's threads.

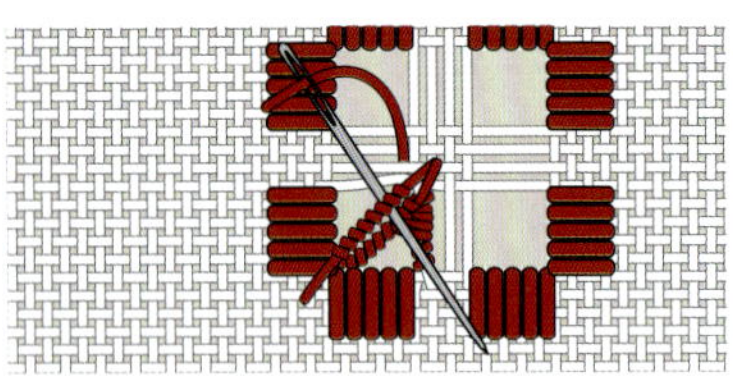

10 Turn the work 90° anticlockwise. From above left, slide the needle under the wrapped diagonal.

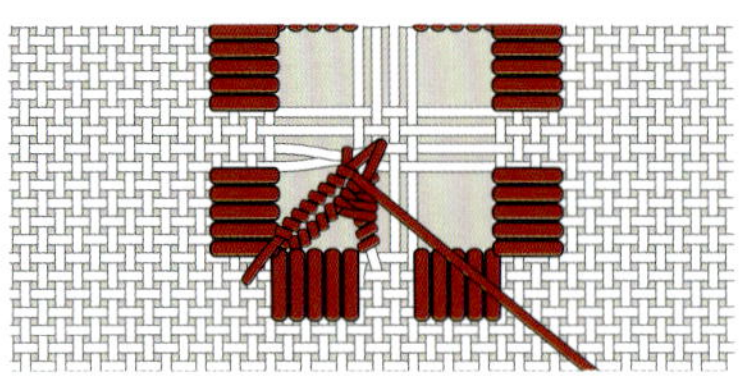

11 Pull the thread to tighten the stitch and pull the bar threads inward slightly.

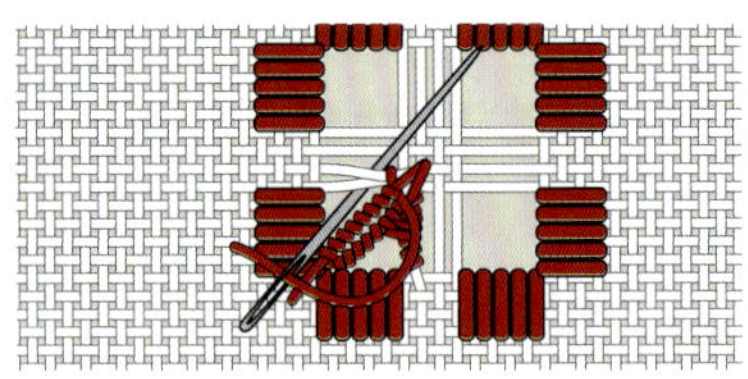

12 From below, slide the needle under the lower two bar threads.

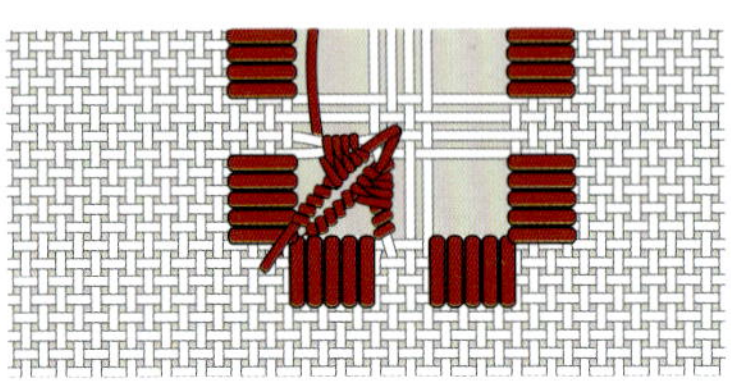

13 Weave back and forth for the same distance as the previous one, ensuring the sides have smooth curves.

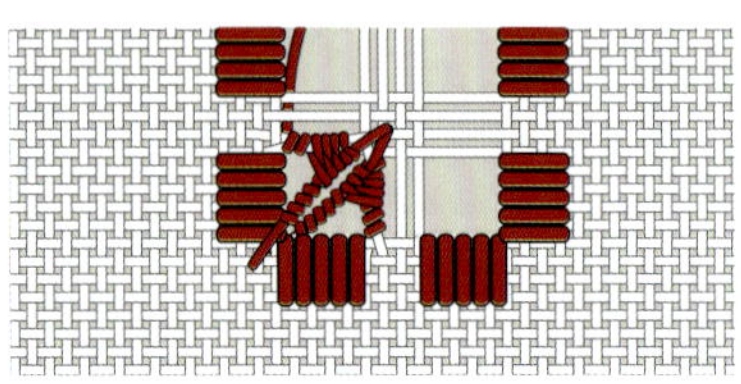

14 Wrap the rest of the bar and bring the thread out in the next quadrant.

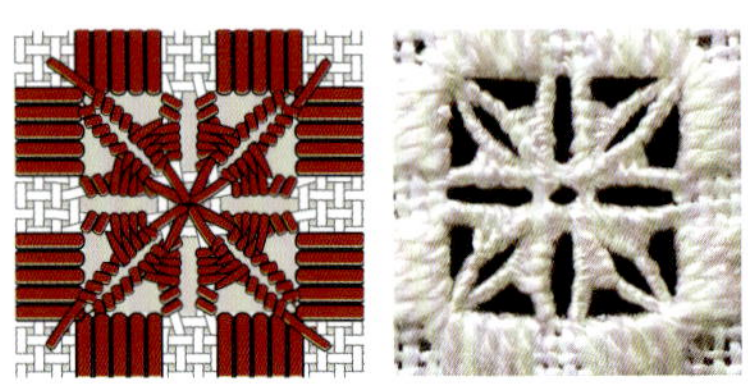

15 Repeat the two eighth crosses in each quadrant.

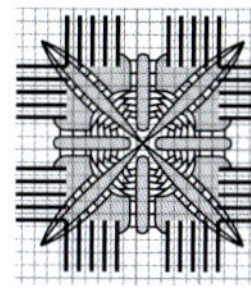

greek eighth cross

Each section is half the width of a Greek quarter cross, giving it the name Greek eighth cross.

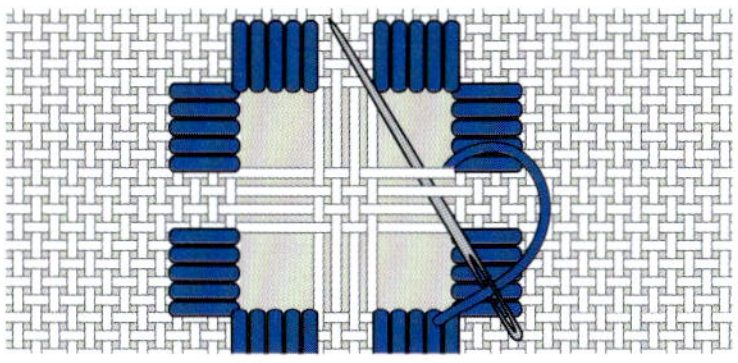

1 Bring the needle out of the fabric below a bar as shown. From below, slide the needle under the upper two fabric threads.

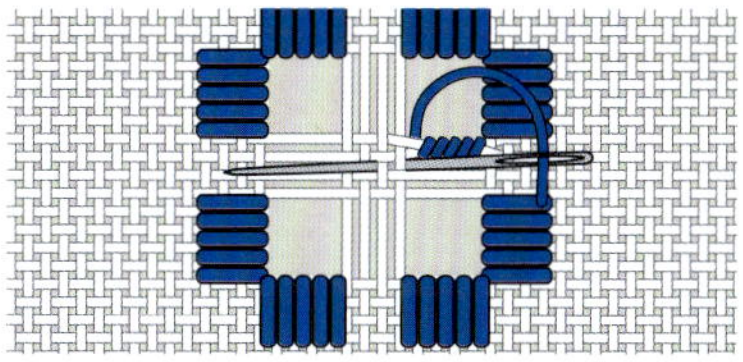

2 Moving left, keep wrapping. When there is space for one more stitch, insert the needle above the wrapped bar. Bring it out in the middle of the woven square.

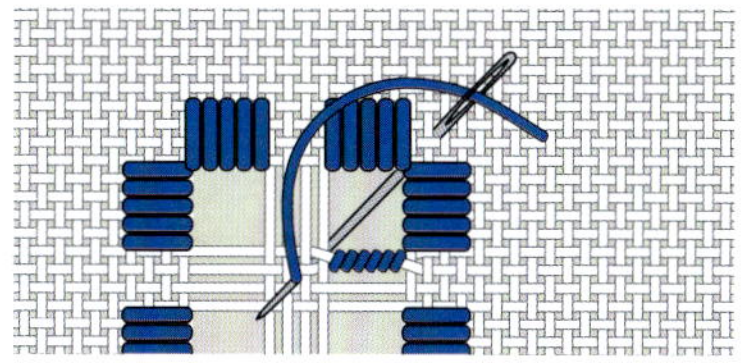

3 Working in the top right quadrant, insert the needle in the front of the far corner, two threads away from the cut edges. Bring it out again in the woven square's centre.

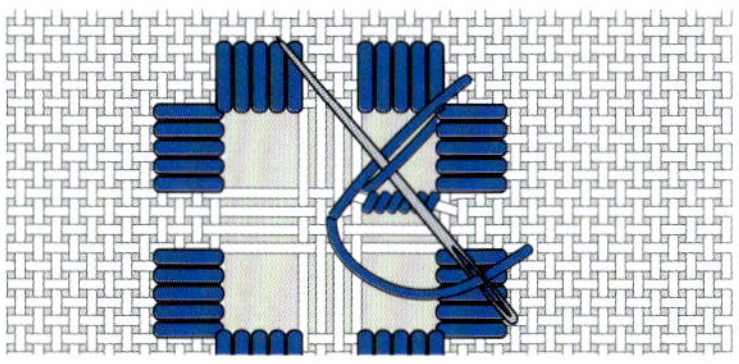

4 Pull the needle through to tighten the stitches. Keeping the tension, from above, slide the needle under the diagonal stitch which sits beneath the fabric.

❶ *The diagonal stitch becomes one side of the eighth cross.*

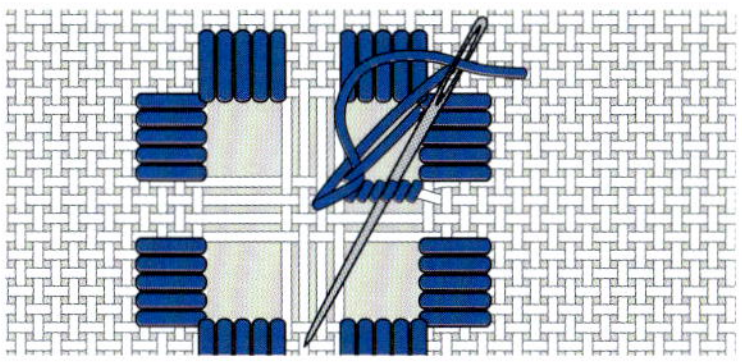

5 From above, slide the needle under the wrapped threads, making sure both diagonal stitches stay tight.

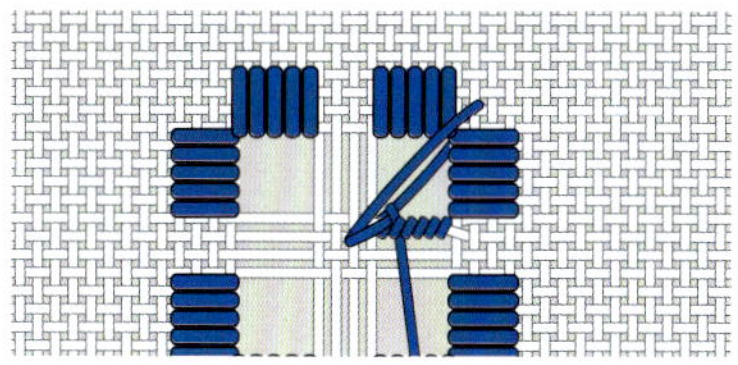

6 Pull the thread to tighten the stitch in towards the woven square, allowing the diagonal to pull inward slightly, and no more.

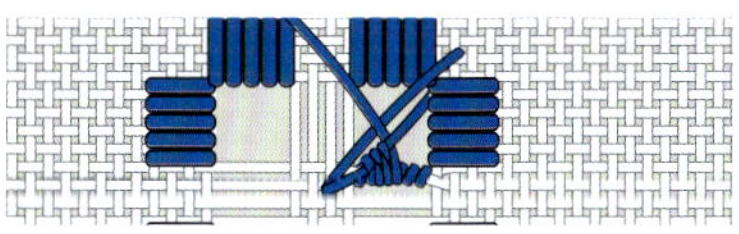

7 Continue to weave back and forth, so just over half the wrapped bar is covered, ensuring the sides have smooth curves and no bumps.

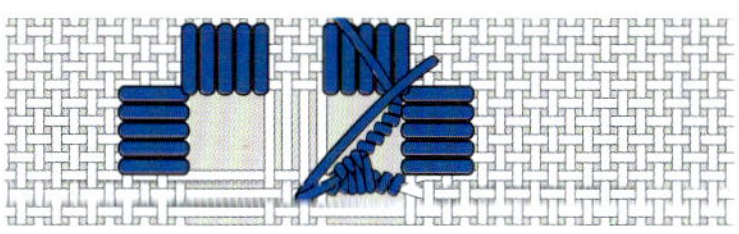

8 Wrap the remainder of the diagonal stitch, and bring the thread out on the far side of the other diagonal stitch.

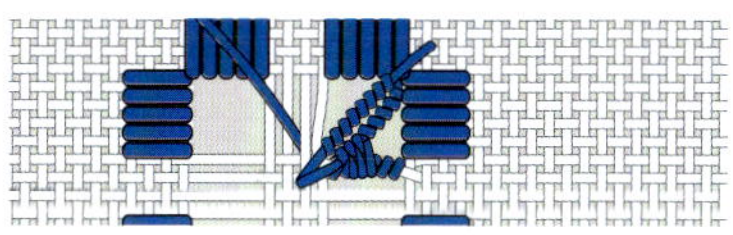

9 Wrap the upper diagonal stitch and bring the thread out in the middle of the adjacent bar's threads.

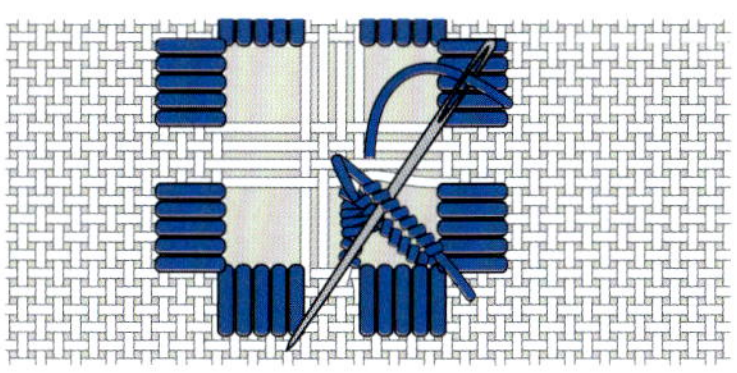

10 Turn the work 90° clockwise. From above right, slide the needle under the wrapped diagonal.

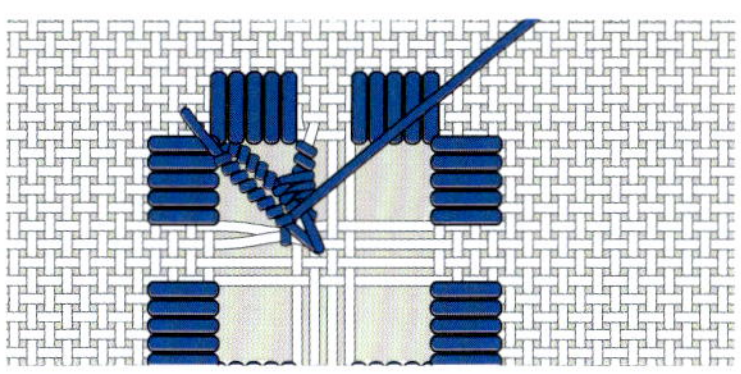

11 Pull the thread to tighten the stitch and pull the bar threads inward slightly.

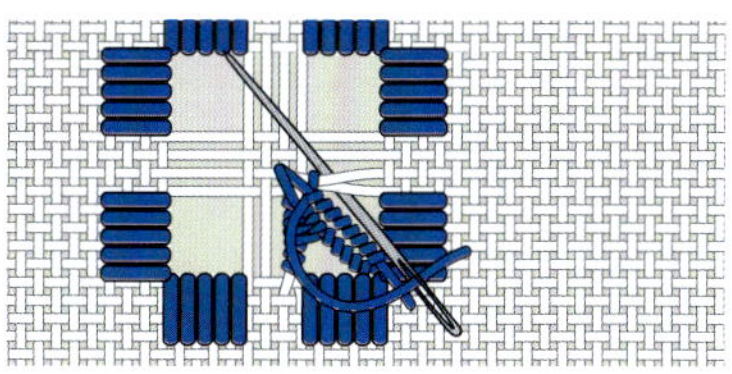

12 From below, slide the needle under the lower two bar threads.

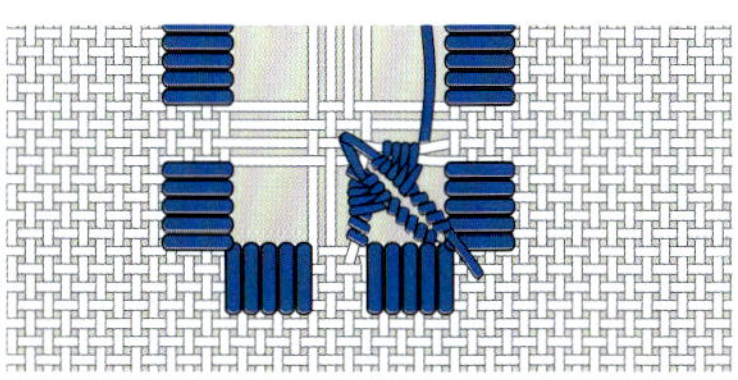

13 Weave back and forth for the same distance as the previous one, ensuring the sides have smooth curves.

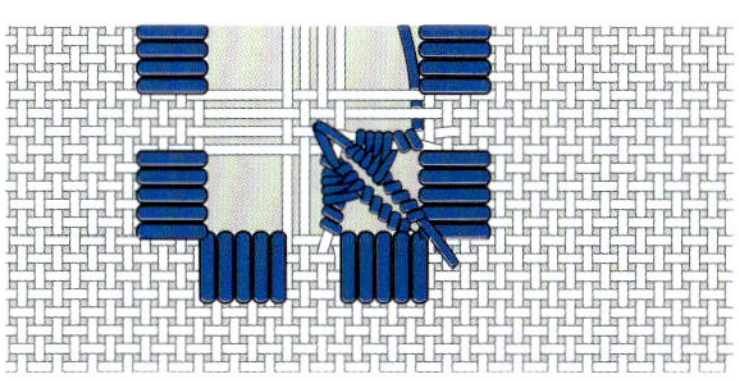

14 Wrap the rest of the bar and bring the thread out in the next quadrant.

15 Repeat the two eighth crosses in each quadrant.

L

CONTEMPORARY

greek cross border *also known as Greek cross ribbon*

Greek crosses can be worked in rows to fill long narrow cutwork areas. The shape shown will be worked in two rows: one on the inside of the corner, and one on the outside.

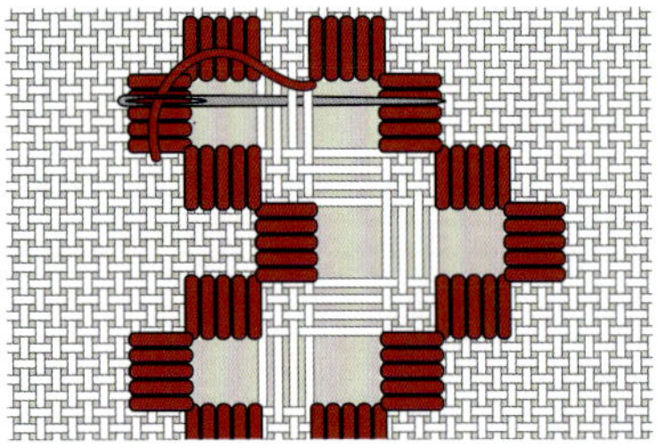

1 Bring the needle out at the top right end of a line of bars, beside the bar. From the left, slide the needle under the two fabric threads closest to where the thread came out.

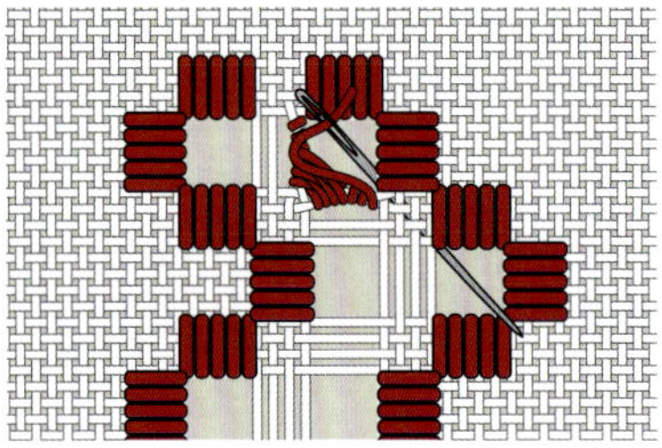

2 Work a quarter cross in the corner between the bar and the next bar. Take the needle behind the intervening woven square and bring it up beside the next bar.

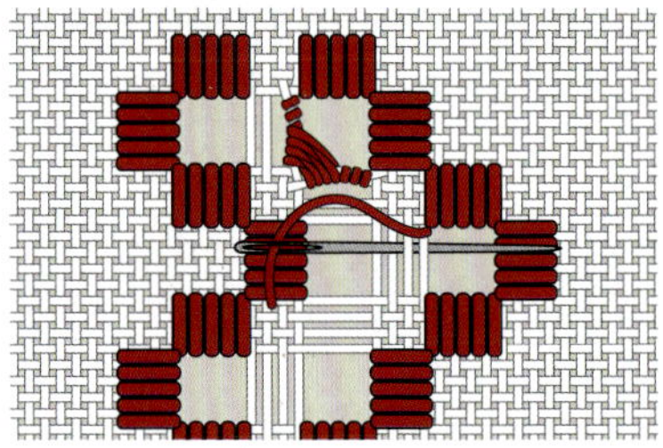

3 From the left, slide the needle under the two closest threads.

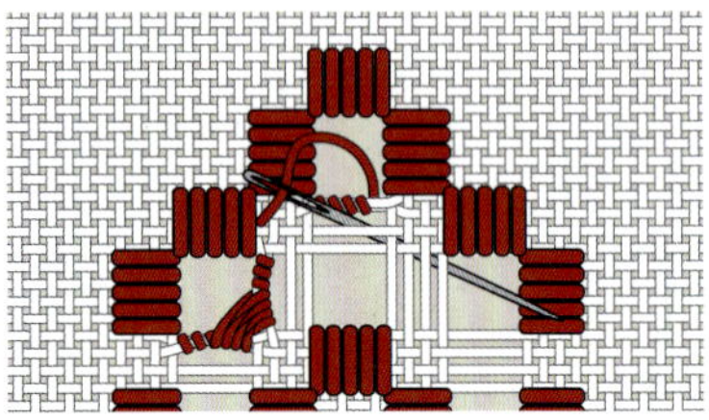

4 Wrap the rest of the bar. Turn the work 90° anticlockwise. Pass the needle behind the woven square and bring it up beside the next bar.

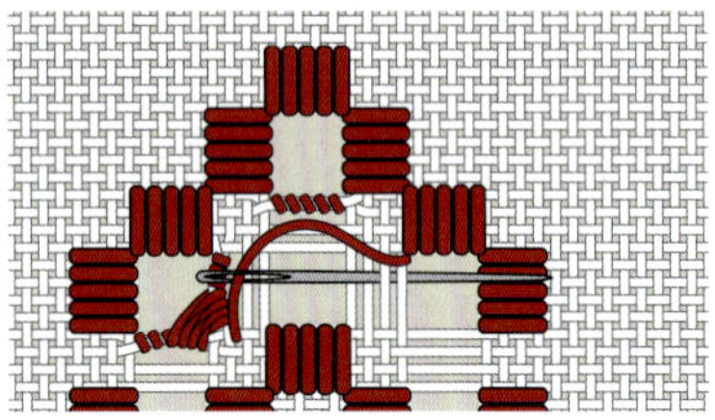

5 From the left, slide the needle under the two fabric threads closest to where the thread came out.

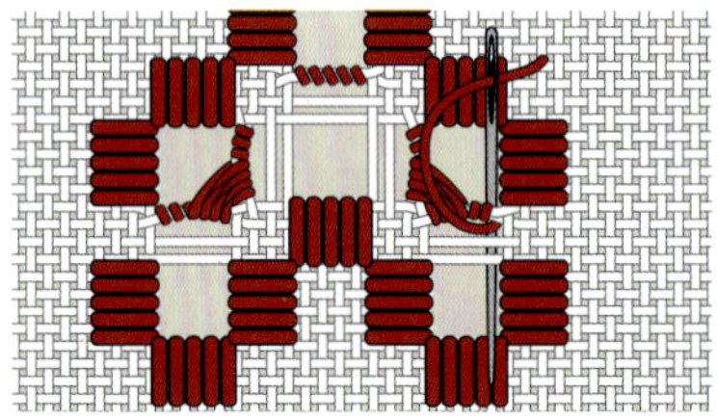

6 Work a quarter cross in the corner between the bar and the next bar. To start the new row, bring the needle out on the other side of the bar.

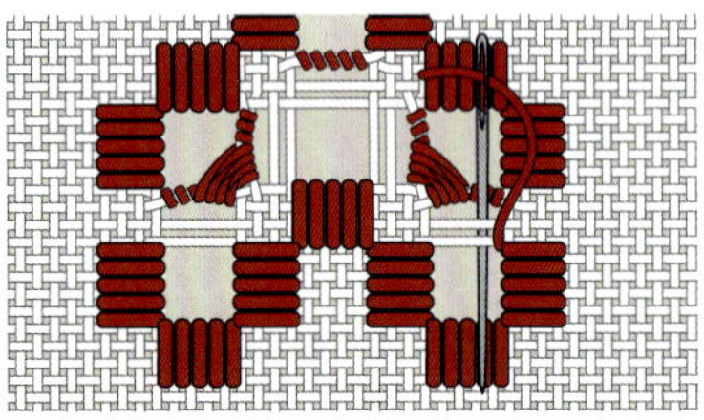

7 From above, slide the needle under the lower two fabric threads.

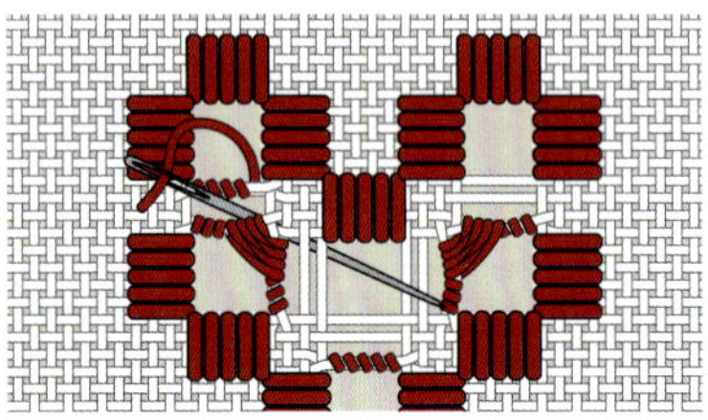

8 Turn the work 180°. Wrap the rest of the bar. Pass the needle behind the intervening woven square and bring it up beside the next bar.

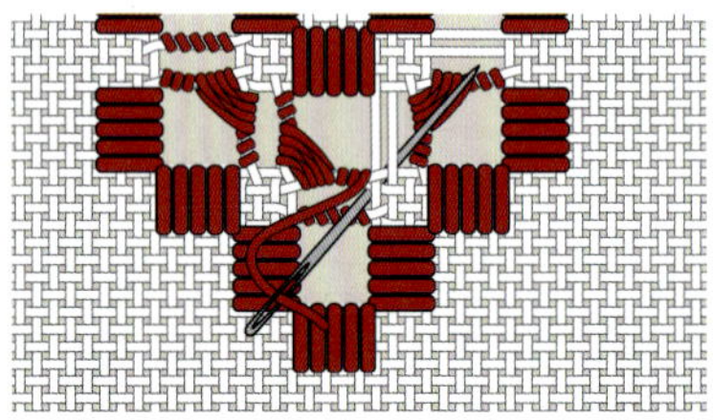

9 Work a quarter cross in the corner between the bar and the next bar. Take the needle behind the intervening woven square and bring it up beside the next bar.

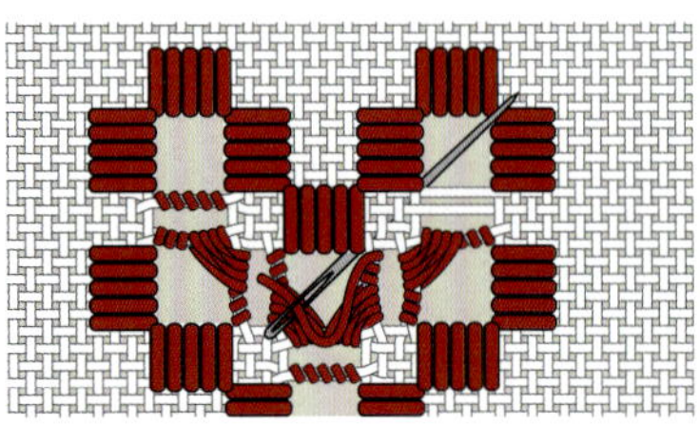

10 Work another quarter cross between the two bars. Pass the needle behind the woven square and bring it up beside the final bar.

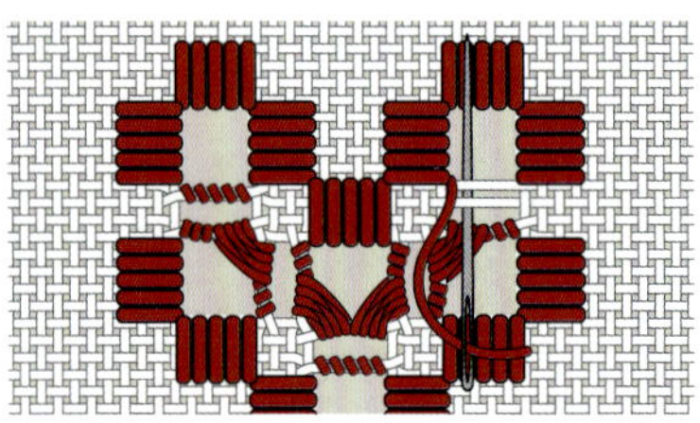

11 From below, slide the needle under the two threads.

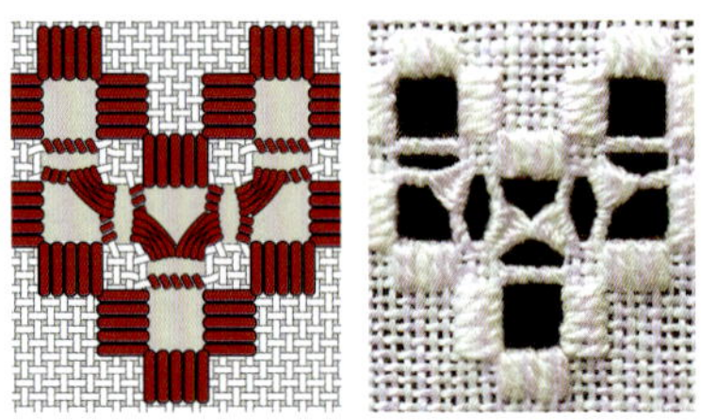

12 Wrap the remainder of the bar and finish the thread in the back of the satin stitching, on the back.

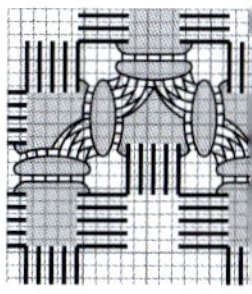

greek cross border *also known as Greek cross ribbon*

Greek crosses can be worked in rows to fill long narrow cutwork areas. The shape shown will be worked in two rows: one on the inside of the corner, and one on the outside.

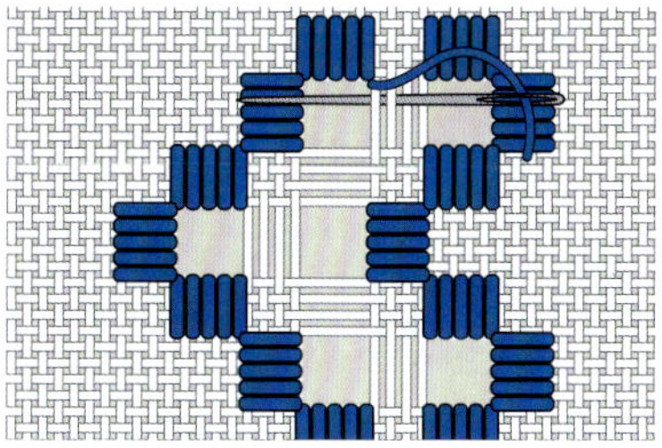

1 Bring the needle out at the top left end of a line of bars, beside the bar. From the right, slide the needle under the two fabric threads closest to where the thread came out.

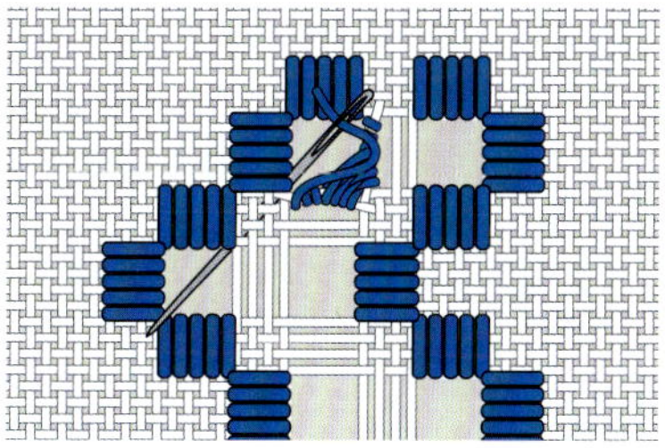

2 Work a quarter cross in the corner between the bar and the next bar. Take the needle behind the intervening woven square and bring it up beside the next bar.

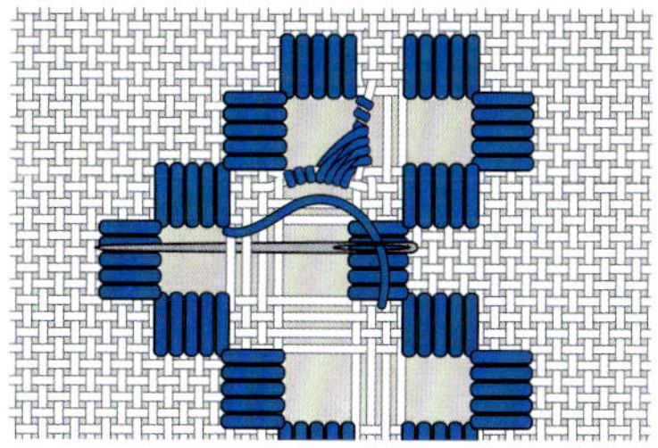

3 From the right, slide the needle under the two closest threads.

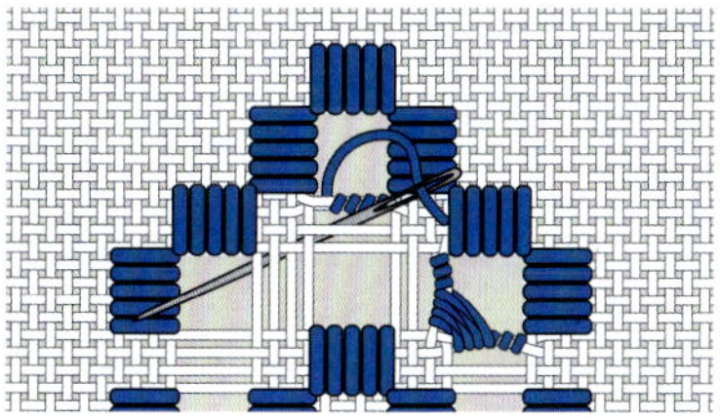

4 Wrap the rest of the bar. Turn the work 90° clockwise. Pass the needle behind the woven square and bring it up beside the next bar.

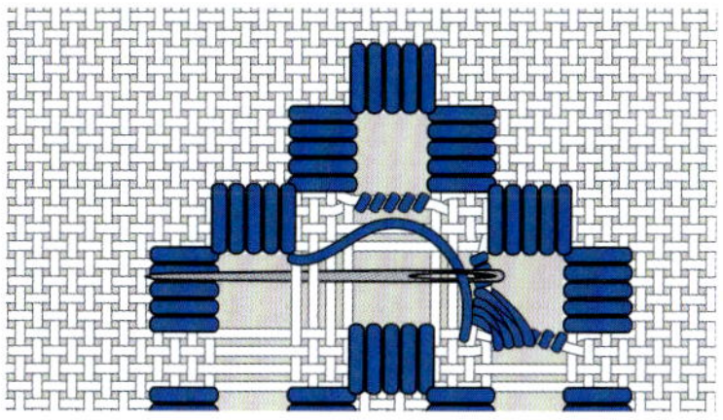

5 From the right, slide the needle under the two fabric threads closest to where the thread came out.

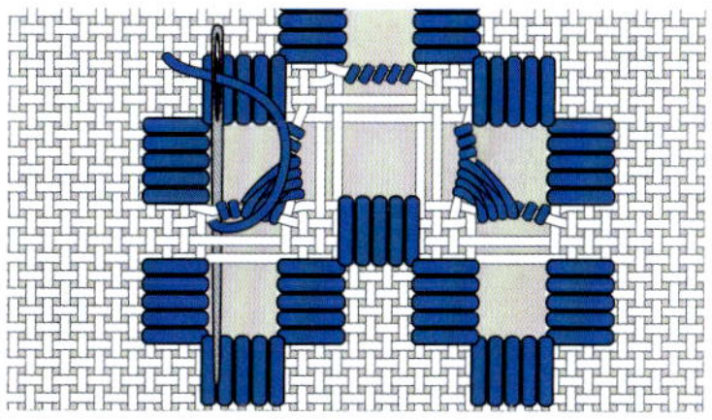

6 Work a quarter cross in the corner between the bar and the next bar. To start the new row, bring the needle out on the other side of the bar.

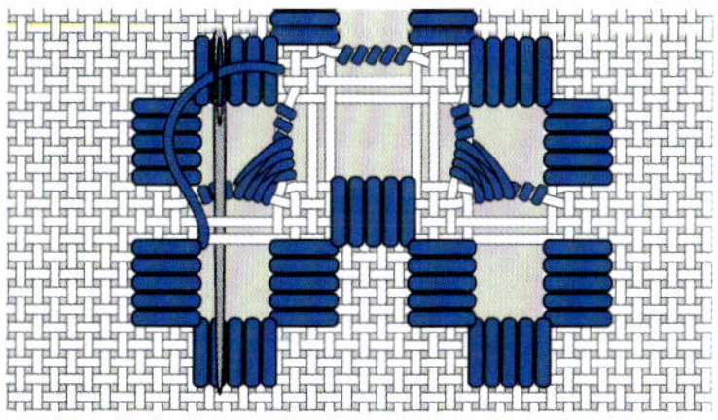

7 From above, slide the needle under the lower two fabric threads.

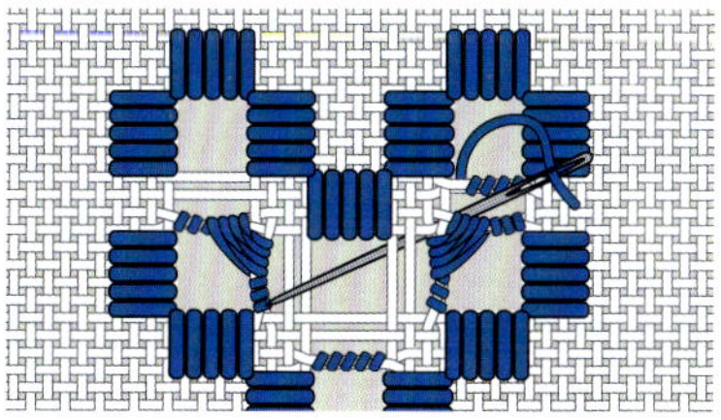

8 Turn the work 180°. Wrap the rest of the bar. Pass the needle behind the intervening woven square and bring it up beside the next bar.

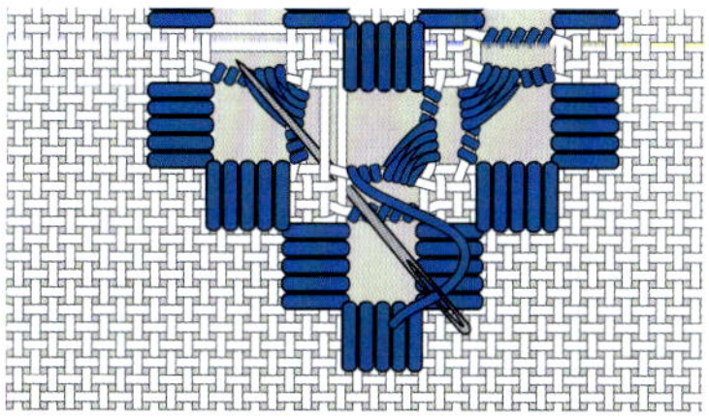

9 Work a quarter cross in the corner between the bar and the next bar. Take the needle behind the intervening woven square and bring it up beside the next bar.

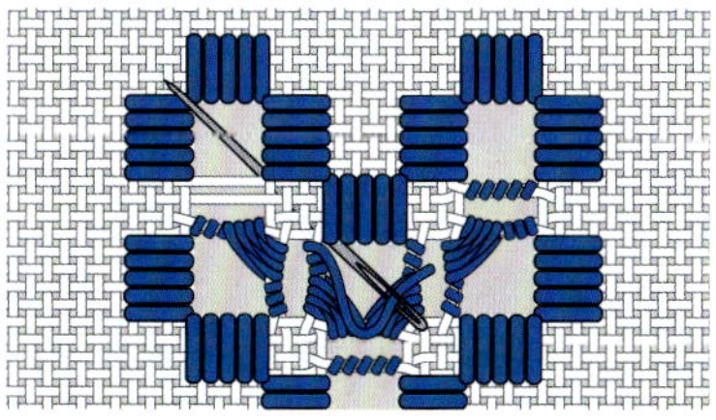

10 Work another quarter cross between the two bars. Pass the needle behind the woven square and bring it up beside the final bar.

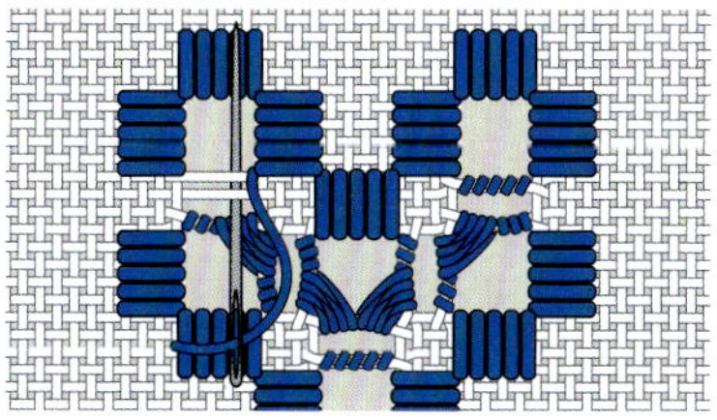

11 From below, slide the needle under the two threads.

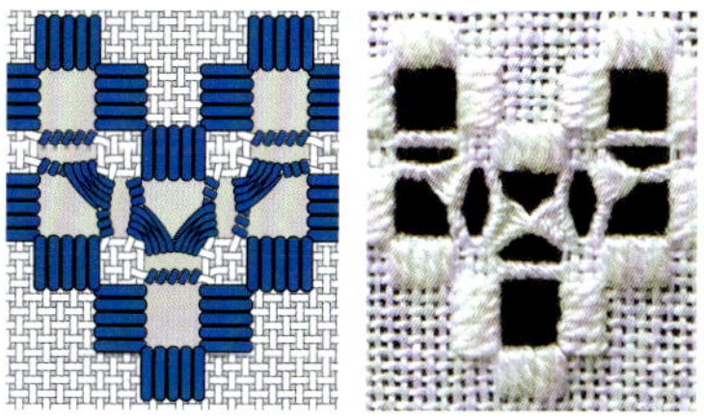

12 Wrap the remainder of the bar and finish the thread in the back of the satin stitching, on the back.

greek cross circlet

This motif is worked using quarter crosses. It can be worked in the satin stitch shape as shown or as part of a cutwork area.

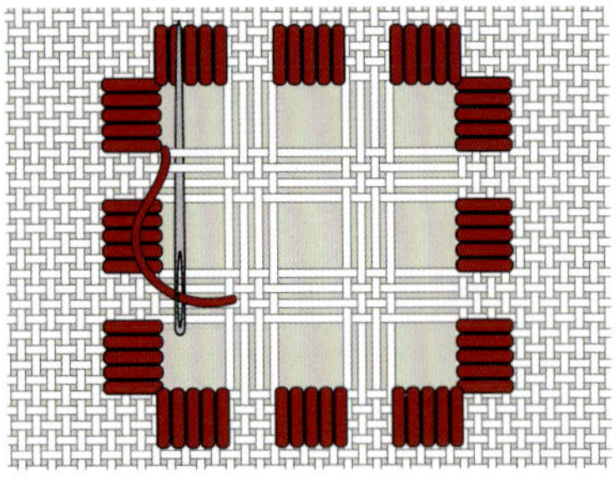

1 Bring the needle out in the top left corner open square, and slide it under the top two threads of the uppermost horizontal bar.

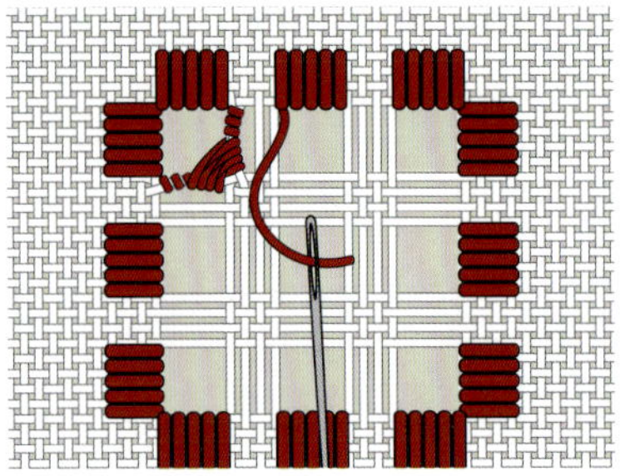

2 Work a quarter cross in the corner between the bar and the next bar. Bring the needle up in the next open square.

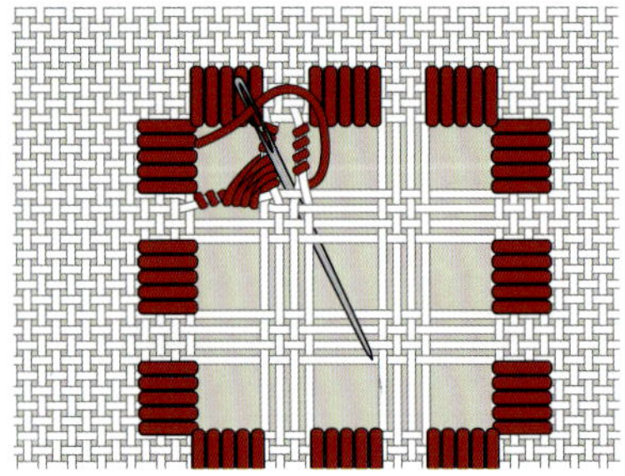

3 Wrap the two uncovered threads of the bar. Take the needle behind the woven square to come out in the centre open square.

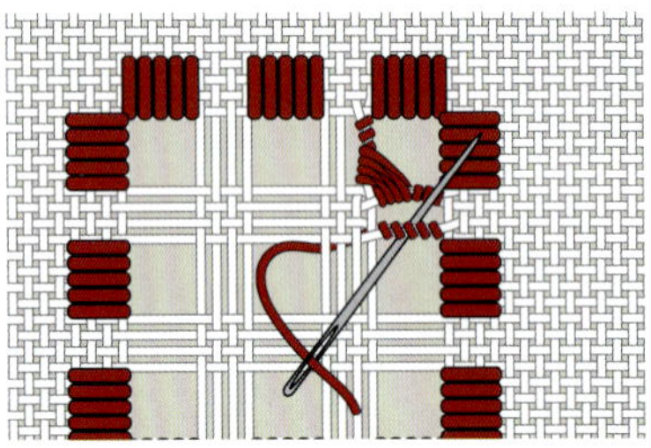

4 Turn the work 90° clockwise. From below, slide the needle under the wrapped bar.

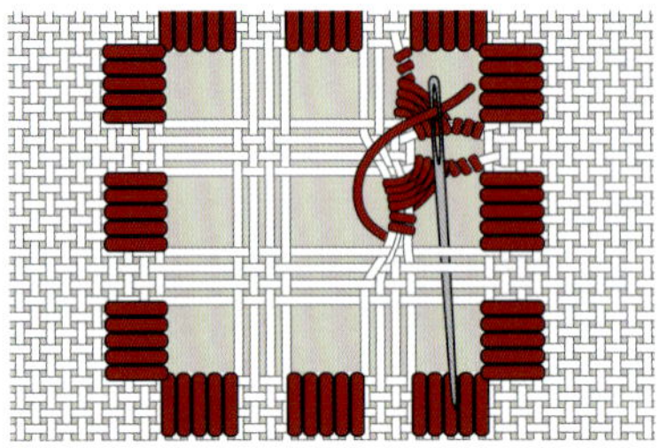

5 Continue working a quarter cross between the two bars, ensuring that all four threads of the vertical bar are included, rather than just the usual two. To move to the next bar, slide the needle under the upper two threads of the adjacent horizontal bar.

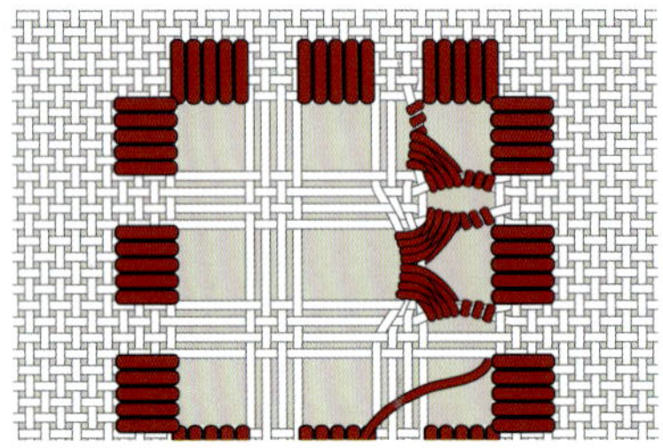

6 Work a quarter cross in the adjacent corner, using only the two threads of the adjacent horizontal bar, as normal.

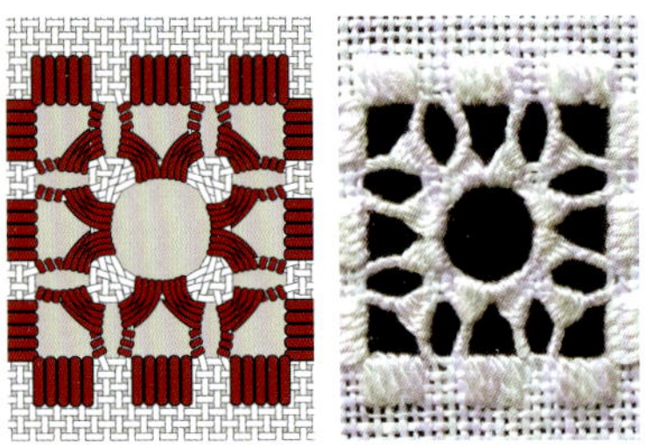

7 Repeat Steps 1 to 6 for the remaining sides.

greek cross circlet

This motif is worked using quarter crosses. It can be worked in the satin stitch shape as shown or as part of a cutwork area.

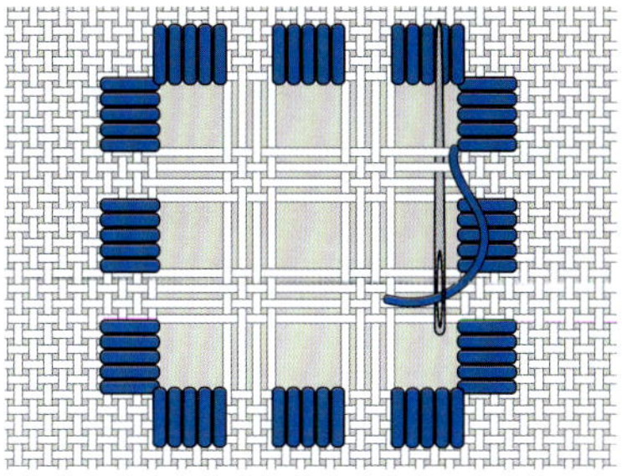

1 Bring the needle out in the top right corner open square, and slide it under the top two threads of the uppermost horizontal bar.

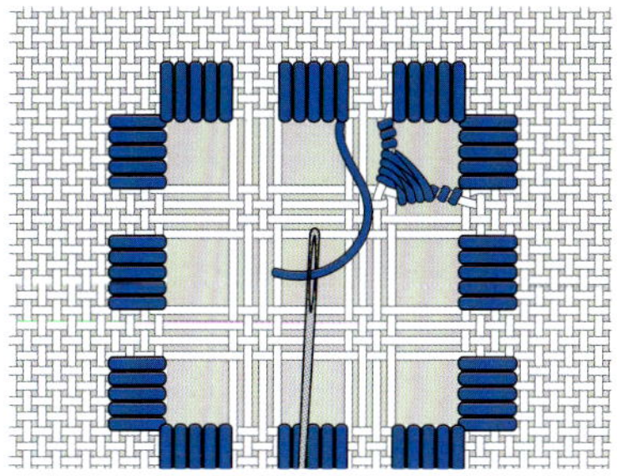

2 Work a quarter cross in the corner between the bar and the next bar. Bring the needle up in the next open square.

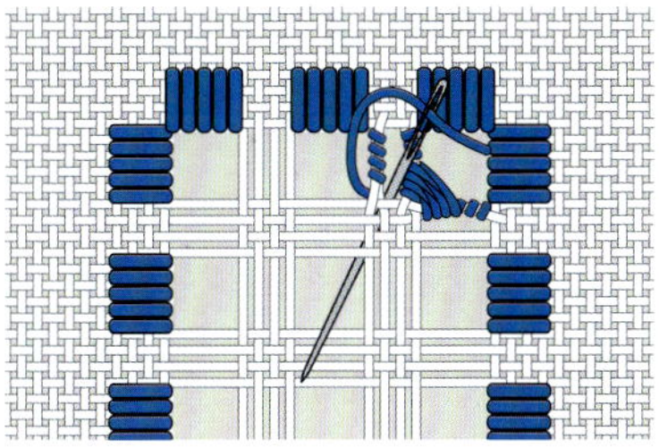

3 Wrap the two uncovered threads of the bar. Take the needle behind the woven square to come out in the centre open square.

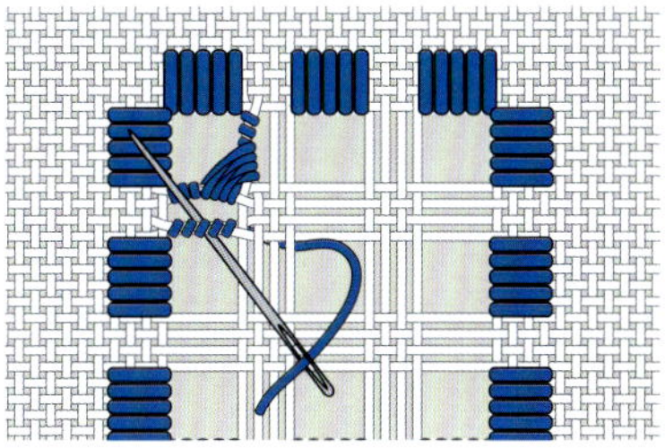

4 Turn the work 90° anticlockwise. From below, slide the needle under the wrapped bar.

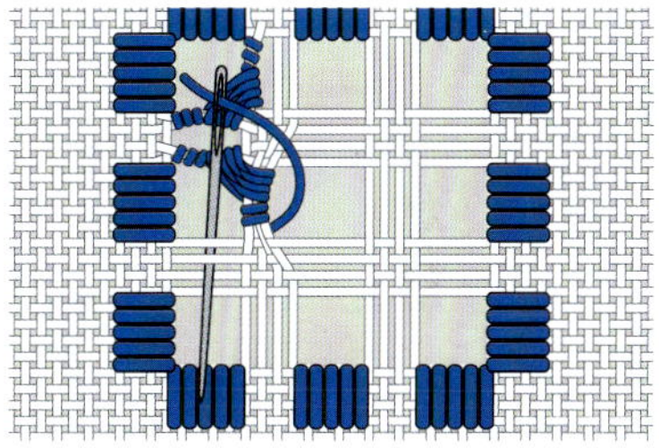

5 Continue working a quarter cross between the two bars, ensuring that all four threads of the vertical bar are included, rather than just the usual two. To move to the next bar, slide the needle under the upper two threads of the adjacent horizontal bar.

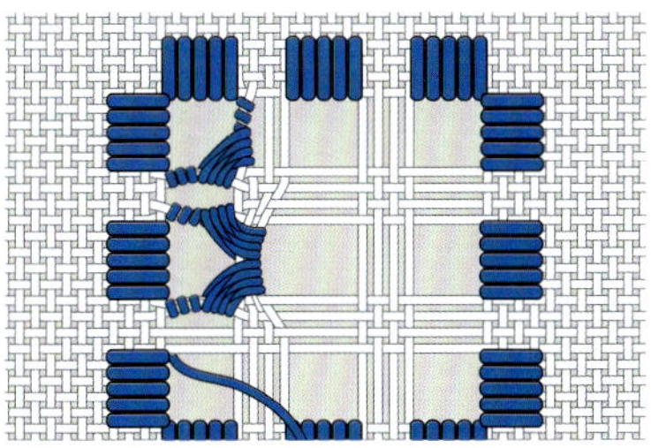

6 Work a quarter cross in the adjacent corner, using only the two threads of the adjacent horizontal bar, as normal.

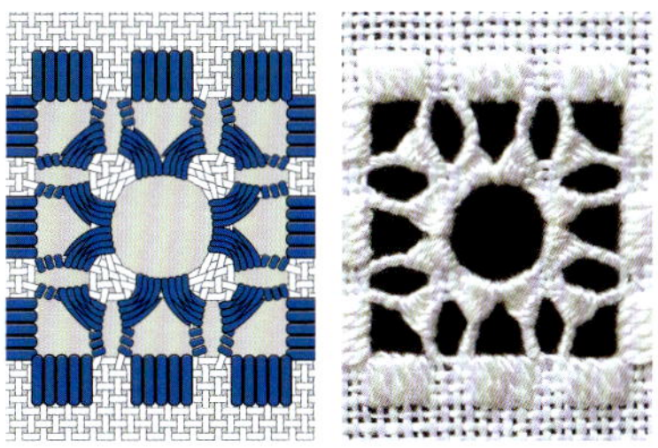

7 Repeat Steps 1 to 6 for the remaining sides.

L

heavy greek cross

This Greek cross variation uses full-width rather than half-width bars, resulting in a slightly heavier version of the stitch.

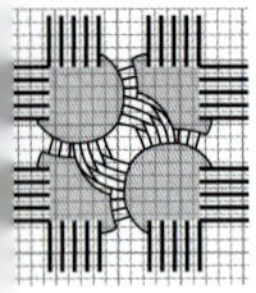

CONTEMPORARY

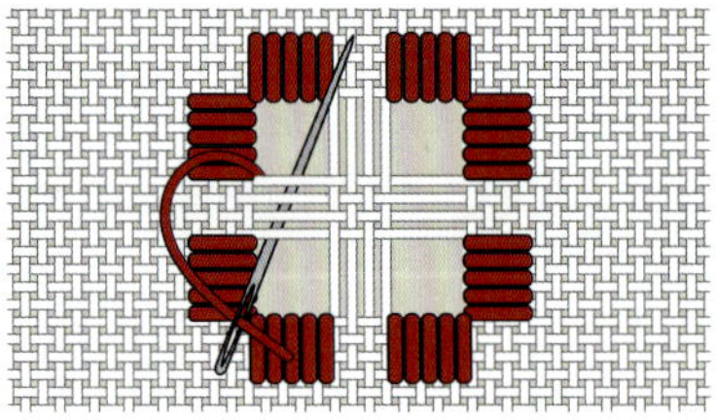

1 Bring the needle out of the fabric above a bar as shown. From below, slide the needle under the bar.

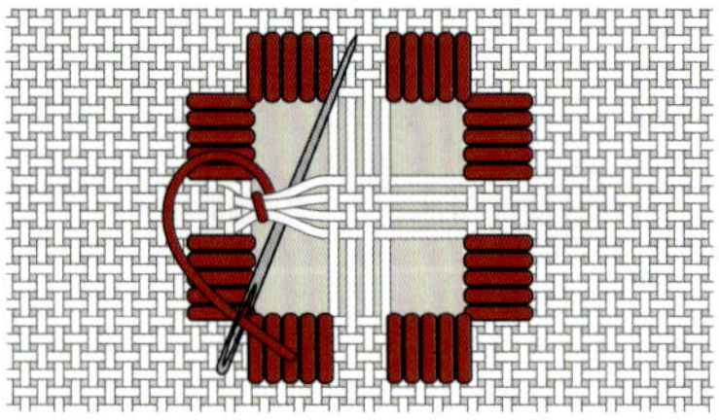

2 Tighten the stitch around the fabric threads. Moving right and from below, slide the needle under the bar again.

3 Keep wrapping tightly. When there is space for one more stitch, take the needle under the woven fabric square and bring it out in the upper right quadrant.

❶ *The wraps should lie next to each other on the bar and not overlap. They do not need to be tightly packed.*

4 Turn the work 45° anticlockwise. From above, slide the needle under the wrapped bar.

5 Pull the needle through and down to snugly tighten the stitch. From below, slide the needle under the upper bar as before.

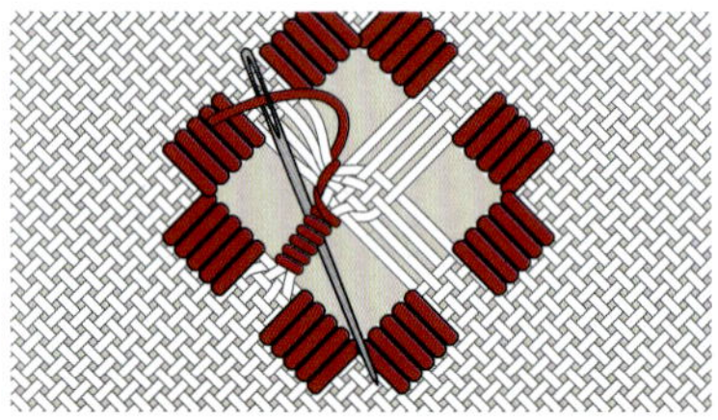

6 Pull the needle through and tighten the stitch. From above, slide the needle under the wrapped bar.

❶ *Pull the stitches to tighten them and pull the two bars together.*

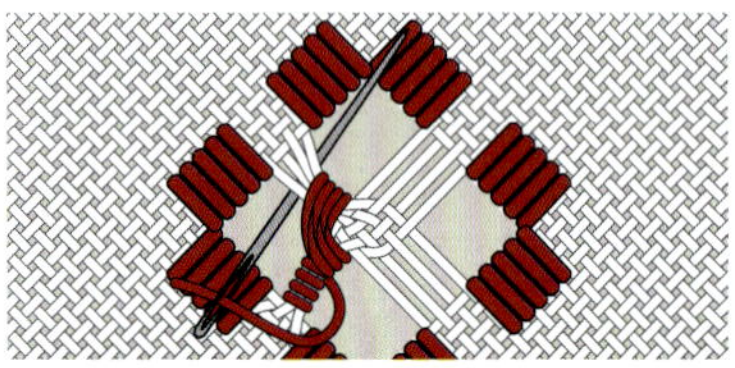

7 Weave between the two bars, until just over half the bars are covered. Finish with the needle underneath the upper bar.

❶ *Each stitch should be longer than the previous ones. They should not overlap. There should be a smooth curve at the sides.*

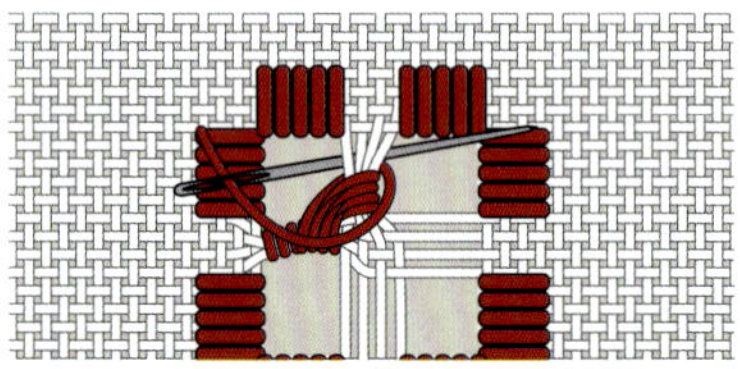

8 Pull the needle through. Turn the work 45° clockwise. From the left, slide the needle under the unwrapped bar again.

9 Wrap the remainder of the bar, and take the needle to the back.

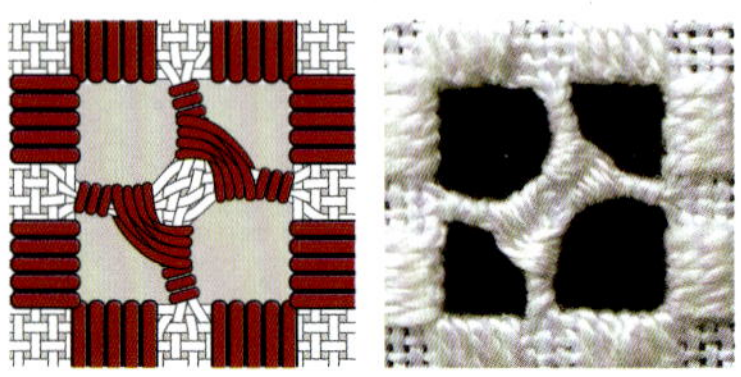

10 Take the thread behind the satin stitch. Work the motif in the opposite corner to complete the square.

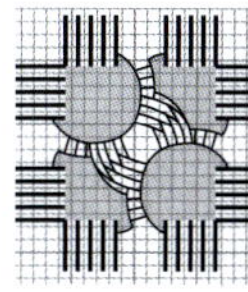

heavy greek cross

This Greek cross variation uses full-width rather than half-width bars, resulting in a slightly heavier version of the stitch.

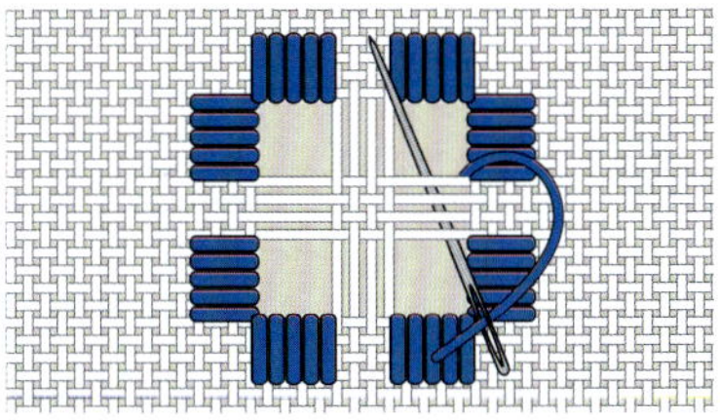

1 Bring the needle out of the fabric above a bar as shown. From below, slide the needle under the bar.

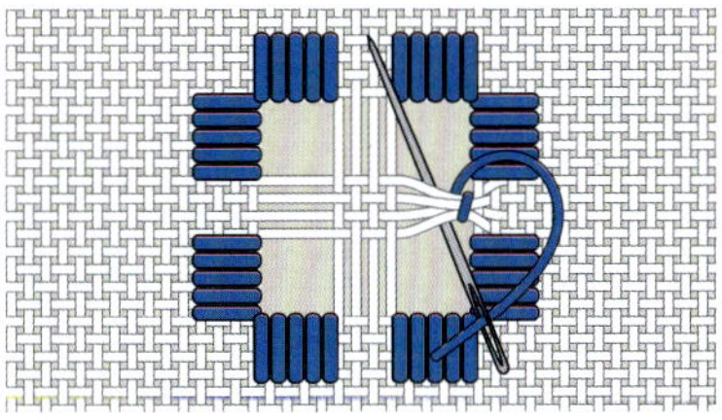

2 Tighten the stitch around the fabric threads. Moving left and from below, slide the needle under the bar again.

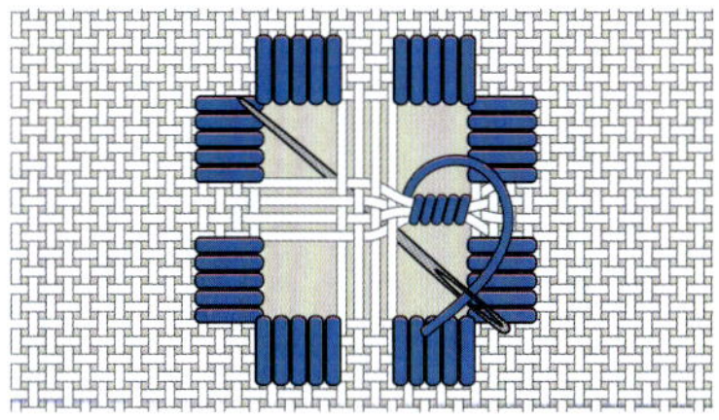

3 Keep wrapping tightly. When there is space for one more stitch, take the needle under the woven fabric square and bring it out in the upper left quadrant.

❶ *The wraps should lie next to each other on the bar and not overlap. They do not need to be tightly packed.*

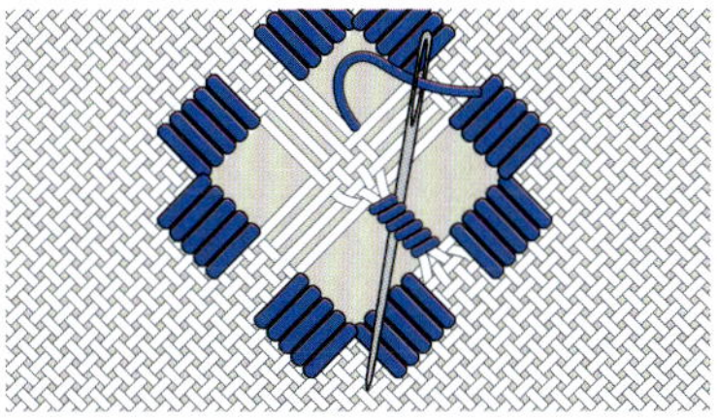

4 Turn the work 45° clockwise. From above, slide the needle under the wrapped bar.

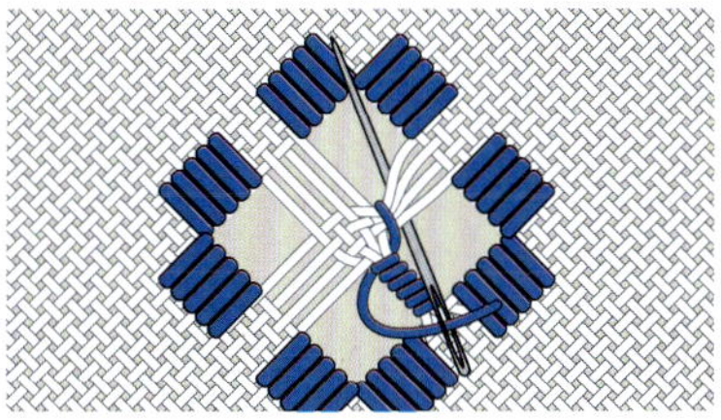

5 Pull the needle through and down to snugly tighten the stitch. From below, slide the needle under the upper bar as before.

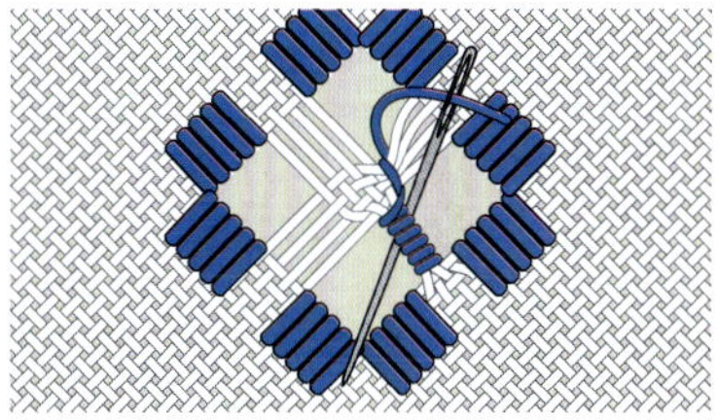

6 Pull the needle through and tighten the stitch. From above, slide the needle under the wrapped bar.

❶ *Pull the stitches to tighten them and pull the two bars together.*

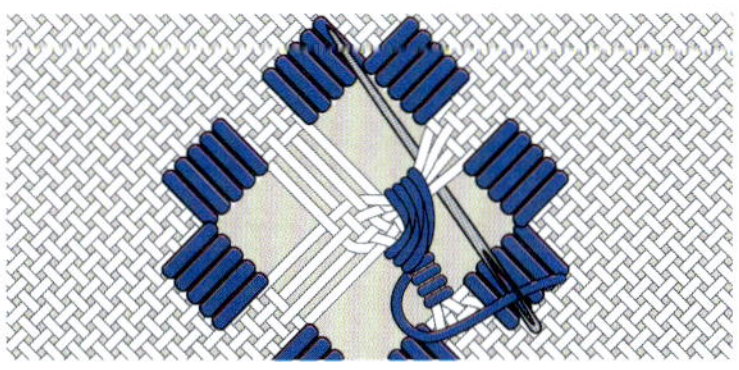

7 Weave between the two bars, until just over half the bars are covered. Finish with the needle underneath the upper bar.

❶ *Each stitch should be longer than the previous ones. They should not overlap. There should be a smooth curve at the sides.*

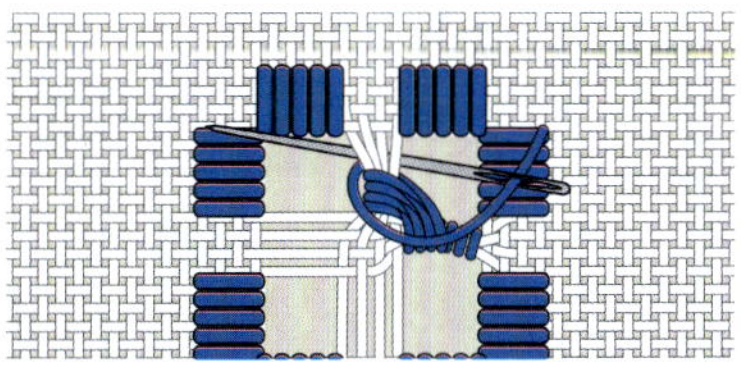

8 Pull the needle through. Turn the work 45° anticlockwise. From the right, slide the needle under the unwrapped bar again.

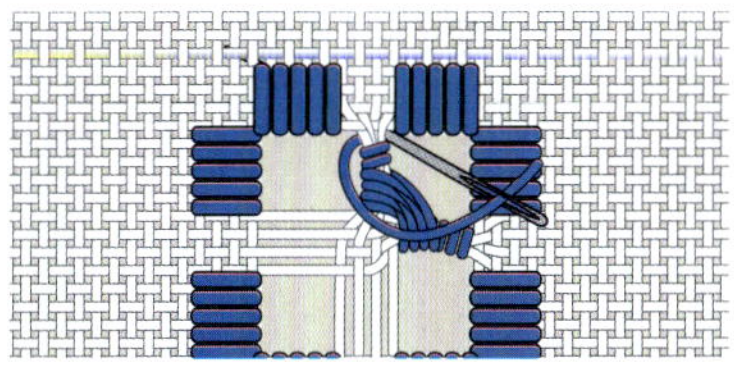

9 Wrap the remainder of the bar, and take the needle to the back.

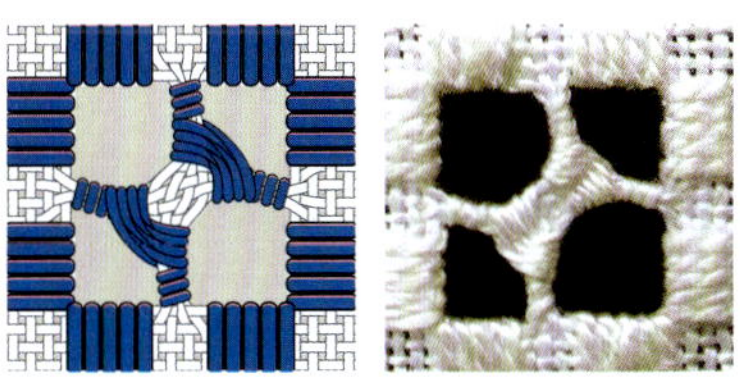

10 Take the thread behind the satin stitch. Work the motif in the opposite corner to complete the square.

L

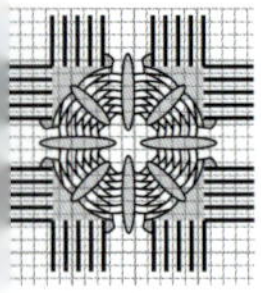

CONTEMPORARY

maltese flower

This pretty flower stitch is a variation on a Greek quarter cross. It is fiddly and difficult, but worth mastering.

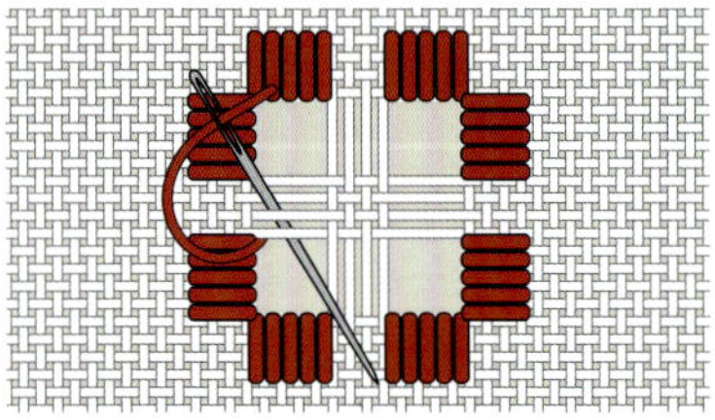

1 Bring the needle out below the left bar. From above, slide the needle under the lower two fabric threads.

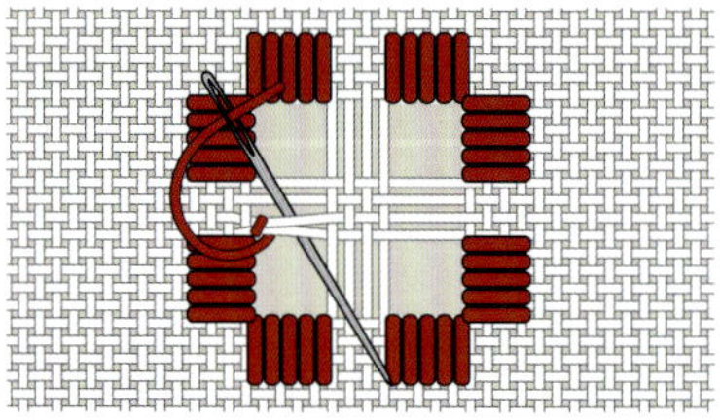

2 Tighten the stitch around the fabric threads. Moving right and from above, slide the needle under the same two fabric threads.

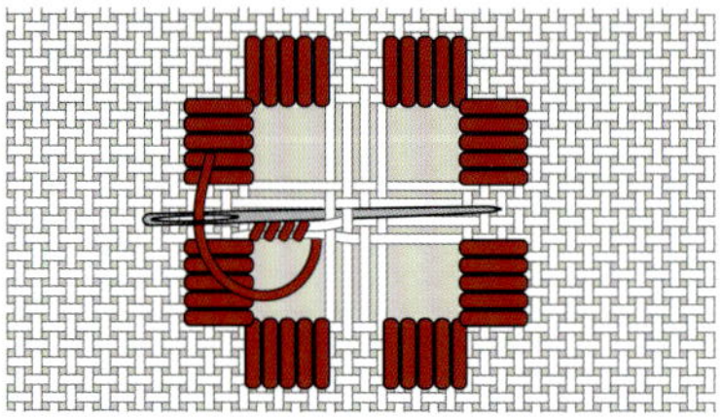

3 Keep wrapping tightly. When there is space for one more stitch, insert the needle above the wrapped bar. Bring it out in the woven square's centre.

❶ *The wraps should lie next to each other on the bar and not overlap. They do not need to be tightly packed.*

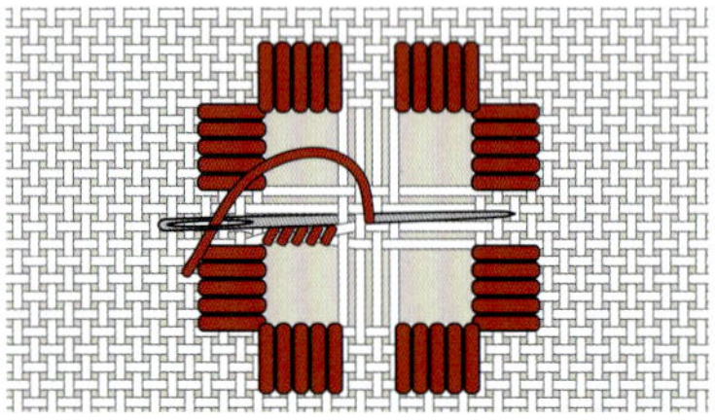

4 Pull the needle through. Insert it two threads to the left and bring it out in the centre again.

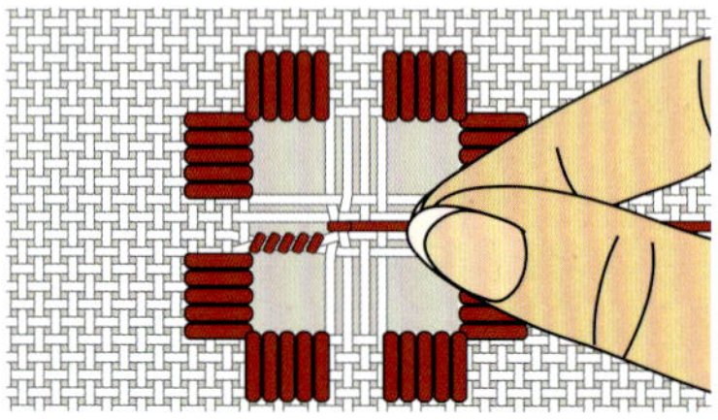

5 Pull the needle through and tighten the stitch to bring the fabric threads together.

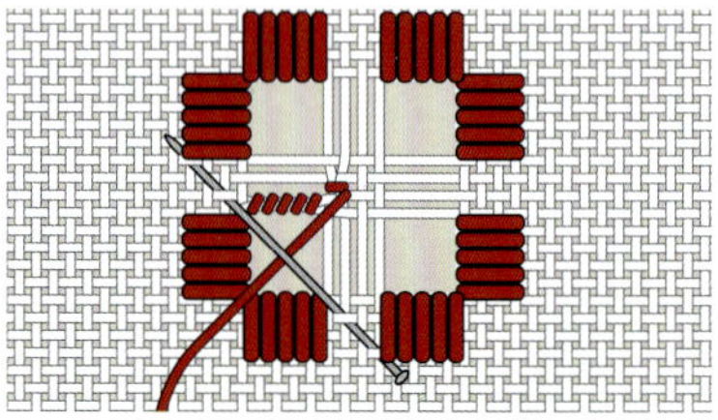

6 Lay the thread across the quadrant where the wrapped bar is. Use a pin to pin down the thread, across the middle of the quadrant.

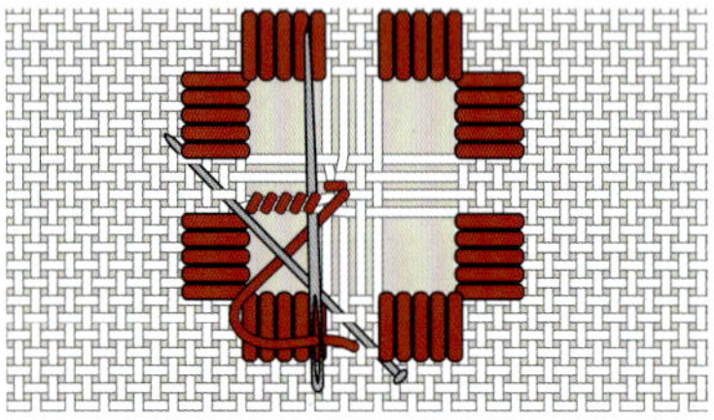

7 From below, take the needle under the wrapped bar, close to the centre.

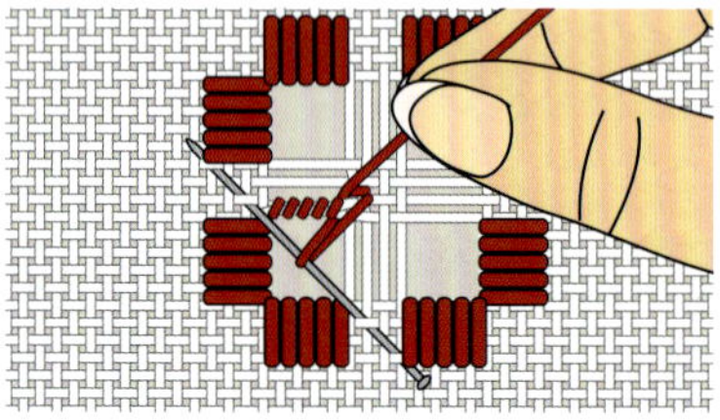

8 Pull the needle through. Pull the thread in snug against the centre woven square.

❶ *Keep the pin in place.*

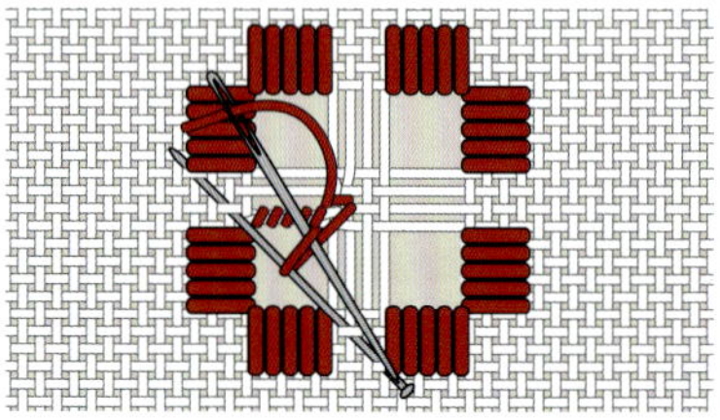

9 From above, slide the needle under the closer of the threads on the pin.

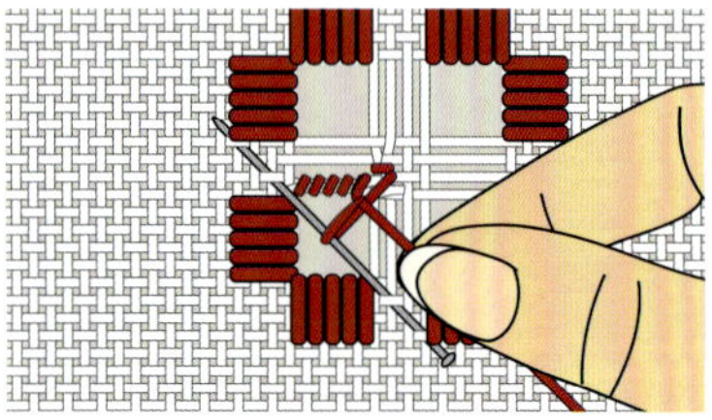

10 Pull the stitch in snug towards the woven centre square.

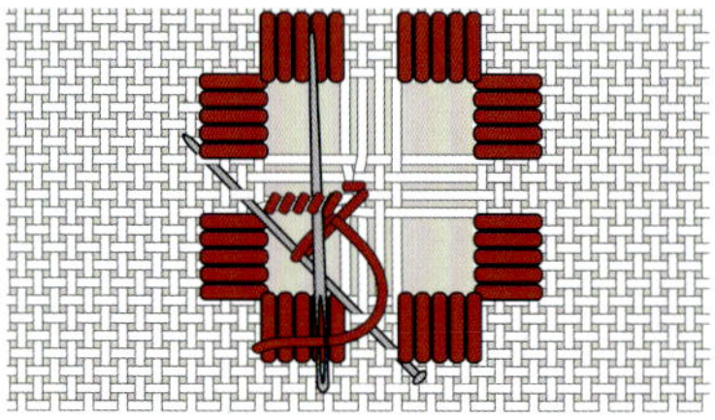

11 From below, slide the needle under the wrapped bar.

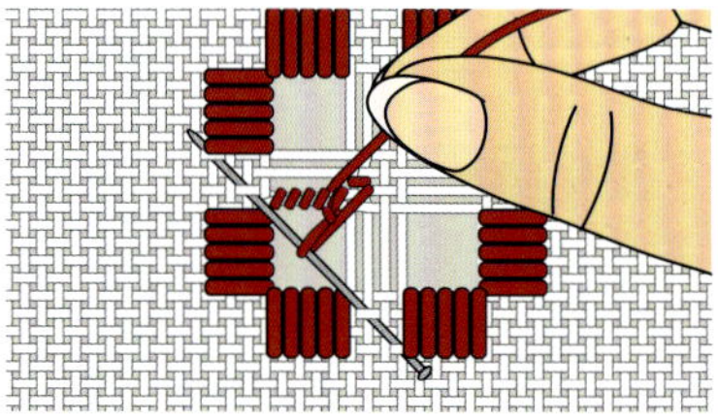

12 Pull the stitch in snug towards the woven centre square.

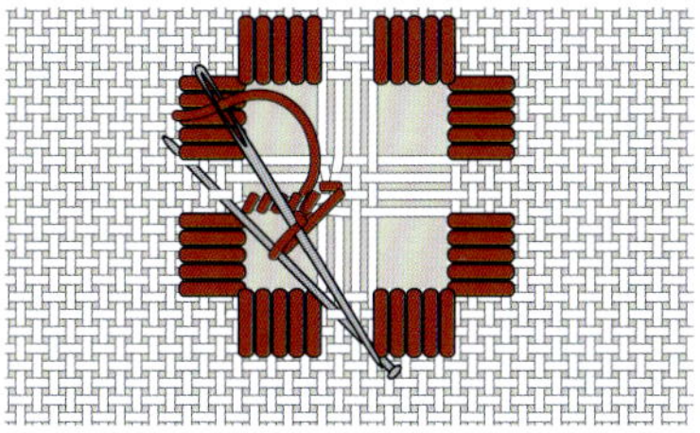

13 From above, slide the needle under the closer of the threads on the pin.

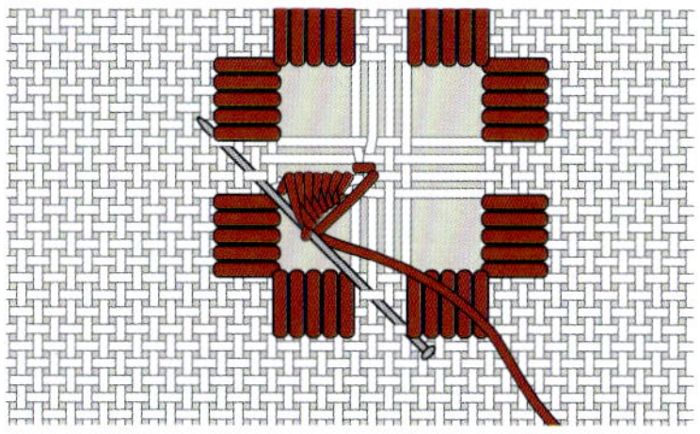

14 Continue weaving between the bar and the thread, pulling the stitches in close to the previous ones. Allow the stitches to loosen off in tension to create a triangular shape.

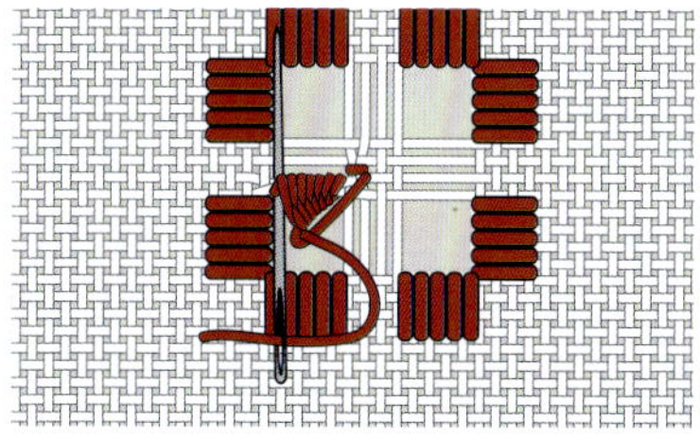

15 Continue weaving. Finish with a stitch under the wrapped bar. When the bar and the pinned thread are full, remove the pin.

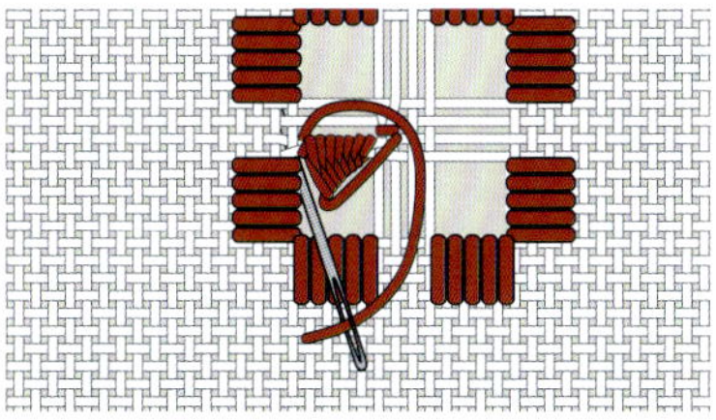

16 Take the needle over the wrapped bar and to the back.

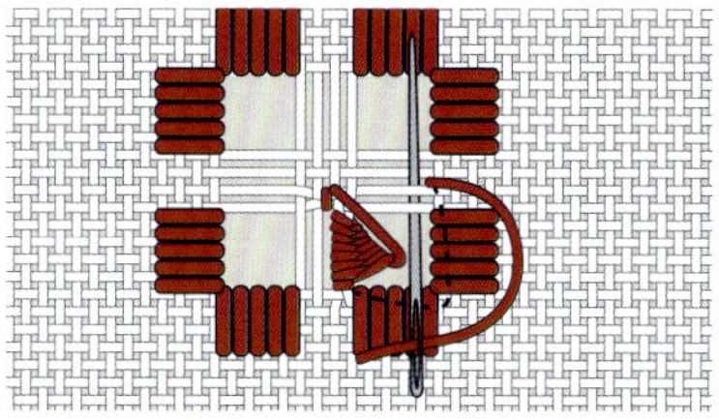

17 Take the thread through the back of the satin stitch to the middle of the bar on the far side of the quadrant. Turn the work 90° anticlockwise. From below, slide the needle under the bottom two threads of the bar.

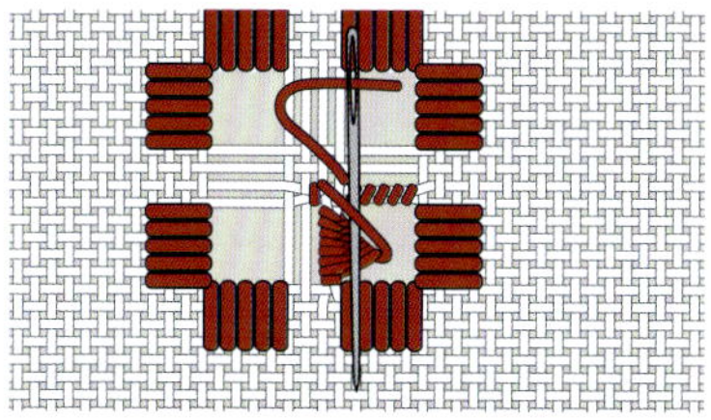

18 Wrap the rest of the bar then slide the needle under the thread that used to be pinned, from above.

❶ *This part of the method can be quite tricky as the centre stitch is no longer pinned. Go slowly and carefully. Alternatively, put the pin back in place to help stabilise.*

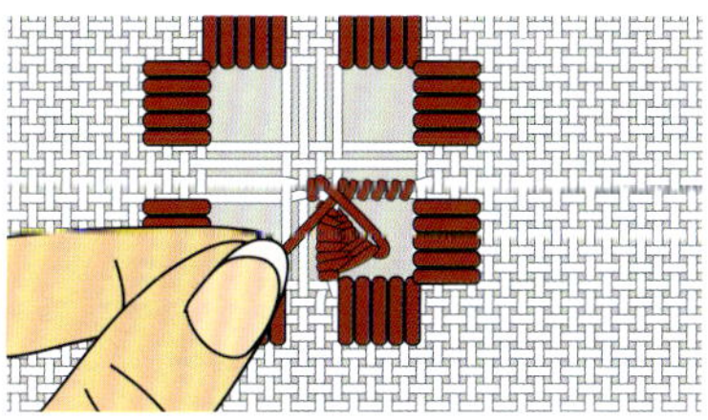

19 Pull the thread in snug against the centre woven square.

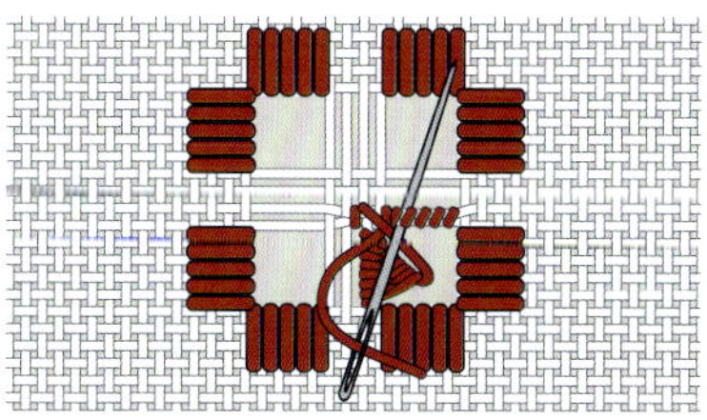

20 From below, slide the needle under the wrapped bar.

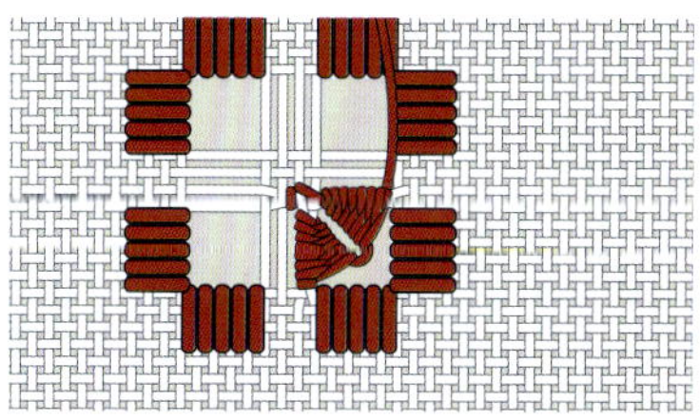

21 Weave back and forth between the wrapped bar and the thread that used to be pinned.

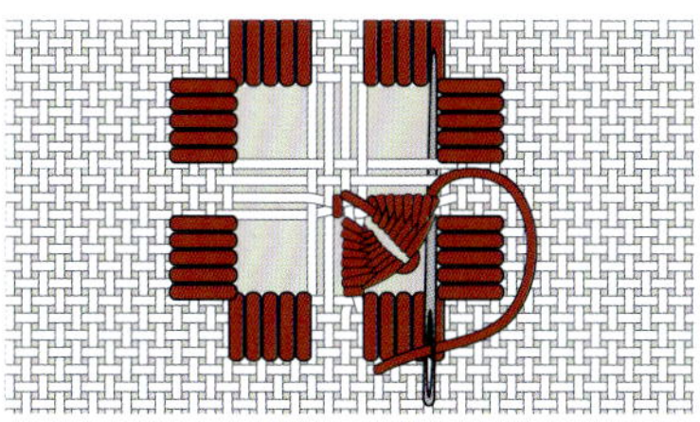

22 When the bar and the thread are full, take the needle under the bar and bring it out in the next quadrant.

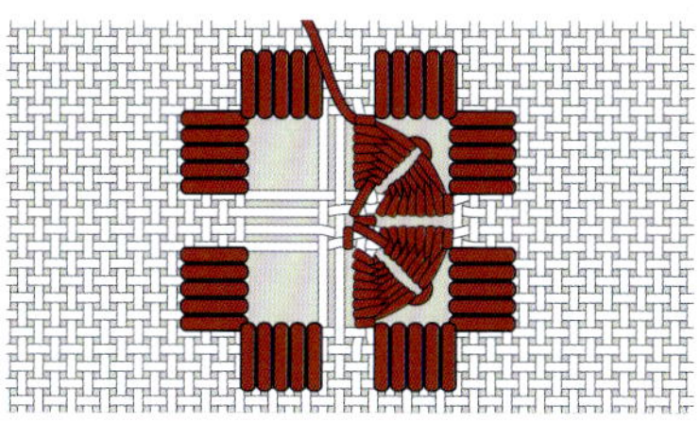

23 Cycle through the steps to complete the next quadrant similarly, turning the work as required.

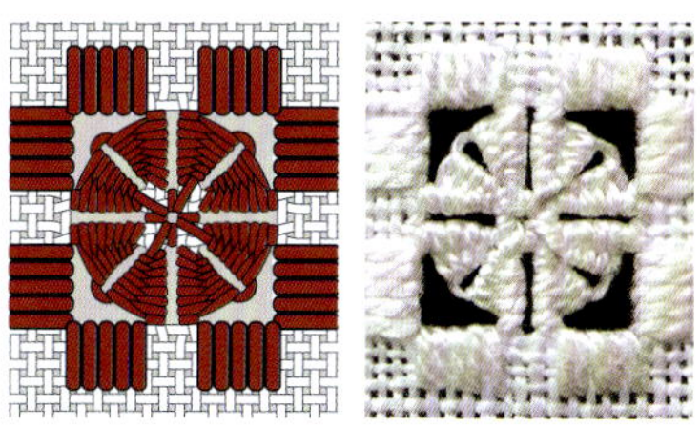

24 Work the two final quadrants in the same way.

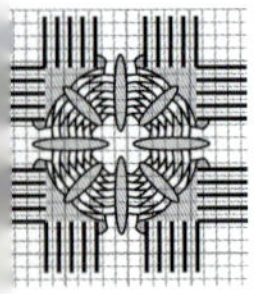

maltese flower

This pretty flower stitch is a variation on a Greek quarter cross. It is fiddly and difficult, but worth mastering.

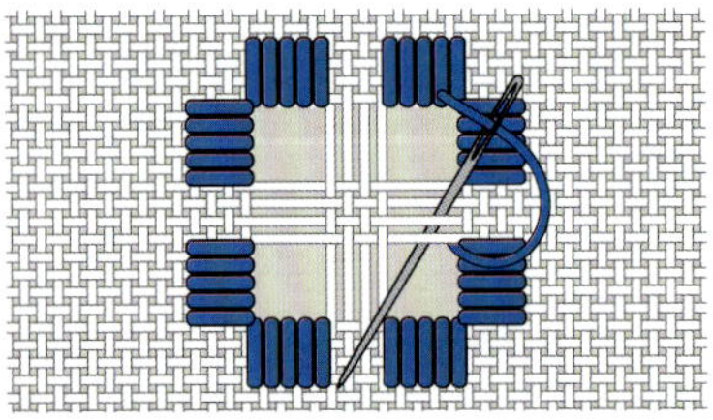

1 Bring the needle out of the fabric in the centre of a bar as shown. From below, slide the needle under the lower two fabric threads.

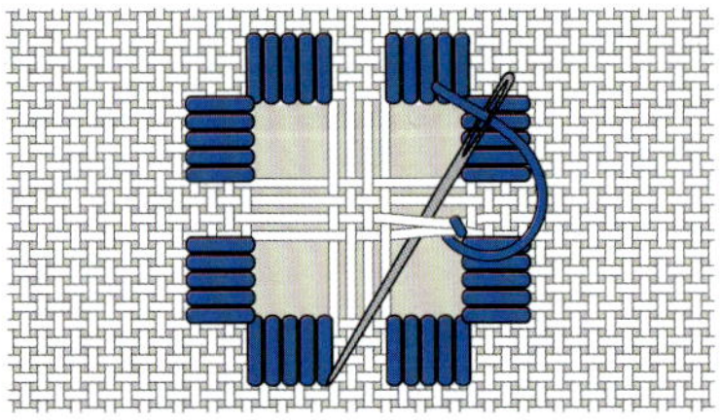

2 Tighten the stitch around the fabric threads. Moving left and from below, slide the needle under the same two fabric threads.

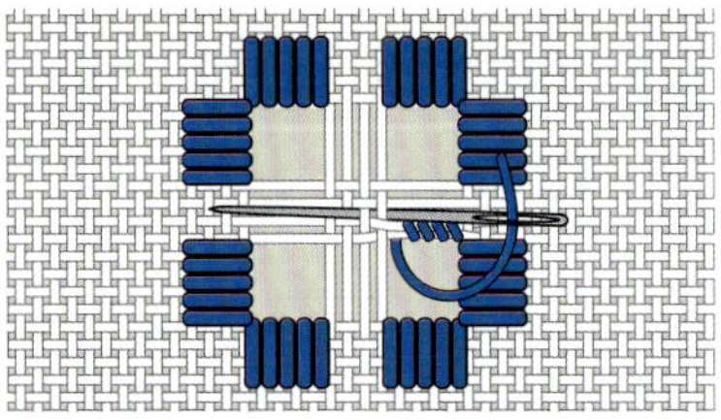

3 Keep wrapping tightly. When there is space for one more stitch, insert the needle above the wrapped bar. Bring it out in the woven square's centre.

❶ *The wraps should lie next to each other on the bar and not overlap. They do not need to be tightly packed.*

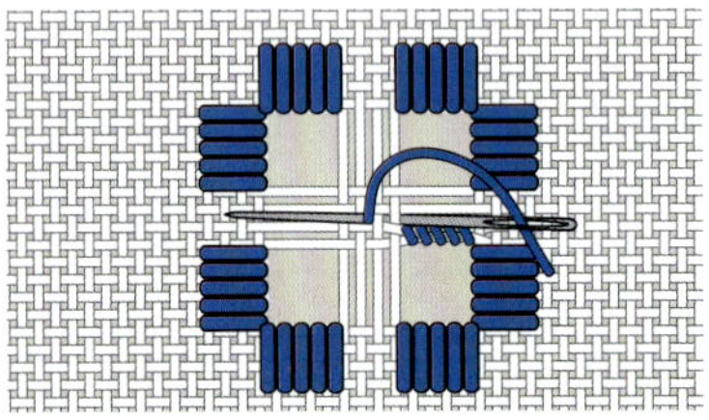

4 Pull the needle through. Insert it two threads to the right and bring it out in the centre again.

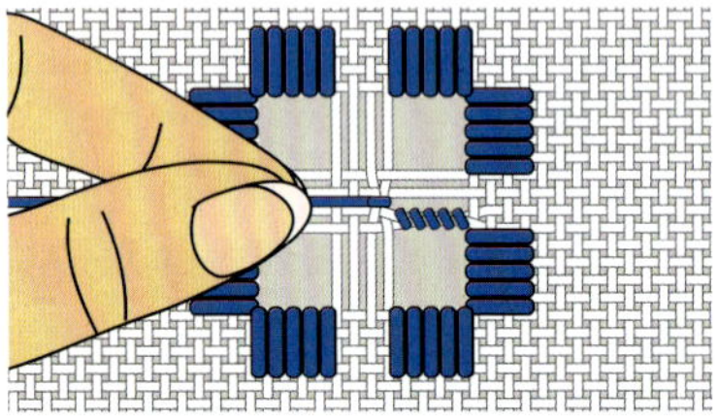

5 Pull the needle through and tighten the stitch to bring the fabric threads together.

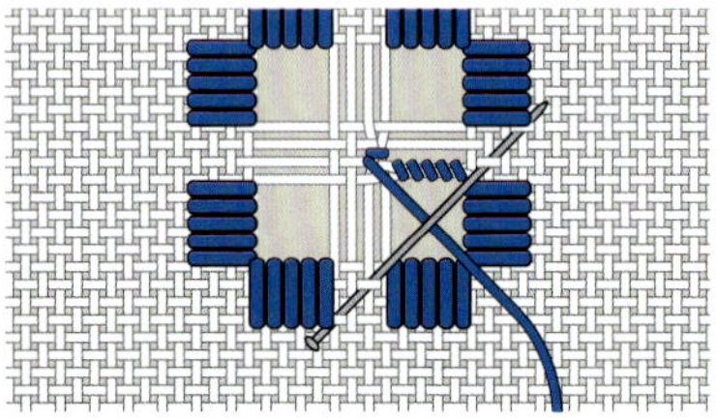

6 Lay the thread across the quadrant where the wrapped bar is. Use a pin to pin down the thread, across the middle of the quadrant.

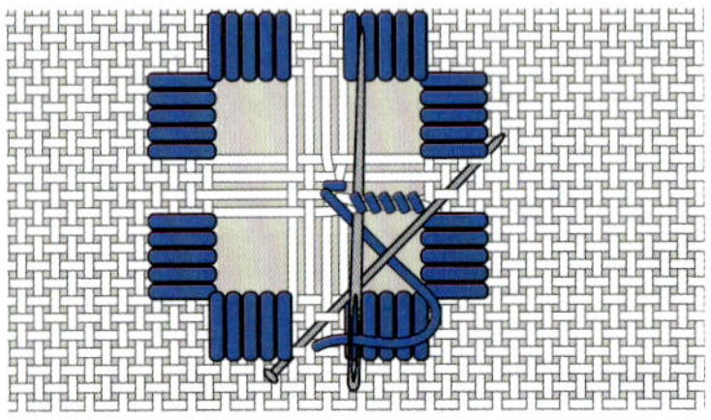

7 From below, take the needle under the wrapped bar, close to the centre.

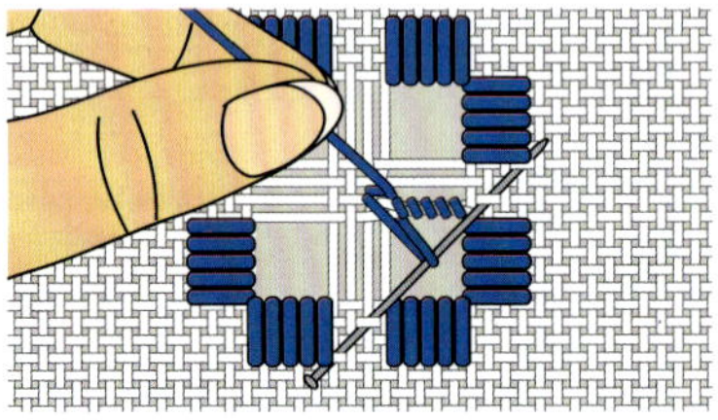

8 Pull the needle through. Pull the thread in snug against the centre woven square.

❶ *Keep the pin in place.*

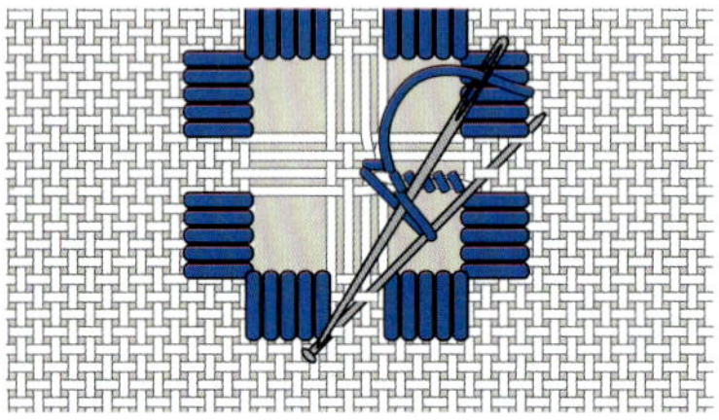

9 From above, slide the needle under the closer of the threads on the pin.

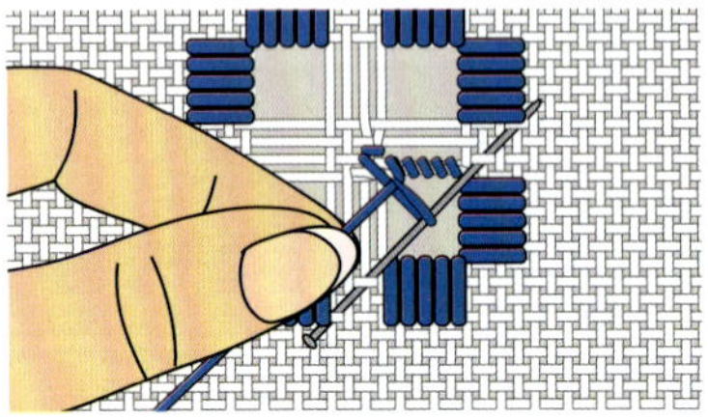

10 Pull the stitch in snug towards the woven centre square.

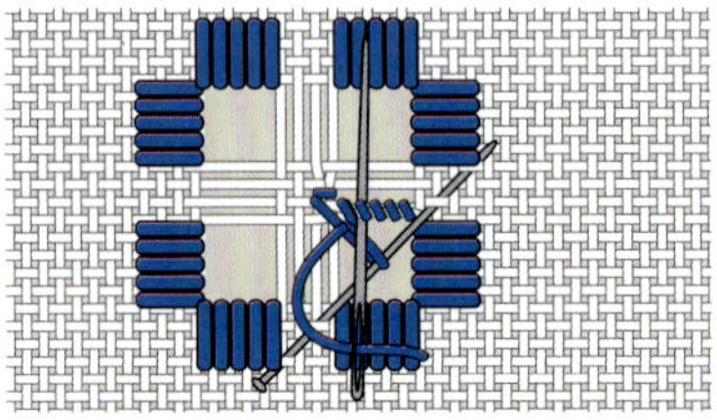

11 From below, slide the needle under the wrapped bar.

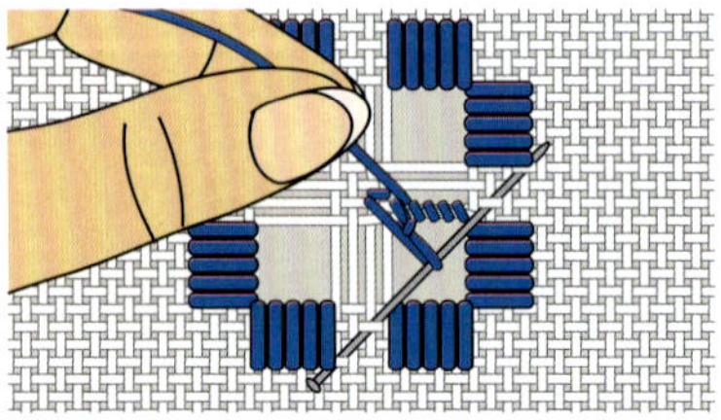

12 Pull the stitch in snug towards the woven centre square.

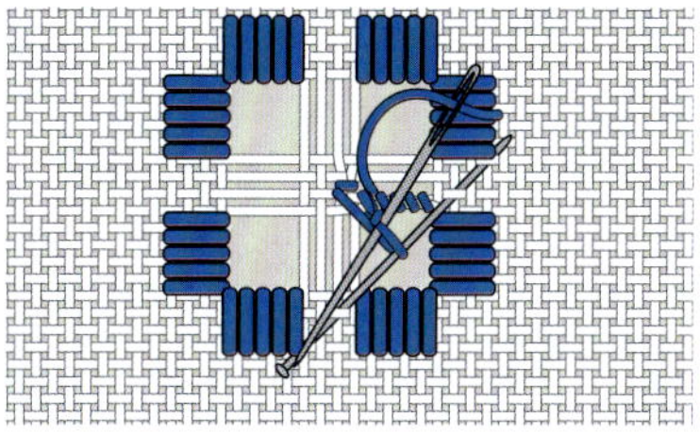

13 From above, slide the needle under the closer of the threads on the pin.

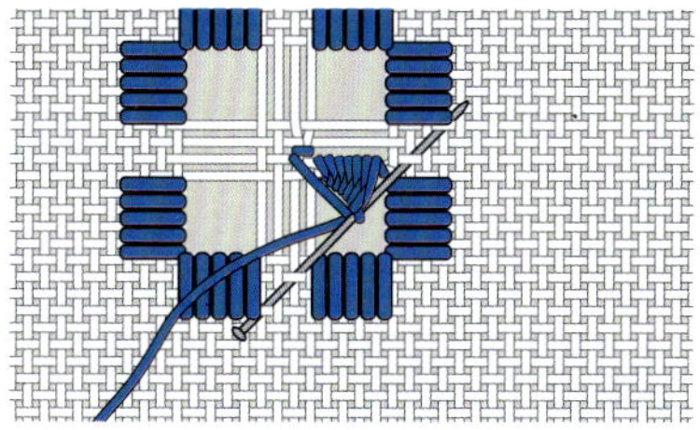

14 Continue weaving between the bar and the thread, pulling the stitches in close to the previous ones. Allow the stitches to loosen off in tension to create a triangular shape.

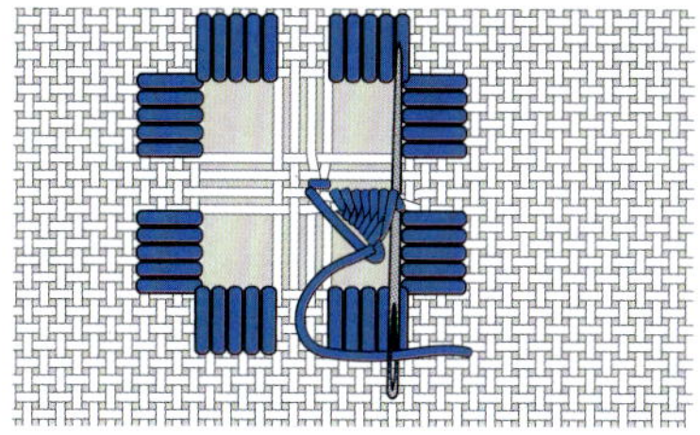

15 Continue weaving. When the bar and the pinned thread are full, remove the pin. Finish with a stitch under the wrapped bar.

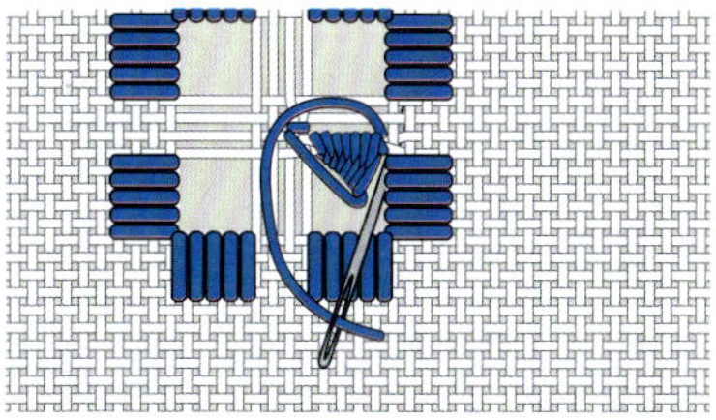

16 Take the needle over the wrapped bar and to the back.

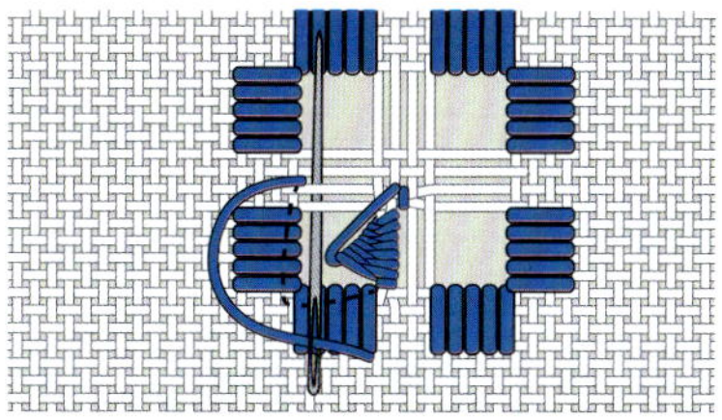

17 Take the thread through the back of the satin stitch to the middle of the bar on the far side of the quadrant. Turn the work 90° clockwise. From below, slide the needle under the bottom two threads of the bar.

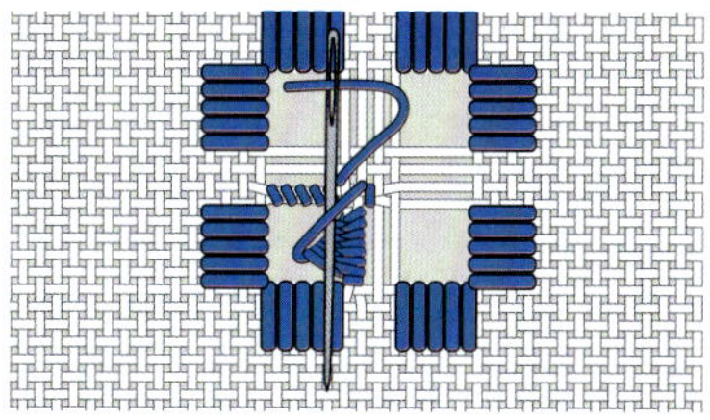

18 Wrap the rest of the bar then slide the needle under the thread that used to be pinned, from above.

❶ *This part of the method can be quite tricky as the centre stitch is no longer pinned. Go slowly and carefully. Alternatively, put the pin back in place to help stabilise.*

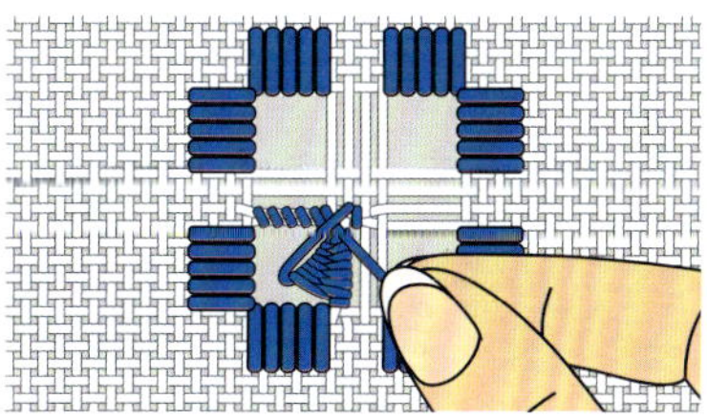

19 Pull the thread in snug against the centre woven square.

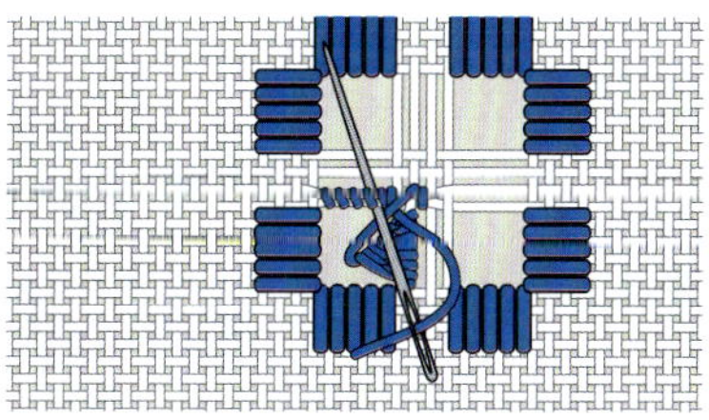

20 From below, slide the needle under the wrapped bar.

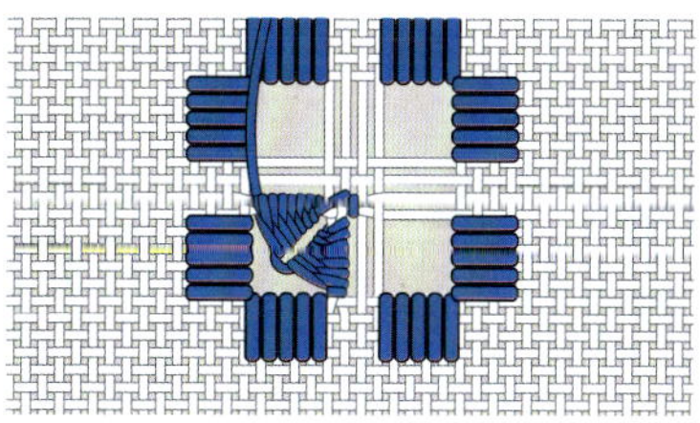

21 Weave back and forth between the wrapped bar and the thread that used to be pinned.

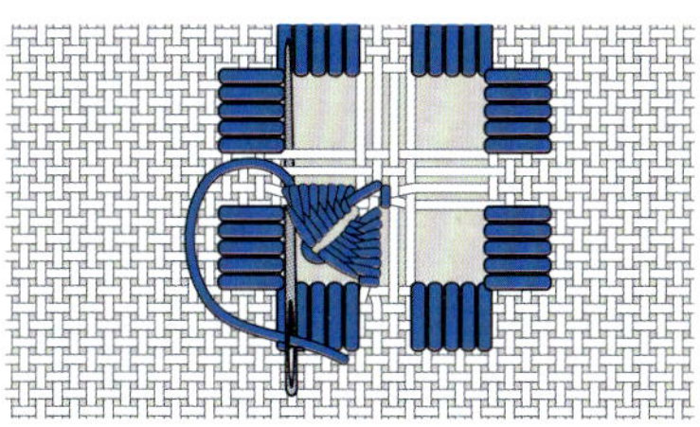

22 When the bar and the thread are full, take the needle under the bar and bring it out in the next quadrant

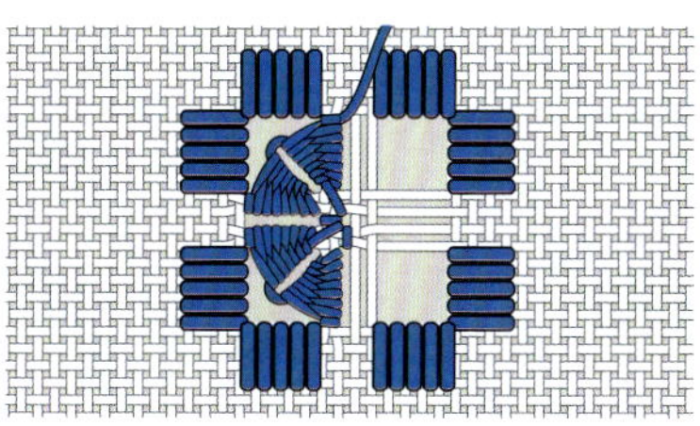

23 Cycle through the steps to complete the next quadrant similarly, turning the work as required.

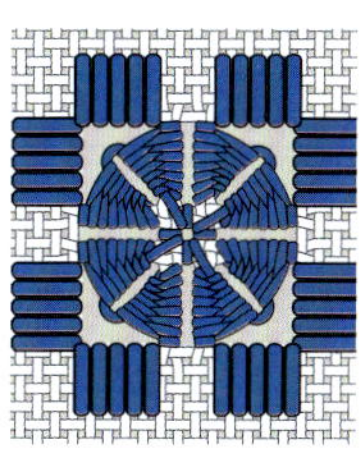

24 Work the two final quadrants in the same way.

woven fan

Woven fans are closely related to Greek crosses. Whereas Greek crosses use the fabric threads as spokes for weaving, woven fans introduce twisted spokes as framework for the weaving. Some also use the fabric threads as part of the framework, and some do not.

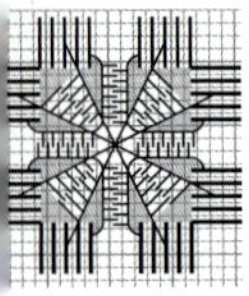

CONTEMPORARY

two spokes

Use this method for working with two foundation spokes in a multiple hole square.

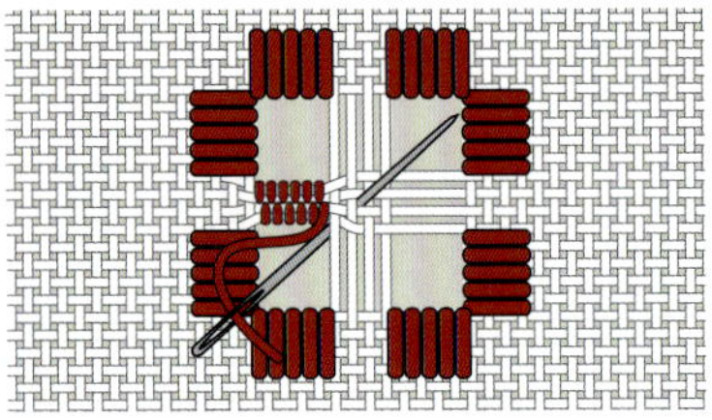

1 Work the first bar at the left-hand side, then bring the needle out in the centre of the woven square.

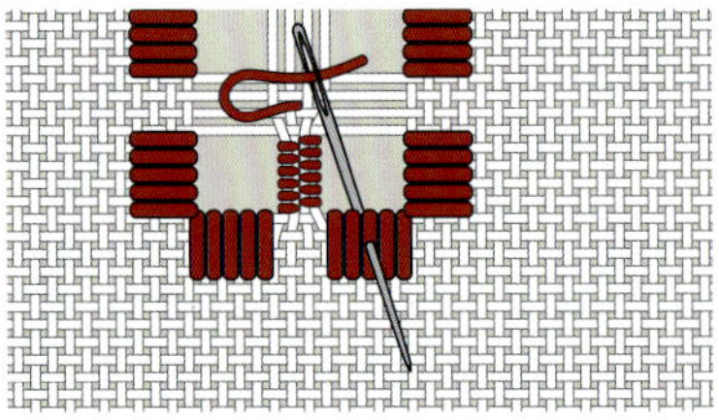

2 Turn the work 90° anticlockwise. Insert the needle in the lower right open square, and bring it out centrally in the lower satin stitch, piercing the centre stitch.

❗ *How far away these stitches are from the corner determines how wide the fan will be. The further apart, the wider the fan; closer will be narrower.*

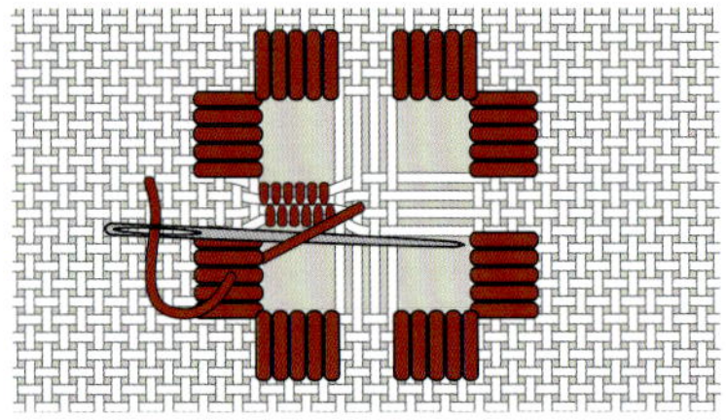

3 Turn the work 90° clockwise. Pull the needle through and tighten the diagonal stitch. From the left, slide the needle under the diagonal stitch.

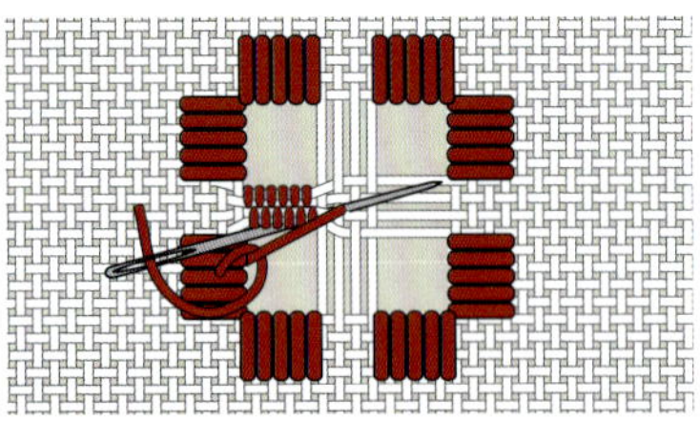

4 Insert the needle above the diagonal, and bring it out in the centre of the woven square.

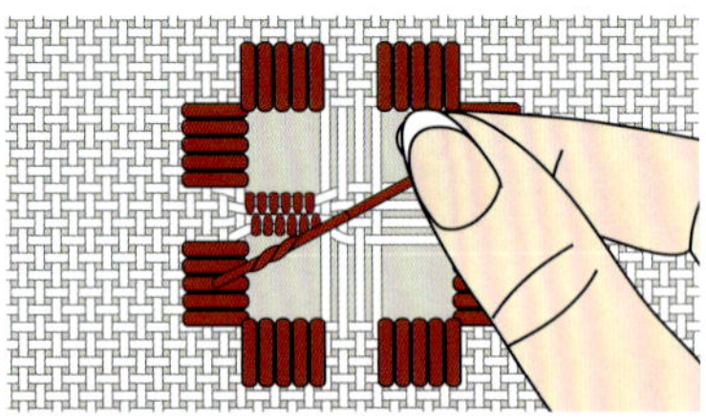

5 Pull the needle through. Pull the thread to intertwine the stitches.

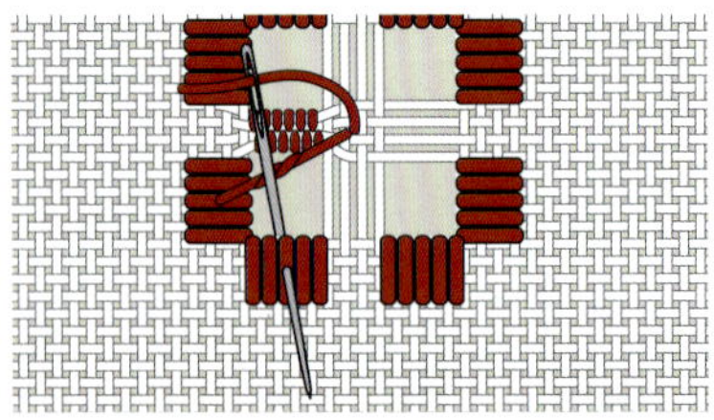

6 Inserting from behind, bring the needle out centrally in the lower satin stitch, piercing the centre stitch.

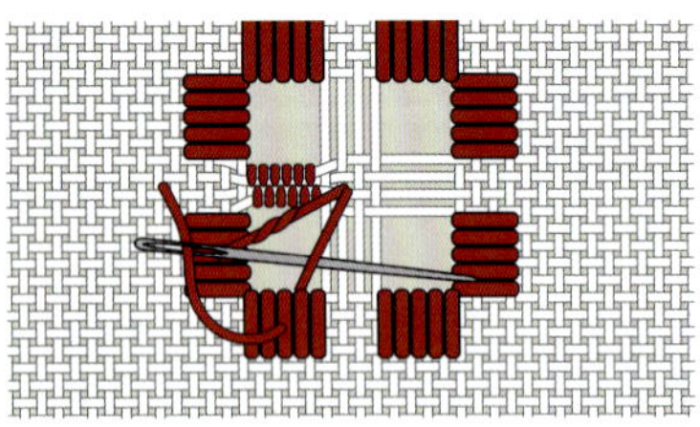

7 From the left, slide the needle under the diagonal stitch.

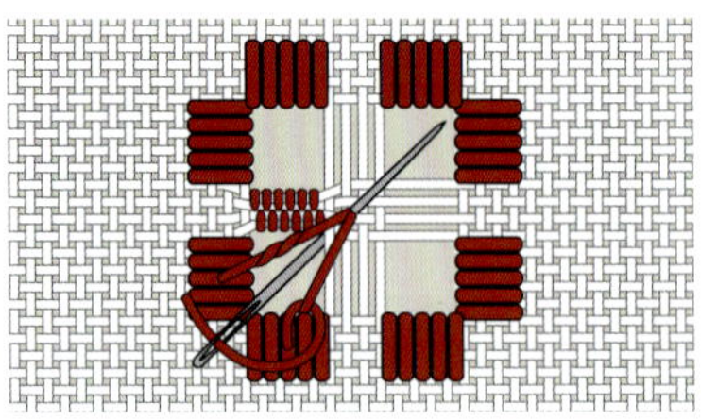

8 Insert the needle between the diagonals, and bring it out in the centre of the woven square.

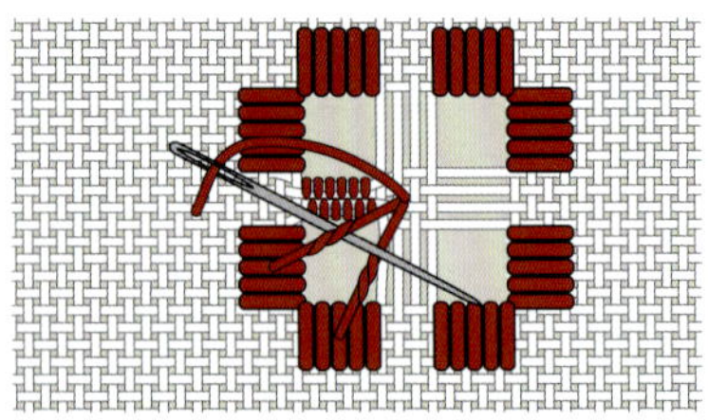

9 Pull the needle through and pull the thread to intertwine the stitches. From the left, slide the needle under the left diagonal.

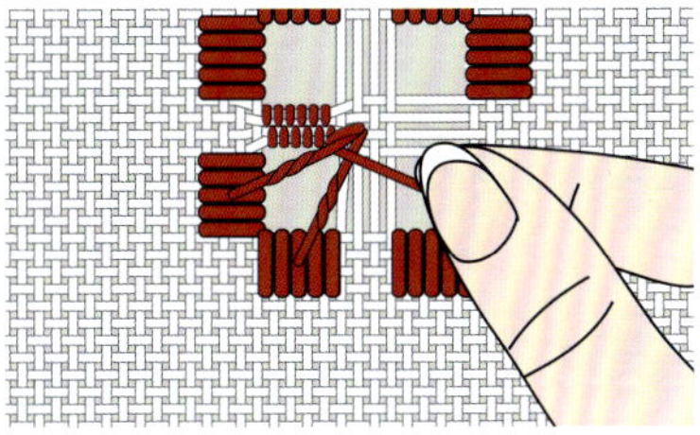

10 Pull the thread to the right and towards the woven centre, to pull the stitches in snug near the apex of the diagonals.

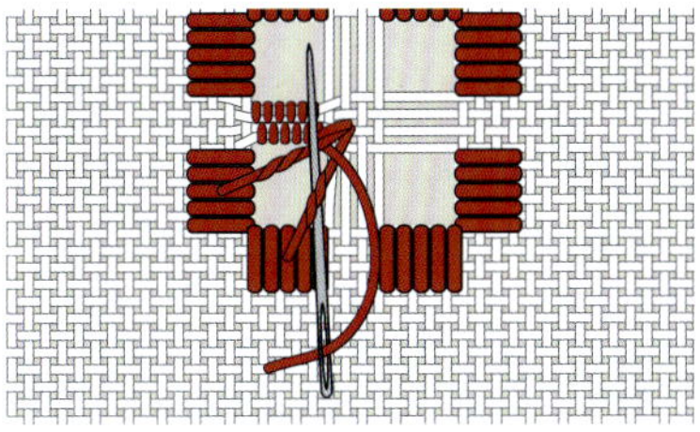

11 From below right, slide the needle under the right diagonal.

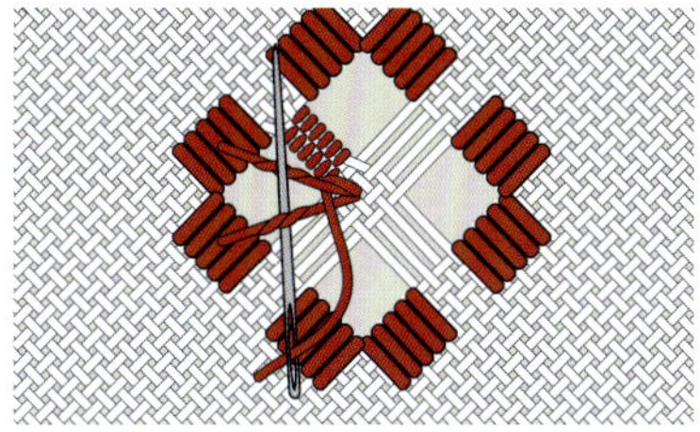

! *If it helps, while weaving the spokes, turn the work 45° so that you're inserting the needle more up and down rather than side to side. It might be more comfortable for the stitches that would otherwise go right to left.*

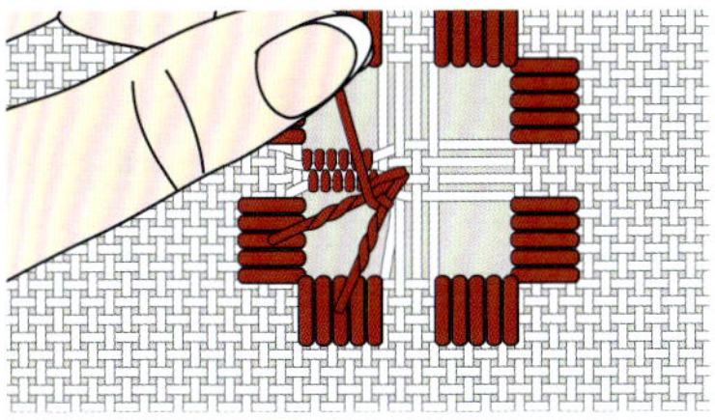

12 Pull the thread to the left and towards the woven centre to bring it snug against the previous stitch.

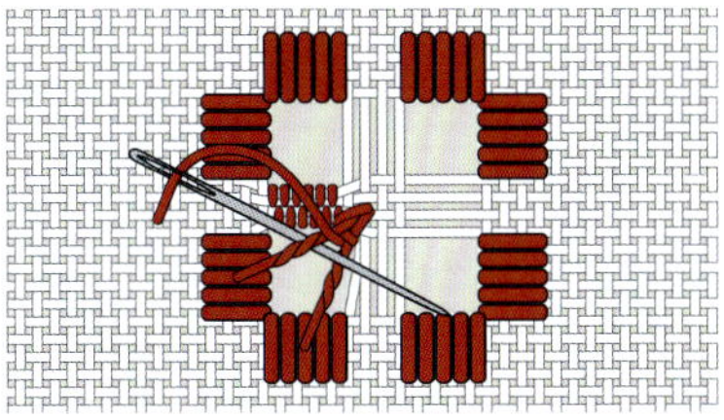

13 From the left, slide the needle under the left diagonal.

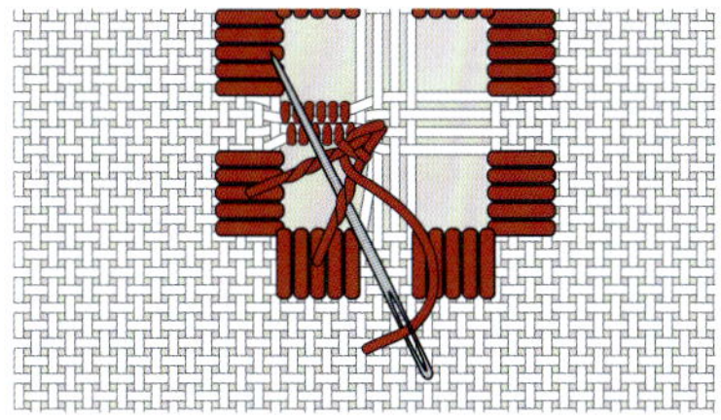

14 Pull the thread in snug against the previous stitches. Slide the needle from right to left under the right diagonal.

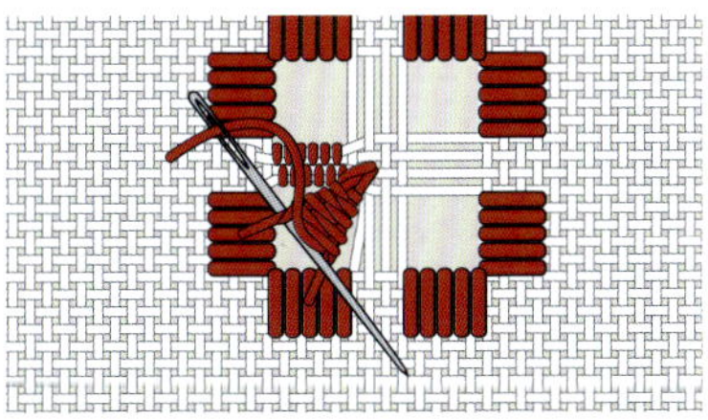

15 Weave back and forth to fill the diagonals, ensuring the stitches lengthen evenly to create a pleasing triangle. Finish the weaving by sliding the needle from left to right under the left diagonal.

! *Even tension will help with shaping. Any stitches that sit out further or tighter than others will look less pleasing. Adjust or re-stitch any stitches that are too loose or too tight.*

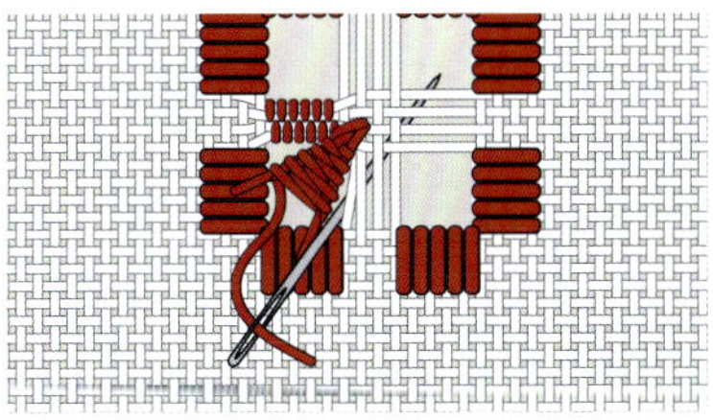

16 Take the needle to the back outside the right diagonal.

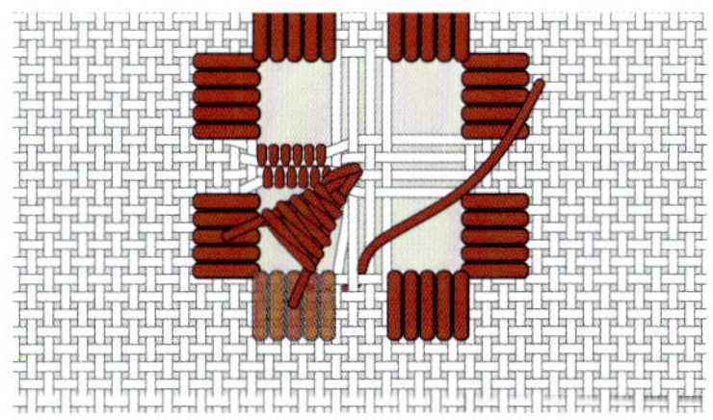

17 On the back, take the thread under the back of the satin stitch and bring it out ready to weave the next bar.

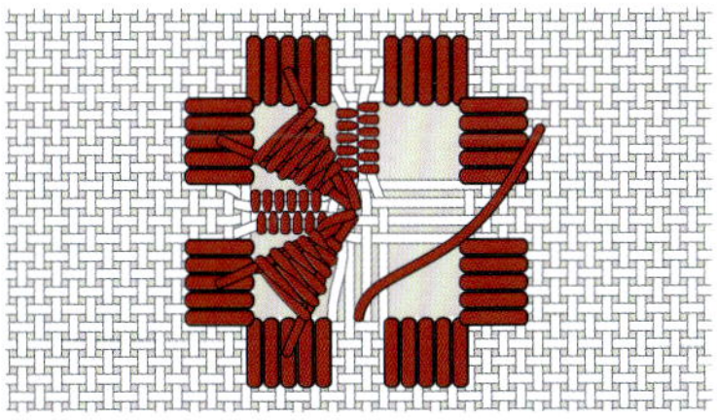

18 Turn the work 90° clockwise and repeat the woven fan.

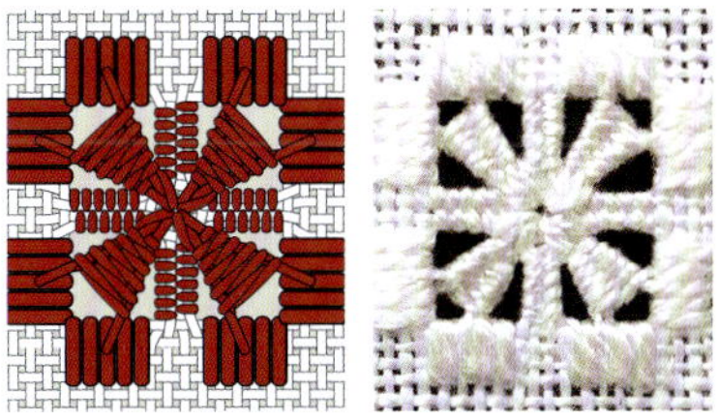

19 Repeat the filling in the remaining two quadrants. Finish the thread in the back of the satin stitch.

R

woven fan

Woven fans are closely related to Greek crosses. Whereas Greek crosses use the fabric threads as spokes for weaving, woven fans introduce twisted spokes as framework for the weaving. Some also use the fabric threads as part of the framework, and some do not.

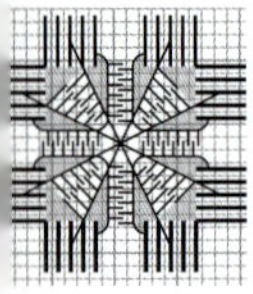

CONTEMPORARY

two spokes

Use this method for working with two foundation spokes in a multiple hole square.

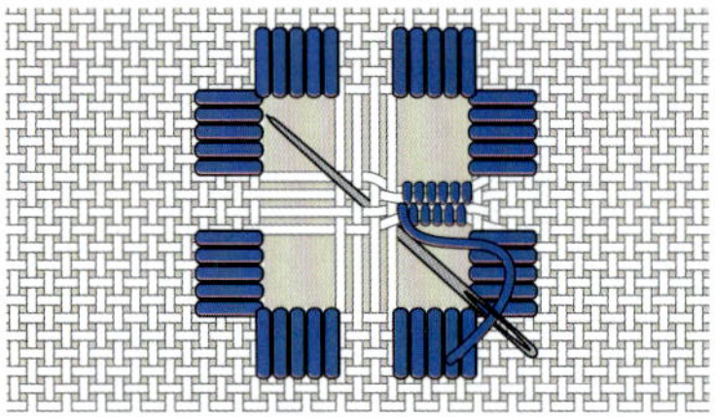

1 Work the first bar at the right-hand side, then bring the needle out in the centre of the woven square.

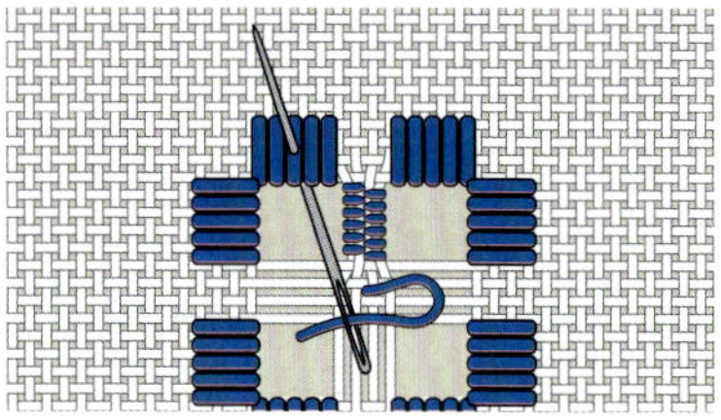

2 Turn the work 90° anticlockwise. Insert the needle in the upper left open square, and bring it out centrally in the upper satin stitch, piercing the centre stitch.

❶ *How far away these stitches are from the corner determines how wide the fan will be. The further apart, the wider the fan; closer will be narrower.*

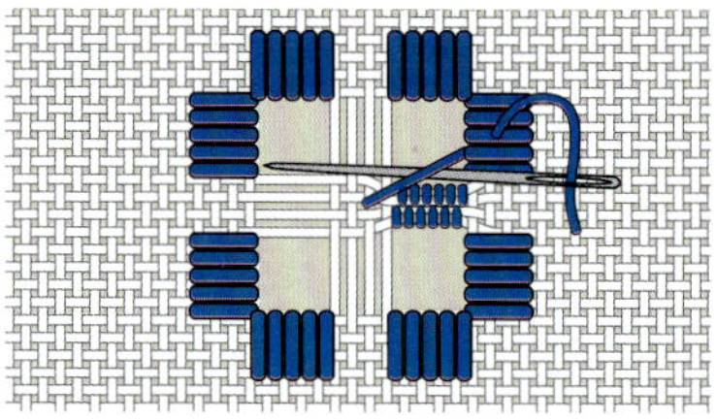

3 Turn the work 90° clockwise. Pull the needle through and tighten the diagonal stitch. From the right, slide the needle under the diagonal stitch.

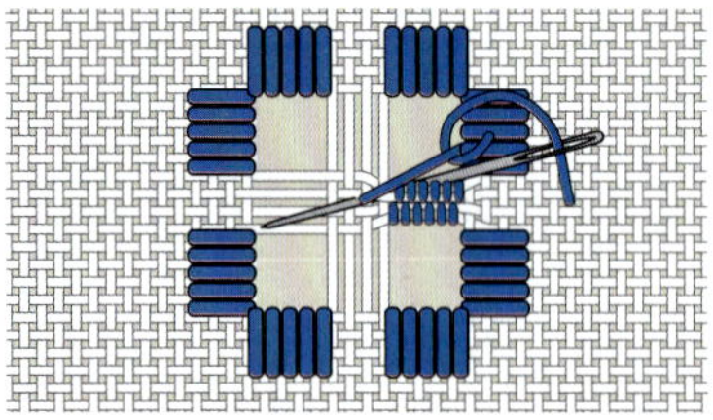

4 Insert the needle below the diagonal, and bring it out in the centre of the woven square.

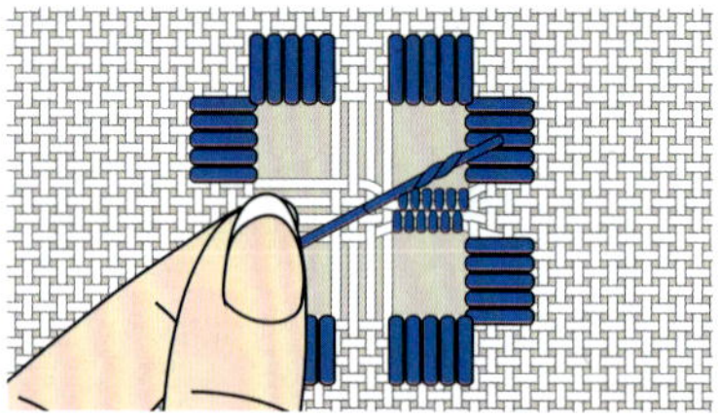

5 Pull the needle through. Pull the thread to intertwine the stitches.

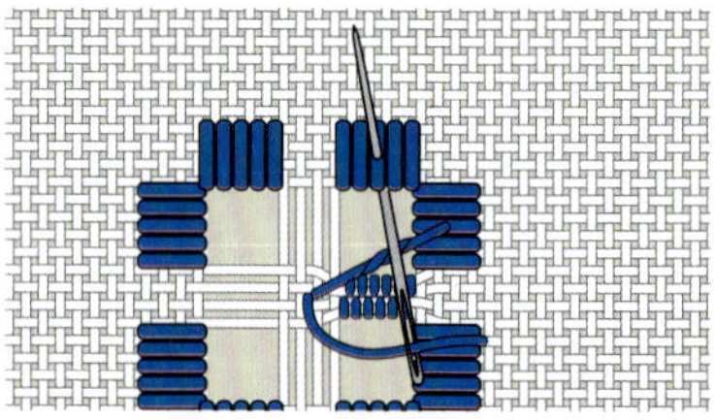

6 Inserting from behind, bring the needle out centrally in the upper satin stitch, piercing the centre stitch.

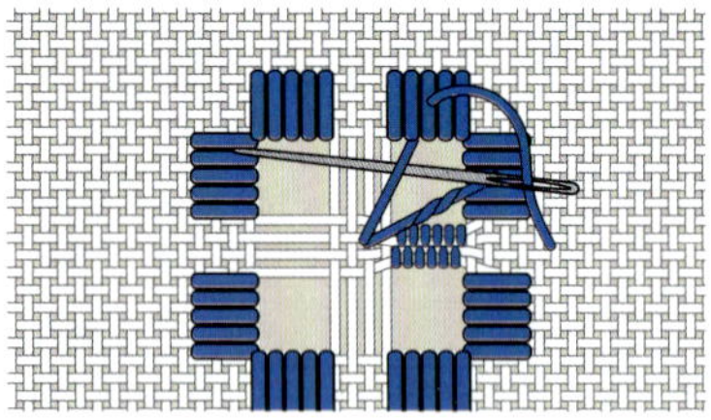

7 From the right, slide the needle under the diagonal stitch.

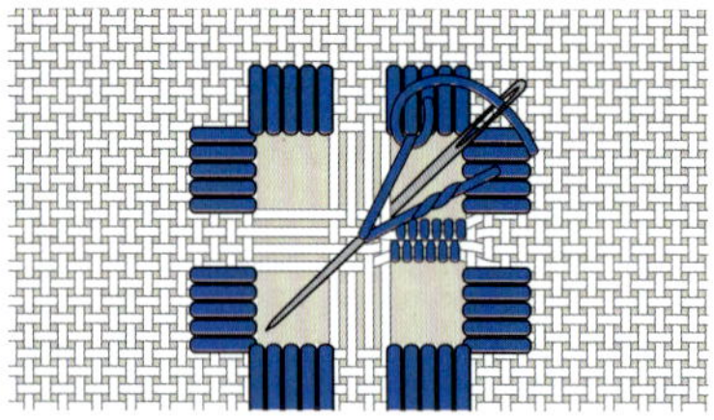

8 Insert the needle between the diagonals, and bring it out in the centre of the woven square.

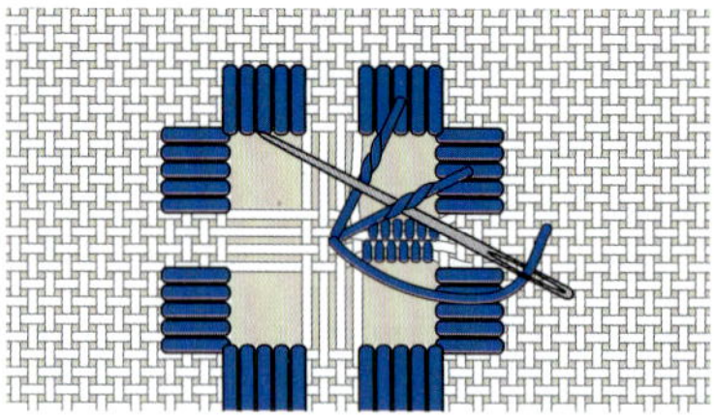

9 Pull the needle through and pull the thread to intertwine the stitches. From the right, slide the needle under the right diagonal.

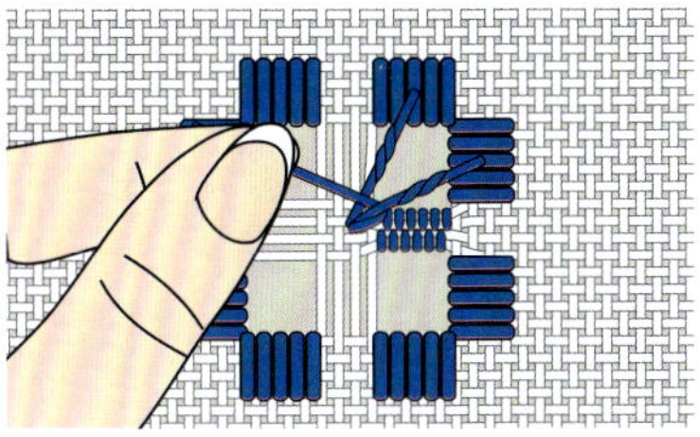

10 Pull the thread to the left and towards the woven centre, to pull the stitches in snug near the apex of the diagonals.

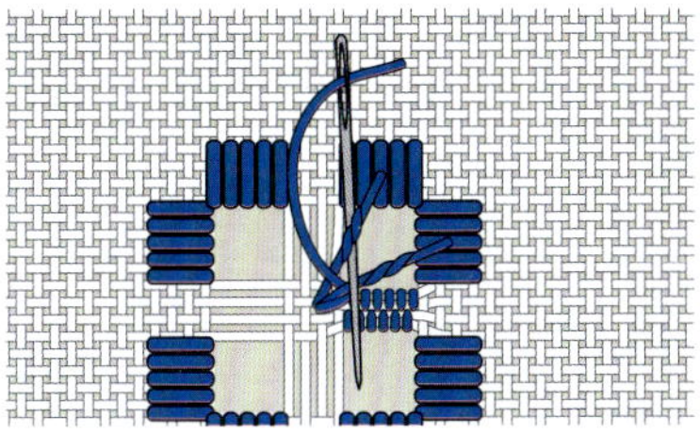

11 From above left, slide the needle under the left diagonal.

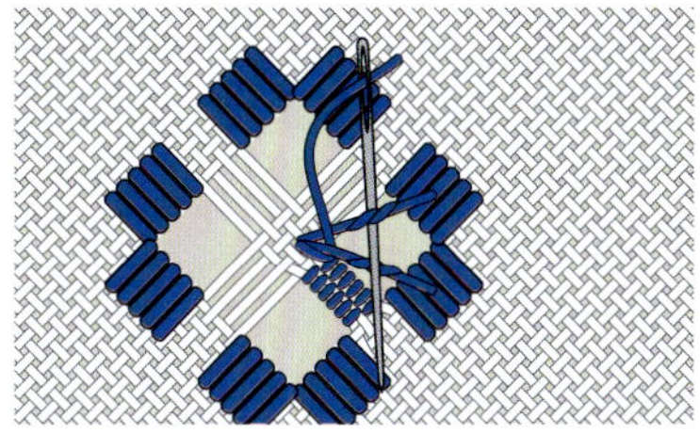

❶ *If it helps, while weaving the spokes, turn the work 45° so that you're inserting the needle more up and down rather than side to side. It might be more comfortable for the stitches that would otherwise go left to right.*

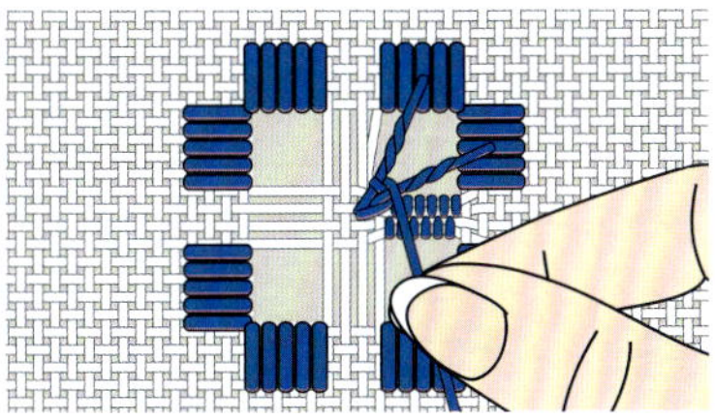

12 Pull the thread to the right and towards the woven centre to bring it snug against the previous stitch.

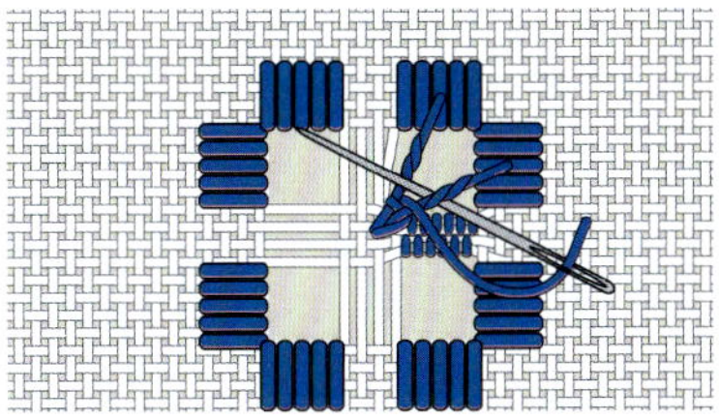

13 From the right, slide the needle under the right diagonal.

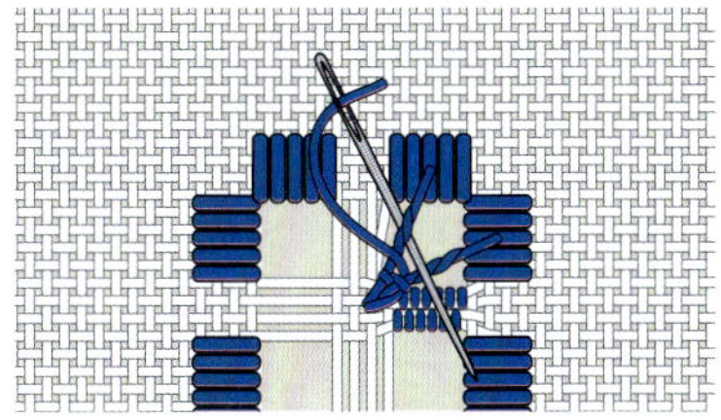

14 Pull the thread in snug against the previous stitches. Slide the needle from left to right under the left diagonal.

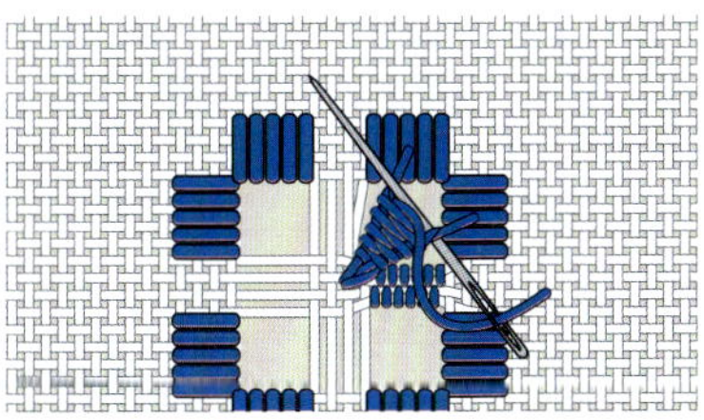

15 Weave back and forth to fill the diagonals, ensuring the stitches lengthen evenly to create a pleasing triangle. Finish the weaving by sliding the needle from right to left under the right diagonal.

❶ *Even tension will help with shaping. Any stitches that sit out further or tighter than others will look less pleasing. Adjust or re-stitch any stitches that are too loose or too tight.*

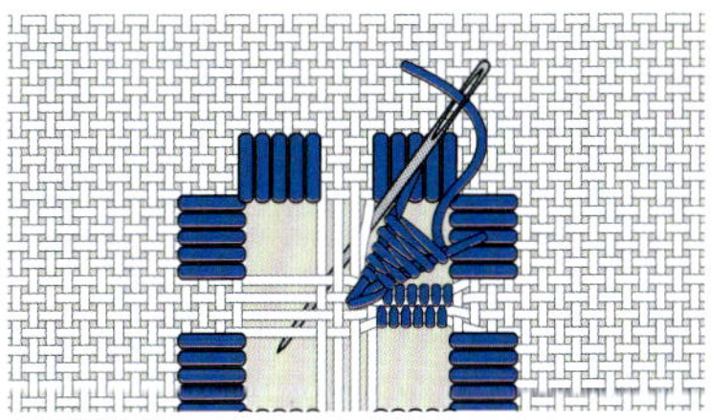

16 Take the needle to the back outside the left diagonal.

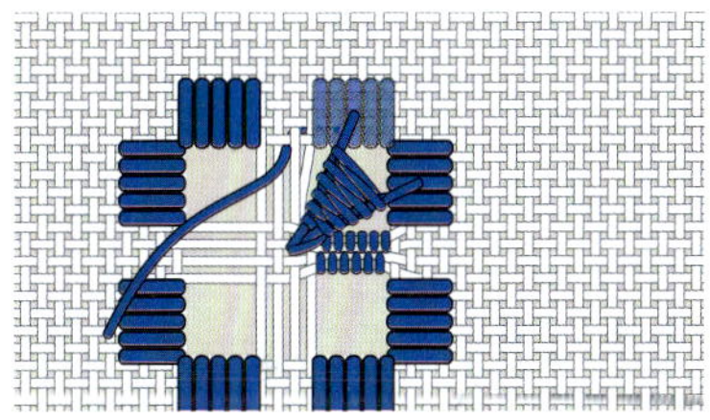

17 On the back, take the thread under the back of the satin stitch and bring it out ready to weave the next bar.

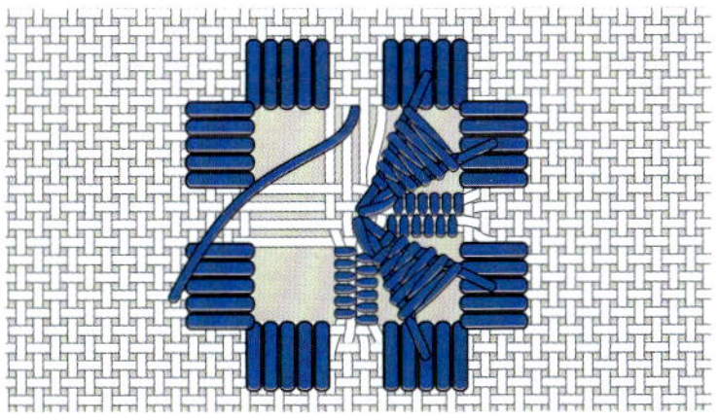

18 Turn the work 90° clockwise and repeat the woven fan.

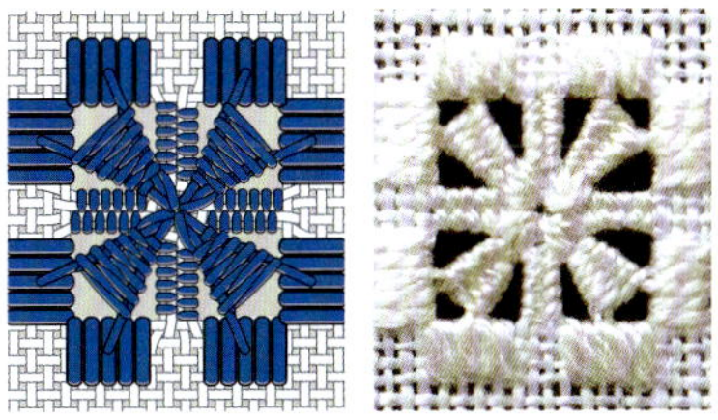

19 Repeat the filling in the remaining two quadrants. Finish the thread in the back of the satin stitch.

woven fan – three spokes

This variation has three spokes instead of two.

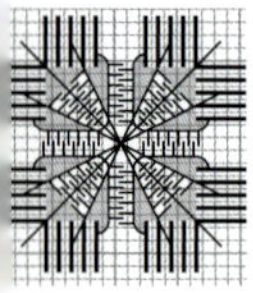

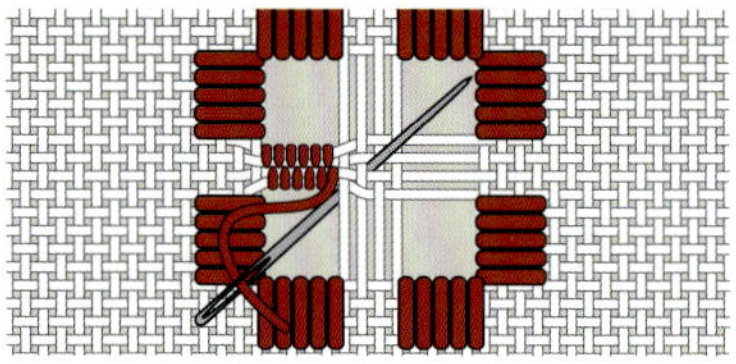

1 Work the first bar at the left-hand side, then bring the needle out in the centre of the woven square.

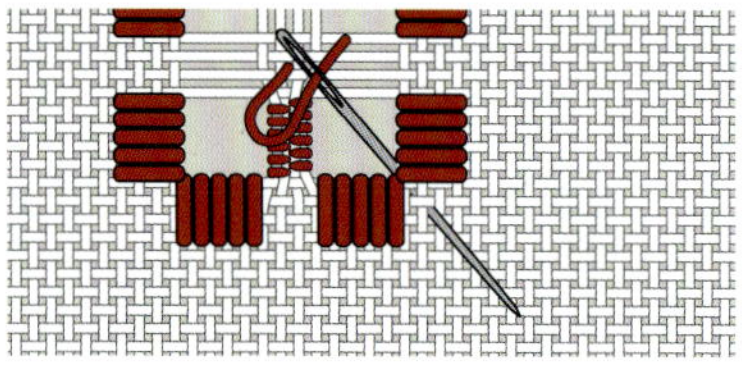

2 Turn the work 90° anticlockwise. Insert the needle in the lower right open square, and bring it out two threads away from the corner.

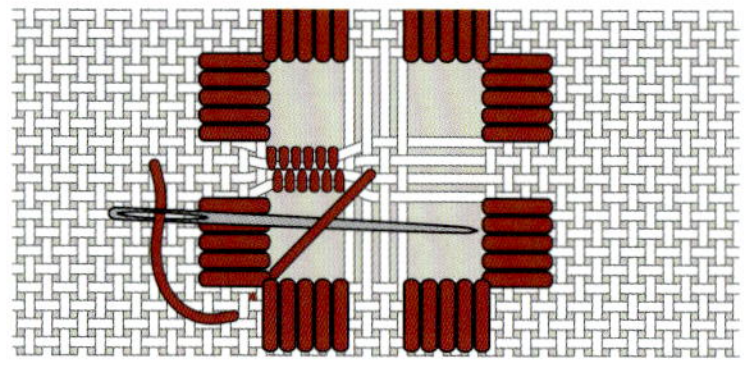

3 Turn the work 90° clockwise. Pull the needle through and tighten the diagonal stitch. From the left, slide the needle under the diagonal stitch.

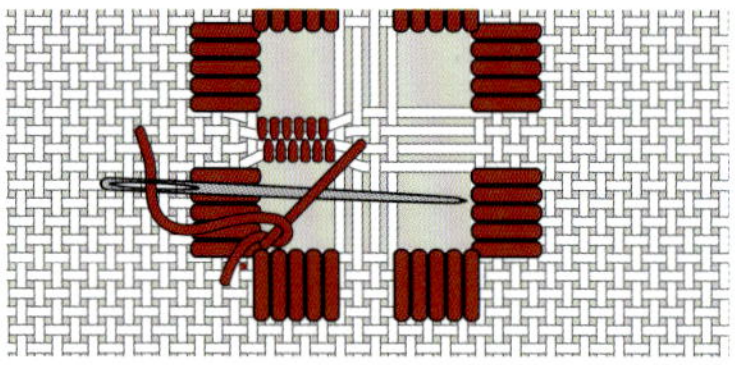

4 From the left, slide the needle under the diagonal stitch again.

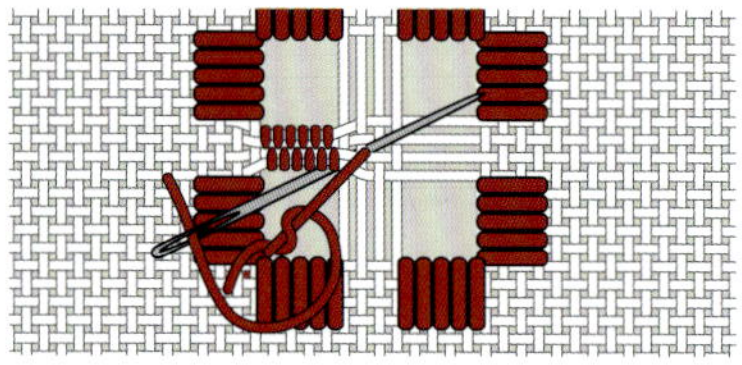

5 Insert the needle above the diagonal. Bring it out in the centre of the woven square.

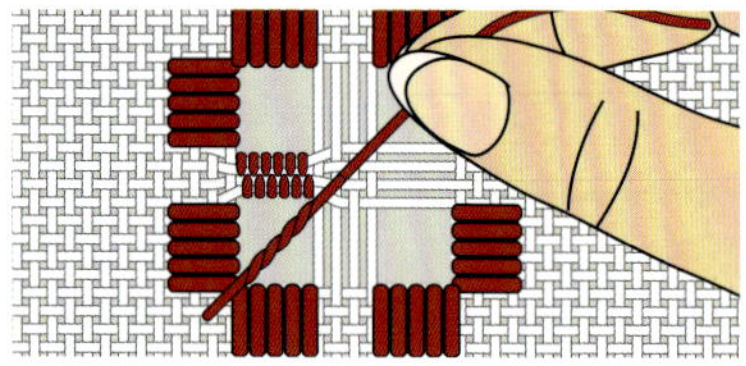

6 Pull the needle through and pull the thread to intertwine the stitches.

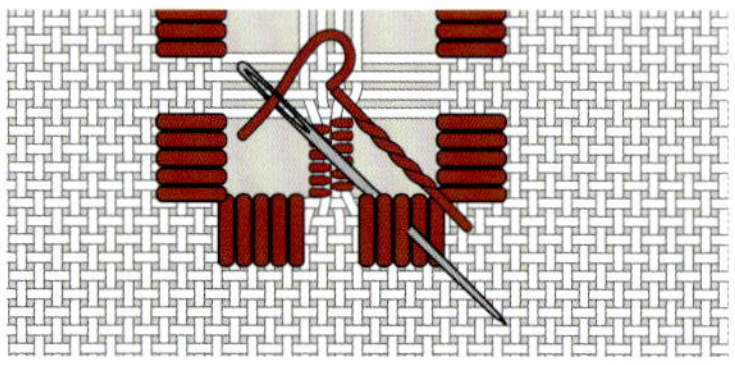

7 Turn the work 90° anticlockwise. Below the diagonal, take the needle under the adjacent satin stitch. Bring it out halfway down the block, two stitches from the corner.

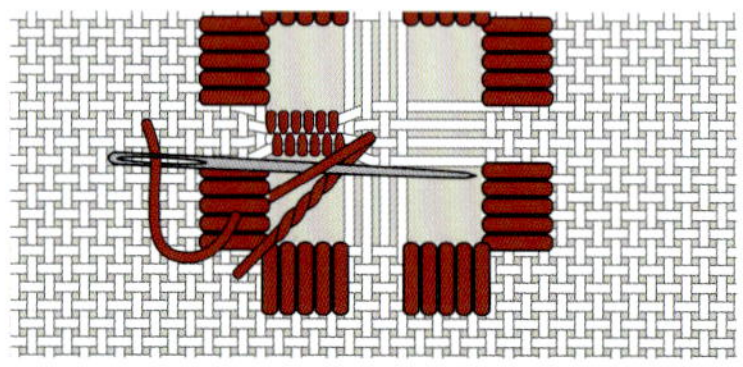

8 Turn the work 90° clockwise. Pull the needle through and tighten the diagonal stitch. Slide the needle from left to right under the diagonal stitch.

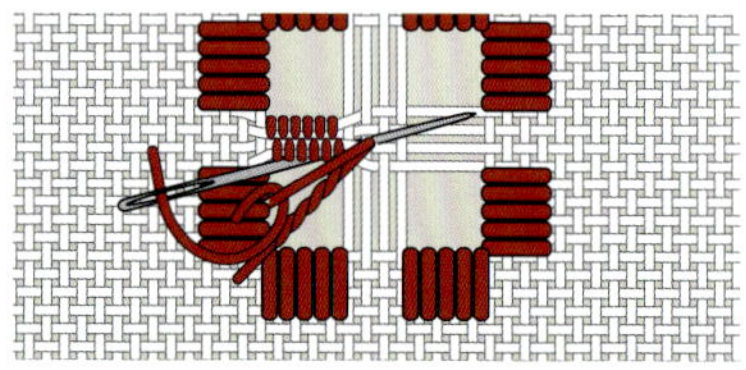

9 Above the diagonal, take the needle under the centre woven square and bring it out in the centre.

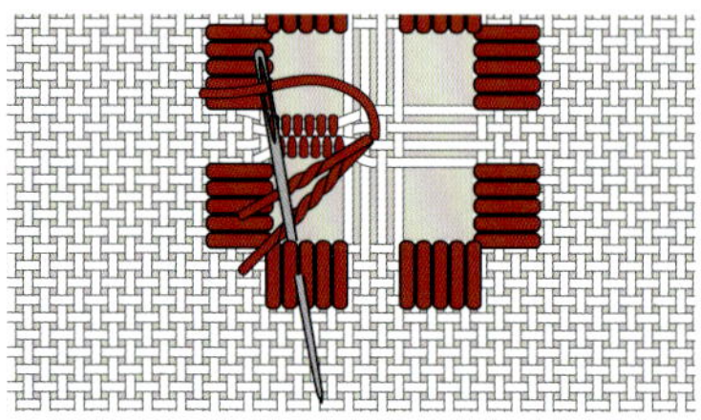

10 Pull the thread to intertwine the stitches. Insert the needle in the back of the lower satin stitch. Bring it out halfway down the block, two stitches from the corner.

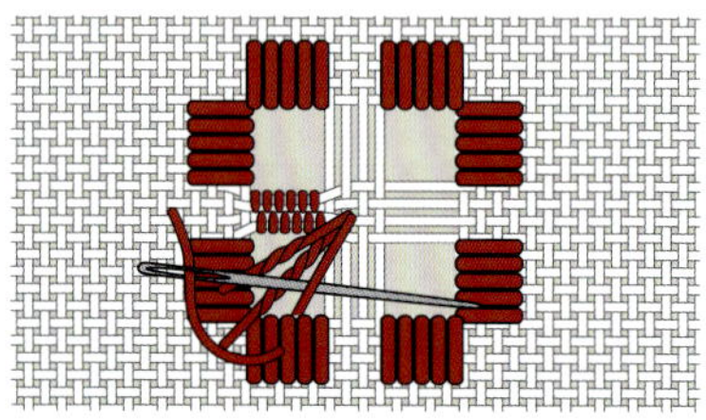

11 Pull the needle through and tighten the diagonal stitch. Slide the needle from left to right under the diagonal stitch.

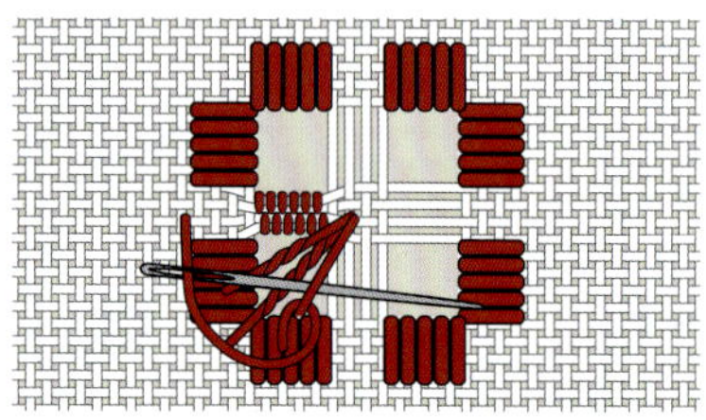

12 Slide the needle from left to right under the diagonal stitch again.

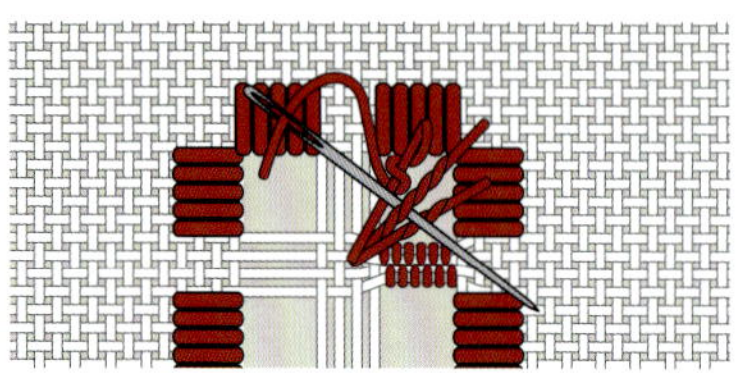

13 Turn the work 180°. Slide the needle from left to right under the middle diagonal.

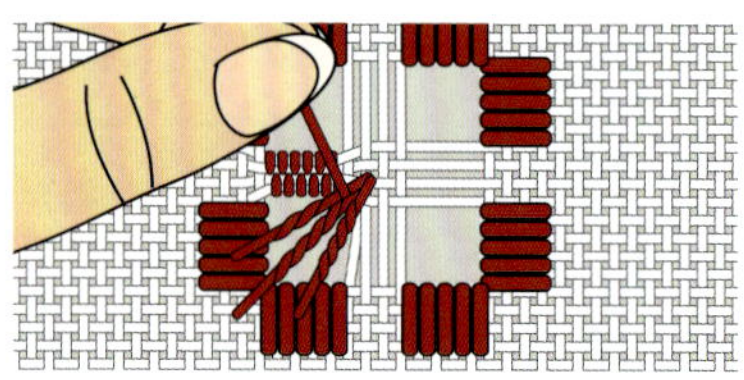

14 Turn the work 180°. Pull to intertwine the stitches, but do not allow the diagonal to be distorted.

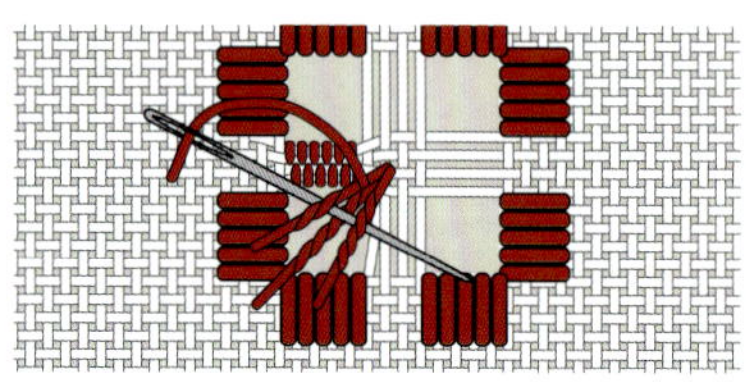

15 Slide the needle from left to right under the outer diagonals.

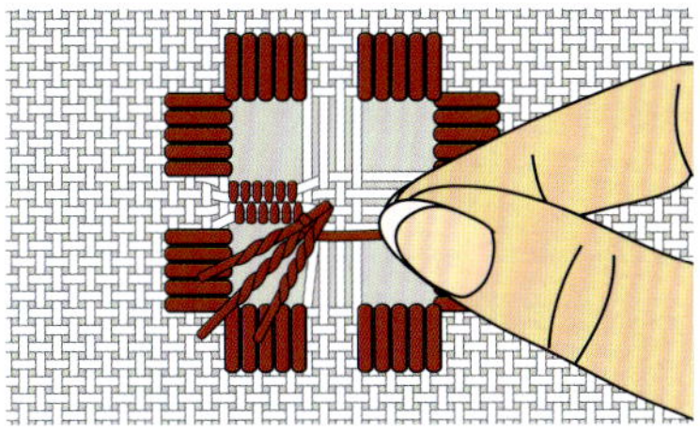

16 Pull the thread to the right and towards the woven centre, to pull the stitches in snug near the apex of the three diagonals.

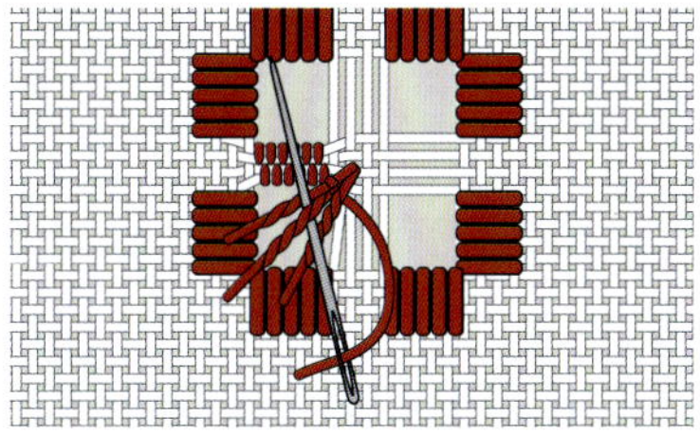

17 Slide the needle from right to left under the middle diagonal.

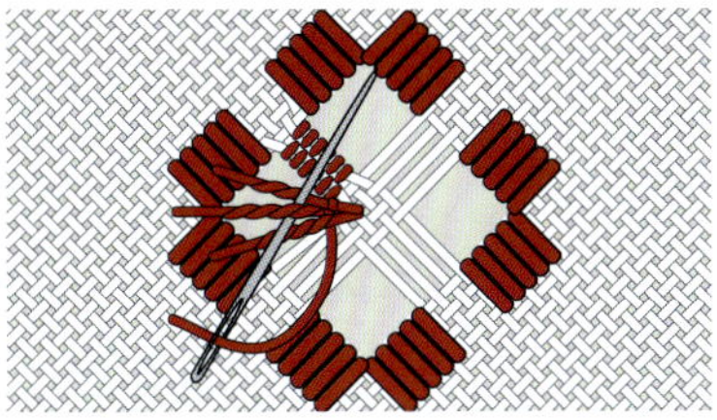

! *If it helps, while weaving the spokes, turn the work 45° so that you're inserting the needle more up and down rather than side to side. It might be more comfortable for the stitches that would otherwise go right to left.*

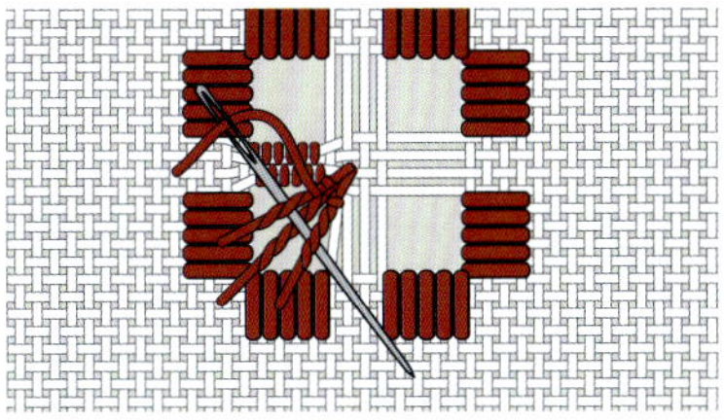

18 Pull the thread left and towards the woven centre, to pull the stitches in snug near the apex of the diagonals. Slide the needle from left to right under the outer two diagonals.

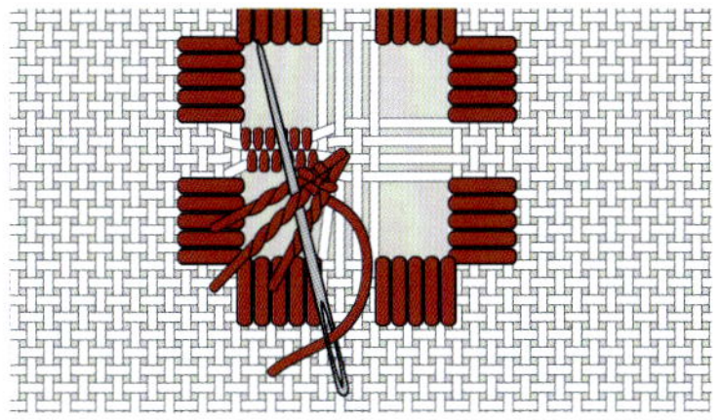

19 Pull the thread in snug against the previous stitches. Slide the needle from right to left under the middle diagonal.

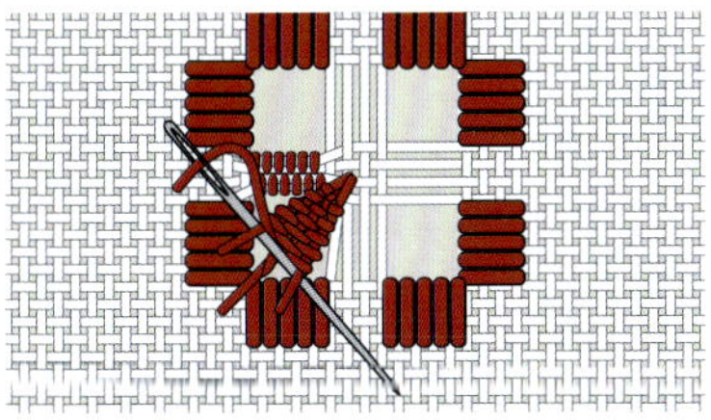

20 Keep weaving back and forth to fill the diagonals, ensuring the stitches lengthen evenly to create a pleasing triangle. Finish by sliding the needle from left to right under the outer diagonals.

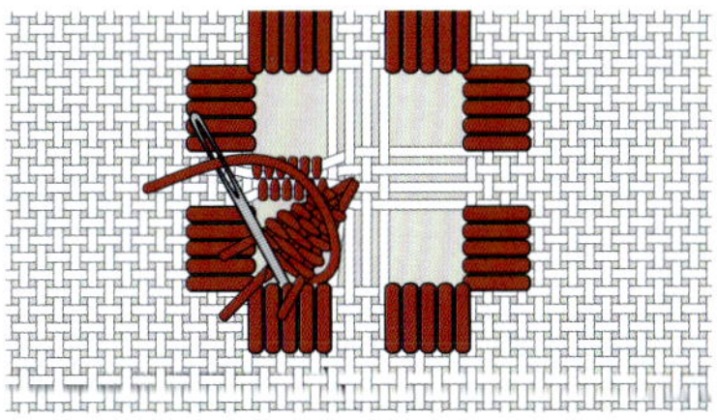

21 Insert the needle between the middle and right diagonals, taking the needle to the back.

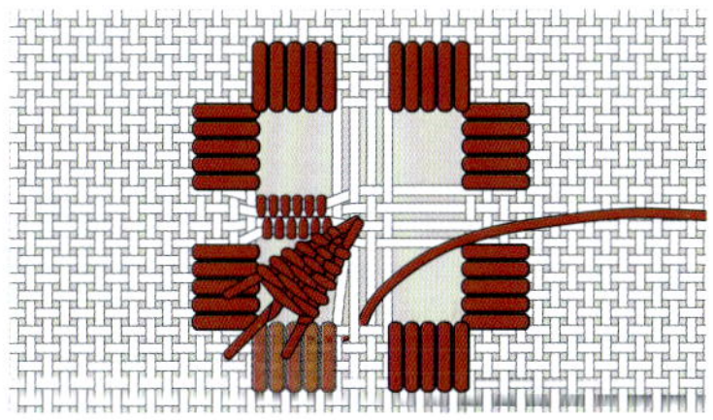

22 On the back, run the needle through the back of the satin stitch and bring it out at the end of the next bar to be woven.

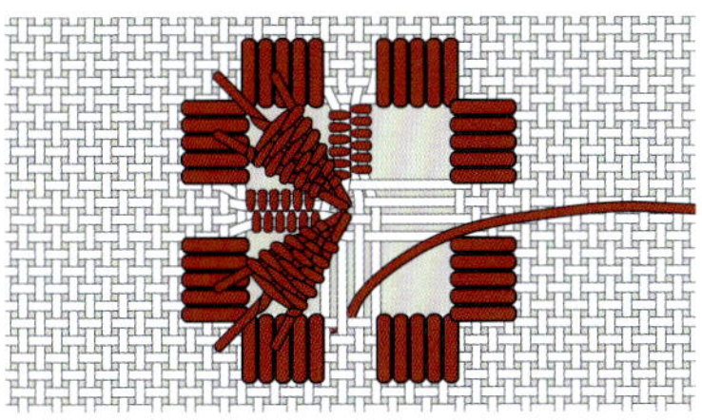

23 Turn the work 90° clockwise and repeat the filling in the next quadrant.

24 Repeat the filling in the remaining two quadrants. Finish the thread in the back of the satin stitch.

R

woven fan – three spokes

This variation has three spokes instead of two.

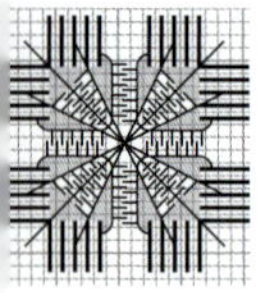

CONTEMPORARY

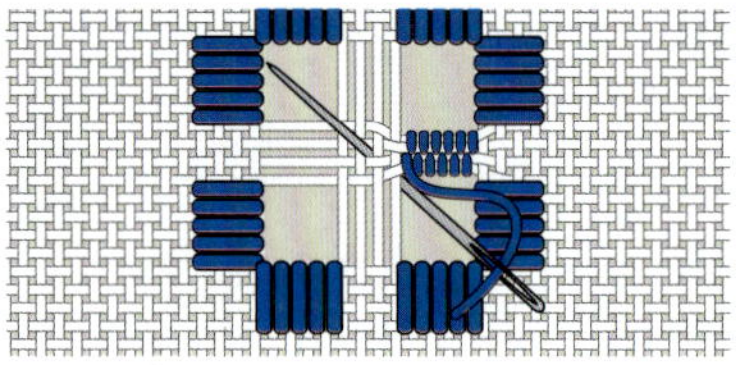

1 Work the first bar at the right-hand side, then bring the needle out in the centre of the woven square.

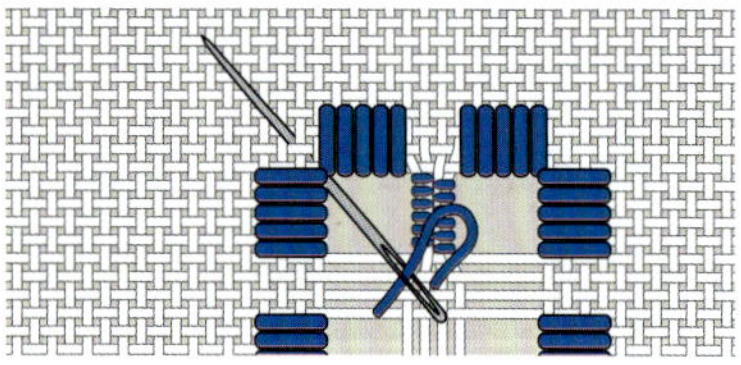

2 Turn the work 90° anticlockwise. Insert the needle in the upper left open square, and bring it out two threads away from the corner.

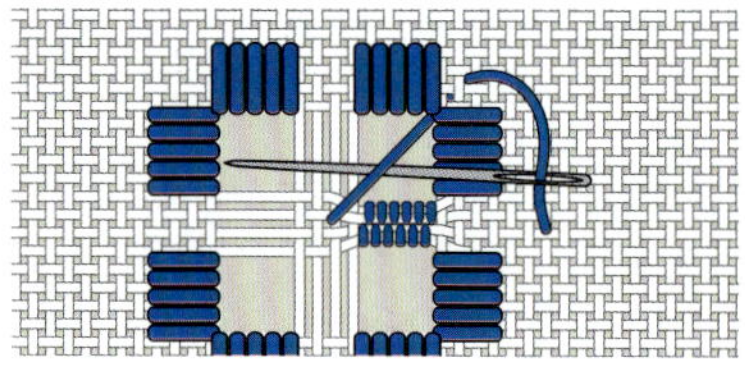

3 Turn the work 90° clockwise. Pull the needle through and tighten the diagonal stitch. From the right, slide the needle under the diagonal stitch.

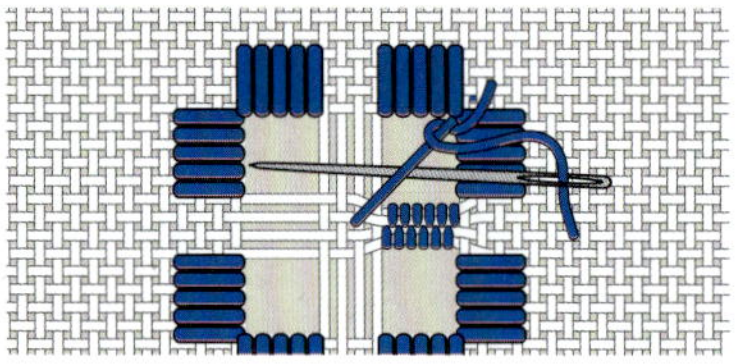

4 From the right, slide the needle under the diagonal stitch again.

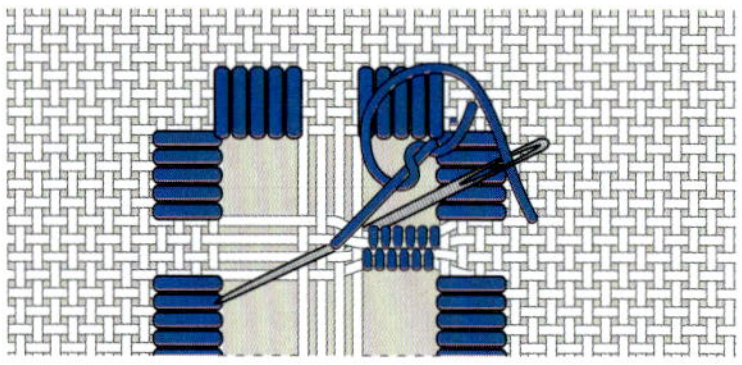

5 Insert the needle below the diagonal. Bring it out in the centre of the woven square.

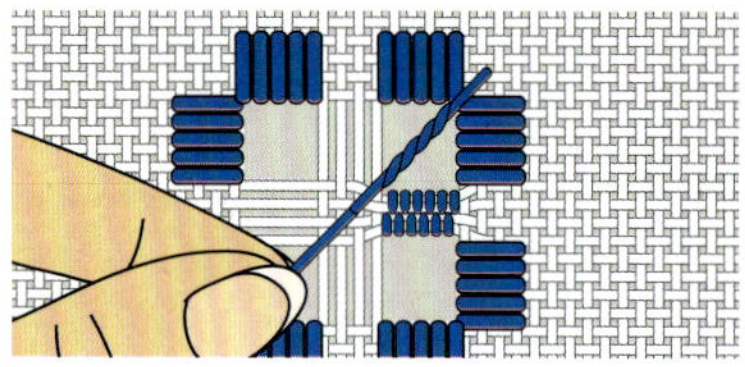

6 Pull the needle through and pull the thread to intertwine the stitches.

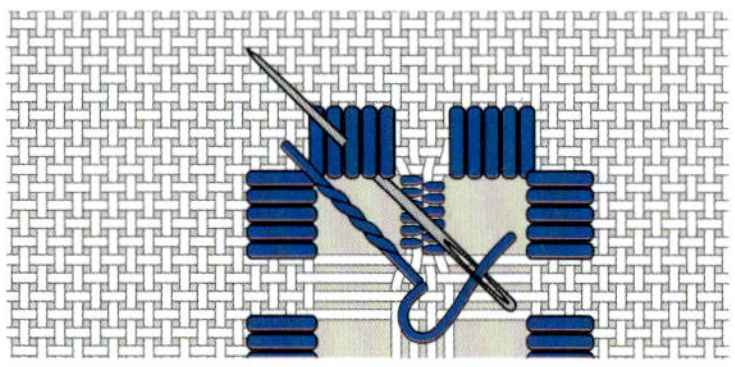

7 Turn the work 90° anticlockwise. Above the diagonal, take the needle under the adjacent satin stitch. Bring it out halfway up the block, two stitches from the corner.

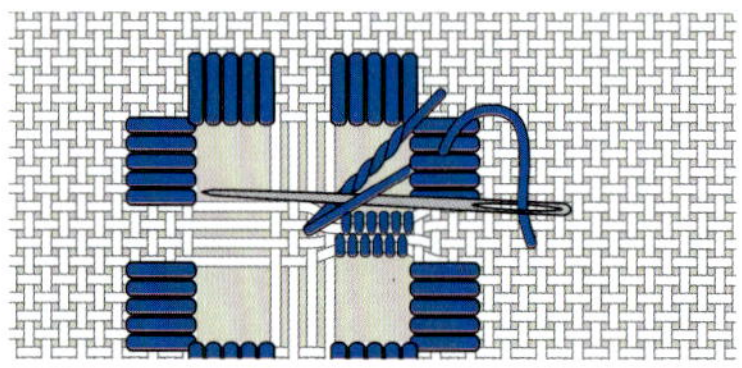

8 Turn the work 90° clockwise. Pull the needle through and tighten the diagonal stitch. Slide the needle from right to left under the diagonal stitch.

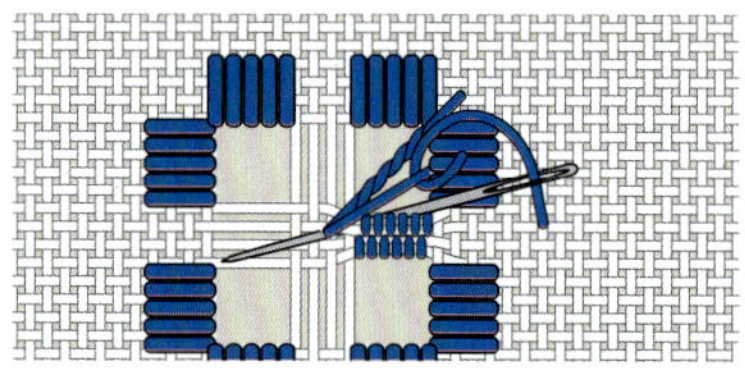

9 Below the diagonal, take the needle under the centre woven square and bring it out in the centre.

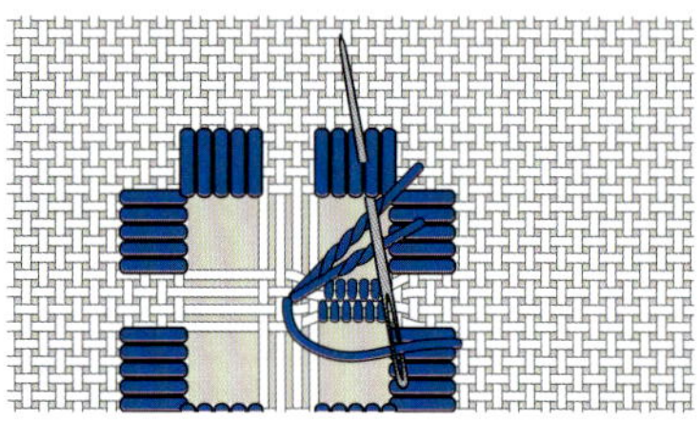

10 Pull the thread to intertwine the stitches. Insert the needle in the back of the upper satin stitch. Bring it out halfway up the block, two stitches from the corner.

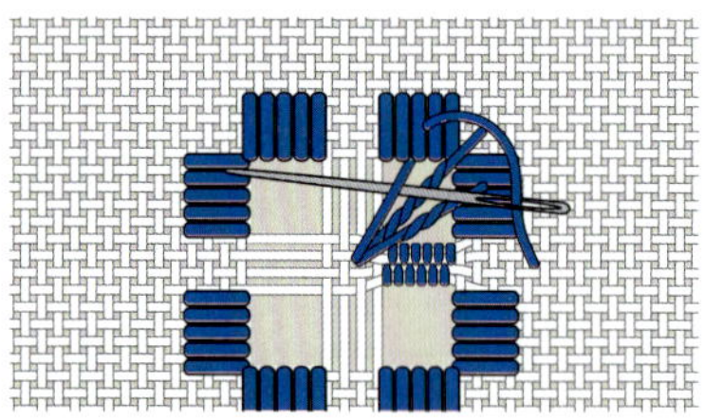

11 Pull the needle through and tighten the diagonal stitch. Slide the needle from right to left under the diagonal stitch.

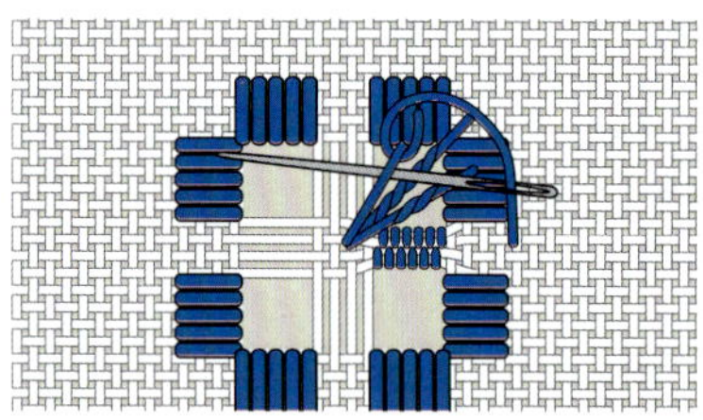

12 Slide the needle from right to left under the diagonal stitch again.

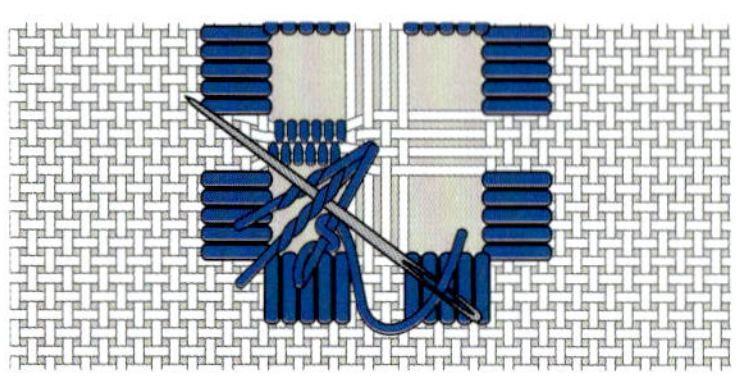

13 Turn the work 180°. Slide the needle from right to left under the middle diagonal.

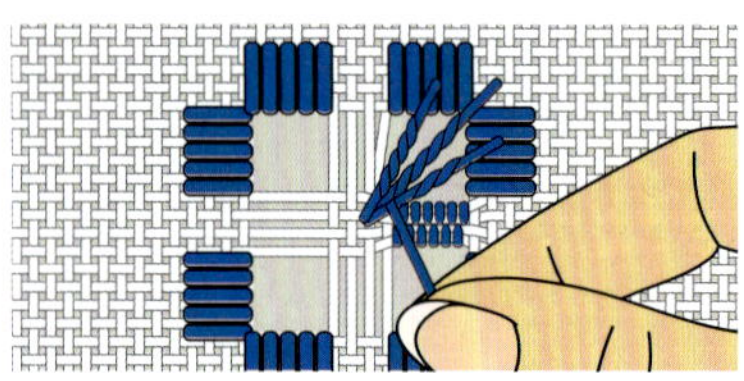

14 Turn the work 180°. Pull to intertwine the stitches, but do not allow the diagonal to be distorted.

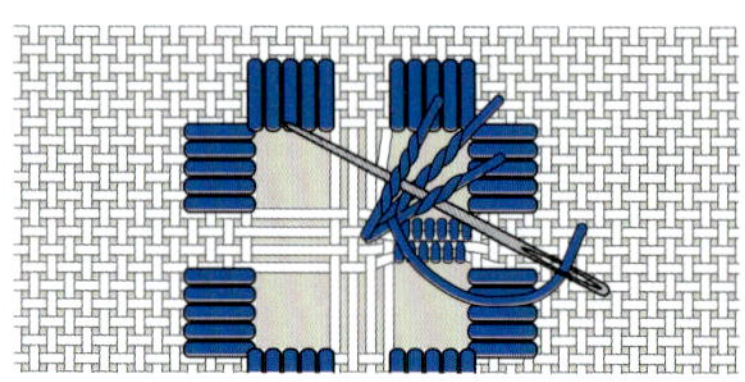

15 Slide the needle from right to left under the outer diagonals.

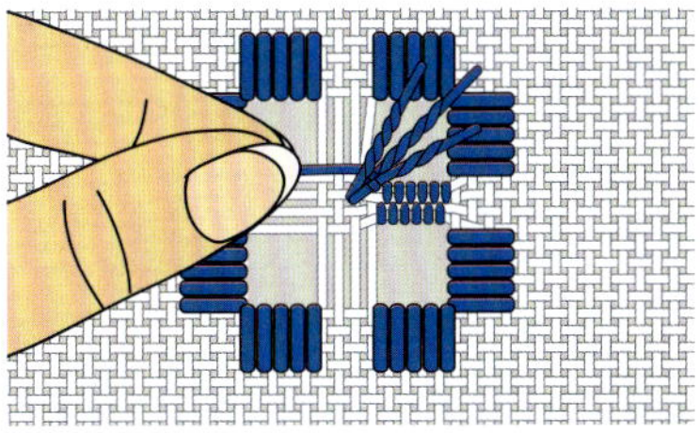

16 Pull the thread to the left and towards the woven centre, to pull the stitches in snug near the apex of the three diagonals.

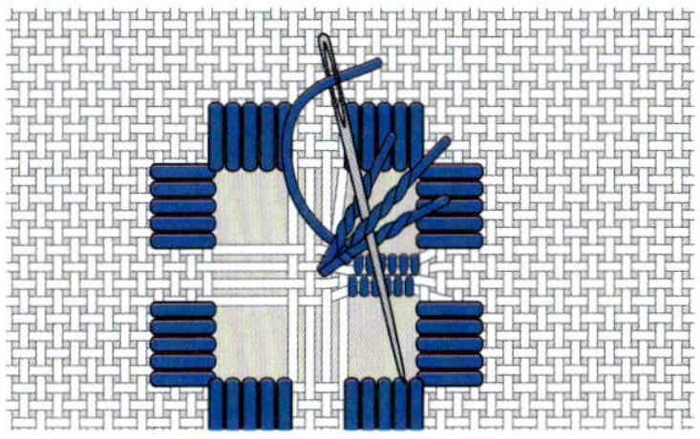

17 Slide the needle from left to right under the middle diagonal.

❶ *If it helps, while weaving the spokes, turn the work 45° so that you're inserting the needle more up and down rather than side to side. It might be more comfortable for the stitches that would otherwise go left to right.*

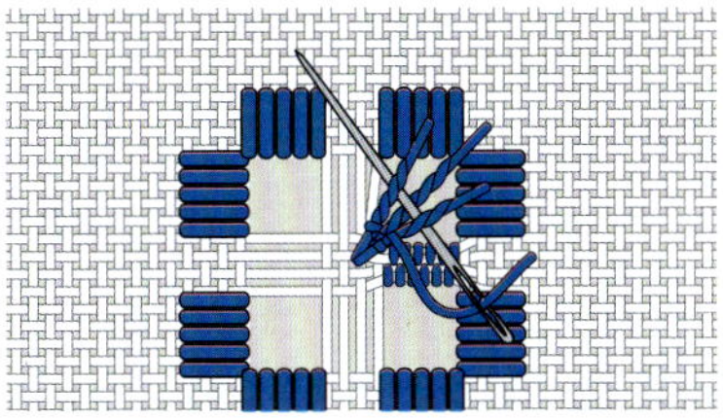

18 Pull the thread right and towards the woven centre, to pull the stitches in snug near the apex of the diagonals. Slide the needle from right to left under the outer two diagonals.

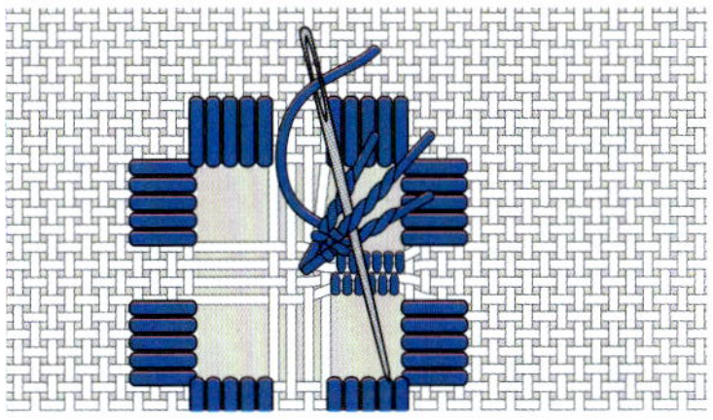

19 Pull the thread in snug against the previous stitches. Slide the needle from left to right under the middle diagonal.

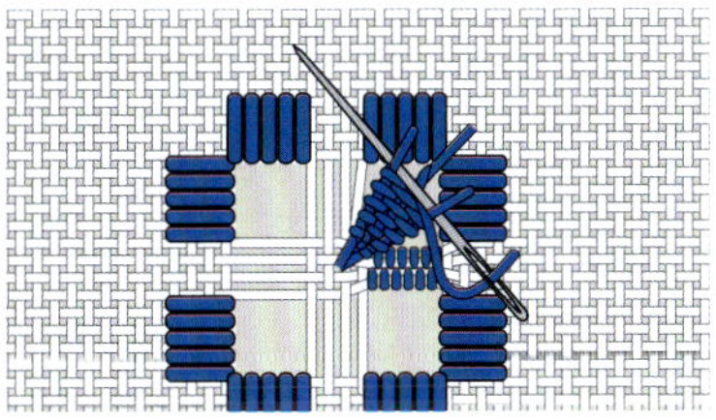

20 Keep weaving back and forth to fill the diagonals, ensuring the stitches lengthen evenly to create a pleasing triangle. Finish by sliding the needle from right to left under the outer diagonals.

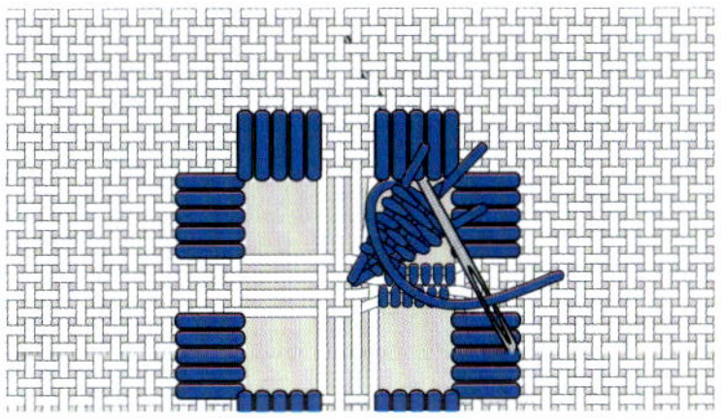

21 Insert the needle between the middle and right diagonals, taking the needle to the back.

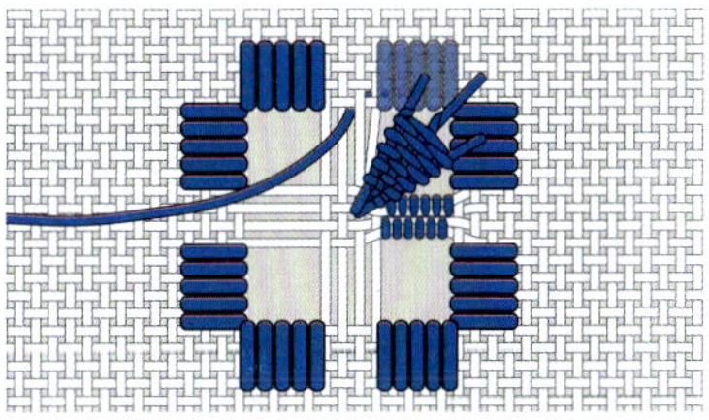

22 On the back, run the needle through the back of the satin stitch and bring it out at the end of the next bar to be woven.

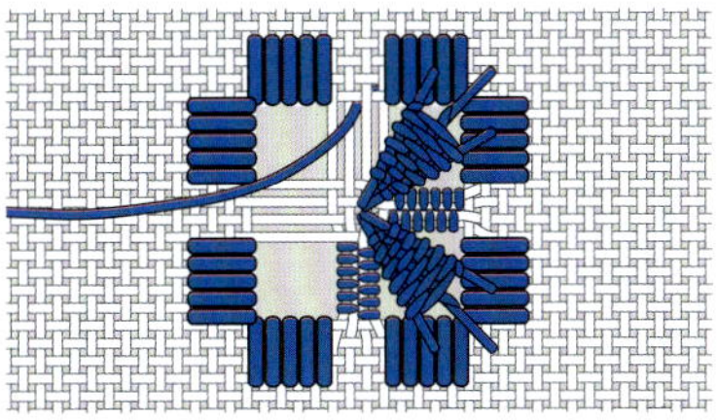

23 Turn the work 90° clockwise and repeat the filling in the next quadrant.

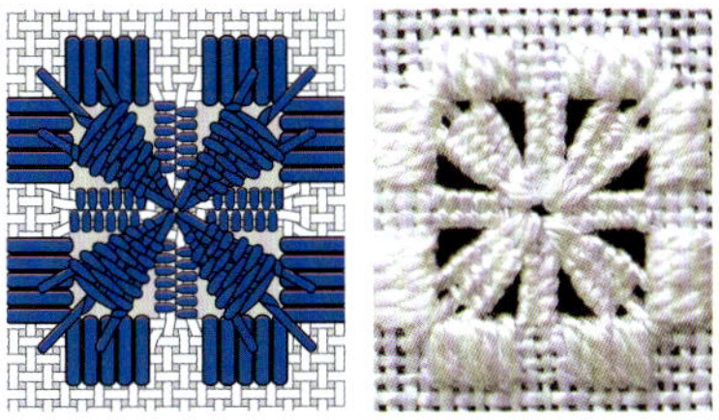

24 Repeat the filling in the remaining two quadrants. Finish the thread in the back of the satin stitch.

stepped fan

Stepped fans can be of varying size, with varying quantities of spokes. Refer to your pattern or project instructions.

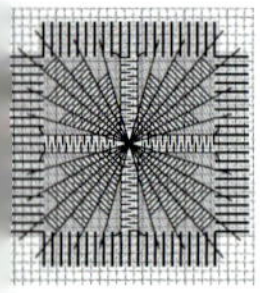

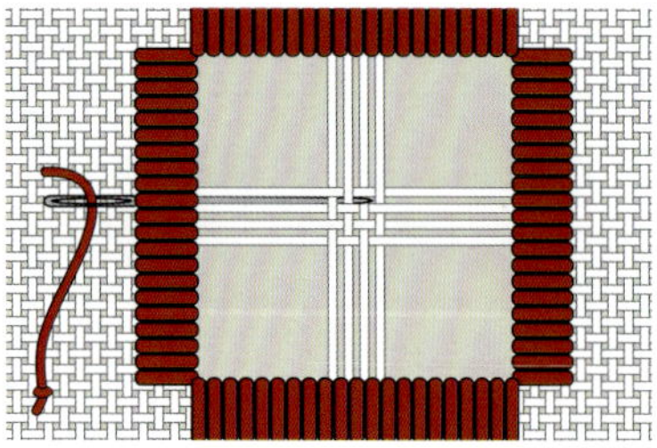

1 Prepare a large square as shown. From the front, insert a needle with a knotted thread at the outer left edge of the satin stitch, and bring it out straight across, one thread above the centre of the woven square.

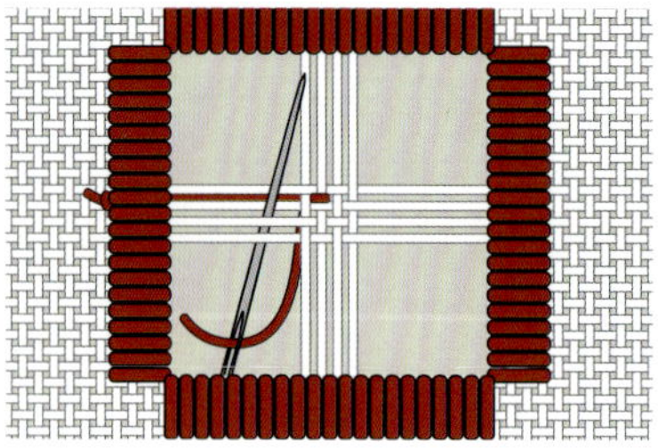

2 Pull the needle through. Insert the needle one thread to the left and bring it out ready to work the bar.

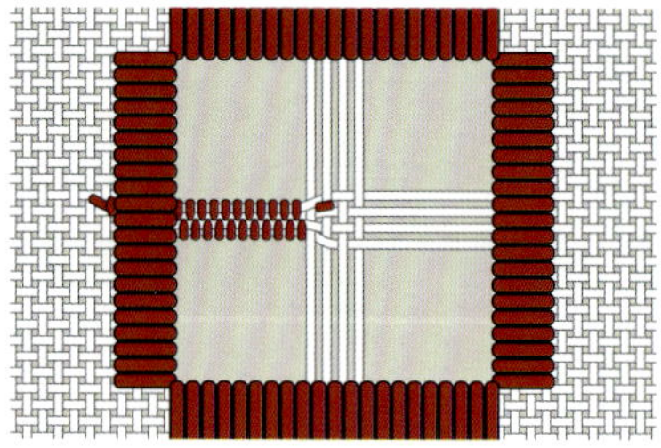

3 Work the bar back to the edge, covering over the laced thread on the back.

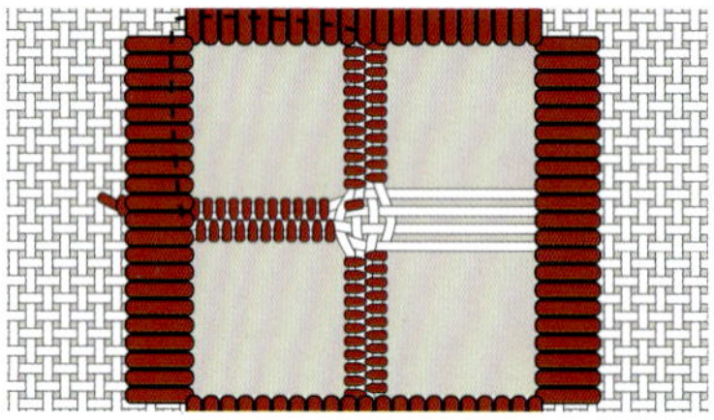

4 Take the thread under the back of the satin stitch around to the next bar and work right across the middle of the square. Finish the thread in the back of the satin stitch.

❶ *Trim the knot from the front of the fabric.*

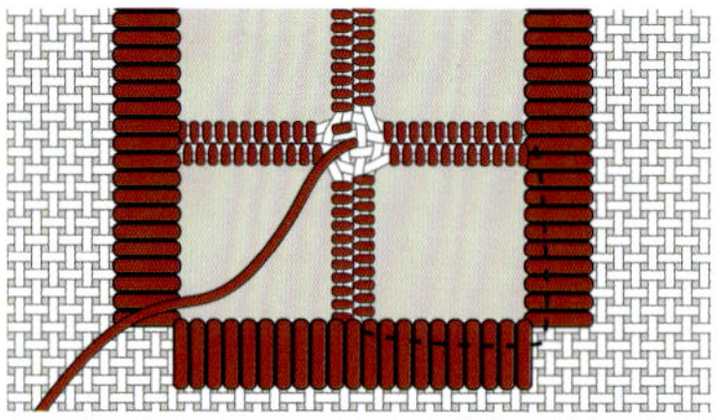

5 Start a long, new thread under the back of the satin stitch. Work the last bar in to the centre. Bring the needle out in the square's centre.

❶ *A new thread helps to ensure you'll have enough for the centre stitching.*

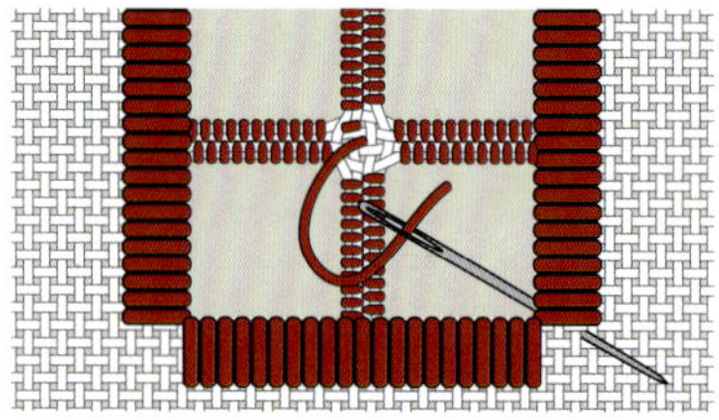

6 Working in the lower right quadrant, bring the needle out one thread down and left from the bottom right end of the right satin stitch.

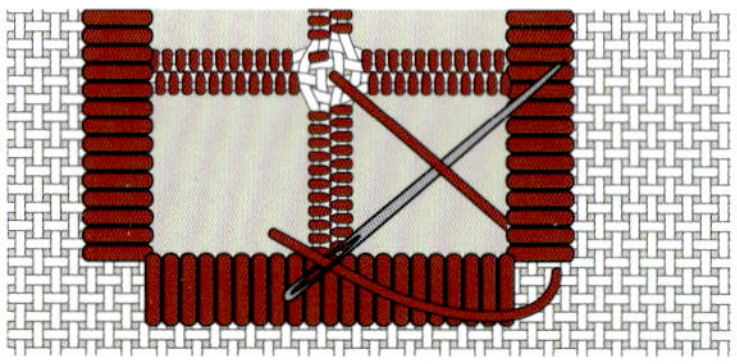

7 Pull the needle through. From below, slide the needle under the diagonal stitch.

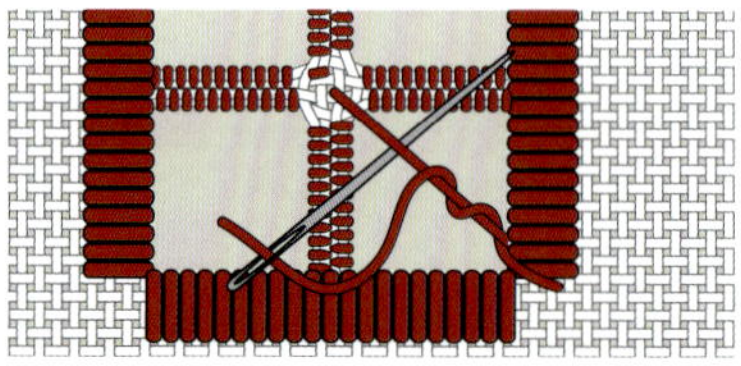

8 Slide the needle under the diagonal stitch twice more.

❶ *If you are working this in a larger square, you may need more twists. You may need fewer for a smaller square.*

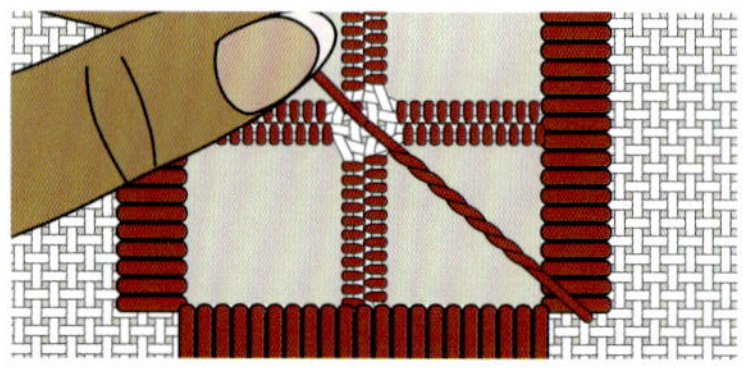

9 Insert the needle below the diagonal. Bring it out in the centre of the woven square. Pull the thread to intertwine the stitches.

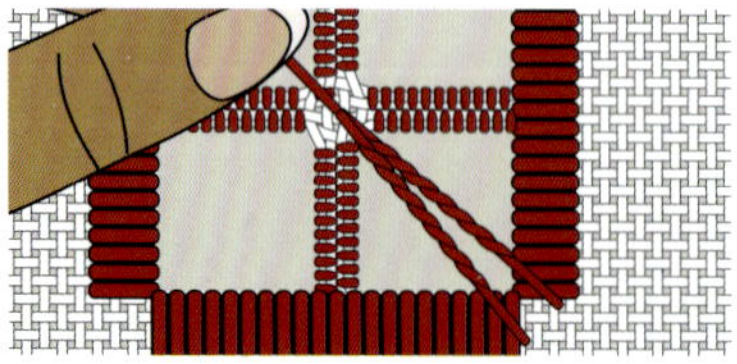

10 Work another twisted diagonal in the same way, to the hole one thread right and up from the bottom right end of the lower satin stitch.

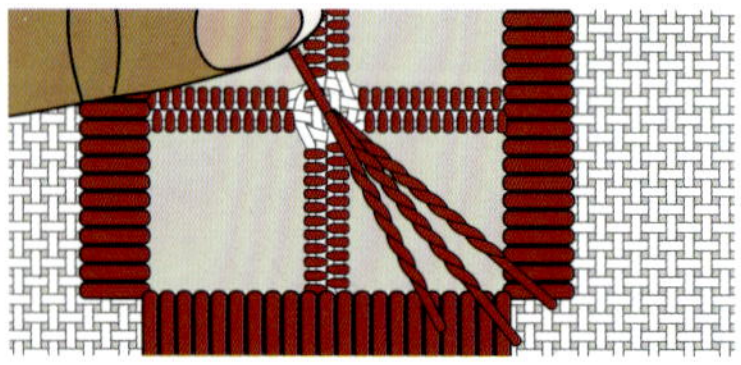

11 Work another twisted diagonal in the bottom satin stitch block, to two threads down from the cut edge, four satin stitches from the right end. Take the needle under the stitch only twice, this time.

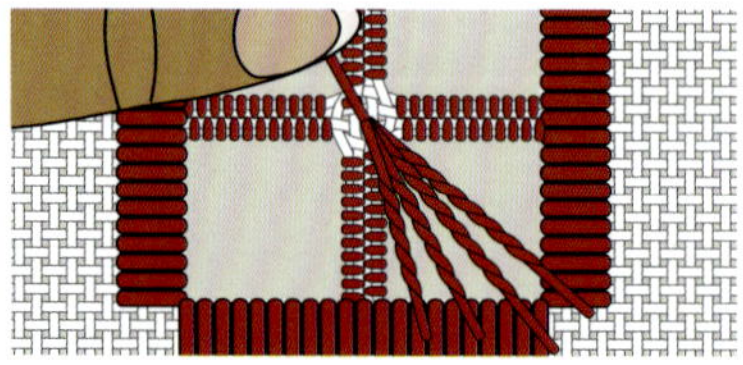

12 Work another twisted diagonal to three threads left of the previous stitch.

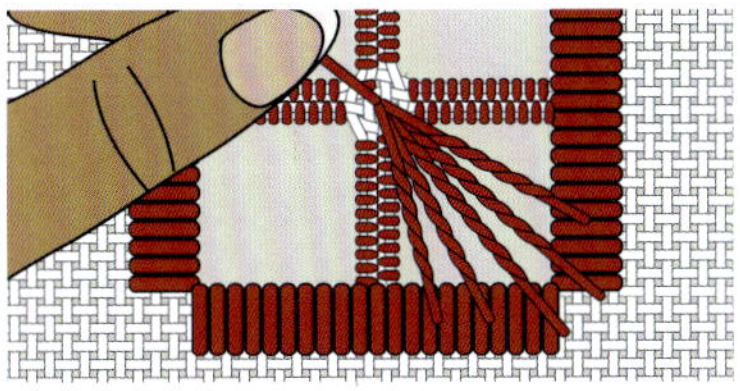

13 Work a fifth twisted diagonal to four satin stitches up from the bottom of the right satin stitch block.

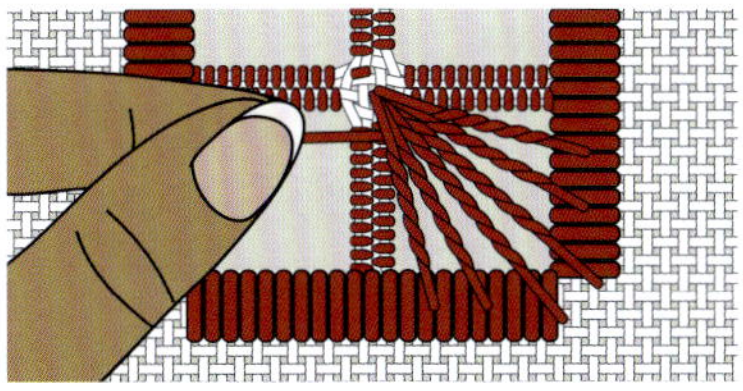

14 Work a sixth diagonal to three satin stitches up from the end of the previous one. Instead of bringing the needle out at the centre, bring it out left of the left-most diagonal.

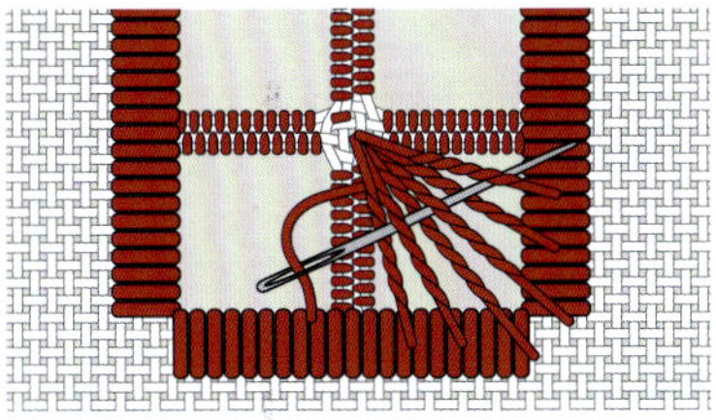

15 From the left, pass the needle over the first diagonal, then under the next, alternating over and under, all the way across.

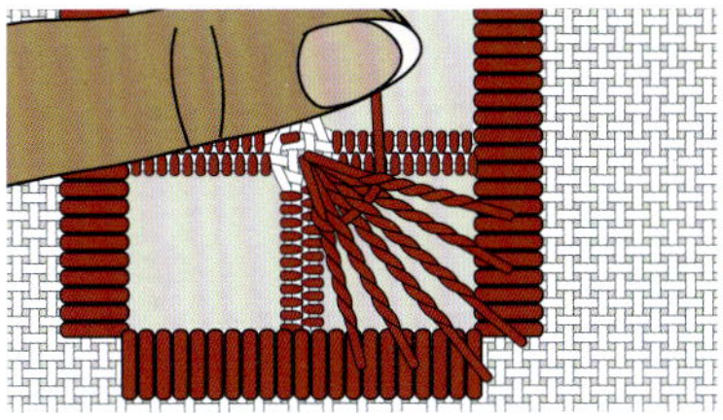

16 Pull the needle through. Pull the stitches towards the centre.

❶ *It will likely be difficult, so you may want to use the point of your needle to help push the thread towards the centre.*

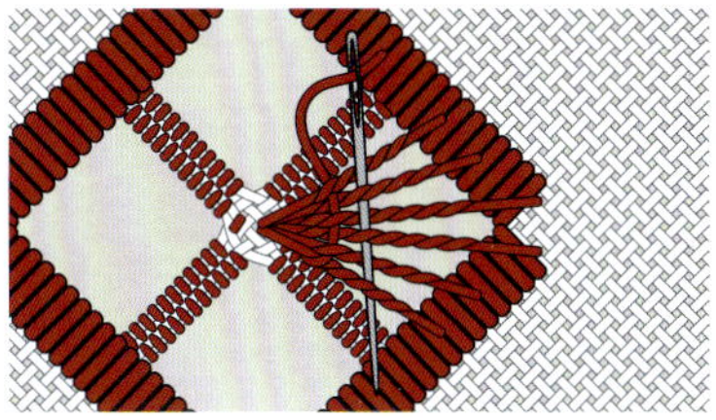

17 Turn the work 45° anticlockwise. From above, slide the needle over the top diagonal, then under the next, alternating over and under, all the way across.

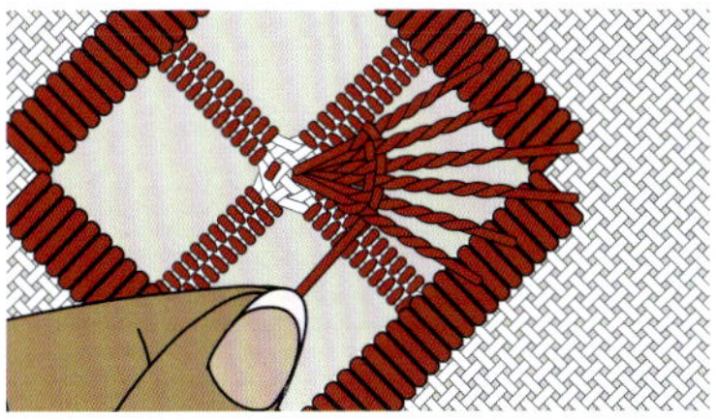

18 Pull the needle through. Pull the stitches towards the centre.

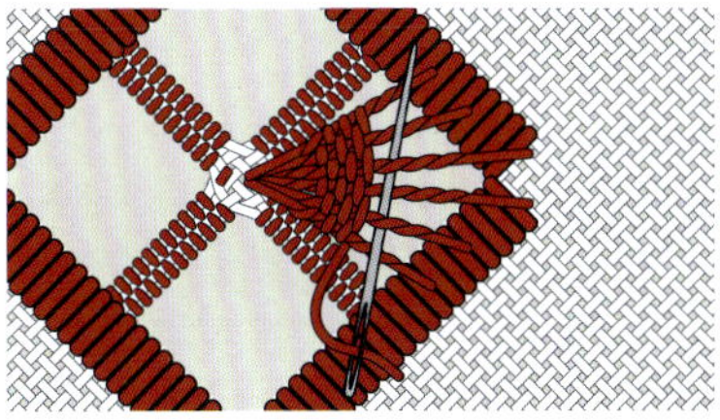

19 Continue weaving back and forth across all six diagonals until three return journeys have been made. Start the fourth, but stop before going under the last diagonal.

❶ *Adjust the row quantities for a larger or smaller square.*

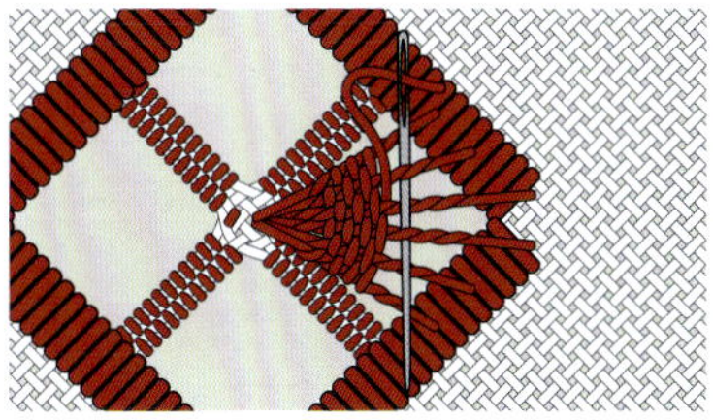

20 Pull the thread through. From above, take the needle under the second diagonal from the top, then over and under the next two.

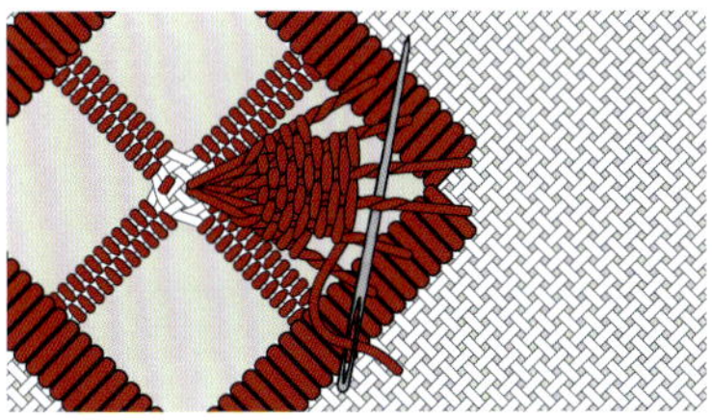

21 Continue weaving back and forth across the four middle diagonals, until three return journeys have been made. Start the fourth by going under the third diagonal from the bottom.

❶ *Adjust row quantities as needed.*

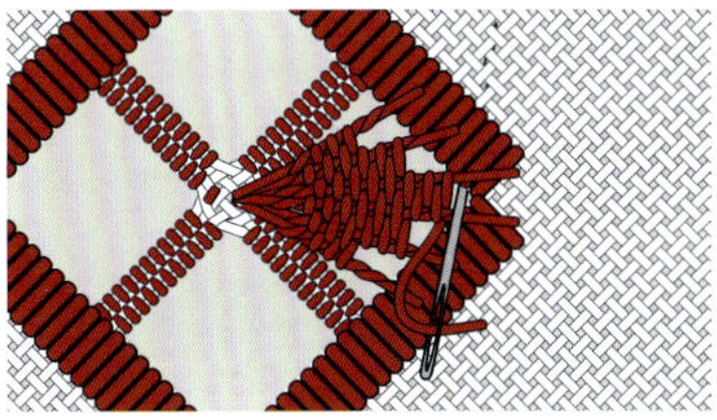

22 Weave back and forth on the middle two diagonals to fill the space. Take the needle to the back.

23 On the back, run the needle under the back of the fan stitching to the centre. Work stepped fans in each of the remaining quadrants and finish the thread in the back of the satin stitch.

❶ *If running the thread under the back of the weaving is difficult, at least go under two or three stitches to catch it.*

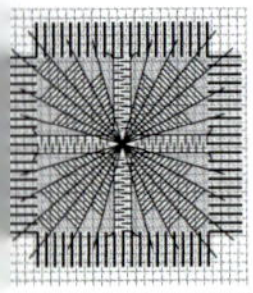

stepped fan

Stepped fans can be of varying size, with varying quantities of spokes. Refer to your pattern or project instructions.

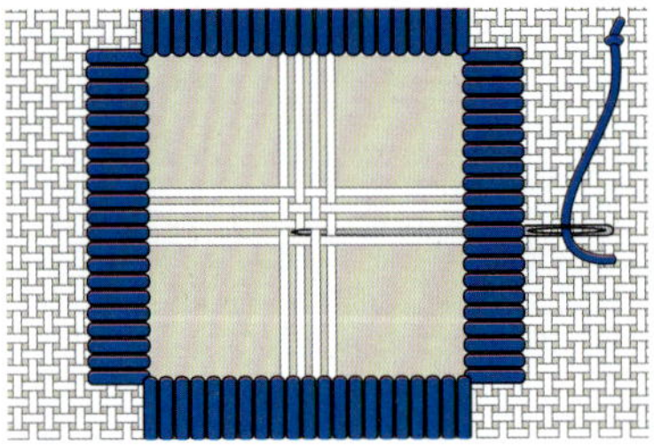

1 Prepare a large square as shown. From the front, insert a needle with a knotted thread at the outer right edge of the satin stitch, and bring it out straight across, one thread below the centre of the woven square.

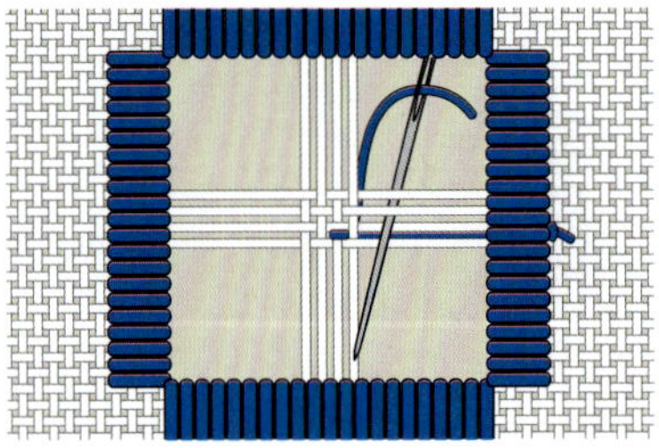

2 Pull the needle through. Insert the needle one thread to the right and bring it out ready to work the bar.

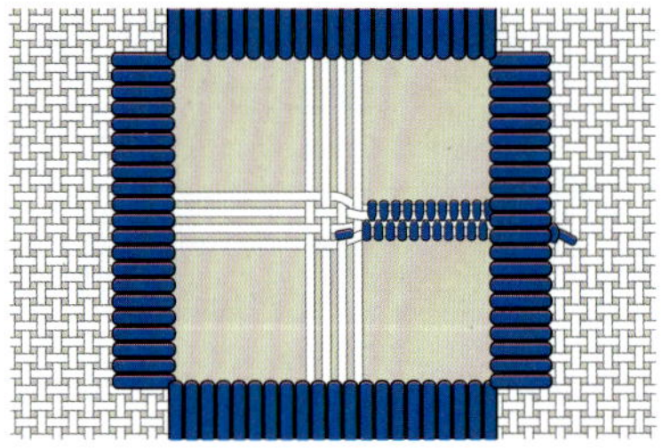

3 Work the bar back to the edge, covering over the laced thread on the back.

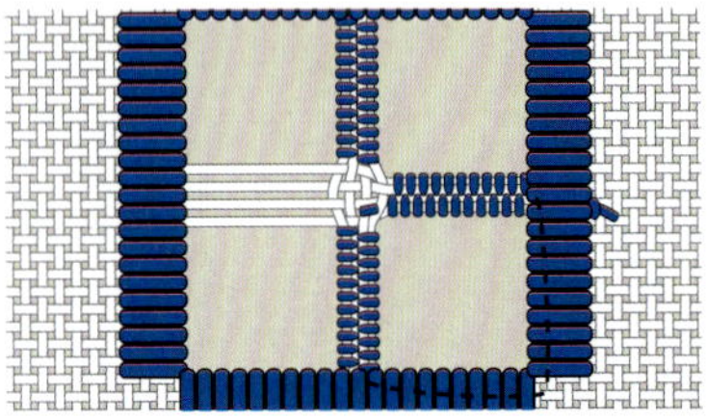

4 Take the thread under the back of the satin stitch around to the next bar and work right across the middle of the square. Finish the thread in the back of the satin stitch.

❶ *Trim the knot from the front of the fabric.*

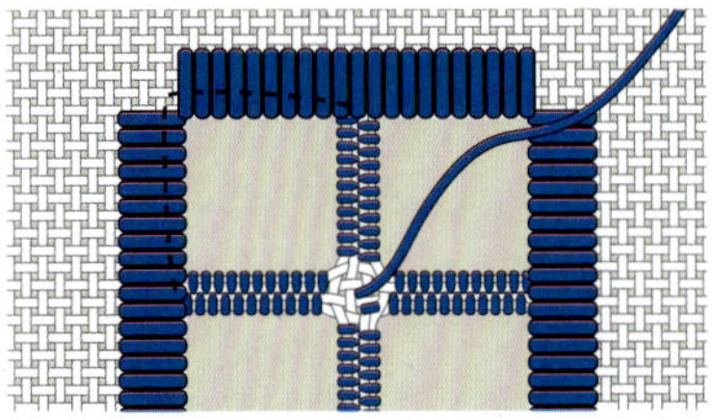

5 Start a long, new thread under the back of the satin stitch. Work the last bar in to the centre. Bring the needle out in the square's centre.

❶ *A new thread helps to ensure you'll have enough for the centre stitching.*

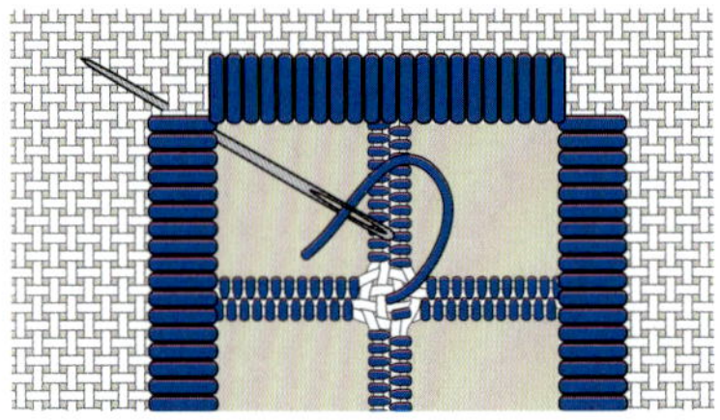

6 Working in the upper left quadrant, bring the needle out one thread up and right from the top left end of the left satin stitch.

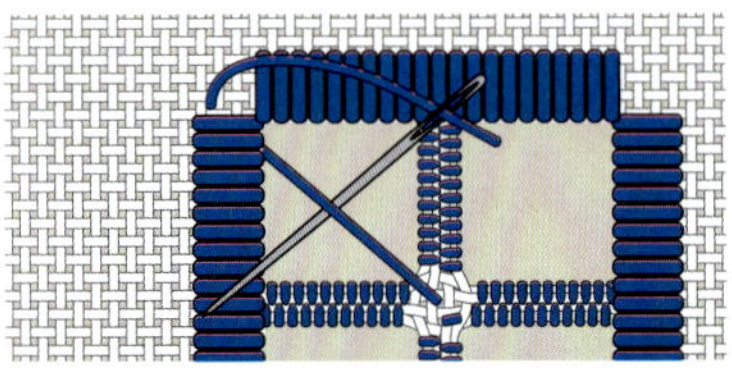

7 Pull the needle through. From above, slide the needle under the diagonal stitch.

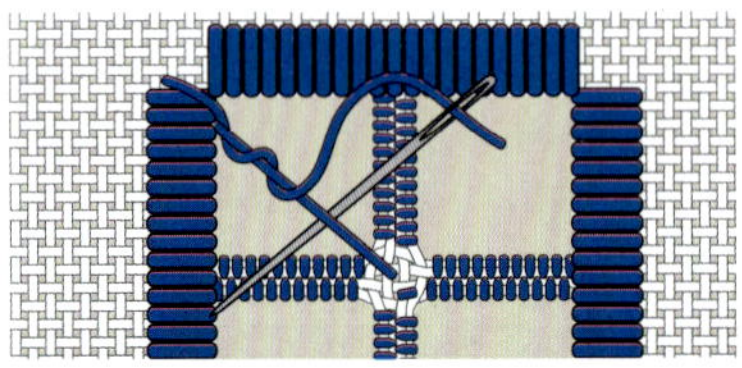

8 Slide the needle under the diagonal stitch twice more.

❶ *If you are working this in a larger square, you may need more twists. You may need fewer for a smaller square.*

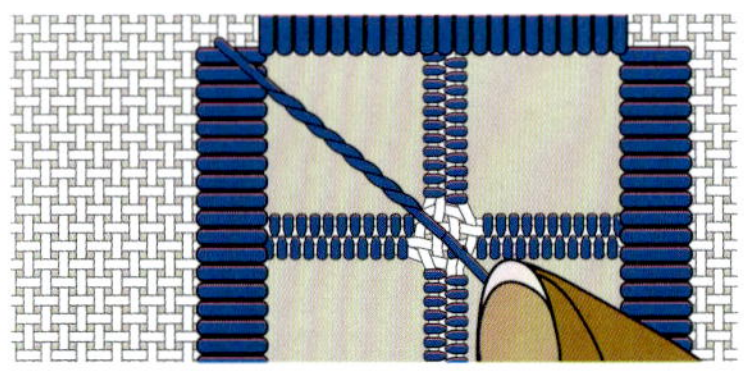

9 Insert the needle above the diagonal. Bring it out in the centre of the woven square. Pull the thread to intertwine the stitches.

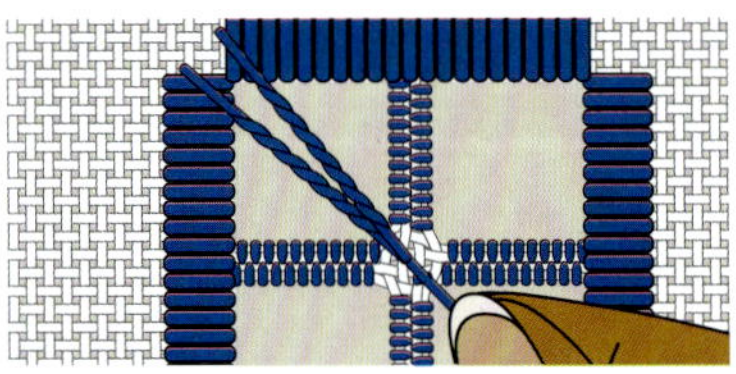

10 Work another twisted diagonal in the same way, to the hole one thread left and down from the upper left end of the top satin stitch.

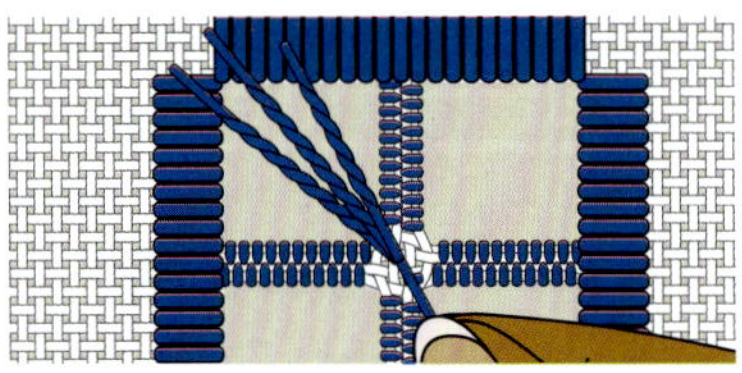

11 Work another twisted diagonal in the top satin stitch block, to two threads up from the cut edge, four satin stitches from the left end. Take the needle under the stitch only twice, this time.

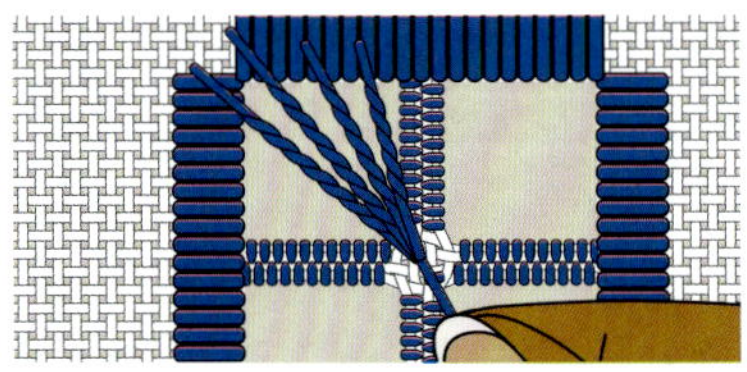

12 Work another twisted diagonal to three threads right of the previous stitch.

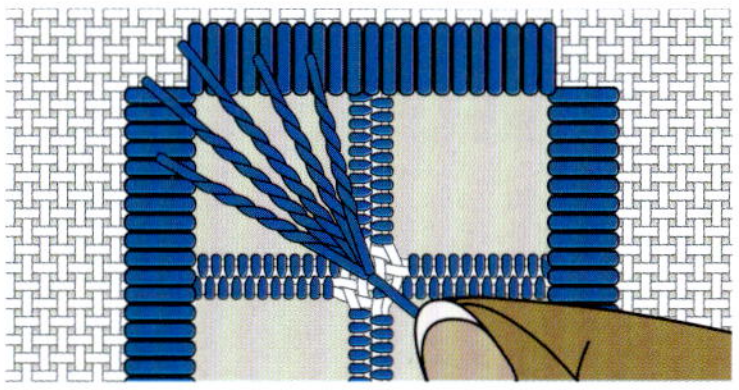

13 Work a fifth twisted diagonal to four satin stitches down from the top of the left satin stitch block.

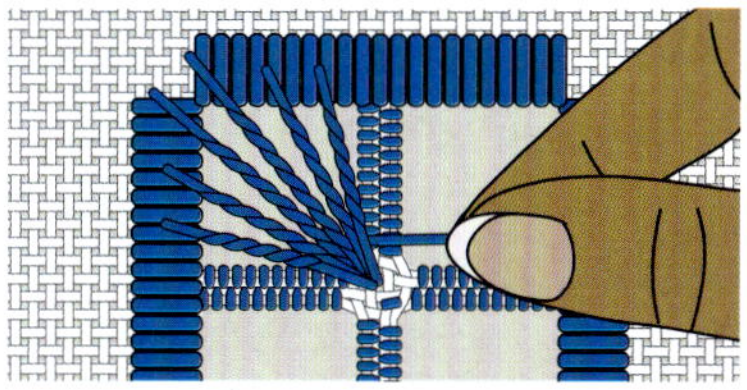

14 Work a sixth diagonal to three satin stitches down from the end of the previous one. Instead of bringing the needle out at the centre, bring it out right of the right-most diagonal.

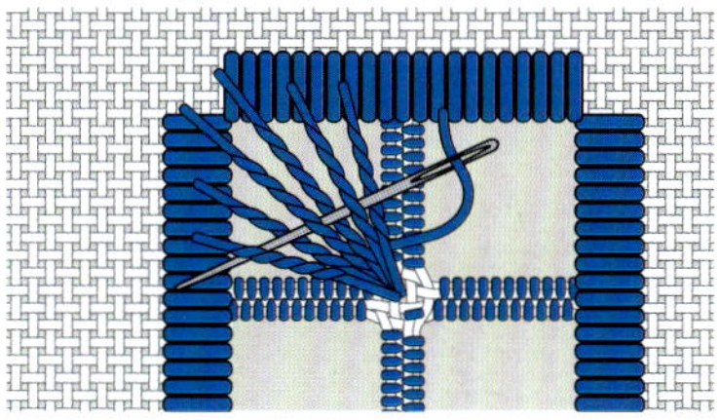

15 From the right, pass the needle over the first diagonal, then under the next, alternating over and under, all the way across.

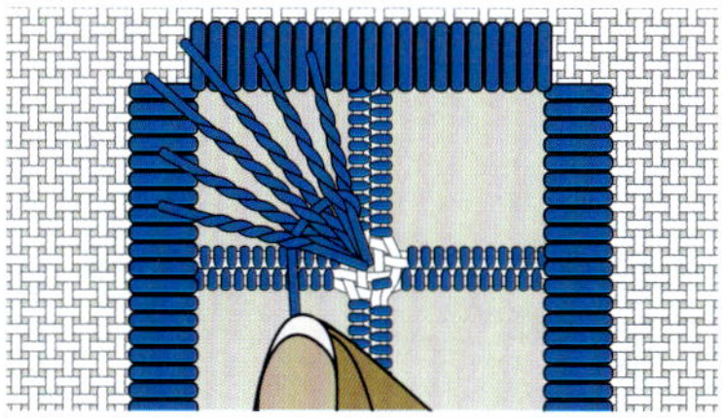

16 Pull the needle through. Pull the stitches towards the centre.

❶ *It will likely be difficult, so you may want to use the point of your needle to help push the thread towards the centre.*

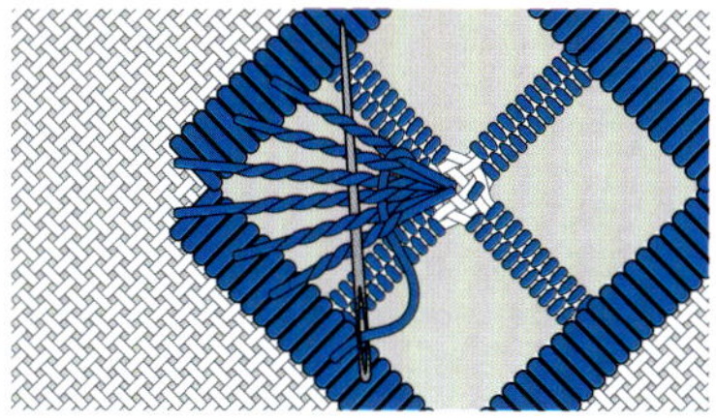

17 Turn the work 45° anticlockwise. From below, slide the needle over the bottom diagonal, then under the next, alternating over and under, all the way across.

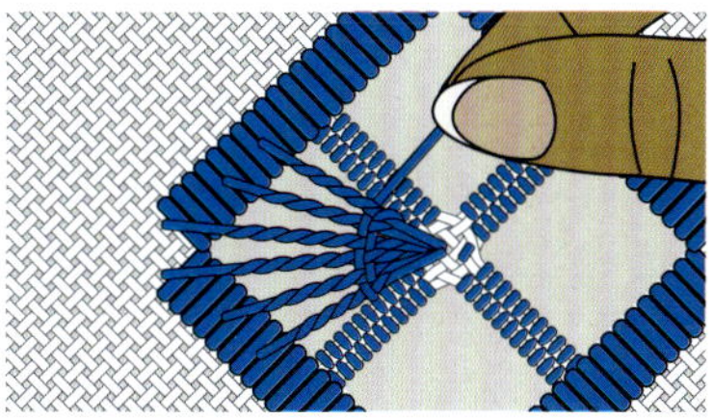

18 Pull the needle through. Pull the stitches towards the centre.

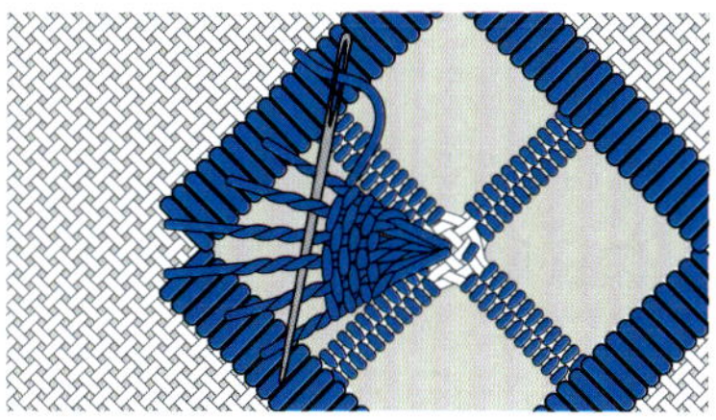

19 Continue weaving back and forth across all six diagonals until three return journeys have been made. Start the fourth, but stop before going under the last diagonal.

❶ *Adjust the row quantities for a larger or smaller square.*

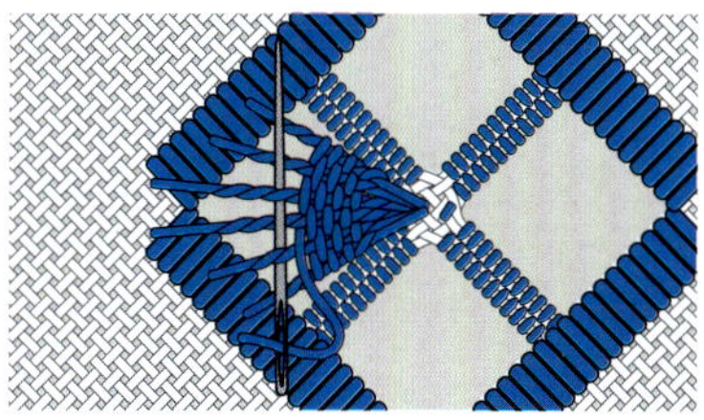

20 Pull the thread through. From below, take the needle under the second diagonal from the bottom, then over and under the next two.

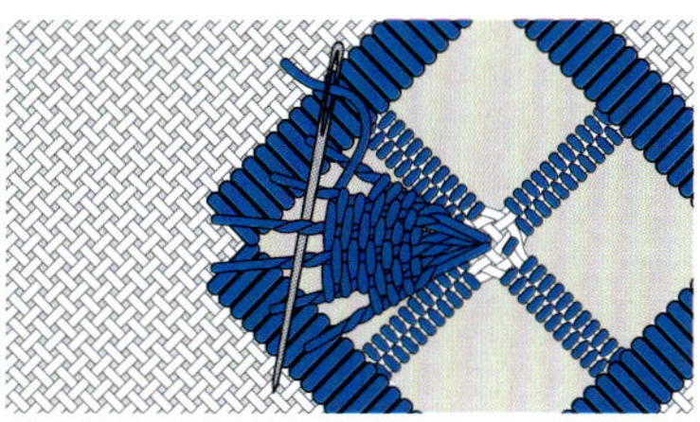

21 Continue weaving back and forth across the four middle diagonals, until three return journeys have been made. Start the fourth by going under the third diagonal from the top.

❶ *Adjust row quantities as needed.*

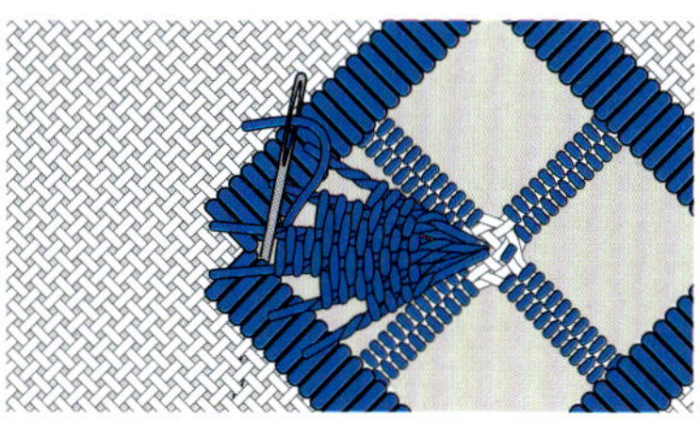

22 Weave back and forth on the middle two diagonals to fill the space. Take the needle to the back.

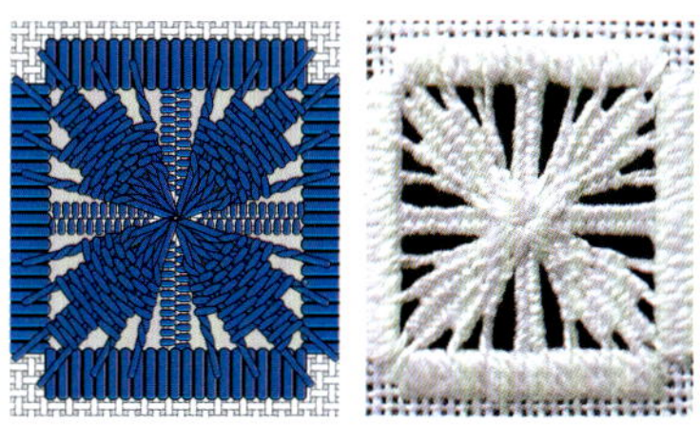

23 On the back, run the needle under the back of the fan stitching to the centre. Work stepped fans in each of the remaining quadrants and finish the thread in the back of the satin stitch.

❶ *If running the thread under the back of the weaving is difficult, at least go under two or three stitches to catch it.*

L

CONTEMPORARY

woven quarter fan

This filling makes use of the fabric threads as foundations for the weaving stitches. It therefore looks much more full than some variations.

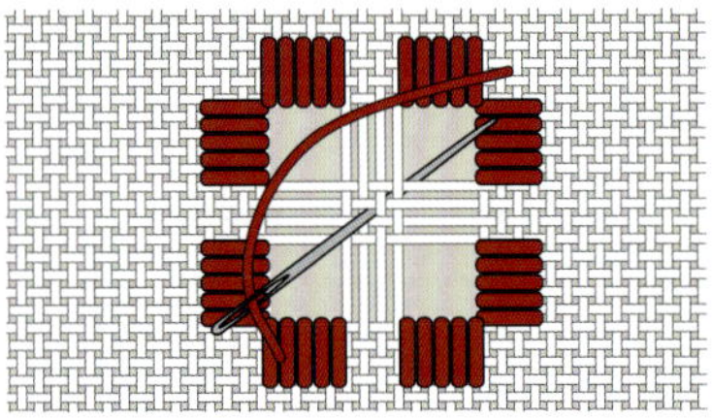

1 Prepare a square as shown. Bring the thread out in the top right corner, two threads away from the cut edges. Insert the needle in the centre of the centre woven square and bring it out below the working thread.

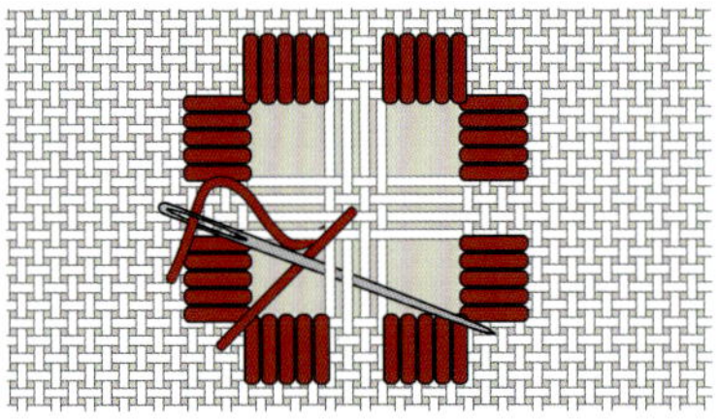

2 Pull the needle through. Turn the work 180°. From the left, take the needle over the diagonal and slide it under the left two threads of the lower vertical bar.

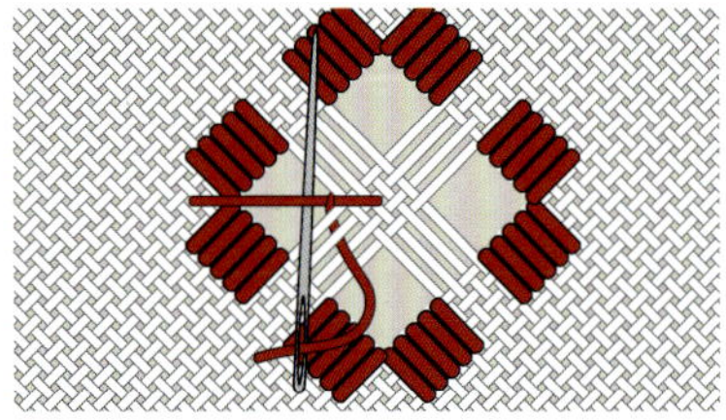

3 Pull the stitch in snug against the woven centre square. Turn the work 45° clockwise. Slide the needle under the centre diagonal, from below.

❶ *Ensure the diagonal stitch stays straight and taut.*

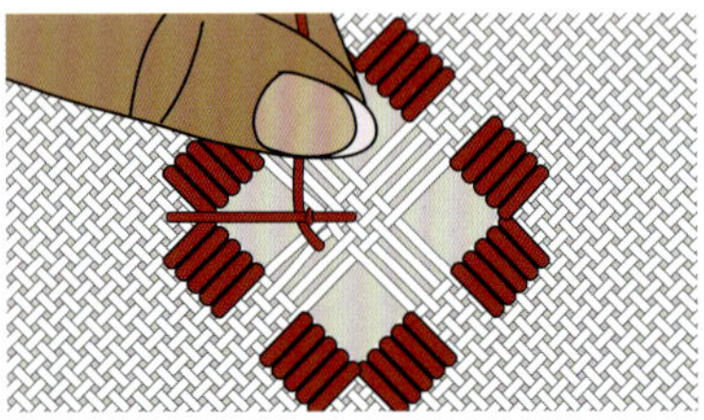

4 Pull to tighten the stitch with firm tension.

❶ *The sides of the fan shouldn't bow inwards; they just need to be firm.*

5 Slide the needle under the lower bar threads, over the diagonal, and under the upper bar threads.

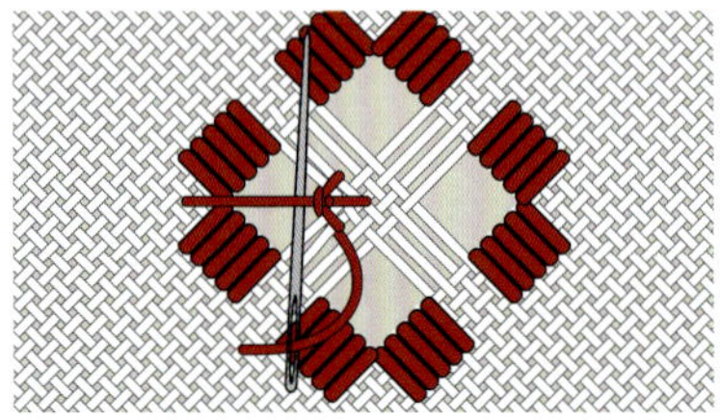

6 Pull the thread to firm up the stitch. From below, slide the needle under the centre diagonal.

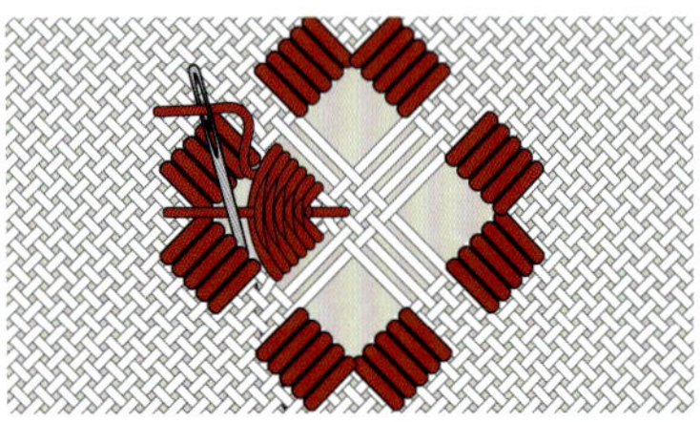

7 Continue, weaving back and forth across the quadrant, keeping the weaving firm, but not pulling the sides inward. To complete the quadrant, take the needle to the back at the lower edge, after going over the centre diagonal.

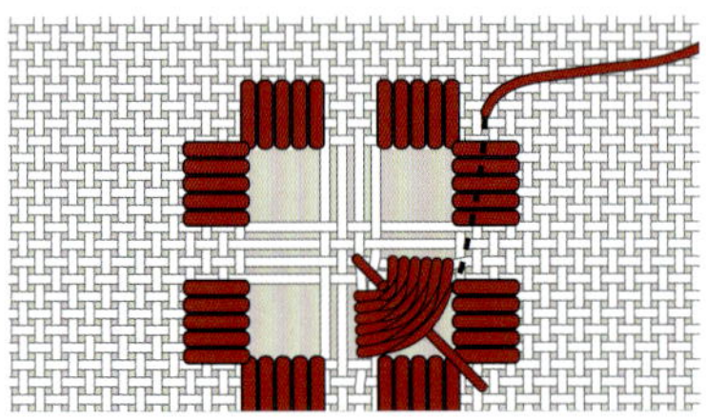

8 Take the thread behind the satin stitch on the back, and bring it out again in the centre of the woven corner of the next quadrant.

9 Complete the three remaining quadrants similarly.

woven quarter fan

R

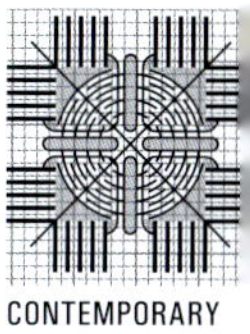

This filling makes use of the fabric threads as foundations for the weaving stitches. It therefore looks much more full than some variations.

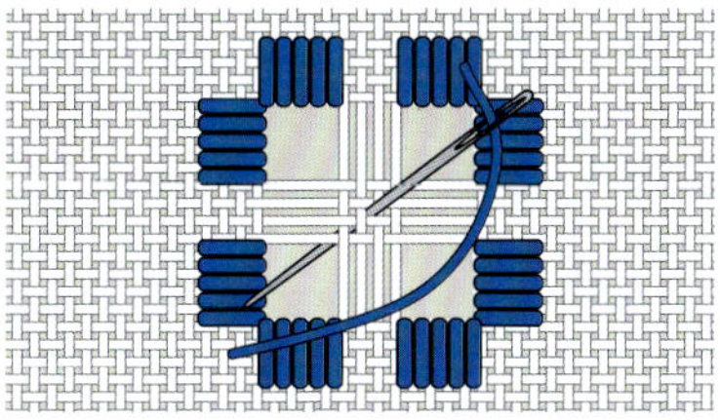

1 Prepare a square as shown. Bring the thread out in the bottom left corner, two threads away from the cut edges. Insert the needle in the centre of the centre woven square and bring it out above the working thread.

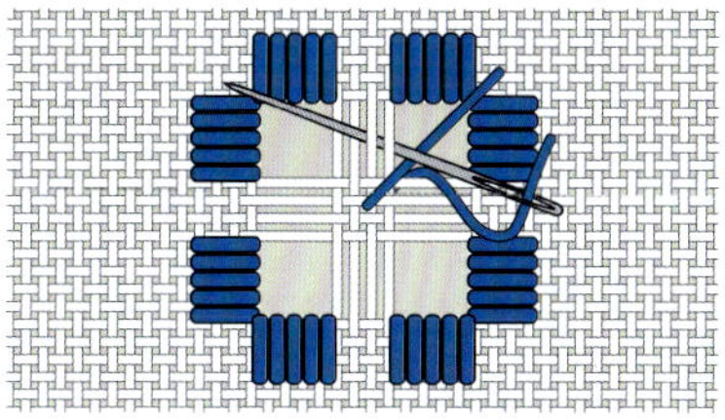

2 Pull the needle through. Turn the work 180°. From the right, take the needle over the diagonal and slide it under the right two threads of the upper vertical bar.

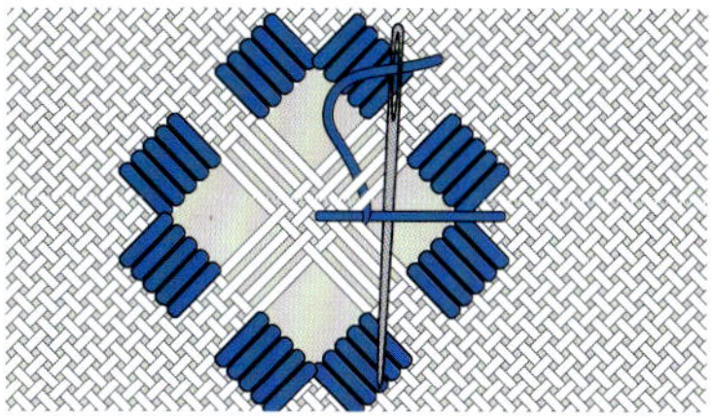

3 Pull the stitch in snug against the woven centre square. Turn the work 45° clockwise. Slide the needle under the centre diagonal, from below.

❶ *Ensure the diagonal stitch stays straight and taut.*

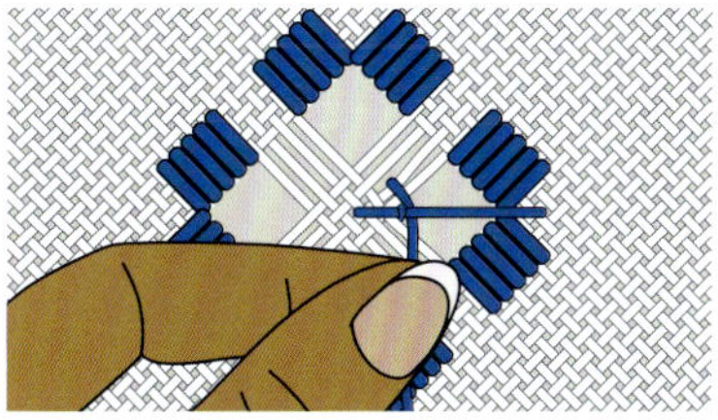

4 Pull to tighten the stitch with firm tension.

❶ *The sides of the fan shouldn't bow inwards; they just need to be firm.*

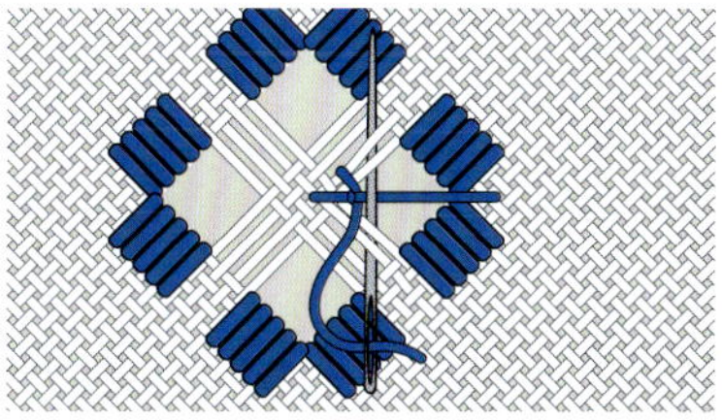

5 Slide the needle under the lower bar threads, over the diagonal, and under the upper bar threads.

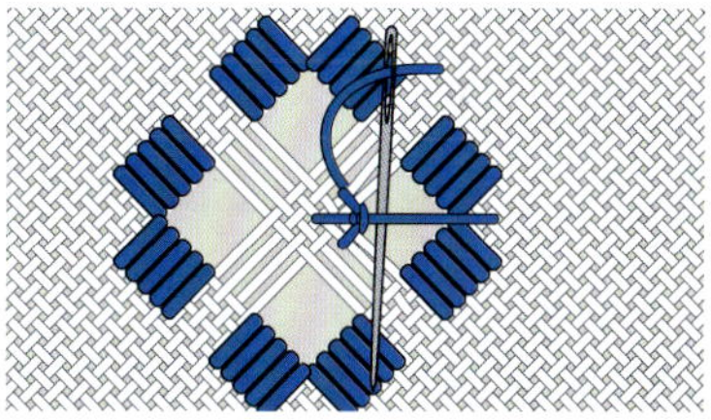

6 Pull the thread to firm up the stitch. From above, slide the needle under the centre diagonal.

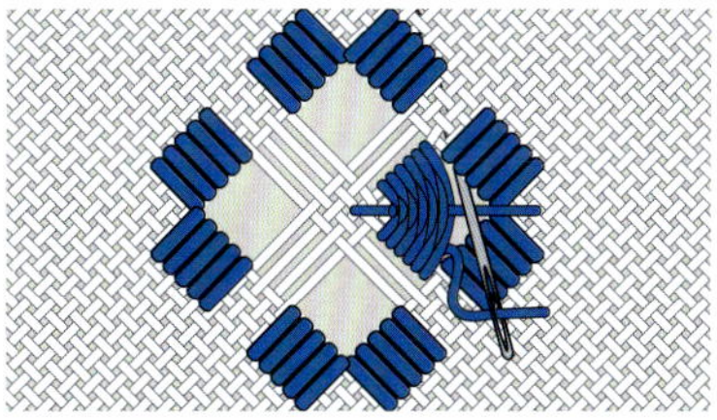

7 Continue, weaving back and forth across the quadrant, keeping the weaving firm, but not pulling the sides inward. To complete the quadrant, take the needle to the back at the upper edge, after going over the centre diagonal.

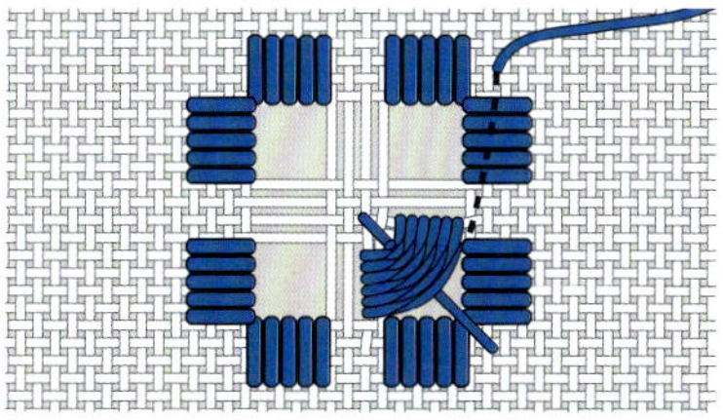

8 Take the thread behind the satin stitch on the back, and bring it out again in the centre of the woven corner of the next quadrant.

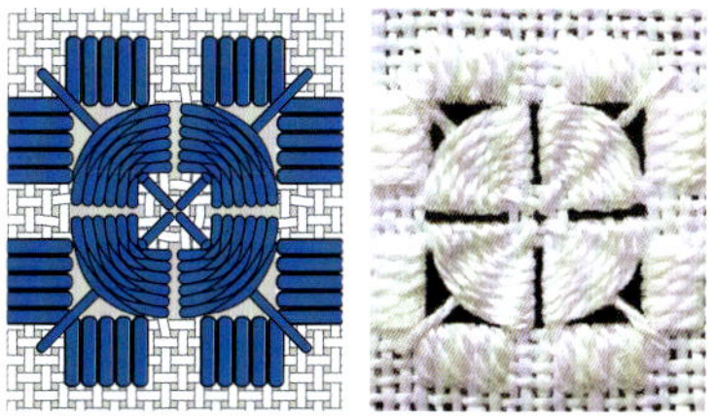

9 Complete the three remaining quadrants similarly.

L

inverse woven fan

also known as inverted woven fan or reverse woven fan

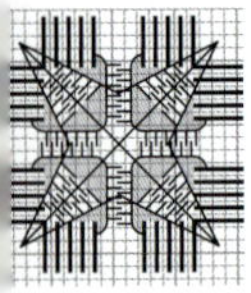

CONTEMPORARY

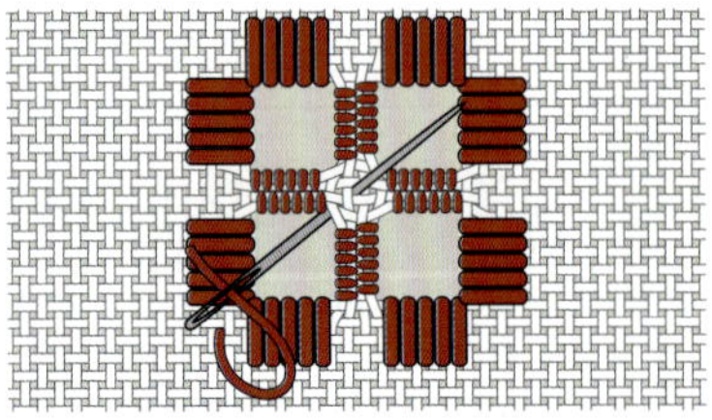

1 Prepare a square as shown with all four bars woven. Bring the thread out in the bottom left corner, two threads away from the cut edges. Bring the needle out in the centre of the woven square.

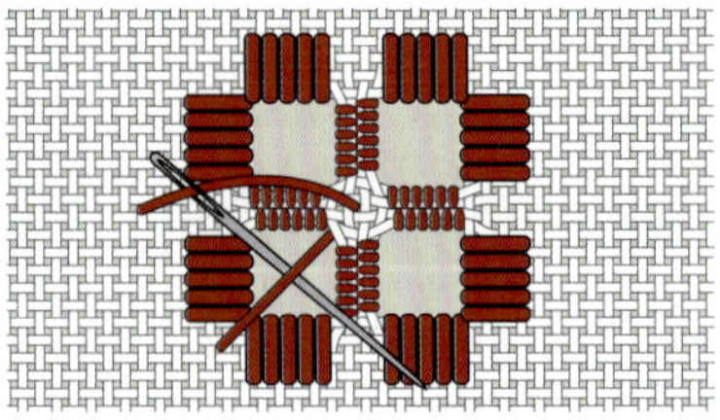

2 Pull the needle through and tighten the stitch. From the left, slide the needle under the diagonal.

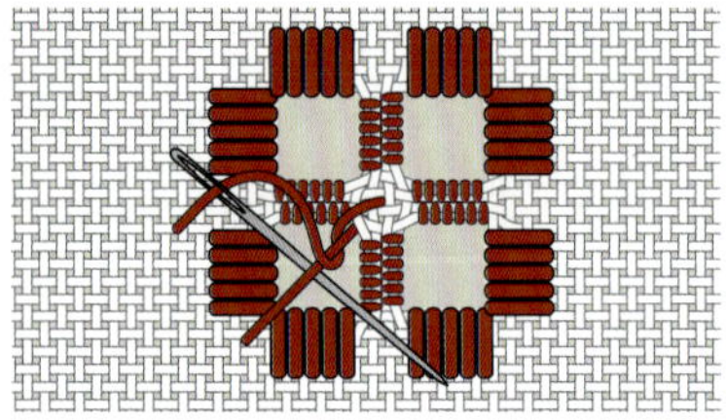

3 From the left, slide the needle under the diagonal again.

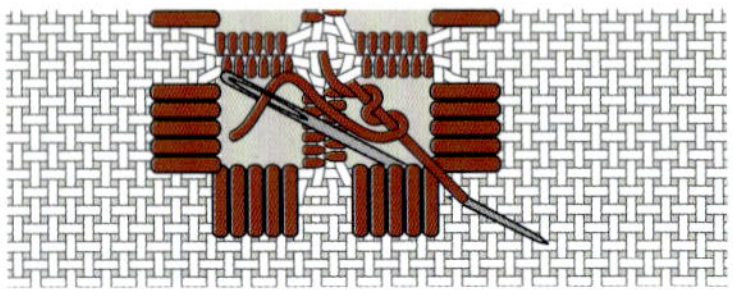

4 Turn the work 90° anticlockwise. Insert the needle below the diagonal and bring it out in the corner again.

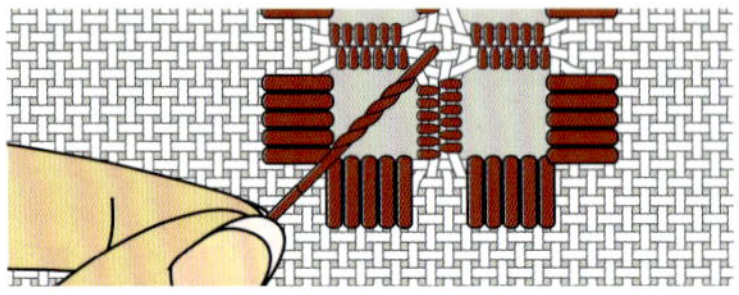

5 Turn the work 90° clockwise. Pull the thread to intertwine the stitches.

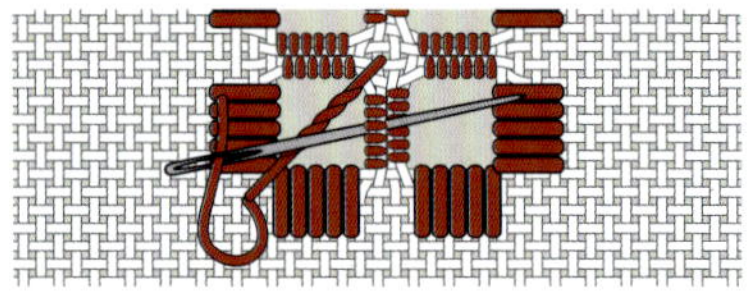

6 Bring the needle out in the centre of the lower vertical bar.

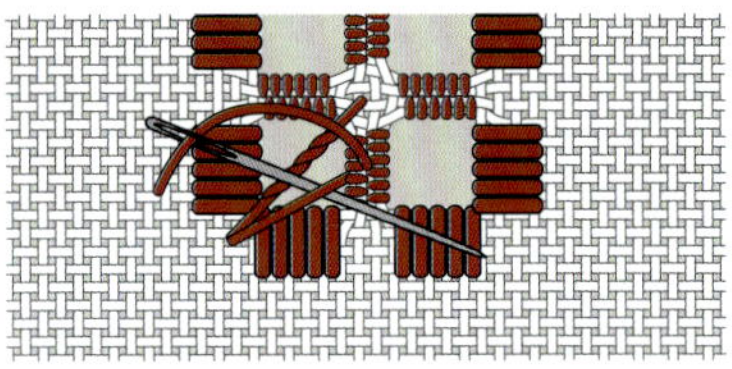

7 Pull the needle through and tighten the stitch. From the left, slide the needle under the diagonal.

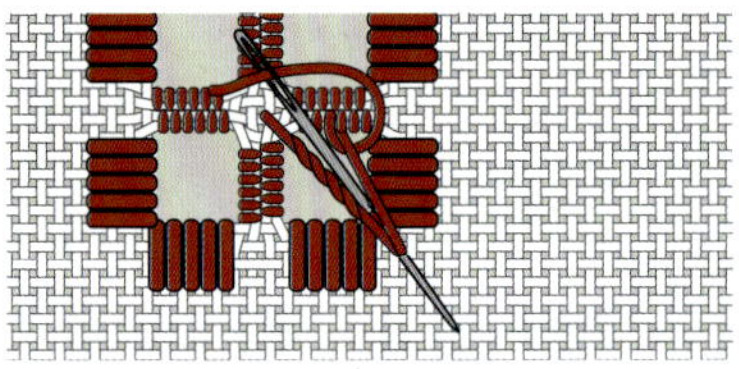

8 Turn the work 90° anticlockwise. Insert the needle between the diagonals and bring it out in the corner again.

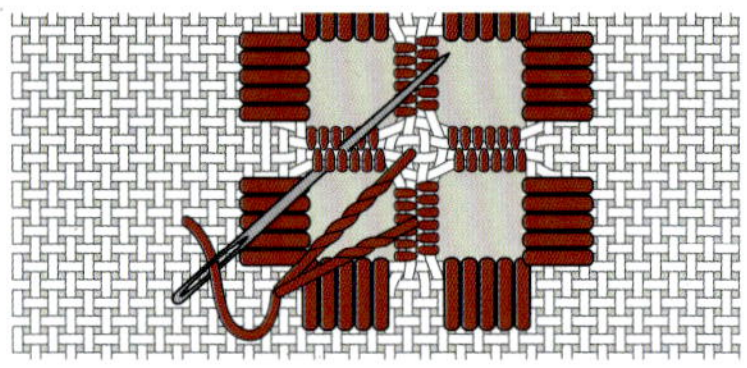

9 Turn the work 90° clockwise. Pull the thread to intertwine the stitches. Bring the needle out in the centre of the left horizontal bar.

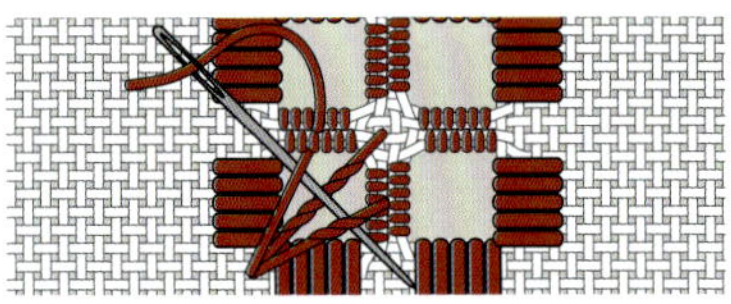

10 Pull the needle through and tighten the stitch. From above, slide the needle under the outer diagonals.

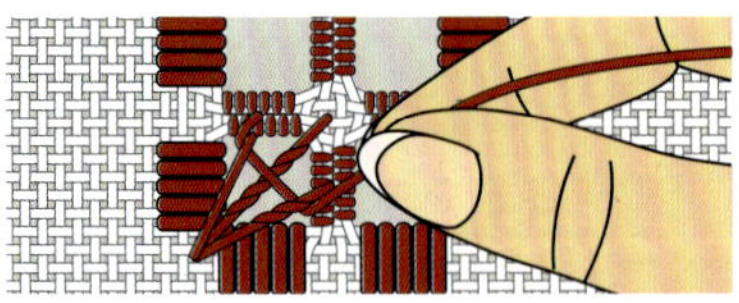

11 Pull the needle through. Keeping the left diagonal straight, pull the thread to tighten the stitch towards the centre.

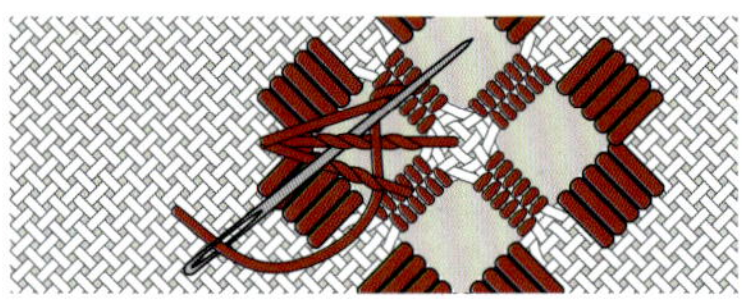

12 Turn the work 45° clockwise. From below, slide the needle under the centre diagonal.

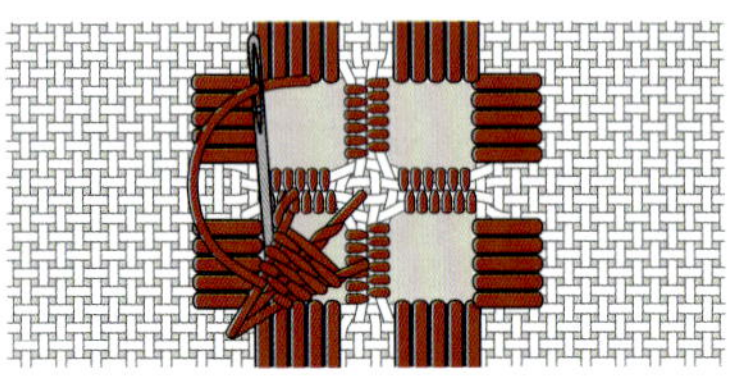

13 Weave back and forth, down to the tip of the fan, with increasing tension. Take the needle to the back in the space to the left of the fan.

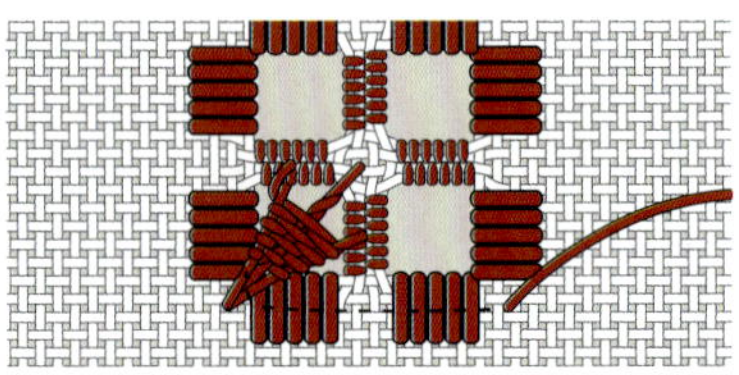

14 Take the thread under the back of the satin stitch and bring it out in another corner ready to work another inverse fan.

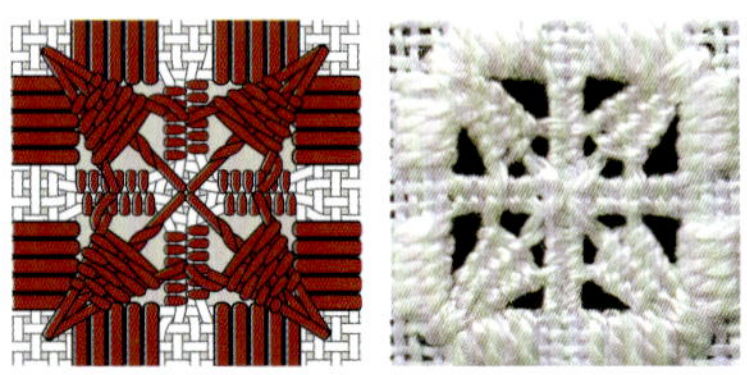

15 Work fans in each of the quadrants.

inverse woven fan *also known as inverted woven fan or reverse woven fan*

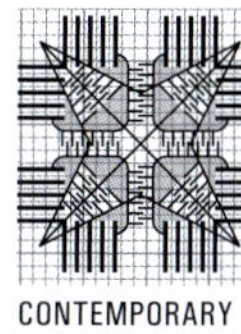

CONTEMPORARY

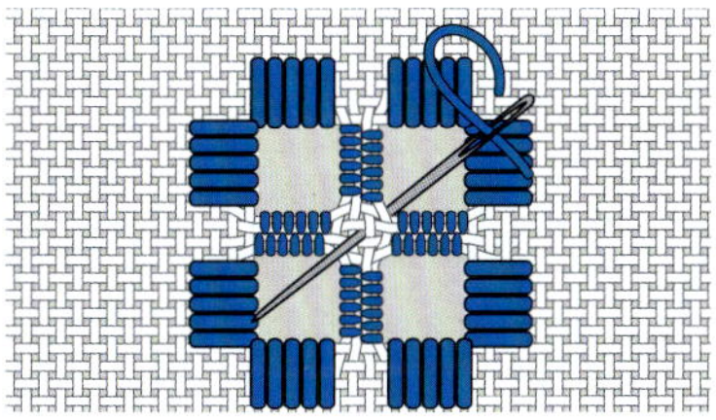

1 Prepare a square as shown with all four bars woven. Bring the thread out in the top right corner, two threads away from the cut edges. Bring the needle out in the centre of the woven square.

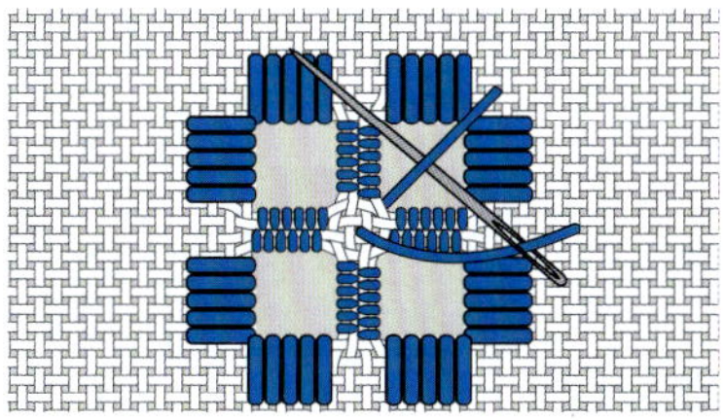

2 Pull the needle through and tighten the stitch. From the right, slide the needle under the diagonal.

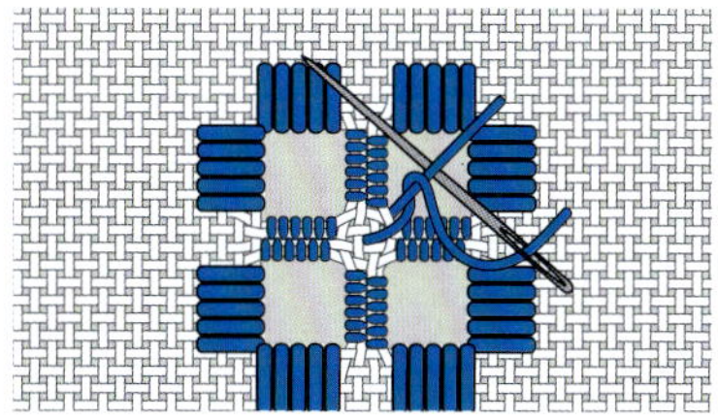

3 From the right, slide the needle under the diagonal again.

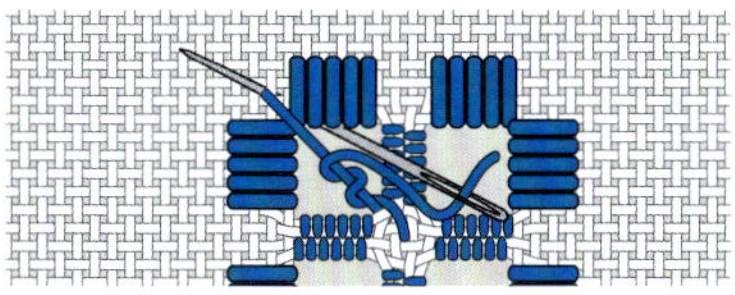

4 Turn the work 90° anticlockwise. Insert the needle above the diagonal and bring it out in the corner again.

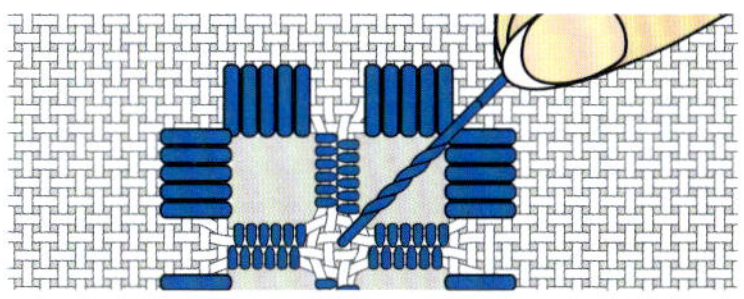

5 Turn the work 90° clockwise. Pull the thread to intertwine the stitches.

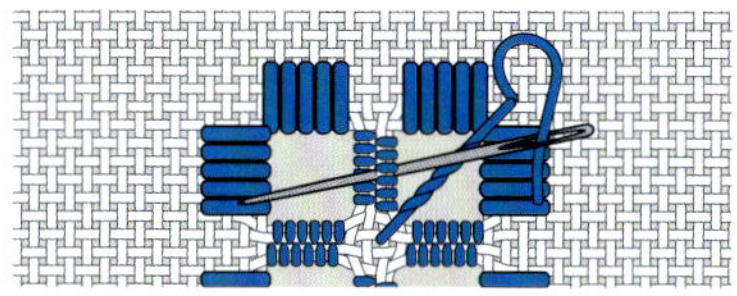

6 Bring the needle out in the centre of the upper vertical bar.

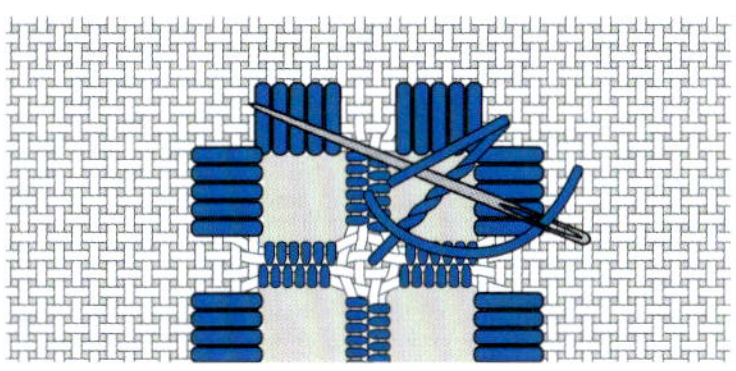

7 Pull the needle through and tighten the stitch. From the right, slide the needle under the diagonal.

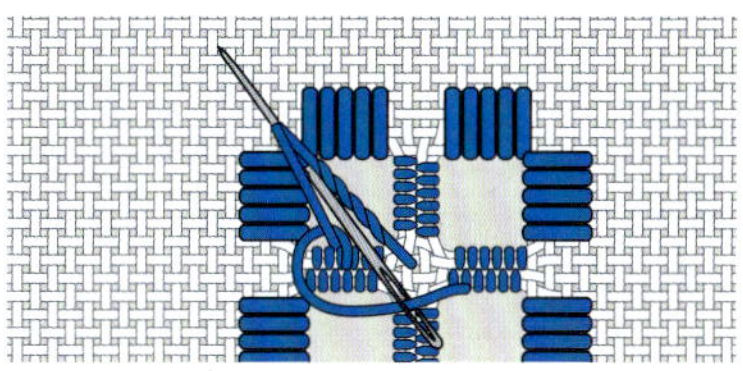

8 Turn the work 90° anticlockwise. Insert the needle between the diagonals and bring it out in the corner again.

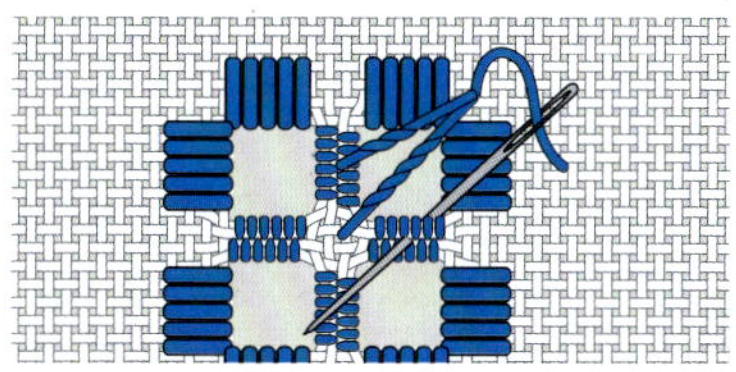

9 Turn the work 90° clockwise. Pull the thread to intertwine the stitches. Bring the needle out in the centre of the right horizontal bar.

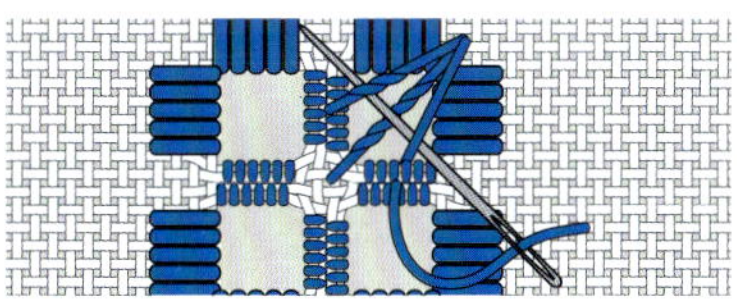

10 Pull the needle through and tighten the stitch. From below, slide the needle under the outer diagonals.

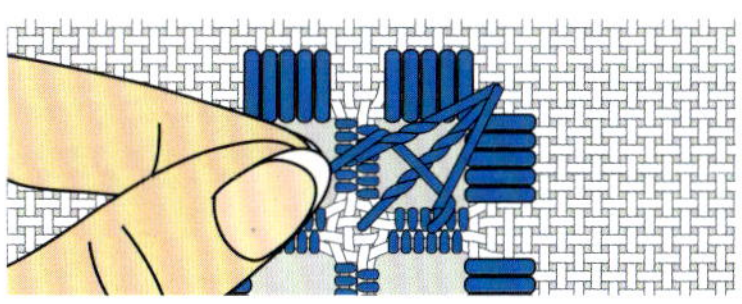

11 Pull the needle through. Keeping the right diagonal straight, pull the thread to tighten the stitch towards the centre.

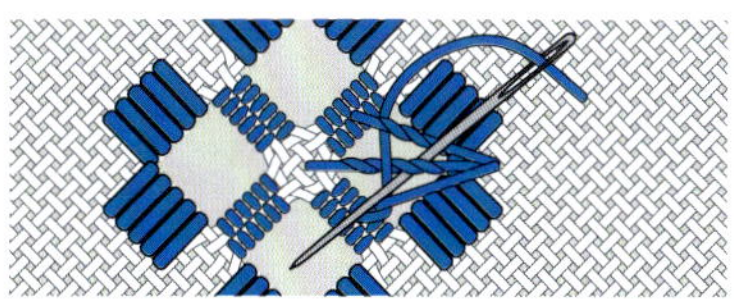

12 Turn the work 45° clockwise. From above, slide the needle under the centre diagonal.

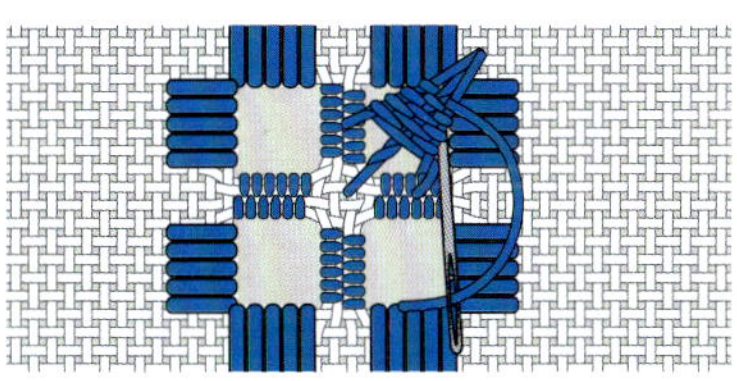

13 Weave back and forth, down to the tip of the fan, with increasing tension. Take the needle to the back in the space to the right of the fan.

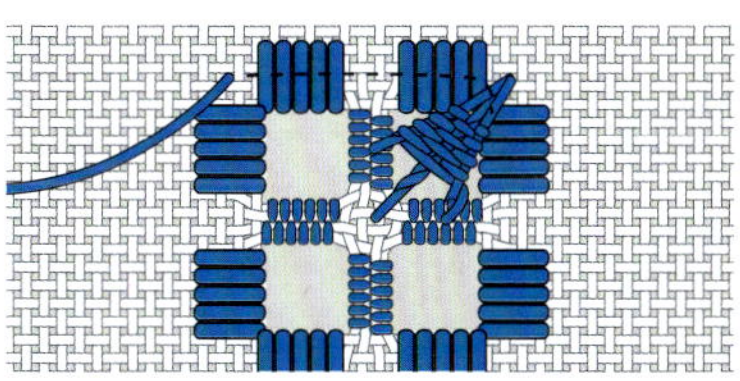

14 Take the thread under the back of the satin stitch and bring it out in another corner ready to work another inverse fan.

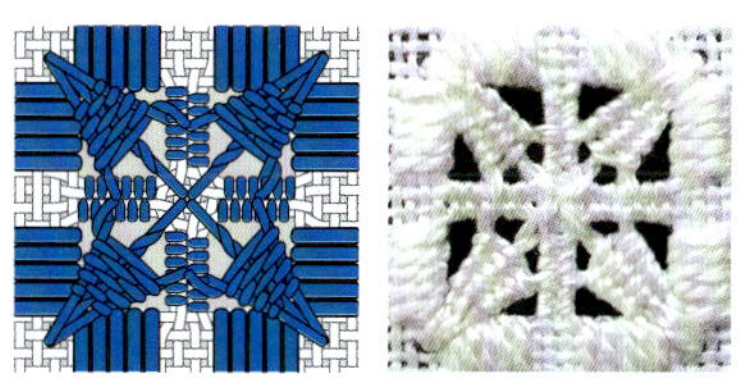

15 Work fans in each of the quadrants.

curled V in a fan

This stitch is a combination of Greek cross, curled V, and woven fan with three spokes.

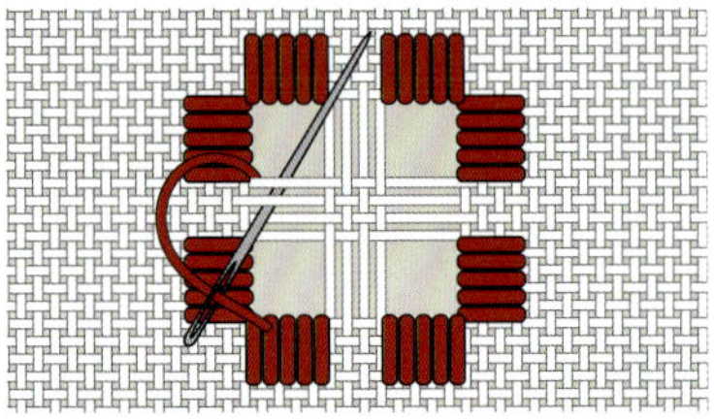

1 Bring the needle out of the fabric above a bar as shown. From below, slide the needle under the upper two threads of the bar.

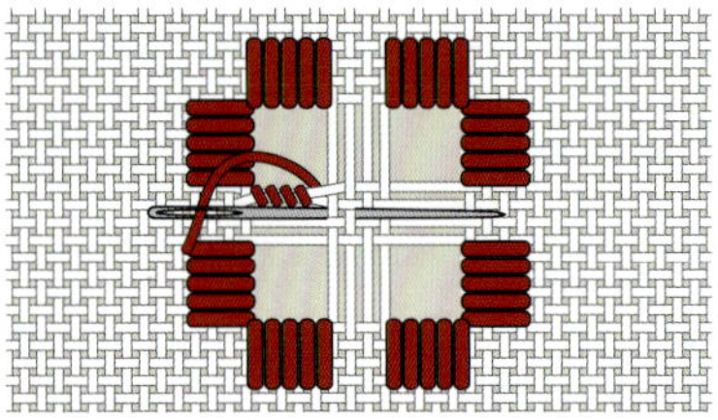

2 Wrap tightly to fill the bar. At the end of the bar, bring the needle out in the woven square's centre.

❶ *The wraps should lie next to each other on the bar and not overlap. They do not need to be tightly packed.*

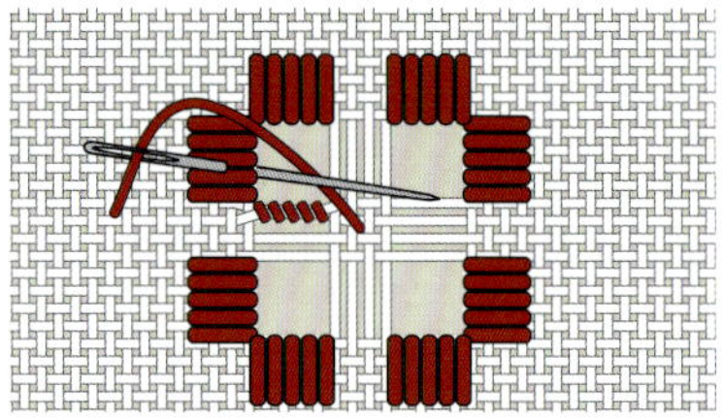

3 Take the needle over to the left edge of the upper left quadrant. Insert it in the centre of the satin stitch, three satin stitches down from the top. Take the needle point over the working thread.

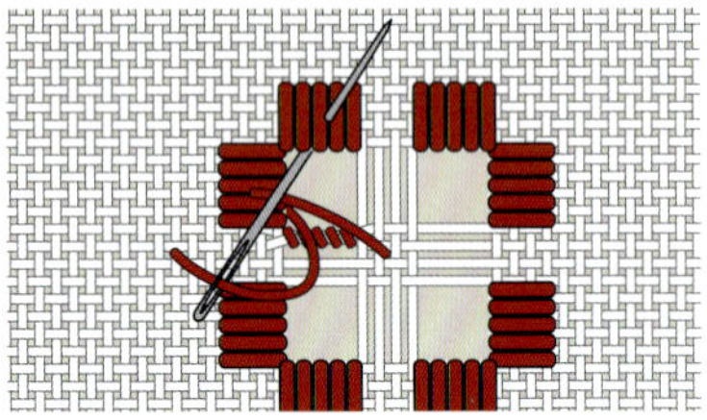

4 Pull the needle through so the stitch curves with gentle tension. Bring the needle out in the centre of the satin stitch at the quadrant's upper edge, three satin stitches from the left.

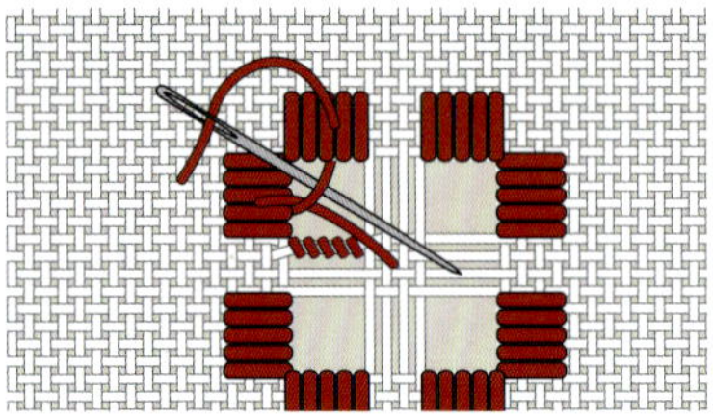

5 Pull the needle through and leave the stitch curving with gentle tension. Slide the needle under the second stitch.

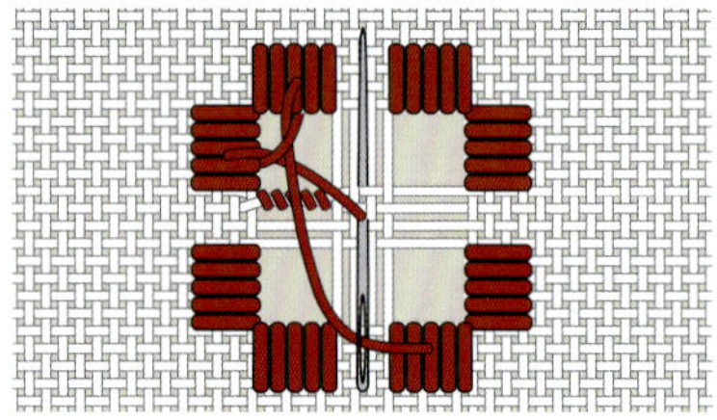

6 Insert the needle in the woven centre and bring it out in the centre of the upper vertical bar.

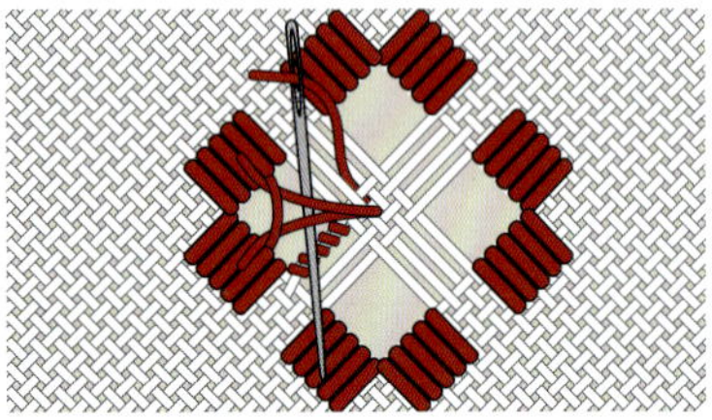

7 Pull the needle through. Turn the work 45° anticlockwise. From above, slide the needle under the V stitches.

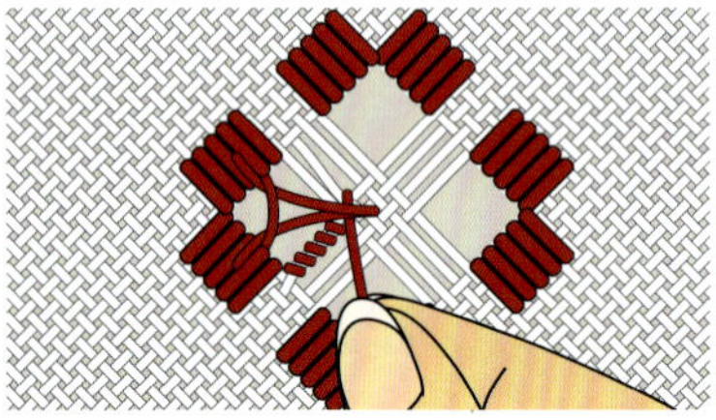

8 Pull the thread to tighten the stitch.

9 From below, slide the needle under the wrapped bar and the lower two threads of the upper bar.

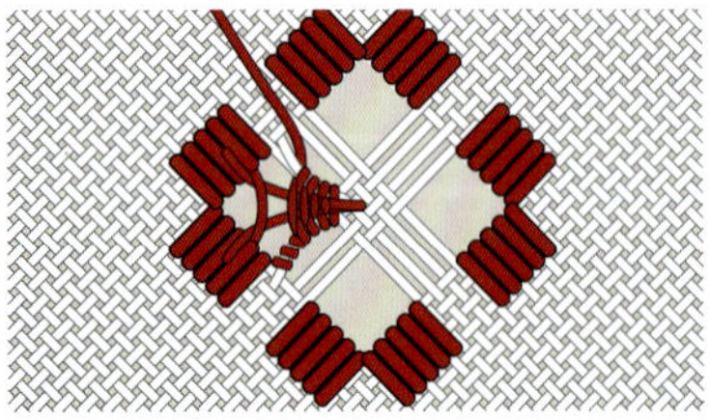

10 Pull the thread to tighten the stitch. Continue weaving back and forth, allowing the bars to curve inwards a little at the edges. Finish with thread at the top.

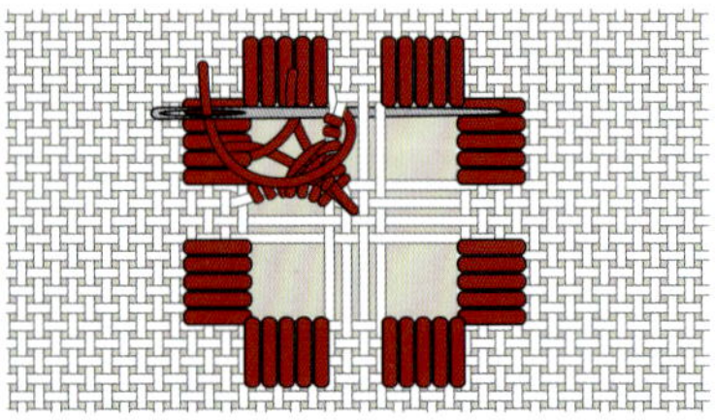

11 Turn the work 45° clockwise. Wrap the rest of the bar, then bring the needle out in the next adjacent quadrant.

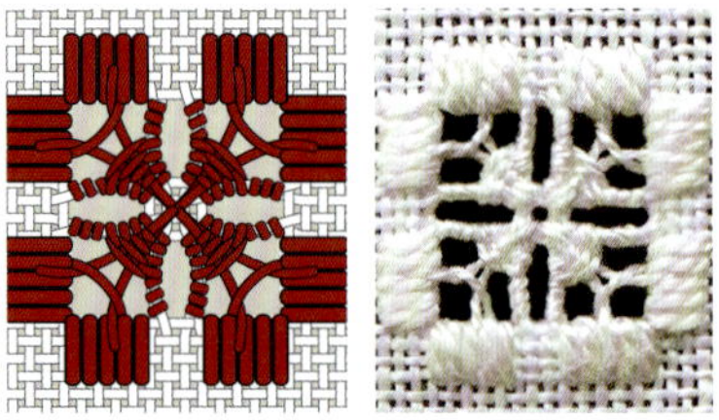

12 Work the same motif in each of the other quadrants.

curled V in a fan

R

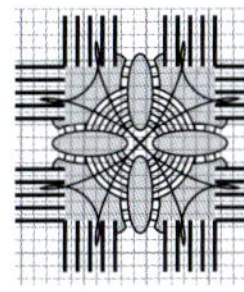

CONTEMPORARY

This stitch is a combination of Greek cross, curled V, and woven fan with three spokes.

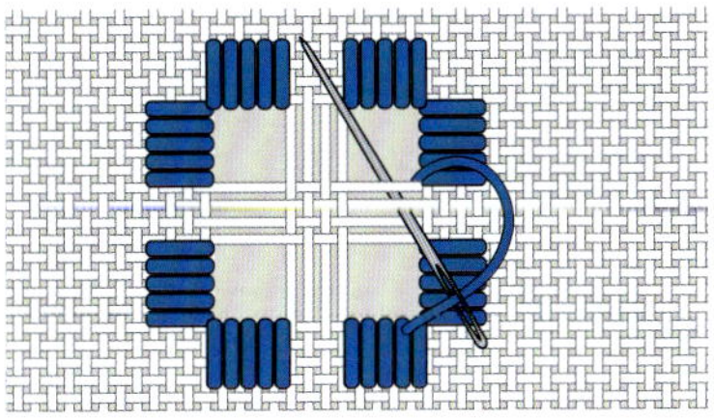

1 Bring the needle out of the fabric above a bar as shown. From below, slide the needle under the upper two threads of the bar.

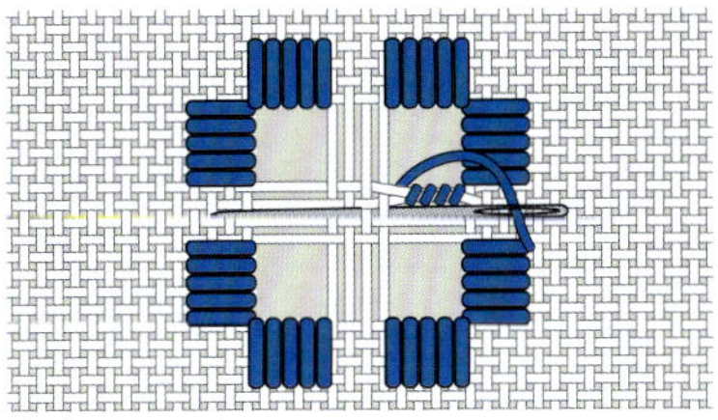

2 Wrap tightly to fill the bar. At the end of the bar, bring the needle out in the woven square's centre.

❶ *The wraps should lie next to each other on the bar and not overlap. They do not need to be tightly packed.*

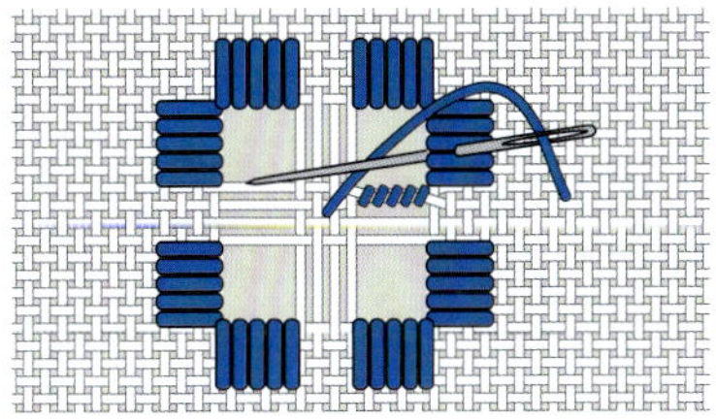

3 Take the needle over to the right edge of the upper right quadrant. Insert it in the centre of the satin stitch, three satin stitches down from the top. Take the needle point over the working thread.

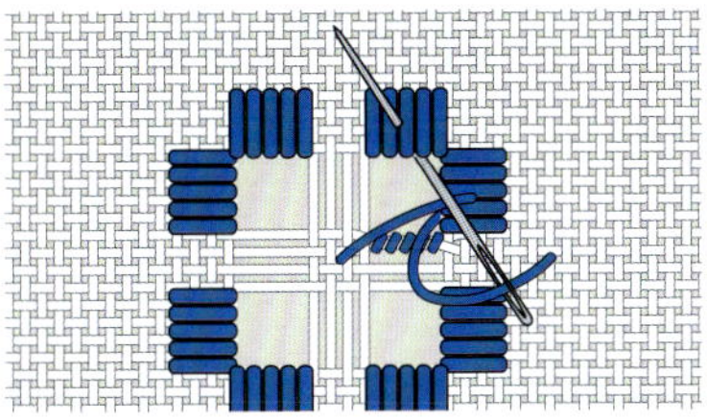

4 Pull the needle through so the stitch curves with gentle tension. Bring the needle out in the centre of the satin stitch at the quadrant's upper edge, three satin stitches from the right.

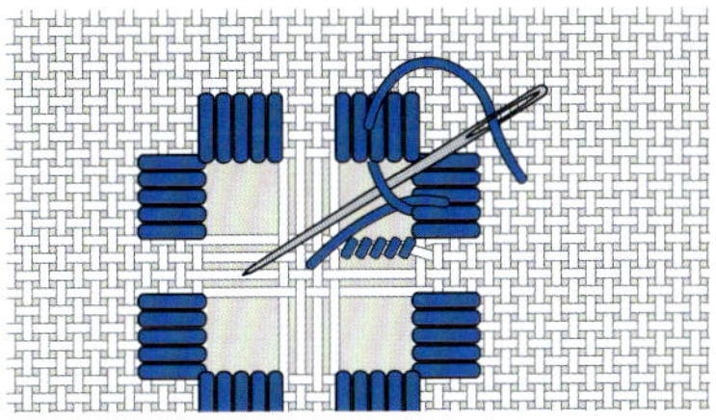

5 Pull the needle through and leave the stitch curving with gentle tension. Slide the needle under the second stitch.

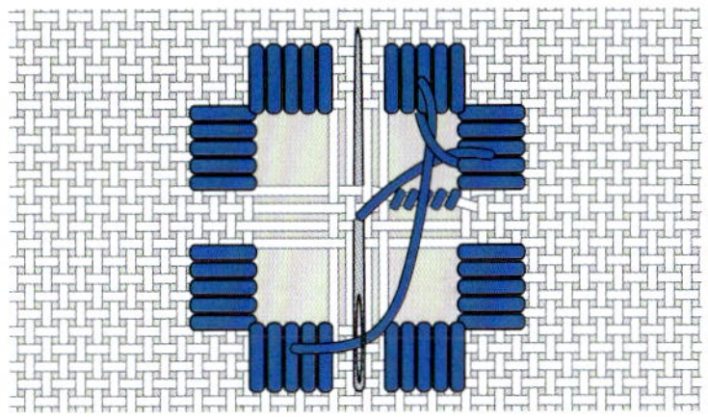

6 Insert the needle in the woven centre and bring it out in the centre of the upper vertical bar.

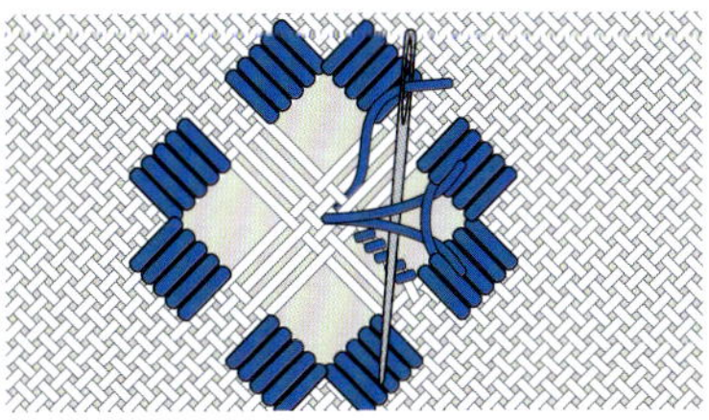

7 Pull the needle through. Turn the work 45° clockwise. From above, slide the needle under the V stitches.

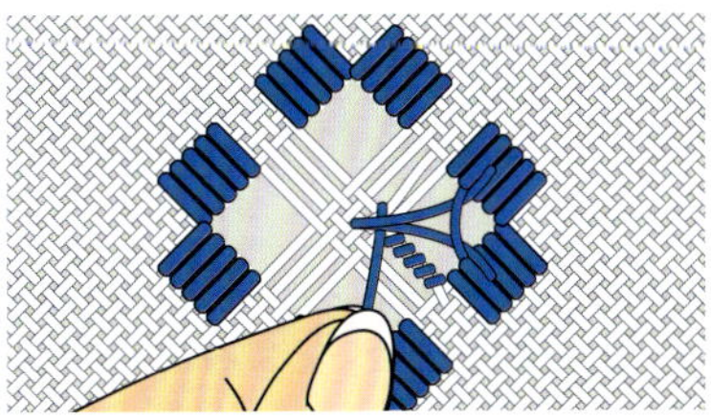

8 Pull the thread to tighten the stitch.

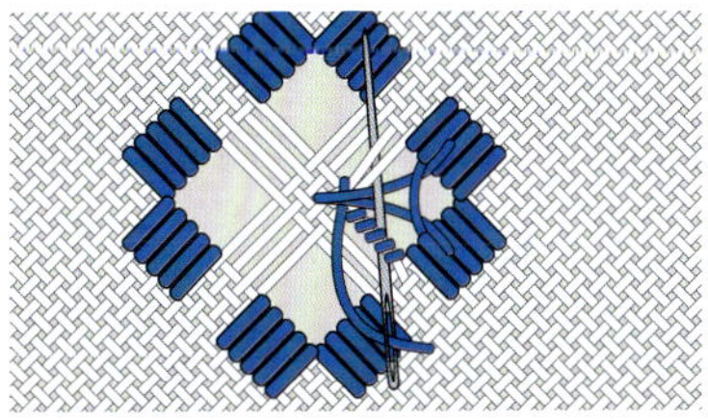

9 From below, slide the needle under the wrapped bar and the lower two threads of the upper bar.

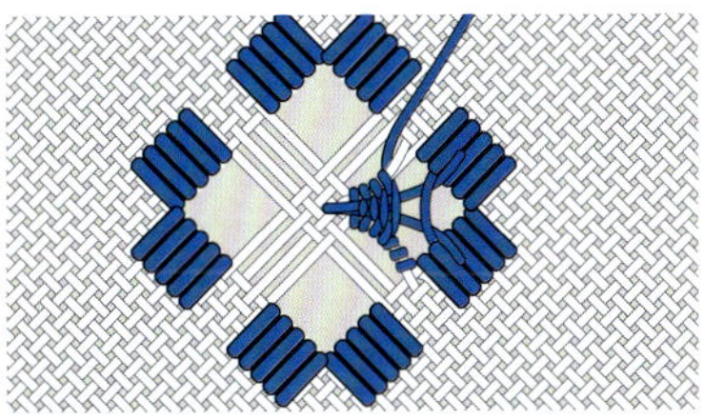

10 Pull the thread to tighten the stitch. Continue weaving back and forth, allowing the bars to curve inwards a little at the edges. Finish with thread at the top.

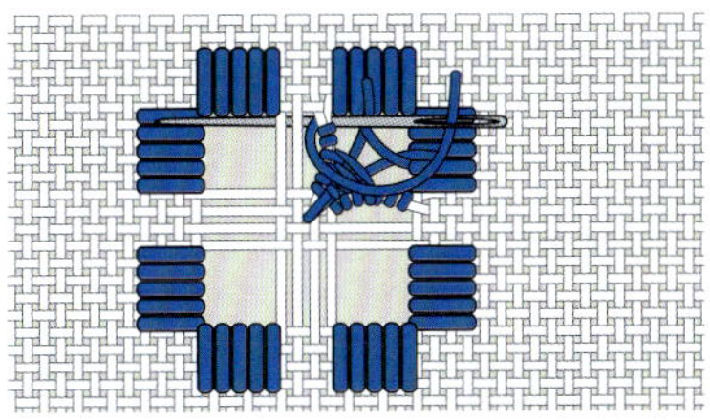

11 Turn the work 45° anticlockwise. Wrap the rest of the bar, then bring the needle out in the next adjacent quadrant.

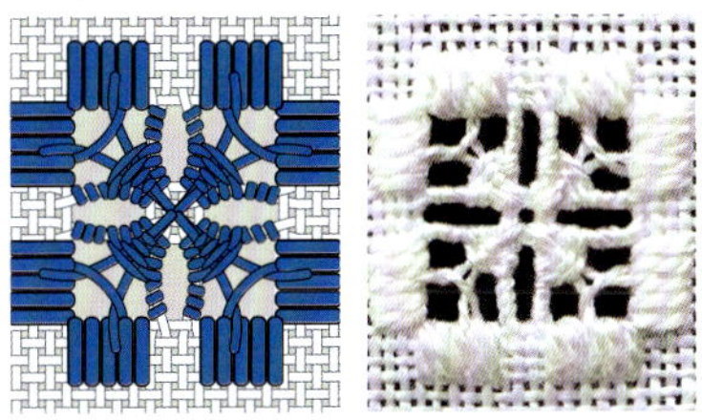

12 Work the same motif in each of the other quadrants.

spider web

Spider webs can be woven, ribbed and whipped. They can be worked singly or as part of larger motifs.

woven spider web – single square

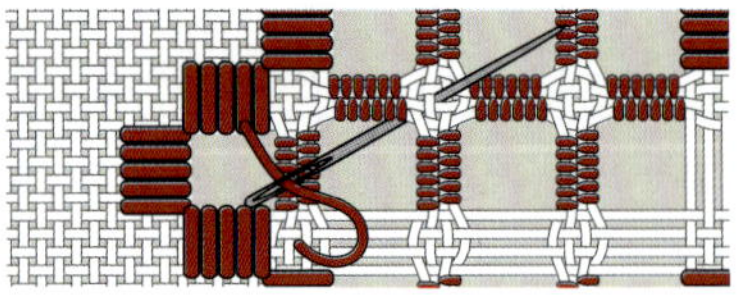

1 After working three sides of the square to be filled, bring the needle out centrally in the adjacent corner woven square. Then bring it out centrally in the opposite woven square.

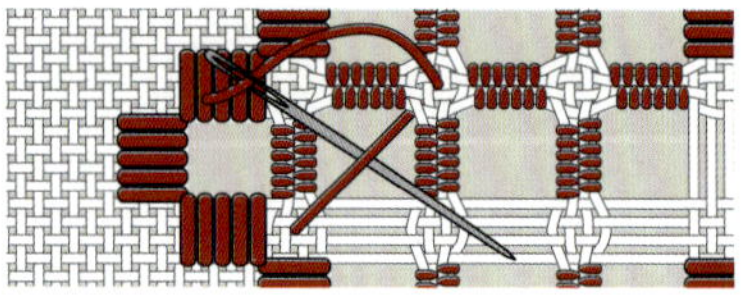

2 Pull the needle through so the stitch sits straight. From above, slide the needle under the diagonal stitch.

3 From above, slide the needle under the diagonal stitch again.

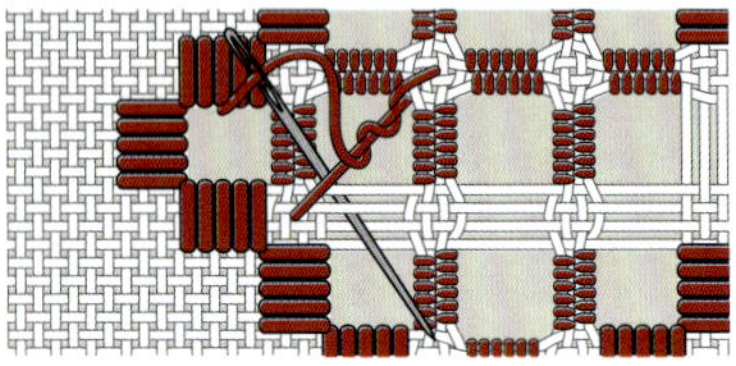

4 Insert the needle above the diagonal stitch, bringing it out in the unwoven bar.

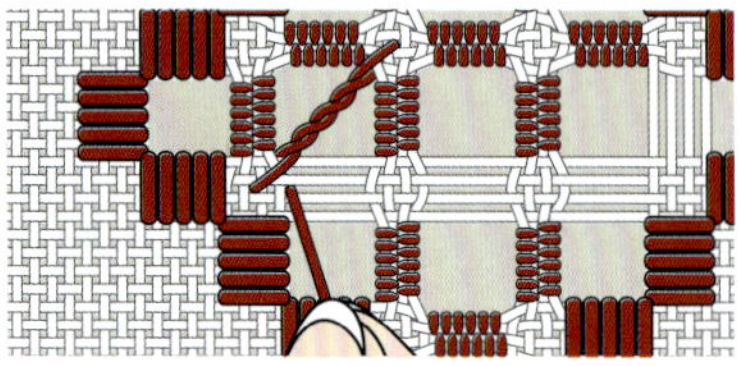

5 Pull the needle through and tighten the stitches to intertwine the twists.

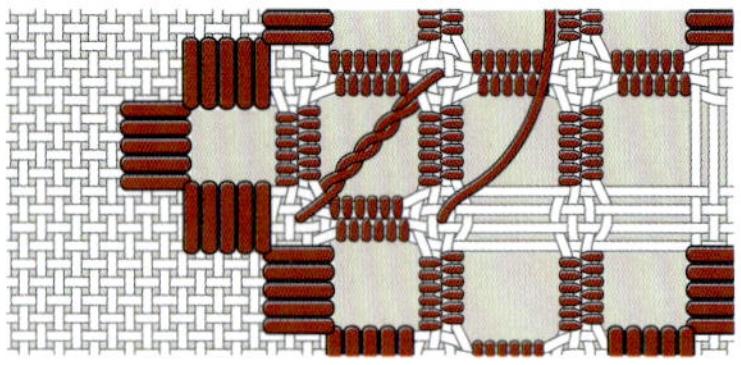

6 Weave the bar then bring the needle out in the centre of the woven square at the end of it.

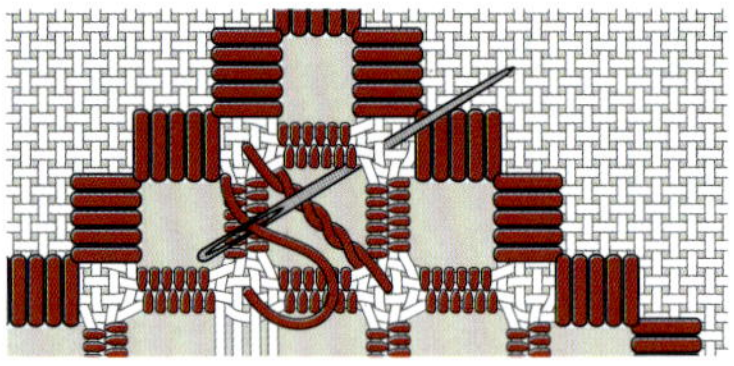

7 Turn the work 90° clockwise. Take the needle over the diagonal stitch and bring it out in the centre of the opposite woven square.

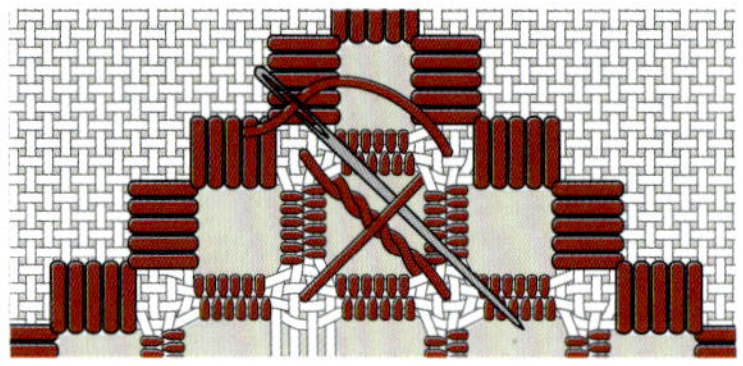

8 Pull the needle through so the stitch sits straight. From above, slide the needle under the diagonal stitch.

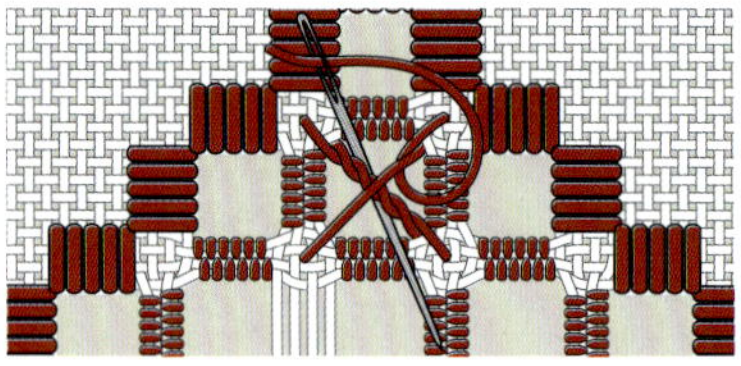

9 From above, slide the needle under the crossing stitches.

10 Pull the needle to intertwine the stitches. Moving in a clockwise direction, pass the needle over the lower left diagonal and under the next.

11 Turn the work 180°. Pass the needle over the next diagonal and under the next.

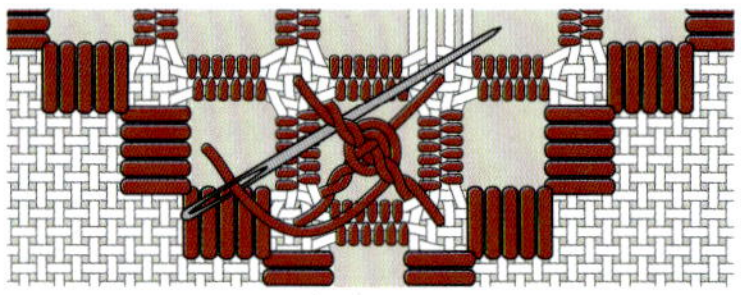

12 With gentle tension, circle the centre again, going over or under each spoke, in the same way as before.

❶ *Be careful not to pull too tight, as the circling stitches are quite unstable.*

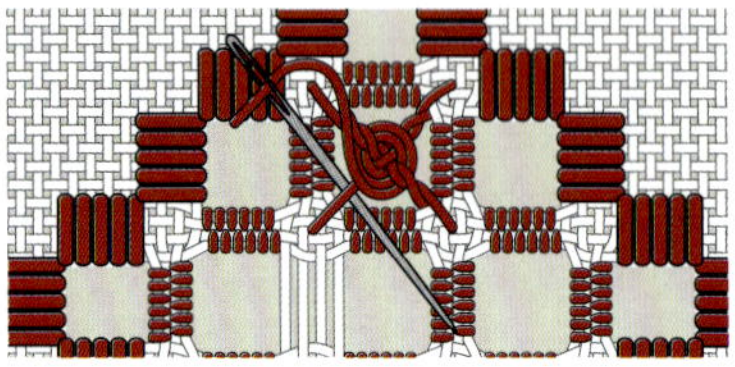

13 Turn the work 180°. From above, slide the needle under the spoke with no twists.

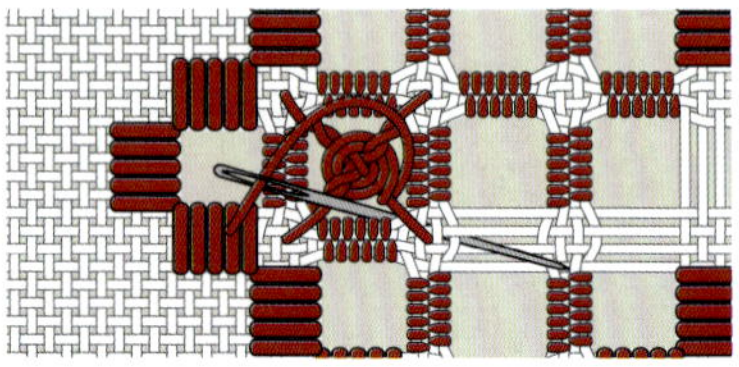

14 Turn the work 90° anticlockwise. Take the needle to the back left of the spoke. Bring it out in the next bar.

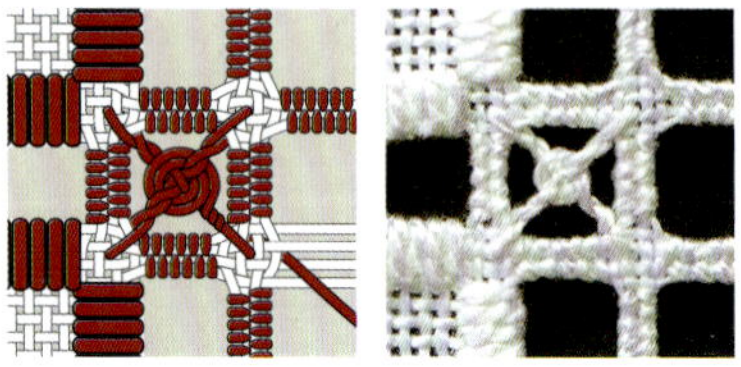

15 Pull to intertwine the stitches. Continue stitching as before.

spider web

Spider webs can be woven, ribbed and whipped. They can be worked singly or as part of larger motifs.

woven spider web – single square

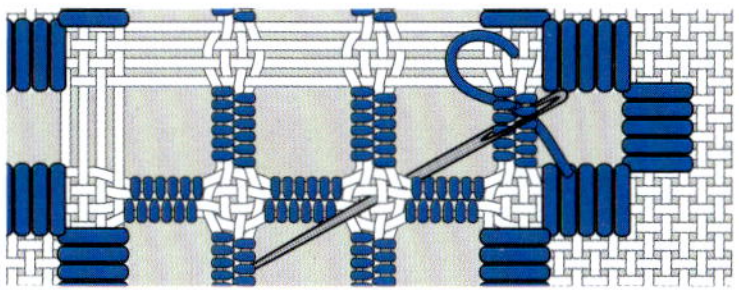

1 After working three sides of the square to be filled, bring the needle out centrally in the adjacent corner woven square. Then bring it out centrally in the opposite woven square.

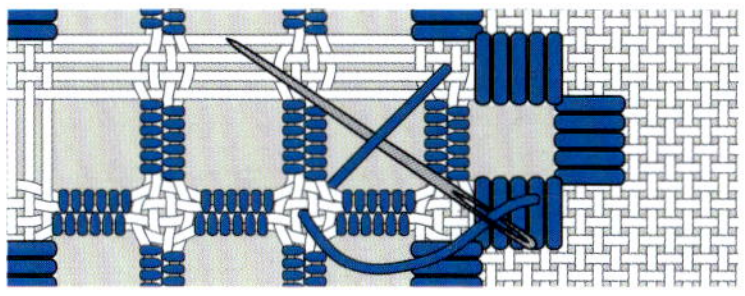

2 Pull the needle through so the stitch sits straight. From below right, slide the needle under the diagonal stitch.

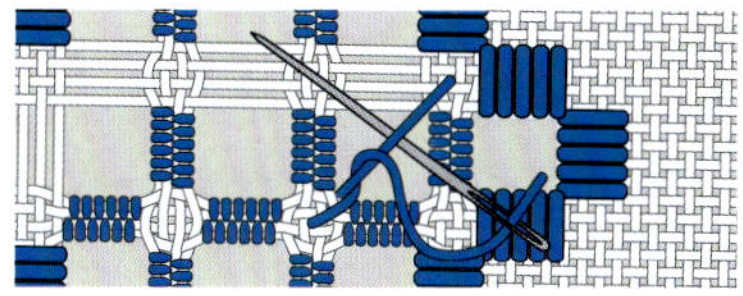

3 From below right, slide the needle under the diagonal stitch again.

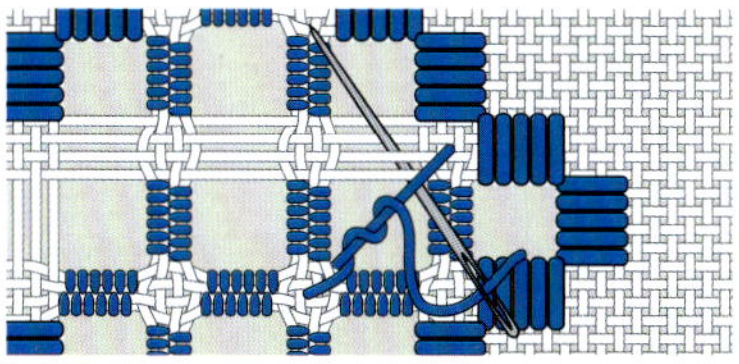

4 Insert the needle below the diagonal stitch, bringing it out in the unwoven bar.

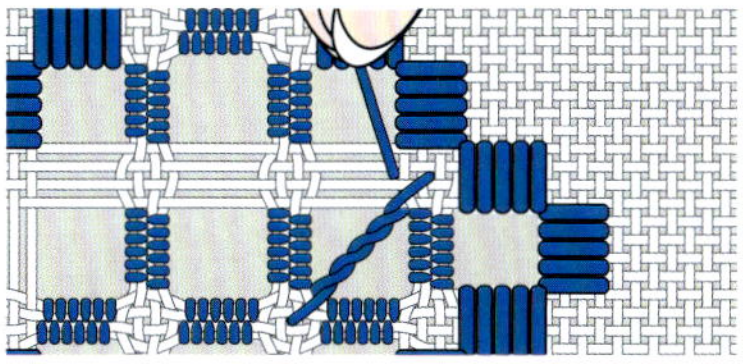

5 Pull the needle through and tighten the stitches to intertwine the twists.

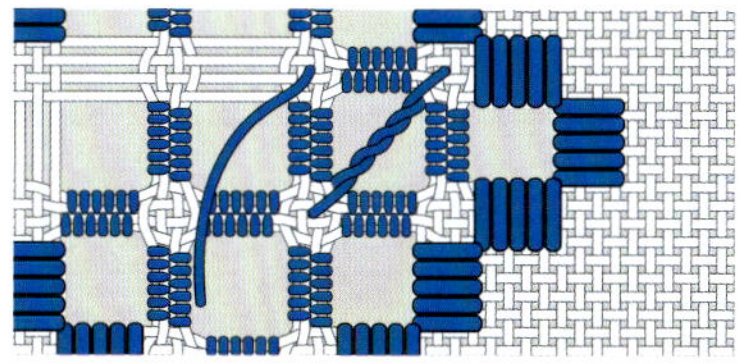

6 Weave the bar then bring the needle out in the centre of the woven square at the end of it.

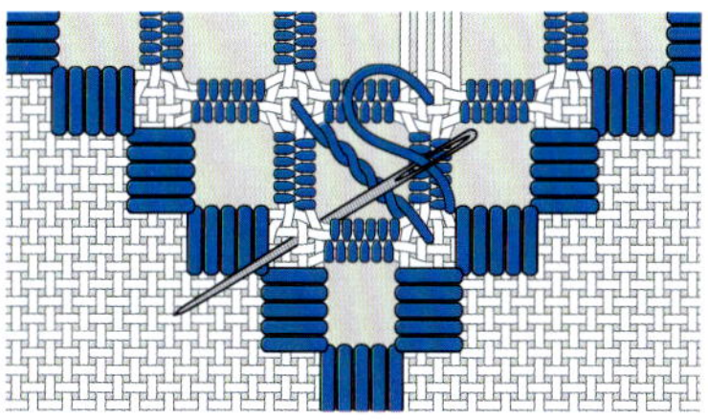

7 Turn the work 90° clockwise. Take the needle over the diagonal stitch and bring it out in the centre of the opposite woven square.

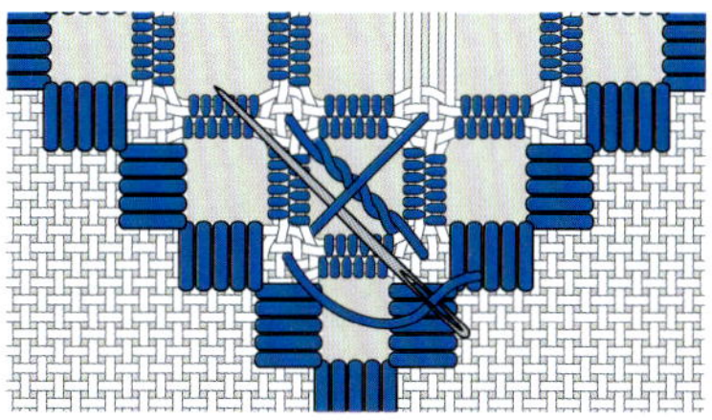

8 Pull the needle through so the stitch sits straight. From below right, slide the needle under the diagonal stitch.

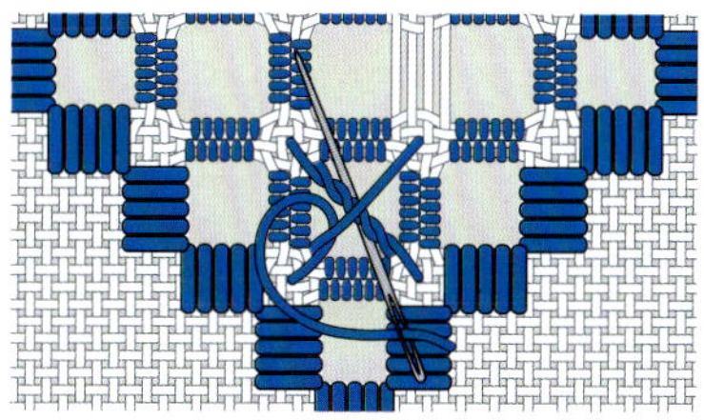

9 From below, slide the needle under the crossing stitches.

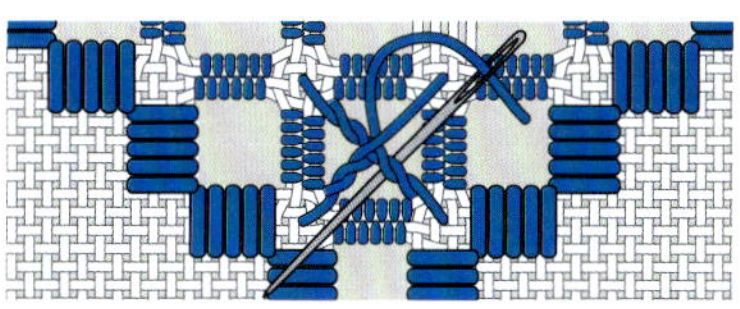

10 Pull the needle to intertwine the stitches. Moving in a clockwise direction, pass the needle over the upper right diagonal and under the next.

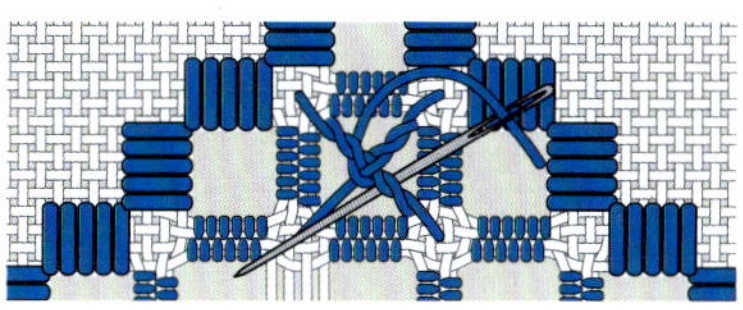

11 Turn the work 180°. Pass the needle over the next diagonal and under the next.

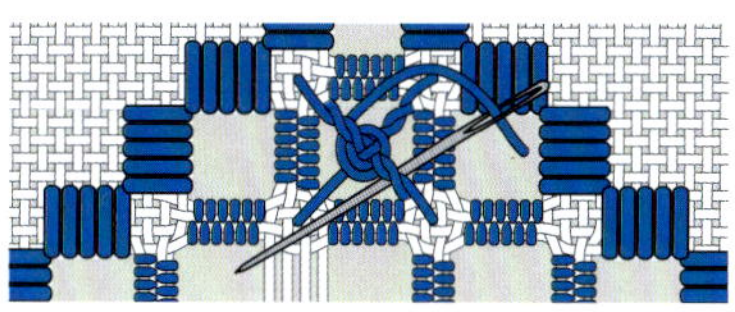

12 With gentle tension, circle the centre again, going over or under each spoke, in the same way as before.

❶ *Be careful not to pull too tight, as the circling stitches are quite unstable.*

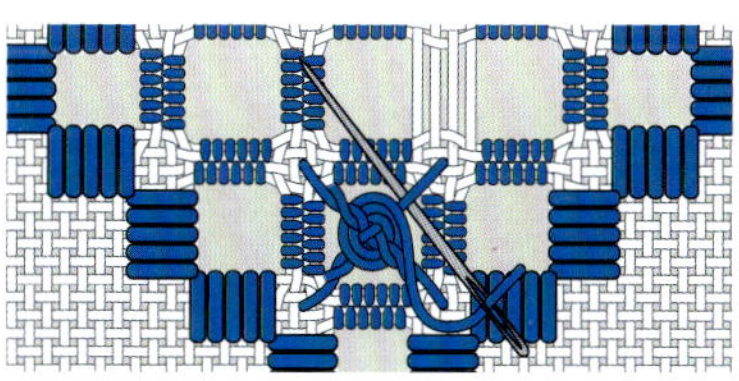

13 Turn the work 180°. From above, slide the needle under the spoke with no twists.

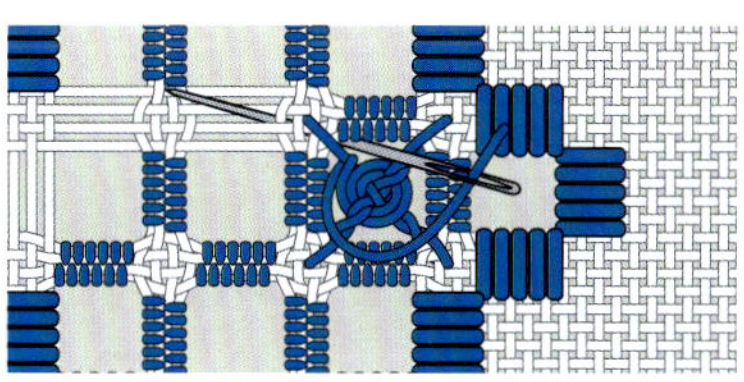

14 Turn the work 90° anticlockwise. Take the needle to the back left of the spoke. Bring it out in the next bar.

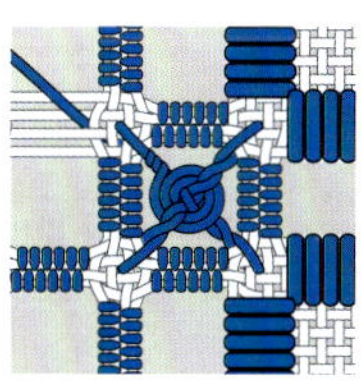

15 Pull to intertwine the stitches. Continue stitching as before.

CONTEMPORARY

woven spider web – three spokes

This stitch is shown worked in a small multiple hole square, but it can also be worked in larger squares. They can be worked singly or in four quadrants together, with woven or wrapped bars.

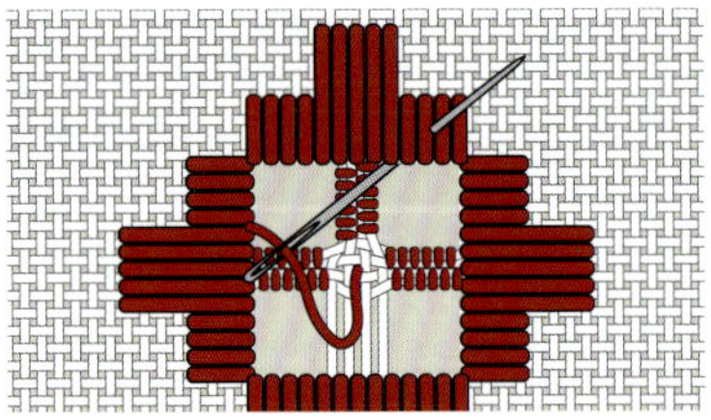

1 Prepare the square as shown. Bring the needle out in the woven square's centre. Bring it out again in the upper satin stitch, two stitches from the corner, halfway up the stitches.

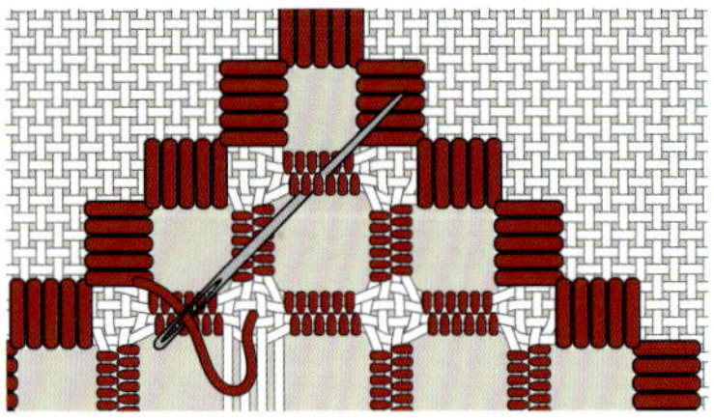

❶ *If working in the middle of an area of cutwork, bring the needle out centrally in the woven bar.*

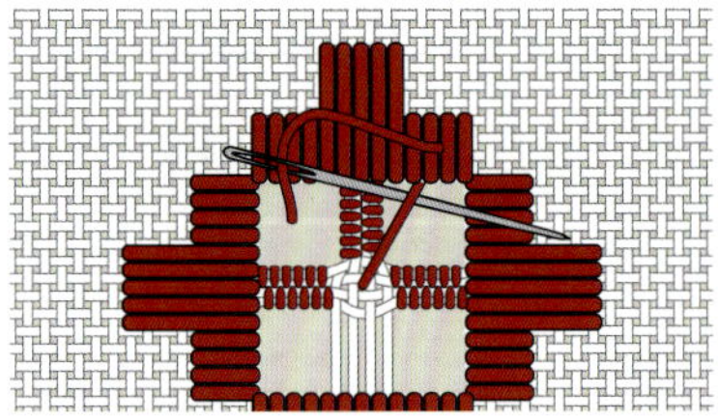

2 Pull the needle through. Slide the needle under the diagonal stitch, from left to right.

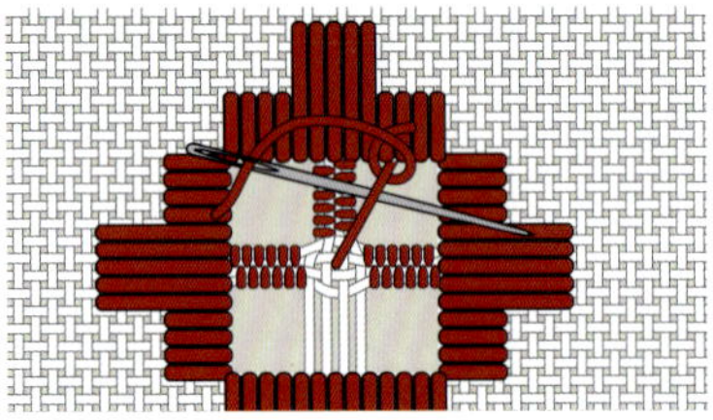

3 Moving down, slide the needle under the diagonal stitch again.

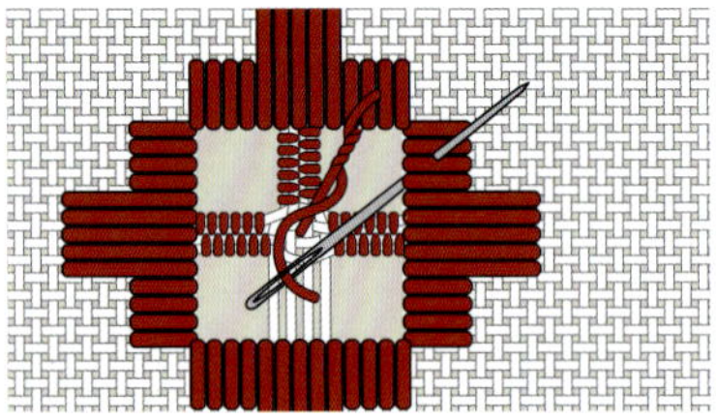

4 Pull to intertwine the stitches. Bring the needle out in the next side, halfway across, two stitches from the corner.

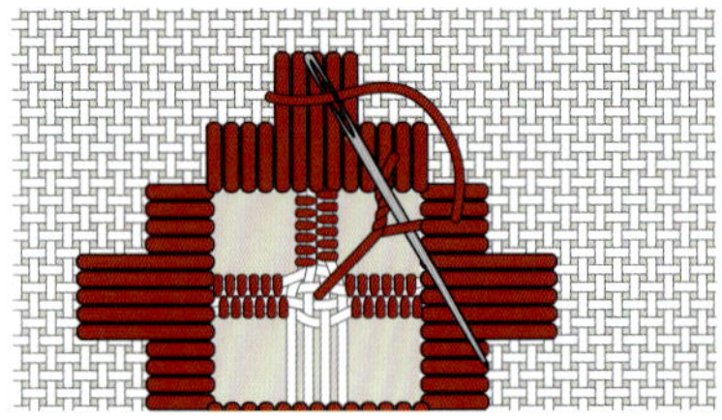

5 Pull the needle through. Slide the needle under the stitch, from above.

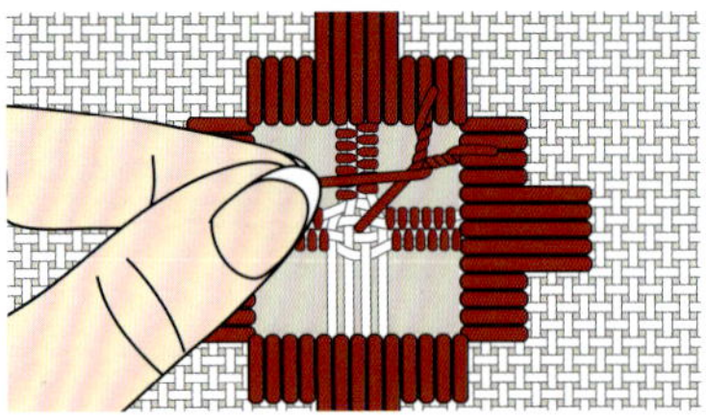

6 Slide the needle under again and pull to intertwine the stitches.

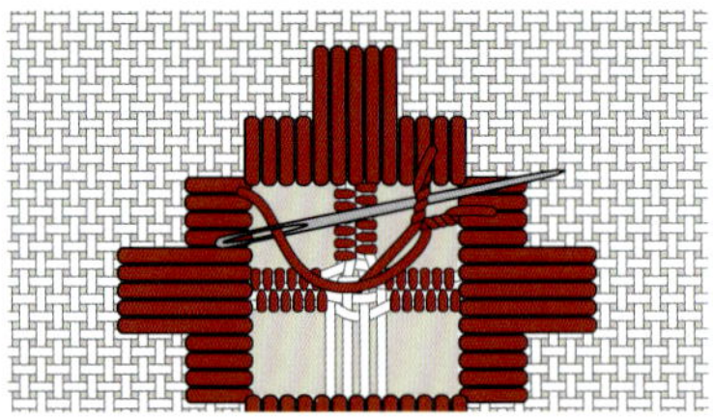

7 Working in a clockwise direction with gentle tension, slide the needle under the Y's left arm, from the left.

8 Take the needle over the right arm of the Y and slide it under the Y stem, from below.

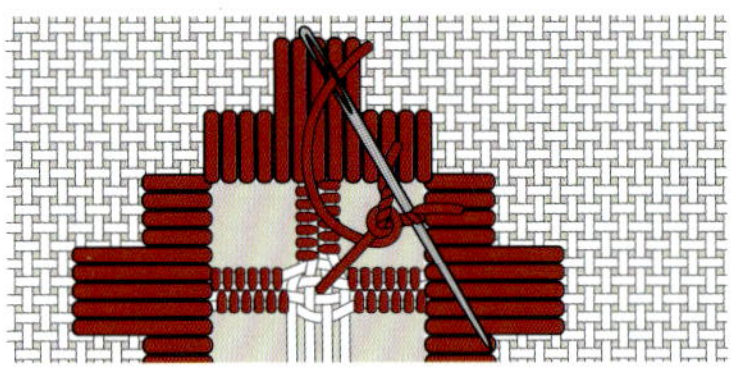

9 Take the needle over the left arm and under the right arm.

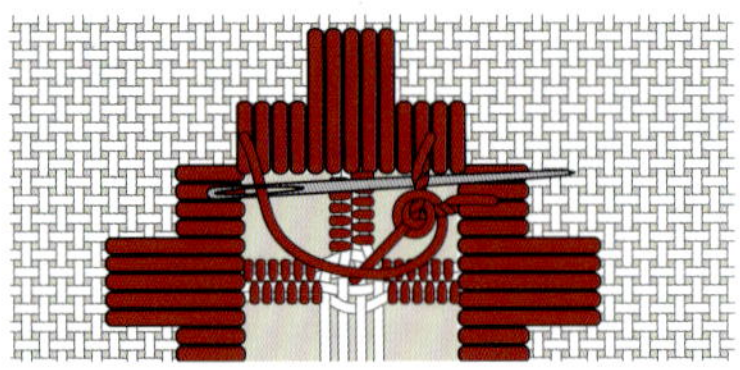

10 Take the needle over the stem and under the left arm.

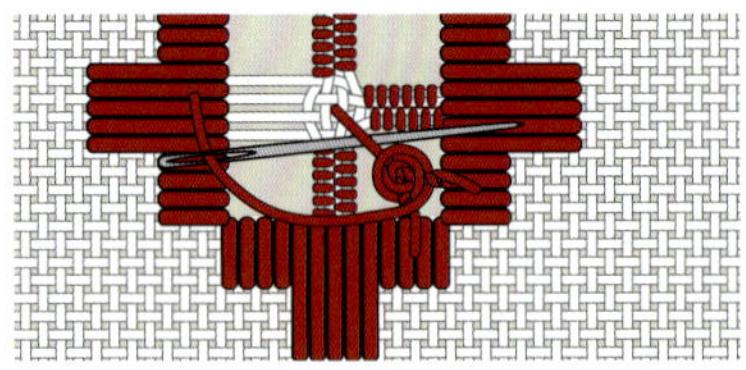

11 Turn the work 90° clockwise. Take the needle over the right arm and under the stem.

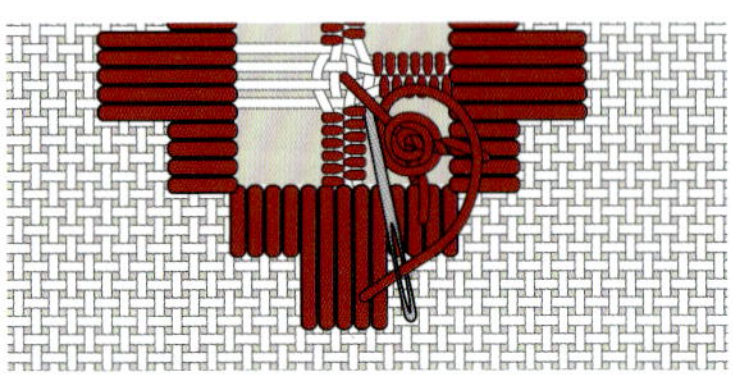

12 Take the needle to the back below the stem.

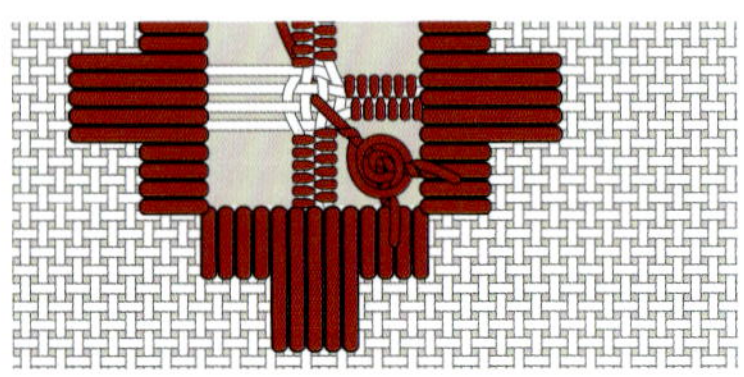

13 Pull the thread to intertwine the stitches.

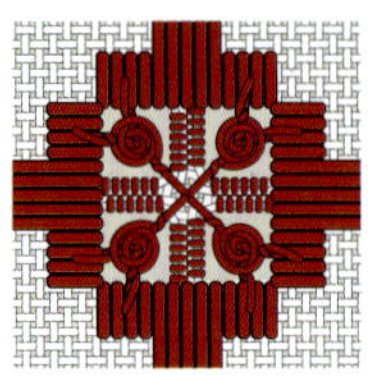

14 Work the motif in the other corners if required.

woven spider web – three spokes

This stitch is shown worked in a small multiple hole square, but it can also be worked in larger squares. They can be worked singly or in four quadrants together, with woven or wrapped bars.

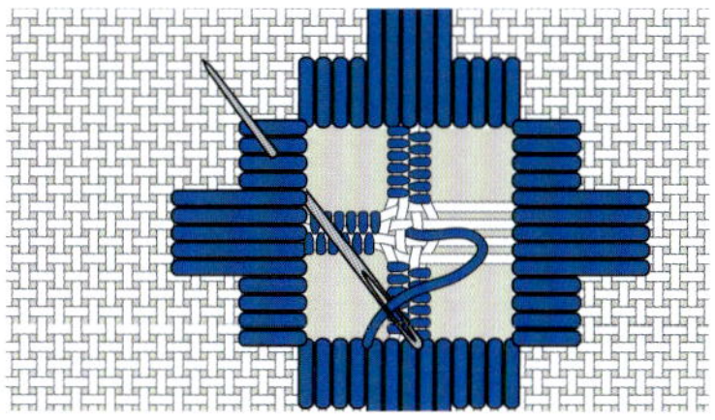

1 Prepare the square as shown. Bring the needle out in the woven square's centre. Bring it out again in the upper satin stitch, two stitches from the corner, halfway up the stitches.

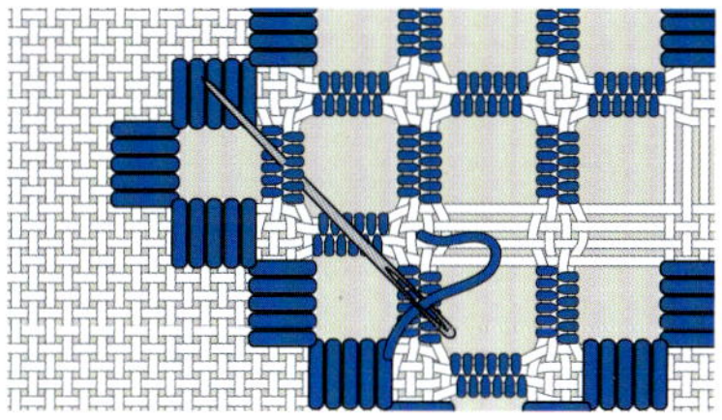

! *If working in the middle of an area of cutwork, bring the needle out centrally in the woven bar.*

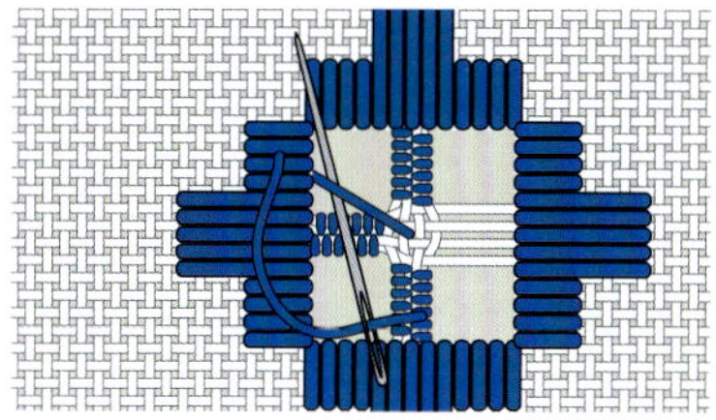

2 Pull the needle through. Slide the needle under the diagonal stitch, from below.

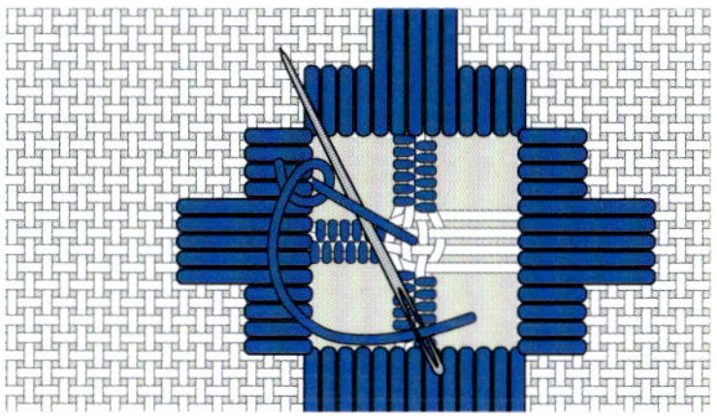

3 Moving right, slide the needle under the diagonal stitch again.

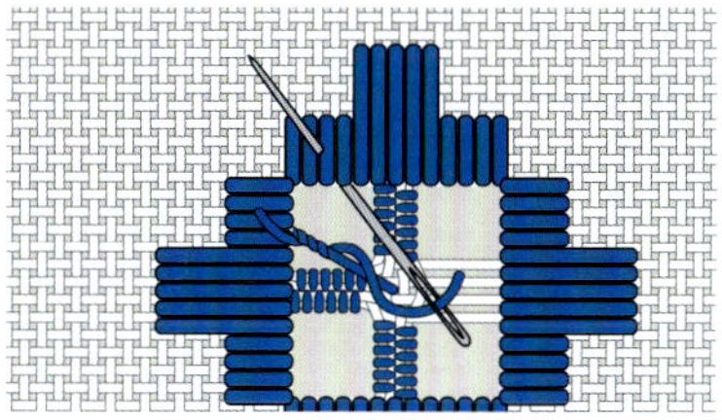

4 Pull to intertwine the stitches. Bring the needle out in the next side, halfway up, two stitches from the corner.

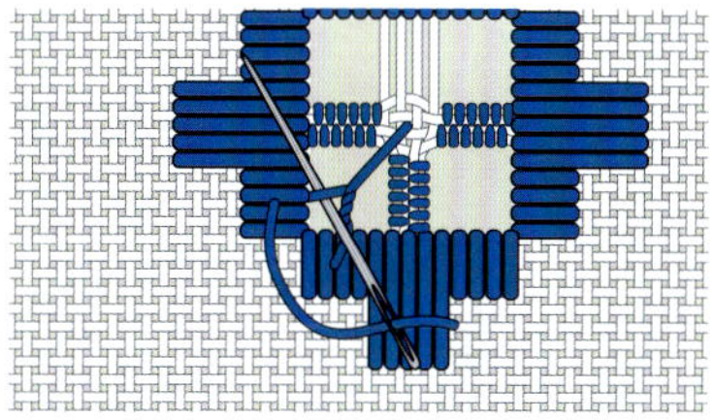

5 Turn the work 90° anticlockwise. Pull the needle through. Slide the needle under the stitch, from below.

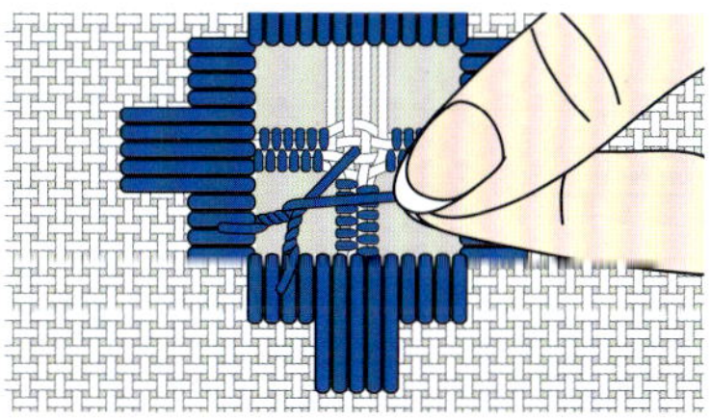

6 Slide the needle under again and pull to intertwine the stitches.

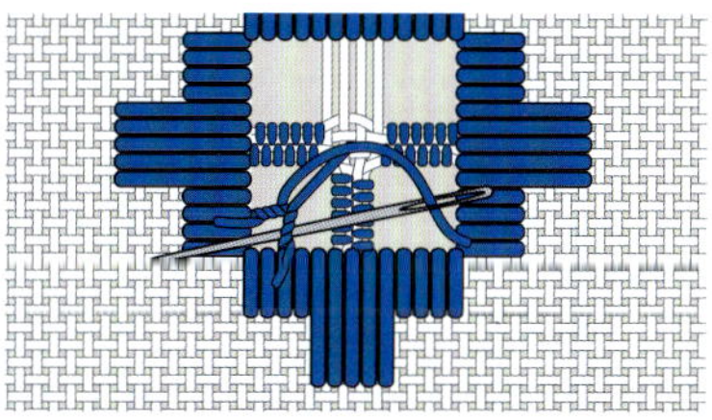

7 Working in a clockwise direction with gentle tension, slide the needle under the Y's left arm, from the right.

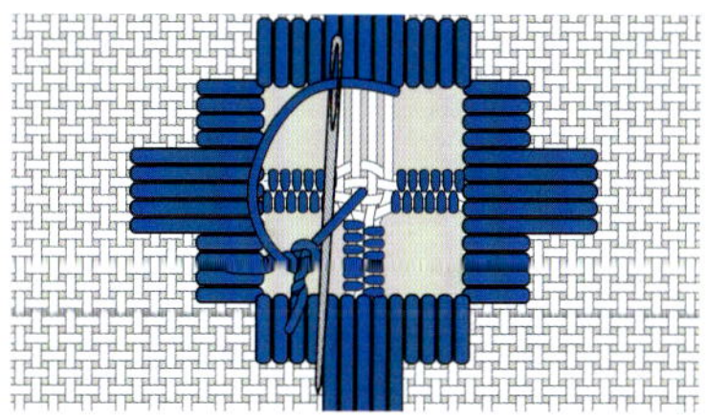

8 Take the needle over the right arm of the Y and slide it under the Y stem, from above.

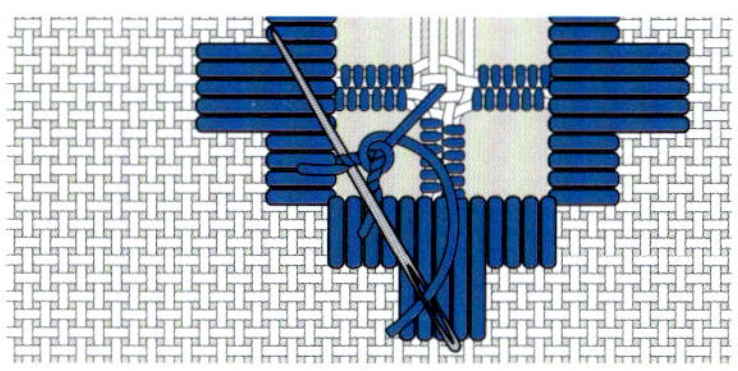

9 Take the needle over the left arm and under the right arm.

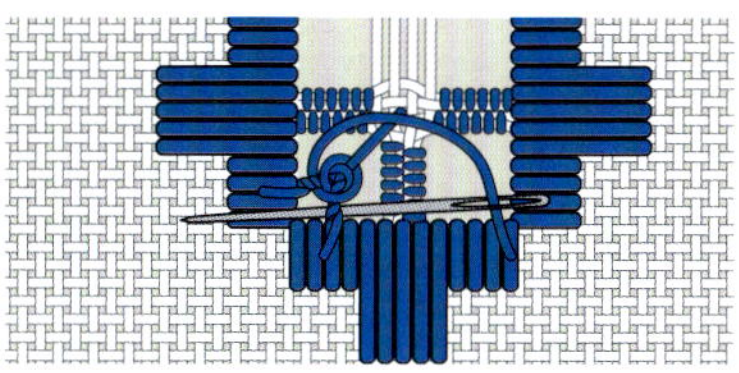

10 Take the needle over the stem and under the left arm.

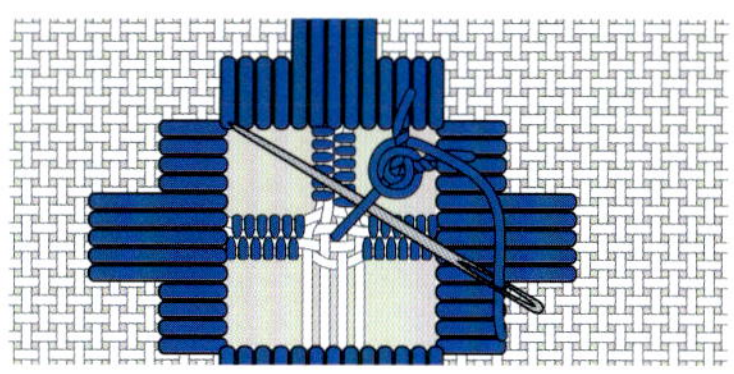

11 Turn the work 180°. Take the needle over the right arm and under the stem.

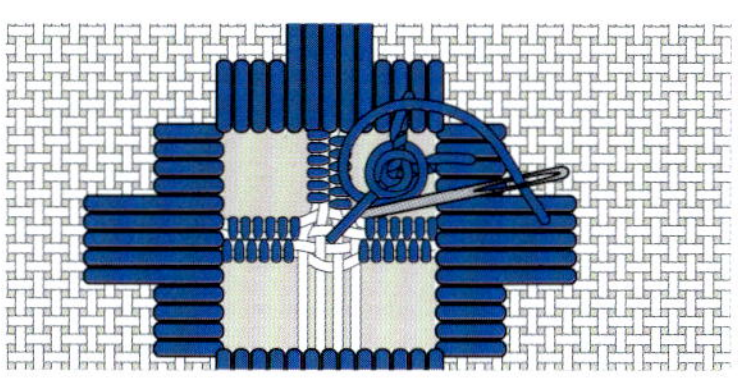

12 Take the needle to the back below the stem.

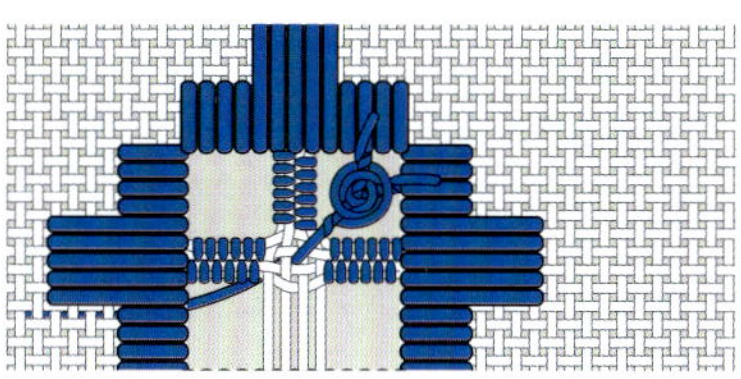

13 Pull the thread to intertwine the stitches.

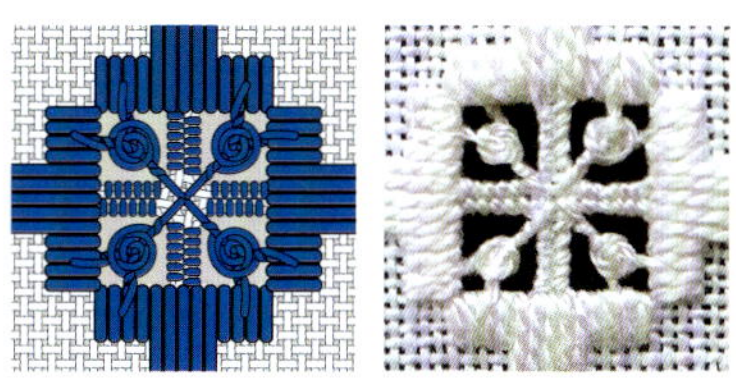

14 Work the motif in the other corners if required.

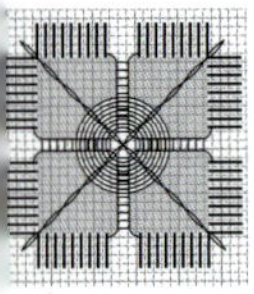

CONTEMPORARY

woven spider web

This is a larger woven spider web than the previous ones; worked over the intersection of woven or wrapped bars. It is sometimes worked in the centre of other filling stitches.

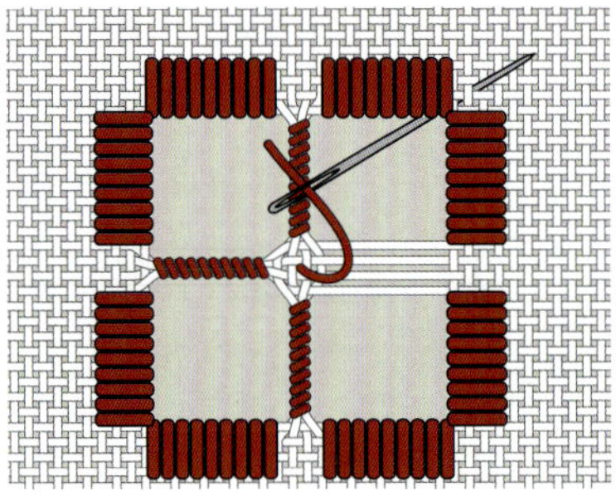

1 In a large square, wrap the bars as shown, then bring the needle out in the woven square's centre. From the back, insert the needle in the corner, two threads away from the edges.

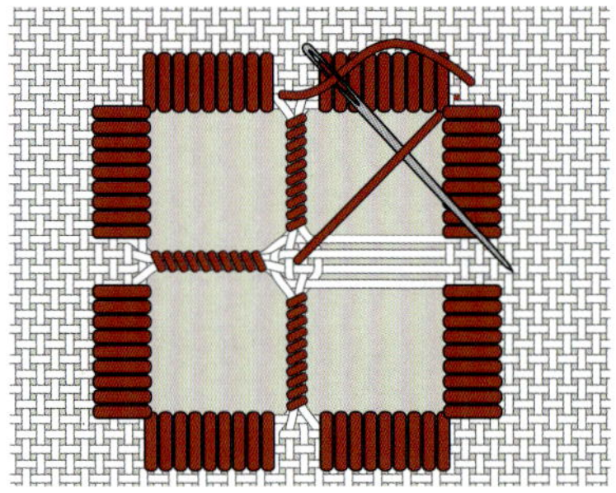

2 Pull the needle through. From above, slide it under the stitch.

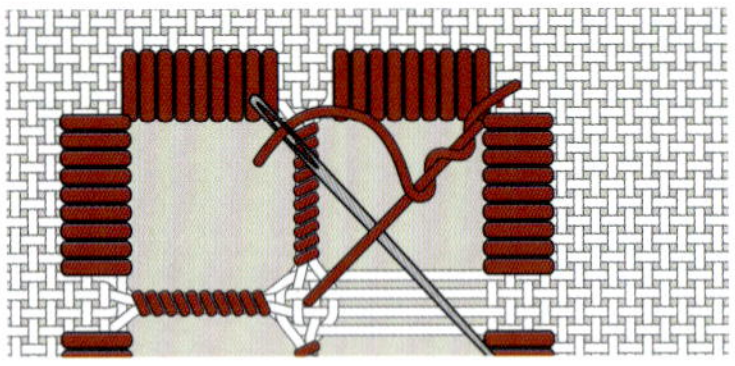

3 Moving towards the centre, slide the needle under the stitch again, twice more.

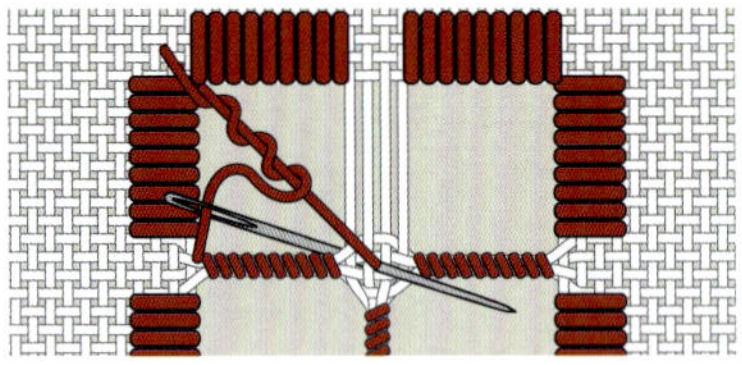

4 Turn the work 90° anticlockwise. Bring the needle out in the centre of the woven square.

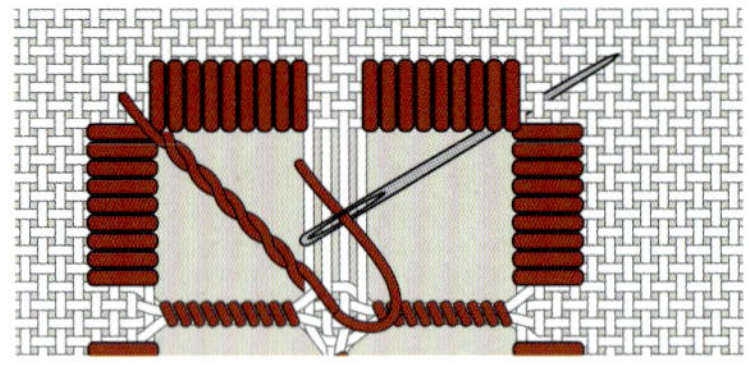

5 Pull to intertwine the stitches. Bring the needle out in the next corner, two threads away from the edge.

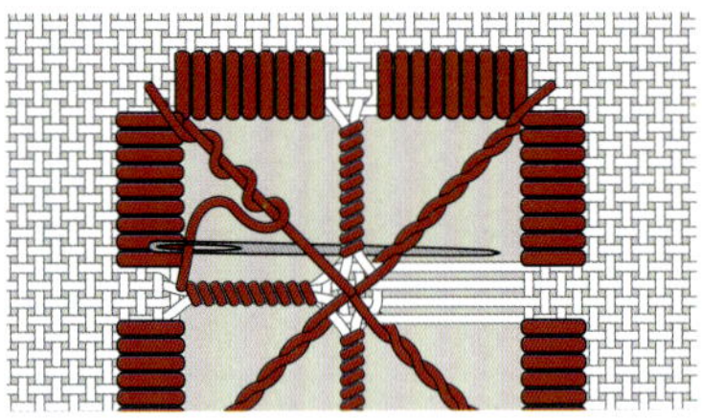

6 Work spokes in each quadrant. Finish by bringing the needle out as if to wrap the final bar.

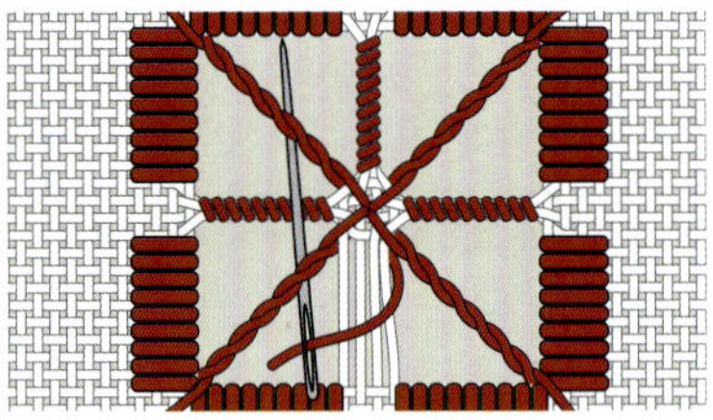

7 Turn the work 90° clockwise. Going around the centre in a clockwise direction, slide the needle under the two left diagonals from below.

8 Pull the thread to bring the stitches in snug to the centre. Slide the needle under the two right diagonals, from above.

9 Pull the thread to bring the stitches in snug to the centre. From the left, slide the needle under the empty bar and the right bar.

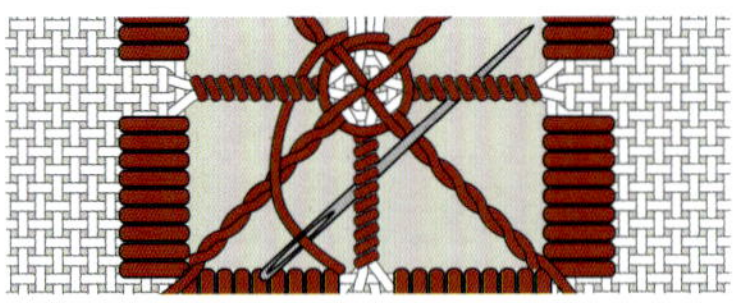

10 Turn the work 180°. Tighten the stitches around the centre. Travelling anticlockwise, take the needle under the next two bars.

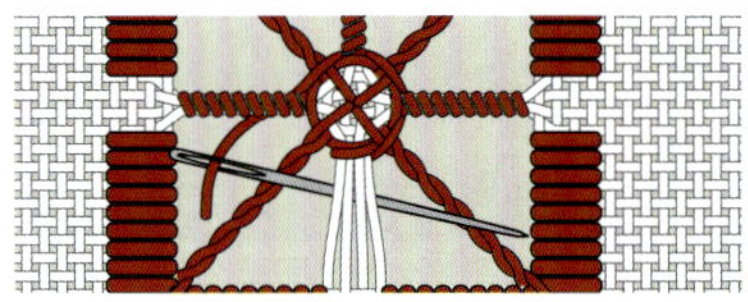

11 Turn the work 180°. Pull the thread to bring the stitches in snug to the centre. Take the needle under the empty bar.

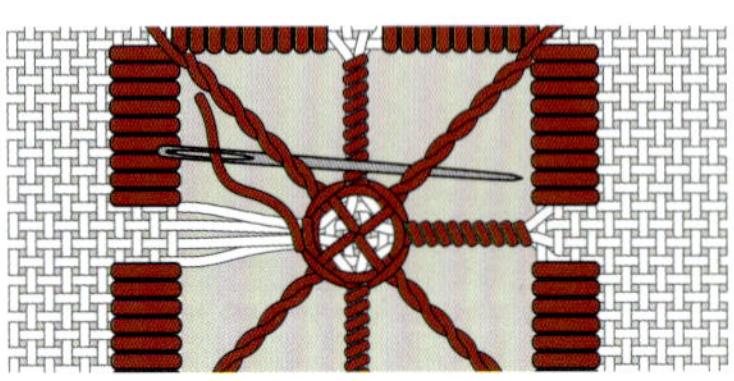

12 Turn the work 90° clockwise. Slide the needle under the two upper diagonals from the left.

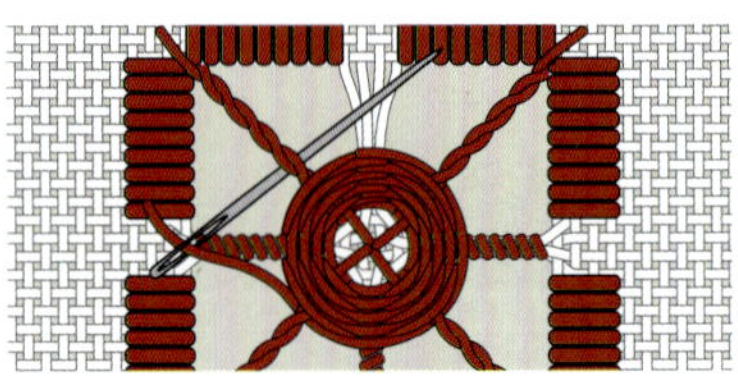

13 Continue turning and weaving the web to the desired size, changing direction at the empty bar each time.

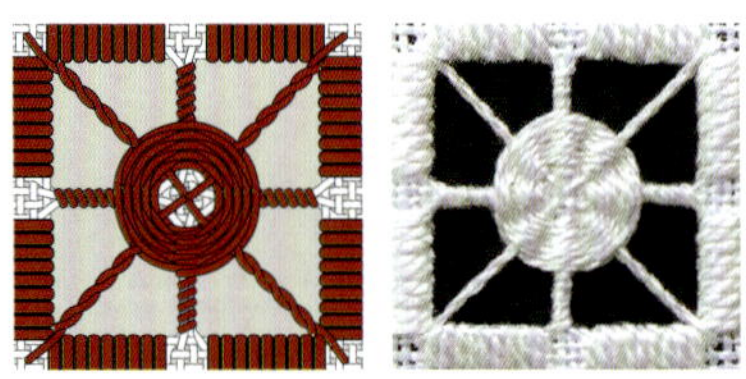

14 Finish a circuit, then wrap the remaining bar. Finish the thread on the back.

woven spider web

This large spider web is worked over the intersection of woven or wrapped bars. It is sometimes worked in the centre of other filling stitches.

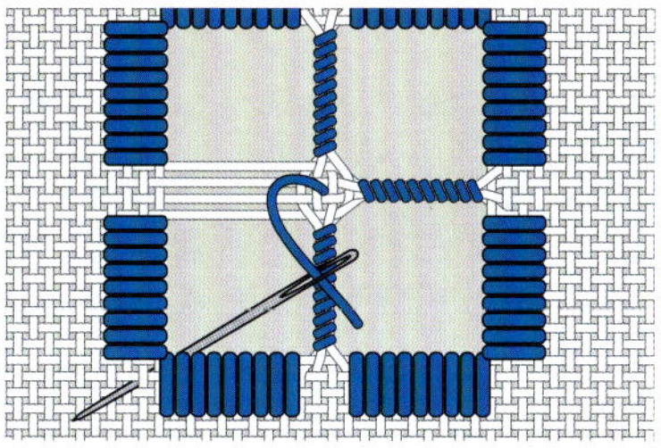

1 In a large square, wrap the bars as shown. Bring the needle out in the centre. From behind, insert it in a corner, two threads from the cut edges.

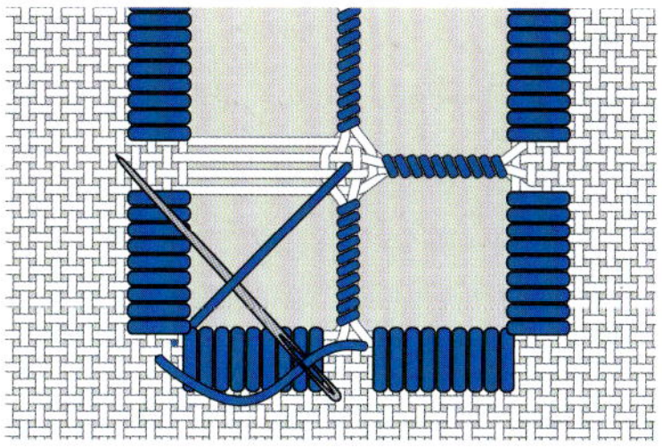

2 Pull the needle through. From below, slide it under the stitch.

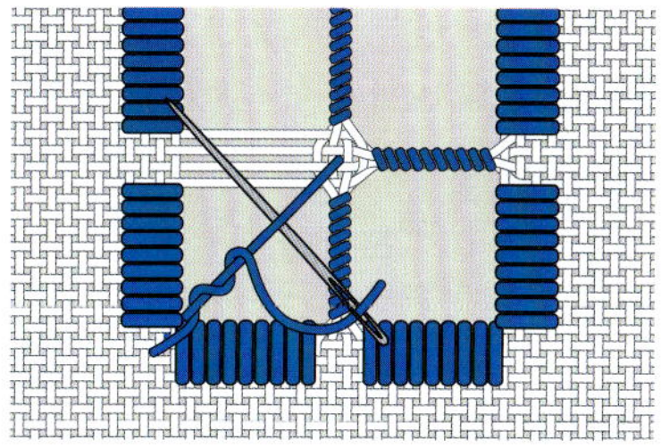

3 Moving towards the centre, slide the needle under the stitch again.

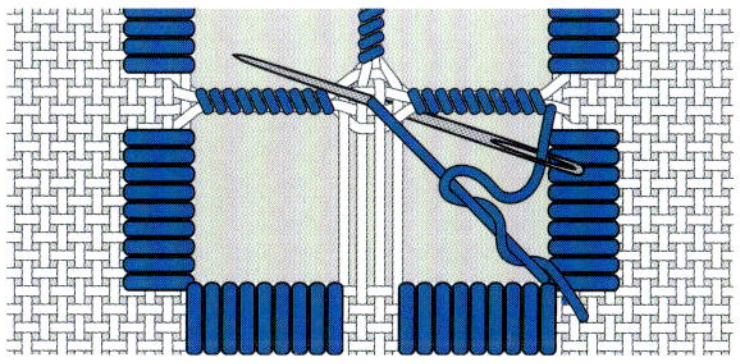

4 Turn the work 90° anticlockwise. Bring the needle out in the centre of the woven square.

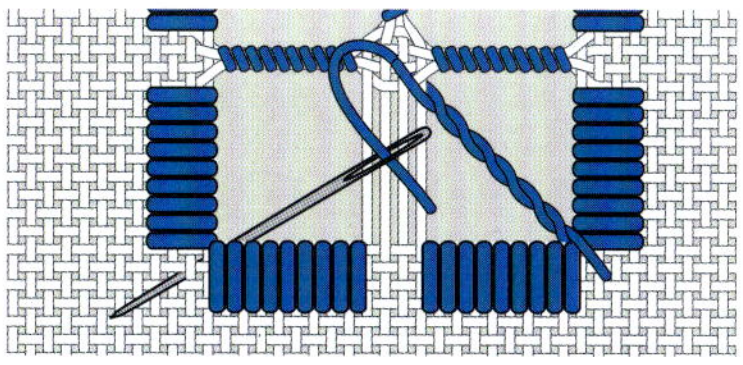

5 Pull to intertwine the stitches. Bring the needle out in the next corner, two threads away from the edge.

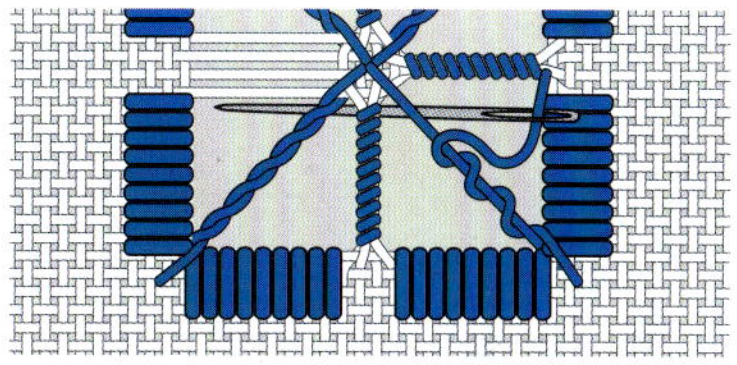

6 Work spokes in each quadrant. Finish by bringing the needle out as if to wrap the final bar.

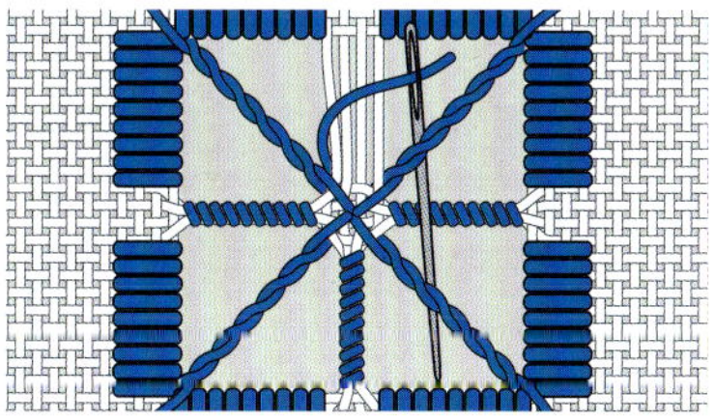

7 Turn the work 90° clockwise. Working in a clockwise direction, slide the needle under the two right diagonals from above.

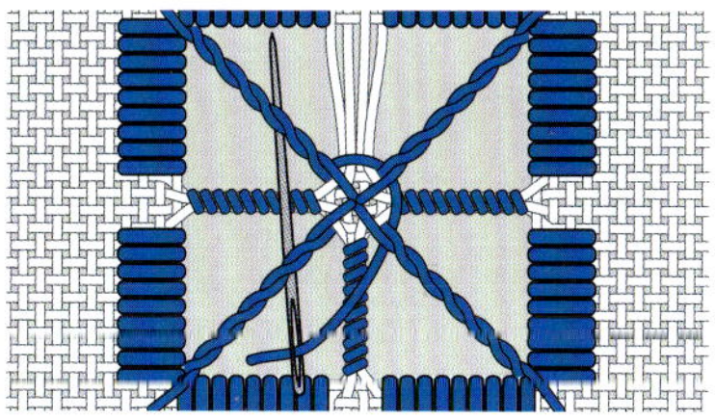

8 Pull the thread to bring the stitches in snug to the centre. Slide the needle under the two left diagonals, from below.

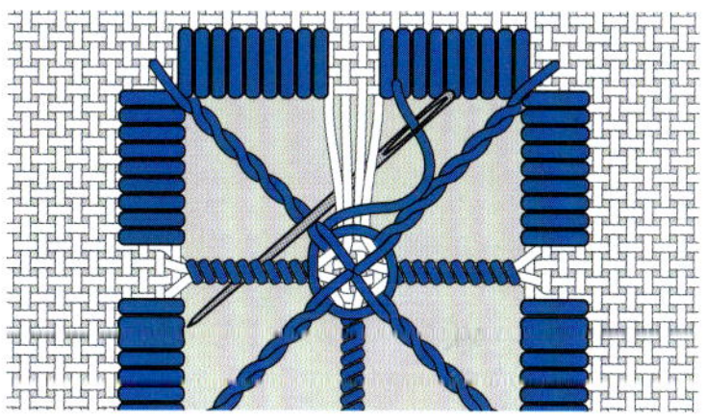

9 Pull the thread to bring the stitches in snug to the centre. From the right, slide the needle under the empty bar and the left bar.

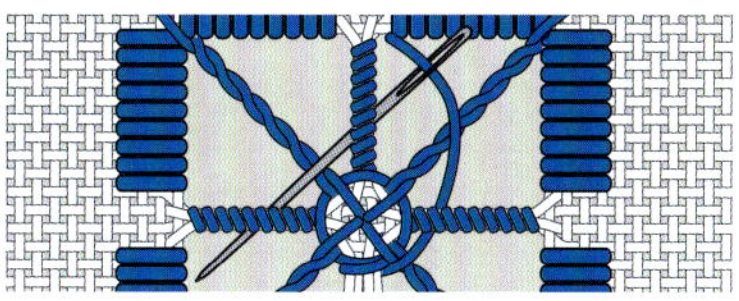

10 Turn the work 180°. Tighten the stitches. Working anticlockwise, take the needle under the next two bars.

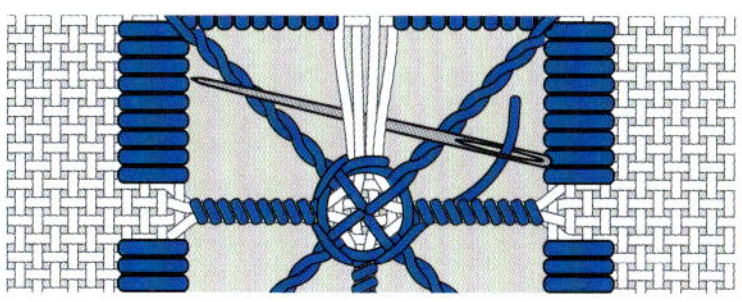

11 Turn the work 180°. Pull the thread in snug to the centre. Take the needle under the empty bar.

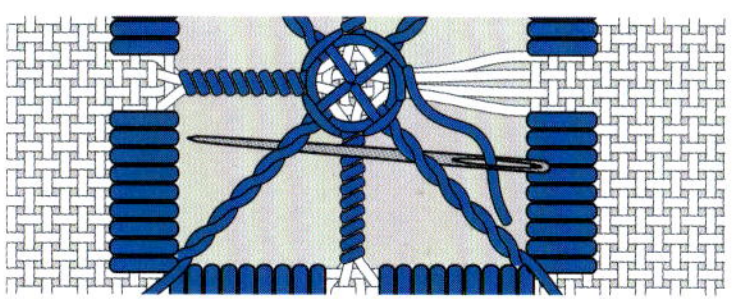

12 Turn the work 90° clockwise. Slide the needle under the two lower diagonals from the right.

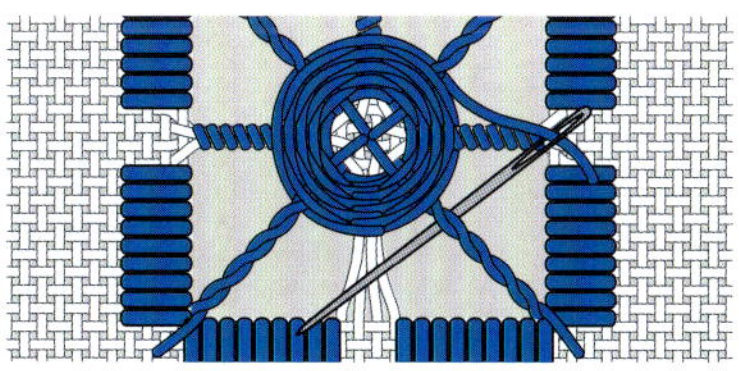

13 Continue turning and weaving the web to the desired size, changing direction at the empty bar each time.

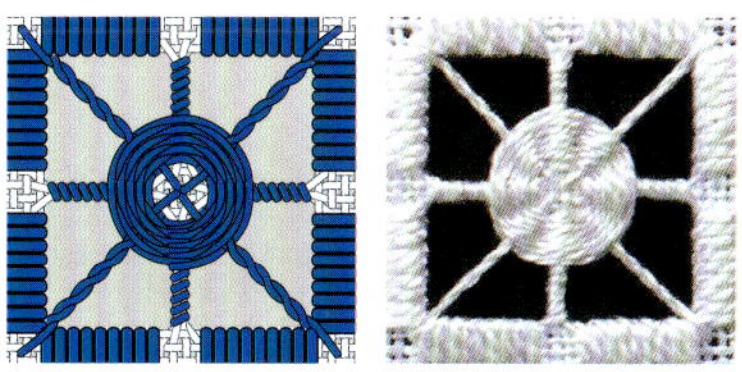

14 Finish a circuit, then wrap the remaining bar. Finish the thread on the back.

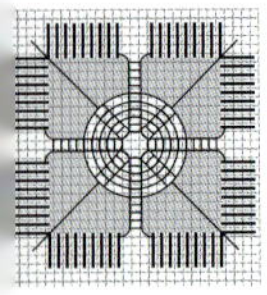

ribbed spider web

This spider web is worked over the intersection of bars. It can be worked in the centre of other filling stitches.

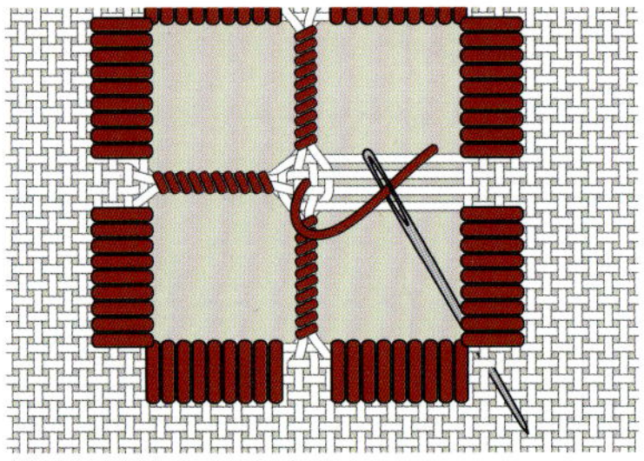

1 In a large square, wrap the bars as shown. Bring the needle out in the woven square's centre, then bring it out in the bottom right corner, two threads away from the edge.

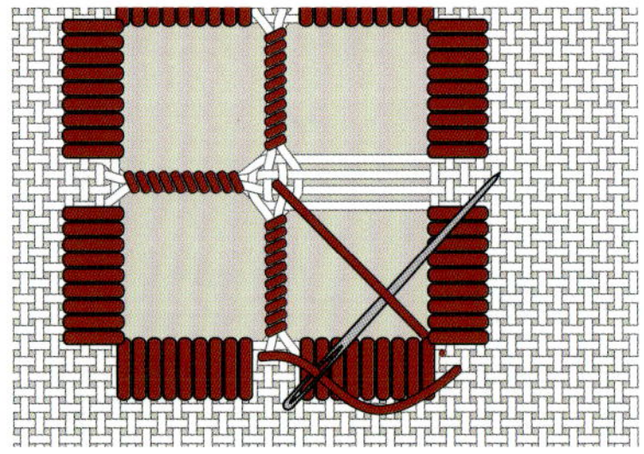

2 Pull the needle through. From below left, slide it under the stitch.
! *If you work the twists the other way for this stitch, they will untwist when you wrap them to make the ribs.*

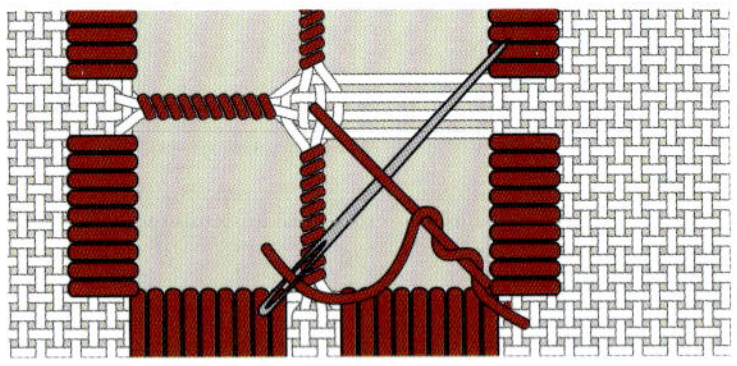

3 Moving towards the centre, slide the needle under the stitch twice more.
! *More twists can be added if desired.*

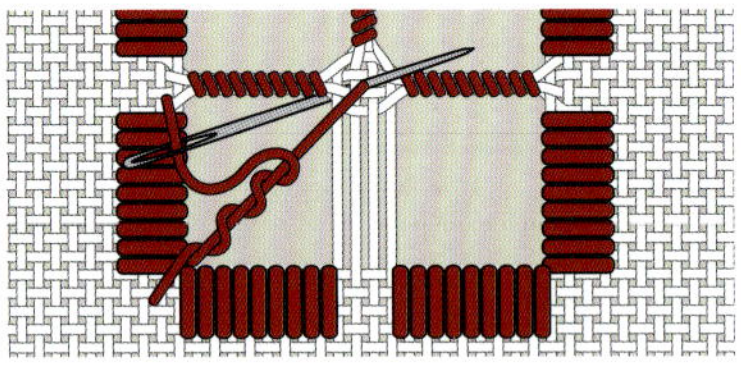

4 Turn the work 90° clockwise. Insert the needle above the diagonal. Bring it out in the woven square's centre.

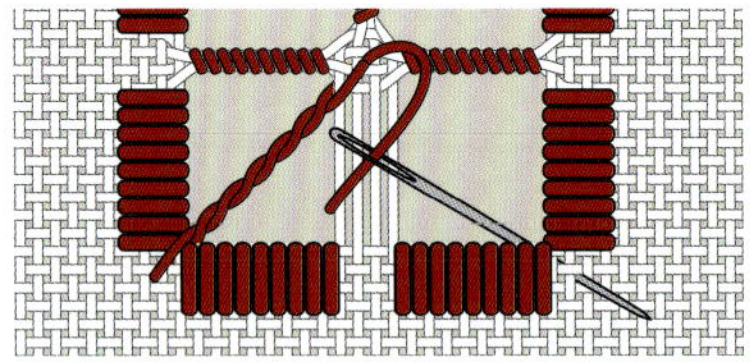

5 Pull to intertwine the stitches. Bring the needle out in the next woven corner, two threads from the edge.

6 Repeat Steps 2 to 5 to work spokes out to each corner. Turn the work as needed. Finish by bringing the needle out as if to wrap the final bar.

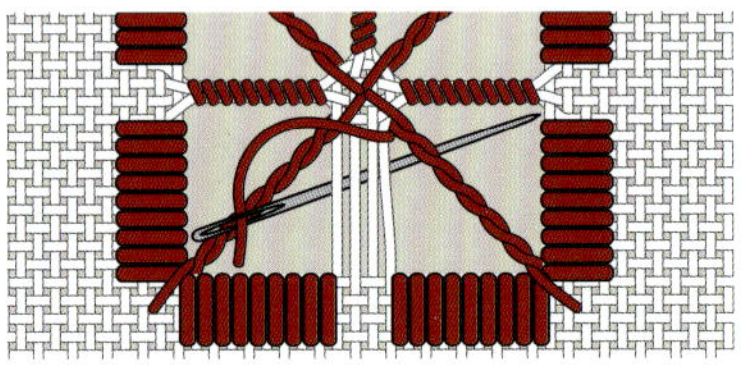

7 Moving anticlockwise, slide the needle, from the left, under the empty bar and the adjacent diagonal.
! *Finish the thread and start a new one under the empty bar, if you know your thread won't finish the web.*

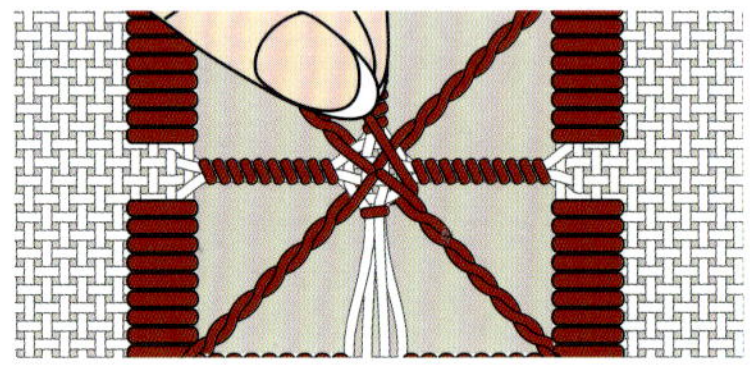

8 Pull the thread towards the centre to tighten the stitch and pull it in snug against the centre.

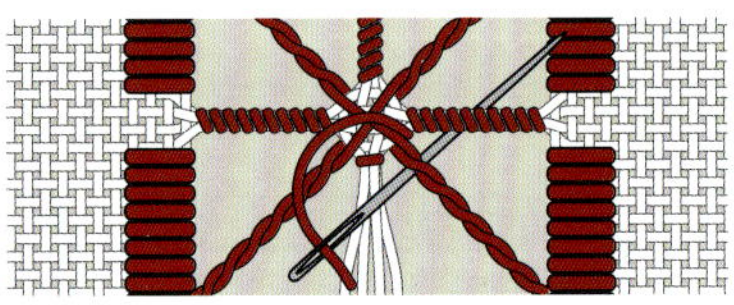

9 From below left, slide the needle under the diagonal and the next bar.
! *Each time, the needle goes under two spokes: the current and next one.*

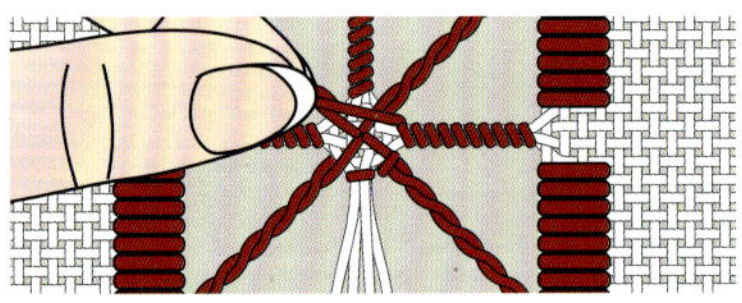

10 Pull the thread towards the centre to tighten the stitch and pull it in snug against the centre.
! *Do this after each stitch.*

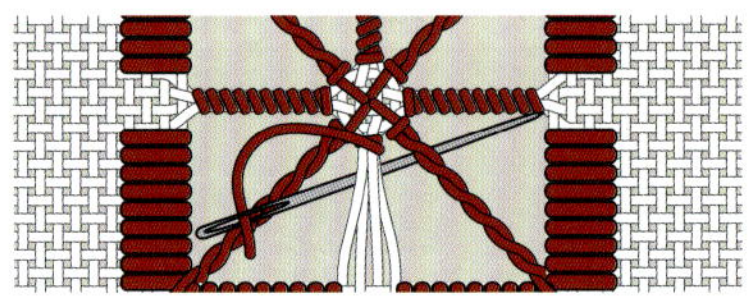

11 Continue around the spokes, turning the work as needed, to create a ribbed web of the desired size.

12 When the web is the desired size and you reach the first spoke again, take the needle under that spoke only.

! *If you're working with woven bars, bring the needle up in the centre of the bar and weave it to finish.*

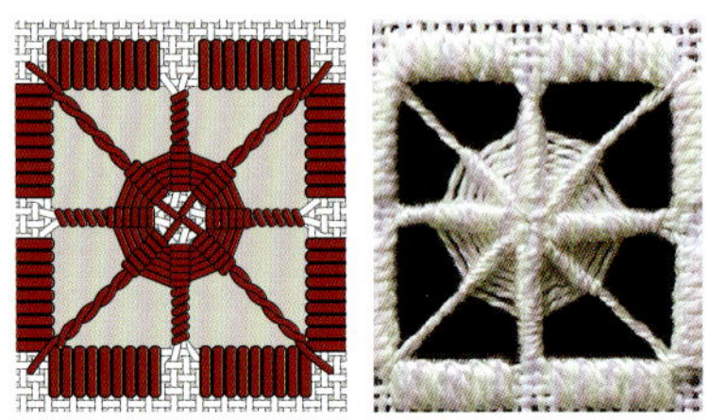

13 Wrap the rest of the spoke and take the needle through to the back to finish the thread.

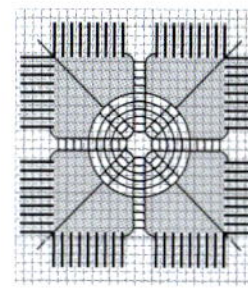

ribbed spider web

This spider web is worked over the intersection of bars. It can be worked in the centre of other filling stitches.

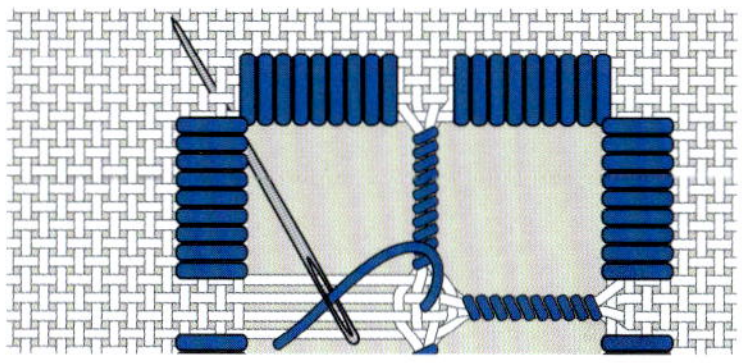

1 In a large square, wrap three bars then bring the needle out in the woven square's centre. From the back, insert the needle in the corner, two threads away from the edge.

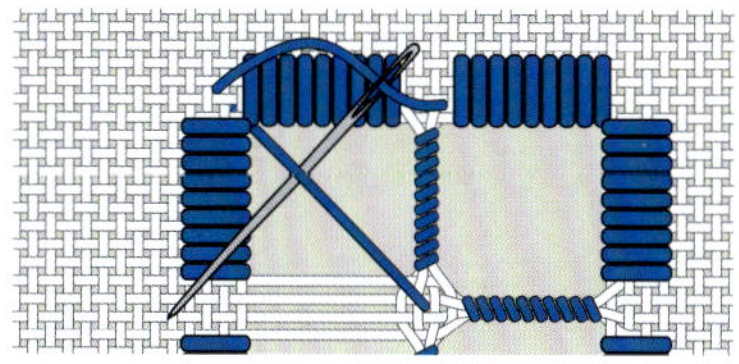

2 Pull the needle through. From above right, slide it under the stitch. ❶ *If you work the twists the other way for this stitch, they will untwist when you wrap them to make the ribs.*

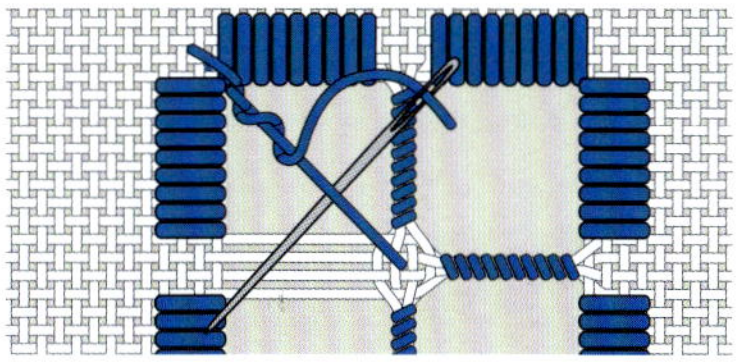

3 Moving towards the centre, slide the needle under the stitch twice more. ❶ *More twists can be added if desired.*

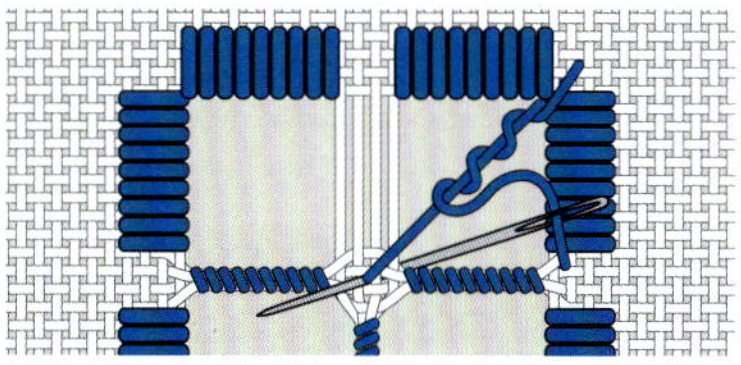

4 Turn the work 90° clockwise. Insert the needle below the diagonal. Bring it out in the woven square's centre.

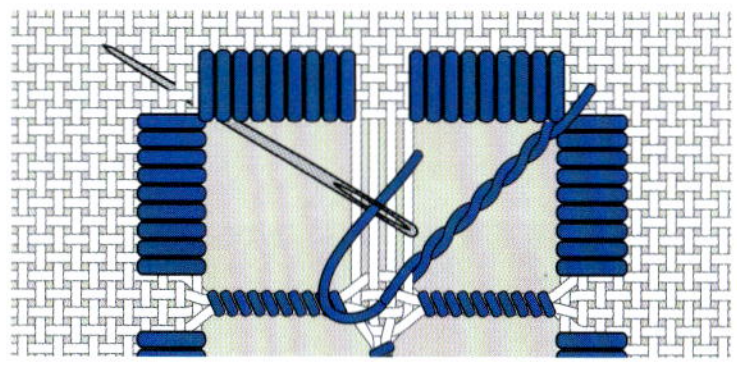

5 Pull to intertwine the stitches. Bring the needle out in the next woven corner, two threads from the edge.

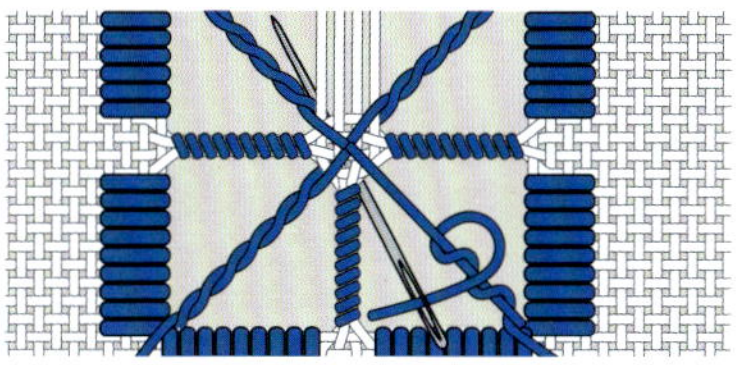

6 Repeat Steps 2 to 5 to work spokes out to each corner. Turn the work as needed. Finish by bringing the needle out ready to wrap the final bar.

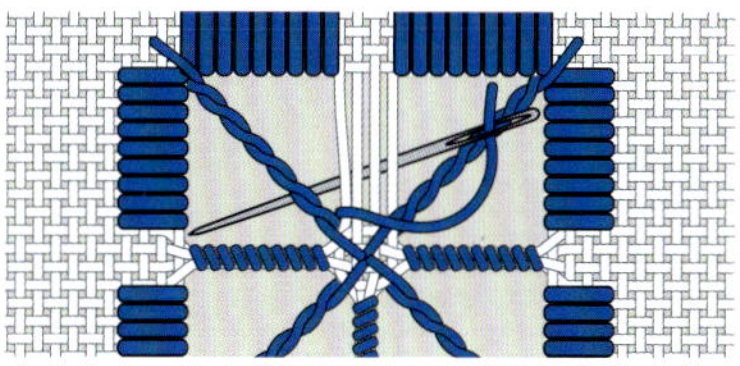

7 Moving anticlockwise, slide the needle, from the right, under the empty bar and the adjacent diagonal. ❶ *Finish the thread and start a new one under the empty bar, if you know your thread won't finish the web.*

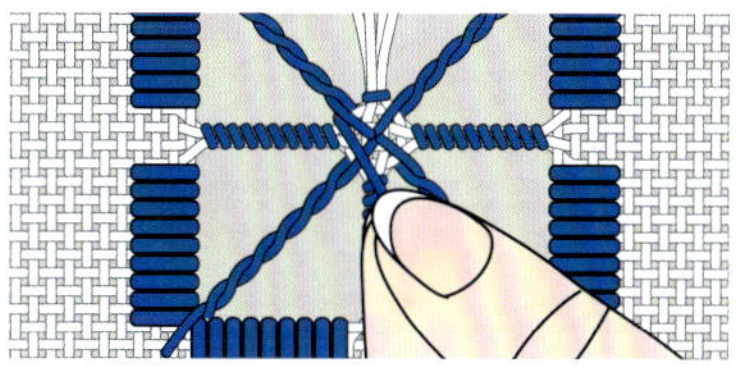

8 Pull the thread towards the centre to tighten the stitch and pull it in snug against the centre.

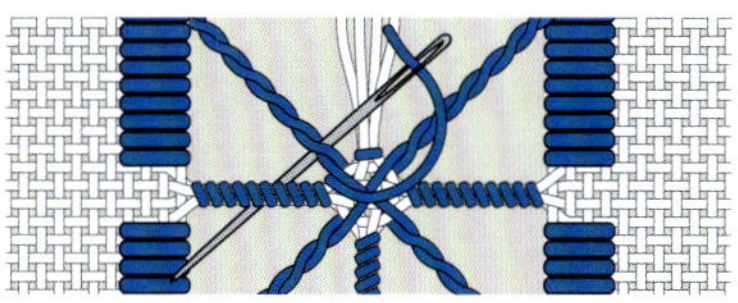

9 From above right, slide the needle under the diagonal and the next bar. ❶ *Each time, the needle goes under two spokes: the current and next one.*

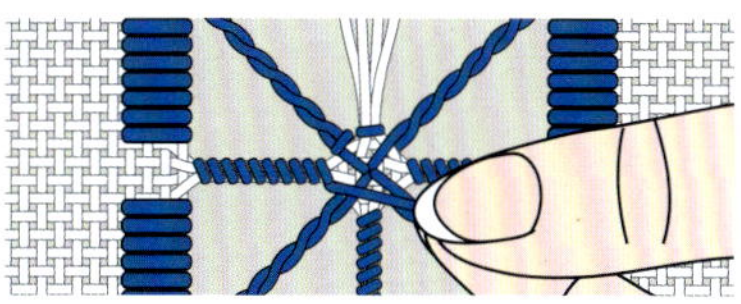

10 Pull the thread to the right to tighten the stitch and pull it in snug against the centre.

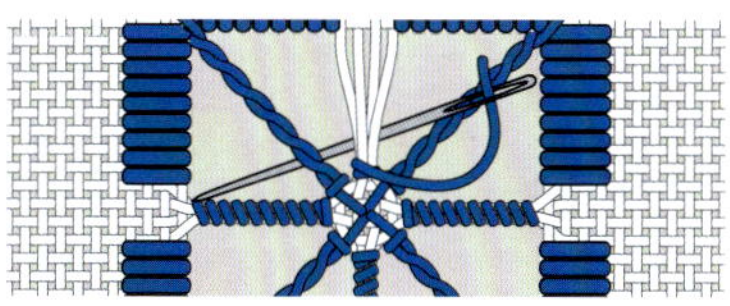

11 Continue around the spokes, turning the work as needed, to create a ribbed web of the desired size.

12 When the web is the desired size and you reach the first spoke again, take the needle under that spoke only.

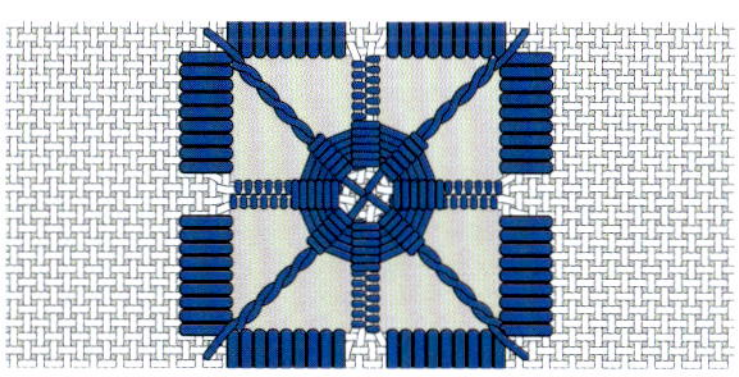

❶ *If you're working with woven bars, bring the needle up in the centre of the bar and weave it to finish.*

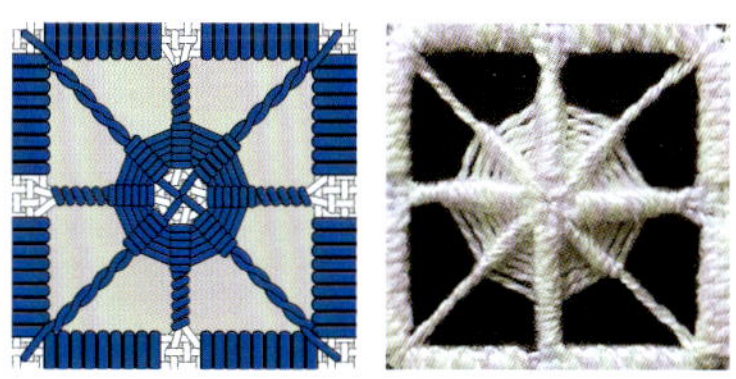

13 Wrap the rest of the spoke and take the needle through to the back to finish the thread.

L

CONTEMPORARY

whipped spider web

This spider web is worked over the intersection of woven or wrapped bars, rather than between them. It can be worked in the centre of other filling stitches.

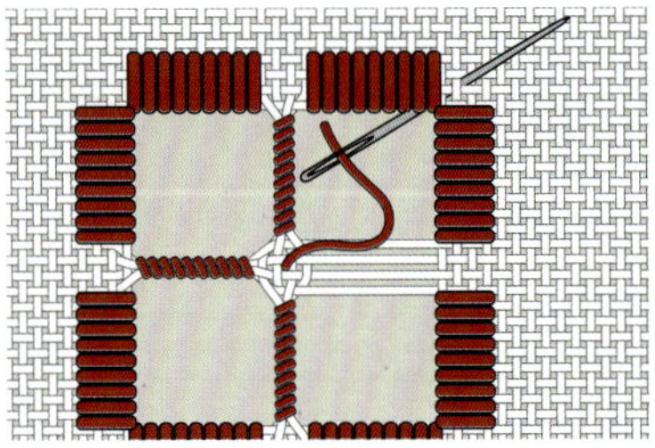

1 In a large square, wrap the bars as shown. Bring the needle out in the woven square's centre, then bring it out in the top right corner, two threads away from the edge.

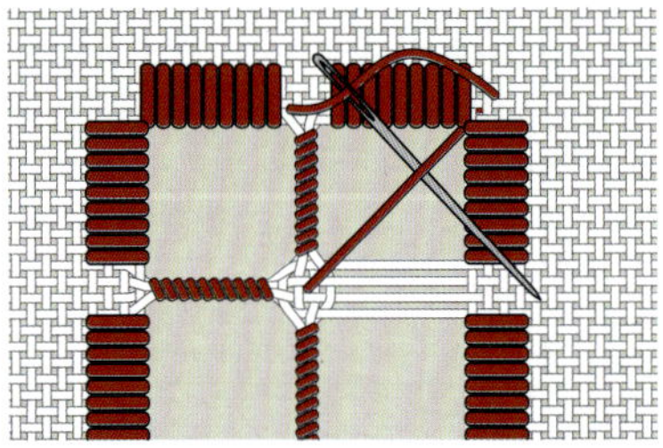

2 Pull the needle through. From above, slide the needle under the stitch.

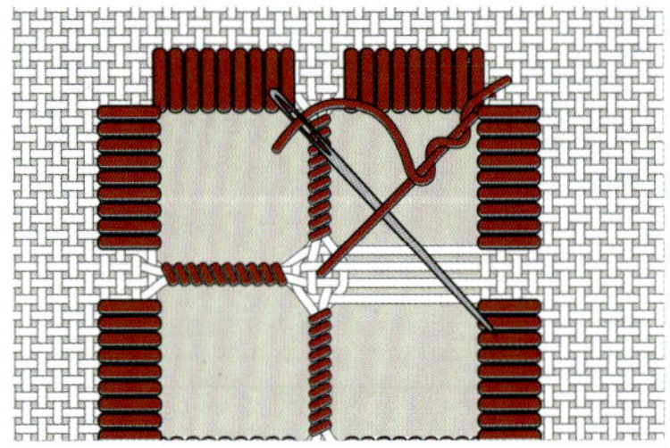

3 Moving towards the centre, slide the needle under the stitch twice more.

❶ *More twists can be added if desired.*

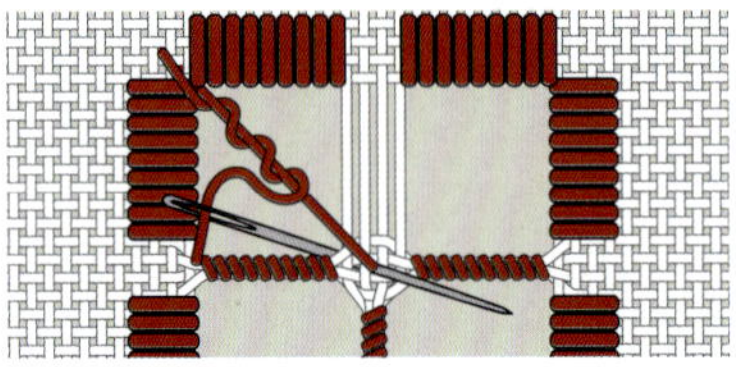

4 Turn the work 90° anticlockwise. Insert the needle below the diagonal and bring the needle out in the centre of the woven square.

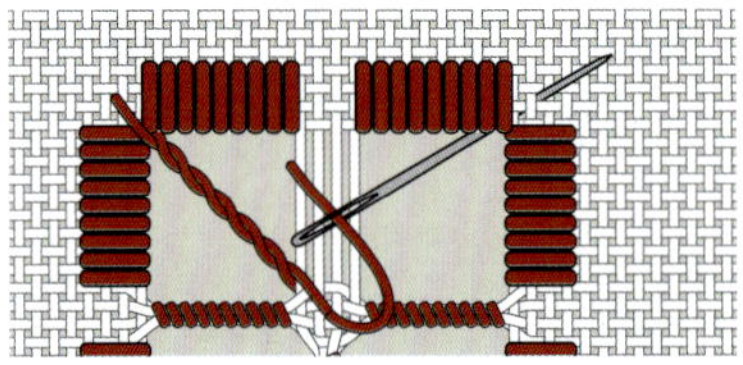

5 Pull to intertwine the stitches. Bring the needle out in the next woven corner, two threads away from the edge.

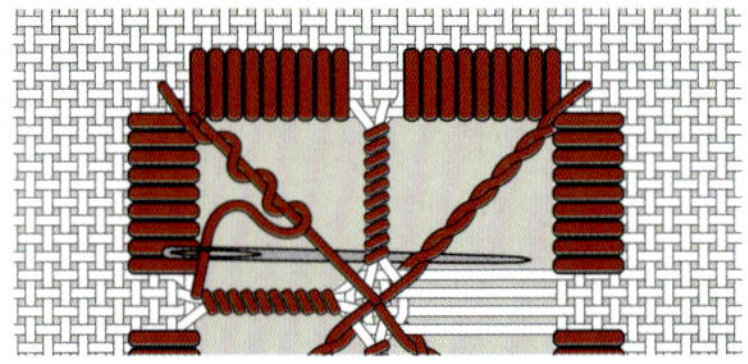

6 Repeat Steps 2 to 5 to work spokes out to each corner. Turn the work as needed. Finish by bringing the needle out as if to wrap the final bar.

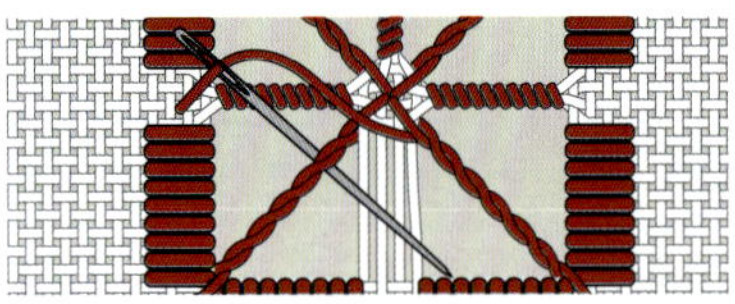

7 Turn the work 90° clockwise. Moving clockwise, from the left, slide the needle under the next diagonal.

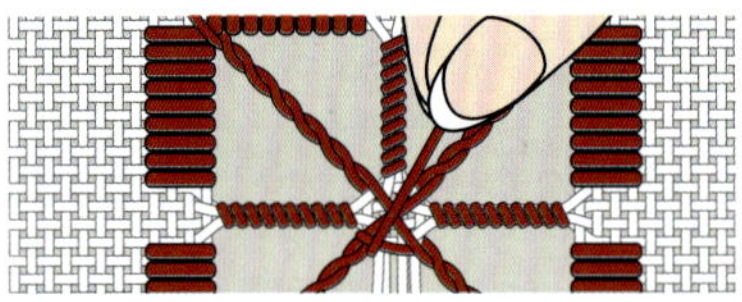

8 Pull the thread up to tighten the stitch snug against the centre.

❶ *Do this after each stitch.*

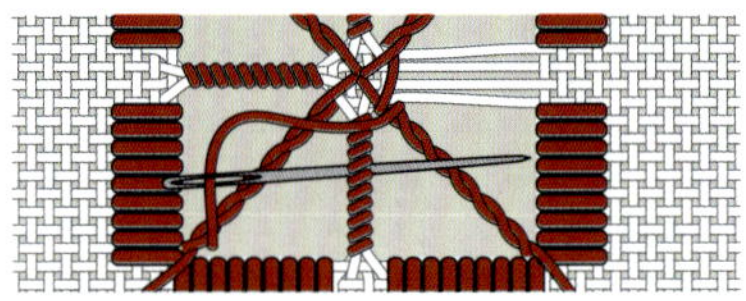

9 Turn the work 90° anticlockwise. From the left, slide the needle under the next wrapped bar.

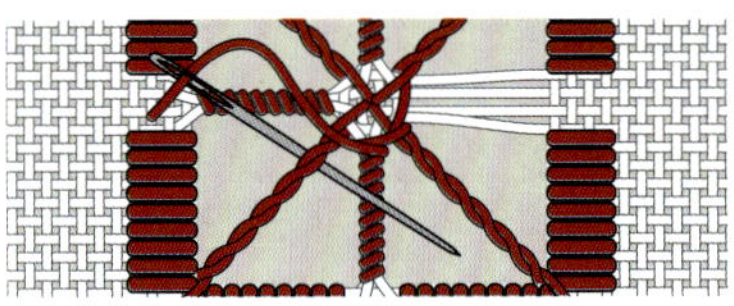

10 Snug the stitch against the centre. Continue around, taking the needle under each spoke, one by one.

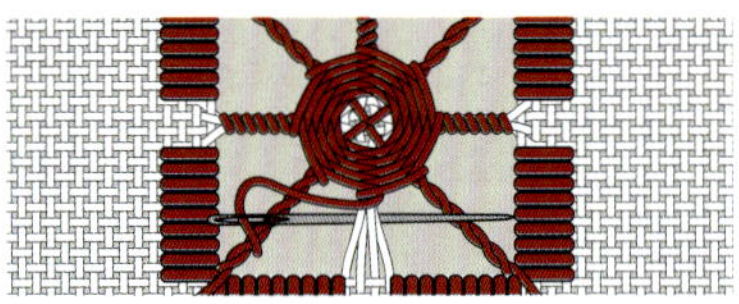

11 When the web is the desired size and you reach the first spoke again, begin wrapping the bar.

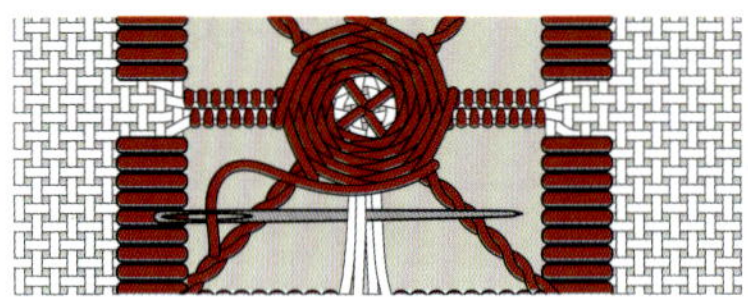

❶ *If you're working with woven bars, bring the needle up in the centre of the bar and weave it to finish.*

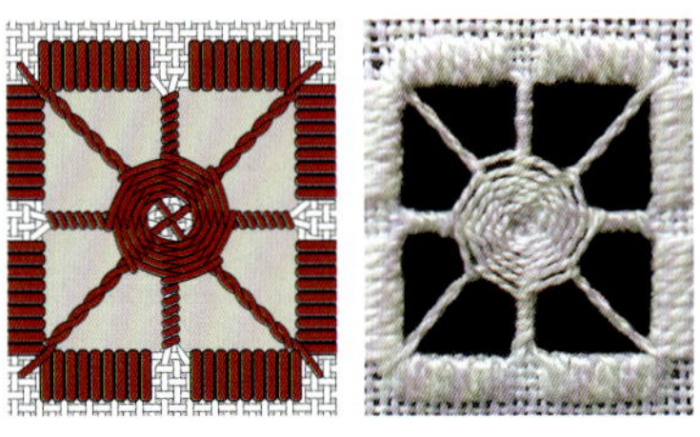

12 Wrap the rest of the bar and take the needle through to the back to finish the thread.

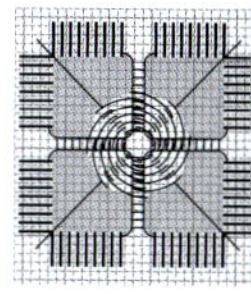

whipped spider web

This spider web is worked over the intersection of woven or wrapped bars, rather than between them. It can be worked in the centre of other filling stitches.

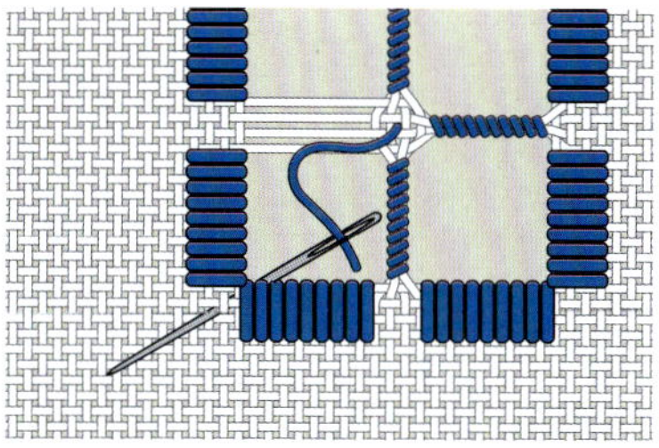

1 In a large square, wrap the bars as shown. Bring the needle out in the woven square's centre, then bring it out in the bottom left corner, two threads away from the edge.

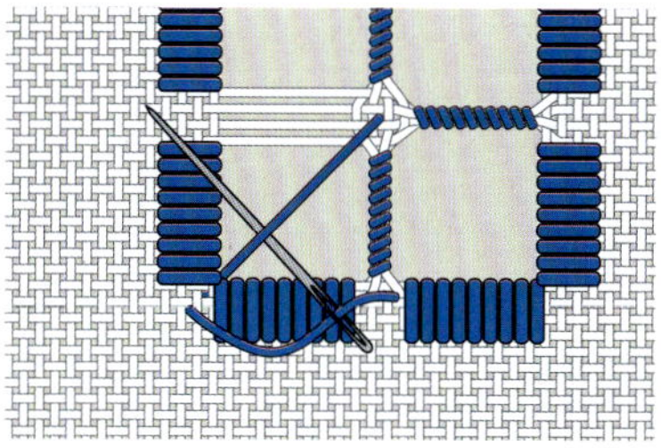

2 Pull the needle through. From below, slide the needle under the stitch.

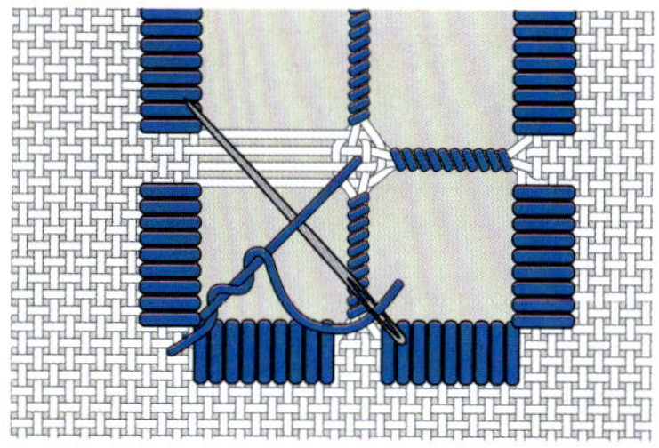

3 Moving towards the centre, slide the needle under the stitch twice more.

❶ *More twists can be added if desired.*

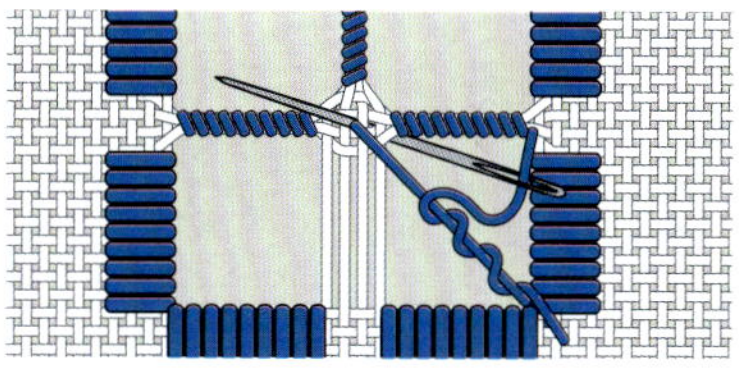

4 Turn the work 90° anticlockwise. Insert the needle above the diagonal and bring the needle out in the centre of the woven square.

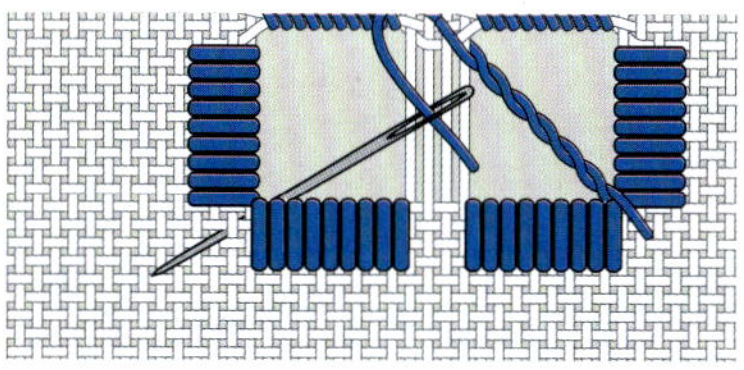

5 Pull to intertwine the stitches. Bring the needle out in the next woven corner, two threads away from the edge.

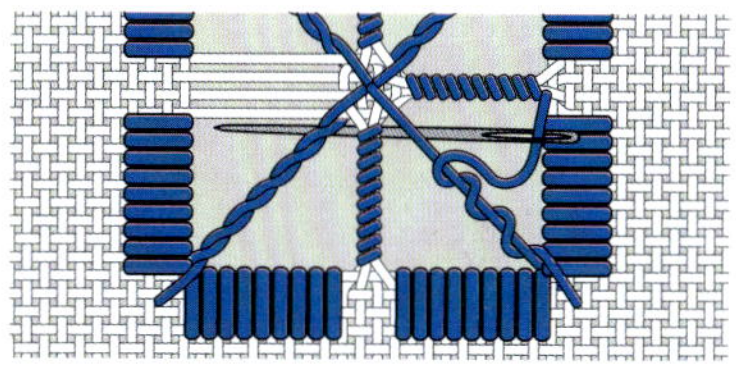

6 Repeat Steps 2 to 5 to work spokes out to each corner. Turn the work as needed. Finish by bringing the needle out as if to wrap the final bar.

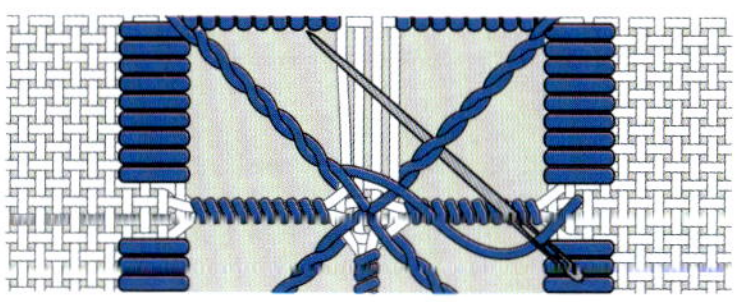

7 Turn the work 90° clockwise. Moving clockwise, from the right, slide the needle under the next diagonal.

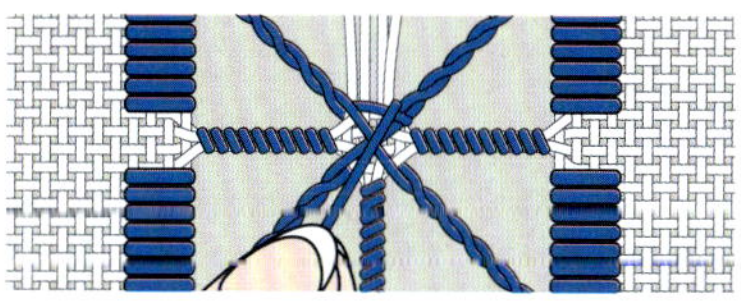

8 Pull the thread down to tighten the stitch snug against the centre.

❶ *Do this after each stitch.*

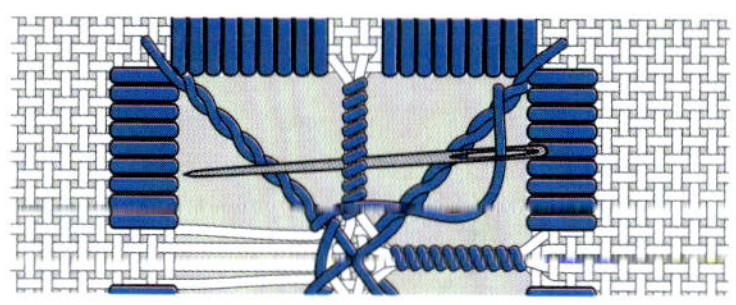

9 Turn the work 90° anticlockwise. From the right, slide the needle under the next wrapped bar.

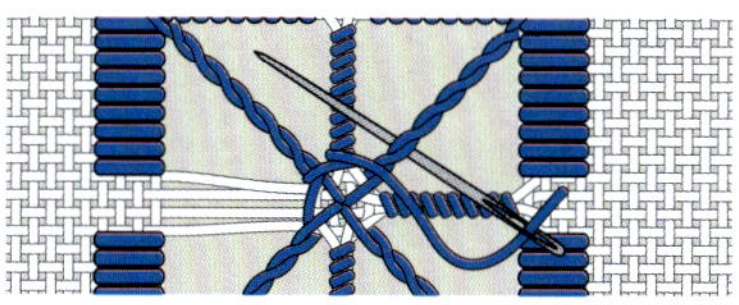

10 Snug the stitch against the centre. Continue around, taking the needle under each spoke, one by one.

11 When the web is the desired size and you reach the first spoke again, begin wrapping the bar.

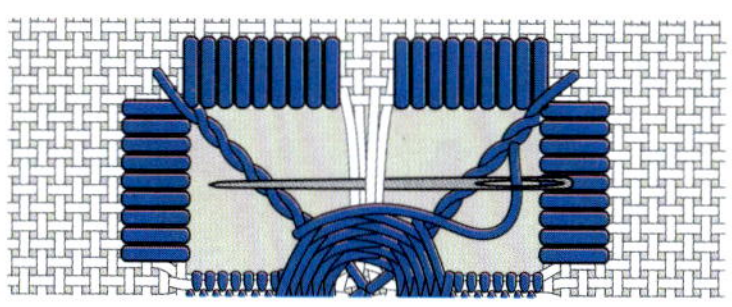

❶ *If you're working with woven bars, bring the needle up in the centre of the bar and weave it to finish.*

12 Wrap the rest of the spoke and take the needle through to the back to finish the thread.

three quarter spider web flower

This motif combines three quarter woven spider webs with a dove's eye.

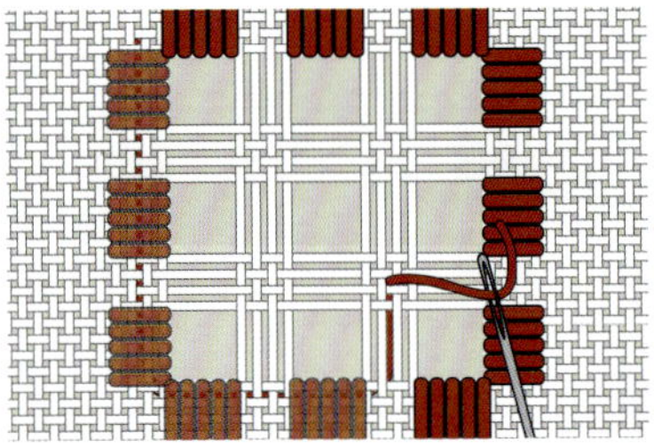

1 Prepare the cutwork area as shown. Run the thread under the back of the satin stitch and bring it out in the middle of the bottom right woven fabric square.

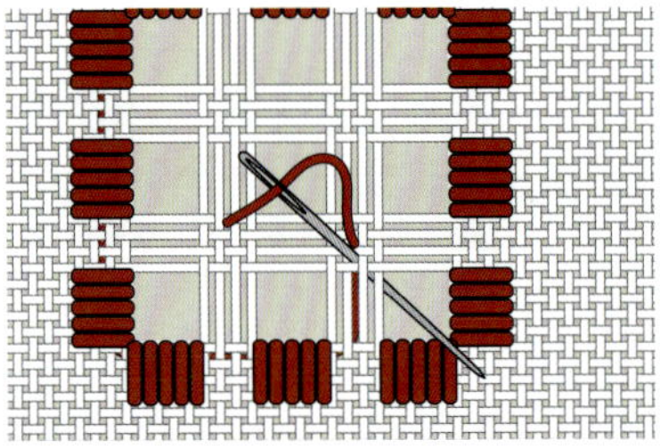

2 Insert the needle one thread down and bring it to the right of the bar that extends down from the woven square.

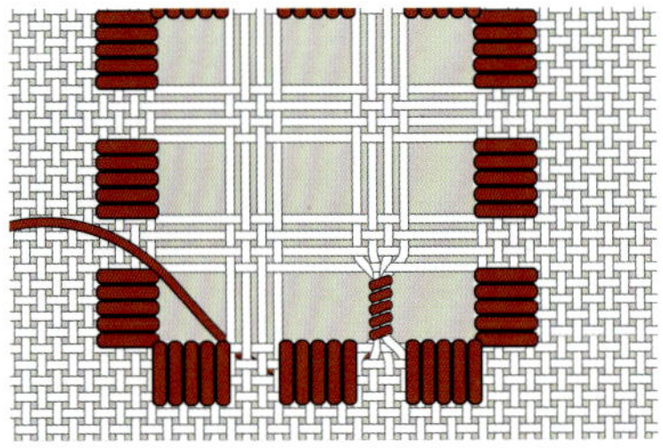

3 Wrap the bar to the edge, then take the needle under the intervening satin stitch on the back, and bring it out ready to stitch the bar to the left of the previous one.

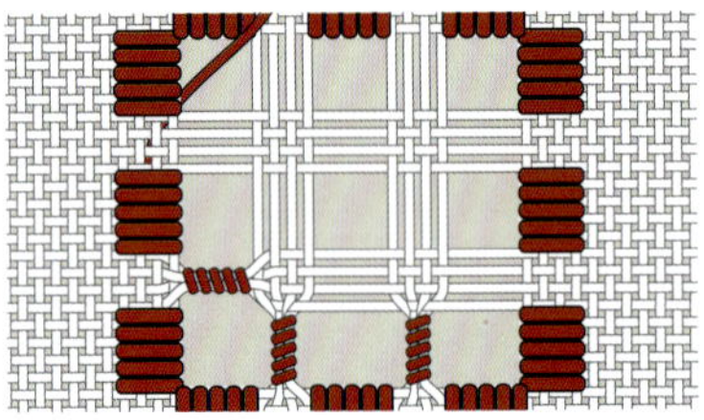

4 Wrap the bar to the first intersection, then the one adjacent to it, towards the edge. Take the needle under the intervening satin stitch on the back, and bring it out ready to stitch the bar above the previous one.

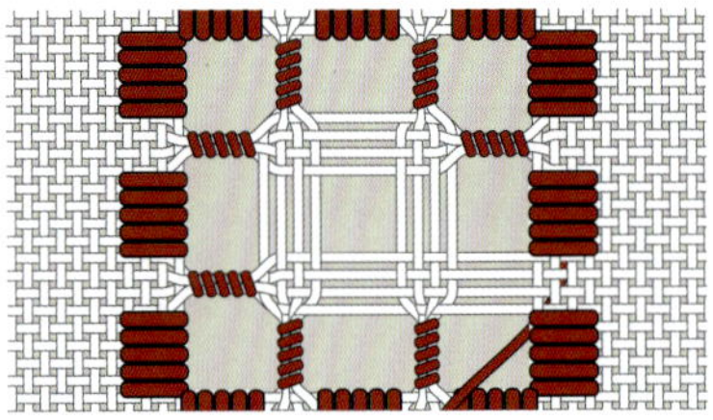

5 Repeat the sequence for the next two corners.

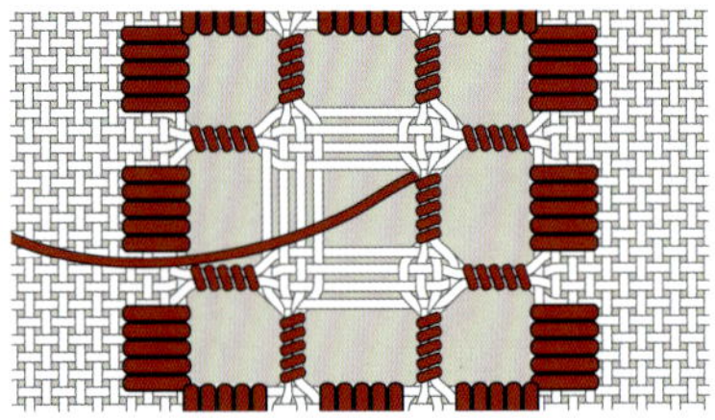

6 Work the remaining outer bar, then the right bar of the centre four.

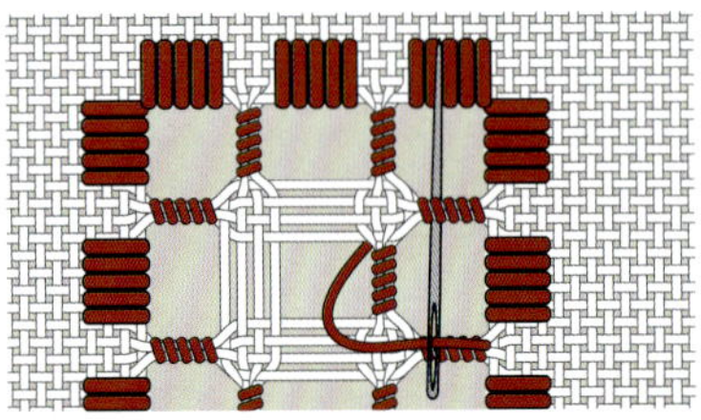

7 Working around the top right intersection of threads, from below, slide the needle under the right bar.

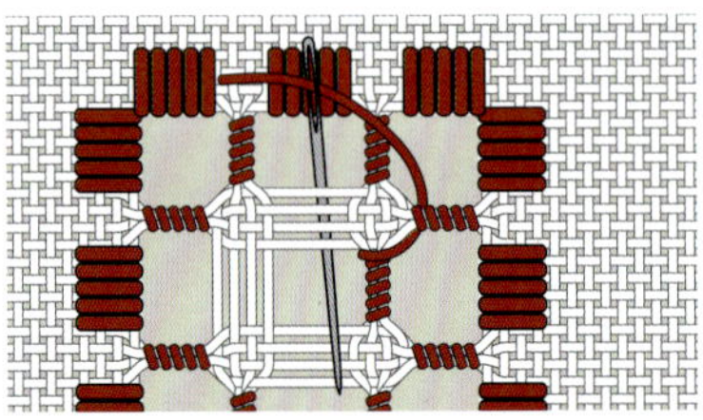

8 From above, slide the needle under the left bar which is not yet wrapped.

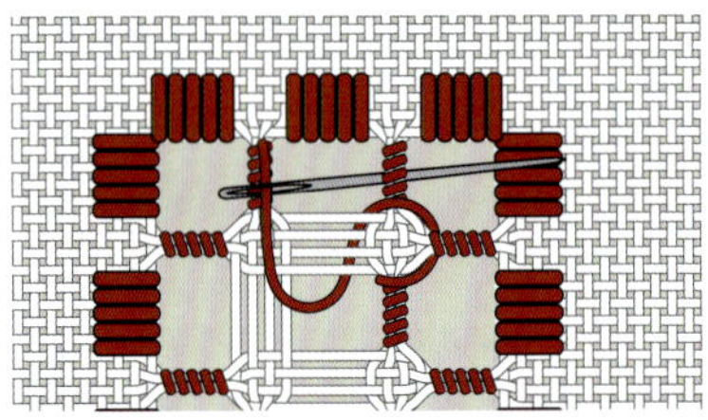

9 Pull the thread in snug around the intersection. From the left, slide the needle under the upper bar.

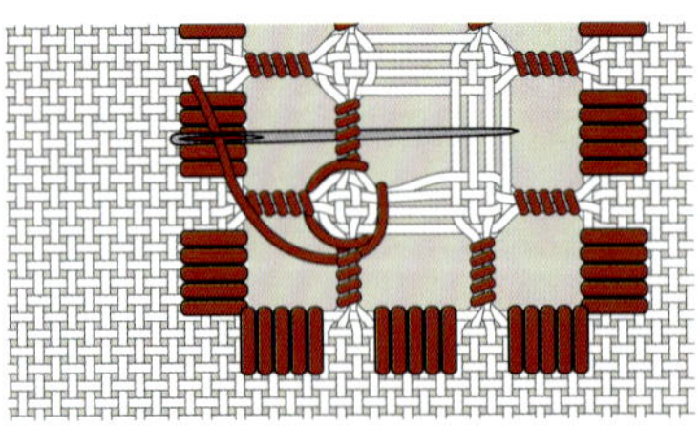

10 Turn the work 180°. From the left, slide the needle under the upper bar.

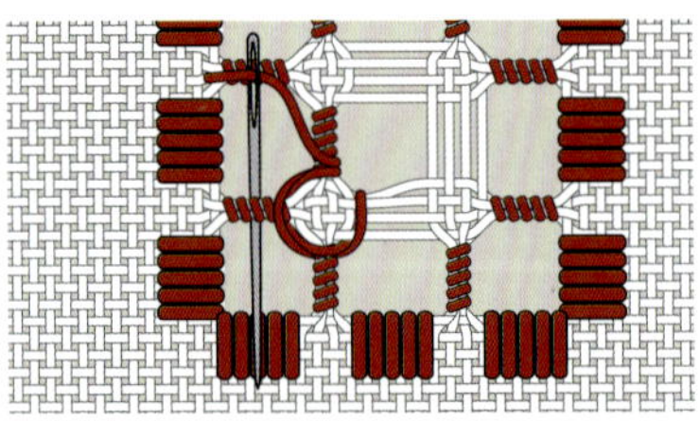

11 Pull the thread in snug around the intersection. From above, slide the needle under the left bar.

12 From below, slide the needle under the right bar which is not yet wrapped.

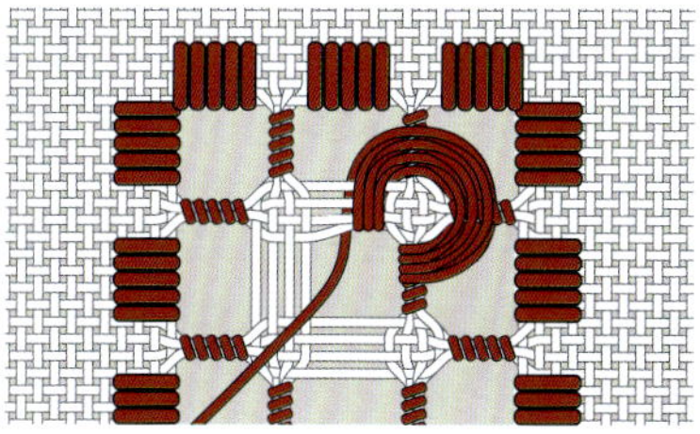

13 Continue weaving back and forth around the intersection, turning the work as necessary, until you have filled half of the bar which is yet to be worked.

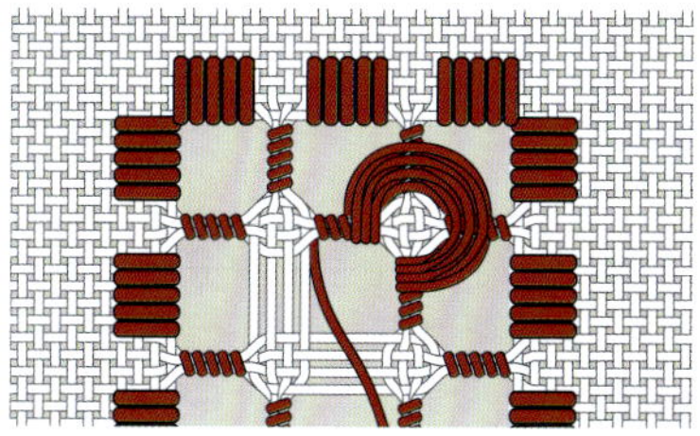

14 Wrap the rest of the bar.

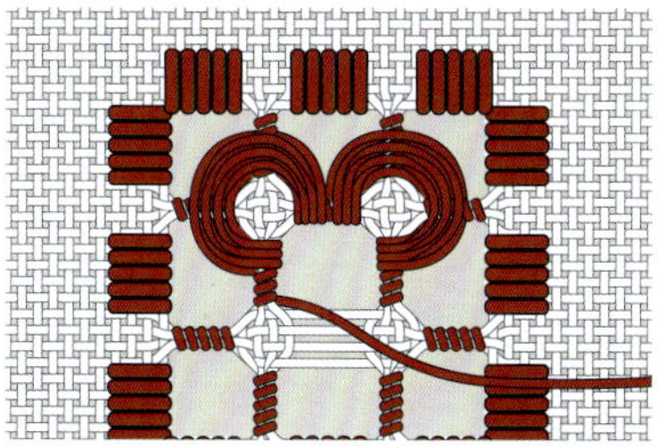

15 Cycle through Steps 7 to 14 to work a three quarter spider web around the outside of the next intersection.

❶ *Use the same quantity of stitches as for the first corner.*

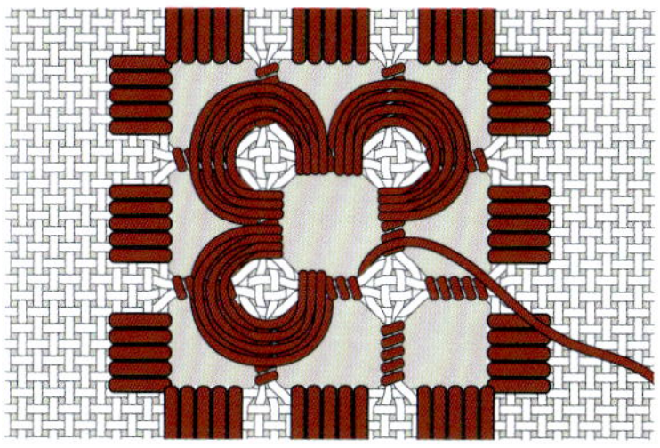

16 Repeat for the next intersection.

17 Work a three quarter spider web around the final intersection.

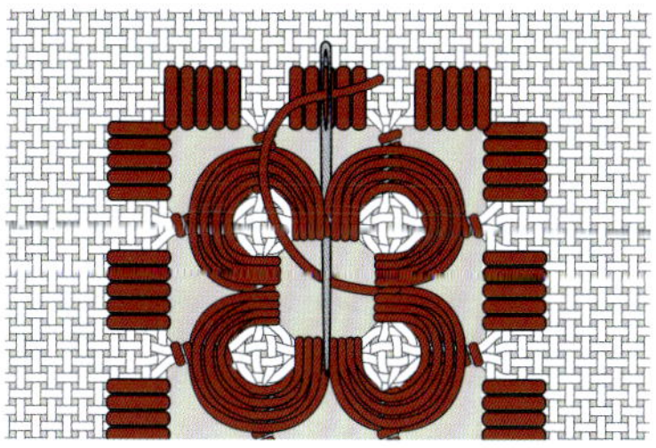

18 Moving around the centre square in an anticlockwise direction, from above, slide the needle under the upper bar. Take the needle point over the curving thread.

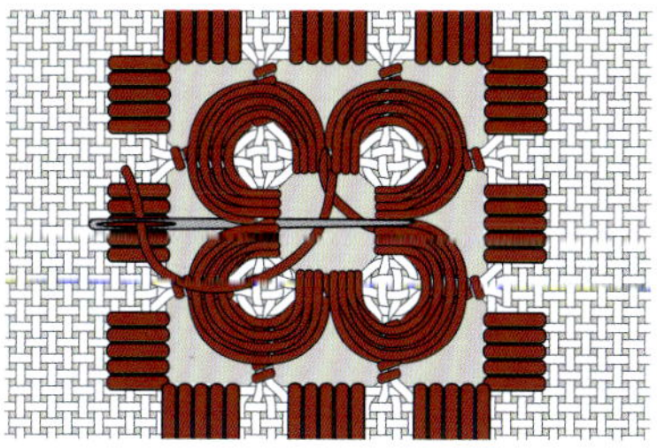

19 Pull the needle through and leave the stitch gently curving. From the left, slide the needle under the left bar. Take the needle point over the curving thread.

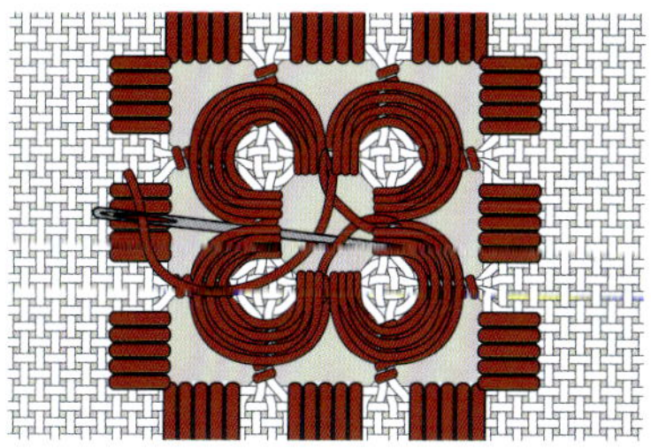

20 Turn the work 90° clockwise. Pull the needle through and leave the stitch gently curving. From the left, slide the needle under the left bar. Take the needle point over the curving thread and under the first dove's eye stitch.

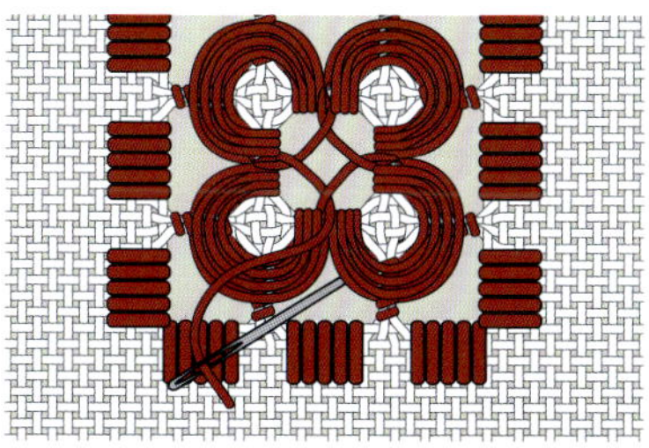

21 Pull the needle through. Take the needle to the back under the lower bar.

22 On the back, finish the thread under the stitching on the inner square.

23 The finished flower motif.

three quarter spider web flower

This motif combines three quarter woven spider webs with a dove's eye.

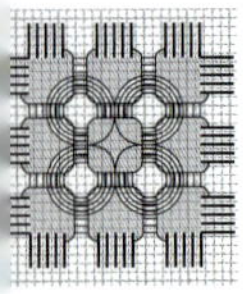

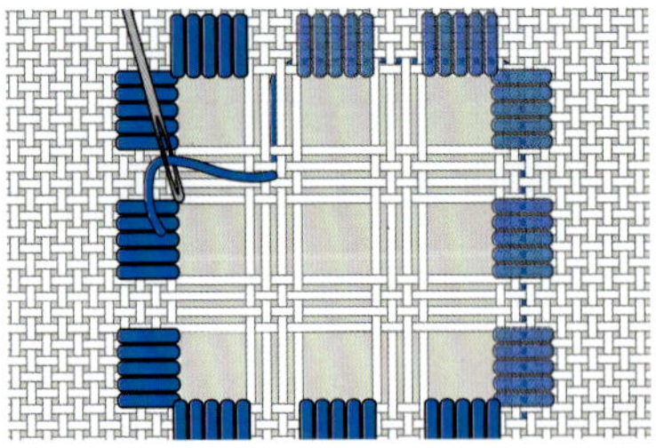

1 Prepare the cutwork area as shown. Run the thread under the back of the satin stitch and bring it out in the middle of the top left woven fabric square.

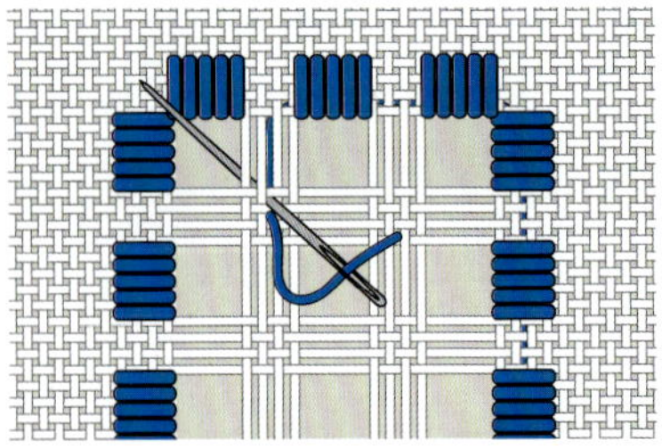

2 Insert the needle one thread up and bring it to the left of the bar that extends up from the woven square.

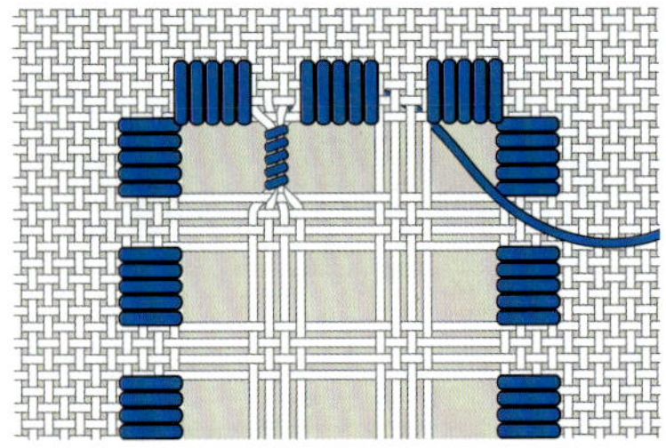

3 Wrap the bar to the edge, then take the needle under the intervening satin stitch on the back, and bring it out ready to stitch the bar to the right of the previous one.

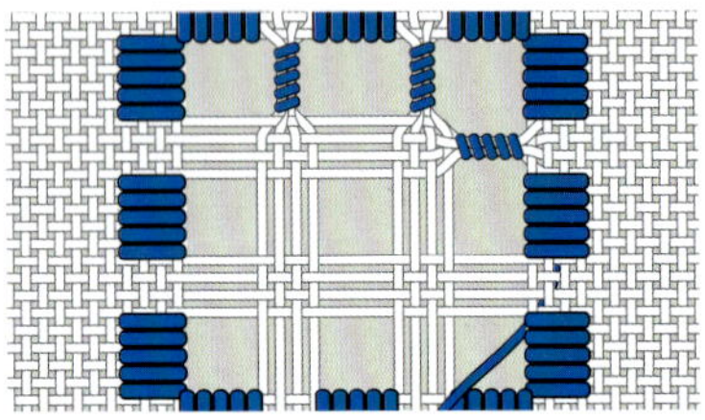

4 Wrap the bar to the first intersection, then the one adjacent to it, towards the edge. Take the needle under the intervening satin stitch on the back, and bring it out ready to stitch the bar above the previous one.

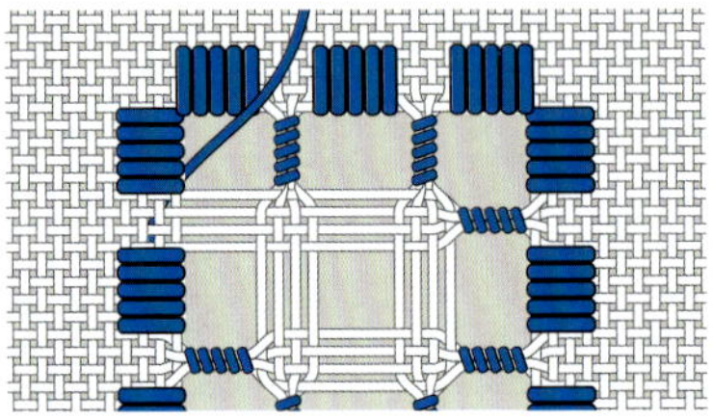

5 Repeat the sequence for the next two corners.

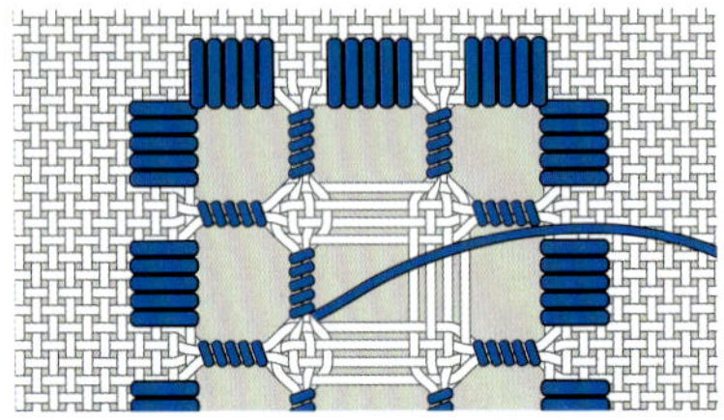

6 Work the remaining outer bar, then the left bar of the centre four.

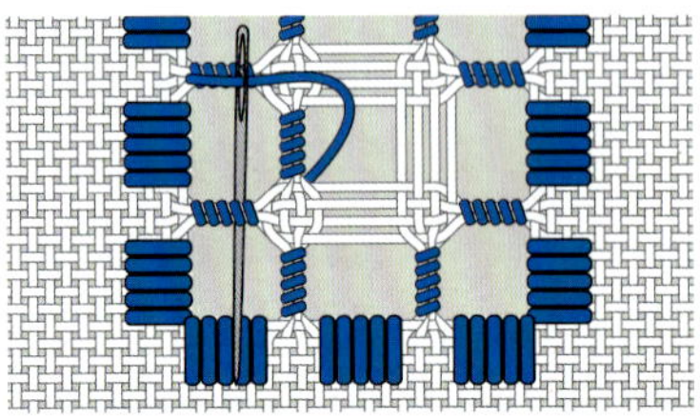

7 Working around the bottom left intersection of threads, from above, slide the needle under the left bar.

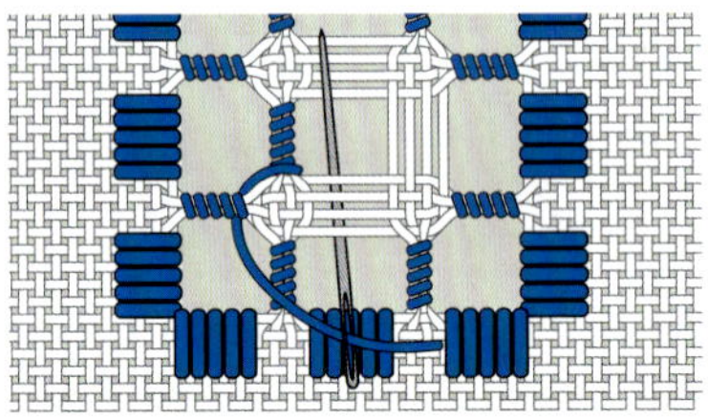

8 From above, slide the needle under the right bar which is not yet wrapped.

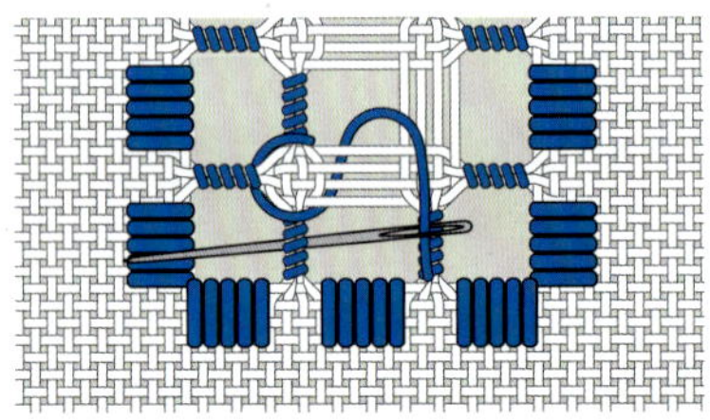

9 Pull the thread in snug around the intersection. From the right, slide the needle under the lower bar.

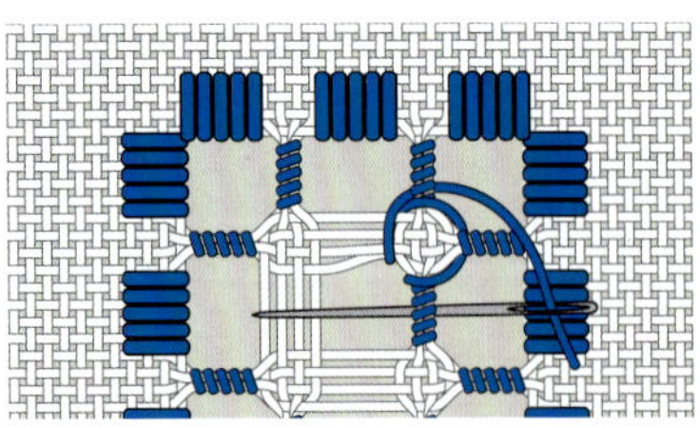

10 Turn the work 180°. From the right, slide the needle under the lower bar.

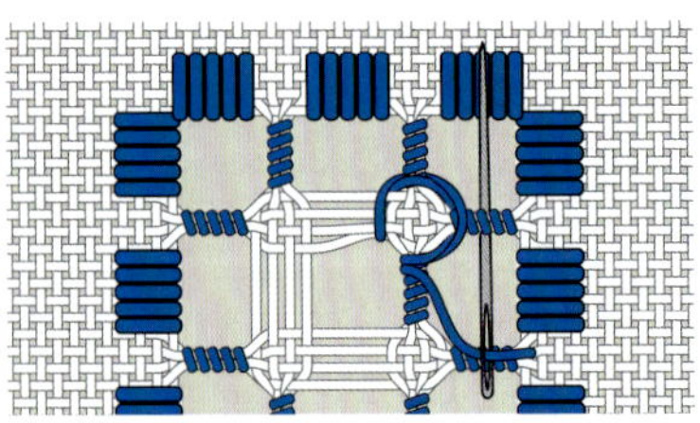

11 Pull the thread in snug around the intersection. From below, slide the needle under the right bar.

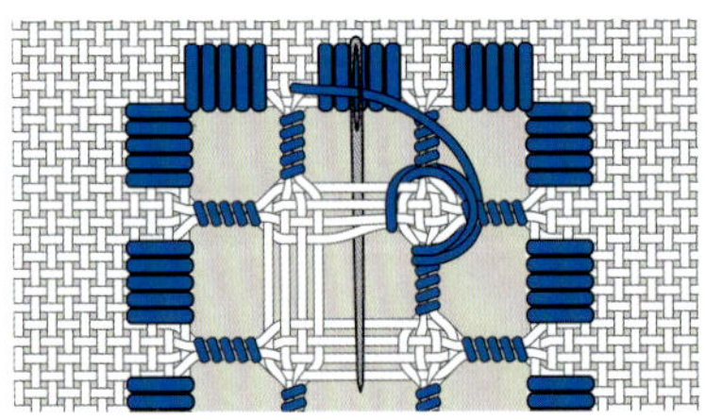

12 From above, slide the needle under the left bar which is not yet wrapped.

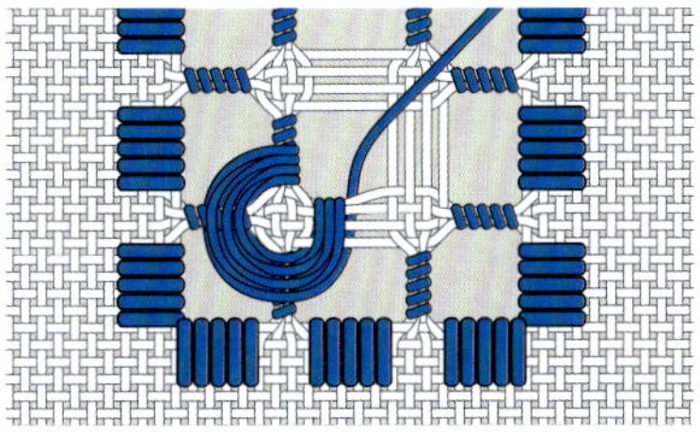

13 Continue weaving back and forth around the intersection, turning the work as necessary, until you have filled half of the bar which is yet to be worked.

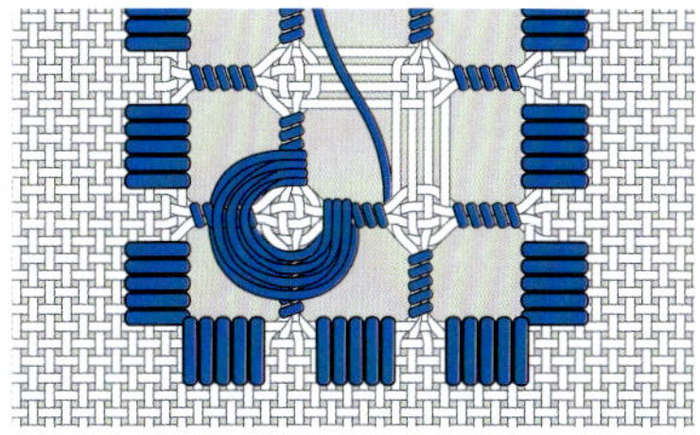

14 Wrap the rest of the bar.

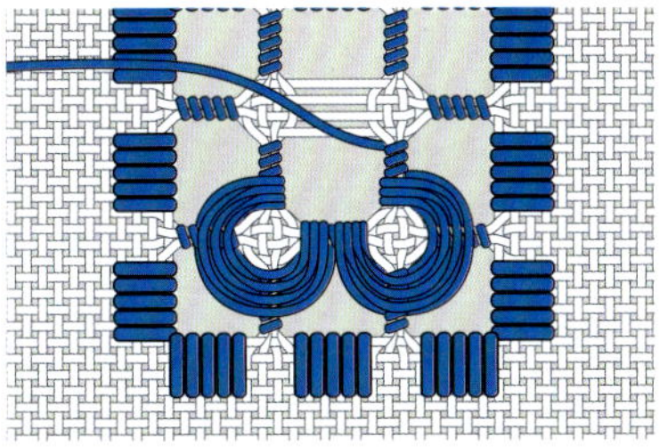

15 Cycle through Steps 7 to 14 to work a three quarter spider web around the outside of the next intersection.

❶ *Use the same quantity of stitches as for the first corner.*

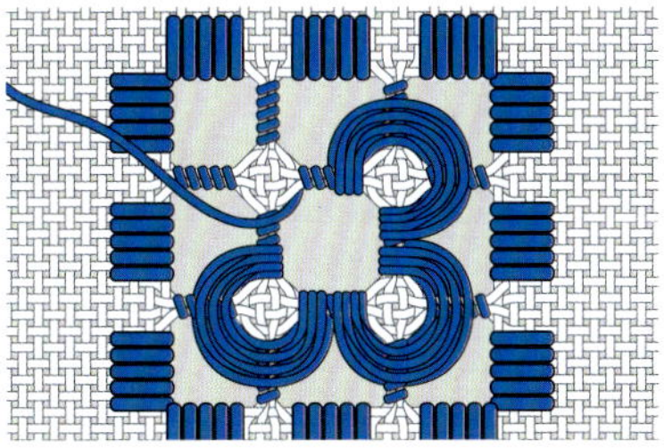

16 Repeat for the next intersection.

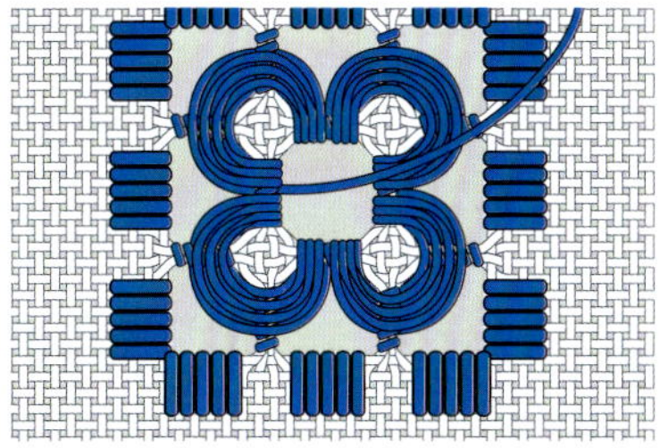

17 Work a three quarter spider web around the final intersection.

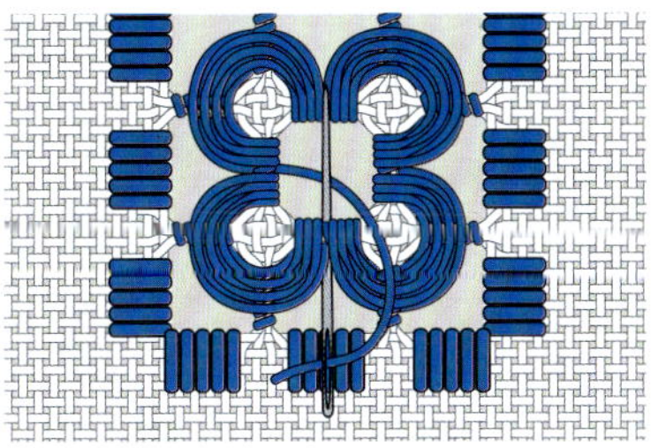

18 Moving around the centre square in an anticlockwise direction, from below, slide the needle under the lower bar. Take the needle point over the curving thread.

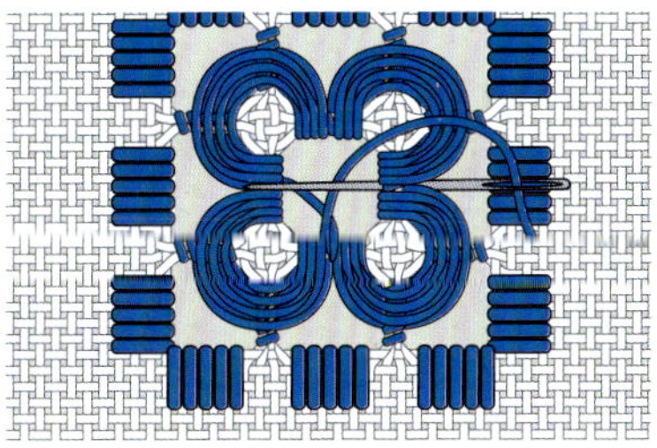

19 Pull the needle through and leave the stitch gently curving. From the right, slide the needle under the right bar. Take the needle point over the curving thread.

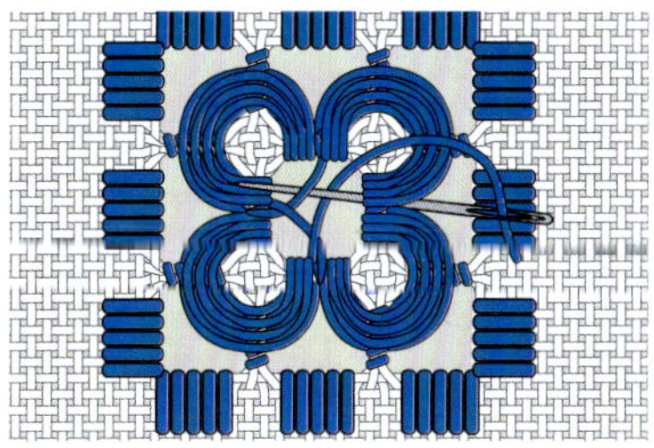

20 Turn the work 90° clockwise. Pull the needle through and leave the stitch gently curving. From the right, slide the needle under the right bar. Take the needle point over the curving thread and under the first dove's eye stitch.

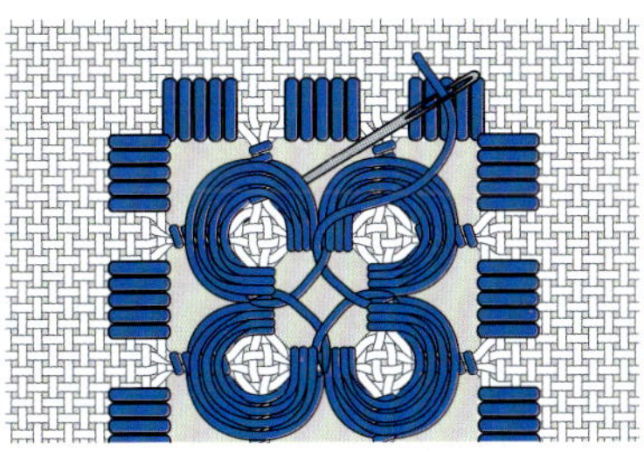

21 Pull the needle through. Take the needle to the back above the upper bar.

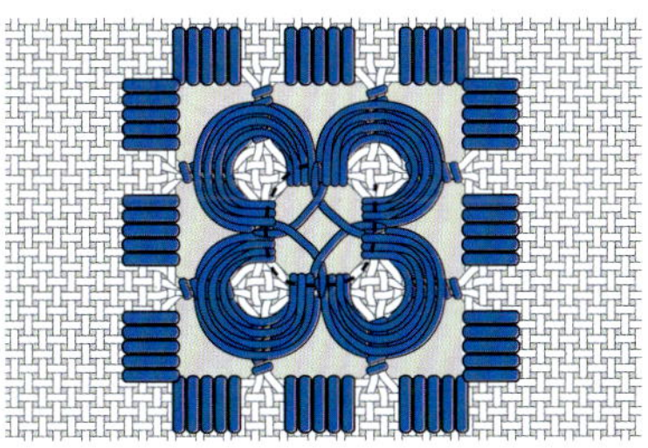

22 On the back, finish the thread under the stitching on the inner square.

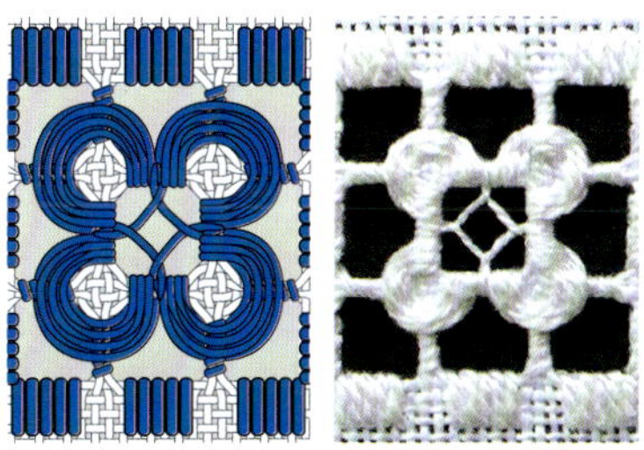

23 The finished flower motif.

buttonhole arc

A single buttonhole arc can be the basis for a number of stitch combinations and variations. They can be worked both clockwise and anticlockwise.

single arc – clockwise stitches

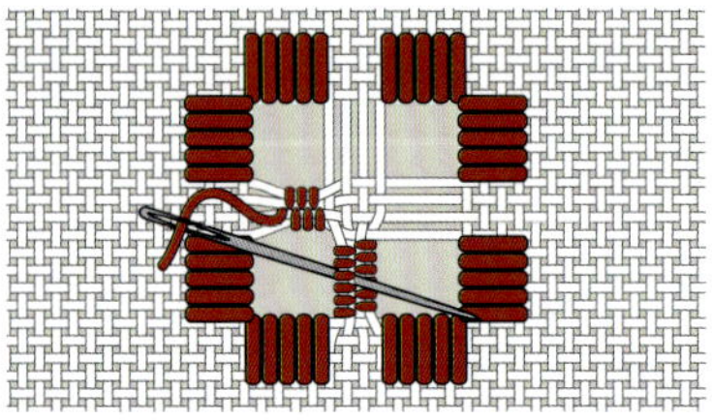

1 Making a left-hand turn, work one and a half woven bars on adjacent sides of a square. Crossing to the full bar, insert the needle in the centre of the bar, from the back.

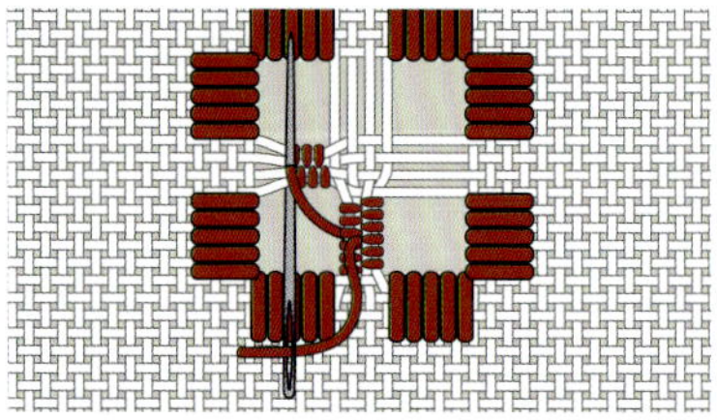

2 Pull the needle through and leave the stitch curving gently; not too tight and not too loose. From behind, insert the needle in the centre of the half-woven bar.

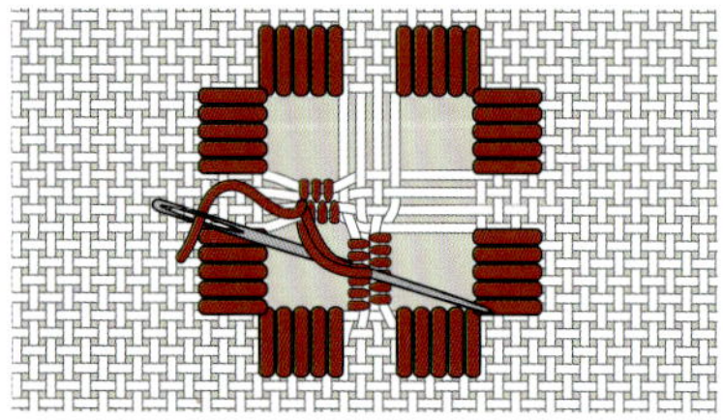

3 Pull the needle through, with a similar tension to the first stitch. From the back, insert the needle in the same place you inserted it the first time.

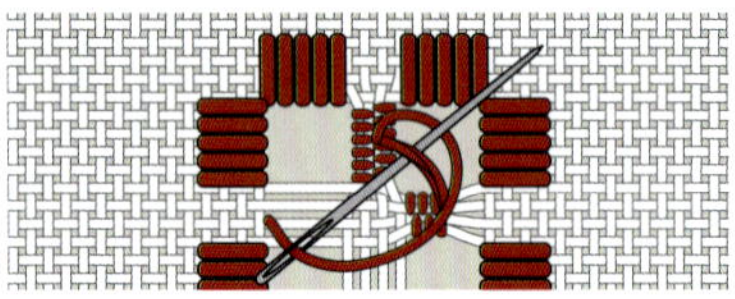

4 Pull the needle through, so that all three stitches have a similar tension. Turn the work 180°. With the needle pointing outward, insert it under the stitches. Take the thread under the needle point.

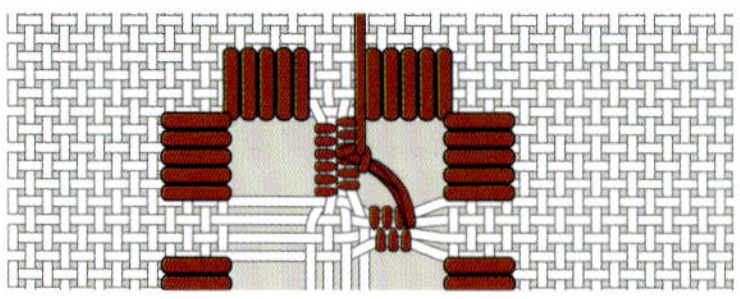

5 Pull the needle through and tighten the buttonhole stitch snugly against the woven bar.

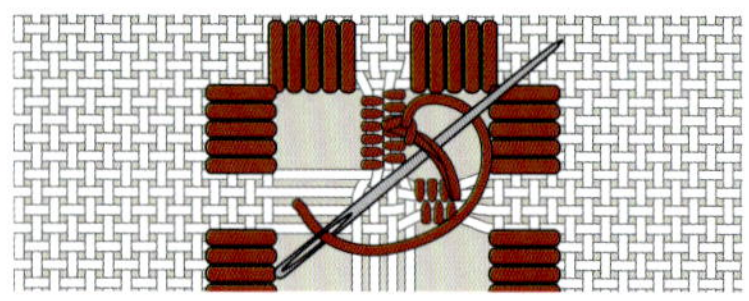

6 Moving back towards the half-woven bar, insert the needle under the curved stitches again. Take the thread under the needle point.

! *The stitches are being added in a clockwise direction.*

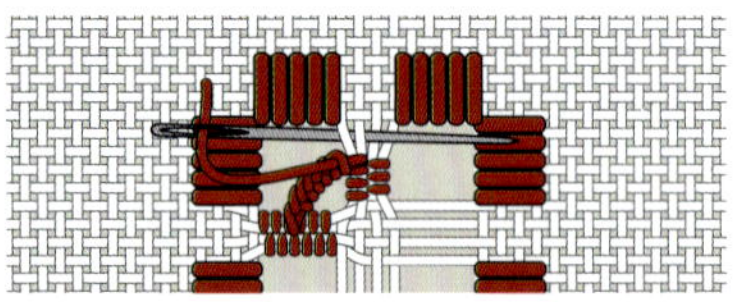

7 Keep working buttonhole stitches to fill the arc. To finish, turn the work 90° anticlockwise and bring the needle out in the centre of the half-woven bar.

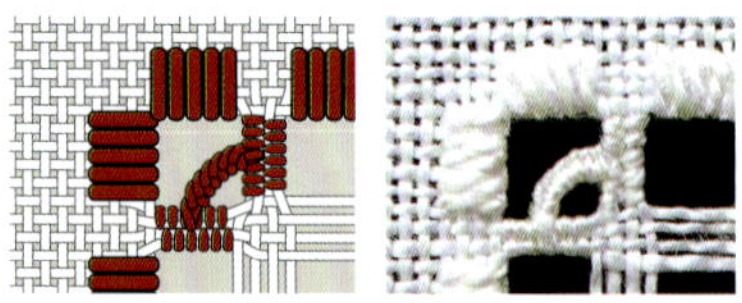

8 Complete the weaving of the bar.

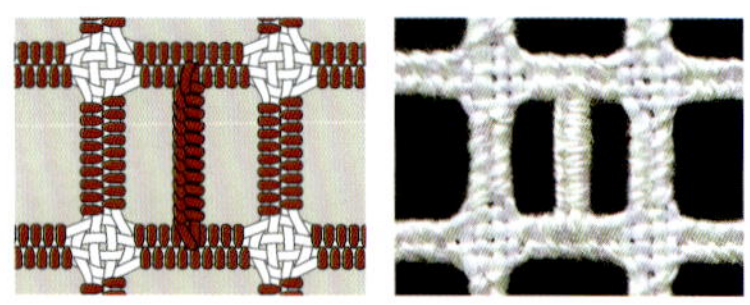

! *When worked straight across between bars, this technique can be use to create buttonholed bars.*

single arc – anticlockwise stitches

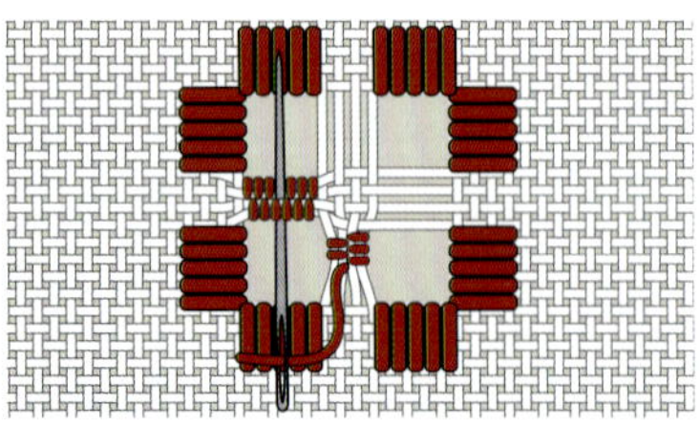

1 Making a right-hand turn, work one and a half woven bars on adjacent sides of a square. Crossing to the full bar, insert the needle in the centre of the bar, from the back.

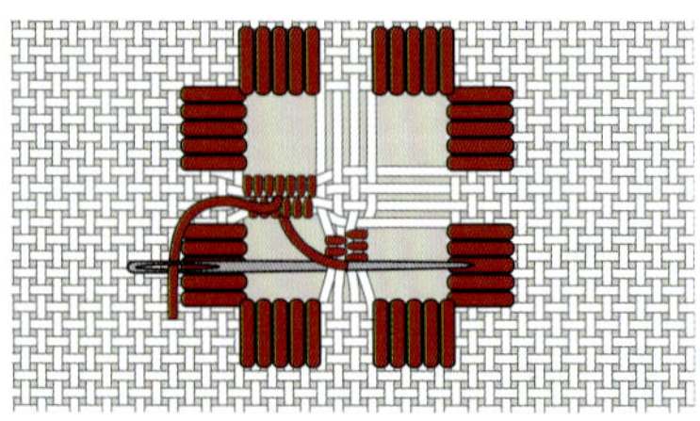

2 Pull the needle through and leave the stitch curving gently; not too tight and not too loose. From behind, insert the needle in the centre of the half-woven bar.

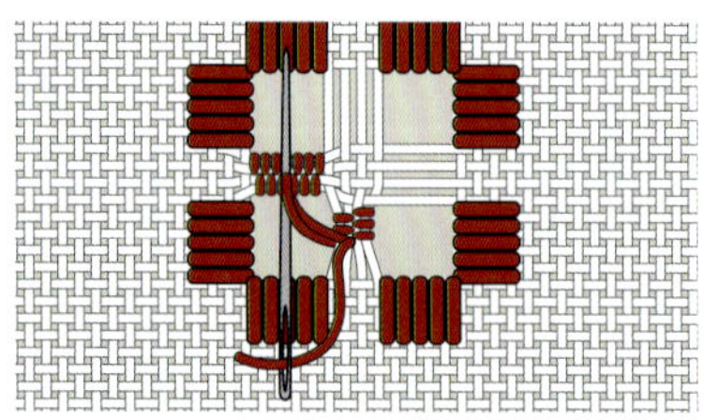

3 Pull the needle through, with a similar tension to the first stitch. From the back, insert the needle in the same place you inserted it the first time.

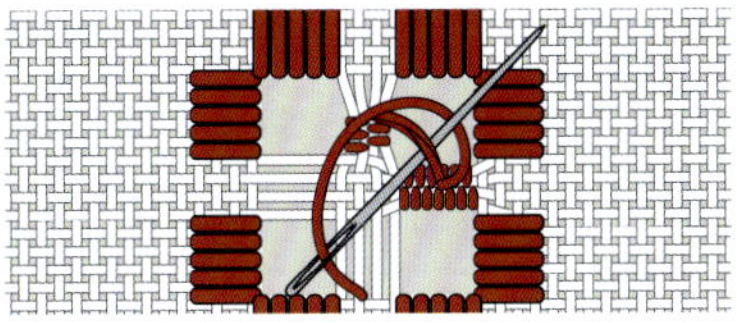

4 Pull the needle through, so that all three stitches have a similar tension. Turn the work 180° . With the needle pointing outward, insert it under the stitches. Take the thread under the needle point.

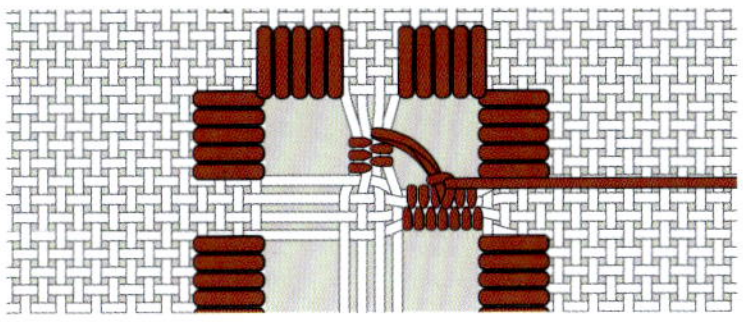

5 Pull the needle through and tighten the buttonhole stitch snugly against the woven bar.

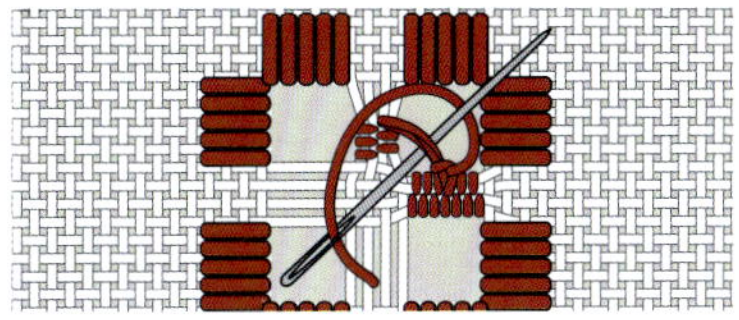

6 Moving back towards the half-woven bar, insert the needle under the curved stitches again. Take the thread under the needle point.

❶ *The stitches are being added in an anticlockwise direction.*

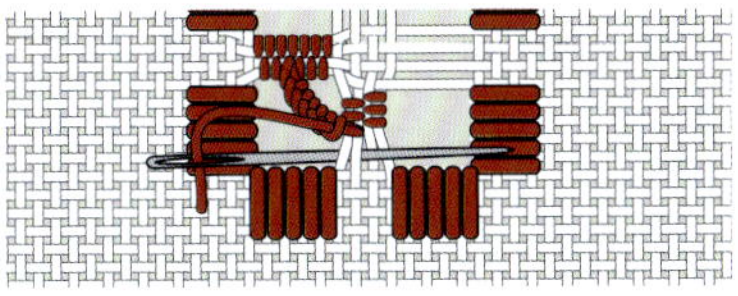

7 Turn the work 180°. Keep working buttonhole stitches to fill the arc. To finish, bring the needle out in the centre of the half-woven bar.

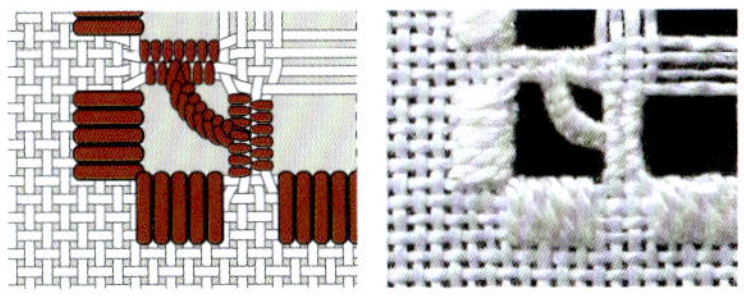

8 Complete the weaving of the bar.

buttonhole circle

also known as buttonhole wheel

Working an arc in each of the satin stitch square's quadrants creates a buttonhole circle.

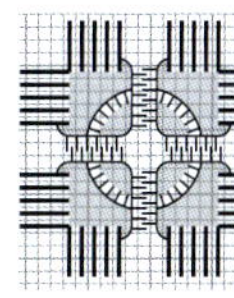

CONTEMPORARY

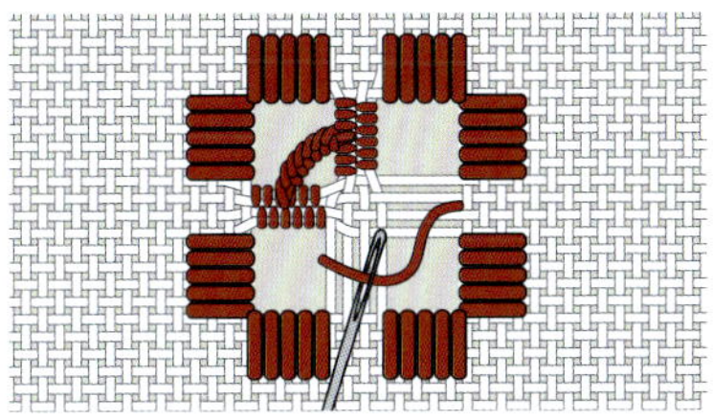

1 Work a clockwise or anticlockwise arc in the first quadrant. Take the thread through the back of the satin stitching, and bring it out ready to work the next woven bar.

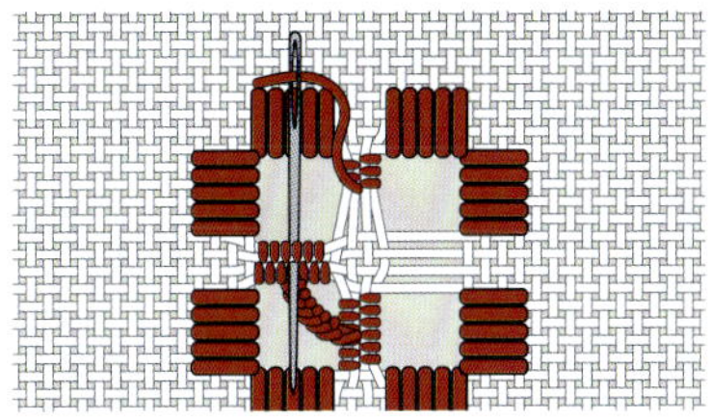

2 Weave half the bar. Turn the work 90° anticlockwise. Crossing to the adjacent full bar, insert the needle in the centre of the bar, from the back.

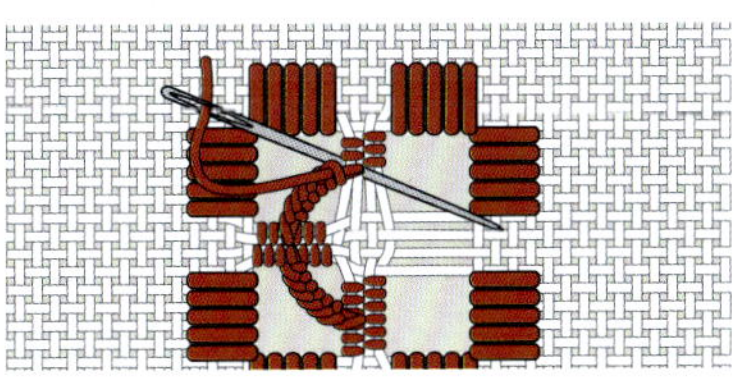

3 Work another single buttonhole arc, working the stitches in a clockwise direction.

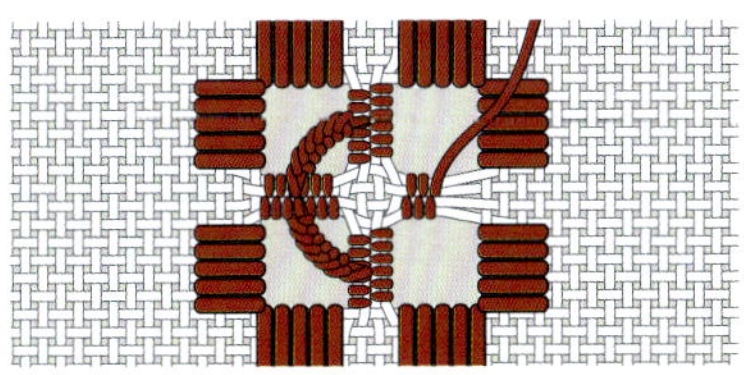

4 Complete the weaving of the bar, then weave half the remaining bar.

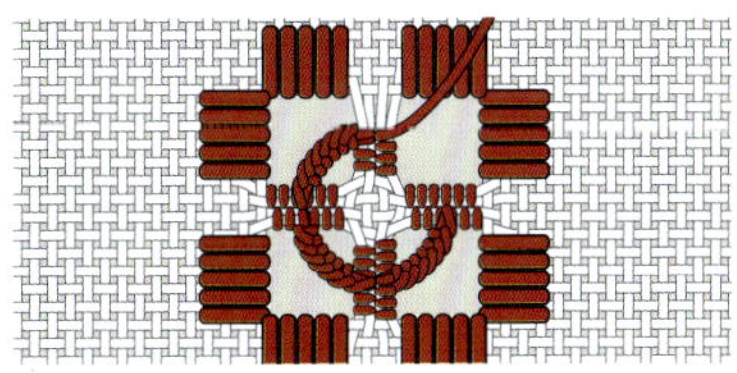

5 Turn the work 90° anticlockwise. Work single arc with clockwise stitches over to the woven bar just completed. Bring the needle out at the centre of the woven bar.

6 Work a single buttonhole arc in the final quadrant, with anticlockwise stitches. Bring the needle out at the centre of the woven bar.

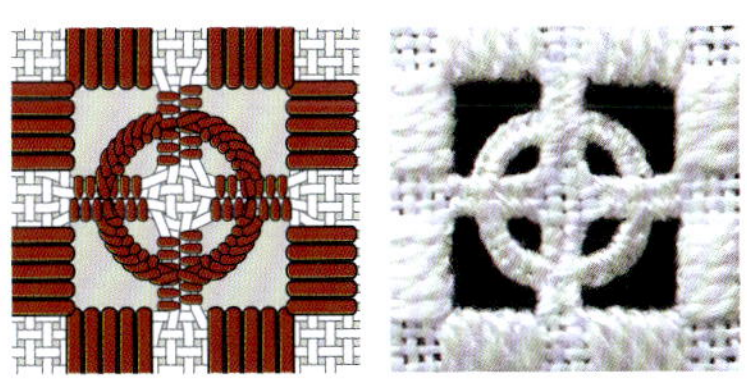

7 Complete the weaving of the bar and finish the thread in the back of the satin stitching.

❶ *If you prefer stitching woven bars in straight lines, use the method for 'Buttonhole arcs with twisted spokes' on pages 186–187 and omit the spokes.*

buttonhole arc

A single buttonhole arc can be the basis for a number of stitch combinations and variations. They can be worked both clockwise and anticlockwise.

single arc – clockwise stitches

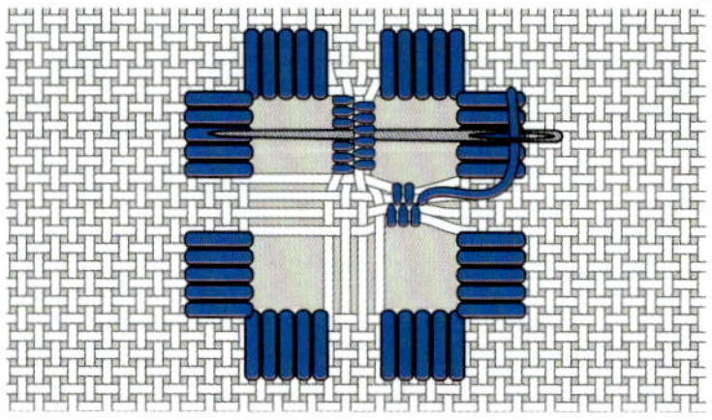

1 From the top, work one and a half woven bars on adjacent sides of the top right quadrant. Crossing to the full bar, insert the needle in the centre of the bar, from the back.

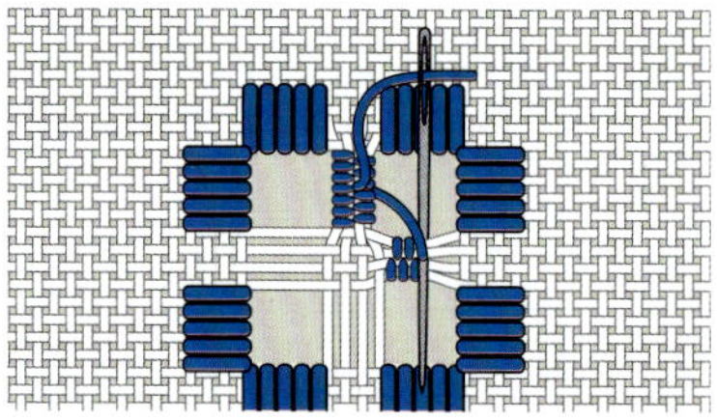

2 Pull the needle through and leave the stitch curving gently; not too tight and not too loose. From behind, insert the needle in the centre of the half-woven bar.

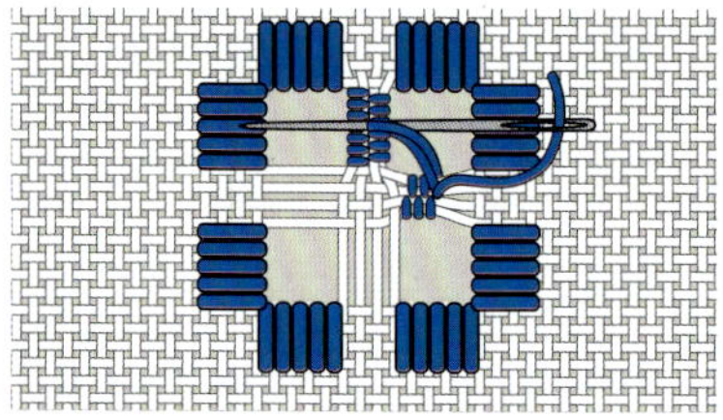

3 Pull the needle through, with a similar tension to the first stitch. From the back, insert the needle in the same place you inserted it the first time.

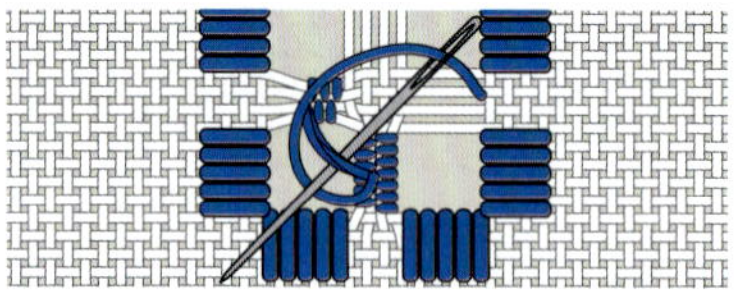

4 Pull the needle through, so that all three stitches have a similar tension. Turn the work 180°. With the needle pointing outward, insert it under the stitches. Take the thread under the needle point.

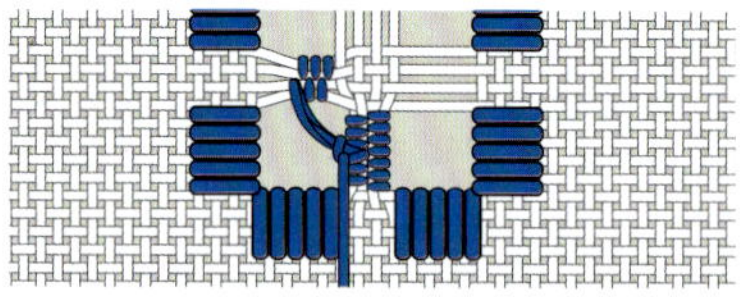

5 Pull the needle through and tighten the buttonhole stitch snugly against the woven bar.

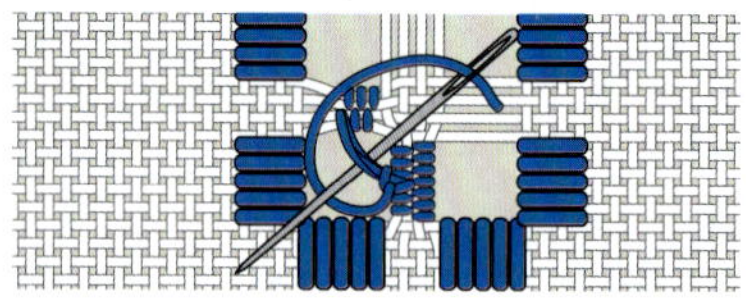

6 Moving back towards the half-woven bar, insert the needle under the curved stitches again. Take the thread under the needle point.

The stitches are being added in a clockwise direction.

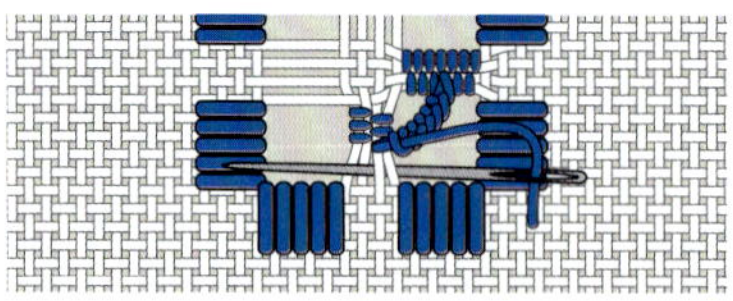

7 Keep working buttonhole stitches to fill the arc. To finish, turn the work 90° anticlockwise and bring the needle out in the centre of the half-woven bar.

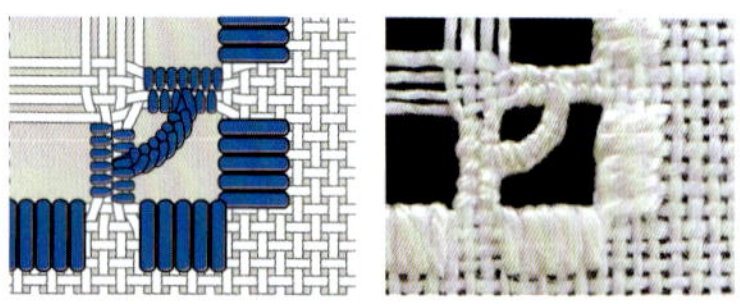

8 Complete the weaving of the bar.

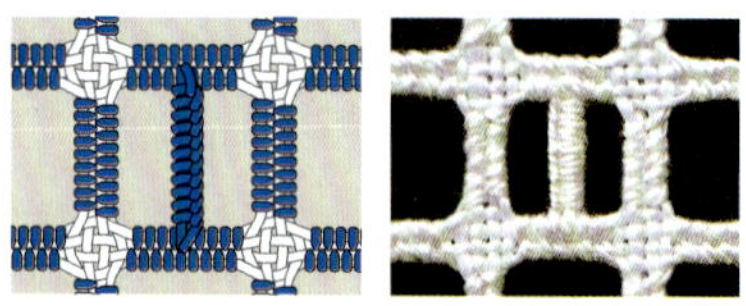

When worked straight across between bars, this technique can be use to create buttonholed bars.

single arc – anticlockwise stitches

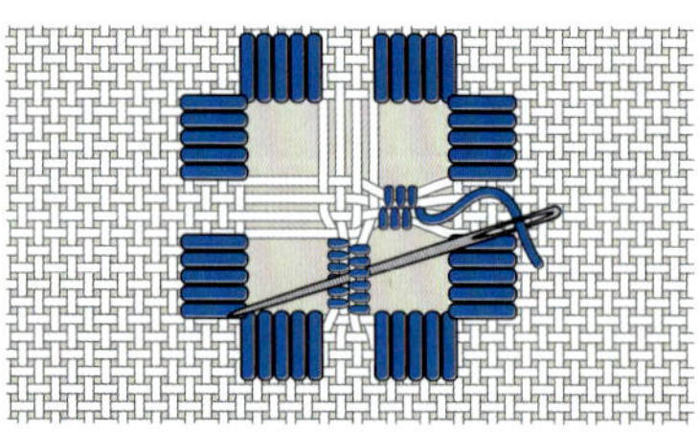

1 Making a right-hand turn, work one and a half woven bars on adjacent sides of a square. Crossing to the full bar, insert the needle in the centre of the bar, from the back.

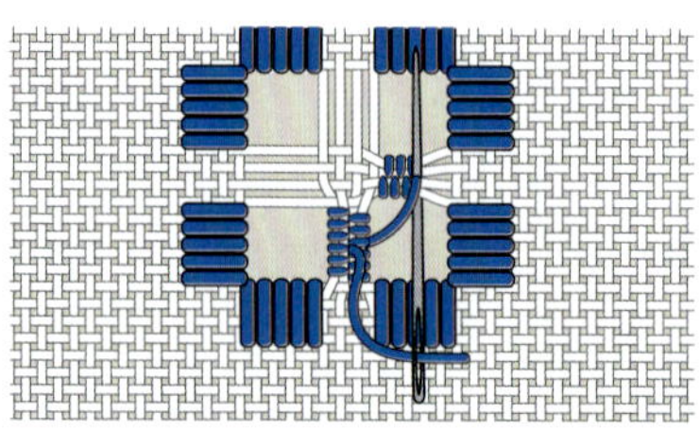

2 Pull the needle through and leave the stitch curving gently; not too tight and not too loose. From behind, insert the needle in the centre of the half-woven bar.

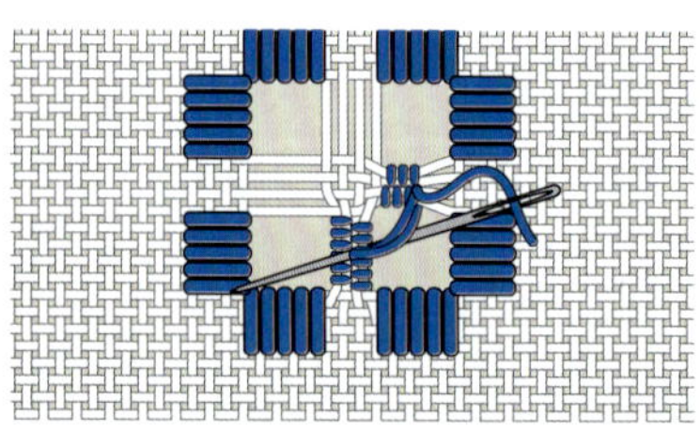

3 Pull the needle through, with a similar tension to the first stitch. From the back, insert the needle in the same place you inserted it the first time.

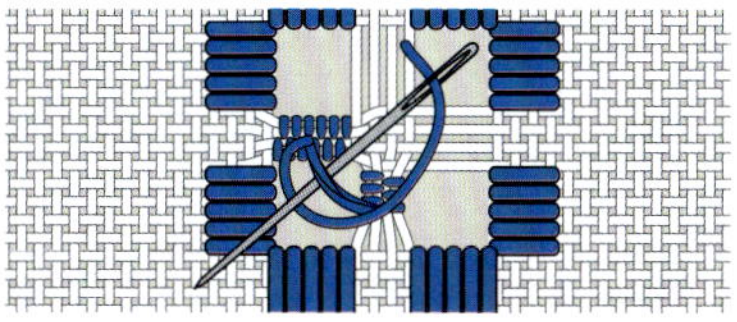

4 Pull the needle through, so that all three stitches have a similar tension. Turn the work 180°. With the needle pointing outward, insert it under the stitches. Take the thread under the needle point.

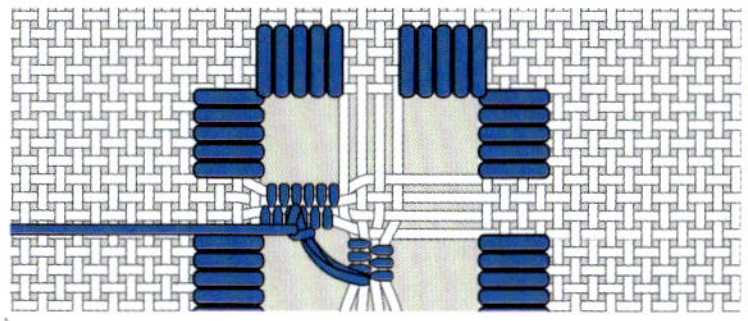

5 Pull the needle through and tighten the buttonhole stitch snugly against the woven bar.

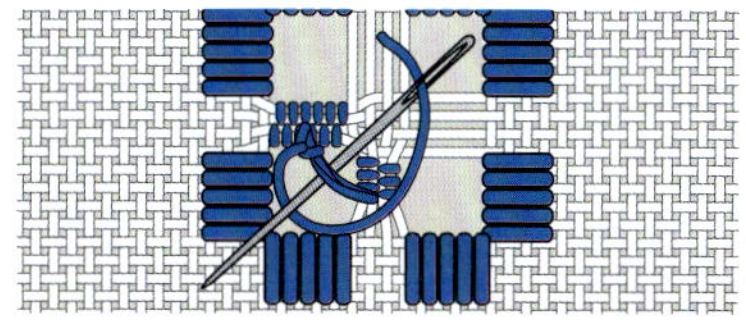

6 Moving back towards the half-woven bar, insert the needle under the curved stitches again. Take the thread under the needle point.

❶ *The stitches are being added in an anticlockwise direction.*

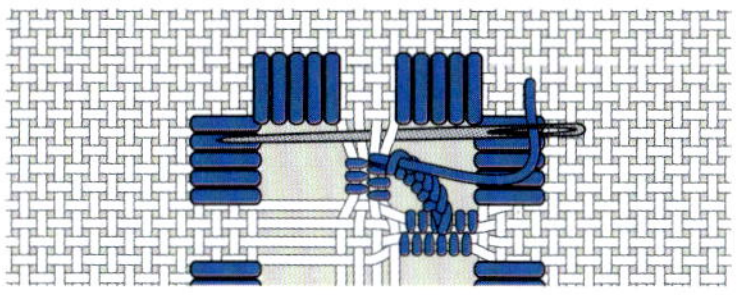

7 Turn the work 180°. Keep working buttonhole stitches to fill the arc. To finish, bring the needle out in the centre of the half-woven bar.

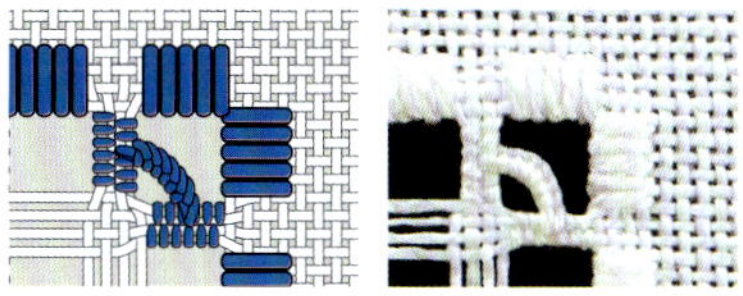

8 Complete the weaving of the bar.

buttonhole circle

also known as buttonhole wheel

Working an arc in each of the satin stitch square's quadrants creates a buttonhole circle.

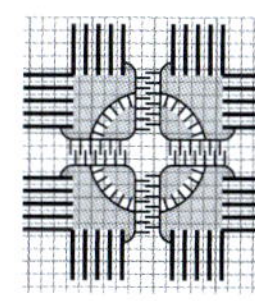

CONTEMPORARY

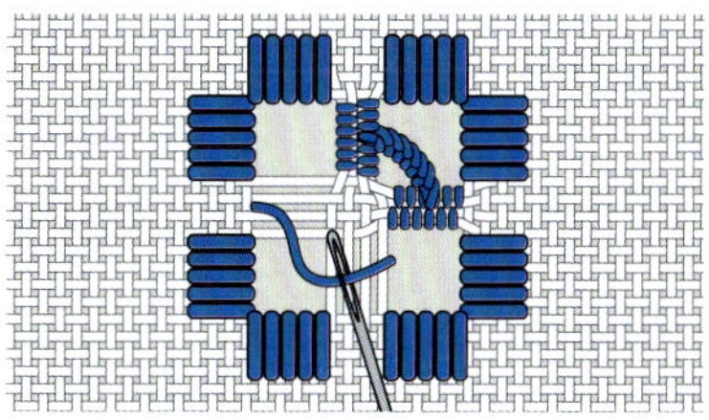

1 Work a clockwise or anticlockwise arc in the first quadrant. Take the thread through the back of the satin stitching, and bring it out ready to work the next woven bar.

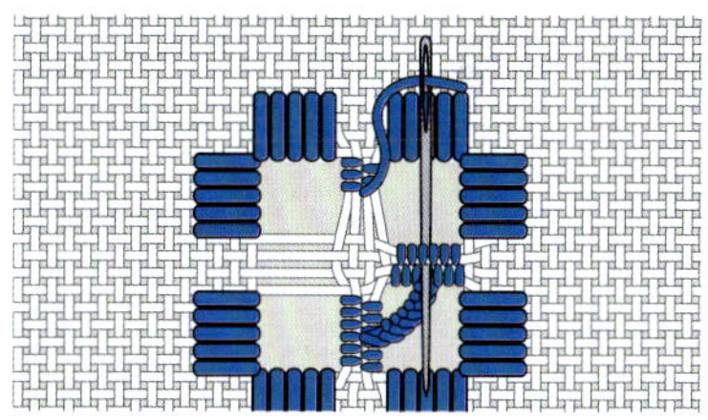

2 Weave half the bar. Turn the work 90° clockwise. Crossing to the adjacent full bar, insert the needle in the centre of the bar, from the back.

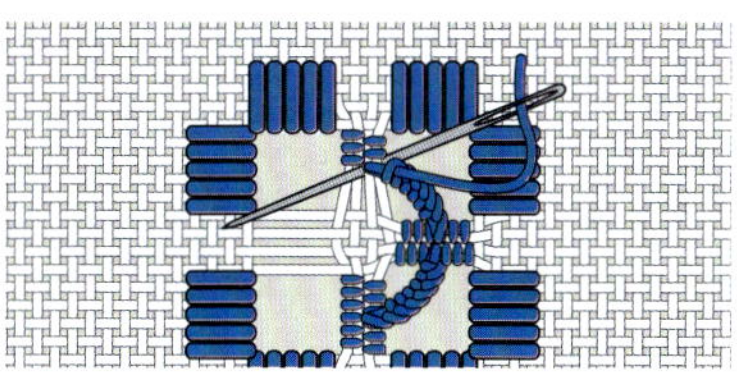

3 Work another single buttonhole arc, working the stitches in an anticlockwise direction.

4 Complete the weaving of the bar, then weave half the remaining bar.

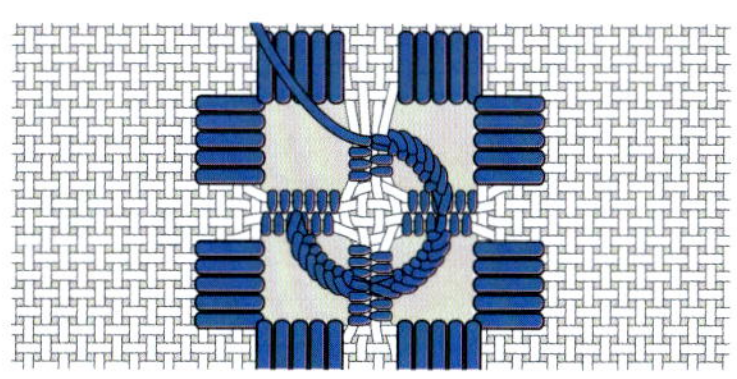

5 Turn the work 90° clockwise. Work single arc with anticlockwise stitches over to the woven bar just completed. Bring the needle out at the centre of the woven bar.

6 Work a single buttonhole arc in the final quadrant, with clockwise stitches. Bring the needle out at the centre of the woven bar.

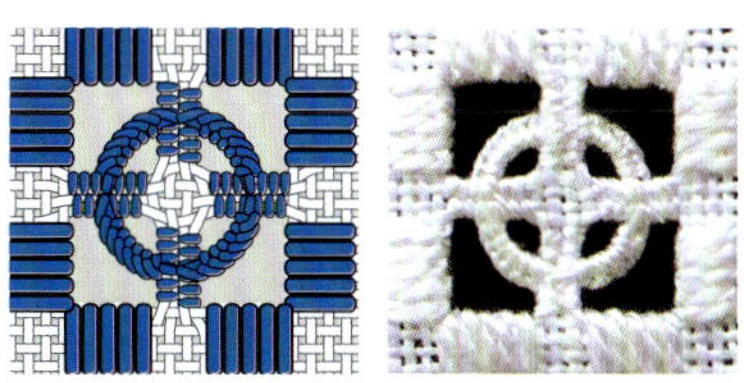

7 Complete the weaving of the bar and finish the thread in the back of the satin stitching.

❶ *If you prefer stitching woven bars in straight lines, use the method for 'Buttonhole arcs with twisted spokes' on pages 188–189 and omit the spokes.*

L

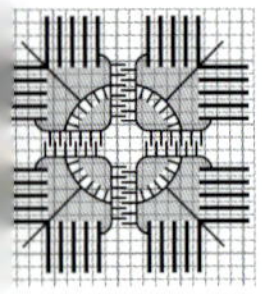

CONTEMPORARY

buttonhole arcs with twisted spokes

This motif can have a single twisted spoke, or ray, as shown here, or multiple.

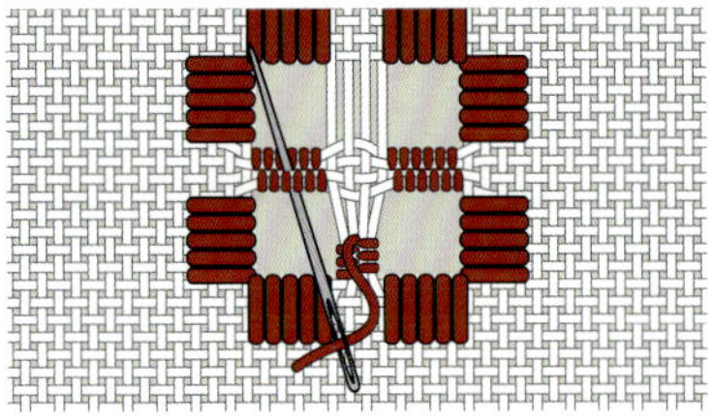

1 Work woven bars across one centre axis. Work half of the next woven bar. Crossing to the adjacent bar on the left, insert the needle in the centre of the bar, from the back.

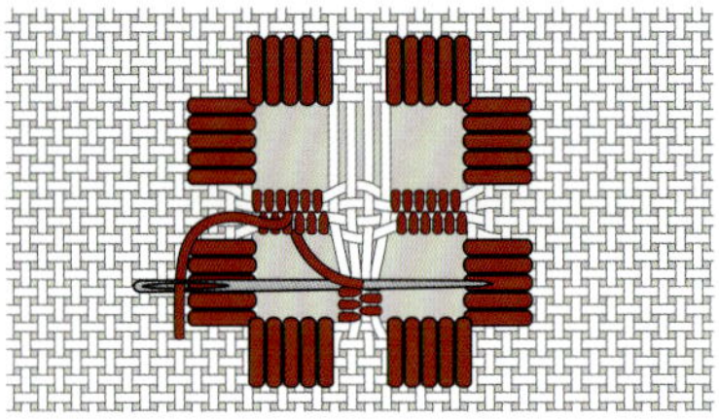

2 Pull the needle through and leave the stitch curving gently. From behind, insert the needle in the centre of the half-woven bar.

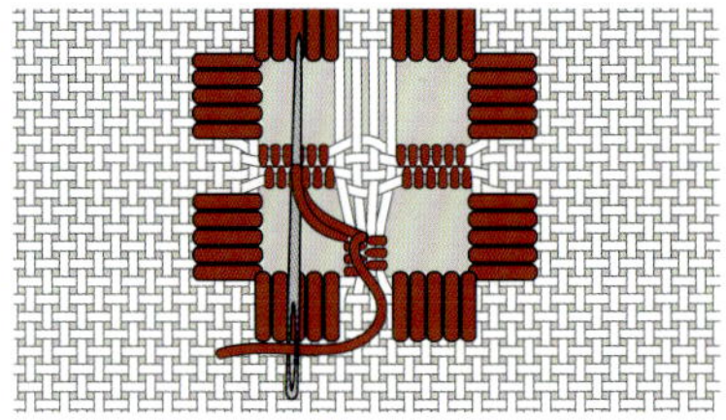

3 Pull the needle through, with a similar tension to the first stitch. From the back, insert the needle in the same place you inserted it the first time.

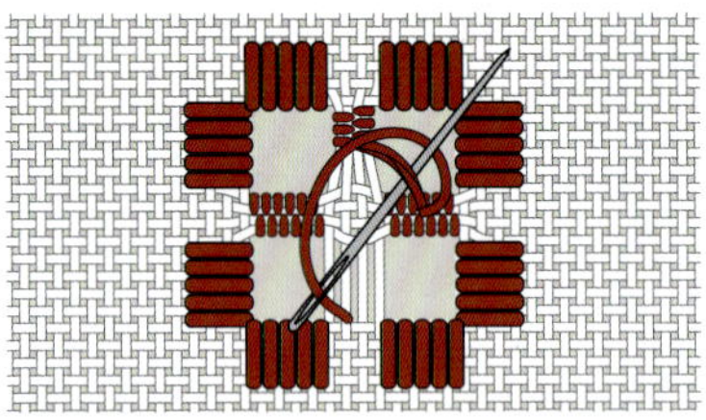

4 Pull the needle through, so that all three stitches have a similar tension. Turn the work 180°. From the centre, insert the needle under the stitches. Take the thread under the needle point.

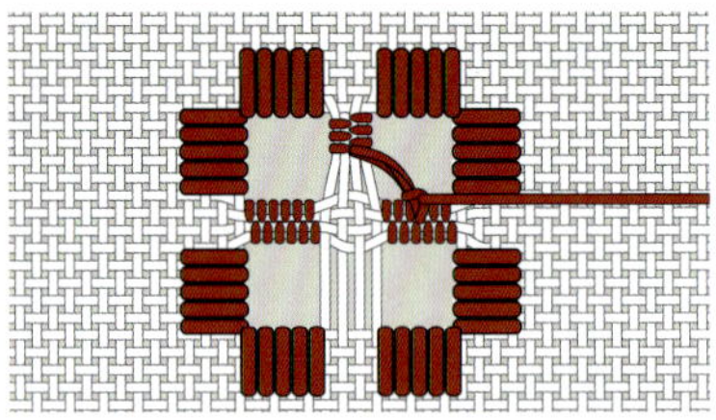

5 Pull the needle through and tighten the buttonhole stitch around the arc stitches, and down towards the woven bar.

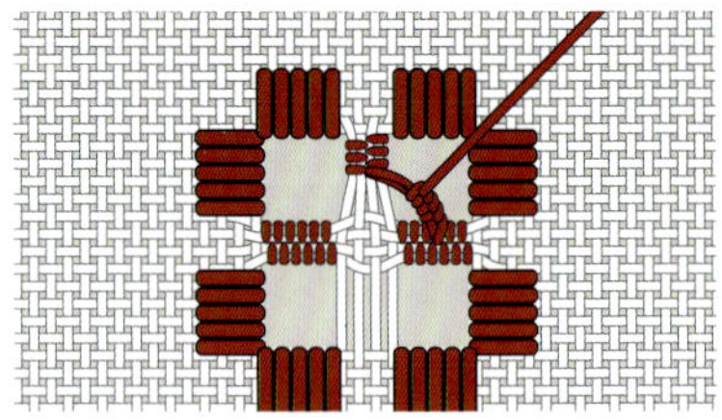

6 Moving back toward the half-woven bar, make three more buttonhole stitches.

The stitches are being added in an anticlockwise direction.

For a larger square and circle, adjust the quantity of buttonhole stitches.

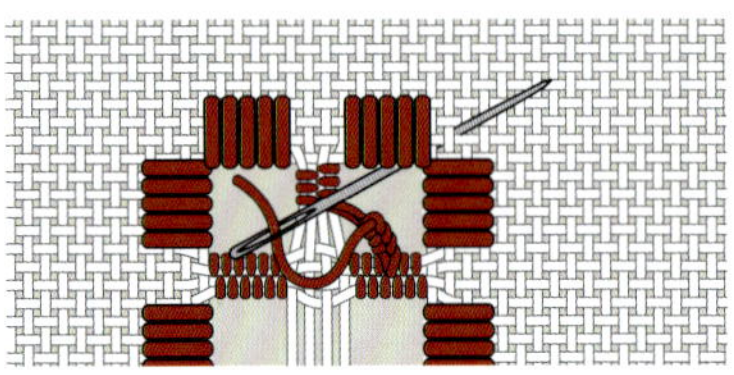

7 From the back, insert the needle in the woven corner, two threads from the cut edge.

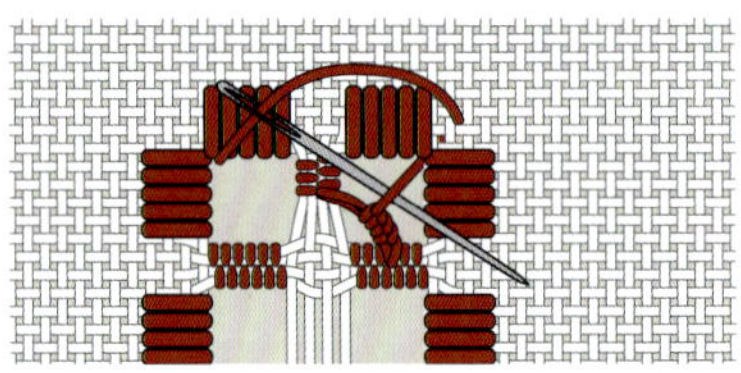

8 Pull the needle through. Tighten the stitch so that it is straight, but doesn't pull on the arc. From above, slide the needle under the stitch.

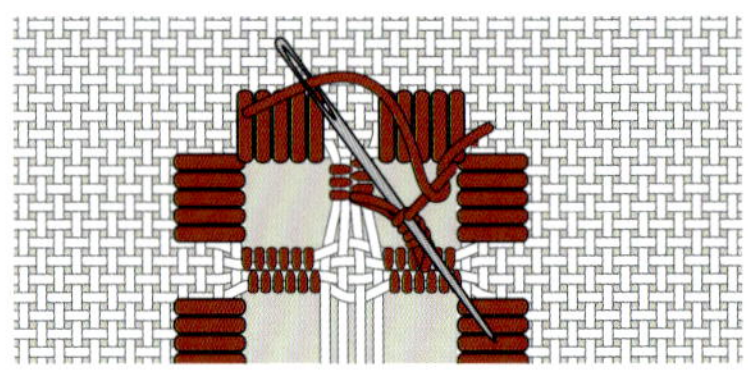

9 From above the diagonal stitch, insert the needle in the back of the 'crook' of the last buttonhole stitch.

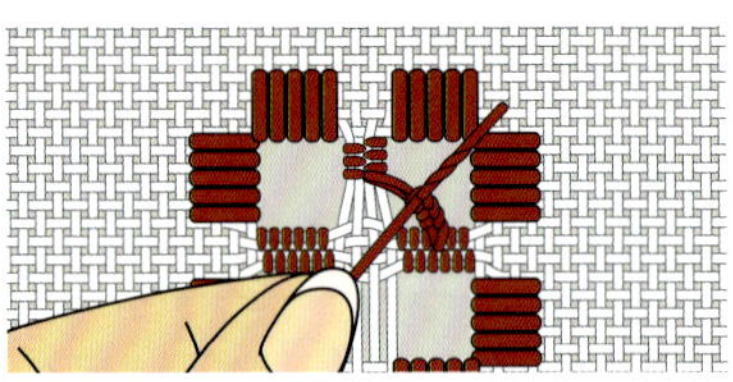

10 Pull the needle through and pull the thread to intertwine the stitches.

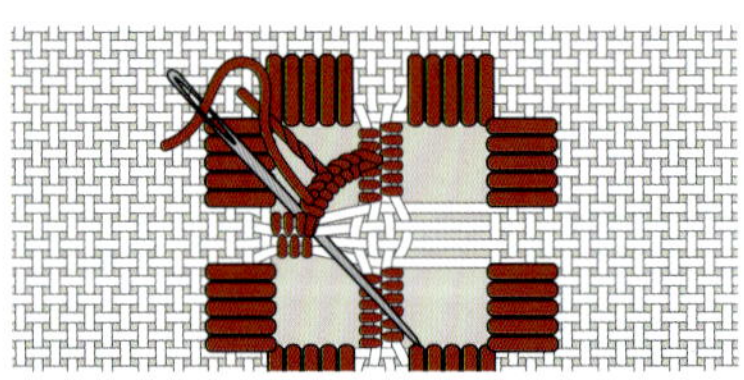

11 Turn the work 90° anticlockwise. Work another three buttonhole stitches, then from the back, insert the needle behind the woven part of the bar, bringing it out ready to continue.

Do not complete the woven bar yet.

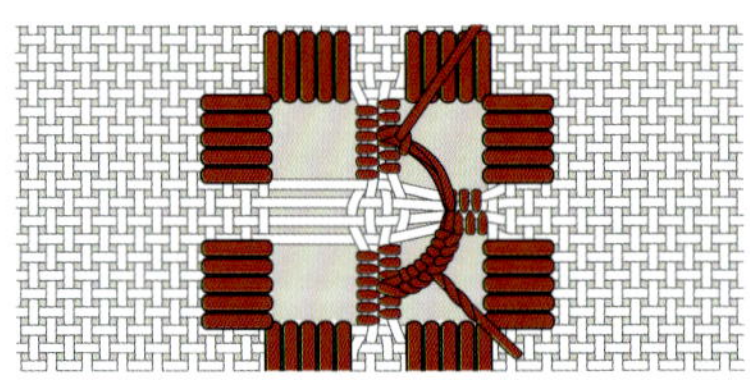

12 Turn the work 180°. Work arc stitches back and forth to the next quadrant's adjacent woven bar. Work a buttonhole stitch and tighten it around the arc stitches, and snug in towards the woven bar.

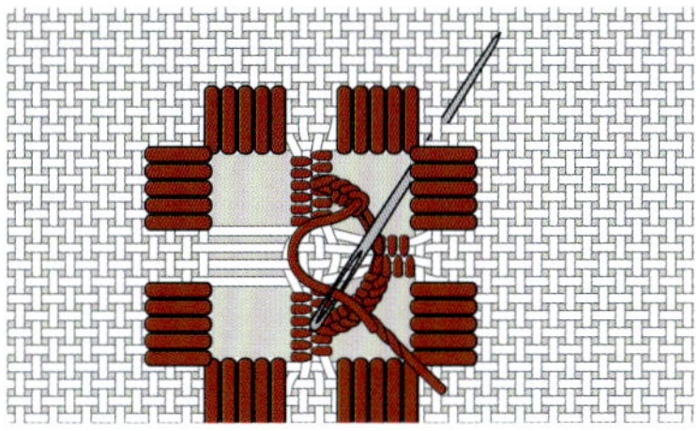

13 Work another three buttonhole stitches. From the back, insert the needle in the woven corner, two threads from the cut edge.

! *The stitches are added in a clockwise direction.*

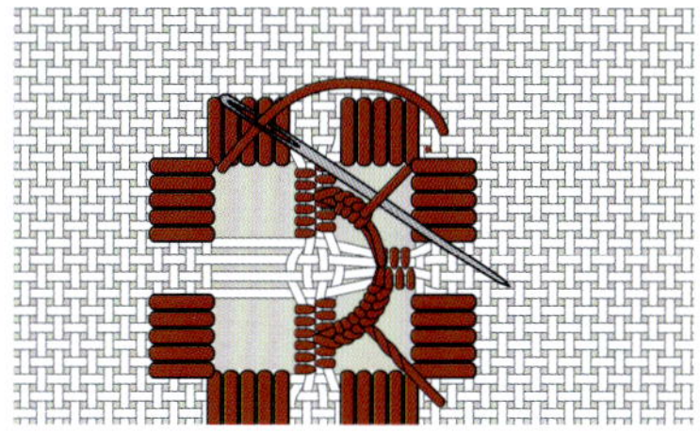

14 Pull the needle through and tighten the stitch so that it is straight, but does not pull on the arc. From the left, slide the needle under the stitch.

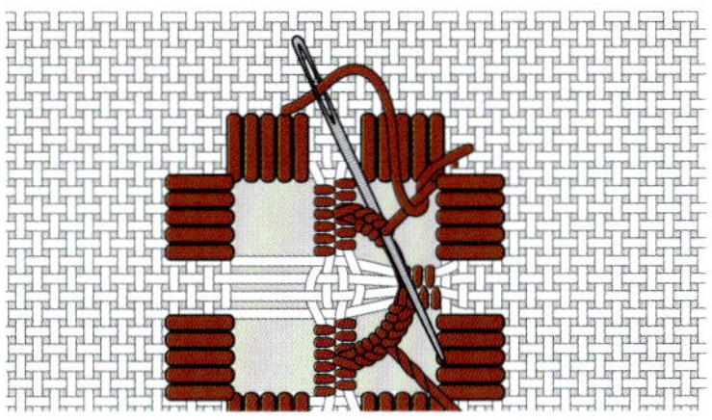

15 From the left of the diagonal stitch, insert the needle in the back of the 'crook' of the last buttonhole stitch.

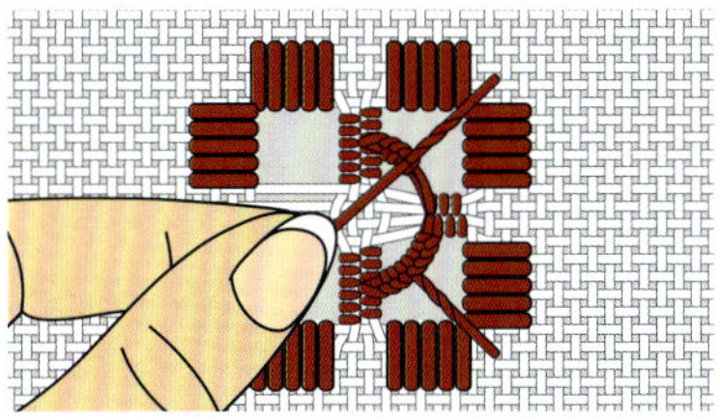

16 Pull the needle through so that the stitches intertwine.

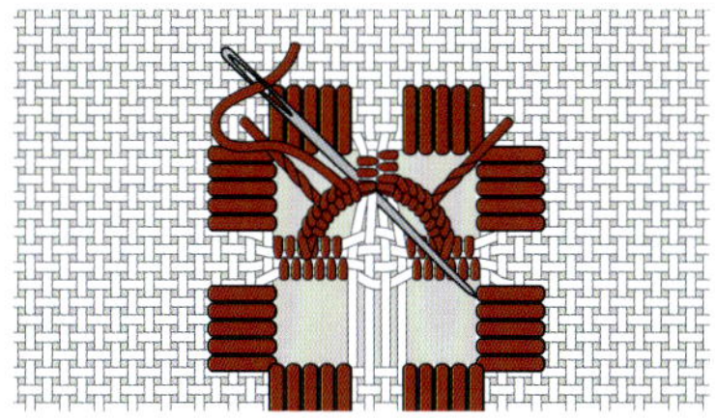

17 Turn the work 90° anticlockwise. Work another three buttonhole stitches, then from the back, insert the needle behind the woven part of the bar, bringing it out ready to continue.

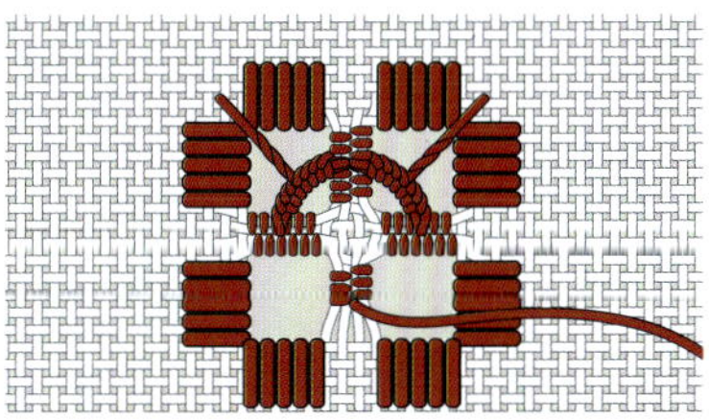

18 Complete the woven bar and work half the next woven bar.

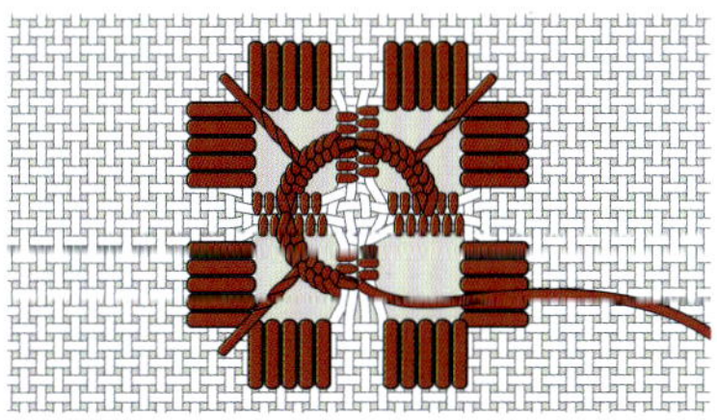

19 Work the left quadrant first, with stitches being added in an anticlockwise direction.

20 Work the right quadrant, with stitches added in a clockwise direction. Finish the woven bar, and the thread in the back of the satin stitch.

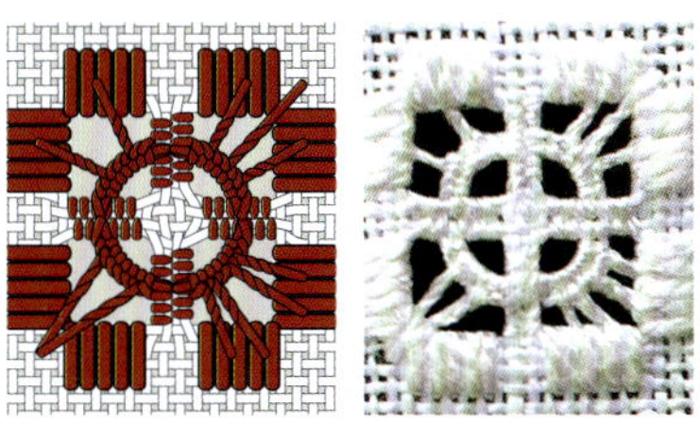

! *This filling stitch can be worked with multiple rays in the corner of each quadrant, examples of which are shown.*

R

buttonhole arcs with twisted spokes

This motif can have a single twisted spoke, or ray, as shown here, or multiple.

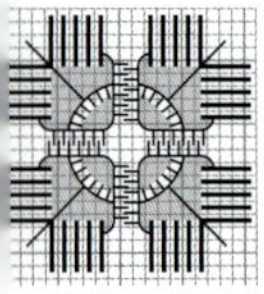

CONTEMPORARY

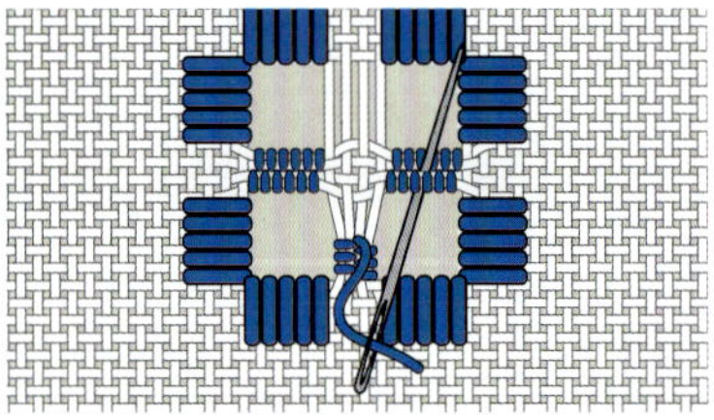

1 Work woven bars across one centre axis. Work half of the next woven bar. Crossing to the adjacent bar on the right, insert the needle in the centre of the bar, from the back.

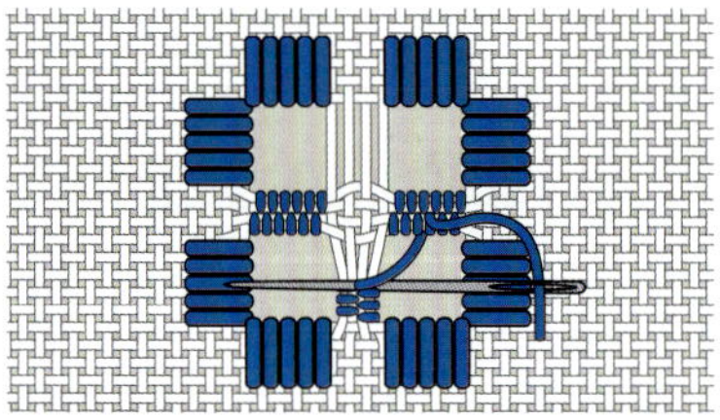

2 Pull the needle through and leave the stitch curving gently. From behind, insert the needle in the centre of the half-woven bar.

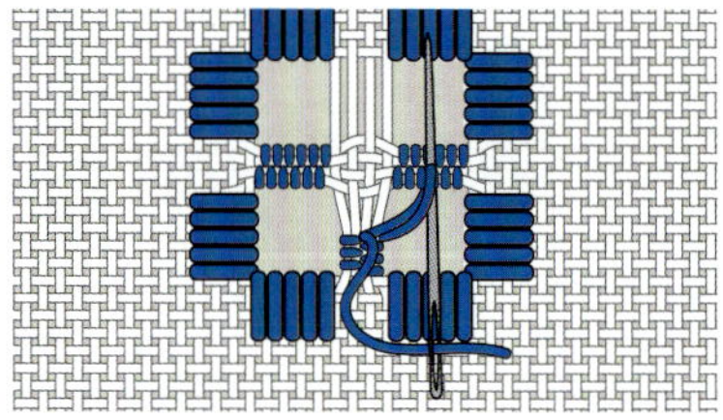

3 Pull the needle through, with a similar tension to the first stitch. From the back, insert the needle in the same place you inserted it the first time.

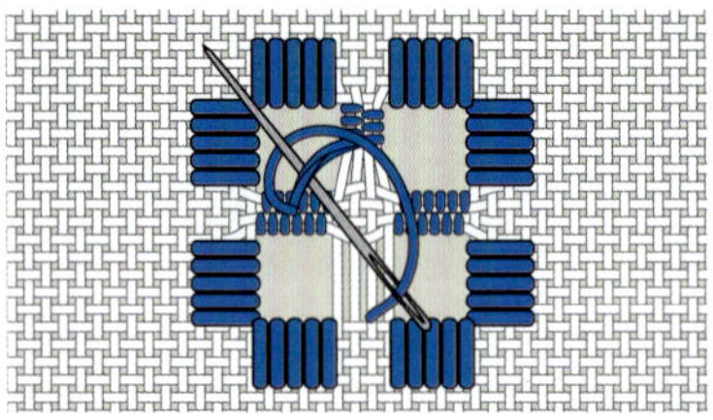

4 Pull the needle through, so that all three stitches have a similar tension. Turn the work 180°. From the centre, insert the needle under the stitches. Take the thread under the needle point.

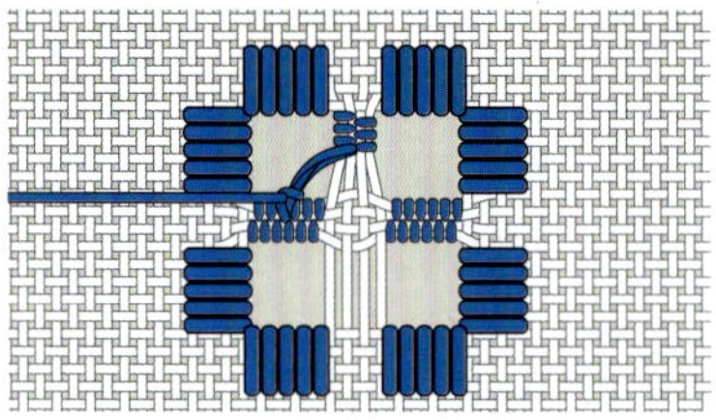

5 Pull the needle through and tighten the buttonhole stitch around the arc stitches, and down towards the woven bar.

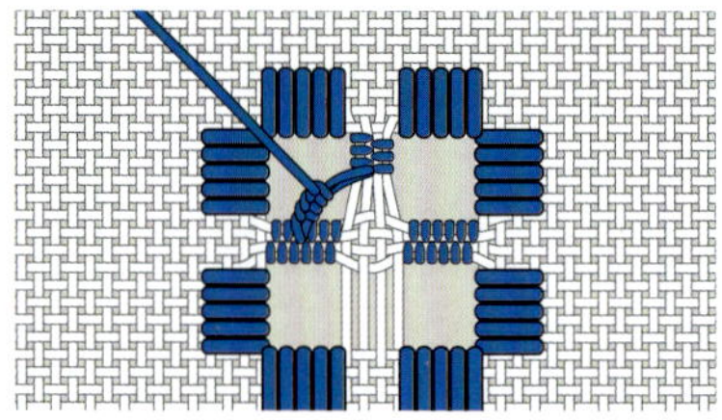

6 Moving back toward the half-woven bar, make three more buttonhole stitches.

❶ *The stitches are being added in a clockwise direction.*

❶ *For a larger square and circle, adjust the quantity of buttonhole stitches.*

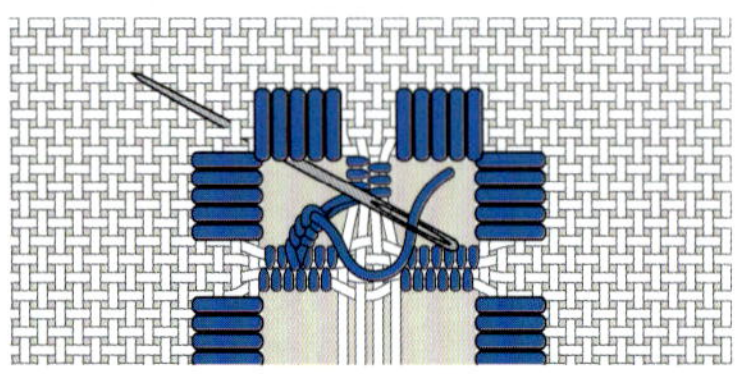

7 From the back, insert the needle in the woven corner, two threads from the cut edge.

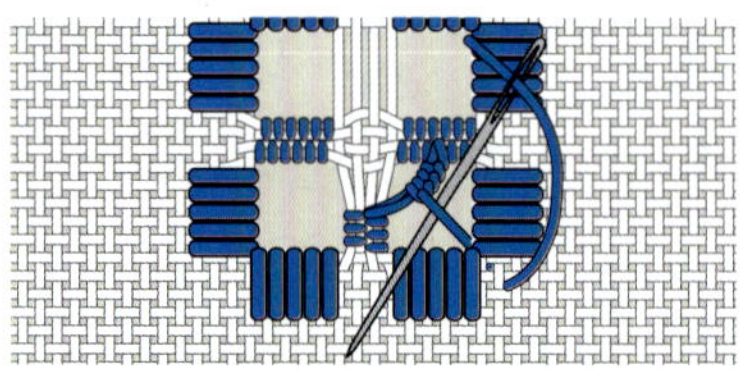

8 Turn the work 180°. Pull the needle through. Tighten the stitch so that it is straight, but doesn't pull on the arc. From above, slide the needle under the stitch.

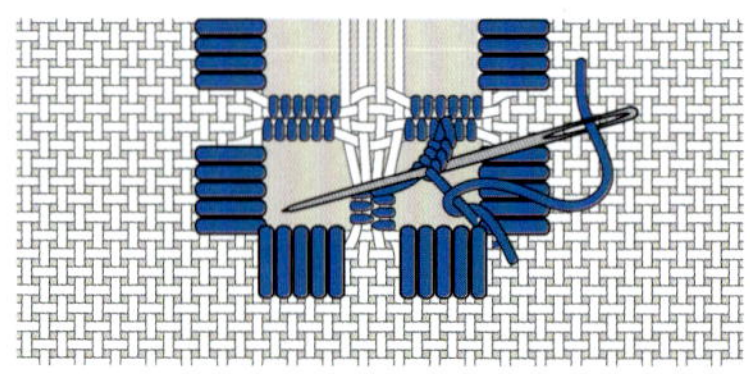

9 From above the diagonal stitch, insert the needle in the back of the 'crook' of the last buttonhole stitch.

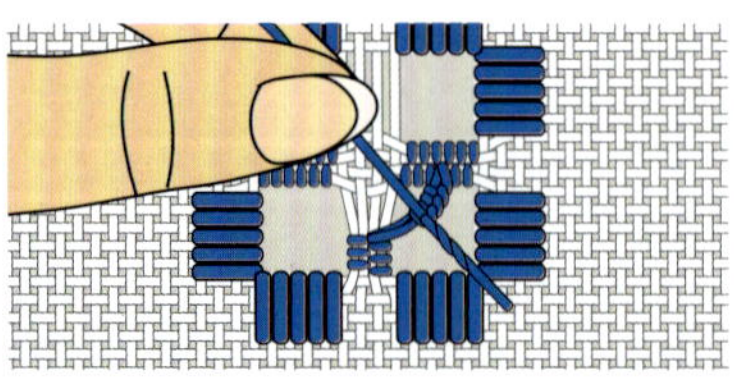

10 Pull the needle through and pull the thread to intertwine the stitches.

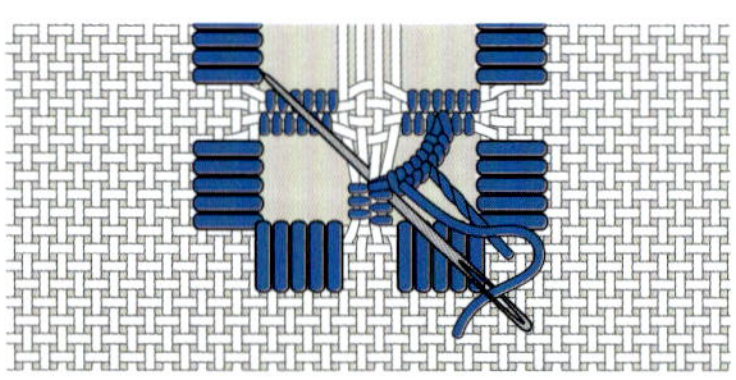

11 Work another three buttonhole stitches, then from the back, insert the needle behind the woven part of the bar, bringing it out ready to continue.

❶ *Do not complete the woven bar yet.*

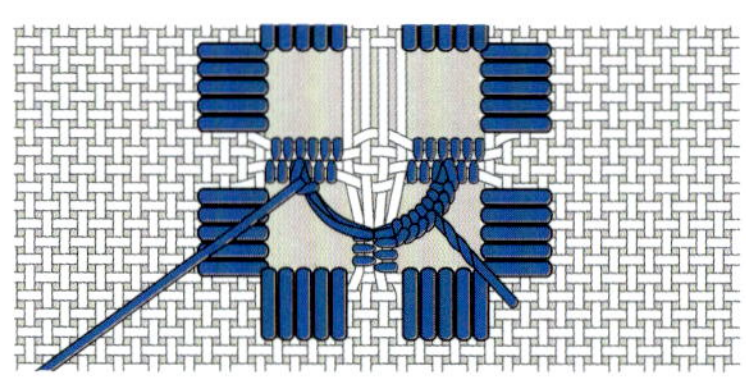

12 Work arc stitches back and forth to the next quadrant's adjacent woven bar. Work a buttonhole stitch and tighten it around the arc stitches, and snug in towards the woven bar.

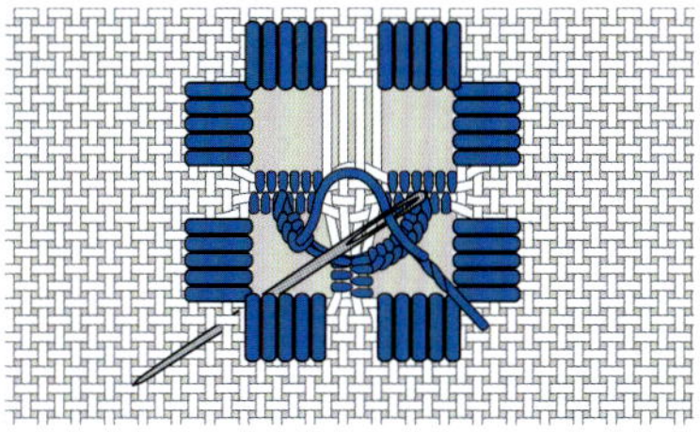

13 Work another three buttonhole stitches. From the back, insert the needle in the woven corner, two threads from the cut edge.

❶ *The stitches are added in a clockwise direction.*

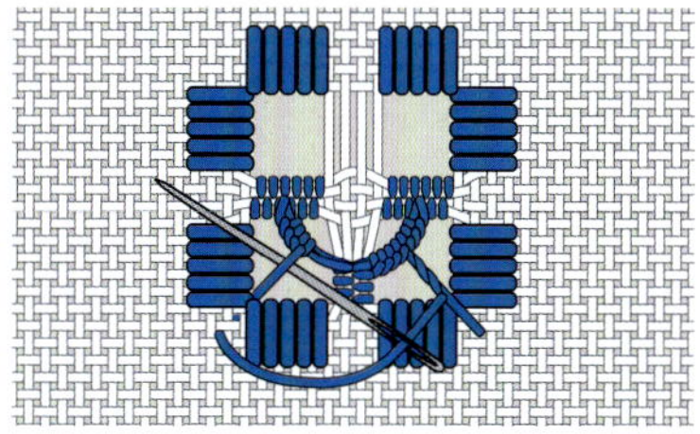

14 Pull the needle through and tighten the stitch so that it is straight, but does not pull on the arc. From the right, slide the needle under the stitch.

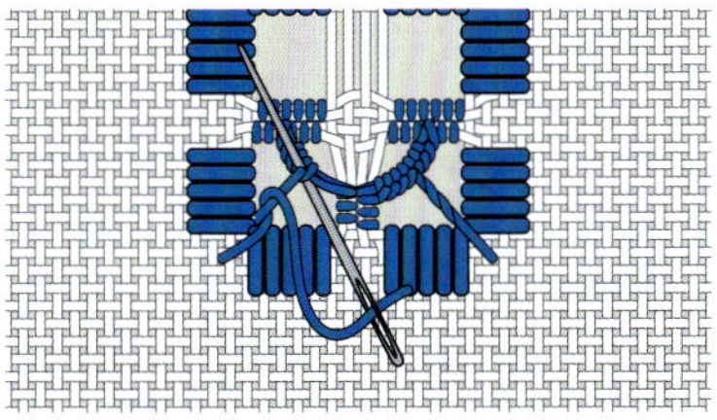

15 From below the diagonal stitch, insert the needle in the back of the 'crook' of the last buttonhole stitch.

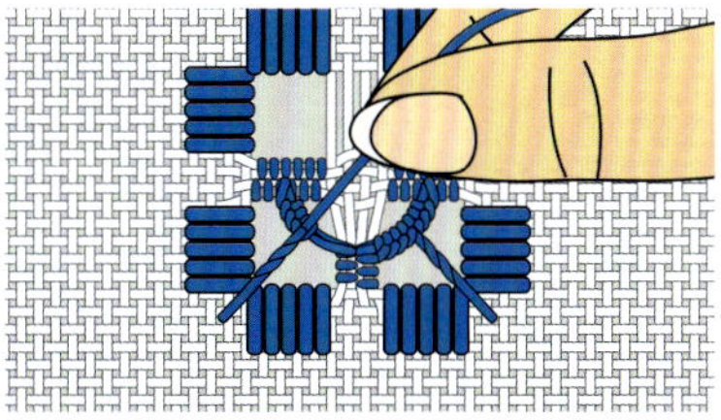

16 Pull the needle through so that the stitches intertwine.

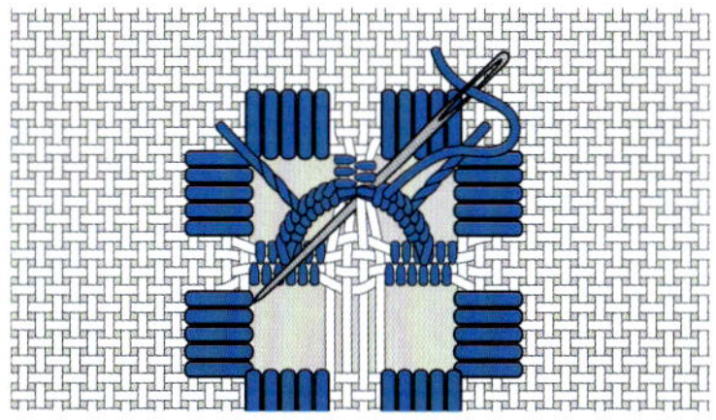

17 Turn the work 180°. Work another three buttonhole stitches, then from the back, insert the needle behind the woven part of the bar, bringing it out ready to continue.

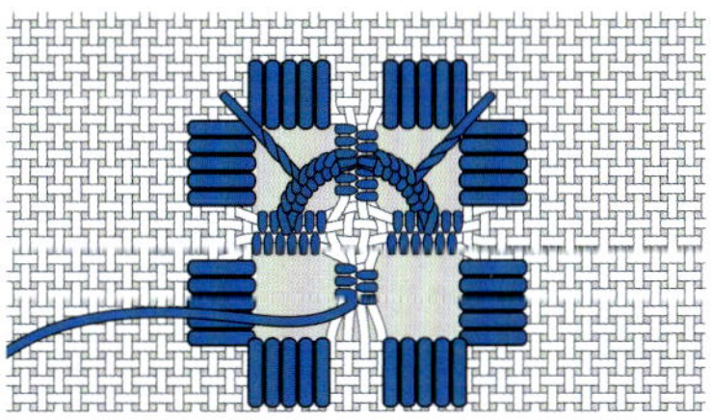

18 Complete the woven bar and work half the next woven bar.

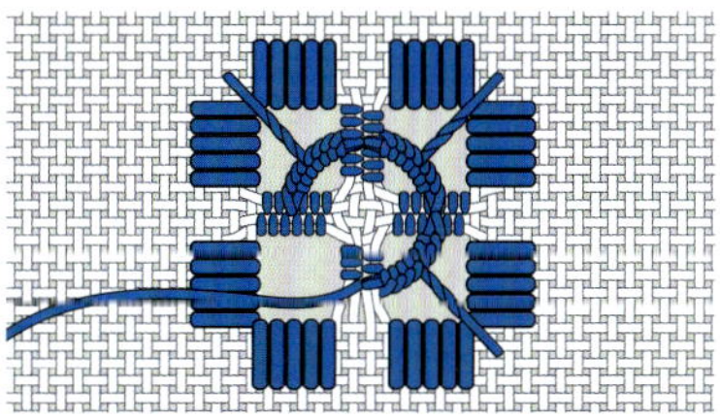

19 Work the left quadrant first, with stitches being added in an anti-clockwise direction.

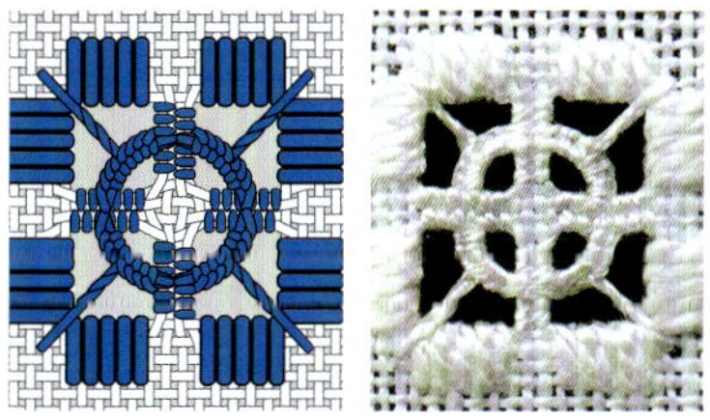

20 Work the right quadrant, with stitches added in a clockwise direction. Finish the woven bar, and the thread in the back of the satin stitch.

❶ *This filling stitch can be worked with multiple rays in the corner of each quadrant, examples of which are shown.*

buttonholed petals

This stitch is very adaptable and many variations are possible. The method shown is for a mid-size square, but it works well in larger squares as well.

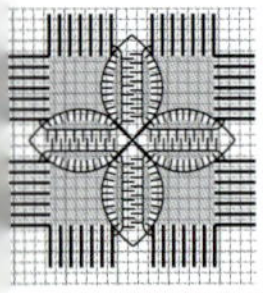

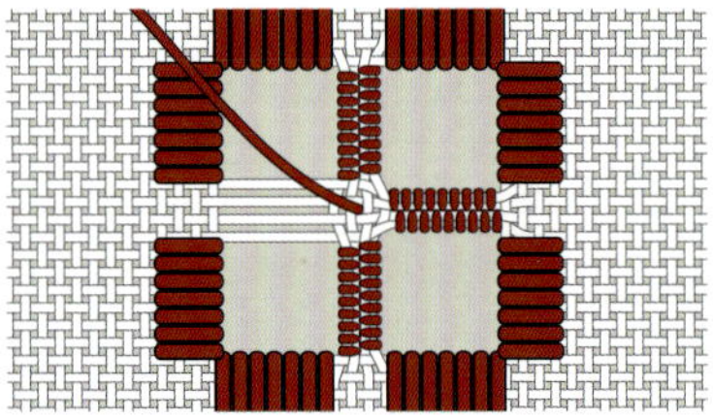

1 Work three woven bars as shown, ending in the centre of the woven square following the third bar.

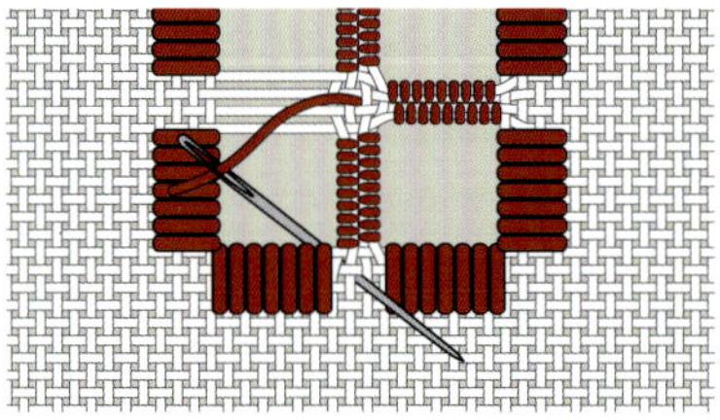

2 Insert the needle in the lower left quadrant, and bring it out two threads below the woven bar's centre.

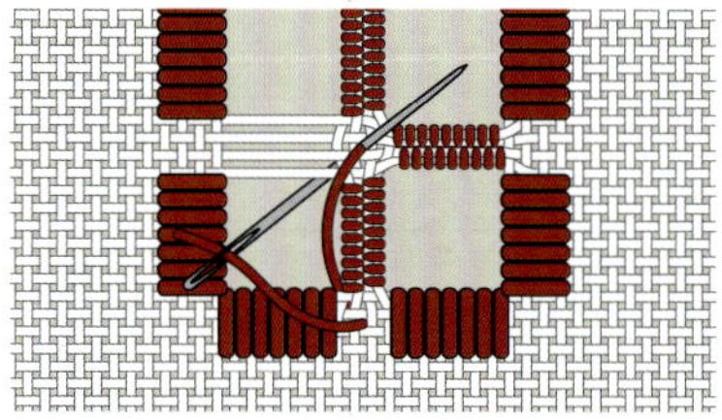

3 Pull the needle through and leave the stitch curving gently. Bring it out in the woven square's centre again.

❶ *The curve of the stitches determines the size of the petal.*

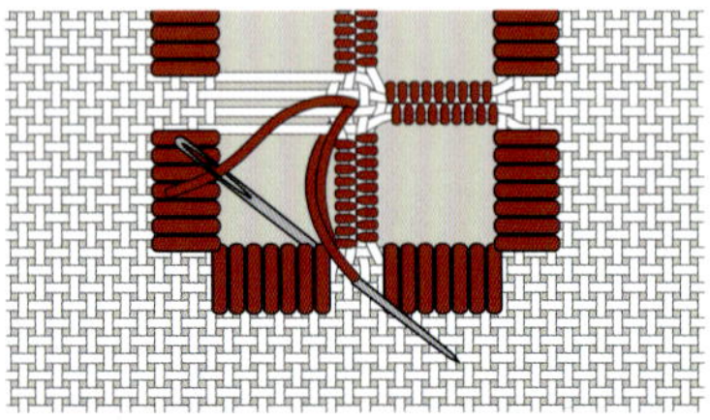

4 Pull the needle through, with a similar tension to the first stitch. Bring the needle out below the woven bar again, in the same hole.

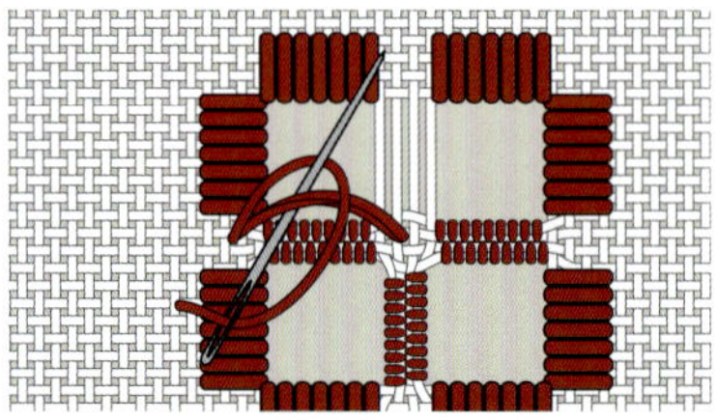

5 Pull the needle through. Turn the work 90° clockwise. From below, insert the needle under the three stitches. Take the thread behind the needle point from left to right.

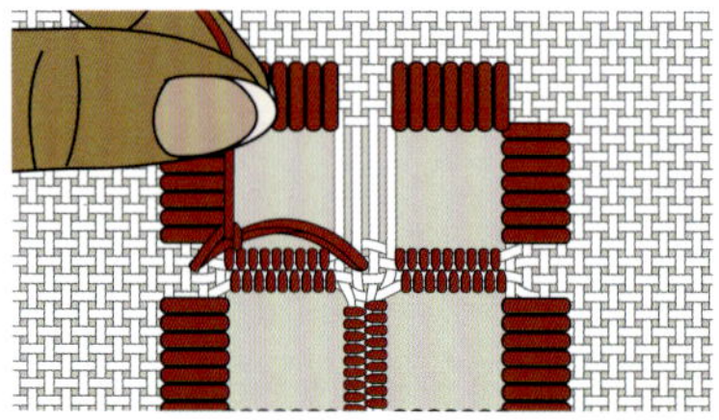

6 Pull the needle through and tighten the stitch to sit snugly around the curved stitches and against the satin stitch.

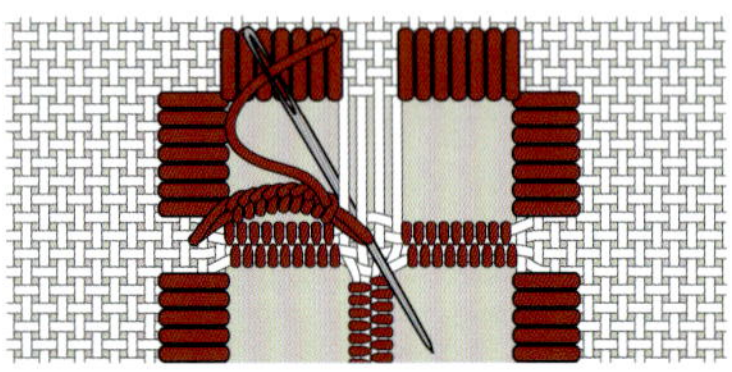

7 Moving right, fill the arc with buttonhole stitches. To complete the arc, bring the needle out in the centre of the woven square.

❶ *Stitches are added in a clockwise direction along the arc.*

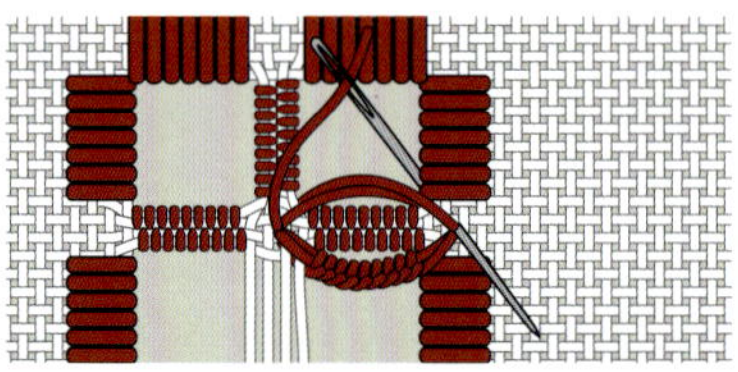

8 Turn the work 180°. Work three curved stitches on the other side of the woven bar, using the same tension as for the previous arc.

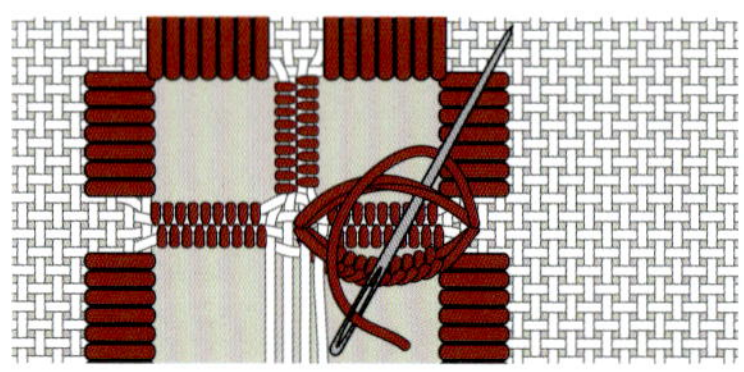

9 Pull the needle through. From below, insert it under the three stitches. Take the thread behind the needle point from right to left.

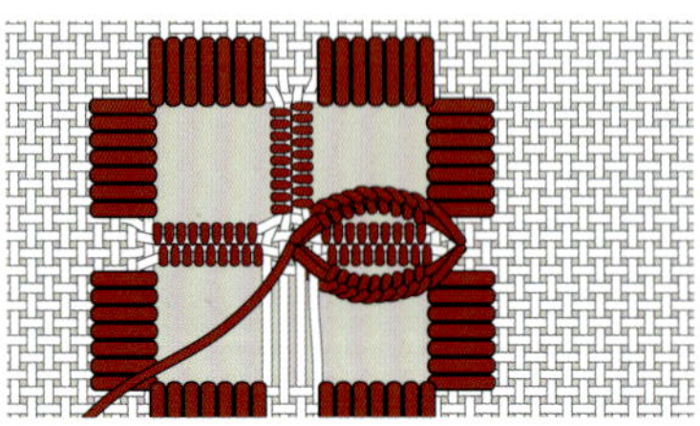

10 Work buttonhole stitches along the arc.

❶ *Stitches are added in an anticlockwise direction, along the arc.*

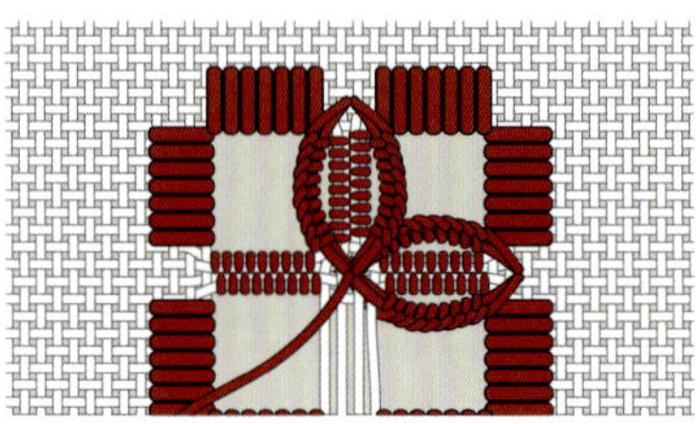

11 Work a petal arc along each side of the next woven bar.

❶ *There will be an overlap of the adjacent petals at the inner end.*

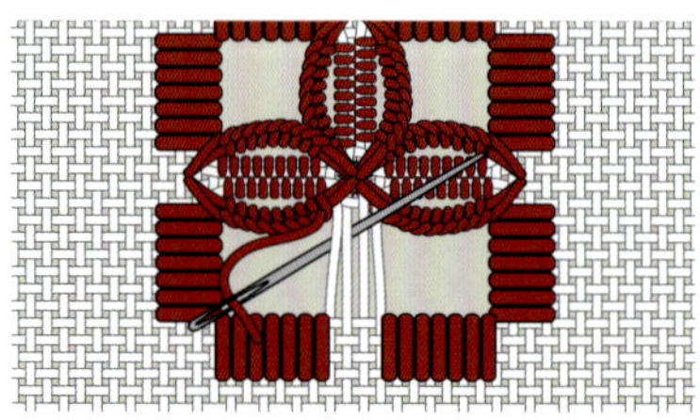

12 Work a petal arc along each side of the next woven bar. To finish the petal and move on, bring the needle out ready to weave the final bar.

13 Weave the bar then bring the needle out two threads down from the bottom of the woven bar.

14 Working from the edge to the centre, work a petal arc along each side of the next woven bar. Finish by running the thread under the back of the satin stitch.

❶ *Instead of working the final petal from the edge to the centre after working the woven bar, you can work the petal from the centre to the edge and then weave the bar inside it, to travel to the edge. It can just be a little harder to squeeze it in inside the buttonholed arcs.*

❶ *This motif has buttonhole arcs in the corners when worked within a framework of woven bars.*

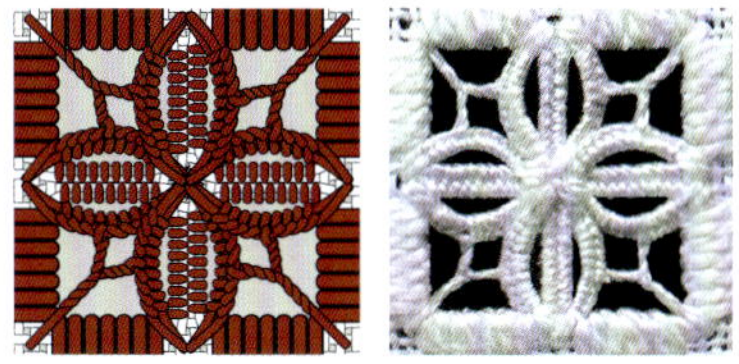

❶ *This motif has inverse twisted Ys (or similar branched stitches) from the arcs to the corners.*

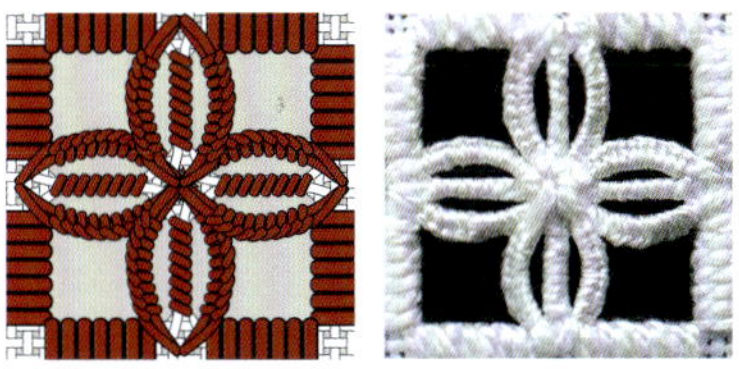

❶ *This motif has wrapped bars in the centre of the petal arcs.*

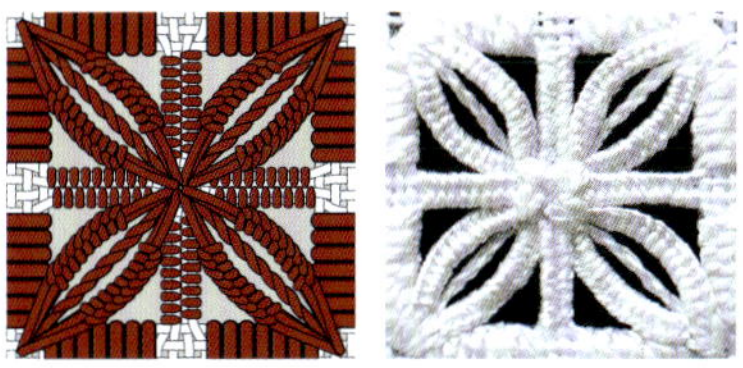

❶ *Work petals on either side of woven, wrapped or twisted diagonals.*

picot on buttonhole stitch

Picots made of chain stitch can be worked on buttonholed petals, arcs or circles.

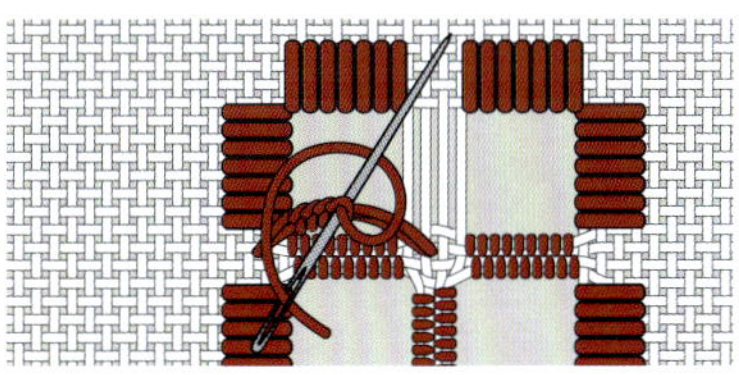

1 Buttonhole along the foundation stitches up to the picot's position. Insert the needle into the last stitch. Take the thread under the needle point.

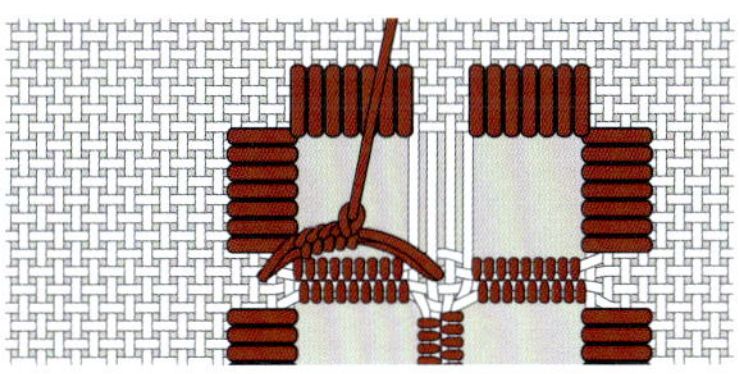

2 Pull the needle through to tighten the stitch close to the buttonhole stitching.

❶ *This creates a chain stitch.*

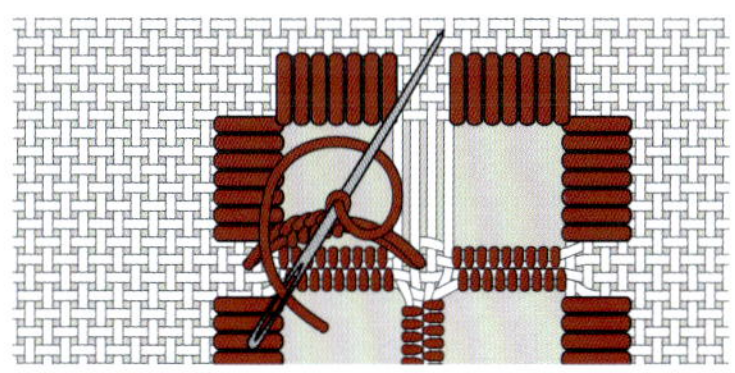

3 Insert the needle into the chain stitch and take the thread under the needle point to create another chain stitch.

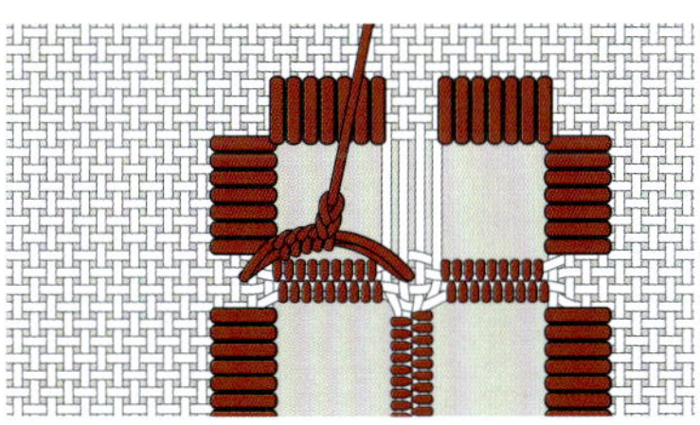

4 Pull the needle through to tighten the stitch.

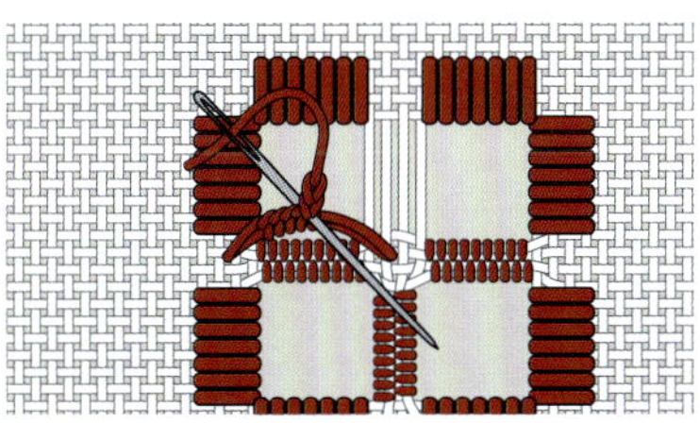

5 Insert the needle in the back of the last buttonhole stitch so that it emerges from it as it would have if no picot had been worked.

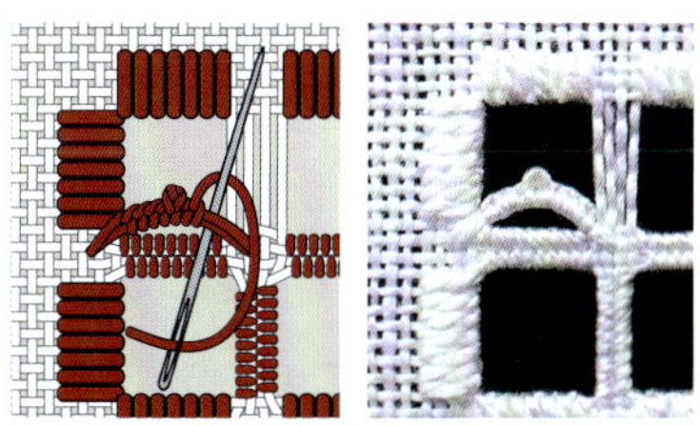

6 Continue buttonholing.

buttonholed petals

This stitch is very adaptable and many variations are possible. The method shown is for a mid-size square, but it works well in larger squares as well.

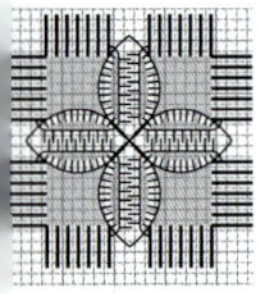

CONTEMPORARY

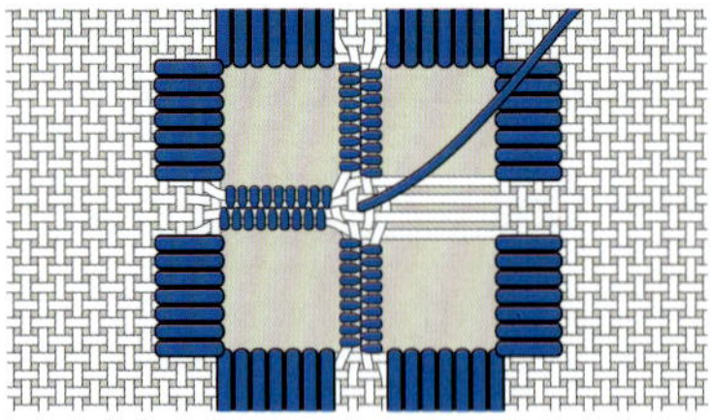

1 Work three woven bars as shown, ending in the centre of the woven square following the third bar.

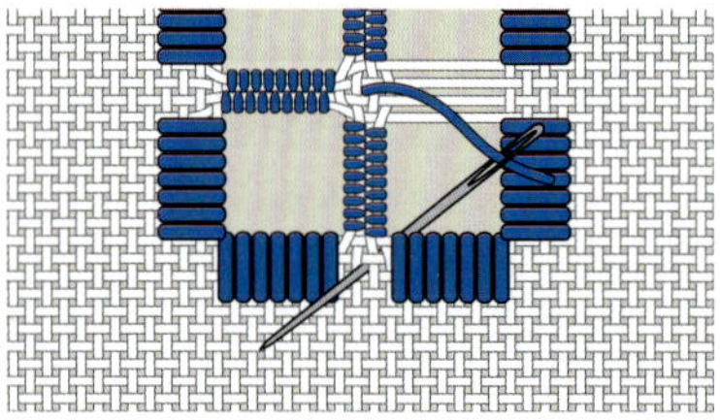

2 Insert the needle in the lower right quadrant, and bring it out two threads down from the bottom of the woven bar.

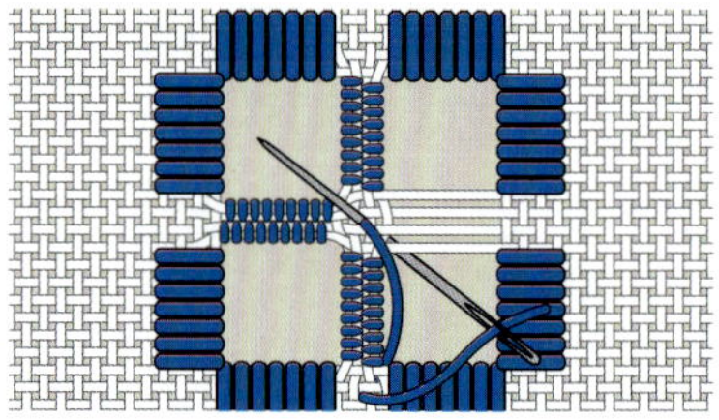

3 Pull the needle through and leave the stitch curving gently. Bring it out in the woven square's centre again.

! *The curve of the stitches determines the size of the petal.*

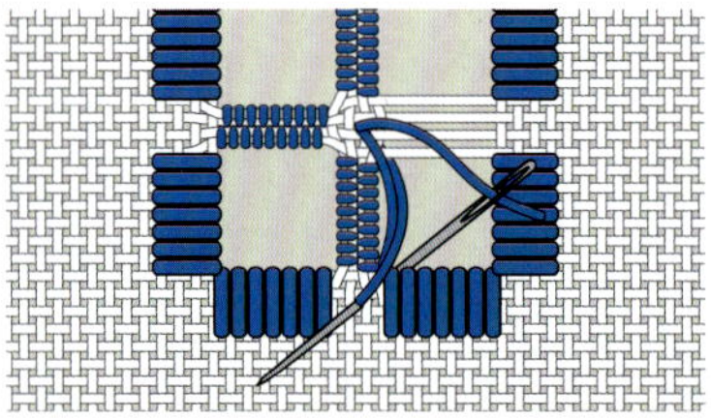

4 Pull the needle through, with a similar tension to the first stitch. Bring the needle out below the woven bar again, in the same hole.

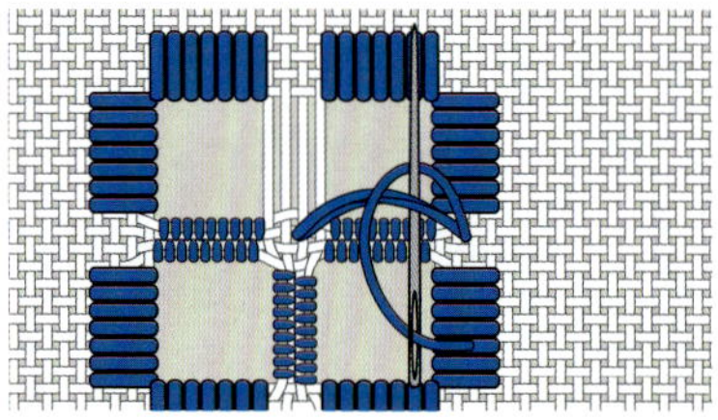

5 Pull the needle through. Turn the work 90° anticlockwise. From below, insert the needle under the three stitches. Take the thread behind the needle point from right to left.

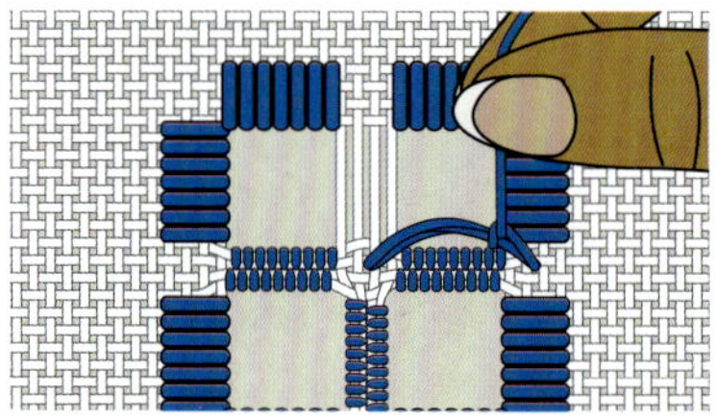

6 Pull the needle through and tighten the stitch to sit snugly around the curved stitches and against the satin stitch.

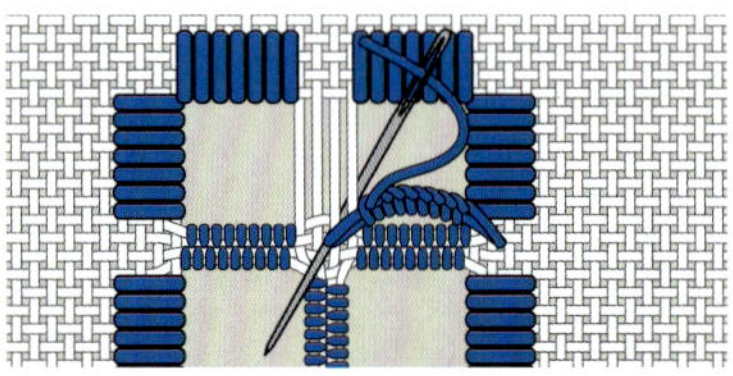

7 Moving right, fill the arc with buttonhole stitches. To complete the arc, bring the needle out in the centre of the woven square.

! *Stitches are added in an anticlockwise direction along the arc.*

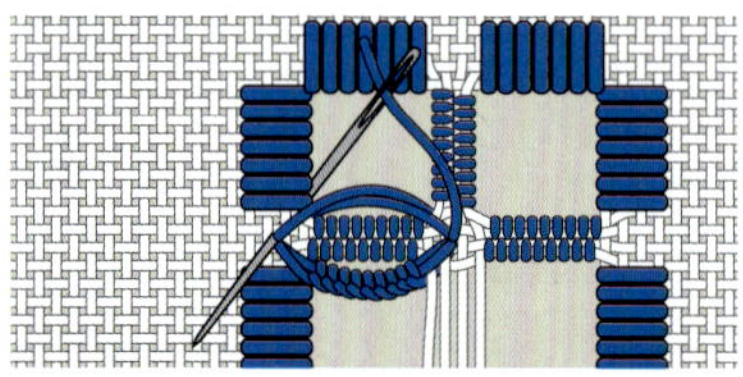

8 Turn the work 180°. Work three curved stitches on the other side of the woven bar, using the same tension as for the previous arc.

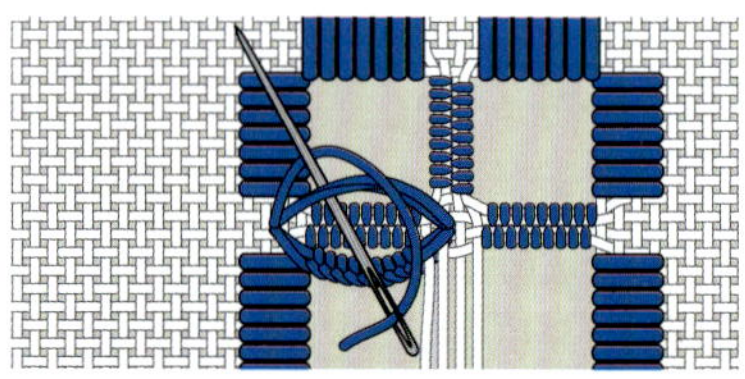

9 Pull the needle through. From below, insert it under the three stitches. Take the thread behind the needle point from left to right.

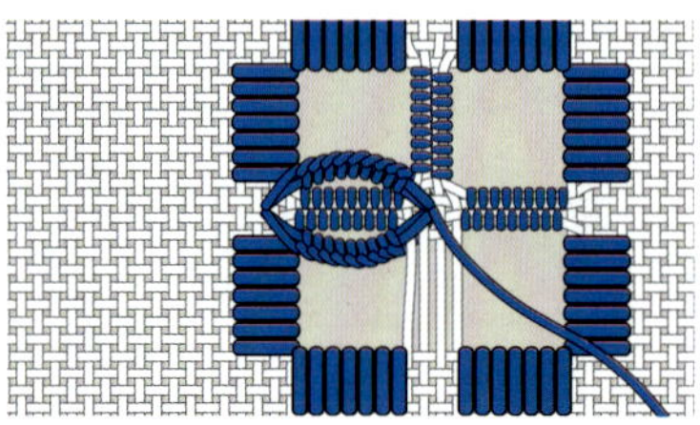

10 Work buttonhole stitches along the arc.

! *Stitches are added in a clockwise direction, along the arc.*

11 Work a petal arc along each side of the next woven bar.

! *There will be an overlap of the adjacent petals at the inner end.*

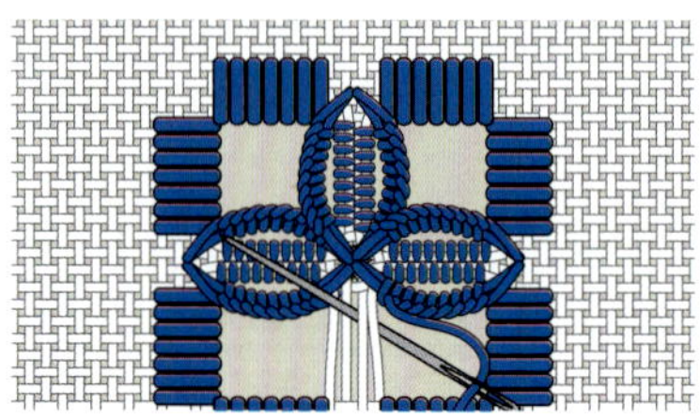

12 Work a petal arc along each side of the next woven bar. To finish the petal and move on, bring the needle out ready to weave the final bar.

13 Weave the bar then bring the needle out two threads down from the bottom of the woven bar.

14 Working from the edge to the centre, work a petal arc along each side of the next woven bar. Finish by running the thread under the back of the satin stitch.

❶ *Instead of working the final petal from the edge to the centre after working the woven bar, you can work the petal from the centre to the edge and then weave the bar inside it, to travel to the edge. It can just be a little harder to squeeze it in inside the buttonholed arcs.*

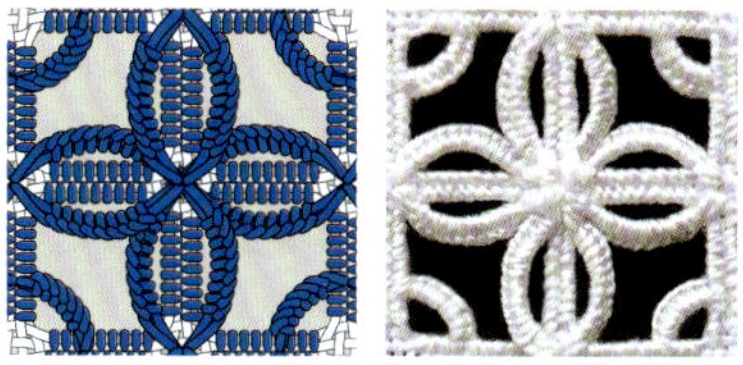

❶ *This motif has buttonhole arcs in the corners when worked within a framework of woven bars.*

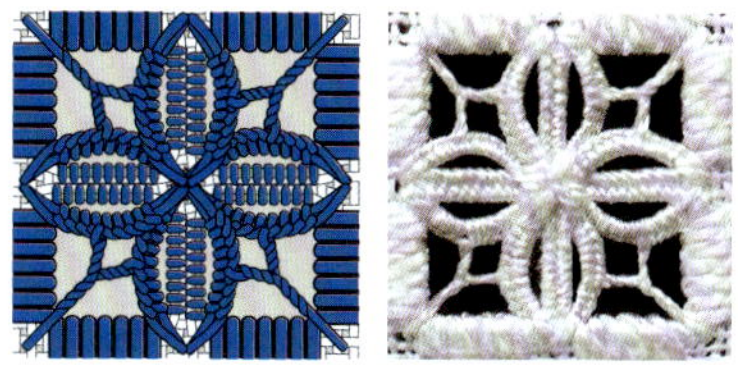

❶ *This motif has inverse twisted Ys (or similar branched stitches) from the arcs to the corners.*

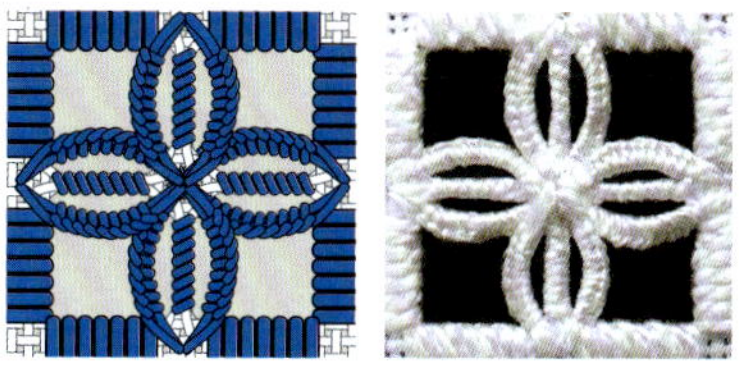

❶ *This motif has wrapped bars in the centre of the petal arcs.*

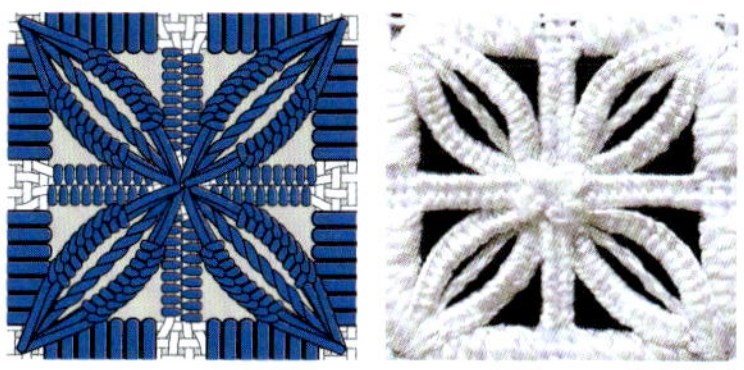

❶ *Work petals on either side of woven, wrapped or twisted diagonals.*

picot on buttonhole stitch

Picots made of chain stitch can be worked on buttonholed petals, arcs or circles.

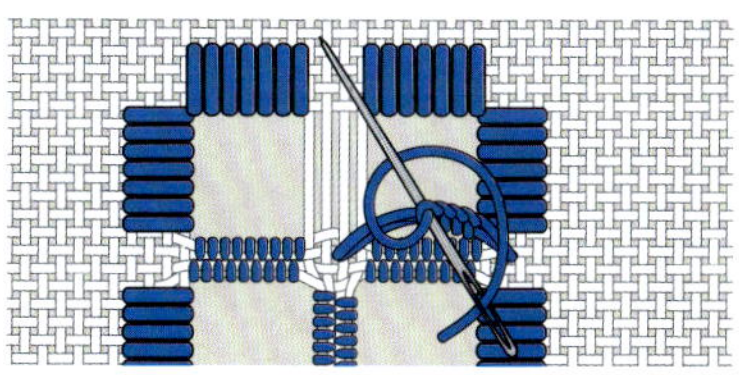

1 Buttonhole along the foundation stitches up to the picot's position. Insert the needle into the last stitch. Take the thread under the needle point.

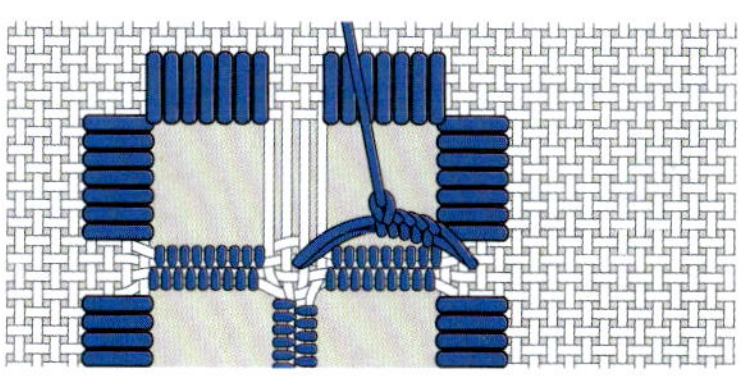

2 Pull the needle through to tighten the stitch close to the buttonhole stitching.

❶ *This creates a chain stitch.*

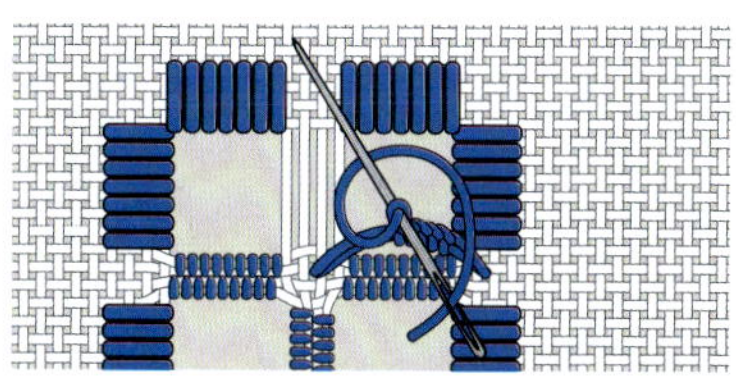

3 Insert the needle into the chain stitch and take the thread under the needle point to create another chain stitch.

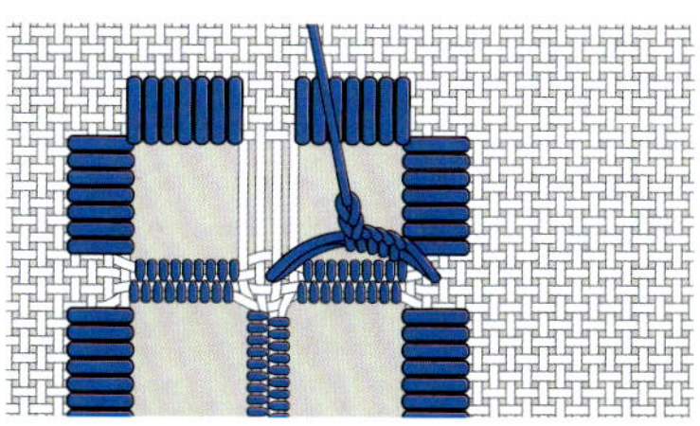

4 Pull the needle through to tighten the stitch.

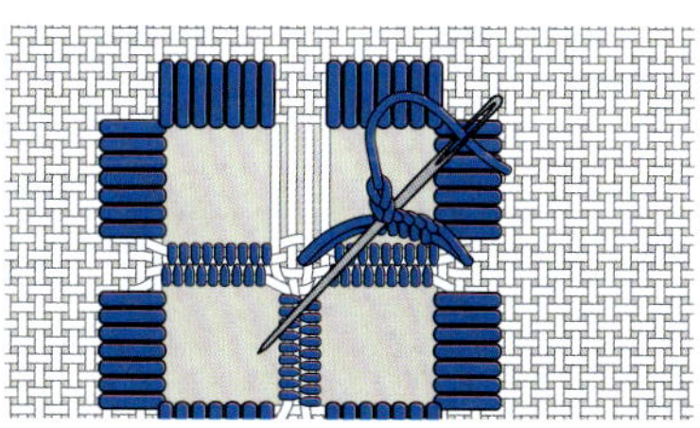

5 Insert the needle in the back of the last buttonhole stitch so that it emerges from it as it would have if no picot had been worked.

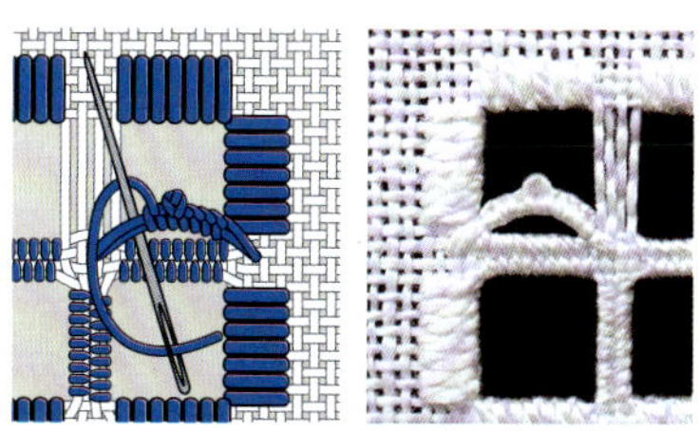

6 Continue buttonholing.

shuttle stitch

This filling uses up and down buttonhole stitch which, in tatting, is formed by a shuttle. It could be substituted in place of any buttonhole stitching.

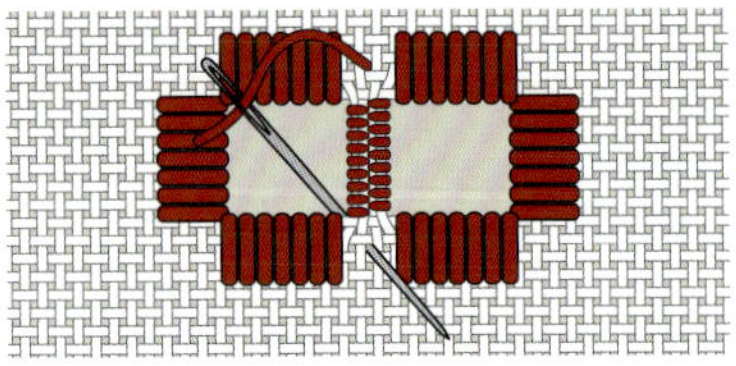

1 Work the bar. Bring the needle out in the centre of the woven square above the bar. Insert the needle in the left quadrant, and bring it out two threads below the woven bar.

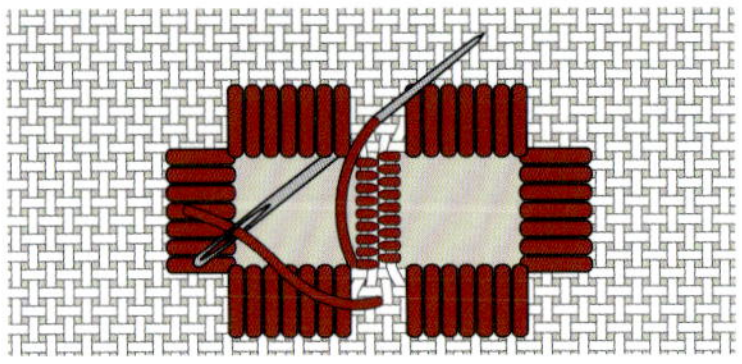

2 Pull the needle through and leave the stitch curving gently. Inserting in the left quadrant again, bring the needle out in the centre of the upper woven square again.

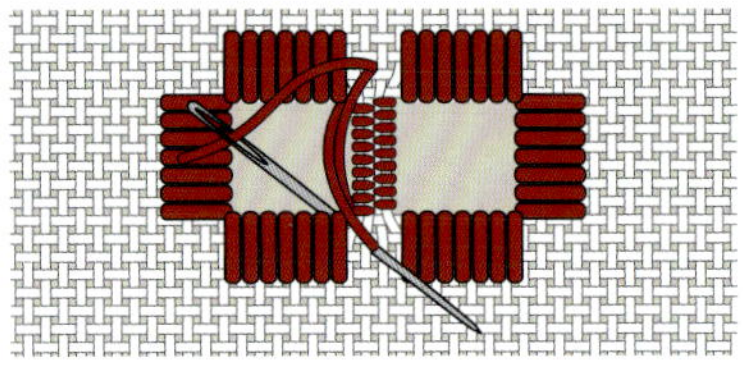

3 Pull the needle through with the same tension as before. Inserting in the left quadrant again, bring the needle out below the woven bar again, in the same hole.

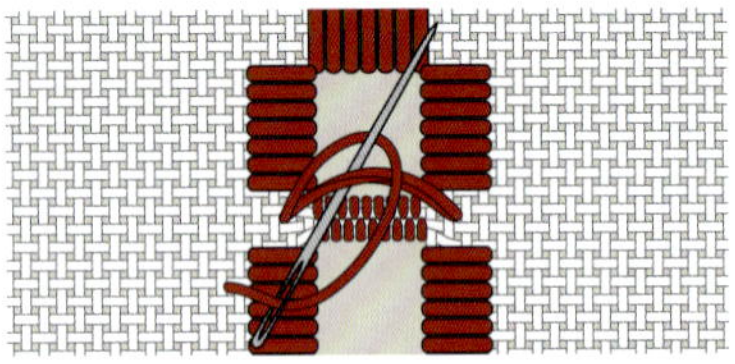

4 Turn the work 90° clockwise. From below, insert the needle under the three stitches. Take the thread behind the needle point from left to right.

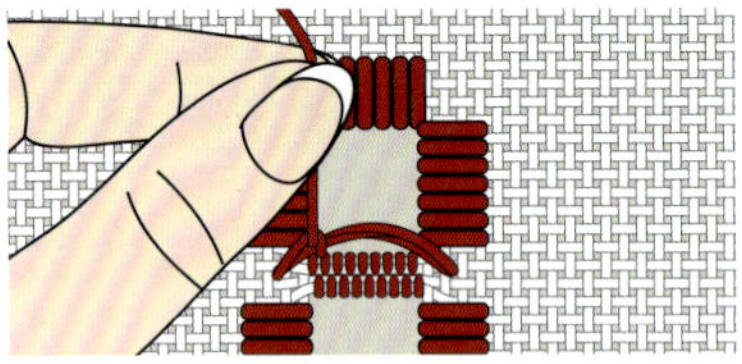

5 Pull the needle through and tighten the stitch snugly around the curved stitches and against the satin stitch.

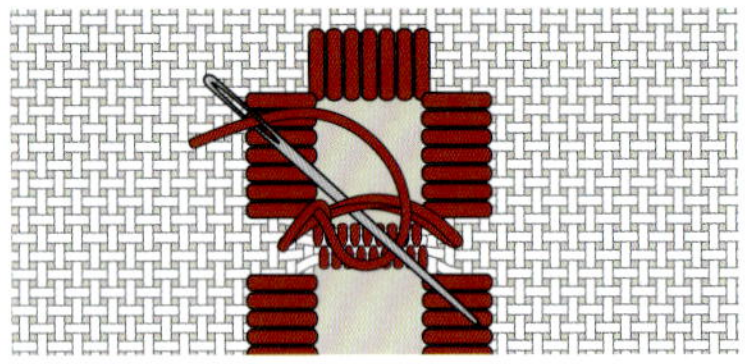

6 Insert the needle under the arc, from above. Take the thread under the needle from left to right.

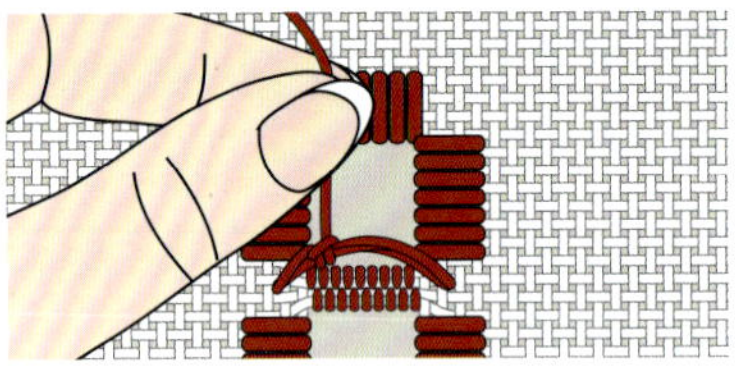

7 Pull the needle through and up to tighten the stitch to sit snugly against the previous stitch.

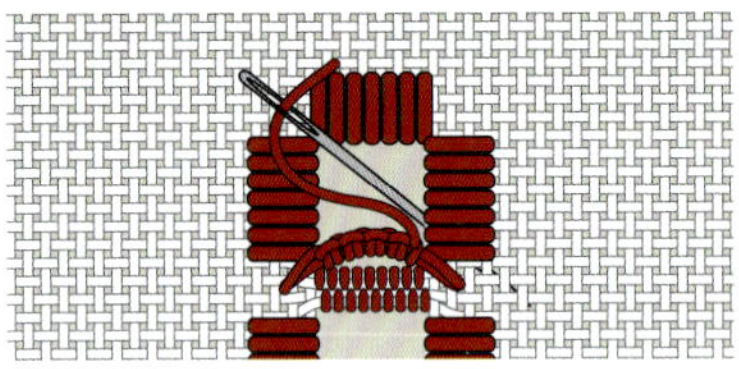

8 Cycle through Steps 4 to 7 to fill the arc. Finish by taking the needle to the back above the arc.

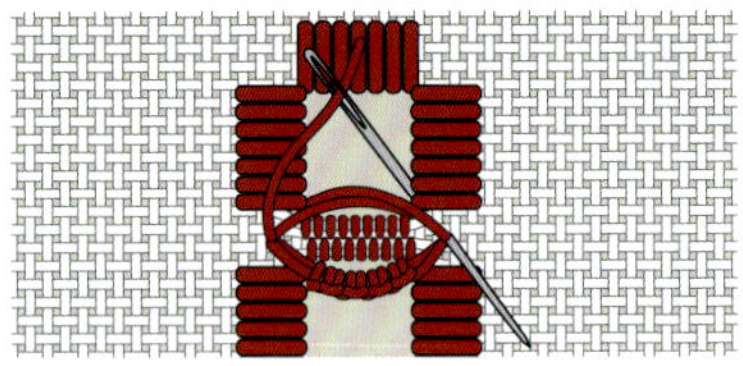

9 Bring the needle out at the end of the arc. Turn the work 180°. Make three stitches back and forth along the upper side.

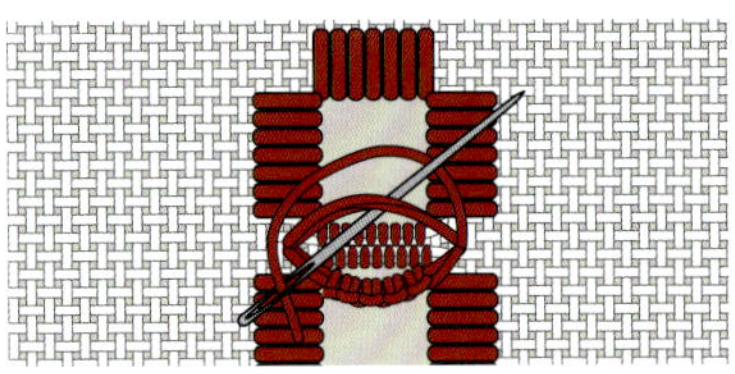

10 From below, insert the needle under the arc. Take the thread behind the needle point from right to left.

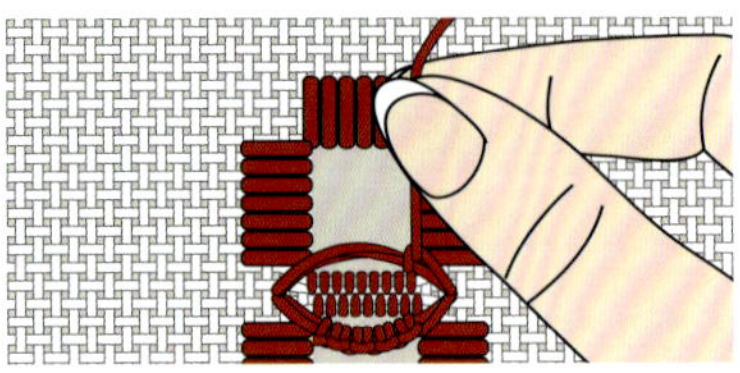

11 Pull the needle through. Tighten the stitch snugly around the arc and against the satin stitch.

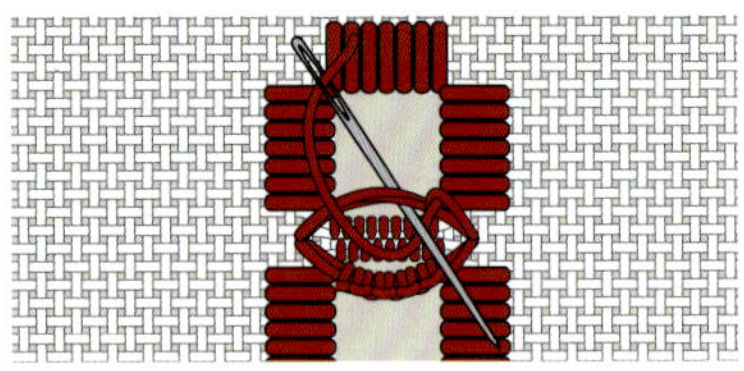

12 Insert the needle under the arc, from above. Take the thread under the needle from right to left.

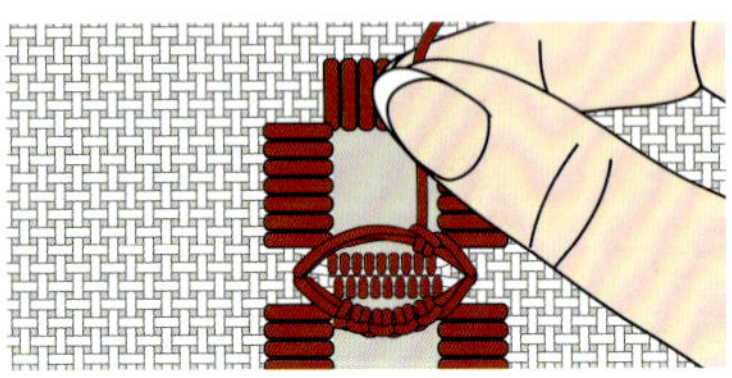

13 Pull the needle through and up to tighten the stitch to sit snugly against the previous stitch.

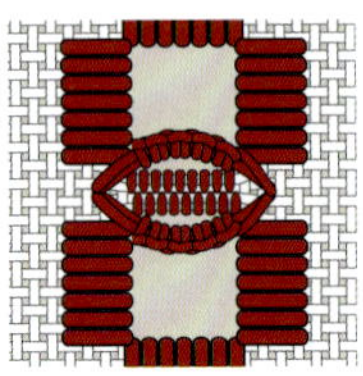

14 Cycle through Steps 10 to 13 to fill the arc. Finish by taking the needle to the back above the arc.

shuttle stitch

This filling uses up and down buttonhole stitch which, in tatting, is formed by a shuttle. It could be substituted in place of any buttonhole stitching.

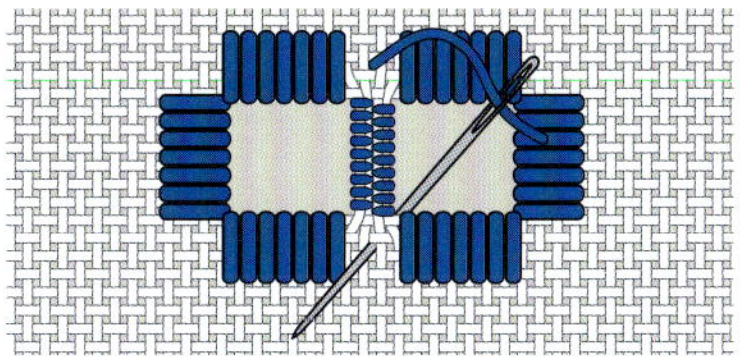

1 Work the bar. Bring the needle out in the centre of the woven square above the bar. Insert the needle in the right quadrant, and bring it out two threads below the woven bar.

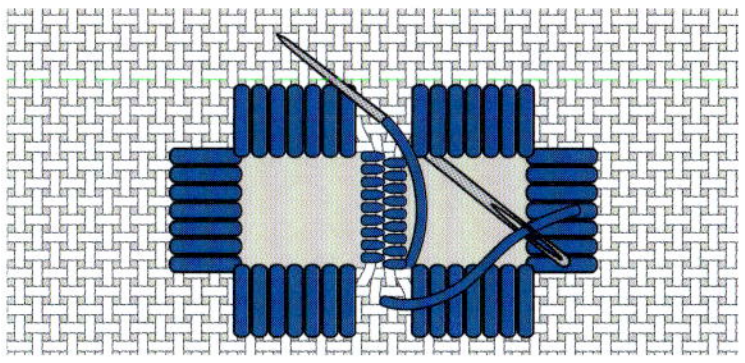

2 Pull the needle through and leave the stitch curving gently. Inserting in the right quadrant again, bring the needle out in the centre of the upper woven square again.

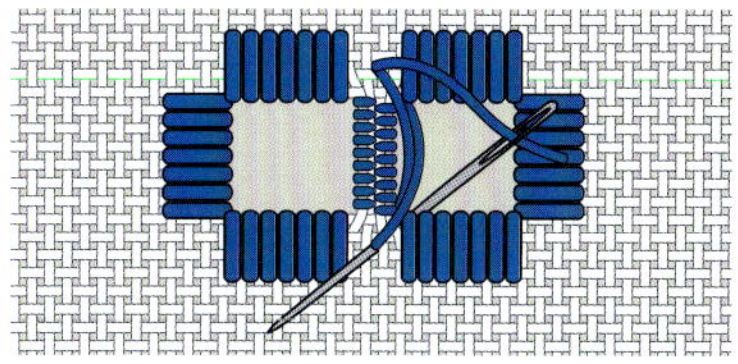

3 Pull the needle through with the same tension as before. Inserting in the right quadrant again, bring the needle out below the woven bar again, in the same hole.

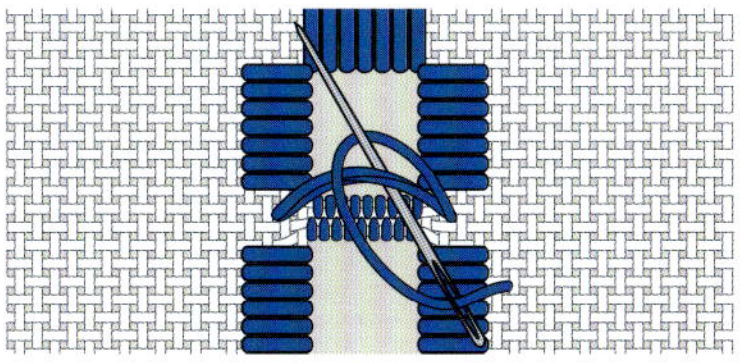

4 Turn the work 90° anticlockwise. From below, insert the needle under the three stitches. Take the thread under the needle point from the right.

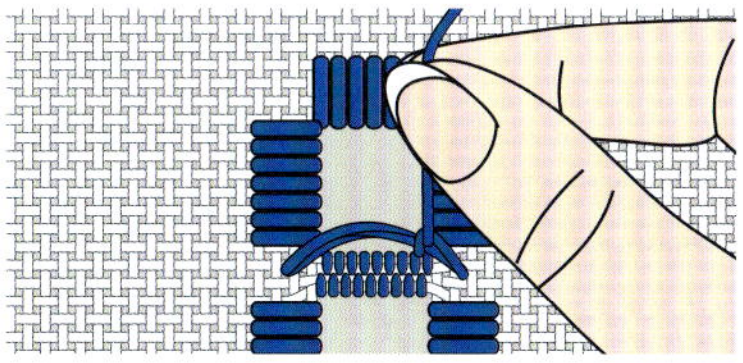

5 Pull the needle through and tighten the stitch snugly around the curved stitches and against the satin stitch.

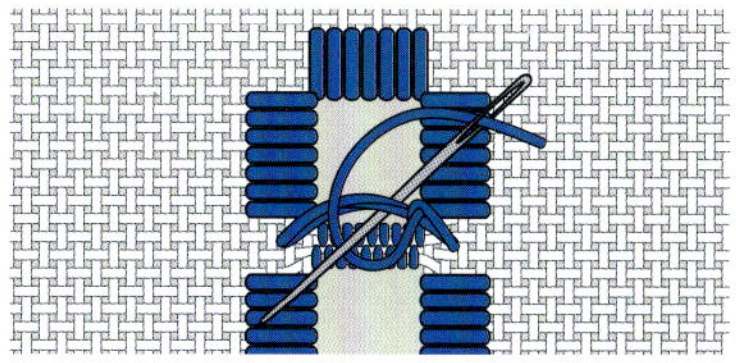

6 Insert the needle under the arc, from above. Take the thread under the needle from right to left.

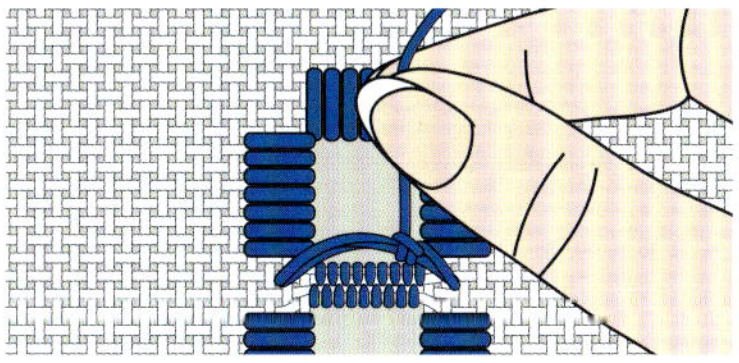

7 Pull the needle through and tighten the stitch to sit snugly against the previous stitch.

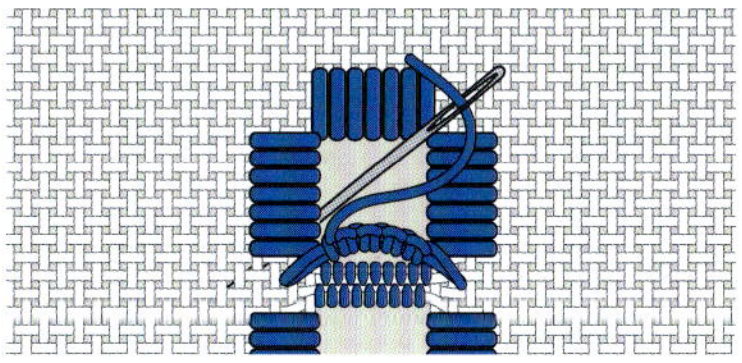

8 Cycle through Steps 4 to 7 to fill the arc. Finish by taking the needle to the back above the arc.

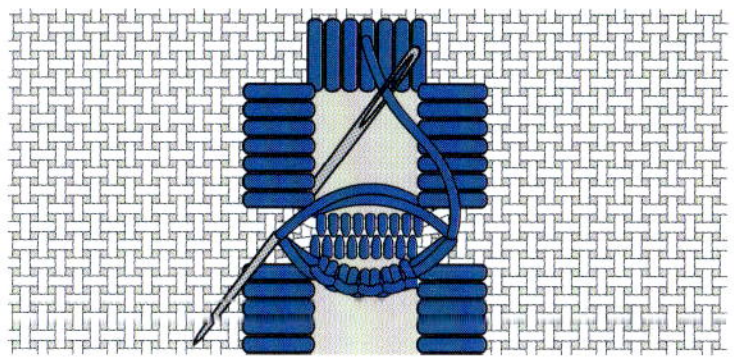

9 Bring the needle out at the end of the arc. Turn the work 180°. Make three stitches back and forth along the upper side.

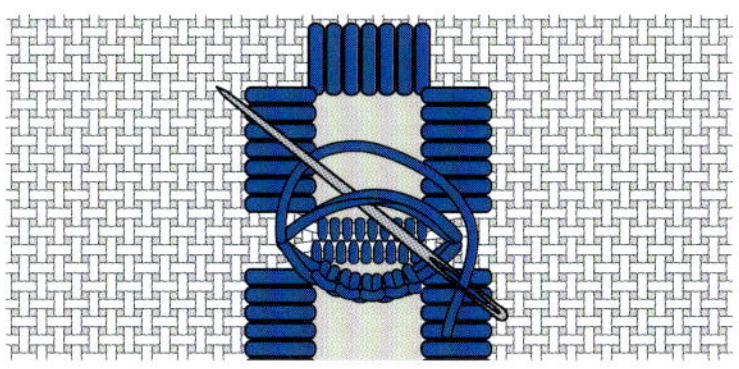

10 From below, insert the needle under the arc. Take the thread behind the needle point from left to right.

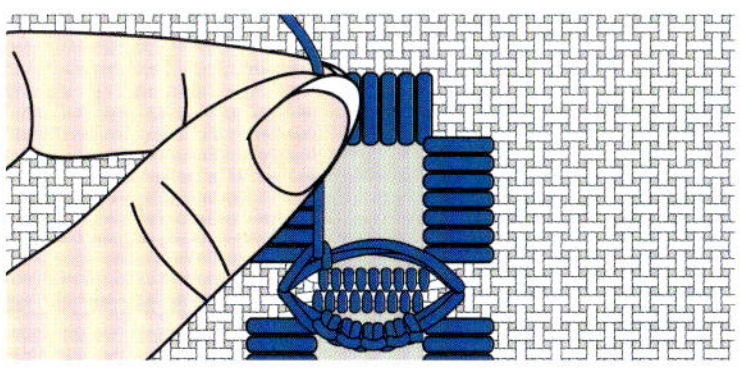

11 Pull the needle through. Tighten the stitch snugly around the arc and against the satin stitch.

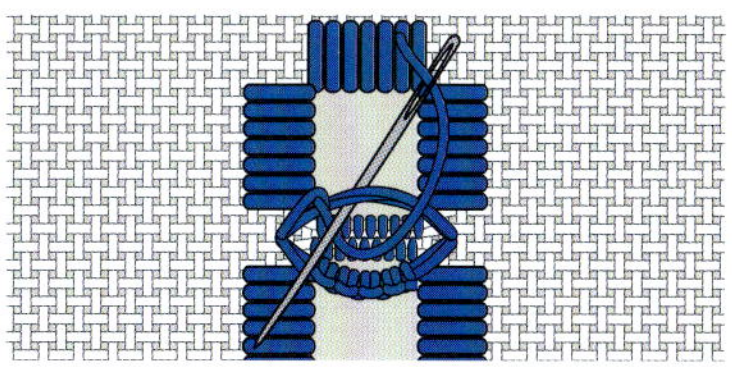

12 Insert the needle under the arc, from above. Take the thread under the needle from left to right.

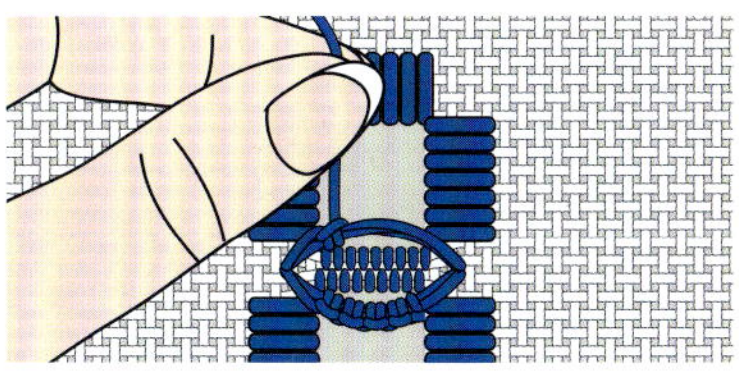

13 Pull the needle through and up to tighten the stitch to sit snugly against the previous stitch.

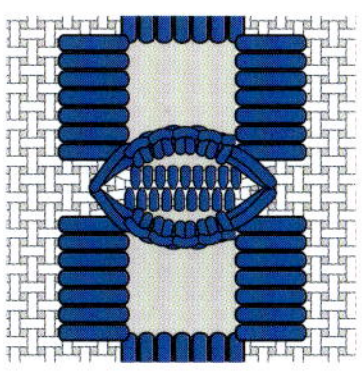

14 Cycle through Steps 10 to 13 to fill the arc. Finish by taking the needle to the back above the arc.

L

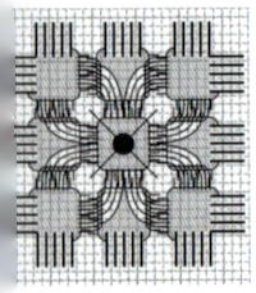

CONTEMPORARY

blanket stitch flower

This motif has many steps, but with care it is not hard to achieve good results.

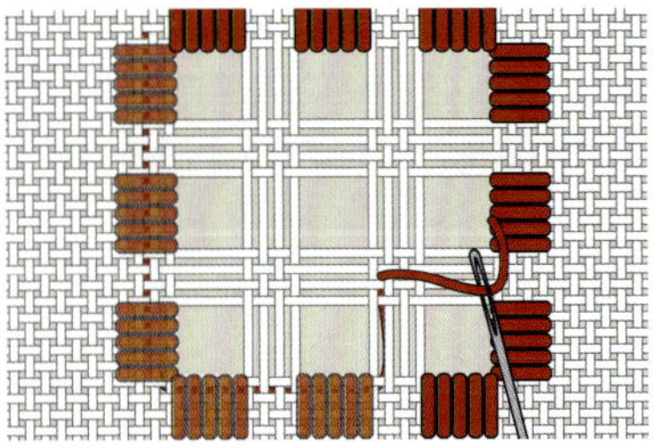

1 Prepare the cutwork area as shown. Run the thread under the back of the satin stitch and bring it out in the bottom right woven square, two threads up and one from the left.

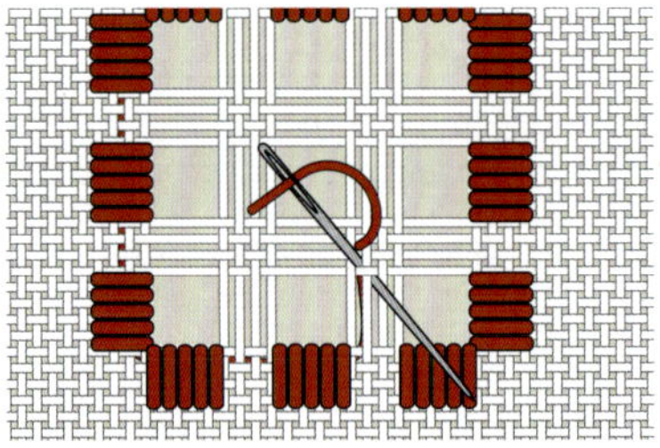

2 Insert the needle one thread down and bring it out in the centre of the bar that extends down from the woven square.

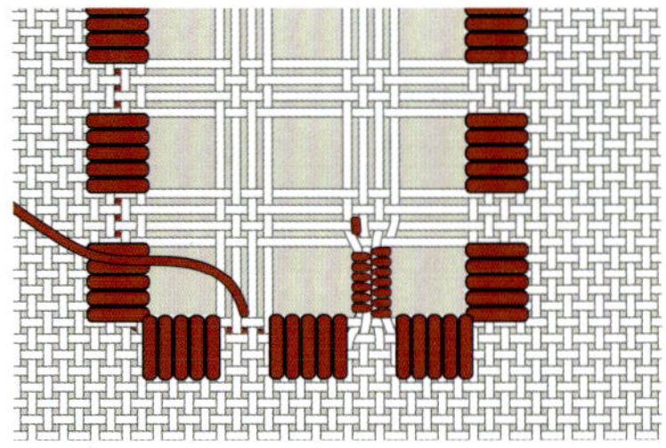

3 Weave the bar. Take the needle under the back of the satin stitch, on the back, and bring it out in the centre of the next bar to the left.

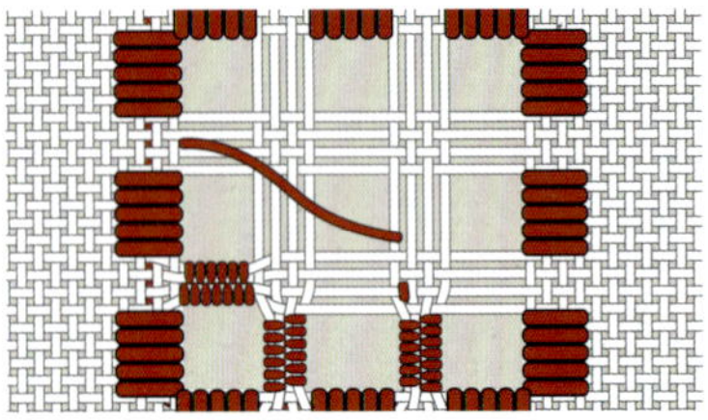

4 Work the next two bars in the bottom left corner. Take the needle through the back of the intervening satin stitch and bring it out ready to start the next bar.

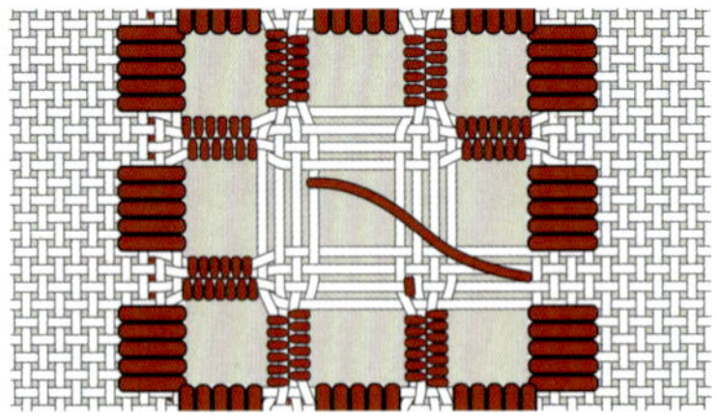

5 Work the next two corners similarly. Finish the thread and start a new, long one. Bring the needle out ready to work the bar.

❶ *A new, long thread will mean there is enough to complete the motif.*

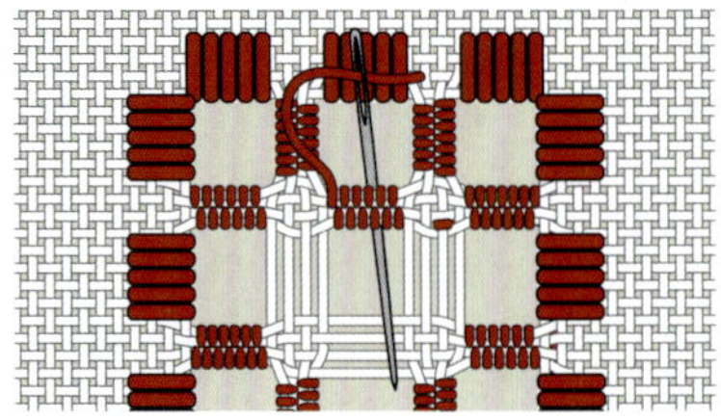

6 Work the bar and then the one between it and the previous bar. Turn the work 90° anticlockwise. To complete the bar, pass the needle behind the bar, from above.

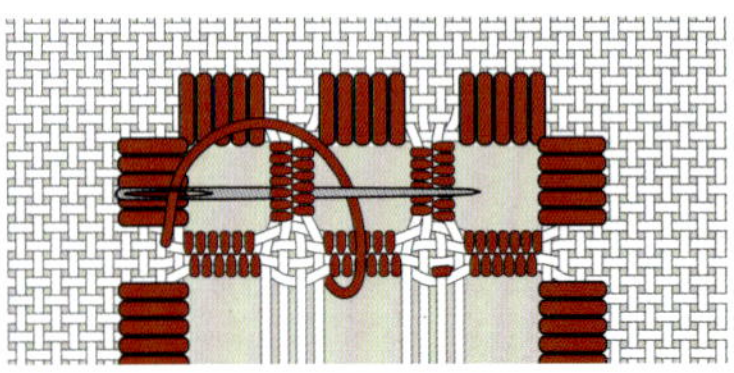

7 From the left, insert the needle under the bar that is up and left from the previous bar. Take the needle over the working thread.

❶ *This creates a blanket stitch.*

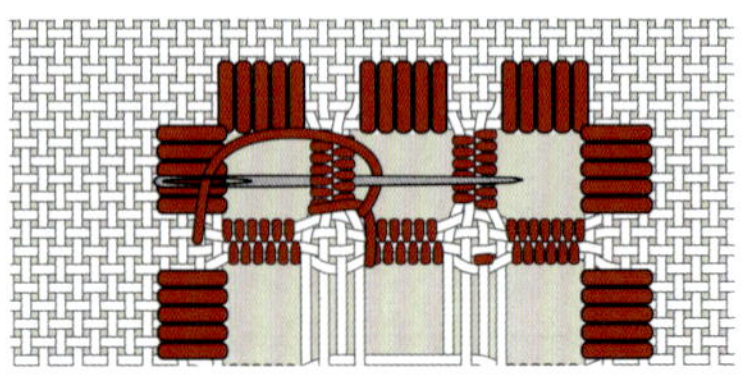

8 Pull the needle through. Tighten the stitch snugly around the intersection of the bars. Moving up, slide the needle under the bar again, taking the needle over the working thread.

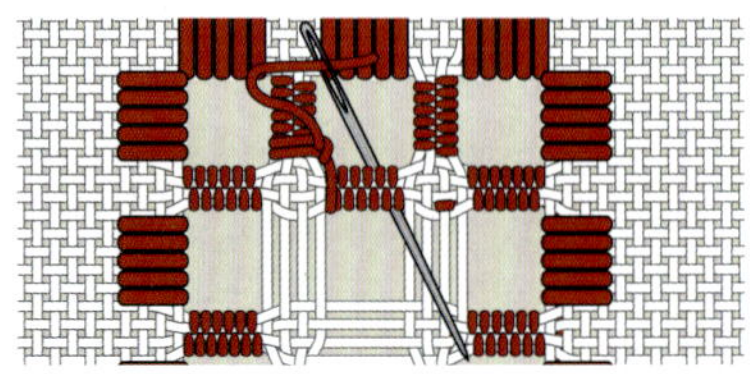

9 Tighten the stitch. From above, slide the needle under the horizontal bar.

❶ *There are two stitches on the vertical bar, and one on the horizontal bar.*

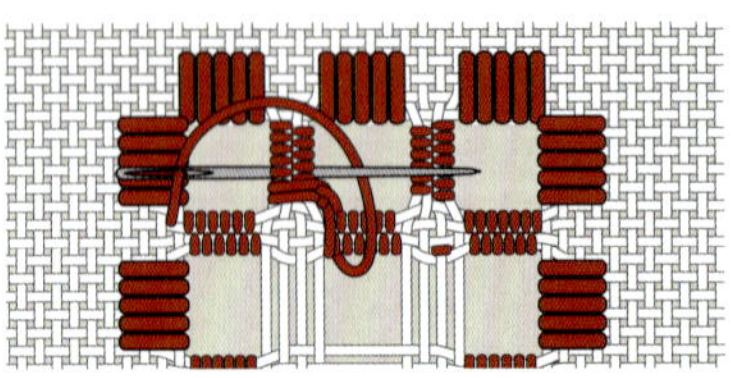

10 From the left, slide the needle under the vertical bar. Take the needle over the working thread.

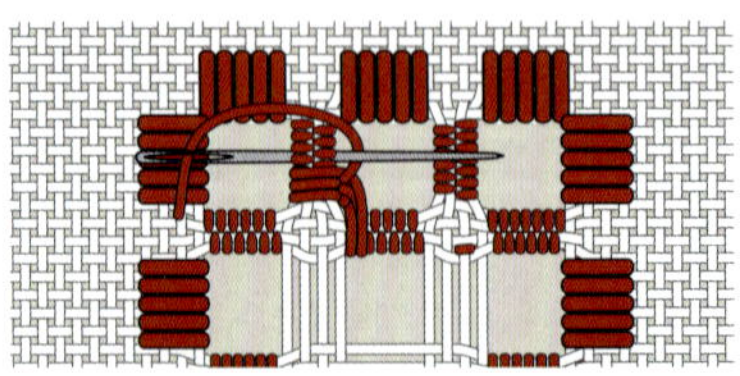

11 Tighten the stitch against the previous one. Moving up, slide the needle under the bar from the left. Take the needle over the working thread.

❶ *Do not allow the stitches to overlap. They should sit next to each other.*

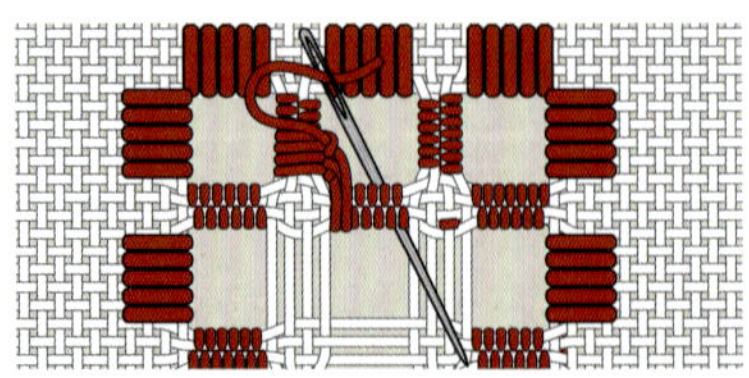

12 Tighten the stitch. From above, slide the needle under the horizontal bar.

❶ *You have four stitches on the vertical bar, and two on the horizontal bar i.e. twice as many on the vertical bar as the horizontal one.*

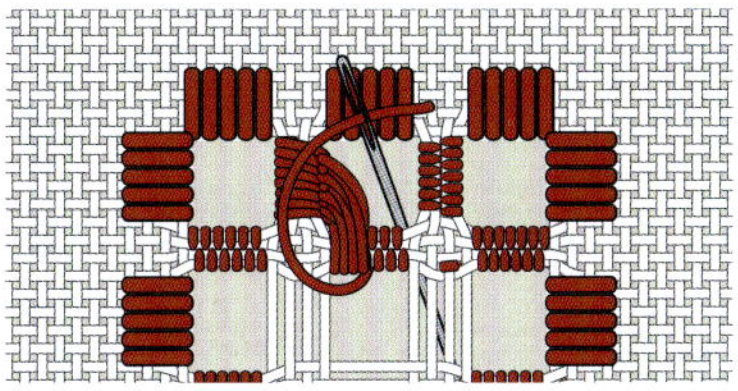

13 Cycle through Steps 10 to 12 to fill the vertical bar and half the horizontal bar. Take the needle to the back above the horizontal bar.

! *There will likely be six to eight stitches on the vertical, and three to four on the horizontal, plus the final one.*

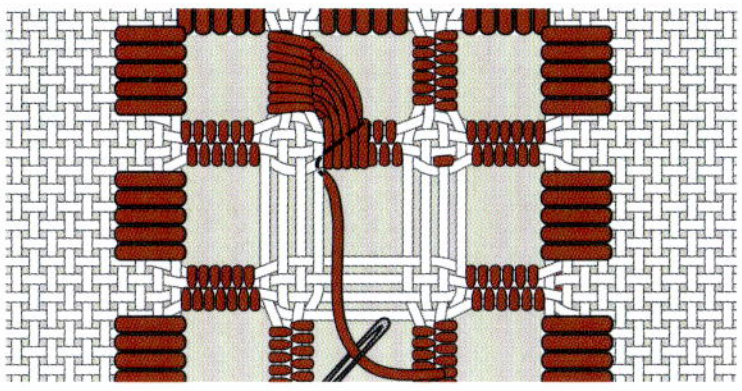

14 Pull the last stitch in snug against the previous stitch. On the back, run the needle through the back of the blanket stitches on the horizontal bar. Bring it out in the corner of the central open square.

! *Use consistent tension for all stitches.*

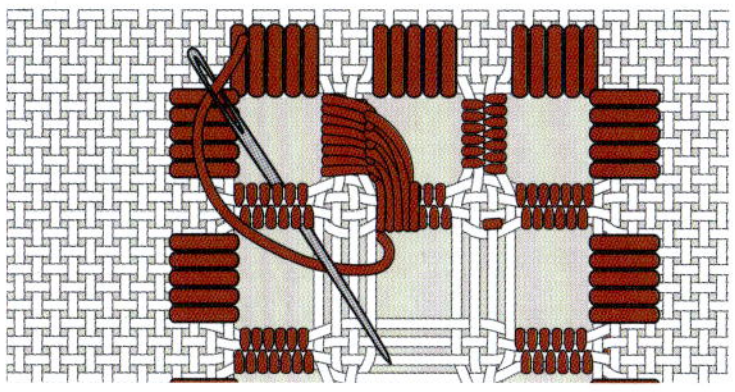

15 From above, insert the needle under the horizontal bar to the left of the one you were previously working on. Take the needle over the working thread.

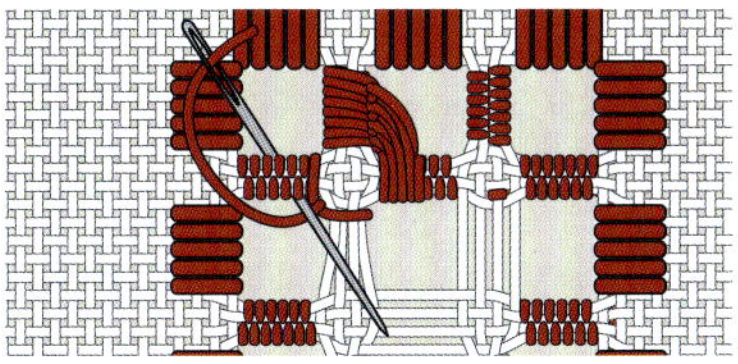

16 Pull the needle through and tighten the stitch snugly around the intersection of the bars. Moving left, slide the needle under the bar again, taking it over the working thread.

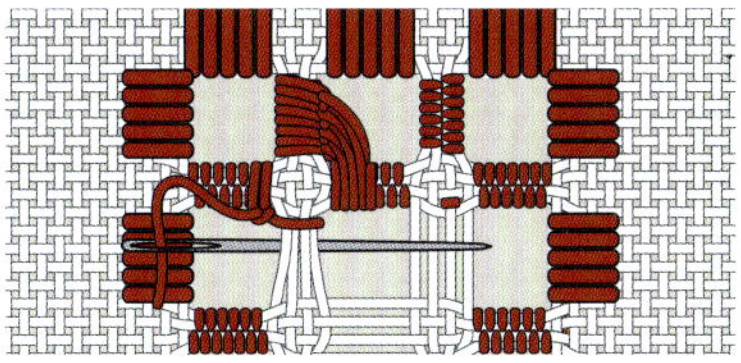

17 Tighten the stitch. From the left, slide the needle under the vertical bar.

! *You have two stitches on the horizontal bar, and one on the vertical.*

18 Cycle through Steps 15 to 17 to fill the horizontal bar, and half the vertical bar. From the left, slide the needle under the bar's left two threads.

! *Work the same quantity of stitches.*

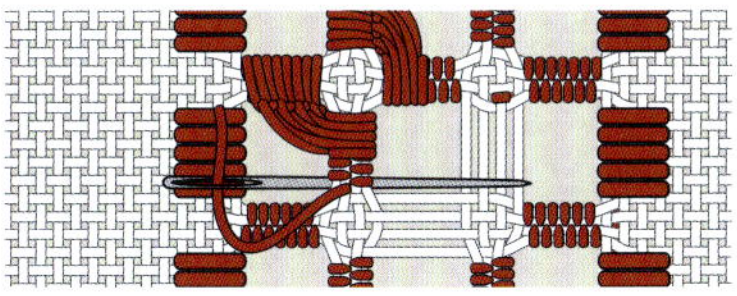

19 Weave the rest of the bar. Finish with a stitch on the left, and bring the needle out in the central open square.

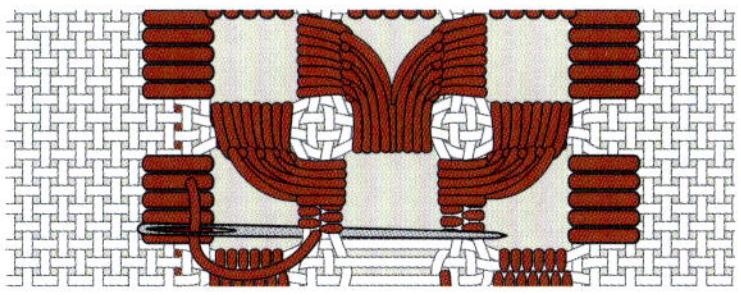

20 Repeat Steps 7 to 19 to work two petals in this corner. Turn the work as required. Bring the needle out in the central open square.

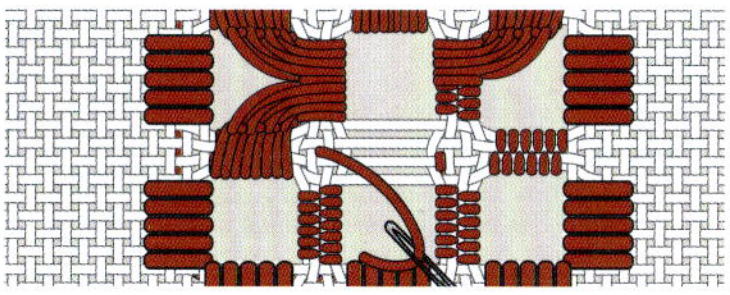

21 Work another petal (Steps 7 to 14). Bring the needle out in the centre of the adjacent woven square.

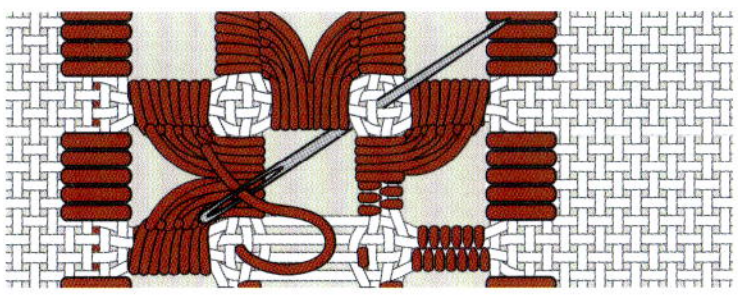

22 Pull the needle through. Bring the needle out in the centre of the opposite woven square.

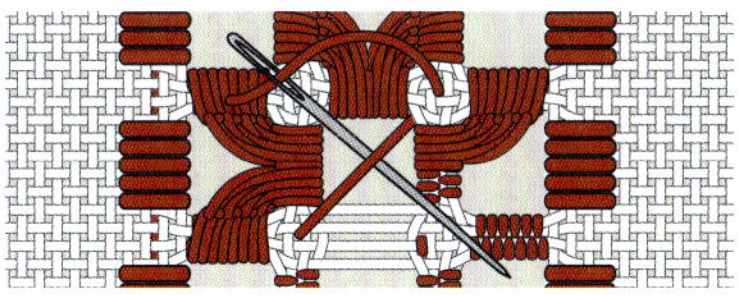

23 Pull the needle through. From above left, slide the needle under the diagonal stitch.

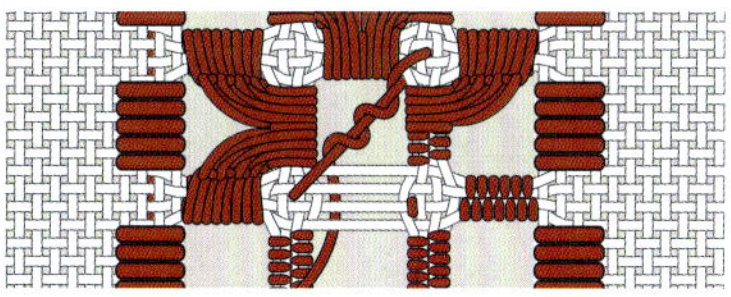

24 Slide the needle under the diagonal again. Take it under the diagonal and the empty bar. Bring it out in the central open square at the base.

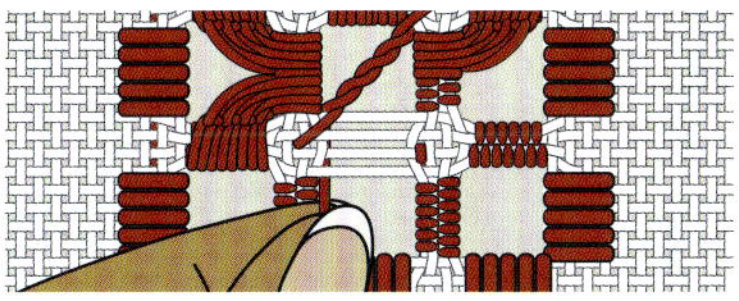

25 Pull the thread downward to intertwine the stitches.

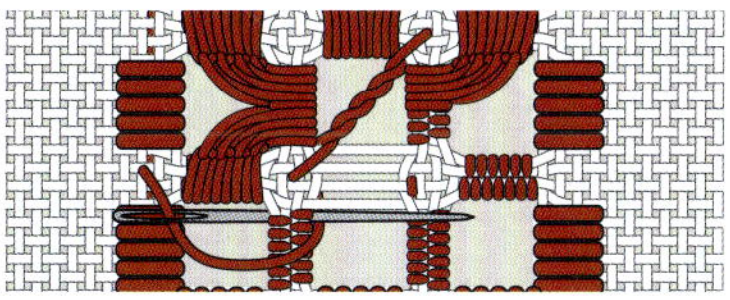

26 From the left, insert the needle under the vertical bar and take the needle over the working thread.

! *This petal starts with the second of the two usual stitches, as following the usual pattern, it would sit badly.*

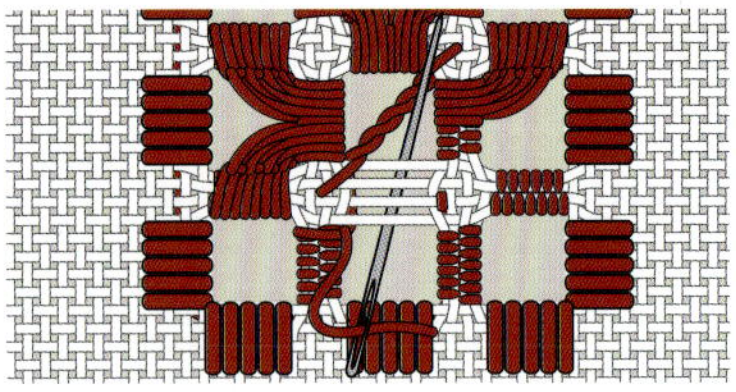

27 Pull the needle through to tighten the stitch snugly against the intersection. Slide the needle under the horizontal stitch, from below.

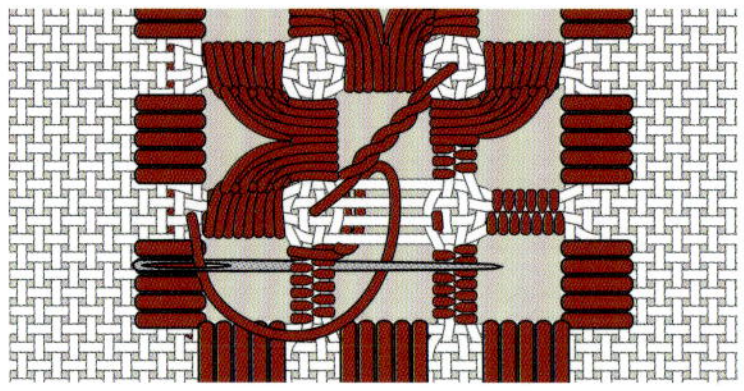

28 From the left, slide the needle under the vertical bar. Take the needle over the working thread.

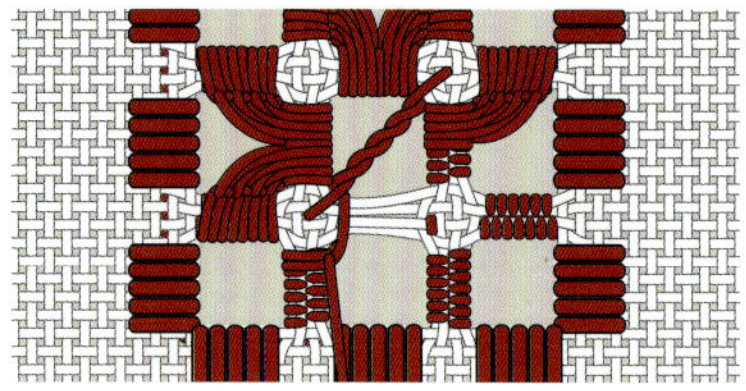

29 Unlike previous petals there is no previous stitch on the horizontal bar to pull in snug against, so pull the stitch in snug against the intersection.

30 Work the rest of petal, then the rest of the bar. Work another petal against the closest side of the next intersection. Bring the needle out in the centre of the woven square.

31 Turn the work 90° clockwise. Take the needle over the diagonal stitch and bring it out in the centre of the opposite woven square.

32 Pull the needle through so the stitch sits straight. From above, slide the needle under the diagonal stitch.

33 From above, slide the needle under the crossing stitches.

34 Pull the needle to intertwine the stitches. Moving in a clockwise direction, pass the needle over the first diagonal and under the next.

35 Turn the work 180°. Pass the needle over the next diagonal and under the next.

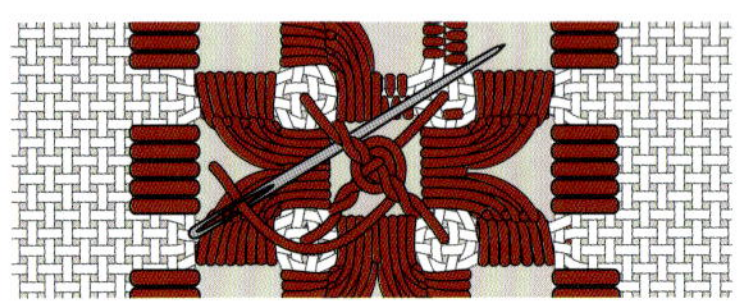

36 With gentle tension, circle the centre again, going over or under each spoke, in the same way as before.

❶ *Be careful not to pull too tight, as the circling stitches are quite unstable.*

37 Turn the work 180°. From above, slide the needle under the spoke with no twists.

38 Turn the work 90° anticlockwise. Take the needle to the back left of the spoke. Bring it out to the right of the bar.

39 Pull to intertwine the stitches. Work a final petal using the method in Steps 27 to 30. To complete the last stitch, take the needle to the back.

40 On the back, run the thread through the back of the first petal and then through the back of the satin stitch, or under the back of the stitching around the centre square.

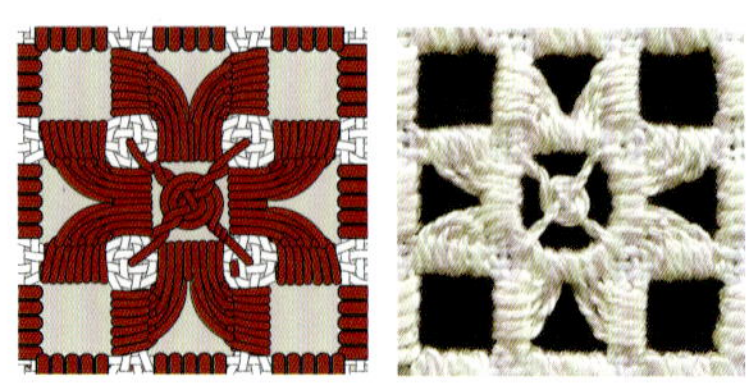

41 The completed blanket stitch flower.

blanket stitch flower

This impressive looking stitch has many steps, however, it is not difficult to achieve good results.

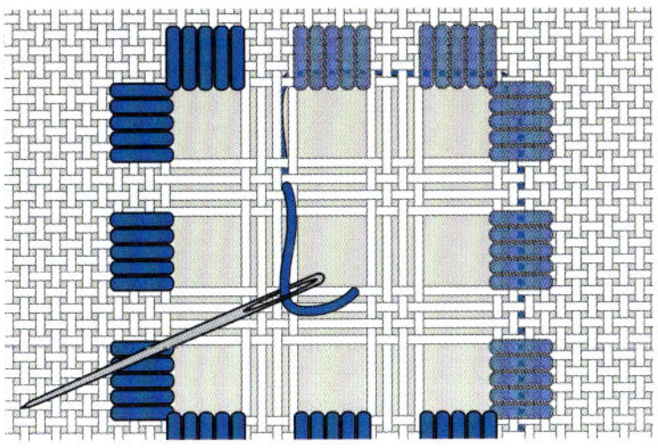

1 Prepare the cutwork area as shown. Run the thread under the back of the satin stitch and bring it out in the top left woven square, two threads down and one from the right.

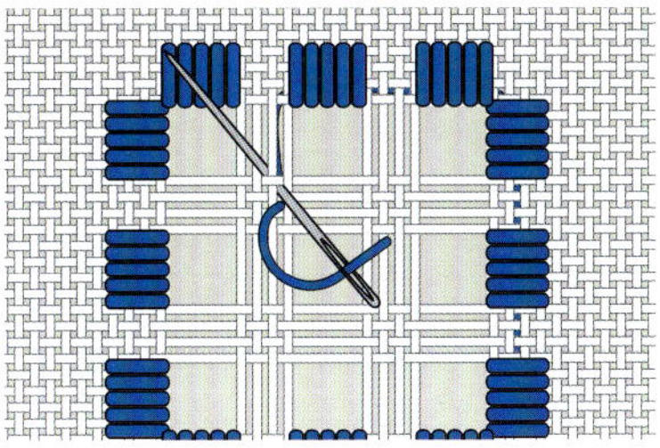

2 Insert the needle one thread up and bring it out in the centre of the bar that extends upward from the woven square.

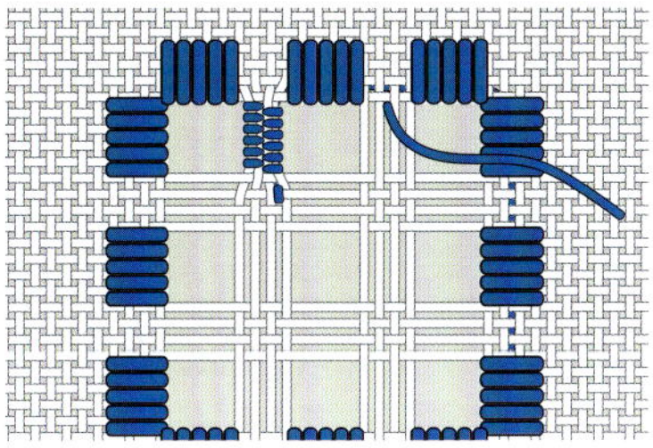

3 Weave the bar. Take the needle under the back of the satin stitch, on the back, and bring it out in the centre of the next bar to the right.

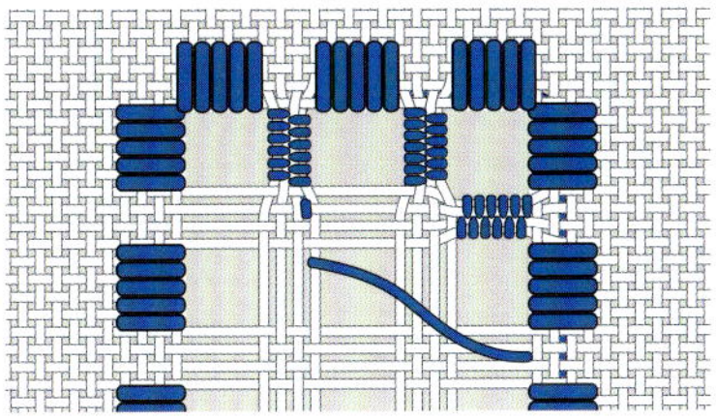

4 Work the next two bars in the top right corner. Take the needle through the back of the intervening satin stitch and bring it out ready to start the next bar.

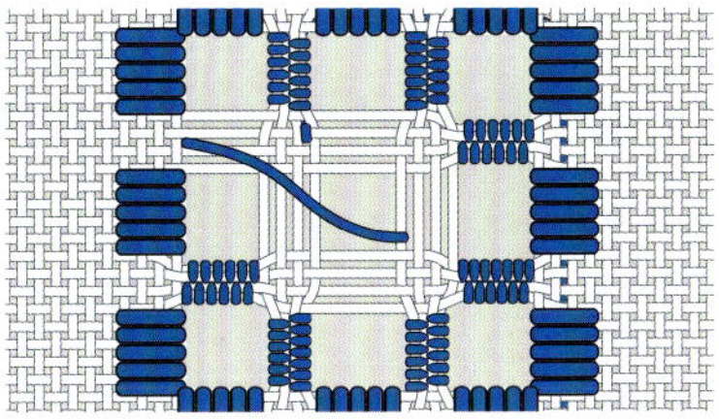

5 Work the next two corners similarly. Finish the thread and start a new, long one. Bring the needle out ready to work the bar.

❶ *A new, long thread will mean there is enough to complete the motif.*

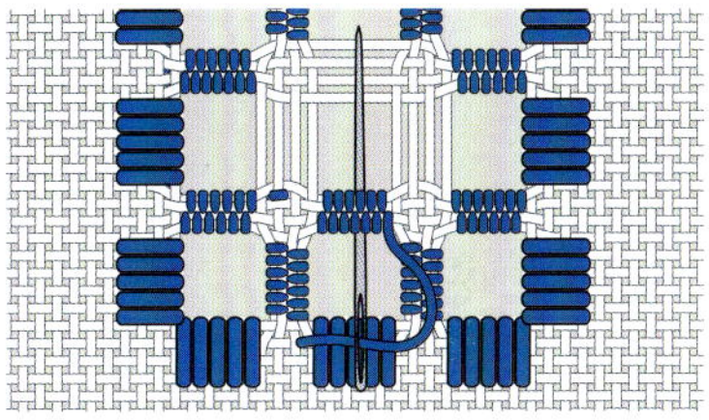

6 Work the bar and then the one between it and the previous bar. Turn the work 90° anticlockwise. To complete the bar, pass the needle behind the bar, from below.

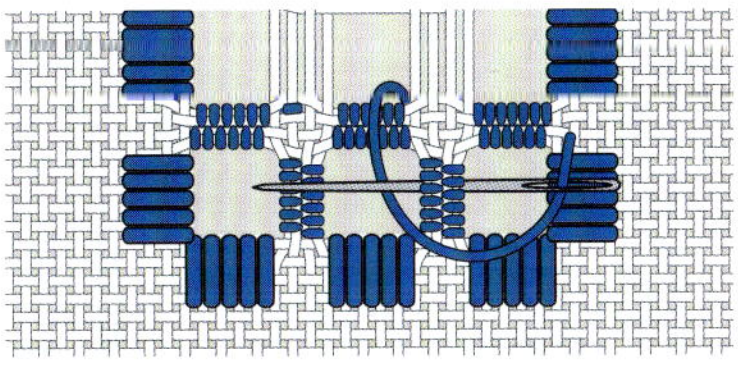

7 From the right, insert the needle under the bar that is down and right from the previous bar. Take the needle over the working thread.

❶ *This creates a blanket stitch.*

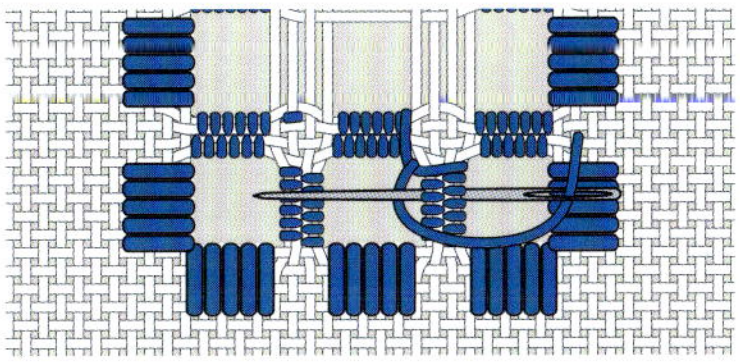

8 Pull the needle through. Tighten the stitch snugly around the intersection of the bars. Moving down, slide the needle under the bar again, taking the needle over the working thread.

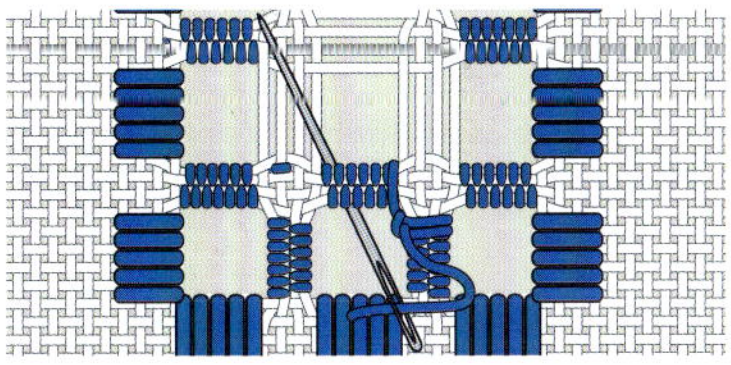

9 Tighten the stitch. From below, slide the needle under the horizontal bar.

❶ *You have two stitches on the vertical bar, and one on the horizontal bar.*

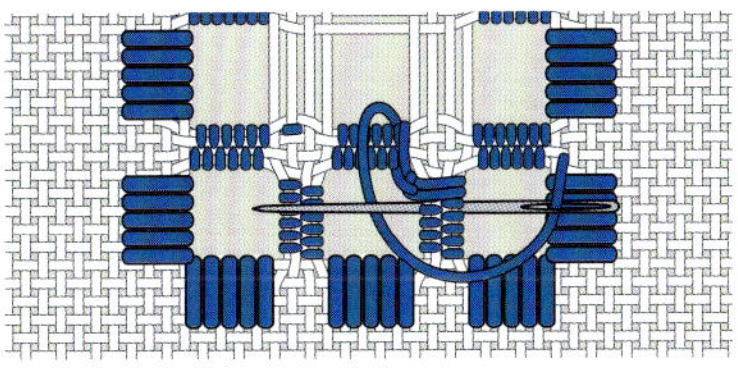

10 From the right, slide the needle under the vertical bar. Take the needle over the working thread.

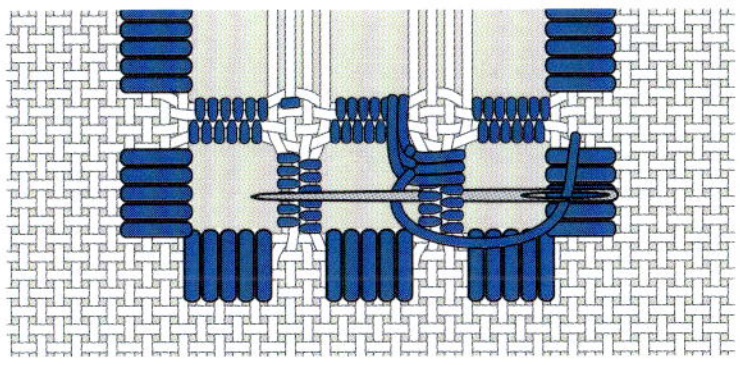

11 Tighten the stitch against the previous one. Moving down, slide the needle under the bar from the right. Take the needle over the working thread.

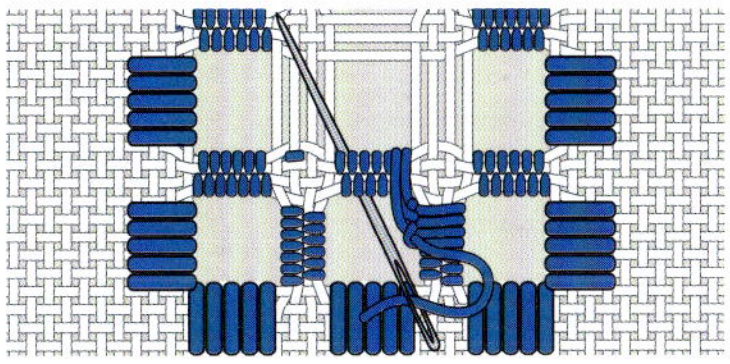

12 Tighten the stitch. From below, slide the needle under the horizontal bar.

❶ *You have four stitches on the vertical bar, and two on the horizontal bar i.e. twice as many on the vertical bar as the horizontal one.*

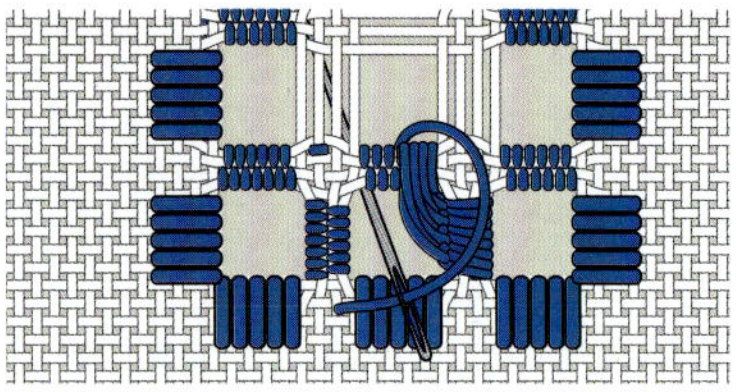

13 Cycle through Steps 10 to 12 to fill the vertical bar, and half the horizontal bar. Take the needle to the back below the horizontal bar.

❶ *There will likely be six to eight stitches on the vertical, and three to four on the horizontal, plus the final one.*

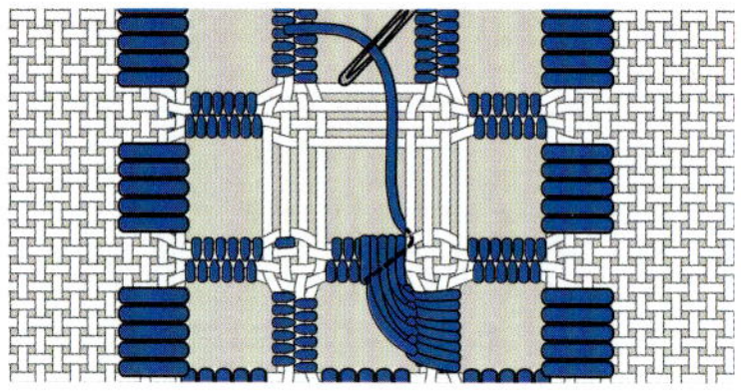

14 Pull the last stitch in snug against the previous stitch. On the back, run the needle through the back of the blanket stitches on the horizontal bar. Bring the needle out in the corner of the central open square.

❶ *Use consistent tension for all stitches.*

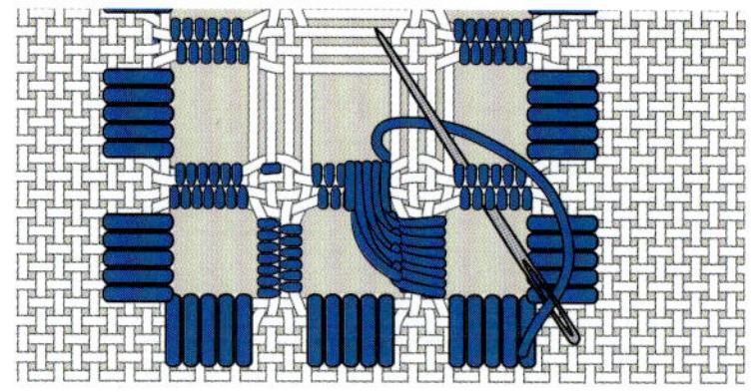

15 From below, insert the needle under the horizontal bar to the right of the one you were previously working on. Take the needle over the working thread.

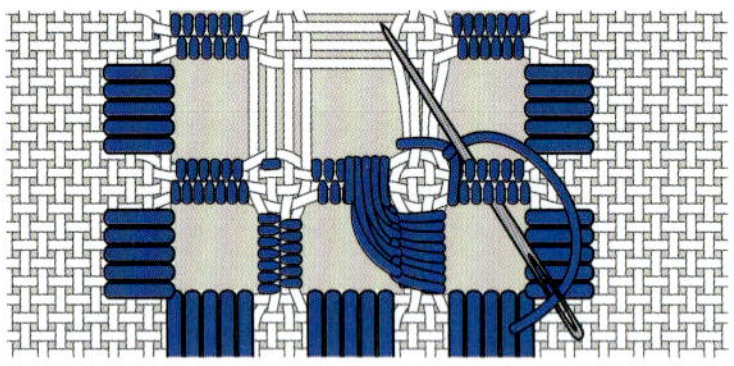

16 Pull the needle through and tighten the stitch snugly around the intersection of the bars. Moving right, slide the needle under the bar again, taking it over the working thread.

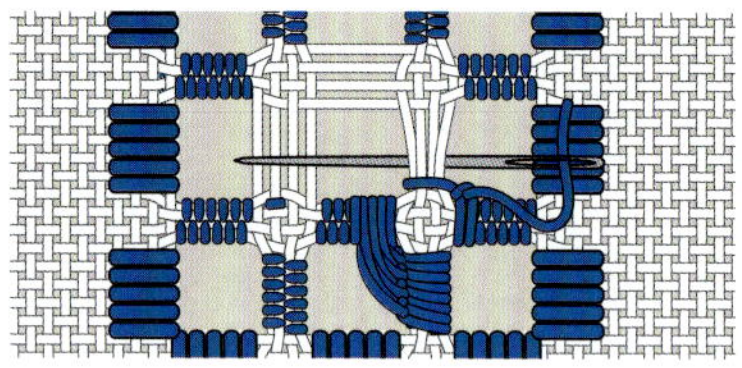

17 Tighten the stitch. From the right, slide the needle under the vertical bar.

❶ *You have two stitches on the horizontal bar, and one on the vertical.*

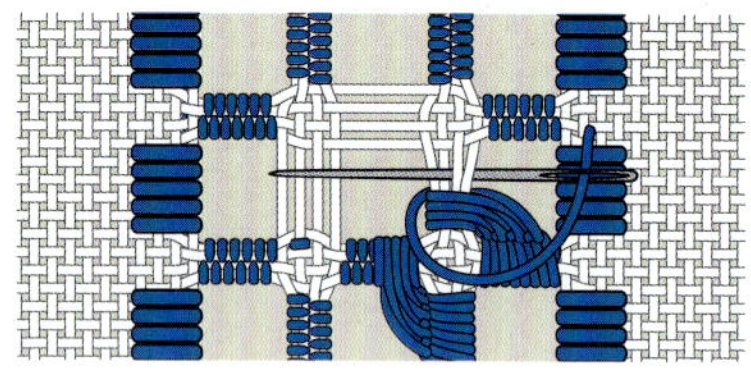

18 Cycle through Steps 15 to 17 to fill the horizontal bar, and half the vertical bar. From the right, slide the needle under the bar's right two threads.

❶ *Work the same quantity of stitches.*

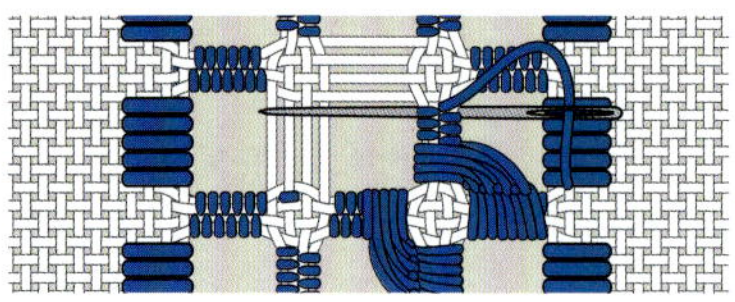

19 Weave the rest of the bar. Finish with a stitch on the right, and bring the needle out in the central open square.

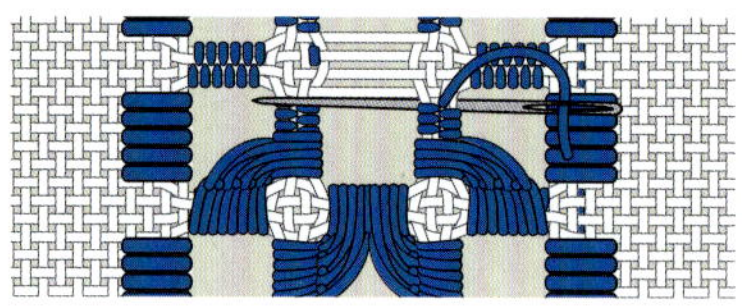

20 Repeat Steps 7 to 19 to work two petals in this corner. Turn the work as required. Bring the needle out in the central open square.

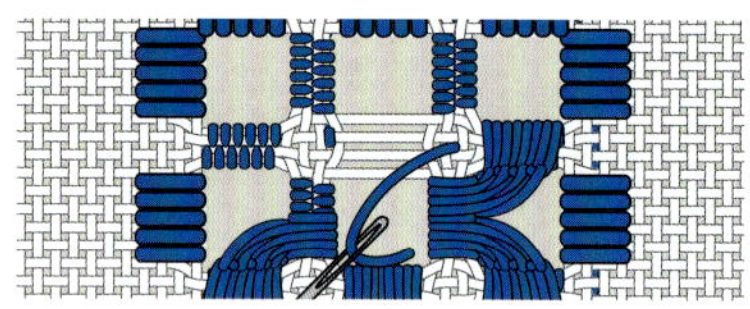

21 Work another petal (Steps 7 to 14). Bring the needle out in the centre of the adjacent woven square.

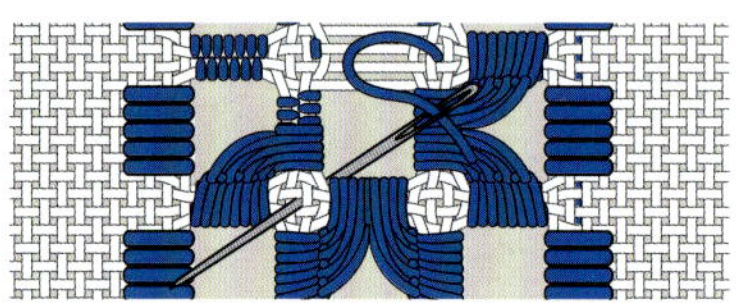

22 Pull the needle through. Bring the needle out in the centre of the opposite woven square.

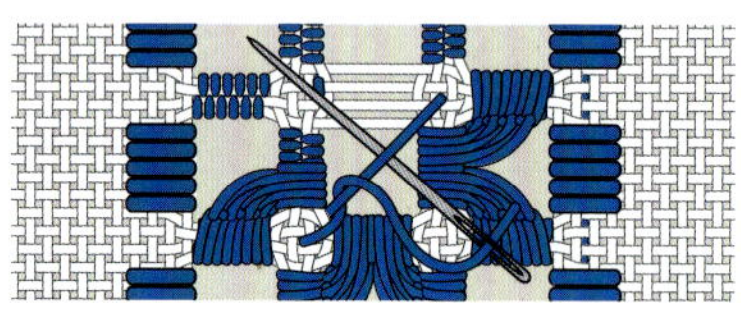

23 Pull the needle through. From below right, slide the needle under the diagonal stitch.

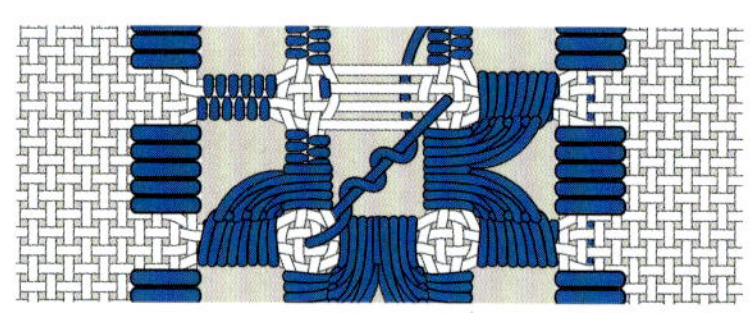

24 Slide the needle under the diagonal again. Take it under the diagonal and the empty bar. Bring it out in the central open square at the top.

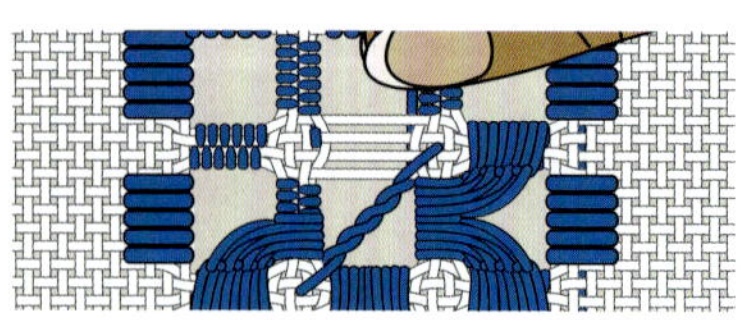

25 Pull the thread upward to intertwine the stitches

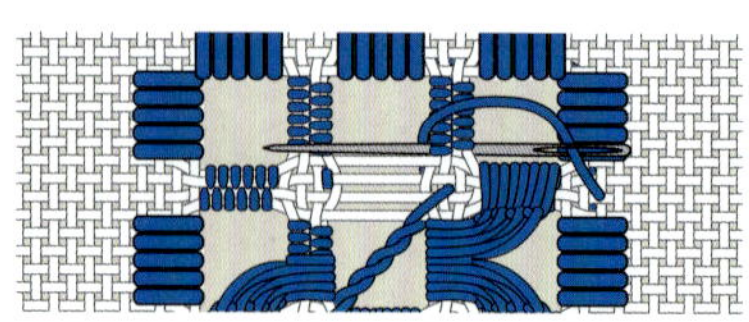

26 From the right, insert the needle under the vertical bar and take the needle over the working thread.

❶ *This petal starts with the second of the two usual stitches, as following the usual pattern, it would sit badly.*

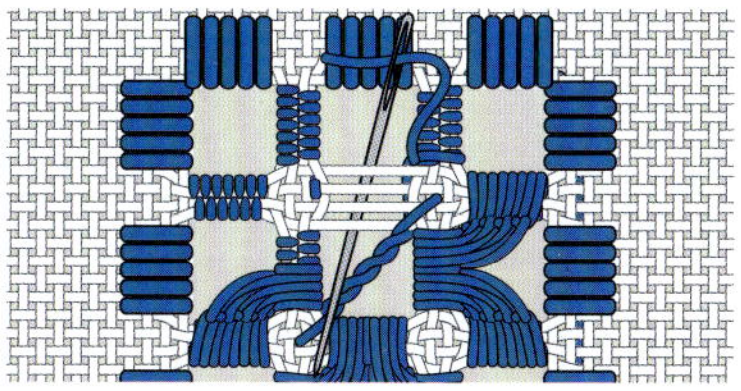

27 Pull the needle through to tighten the stitch snugly against the intersection. Slide the needle under the horizontal stitch, from above.

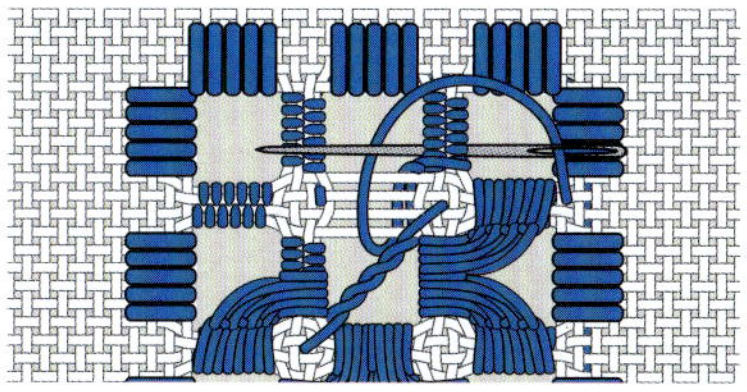

28 From the right, slide the needle under the vertical bar. Take the needle over the working thread.

29 Unlike previous petals there is no previous stitch on the horizontal bar to pull in snug against, so pull the stitch in snug against the intersection.

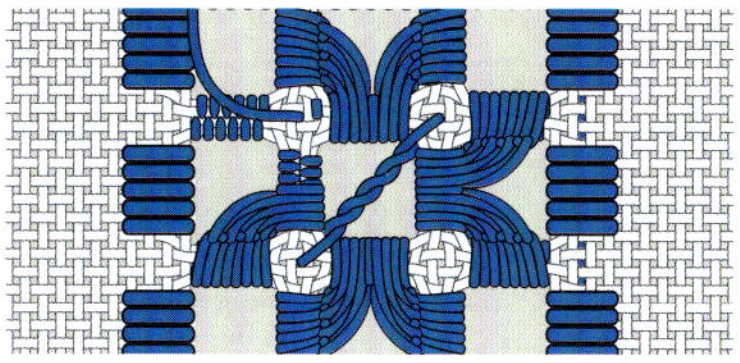

30 Work the rest of petal, then the rest of the bar. Work another petal against the closest side of the next intersection. Bring the needle out in the centre of the woven square.

31 Turn the work 90° clockwise. Take the needle over the diagonal stitch and bring it out in the centre of the opposite woven square.

32 Pull the needle through so the stitch sits straight. From below, slide the needle under the diagonal stitch.

33 From below, slide the needle under the crossing stitches.

34 Pull the needle to intertwine the stitches. Moving in a clockwise direction, pass the needle over the first diagonal and under the next.

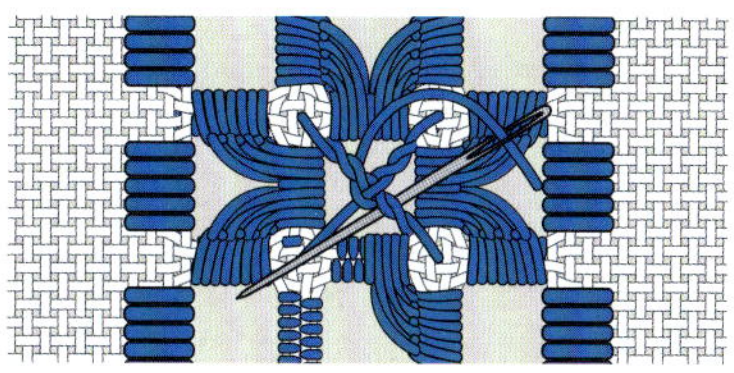

35 Turn the work 180°. Pass the needle over the next diagonal and under the next.

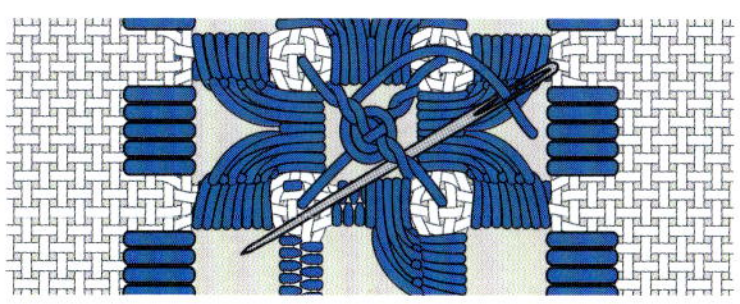

36 With gentle tension, circle the centre again, going over or under each spoke, in the same way as before.

! *Be careful not to pull too tight, as the circling stitches are quite unstable.*

37 Turn the work 180°. From below, slide the needle under the spoke with no twists.

38 Turn the work 90° anticlockwise. Take the needle to the back right of the spoke. Bring it out to the left of the bar.

39 Pull to intertwine the stitches. Work a final petal using the method in Steps 27 to 30. To complete the last stitch, take the needle to the back.

40 On the back, run the thread through the back of the first petal and then through the back of the satin stitch, or under the back of the stitching around the centre square.

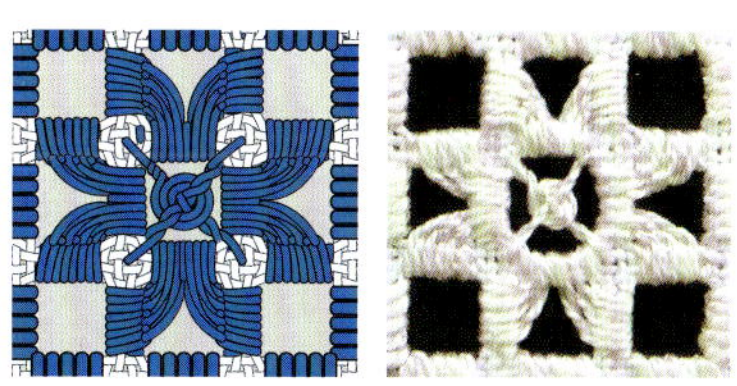

41 The completed blanket stitch flower.

L

buttonholed square

Tension is extremely important for this stitch. Take care to work the buttonhole stitching evenly. A dove's eye is worked in the centre, but other fillings could be substituted.

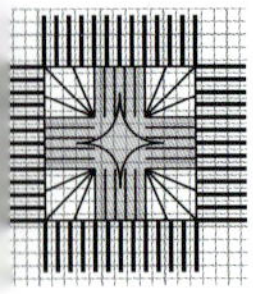

CONTEMPORARY

❗ *I have never previously seen this stitch looking satisfactory, so it was a challenge to devise a good method. Part of the problem is that usually there is a stitch worked in each hole around the square which results in stitches being crammed in. Reducing the quantity of stitches in the corners improves the result. When there are too many stitches it is difficult to maintain good, even tension for all of them.*

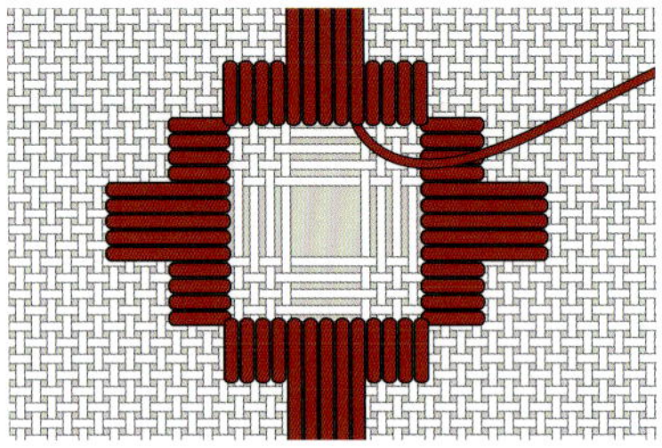

1 Cut the middle four threads on each side and withdraw them. Bring the needle out at the edge of the satin stitch, just left of the top right woven corner.

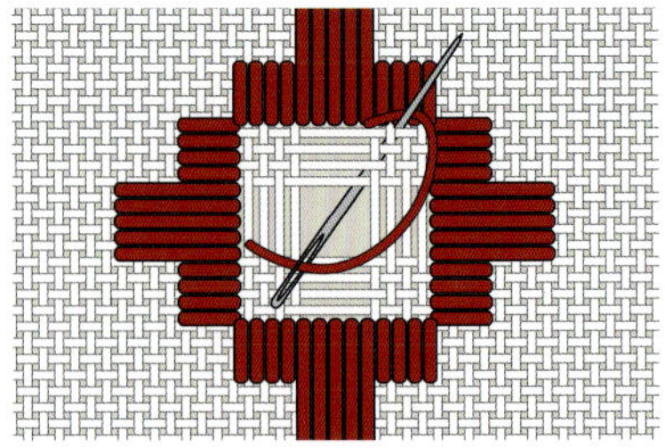

2 Insert the needle in the centre open square, bringing it back out two threads to the right of where it first came out. Take the thread under the needle point from left to right.

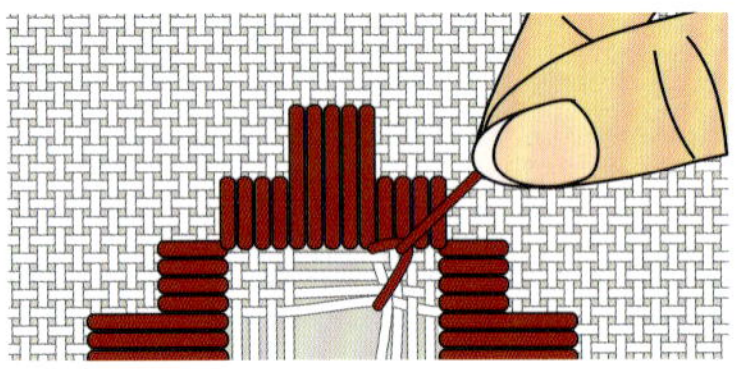

3 Pull the needle through. Pull away from the centre, across the surface of the fabric. This will assist with obtaining a good tension result.

❗ *You can tighten the stitch a lot or a little. Just be consistent throughout.*

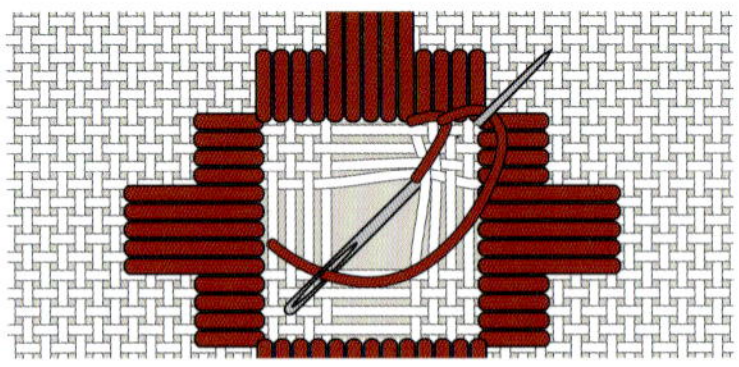

4 Continuing around the square, insert the needle in the centre open square and bring it out two threads further on than before. Take the thread under the needle point from left to right.

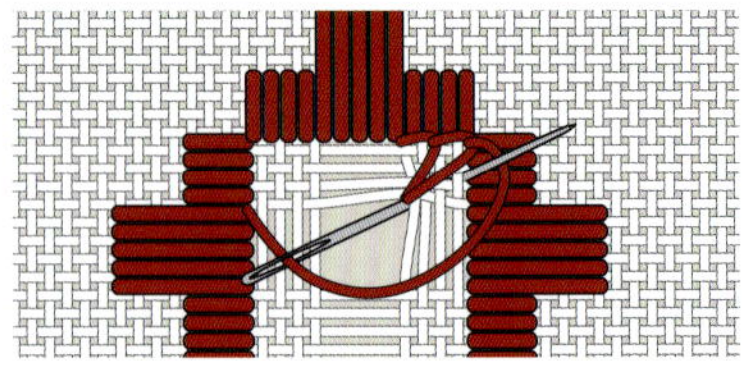

5 Pull the needle through and tighten the stitch as before. Insert the needle in the centre, and bring it out two threads down from the previous time. Take the thread downward under the needle point.

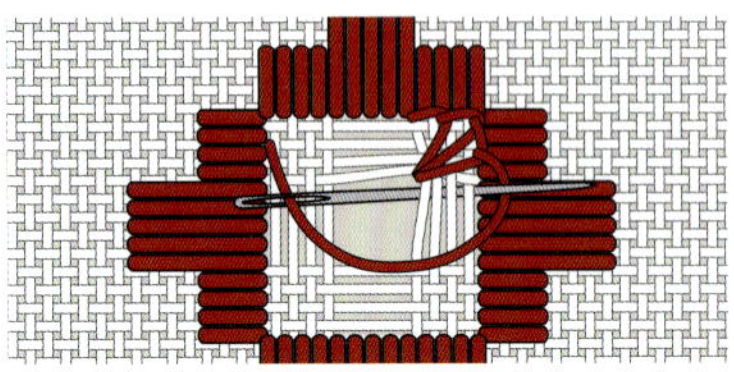

6 Pull the needle through and tighten the stitch. Insert it in the centre, and bring it out two threads lower than before. Take the thread downward under the needle point.

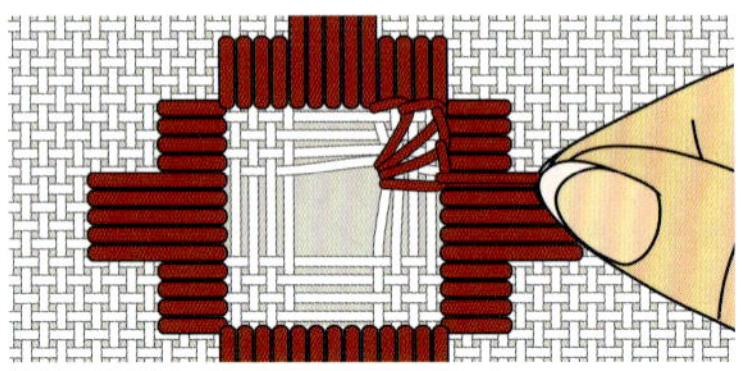

7 Pull the needle through and tighten the stitch.

❗ *Take care to use consistent tension as these fabric threads move more freely because of those that have been removed.*

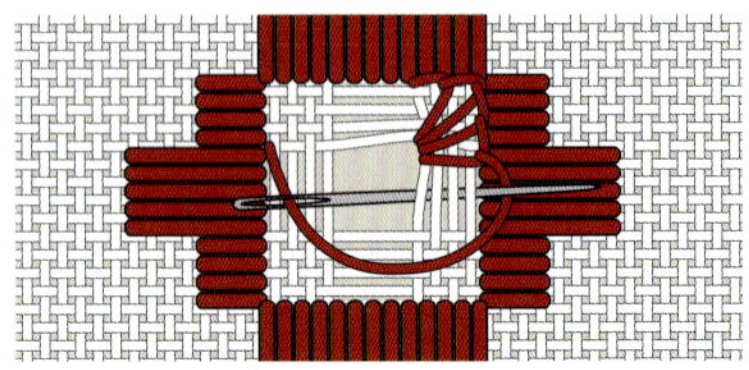

8 Work another buttonhole stitch a little lower.

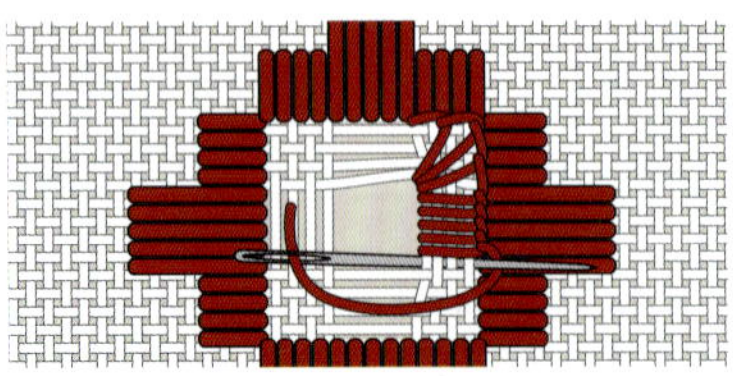

9 Continue working buttonhole stitches towards the next corner.

❗ *Do not cram in the stitches: just enough and not too many.*

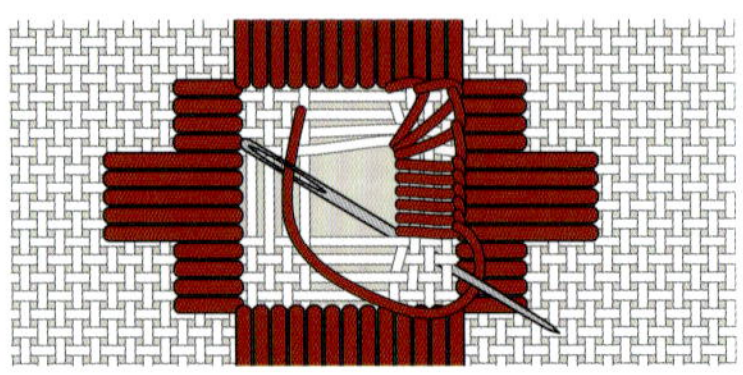

10 Upon reaching the next corner, insert the needle in the inner corner, and bring it at the edge, out two threads down.

11 Continue around the square, up to the last stitch. Slide the needle under the arm of the first stitch, from the outside, in.

❗ *Ensure you use the same quantity of stitches for each of the straight sections.*

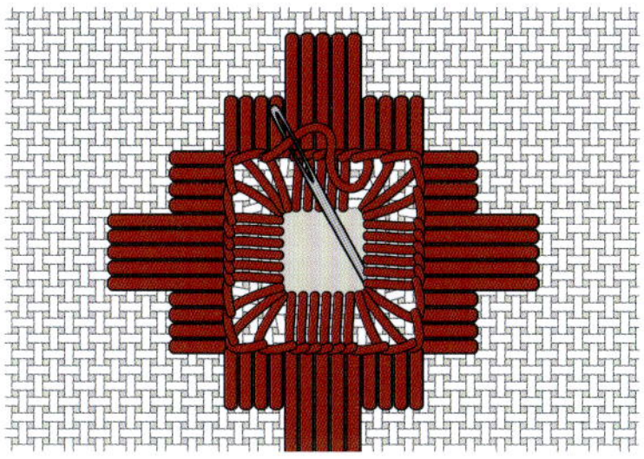

12 Take the needle to the back through the large centre hole.

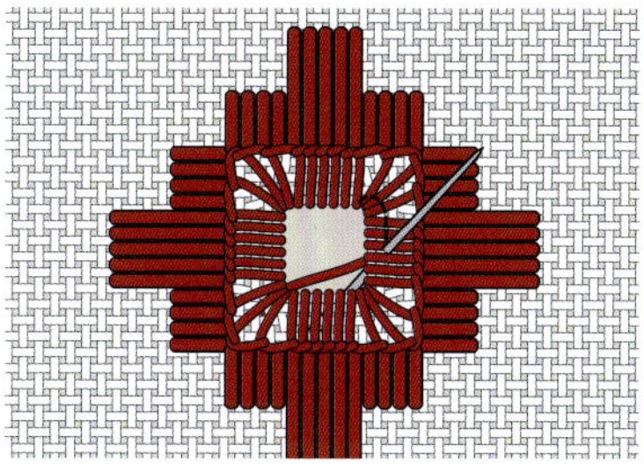

13 On the back, run the needle under the back of the buttonhole stitching and bring it out in the centre of one of the sections of straight buttonhole stitching.

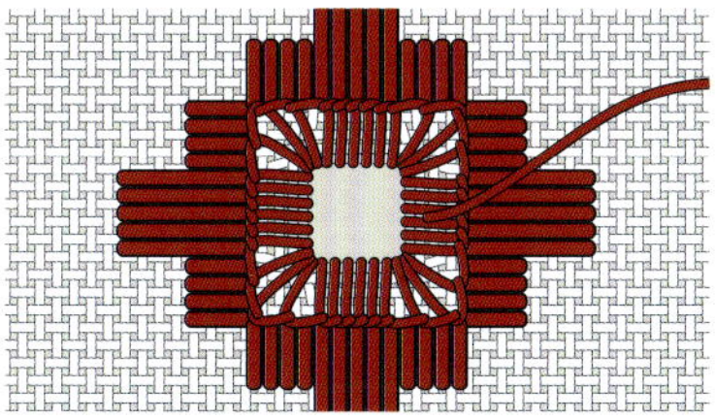

14 Pull the needle through and make sure the last buttonhole stitch sits with the same tension as all the others.

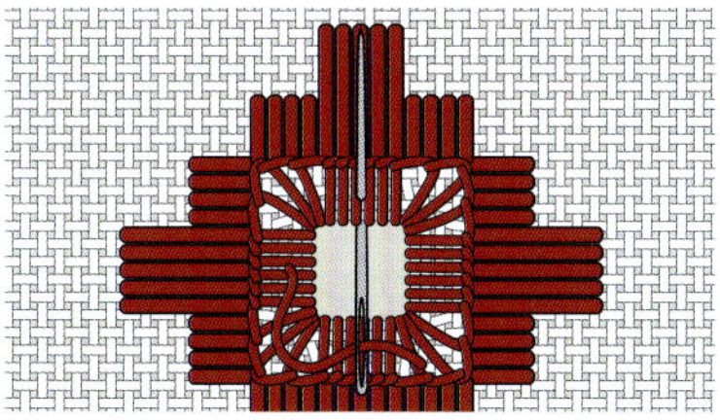

15 Turn the work 180°. Working in a clockwise direction, insert the needle into the centre back of the next straight section of buttonhole.

❶ *The needle is always inserted in the back of the work.*

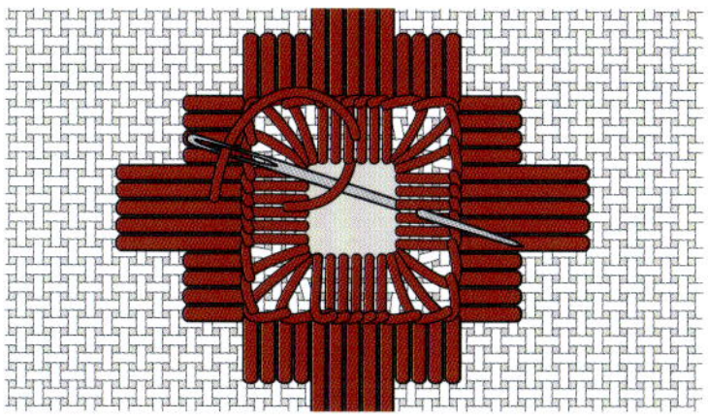

16 Pull the needle through so the stitch gently curves between the two sides. Insert the needle under the previous stitch and into the back of the next straight section of buttonhole.

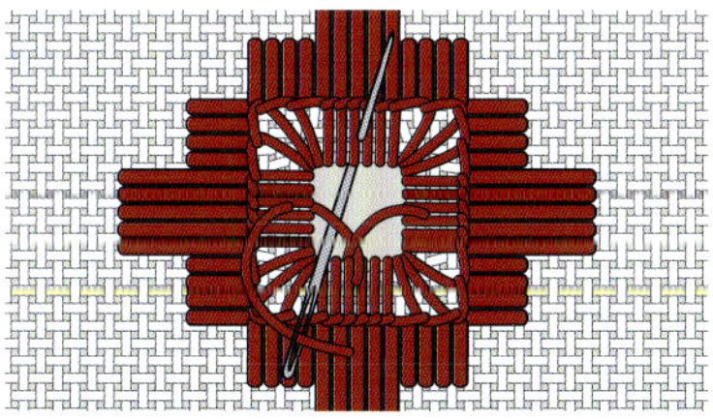

17 Pull the needle through so the stitch gently curves between the two sides. Turn the work 180°. Insert the needle under the previous stitch and into the back of the next straight section of buttonhole.

18 Pull the needle through so the stitch gently curves between the two sides. Take the needle under the previous stitch.

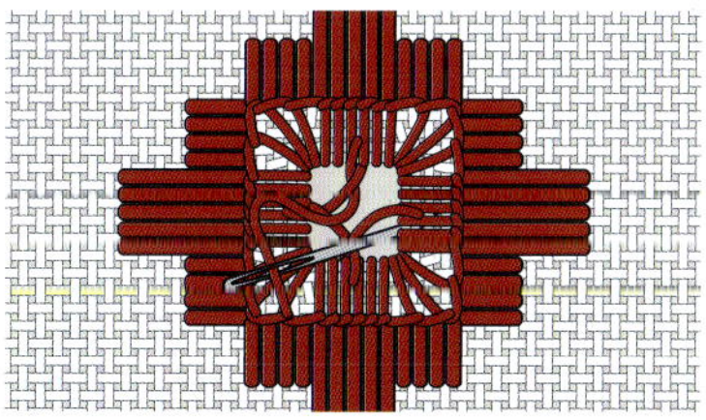

19 Take the needle over the initial curved thread, and to the back.

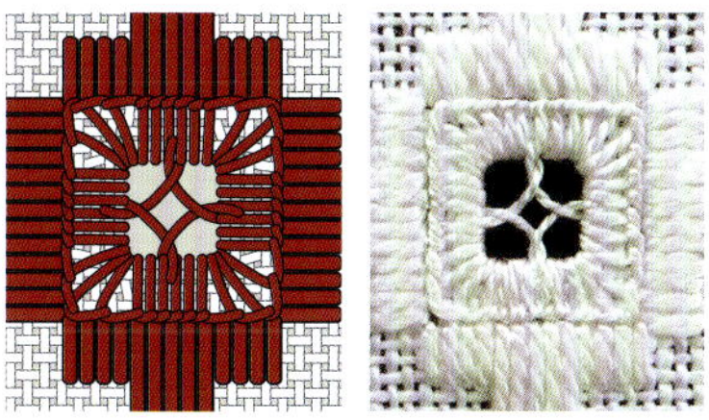

20 Tension the last stitch so it has the same tension as the rest. Finish the thread by running it through the back of some of the buttonhole stitching.

❶ *There is a sister for this motif, where the rolled buttonhole edge sits at the inner edge. I could find no way to make this stitch look acceptable, despite extensive experimentation. It just wasn't possible to have that many stitches on the inner edge and have it look neat.*

buttonholed square

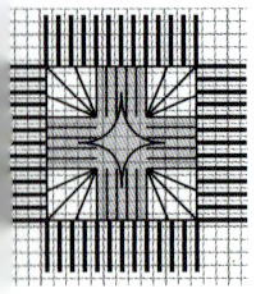

CONTEMPORARY

Tension is extremely important for this stitch. Take care to work the buttonhole stitching evenly. A dove's eye is worked in the centre, but other fillings could be substituted.

❗ *I have never previously seen this stitch looking satisfactory, so it was a challenge to devise a good method. Part of the problem is that usually there is a stitch worked in each hole around the square which results in stitches being crammed in. Reducing the quantity of stitches in the corners improves the result. When there are too many stitches it is difficult to maintain good, even tension for all of them.*

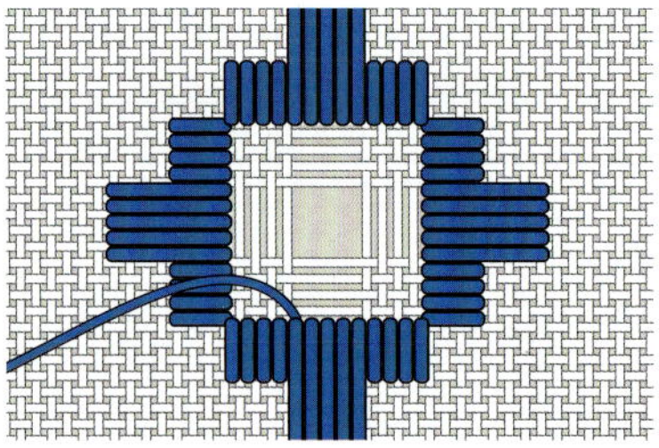

1 Cut the middle four threads on each side and withdraw them. Bring the needle out at the edge of the satin stitch, just right of the bottom left woven corner.

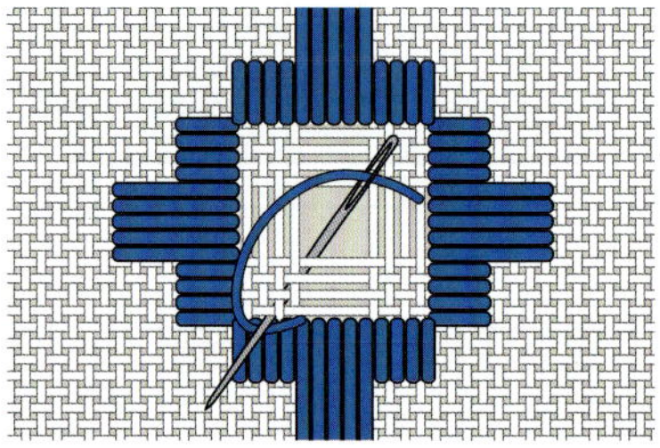

2 Insert the needle in the centre open square, bringing it back out two threads to the left of where it first came out. Take the thread under the needle point from right to left.

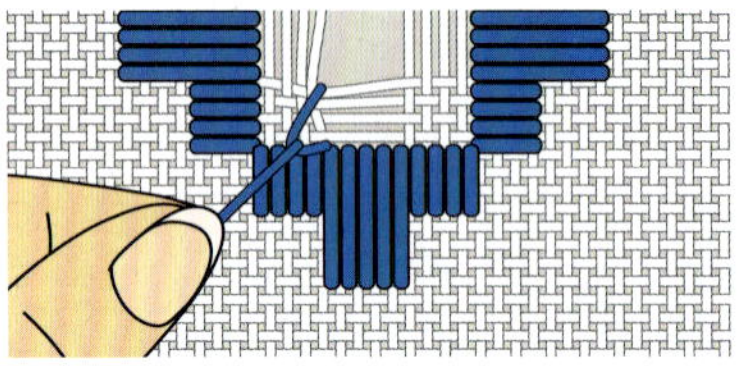

3 Pull the needle through. Pull away from the centre, across the surface of the fabric. This will assist with obtaining a good tension result.

❗ *You can tighten the stitch a lot or a little. Just be consistent throughout.*

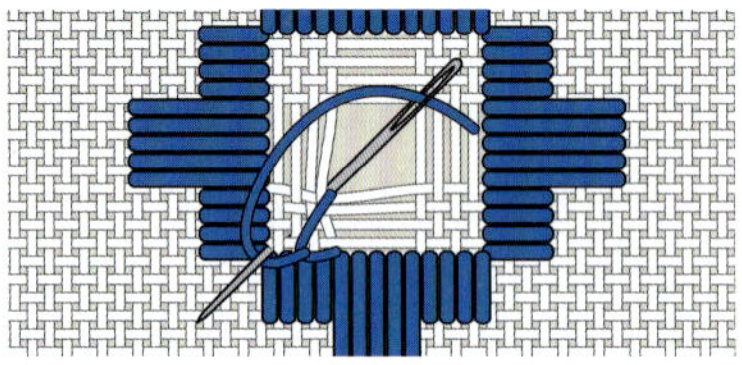

4 Continuing around the square, insert the needle in the centre open square and bring it out two threads further on than before. Take the thread under the needle point from right to left.

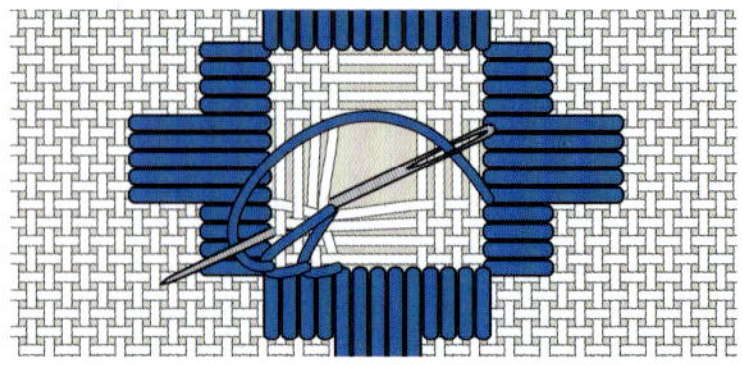

5 Pull the needle through and tighten the stitch as before. Insert the needle in the centre, and bring it out two threads up from the previous time. Take the thread upward under the needle point.

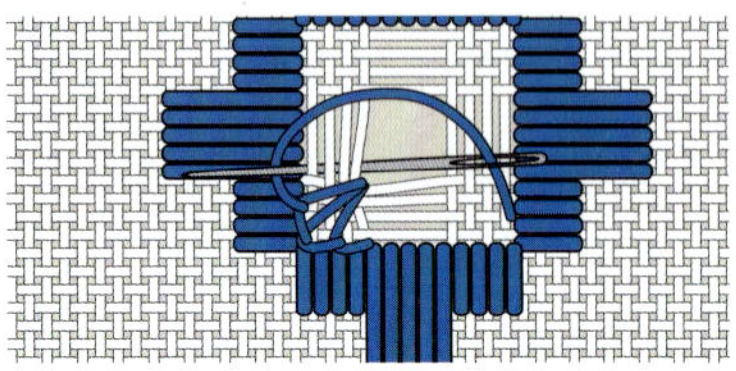

6 Pull the needle through and tighten the stitch. Insert it in the centre, and bring it out two threads higher than before. Take the thread upward under the needle point.

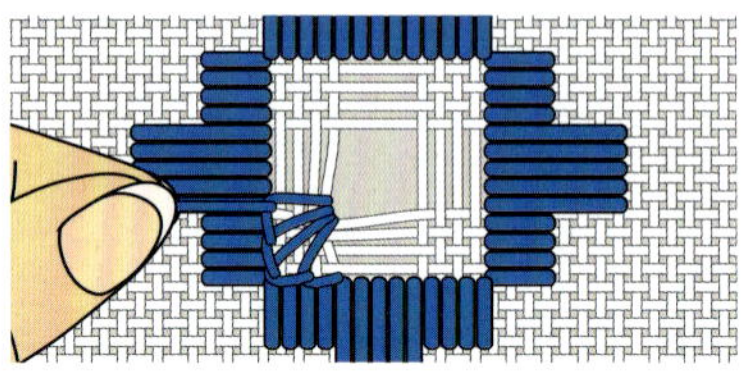

7 Pull the needle through and tighten the stitch.

❗ *Take care to use consistent tension as these fabric threads move more freely because of those that have been removed.*

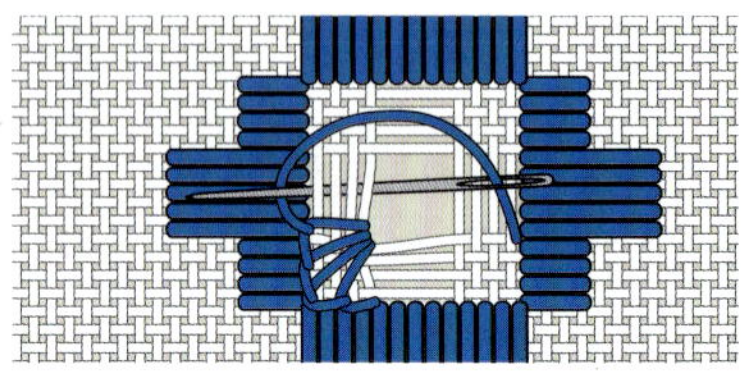

8 Work another buttonhole stitch up a little further.

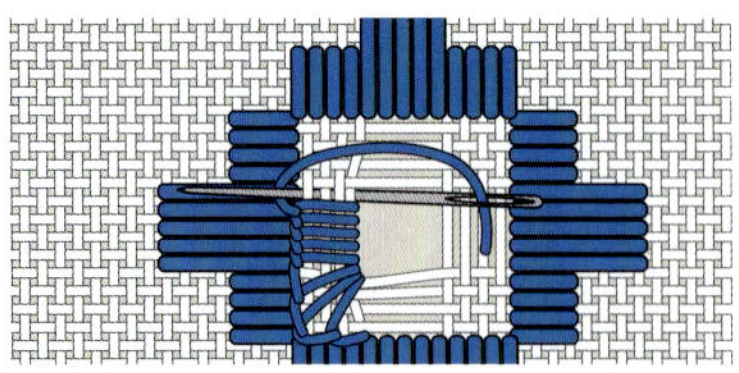

9 Continue working buttonhole stitches towards the next corner.

❗ *Do not cram in the stitches: just enough and not too many.*

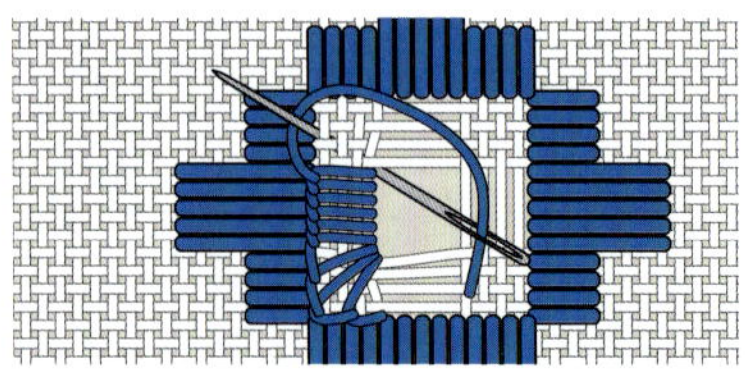

10 Upon reaching the next corner, insert the needle in the inner corner, and bring it at the edge, out two threads up.

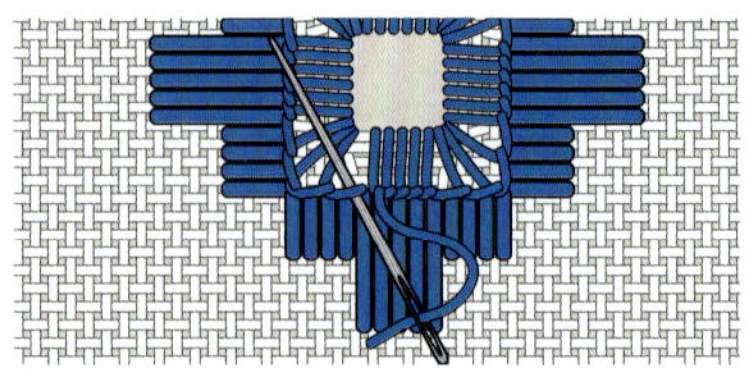

11 Continue around the square, up to the last stitch. Slide the needle under the arm of the first stitch, from the outside, in.

❗ *Ensure you use the same quantity of stitches for each of the straight sections.*

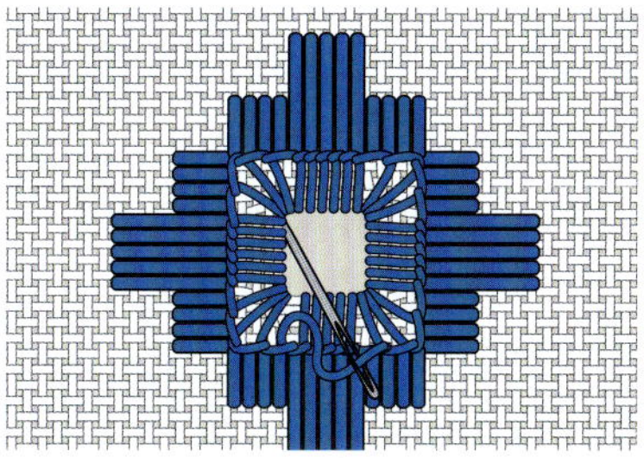

12 Take the needle to the back through the large centre hole.

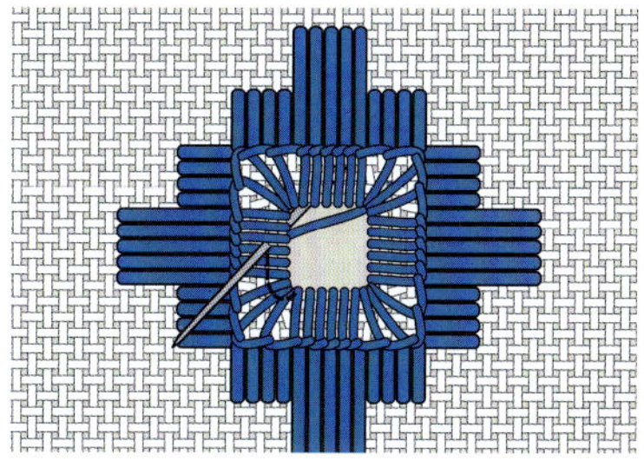

13 On the back, run the needle under the back of the buttonhole stitching and bring it out in the centre of one of the sections of straight buttonhole stitching.

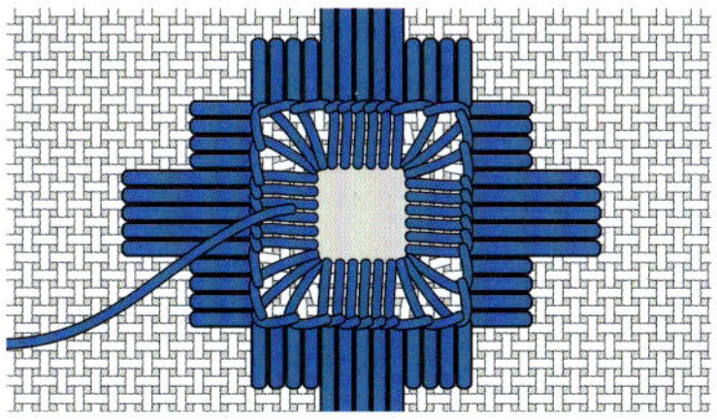

14 Pull the needle through and make sure the last buttonhole stitch sits with the same tension as all the others.

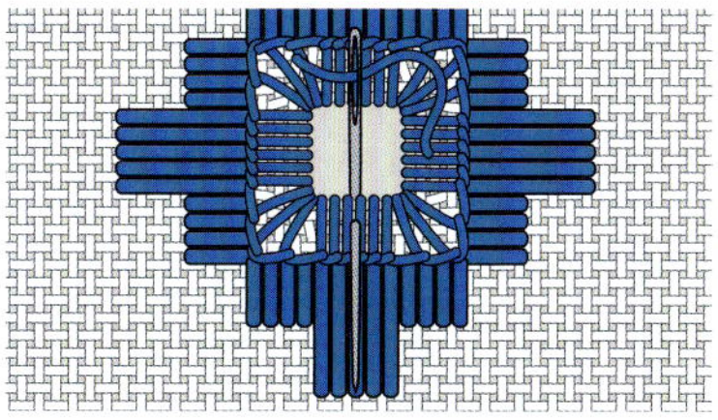

15 Turn the work 180°. Working in a clockwise direction, insert the needle into the centre back of the next straight section of buttonhole.

❶ *The needle is always inserted in the back of the work.*

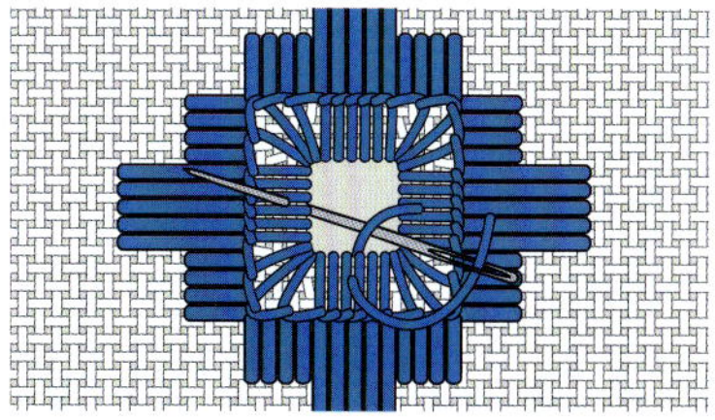

16 Pull the needle through so the stitch gently curves between the two sides. Insert the needle under the previous stitch and into the back of the next straight section of buttonhole.

17 Pull the needle through so the stitch gently curves between the two sides. Turn the work 180°. Insert the needle under the previous stitch and into the back of the next straight section of buttonhole.

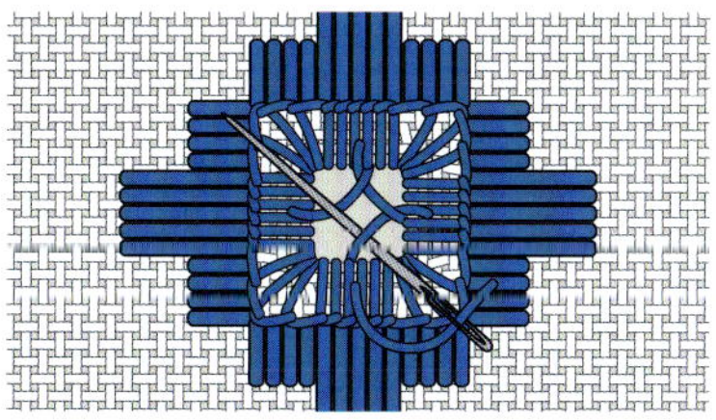

18 Pull the needle through so the stitch gently curves between the two sides. Take the needle under the previous stitch.

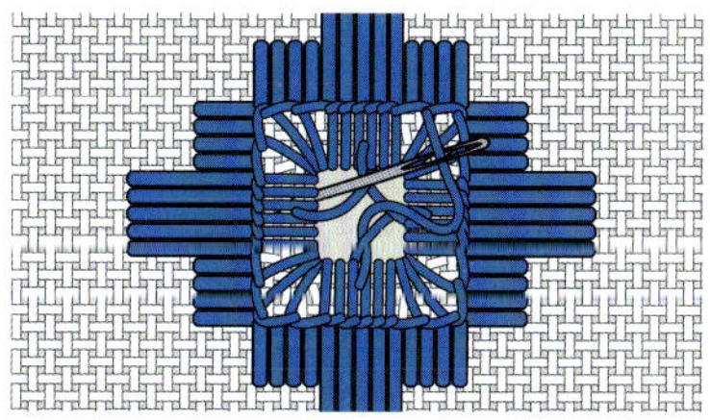

19 Take the needle over the initial curved thread, and to the back.

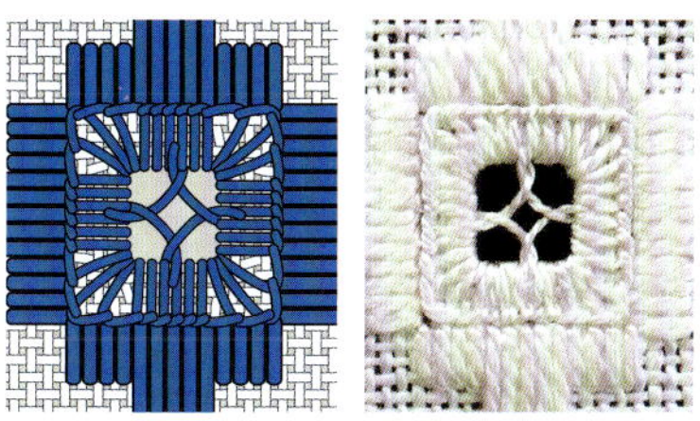

20 Tension the last stitch so it has the same tension as the rest. Finish the thread by running it through the back of some of the buttonhole stitching.

❶ *There is a sister for this motif, where the rolled buttonhole edge sits at the inner edge. I could find no way to make this stitch look acceptable, despite extensive experimentation. It just wasn't possible to have that many stitches on the inner edge and have it look neat.*

buttonhole stitch with dove's eye

This can be worked on wrapped (shown here) or woven bars. It can be in a square like this, or in the midst of a larger area.

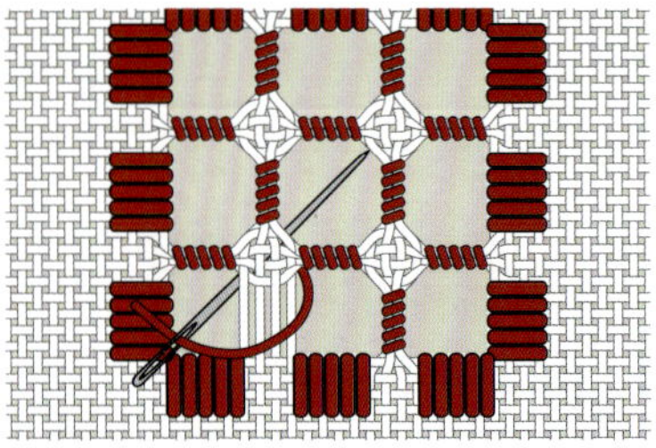

1 Prepare a large square as shown. Wrap all of the bars except one, as shown. Bring the needle out for the final bar. Take it over the bar and diagonally behind the adjacent woven square.

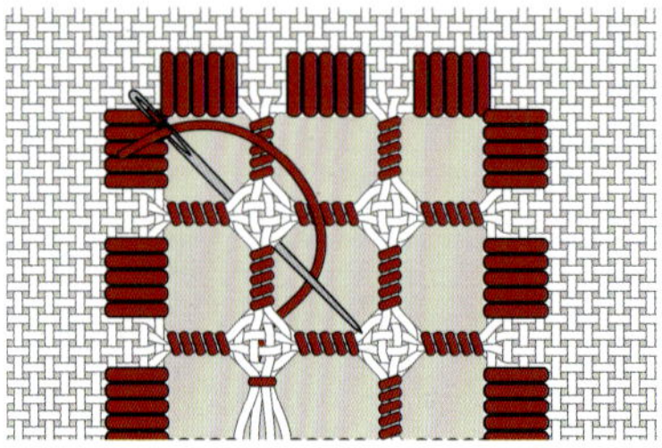

2 Pull the needle through. Moving clockwise, insert the needle under the next woven square, from the outside towards the centre. Take the thread under the needle point from lower left to upper right.

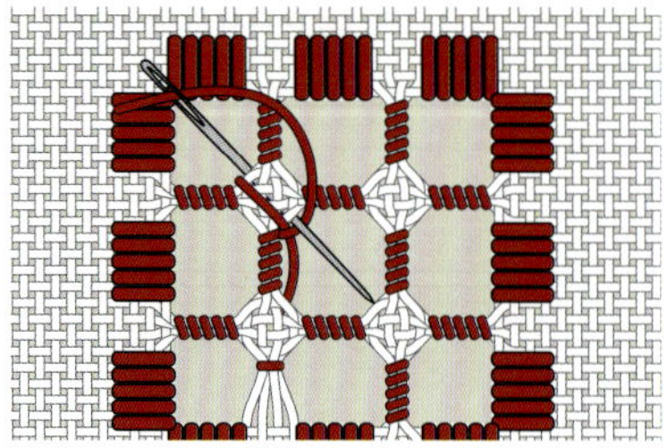

3 Pull the needle through so that the first stitch has a slight curve. Take another stitch next to the first, with the thread under the needle point again.

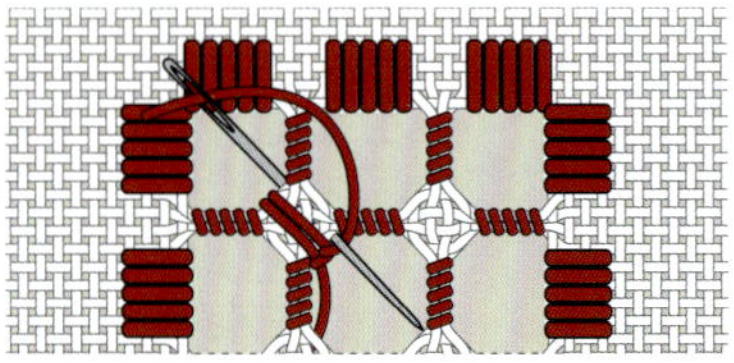

4 Pull the needle through and tighten the stitch around the woven square. Make a third stitch with the thread under the needle point again.

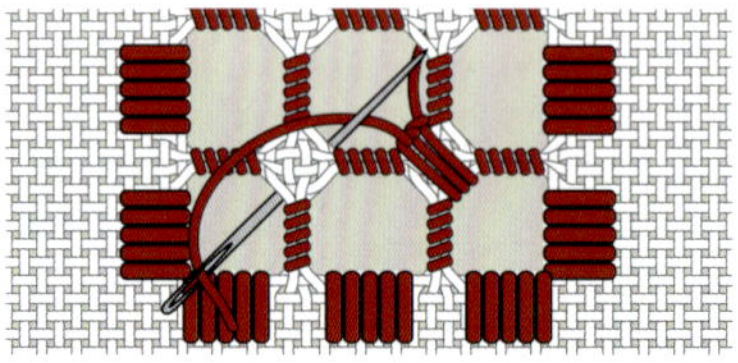

5 Pull the needle through to snug the stitch. Turn the work 180°. Insert the needle under the next woven square, towards the centre. Take the needle over the working thread.

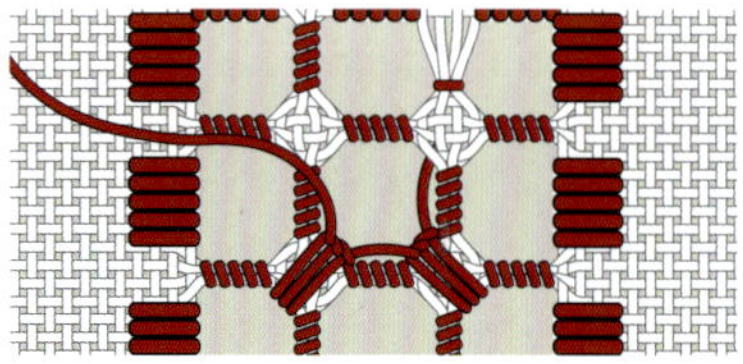

6 Pull the needle through so that the first stitch has a slight curve. Take another two stitches next to the first.

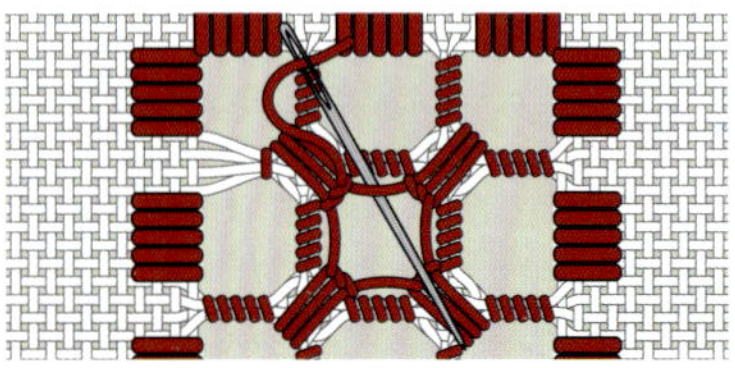

7 Repeat the three buttonhole stitches on the other two corners of the square, turning the work as necessary. Following the last buttonhole stitch insert the needle between the wrapped bar and the first long stitch.

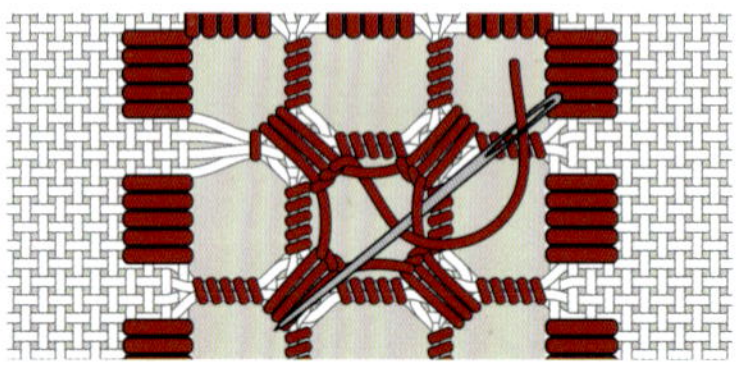

8 Pull the needle through. Moving clockwise, and turning the work as necessary, insert the needle under the next long stitch from the outside. Take it over the working thread.

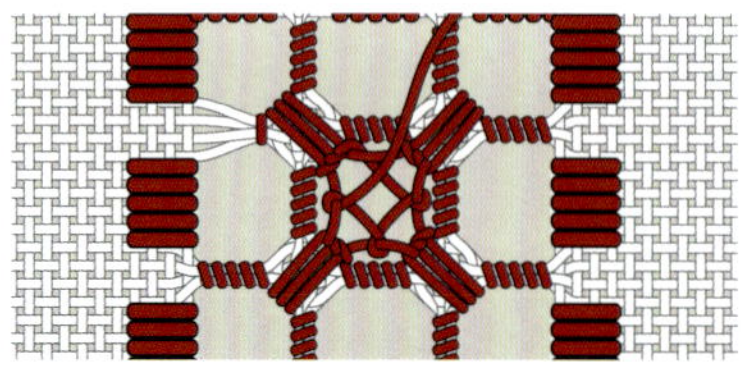

9 Continuing around and turning the work as needed, take the needle under the long buttonhole stitch from the outside, then over the working thread, on each of the next two sides.

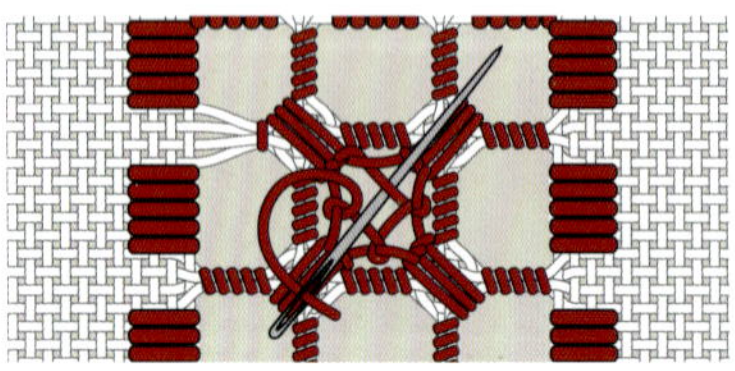

10 Slide the needle under the first section of the dove's eye, from below.

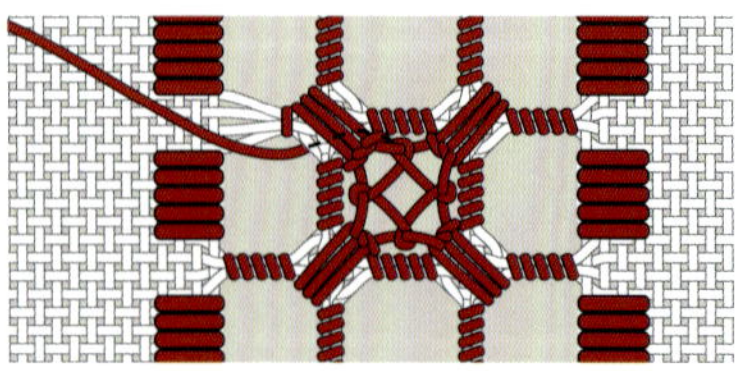

11 Take the needle to the back above the long buttonhole stitch and run it under the back of the corner buttonhole stitches to the bar that has not yet been stitched.

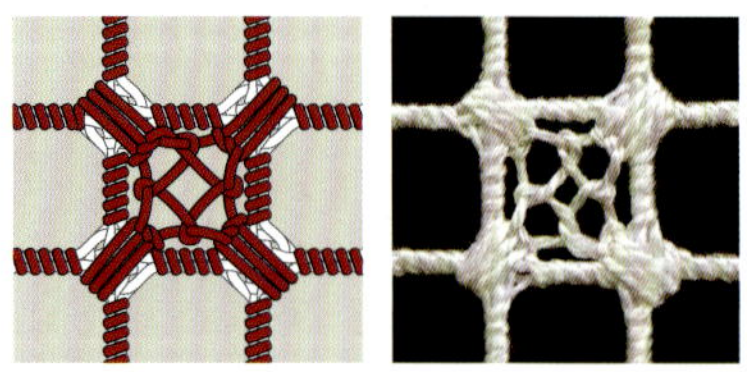

12 Wrap the remaining bar then finish the thread in the back of the satin stitch.

buttonhole stitch with dove's eye

This can be worked on wrapped (shown here) or woven bars. It can be in a square like this, or in the midst of a larger area.

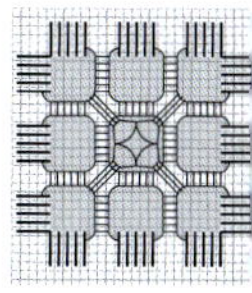

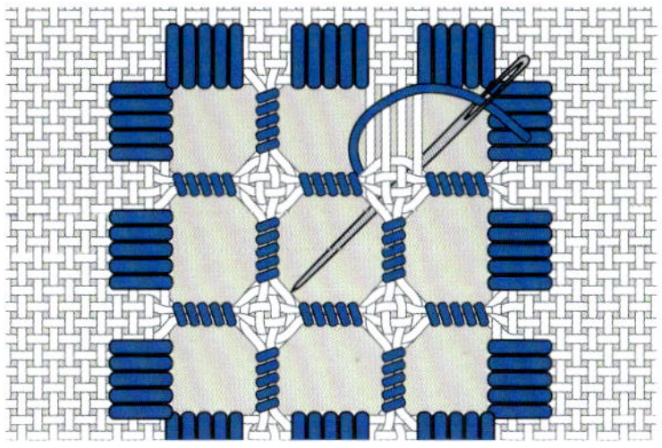

1 Prepare a large square as shown. Wrap all of the bars except one, as shown. Bring the needle out for the final bar. Take it over the bar and diagonally behind the adjacent woven square.

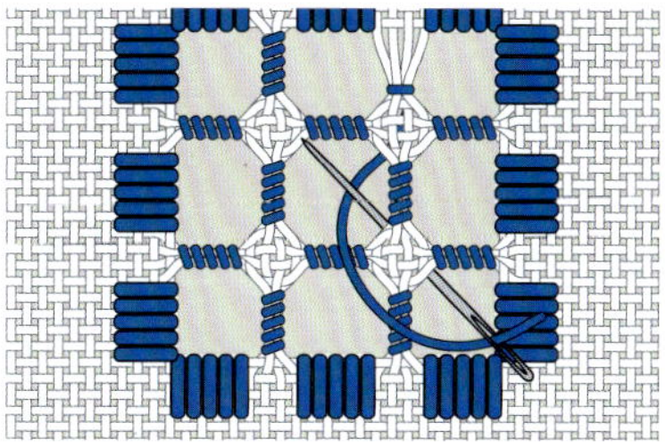

2 Pull the needle through. Moving clockwise, insert the needle under the next woven square, from the outside towards the centre. Take the thread under the needle point from upper right to lower left.

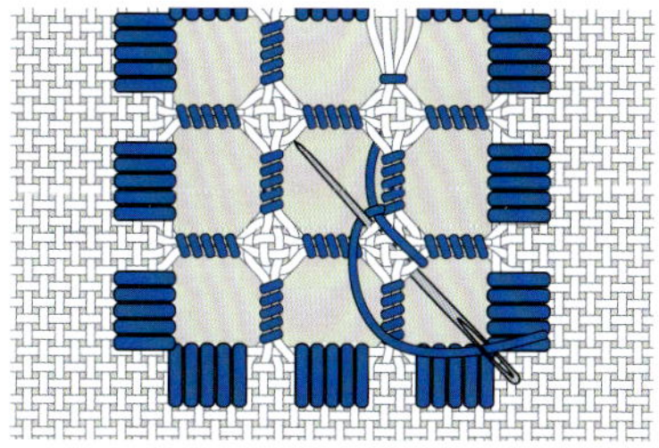

3 Pull the needle through so that the first stitch has a slight curve. Take another stitch next to the first, with the thread under the needle point again.

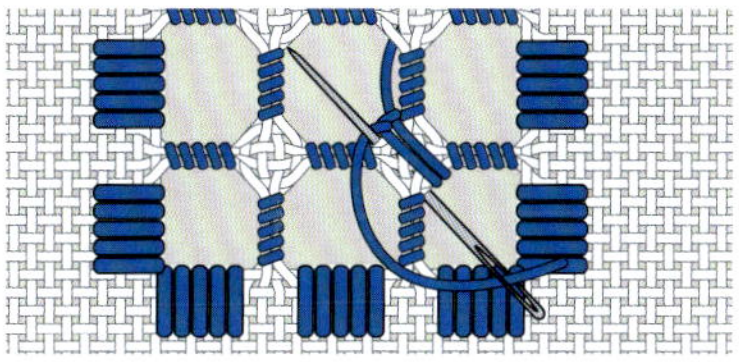

4 Pull the needle through and tighten the stitch around the woven square. Make a third stitch with the thread under the needle point again.

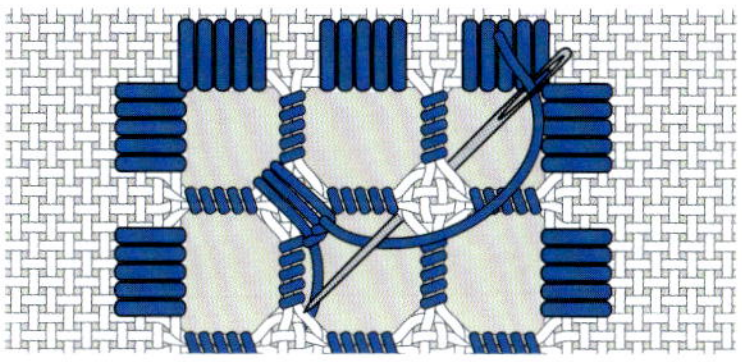

5 Pull the needle through to snug the stitch. Turn the work 180°. Insert the needle under the next woven square, towards the centre. Take the needle over the working thread.

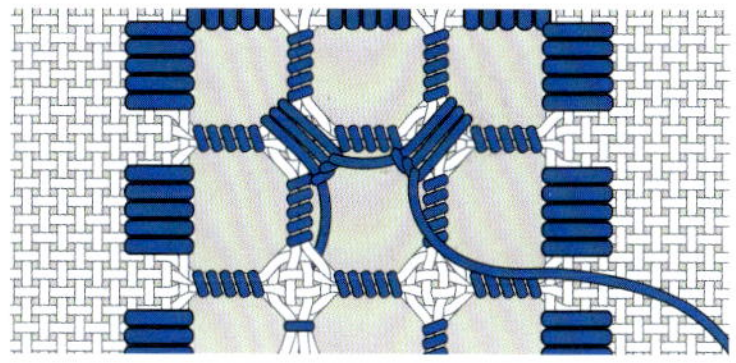

6 Pull the needle through so that the first stitch has a slight curve. Take another two stitches next to the first.

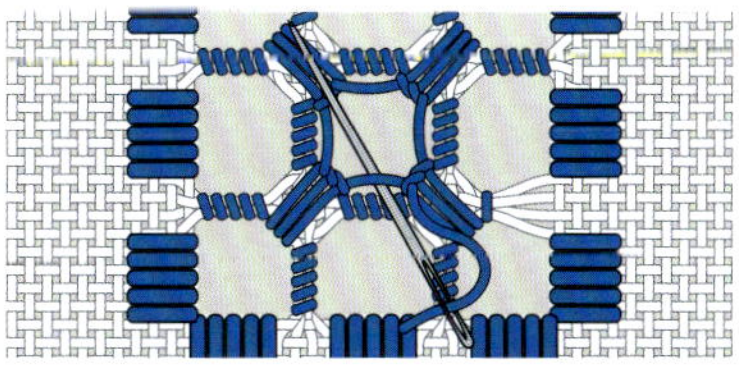

7 Repeat the three buttonhole stitches on the other two corners of the square, turning the work as necessary. Following the last buttonhole stitch insert the needle between the wrapped bar and the first long stitch.

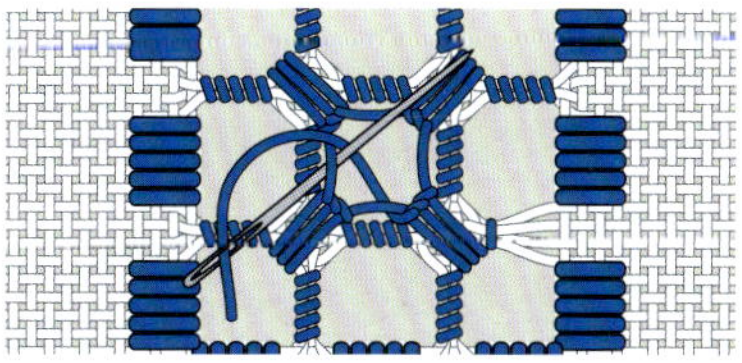

8 Pull the needle through. Moving clockwise, and turning the work as necessary, insert the needle under the next long stitch from the outside. Take it over the working thread.

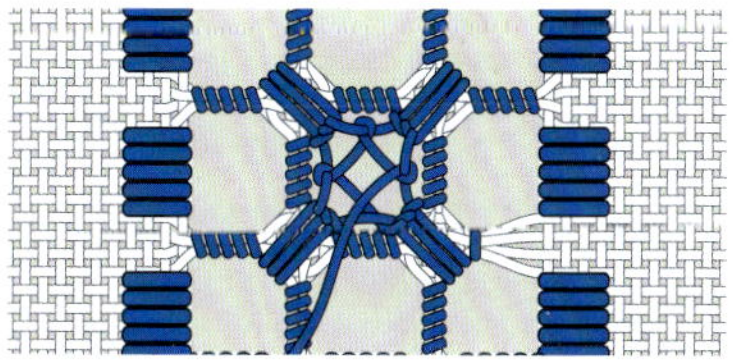

9 Continuing around and turning the work as needed, take the needle under the long buttonhole stitch from the outside, then over the working thread, on each of the next two sides.

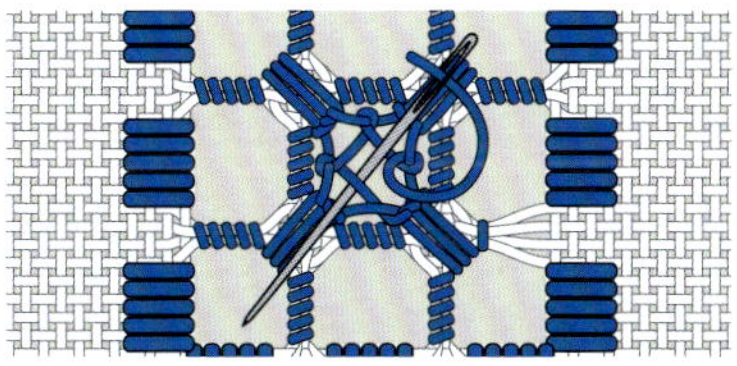

10 Slide the needle under the first section of the dove's eye, from above.

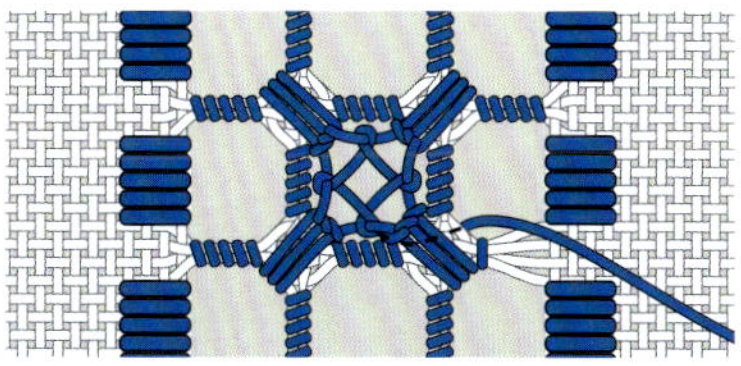

11 Take the needle to the back below the long buttonhole stitch and run it under the back of the corner buttonhole stitches to the bar that has not yet been stitched.

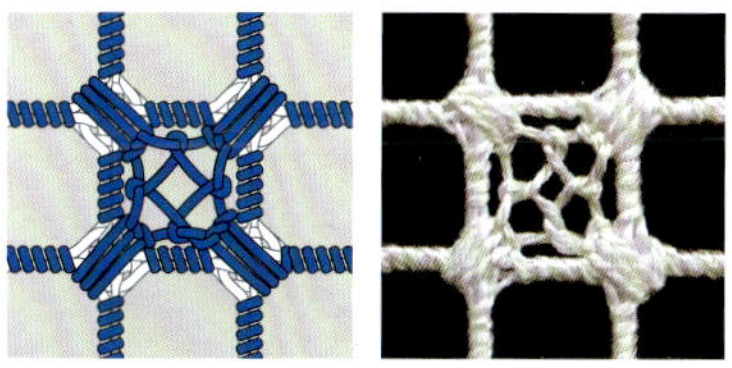

12 Wrap the remaining bar then finish the thread in the back of the satin stitch.

L

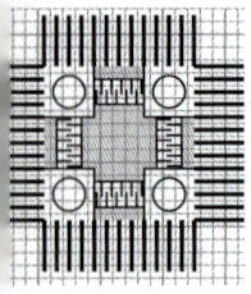

CONTEMPORARY

eyelets as filling stitches

There are three main ways of using eyelets within cutwork: full eyelets in the corners of square cutwork areas, simplified eyelets at the centre of square cutwork areas, and simplified eyelets across cutwork areas as a whole, in the intervening woven squares.

corner eyelets with full-width bars

Woven bars are shown, but they could also be wrapped.

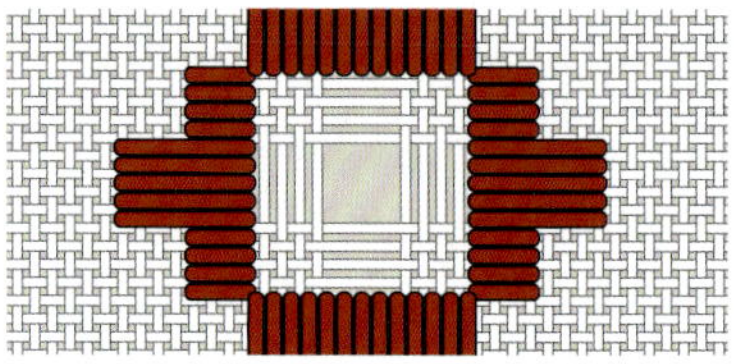

1 Cut and withdraw four threads in the centre of each side, so that woven squares remain in the corners, with fabric threads between them.

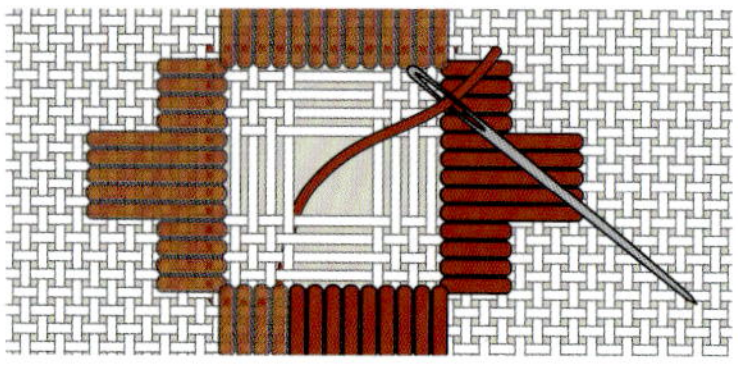

2 Anchor the thread in the back of the satin stitch and bring it out in the bottom left corner of the central open square.

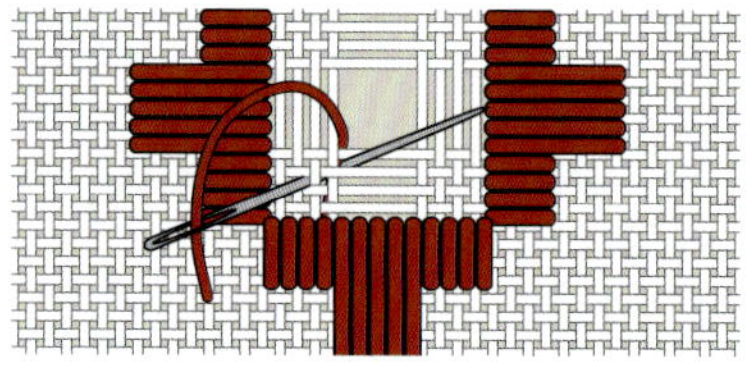

3 Insert the needle into the woven square's centre. Take it behind the thread on the back. Bring it out one thread below where it last emerged.

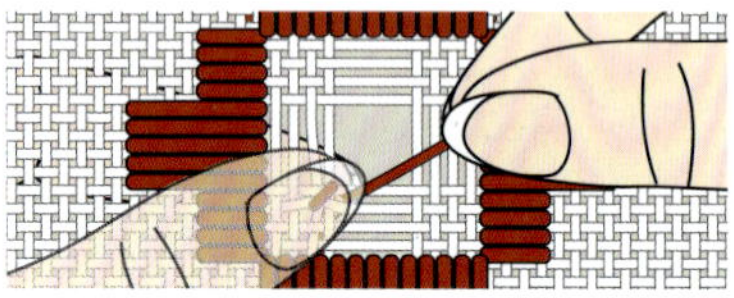

4 Pinch the stitch between your finger and thumb. With the other hand, pull the thread away from the centre to tighten the stitch and enlarge the hole.

❶ *An eyelet is a hole, so pull it open! Even tension makes an evenly shaped hole.*

❶ *Pinching while you pull stabilises the fabric, helping you tighten the stitch well.*

❶ *Never bring the needle out at the centre and insert it at the edge. This pulls the stitches away from the edge and bunches them in the centre, rather than enlarging the centre hole. Eyelet holes should be holes rather than pinpricks.*

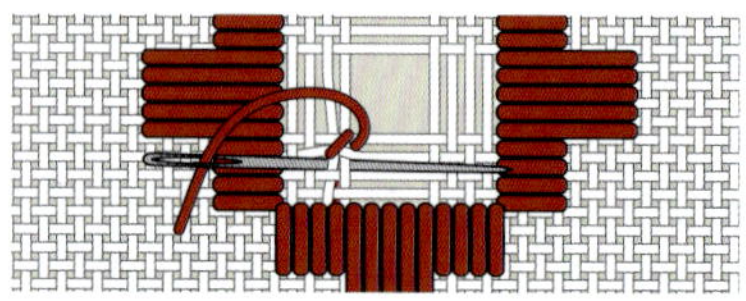

5 Insert the needle in the centre of the eyelet. Take the needle behind the thread on the back, and bring it out again one thread down from where it last emerged.

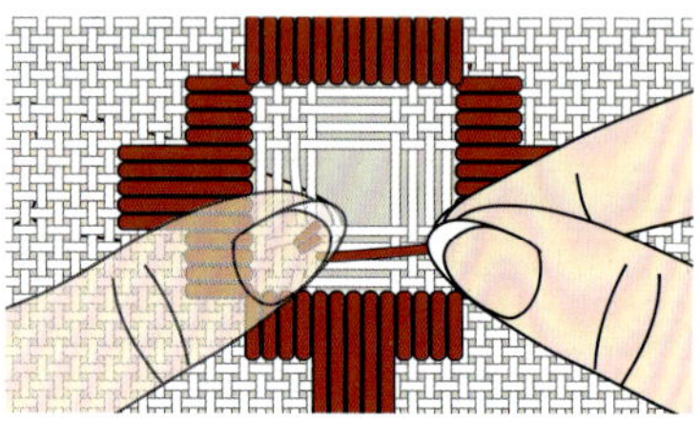

6 Pull the needle through and pinch and pull to tighten the stitch. Insert the needle at the centre and bring it out again one thread further around the edge of the eyelet.

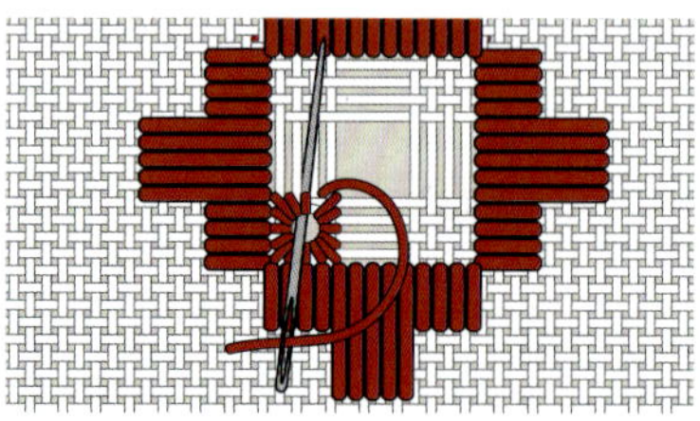

7 Continue around, with five stitches on each side, tightening after each stitch. Turn the work as needed. Complete the final stitch and bring the needle out to weave the adjacent bar.

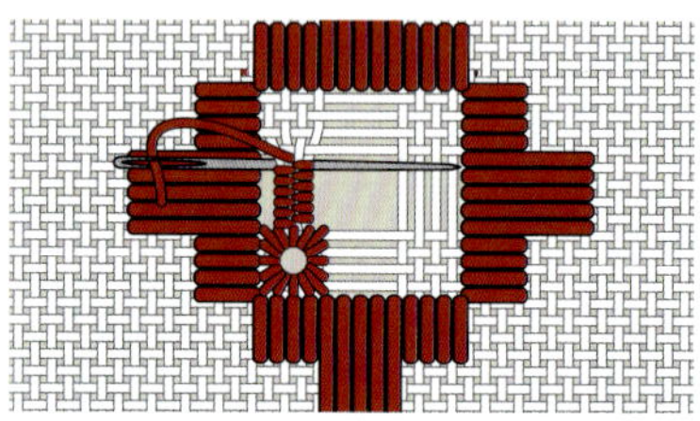

8 Weave the bar, finishing with a stitch on the left, then bring the needle out in the central open square.

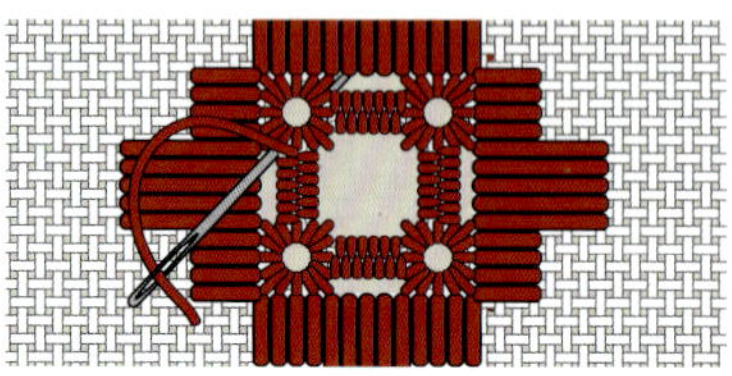

9 Repeat the eyelets and woven bars. Take the thread to the back on completion.

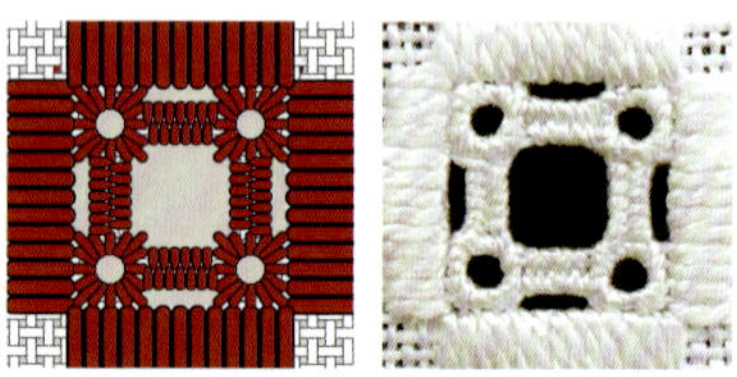

10 Finish the thread on the back under the adjacent satin stitch.

eyelets as filling stitches

There are three main ways of using eyelets within cutwork: full eyelets in the corners of square cutwork areas, simplified eyelets at the centre of square cutwork areas, and simplified eyelets across cutwork areas as a whole, in the intervening woven squares.

corner eyelets with full-width bars

Woven bars are shown, but they could also be wrapped.

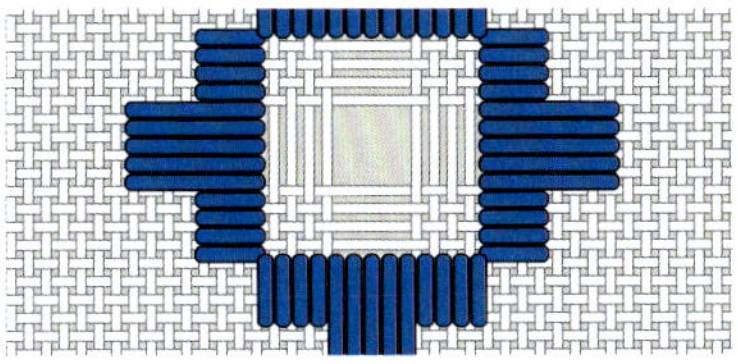

1 Cut and withdraw four threads in the centre of each side, so that woven squares remain in the corners, with fabric threads between them.

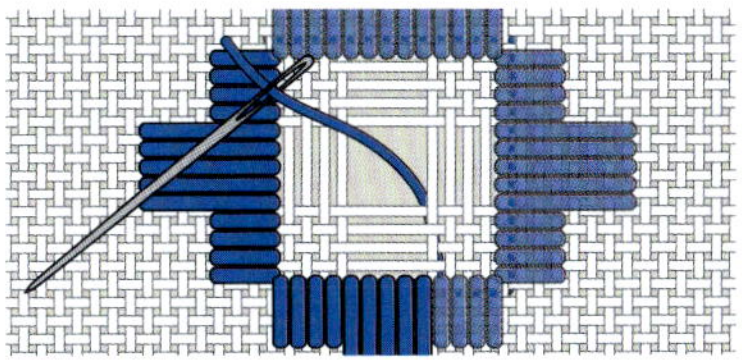

2 Anchor the thread in the back of the satin stitch and bring it out in the bottom right corner of the central open square.

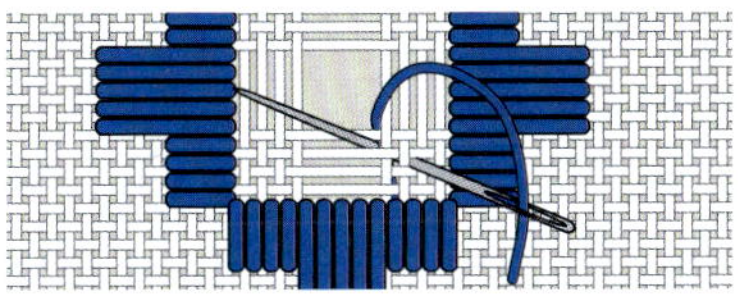

3 Insert the needle into the woven square's centre. Take it behind the thread on the back. Bring it out one thread below where it last emerged.

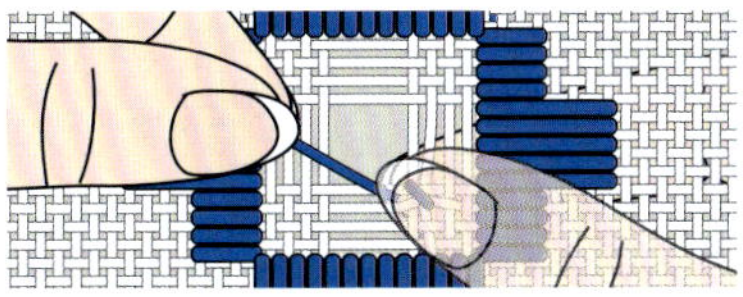

4 Pinch the stitch between your finger and thumb. With the other hand, pull the thread away from the centre to tighten the stitch and enlarge the hole.
❶ An eyelet is a hole, so pull it open! Even tension makes an evenly shaped hole.
❶ Pinching while you pull stabilises the fabric, helping you tighten the stitch well.

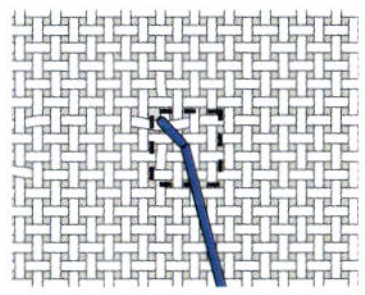

❶ Never bring the needle out at the centre and insert it at the edge. This pulls the stitches away from the edge and bunches them in the centre, rather than enlarging the centre hole. Eyelet holes should be holes rather than pinpricks.

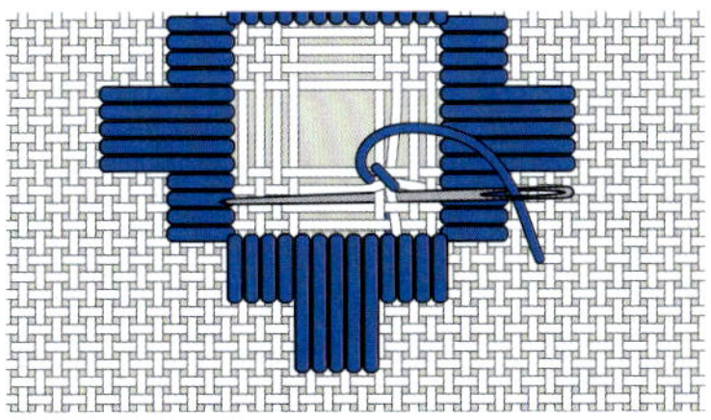

5 Insert the needle in the centre of the eyelet. Take the needle behind the thread on the back, and bring it out again one thread down from where it last emerged.

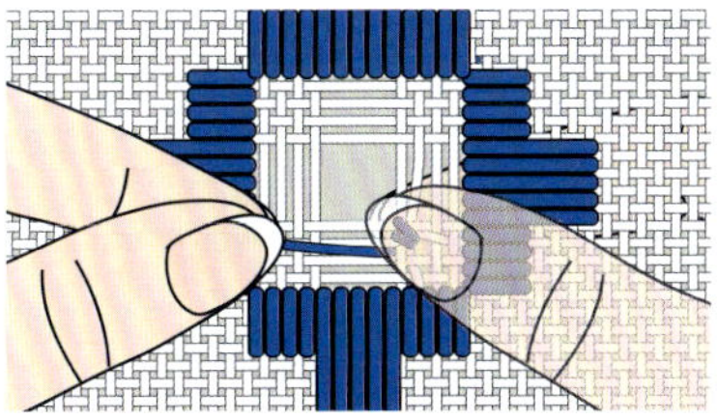

6 Pull the needle through and pinch and pull to tighten the stitch. Insert the needle at the centre and bring it out again one thread further around the edge of the eyelet.

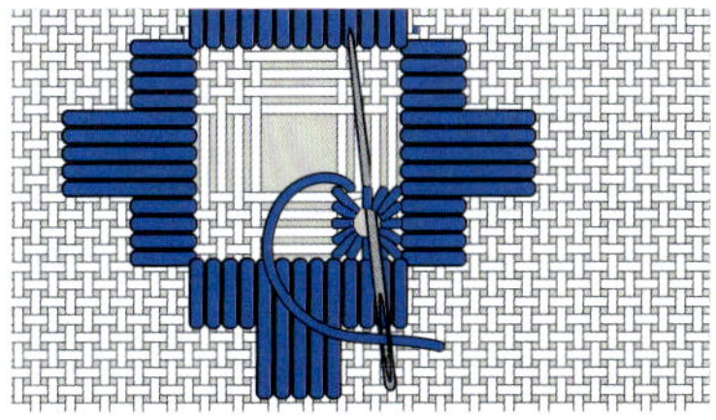

7 Continue around, with five stitches on each side, tightening after each stitch. Turn the work as needed. Complete the final stitch and bring the needle out to weave the adjacent bar.

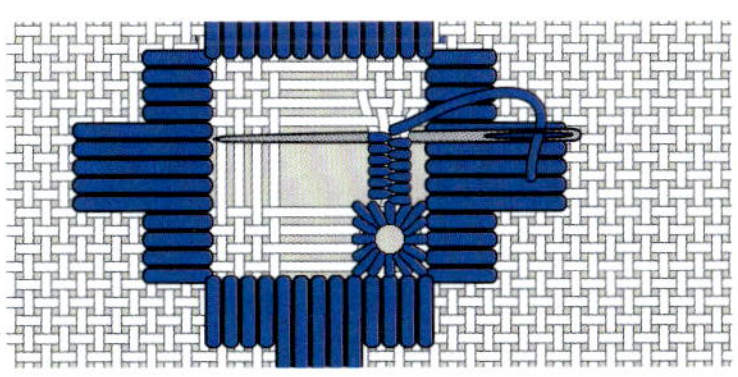

8 Weave the bar, finishing with a stitch on the right, then bring the needle out in the central open square.

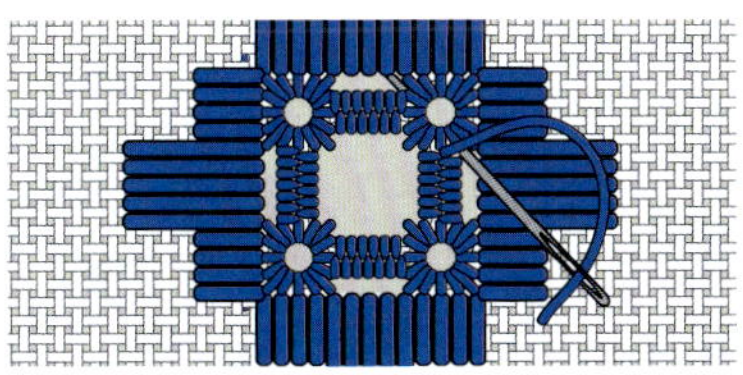

9 Repeat the eyelets and woven bars. Take the thread to the back on completion.

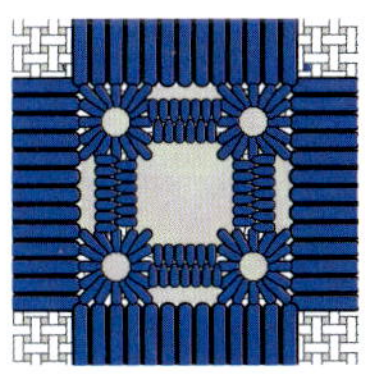

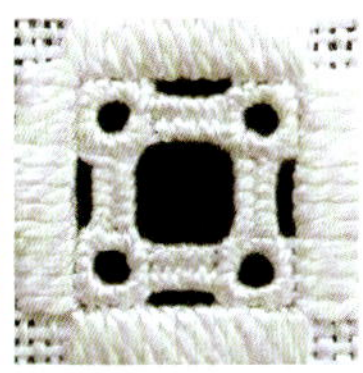

10 Finish the thread on the back under the adjacent satin stitch.

corner eyelets with square filet

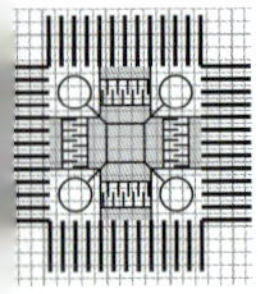

When fillings are worked where the anchoring points are in the corners of the large square, such as with square filets or spider webs, they should be worked first, before the eyelets and woven bars are completed.

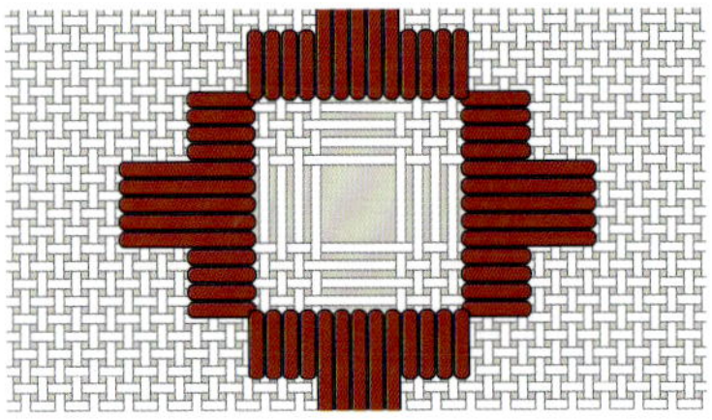

1 Cut and withdraw four threads in the centre of each side, so that woven squares remain in the corners, with fabric threads between them.

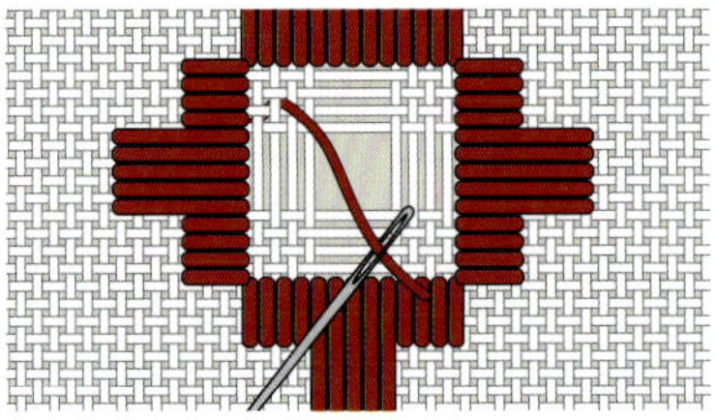

2 Anchor the thread in the back of the satin stitch and bring it out in the centre of the top left woven square.

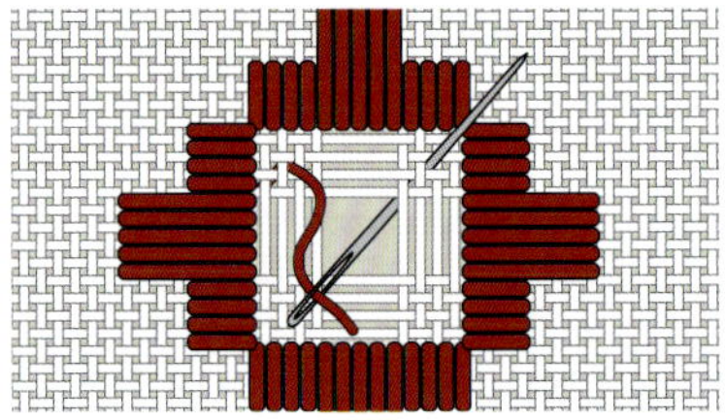

3 Working clockwise, insert the needle in the centre back of the next woven square.

! *Always insert the needle in the back.*

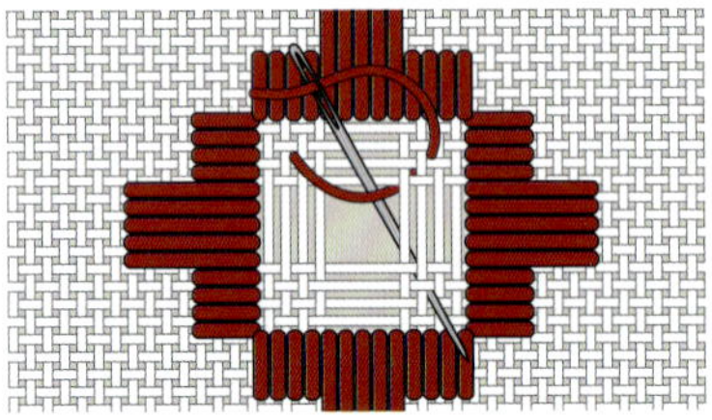

4 Pull the needle through. Insert the needle under the previous stitch and into the centre back of the next woven square.

! *Make sure the square filet is worked tighter than normal as it will loosen off when you work the eyelets.*

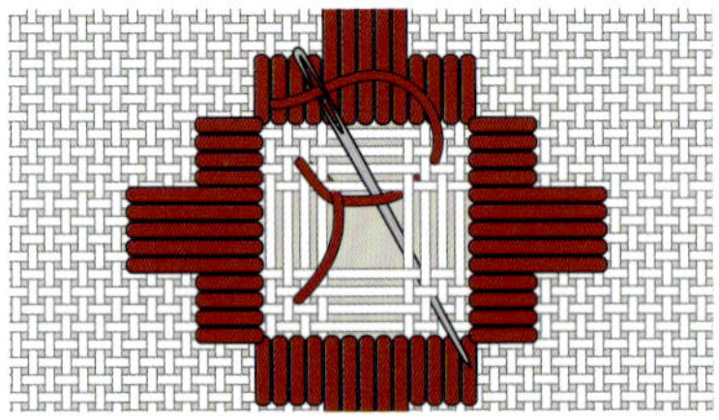

5 Pull the needle through. Turn the work 90° anticlockwise. Insert the needle under the previous stitch and into the centre back of the next woven square.

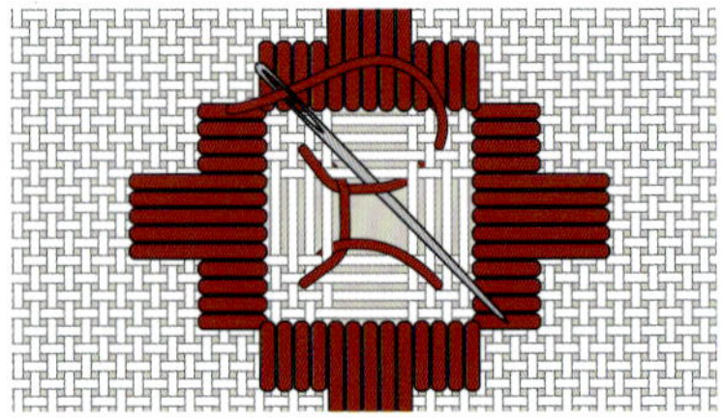

6 Pull the needle through. Turn the work 90° anticlockwise. Slide the needle under the previous stitch.

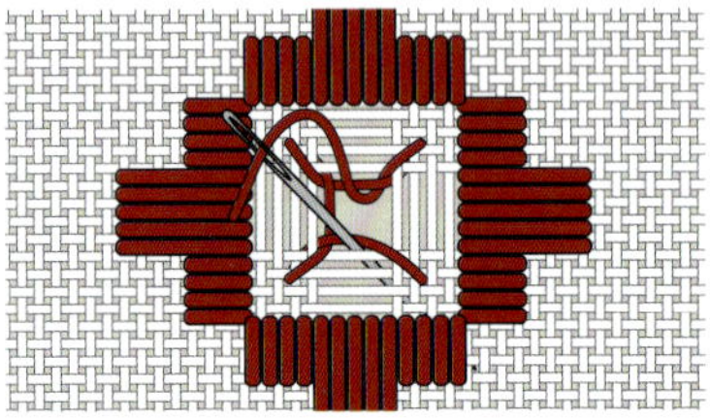

7 Take the needle over the initial stitch, then to the back.

! *The thread needs to come out in the same place it was just inserted, so in the next step it will be anchored on the back to allow it to come out of the same hole without simply undoing the stitch.*

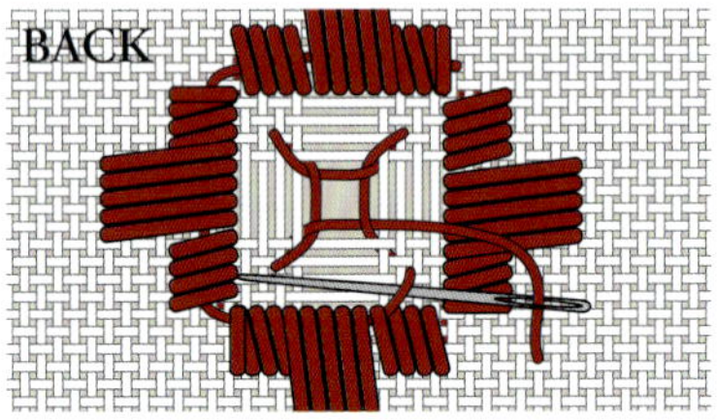

8 On the back, slide the needle under the thread leading from the tail to the stitching.

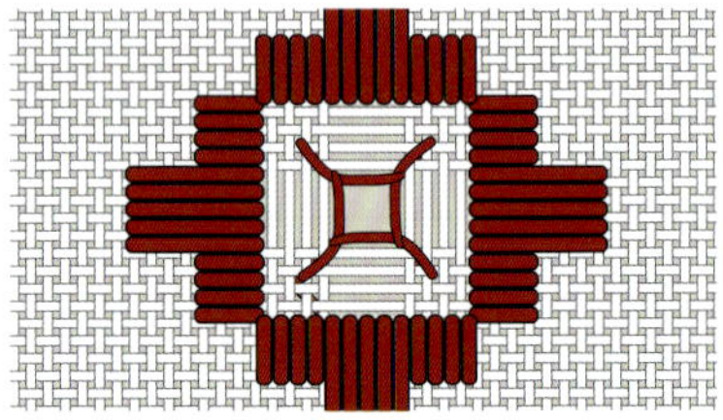

! *Before you go any further, make sure the square filet is quite tight. It will loosen off once you stitch the eyelets, at which point it will not be possible to tighten it. If you need to tighten the square filet, do it now before it is too late.*

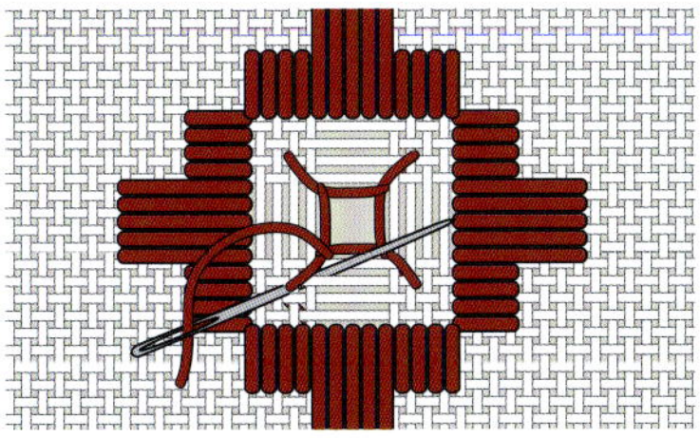

9 Working from the front, bring needle out in the same corner, below the square filet. Insert the needle into the woven square's centre. Take it behind the threads on the back. Bring it out one thread below where it last emerged.

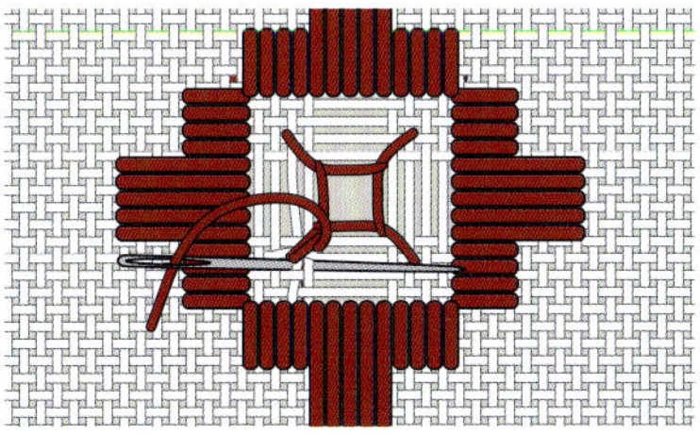

10 Pull the needle through and pinch and pull to tighten the stitch. Insert the needle in the centre of the eyelet. Take the needle behind the threads on the back, and bring it out again one thread down from where it last emerged.

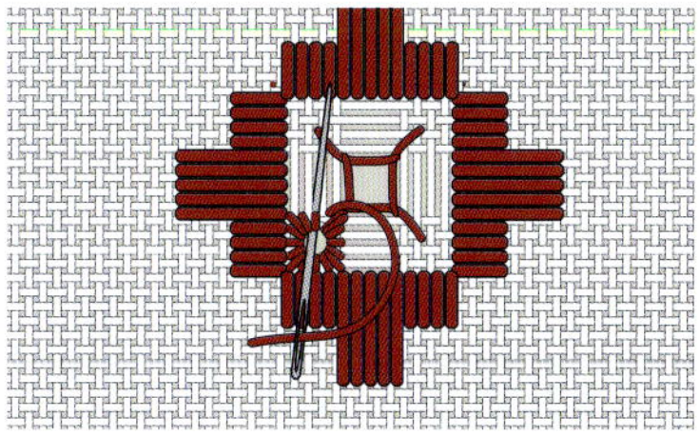

11 Continue around, with five stitches on each side, tightening after each stitch. Turn the work as needed. Complete the final stitch and bring the needle out to weave the adjacent bar.

! *Pull the eyelet stitches tightly as an eyelet should be a hole, not a pinprick.*

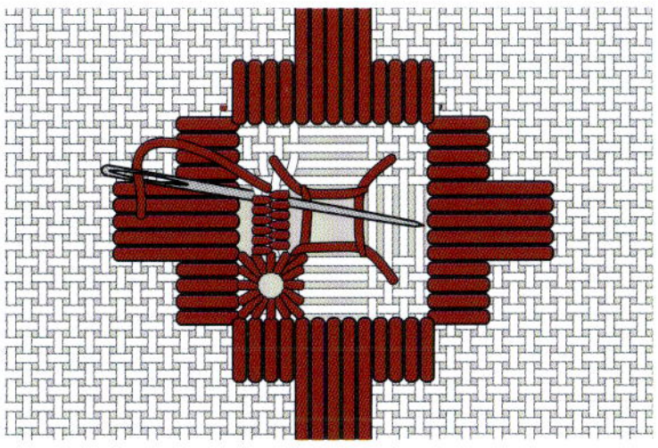

12 Weave the bar, finishing with a stitch on the left, then bring the needle out in the central open square, below the next corner stitches of the square filet.

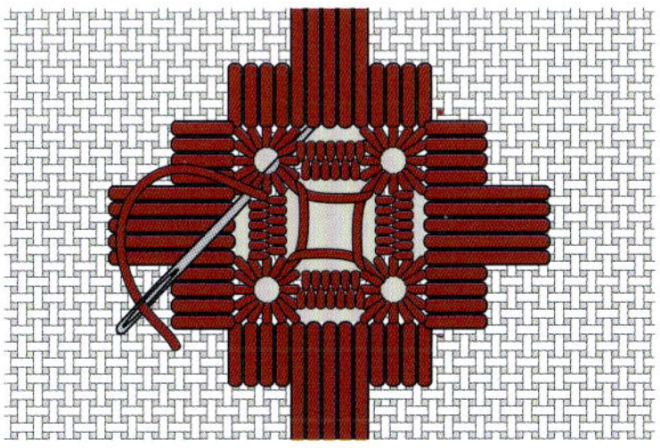

13 Repeat the eyelets and woven bars, going around the square filet corner stitches. Take the thread to the back on completion.

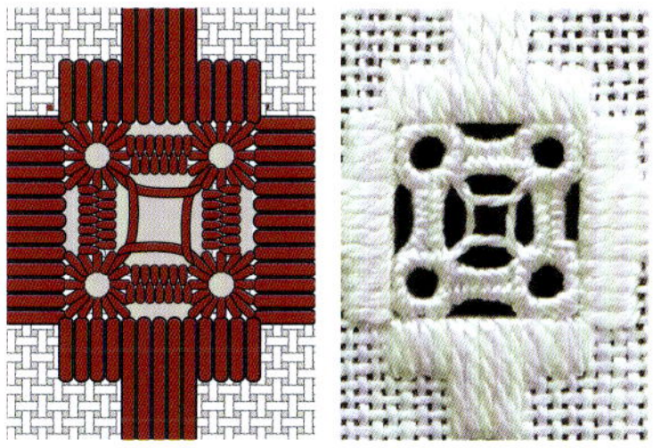

14 Finish the thread on the back under the adjacent satin stitch.

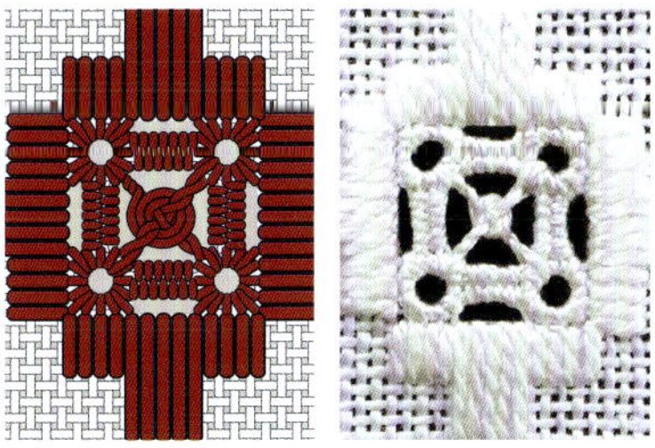

! *Spider webs can be worked similarly, with the spider web completed before the eyelet.*

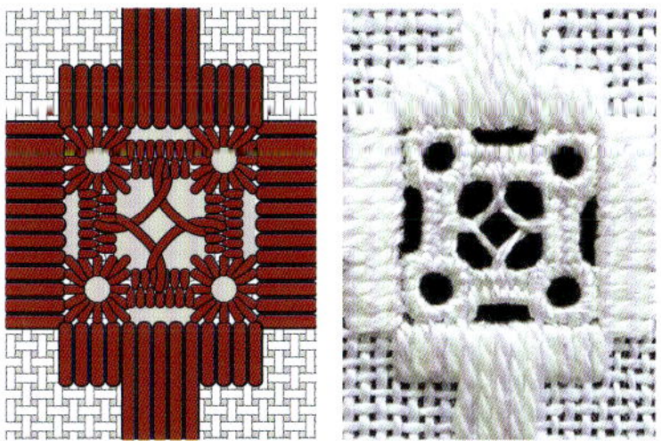

! *Dove's eyes can be worked while weaving the fourth bar of the motif.*

corner eyelets with square filet

When fillings are worked where the anchoring points are in the corners of the large square, such as with square filets or spider webs, they should be worked first, before the eyelets and woven bars are completed.

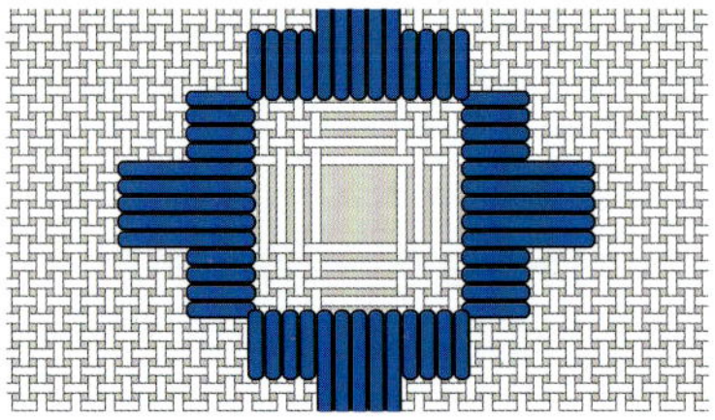

1 Cut and withdraw four threads in the centre of each side, so that woven squares remain in the corners, with fabric threads between them.

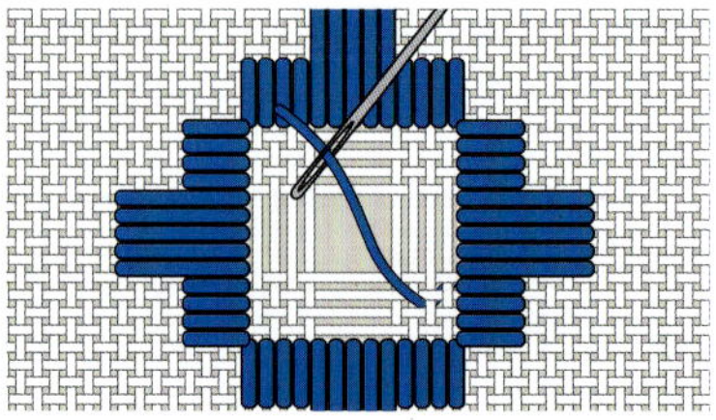

2 Anchor the thread in the back of the satin stitch and bring it out in the centre of the bottom right woven square.

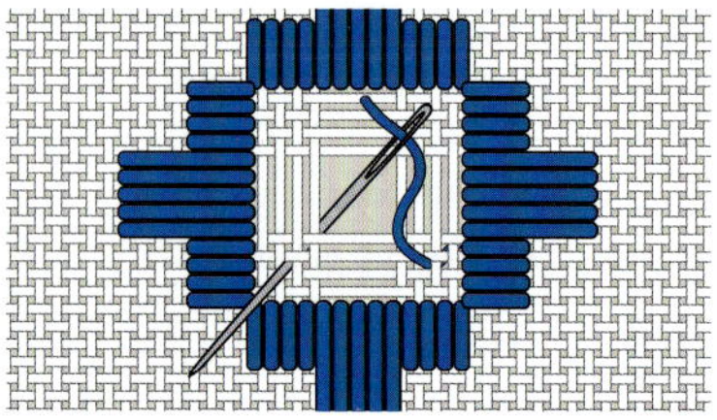

3 Working clockwise, insert the needle in the centre back of the next woven square.

❶ *Always insert the needle in the back.*

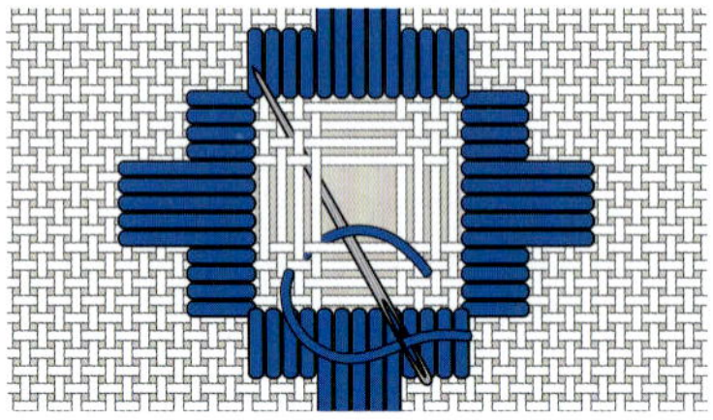

4 Pull the needle through. Insert the needle under the previous stitch and into the centre back of the next woven square.

❶ *Make sure the square filet is worked tighter than normal as it will loosen off when you work the eyelets.*

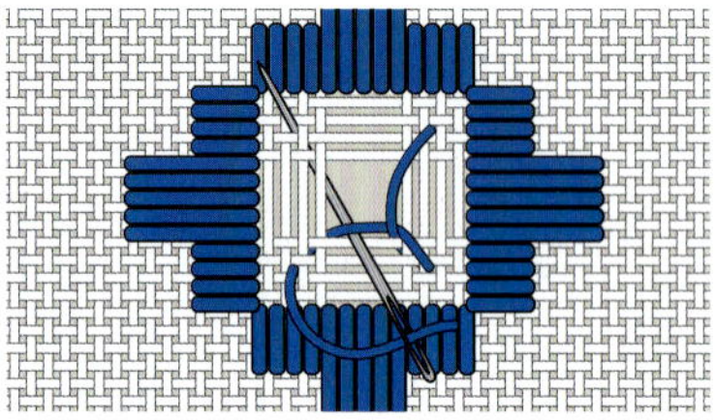

5 Pull the needle through. Turn the work 90° anticlockwise. Insert the needle under the previous stitch and into the centre back of the next woven square.

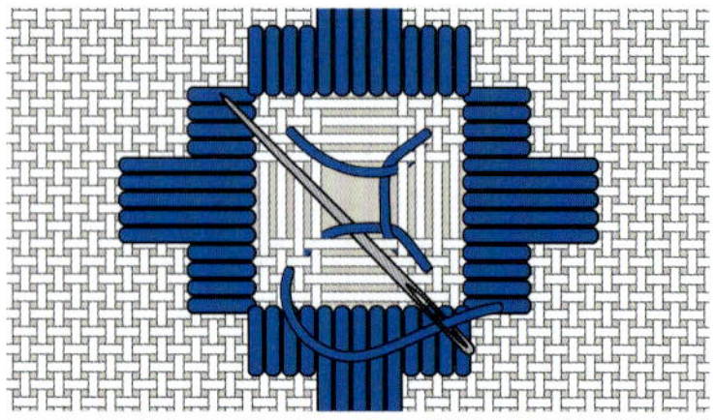

6 Pull the needle through. Turn the work 90° anticlockwise. Slide the needle under the previous stitch.

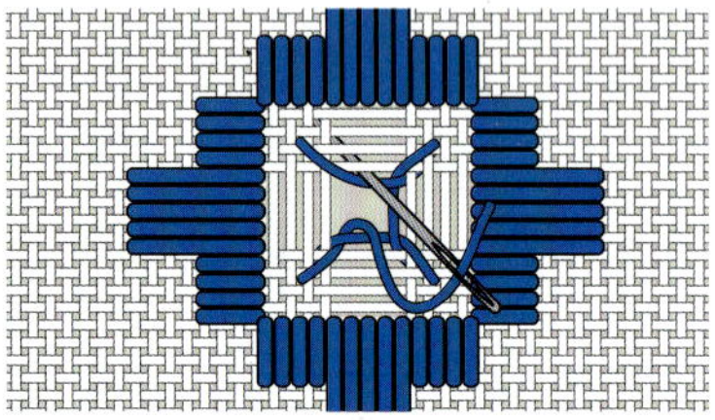

7 Take the needle over the initial stitch, then to the back.

❶ *The thread needs to come out in the same place it was just inserted, so in the next step it will be anchored on the back to allow it to come out of the same hole without simply undoing the stitch.*

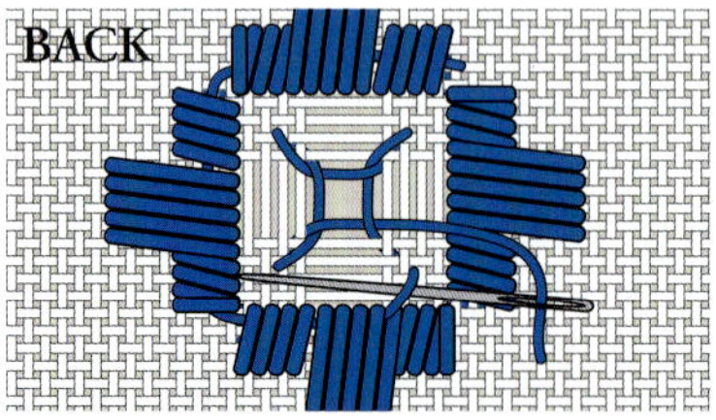

8 On the back, slide the needle under the thread leading from the tail to the stitching.

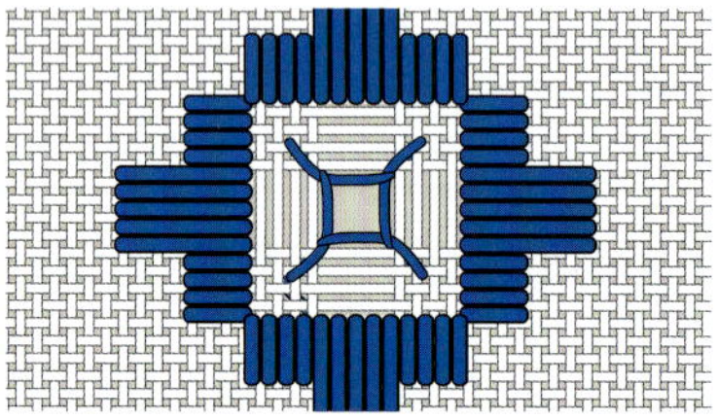

❶ *Before you go any further, make sure the square filet is quite tight. It will loosen off once you stitch the eyelets, at which point it will not be possible to tighten it. If you need to tighten the square filet, do it now before it is too late.*

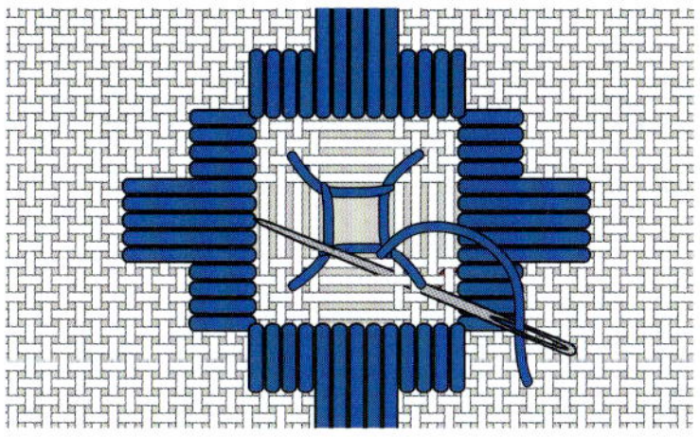

9 Working from the front, bring the needle out in the same corner, below the square filet. Insert the needle into the woven square's centre. Take it behind the threads on the back. Bring it out one thread below where it last emerged.

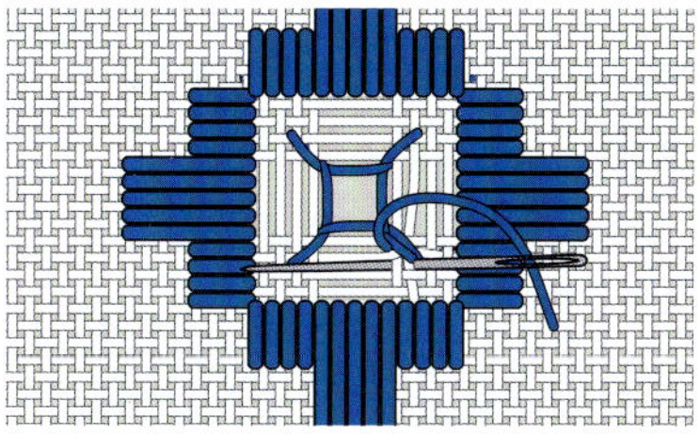

10 Pull the needle through and pinch and pull to tighten the stitch. Insert the needle in the centre of the eyelet. Take the needle behind the threads on the back, and bring it out again one thread down from where it last emerged.

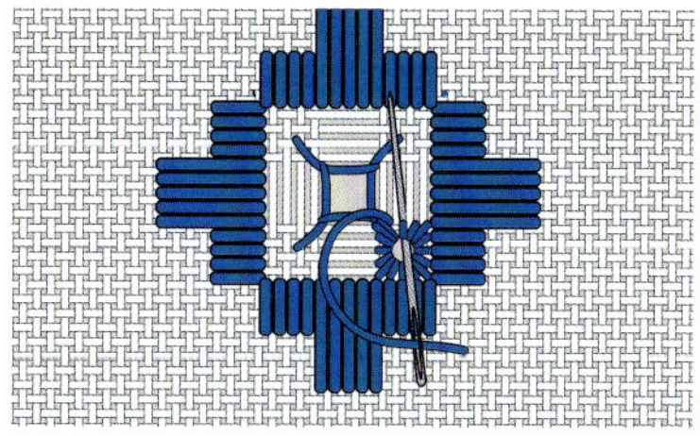

11 Continue around, with five stitches on each side, tightening after each stitch. Turn the work as needed. Complete the final stitch and bring the needle out to weave the adjacent bar.

❶ *Pull the eyelet stitches tightly as an eyelet should be a hole, not a pinprick.*

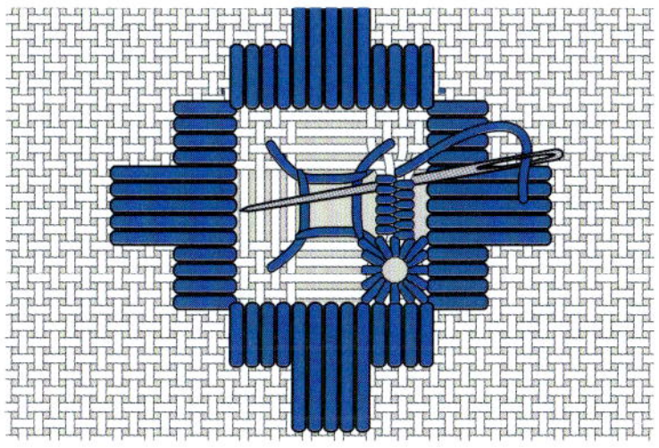

12 Weave the bar, finishing with a stitch on the right, then bring the needle out in the central open square, below the next corner stitches of the square filet.

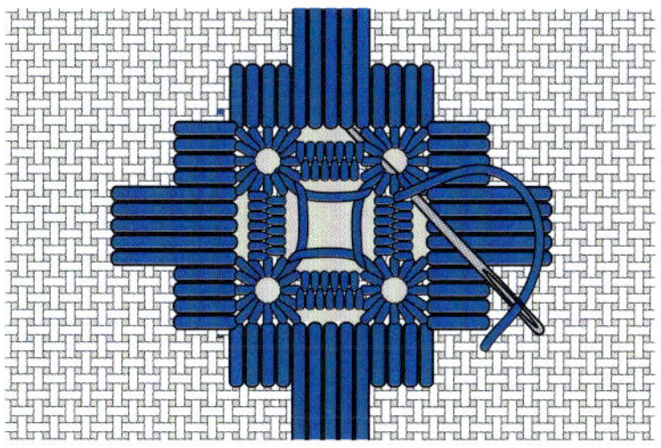

13 Repeat the eyelets and woven bars, going around the square filet corner stitches. Take the thread to the back on completion.

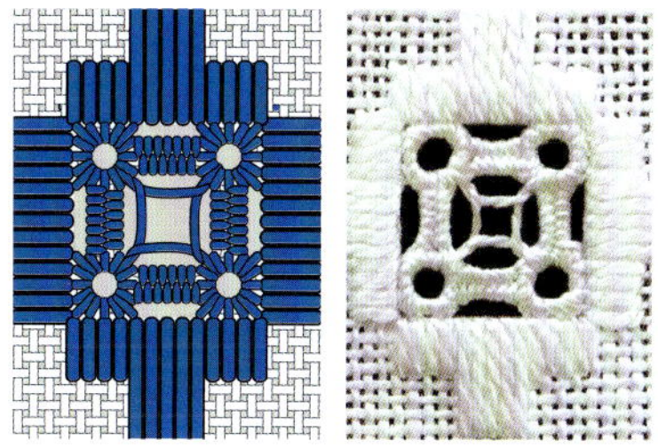

14 Finish the thread on the back under the adjacent satin stitch.

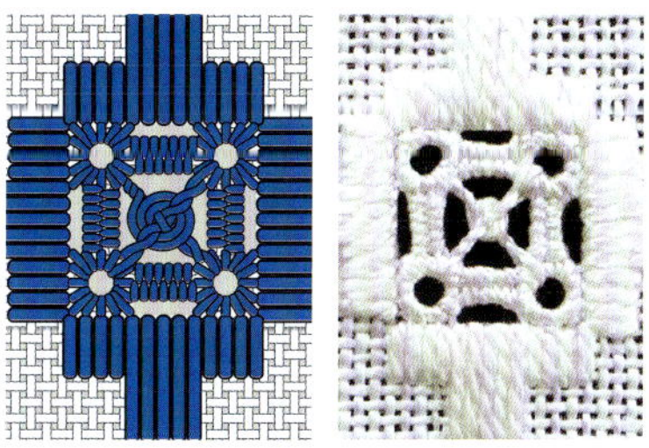

❶ *Spider webs can be worked similarly, with the spider web completed before the eyelet.*

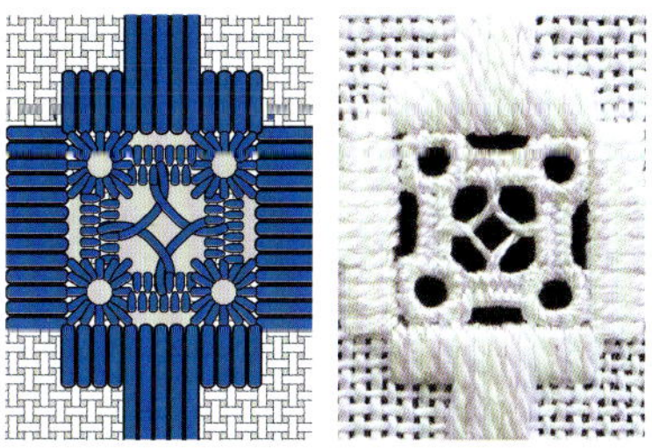

❶ *Dove's eyes can be worked while weaving the fourth bar of the motif.*

corner eyelets with divided wrapped bars

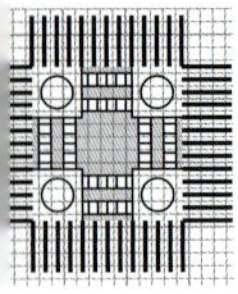

CONTEMPORARY

When working with divided bars, the process is a little different to working with full-width bars. Wrapped bars are shown here, but they could also be woven.

1 Cut and withdraw four threads in the centre of each side, so that woven squares remain in the corners, with fabric threads between them.

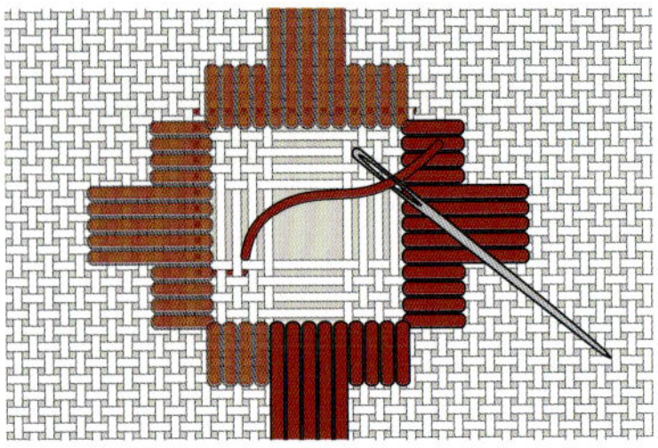

2 Anchor the thread in the back of the satin stitch and bring it out centrally at the bottom of the left bar.

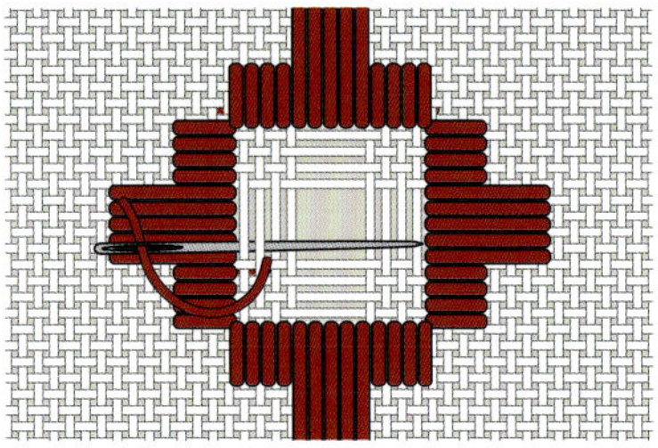

3 Slide the needle under the left two threads of the bar, from the left.

❶ *Wrapping only two threads is half the width of a regular bar.*

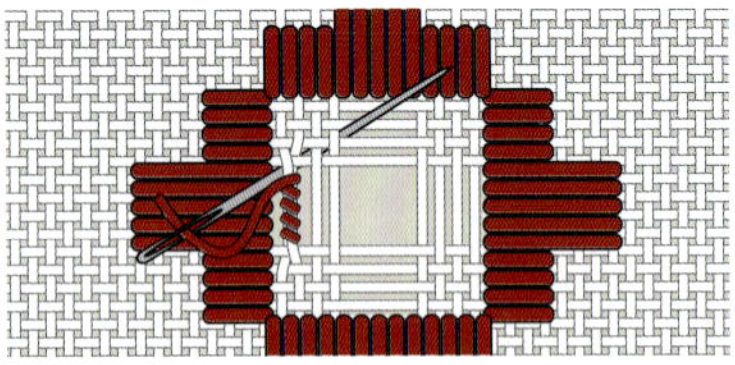

4 Pull the thread to tighten the stitch and continue tightly wrapping the half-width bar. To complete it and move to the next, pass the needle behind the woven square and bring it out centrally in the next bar.

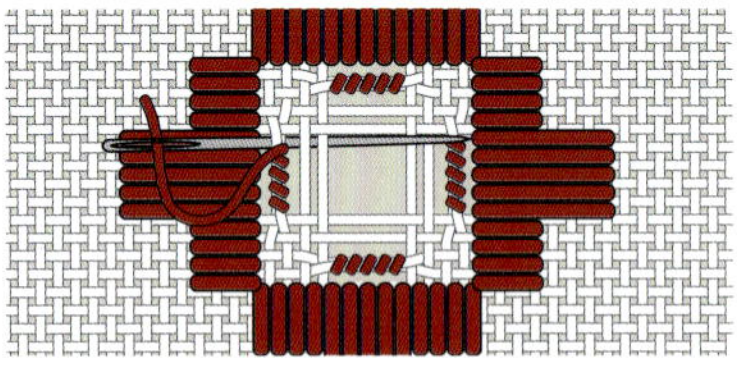

5 Wrap half-width bars along each side's outside edge, turning the work as needed. To move on, bring the needle out in the closest corner of the central open square.

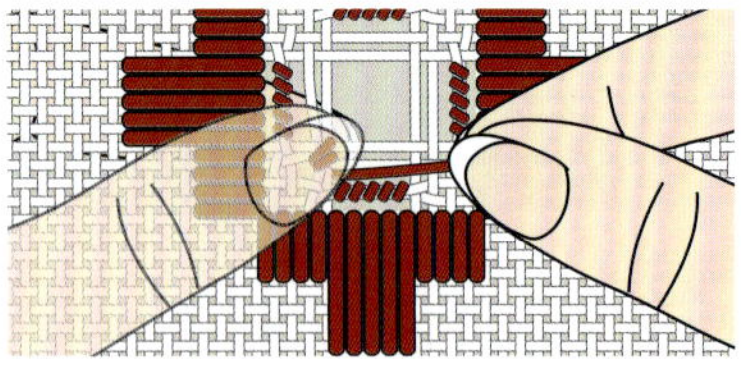

6 Work Steps 3 to 6 of 'Corner eyelets with full-width bars' shown on page 208.

❶ *As you go, work over the stitches that span the back of the eyelet areas.*

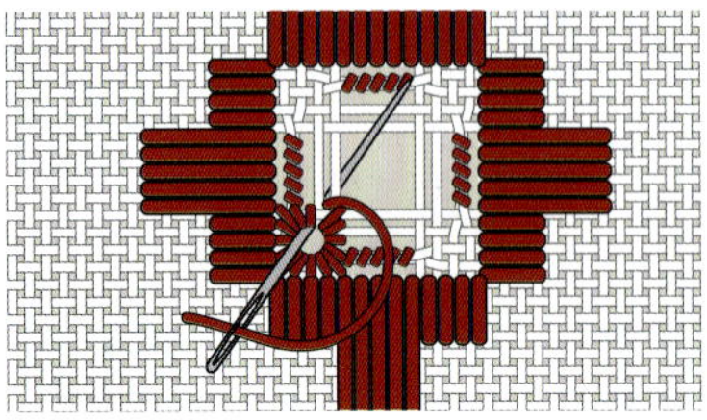

7 Continue around, with five stitches on each side, tightening after each stitch. Turn the work as needed, to make needle insertion easier. Complete the final stitch and bring the needle out in the closest corner of the central open square.

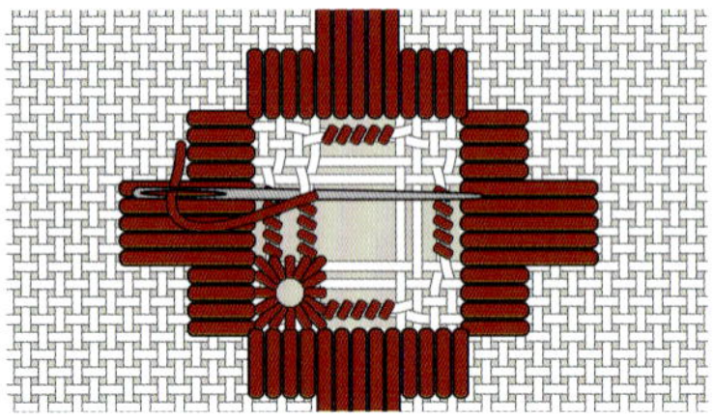

8 Wrap the bar, then bring the needle out in the central open square.

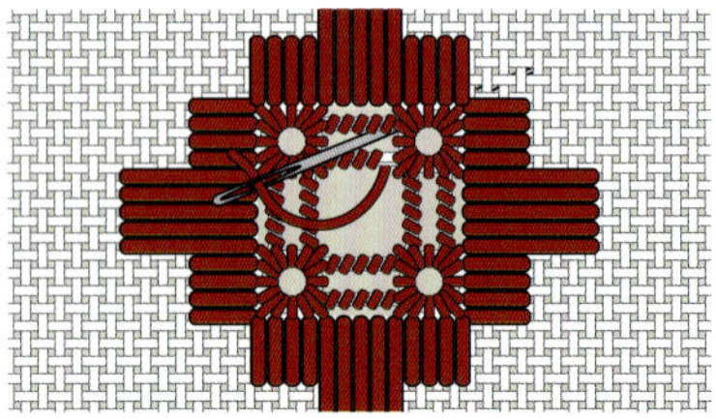

9 Repeat the eyelets and wrapped half-width bars, turning the work as required. Take the thread to the back on completion.

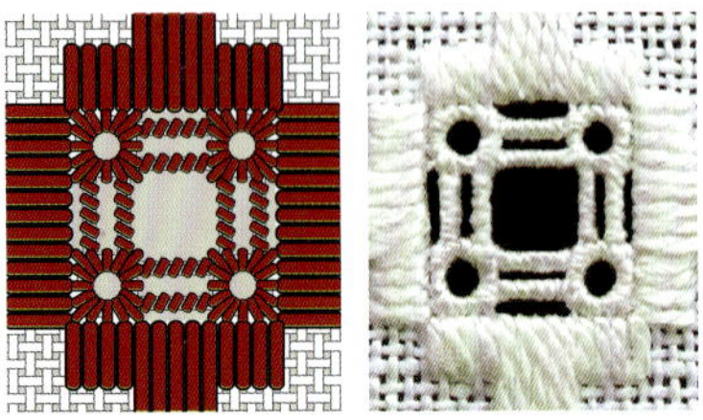

10 Finish the thread on the back by running it under the back of the adjacent satin stitch.

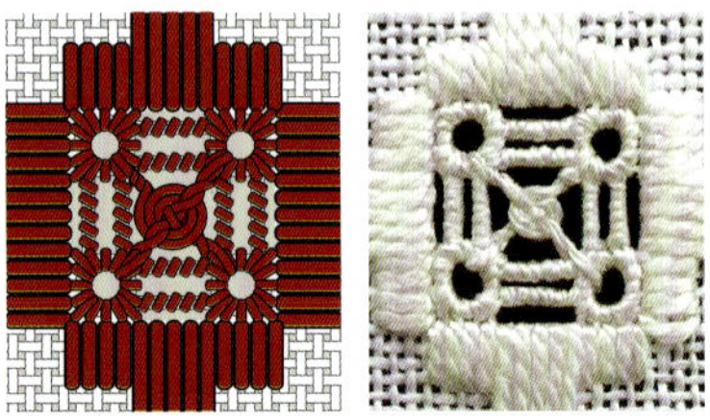

❶ *Filling stitches can be worked in the centre as part of the stitching process.*

corner eyelets with divided wrapped bars

When working with divided bars, the process is a little different to working with full-width bars. Wrapped bars are shown here, but they could also be woven.

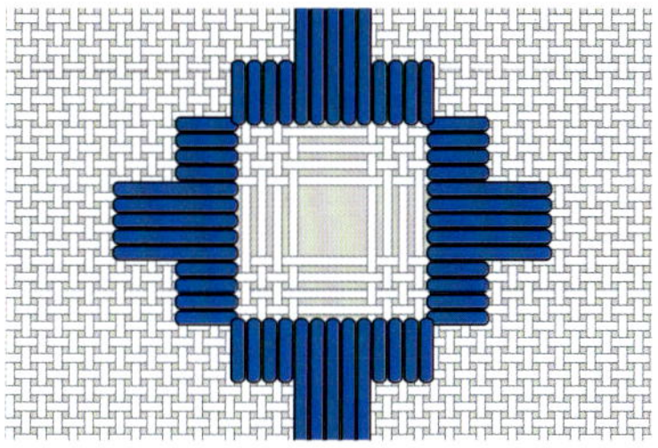

1 Cut and withdraw four threads in the centre of each side, so that woven squares remain in the corners, with fabric threads between them.

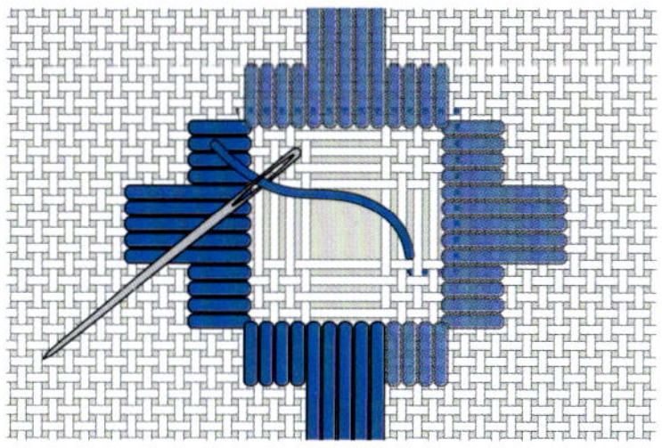

2 Anchor the thread in the back of the satin stitch and bring it out centrally at the bottom of the right bar.

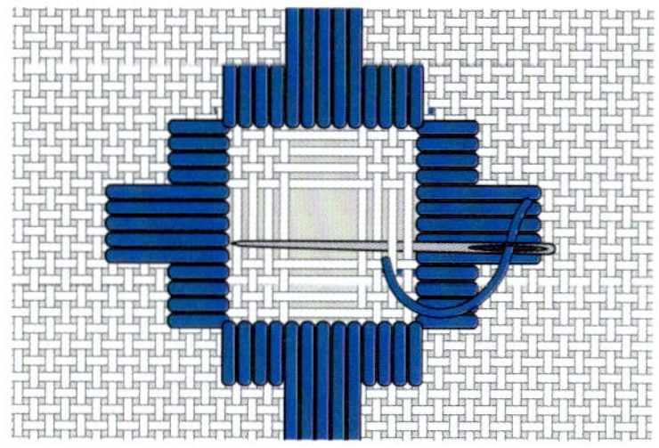

3 Slide the needle under the right two threads of the bar, from the right.

❶ *Wrapping only two threads is half the width of a regular bar.*

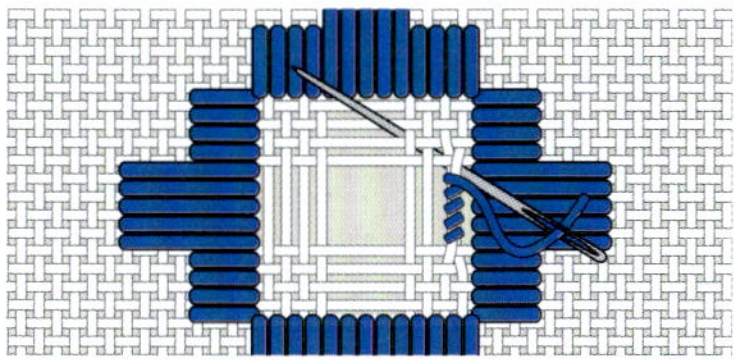

4 Pull the thread to tighten the stitch and continue tightly wrapping the half-width bar. To complete it and move to the next, pass the needle behind the woven square and bring it out centrally in the next bar.

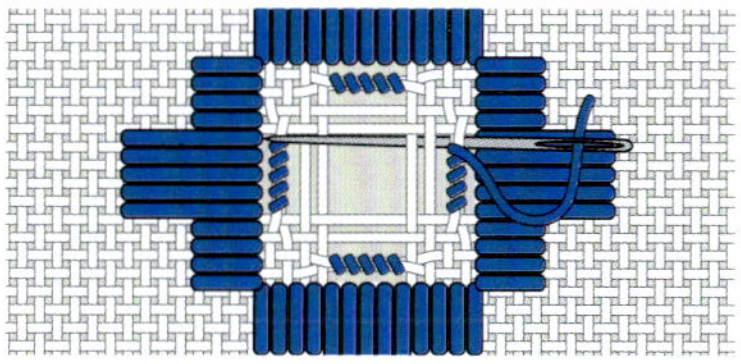

5 Wrap half-width bars along each side's outside edge, turning the work as needed. To move on, bring the needle out in the closest corner of the central open square.

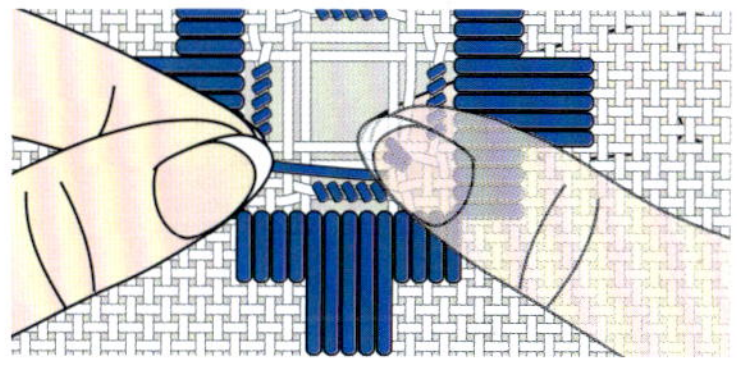

6 Work Steps 3 to 6 of 'Corner eyelets with full-width bars' shown on page 209.

❶ *As you go, work over the stitches that span the back of the eyelet areas.*

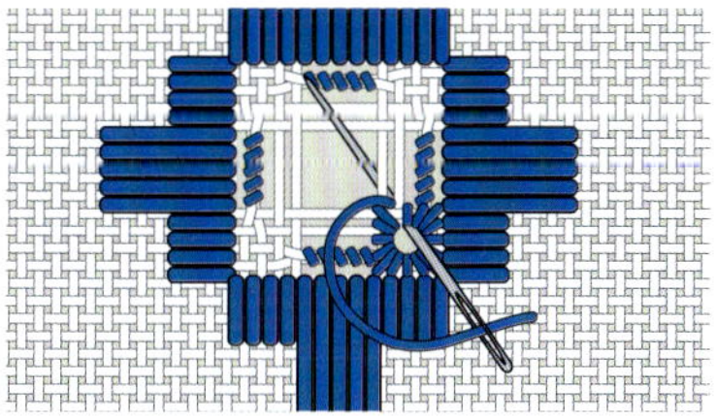

7 Continue around, with five stitches on each side, tightening after each stitch. Turn the work as needed, to make needle insertion easier. Complete the final stitch and bring the needle out in the closest corner of the central open square.

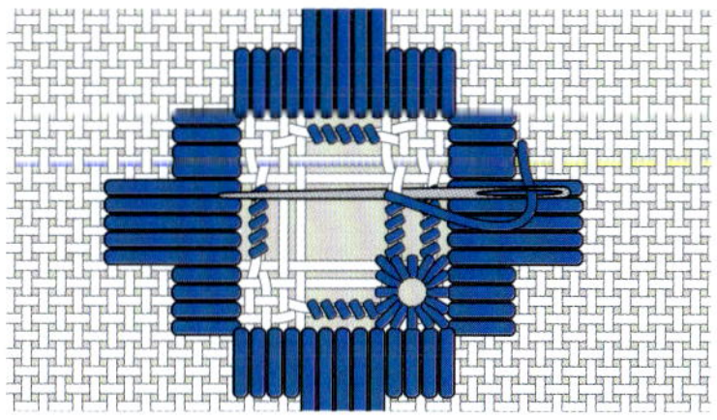

8 Wrap the bar, then bring the needle out in the central open square.

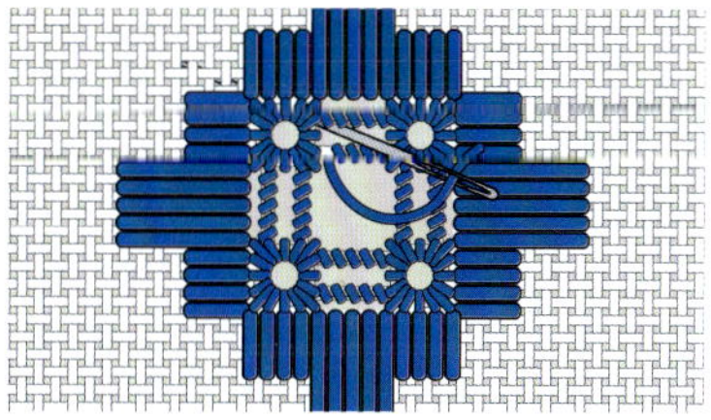

9 Repeat the eyelets and wrapped half-width bars, turning the work as required. Take the thread to the back on completion.

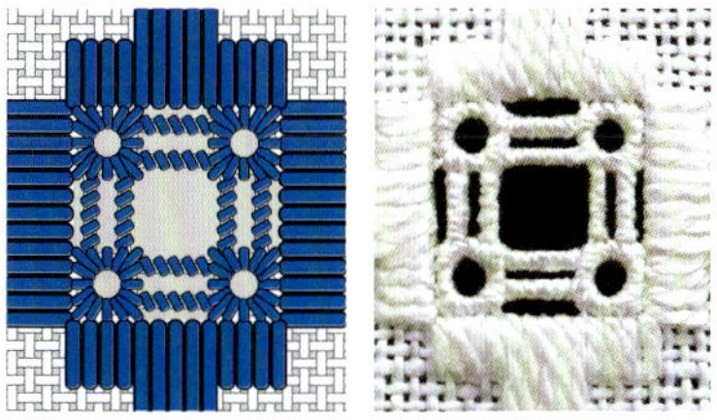

10 Finish the thread on the back by running it under the back of the adjacent satin stitch.

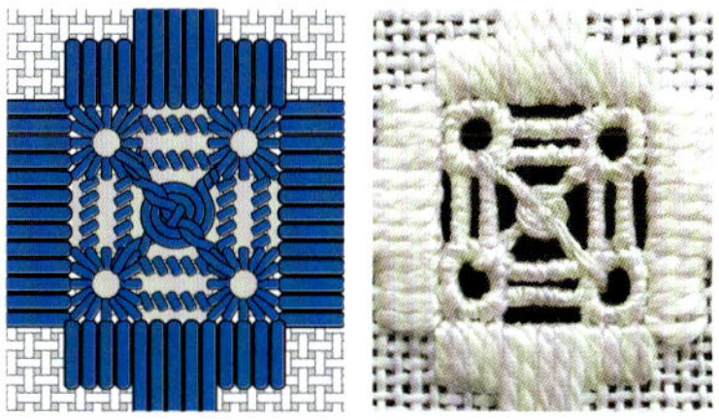

❶ *Filling stitches can be worked in the centre as part of the stitching process.*

L

CONTEMPORARY

simplified eyelets at intersections

In cutwork areas, any woven fabric square between bars can have a simplified eyelet worked in them. It is a simple process that easily adds laciness to a design. They can be worked in the centre of large cutwork squares, or across a whole area of cutwork.

Simplified eyelets at intersections are worked as late in the process as possible so as not to distort the surrounding fabric threads. Whether using straight or zig-zagging lines for the weaving or wrapping, the eyelets are worked on the second pass through an area i.e. the second time you come to the intersection, not the first time. Generally, when three of the bars leading to the intersection have been worked, that is the time to work the eyelet.

In planning the path for the eyelet stitching, you want to end up with the final stitches against the bar you're about to stitch. It does not matter whether you move around the square in a clockwise or anticlockwise direction when making your stitches.

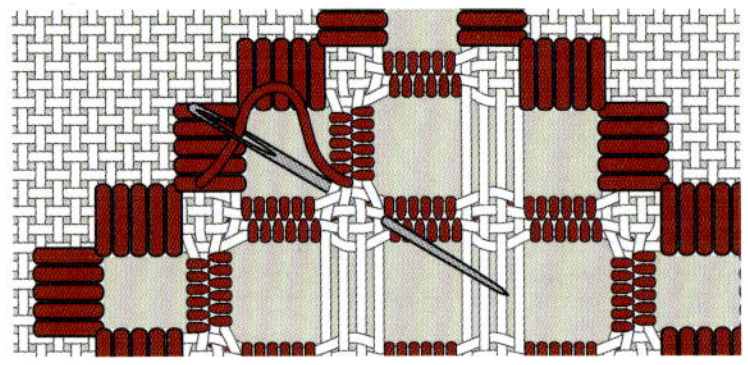

1 When you reach the intersection for the eyelet, finish the previous bar by passing the needle behind the woven square and bringing it out at the centre of the end of the adjacent bar on the opposite side.

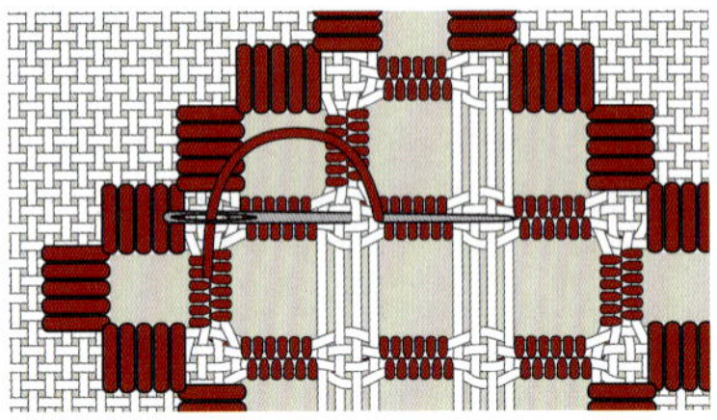

2 Pull the needle through. Insert the needle in the centre of the woven square and bring it out in the same hole as previously.

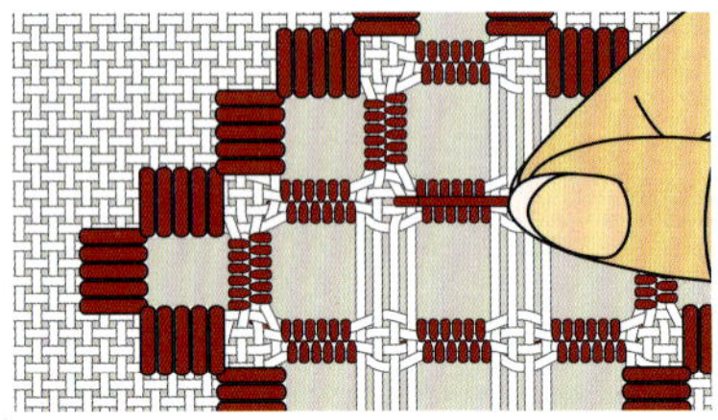

3 Pull the needle through. Pull the thread away from the centre to tighten the stitch and begin making the hole.

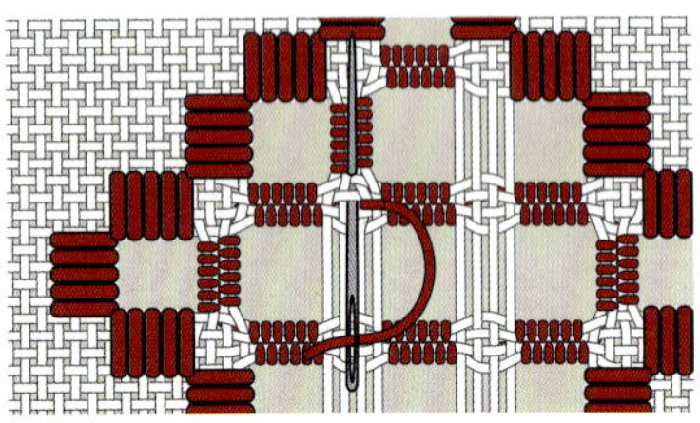

4 Insert the needle in the centre and bring it out at the centre of the end of the just completed bar.

Each side will have two stitches.

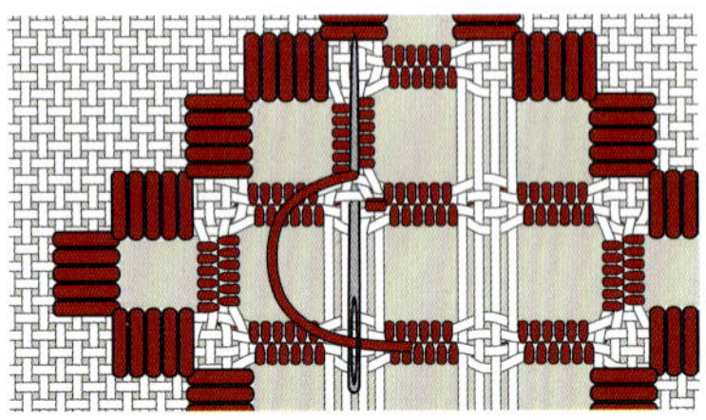

5 Pull the needle through. Insert the needle in the centre of the woven square and bring it out in the same place as previously.

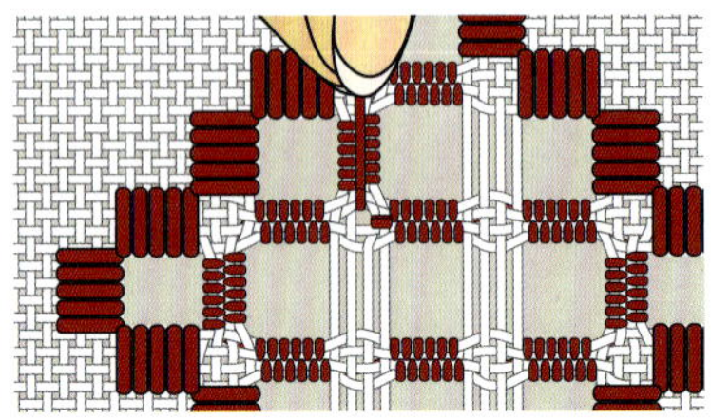

6 Pull the needle through. Pull the thread away from the centre to tighten the stitch and open the hole further.

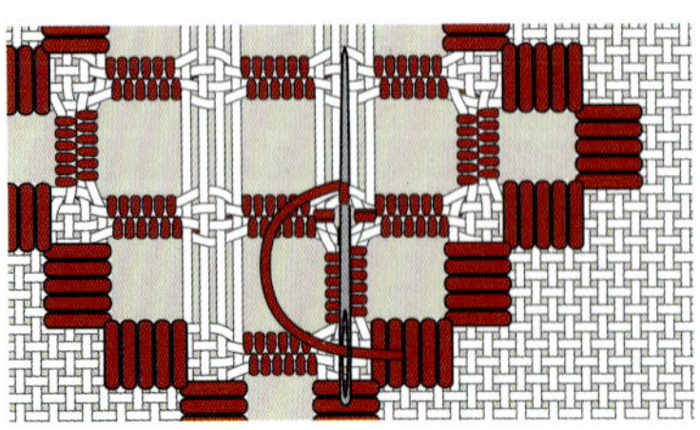

7 Continue around the eyelet, making two stitches in each side and tightening them. Turn the work as necessary. To complete the eyelet, bring the needle out ready to work the next bar.

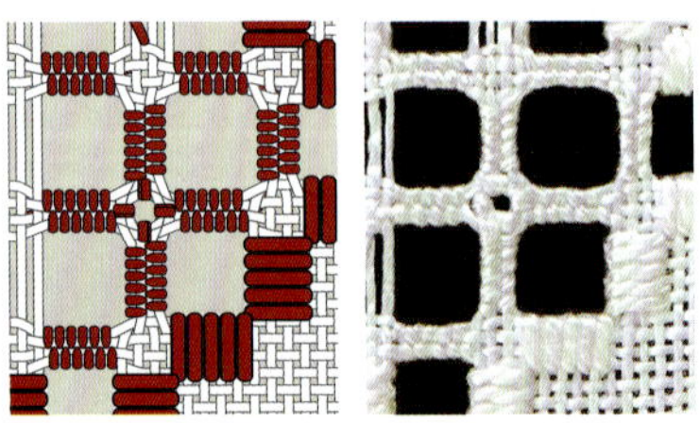

8 The completed eyelet. Work bars and additional eyelets as desired.

These eyelets are not usually worked adjacent to satin stitching, but if they fit there, there's no reason why they can't be!

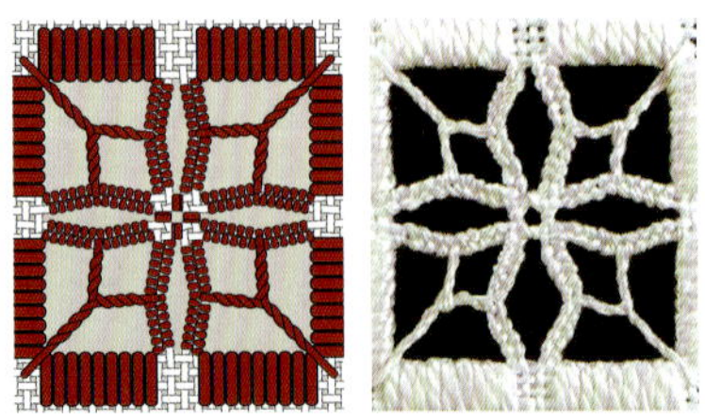

These simplified eyelets can be worked in the centre of motifs in large squares.

simplified eyelets at intersections

In cutwork areas, any woven fabric square between bars can have a simplified eyelet worked in them. It is a simple process that easily adds laciness to a design. They can be worked in the centre of large cutwork squares, or across a whole area of cutwork.

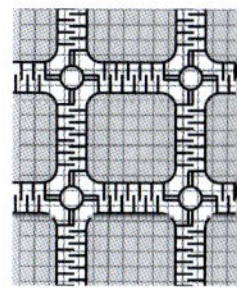

❶ *Simplified eyelets at intersections are worked as late in the process as possible so as not to distort the surrounding fabric threads. Whether using straight or zig-zagging lines for the weaving or wrapping, the eyelets are worked on the second pass through an area i.e. the second time you come to the intersection, not the first time. Generally, when three of the bars leading to the intersection have been worked, that is the time to work the eyelet.*

❶ *In planning the path for the eyelet stitching, you want to end up with the final stitches against the bar you're about to stitch. It does not matter whether you move around the square in a clockwise or anticlockwise direction when making your stitches.*

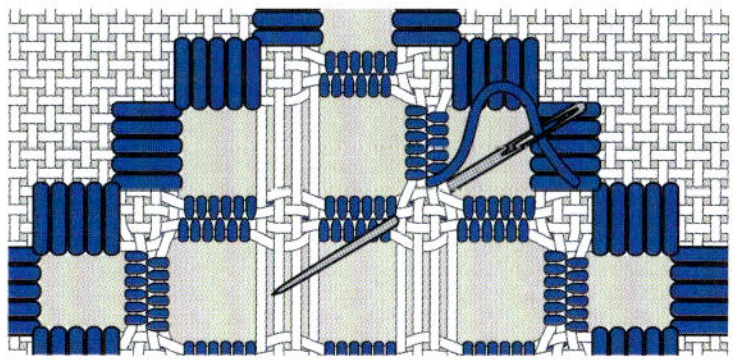

1 When you reach the intersection for the eyelet, finish the previous bar by passing the needle behind the woven square and bringing it out at the centre of the end of the adjacent bar on the opposite side.

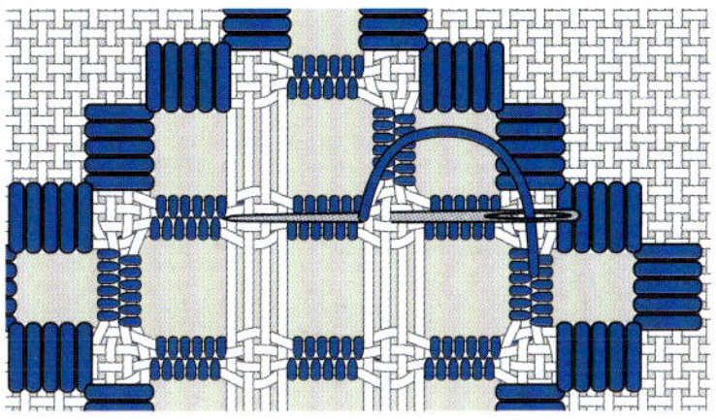

2 Pull the needle through. Insert the needle in the centre of the woven square and bring it out in the same place as previously.

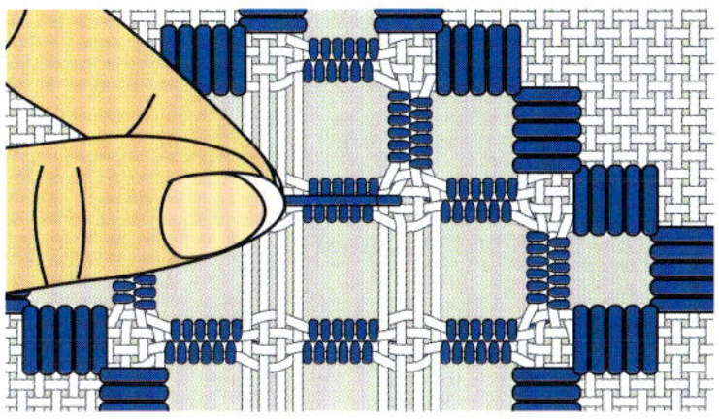

3 Pull the needle through. Pull the thread away from the centre to tighten the stitch and begin making the hole.

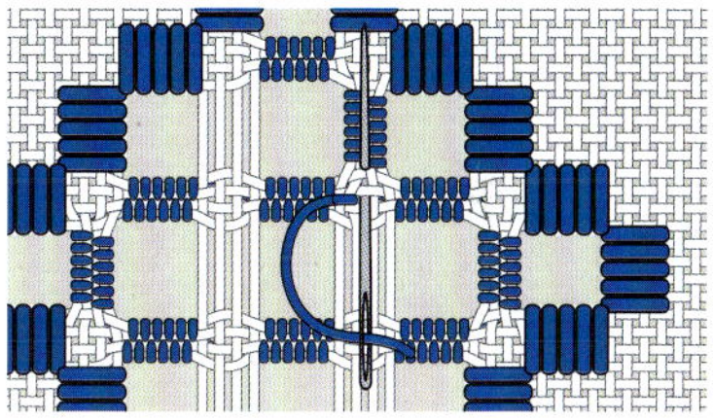

4 Insert the needle in the centre and bring it out at the centre of the end of the just completed bar.

❶ *Each side will have two stitches.*

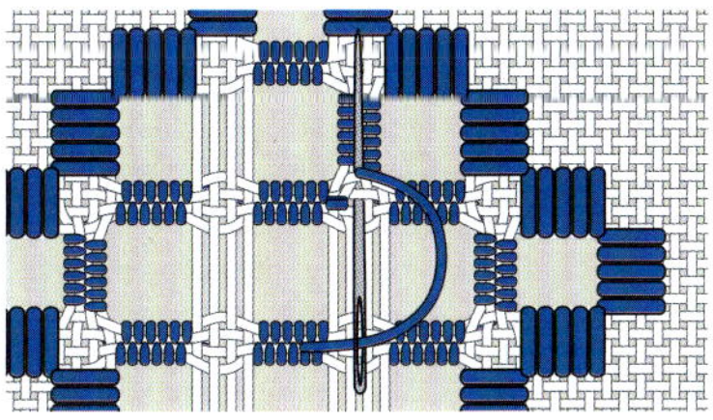

5 Pull the needle through. Insert the needle in the centre of the woven square and bring it out in the same place as previously.

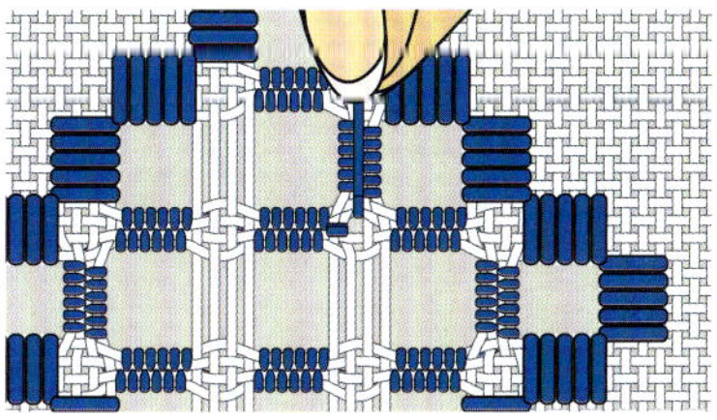

6 Pull the needle through. Pull the thread away from the centre to tighten the stitch and open the hole further.

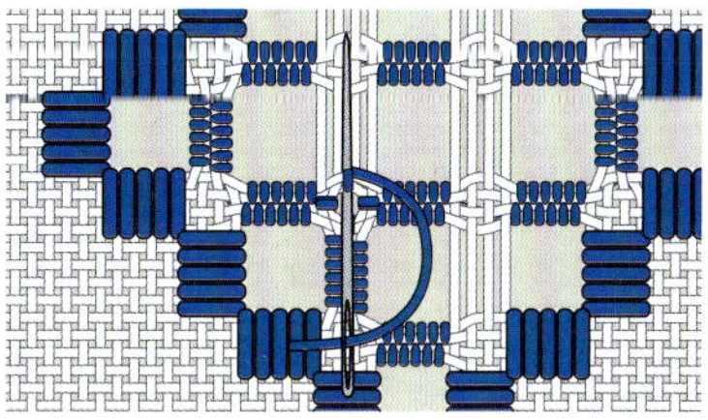

7 Continue around the eyelet, making two stitches in each side and tightening them. Turn the work as necessary. To complete the eyelet, bring the needle out ready to work the next bar.

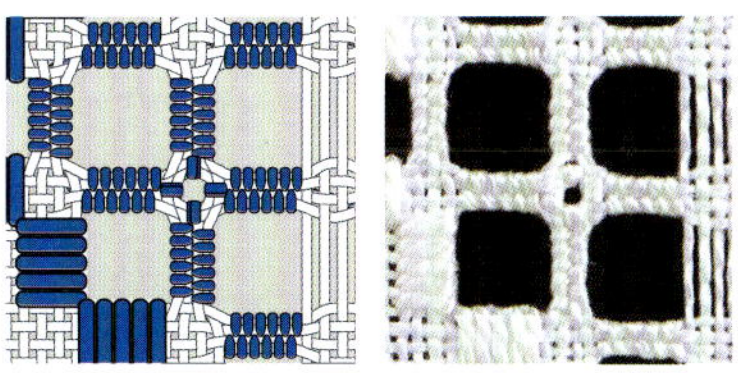

8 The completed eyelet. Work bars and additional eyelets as desired.

❶ *These eyelets are not usually worked adjacent to satin stitching, but if they fit there, there's no reason why they can't be!*

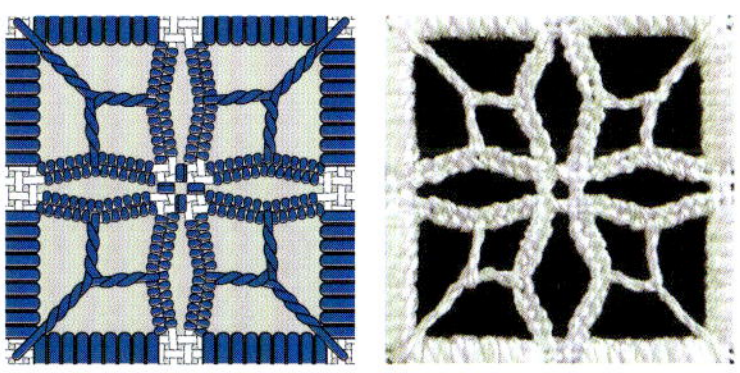

❶ *These simplified eyelets can be worked in the centre of motifs in large squares.*

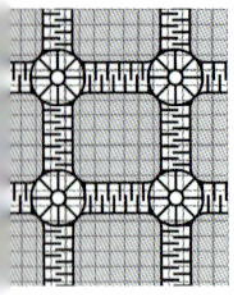

buttonhole eyelets at intersections

Buttonhole eyelets can be worked with a stitch between every fabric thread. However, it looks just as effective and is much easier if you only work a stitch between every second fabric thread.

❶ *Buttonhole eyelets at intersections are worked as late in the process as possible so as not to distort the surrounding fabric threads. Whether using straight or zig-zagging lines for the weaving or wrapping, the eyelets are worked on the second pass through an area i.e. the second time you come to the intersection, not the first time. Generally, when three of the bars leading to the intersection have been worked, that is the time to work the eyelet.*

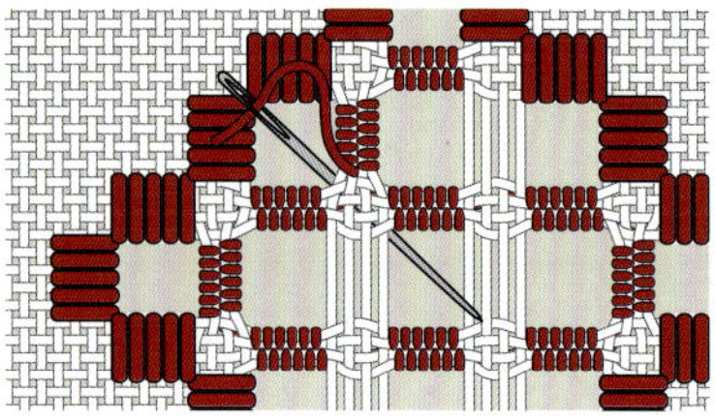

1 When you reach the intersection for the eyelet, finish the previous bar by bringing the needle out on the opposite side of the woven square.

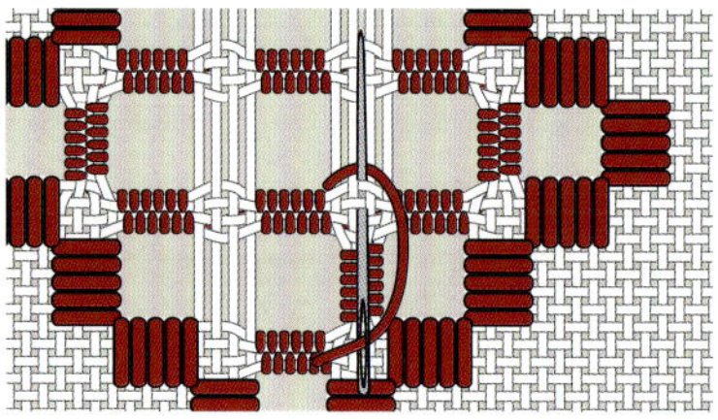

2 Turn the work 180°. Insert the needle in the centre of the woven square. Working clockwise, bring it out two threads to the right. Take the thread behind the needle point from left to right.

❶ *You can go clockwise or anticlockwise. Just be consistent throughout.*

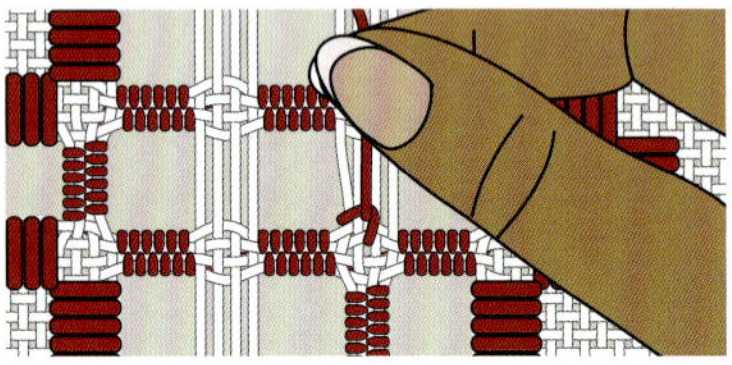

3 Pull the needle through. Pull the thread away from the centre, across the surface of the fabric, to tighten the stitch and begin making the hole.

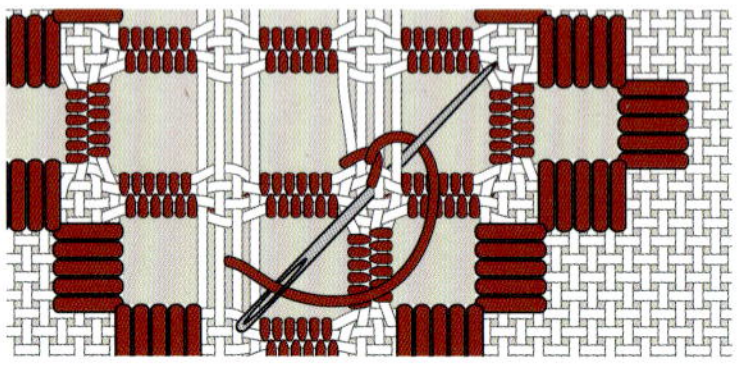

4 Insert the needle in the centre and bring it out two threads further on than the last time. Take the thread behind the needle point from left to right.

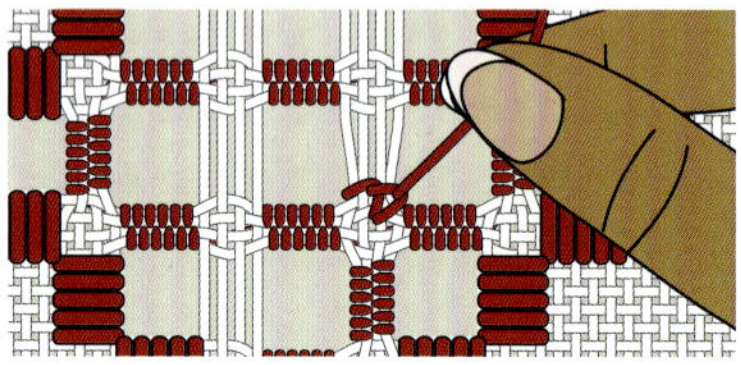

5 Pull the needle through. Pull the thread away from the centre, across the surface of the fabric, to tighten the stitch and enlarge the hole.

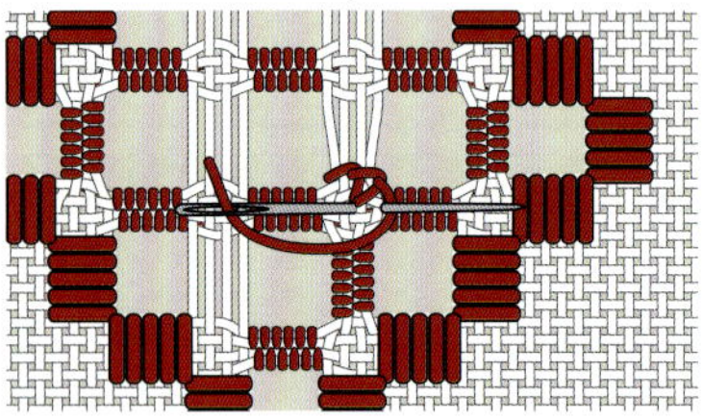

6 Insert the needle in the centre and bring it out two threads further on than the last time. Take the thread behind the needle point from top to bottom.

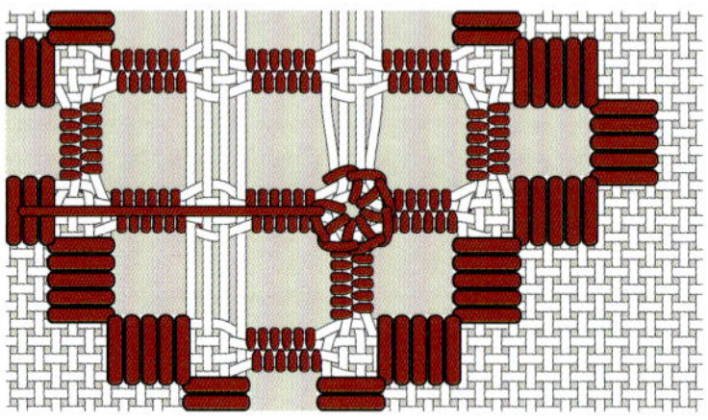

7 Continue around the eyelet, Pulling each stitch tight as you go, stopping before the last stitch.

8 Slide the needle under the first stitch, from the outside, towards the centre.

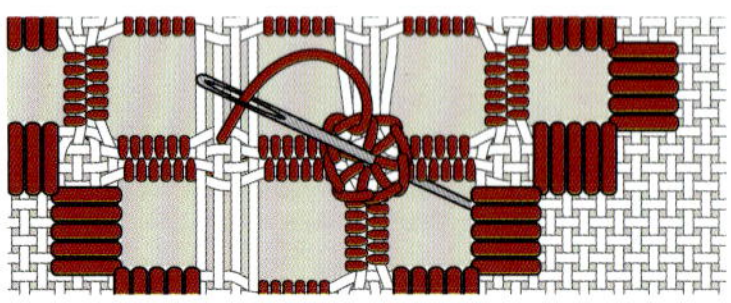

9 Take the needle to the back through the centre hole.

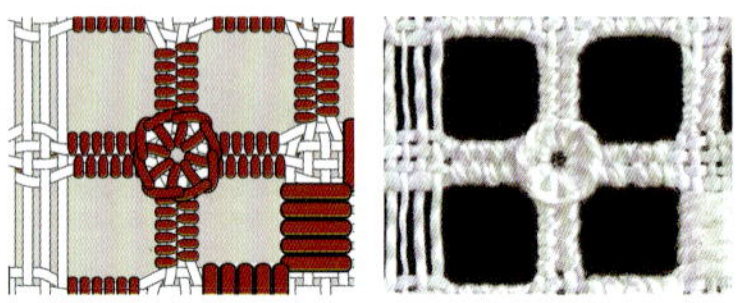

10 Pull the needle through and tighten the last stitch so that it sits and has the same tension as all the rest. Work the next woven bar.

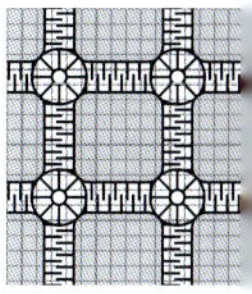

buttonhole eyelets at intersections

Buttonhole eyelets can be worked with a stitch between every fabric thread. However, it looks just as effective and is much easier if you only work a stitch between every second fabric thread.

❶ *Buttonhole eyelets at intersections are worked as late in the process as possible so as not to distort the surrounding fabric threads. Whether using straight or zig-zagging lines for the weaving or wrapping, the eyelets are worked on the second pass through an area i.e. the second time you come to the intersection, not the first time. Generally, when three of the bars leading to the intersection have been worked, that is the time to work the eyelet.*

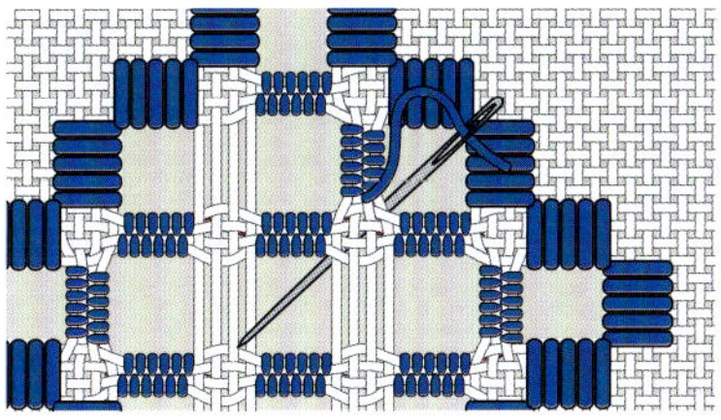

1 When you reach the intersection for the eyelet, finish the previous bar by bringing the needle out on the opposite side of the woven square.

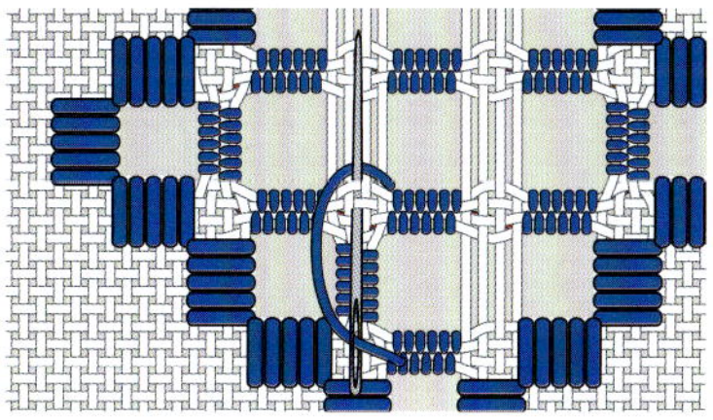

2 Turn the work 180°. Insert the needle in the centre of the woven square. Working anticlockwise, bring it out two threads to the left. Take the thread behind the needle point from right to left.

❶ *You can go clockwise or anticlockwise. Just be consistent throughout.*

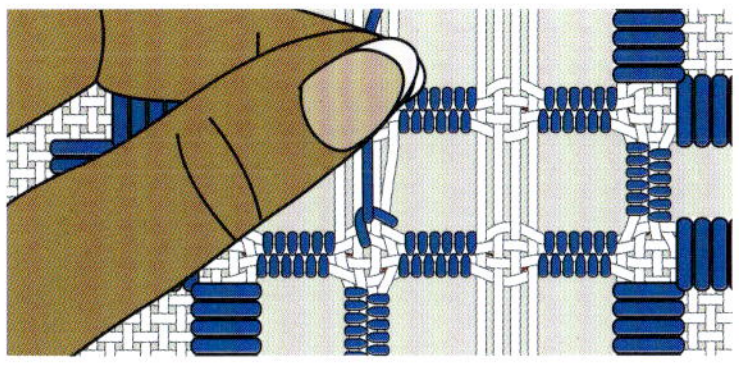

3 Pull the needle through. Pull the thread away from the centre, across the surface of the fabric, to tighten the stitch and begin making the hole.

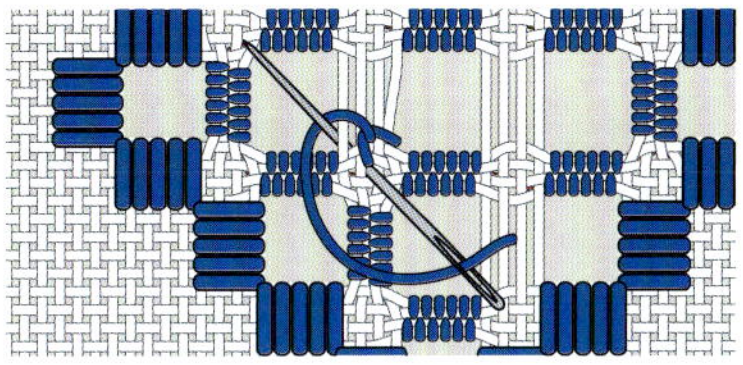

4 Insert the needle in the centre and bring it out two threads further on than the last time. Take the thread behind the needle point from right to left.

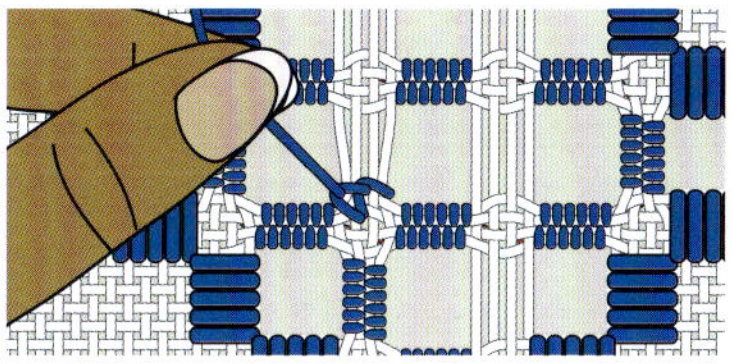

5 Pull the needle through. Pull the thread away from the centre, across the surface of the fabric, to tighten the stitch and enlarge the hole.

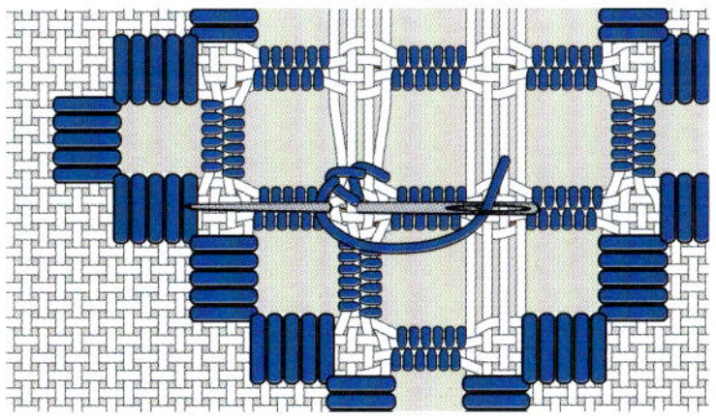

6 Insert the needle in the centre and bring it out two threads further on than the last time. Take the thread behind the needle point from top to bottom.

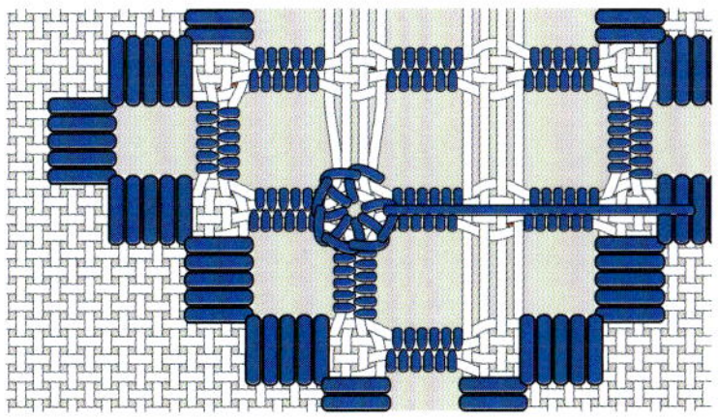

7 Continue around the eyelet, Pulling each stitch tight as you go, stopping before the last stitch.

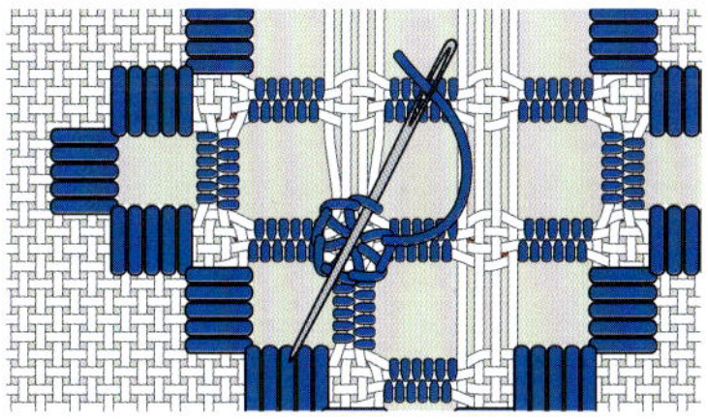

8 Slide the needle under the first stitch, from the outside, towards the centre.

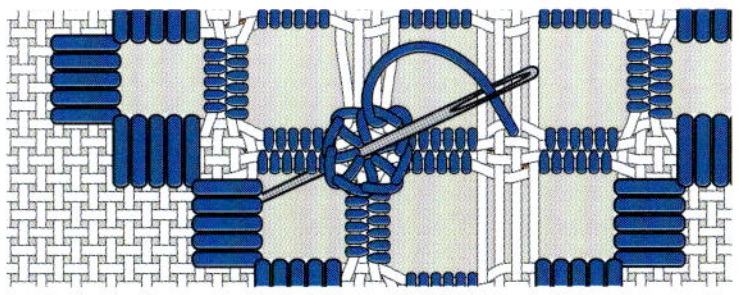

9 Take the needle to the back through the centre hole.

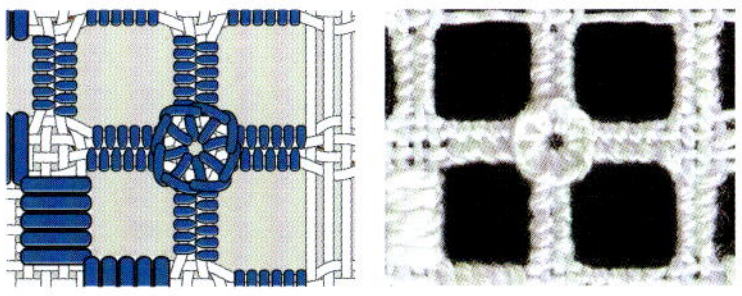

10 Pull the needle through and tighten the last stitch so that it sits and has the same tension as all the rest. Work the next woven bar.

diamond filling

Tension of the twists is very important in this stitch, so take care to have them sitting well.

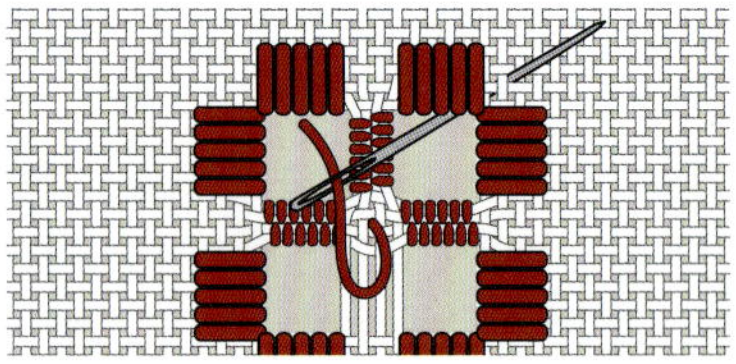

1 Weave three bars and bring the needle out in the woven square's centre. Take it to the far side of the top right quadrant and bring the needle out two threads away from each edge.

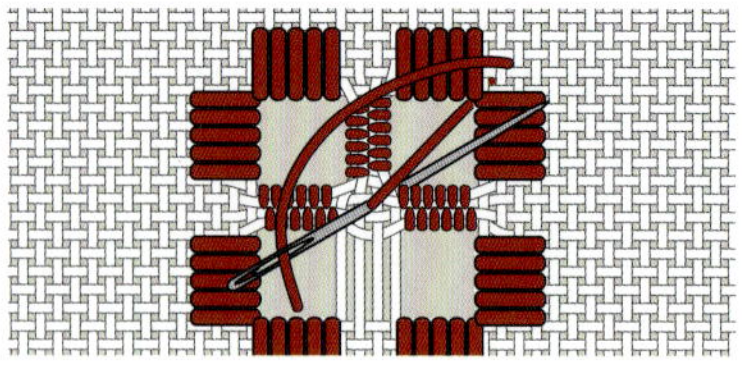

2 Insert the needle in the centre and bring the needle out below the two stitches.

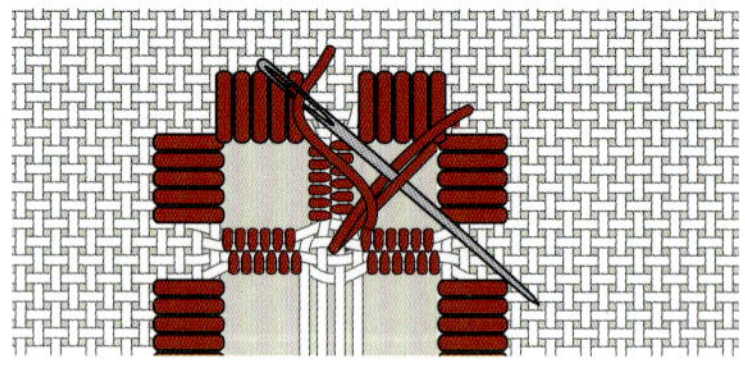

3 From above, slide the needle under the first stitch.

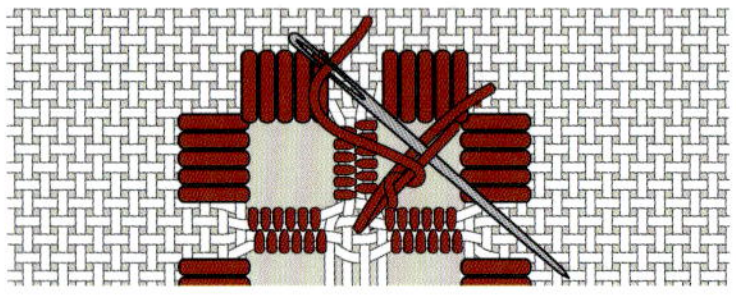

4 From above, slide the needle under the stitch again.

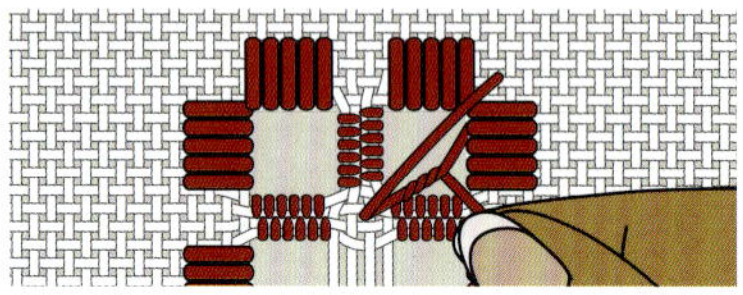

5 Pull the thread to intertwine the stitches.

❶ *Throughout the process of stitching this motif, regularly pull to intertwine.*

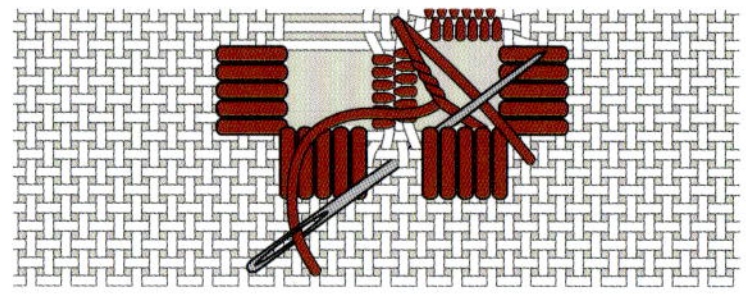

6 Turn the work 90° clockwise. Insert the needle two threads away from the end of the closest woven bar. Bring it out above the working thread.

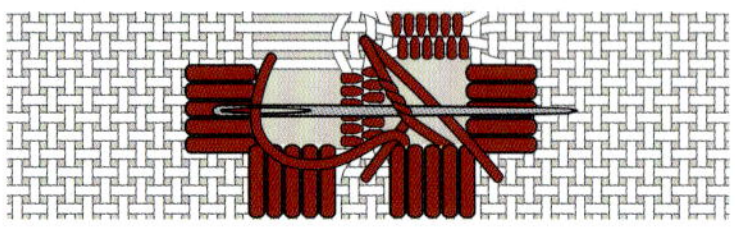

7 Above the side arm and from the left, slide the needle under the twisted section of the diagonal.

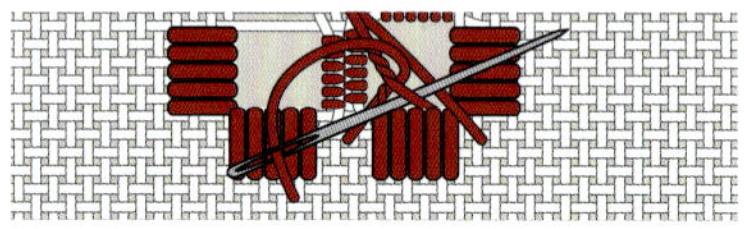

8 Pull the thread to intertwine the stitches. From the left, slide the needle under the diagonal's lower part.

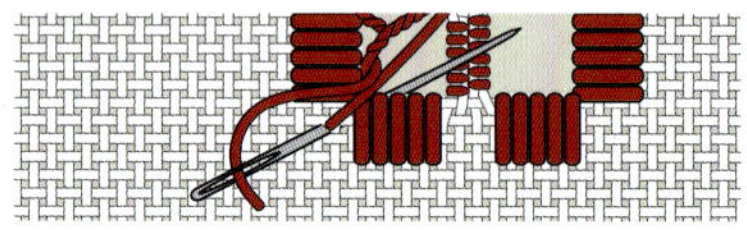

9 Turn the work 90° clockwise. Insert the needle in the corner, bringing it out below the lower diagonal.

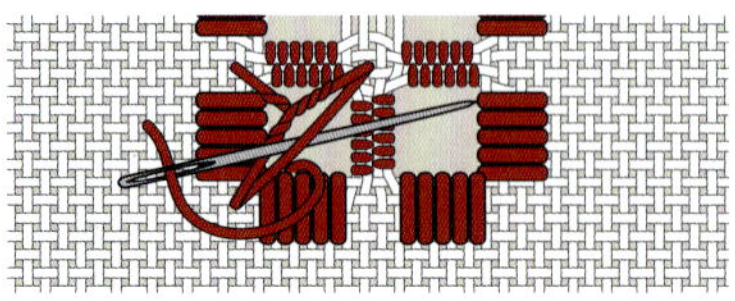

10 From the left, slide the needle under the lower diagonal.

11 From above, take the needle under the diagonal. Bring it out two threads below the closest bar's end.

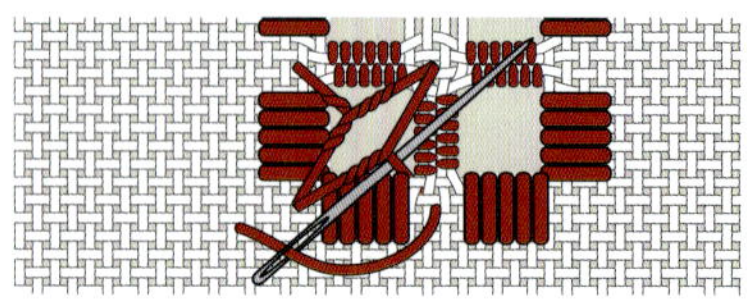

12 Pull the needle through and intertwine the stitches. From below, slide the needle under the side arm.

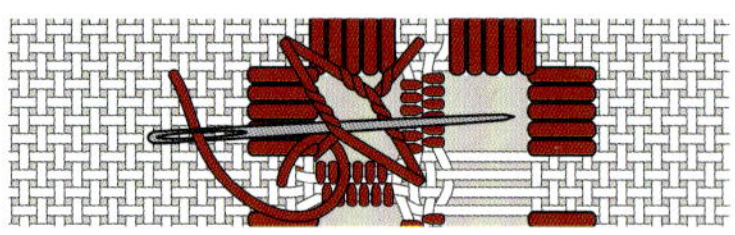

13 Turn the work 90° clockwise. From the left, slide the needle the twisted section of the diagonal.

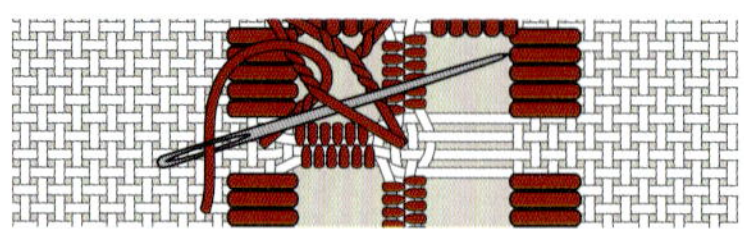

14 Pull to intertwine the stitches. From the left, slide the needle under the lower part of the diagonal.

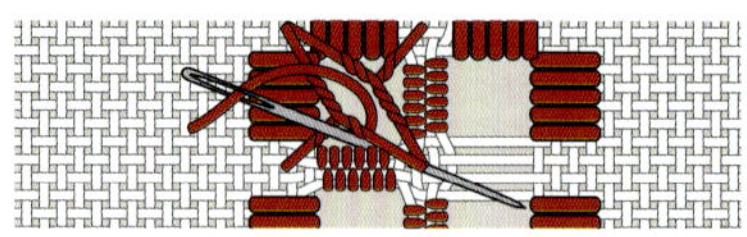

15 Insert the needle below the diagonal. Bring it out in the centre of the woven square.

16 Pull the needle through and intertwine the stitches. Work diamonds in each of the other quadrants.

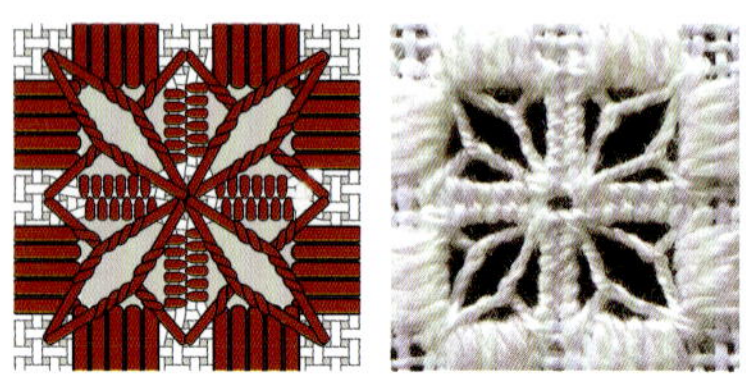

17 Upon completing the final diamond, weave the remaining bar.

diamond filling

Tension of the twists is very important in this stitch, so take care to have them sitting well.

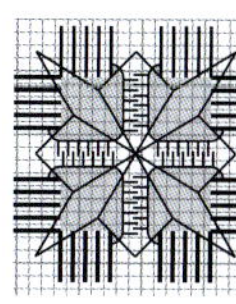

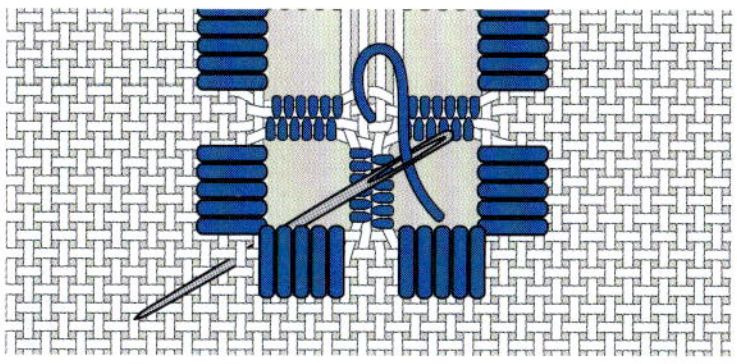

1 Weave three bars and bring the needle out in the woven square's centre. Take it to the far side of the lower left quadrant and bring the needle out two threads away from each edge.

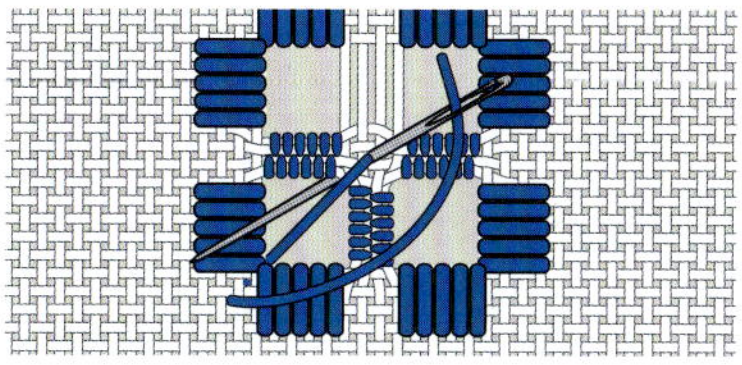

2 Insert the needle in the centre and bring the needle out above the two stitches.

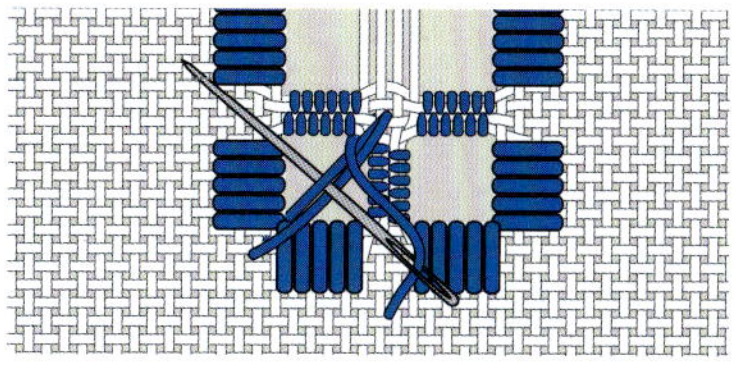

3 From below, slide the needle under the first stitch.

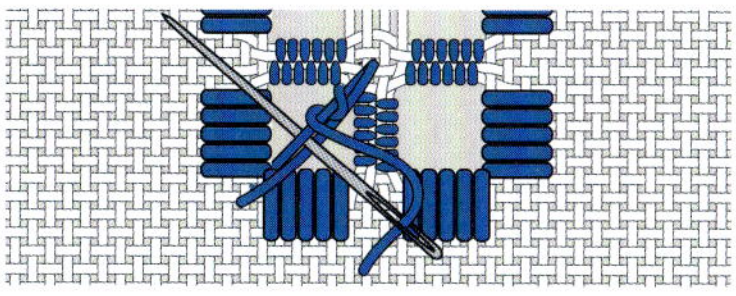

4 From below, slide the needle under the stitch again.

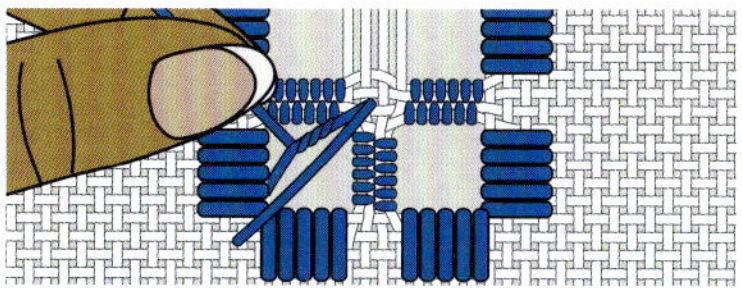

5 Pull the thread to intertwine the stitches.

❶ *Throughout the process of stitching this motif, regularly pull to intertwine.*

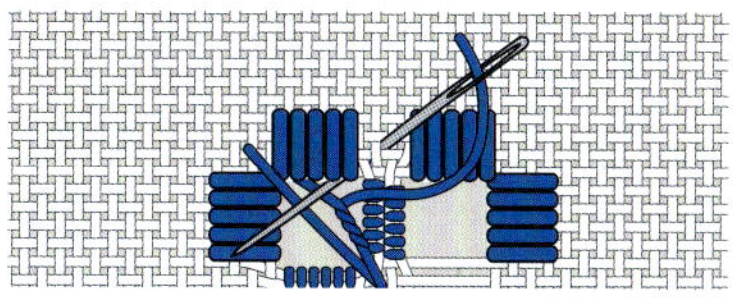

6 Turn the work 90° clockwise. Insert the needle two threads away from the end of the closest woven bar. Bring it out above the working thread.

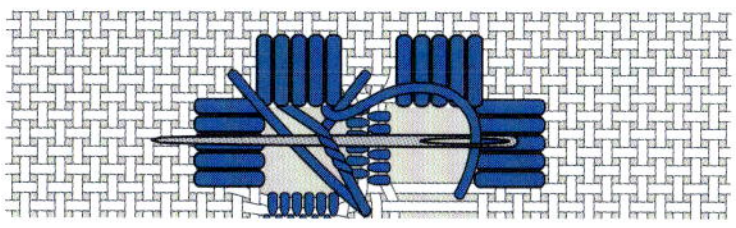

7 Above the side arm, and from the right, slide the needle under the twisted section of the diagonal.

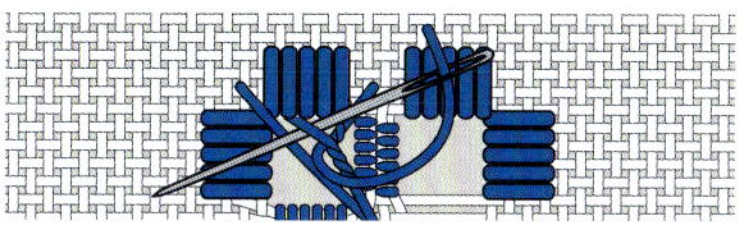

8 Pull the thread to intertwine the stitches. From the right, slide the needle under the diagonal's upper part.

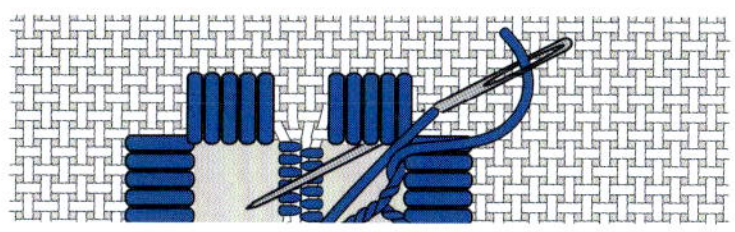

9 Turn the work 90° clockwise. Insert the needle in the corner, bringing it out below the upper diagonal.

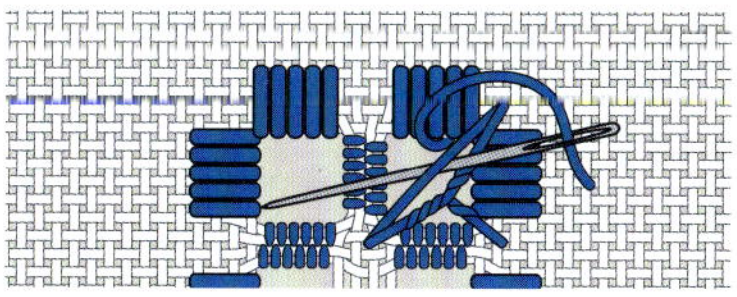

10 From the right, slide the needle under the upper diagonal.

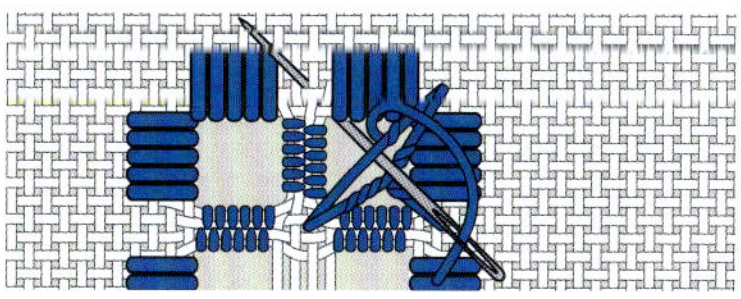

11 From below, take the needle under the diagonal. Bring it out two threads above the closest bar's end.

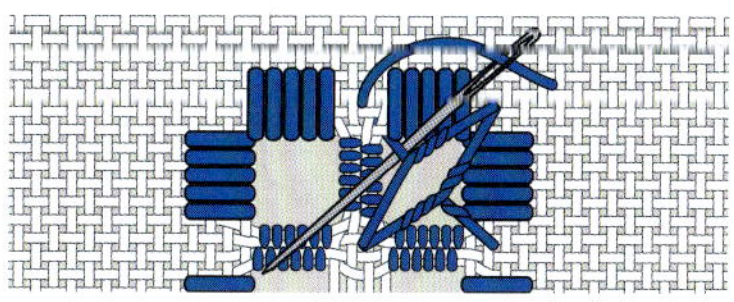

12 Pull the needle through and intertwine the stitches. From above, slide the needle under the side arm.

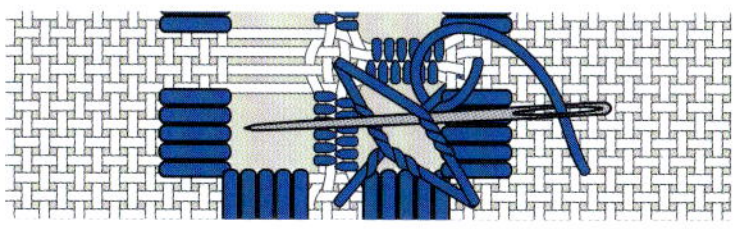

13 Turn the work 90° clockwise. From the right, slide the needle the twisted section of the diagonal.

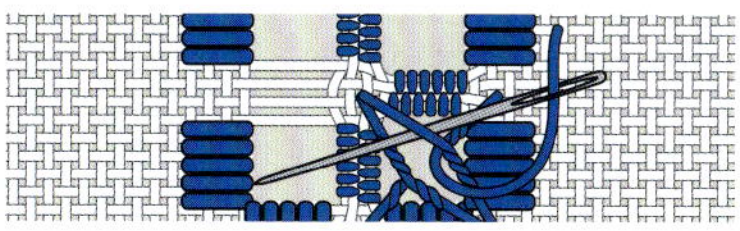

14 Pull to intertwine the stitches. From the right, slide the needle under the upper part of the diagonal.

15 Insert the needle above the diagonal. Bring it out in the centre of the woven square.

16 Pull the needle through and intertwine the stitches. Work diamonds in each of the other quadrants.

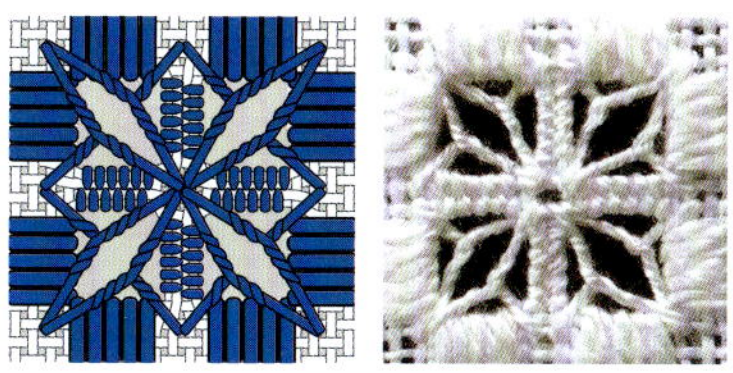

17 Upon completing the final diamond, weave the remaining bar.

drunkard's path

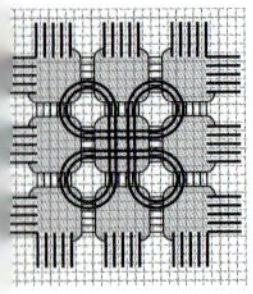

This filling uses two thicknesses of thread: the thinner thread for the wrapped bars, and the thicker thread for the decorative interlacing.

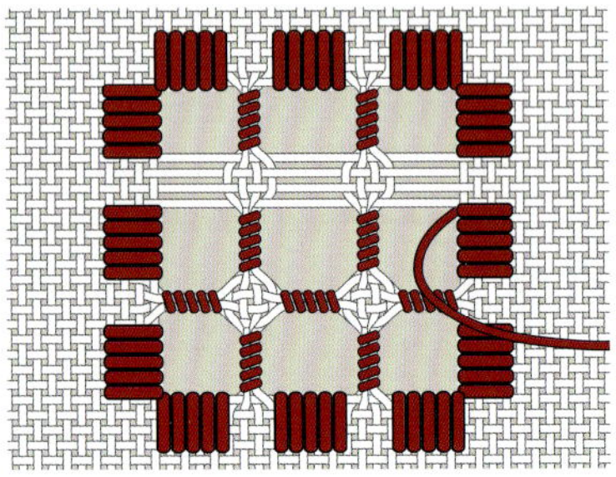

1 Prepare a large square as shown. Wrap three lines of the bars, and bring the needle out below the bar, at the right end of the top line, ready to wrap.

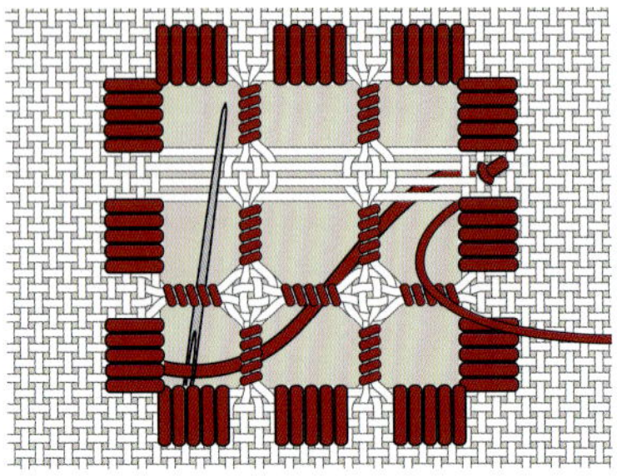

2 Insert a knotted length of thicker thread, from the front, in the fabric at the right end of the line. Bring it out below the line in the far left square.

❶ *The thicker thread is just parked here for now.*

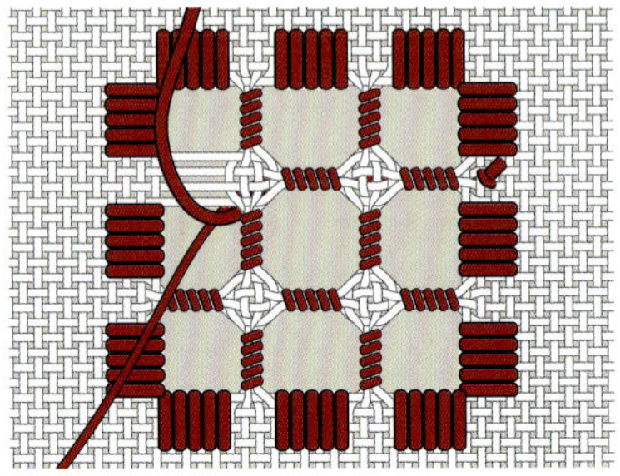

3 Wrap the two bars with the thinner thread, covering the thick thread on the back with the wraps. Bring the thread out ready to stitch the last bar.

❶ *The thinner thread is just parked here for now.*

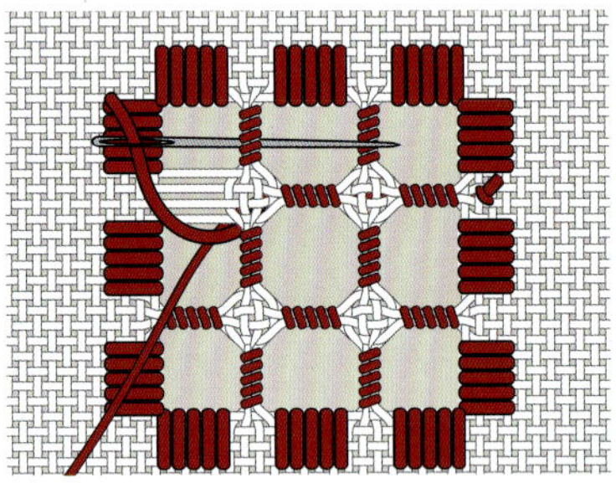

4 Resuming with the thicker thread, slide the needle under the top left vertical bar, from the left.

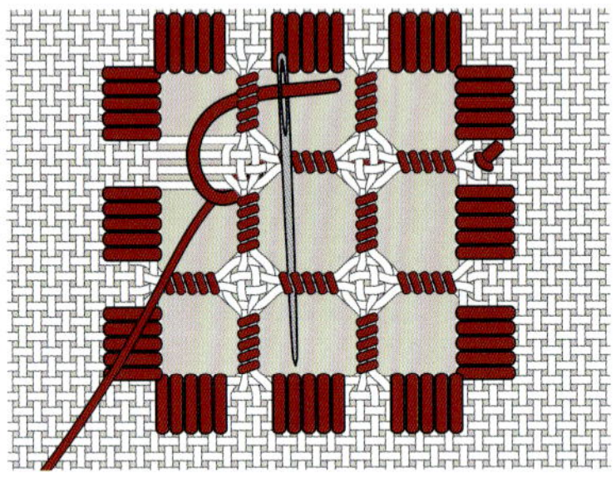

5 Heading down, slide the needle over the upper middle horizontal bar, and under the lower middle horizontal bar.

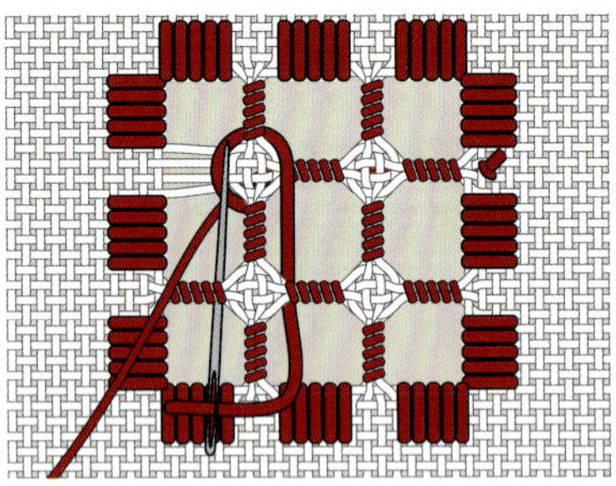

6 Pull the thread in snug to the intersection that it goes around. Heading up, slide the needle under the lower left horizontal bar.

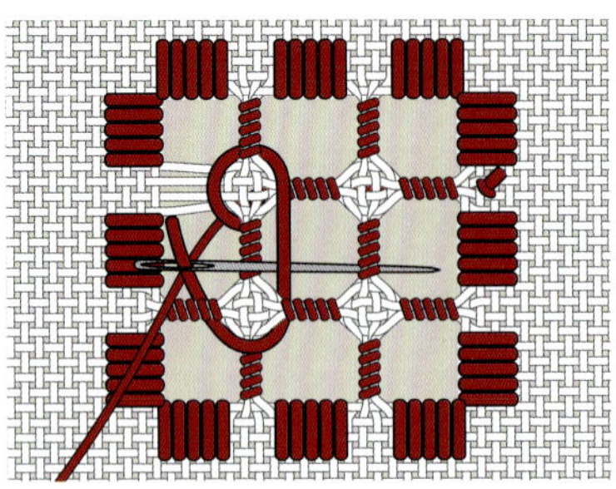

7 Pull the thread in snug. Heading to the right, take the needle over the left middle vertical bar, and slide it under the thread and the right middle vertical bar.

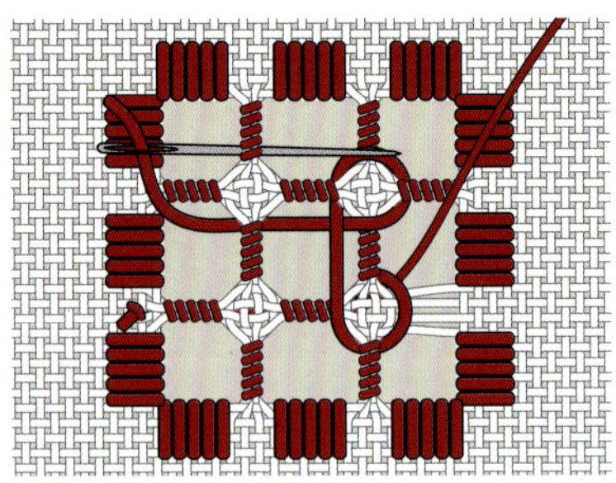

8 Turn the work 180°. Pull the thread in snug. Take the needle over the left upper horizontal bar, and slide it under the top left vertical bar.

9 Heading down, take the needle over the upper middle horizontal bar, and slide it under the thread and the lower middle horizontal bar.

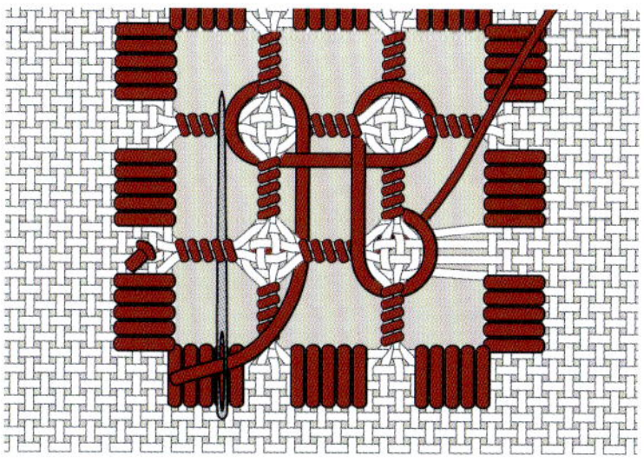

10 Pull the thread in snug. Heading up, slide the needle under the lower left horizontal bar.

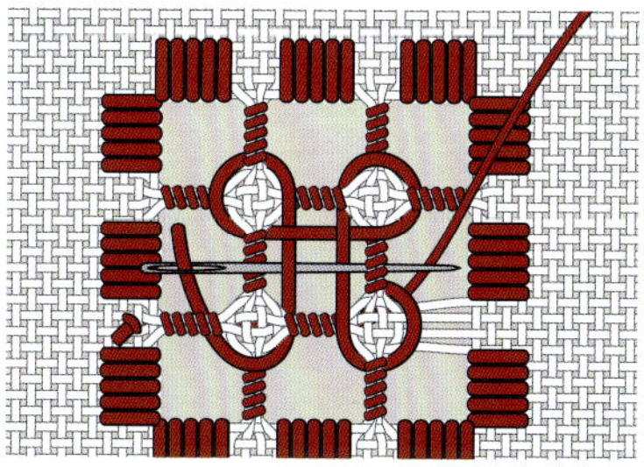

11 Pull the thread in snug. Heading to the right, take the needle over the left middle vertical bar, and slide it under the first thread, over the next thread, and under the right middle horizontal bar.

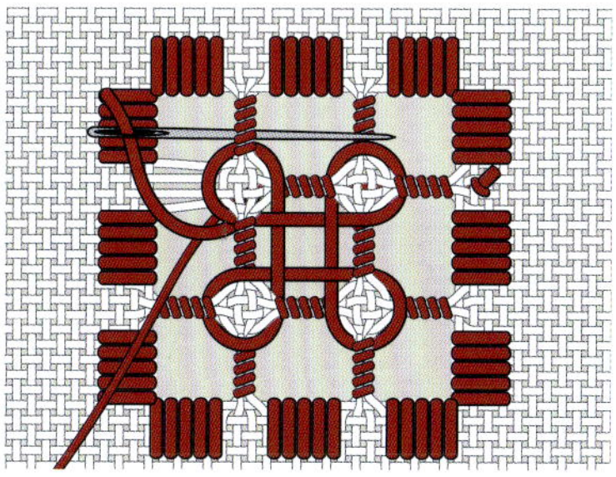

12 Turn the work 180°. Pull the thread in snug. Take the needle over the left upper horizontal bar, and slide it under the top left vertical bar.

This starts the second circuit, which should sit next to the first circuit.

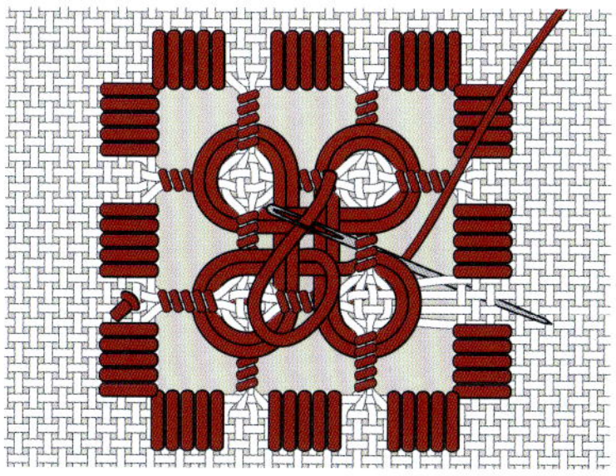

13 Continue on, turning the work as required, and following the previous path, using the same crossing patterns as before. To finish the thick thread, complete the path, and bring the needle out in the fabric at the right end of the line.

The second circuit should sit next to the first, and not overlap the first threads.

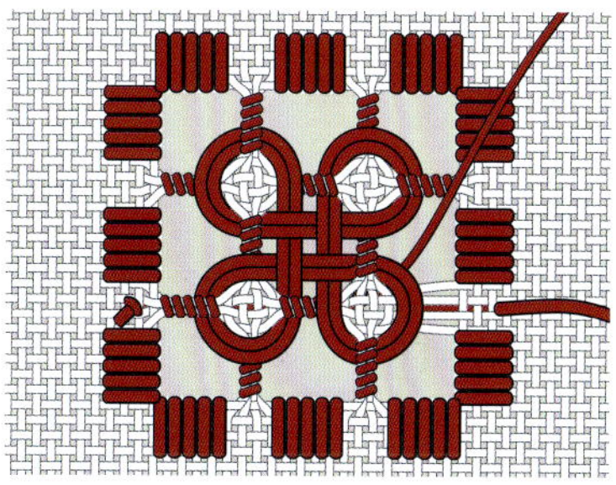

14 Pull the needle through and leave the thread parked there for the time being.

15 Resuming with the thinner thread, wrap the final bar. Finish the thread in the back of the satin stitch, and trim the end of the thicker thread, and the knot from the beginning.

R drunkard's path

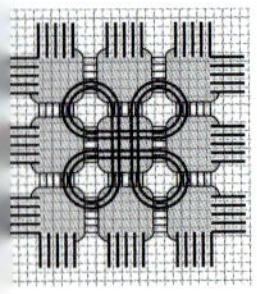

CONTEMPORARY

This filling uses two thicknesses of thread: the thinner thread for the wrapped bars, and the thicker thread for the decorative interlacing.

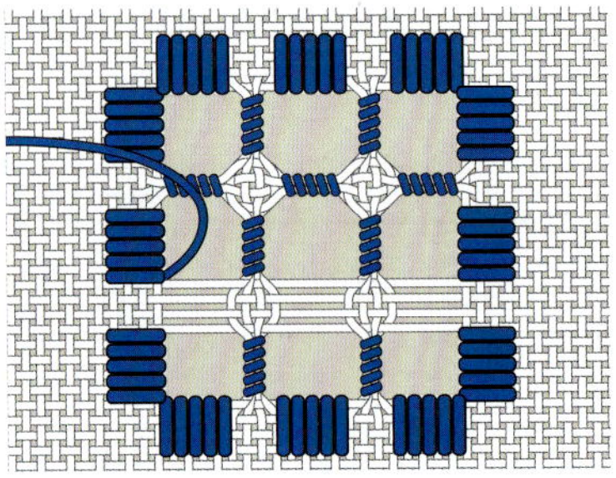

1 Prepare a large square as shown. Wrap three lines of the bars, and bring the needle out above the bar, at the left end of the bottom line, ready to wrap.

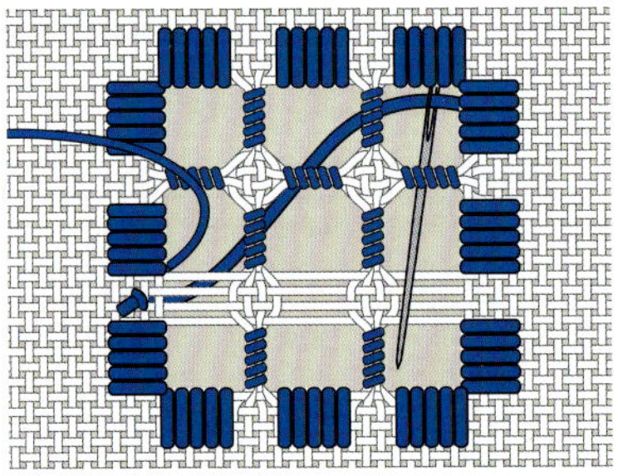

2 Insert a knotted length of thicker thread, from the front, in the fabric at the left end of the line. Bring it out above the line in the far right square.

❶ *The thicker thread is just parked here for now.*

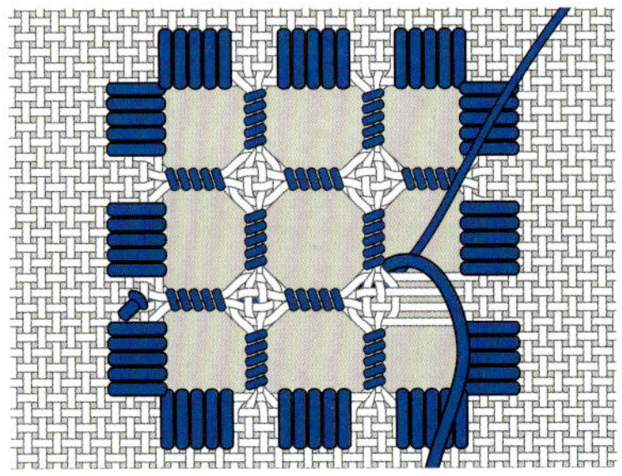

3 Wrap the two bars with the thinner thread, covering the thick thread on the back with the wraps. Bring the thread out ready to stitch the last bar.

❶ *The thinner thread is just parked here for now.*

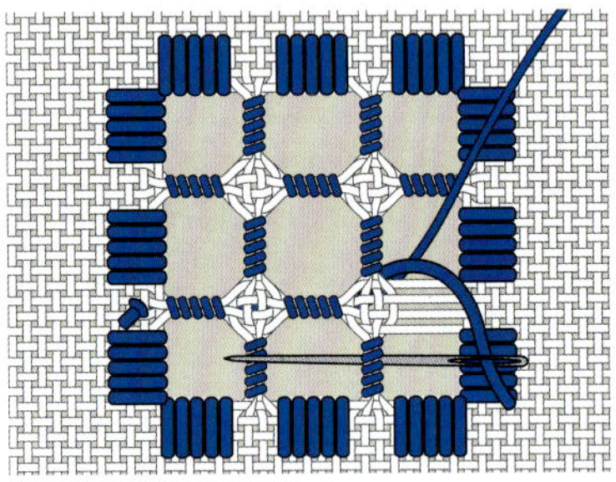

4 Resuming with the thicker thread, slide the needle under the bottom right vertical bar, from the right.

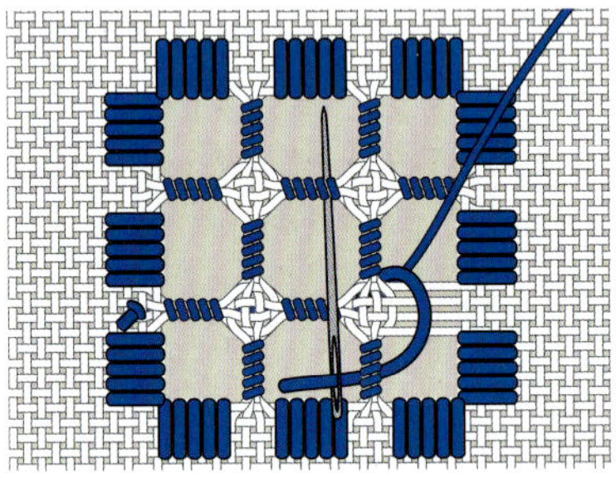

5 Heading up, slide the needle over the lower middle horizontal bar, and under the upper middle horizontal bar.

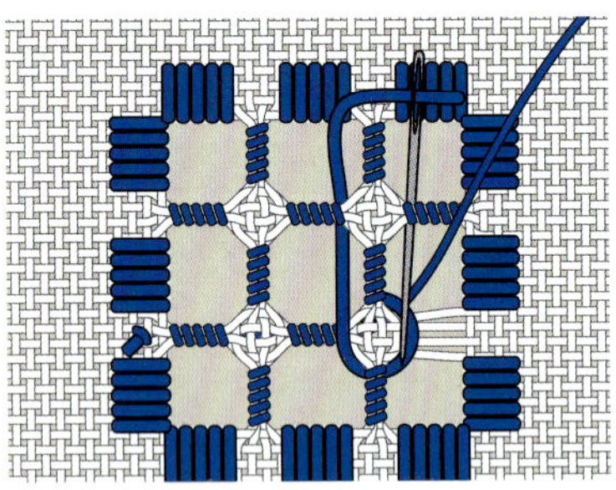

6 Pull the thread in snug to the intersection that it goes around. Heading down, slide the needle under the upper right horizontal bar.

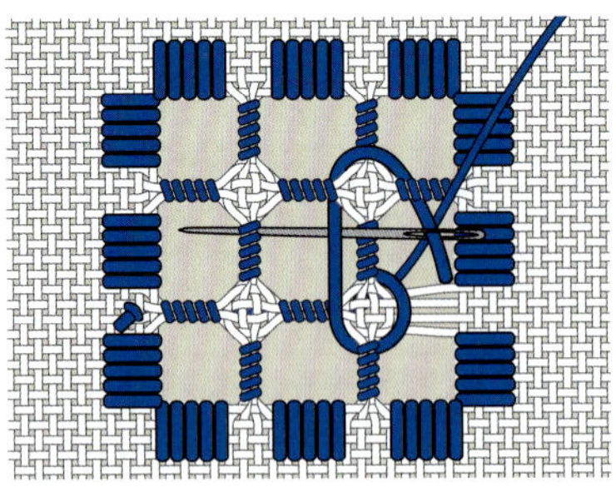

7 Pull the thread in snug. Heading to the left, take the needle over the right middle vertical bar, and slide it under the thread and the left middle vertical bar.

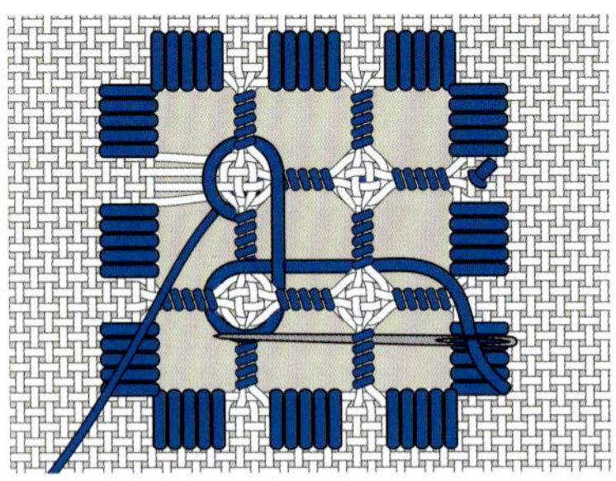

8 Turn the work 180°. Pull the thread in snug. Take the needle over the right lower horizontal bar, and slide it under the bottom right vertical bar.

9 Heading up, take the needle over the lower middle horizontal bar, and slide it under the thread and the upper middle horizontal bar.

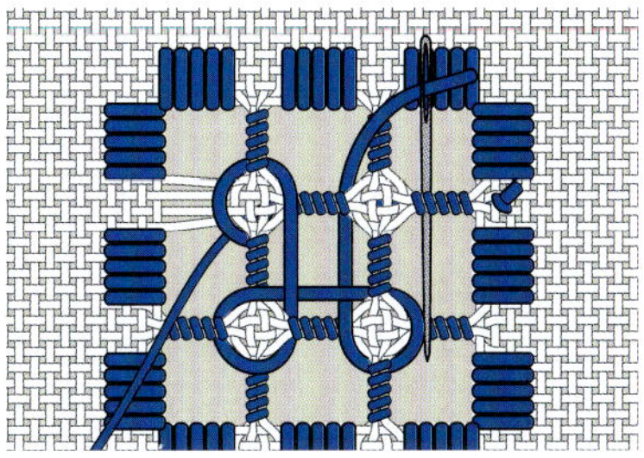

10 Pull the thread in snug. Heading down, slide the needle under the upper right horizontal bar.

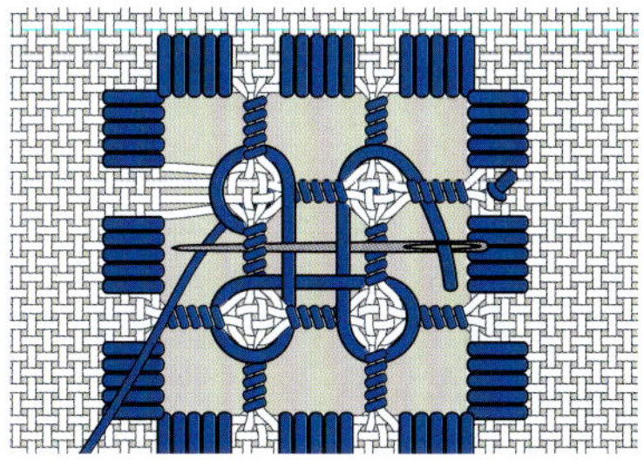

11 Pull the thread in snug. Heading to the left, take the needle over the right middle vertical bar, and slide it under the first thread, over the next thread, and under the left middle vertical bar.

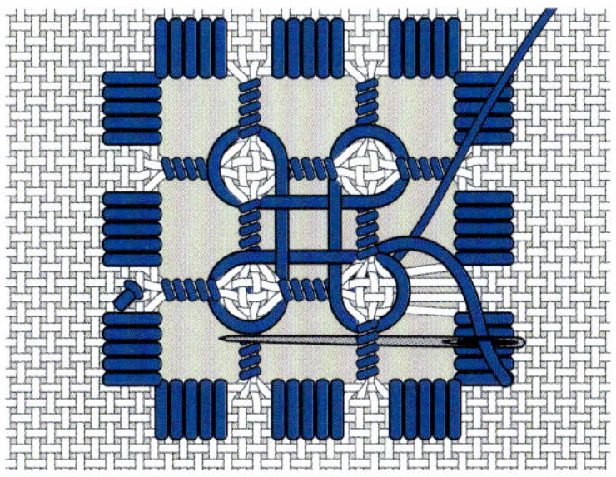

12 Turn the work 180°. Pull the thread in snug. Take the needle over the right lower horizontal bar, and slide it under the bottom right vertical bar.

! *This starts the second circuit, which should sit next to the first circuit.*

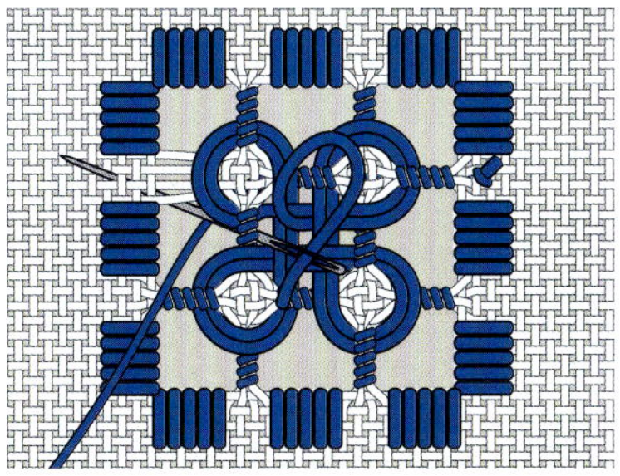

13 Continue on, turning the work as required, and following the previous path, using the same crossing patterns as before. To finish the thick thread, complete the path, and bring the needle out in the fabric at the left end of the line.

! *The second circuit should sit next to the first, and not overlap the first threads.*

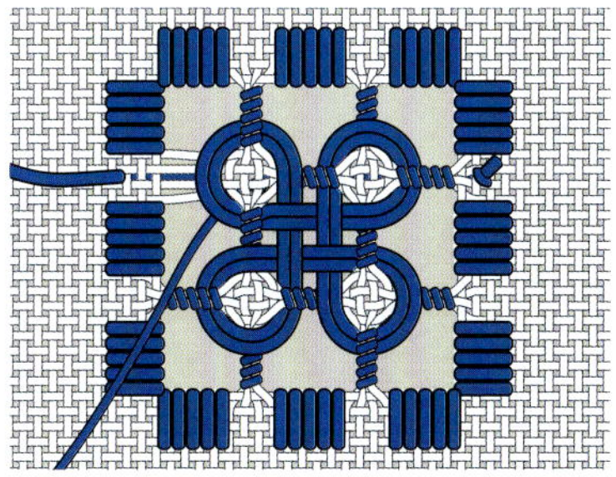

14 Pull the needle through and leave the thread parked there for the time being.

15 Resuming with the thinner thread, wrap the final bar. Finish the thread in the back of the satin stitch, and trim the end of the thicker thread, and the knot from the beginning.

L

festoon stitch

also known as circled dove's eye

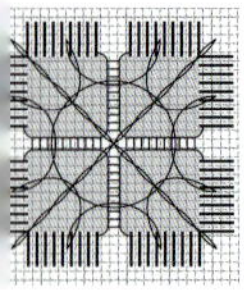

CONTEMPORARY

This is a stitch where tension is really important. If you don't get a good result the first time, adjust your tension for the looped stitches.

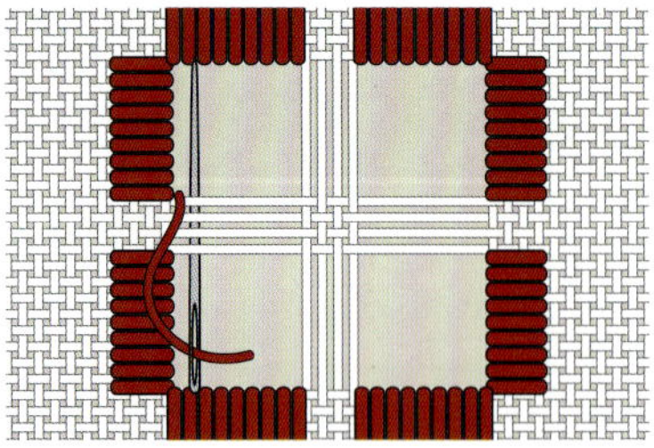

1 Prepare a large square as shown. Bring the needle out above the left bar. From below, slide the needle under all four threads.

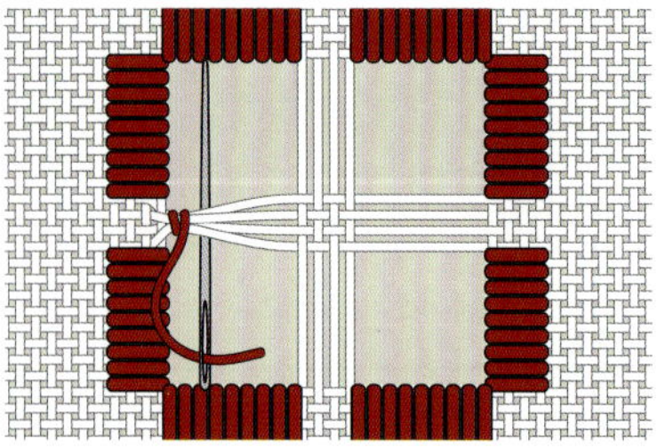

2 Pull the needle through and tighten the stitch. Moving right, and from below, slide the needle under the stitches again.

! *The wraps should lie next to each other on the bar and not overlap. They do not need to be tightly packed.*

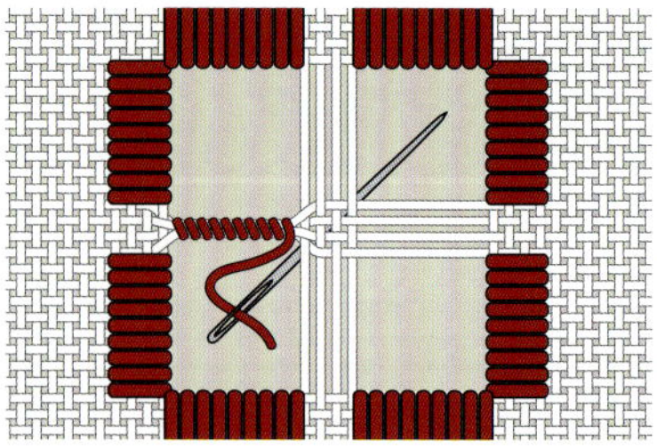

3 Tightly wrap the rest of the bar, then pass the needle behind the woven square and bring it out above the next bar to the right.

! *The bars are worked straight across, rather than turning the corner, as this helps to keep them aligned.*

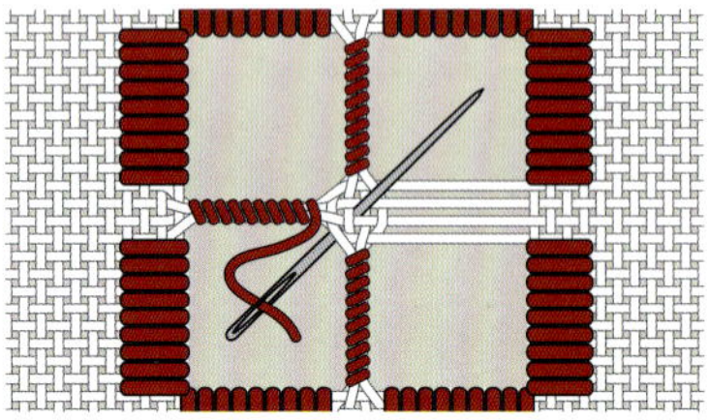

4 Wrap the next bar then run the thread under the back of the satin stitch. Wrap the next bar and bring the needle out in the centre of the woven square.

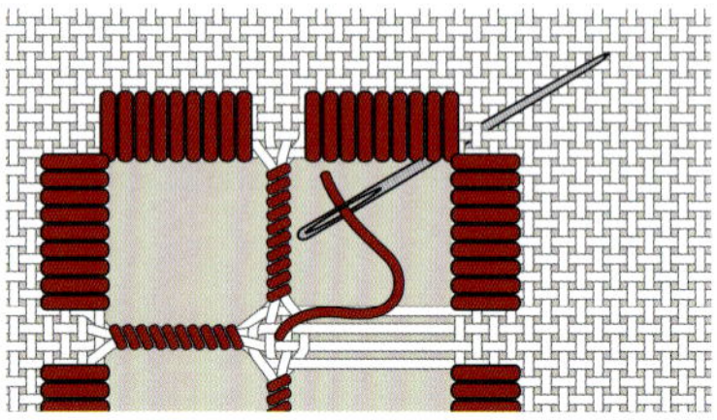

5 Pull the needle through. Bring the needle out in the top right corner, two threads away from the edge.

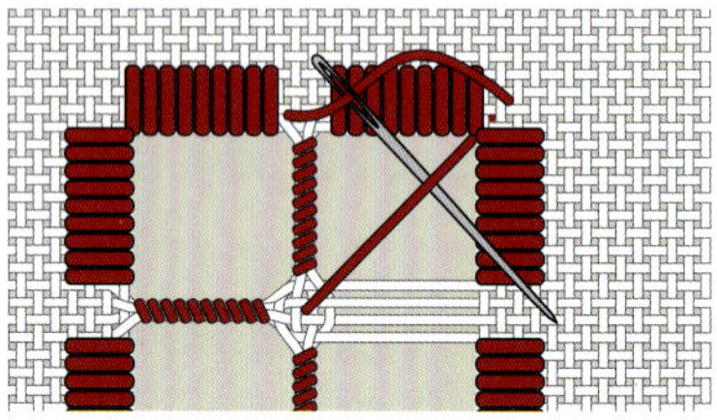

6 Pull the needle through. From above, slide the needle under the stitch.

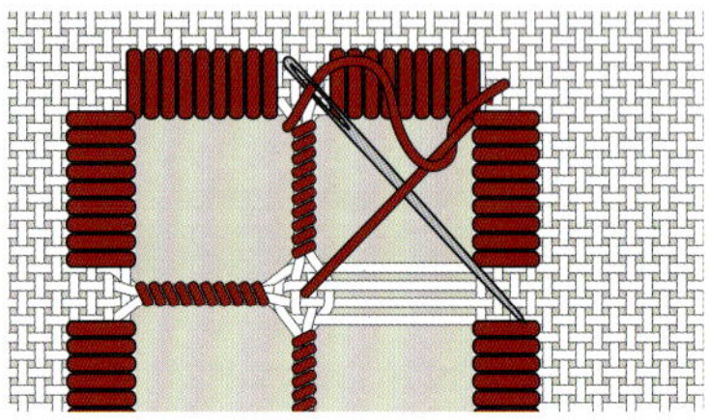

7 Moving towards the centre, slide the needle under the stitch again.

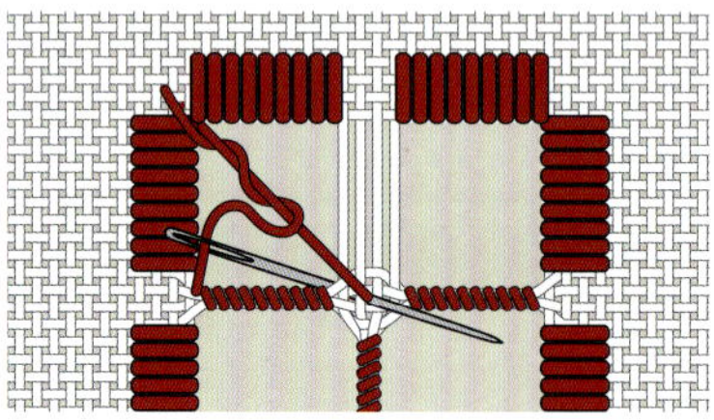

8 Turn the work 90° anticlockwise. Bring the needle out in the centre of the woven square.

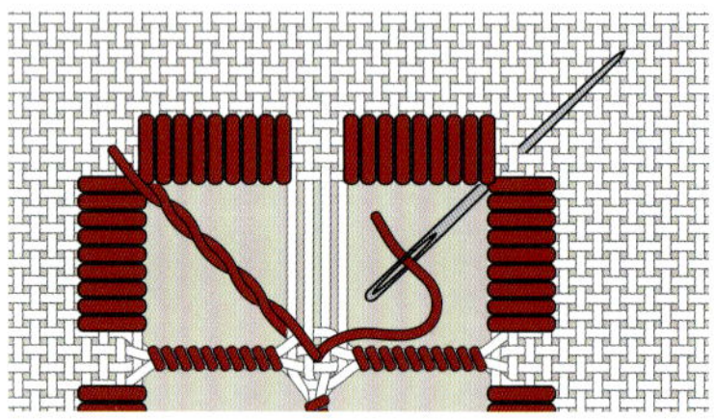

9 Pull the needle to intertwine the stitches. Bring the needle out in the next woven corner, two threads away from the edge.

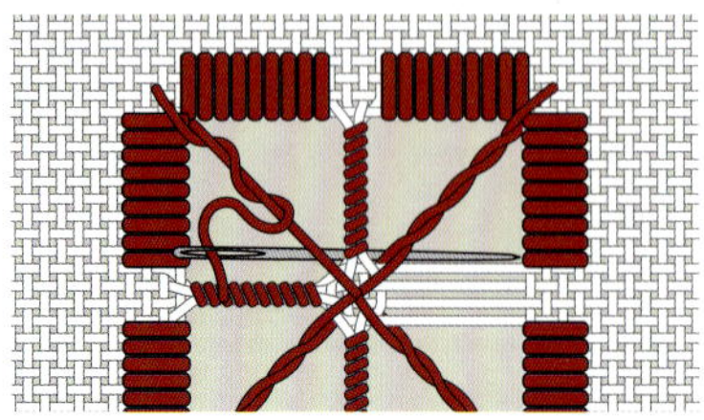

10 Repeat Steps 6 to 8 to work spokes out to each corner. Turn the work as needed. To finish, bring the needle out ready to wrap the final bar.

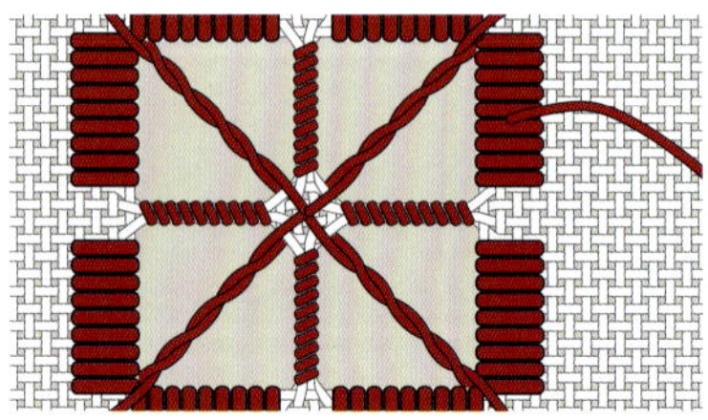

11 Wrap the final bar. Take the needle through the back of the satin stitch. Bring it out in the centre of the satin stitch above right, four threads up.

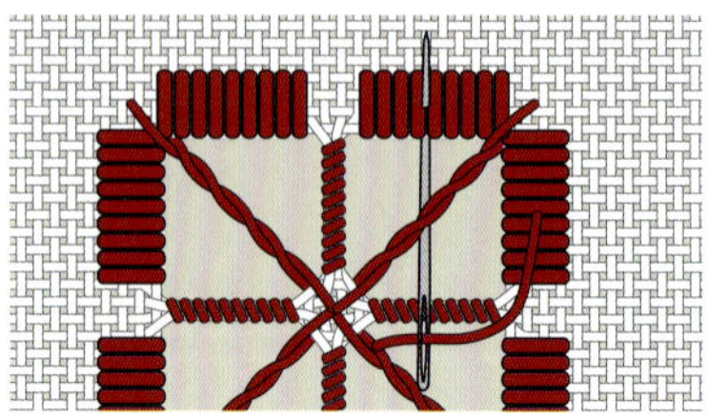

12 From below, slide the needle under the diagonal. Bring it out in the centre of the next block of satin stitch, five threads from the corner.

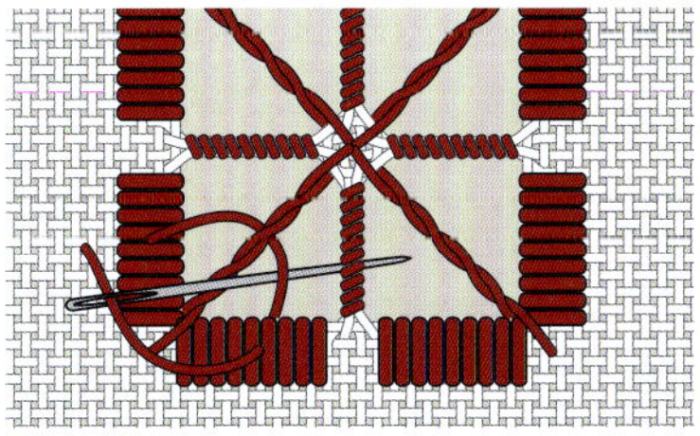

13 Pull the needle through so that the stitch curves gently. Turn the work 180°. From the left, take the needle under the curved stitch and the next wrapped bar.

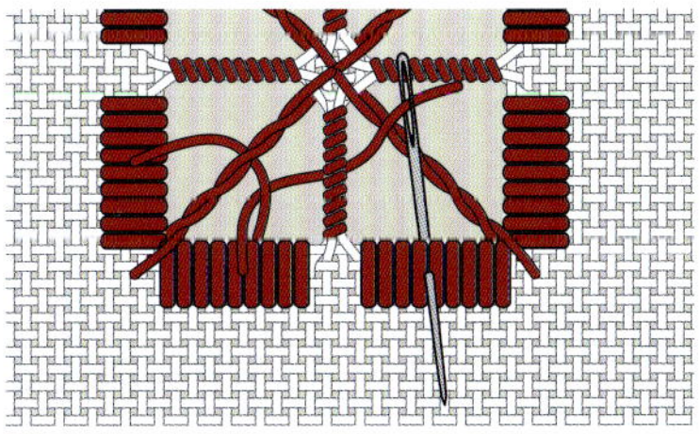

14 Bring the needle out in the centre of the next satin stitch block, five threads from the corner.

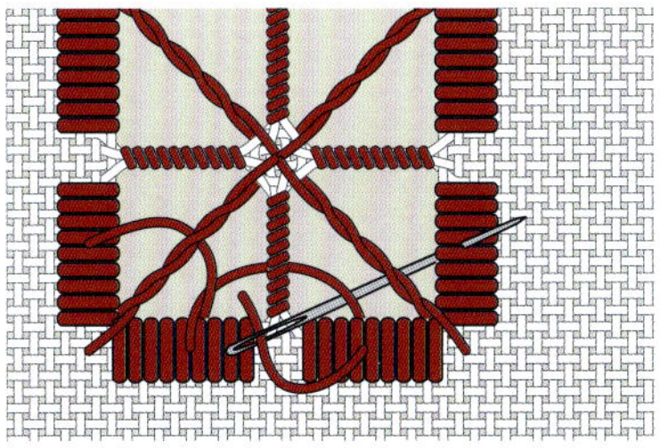

15 Pull the needle through so that the stitch curves gently. Take the needle under the curved stitch and the closest diagonal. Bring it out in the centre of the next satin stitch block, five threads from the corner.

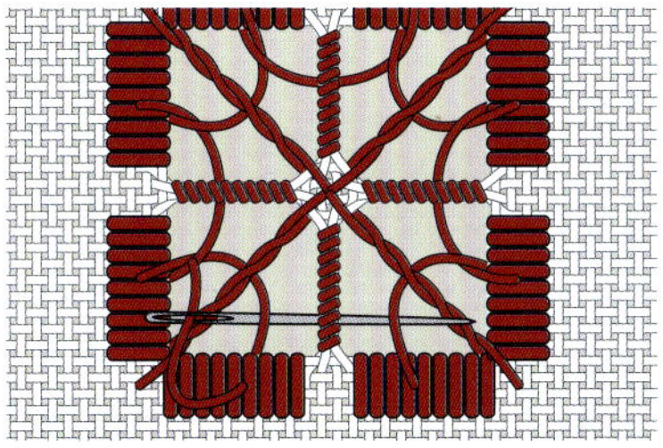

16 Cycle through Steps 13 to 15, turning the work as necessary. Pull the needle through. Slide the needle under the previous curve, under the wrapped bar, and under the next curved stitch.

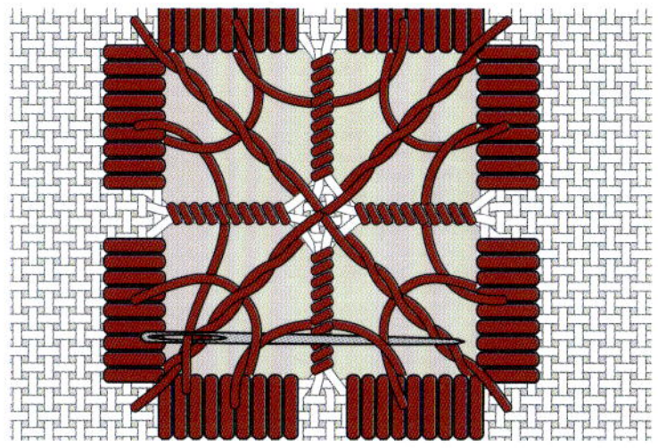

17 Turn the work 90° clockwise. Slide the needle under the intersection of the first two curved stitches, over the wrapped bar, and under the next curved stitches' intersection.

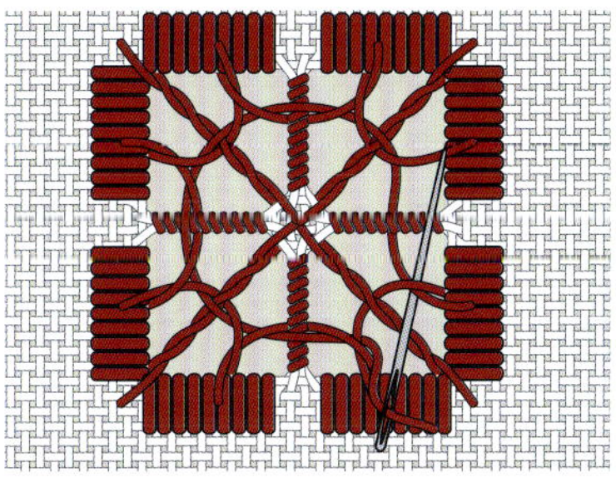

18 Repeat this for the next two sides. On the last side, slide the needle under the first curved stitches' intersection on the next side.

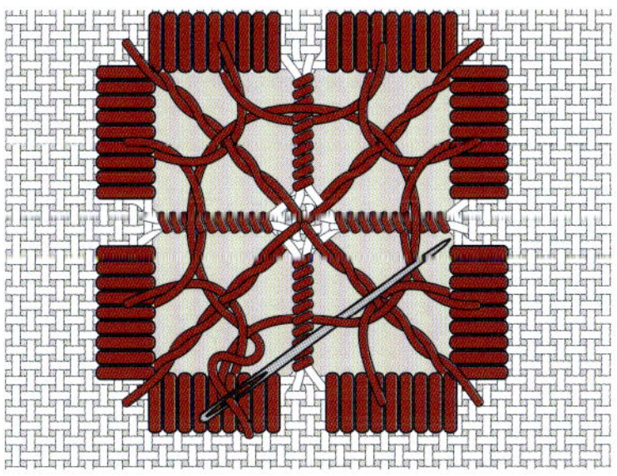

19 Turn the work 90° clockwise. Take the needle over the wrapped bar, and from below, slide it under the thread coming from under the wrapped bar.

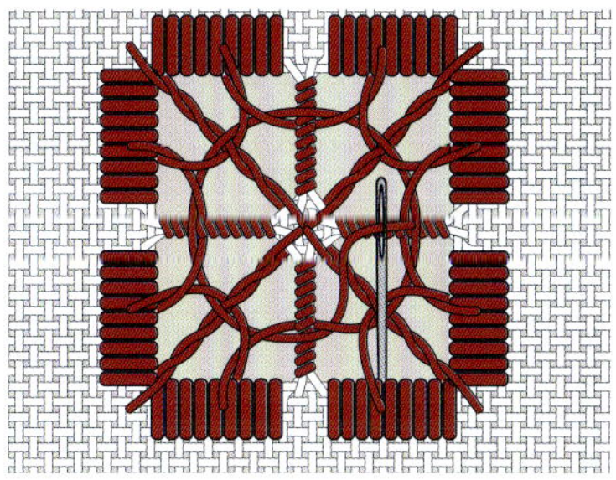

20 Take the needle over the very first curved stitch and through to the back.

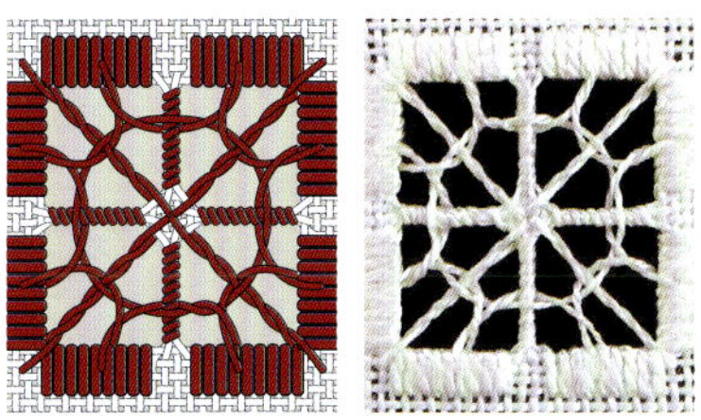

21 Adjust the tension of any of the stitches that aren't sitting quite right, and then finish off the thread by running it under the back of the satin stitch, on the back.

❶ *The looser the stitches are in the first circuit, the smaller the circle will be in the next circuit. The tighter the stitches are in the first circuit, the larger the circle will be in the next circuit.*

❶ *This stitch can be worked with a spider web (of any type). Work the spokes then the spider web. By working the first festoon circuit with tighter tension the circle of the second circuit can be enlarged to fit around the web.*

festoon stitch

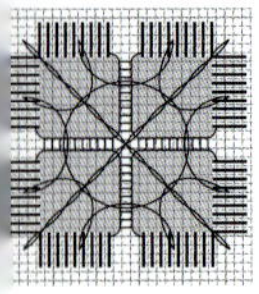

CONTEMPORARY

also known as circled dove's eye

This is a stitch where tension is really important. If you don't get a good result the first time, adjust your tension for the looped stitches.

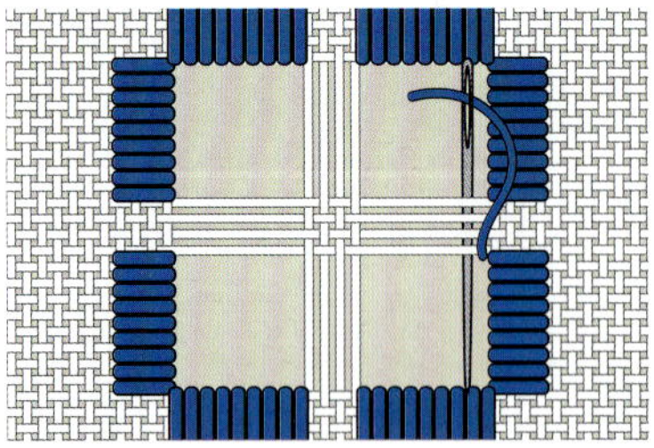

1 Prepare a large square as shown. Bring the needle out below the right bar. From above, slide the needle under all four threads.

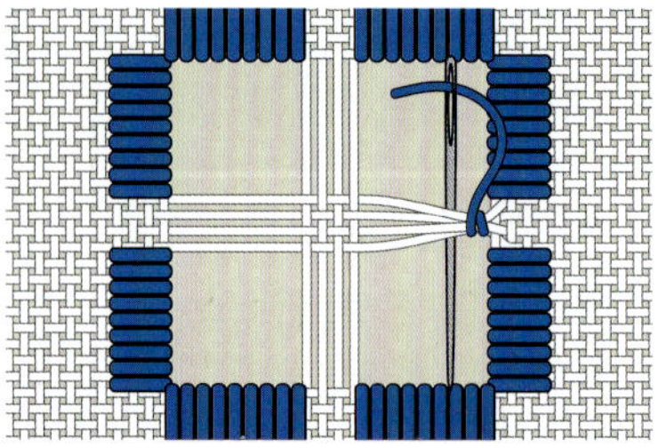

2 Pull the needle through and tighten the stitch. Moving left, and from above, slide the needle under the stitches again.

❶ *The wraps should lie next to each other on the bar and not overlap. They do not need to be tightly packed.*

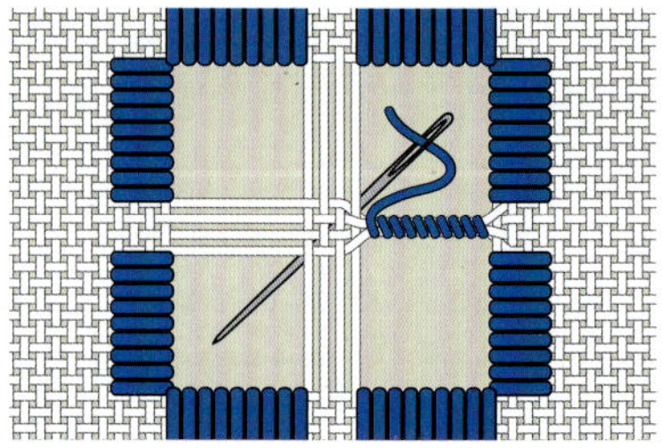

3 Tightly wrap the rest of the bar, then pass the needle behind the woven square and bring it out below the next bar to the right.

❶ *The bars are worked straight across, rather than turning the corner, as this helps to keep them aligned.*

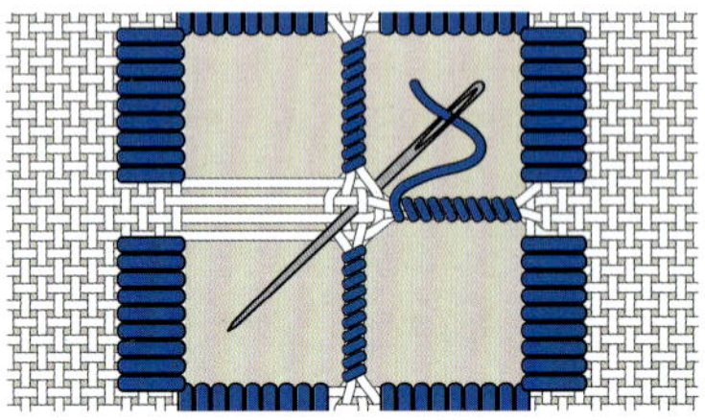

4 Wrap the next bar then run the thread under the back of the satin stitch. Wrap the next bar and bring the needle out in the centre of the woven square.

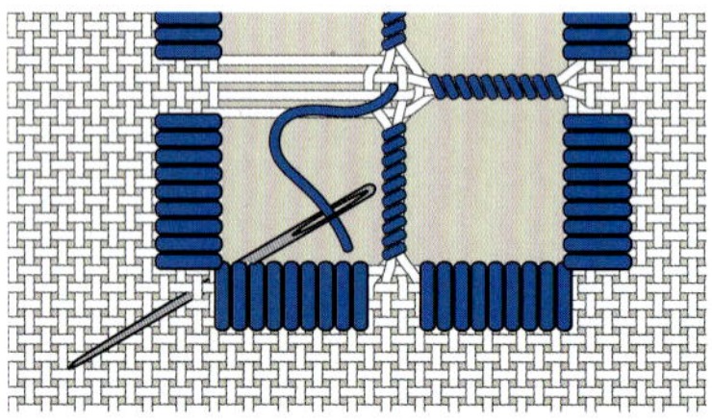

5 Pull the needle through. Bring the needle out in the bottom right corner, two threads away from the edge.

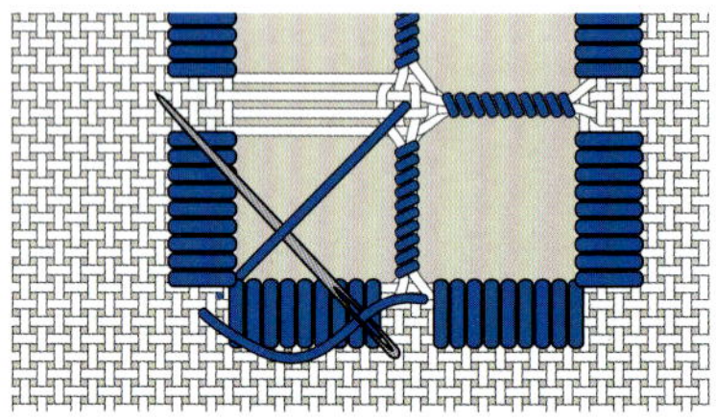

6 Pull the needle through. From below, slide the needle under the stitch.

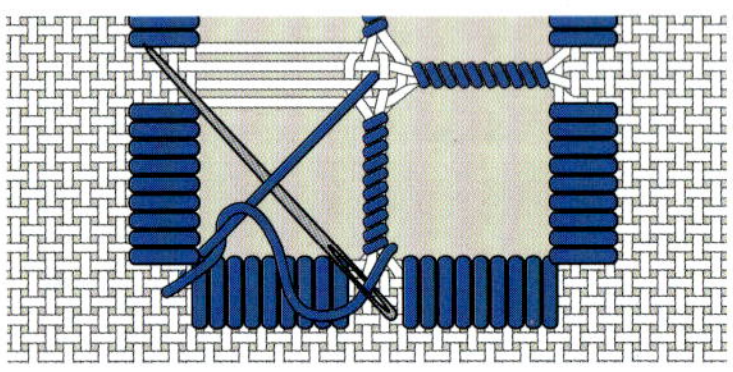

7 Moving towards the centre, slide the needle under the stitch again.

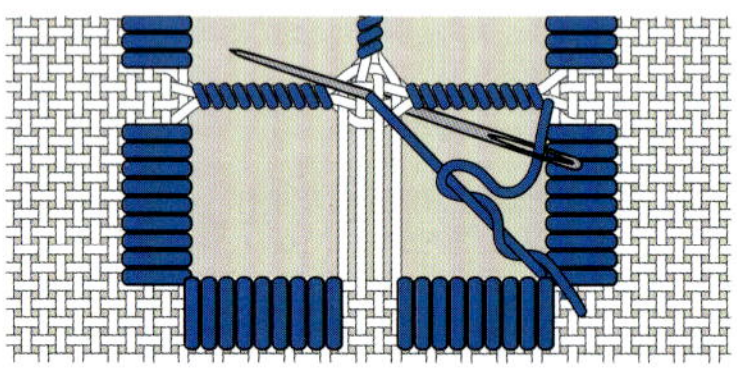

8 Turn the work 90° anticlockwise. Bring the needle out in the centre of the woven square.

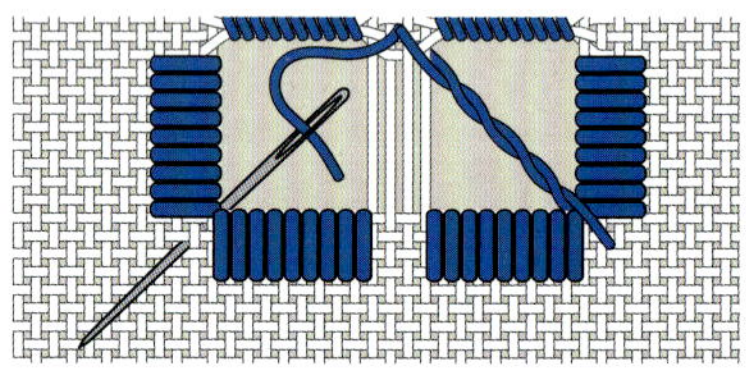

9 Pull the needle to intertwine the stitches. Bring the needle out in the next woven corner, two threads away from the edge.

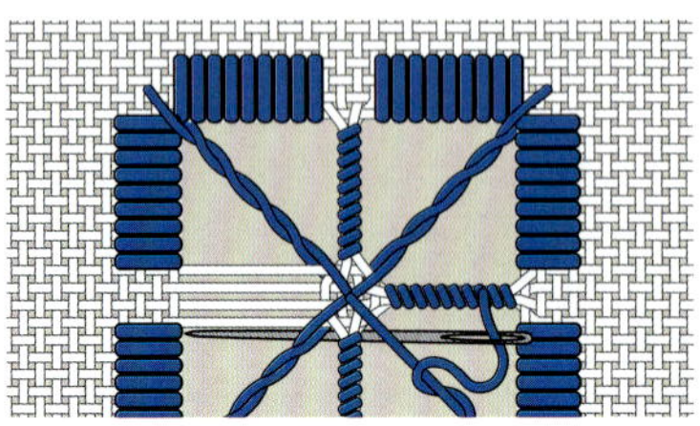

10 Repeat Steps 6 to 8 to work spokes out to each corner. Turn the work as needed. To finish, bring the needle out ready to wrap the final bar.

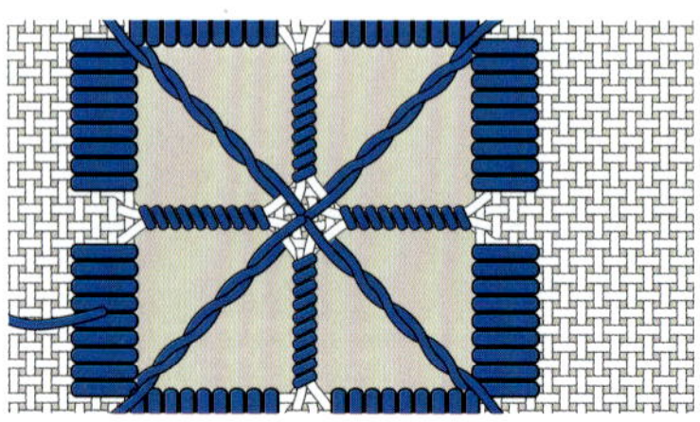

11 Wrap the final bar. Take the needle through the back of the satin stitch. Bring it out centrally in the satin stitch left, down, four threads down.

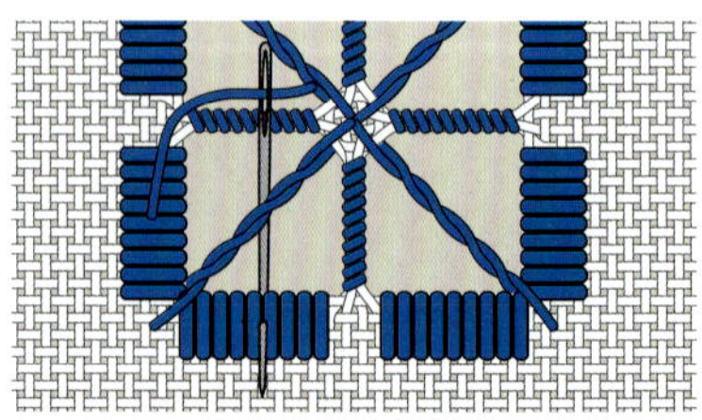

12 From above, slide the needle under the diagonal. Bring it out in the centre of the next block of satin stitch, five threads from the corner.

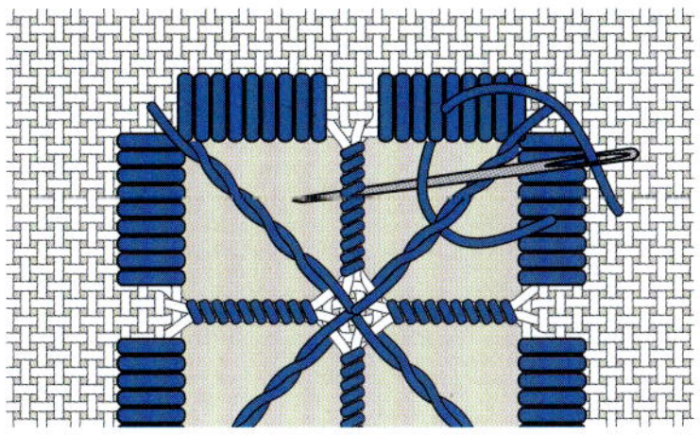

13 Pull the needle through so that the stitch curves gently. Turn the work 180°. From the right, take the needle under the curved stitch and the next wrapped bar.

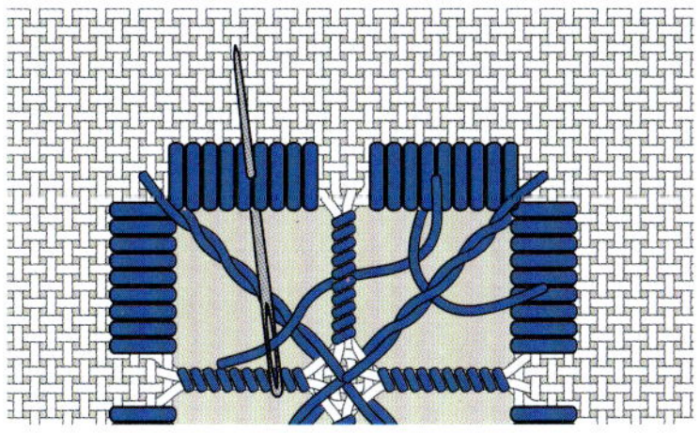

14 Bring the needle out in the centre of the next satin stitch block, five threads from the corner.

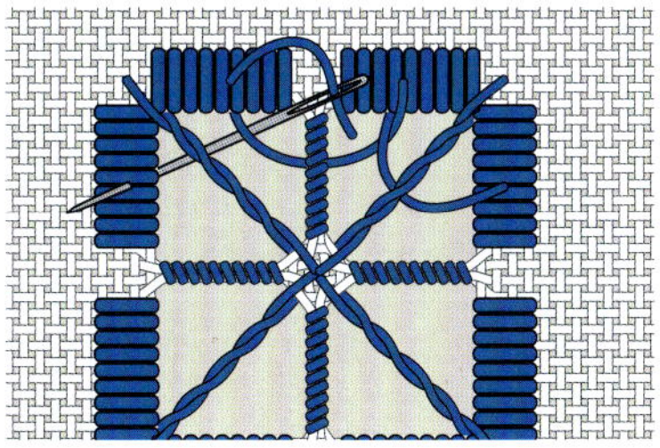

15 Pull the needle through so that the stitch curves gently. Take the needle under the curved stitch and the closest diagonal. Bring it out in the centre of the next satin stitch block, five threads from the corner.

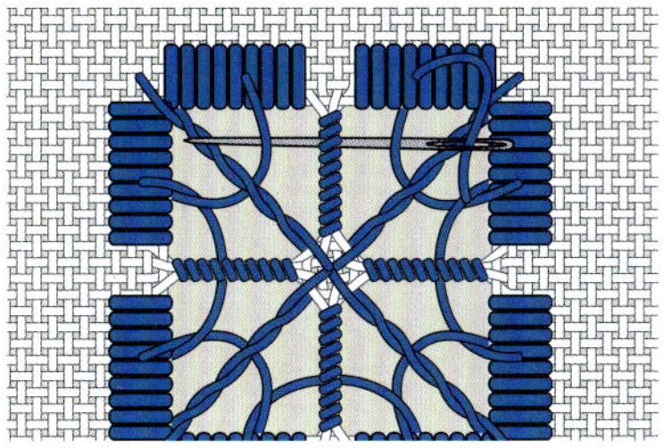

16 Cycle through Steps 13 to 15, turning the work as necessary. Pull the needle through. Slide the needle under the previous curve, under the wrapped bar, and under the next curved stitch.

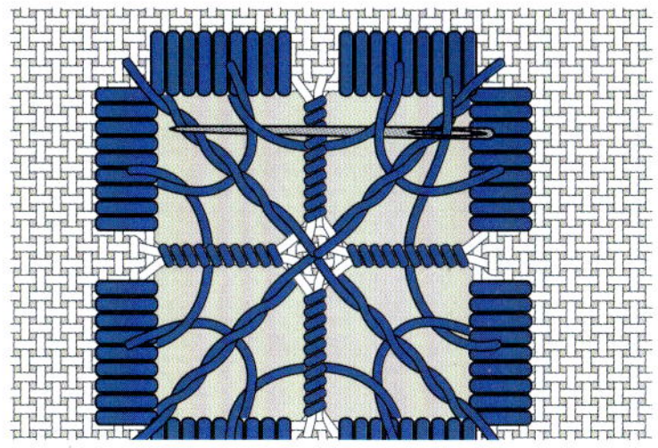

17 Turn the work 90° clockwise. Slide the needle under the intersection of the first two curved stitches, over the wrapped bar, and under the next curved stitches' intersection.

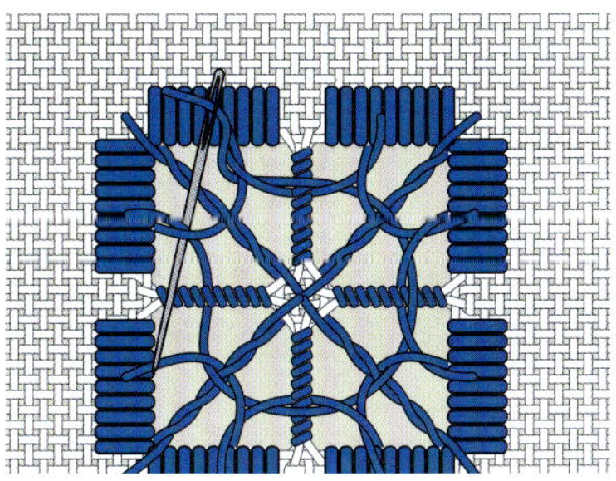

18 Repeat this for the next two sides. On the last side, slide the needle under the first curved stitches' intersection on the next side.

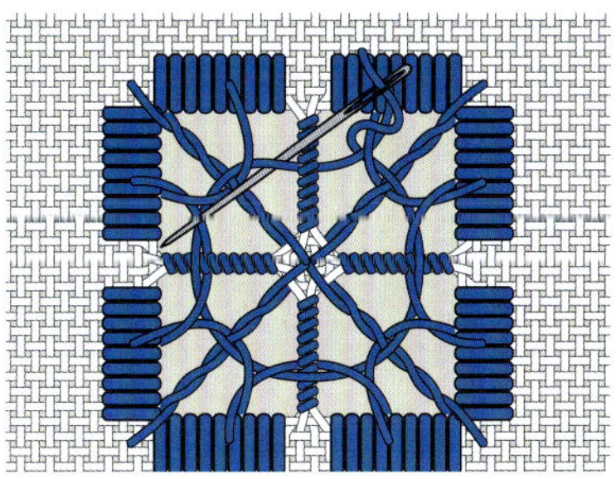

19 Turn the work 90° clockwise. Take the needle over the wrapped bar, and from above, slide it under the thread coming from under the wrapped bar.

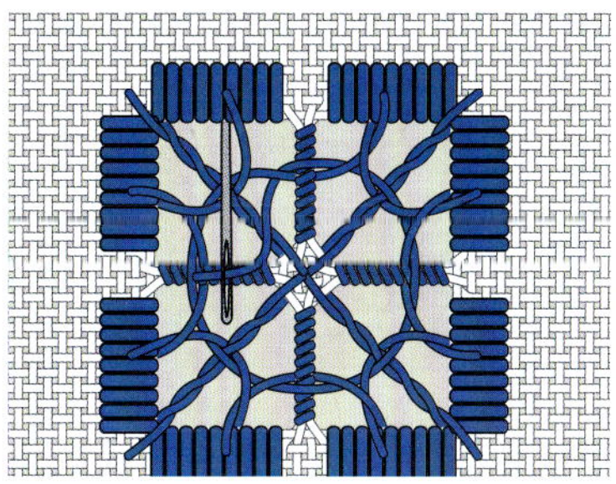

20 Take the needle over the very first curved stitch and through to the back.

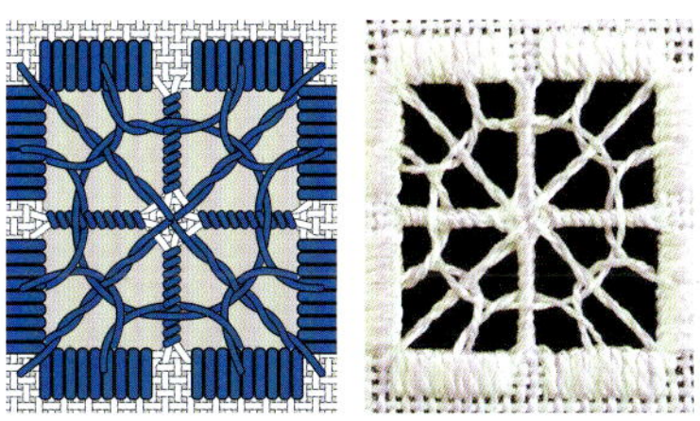

21 Adjust the tension of any of the stitches that aren't sitting quite right, and then finish off the thread by running it under the back of the satin stitch, on the back.

❶ *The looser the stitches are in the first circuit, the smaller the circle will be in the next circuit. The tighter the stitches are in the first circuit, the larger the circle will be in the next circuit.*

❶ *This stitch can be worked with a spider web (of any type). Work the spokes then the spider web. By working the first festoon circuit with tighter tension the circle of the second circuit can be enlarged to fit around the web.*

flower filling

Tension is very important for this stitch. It may take some practice to get it right.

CONTEMPORARY

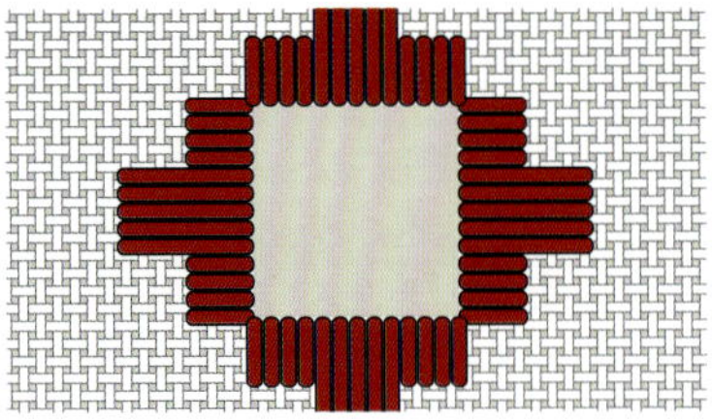

1 Prepare a satin stitch square as shown, cutting and removing all the threads within.

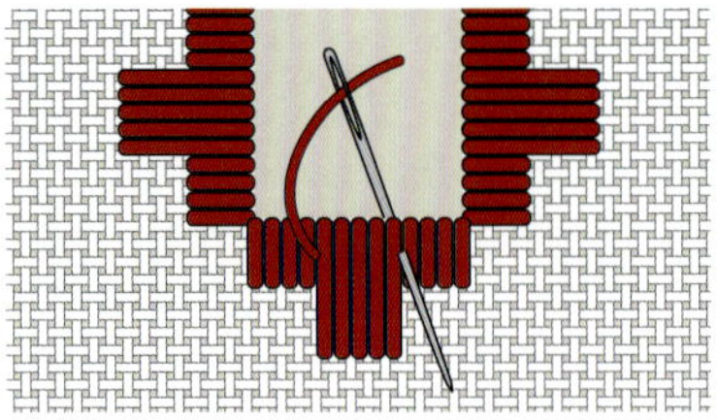

2 Bring the needle out in the bottom satin stitch, two threads from the cut edge, four stitches from the left. Insert it in the open square and bring it out five stitches to the right.

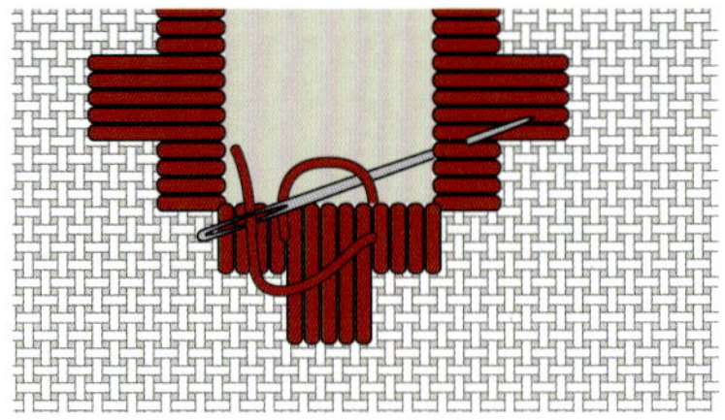

3 Pull the needle through so the curves gently. Slide it under the stitch. Bring it out in the next side, two threads from the cut edge, four stitches up from the bottom.

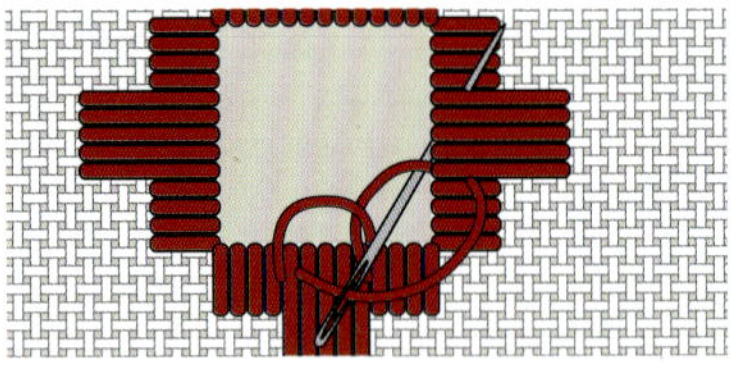

4 Pull the needle through to create a curved stitch. Insert the needle in the curve, and bring it out five stitches further up.

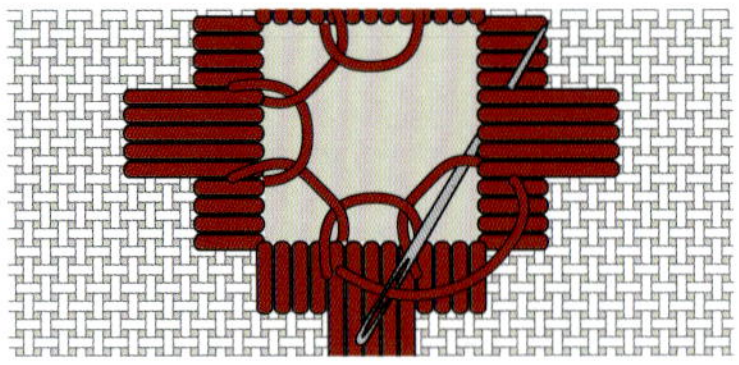

5 Pull the needle through, creating a curved stitch. Turning the work, repeat the stitches on the next two sides.

❶ *The looser these stitches, the smaller the circling stitch, and vice versa.*

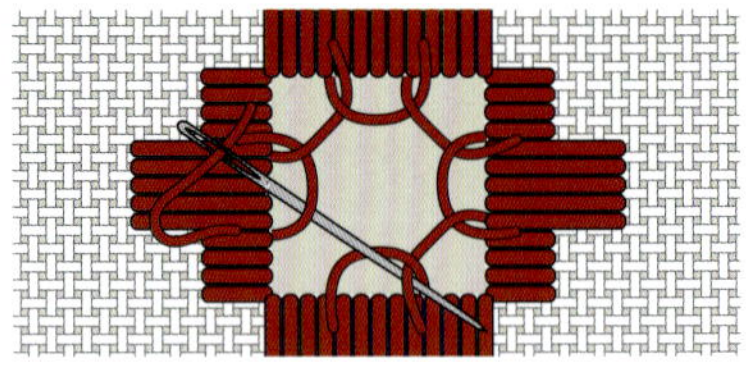

6 Pull the needle through to create a curved stitch. Turn the work 180°. Slide the needle under the curved stitch, over the first stitch, and under the left side of the second stitch.

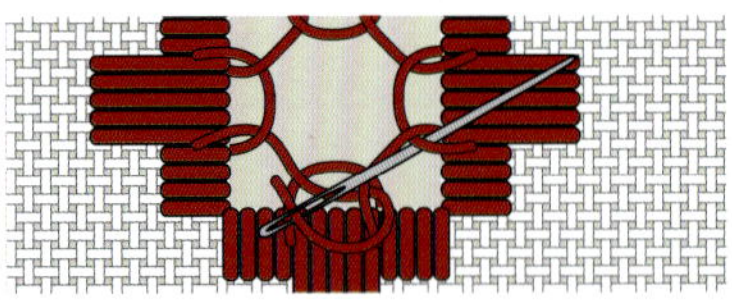

7 Slide the needle under the left side of the next stitch.

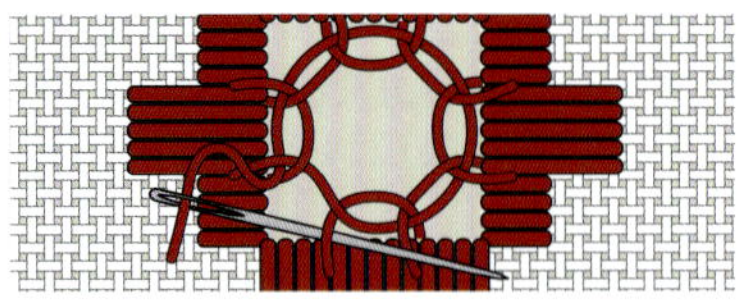

8 Continue, anticlockwise, sliding the needle under the left side of each stitch, finishing with the first one.

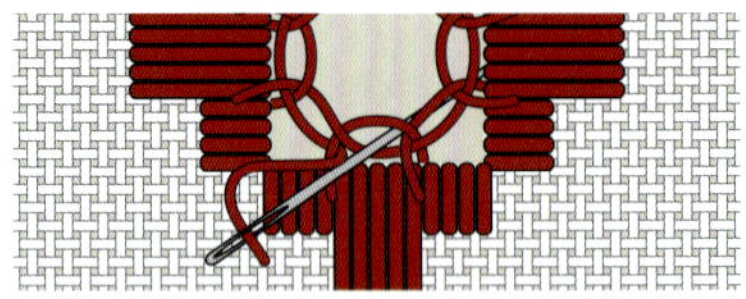

9 Take the needle through to the back between the first curved stitch and the circling stitch.

CONTEMPORARY

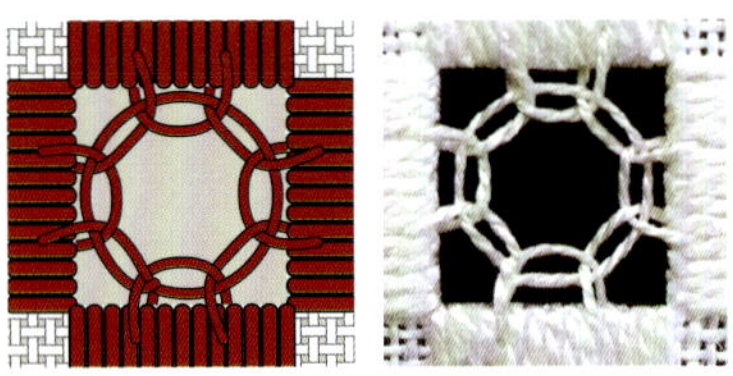

❶ *At this point, if you finish the thread in the back of the satin stitch, it is a Double Circular Web.*

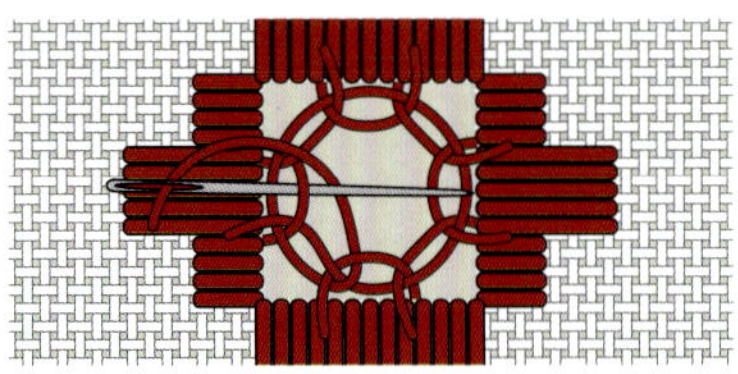

10 Bring the needle up in the centre. From the left, slide it under the curved stitch on the left side. Take it over the working thread.

11 Pull the needle through so the stitch curves gently. Turn the work and repeat twice more, then take the needle under the first inner curve.

12 Pull the needle through. Take the needle to the back between the first curve and the circling stitch.

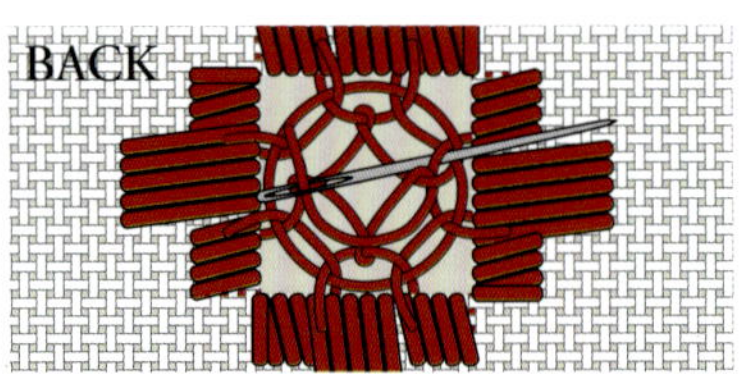

13 Adjust the stitches to sit evenly. On the back, from the left, take the needle under the first curve. Finish in the back of the satin stitch.

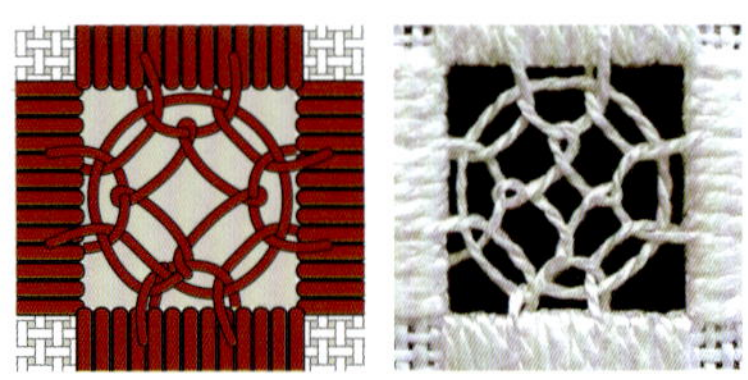

14 The completed flower filling.

flower filling

Tension is very important for this stitch. It may take some practice to get it right.

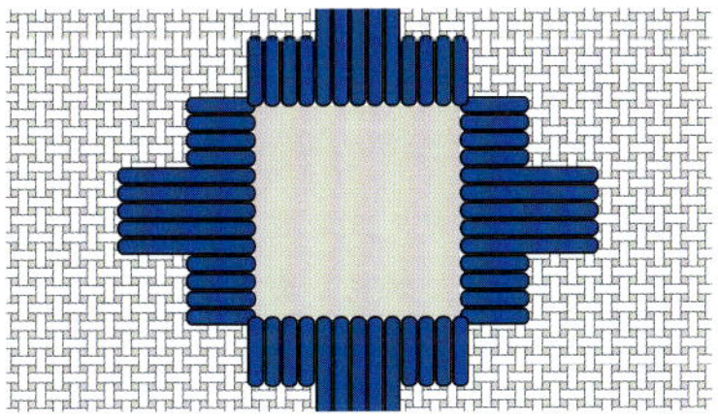

1 Prepare a satin stitch square as shown, cutting and removing all the threads within.

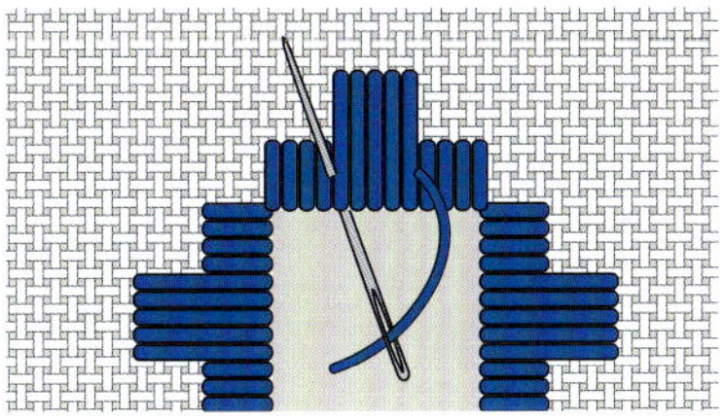

2 Bring the needle out in the top satin stitch, two threads from the cut edge, four stitches from the right. Insert it in the open square and bring it out five stitches to the left.

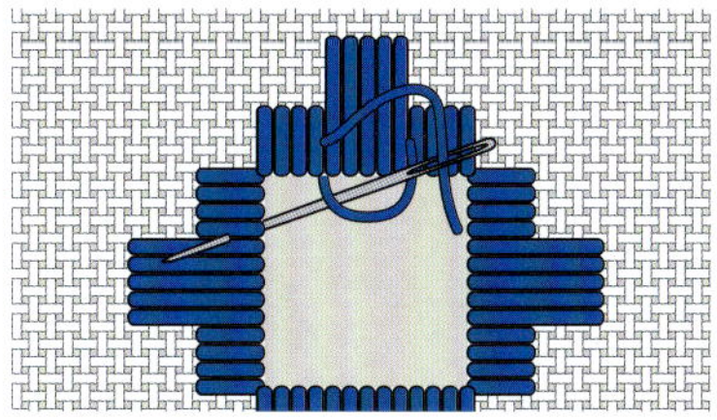

3 Pull the needle through so the curves gently. Slide it under the stitch. Bring it out in the next side, two threads from the cut edge, four stitches down from the top.

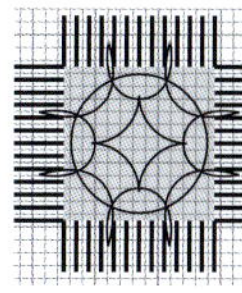

CONTEMPORARY

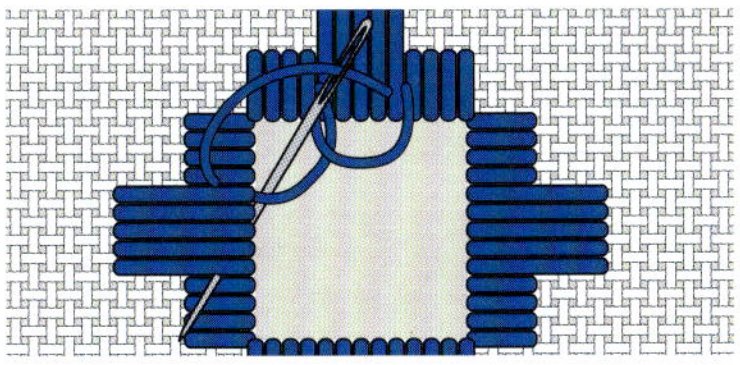

4 Pull the needle through to create a curved stitch. Insert the needle in the curve, and bring it out five stitches further down.

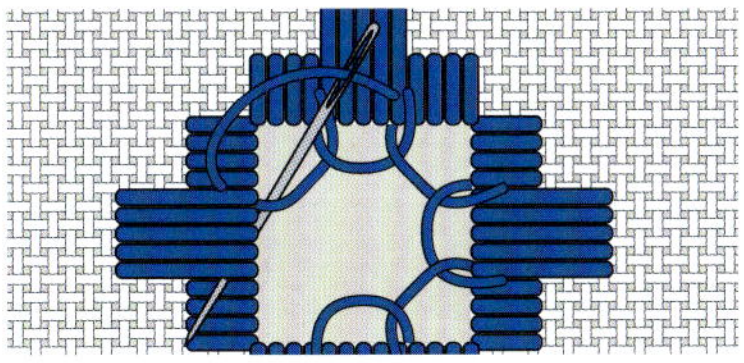

5 Pull the needle through, creating a curved stitch. Turning the work, repeat the stitches on the next two sides.

❶ *The looser these stitches, the smaller the circling stitch, and vice versa.*

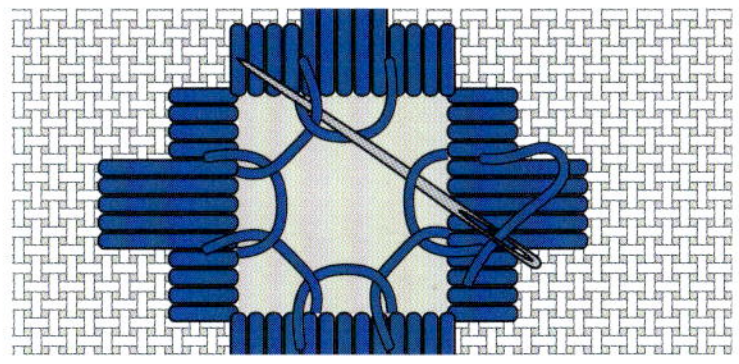

6 Pull the needle through to create a curved stitch. Turn the work 180°. Slide the needle under the curved stitch, over the first stitch, and under the right side of the second stitch.

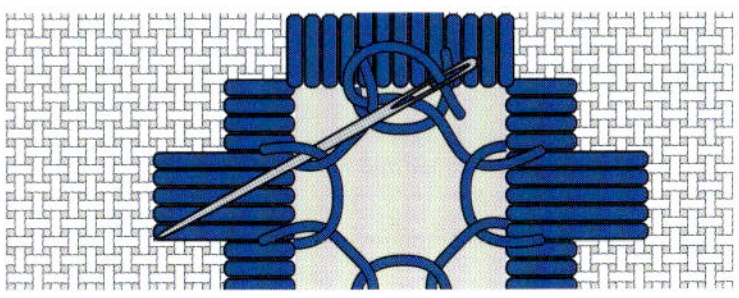

7 Slide the needle under the right side of the next stitch.

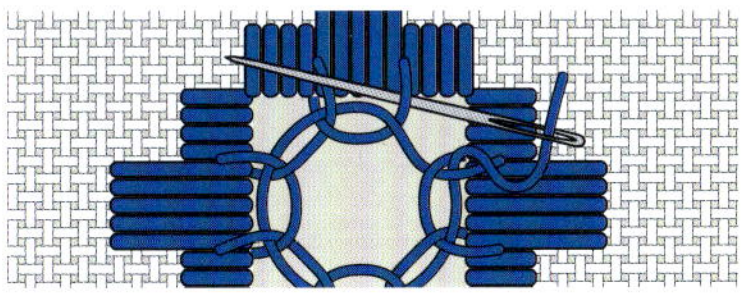

8 Continue, anticlockwise, sliding the needle under the right side of each stitch, finishing with the first one.

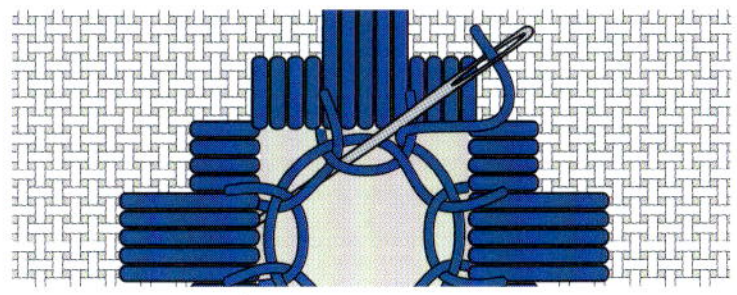

9 Take the needle through to the back between the first curved stitch and the circling stitch.

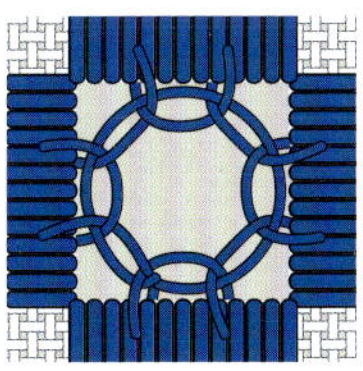

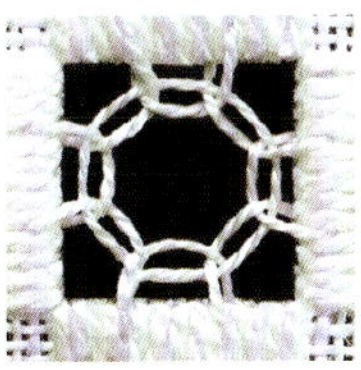

❶ *At this point, if you finish the thread in the back of the satin stitch, it is a Double Circular Web.*

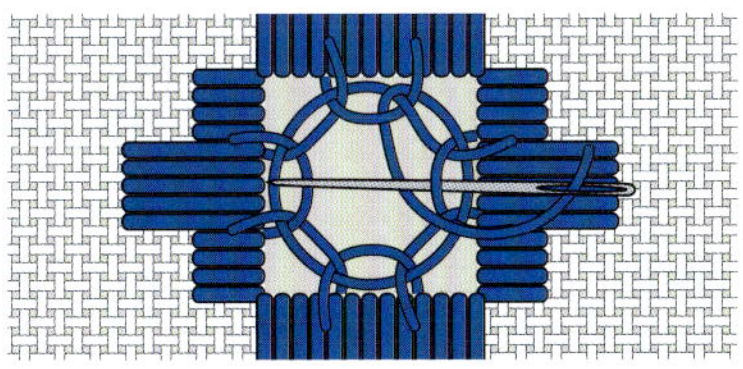

10 Bring the needle up in the centre. From the right, slide it under the curved stitch on the right-hand side. Take it over the working thread.

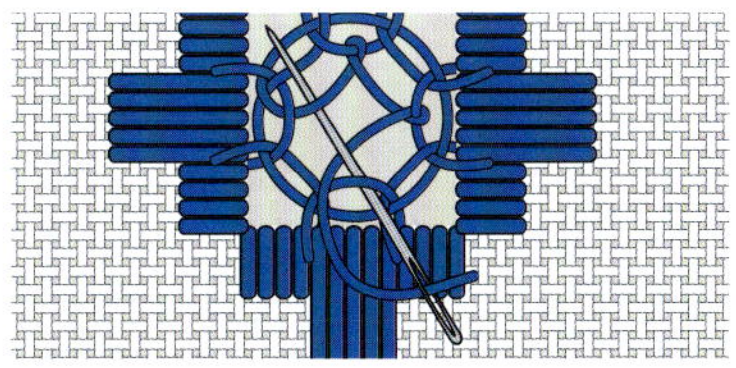

11 Pull the needle through so the stitch curves gently. Turn the work and repeat twice more, then take the needle under the first inner curve.

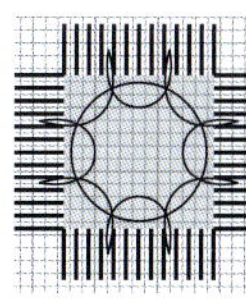

CONTEMPORARY

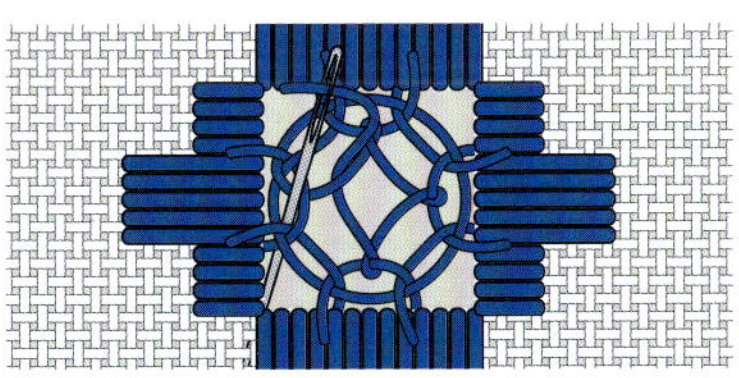

12 Pull the needle through. Take the needle to the back between the first curve and the circling stitch.

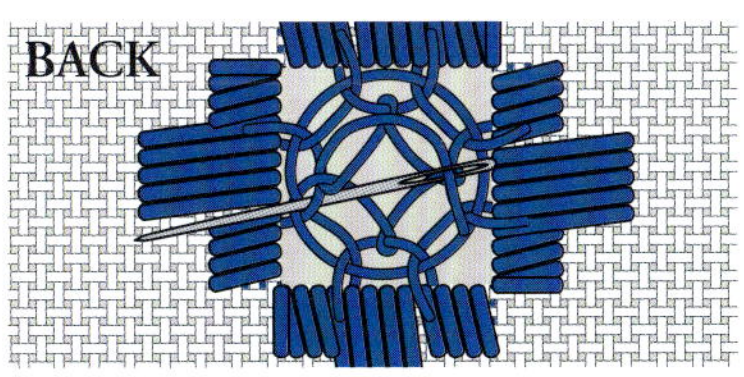

13 Adjust the stitches to sit evenly. On the back, from the right, take the needle under the first curve. Finish in the back of the satin stitch.

14 The completed flower filling.

L

wheel filling

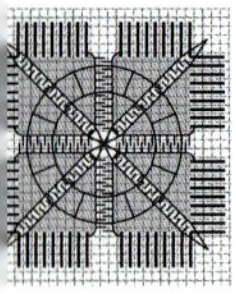

TRADITIONAL

This filling is worked as a feature stitch in a large opening. It looks complicated but is simpler than perhaps expected.

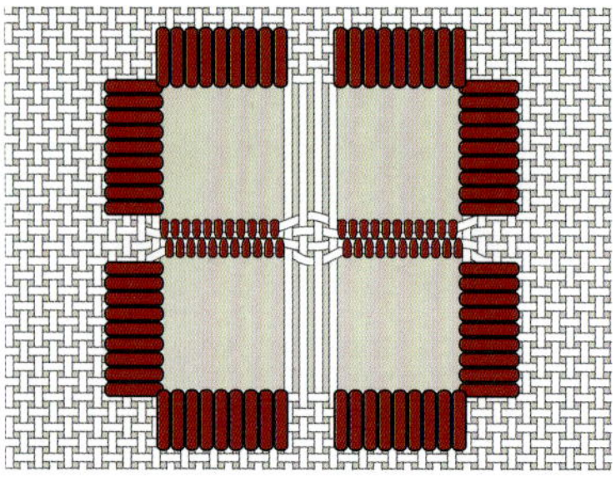

1 Prepare a large square as shown. Weave from one side to the other along two of the bars.

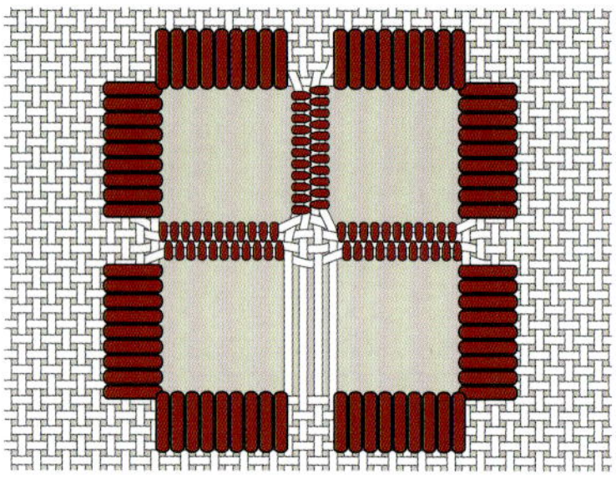

2 On the back, take the thread behind the intervening satin stitch. Work the next bar in to the centre.

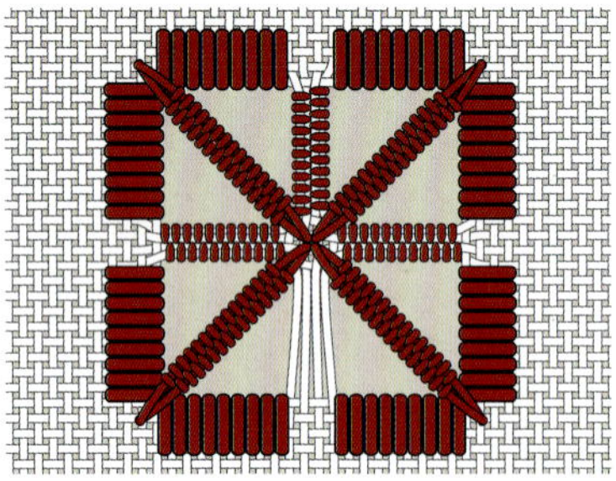

3 From the centre, work woven diagonals out to each corner, anchoring the outer ends two threads out from the cut corner.

❶ *'Woven diagonal' instructions on page 72.*

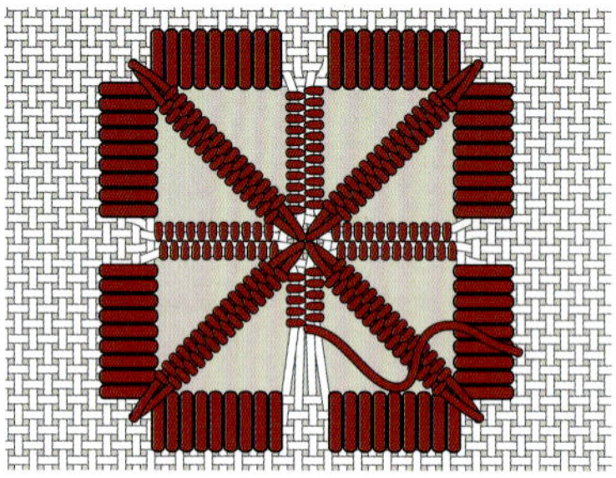

4 Work half of the final bar.

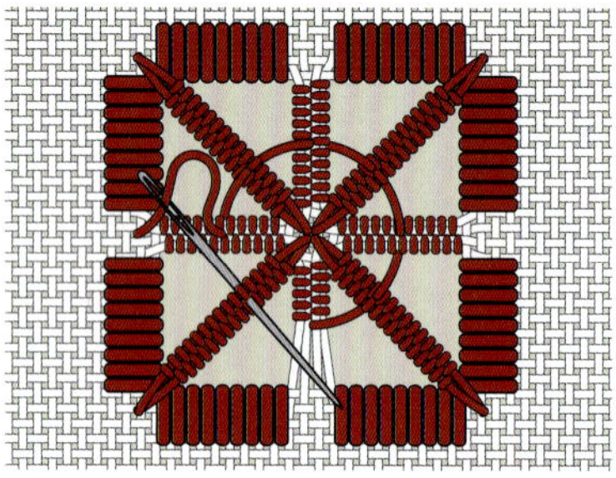

5 Working in an anticlockwise direction, insert the needle in the back of each of the bars in turn, the same distance from the centre as where the row started.

❶ *Turn the work as necessary.*

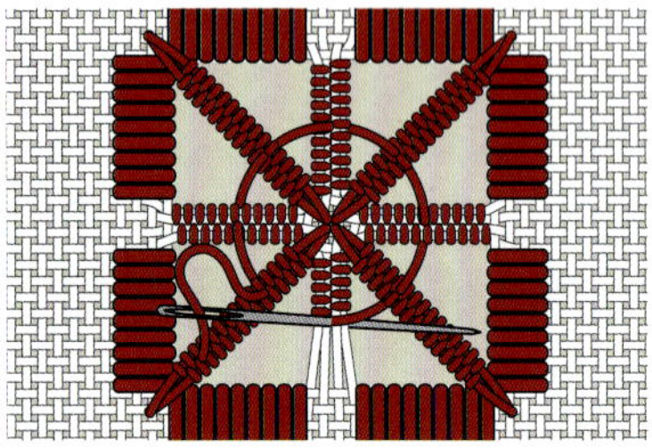

6 Insert the needle in the final bar from front to back.

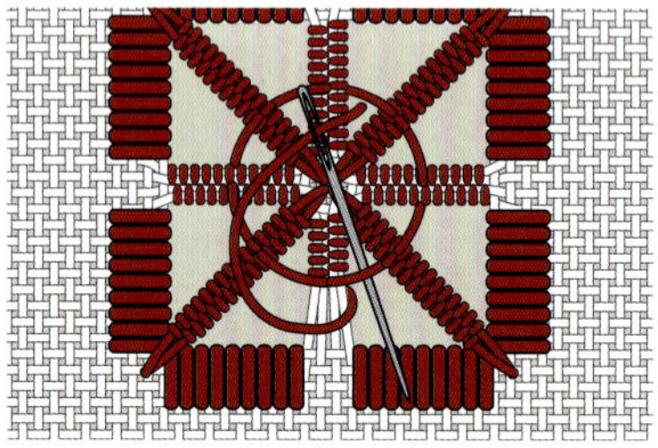

7 Pull the needle through. From above, slide the needle under the first laced segment of the circle.

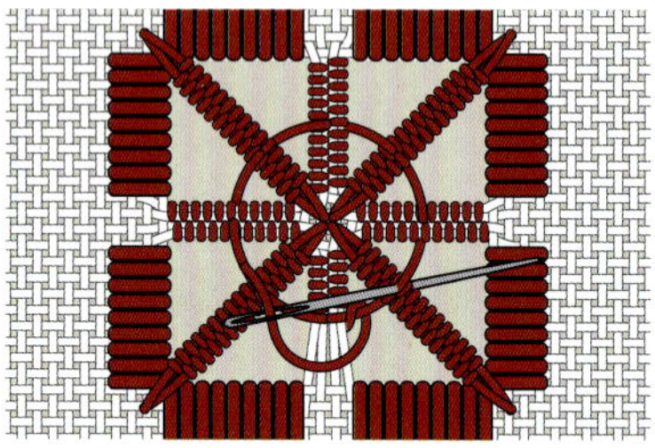

8 From the front, insert the needle in the next bar, so that the needle comes out outside the circle.

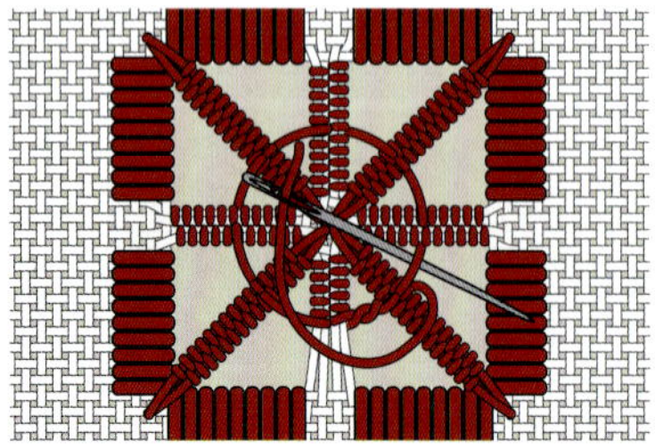

9 Pull the needle and thread to intertwine the stitches. From above left, slide the needle under the next segment.

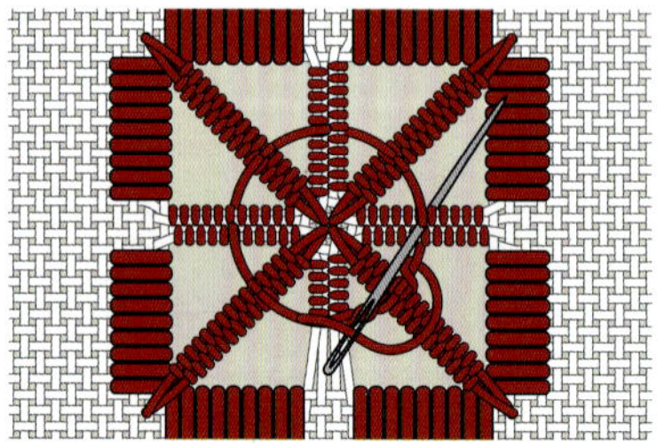

10 From the front, insert the needle in the next bar, so that it comes out in the next section outside the circle.

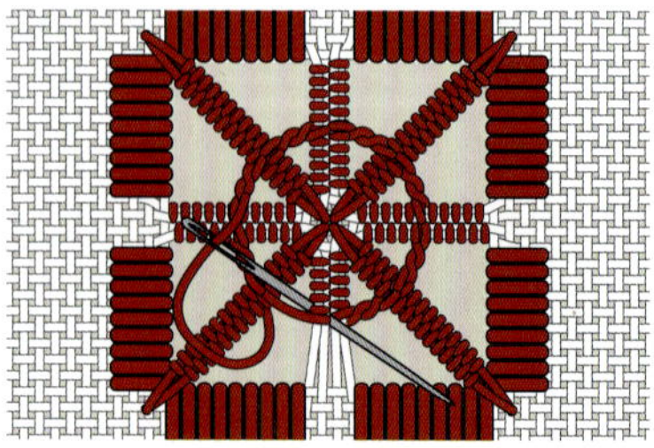

11 Continue around the circle. For the last segment, insert the needle from inside the circle, into the back of the final bar.

12 Weave to nearly the end of the bar.

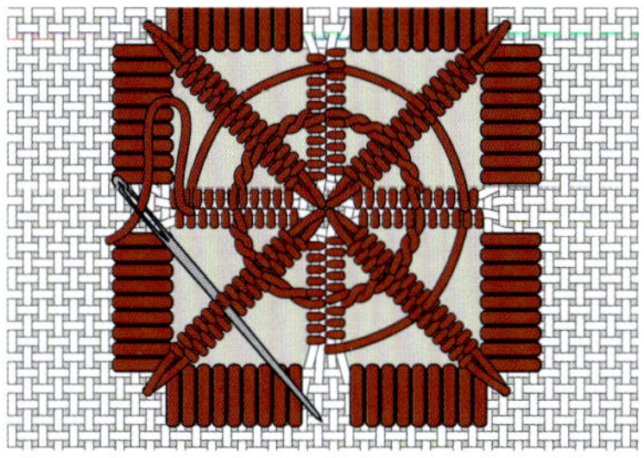

13 Working in an anticlockwise direction, insert the needle in the back of each of the bars in turn, the same distance from the centre as where the row started.

❶ *Turn the work as necessary.*

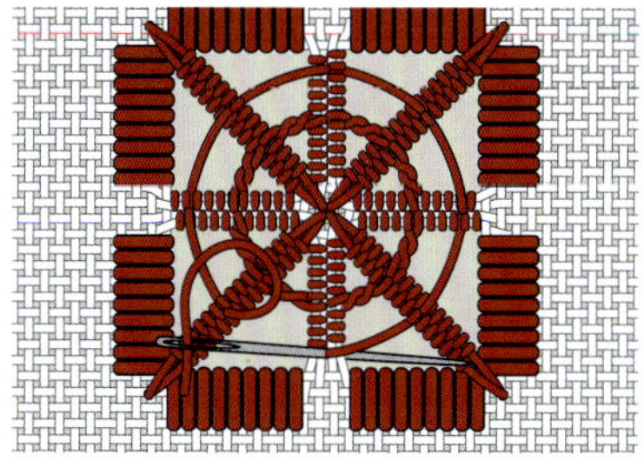

14 Insert the needle in the final bar from front to back.

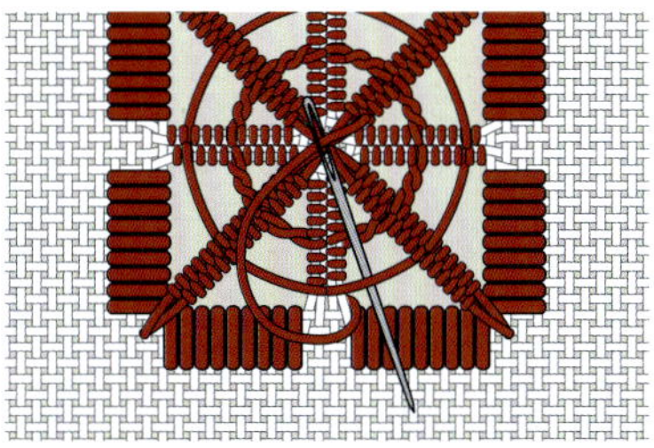

15 Pull the needle through. From above, slide the needle under the first laced segment of the circle.

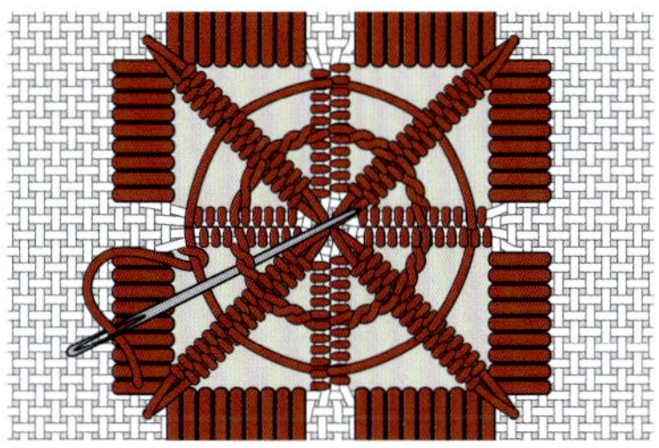

16 Turn the work 90° clockwise. From the left, slide the needle under the corresponding segment of the inner circle.

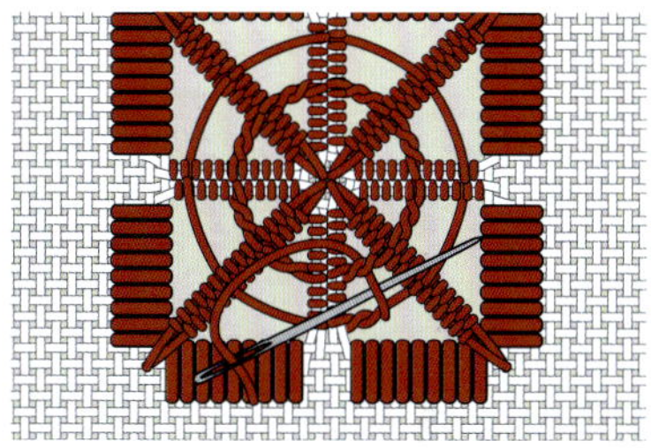

17 Intertwine the stitches. Turn the work 90° anticlockwise. From the left, slide the needle under the stitch between the two circles.

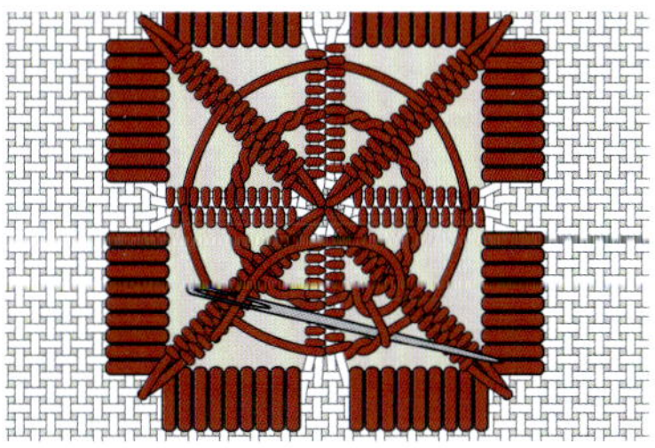

18 From above left, slide the needle under the intersection of the stitch between the circles and the outer circle.

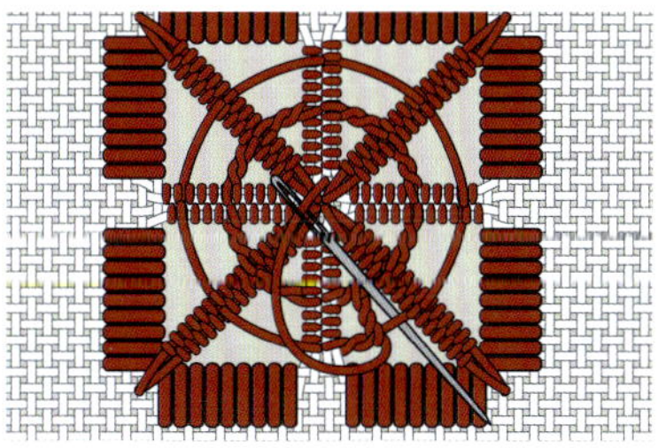

19 Intertwine the stitches. From above left, slide the needle under the second section of the outer circle segment.

❶ *When you intertwine these stitches, do not pull the circles together.*

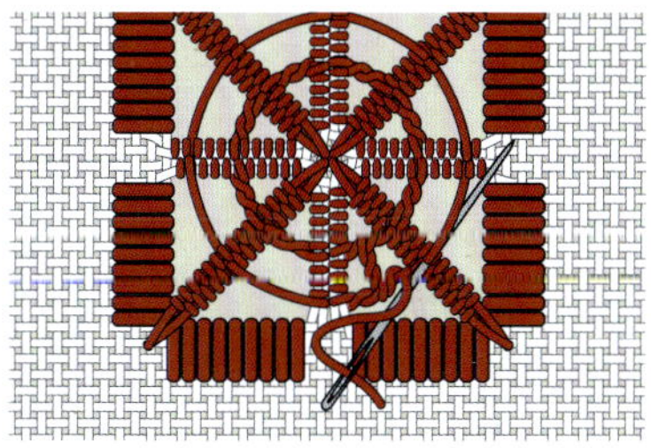

20 From the front, insert the needle in the next bar, so that it comes out in the next section outside the circle.

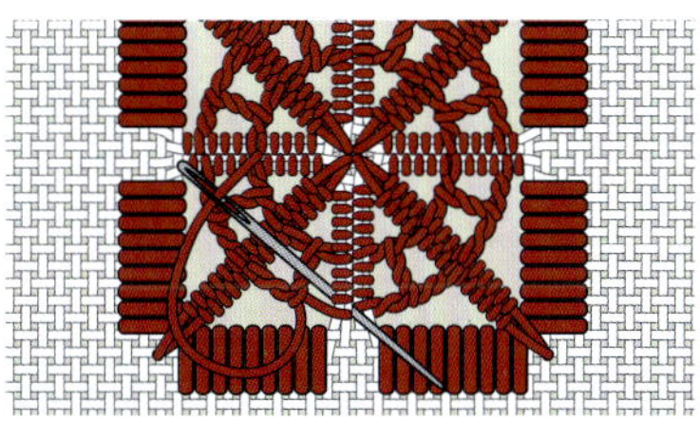

21 Continue around the circle in the same way. For the second part of the last segment, insert the needle from inside the circle, into the back of the final bar.

22 Complete the bar's final section of weaving outside the circle and finish the thread underneath the back of the satin stitch.

R

wheel filling

This filling is worked as a feature stitch in a large opening. It looks complicated but is simpler than perhaps expected.

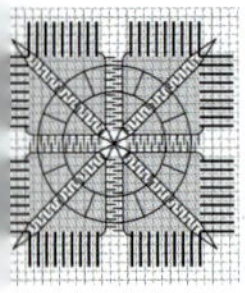

TRADITIONAL

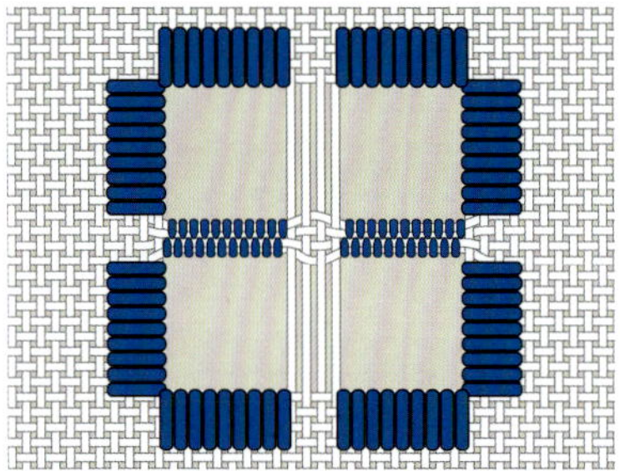

1 Prepare a large square as shown. Weave from one side to the other along two of the bars.

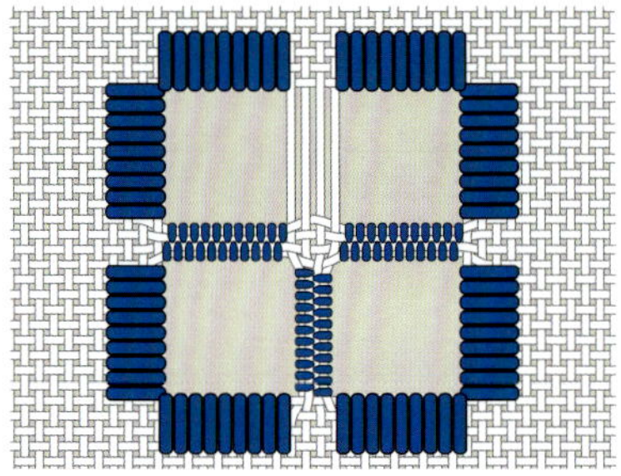

2 On the back, take the thread behind the intervening satin stitch. Work the next bar in to the centre.

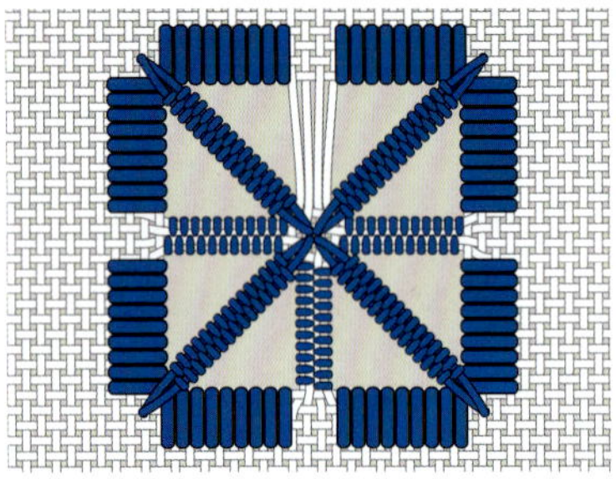

3 From the centre, work woven diagonals out to each corner, anchoring the outer ends two threads out from the cut corner.

❶ *'Woven diagonal' instructions on page 73.*

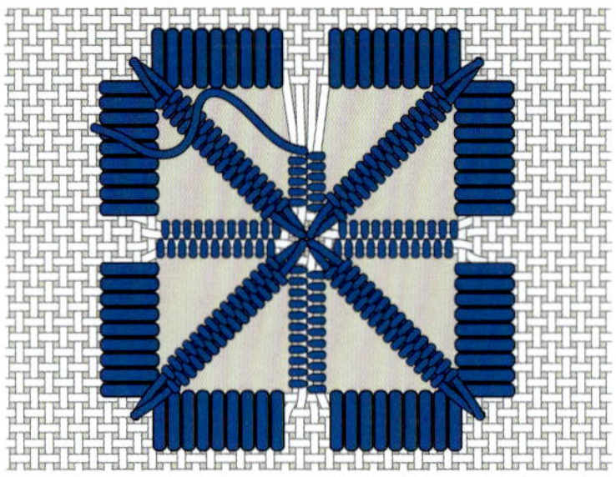

4 Work half of the final bar.

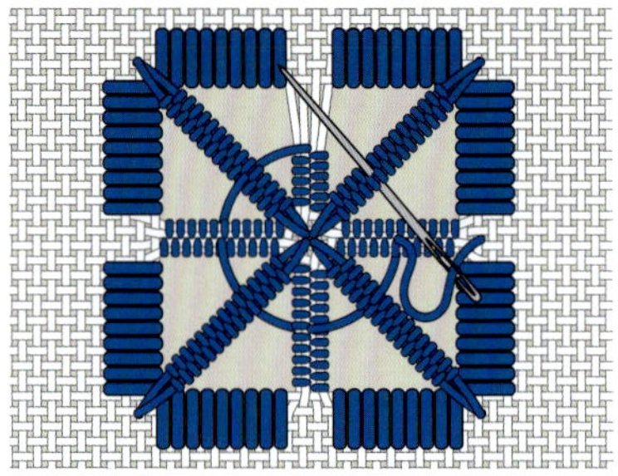

5 Working in an anticlockwise direction, insert the needle in the back of each of the bars in turn, the same distance from the centre as where the row started.

❶ *Turn the work as necessary.*

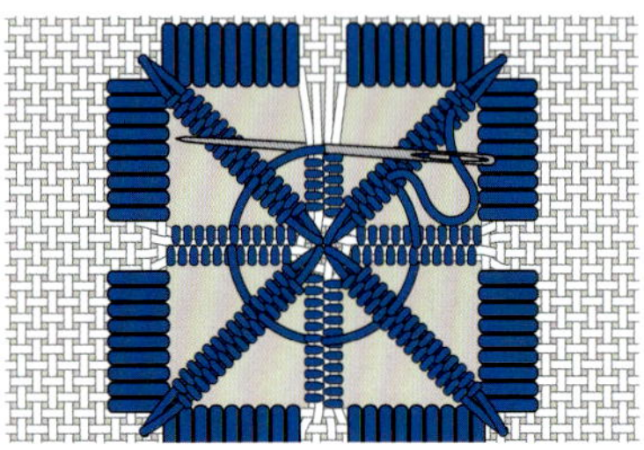

6 Insert the needle in the final bar from front to back.

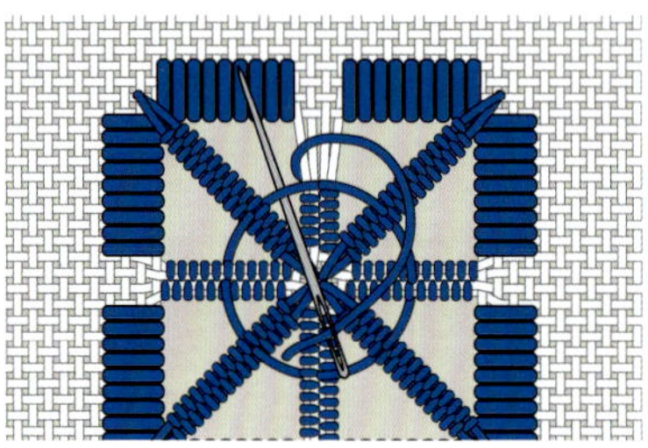

7 Pull the needle through. From below, slide the needle under the first laced segment of the circle.

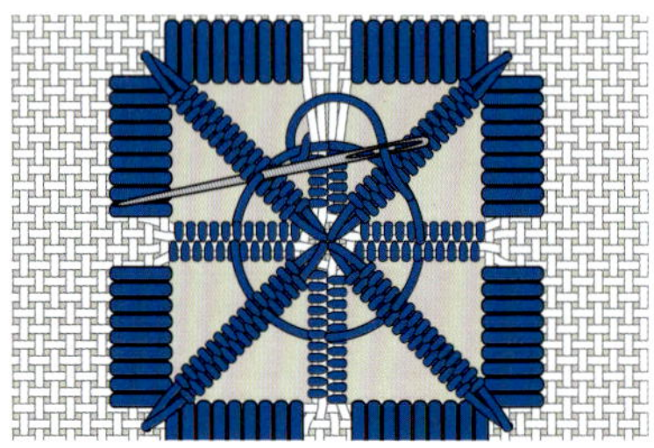

8 From the front, insert the needle in the next bar, so that the needle comes out outside the circle.

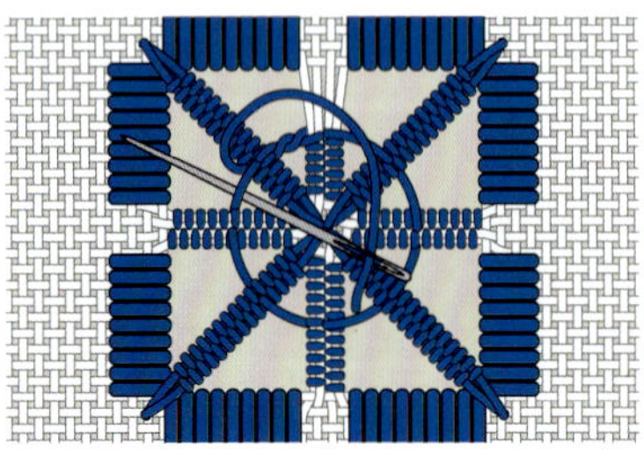

9 Pull the needle and thread to intertwine the stitches. From below right, slide the needle under the next segment.

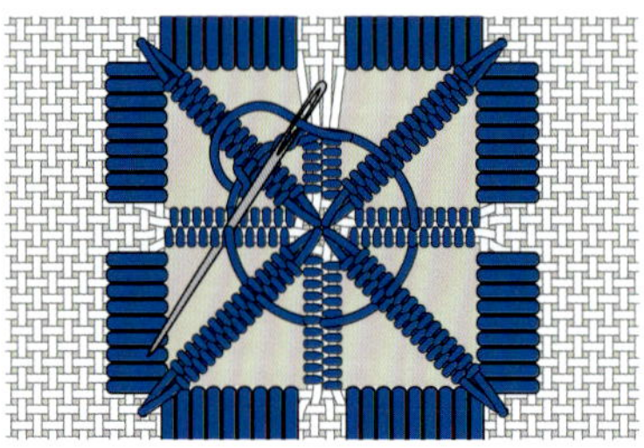

10 From the front, insert the needle in the next bar, so that it comes out in the next section outside the circle.

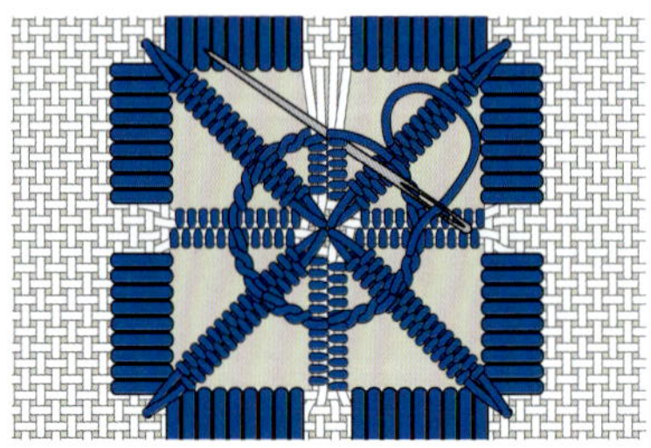

11 Continue around the circle. For the last segment, insert the needle from inside the circle, into the back of the final bar.

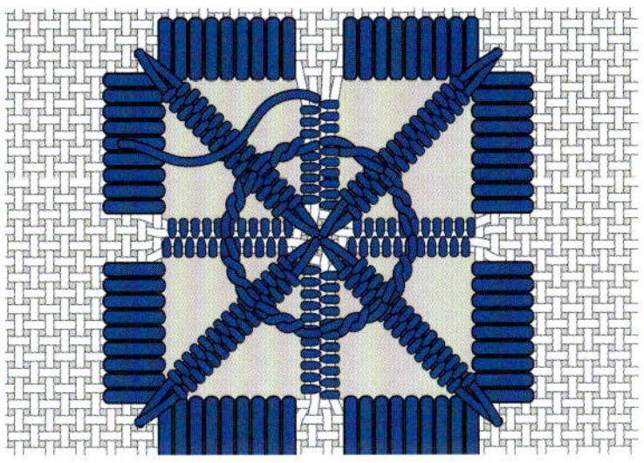

12 Weave to nearly the end of the bar.

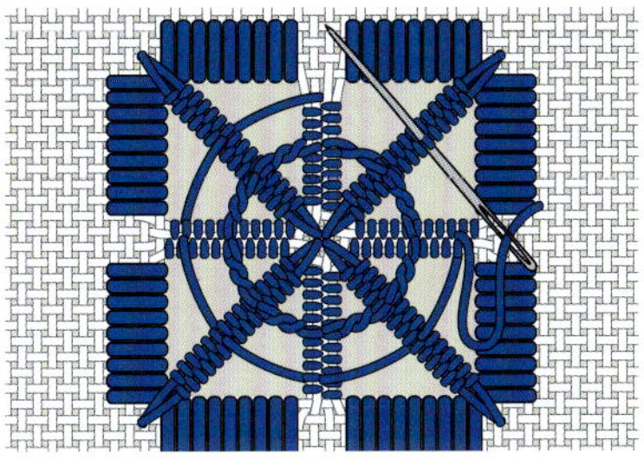

13 Working in an anticlockwise direction, insert the needle in the back of each of the bars in turn, the same distance from the centre as where the row started.

❶ *Turn the work as necessary.*

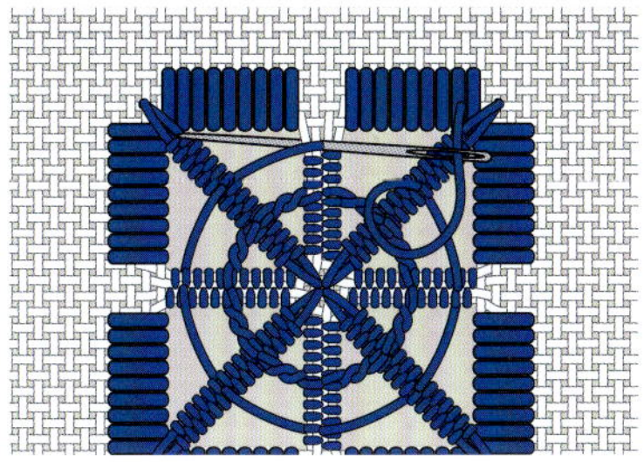

14 Insert the needle in the final bar from front to back.

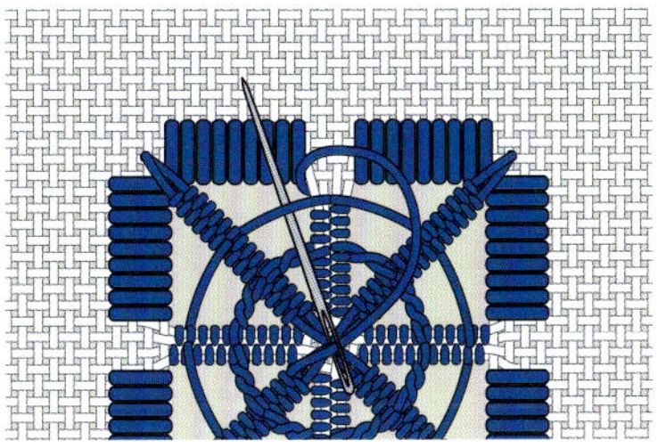

15 Pull the needle through. From below, slide the needle under the first laced segment of the circle.

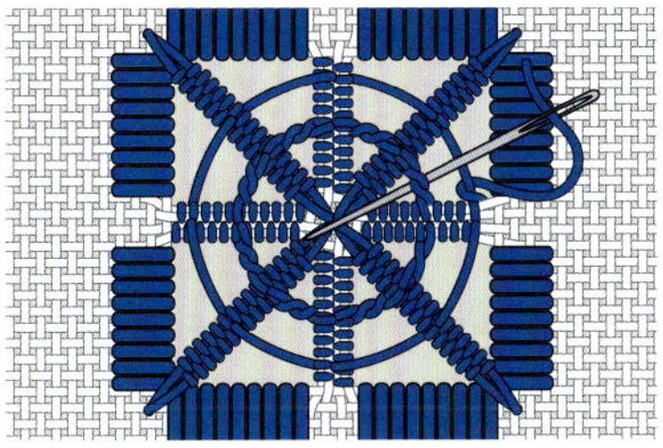

16 Turn the work 90° clockwise. From the right, slide the needle under the corresponding segment of the inner circle.

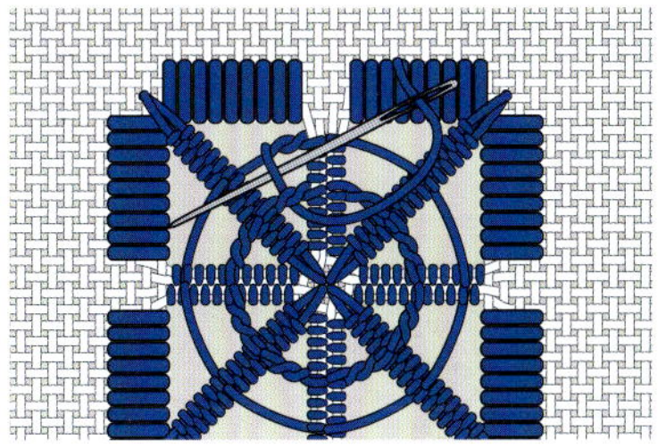

17 Intertwine the stitches. Turn the work 90° anticlockwise. From the right, slide the needle under the stitch between the two circles.

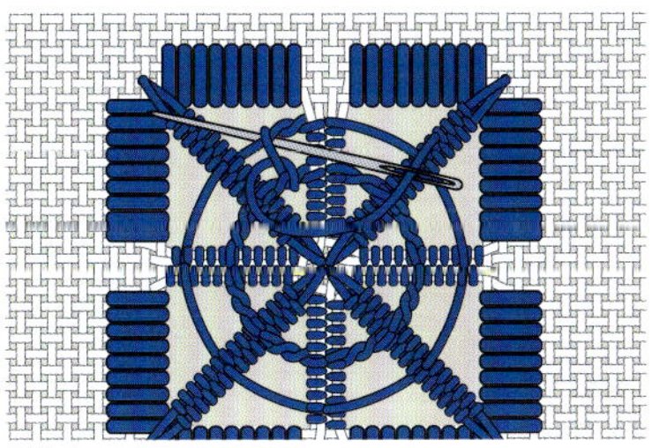

18 From below right, slide the needle under the intersection of the stitch between the circles, and the outer circle.

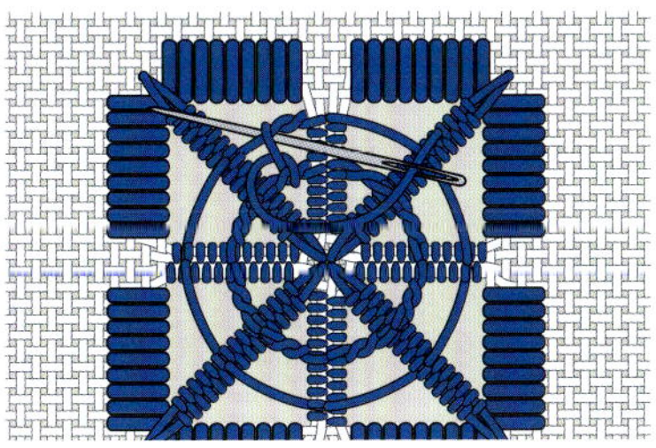

19 Intertwine the stitches. From below right, slide the needle under the second section of the outer circle segment.

❶ *When you intertwine these stitches, do not pull the circles together.*

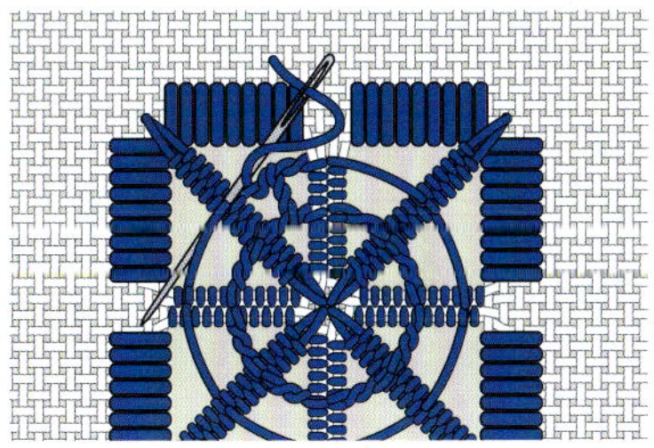

20 From the front, insert the needle in the next bar, so that it comes out in the next section outside the circle.

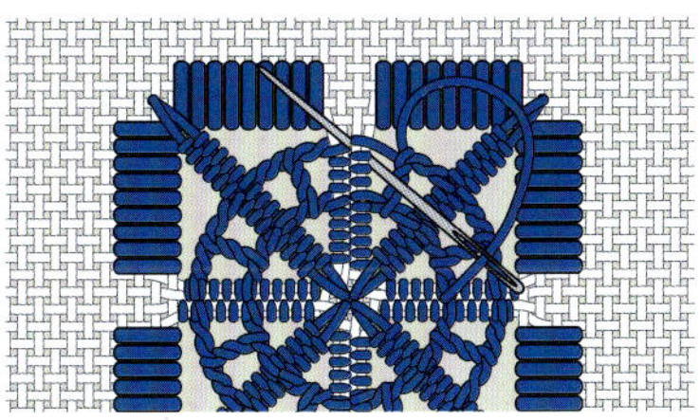

21 Continue around the circle in the same way. For the second part of the last segment, insert the needle from inside the circle, into the back of the final bar.

22 Complete the bar's final section of weaving outside the circle and finish the thread underneath the back of the satin stitch.

L

edelweiss

CONTEMPORARY

This stitch is a combination of a ribbed spider web and Greek quarter crosses.

❗ *Tension is crucial for this stitch, as is the thickness of the thread compared to the size of the whole motif.*

If your motif requires six or more threads to be removed from the square's quadrants, use the thicker satin stitching thread rather than the thinner, filling stitch thread. A thinner thread means more stitches are needed to fill the space. More stitches make it harder to get a smooth result, because some will end up overlapping or with loose tension.

You will need long thread lengths for this motif. If you can see it will not be long enough, lace it to the edge at the completion of Step 7, finishing it in the back of the satin stitch. Start a new thread similarly and lace it to the centre behind the unwrapped bar ready to continue.

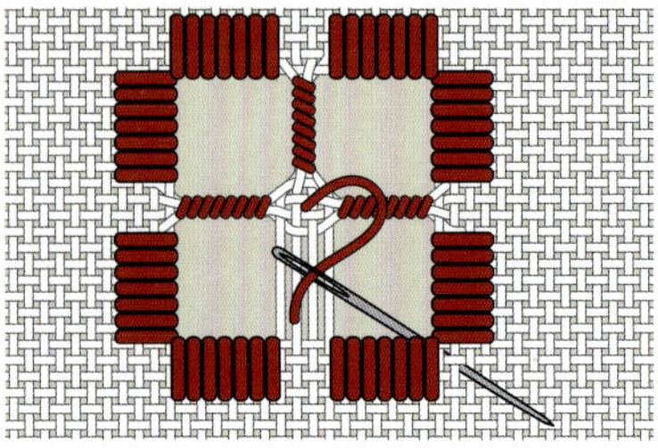

1 In a large square, wrap the bars as shown. Bring the needle out in the woven square's centre. From the back, insert it in the lower right corner, two threads from the edge.

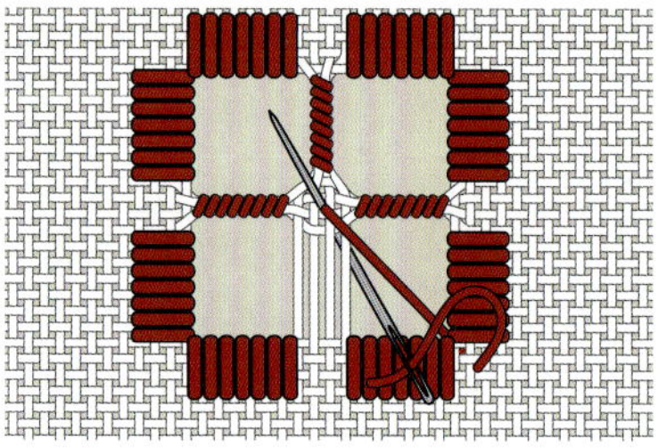

2 Pull the needle through, then bring it out in the centre.

3 Pull the needle through and bring it out in the corner, two threads away from the edge.

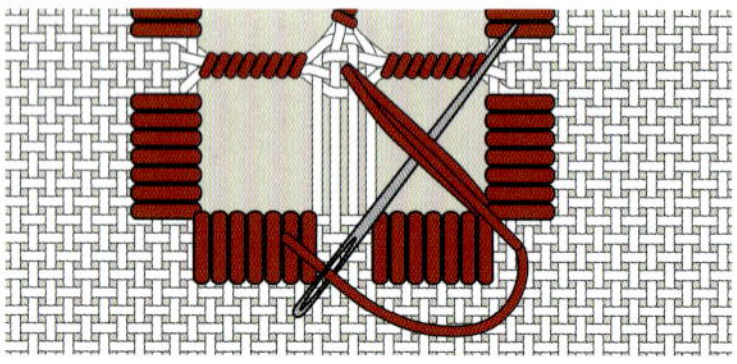

4 Pull the needle through. Slide the needle from left to right under the diagonal threads.

5 Wrap all the way along the diagonal threads, then bring the needle out in the centre again.

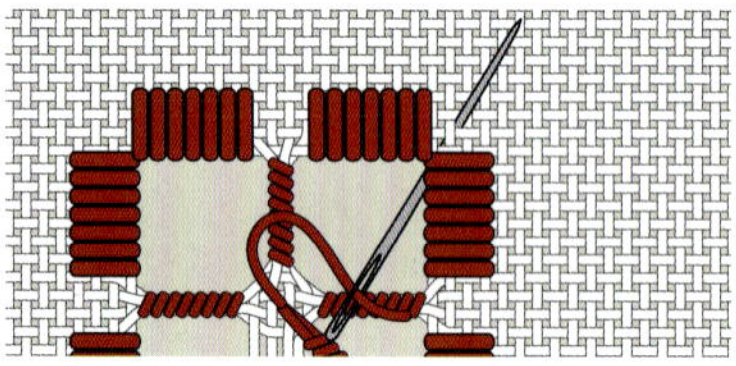

6 Move to the upper right quadrant and bring the needle out in the corner, two threads away from the edge.

7 Repeat the wrapped diagonals in each of the corners. Bring the needle out past the next bar.

❗ *If the thread is not long enough to finish the motif, lace it to the edge, finish it, and start a new one after this step.*

8 Pull the needle through. Working in an anticlockwise direction, take the needle under the bar and the next diagonal.

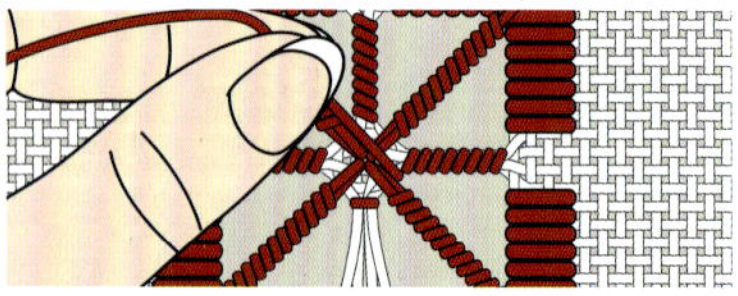

9 Pull the needle through and towards the centre to bring the stitch in snugly.

❗ *Pull towards the centre after each stitch. This foundation needs to be very firm.*

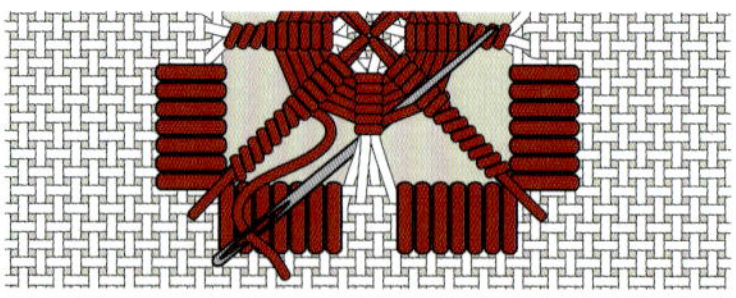

10 Continue working a ribbed spider web. When the web covers half the bars' length and a circuit is complete, take the needle under the next bar and the outermost stitch between that bar and next diagonal.

❗ *The web should be firm and solid. If not, the stitches should be tighter.*

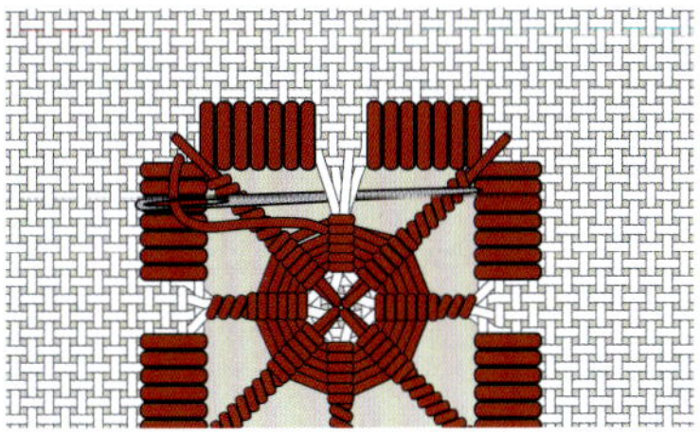

11 Pull the needle through. Turn the work 180°. From the left, slide the needle under the bar.

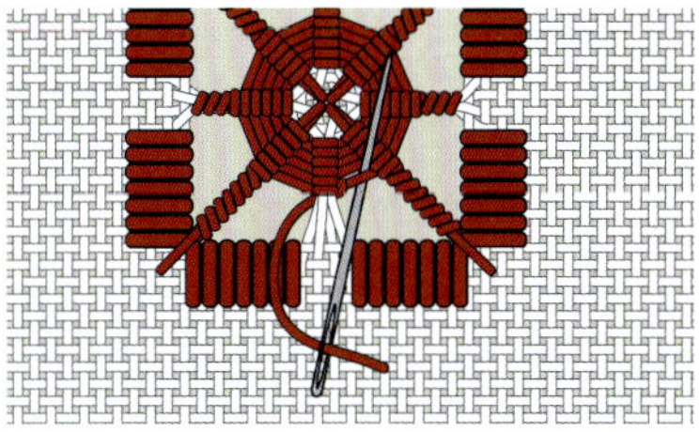

12 Pull the needle to tighten the stitch. Turn the work 180°. From below, slide the needle under the outermost web stitch.

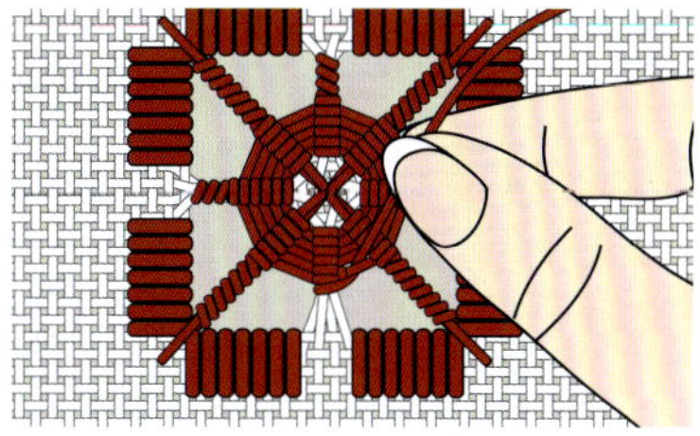

13 Pull the thread to tighten the stitch and pull the bar to the right.

14 Continue weaving between the bar and the stitch. After each stitch towards the web, pull tightly to continue curving the bar.

❶ *As you stitch, the tight weaving stitches will pull the outer part of the bar towards the web, causing the bar to bow slightly outward. When this happens the stitch is working well.*

❶ *Take care that the stitches sit neatly and do not overlap previous ones.*

15 When the web stitch is filled, take the needle under the diagonal, and under the outer stitch in the next section along.

❶ *You may get a small gap forming between the quarter cross and the web. If the web's stitches are firm enough, this should be minimised.*

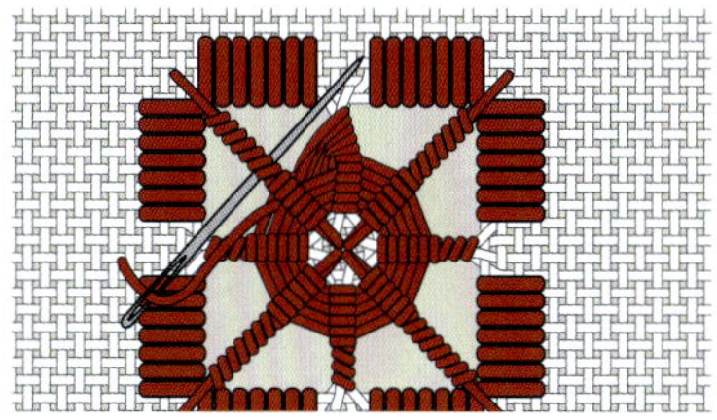

16 Pull the needle through. Turn the work 180°. From the left, take the needle under the diagonal.

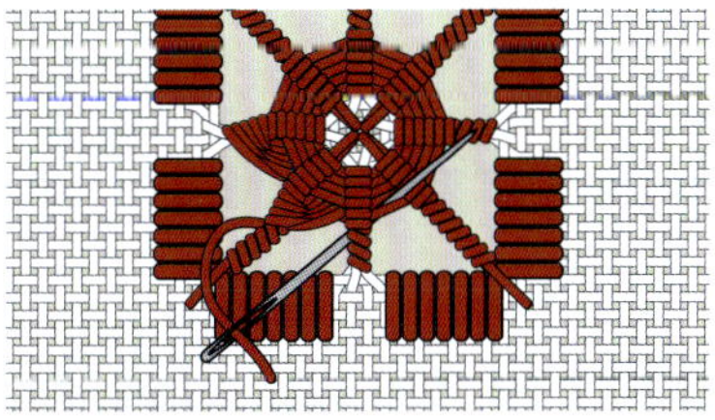

17 Turning the work as required, and with firm tension, weave back and forth between the diagonal and the outermost web stitch. Take the needle under the next bar and the next section's outermost web stitch.

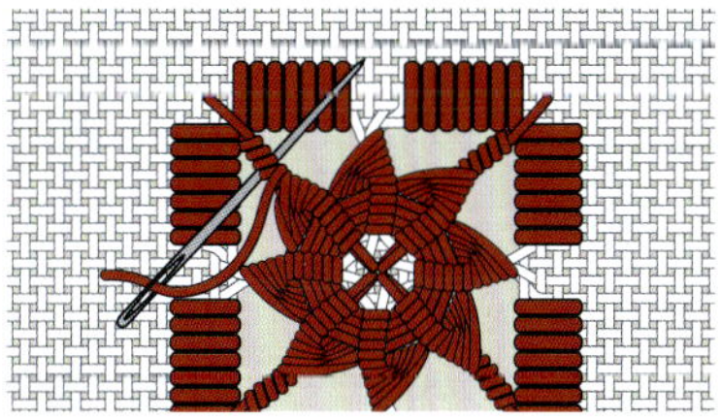

18 Continue around the circle, working quarter crosses. To complete the motif, slide the needle under the final diagonal from below left.

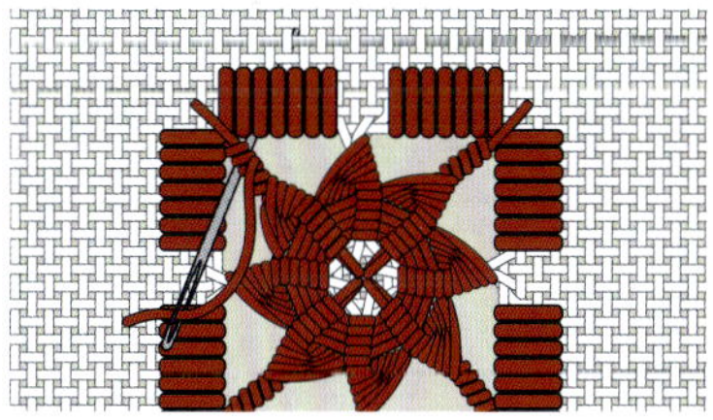

19 Tighten the stitch so it merges in with the other wraps. Take the needle to the back below the diagonal, and finish the thread in the back of the satin stitch.

20 The completed motif.

❶ *This is a motif where tension is crucial for getting the stitches to sit well. Do not be afraid to practice so that your stitching improves. When I was writing the instructions for this stitch, I stitched sample after sample for some days before being happy with them.*

R

edelweiss

This stitch is a combination of a ribbed spider web and Greek quarter crosses.

CONTEMPORARY

❶ *Tension is crucial for this stitch, as is the thickness of the thread compared to the size of the whole motif.*

If your motif requires six or more threads to be removed from the square's quadrants, use the thicker satin stitching thread rather than the thinner, filling stitch thread. A thinner thread means more stitches are needed to fill the space. More stitches make it harder to get a smooth result, because some will end up overlapping or with loose tension.

You will need long thread lengths for this motif. If you can see it will not be long enough, lace it to the edge at the completion of Step 7, finishing it in the back of the satin stitch. Start a new thread similarly and lace it to the centre behind the unwrapped bar ready to continue.

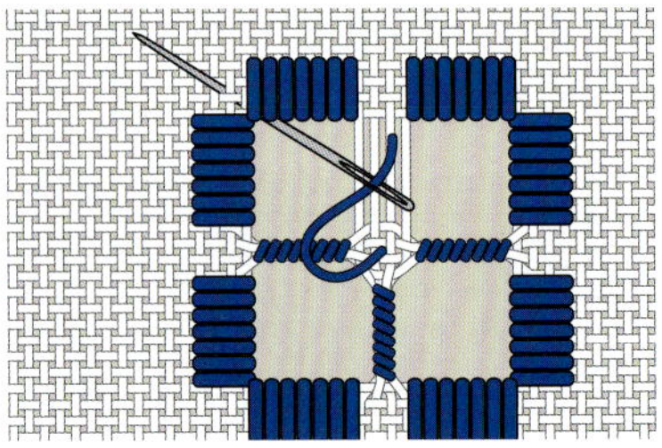

1 In a large square, wrap the bars as shown. Bring the needle out in the woven square's centre. From the back, insert it in the upper left corner, two threads from the edge.

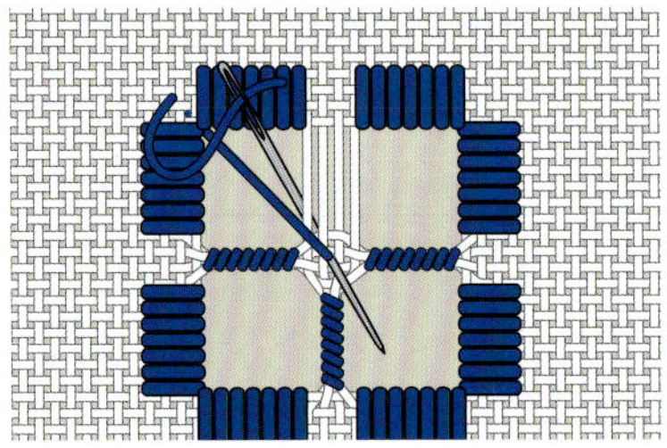

2 Pull the needle through, then bring it out in the centre.

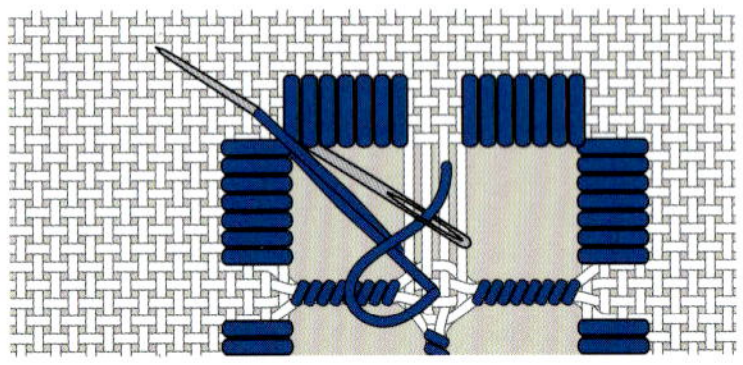

3 Pull the needle through and bring it out in the corner, two threads away from the edge.

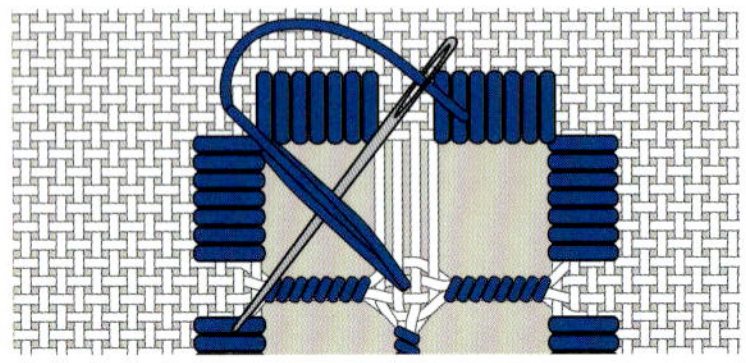

4 Pull the needle through. Slide the needle from right to left under the diagonal threads.

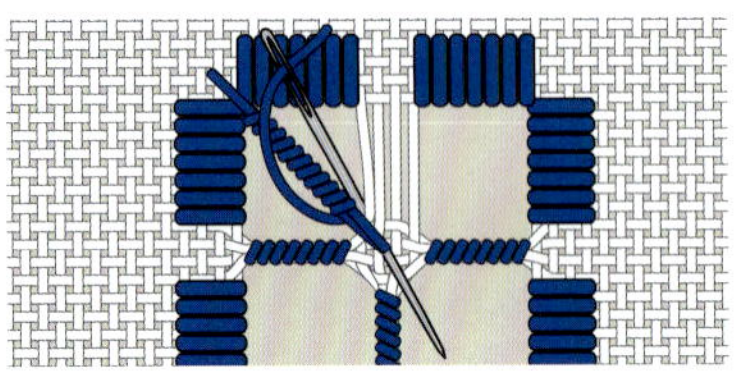

5 Wrap all the way along the diagonal threads, then bring the needle out in the centre again.

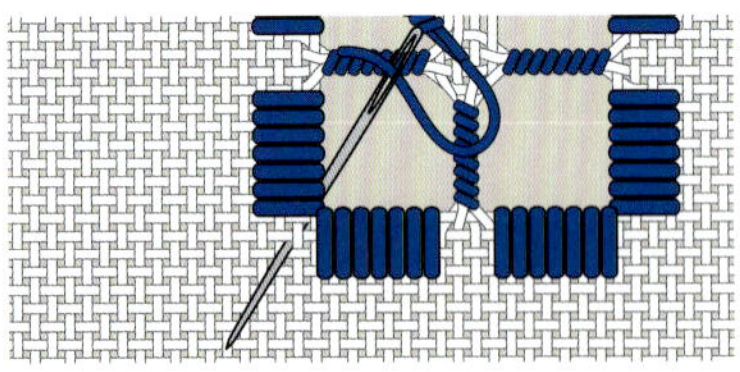

6 Move to the lower left quadrant and bring the needle out in the corner, two threads away from the edge.

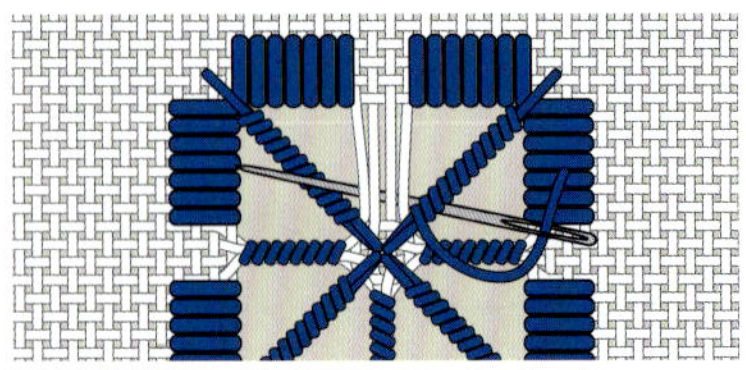

7 Repeat the wrapped diagonals in each of the corners. Bring the needle out past the next bar.

❶ *If the thread is not long enough to finish the motif, lace it to the edge, finish it, and start a new one after this step.*

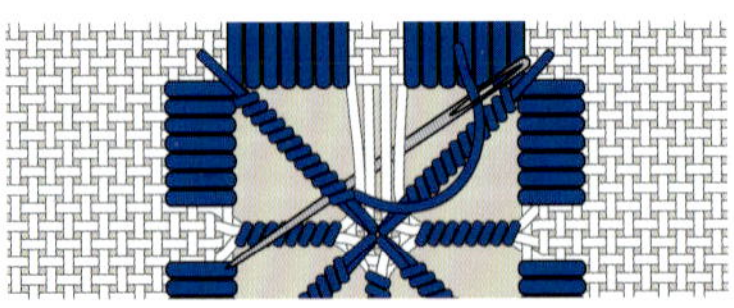

8 Pull the needle through. Working in an anticlockwise direction, take the needle under the bar and the next diagonal.

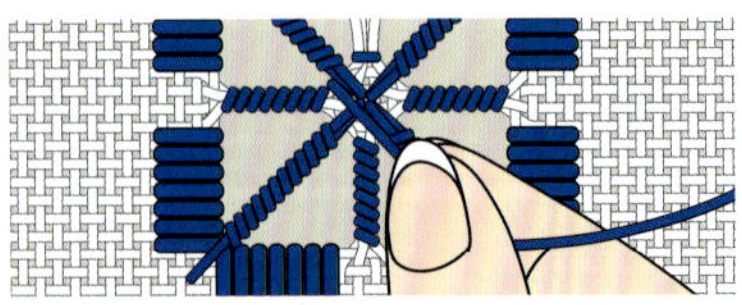

9 Pull the needle through and towards the centre to bring the stitch in snugly.

❶ *Pull towards the centre after each stitch. This foundation needs to be very firm.*

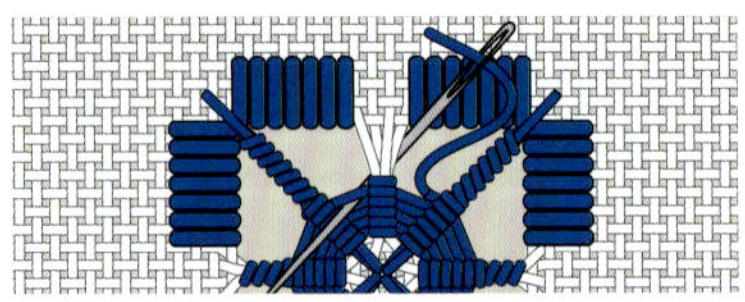

10 Continue working a ribbed spider web. When the web covers half the bars' length and a circuit is complete, take the needle under the next bar and the outermost stitch between that bar and next diagonal.

❶ *The web should be firm and solid. If it isn't, the stitches need to be tighter.*

11 Pull the needle through. Turn the work 180°. From the right, slide the needle under the bar.

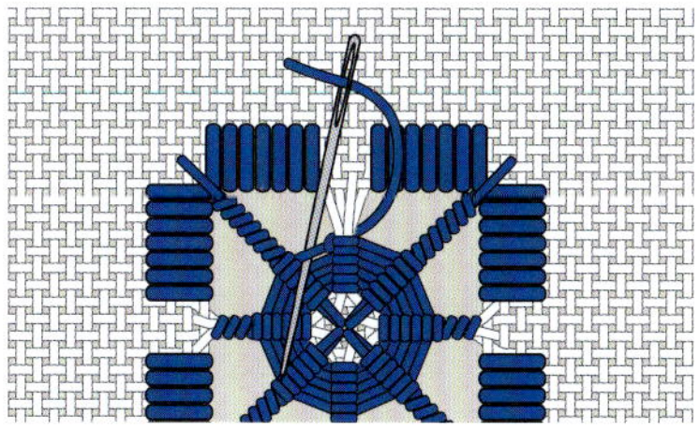

12 Pull the needle to tighten the stitch. Turn the work 180°. From above, slide the needle under the outermost web stitch.

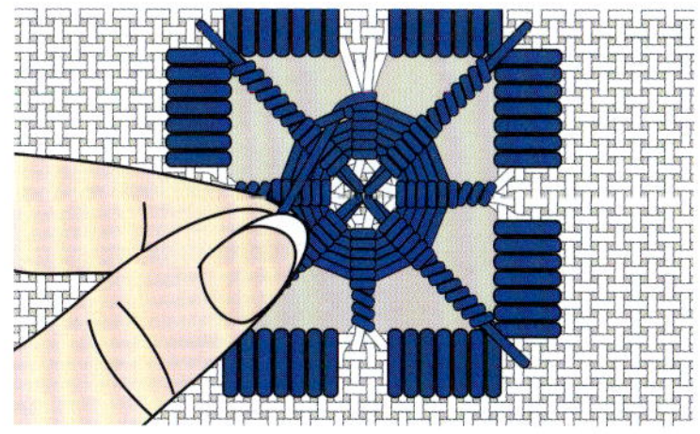

13 Pull the thread to tighten the stitch and pull the bar to the left.

14 Continue weaving between the bar and the stitch with firm tension to fill the space.

❶ *As you stitch, the tight weaving stitches will pull the outer part of the bar towards the web, causing the bar to bow slightly outward. When this happens the stitch is working well.*

❶ *Take care that the stitches sit neatly and do not overlap previous ones.*

15 When the web stitch is filled, take the needle under the diagonal, and under the outer stitch in the next section along.

❶ *You may get a small gap forming between the quarter cross and the web. If the web's stitches are firm enough, this should be minimised.*

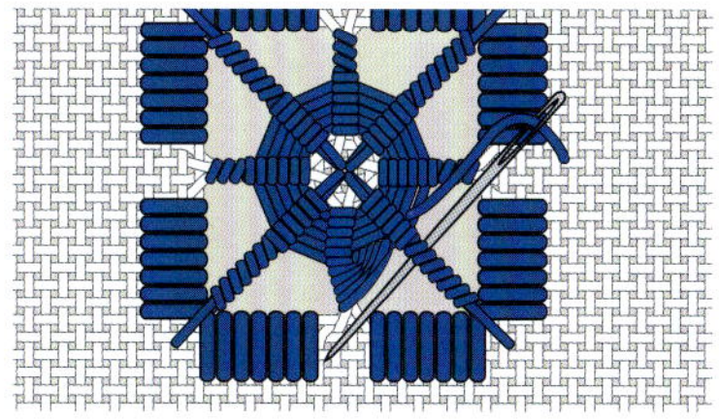

16 Pull the needle through. Turn the work 180°. From the right, take the needle under the diagonal.

17 Turning the work as required, and with firm tension, weave back and forth between the diagonal and the outermost web stitch. Take the needle under the next bar and the next section's outermost web stitch.

18 Continue around the circle, working quarter crosses. To complete the motif, slide the needle under the final diagonal from above right.

19 Tighten the stitch so it merges in with the other wraps. Take the needle to the back below the diagonal, and finish the thread in the back of the satin stitch.

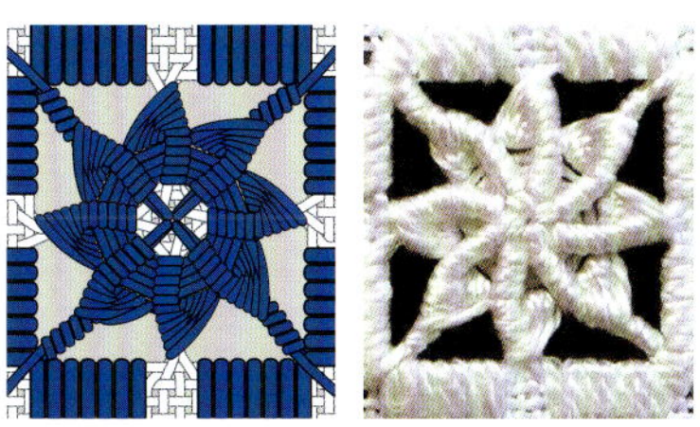

20 The completed motif.

❶ *This is a motif where tension is crucial for getting the stitches to sit well. Do not be afraid to practice so that your stitching improves. When I was writing the instructions for this stitch, I stitched sample after sample for some days before being happy with them.*

L

queen anne's lace

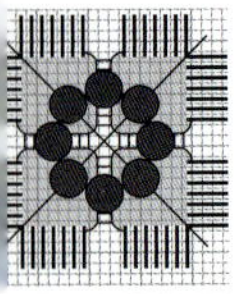

CONTEMPORARY

Consistency is key in this motif. You will need to use good tension for wrapping the bars, twisting the threads, working and spacing the ring knots, and working the spider webs. You will need consistent quantities of twists for the diagonals and circling stitches for the webs.

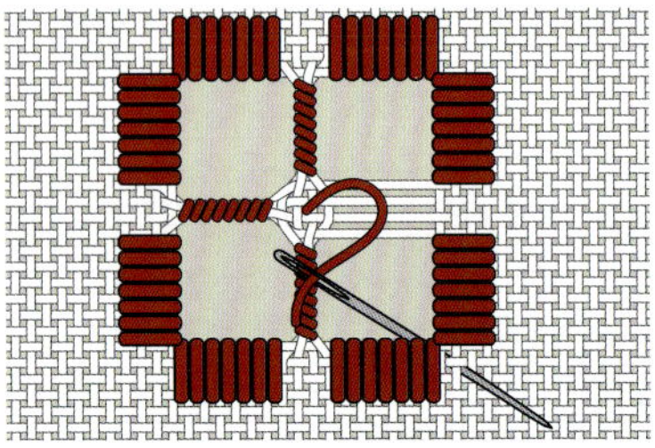

1 In a large square, wrap the bars as shown. Bring the needle out in the woven square's centre. From the back, insert the needle in the lower right corner, two threads from the edge.

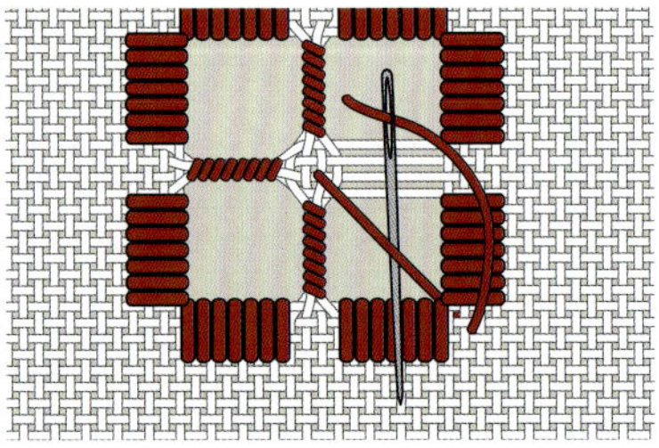

2 Pull the needle through, then slide it under the stitch from above.

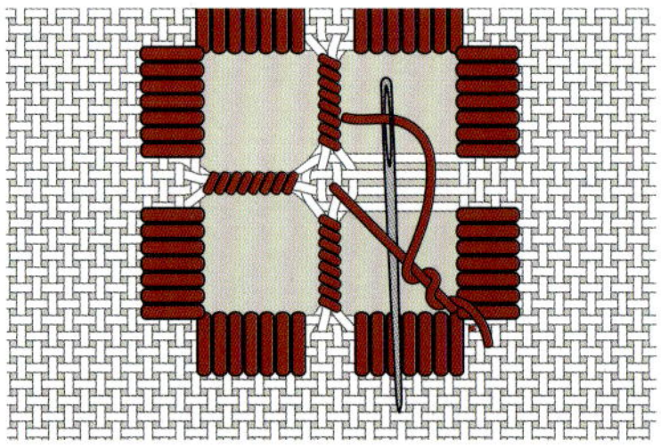

3 Slide the needle under, twice more.

! *If working in a larger square than the one shown (this one has six removed in each quadrant), you may need to slide it under an additional time.*

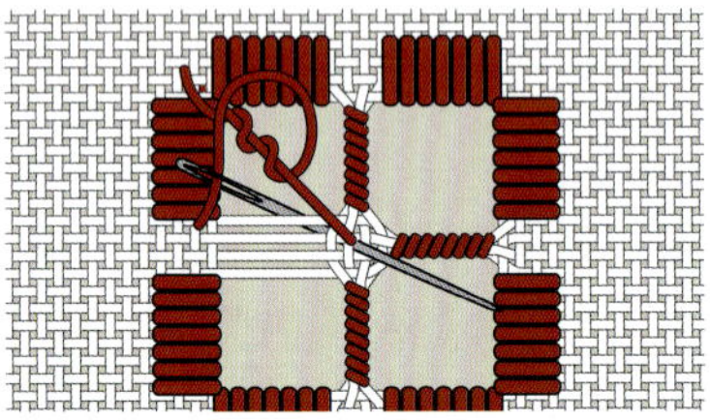

4 Turn the work 180°. Insert the needle below the diagonal and bring it out in the centre.

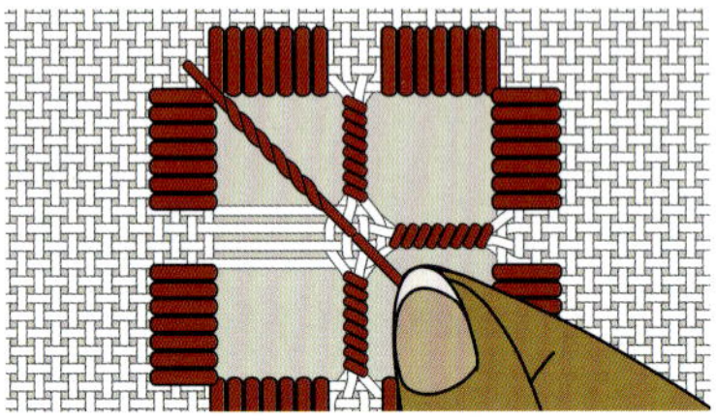

5 Pull the needle through. Pull the thread to intertwine the stitches.

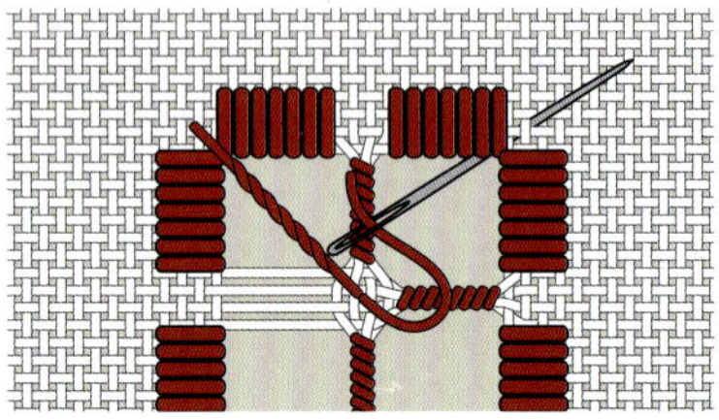

6 Going around the square in a clockwise direction, from the back, insert the needle in the next corner.

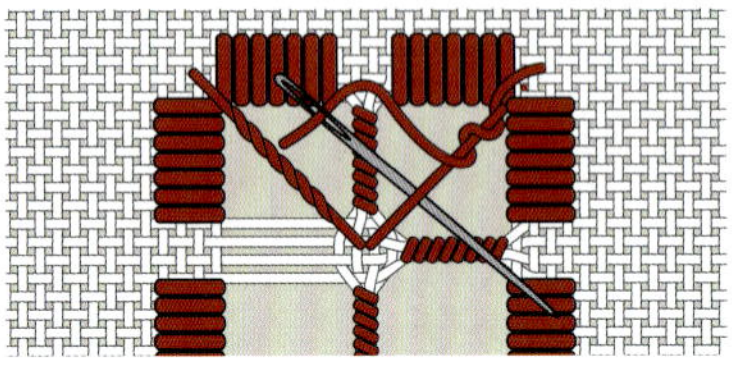

7 Pull the needle through. Slide it under the stitch from above left, three times.

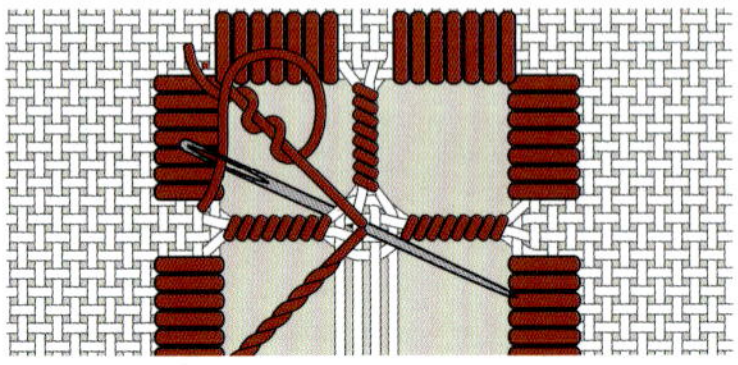

8 Turn the work 90° anticlockwise. Insert the needle below the diagonal and bring it out in the centre.

9 Pull the needle through and intertwine the stitches. Repeat the diagonals in the two remaining quadrants, turning the work as needed. To finish, insert the needle below the diagonal and bring it out on the far side of the non-wrapped bar.

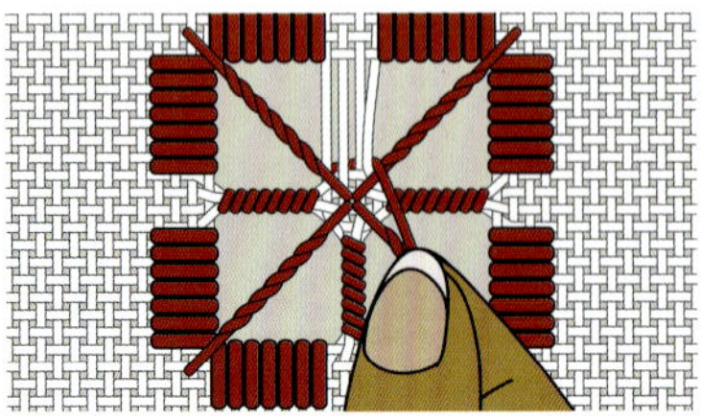

10 Pull the needle through. Pull the thread down and to the right to intertwine the stitches and to pull it snug into the centre.

11 Wrap just over half the bar.

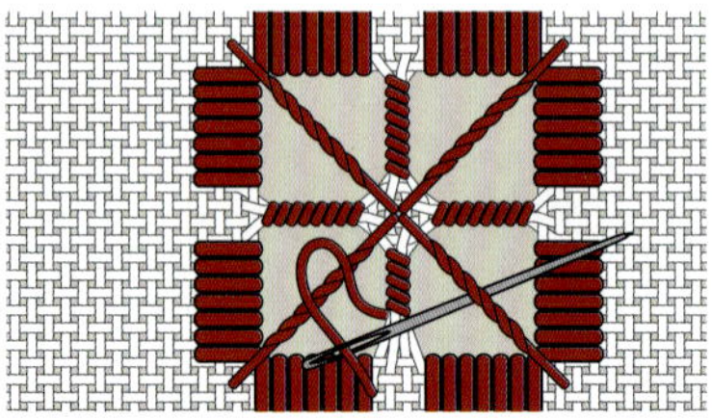

12 Pull the needle through. Turn the work 180°. From below, insert the needle under the diagonal to the right of the half-wrapped bar.

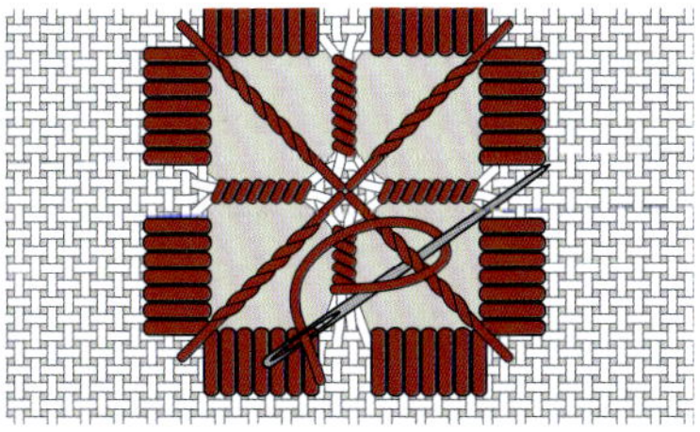

13 Positioning the needle a little less than halfway along the diagonal stitch, wrap the thread around the needle point in an anticlockwise direction.

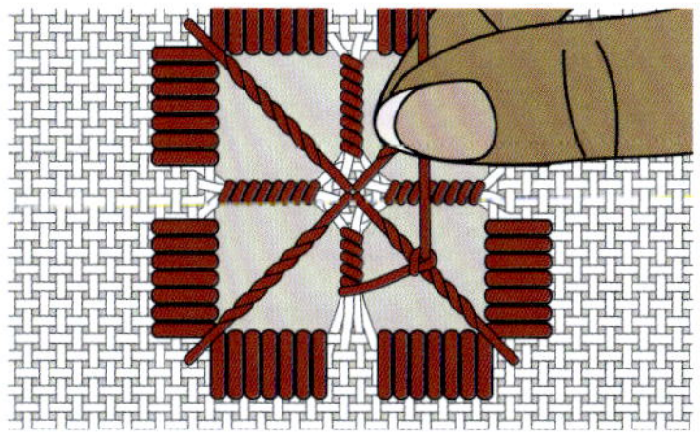

14 Pull the needle through. As the knot around the diagonal starts to tighten, pull directly upward, perpendicular to the fabric.

❶ *This helps to tighten the knot into the correct position, with good tension in the thread leading to the knot.*

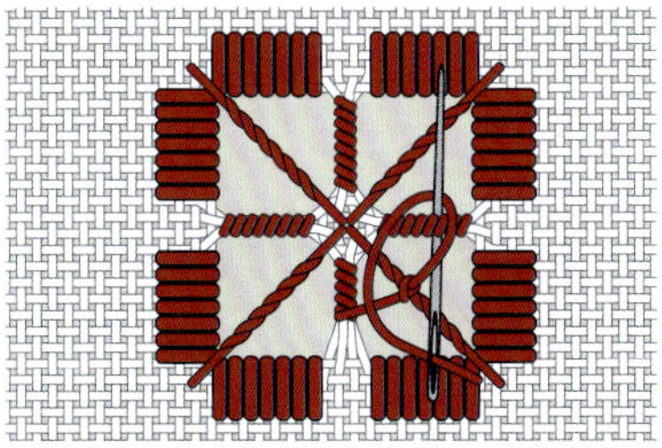

15 Moving in an anticlockwise direction, insert the needle under the next wrapped bar, a little over halfway along.

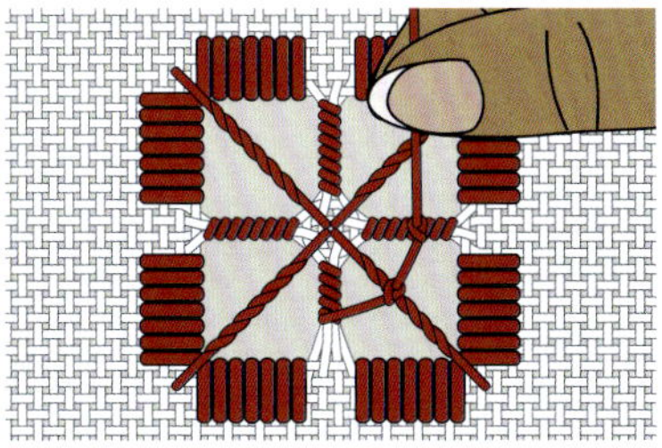

16 Pull the needle through and tighten the knot, carefully positioning it by pulling the thread through until the knot starts to tighten and then directly up.

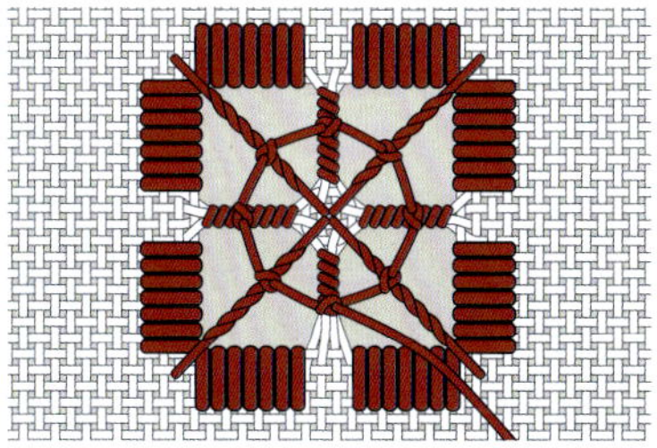

17 Continue around the spokes, turning the work as needed, working a knot on each one. The final knot is worked over the half-wrapped bar.

❶ *Adjust the position of any of the knots as required.*

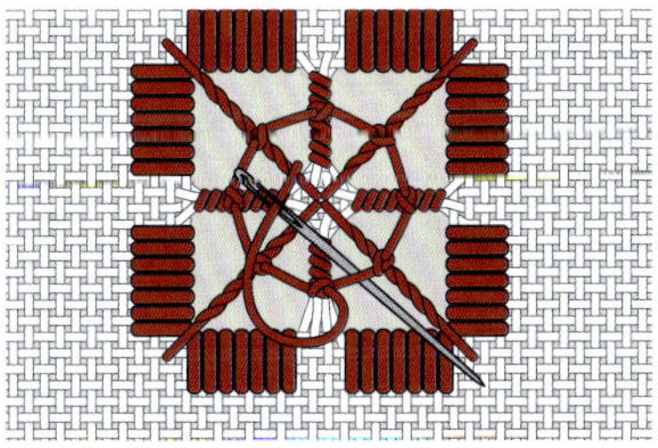

18 Slide the needle under the next section of the ring, from left to right.

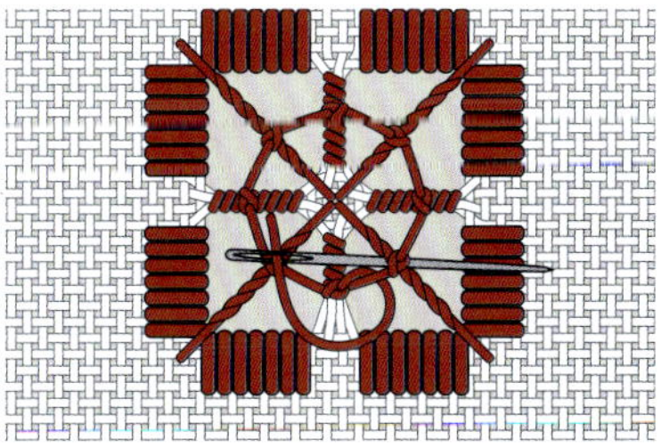

19 Slide the needle under the next knotted intersection from left to right.

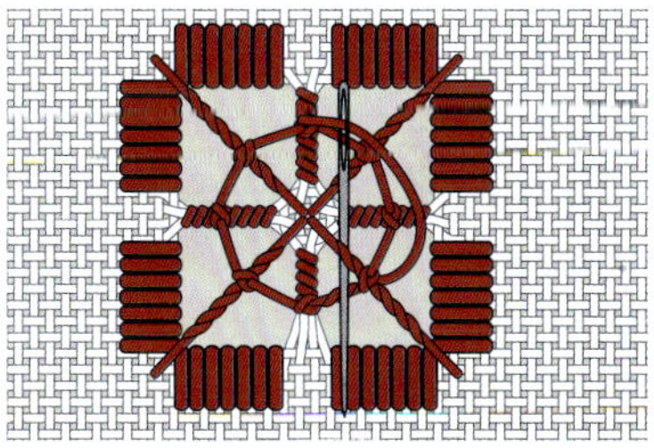

20 Pull the thread to intertwine the stitches. Slide the needle under the upper section of the twisted diagonal, from above.

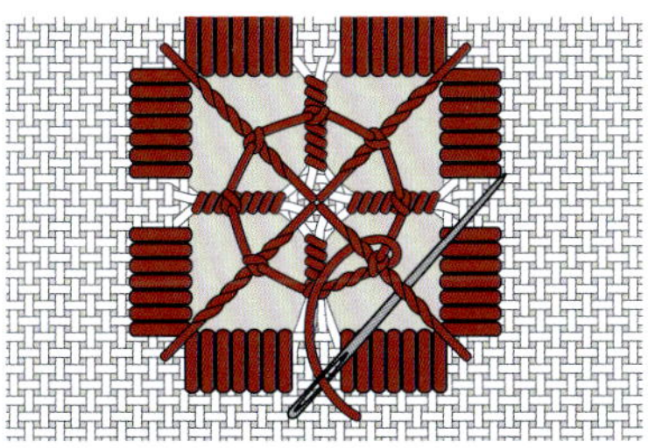

21 Slide the needle under the lower section of the twisted diagonal, from below.

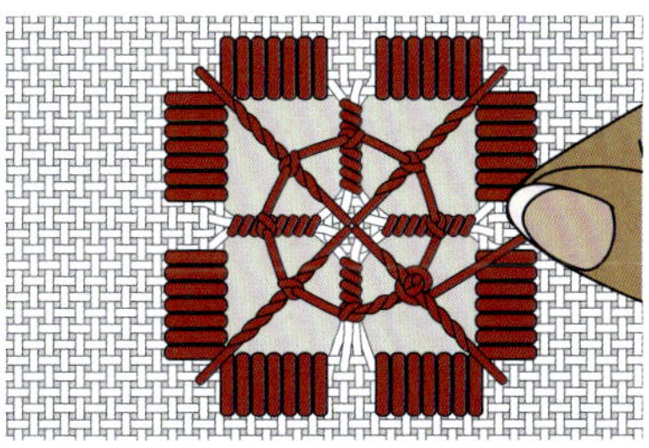

22 Pull the thread in tight around the intersection.

23 Slide the needle under the upper section of the twisted diagonal, from above.

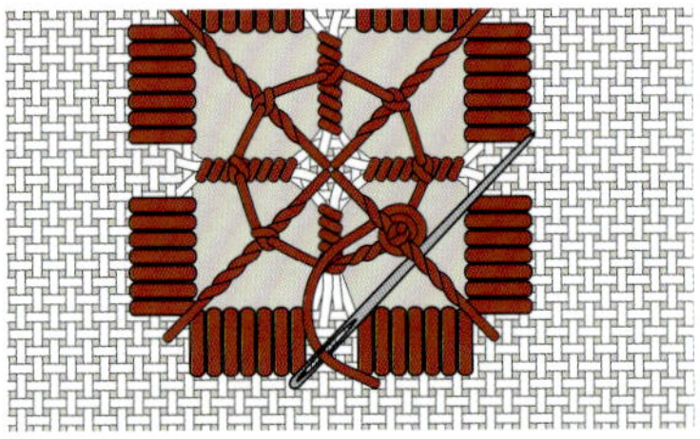

24 Pull the thread in snug. Slide the needle under the lower section of the twisted diagonal, from below.

❶ *Do not allow the thread to overlap the previous circuit.*

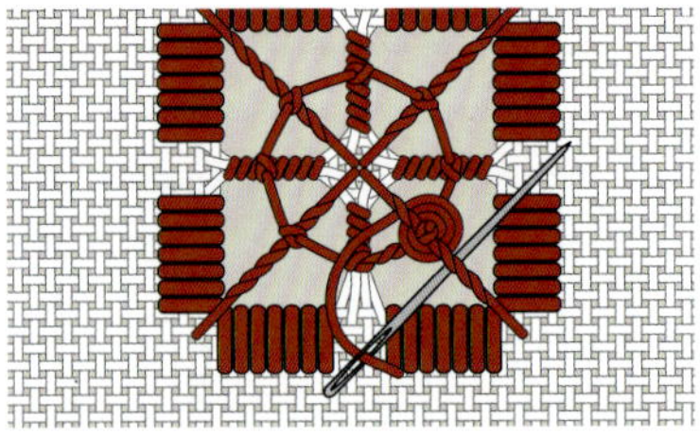

25 Circle the intersection once or twice more taking care that none of the circling stitches overlap.

❶ *When working with a larger square you may need additional circuits. Use a consistent quantity throughout.*

26 From the left, slide the needle under the upper part of the ring stitch in the same section as the spider web.

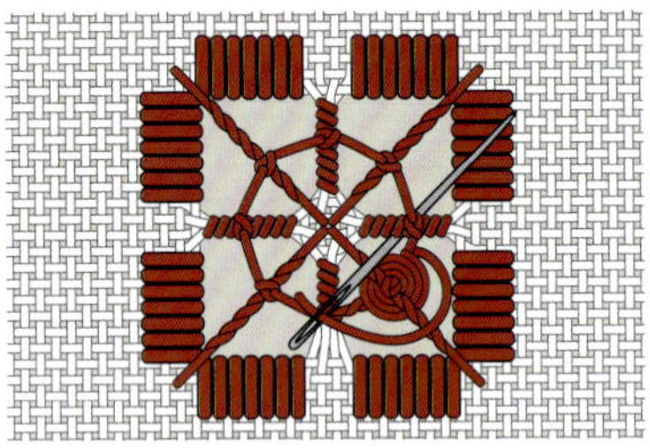

27 From below left, slide the needle under the intersection of the knotted ring and next wrapped bar.

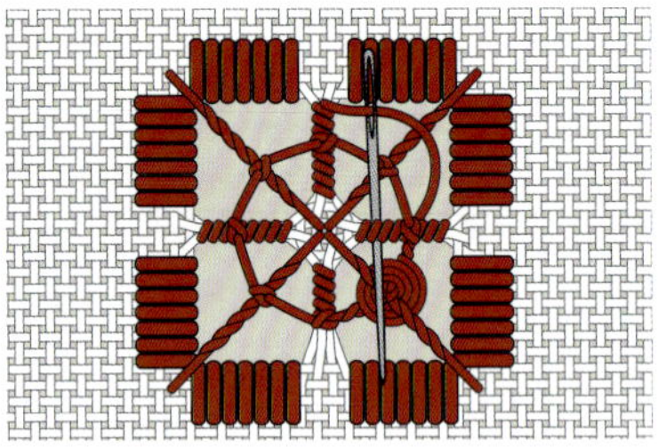

28 Pull to intertwine the stitches. From above, slide the needle under the inner section of the wrapped bar.

29 Slide the needle under the outer section of the wrapped bar, from below.

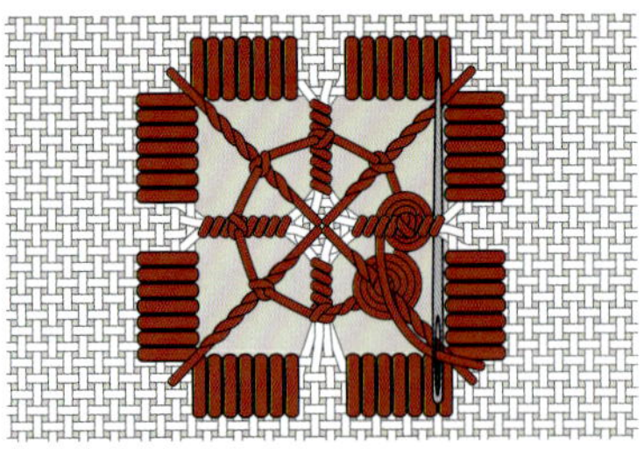

30 Tighten the first circuit of the intersection, to bring it in snug, then make the same quantity of circuits as before.

31 From below left, slide the needle under the upper part of the ring stitch in the same section as the spider web.

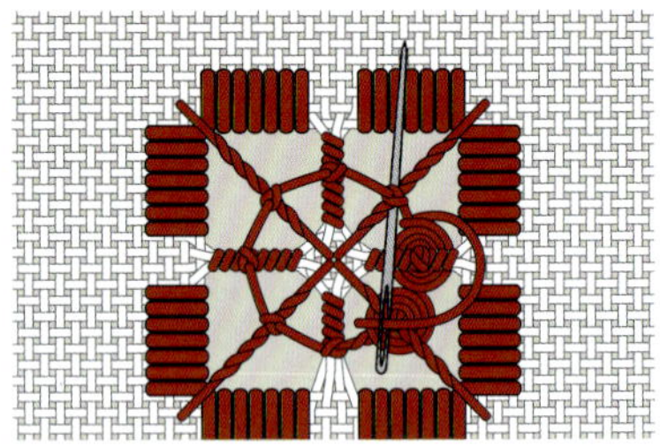

32 From below, slide the needle under the intersection of the knotted ring and next diagonal.

33 Continue around the ring, working spider webs. Turn the work as needed for ease of needle insertion. When you have circled the last web the required quantity of times, slide the needle under the half-wrapped bar, from below.

34 Make more wrap stitches to fill the space and reach the motif's edge. Take the thread to the back and finish it under the back of the satin stitch.

❶ *These stitches wrap the other way compared to the ones at the inner end of the bar.*

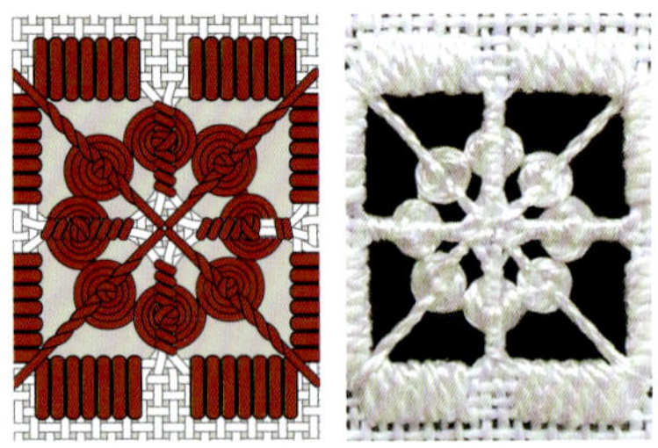

35 The completed motif.

queen anne's lace

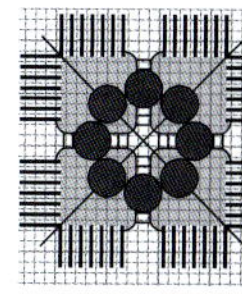

Consistency is key in this motif. You will need to use good tension for wrapping the bars, twisting the threads, working and spacing the ring knots, and working the spider webs. You will need consistent quantities of twists for the diagonals and circling stitches for the webs.

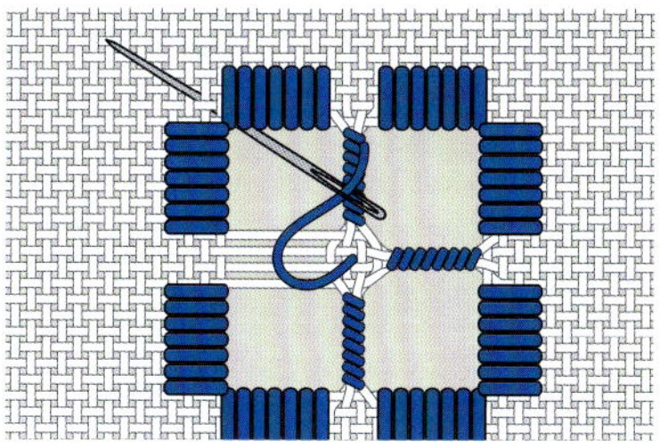

1 In a large square, wrap the bars as shown. Bring the needle out in the woven square's centre. From the back, insert the needle in the upper left corner, two threads from the edge.

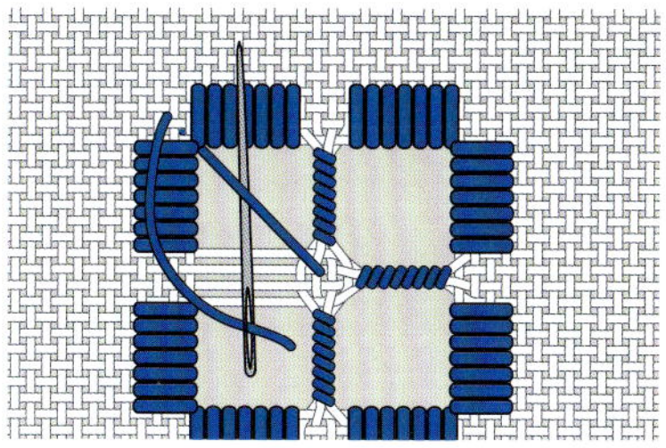

2 Pull the needle through, then slide it under the stitch from below.

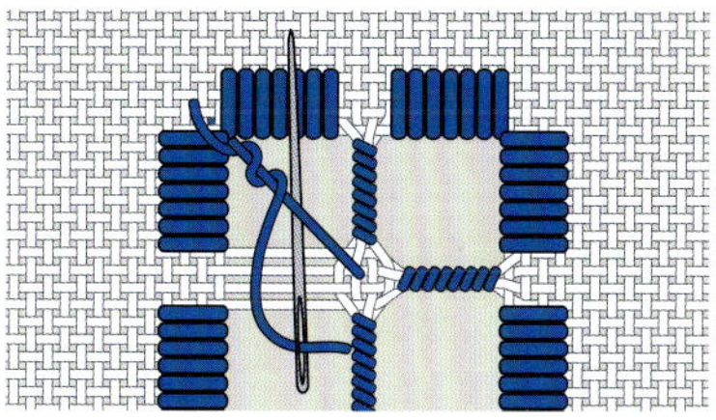

3 Slide the needle under, twice more.
❶ *If working in a larger square than the one shown (this one has six removed in each quadrant), you may need to slide it under an additional time.*

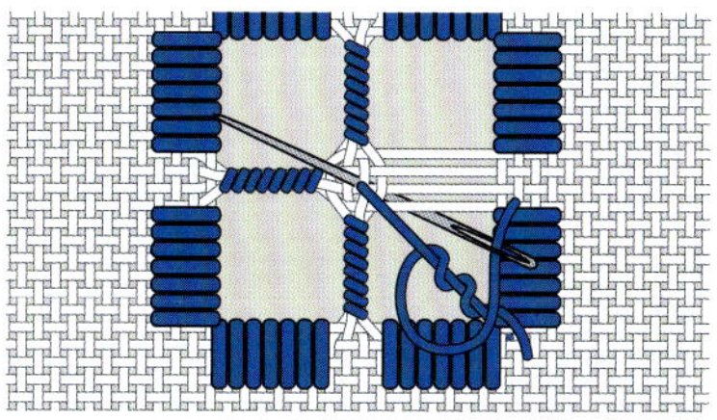

4 Turn the work 180°. Insert the needle above the diagonal and bring it out in the centre.

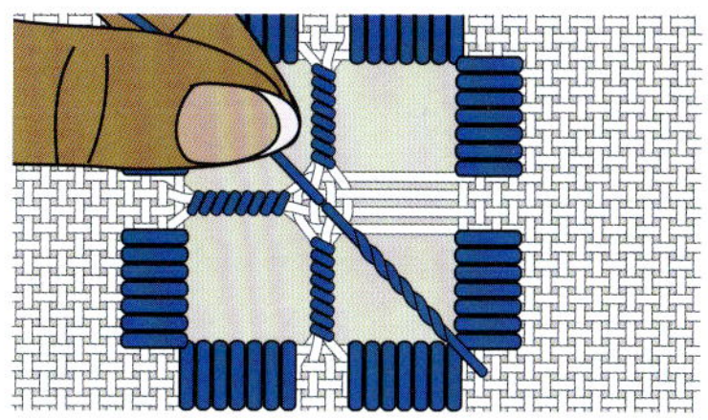

5 Pull the needle through. Pull the thread to intertwine the stitches.

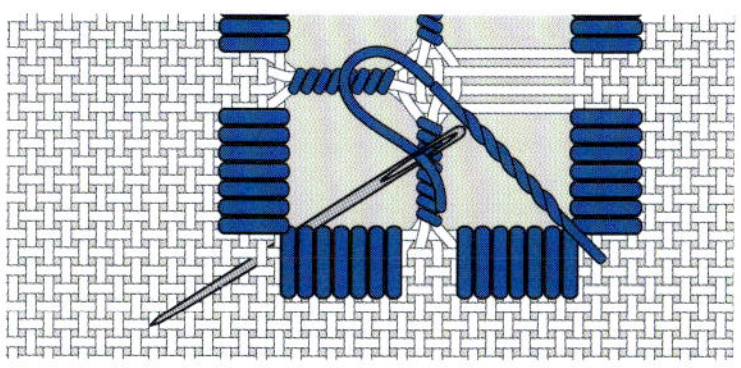

6 Moving in an anticlockwise direction, from the back, insert the needle in the next corner.

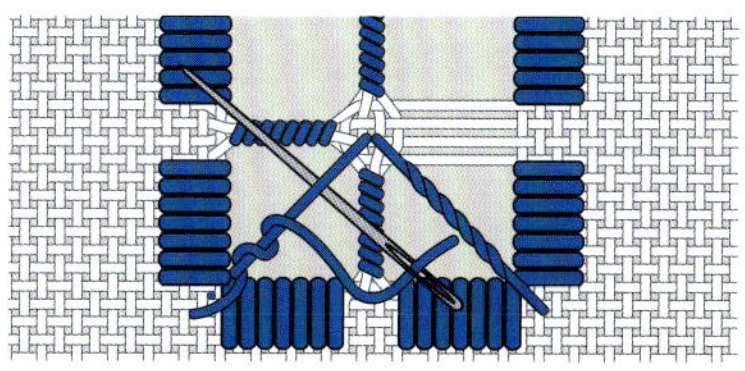

7 Pull the needle through. Slide it under the stitch from below right, three times.

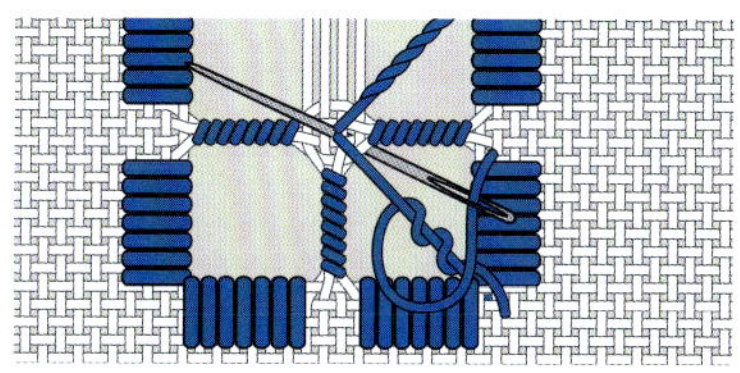

8 Turn the work 90° anticlockwise. Insert the needle below the diagonal and bring it out in the centre.

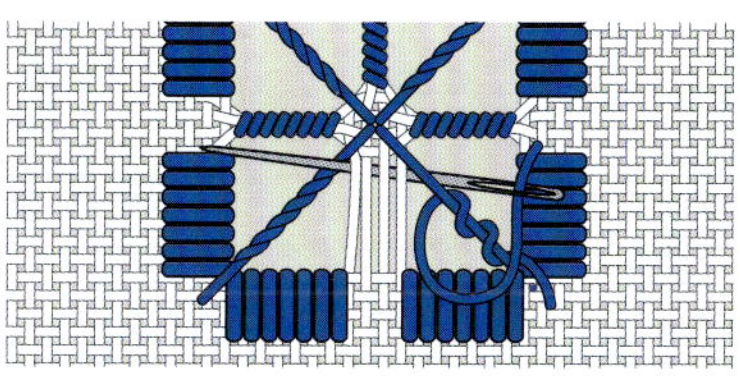

9 Pull the needle through and intertwine the stitches. Repeat the diagonals in the two remaining quadrants, turning the work as needed. To finish, insert the needle below the diagonal and bring it out on the far side of the non-wrapped bar.

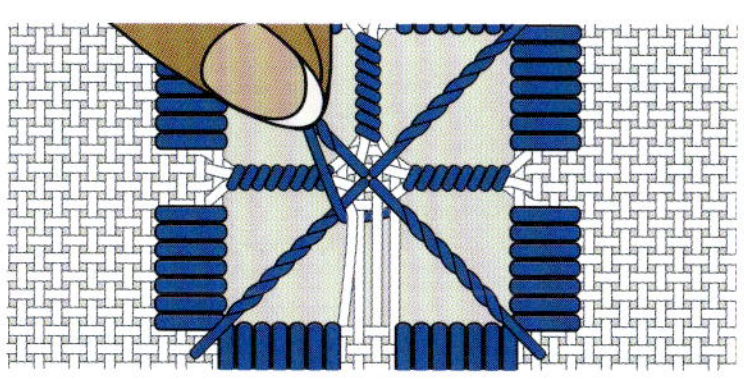

10 Pull the needle through. Pull the thread up and to the left to intertwine the stitches and to pull it snug into the centre.

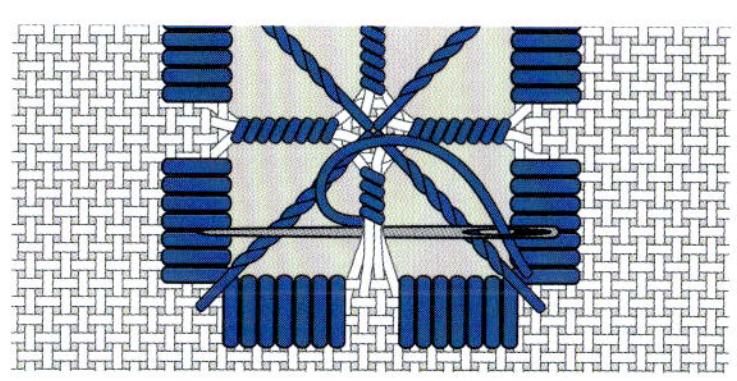

11 Wrap just over half the bar.

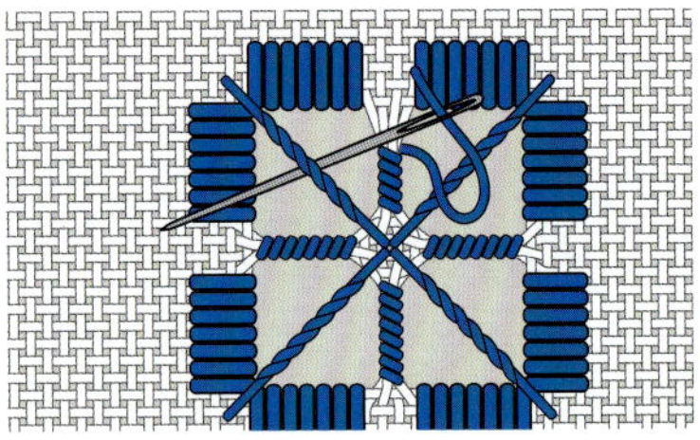

12 Pull the needle through. Turn the work 180°. From above, insert the needle under the diagonal to the left of the half-wrapped bar.

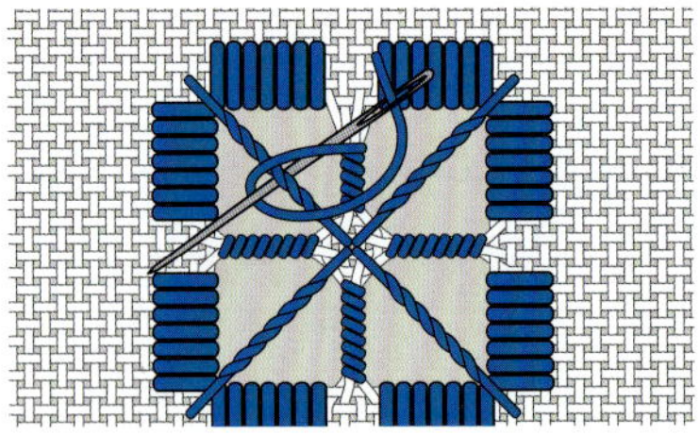

13 Positioning the needle a little less than halfway along the diagonal stitch, wrap the thread around the needle point in an anticlockwise direction.

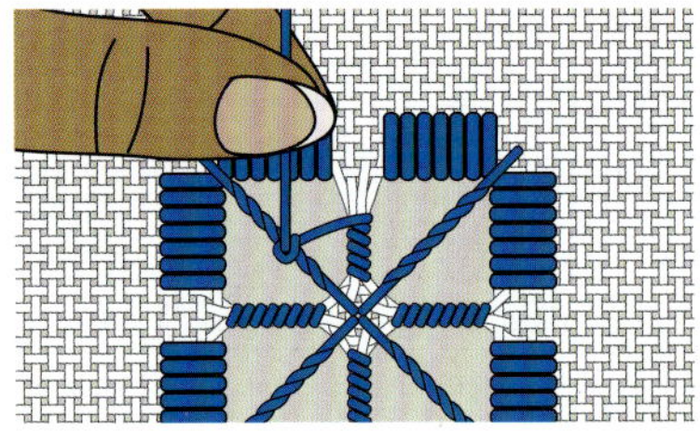

14 Pull the needle through. As the knot around the diagonal starts to tighten, pull directly upward, perpendicular to the fabric.

❶ *This helps to tighten the knot into the correct position, with good tension in the thread leading to the knot.*

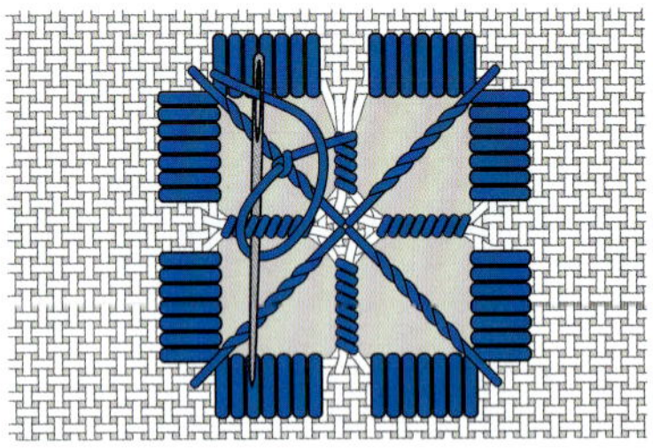

15 Moving in an anticlockwise direction, insert the needle under the next wrapped bar, a little over halfway along.

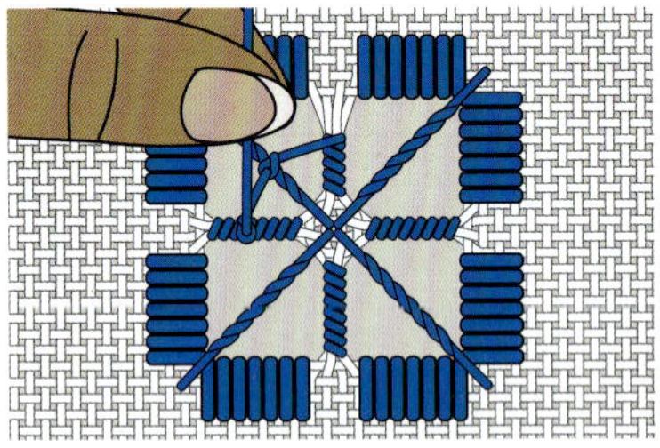

16 Pull the needle through and tighten the knot, carefully positioning it by pulling the thread through until the knot starts to tighten and then directly up.

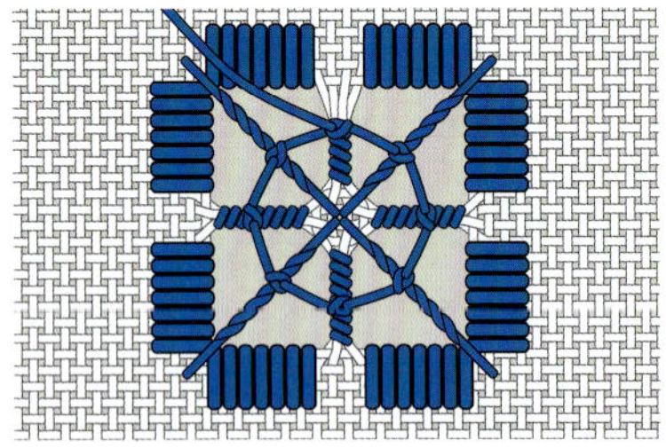

17 Continue around the spokes, turning the work as needed, working a knot on each one. The final knot is worked over the half-wrapped bar.

❶ *Adjust the position of any of the knots as required.*

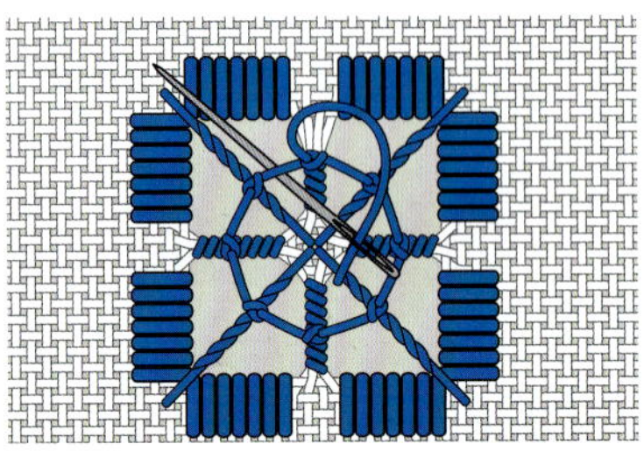

18 Slide the needle under the next section of the ring, from right to left.

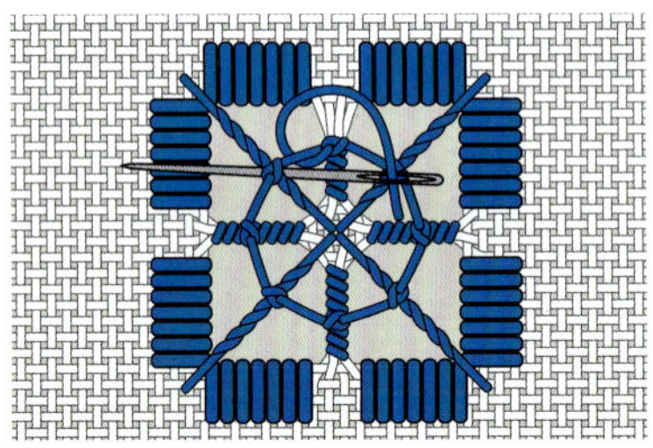

19 Slide the needle under the next knotted intersection from right to left.

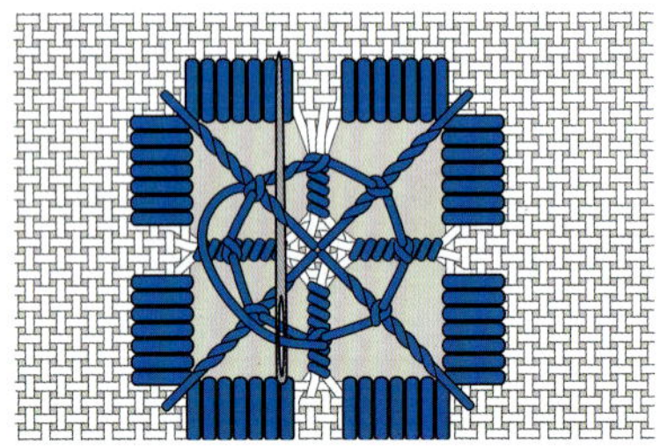

20 Pull the thread to intertwine the stitches. Slide the needle under the lower section of the twisted diagonal, from below.

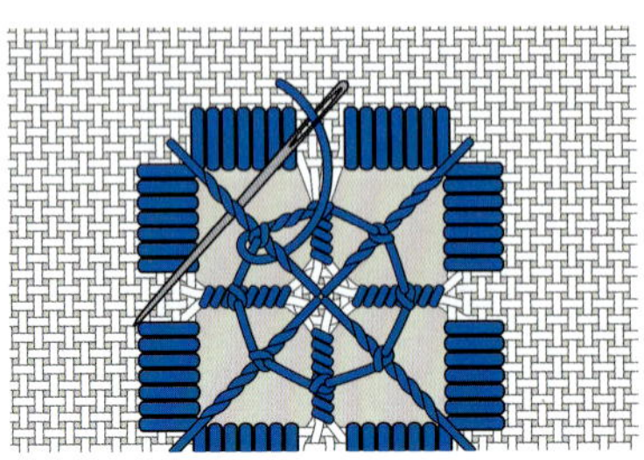

21 Slide the needle under the upper section of the twisted diagonal, from above.

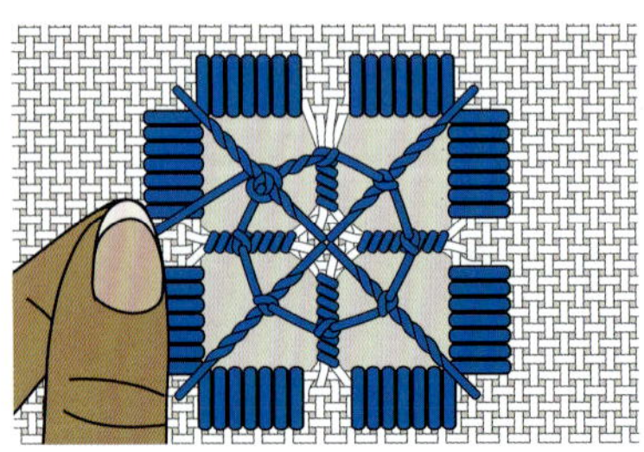

22 Pull the thread in tight around the intersection.

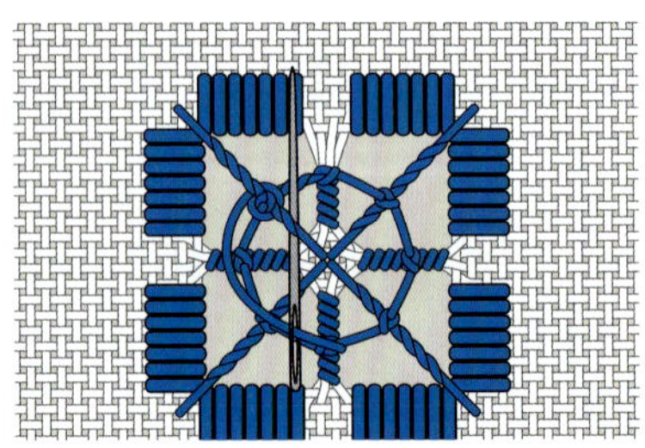

23 Slide the needle under the lower section of the twisted diagonal, from below.

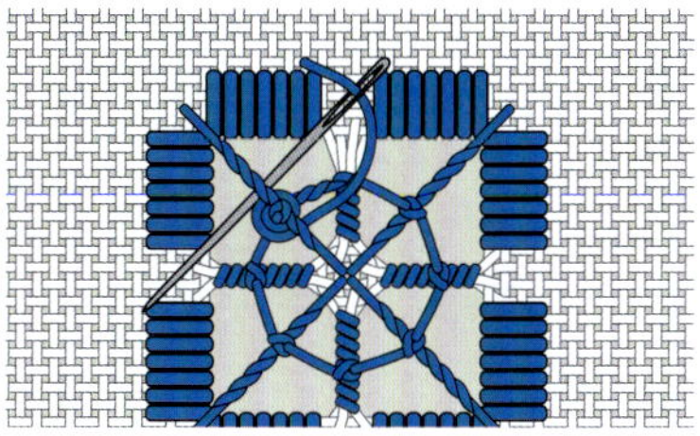

24 Pull the thread in snug. Slide the needle under the upper section of the twisted diagonal, from above.

! *Do not allow the thread to overlap the previous circuit.*

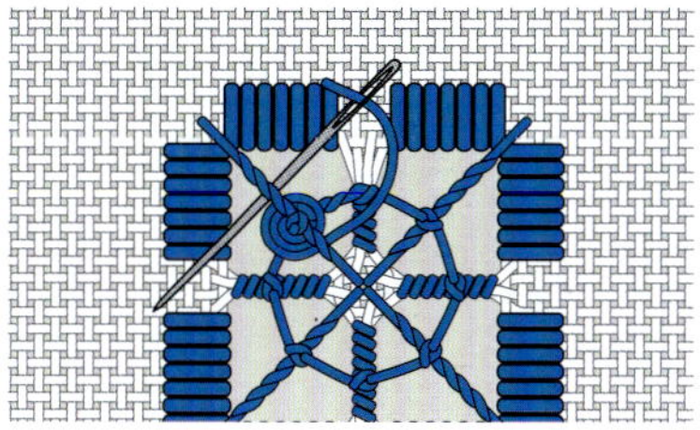

25 Circle the intersection once or twice more taking care that none of the circling stitches overlap.

! *When working with a larger square you may need additional circuits. Use a consistent quantity throughout.*

26 From the right, slide the needle under the lower part of the ring stitch in the same section as the spider web.

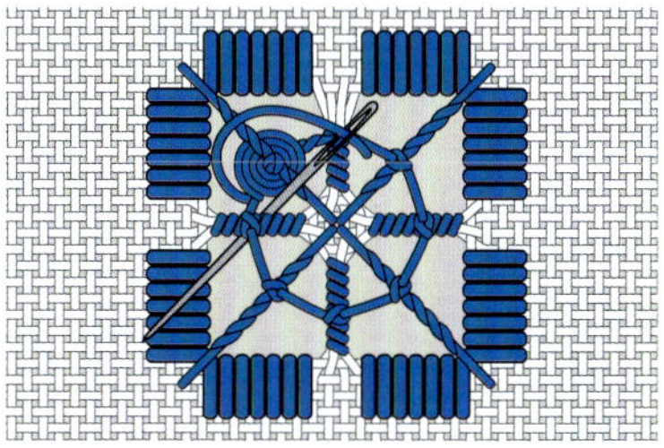

27 From above right, slide the needle under the intersection of the knotted ring and next wrapped bar.

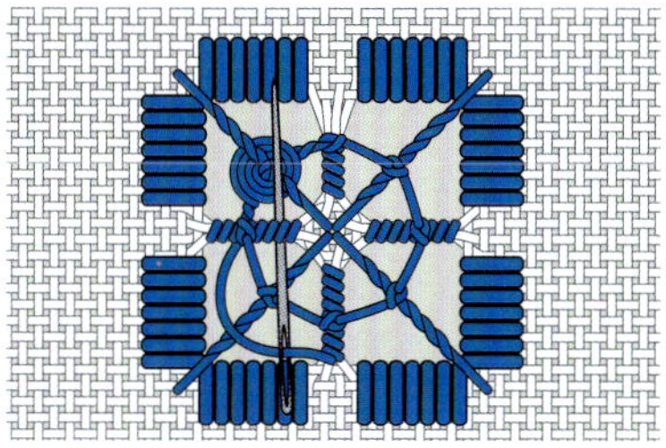

28 Pull to intertwine the stitches. From below, slide the needle under the inner section of the wrapped bar.

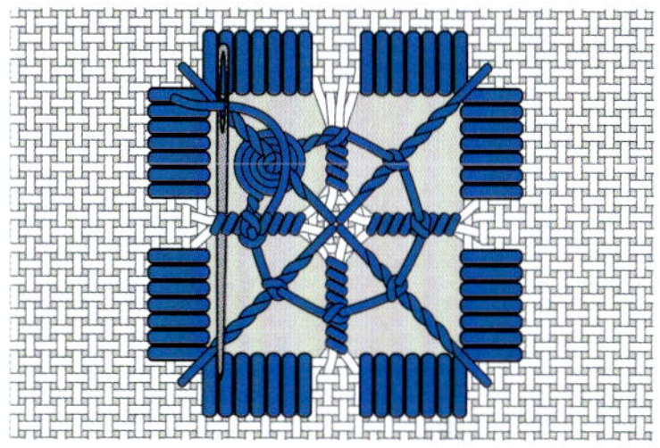

29 Slide the needle under the outer section of the wrapped bar, from above.

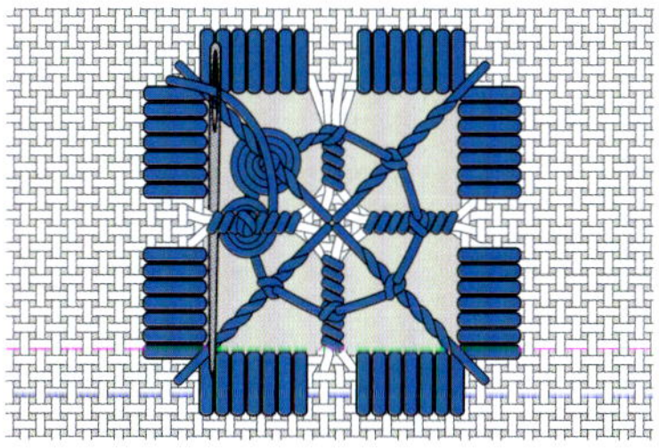

30 Tighten the first circuit of the intersection, to bring it in snug, then make the same quantity of circuits as before.

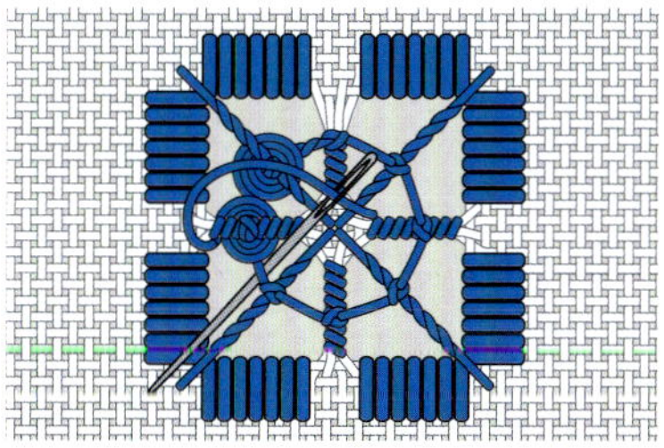

31 From above right, slide the needle under the lower part of the ring stitch in the same section as the spider web.

32 From above, slide the needle under the intersection of the knotted ring and next diagonal.

33 Continue around the ring, working spider webs. Turn the work as needed for ease of needle insertion. When you have circled the last web the required quantity of times, slide the needle under the half-wrapped bar, from above.

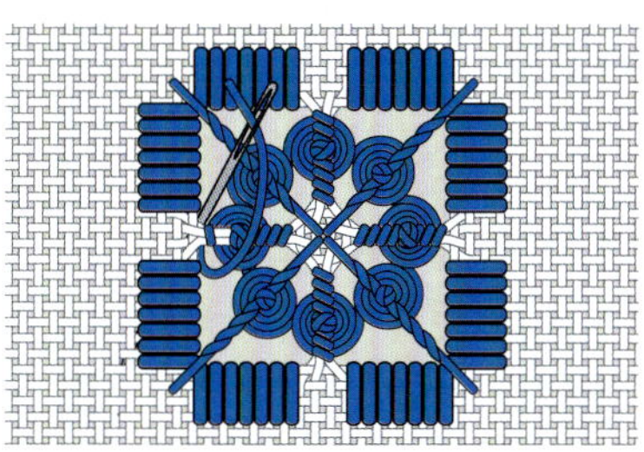

34 Make more wrap stitches to fill the space and reach the motif's edge. Take the thread to the back and finish it under the back of the satin stitch.

! *These stitches wrap the other way compared to the ones at the inner end of the bar.*

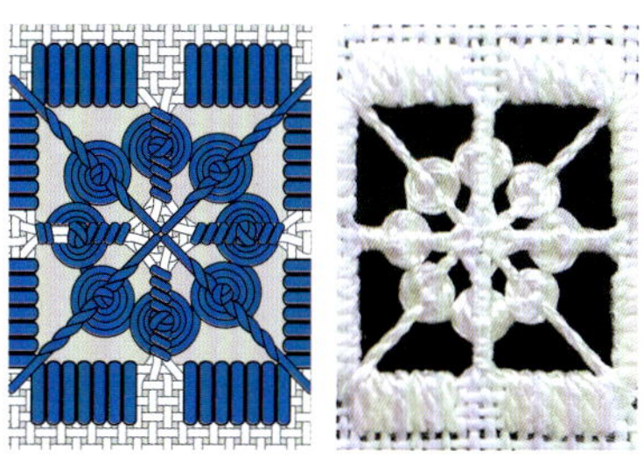

35 The completed motif.

L

bullion flower

CONTEMPORARY

This motif is worked on the intersection of bars (woven or wrapped) to create a three dimensional flower. Bullion knots can be worked with either clockwise or anticlockwise wraps. I find that anticlockwise gives a better result for this motif as it creates thicker, more pronounced bullions.

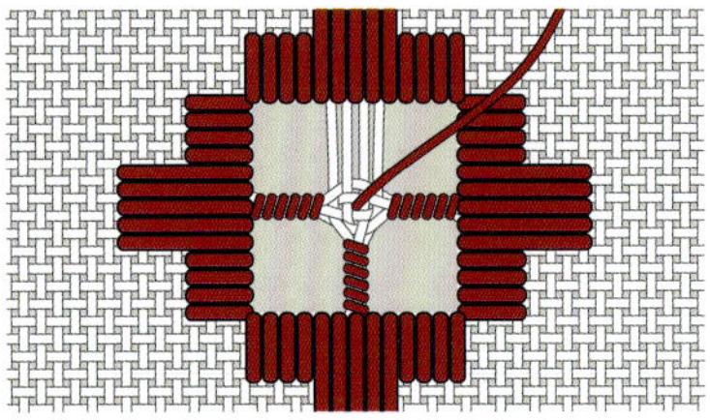

1 When three of the four bars leading to the intersection have been stitched, you can work the flower. Bring the thread out in the centre of the woven square.

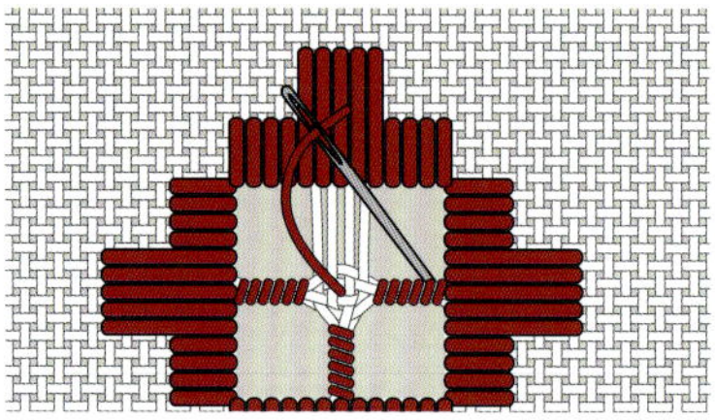

2 Take the needle to the back in one of the open quadrants.

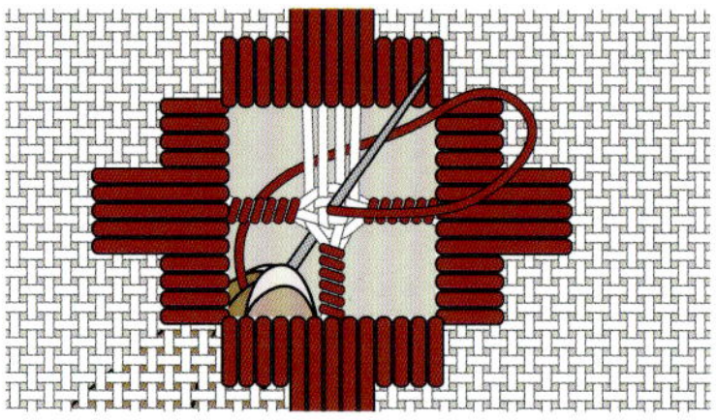

3 From the back, insert the needle into the centre of the woven square.

❶ *Do not pull it through; leave it sitting in the fabric.*

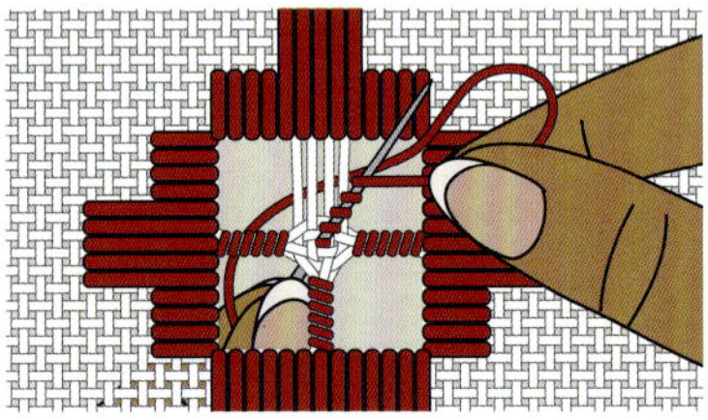

4 With the needle's eye in one hand, position the needle so that most of it is above the fabric. With the large loop of thread in the other hand, wrap the loop thread around the needle in an anticlockwise manner.

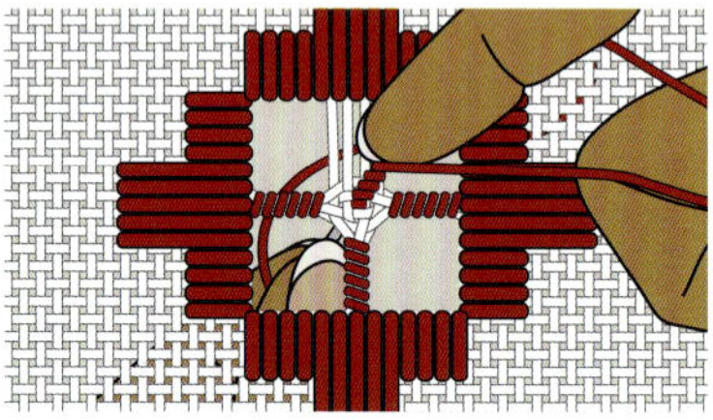

5 Push the wraps down to the surface of the fabric.

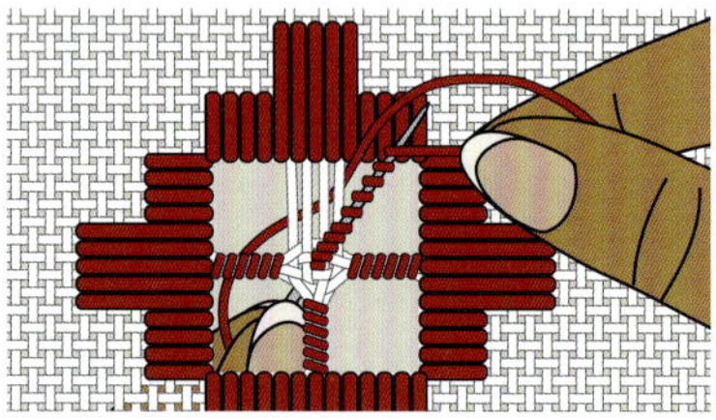

6 Add more wraps.

❶ *The quantity of wraps you use will affect the size of the bullion petal. The more wraps, the larger the bullion petal. I used ten for my sample.*

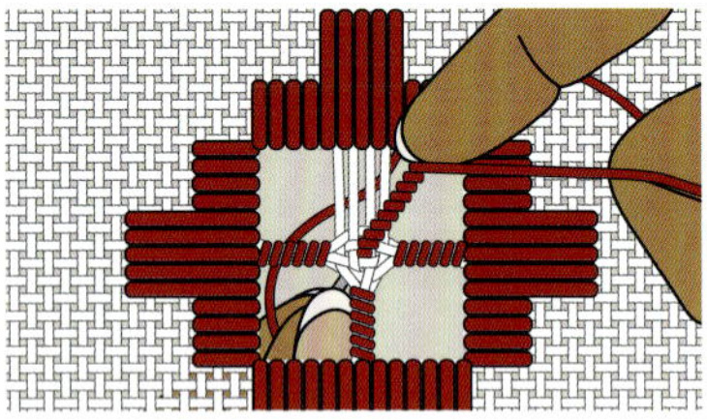

7 Push the wraps down again.

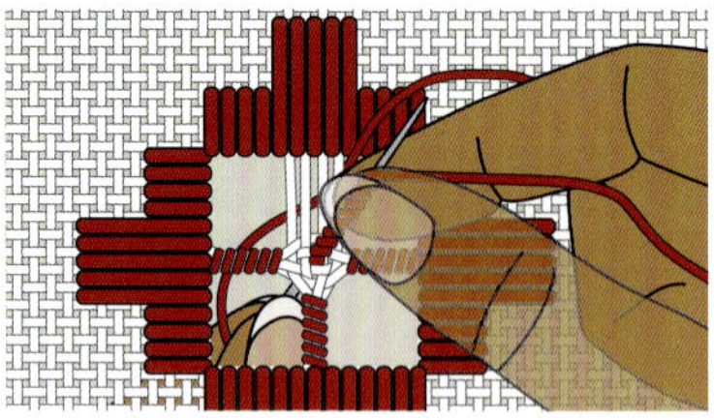

8 Tensioning the working thread with fingers other than your forefinger and thumb, gently hold the wraps on the needle with your forefinger and thumb.

❶ *Don't hold the wraps tight. You're only trying to stop them unravelling. If you hold the needle tight, it will be harder to pull it through the wraps.*

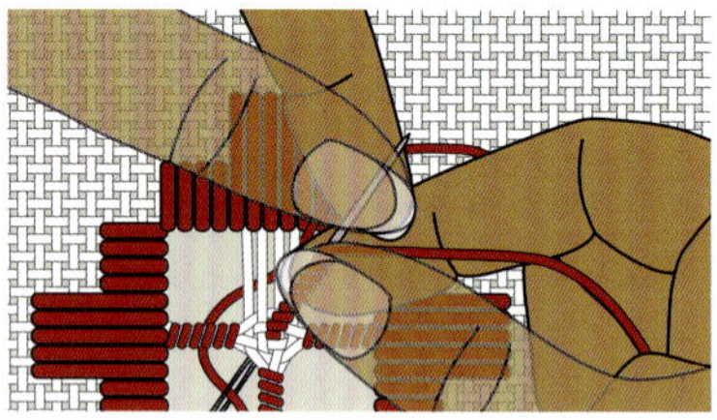

9 Bring your other hand from up below and gently ease the needle through the wraps.

❶ *It is fine to let go of the needle underneath the fabric. It isn't going anywhere!*

❗ *Because a tapestry needle has a relatively large eye, it may be difficult to pull the needle through. It may help to turn your fingers covering the wraps in a clockwise direction to slightly loosen the wraps.*

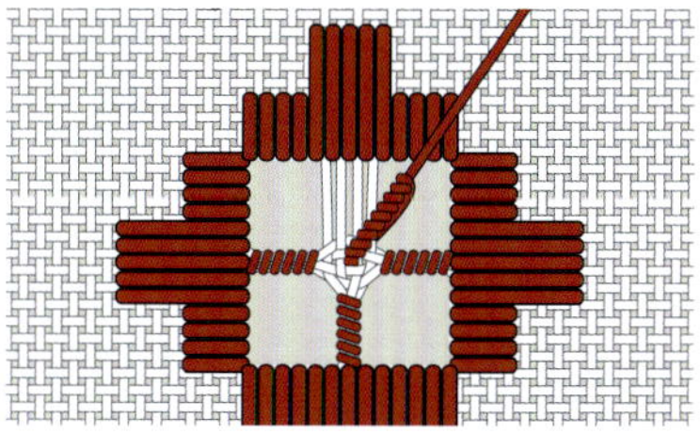

10 Continue pulling the working thread, until the loop is the length of the wraps.

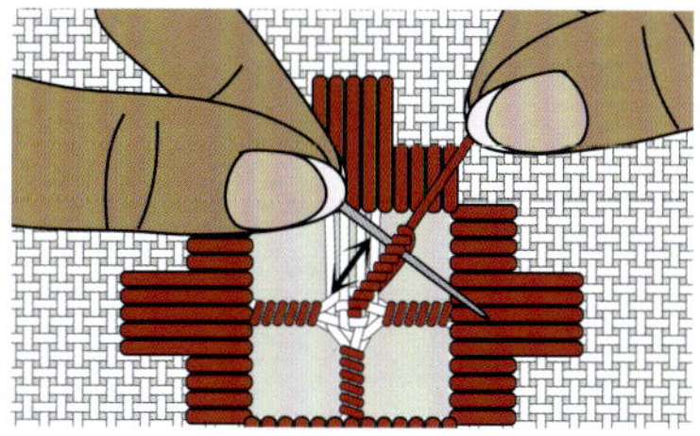

❗ *If the wraps don't sit nicely, insert the needle into the loop and gently stroke back and forth inside it, while pulling the working end of the thread.*

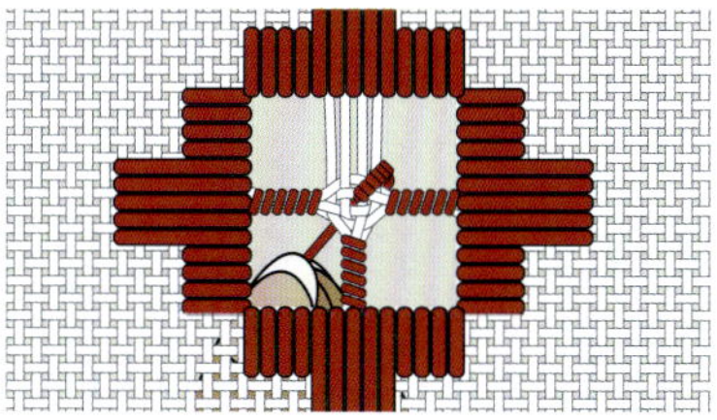

11 Take the needle to the back through the same quadrant. Pull the needle through and down. You will have a large loop for the last wrap.

❗ *This isn't a mistake! It will happen so don't feel bad when it does!*

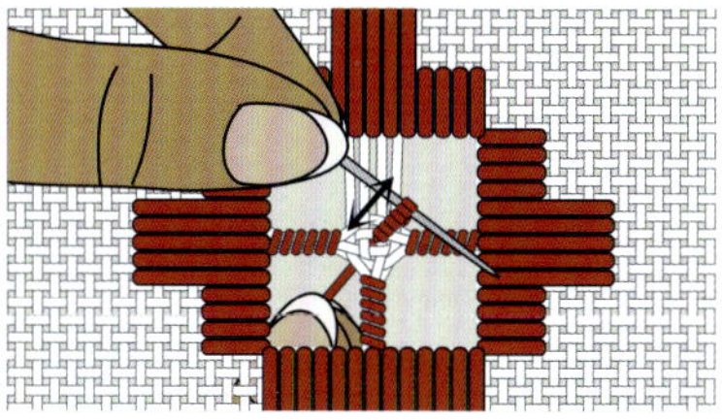

12 Insert the needle in the loop and pull it up and down while pulling on the working thread.

❗ *This will ease the extra length through so that the loop looks neat.*

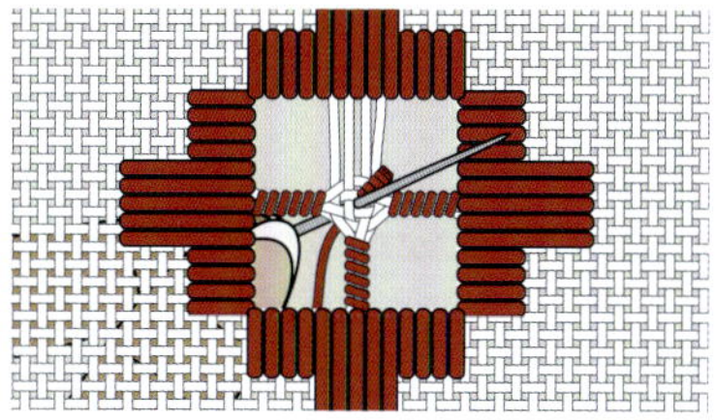

13 When the loop and all its wraps sit nicely, bring the needle to the front through the centre of the woven square, ready to begin the next petal.

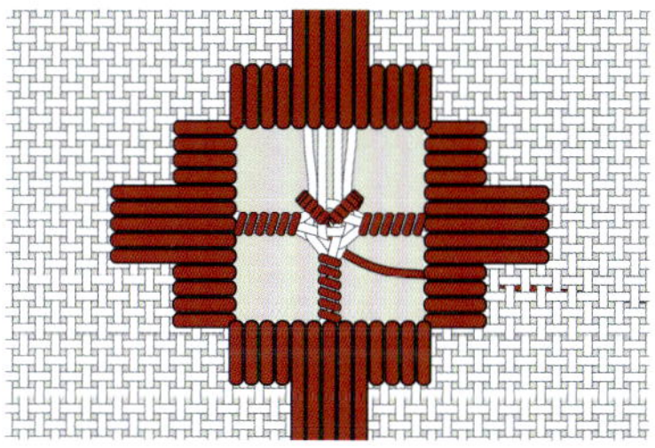

14 Turn the work and stitch another petal, with the same quantity of wraps, on the opposite side of the unwrapped bar.

❗ *Finishing the sequence of petals with one on the same side as the not-yet-wrapped bar would mean that the thread on the back would sit poorly – also causing the petal to not look quite right – when the motif is finished. Finishing with one of the petals on the far side from the not-yet-wrapped bar means it will sit much better.*

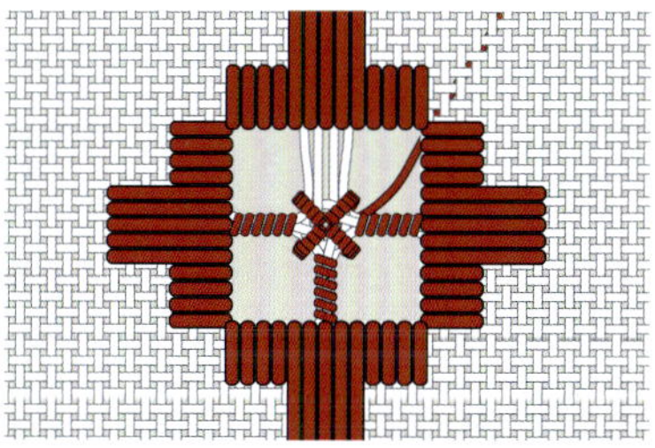

15 Turn the work as necessary and work a petal in each of the remaining quadrants.

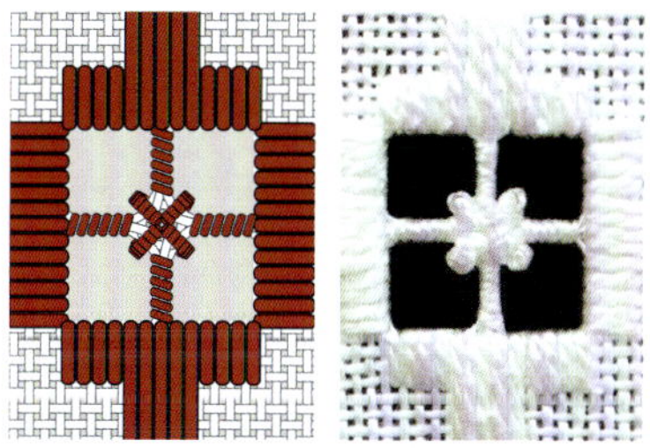

16 To complete the motif, wrap the final bar and finish the thread in the back of the satin stitch.

bullion flower

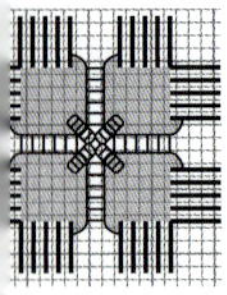

This motif is worked on the intersection of bars (woven or wrapped) to create a three dimensional flower. Bullion knots can be worked with either clockwise or anticlockwise wraps. I find that anticlockwise gives a better result for this motif as it creates thicker, more pronounced bullions.

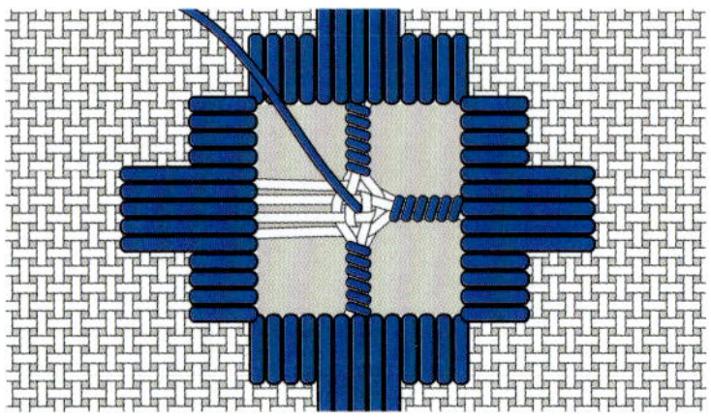

1 When three of the four bars leading to the intersection have been stitched, you can work the flower. Bring the thread out in the centre of the woven square.

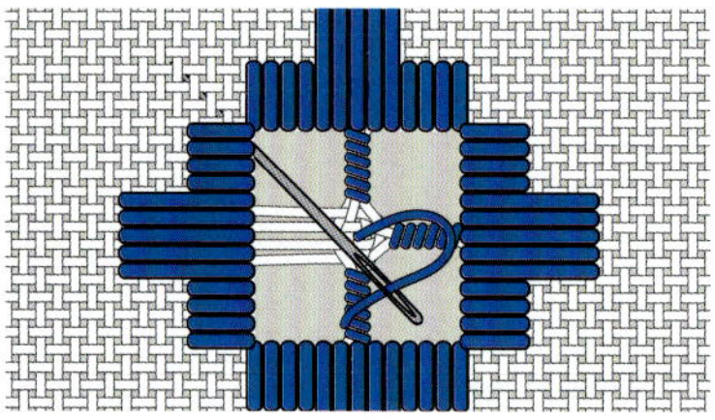

2 Take the needle to the back in one of the open quadrants.

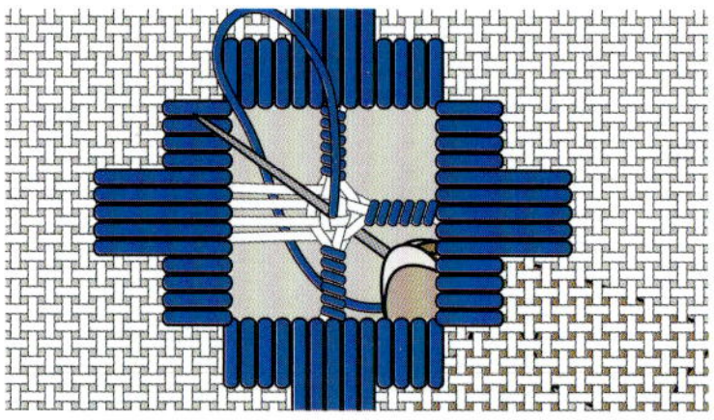

3 From the back, insert the needle into the centre of the woven square.

! *Do not pull it through; leave it sitting in the fabric.*

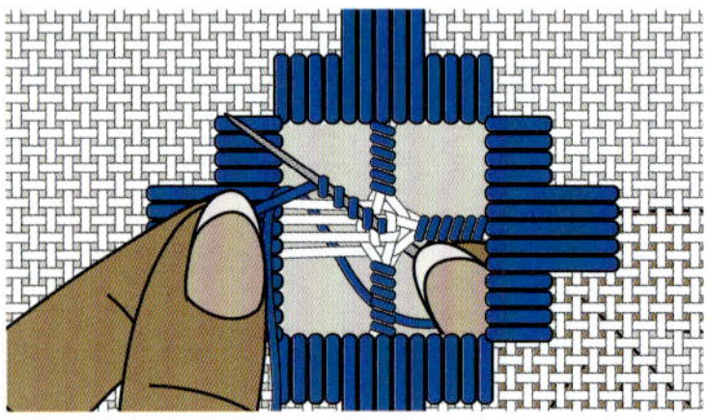

4 With the needle's eye in one hand, position the needle so that most of it is above the fabric. With the large loop of thread in the other hand, wrap the loop of thread around the needle in an anticlockwise manner.

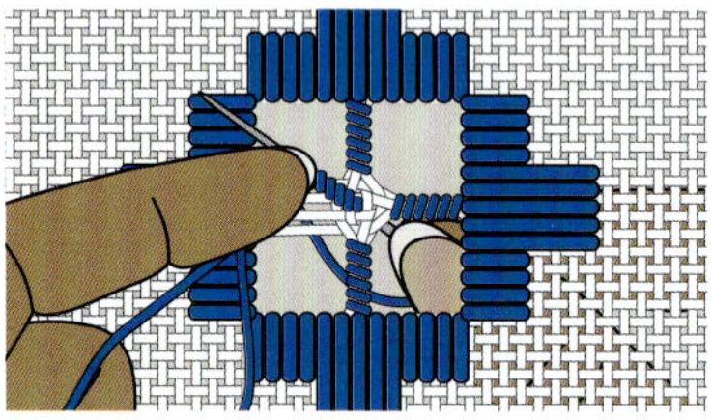

5 Push the wraps down to the surface of the fabric.

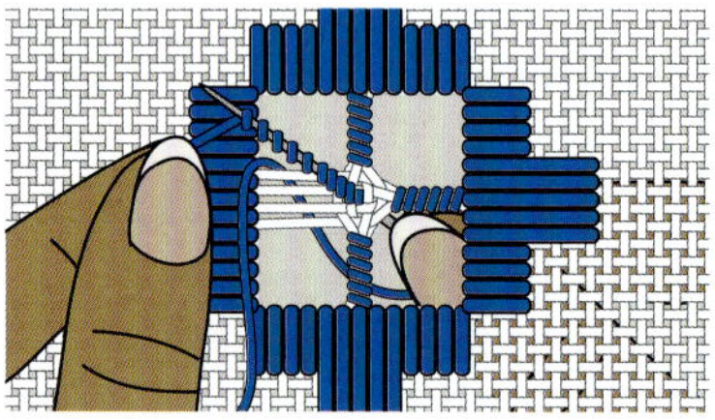

6 Add more wraps.

! *The quantity of wraps you use will affect the size of the bullion petal. The more wraps, the larger the bullion petal. I used ten for my sample.*

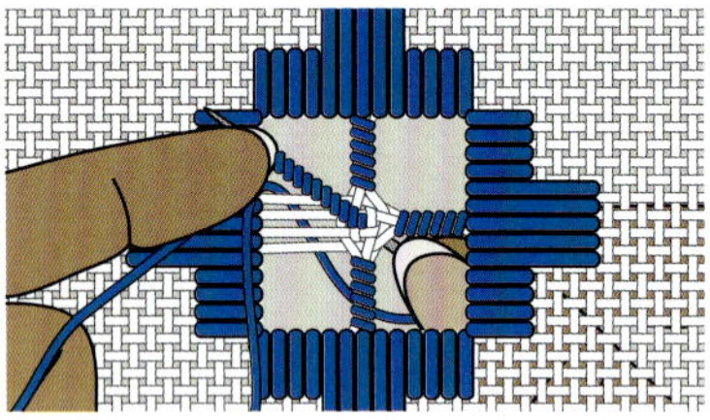

7 Push the wraps down again.

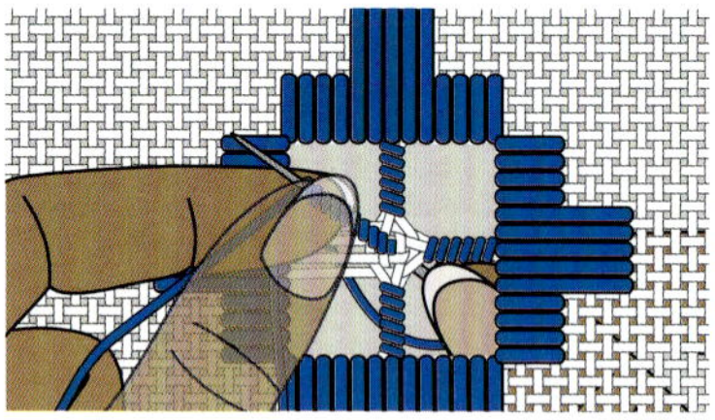

8 Tensioning the working thread with fingers other than your forefinger and thumb, gently hold the wraps on the needle with your forefinger and thumb.

! *Don't hold the wraps tight. You're only trying to stop them unravelling. If you hold the needle tight, it will be harder to pull it through the wraps.*

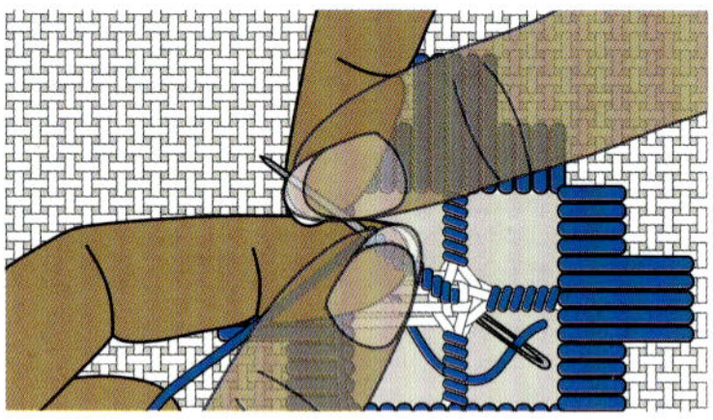

9 Bring your other hand from up below and gently ease the needle through the wraps.

! *It is fine to let go of the needle underneath the fabric. It isn't going anywhere!*

❗ *Because a tapestry needle has a relatively large eye, it may be difficult to pull the needle through. It may help to turn your fingers covering the wraps in a clockwise direction to slightly loosen the wraps.*

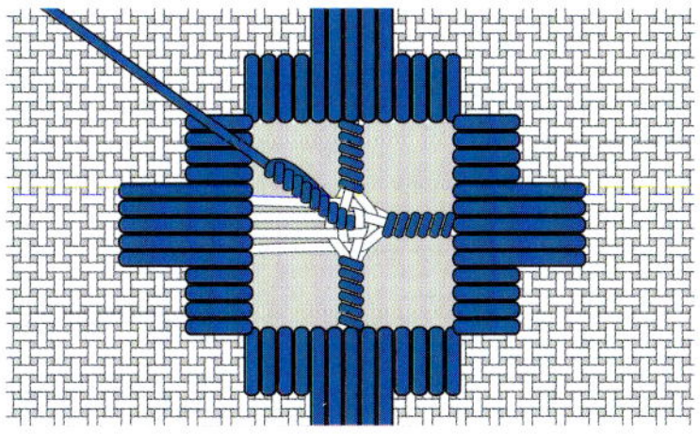

10 Continue pulling the working thread, until the loop is the length of the wraps.

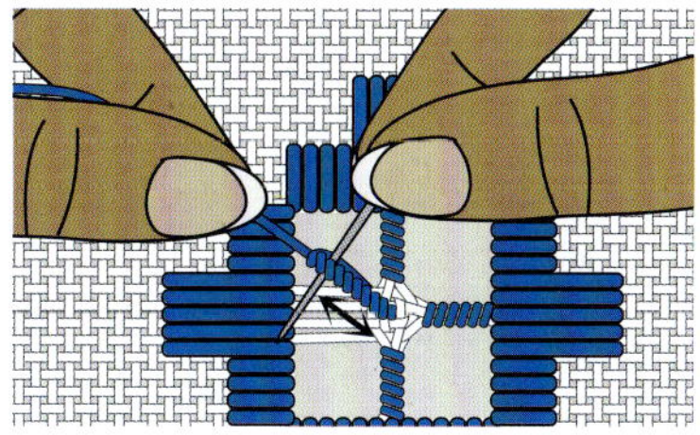

❗ *If the wraps don't sit nicely, insert the needle into the loop and gently stroke back and forth inside it, while pulling the working end of the thread.*

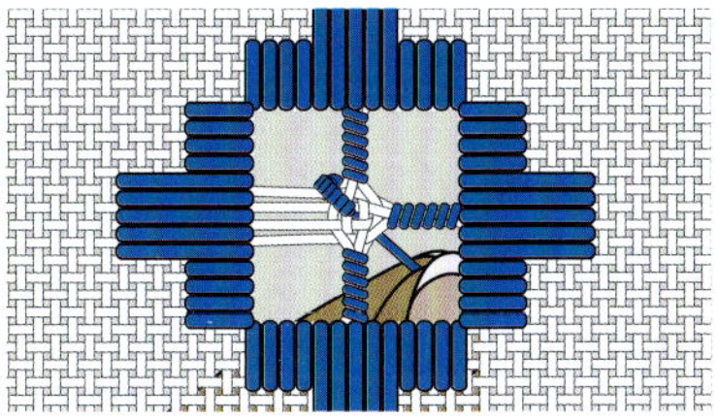

11 Take the needle to the back through the same quadrant. Pull the needle through and down. You will have a large loop for the last wrap.

❗ *This isn't a mistake! It will happen so don't feel bad when it does!*

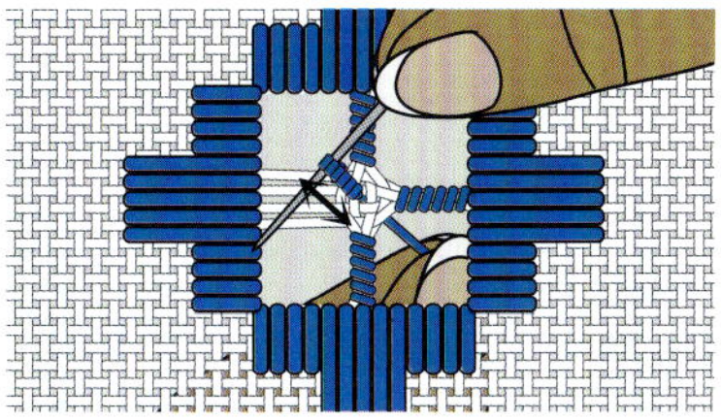

12 Insert the needle in the loop and pull it up and down while pulling on the working thread.

❗ *This will ease the extra length through so that the loop looks neat.*

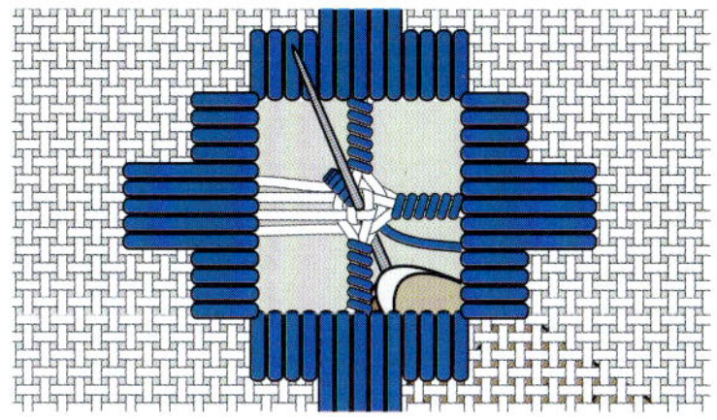

13 When the loop and all its wraps sit nicely, bring the needle to the front through the centre of the woven square, ready to begin the next petal.

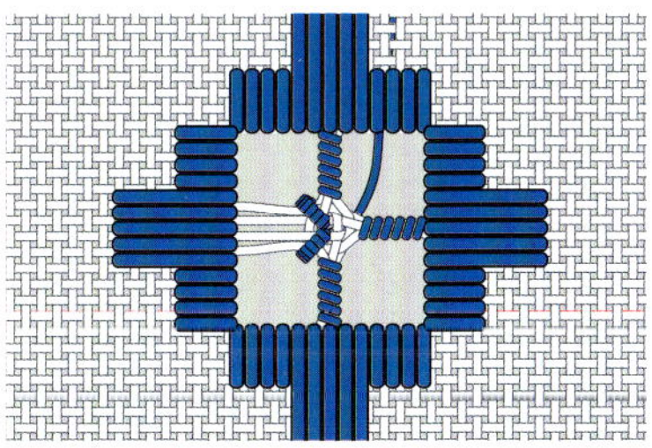

14 Turn the work and stitch another petal, with the same quantity of wraps, on the opposite side of the unwrapped bar.

❗ *Finishing the sequence of petals with one on the same side as the not-yet-wrapped bar would mean that the thread on the back would sit poorly – also causing the petal to not look quite right – when the motif is finished. Finishing with one of the petals on the far side from the not-yet-wrapped bar means it will sit much better.*

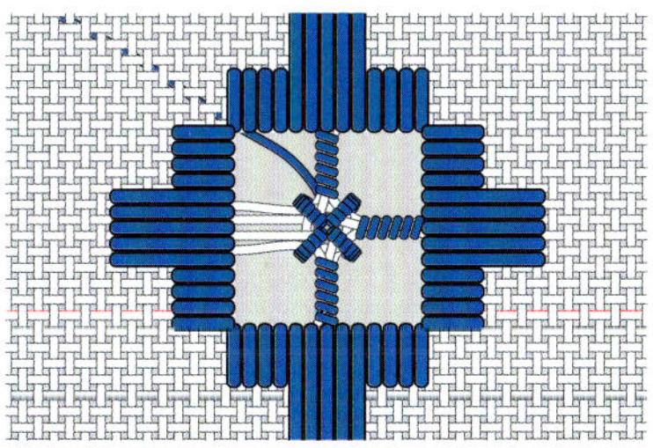

15 Turn the work as necessary and work a petal in each of the remaining quadrants.

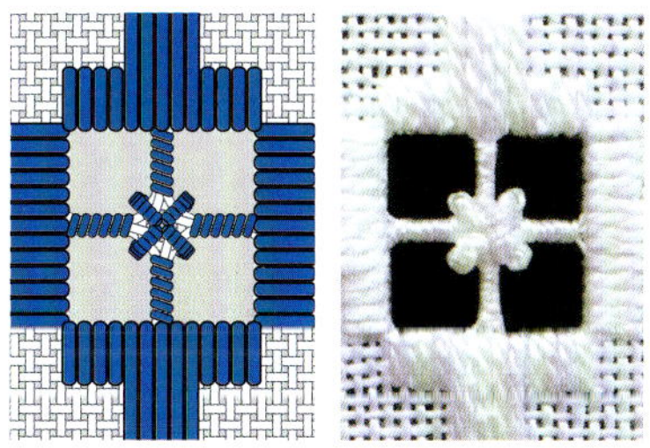

16 To complete the motif, wrap the final bar and finish the thread in the back of the satin stitch.

L

chain stitch flower

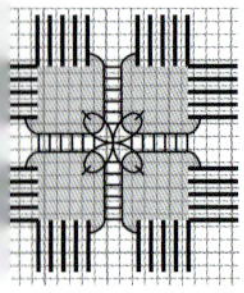

CONTEMPORARY

This motif is worked on the intersection of bars (woven or wrapped) to create a flower. The key to this stitch is to not pull the chain stitches too tight. If you do, they'll just disappear and won't be effective.

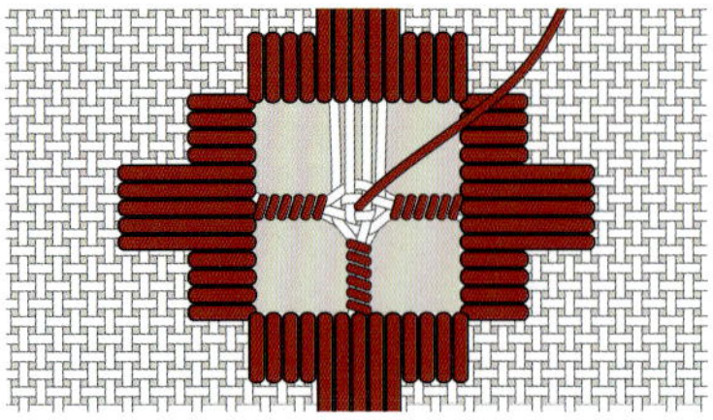

1 When three of the four bars leading to the intersection have been stitched, you can work the flower. Bring the thread out in the centre of the woven square.

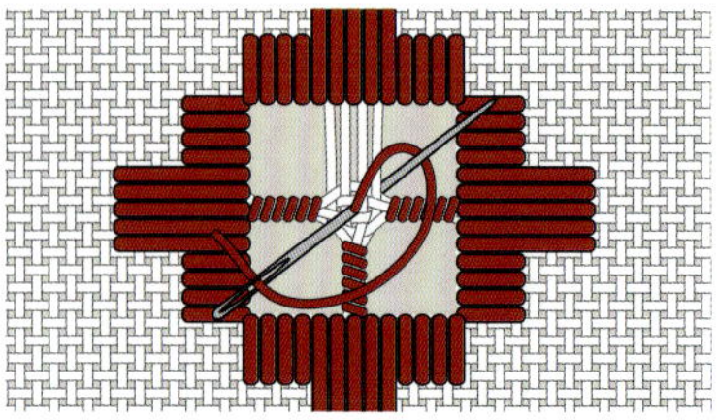

2 Insert the needle back in the centre of the woven square. Take the thread under the needle point.

It doesn't matter if the thread goes left to right or right to left.

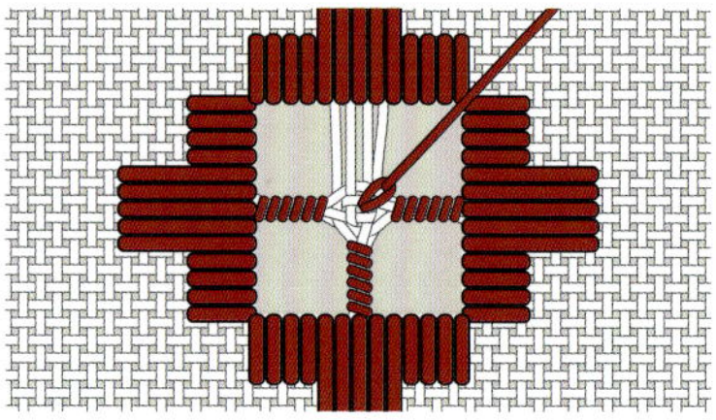

3 Pull the needle through to gently tighten the chain.

The sides of the chain should curve gently.

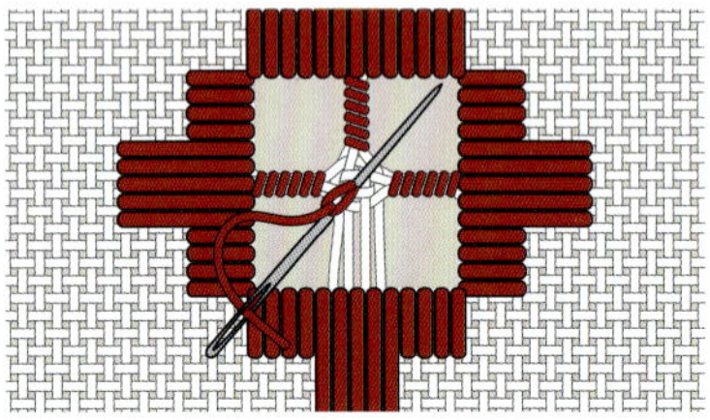

4 Turn the work 180°. Insert the needle under the chain stitch and bring it out again in the centre of the woven square.

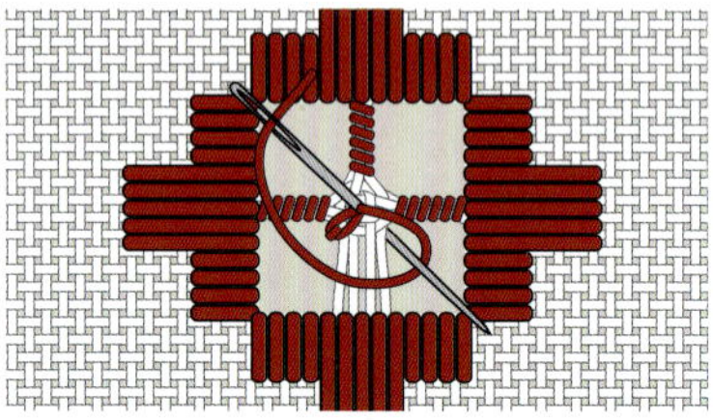

5 Pull the needle through. Tighten the stitch so that it gently goes over the end of the chain. Insert the needle in the centre again, pointing towards the quadrant on the other side of the unwrapped bar. Take the thread under the needle point.

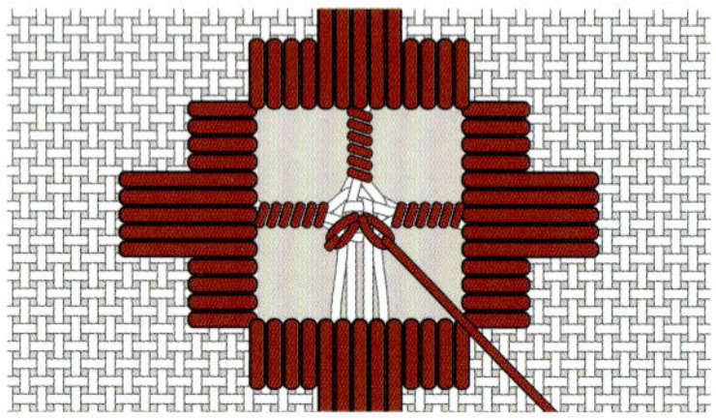

6 Pull the needle through to gently tighten the chain.

Finishing the sequence of petals with one on the same side as the not-yet-wrapped bar would mean that the thread on the back would sit poorly – also causing the petal to not look quite right – when the motif is finished. Finishing with one of the petals on the far side from the not-yet-wrapped bar means it will sit much better.

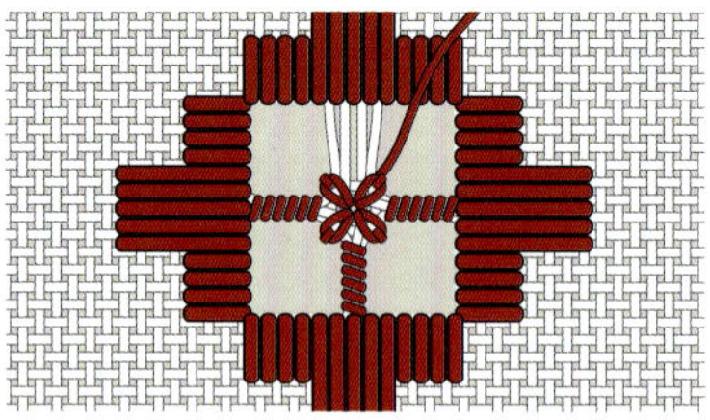

7 Take the needle to the back, and then turning the work as required, work chains in the other two quadrants.

Do not pull the anchoring stitches over the end of the chain too tight.

8 Take the thread under the back of stitching on the centre woven square to anchor it, then wrap the final bar and finish the thread in the back of the satin stitch.

chain stitch flower

This motif is worked on the intersection of bars (woven or wrapped) to create a flower. The key to this stitch is to not pull the chain stitches too tight. If you do, they'll just disappear and won't be effective.

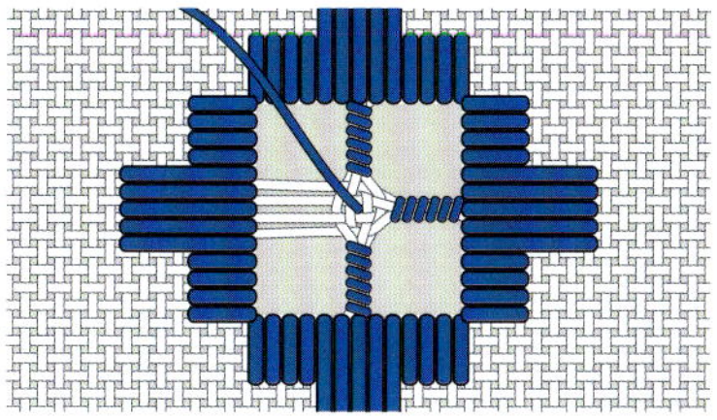

1 When three of the four bars leading to the intersection have been stitched, you can work the flower. Bring the thread out in the centre of the woven square.

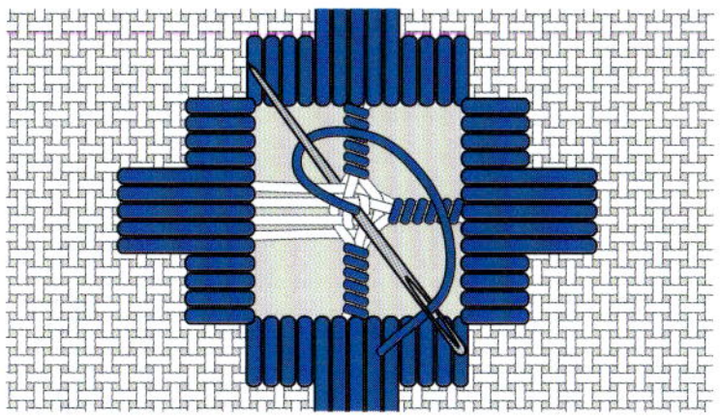

2 Insert the needle back in the centre of the woven square. Take the thread under the needle point.

❶ *It doesn't matter if the thread goes left to right or right to left.*

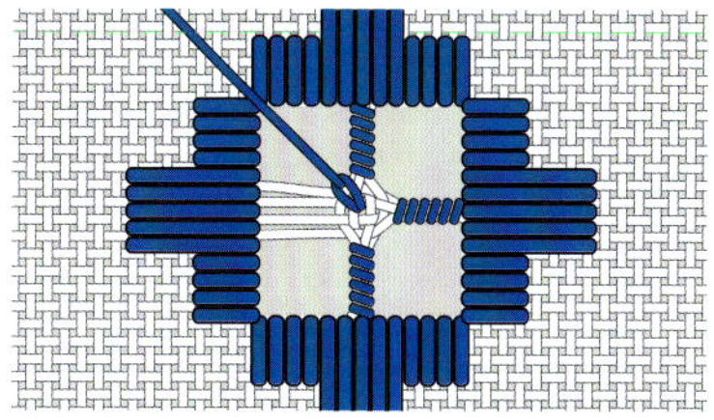

3 Pull the needle through to gently tighten the chain.

❶ *The sides of the chain should curve gently.*

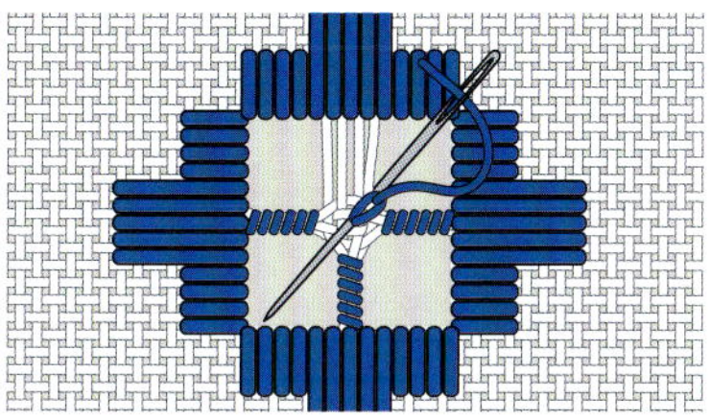

4 Turn the work 90° clockwise. Insert the needle under the chain stitch and bring it out again in the centre of the woven square.

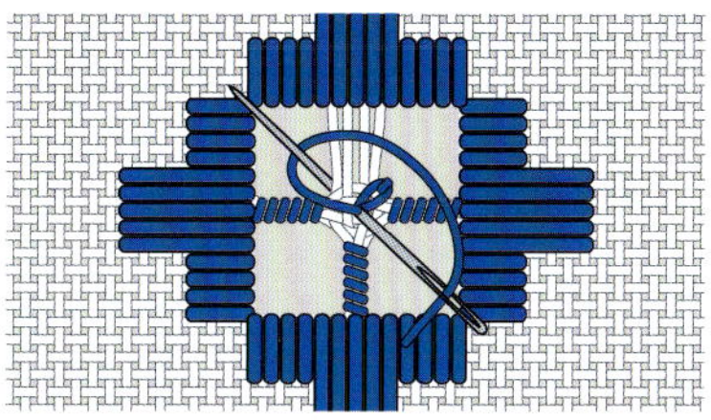

5 Pull the needle through. Tighten the stitch so that it gently goes over the end of the chain. Insert the needle in the centre again, pointing towards the quadrant on the other side of the unwrapped bar. Take the thread under the needle point.

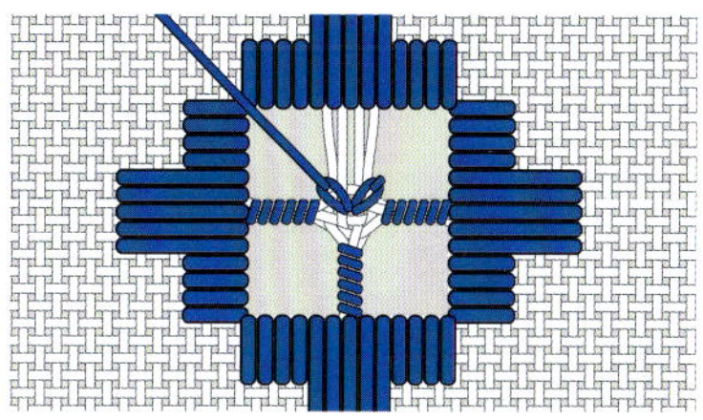

6 Pull the needle through to gently tighten the chain.

❶ *Finishing the sequence of petals with one on the same side as the not-yet-wrapped bar would mean that the thread on the back would sit poorly – also causing the petal to not look quite right – when the motif is finished. Finishing with one of the petals on the far side from the not-yet-wrapped bar means it will sit much better.*

7 Take the needle to the back, and then turning the work as required, work chains in the other two quadrants.

❶ *Do not pull the anchoring stitches over the end of the chain too tight.*

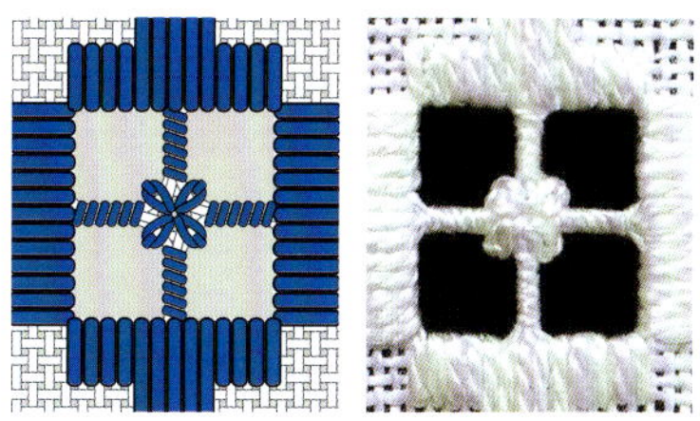

8 Take the thread under the back of stitching on the centre woven square to anchor it, then wrap the final bar and finish the thread in the back of the satin stitch.

L lacy daisy

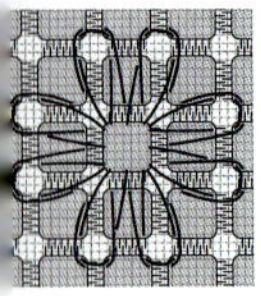

CONTEMPORARY

This motif is a flower worked over a large area of woven bars. It can be worked in its own cutwork shape as shown here, or incorporated into a larger area of cutwork.

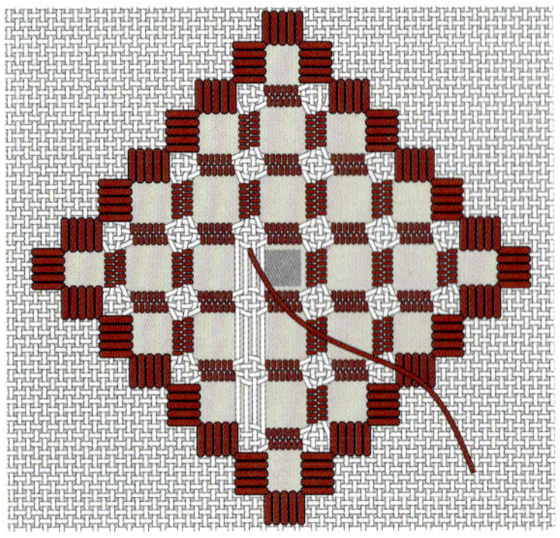

1 Prepare a diamond as shown. Bring the thread out ready to weave the next bar.

! *The centre is indicated with a grey square to help with positioning.*

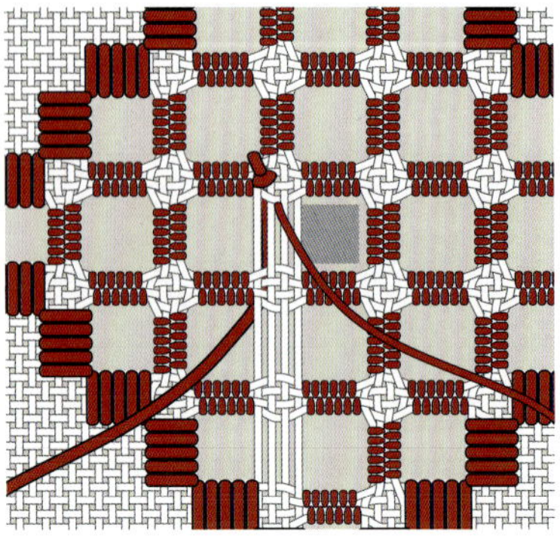

2 Thread the needle with the thicker thread, with a knot in the end. Insert the needle into the front of the woven square at the end of the stitching. Bring it out beside the end of the next bar.

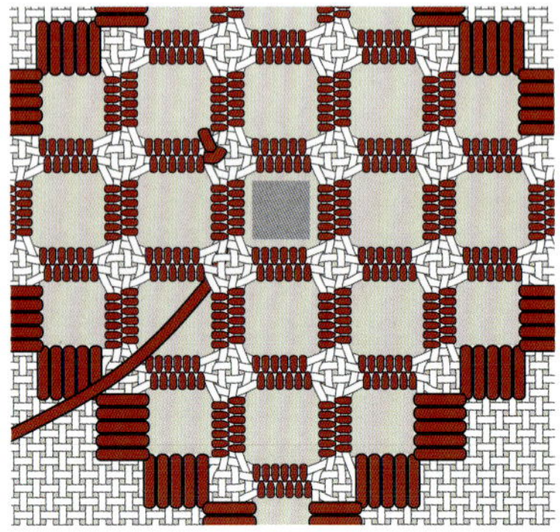

3 Picking up the thinner thread, weave the bar, including the thick thread in the back. Weave the remaining two bars without the thicker thread. Finish the thinner thread in the back of the satin stitching.

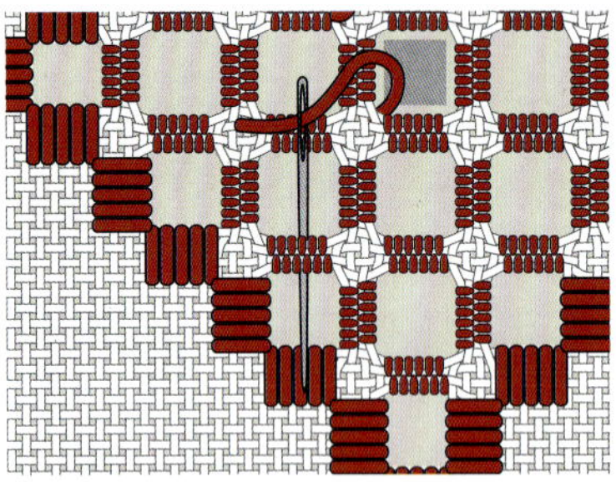

4 Thread the needle with the thicker thread. Bring it out in the diamond's centre square. Take it over the centre square's bottom left woven corner, and slide it under the horizontal bar which is down and to the left.

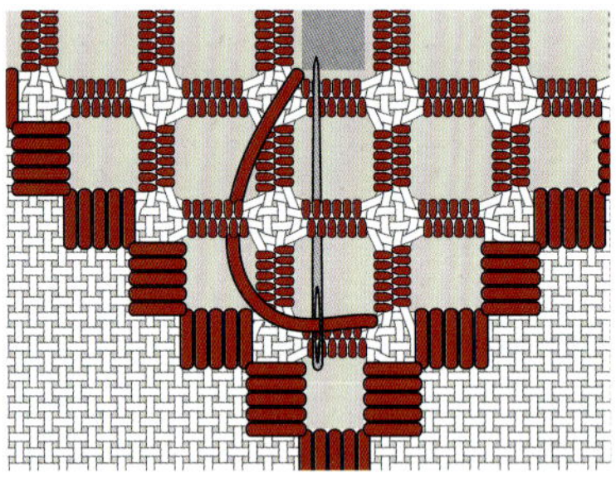

5 From below, slide the needle under the horizontal bar to the right of the previous one.

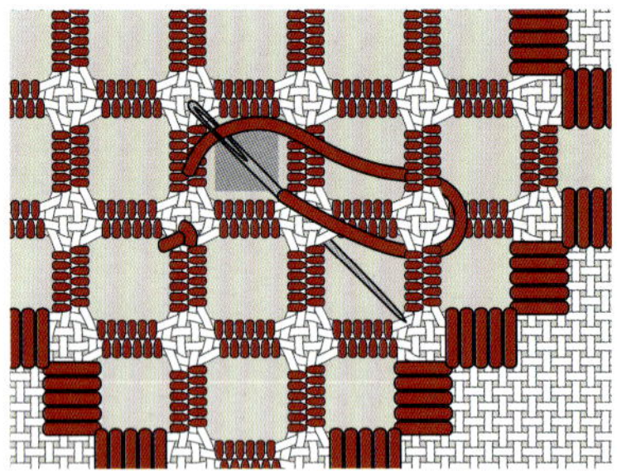

6 Turn the work 90° anticlockwise. Pull the thread to bring it in close around the bars. From above left, slide the needle under the centre square's bottom right woven corner.

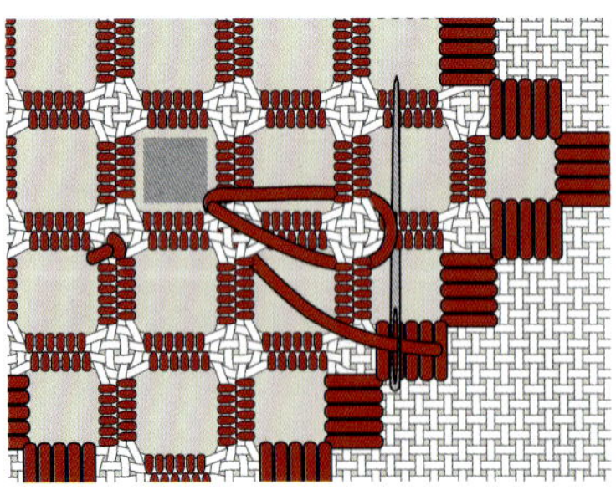

7 From below, slide the needle under the second horizontal bar right of the centre.

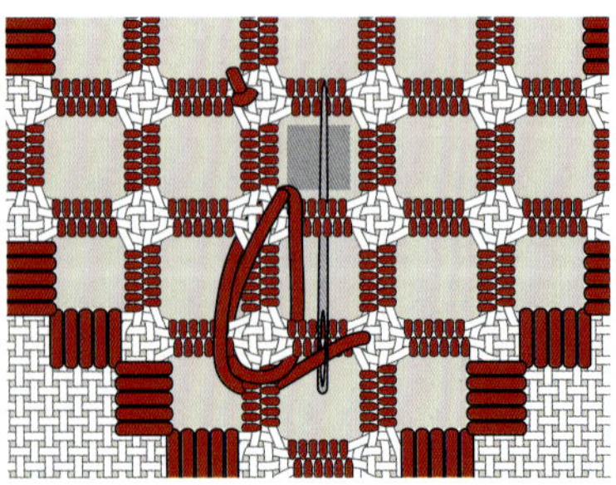

8 Turn the work 90° clockwise. Pull the thread to bring it in close around the bars. From below, slide the needle under the horizontal bar below the centre square.

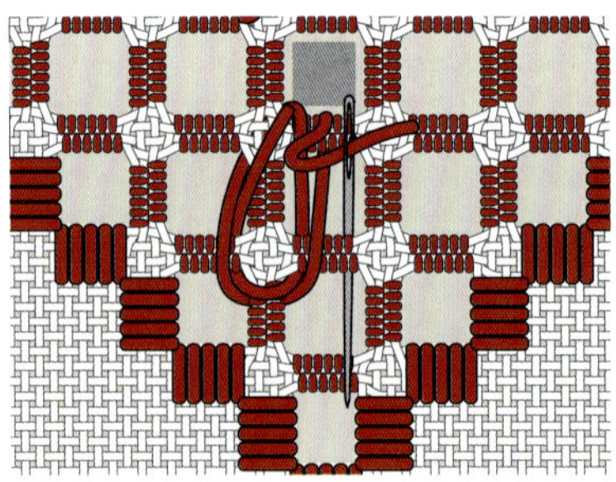

9 From above, slide the needle under the horizontal bar below the previous one.

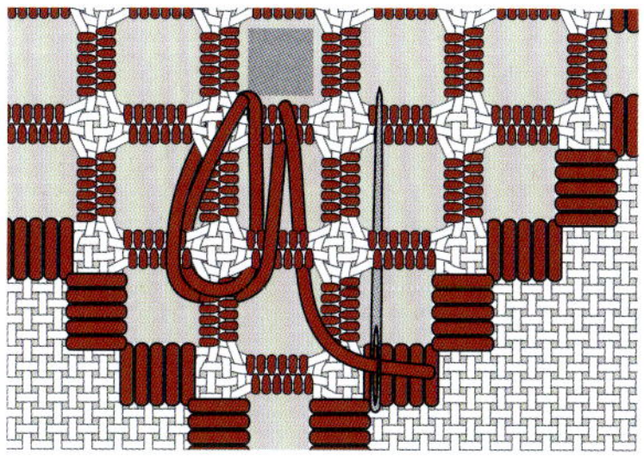

10 Pull the thread to bring it in close around the bars. From below, slide the needle under the horizontal bar to the right of the previous one.

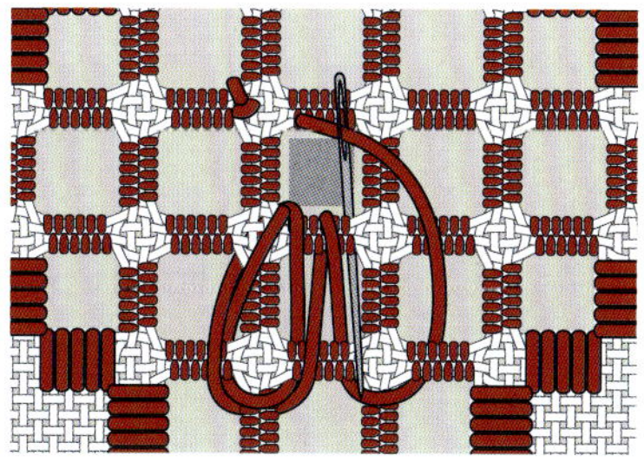

11 From above, slide the needle under the horizontal bar below the centre square. Bring the needle out between the thread and the vertical bar.

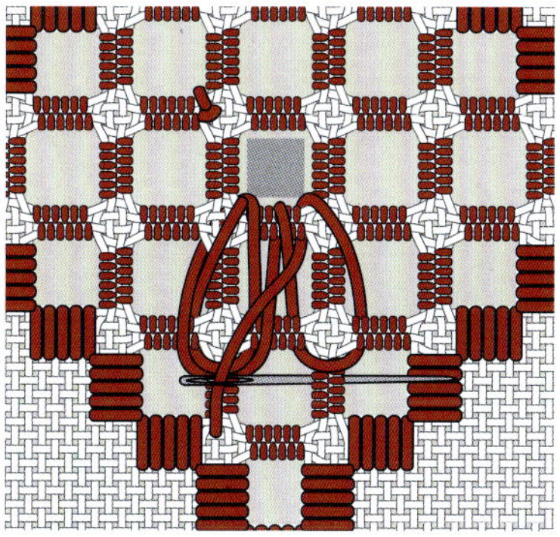

12 Pull the thread to bring it in close around the bars. From the left, slide the needle under the vertical bar below the current petal.

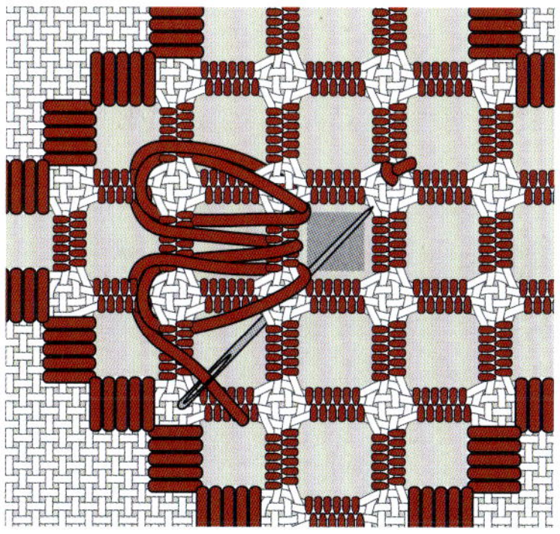

13 Turn the work 90° clockwise. From below left, slide the needle under the centre square's bottom left woven corner.

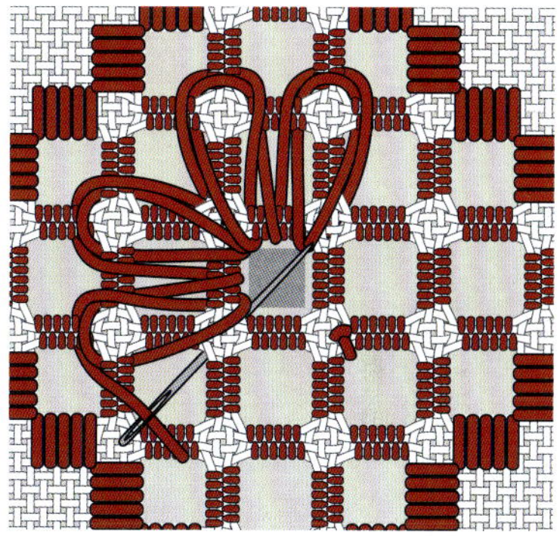

14 Cycle through Steps 4 to 13, turning the work as necessary.

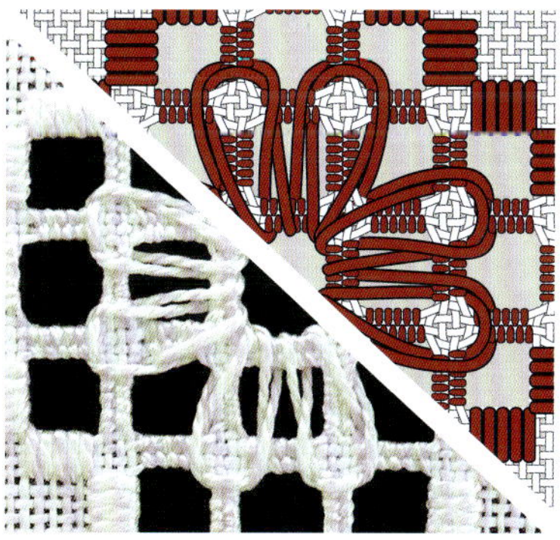

15 Repeat for the two remaining quadrants. On completion, take the thread to the back. Run it under the thick stitches on the centre square. Trim the knot from the beginning of the thread.

R

lacy daisy

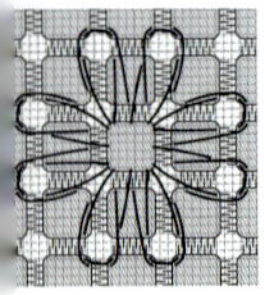

CONTEMPORARY

This motif is a flower worked over a large area of woven bars. It can be worked in its own cutwork shape as shown here, or incorporated into a larger area of cutwork.

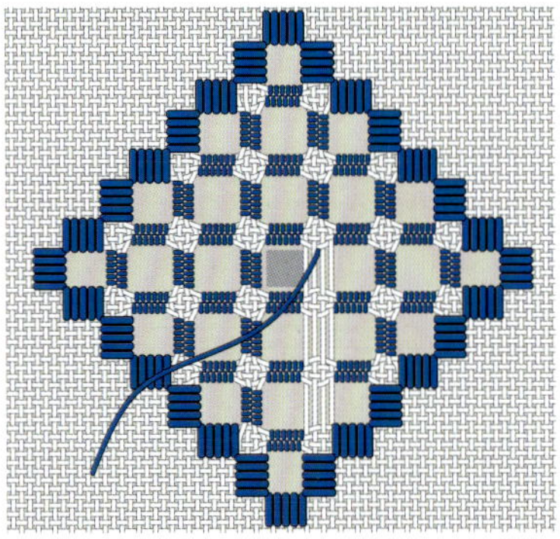

1 Prepare a diamond as shown. Bring the thread out ready to weave the next bar.

❶ *The centre is indicated with a grey square to help with positioning.*

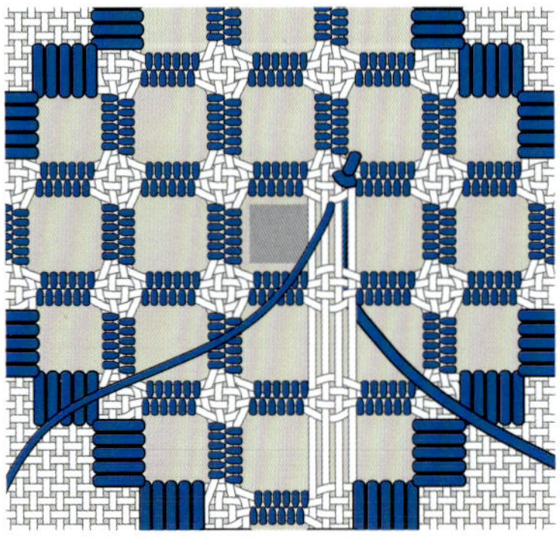

2 Thread the needle with the thicker thread, with a knot in the end. Insert the needle into the front of the woven square at the end of the stitching. Bring it out beside the end of the next bar.

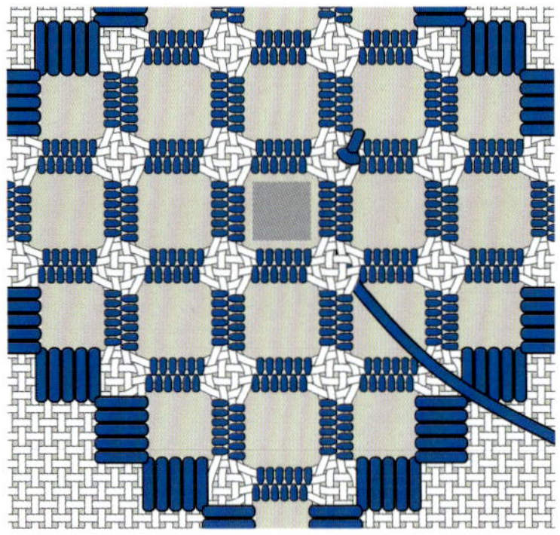

3 Picking up the thinner thread, weave the bar, including the thick thread in the back. Weave the remaining two bars without the thicker thread. Finish the thinner thread in the back of the satin stitching.

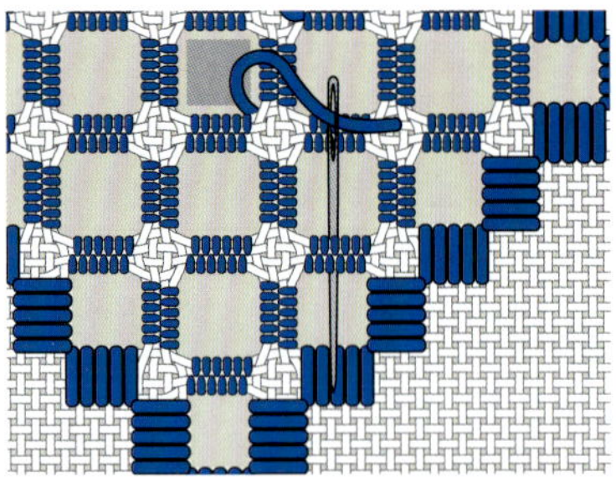

4 Thread the needle with the thicker thread. Bring it out in the diamond's centre square. Take it over the centre square's bottom right woven corner, and slide it under the horizontal bar which is down and to the right.

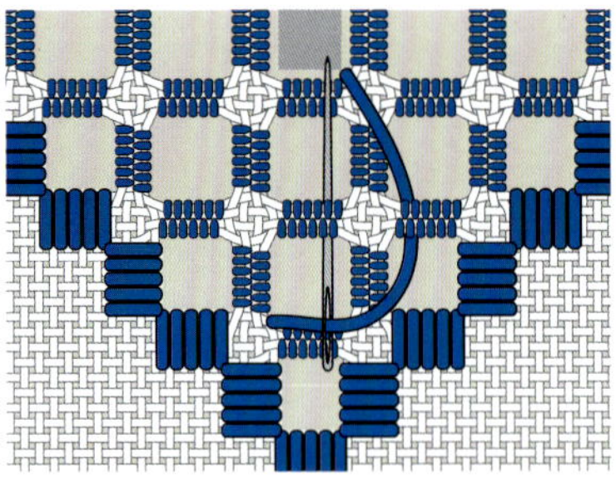

5 From below, slide the needle under the horizontal bar to the left of the previous one.

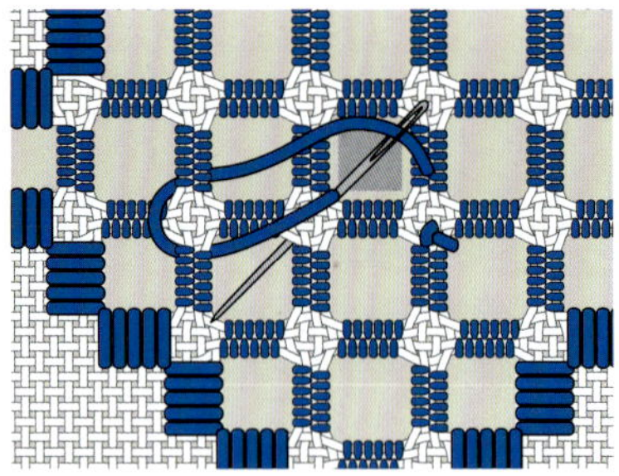

6 Turn the work 90° clockwise. Pull the thread to bring it in close around the bars. From above right, slide the needle under the centre square's bottom left woven corner.

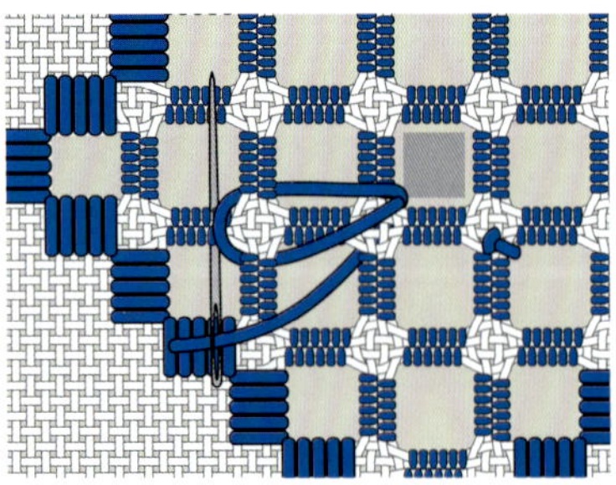

7 From below, slide the needle under the second horizontal bar left of the centre.

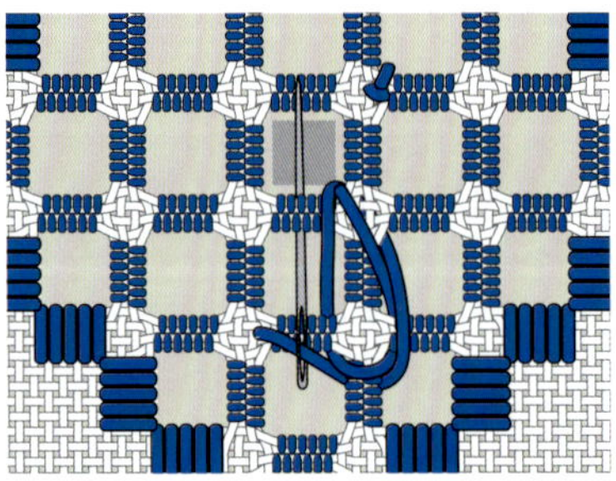

8 Turn the work 90° anticlockwise. Pull the thread to bring it in close around the bars. From below, slide the needle under the horizontal bar below the centre square.

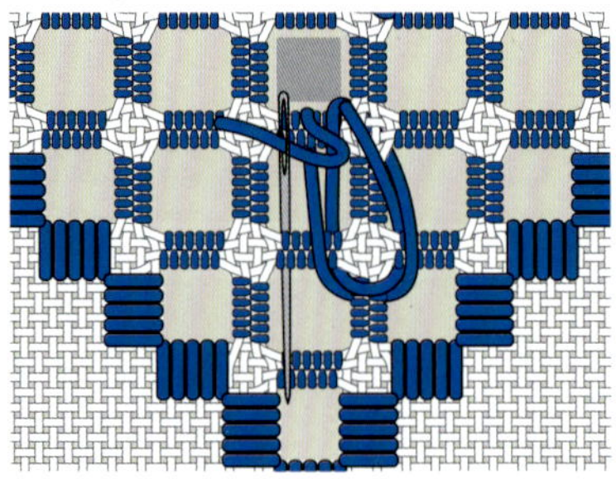

9 From above, slide the needle under the horizontal bar below the previous one.

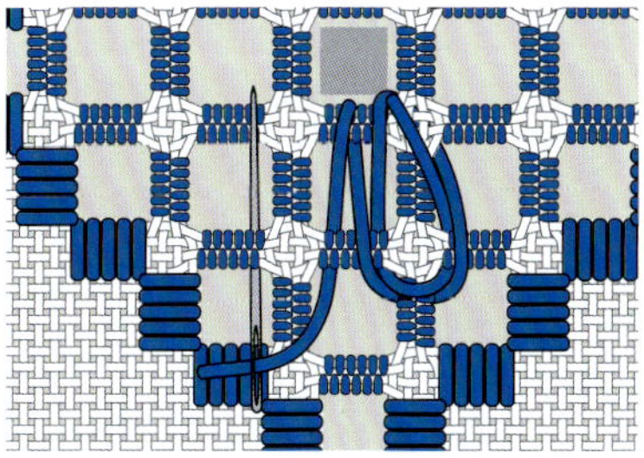

10 Pull the thread to bring it in close around the bars. From below, slide the needle under the horizontal bar to the left of the previous one.

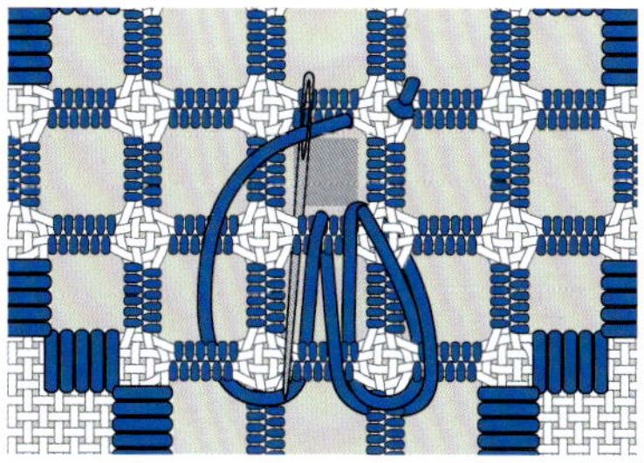

11 From above, slide the needle under the horizontal bar below the centre square. Bring the needle out between the thread and the vertical bar.

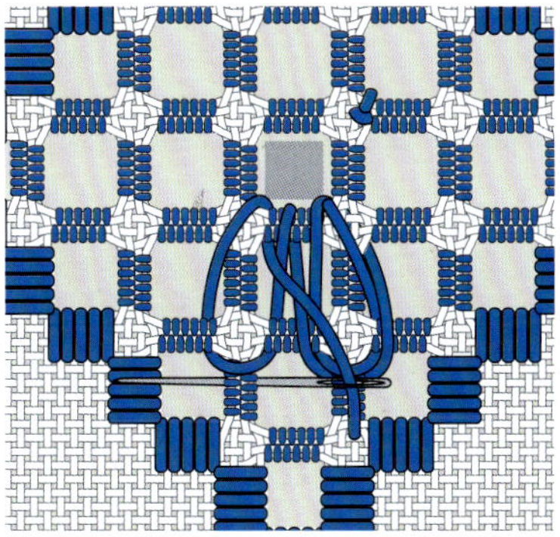

12 Pull the thread to bring it in close around the bars. From the right, slide the needle under the vertical bar below the current petal.

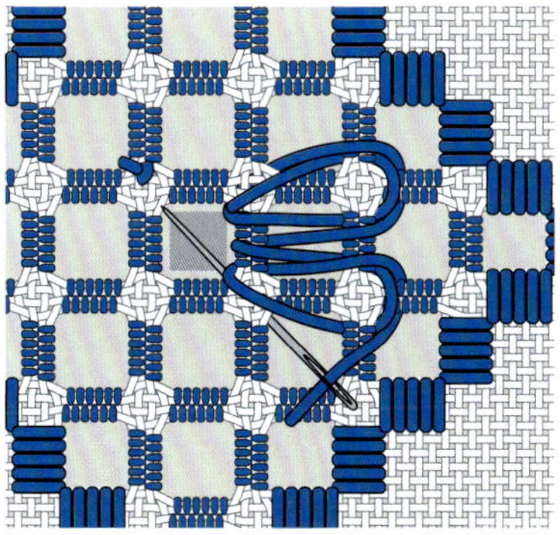

13 Turn the work 90° anticlockwise. From below right, slide the needle under the centre square's bottom right woven corner.

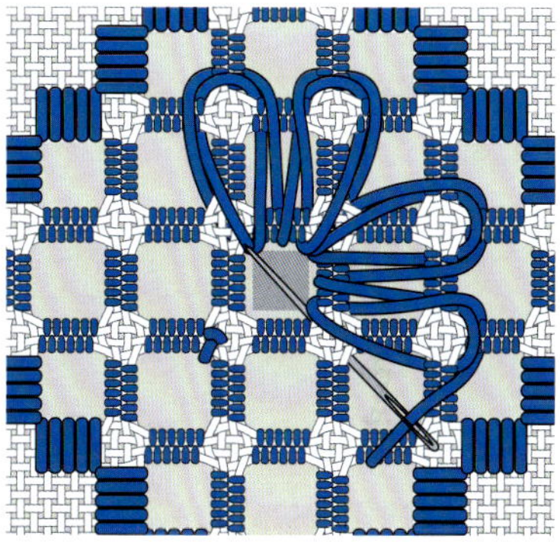

14 Cycle through Steps 4 to 13, turning the work as necessary.

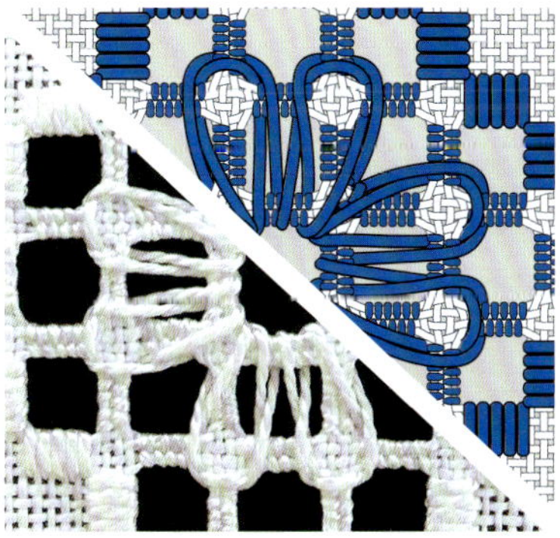

15 Repeat for the two remaining quadrants. On completion, take the thread to the back. Run it under the thick stitches on the centre square. Trim the knot from the beginning of the thread.

soleil stitch

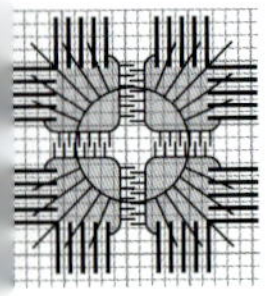

CONTEMPORARY

This stitch can be worked with the rays spaced apart (*soleil* means sun), as shown here, or with a stitch between each satin stitch for a more solid effect, which works well with overdyed threads.

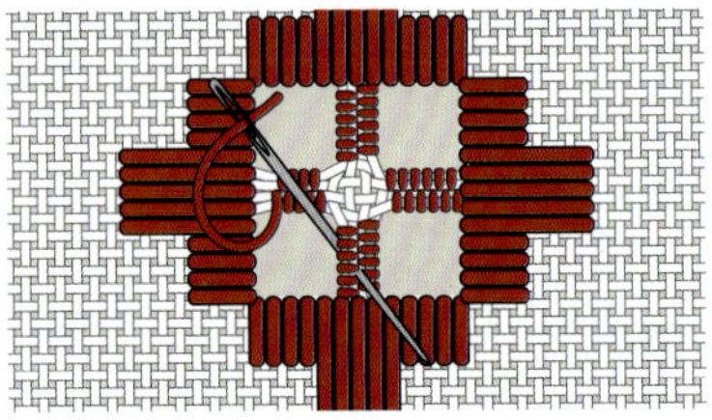

1 Work three bars, then about half of the final bar. Insert the needle in the back of the adjacent bar, two thirds of the way along.

❶ *The further out along the bar, the larger the open circle in the centre.*

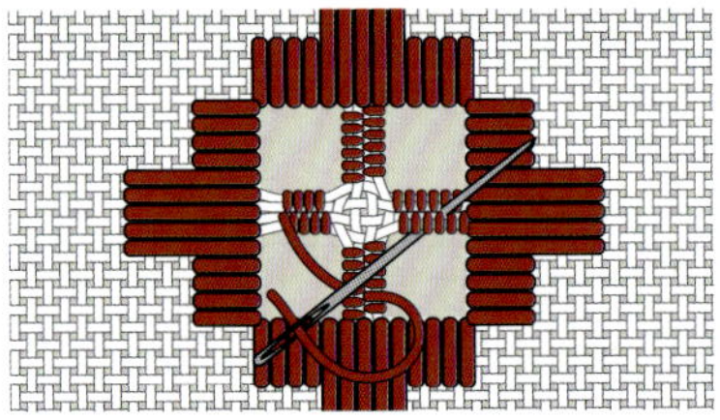

2 Pull the needle through and leave the stitch curving gently. Continuing around in the same direction, insert the needle in the back of the next bar, about half of the distance from the centre.

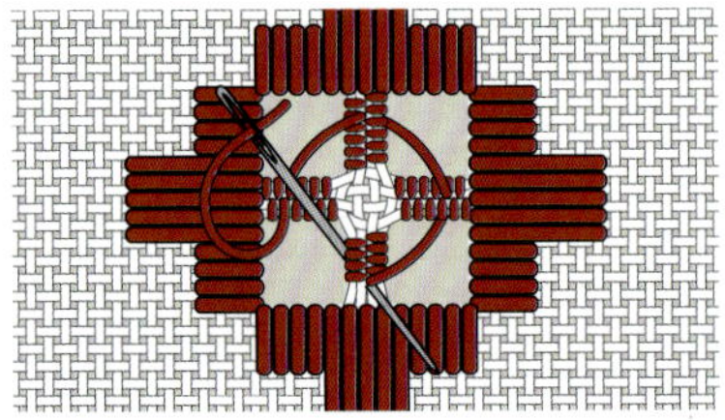

3 Pull the needle through and leave the stitch curving gently. Repeat for the next two bars, turning the work as required.

4 Pull the needle through and leave the stitch curving gently. Heading back around the circle, insert the needle in the back of the bar, through the same hole as before.

5 Continue around the circle, back to the beginning, turning the work as required.

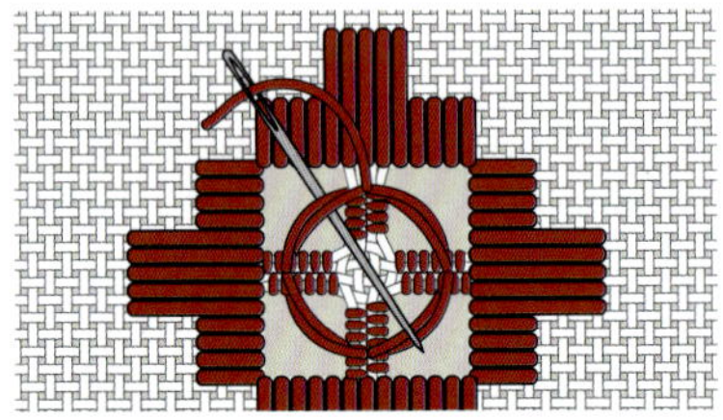

6 Pull the needle through and pass the needle under the circling threads in the first quadrant, from the outside to the inside.

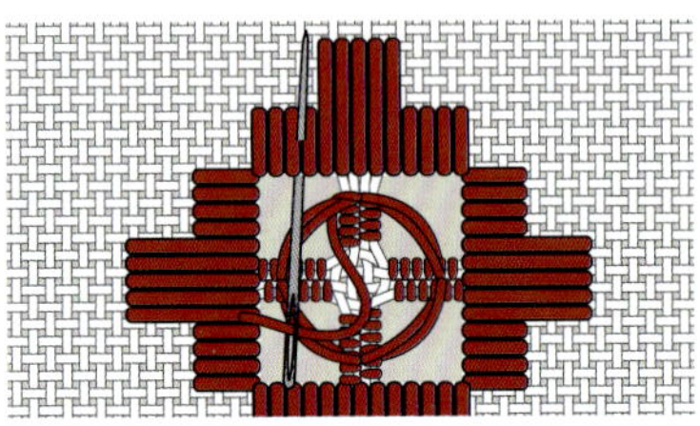

7 Insert the needle in the back of the satin stitch at the top of the square, bringing it out three threads from the left, halfway down.

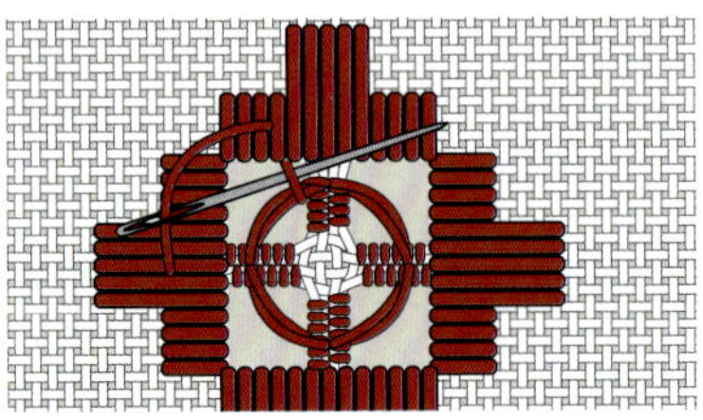

8 Pull the needle through. Slide the needle under the stitch from the left.

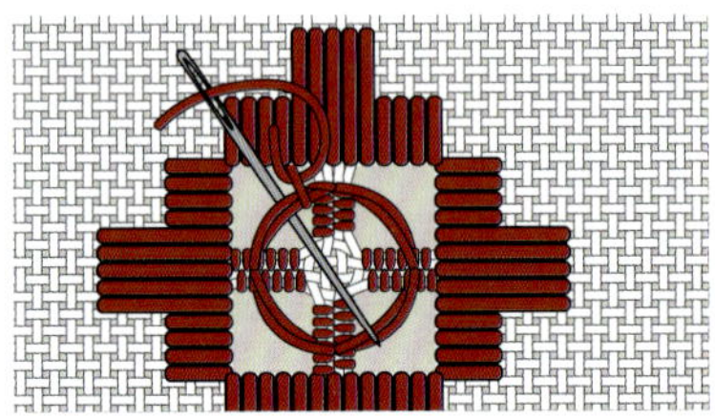

9 Slide the needle under the circling stitches from above, left of the stitch.

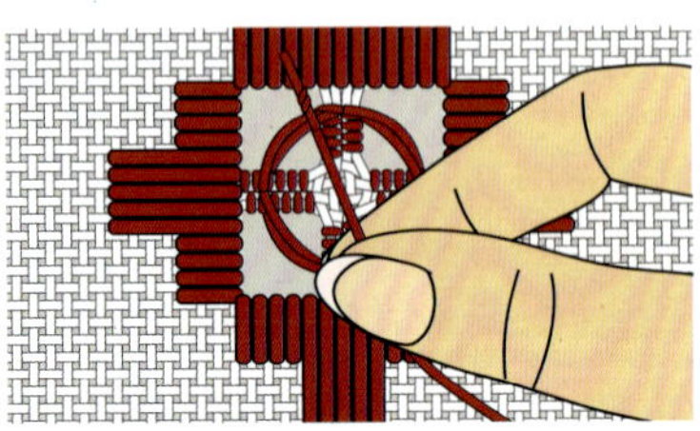

10 Pull the thread toward the centre to intertwine the stitches.

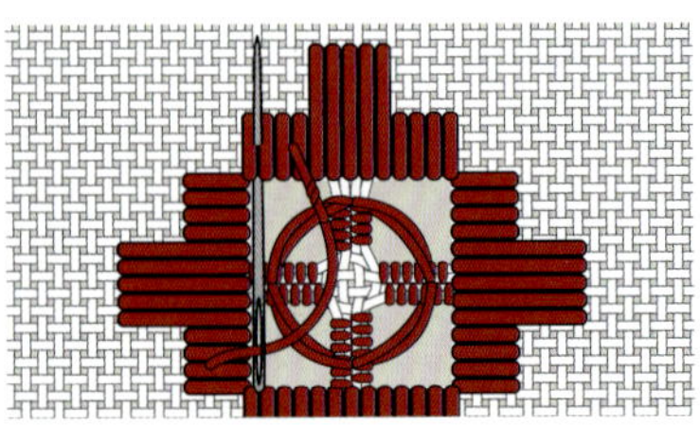

11 Insert the needle in the back of the satin stitch, bringing it out two threads to the left of where it previously came out.

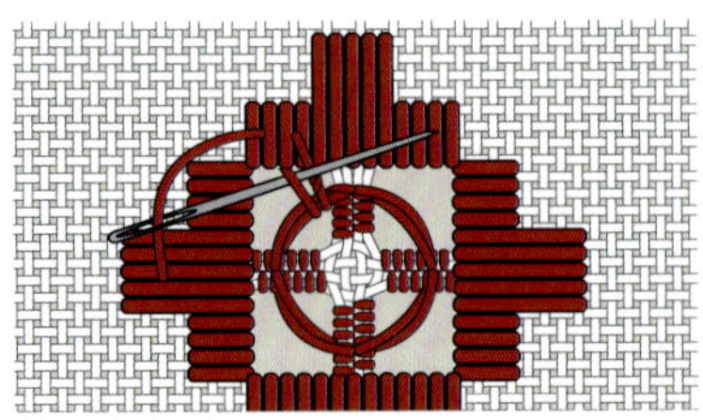

12 Pull the needle through. Slide the needle under the stitch from the left.

Soleil stitch was devised by Marianne Mäder and is published here for the first time. Marianne loves colour, so I have used colour for this sample.

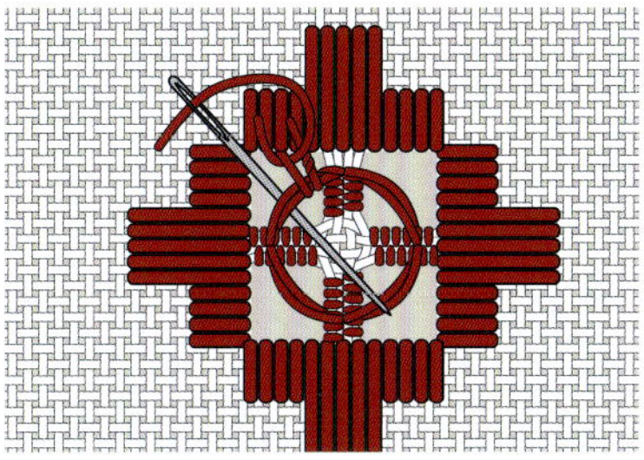

13 Slide the needle under the circling stitches from above, left of the stitch.

❶ *When working in a larger square, you may find that the longer stitches require another twist.*

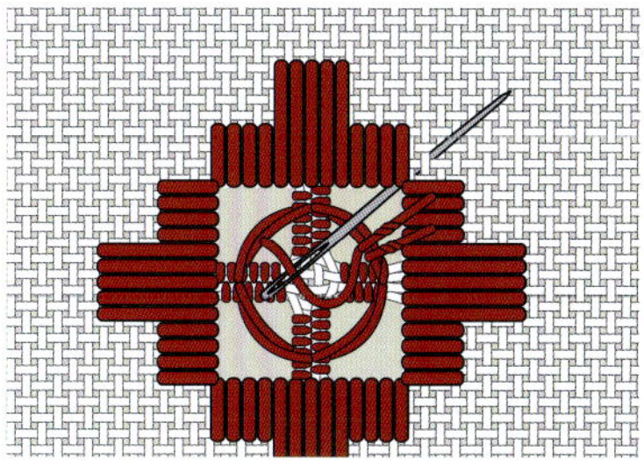

14 Turn the work 90° clockwise. Pull the thread toward the centre to intertwine the stitches. Inserting from the back, bring the needle out in the woven corner, two threads away from the cut edges.

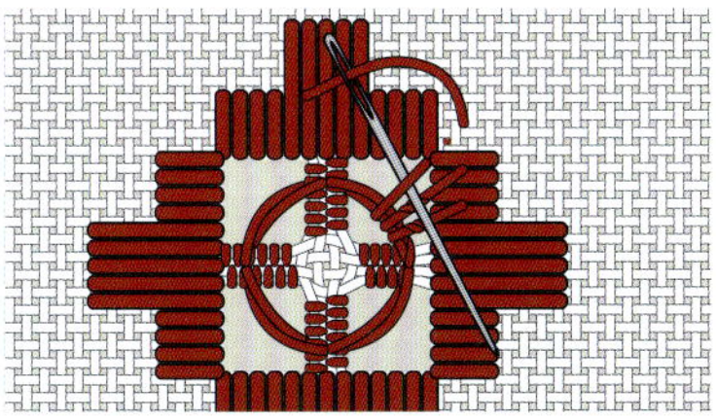

15 Pull the needle through. Slide the needle under the stitch from the left.

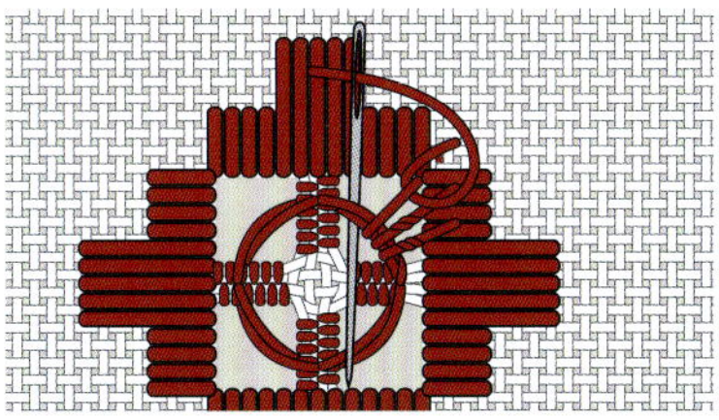

16 Slide the needle under the circling stitches from above, left of the stitch.

17 Pull the thread to intertwine the stitches. Work two more twisted rays on the next side of the quadrant; one stitch from the corner, and three stitches from the corner. To finish, pass the needle behind the woven bar, bringing it out in the next quadrant, inside the circle.

18 Repeat the rays in each of the other three quadrants following Steps 7 to 17. On completion of the final ray, bring the thread out ready to complete the woven bar.

19 Weave the bar and finish the thread in the back of the satin stitch.

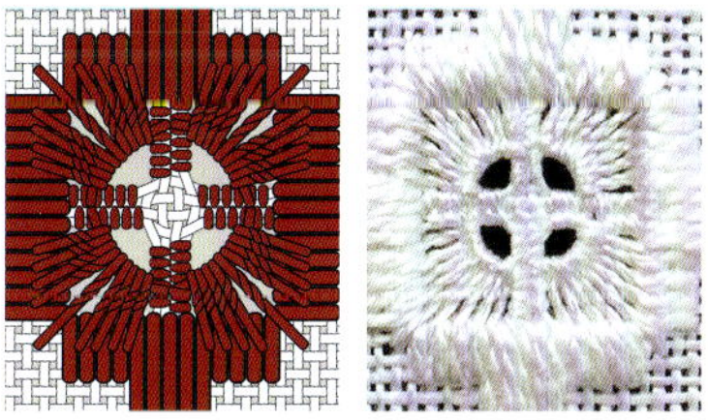

❶ *By working a twisted stitch between each satin stitch around the edge of the motif, the filling becomes more solid, to make Full Soleil Stitch. This can look particularly attractive when worked in an overdyed thread.*

R

soleil stitch

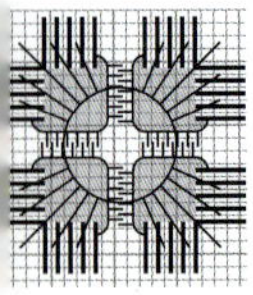

CONTEMPORARY

This stitch can be worked with the rays spaced apart (*soleil* means sun), as shown here, or with a stitch between each satin stitch for a more solid effect, which works well with overdyed threads.

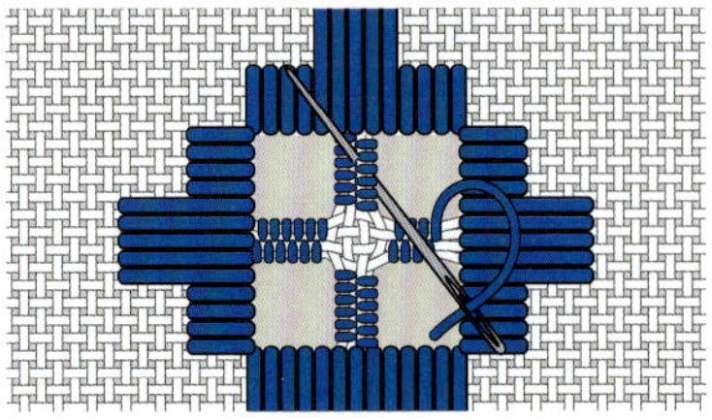

1 Work three bars, then about half of the final bar. Insert the needle in the back of the adjacent bar, two thirds of the way along.

❶ *The further out along the bar, the larger the open circle in the centre.*

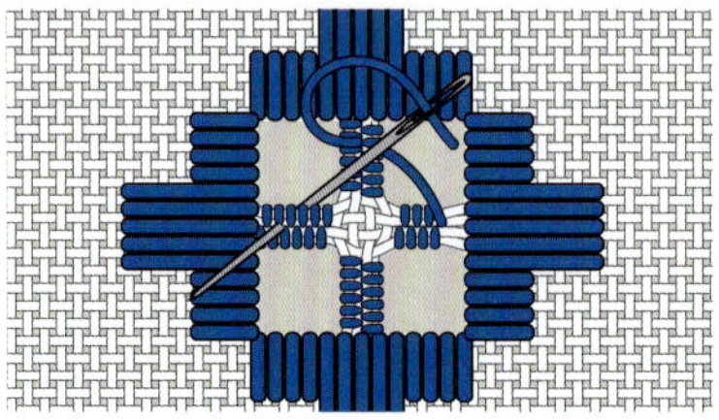

2 Pull the needle through and leave the stitch curving gently. Continuing around in the same direction, insert the needle in the back of the next bar, about half of the distance from the centre.

3 Pull the needle through and leave the stitch curving gently. Repeat for the next two bars, turning the work as required.

4 Pull the needle through and leave the stitch curving gently. Heading back around the circle, insert the needle in the back of the bar, through the same hole as before.

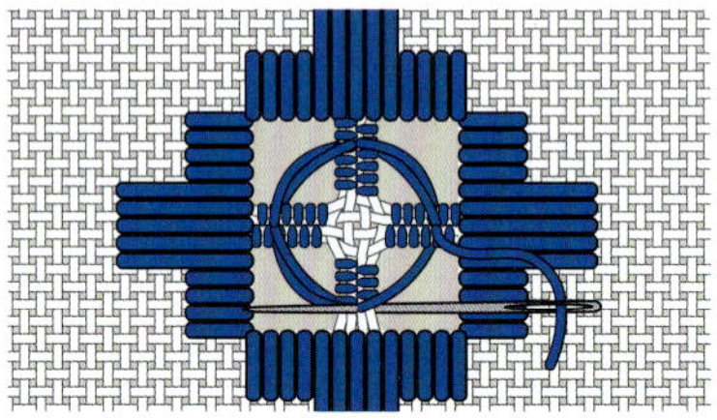

5 Continue around the circle, back to the beginning, turning the work as required.

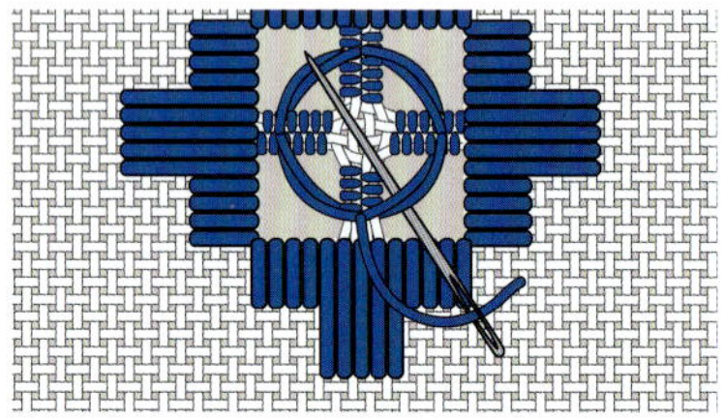

6 Pull the needle through and pass the needle under the circling threads in the first quadrant, from the outside to the inside.

7 Insert the needle in the back of the satin stitch at the bottom of the square, bringing it out three threads from the right, halfway down.

8 Pull the needle through. Slide the needle under the stitch from the right.

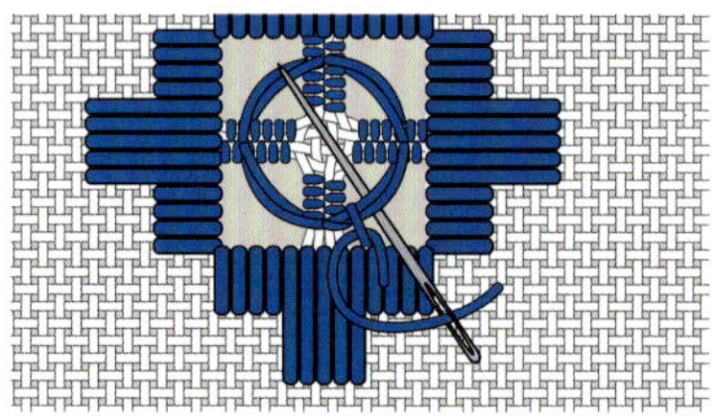

9 Slide the needle under the circling stitches from below, right of the stitch.

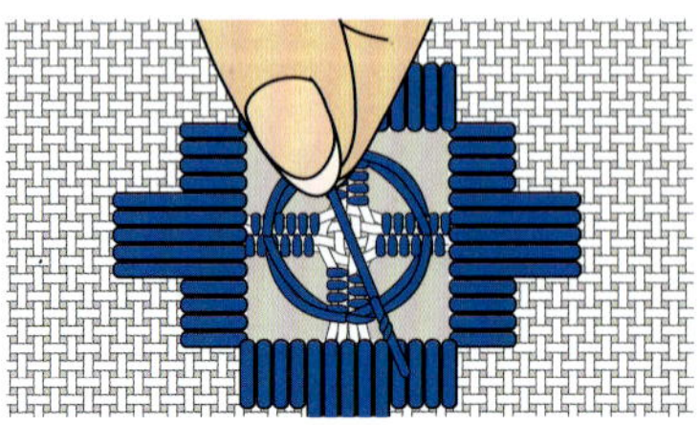

10 Pull the thread toward the centre to intertwine the stitches.

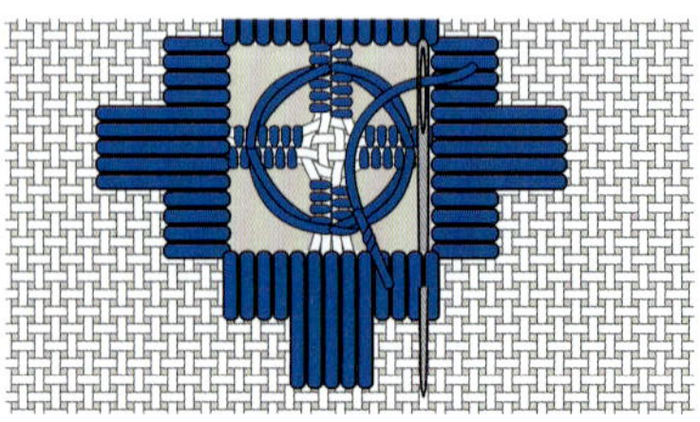

11 Insert the needle in the back of the satin stitch, bringing it out two threads to the right of where it previously came out.

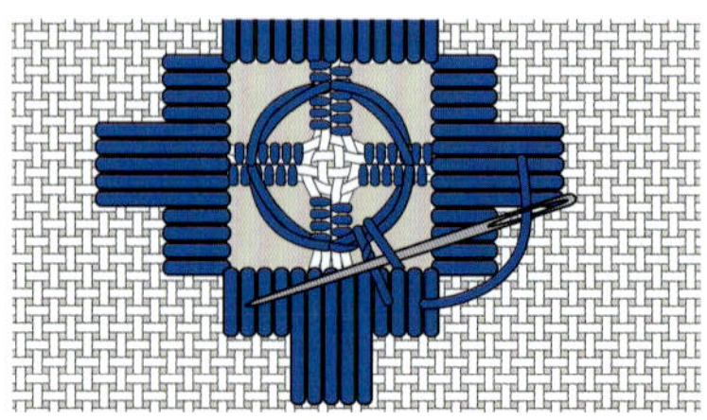

12 Pull the needle through. Slide the needle under the stitch from the right.

Soleil stitch was devised by Marianne Mäder and is published here for the first time. Marianne loves colour, so I have used colour for this sample.

13 Slide the needle under the circling stitches from below, right of the stitch.

When working in a larger square, you may find that the longer stitches require another twist.

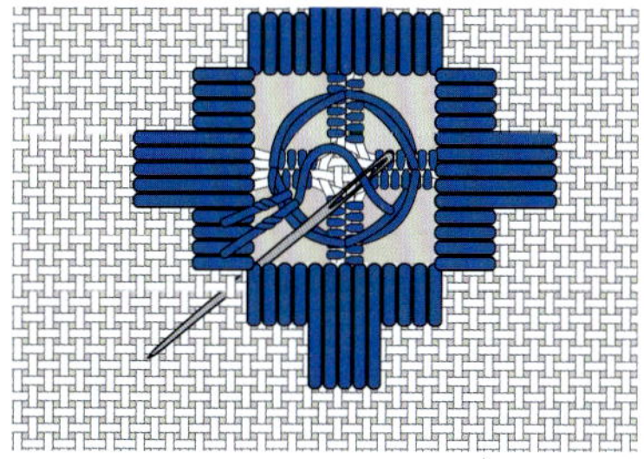

14 Turn the work 90° clockwise. Pull the thread toward the centre to intertwine the stitches. Inserting from the back, bring the needle out in the woven corner, two threads away from the cut edges.

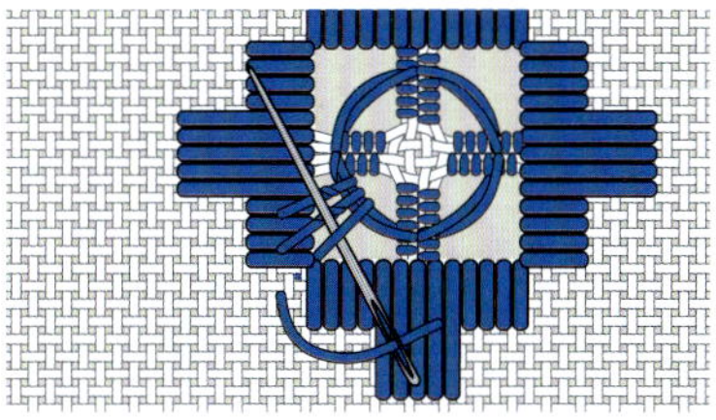

15 Pull the needle through. Slide the needle under the stitch from below.

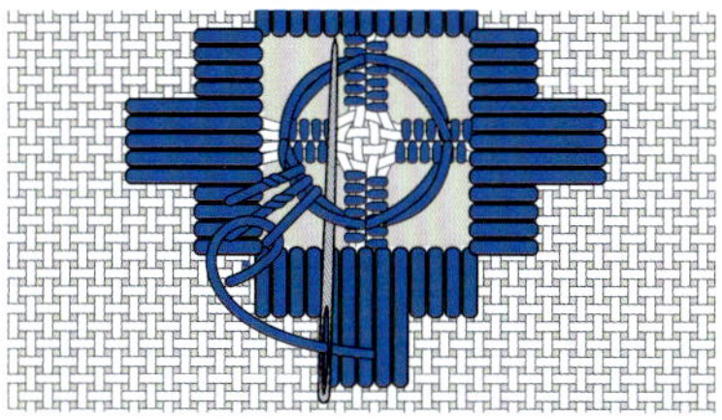

16 Slide the needle under the circling stitches from below, right of the stitch.

17 Pull the thread to intertwine the stitches. Work two more twisted rays on the next side of the quadrant; one stitch from the corner, and three stitches from the corner. To finish, pass the needle behind the woven bar, bringing it out in the next quadrant, inside the circle.

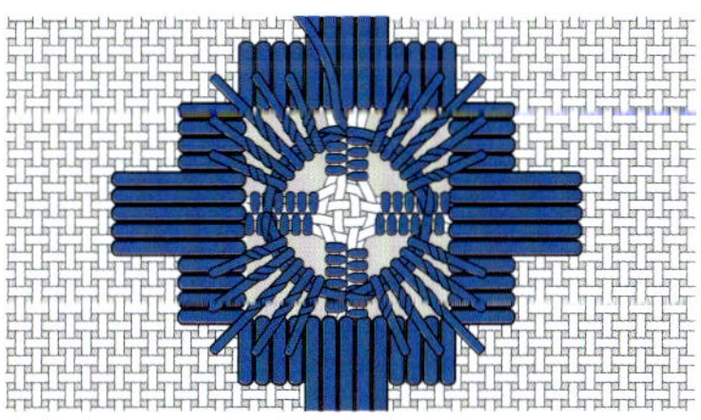

18 Repeat the rays in each of the other three quadrants following Steps 7 to 17. On completion of the final ray, bring the thread out ready to complete the woven bar.

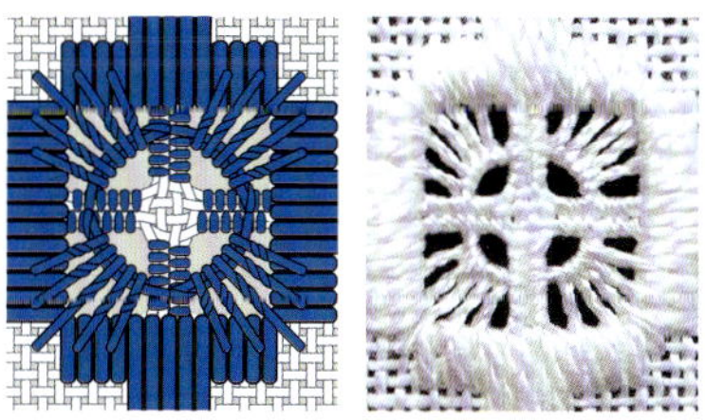

19 Weave the bar and finish the thread in the back of the satin stitch.

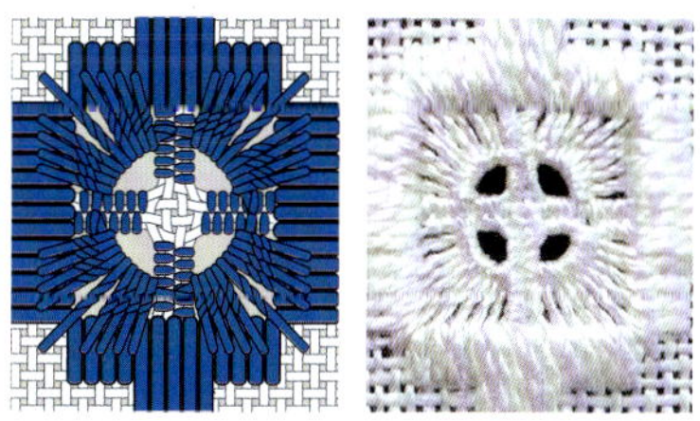

By working a twisted stitch between each satin stitch around the edge of the motif, the filling becomes more solid, to make Full Soleil Stitch. This can look particularly attractive when worked in an overdyed thread.

L

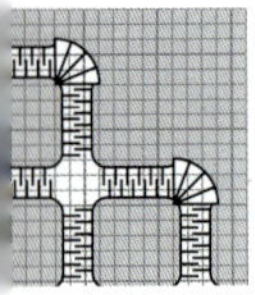

CONTEMPORARY

lacy buttonhole edge

This delicate lacy edging is unstable, so therefore requires extra strengthening before stitching. The sample method uses three rows, but it can be worked with any number of rows.

cutting and withdrawing the threads

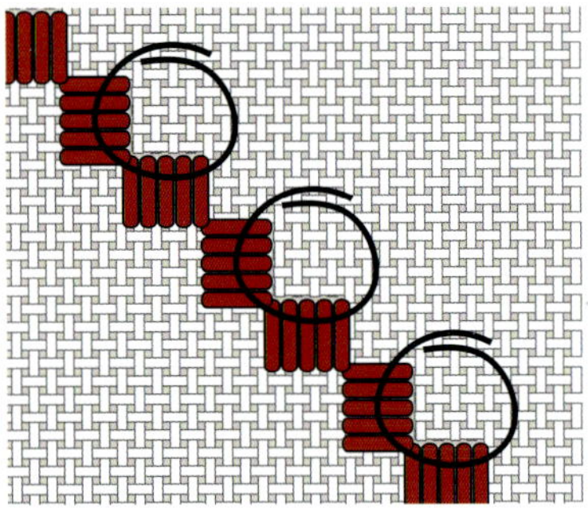

1 At the inner edge of where the lacy edge will be worked, there is a line of satin stitch blocks. Cut the threads along the outer edge of the satin stitch blocks.

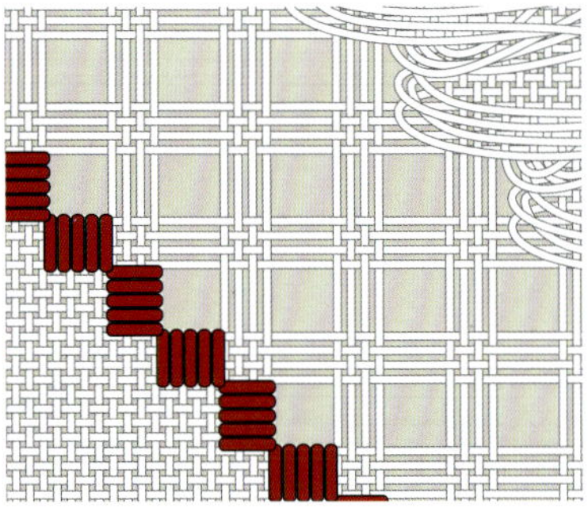

2 Carefully draw back the threads so that there are four rows of fabric threads for working on.

❶ *You will need four rows withdrawn for three rows of stitching.*

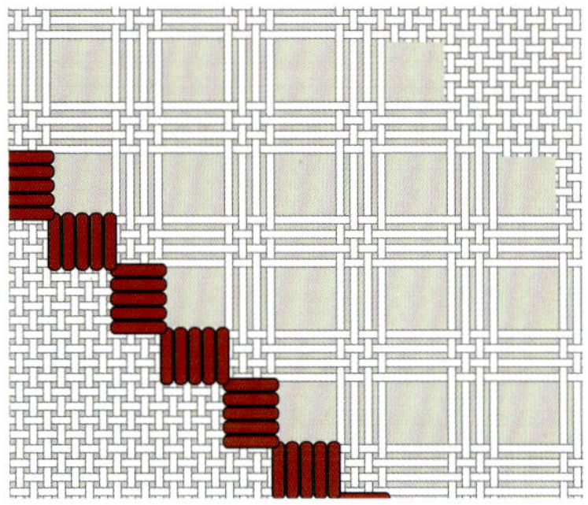

3 Trim the withdrawn threads at the edge of the cutwork area.

❶ *The more threads you remove, the more unstable the fabric becomes. Only remove what you're about to stitch over.*

lacing the back

The corners are weak as the cut threads are interwoven over only a very short distance. A web of threads laced across the back helps to strengthen them. Use thread that is a similar colour and thickness to the fabric. If an appropriate weight or colour is unavailable, use a thread from the side of the fabric.

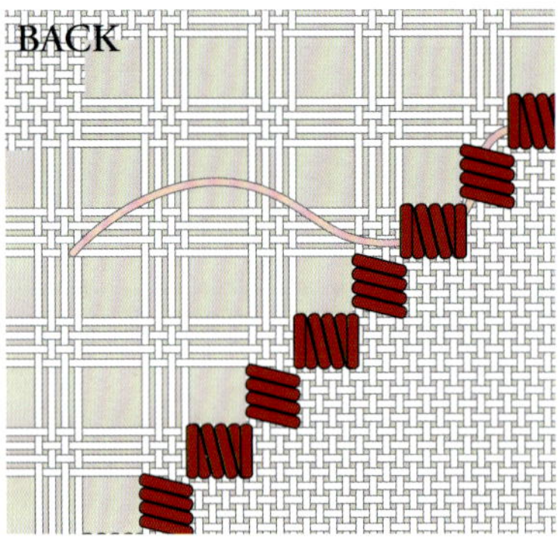

1 With the back of the work facing, fasten a long thread in the back of the satin stitch blocks.

❶ *Shown here as a different colour to the fabric for illustration purposes only.*

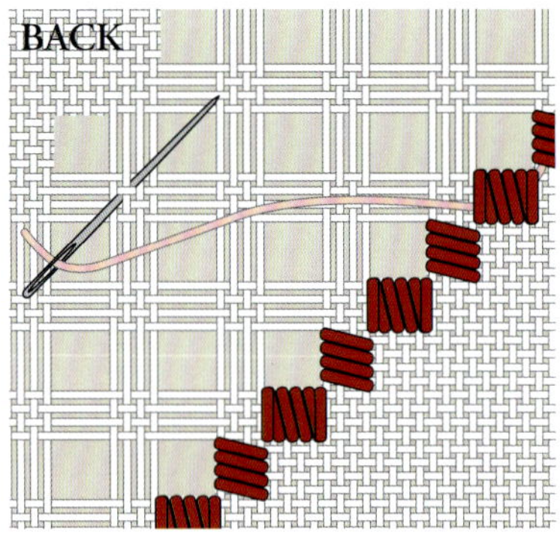

2 Count left four woven squares. In the fourth square, insert the needle three threads from the right and halfway up. Bring it out one thread up and right.

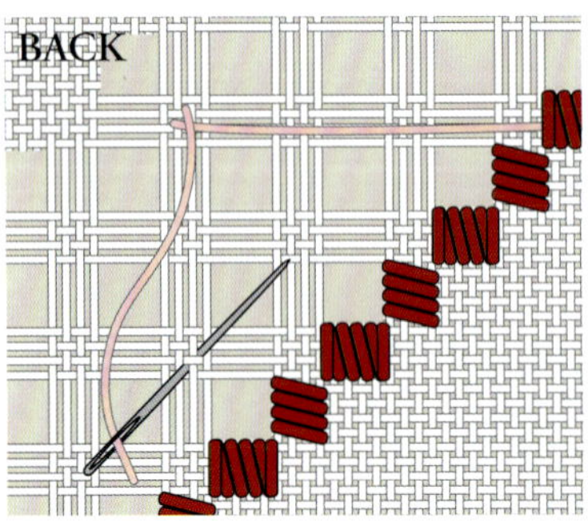

3 Pull the needle through. Two woven squares down, insert the needle three threads down, halfway across. Bring it out one up and right.

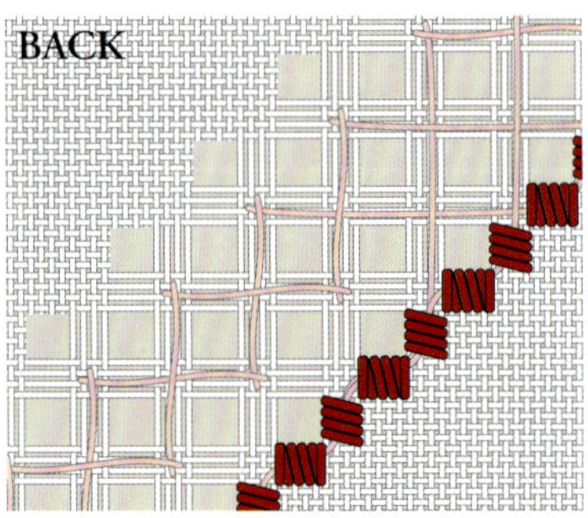

4 Build up two rows of strengthening threads around the edge of the stitching area. Anchor the ends of the thread in the satin stitch.

❶ *To start or finish a thread, secure it in the adjacent kloster blocks.*

❶ *The threads should lie taut on the back of the fabric, but not so tight that they pucker the fabric. Regularly lay your work on a flat surface to check the tension.*

stitching the edge

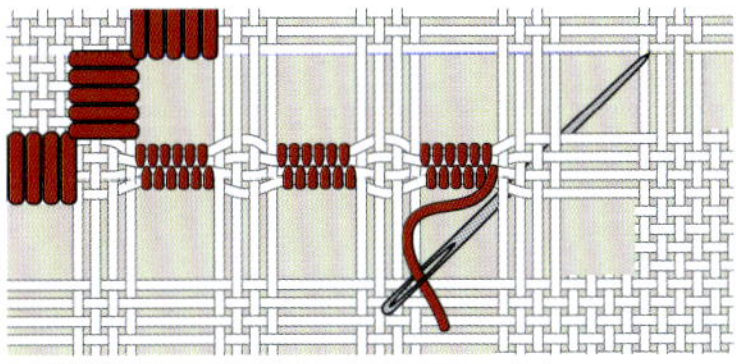

1 Weave the bars using the straight lines method, taking care to catch in the laced threads on the back into one side of the stitching, as you go. When you reach an outer corner, take the thread behind the woven square to the opposite corner.

❶ *The work has been turned 90° clockwise from when you were working on the front before.*

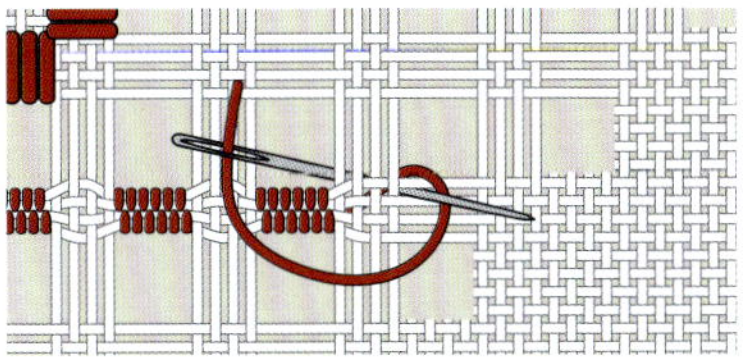

2 Pull the needle through. Insert the needle in the corner above left of the woven square, bringing it out between the top thread and the next one down the far side of the woven square. Take the thread behind the needle point from top to bottom.

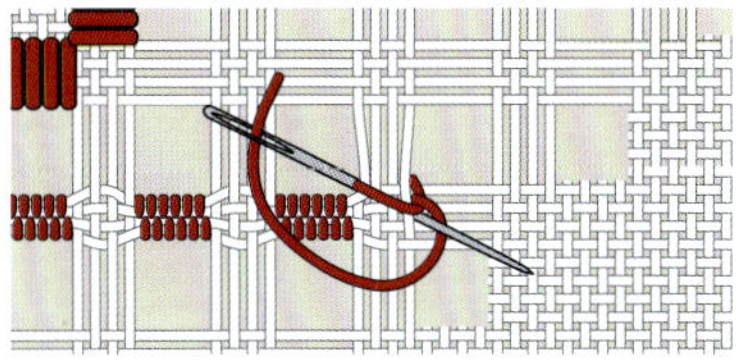

3 Pull the needle through and tighten the stitch so that it has gentle tension. Insert the needle in the inner corner, bringing it out one thread further down than the last stitch.

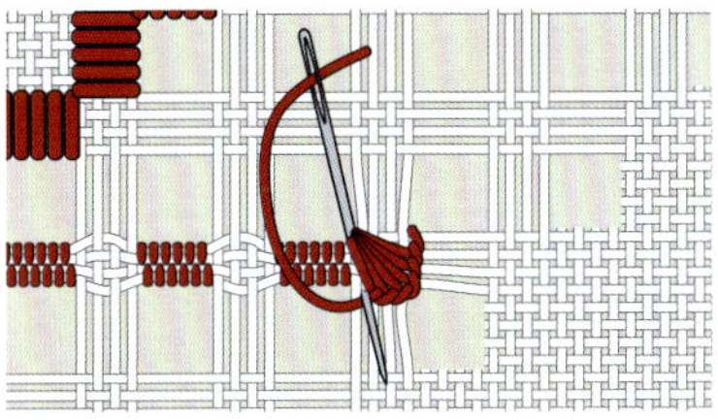

4 Working clockwise, continue working buttonhole stitches around the two outer edges of the woven square, pivoting in the inner corner. The last buttonhole stitch is between the last and second last threads around the edge.

❶ *Make sure the stitches sit next to each other at the inner corner and don't overlap.*

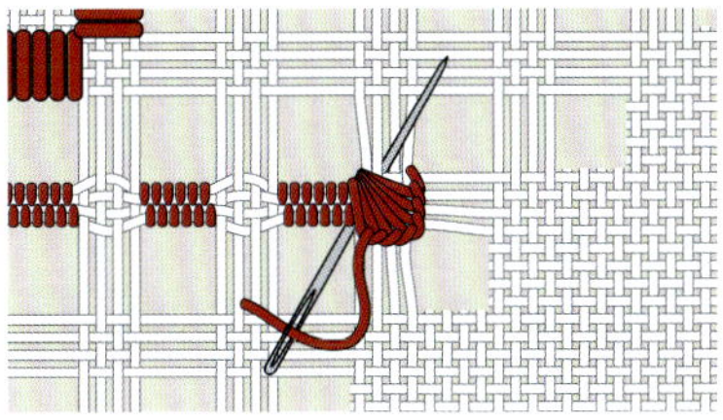

5 To finish the corner take the needle behind it and bring it out in the middle of the next bar, ready to begin weaving.

❶ *To be really neat here, turn the work over to the back and pass the needle through the back of the buttonhole stitches, then bring it out ready to weave the next bar.*

❶ *Around the outer edge of the corner there should be a stitch in between each of the fabric's threads. Do not skip any holes.*

❶ *For added strength, always stitch the buttonhole corner back towards the previously woven bar as this creates two stitches that pass diagonally behind the length of the corner to strengthen it. The corner will not be as strong if the buttonhole is stitched in the same direction as the needleweaving.*

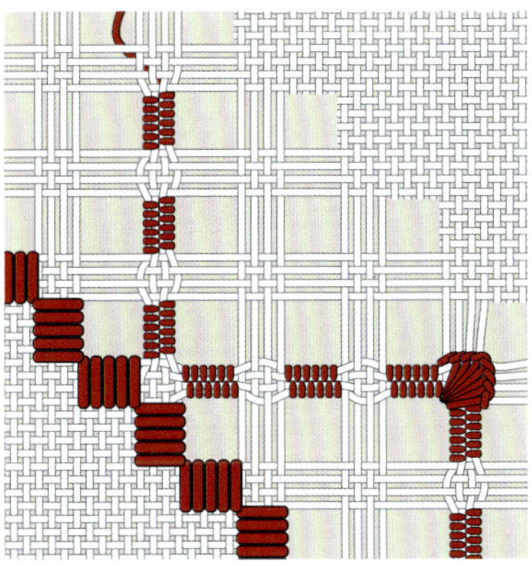

6 Weave bars back to the satin stitch, then turn the corner and work outward again.

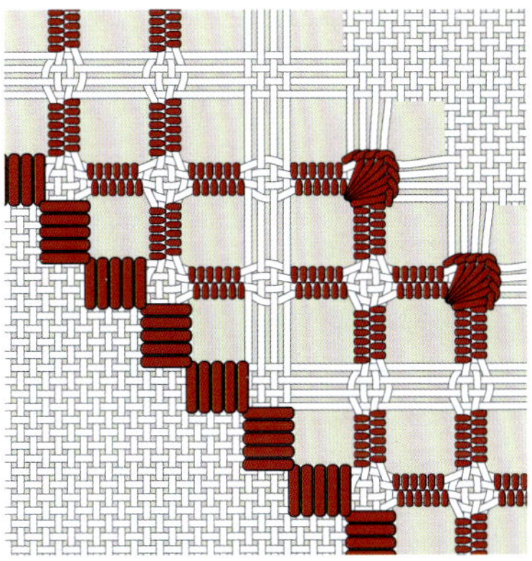

7 Continue weaving bars and buttonholing corners, according to your pattern. Use a new thread to work another row.

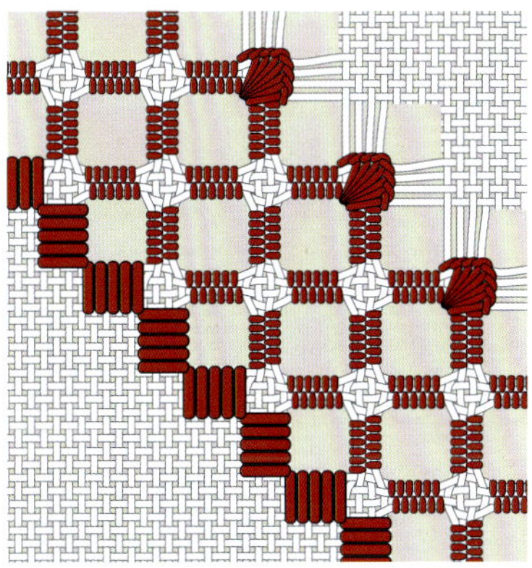

8 Work additional rows similarly.

Continued overleaf.

straight sides

When stitching a lacy buttonhole edge along a straight side, you will need to carefully plan your stitching order according to the shape of the edge. Draw a diagram and work out the order before you begin stitching. The buttonhole corners should be stitched as they are encountered. I like to work them pointing towards the outer edge.

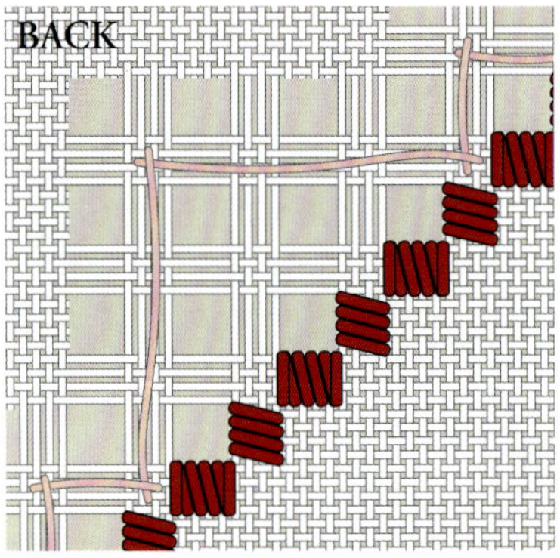

The diagram above shows a possible lacing solution for strengthening.

It is the outer corners that are the weakest point and therefore need the most strengthening.

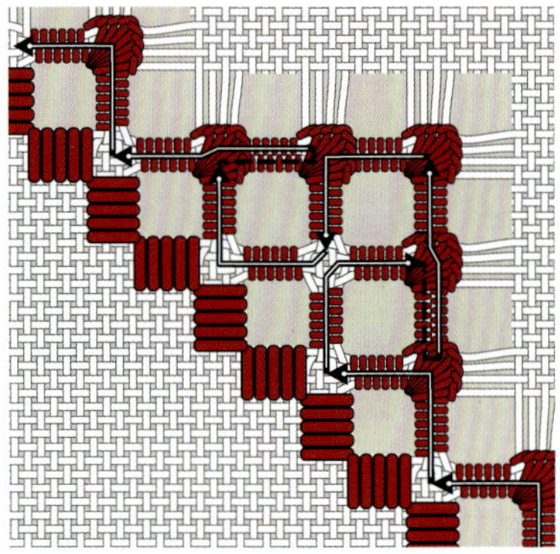

In the diagram above, the arrow lines show a possible stitching path.

The black and white arrow line shows the stitching path. The dotted black sections are laced along the back.

cutting out

Cutting a piece out of the fabric is the final step in Hardanger embroidery. When cutting a piece from the surrounding fabric, work slowly and with great care. As it is the final step, it would be a great pity to make a mistake!

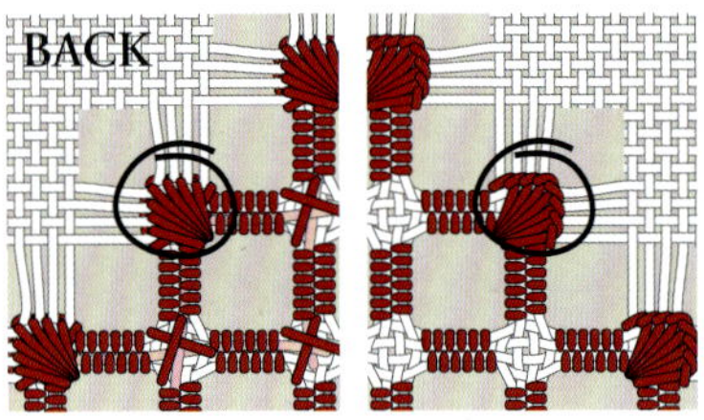

Always work from the back (shown left). If you work from the front (shown right) you will not be able to see where to cut because the rolled buttonhole edge obscure it. Always have the embroidery on the right and the scissors on the left. Scissor blades cut more closely when positioned this way (unless you are working with left-handed scissors, in which case they are the opposite).

Make sure your scissors have sharp blades. Blunt blades give a poor cut.

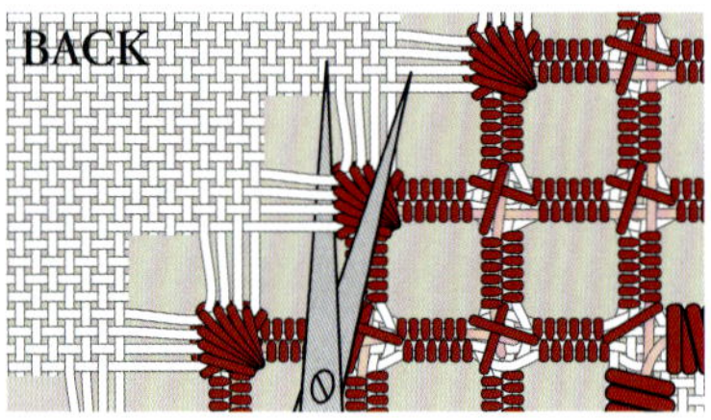

1 With the back of the work facing, slip the lower scissor point under a group of four threads. As you slide it in, position the lower blade so that it sits between the fabric threads and the rolled buttonhole edge below the fabric. Give the scissors a wiggle to see if any stitching is caught on the blade. When you are satisfied that all is well, return the point of the scissors to the surface and carefully snip through the four threads.

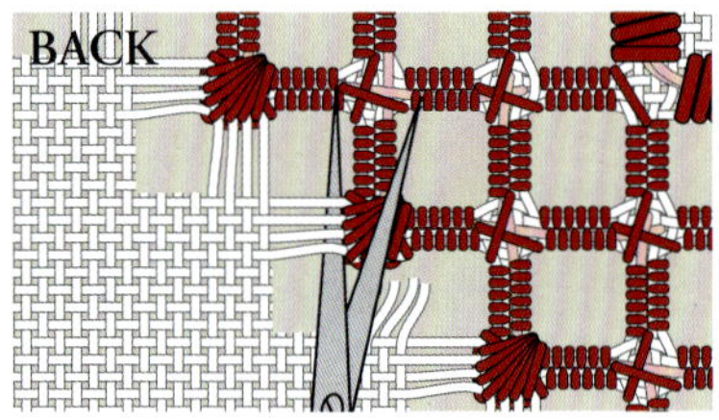

2 Turn the work and move to the next group of four threads and cut again.

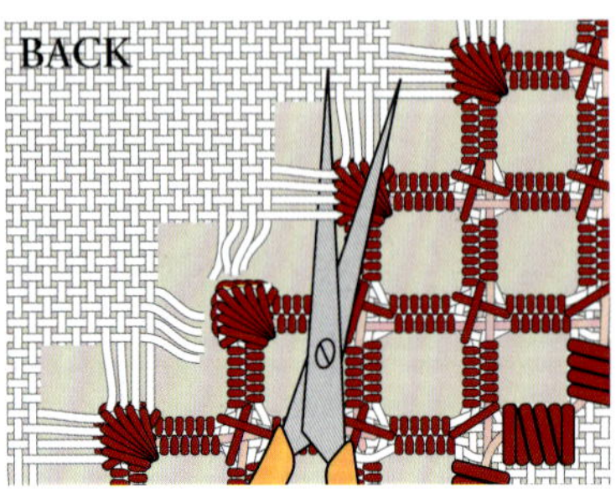

3 Continue slowly around the whole piece until it has all been cut from the surrounding fabric.

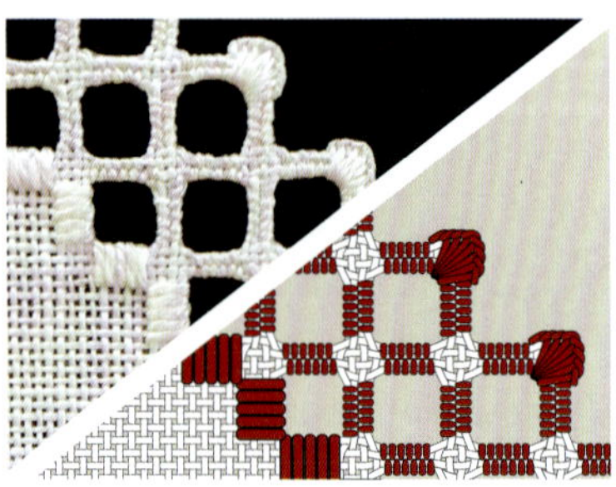

4 Turn back to the front for the final result.

top tip cutting out

Take your time!

It is very tempting to rush the cutting out to get it finished! Don't take the chance of spoiling all the hard work you have done by making a difficult to repair mistake, right at the end.

Go slowly and carefully.

lacy buttonhole edge

This delicate lacy edging is unstable, so therefore requires extra strengthening before stitching. The sample method uses three rows, but it can be worked with any number of rows.

cutting and withdrawing the threads

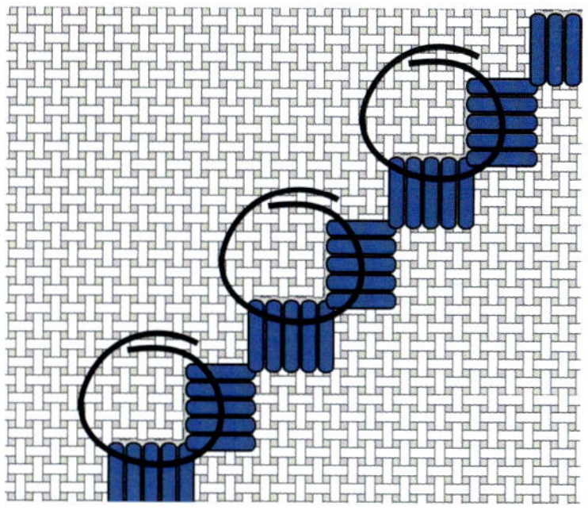

1 At the inner edge of where the lacy edge will be worked, there is a line of satin stitch blocks. Cut the threads along the outer edge of the satin stitch blocks.

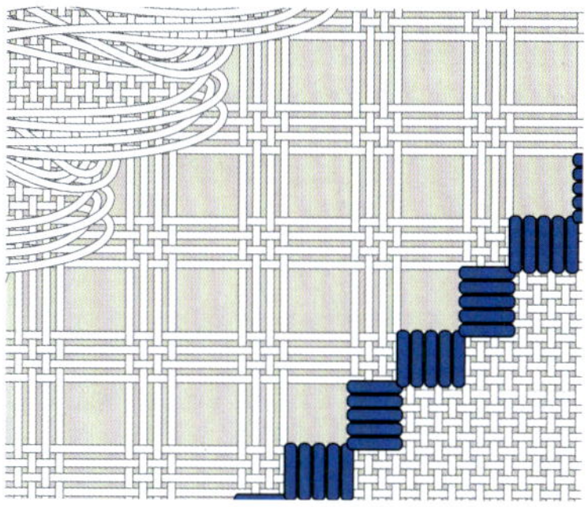

2 Carefully draw back the threads so that there are four rows of fabric threads for working on.

❶ *You will need four rows withdrawn for three rows of stitching.*

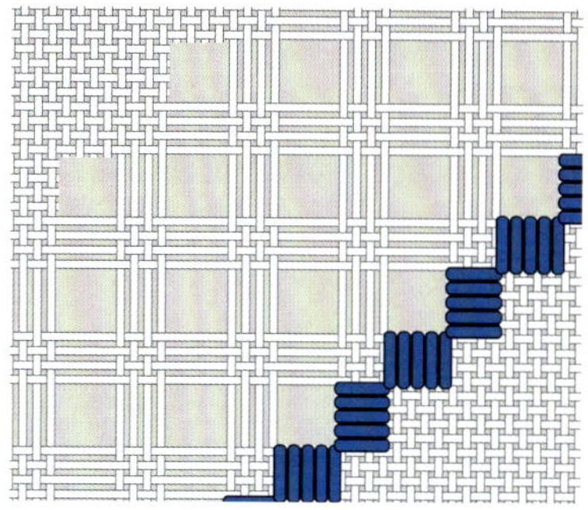

3 Trim the withdrawn threads at the edge of the cutwork area.

❶ *The more threads you remove, the more unstable the fabric becomes. Only remove what you're about to stitch over.*

lacing the back

The corners are weak as the cut threads are interwoven over only a very short distance. A web of threads laced across the back helps to strengthen them. Use thread that is a similar colour and thickness to the fabric. If an appropriate weight or colour is unavailable, use a thread from the side of the fabric.

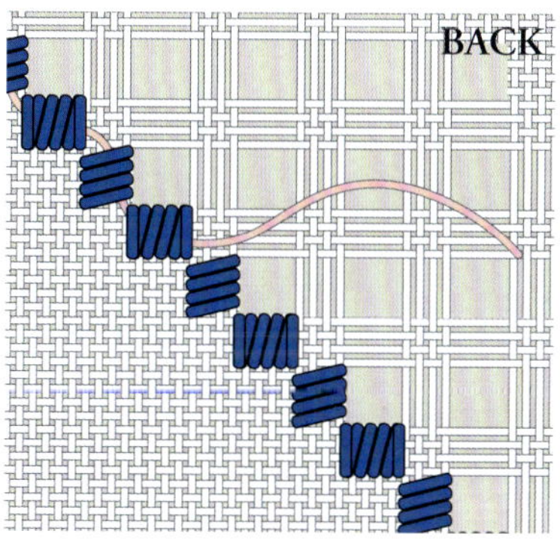

1 With the back of the work facing, fasten a long thread in the back of the satin stitch blocks.

❶ *Shown here as a different colour to the fabric for illustration purposes only.*

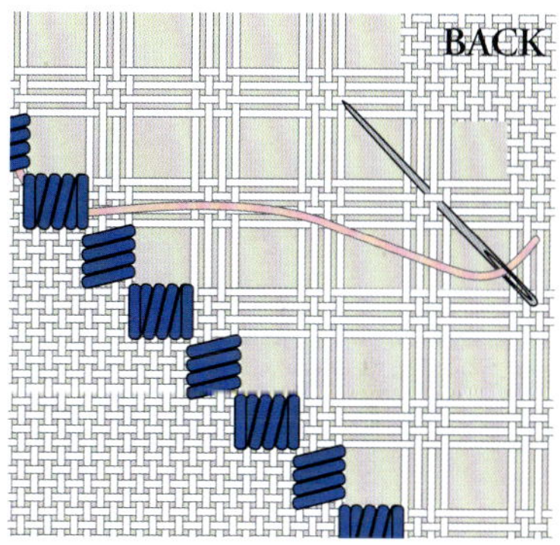

2 Count right four woven squares. In the fourth square, insert the needle three threads from the left and halfway up. Bring it out one thread up and left.

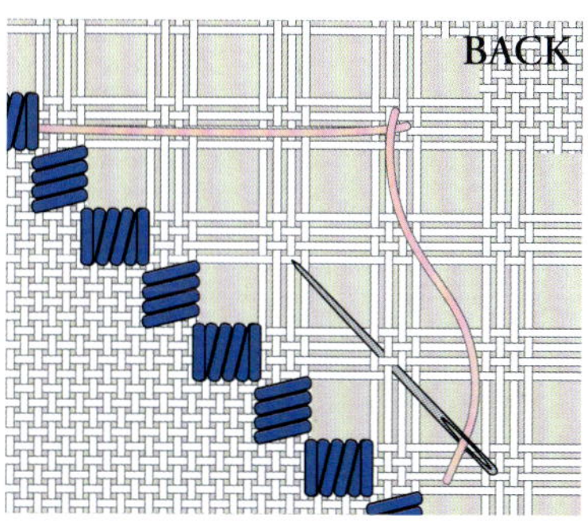

3 Pull the needle through. Two woven squares down, insert the needle three threads down, halfway across. Bring it out one up and left.

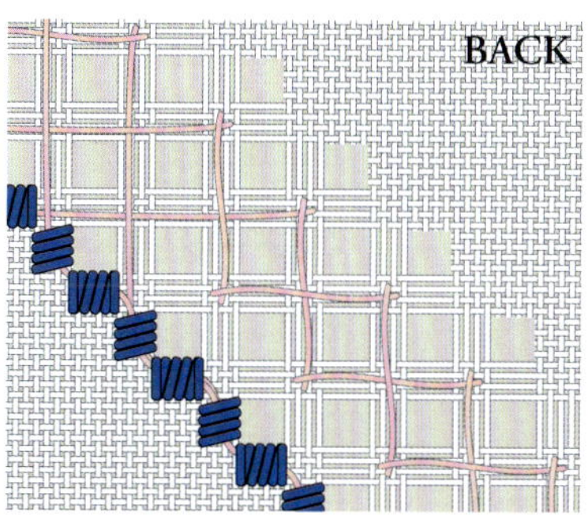

4 Build up two rows of strengthening threads around the edge of the stitching area. Anchor the ends of the thread in the satin stitch.

❶ *To start or finish a thread, secure it in the adjacent kloster blocks.*

❶ *The threads should lie taut on the back of the fabric, but not so tight that they pucker the fabric. Regularly lay your work on a flat surface to check the tension.*

Continued overleaf.

stitching the edge

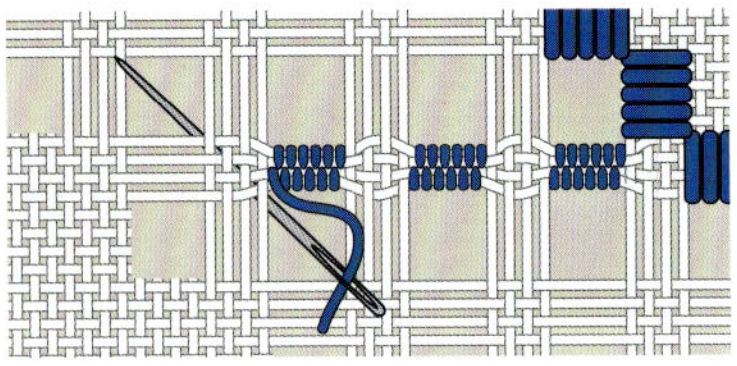

1 Weave the bars using the straight lines method, taking care to catch in the laced threads on the back into one side of the stitching, as you go. When you reach an outer corner, take the thread behind the woven square to the opposite corner.

❶ *The work has been turned 90° anticlockwise from when you were working on the front before.*

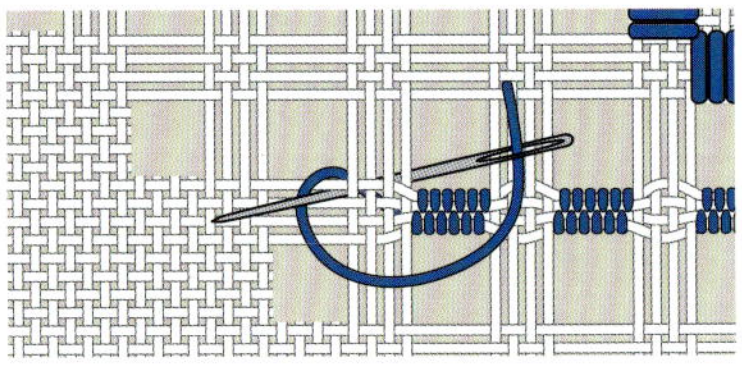

2 Pull the needle through. Insert the needle in the corner above right of the woven square, bringing it out between the top thread and the next one down the far side of the woven square. Take the thread behind the needle point from top to bottom.

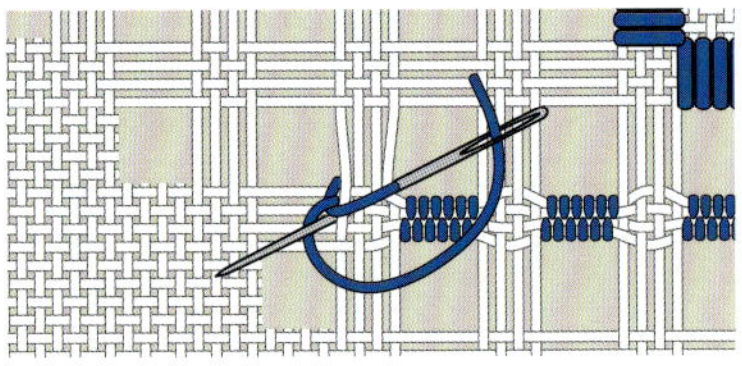

3 Pull the needle through and tighten the stitch so that it has gentle tension. Insert the needle in the inner corner, bringing it out one thread further down than the last stitch.

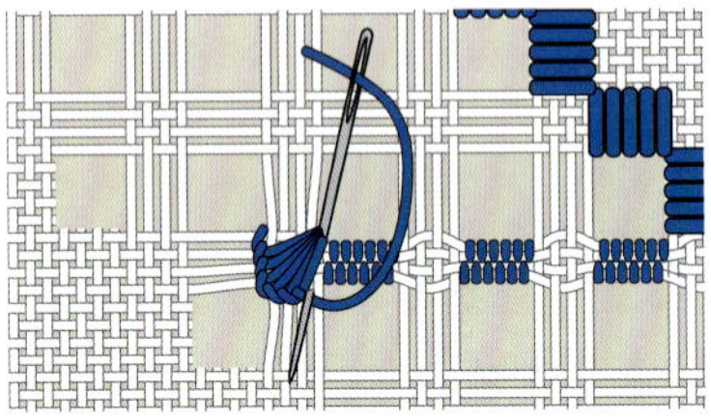

4 Working anticlockwise, continue working buttonhole stitches around the two outer edges of the woven square, pivoting in the inner corner. The last buttonhole stitch is between the last and second last threads around the edge.

❶ *Make sure the stitches sit next to each other at the inner corner and don't overlap.*

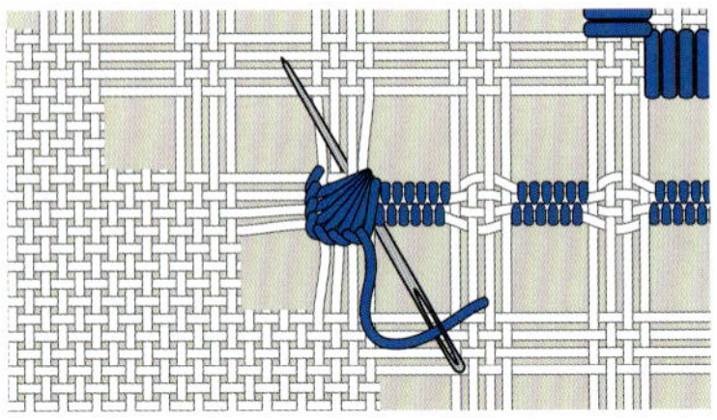

5 To finish the corner take the needle behind it and bring it out in the middle of the next bar, ready to begin weaving.

❶ *To be really neat here, turn the work over to the back and pass the needle through the back of the buttonhole stitches, then bring it out ready to weave the next bar.*

❶ *Around the outer edge of the corner there should be a stitch in between each of the fabric's threads. Do not skip any holes.*

❶ *For added strength, always stitch the buttonhole corner back towards the previously woven bar as this creates two stitches that pass diagonally behind the length of the corner to strengthen it. The corner will not be as strong if the buttonhole is stitched in the same direction as the needleweaving.*

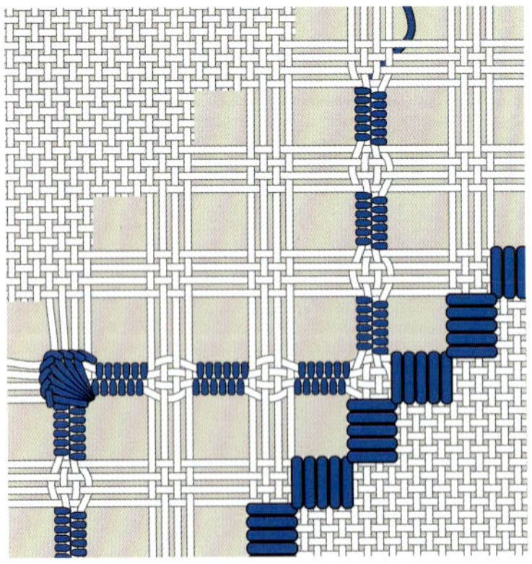

6 Weave bars back to the satin stitch, then turn the corner and work outward again.

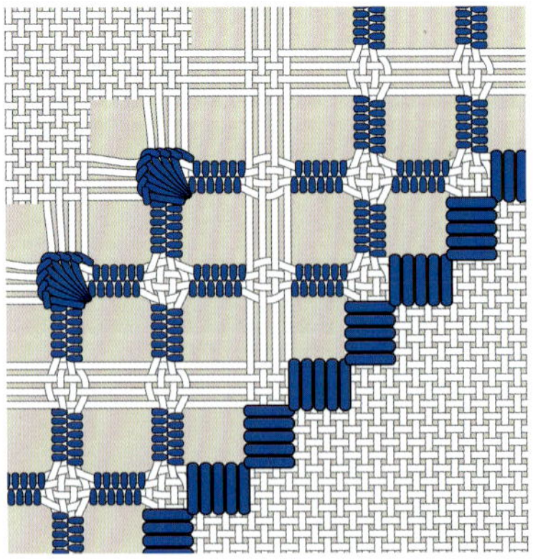

7 Continue weaving bars and buttonholing corners, according to your pattern. Use a new thread to work another row.

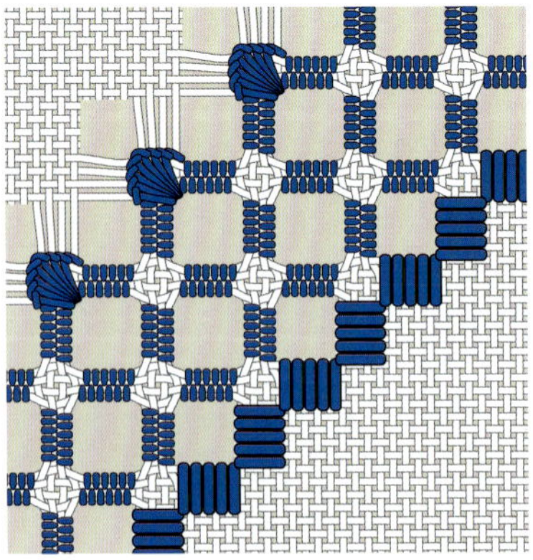

8 Work additional rows similarly.

straight sides

❶ *When stitching a lacy buttonhole edge along a straight side, you will need to carefully plan your stitching order according to the shape of the edge. Draw a diagram and work out the order before you begin stitching. The buttonhole corners should be stitched as they are encountered. I like to work them pointing towards the outer edge.*

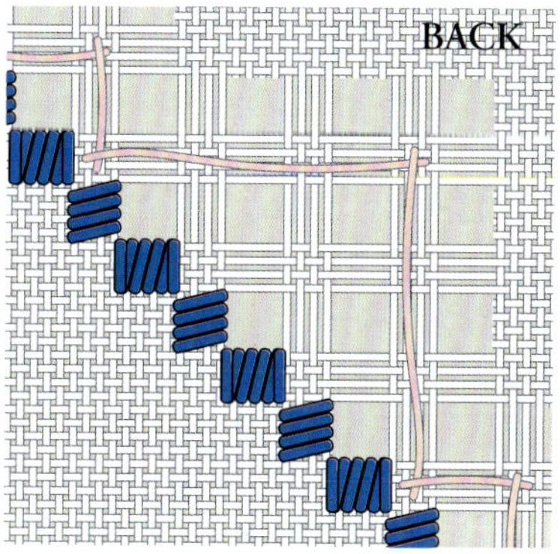

The diagram above shows a possible lacing solution for strengthening.

❶ *It is the outer corners that are the weakest point and therefore need the most strengthening.*

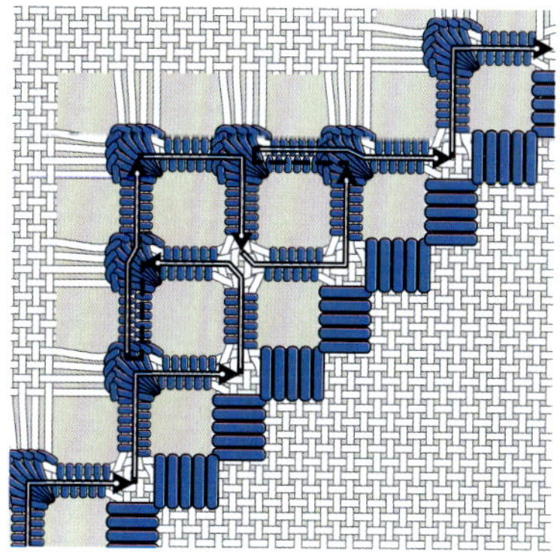

In the diagram above, the arrow lines show a possible stitching path.

❶ *The black and white arrow line shows the stitching path. The dotted black sections are laced along the back.*

cutting out

Cutting a piece out of the fabric is the final step in Hardanger embroidery. When cutting a piece from the surrounding fabric, work slowly and with great care. As it is the final step, it would be a great pity to make a mistake!

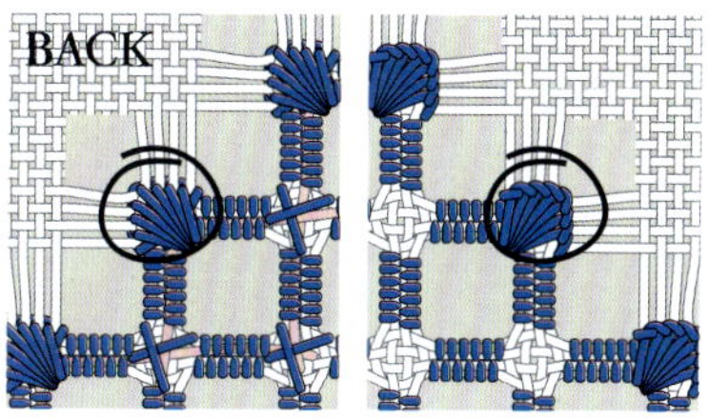

❶ *Always work from the back (shown left). If you work from the front (shown right) you will not be able to see where to cut because the rolled buttonhole edge obscure it. Always have the embroidery on the right and the scissors on the left, even though as a right-hander, this may feel awkward. Scissor blades cut more closely when positioned this way.*

❶ *Make sure you are using scissors with sharp blades. Blunt blades will give a poor cut.*

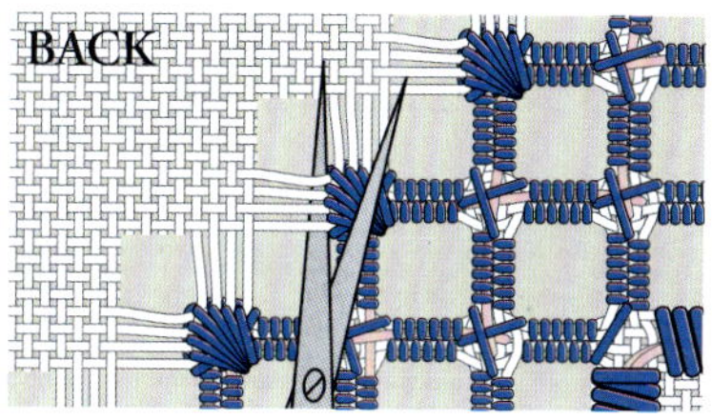

1 With the back of the work facing, slip the lower scissor point under a group of four threads. As you slide it in, position the lower blade so that it sits between the fabric threads and the rolled buttonhole edge below the fabric. Give the scissors a wiggle to see if any stitching is caught on the blade. When you are satisfied that all is well, return the point of the scissors to the surface and carefully snip through the four threads.

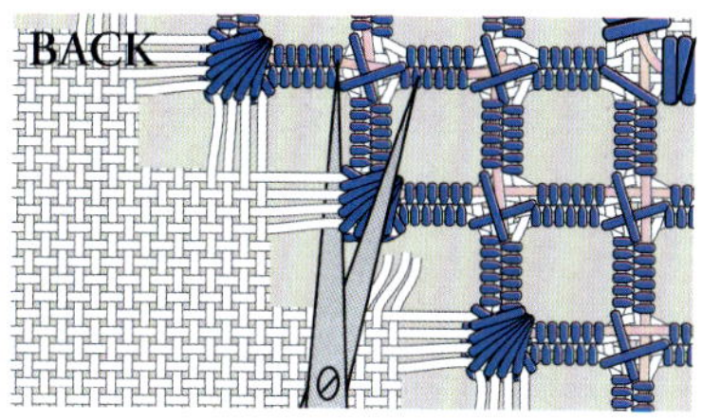

2 Turn the work and move to the next group of four threads and cut again.

❶ *Work slowly! It is very tempting to rush this final stage. Don't take the chance of spoiling all the hard work you have put in by making a difficult to repair mistake at this point.*

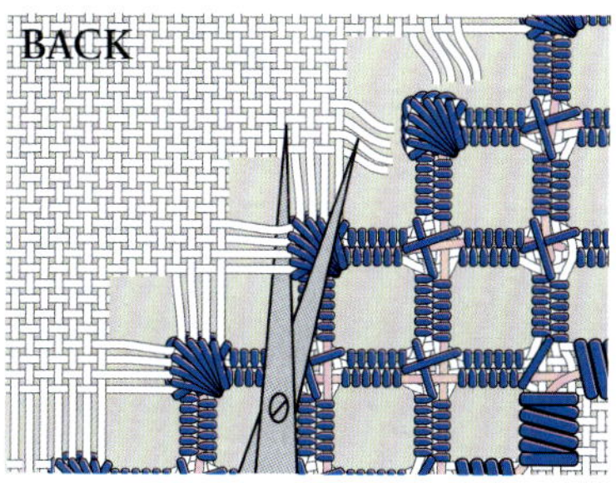

3 Continue slowly around the whole piece until it has all been cut from the surrounding fabric.

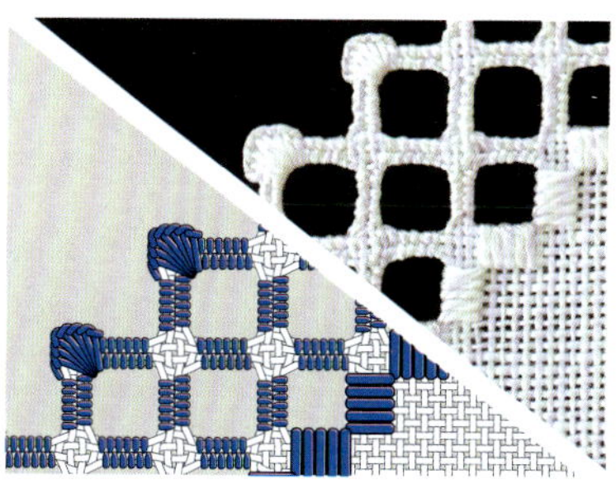

4 Turn back to the front for the final result.

top tip cutting out

Take your time!

It is very tempting to rush the cutting out to get it finished! Don't take the chance of spoiling all the hard work you have done by making a difficult to repair mistake, right at the end.

Go slowly and carefully.

sampler

This sampler was worked on 28 count linen to make it as accessible as possible to as many stitchers as possible. You could change the scale and work it with a higher or lower count if you wish. If you change the fabric count, you will also need to change the thread thicknesses, beads and needles accordingly.

size approx 64 x 30 cm / 25 x 12 in

design thread dimensions
296 (w) x 624 (h) threads

materials and equipment

- 75 cm (30 in) 28 count Vaupel and Heilenbeck Article 900/300 linen banding, off white
- 5 reels Londonderry linen thread, 30/3, ivory
- 5 reels Londonderry linen thread, 50/3, ivory
- Miyuki delica beads size 11/0, DB203; or Mill Hill seed beads, size 11, 03021
- No 24 tapestry needle
- No 26 tapestry needle
- sewing machine thread, pale colour, and to match fabric

❶ *A note on thread: I use linen thread as it was traditionally used for Hardanger. Its natural tendency to crease assists me when working pulled and drawn thread stitches, as when you crease the thread in place, it holds its tension better. You can use pearl cotton if preferred. You will need 2 balls each of Pearl 8 and Pearl 12, in DMC colour 712 to match the fabric.*

A small version of the chart showing the band numbers. The full chart is shown, in parts, much larger, on following pages. It is put together as shown above, with the greyed sections indicating an overlap.

preparation

1 Zig-zag, overcast, overlock or serge the ends of the fabric to prevent fraying as you stitch.

2 Fold the fabric in half along the length of the fabric. From the top end of the fabric, measure 8 cm (3 in) down the centre fold. Mark with a pin.

3 Using a long length of pale coloured sewing machine thread, bring the needle out at the pin and tack (baste) over and under groups of four threads to the bottom of the fabric. Secure the ends with a few back stitches.

4 With a new thread, insert the needle at the bottom of the top tacked stitch. Leaving a tail at the centre, tack under and over groups of four threads, out to the right edge of the fabric. Thread the tail into the needle and work over and under groups of four threads out to the left edge of the fabric. Secure the ends with a few back stitches.

5 Count down nine groups of four threads (36 threads). At the end of the ninth group, repeat the tacking across.

❶ *Each of these horizontal lines of tacking will be at the top of a line of four-sided stitch.*

6 Repeat this tacking 17 groups of four (68 threads) further down. Then nine groups (36 threads), 29 groups (116 threads), nine groups (36 threads), 19 groups (76 threads), nine groups (36 threads), 45 groups (180 threads), and then nine groups (36 threads).

7 You can also repeat the vertical line of tacking down the sides of the stitching area, if desired. Count 37 groups of four (148 threads) out to either side of the centre line and work a vertical line of tacking.

foundation embroidery

❶ *Follow the chart for stitch placement. Do not make assumptions about the size or placement of motifs.*

❶ *All satin stitch is worked using the 30/3 thread. All other stitching is worked in the 50/3 thread. Any exceptions to this are clearly marked. The fillings are worked after all the other stitching has been completed.*

❶ *Use the No 24 tapestry needle for the foundation embroidery.*

band 1 Work the satin stitch squares (p *22*, **23**), the end blocks, and stepped triangles (p *24*, **25**), taking care to position all satin stitch near the ends correctly. There is altered positioning to get them to align with the sides neatly. Work the four-sided stitch (p *30*, **31**) above and below the band.

band 2 Work the satin stitch (p *16*, **18**) diamond motifs, starting with the middle one and working outward. Work the cable stitch (p *28*, **29**) between the diamonds. Work the satin stitch half-stars (p *26*, **27**) at the top and bottom edges of the band. Nestle the eyelets (p *32*, **33**) around the stars.

band 3 Work as for Band 1.

band 4 Work the satin stitch star in the centre of the band. Moving out, work the cable stitch diamond. Work the satin stitch inner and outer edge of the centre diamond and the side diamonds. Work the remaining cable stitch. Work the satin stitch stars in the side diamonds. Satin stitch the triangular motifs at the band's top and bottom edges. Work the eyelets near the stars.

band 5 Work as for Band 1.

band 6 Work the satin stitch diamond in the centre. Work the cable stitch lines near the top and the bottom edges of the band. Nestle the satin stitch diamonds and part diamonds in the spaces created by the cable stitch. Work the eyelets between the cable stitch and the diamonds.

band 7 Work as for Band 1.

band 8 Work the diamond of stepped satin stitch triangles in the centre. Work the cable stitch around it. Work the two satin stitch diamonds around that. Work the inner and outer adjacent cable stitch. Work the part repeats of the whole central motif at the sides. Work the diagonal lines of diamonds made from stepped satin stitch triangles, nestled in the spaces at the top and bottom edges of the band. Work the cable stitch, then the satin stitch half-

3
4
5

Bands 1 to 4

stars. Work the eyelets nestled around the half-stars, and on either side of the lines of stepped triangle diamonds.

band 9 Work as for Band 1.

filling stitches

❶ *On the chart, the areas where threads are removed are shown in grey. Cut and withdraw the threads in each cutwork area just before stitching, to destabilise the fabric as little as possible.*

❶ *Stitch instruction page references are italic for left-handers and bold for right-handers. Those for both are regular font.*

❶ *On the stitching order diagrams, purple paths are for all stitchers. Red is for left-handers, and blue is for right-handers. Where there is a dot, start there and work from light to dark along the path. Where there is no dot, start as directed and progress from light to dark.*

❶ *Use the No 24 tapestry needle for everything except the beading. Change to the No 26 for adding the beads.*

band 1

Cutting Cut and withdraw all but the middle four threads in each square.

Stitching A: Rosette (p *86*, **88**). B: Woven bars (p *44*, **48**), wide woven petals (p *74*, 75). C: Edelweiss, worked with 30/3 thread (p *236*, **238**). D: Festoon stitch (p *226*, **228**).

band 2

Cutting Cut and withdraw all the threads that meet the

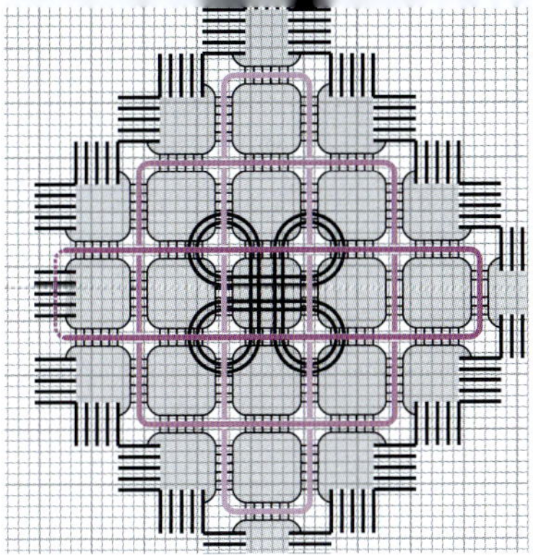

Band 2, A *Left-handers start in top left of each path. Right-handers start in bottom right of each path.*

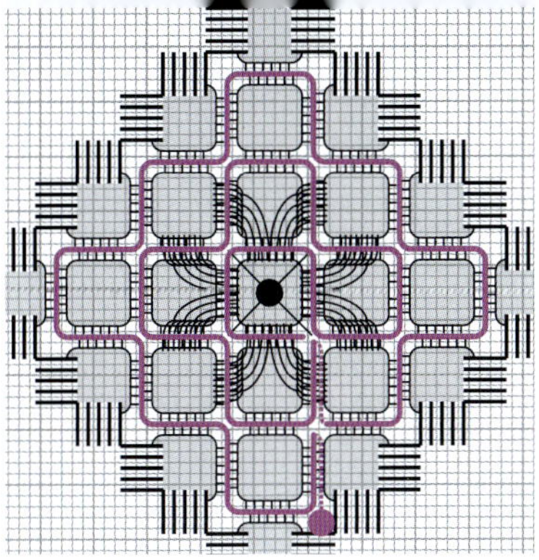

Band 2, B *Dotted lines indicate lacing behind. Left-handers turn the diagram 180°.*

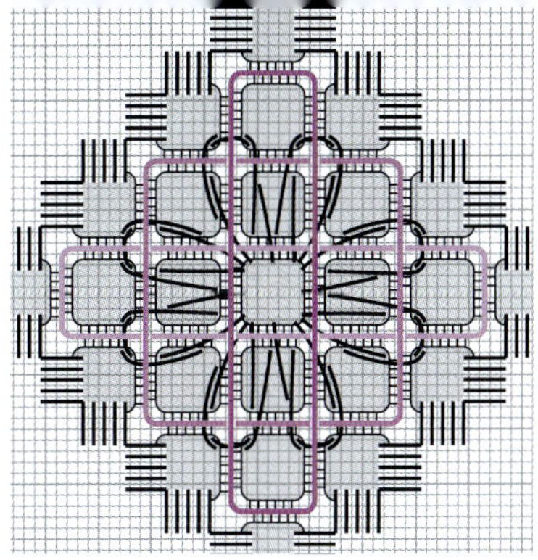

Band 2, C *Left-handers start in bottom left of each path. Right-handers start in bottom right of each path.*

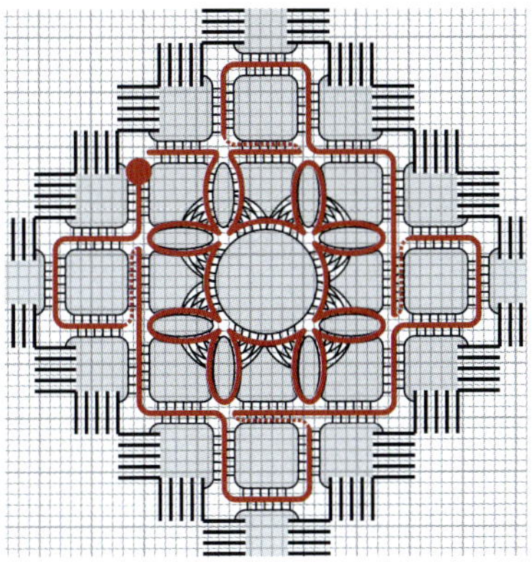

Band 2, D *Dotted lines indicate lacing behind.*

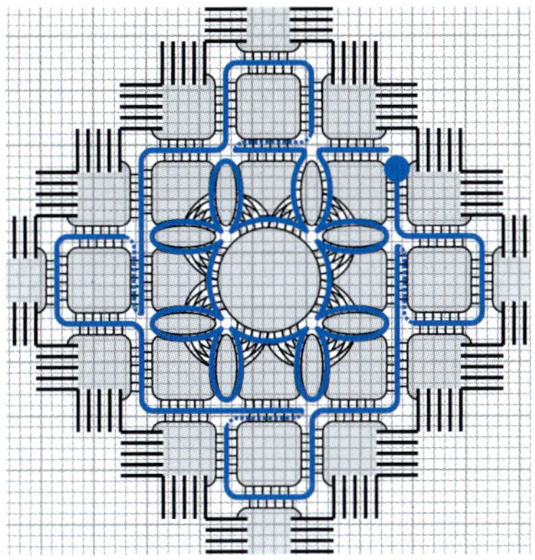

Band 2, D *Dotted lines indicate lacing behind.*

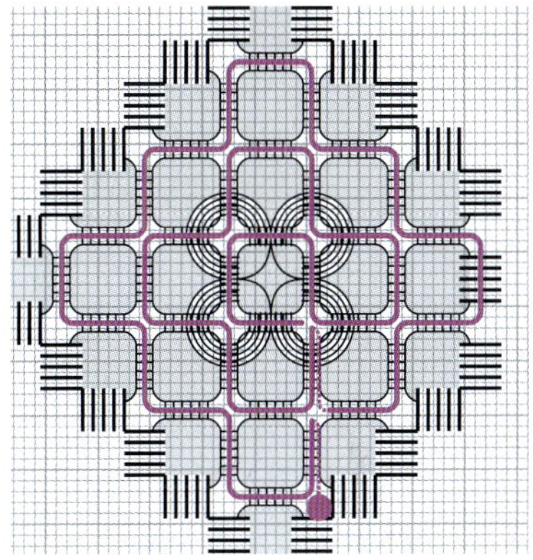

Band 2, E *Dotted lines indicate lacing behind. Left-handers turn the diagram 180°.*

ends of the satin stitches, within the diamonds.

Stitching Use the stitching order diagrams, above, for the cutwork areas. A: Wrapped bars (p *52*, **56**) with Drunkard's path (p *222*, **224**) in the centre. B: Woven bars (p *46*, **50**) with Blanket stitch flower (p *196*, **199**) in the centre. C: Woven bars (p *44*, **48**) with Lacy daisy (p *252*, **254**) in the centre. D: Woven bars (p *46*, **50**) with a Greek cross circlet (p *142*, **143**) in the centre. E: Wrapped bars (p *54*, **58**) with a Three quarter spider web flower (p *178*, **180**) in the centre.

band 3

Cutting Cut and withdraw all but the middle four threads in each square, except for D. For D, on each side leave two, cut six, leave four, cut six, leave two.

Stitching A: Dove's eye cobweb (p *102*, **104**). B: Whipped spider web (p *176*, **177**). C: Ribbed spider web (p *174*, **175**). D: Greek quarter crosses (p *134*, **136**) worked as shown in the stitching order diagram, right.

band 4

Cutting Cut and remove all threads in A, D, H and K. Cut and withdraw the middle four threads in B, C, I and J. Cut and withdraw according to the cutting diagram for E and G (see next page). Cut and withdraw all the threads that meet the ends of satin stitches in F.

Stitching A: Double twist square filet (p *116*, **117**). B: Corner eyelets with full-width bars (p *208*, **209**). C: Corner eyelets with square filet (p *210*, **212**). D: Dove's eye with cross (p *98*, **100**). E: Wrapped grouped zig-zagging line (p *66*). F: Simplified eyelets at intersections (p *216*, **217**) and a mix of Greek cross variations (p *134*, **136**). Follow the stitching order diagram (see next page) and make use of the 'extra' stitch (p *135*, **137**) where needed. Note the placement of simplified eyelets on some, but not all, intersections. G: Woven grouped zig-zagging line (p *64*). H: Dove's eye with cross (p *98*, **100**). I: Corner eyelets (p *210*, **212**) with dove's eye (p *92*, **94**). J: Corner eyelets (p *210*, **212**) with spider web (p *168*, **169**). K: Double twist square filet (p *116*, **117**).

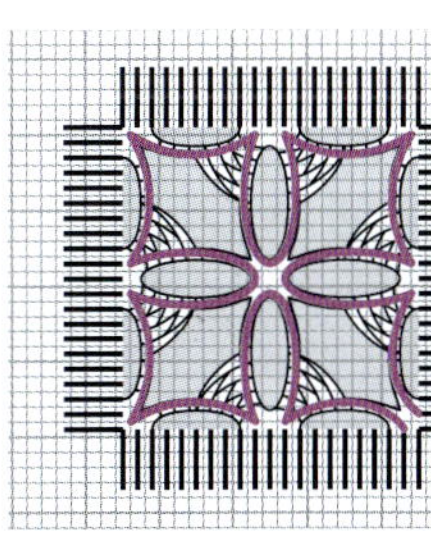

Band 3, D *Left-handers turn the diagram 180°.*

band 5

Cutting Cut and withdraw all but the middle four threads in each square.

Stitching A: Buttonhole arcs with twisted spokes (p *186*, **188**). B: Buttonholed petals (p *190*, **192**). C: Buttonholed petals (p *190*, **192**) with inverse twisted Ys (p *82*, **84**). D: Queen Anne's lace (p *240*, **243**).

Band 4, E and G Cut at the purple lines. Withdraw the threads between the cuts. Turn 180° for Band 4, G.

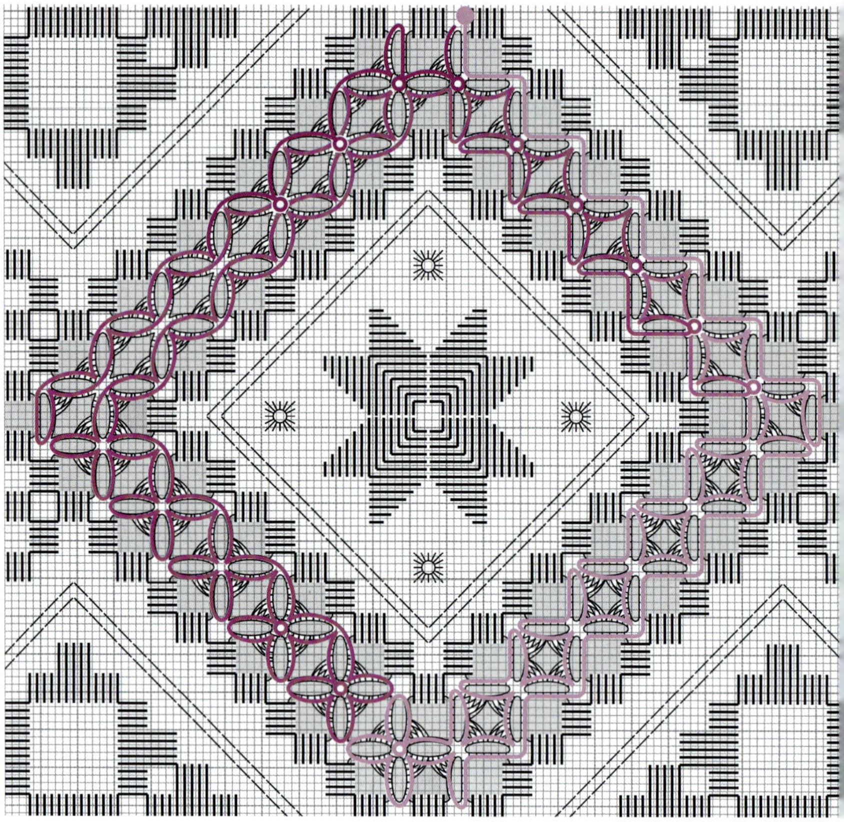

▶ *Band 4, F Don't forget to work the eyelets on the last pass through their intersections!*

band 6

Cutting Cut and withdraw all the threads that meet the ends of the satin stitches within the cutwork areas.

Stitching A: Wrapped bars (p *54*, **58**). B: Woven bars (p *46*, **50**) with side-on bead picots (p *132*, **133**). C: Woven bars (p *46*, **50**) with end-on bead picots (p *132*, **133**). D: As for A. E: Work half the Woven bar (p *44*, **48**) then work Twisted Ys (p *80*, **81**) out to the corners on each side of the bar. Complete the bar. F: Woven bars (p *44*, **48**), Dove's eyes (p *92*, **94**), Beaded diamonds (p *118*, **119**), Looped picots (p *126*, **127**), and Buttonhole eyelets at intersections (p *218*, **219**). Follow the stitching order diagram below. G: Woven bars (p *44*, **48**), Nutmeg stitch (p *120*, **121**), Knotted picots (p *122*, **124**), and Simplified eyelets at intersections (p *216*, **217**). Follow the stitching order diagrams below. H: Woven bars (p *44*, **48**), Beaded square (p *118*, **119**), Square filet (p *114*, **115**), Chain stitch picots (p *130*, **131**), Buttonhole eyelet at intersections (p *218*, **219**). Follow the stitching order diagrams on the opposite page. I: As for E. J: As for A. K: Woven bars (p *46*, **50**) with end-on bead picots (p *132*, **133**). L: Woven bars (p *46*, **50**) with side-on bead picots (p *132*, **133**). M: As for A.

band 7

Cutting A: Cut and withdraw all but the middle four threads. B, C and D: On each side, cut four, leave four, cut four, leave four, cut four. Withdraw the cut threads.

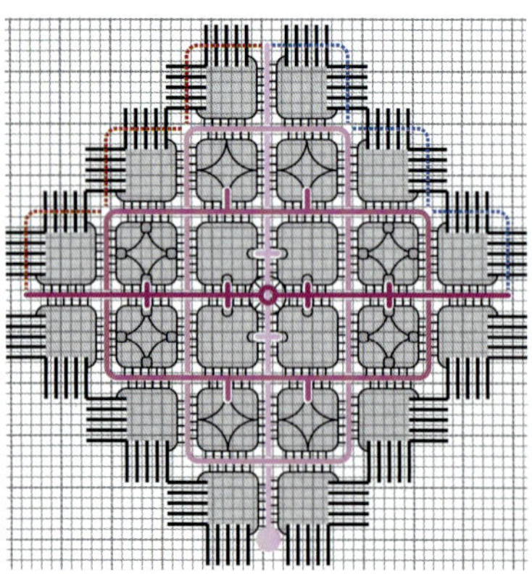

Band 6, F The path indicates when fillings are added. Left-handers work circuits anticlockwise. Right-handers go clockwise.

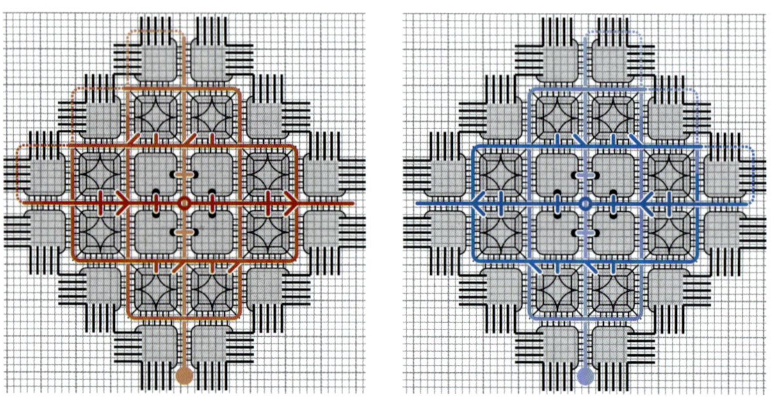

Band 6, G The path indicates when fillings are added.

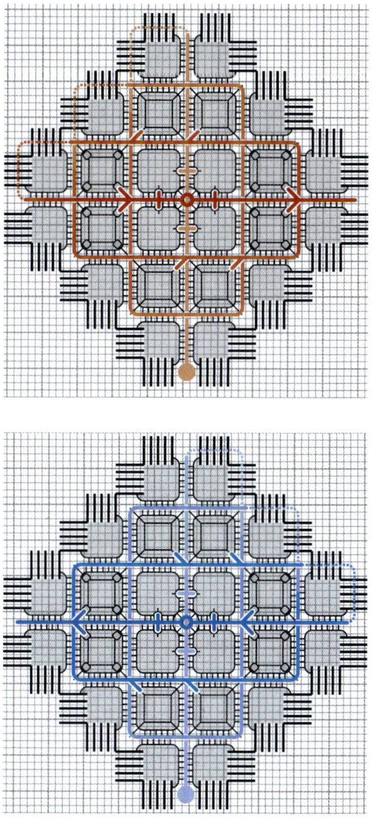

Band 6, H The path indicates when fillings are added.

Stitching A: Wrapped divided bars (p *69*, **71**) with Dove's eyes (p *92*, **94**). B: Wrapped bars (p *54*, **58**), Dove's eye in a wrapped circle (p *106*, **108**). Follow the stitching order diagrams below. C: Buttonhole stitch with dove's eye (p *206*, **207**). D: Use the centre of Dove's eye in a wrapped circle (p *106*, **108**), with Greek quarter crosses (p *134*, **136**). Follow the stitching order diagrams below.

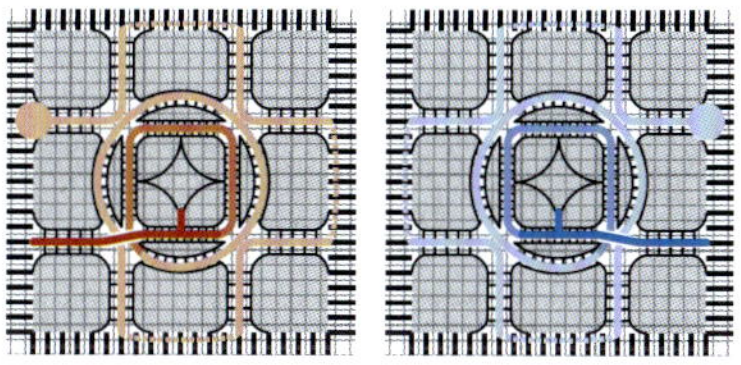

Band 7, B

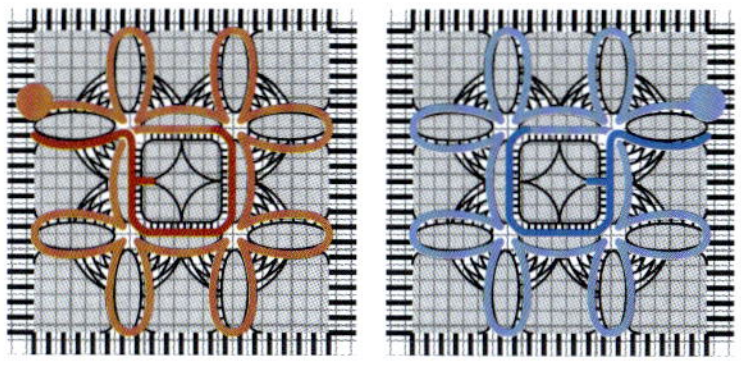

Band 7, D

Bands 5 to 9

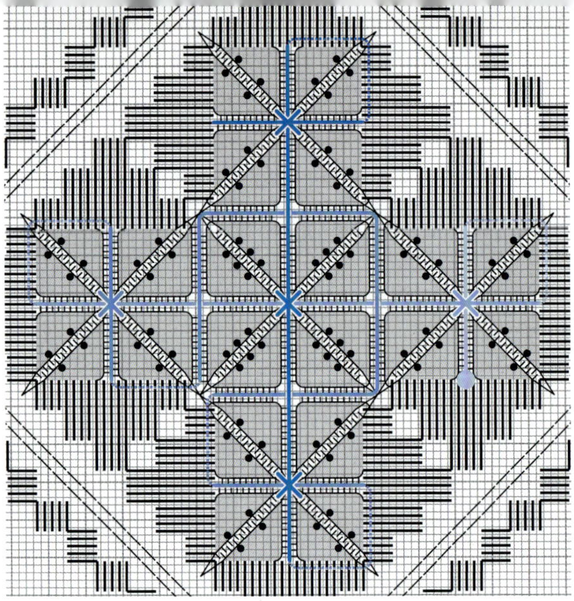

***Band 8, Q** The path indicates when fillings are added.*

band 8

Cutting A, B, C, E, F, G, H, I, J, K, M, N, S, T, U, W, Y, Z, BB, DD, EE, FF: Cut and withdraw all but the middle four threads in each square. D, L, V, CC: Cut and remove all threads. X, AA: Cut and withdraw the four middle threads in each square. O, P, Q, R: Cut and withdraw all the threads that meet the ends of the satin stitches within the cutwork areas.

Stitching A: Woven fan with two spokes (p *150*, **152**). B: Diamond filling (p *220*, **221**). C: Wrapped divided bars (p *69*, **71**). D: Ringed crossed dove's eye (p *112*, **113**). E: Buttonhole circle (p *183*, **185**) with picots (p *191*, **193**). F: Curled V with no twist (p *90*, **91**). G: Greek eighth cross (p *138*, **139**). H: Curled V in a fan (p *166*, **167**). I: Curled V with single twist (p *90*, **91**). J: Greek cross (p *135*, **137**). K: Heavy Greek cross (p *144*, **145**). L: Flower filling (p *230*, **231**). M: Curled V with double twist (p *90*, **91**). N: Woven fan with three spokes (p *154*, **156**). O: Woven bars (p *44*, **48**), Twisted Ys (p *80*, **81**), Woven spider web in a single square (p *168*, **169**). Work this cutwork area in two zig-zagging lines along its length: the left line and the right line. Work the right line first, so that the arms of the twisted Ys have something to be worked into when working the second line. P: Wrapped bars (p *54*, **58**), Woven bars (p *46*, **50**) and Simplified eyelet at intersections (p *216*, **217**). Work the outer line of woven bars first. Then work the inner line of wrapped bars, with simplified eyelets at the intersections between the woven and wrapped bars. Q: Woven bars (p *44*, **48**), Woven diagonals (p *72*, **73**), and Knotted picots (p *122*, **124**). Follow the stitching order diagrams above. R: Woven bars (p *46*, **50**), Triangular dove's eyes (p *96*, **97**), Woven spider web with three spokes (p *170*, **171**). Work this cutwork area in two zig-zagging lines along its length: the left line and the right line. Work the left line first, so that the arms of the filling stitches have something to be worked into when working the second line. S: Inverse woven fan (p *164*, **165**). T: Dove's eyes with wrapped bars (p *110*, **111**). U: Buttonhole circle (p *183*, **185**). V: Enclosed square filet (p *116*, **117**). W: Wrapped bars (p *52*, **56**) with Chain stitch flower (p *250*, **251**). X: Reverse Greek cross (p *135*, **137**). Y: Soleil stitch (p *256*, **258**) with a ray between each satin stitch. Z: Woven quarter fan (p *162*, **163**). AA: Corner eyelets with divided wrapped bars (p *214*, **215**). BB: Twisted Ys (p *80*, **81**) with wrapped divided bars (p *69*, **71**). CC: Double twist square filet (p *116*, **117**). DD: Wrapped bars (p *52*, **56**) with bullion flower (p *246*, **248**). EE: Soleil stitch (p *256*, **258**). FF: Maltese flower (p *146*, **148**).

band 9

Cutting Cut and withdraw all but the middle four threads in each square.

Stitching A: Woven spider web (p *172*, **173**). B: Stepped fan (p *158*, **160**). C: Wheel filling (p *232*, **234**). D: Woven bars (p *44*, **48**), Woven petals (p *72*, **73**).

finishing

1 Measure 5 cm (2 in) from the end of the stitching at each end. Trim the fabric at this point.

2 With the back facing, fold 1 cm (⅜ in) in, and then another 1 cm (⅜ in), at each end.

3 Using machine sewing thread to match the fabric, sew a hem 2 mm (1/16 in) from the inside edge of the hem.

❶ *If you don't have a sewing machine, you can neatly whip stitch the hems, or alternatively, decoratively hemstitch them.*

4 Remove any tacking.

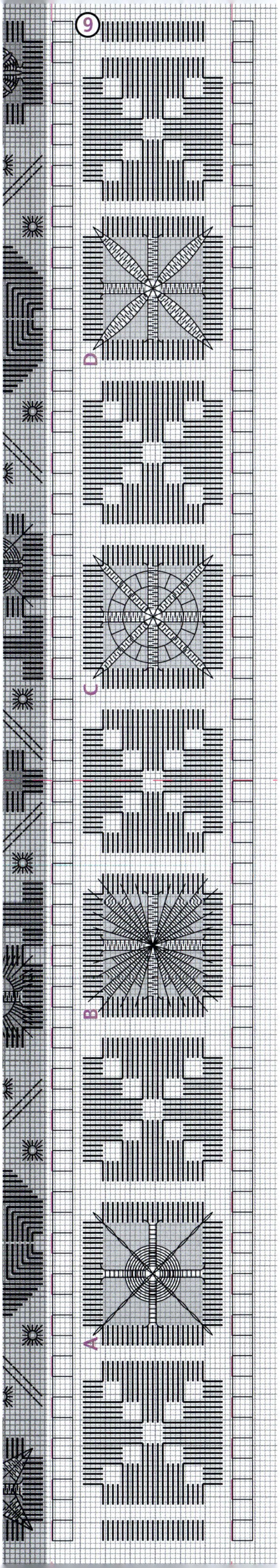

appendix: decoding fillings

Sometimes you will see a filling that you want to make, but you cannot find instructions, or the instructions you can find are not helpful. So, what can you do?

While researching this book I saw stitch instructions that were not very helpful. Some had a finished example and just one diagram showing the stitch part way through. Some had cursory text accompanying them. Often these motifs were found in very old, out-of-print, copyright-expired books. There just wasn't enough information provided. In these cases, you need a plan of attack.

combine and adapt instructions

The illustration shown right is from Therese de Dillmont's *Openwork Embroidery*, which is out of copyright. By putting together the instructions for wrapped bars (p *52*, **56**), twisted spokes (p *76*, 77), woven fans with three spokes (p *154*, **156**) and wheel filling (p *232*, **234**), this motif could be created. Experimentation would still be needed to get it right, but using the knowledge of those motifs, one could create this motif.

The motif shown right uses unusual placement of bars within a satin stitch square, and different types of buttonholed arcs. It is unusual to have woven bars (p *44*, **48**) right at the edge of the motif, and the satin stitch has been positioned in a particular way to accommodate it. In the corners are buttonhole arcs (p *182*, **184**), and buttonholed petals (p *190*, **192**) are worked beside the centre axes.

use what you know and experiment

This illustration is from Therese de Dillmont's *Hardanger Embroideries. Series 1*, which is out of copyright. The project provided this photograph and the instructions "do the little rosettes that ornament the openwork..." There are no instructions provided elsewhere in the book for this stitch. Fortunately, I knew how to do lacy daisy (p *252*, **254**), but if I hadn't, then I would have had to make observations and then experiment with a needle and thread.

Firstly, I would have noted that it uses thick thread, as is used for the satin stitch (or thicker!). I then would have set up a cutwork mesh of threads on my fabric, and set about trying to create the same look.

Decoding, understanding and reproducing filling stitches takes time and practice. When I was working out stitching methods for this book, the first try was never the only try! For example, for diagonal stitches, I might try a single stitch to wrap, triple stitches to wrap or weave, multiple stitches to wrap or weave, or a twisted stitch, to see what worked best. I would try many variations until I was satisfied that I had achieved the best result.

When trying to figure out something new, you likely won't get it right the first time, but keep trying until you do!

filling stitch pictorial index

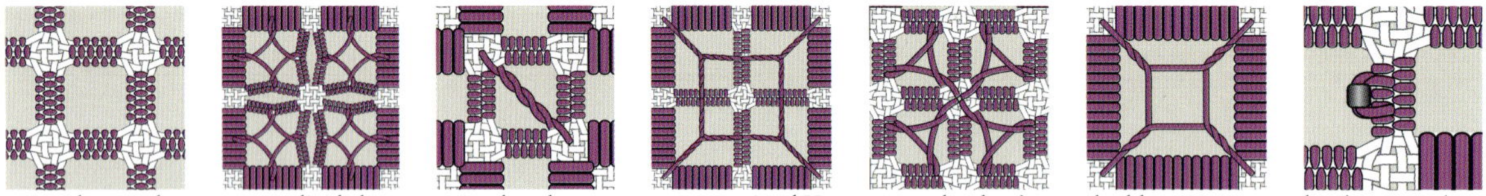

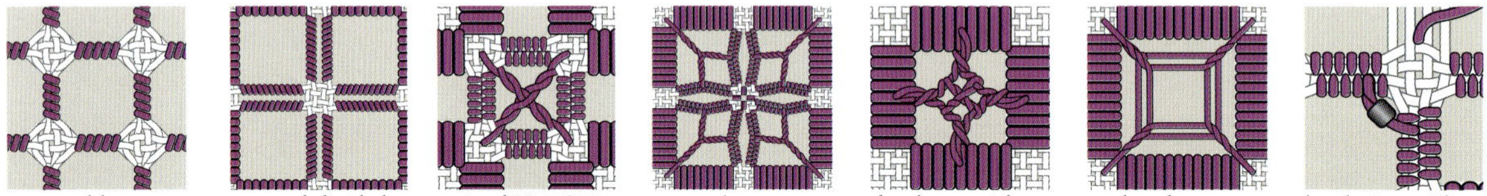

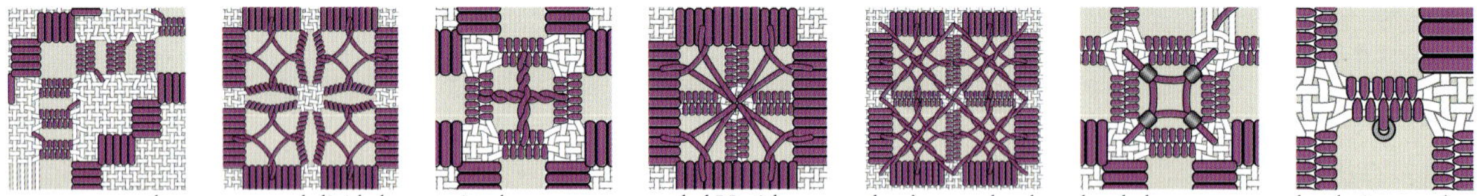

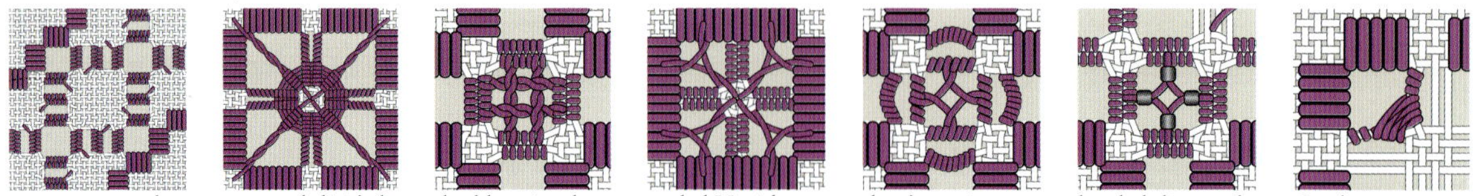

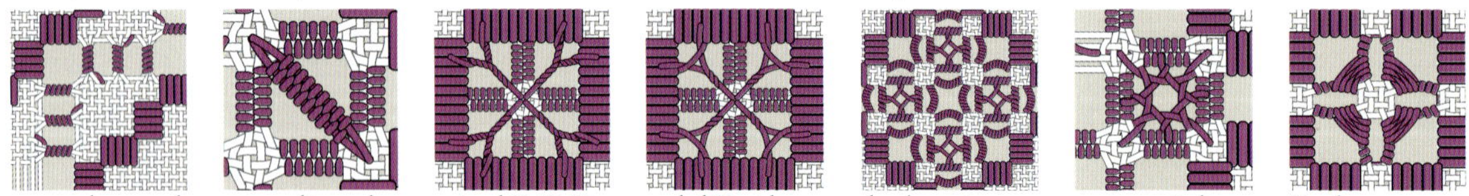

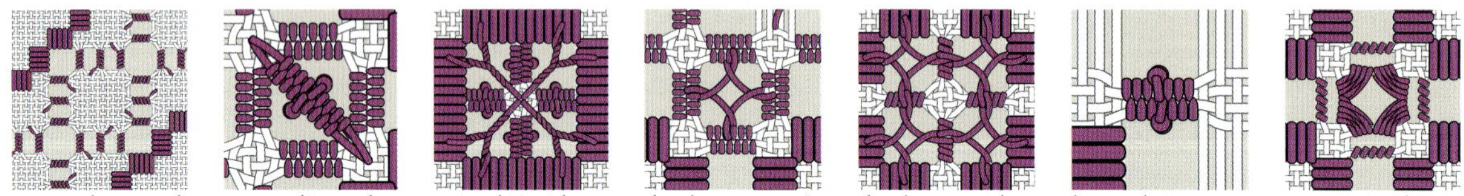

Some fillings have names and others have descriptions. Numbers in *italics* indicate left-handed instructions; numbers in **bold** indicate right-handed instructions. Numbers in roman (regular) typeface are for both.

reverse Greek cross in a circle *135*, **137**

stepped fan *158*, **160**

whipped spider web *176*, **177**

buttonholed petals and arcs *191*, **193**

buttonhole stitch with dove's eye *206*, **207**

buttonhole eyelets at intersections *218*, **219**

edelweiss *236*, **238**

Greek eighth cross *138*, **139**

woven quarter fan *162*, **163**

three quarter spider web flower *178*, **180**

buttonholed petals with inverse twisted Ys *191*, **193**

corner eyelets with full-width bars *208*, **209**

diamond filling *220*, **221**

Queen Anne's lace *240*, **243**

Greek cross border *140*, **141**

inverse woven fan *164*, **165**

buttonhole arc *182*, **184**

buttonholed petals with wrapped bars *191*, **193**

corner eyelets with square filet *210*, **212**

drunkard's path *222*, **224**

bullion flower *246*, **248**

Greek cross circlet *142*, **143**

curled V in a fan *166*, **167**

buttonholed bar *182*, **184**

diagonal buttonholed petals *191*, **193**

corner eyelets with spider web *211*, **213**

festoon stitch *226*, **228**

chain stitch flower *250*, **251**

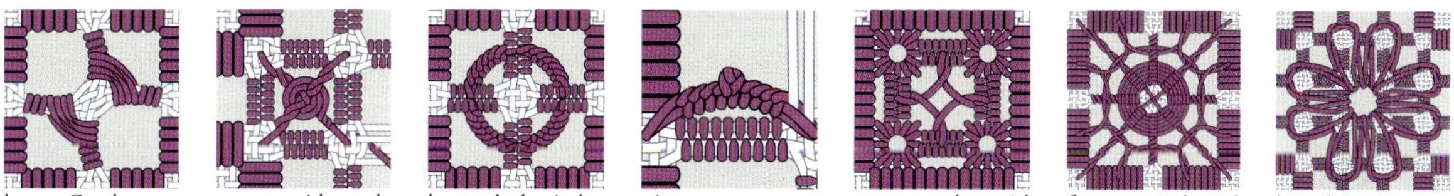

heavy Greek cross *144*, **145**

woven spider web, single square *168*, **169**

buttonhole circle *183*, **185**

picot on buttonhole stitch *191*, **193**

corner eyelets with dove's eye *211*, **213**

festoon stitch with spider web *227*, **229**

lacy daisy *252*, **254**

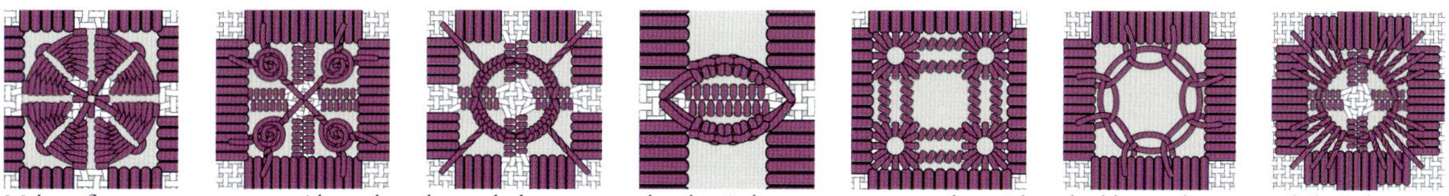

Maltese flower *146*, **148**

woven spider web, three spokes *170*, **171**

buttonhole arcs with twisted spokes *186*, **188**

shuttle stitch *194*, **195**

corner eyelets with divided wrapped bars *214*, **215**

double circular web *230*, **231**

soleil stitch, spaced *256*, **258**

woven fan, two spokes *150*, **152**

woven spider web *172*, **173**

buttonhole arcs w/ twisted spokes, variations *187*, **189**

blanket stitch flower *196*, **199**

cnr eyelets w/ div. wrap. bars w/ spider web *214*, **215**

flower filling *230*, **231**

soleil stitch, full *257*, **259**

woven fan, three spokes *154*, **156**

ribbed spider web *174*, **175**

buttonholed petals *190*, **192**

buttonholed square *202*, **204**

simplified eyelets at intersections *216*, **217**

wheel filling *232*, **234**

lacy buttonhole edge *260*, **264**

index

Numbers in *italics* indicate left-handed instructions; numbers in **bold** indicate right-handed instructions.